2/08

BARRON'S

NINTH EDITION

BEST BUYS
in College Education

Lucia Solórzano

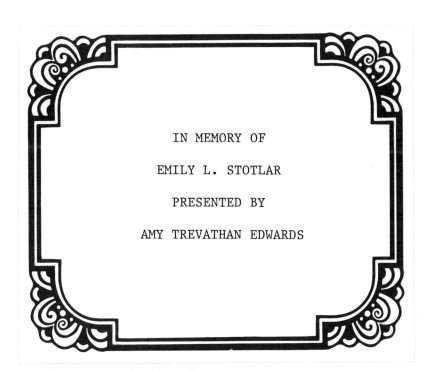

All inquiries should be addressed to:
Barron's Educational Series, Inc.
250 Wireless Boulevard
Hauppauge, New York 11788
www.barronseduc.com

ISBN-13: 978-0-7641-3369-5
ISBN-10: 0-7641-3369-1

International Standard Serial No. 1539-9680

PRINTED IN THE UNITED STATES OF AMERICA
9 8 7 6 5 4 3 2 1

Contents

Introduction iv

Five "Quick Lists" to Help Target Your Choices x

    1. Colleges with 20,000 or More Full-time Undergraduates x

    2. Colleges with 1000 or Fewer Full-time Undergraduates x

    3. Colleges with Tuition and Fees of $15,000 or Less xi

    4. Colleges with Predominantly Single-Sex Enrollments xi

    5. Colleges with Chapters of Phi Beta Kappa xii

Profiles of the Colleges 1

Alphabetical Index of the Colleges 707

Introduction

For about 1.5 million high school seniors every year, choosing the right college is the first major life decision they will make, preceding the choice of a career, a spouse, a home, or a community in which to live. Perhaps this is the year for you, or for a son or daughter. In many cases, the choice of college determines how these other decisions will be made, so that picking THE right school is one of the most important, overwhelming, pressure-filled, confusing, and nerve-wracking ordeals a student will ever encounter. The problem is further complicated by three myths that dominate the process: (1) there is only one right college for every student, (2) to be any good, the college must be well known, and (3) if the college is any good, it will be very expensive.

Barron's Best Buys in College Education is a guide to 247 myth-breakers, schools that breach the supposed link between college price and college quality. Although some of them are better known than others, all deserve recognition where it counts: in the performance of their faculties, the depth and comprehensiveness of their curricula, the preparation of their students for lives after graduation, and the prices they charge for their services. These "best buys" run the gamut from sprawling state universities of more than 20,000 undergraduates to private colleges whose enrollments seem more like extended families; from service academies where students pay initial fees of only $2200 to $3000—and receive monthly wages while attending—to colleges whose tuition, fees, room, and board exceeding $36,000 stretch the definition of a "best buy" until you look at what colleges of similar student quality and graduate-school placement records are charging.

With the average tuition at a private 4-year college exceeding $21,000 in the 2005–2006 academic year, and rising at a rate of 6% a year, parents who remember what they paid for their bachelor's degrees are likely to experience "sticker shock" in the college market of the twenty-first century. *Barron's Best Buys* looks beyond the nation's best-known and most expensive 4-year colleges to discover schools where the education dollar goes further, often with results that give their more prestigious peers a good run for their money.

How the Best Buys Were Selected

In the summer of 2005, 265 4-year colleges and universities were chosen as prospective "best buys," based on their tuition rates as compared not only with the national average for schools of the same type but also with the rates for similar schools in that region or schools of comparative selectivity or academic emphasis. The idea was to tap institutions in every state and of nearly every size, religious affiliation, student quality, and academic orientation to obtain a final list of 245 to 265 that presented the best values to suit a wide range of student abilities and interests.

Questionnaires or copies of the institution's profile that appeared in the eighth edition of *Barron's Best Buys* were sent to the dean of students and to students at each of the 265 colleges and universities, including undergraduates at the campus newspaper, and in a representative sampling selected by the dean. Statistical data for these prospective best buys were obtained from questionnaires sent in fall 2005 by Barron's Educational Series for the 2006 *Profiles of American Colleges*. In the case of some of the schools initially selected, none of the undergraduates returned the questionnaires or those who did gave generally negative ratings of the college. Other institutions proved too expensive or had graduation rates or other statistical indices of quality that were too low when compared with corresponding factors at similar schools. Still others failed to provide current information. The final 247 represent the best combination of sound data and student satisfaction.

For the most part, these 247 are places where tuition and required fees in 2005–2006 did not exceed $30,000, where at least two-thirds of the faculties held Ph.D.'s or the highest other terminal degrees in their respective fields, and where at least half of the entering freshmen graduated in 4 or 5 years. However, college quality is not a factor that can be evaluated just by numbers, and several colleges and universities that fall below some of these thresholds have been included.

In all cases, the opinions of students weighed heavily in the final decision of whether or not a particular college qualified as a "best buy." For example, some members of the final 247 offer extremely low tuition rates but have faculties who, judged by their credentials, do not appear to be top-notch. However, according to their students, these professors provide a great deal of personal attention and push undergraduates to excel. At other colleges, well-designed and well-executed curricula or educational philosophies give their programs a spark that motivates previously disinterested learners. As might be expected, not every college turned out to be the perfect choice for all its students. In the 247 colleges that became examples of *Barron's Best Buys*, however, either the qualitative data were too strong to ignore or else a majority of the students surveyed, while mindful of their institution's shortcomings, were satisfied with the quality of academics provided and felt that, if confronted with the same decision again, they would attend that college or university.

What the Data Capsules Tell

The statistical capsule at the beginning of each profile enables a reader to determine very quickly whether the college meets certain "acceptable" criteria that he or she has set, such as location, size, or academic standing of the student body. Data not provided by the colleges are indicated as "NA." Data that are not applicable, such as room and board rates at a commuter university or tuition at a service academy, are indicated as "N/App."

Setting gives a first impression of the environment in which a college is located: rural, small town or city, suburban, or urban.

Control tells whether the college is state supported (or underwritten by Uncle Sam in the case of the service academies) or is privately endowed. Many private colleges maintain some religious affiliation, in which case this information follows in parentheses. Some colleges are religious in history and tradition only; others may require chapel attendance. These differences are reflected in the profiles.

Figures for **undergraduate** and **graduate enrollments** are for full-time students only in the 2005–2006 school year. In a very few cases, numbers are from the 2004–2005 school year or include both full-time and part-time students if that was the only data available. Figures for part-time students generally follow in parentheses if their numbers are so large in comparison to the full-time enrollment that this information helps students to judge more accurately the college's size.

Student/faculty ratio, the ratio of full-time students to full-time faculty, gives a very general idea of the chances for personal attention from faculty members. However, these numbers do not take into account either the lectures of 400+ students and/or the busy research-oriented professors at many larger universities or, at the other extreme, the extra efforts extended by many professors to establish one-to-one relationships with students. The profiles offer these insights.

Freshman profile contains data on the standardized test scores and high school class ranks of the freshmen who entered in fall 2005. Wherever possible, a distribution of test scores is given, enabling a prospective student to tell instantly how his or her performance compares with that of the most recent freshman class. If a student's test scores rank in the top 5%, for example, will the college provide sufficient challenge through either its regular curriculum or an honors program? If, on the other hand, the student's marks are in the lower quartile, are academic support services available or is the student willing to work harder than his or her classmates to succeed? **The SAT scores presented are for the SAT I verbal and mathematics tests that were taken by students who enrolled as freshmen in fall 2005. These students were the last entering class to take the old 2-part SAT I test. In March of 2005 high school students planning to attend college took a new version of the SAT that includes 3 sections instead of 2, the 3 being critical reading, mathematics, and writing. Since fall 2005 freshmen did not submit scores from the new 3-part test; only scores from the old SAT I verbal and mathematics tests are included in this edition's data capsule.** For a majority of the colleges profiled, statistics on class rank show the percentages who graduated in both the top tenth and the upper fifth, or in some cases, the upper fourth of the high school class. When a school did not supply data for the top tenth, figures for the upper fifth and upper two-fifths are listed instead.

Faculty profile shows the percentage of full-time faculty with doctorates or the highest professional degrees in their fields. However, while a high figure may connote academic expertise, it says nothing about other important qualities such as excellence in teaching, interest in students, or accessibility after classes, information that the profiles provide.

Figures for **tuition and fees** are for the 2005–2006 school year and include a year's tuition for full-time students plus all fees that must be paid in order to enroll. Not included are special fees for science laboratories, music lessons, or similar items. Figures for **room and board** also are for the 2005–2006 school year.

Freshman financial aid shows the percentage of freshmen who received some form of financial assistance in the 2005–2006 school year or, in a few cases, the most recent year for which data were available. On the questionnaire sent for the 2006 *Profiles of American Colleges*, each institution was asked to list the average amounts of aid that might be granted to a freshman from the following sources: need-based scholarships or need-based grants, need-based self-help aid, such as loans and jobs, non-need-based athletic scholarships, and other non-need-based awards and non-need-based scholarships. The **average scholarship or grant** figures indicate money that a student does not need to pay back. However, this figure is only an average amount and may not represent all the funds available to an individual based on financial need and/or academic merit. Therefore *no* college should be discounted just because the figures listed for average scholarship or grant do not equal what a student feels he or she needs in order to attend.

Students planning to earn extra money during the college years can get an idea of the part-time job opportunities available on campus from the data given for **campus jobs** and **average earnings** in the 2005–2006 school year.

The final elements of the capsule include the **application deadline** for fall entry for both early decision or early action if that is an option and regular admission, and the **financial aid deadline,** the date by which a student's financial aid forms must be completed to be considered for aid for fall entry. It *always* is a good idea for students to double check with the college or university concerning the deadline date by which applications for admission must be submitted since deadlines often vary from year to year. And though most colleges list deadlines for submitting financial-aid materials, students are always advised to submit their aid requests as soon as possible after the first of the year since aid money is often allotted quickly. An **admissions information** telephone number and wherever available a toll-free number, E-mail address, and web site address are listed for students with additional questions or seeking more information.

Below the capsule and preceding the more detailed information in each profile is a brief description of a salient feature or characteristic of the college. Here the focus is on one factor that makes the school unique—perhaps a matter of geography, history, or orientation, or an unusual program or curriculum—whatever distinguishes it from other colleges of the same size or general type.

What Each Profile Reveals

Each profile is organized around the same basic components: **student body, academics, facilities, special programs, campus life, cost cutters, rate of return, payoff,** and **bottom line.**

Student body provides a statistical profile of the undergraduate enrollment, as well as students' descriptions of their peers. When provided by the college, the data show the geographic, racial, and ethnic origins of the undergraduate student body, the percentage who are members of various religious affiliations, usually just in the cases of colleges and universities with religious affiliations, and the percentage from public or from private or parochial schools. Across the board, just about every college with a predominantly white student body has undertaken special initiatives to increase the number of minority undergraduates. However, problems with diversification continue on most campuses, with students reporting, unless otherwise noted, a lack of real integration between majority and minority groups outside of the classroom.

The **academics** section includes a wide range of curriculum-related matters: the range of degrees offered, school calendar, average class sizes, general-education requirements (broader coursework mandated in addition to the major), and student views on the quality of the faculty as well as on the strongest and weakest academic programs offered. Numbers are provided for both the full-time and the part-time faculties on campus, as well as for the percentage who are women. Students weighing these numbers should note that, while a large number of part-timers can mean a strong contingent of working professionals bringing knowledge from the front-lines of particular fields, it can also mean faculty who are harder to reach outside of the classroom and who have less commitment to the overall academic and social life of the campus.

Facilities examines the library as a place both to study and to conduct research; the term "volumes" includes not only formally published books but also other bound volumes of printed materials. The number of periodicals represents current subscriptions. This section also describes the campus computer facilities. For the most part, undergraduate respondents recommended that a freshman consider bringing his or her own computer to college for convenience, either to avoid a trip to the main laboratory in zero degree weather or to be able to work during the wee hours of the morning when many campus labs are closed. Before purchasing a computer, however, a student should check with the college or university to which he or she has been accepted to learn whether the institution recommends a particular brand of computer, or perhaps advises waiting to buy one at a discount on campus. In any case, students agreed, a personal computer is nice but certainly is not necessary for a successful 4 or 5 years at most colleges.

Special programs lists off-campus experiences designed to enrich a student's time on campus. While most of the options for study abroad cost more than staying on campus, financial aid usually is adjusted to compensate for these higher expenses. Within the United States, many colleges offer 3-2 programs, so called because a student spends 3 years at his or her home campus and 2 years at another institution to earn bachelor's degrees from both. For example, many smaller colleges have 3-2 programs in engineering. Washington Semester programs, in which undergraduates spend a term in the nation's capital, are popular, as is cross registration for courses at area colleges and universities. Not included in the profiles, unless exceptional, are general programs that nearly all colleges provide, such as honors programs for top students, academic support services for those in need of special help, or academic pacts that allow a student to pay reduced fees at a public university in a neighboring state if the home university does not offer a particular academic program. Students interested in these features should seek information from the individual college or university.

Campus life provides information on the percentage of undergraduates who reside on campus and describes a typical weekend, exploring the predominance of Greek life and alternative social activities, special clubs, and community service; sporting events, through either the National Collegiate Athletic Association (NCAA) or the National Association of Intercollegiate Athletics (NAIA); and favorite getaways. Popular student groups or activities common to most campuses, such as the student government or student activities boards, weekend movies, concerts, or lecture series are not mentioned in every profile. Also excluded from individual profiles is discussion of the widespread use of alcohol and, to a lesser extent, other drugs on most college campuses, the exceptions being service academies and a handful of very religious schools. Students also provide their assessment of whether crime is a problem on their campus and what safety measures have been taken. Undergraduates report that "date rape" is a rising concern on most campuses, and many colleges either have educational programs in place or are starting them.

Joining a fraternity or sorority should be viewed as both a social and a financial decision. These groups can make a large campus seem more intimate or can provide at smaller colleges a core group of friends and an active social life. On the other hand, they also can "empty your wallet if you're not careful," a member advises. Therefore, students stretching their finances to afford a particular college should weigh carefully the predominance of Greek life on campus, its importance to their social happiness, and its impact on the pocketbook.

The **cost cutters** section provides information on the percentages of freshmen and other undergraduates who received financial aid in the 2005–2006 school year or most recent year for which data is available, the average freshman aid package, and a breakdown of the total award into scholarships or grants, and self-help aid, plus a figure, provided by the college, indicating the average financial indebtedness of a recent graduate. Although this figure for student debt is just an average, it should be considered in terms of whether the education offered at a particular college, along with the opportunities it provides for a good job with career advancement or for acceptance into a first-rate graduate or professional school, is worth the thousands of dollars of debt that may be incurred. For some, a high figure will seem acceptable; for others, it will not.

The bulk of the section lists special institutional scholarships available to students, excluding those offered through the Reserve Officer Training Corps (ROTC) or the National Merit Scholars programs available on most campuses. In all cases, students should double-check the amounts listed for various scholarships, as some awards increase in value annually along with tuition while others remain the same. Many of the scholarships listed use such criteria as grade point average, class rank and standardized test scores for deciding which students receive the awards. During the 2005–2006 school year, many colleges and universities were revising their scholarship criteria to reflect the change in the SAT discussed earlier in this introduction. Most of the scholarships listed were using criteria based on just the math and critical reading portions of the new SAT and not the writing section. Students interested in particular scholarships that use the SAT as criteria should double check on which measures each college or university is using at the time they apply. Also listed in this section are various tuition payment plans offered, as well as the availability of cooperative education programs that let a student alternate a term of study with a term of paid employment.

Figures given for the portion of all freshmen and continuing students receiving some form of financial aid include undergraduates getting merit-based and/or need-based aid from sources provided solely by the college or university, as well as funds from the coffers of each state and that great granduncle of us all, Uncle Sam. Every year, students at the nation's 2- and 4-year colleges share in the annual distribution of more than $80 billion in federal financial aid, an increasing portion of that loans that students and their families must repay. Federal student aid in the form of need-based grants, loans, work-study programs, and education tax credits is the largest source of help available, comprising two-thirds of the total aid provided. By comparison, institutional aid accounts for about a fifth of the total pool. Therefore, ALL students, regardless of family income, should apply for federal financial aid as well as any institutional programs for which they are eligible. Bright students with need will find their financial aid packages tilted more heavily toward scholarships or need-based grants that they do not have to pay back; less able students will carry more loans and work commitments. Advises a recent graduate from Virginia: "To students hesitant about applying to a college because of the high cost of attending, I say, 'Don't be.' Those who qualify for aid, grants, and/or scholarships will find that almost any college can offer both the right price and the right education." Other students may cut costs further by using advanced placement credits or attending college during the summer and thereby shortening the time required to complete a bachelor's degree, or by going to a lower-cost community college for the first 2 years and transferring to a more expensive school for the junior and senior years.

A "cost booster" not mentioned in every profile that continues to catch new students off guard is the extra expenses associated with going to college. Foremost among them is the price of books. After 12 years of having textbooks provided free by the school system, most students are taken aback by average yearly costs for books and other supplies exceeding $900, even more for science and art majors, and are often dismayed to learn that they cannot sell back their books or, in doing so, will receive just a fraction of the original cost. Other expenses that can add to the college tab are those spent over many months for beer and late-night pizzas or transportation for trips home or for off-campus excursions.

The remaining three sections are fairly straightforward. **Rate of return** takes a peek at student success and satisfaction on campus by looking at the percentage of entering freshmen who return for the sophomore year and the percentage who go on to graduate in 4, 5, or, in a growing number of cases, 6 years. Fewer students are graduating in the traditional 4-year period. A study by the National Institute of Independent Colleges and Universities found just 41% of students who were enrolled in a 4-year degree program completed a bachelor's degree within 6 years; of those who entered college directly from high school and attended full-time, the completion rate was somewhat higher—about 46% after 6 years. Many students take a year off to work or to travel or, on a less positive note, change their majors so many times that they add on another year—and another year's tuition—to meet each new set of course requirements. Also, more and more students are finding it increasingly difficult to combine in 4 years both general-education requirements and extensive courseloads in some preprofessional majors. Moreover, if required classes fill up too soon, students often have no choice but to extend their college stay—and their tuition payments. Students weighing the comparative values of 2 colleges should consider not only the annual tuition rate of each but also how long a majority of entering freshmen take to earn a bachelor's degree from each school. It may turn out that a college with the more expensive yearly tuition rate will actually cost less over 4 years than a less expensive college where a majority of students need 5 or 6 years to finish.

Payoff, with figures on both the most popular majors and the percentages of students headed directly to graduate or professional schools or into the job market, enables a student to match his or her academic focus with that of an individual college. For example, if you're planning to attend graduate school but more than 90% of a particular college's alumni immediately enter the job market, you may be happier at a school more concerned with graduate-school preparation. If your heart is set on settling in California, choosing a college that sends most of its graduates into jobs in the Midwest may well lead to disappointment.

Finally, **bottom line** is just that: a brief sum-up of each particular college experience or advice to future students from current undergraduates or recent alumni.

How This Book Can Help You

If you already have a clear idea of the kind of school you want, turn to the five lists immediately following this introduction. Here you will find the names of colleges and universities that meet each of five different criteria students often use in initially narrowing their college choices: full-time undergraduate enrollment over 20,000 students, full-time undergraduate enrollment under 1000 students, tuition and fees (not including room and board) under $15,000, an either all-male or all-female undergraduate student body, and membership in Phi Beta Kappa, the national honor society that recognizes high-quality programs in the liberal arts. Reading the profiles for the colleges listed under these headings may disclose some schools that appear right for you.

But suppose that your primary concerns fall under none of these headings. In that case, use a different approach. Note that the profiles are arranged alphabetically by state and that they follow the same format, making it easier to locate specific items of information quickly and to draw comparisons between similar colleges in different states. For example, if you are considering schools within a certain price range or a particular part of the country, with perhaps a lively Greek presence or exceptional program in biology, flipping to the same section in several profiles should help to get your selection process started. Or maybe simply reading the data capsules or first paragraphs for some randomly selected colleges will reveal an academic program or an approach to learning that intrigues you.

Hopefully, *Barron's Best Buys in College Education* may ultimately lead you, the student, to a college, described in this book, where you apply, are accepted, and discover just the right academic major, faculty mentor, and circle of friends that together add up to a very happy and successful college experience. Or, after reading the guide, you may decide to apply to a more expensive college or another school not listed. Either route will be fine as long as it leads to the college that is right for you, not your mother or your father or your friends or your college counselor.

The choice of a college will remain one of life's major decisions, but it does not have to be a traumatic one. *Barron's Best Buys in College Education* is a testament to the experiences of thousands of once-uncertain high school seniors who found happiness and academic challenge at colleges that do not charge top dollar for top-quality educational programs. After matching your personal interests and criteria with those of students already on these 247 campuses, hopefully, you will experience an equally satisfying outcome.

Five "Quick Lists" to Help Target Your Choices

As you begin your search for a suitable college, you may already have some idea of the kind of school you are looking for: very large or very small, very strong in the liberal arts, single-sex (or nearly so), or maybe as low as colleges go in terms of tuition. The following "quick lists" provide the names of colleges in *Barron's Best Buys* that (1) enroll at least 20,000 full-time undergraduates, (2) enroll fewer than 1000, (3) cost $15,000 or less a year for tuition and required fees (no room or board included), (4) have all-male or all-female student bodies (or practically so), or (5) have chapters of Phi Beta Kappa, the national honorary society for excellence in the liberal arts. A number of colleges appear on more than one list.

1. Colleges with 20,000 or More Full-time Undergraduates

The Ohio State University, Columbus (OH)	33,817	Rutgers University, Brunswick/Piscataway (NJ)	24,242
University of Texas, Austin (TX)	33,682	University of California, Los Angeles (CA)	23,850
The Pennsylvania State University (PA)	33,208	University of Colorado, Boulder (CO)	23,539
Texas A&M University (TX)	33,131	University of Washington (WA)	23,216
University of Illinois, Urbana-Champaign (IL)	29,905	The University of Georgia (GA)	22,735
Purdue University (IN)	29,196	University of California, Davis (CA)	22,735
Indiana University, Bloomington (IN)	27,974	University of California, Berkeley (CA)	21,771
Brigham Young University (UT)	27,460	Virginia Polytechnic Institute and State University (VA)	21,085
University of Wisconsin, Madison (WI)	27,441	Temple University (PA)	20,936
University of Arizona (AZ)	24,595	University of California, San Diego (CA)	20,339
University of Michigan, Ann Arbor (MI)	24,446	University of MIssouri, Columbia (MO)	19,979

2. Colleges with 1000 or Fewer Full-time Undergraduates

Illinois College (IL)	1009	Hollins University (VA)	790
Bluffton College (OH)	1005	Oglethorpe University (GA)	784
Hanover College (IN)	1004	Albertson College (ID)	761
Hendrix College (AR)	1001	Randolph-Macon Woman's College (VA)	760
Ripon College (WI)	953	Prescott College (AZ)	723
Quincy University (IL)	927	New College of Florida (FL)	692
Goshen College (IN) (full/part-time)	922	Blackburn College (IL)	590
The Cooper Union for the Advancement of Science and Art (NY)	919	Converse College (SC)	571
		Coker College (SC)	560
Hiram College (OH)	900	Lyon College (AR)	458
Bethany College (WV)	895	Christendom College (VA)	372
Saint Joseph's College (IN)	886	Thomas Aquinas College (CA)	359
Centenary College of Louisiana (LA)	882	Alaska Pacific University (AK)	336
Agnes Scott College (GA)	879	Franklin W. Olin College of Engineering (MA)	286
Wabash College (IN)	871	Shimer College (IL)	93
Warren Wilson College (NC)	820	Webb Institute (NY)	80

3. Colleges with Tuition and Fees of $15,000 or Less
(nonresident charges are given for public institutions)

University of North Florida (FL)	$14,911
University of Mary Washington (VA)	$14,776
The Evergreen State College (WA)	$14,747
Drury University (MO)	$14,687
Texas A&M University (TX)	$14,679
Bethany College (WV)	$14,370
Montana Tech of the University of Montana (MT)	$14,070
University of Montana (MT)	$13,932
Lyon College (AR)	$13,905
University of Kansas (KS)	$13,866
University of Arizona (AZ)	$13,678
University of Utah (UT)	$13,528
University of Alabama (AL)	$13,516
University of North Carolina, Asheville (NC)	$13,325
Appalachian State University (NC)	$13,178
University of Idaho (ID)	$12,738
University of Nevada, Reno (NV)	$12,737
Blackburn College (IL)	$12,733
North Dakota State University (ND)	$12,590
University of Northern Colorado (CO)	$12,381
California Polytechnic State University San Luis Obispo (CA)	$12,381
State University of New York at Binghamton (NY)	$12,098
State University of New York at Geneseo (NY)	$11,780
State University of New York at Albany (NY)	$11,760
Hawaii Pacific University (HI)	$11,630
State University of New York at Potsdam (NY)	$11,549
State University of New York, College of Environmental Science and Forestry (NY)	$11,454
Hunter College, City University of New York (NY)	$11,147
Shepherd University (WV)	$10,618
New Mexico Institute of Mining and Technology (NM)	$10,463
Grove City College (PA)	$10,440
York College of Pennsylvania (PA)	$10,050
Truman State University (MO)	$10,042
University of Wyoming (WY)	$9816
South Dakota School of Mines & Technology (SD)	$9744
University of Minnesota, Morris (MN)	$9722
U.S. Merchant Marine Academy (NY) (freshman fees)	$6516
Brigham Young University (UT) (non-LDS)	$5116
U.S. Coast Guard Academy (CT) (initial fees)	$3000
U.S. Military Academy (NY) (initial fees)	$2400–$3000
U.S. Air Force Academy (CO) (initial fees)	$2500
U.S. Naval Academy (MD) (initial fees)	$2200
The Cooper Union for the Advancement of Science and Art (NY)	$1450
Berea College (KY)	$516
College of the Ozarks (MO)	$330
Franklin W. Olin College of Engineering (MA)	$0
Webb Institute (NY)	$0

4. Colleges with Predominantly Single-Sex Enrollments

Women's		Men's	
College of St. Catherine (MN)	2362		
College of St. Benedict (MN)	1993	St. John's University (MN)	1845
Alverno College (WI)	1515	Hampden-Sydney College (VA)	1062
Saint Mary's College (IN)	1366	Wabash College (IN)	871
Mary Baldwin College (VA)	1074		
Agnes Scott College (GA)	879		
Hollins University (VA)	790		
Randolph-Macon Woman's College (VA)	760		
Converse College (SC)	571		

5. Colleges with Chapters of Phi Beta Kappa

Birmingham-Southern College (AL)

University of Alabama (AL)

Hendrix College (AR)

University of Arizona (AZ)

University of California, Berkeley (CA)

University of California, Davis (CA)

University of California, Los Angeles (CA)

University of California, San Diego (CA)

University of California, Santa Cruz (CA)

University of Colorado, Boulder (CO)

University of Denver (CO)

University of Connecticut (CT)

University of Delaware (DE)

Eckerd College (FL)

Agnes Scott College (GA)

University of Georgia (GA)

University of Idaho (ID)

Augustana College (IL)

Illinois College (IL)

Illinois Wesleyan University (IL)

Knox College (IL)

University of Illinois, Chicago (IL)

University of Illinois, Urbana-Champaign (IL)

DePauw University (IN)

Earlham College (IN)

Indiana University, Bloomington (IN)

Purdue University (IN)

Valparaiso University (IN)

Wabash College (IN)

Coe College (IA)

Cornell College (IA)

Drake University (IA)

Grinnell College (IA)

Luther College (IA)

University of Iowa (IA)

University of Kansas (KS)

Centre College (KY)

University of Maine (ME)

St. Mary's College (MD)

Albion College (MI)

Alma College (MI)

Hope College (MI)

Kalamazoo College (MI)

University of Michigan, Ann Arbor (MI)

College of St. Catherine (MN)

Gustavus Adolphus College (MN)

Hamline University (MN)

Macalester College (MN)

St. Olaf College (MN)

Millsaps College (MS)

Saint Louis University (MO)

Truman State University (MO)

University of Missouri, Columbia (MO)

University of New Hampshire (NH)

Rutgers University, Brunswick/Piscataway (NJ)

Elmira College (NY)

Hofstra University (NY)

Hunter College, City University of New York (NY)

State University of New York, Albany (NY)

State University of New York, Binghamton (NY)

State University of New York, Geneseo (NY)

University of North Carolina, Chapel Hill (NC)

Hiram College (OH)

Marietta College (OH)

Miami University (OH)

The Ohio State University (OH)

University of Tulsa (OK)

University of Oregon (OR)

Willamette University (OR)

Saint Joseph's University (PA)

The Pennsylvania State University (PA)

Temple University (PA)

University of Pittsburgh (PA)

Washington and Jefferson College (PA)

University of Rhode Island (RI)

Furman University (SC)

University of South Carolina, Columbia (SC)

Wofford College (SC)

Rhodes College (TN)

Sewanee, The University of the South (TN)

University of Tennessee, Knoxville (TN)

Austin College (TX)

Rice University (TX)

Southwestern University (TX)

Texas A&M University (TX)

Texas Christian University (TX)

Trinity University (TX)

University of Dallas (TX)

University of Texas, Austin (TX)

University of Utah (UT)

University of Vermont (VT)

The College of William and Mary (VA)

Hampden-Sydney College (VA)

Hollins University (VA)

Mary Baldwin College (VA)

Randolph-Macon College (VA)

Randolph-Macon Woman's College (VA)

University of Mary Washington (VA)

University of Virginia (VA)

Virginia Polytechnic Institute (VA)

Washington and Lee University (VA)

University of Puget Sound (WA)

University of Washington (WA)

Whitman College (WA)

Beloit College (WI)

Marquette University (WI)

Ripon College (WI)

University of Wisconsin, Madison (WI)

University of Wyoming (WY)

Alabama

Birmingham-Southern College

Birmingham, Alabama 35254

Setting: Urban
Control: Private (United Methodist)
Undergraduate enrollment: 564 men, 730 women
Graduate enrollment: 20 men, 16 women
Student/faculty ratio: 13:1
Freshman profile: 10% scored over 700 on SAT I verbal; 40% scored 600–700; 35% 500–599; 15% below 500. 10% scored over 700 on SAT I math; 38% scored 600–700; 40% 500–599; 12% below 500. 28% scored above 28 on the ACT; 16% scored 27–28; 26% 24–26; 22% 21–23; 8% below 21. 33% graduated in top tenth of high school class; 61% in upper fifth.

Faculty profile: 94% Ph.D.'s
Tuition and fees: $21,450
Room and board: $7044
Freshman financial aid: 98%; average scholarship or grant: $3475 need-based; $8180 non-need-based
Campus jobs: 20%; average earnings: $750/year
Application deadline: Jan. 15
Financial aid deadline: Mar. 1
Admissions information: (205) 226-4696; (800) 523-5793
    e-mail: ssalmon@bsc.edu
    web site: www.bsc.edu

Thirty years or so ago, few students would have considered Birmingham-Southern College, 3 miles west of downtown Birmingham, Alabama, a secure educational investment. The school's steadily declining enrollment had sunk below 750 students, and administrators faced a dilemma confronting many schools at the time: to boost enrollment quickly by lowering standards, throwing out the liberal arts, and giving students more of the job-related courses they wanted or to hang tough and strengthen the arts and sciences while improving key preprofessional programs. In the case of Birmingham-Southern, whose hyphenated name recalls the merger of the two schools that joined as one in 1918, administrators opted for merger again, this time blending the liberal arts tradition with new preprofessional programs in a curriculum that students consider one of the best bets around.

Total charges of $28,494 for tuition, fees, room, and board in the 2005–2006 school year make Birmingham-Southern one of the more expensive small colleges in the Southeast. But a rock-solid reputation for getting its well-prepared graduates into professional and graduate schools also has made Birmingham-Southern a financial winner compared to schools of similar size and academic emphasis around the country. "Students come here to learn and to prepare themselves for postgraduate work, so their intention is to succeed and do well in their studies," says a senior. "I plan to attend law school next year, and I could not feel better prepared, thanks to the education I have received here."

Student body: Students seeking a bit of ivy in the South had nevertheless best be prepared: 75% of the student body still hail from Alabama, with 93% of the rest also from the South. Altogether, 33 states and 8 foreign countries are represented. Although the school remains affiliated with the United Methodist Church, only 30% of the students are Methodist. Just over a third are graduates of private high schools. Seven percent of the students are African-American; 3% are Asian-American; 1% Hispanic and less than 1% Native American. Thirty-five students are foreign nationals. Students tend to be more conservative than liberal on many political and economic issues, although as one Alabaman observes, "comparatively speaking, BSC is one of the more liberal colleges in the immediate area." However, the term "southern comfort" doesn't describe the academic pace. Most students have a preprofessional focus in their studies and tend to be competitive, although far from cutthroat. "The goal-oriented nature of most students makes individual achievement a source of peer respect," says a philosophy major headed to medical school. "Even nonrelated majors know what grade point average is needed to get into graduate school in English or what a good MCAT score is." Students are quick to point out, however, that while academically driven, they also know when to "let loose and relax."

Academics: Birmingham-Southern offers bachelor's degrees in 32 disciplines plus 13 interdisciplinary majors ranging from international business to musical theater. Individualized majors also are possible. A master of arts in public and private management and a master of music in composition, piano, organ, and voice are the sole graduate degrees. The academic year is divided into 2 semesters and a January interim term. Average class size is 21, but sizes range from 5 in an advanced physics class to 50 in General Chemistry, although there are 2 lab sections.

Birmingham-Southern's general education program allows students to choose coursework from 6 broad areas of subject matter: behavioral and social sciences; business; education; fine and performing arts; humanities; and mathematics and natural and physical sciences. In choosing their classes, students must meet academic expectations defined as different kinds of foundations, for example, first-year foundations (courses directed at the freshman learner), disciplinary foundations (courses that cover the breadth of the arts and sciences), and skill foundations (courses that demonstrate competency in creative art, a foreign language, mathematics, and writing). In addition, undergraduates must complete an intercultural foundation through a course that examines an ethnic minority American culture or a foreign culture, a scholarship foundation in the form of a scholarly senior seminar, interim or independent study, and an intellectual and cultural foundation met by attending over a student's 4 years at least 40 approved cultural and intellectual programs held on campus and in the community. Students earning bachelor of science and bachelor of arts degrees must fulfill more foundation requirements than those earning bachelors of music, music education, and fine arts.

All but 8 of the 109 full-time faculty and all of the 35 part-time members teach undergraduates. Forty-one percent are women. Students rate their professors at the end of each semester, and, for the most part, the reviews are excellent. "The faculty overall is wonderful," says one senior. "Its members are very open to student opinion and interaction, and many get involved in all aspects of the college, such as coaching intramurals, judging contests, and living in the dorms."

Because of BSC's strong track record in getting students admitted to medical school, biology wins raves as a major that emphasizes personal attention and opportunities for undergraduate research. The chemistry and physics programs also are strong. The opening in 2002 of a new $24 million, 104,000 square foot science center has made these disciplines even more impressive. Political science is known for demanding clear and organized thinking from its students and providing in return top-ticket professors with plenty of previous and current real-life political experience. The history faculty likewise brings to the classroom multiple areas of expertise as well as hands-on experience overseas. The music and theater arts majors expect quality performance from their students and faculty, and get it. English is noted for its individual attention, which helps to develop strong writing skills in all students. Notes a major: "The professors are not only extremely insightful but also friendly, interesting, and provocative."

Although nearly a fifth of the students major in business administration, many nonmajors consider the department weaker than its liberal-arts counterparts. Students say it needs to attract more demanding faculty and, in turn, more of the brightest undergraduates around campus. Programs in philosophy, computer science, and physics could use more professors.

Facilities: Renovation of the popular Charles Andrew Rush Learning Center/N.E. Miles Library nearly a decade ago provided more research carrels and private rooms for those who prefer to study in silence. Holdings of 277,000 volumes plus subscriptions to 1215 periodicals are enhanced by a computerized system that lists materials at Rush and other libraries in Birmingham. "Each time I click on," says a political science major, "the school has gotten more resources." For missing publications, students use the Internet, interlibrary loan or make a trip to the library at the University of Alabama at Birmingham or Samford University, or to the Birmingham Public Library.

More than 880 college-owned computers are available to students in 9 classroom labs, 7 residential labs, 5 small departmental labs, and all science labs. Computer hookups in individual dorm rooms and Greek houses also are available. The college strongly recommends that students have their own personal computers, and the vast majority do. In the 2005–2006 school year, 92% of BSC students owned their own computers. Wireless access also was planned for common areas in the library, the Norton Campus Center, and the plaza/fountain area in the spring of 2006.

Special programs: Opportunities to study abroad are offered for an academic year, semester, or summer in England, France, Africa, and Latin America, or wherever else students request. Would-be scientists can spend 5 months at Oak Ridge National Laboratory in Tennessee or study marine science on Dauphin Island off the coast of Alabama. Those preferring to travel a shorter distance may take courses at any of 4 area institutions. Dual-degree programs in engineering are offered with Auburn, Columbia, and Washington universities and at the University of Alabama at Birmingham, in nursing with Vanderbilt University, and in environmental studies with Duke University. An interdisciplinary program in leadership studies enables students interested in the field to take specially designated courses and seminars as well as complete a community service project.

Campus life: Eighty-five percent of BSC's students live in single-sex housing on the 192-acre campus, and when they're not studying, most are enjoying band parties sponsored by 1 of the 6 national fraternities or 7 national sororities on campus or attending a Panthers basketball or soccer game. Going Greek is very big at BSC, with 54% of the men and 60% of the women involved in fraternity and sorority life. A new fraternity row was dedicated in March 2003. In September 2003, Birmingham-Southern became a member of NCAA Division I after nearly 5 decades and 3 national championships in NAIA competition. The college offers 6 varsity sports for men and 8 for women; 40% of the student body take part in the 17 intramural sports open to each sex. Large numbers of students also turn out for popular clubs such as Southern Volunteer Services, through which about three-quarters of the students provide help to the needy. Although students say the potential for crime exists on campus, incidents rarely occur and have been kept in check by security phones around campus and combination locks at the dorms. "Security takes on a Dad-like role," says one senior. The fact that there is a single, gated—and guarded—entrance to the fenced campus also restricts entrance by strangers. "When I enter the gates I feel like I am entering my own little world," says a junior, "and when that world seems too small, the exciting city of Birmingham lies just outside."

Off-campus excitement includes football games at Auburn University or the University of Alabama, Tuscaloosa, the Southside bars and restaurants, the city zoo and botanical gardens, and mountain biking and hiking at Oak Mountain State Park. Atlanta is a 2-hour drive, New Orleans, 5 hours.

Cost cutters: Ninety-eight percent of all BSC's undergraduates received financial aid in the 2005–2006 school year; 42% were on need-based assistance. The average financial aid package for fall 2005 freshmen included a need-based scholarship or grant averaging $3475 and need-based self-help aid such as loans and jobs averaging $4125. Non-need-based athletic scholarships for first-year students averaged $15,420. Other non-need-based awards and scholarships averaged $8180. The average 2005 graduate had debts of $17,972.

Entering freshmen can compete for a wide range of hefty, renewable scholarships. At least 15 full-tuition scholarships are available, including the highly coveted McWane Honors Award, which provides a full tuition scholarship plus an $11,000 annual stipend that supports summer travel, foreign study, internships, and other diverse academic experiences. Presidential Scholarships are awarded in amounts ranging from $9000–$12,000 to high-achieving students, generally according to their intended field of study. To be considered for the wide range of Distinguished Scholars Awards offered, students should rank within the top 10% of their high school graduating class and have combined critical reading and math SATs between 1300 and 1600 or an ACT composite between 30 and 36. Students also must complete an interview and essay during an Honors Day Scholarship Competition, held in late February or early March. Candidates also are encouraged to have submitted their application for admission by December 1 if possible. Other academic scholarships are available to students with slightly lower class rank and standardized test scores.

Rate of return: Eighty-four percent of entering freshmen return for the sophomore year. Sixty-nine percent graduate in 4 years; 77%, in 5 years; 79% in 6.

Payoff: Business administration was the favorite among 2005 degree recipients, accounting for 17% of all graduates. Education and English majors placed next, claiming 11% and 8% of the graduates respectively. Just over 40% of recent graduates took jobs upon receiving their degrees, many in such fields as insurance, banking, and marketing at corporations primarily in Alabama, Washington, D.C., or New York. Forty-eight percent of recent graduates enrolled in graduate school within 6 months of commencement.

Bottom line: Says a chemistry major: "Birmingham-Southern is a good place to stand out as an individual and to meet other serious students with similar interests." Although students at times find the small size stifling, they also view it as the most positive aspect of campus life, in terms of the close faculty-student and student-student friendships that develop.

Spring Hill College

Mobile, Alabama 36608

Setting: Suburban
Control: Private (Roman Catholic)
Undergraduate enrollment: 430 men, 744 women
Graduate enrollment: 7 men, 13 women
Student/faculty ratio: 16:1
Freshman profile: 4% scored over 700 on SAT I verbal; 25% scored 600–700; 41% 500–599; 30% below 500. 3% scored over 700 on SAT I math; 28% scored 600–700; 30% 500–599; 39% below 500. 6% scored above 28 on the ACT; 15% scored 27–28; 23% 24–26; 32% 21–23; 24% below 21. 19% graduated in top tenth of high school class; 31% in upper fifth.
Faculty profile: 85% Ph.D.'s

Tuition and fees: $20,948
Room and board: $7730
Freshman financial aid: 97%; average scholarship or grant: $11,354 need-based; $8690 non-need-based
Campus jobs: 31%; average earnings: $1452/year
Application deadline: Priority date: Jan. 15; regular: July 1
Financial aid deadline: Mar. 1
Admissions information: (251) 380-3030; (800) 742-6704
  e-mail: admit@shc.edu
  web site: www.shc.edu

Imagine a semitropical climate with Gulf Coast breezes that make sailing, rowing, and tennis popular sports, and the beach a relaxing retreat just 1 hour away. Add an 18-hole golf course and a campus quadrangle listed on the National Register of Historic Places, fortunately spared the eye of Hurricane Katrina in September 2005, so damage to the campus was minimal. If this were a resort, an annual fee of just under $29,000, including bed and board, might send one dashing off to the nearest travel agent. But place all of these amenities within the framework of a rigorous and value-oriented Roman Catholic Jesuit education, and students attending Spring Hill College in Mobile, Alabama, have an experience rich in social, moral, academic, athletic, and spiritual growth for a price even the most cost-conscious freshman won't mind having some fun with.

Student body: Fifty-two percent of Spring Hill's students are Catholic, 70% in a recent year were graduates of private high schools. Forty-six percent are from Alabama, with most of the out-of-staters also from south of the Mason-Dixon line. Altogether, 36 states and 8 foreign countries have students on campus. Minority students constitute 24% of enrollment; most of that number, 16%, are African-American, 6% are Hispanic and 1% each Asian-American and Native American. Foreign nationals also account for 1%. With a total undergraduate enrollment of less than 1200, students simply find the school too small to break into isolated groups. Most undergraduates tend to be fairly conservative in their viewpoints, goal-oriented, and serious about their studies, but not all. Observes a resident assistant: "Many take the academics of our school lightly. This is not an easy school to succeed in. You have to study and many don't. The college life of partying causes them to neglect their academics." Few of these party lovers last much beyond their freshman year, and generally won't be found in the more competitive science and premed majors.

Academics: Spring Hill, which began its first semester in May 1830 with teachers and funding from France, offers the bachelor's degree in more than 40 disciplines and masters degrees in business administration, teaching and education, liberal arts and theology. The academic year is divided into 2 semesters. For freshmen and sophomores, class size usually hovers around 30 members in the core classes, though 48 are enrolled in Principles of Biology. Juniors and seniors find more classes have between 7 and 15 students, with just 3 enrolled in physical chemistry. Among the most crowded classes are those that fulfill the traditional Jesuit core curriculum required of all students, encompassing courses from a wide range of disciplines, including 9 hours each of philosophy and theology. The core fulfills 60 of the 128 semester hours needed to graduate. Says a junior: "The professors teach core classes with the same enthusiasm and severity as one would expect in one's major-concentration classes." Thinking and writing are stressed in the core and throughout the curriculum. The junior continues: "When students leave Spring Hill, they can think, write well, and speak effectively, and they have a well-rounded educational background."

All of the 72 full-time and all but 9 of the 70 part-time faculty teach undergraduates. Forty-four percent of the pool are women. "The faculty have a genuine care and respect for us as students and adults," says a junior. They also encourage ideas different from their own and are receptive to student proposals for independent projects and new organizations. The closeness that develops between faculty and students motivates many undergraduates to do better. Says a senior: "It is hard to look a professor you've known since freshman year in the eye when you haven't done your assignment. You know you've let the professor down."

The business faculty, in particular, receive high marks for creativity in teaching methods. Philosophy and theology both boast thought-provoking, dedicated professors. Members of the political science faculty, says a major, reflect "a genuine love of what they teach." The sciences, biology and chemistry, also are especially strong in preparing students for medical school and other advanced study after college. Marine biology benefits from both great faculty and the college's location on the Gulf Coast. Nursing offers plenty of valuable hands-on experience every semester during clinicals at 4 local hospitals.

Students consider the fine and performing arts department "almost nonexistent" and in need of more financial support. Majors are offered in studio art, art business, art therapy, graphic design, and theater, though courses in music appreciation, guitar performance, chorale, and noncredit, private study in keyboard or voice are available to music lovers. Adds an art therapy major: "I wish that the art department had more funding for more supplies for the students and possibly more faculty to teach a more diverse range of classes." There also is no major in physics or sociology. A language major in Hispanic studies is available, but a minor only is offered in French and Spanish.

Facilities: The summer of 2004 marked the opening of Spring Hill's new library—and not a semester too soon. Thomas Byrne Memorial Library was "a great place to study as long as you didn't need to find something there," recalls a history major. The stacks were off limits to students and only librarians could retrieve sources. Not anymore. The new Marnie and John Burke Memorial Library is made for browsing with seating for 350 students in both group and individual study areas. The latest information technology incorporated into the structure has eliminated the need for students to make trips to the University of South Alabama for additional resources. The in-house collection stands at nearly 177,000 volumes and 547 periodicals. A course-related bibliographic instruction program, modeled after one developed at Earlham College, involves faculty and librarians in the development of assignments to hone students' research skills and their use of library materials and computerized aids.

Burke Library also is the new home of Information Technology Services on campus. The lower level of the new structure contains 2 computer lab/classrooms plus a distance education classroom. The first floor has a late night study lab. Altogether, about 160 Windows-based and Macintosh computers are available in labs around campus. The library, along with the Eisele Outdoor Learning Center, is among assorted places on campus that are wireless. Student rooms also are equipped with hookups for personal computers.

Special programs: Students can earn 6 semester credits in Spanish by spending a summer in a Spanish American country. Other summer study programs are available in various English-speaking countries and in Paris, Madrid, and Urbino, Italy; programs coordinated by other institutions are offered throughout the school year. Additional off-campus options include: marine biology courses at Dauphin Island, Alabama, internships during a semester in Washington, D.C., 3-2 engineering programs with the universities of Florida and Alabama/Birmingham and with Auburn, Texas A & M, and Marquette universities; and 3-2 occupational therapy and physical therapy programs with Rockhurst and Nova Southeastern universities. For students concerned about life after Spring Hill, the college offers a 4-year academic and career development program. In the freshman year, students attend a seminar to assist them in the transition from high school to college; sophomore year they are assigned a mentor from the Mobile community who works in their field of interest; as juniors, students may complete an internship in their career area; senior year, résumé guidance, job fairs, and networking socials set students on their way.

Campus life: Upon entering Spring Hill's 450-acre campus, there is no mistaking the Jesuit influence. St. Joseph's Chapel, whose Gothic arches flank the quadrangle on the north, is a prominent campus landmark. According to the charter of the college, the president and a significant number of the board of trustees must be Jesuits, and although the number of Jesuits on campus has declined, their influence far exceeds their physical presence. Their support of students and energetic involvement in many campus activities is a constant reminder of the school's emphasis on spiritual and moral development. Students are quick to point out, however, that the approach is one of learning by example rather than by theological indoctrination. Says a student: "I am a Southern Baptist and could not imagine feeling more comfortable anywhere else."

Seventy-two percent of the undergraduates reside on campus, and most remain there at week's end. Fourteen percent of the men and 23% of the women belong to 2 national fraternities and 4 national sororities. Nonmembers often are invited to Greek parties, or have their choice of several appealing alternative activities, among them SHORES, Spring Hill Ocean Research and Exploration Society, which does just that, and SHAPe, Spring Hill Awakening Program, which sponsors semester retreats. The college also provides bus transportation to Saturday-night gatherings off campus. Crime is not much of a problem as several precautionary steps are regularly taken. After dark each night, the back gates are locked and anyone still desiring to go through campus must enter through the main security gates. Notes a sophomore:

"There are 3 security guards on duty and we call them 'the squirrel patrol,' because they don't have anything to do other than chase squirrels." Students who do not feel safe walking alone after dark may call a security officer to escort them.

Seven men's and 8 women's NAIA intercollegiate sports involve a third of the men and under a fifth of the women. Badger basketball attracts the best crowds, though soccer and baseball also draw well in their seasons. Intramurals are a way of life, and a majority play the 12 sports provided. Club sports, including rugby and lacrosse, also are popular.

Those in need of a change of scene often make the hour drive to the beach. New Orleans is a 2-hour drive from campus.

Cost cutters: Ninety-seven percent of all undergraduates received financial aid in the 2005–2006 school year. Seventy percent of the freshmen and 64% of the continuing students received need-based assistance. The average freshman award for a first-year student with need included a need-based scholarship or grant averaging $11,354 and need-based self-help aid such as loans and jobs averaging $4630. Non-need-based athletic scholarships for first-year students averaged $3926; other non-need-based awards and scholarships averaged $8690. The average financial indebtedness of a 2005 graduate was $16,646. High-achieving entering freshmen may compete in mid February for a wide range of merit scholarships, including 4 much coveted Spring Hill Scholars awards that for fall 2006 paid $27,500 to first-year students who had demonstrated academic excellence, leadership, and service. Other academic scholarships range in value from $10,000 to $17,500.

Rate of return: Eighty-one percent of the first-year students return for a second year. Forty-eight percent go on to graduate in 4 years; 58% in 5 years.

Payoff: Majors in 3 fields accounted for nearly half of the degrees awarded in 2005: 20% specialized in business administration, 12% in biology, and 11% in communication arts. About 70% of the graduates in a recent year entered the job market within months of commencement, many with firms such as 3-M Company or with the Internal Revenue Service. More than a third pursue advanced degrees, at least part-time while working.

Bottom line: Students who succeed best at Spring Hill are comfortable in a close-knit community where individuals are valued. Advises a southerner: "A student who is serious about his or her studies and who recognizes that college is more than just studying or just partying will benefit most from his or her time at Spring Hill."

University of Alabama, Tuscaloosa

Tuscaloosa, Alabama 35487

Setting: Small city
Control: Public
Undergraduate enrollment: 7421 men, 8411 women
Graduate enrollment: 1344 men, 1404 women
Student/faculty ratio: 23:1
Freshman profile: 8% scored over 700 on SAT I verbal; 29% scored 600–700; 39% 500–599; 24% below 500. 9% scored over 700 on SAT I math; 26% scored 600–700; 42% 500–599; 23% below 500. 13% scored above 28 on the ACT; 11% scored 27–28; 20% 24–26; 30% 21–23; 26% below 21. 24% graduated in top tenth of high school class; 39% in upper fifth.

Faculty profile: 90% Ph.D.'s
Tuition and fees: $4864 in-state; $13,516 out-of-state
Room and board: $5024
Freshman financial aid: 72%; average scholarship or grant: $3476 need-based; $6795 non-need-based
Campus jobs: NA; average earnings: $3110/year
Application deadline: Mar. 1 (priority date); regular: Apr. 1
Financial aid deadline: Mar. 1 (scholarship priority: Dec. 1)
Admission information: (205) 348-5666; (800) 933-BAMA
e-mail: admissions@ua.edu
web site: www.gobama.ua.edu

If the term "'Bama bound" sounds like something a conductor would yell, then more top students are "hopping aboard" for a 175-year-old educational journey that is very southern in its pace and traditions, and years behind the times in terms of tuition. For just under $5000 a year for Alabama residents and about $13,500 for everyone else, students can study 21st-century engineering and accounting amid white-columned buildings from the Old South, 4 of which survived the torching of the campus by Union troops in the Civil War. A student can dress for football and stroll about campus in derby hat and cane to signify membership in Jasons, a prestigious senior men's honor society, or simply behave like a good ole boy, tossing a Frisbee or sunning on the grassy quad. "I love it here," enthuses a Pennsylvanian.

Student body: Alabama's undergraduate student body is 82% white Americans, 12% African-Americans, 2% Hispanics, 1% Asian-Americans, and 1% Native Americans. Two percent are foreign nationals from 79 countries. To help foster greater diversity, the university recently established an administrative unit to focus on the issues of diversity and inclusiveness. Eighty-nine percent are graduates of public schools. 'Bama students consider themselves to be outgoing and energetic, conservative (most are Republicans) and competitive, within reason, always maintaining a sense of appearance and decorum. "Socially, UA seems different from other schools," observes a southerner from outside Alabama. "People don't dance at the popular bars on 'the Strip.' Generally guys don't approach girls. Values held are traditional, especially in the area of race relations." For many students, attending 'Bama is a family tradition, with 80% of the undergraduates coming from in-state, though all 50 states have their 'Bama grads-to-be. Ninety percent of the out-of-staters, however, are southern. Bright students fight a stereotype of 'Bama being, in the words of 1 junior, a "bland state school," an image that many even bring with them when they arrive. Says the junior, now a quantitative finance major: "Some of the undergraduates are more interested in football and partying than in obtaining a degree. I was not expecting to meet any geniuses when I chose to come here, but the intellectual capability of the majority of undergraduates is impressive."

Academics: The University of Alabama, which admitted its first students in 1831, confers degrees through the doctorate in 8 undergraduate schools and colleges and 10 graduate schools or divisions. Students can choose from about 80 undergraduate majors and over 130 graduate-degree programs. The academic year is divided into 2 semesters plus a 3-week May interim term offering time for intensive study, internships, or travel. Popular introductory classes like Introductory Biology for Non-Majors may enroll 330 students. Some higher-level courses have 150, but the average is closer to 25. Honors courses are usually quite small, rarely more than a dozen students, and the professor in each of 77 recent fall classes taught to just 1 student.

General education requirements encompass core courses in freshman composition and upper-level writing, mathematics, social and natural sciences, humanities, and foreign language or computer science. Students accustomed to southern hospitality aren't surprised to find a faculty that is friendly as well as accessible through flexible office hours and e-mail, which many answer promptly. Three-fourths of the 922 full-time professors and just over half of the 226 part-timers teach undergraduates though just over a fourth of the introductory courses—28%—are taught, at least in part, by graduate students. That figure represents a 20% drop from several years ago. Forty percent of the faculty members are women. Most students manage to have a sampling of excellent teachers especially in the honors program as well as a few bad ones during their time on campus. A senior sums up his experience this way: "Most of my time has been spent with professors who not only know their material but have a genuine interest in their students knowing it, too."

Among students, the Culverhouse College of Commerce and Business Administration ranks highly because of its great faculty, well-designed curriculum, and outstanding facilities including, says an admiring public relations major, "2 newly renovated buildings that are technologically loaded," and wireless. A recent survey of accounting faculty nationwide ranked the college's School of Accounting 11th in the nation and 1st in the Southeast. The prehealth and prelaw programs specialize in excellent faculty advising, something students bound for the highly competitive professional schools in these fields appreciate. The College of Communication and Information Sciences is especially large and can offer students a wide range of concentrations from advertising and public relations to speech communication, journalism, and telecommunication and film. Extensive facilities, skilled instructors, and many student clubs enhance the broad curricula. Noted a communication studies major recently: "The debate team holds 14 national championship titles, which is 2 more than the football team." The College of Engineering features small classes and "faculty members who care about their students' well-being," says a chemical engineering major. While many liberal arts majors tend to fade beside the better funded professional programs, English and history shine, with dedicated faculty willing to work 1-on-1 with students and several honors courses and seminars available. The American studies program also is distinctive.

Other liberal arts departments, such as Spanish, where many courses have been taught by graduate students and the emphasis has been on literature rather than conversation and culture, disappoint some students. Political science uses too many graduate students as primary instructors; math, too many professors who have difficulty speaking intelligible English. Too many programs in the College of Arts and Sciences, concludes a finance major, "are over-extended, ill-advised, and under-funded." The College of Education also needs more financial support, especially its library.

Facilities: Amelia Gayle Gorgas Library and 6 discipline-specific facilities, including 4 built in the last dozen years, boast 2.5 million volumes plus 23,222 periodicals. More than a dozen computer terminals linked to the computerized catalog Amelia are located on each of the library floors, enabling students to locate holdings at any of the branch facilities on campus as well as listings at all Alabama universities. Students engaged in particularly in-depth research can turn to Amelia for access to the 3.5-million-volume Center for Research Libraries in Chicago, which makes its materials available to member research libraries through database and interlibrary loan. Laptops are available for checkout and use within Gorgas library.

'Bama students have access to more than 70 computer labs with 1500 PCs of varying makes spread among residence halls, libraries, and departmental buildings. Most close at midnight or 2 a.m.; not many are open around the clock. Says a junior: "During finals and midterms it gets hectic because plenty of students procrastinate—myself included." All residence halls have wired Internet access and many university buildings besides the main library provide public wireless access.

Special programs: The Blount Undergraduate Initiative started in 1999 provides an intensive liberal arts education in a living/learning environment for a limited number of entering freshmen and in academic house-based seminars for upperclassmen. Qualified students are admitted based on competitive applications and pay the regular tuition rate. Students in 'Bama's New College may design their own individualized curricula called depth studies. The Computer-Based Honors Program lets outstanding students, who are accepted as freshmen, do computer-related research in their chosen fields of study. A 5-year bachelor's-master's degree in business is another option. An International Honors Program is open to qualified undergraduates who wish to combine learning about foreign countries and cultures with language study and overseas travel. Study-abroad opportunities for all students are offered in 28 countries, including exchange programs in Germany, Japan, Belgium, and England. Internships are offered in the nation's capital, in the state capital, and at numerous firms in the Southeast and as far north as New York. Cross registration with Stillman College, a small Presbyterian school in Tuscaloosa, also is possible.

Campus life: Thirty percent of the undergraduates live on the 1000-acre campus in the heart of Tuscaloosa, a city of 78,000 in west-central Alabama. Students say they feel safe walking the campus at night, with numerous parking lot attendants, lights, and "blue phones" close at hand in case they need to notify police quickly. If the academics are sometimes relaxed at Alabama, students describe the social life as "intense." Greek life in particular is very big, involving 19% of the men and 26% of the women in 1 local and 26 national fraternities and 1 local and 20 national sororities. Fraternities and sororities remain segregated by student preference, not mandate, with traditionally black fraternities located on a different row from those for whites. In the 2005–2006 school year, a Greek Excellence Awards program was started that expects each Greek organization to assess its progress annually in 6 major areas, including multicultural programming.

Undergraduates not involved in Greek life tend to feel left out, although the bars on "the Strip," right off campus, are popular watering holes for those of age. The Student Government Association, once the powerful grooming place for aspiring Alabama politicians, was reinstituted in 1996 after its dissolution as a governing body 5 years before. Jasons, a traditional senior men's honor society, admits 40 members each year, though it is not chartered by the university because of its single-sex nature. The analogous women's honor society is The XXXI.

Fall weekends revolve around football with current students joining alumni in packing 83,818-seat (soon to be 91,000-seat) Bryant-Denny Stadium to cheer on "the Crimson Tide." "School spirit is tremendous," says a senior, "and life centers around those games. Granted, not everyone is a football fan...but you would be surprised how contagious football fever can be." Fraternities and sororities host band parties the nights before Saturday games, as well as game nights, for Greek members and their invited guests. Basketball and women's gymnastics also boast large followings. Altogether, the university fields 9 intercollegiate sports for men and 12 for women, and at least 16 intramural sports for each sex. Two-thirds of the men and a fourth of the women participate in intramurals.

Dates are important at Alabama, to the degree that some students will forgo a football game or band party rather than go alone. In warmer weather, students with or without dates can head for Lake Tuscaloosa to do some water skiing. Longer drives include Birmingham, 45 minutes away, and Atlanta, about 4 hours' distance.

Cost cutters: Seventy-two percent of fall 2005 freshmen received some form of financial aid, along with 73% of continuing students. About a third of all undergraduates were on need-based aid. The average aid package for freshmen with financial need included a need-based scholarship or grant averaging $3476 and need-based self-help aid such as loans and jobs averaging $3347. Non-need-based athletic scholarships for first-year students averaged $12,829. Other non-need-based awards and scholarships averaged $6795. Average indebtedness for a 2005 graduate totaled $18,989.

As the university has raised its admission and retention standards, it has also provided more endowed scholarships and fellowships to attract and keep superior students. Academic Elite Scholarships pay a minimum of $8500 a year to students with GPAs of at least 3.8, ACTs of 32, or combined math and critical reading SATs of 1400, and significant achievement in academics, extracurricular activities, leadership, and service. Students must complete and submit an essay by Dec. 1 to be considered. Automatic in-state and out-of-state scholarships pay from $1250 a year to full tuition, depending on a student's standardized test scores and grade point average. Computer-Based Honors Program awards pay $4600 a year. An Academic Walk-On program allows top students who enter without scholarships to earn such support after 3 semesters of distinguished academic achievement. A cooperative education program is available in all majors except teacher education, at firms located mainly in Alabama and the surrounding southeastern states. Just about any way a parent or student can pay, the university will take the money. Credit card, electronic bank transfer, payment by installment—they all look green to the bursar.

Rate of return: Eighty-six percent of entering freshmen return for the sophomore year. Thirty-five percent go on to graduate in 4 years; 57% in 5 years; 63% in 6.

Payoff: Among 2005 graduates, 3 business-related disciplines of marketing, finance, and management represented the largest portion of bachelor's degrees awarded at 7% each. Major employers of Alabama grads include Dow Chemical, Russell Corporation, Lever Brothers, and other businesses, as well as healthcare providers, school boards, and government agencies. Altogether, almost 600 companies and organizations from across the nation send representatives to recruit at 'Bama, although many more firms do so "in absentia." Smaller percentages of graduates pursue advanced degrees in fields such as business, law, and medicine.

Bottom line: Students who stand to benefit most from being 'Bama bound have a respect and appreciation for southern values and traditions and, within that frame of mind, the will to study, keeping a balance with other exciting aspects of campus life. Says a senior: "It is entirely possible to slide through 4 years of mediocre classwork, learn only what is required, and graduate. But it is also possible to obtain an *excellent* education from this university…This school has tremendous academic potential for those students willing to challenge themselves and make the most of it."

Alaska Pacific University

Anchorage, Alaska 99508

Setting: Small city
Control: Private
Undergraduate enrollment: 126 men, 210 women (244 part-time)
Graduate enrollment: 24 men, 54 women
Student/faculty ratio: 9:1
Freshman profile: 0% scored over 700 on SAT I verbal; 12% scored 600–700; 48% 500–599; 40% below 500. 4% scored over 700 on SAT I math; 12% scored 600–700; 32% 500–599; 52% below 500. 6% scored above 28 on the ACT; 6% scored 27–28; 28% 24–26; 22% 21–23; 38% below 21. 39% graduated in top fifth of high school class; 61% in upper two-fifths.

Faculty profile: 68% Ph.D.'s
Tuition and fees: $18,342
Room and board: $6800
Freshman financial aid: 90%; average scholarship or grant: $6725 need-based
Campus jobs: 18%; average earnings: $1326/year
Application deadline: Early decision: Dec. 1, regular: Feb. 1
Financial aid deadline: Mar. 15 (priority)
Admissions information: (907) 564-8248; (800) ALASKA-U (252-7528)
e-mail: admissions@alaskapacific.edu
web site: www.alaskapacific.edu

Alaska Pacific University, based in Anchorage, Alaska, may be out of the geographic mainstream, but its curriculum couldn't be more on target. At APU, founded in 1957, 2 years before Alaska became a state, the focus is on active learning, with an emphasis on *how* students learn as much as on *what* they learn. The approach called "directed study" is intended to make students, over their 4 or 5 years, take increasing amounts of responsibility for their own education. The process includes a freshman orientation course, a sophomore seminar, and junior practicum, all building toward a senior project in the student's major, which is related to his or her postgraduate plans. This approach places the university at the edge of wide, largely unexplored worlds of learning, in much the same way that Americans from the lower 48 states approach what has been called "the last Great Frontier." And though the costs of living in and traveling to and from Alaska must figure into any decision to earn a bachelor's degree at APU, a basic tuition rate of just over $18,000 in the 2005–2006 school year is enough to cause any academic explorer with a sense of adventure to start packing.

Student body: "For its size, APU has a very racially and ethnically diverse population," boasts a student from the lower 48, which statistics bear out. The undergraduate student body is about two-thirds white American, 19% Native American or Alaskan Native, 5% African-American, and 3% each Hispanic and Asian-American, with 2 foreign-national students from 2 countries. Sixty-nine percent call Alaska home, with students from 39 other states giving "the last Great Frontier" a try. Among out-of-staters, the largest portion come from the West. The average age of students is higher than at more traditional colleges: 21 years for freshmen and 30 for all undergraduates. Because the enrollment is so small, students come to consider their classmates as family, with all the good and bad aspects of such relationships. Many are liberal in their thinking, outdoorsy, and energetic. Alaska Pacific is a place where students come to shape their own personal and academic destinies, with little outward competition between classmates. Says a senior from the Midwest: "We are a small school in Alaska, we all have to get along. The winters alone require this."

Academics: APU offers bachelor's degrees in 11 majors contained within 6 areas: education (K-8), psychology, business administration, environmental science, outdoor studies, and liberal studies. The university also offers master's degree programs in 9 fields.

The university follows a semester calendar that consists of a 4-week block when a single course in taken and an 11-week session, in which most students take 3 classes. Some courses meet for the entire 15 weeks. The average class size for undergraduates is 9, with the largest class, in applied statistics, recently enrolling 26. In addition to specific courses required for the active learning program, students must take a lab science, a course in social and behavioral sciences, and 1 in ethics or religion, plus 2 classes in humanities and 1 in American sign language. Also, a course each must be taken in writing, speech, and quantitative skills to meet competency expectations.

Alaska Pacific's faculty consists of 44 full-time members and 40 part-time; all but 6 members of the full-time faculty and all but 4 of the part-time teach undergraduates. Thirty-nine percent are women. The figures include 30 to 35 adjunct faculty members employed each semester, largely to teach courses in programs for older returning students. There is nothing provincial about these professors; faculty members boast advanced degrees from Harvard, Stanford, and other highly prestigious universities around the United States. But there are few research snobs among the bunch, with one student describing them as "a very personalized and supportive faculty who are friends as well as mentors."

Professors with close ties to the working world who give their students the same opportunity to become involved make APU's top departments strong. Students in elementary education spend lots of time in the local schools under the tutelage of watchful academic advisers. The outdoors studies and environmental science programs both benefit from the school's emphasis on experiential learning and the great wild setting in which to do it. "The faculty is outstanding," says an environmental science major, "but large amounts of effort are required by the student. The faculty won't hold your hand."

Some students consider the liberal studies program to be the weakest, lacking the structure and vision offered by the other areas. The program, which relies on students to design their own interdisciplinary majors, works best for the most self-directed learners, which not all students are. To insure student success in the program, prospective majors are asked to apply to the department in their sophomore year. Also, the total number of majors offered at APU, 11, is also quite small so a number of programs available at larger schools are not present here.

Facilities: Students from APU share use of the Anchorage Higher Education Consortium Library, located adjacent to campus at the University of Alaska at Anchorage. The consortium library contains more than 760,000 bound volumes and 3430 periodicals. On its own campus, APU offers microform and computer database catalogs of the holdings of the Consortium Library and the Western Library Network.

Computers, recently numbering about 40 PC's, are located in Grant Hall, the major academic center on campus. Computers in the academic center are open until 10 p.m. Another lab in the dormitory is open any time to dorm residents. Because a fair number of students own their own units, there is almost no wait to use the computers in the labs. Internet and Web access is provided free to all enrolled students.

Special programs: Alaska Pacific offers exchange programs with sister colleges in Japan, China, Taiwan, Australia, and Russia. Students also may spend up to 2 nonsequential semesters at any of 5 other small U.S. colleges in the recently established Eco League. The league includes small schools such as College of the Atlantic in Maine and Prescott College in Arizona that offer strong programs related to the outdoors and the environment. Right on campus, APU provides moose avoidance workshops, designed to help new students decide when it's safe to pass a moose on a campus trail—and when to find an alternate route. A bachelor's degree program in a handful of fields is specially designed for adult students with 30 semester-hours of college behind them who want to graduate within 2 years. A Rural Alaska Native Adult program offers distance learning degree programs in the same disciplines to students who live and work in rural Alaska.

Campus life: The fact that there are no fraternities or sororities or intercollegiate sports, and very few campus parties does little to dampen the unconventional APU spirit. In fact, most students did not come seeking those traditional campus features. Says a student from Colorado: "I was lured to APU by one simple fact: it is located in Alaska. Students here mainly spend their free time outside exploring the natural beauty." About a fifth of the undergraduates live on the heavily wooded 200-acre campus located in midtown Anchorage (pop. 260,000). Students may choose to live in residence halls or in 1 of several theme houses. Their variety most recently included a co-op house and the Nordic ski house. Students generally keep busy in activities ranging from drama to moose nugget baseball. The widely divergent COLORS, a club supporting racial and ethnic diversity, the Environmental Club, and the Psychology Club are very popular with all students eager to learn new ways. Although there is little to no campus crime, some students have wished security were a bit better with more lighting along darkened pathways. Safety signs scattered around campus typically read, "Moose in area," or "No sledding." Off campus in Anchorage, law enforcement receives more calls about moose and bears than for holdups and a variety of other more common urban offenses.

There are 2 intramural sports for men and 2 for women, while Ultimate sledding draws its own share of adventurers. Many students also attend hockey games, both semipro and next door at the University of Alaska. "Anchorage's night life is not that of Los Angeles or New York," says a student, "but the place can certainly keep you busy." However, sun worshippers may have a hard time coping during the long winter months. In January, the range of daylight in Anchorage is 5.5 hours, in June, 19. However, Anchorage is not Nome. The average January high is 20 degrees. As a university publication notes, winter is the dominant season throughout the school year.

For the fitness buff, the campus has 10 miles of running, cross-country skiing, and biking trails plus a small lake for boating and kayaking. For great escapes, the APU outdoor program offers numerous student-run trips a year, ranging from major expeditions like a trip to Mount McKinley base camp to short, late night cross-country ski and ice cream runs.

Cost cutters: Ninety percent of the first-year students and 83% of the rest received some kind of financial assistance for the 2005–2006 school year. Need-based aid went to 67% of the first years and 60% of the continuing students. The average financial award for first-year students with financial need included a need-based scholarship or grant averaging $6725 and need-based self-help aid such as loans and jobs averaging $5324. The average financial indebtedness of a 2005 graduate was $17,775. A number of scholarships, many based on students' talents, academic interests, and background, are available. The cost of living in Anchorage is comparable to living in Seattle, Chicago, or Dallas, and not as expensive as some students anticipate.

Rate of return: Fifty-one percent of full-time freshmen return for the sophomore year. Seventeen percent of entering freshmen graduate in 4 years; 31% in 5 years; 36% in 6.

Payoff: Twenty-three percent of the 2005 graduates earned bachelor's degrees in outdoor studies; 21% followed with degrees in education (K–8), 16% in environmental science. The vast majority of APU graduates take jobs right in Anchorage or move down to the West Coast. Most of those who go on for further education enter business school.

Bottom line: Alaska Pacific University is made for independent-minded students who want to assume the responsibility for their own education, under the guidance of interested faculty members. However, studying in Alaska provides its own special set of challenges outside the classroom, most notably its distance from the lower 48 states and lengthy hours of darkness during the winter, which students must be willing to embrace with a love of the great wilderness and sense of adventure.

Arizona

Prescott College

Prescott, Arizona 86305

Setting: Small town
Control: Private
Undergraduate enrollment: 256 men, 467 women
Graduate enrollment: 52 men, 118 women
Student/faculty ratio: 7:1
Freshman profile: 17% scored over 699 on SAT I verbal; 34% scored 600–699; 33% 500–599; 16% below 500. 6% scored over 699 on SAT I math; 22% scored 600–699; 47% 500–599; 25% below 500. 7% scored above 29 on the ACT; 56% scored 24–29. 35% 18–23; 2% below 18. 12% ranked in top tenth of high school graduating class; 31% in upper fourth.

Faculty profile: 58% Ph.D.'s
Tuition and fees: $19,400
Room and board: N/App
Freshman financial aid: 56%; average scholarship or grant: $4627 need-based
Campus jobs: NA; average earnings: NA
Application deadline: Priority: Mar. 1; regular: Aug. 15
Financial aid deadline: None (Preferred: Feb. 15)
Admissions information: (928) 350-2100; (800) 628-6364
   e-mail: admissions@prescott.edu
   web site: www.prescott.edu

The 4 acres of land and buildings known as Prescott College in the mountains of central Arizona aren't remarkable because of their award-winning architecture or high-tech classrooms, because they have little of either. But that doesn't bother the 723 undergraduates whose academic gaze is focused well beyond the campus borders. For them, the deserts and mountains of the Southwest are their state-of-the-art classroom, as students participate in extensive field trips to see firsthand what they are reading about and discussing. Here, for every hour a student spends poring over books in a classroom or in the library, many others are spent rafting down the Colorado River to study firsthand the geology of the Grand Canyon or perching on the side of a mountain in a rock-climbing course. Further afield, they can study wetlands ecology at a facility in Kino Bay, Mexico. At Prescott, students learn by doing, and for a price in 2005–2006 of $19,400 a year students do—and learn—a lot.

Student body: Among students interested in an unusually outdoor, largely self-designed education, the word is out about Prescott, way beyond the bounds of the Southwest. Just a third of the students are from Arizona. The largest portion of the nonresidents come from far, far east of the Grand Canyon, in the northeastern United States. Altogether, in a recent year, students represented 43 states and 3 foreign countries. Three percent of the undergraduates are Native Americans, 5.5% Hispanics, and 1% each are African-Americans and Asian-Americans. Only 1 undergraduate in the 2005–2006 school year was a foreign national. The ethnicity of 9% was unknown or not reported. The average age of undergraduates is 28; 49% are 25 or older, and many of the younger students sport "dreads, multiple piercings, and dogs," says an older senior. Students who seek out Prescott's approach to learning are more like undergraduates of the sixties than the 21st century with an open-mindedness toward new ideas and a strong sense of social responsibility. For them, being environmentally aware means much more than putting aluminum, glass, and newspaper in their proper recycling bins. Their commitment can call for more aggressive actions, such as lobbying through writing editorials or picketing to protest an issue, such as ranchers killing coyotes. "Everyone here is very enthusiastic about what he or she is doing, no matter how serious or unusual it may be," notes a junior. As individualistic and self-directed as students are, however, there is a definite spirit of cooperation on campus, with students serving as equal voting members along with faculty and staff at committee meetings.

Academics: Prescott College was established in 1966 but in late 1974 declared bankruptcy, losing its original 600-acre campus, its accreditation, and all but 50 of its students. Rather than close a school they believed in, a dedicated team of faculty members and administrators fought back, taking dramatic pay cuts and teaching as best they could without a campus. Today, Prescott has regained its accreditation and more than doubled enrollment in its resident degree program in just the last few years, and has been looking to acquire land to build an ecologically sound campus. Throughout the struggle, though, Prescott's commitment to experiential learning with an environmental emphasis has remained the same. Along with recently added master's degrees and a doctorate in education, Prescott awards the bachelor's degree in 4 interdisciplinary areas, environmental studies, adventure education, integrative studies, and arts and letters, as well as in education and independent studies. Each of the 4 broad areas has several fields of concentration around which students may design their own programs of study.

The academic year is divided into a one-month block followed by a 3-month quarter, which together equals a traditional semester in length. The block periods allow for in-depth study of a single subject. Students generally take 3 classes or 2 classes and an independent study during each quarter. Average class size for undergraduates is 10, with the range rarely above 13 or below 6. In fact, if any teacher or student wants to put more than 12 students in a course, the class can vote on whether to admit the additional members.

Students need to demonstrate college-level competency in only 2 areas besides their major: writing and mathematics. Each new student also must attend a 3-week wilderness orientation program in which they backpack to an area such as the Grand Canyon or southwestern mountains and canyons to learn more about the school and themselves. A Prescott education is built on individual initiative. Faculty and student-written evaluations replace grades, unless a student requests them. All students design their own curricula by writing contracts with faculty. Third-year students develop their own graduation program, which must, however, be approved by a review committee. Students keep a portfolio for each class, which contains class notes, syntheses of assigned readings, and a field journal if there are trips, as well as a daily or weekly record of personal thoughts and feelings about the course. The portfolio may take the place of tests and exams though exams may be required in some courses. While students do spend time in the classroom, they also spend a lot of time out of it in internships, independent study projects, and other off-campus activities.

The faculty of 87 has 50 full-time members and is 39% female. Professors are respected as both passionate and creative scholars and friends who came to be part of a community. Notes a senior from the East: "The faculty are here to learn, as well as teach. They believe in the mission of the college, which is to create self-motivated, independent, and creative adults." Students' chief complaint is that sometimes excellent faculty members leave because of low salaries and limited financial support for facilities.

Of the 4 interdisciplinary programs offered, students rate adventure education at the top, largely because of its highly experienced and involved faculty. The program focuses on leadership training, experiential education, rock climbing, ski touring, backpacking, mountaineering, whitewater and sea kayaking, rafting, and mountain search and rescue and is extremely selective. New students often are unable to enroll in adventure education courses in their first year. Environmental studies also is superb, with faculty drawing on their own diverse experiences as well as providing students with plenty of field trips and internships with the National Park Service and other institutions. The human development program within integrative studies and the fine arts focus within arts and letters also are considered first-rate.

Students and administrators agree on the common weak point: the lack of lab facilities, which prohibits work in the hard sciences or other technical areas.

Facilities: The new Crossroads Center, which opened in 2005, offers a more integrated approach to the library, combining traditional library features with other technological and social functions. The 22,000-square-foot facility was designed to serve as both a teaching and community center. It includes the new library, dubbed an "information commons," classrooms, meeting rooms, and various technological/multimedia offices as well as a café and outdoor amphitheater and designated "quiet" spaces and social spaces. Actual holdings of the new center and existing library are limited, almost 23,300 volumes and 262 periodicals. A Cat computerized system helps search for books, an interlibrary loan program acquires them through the major libraries of Arizona and the rest of the United States, and a much-adored librarian/"miracle worker," as an arts and letters major put it, will "find anything you desire, given enough time." Various CD-ROM disks, online services, and the Internet also assist in the search.

Computers contained in the new Crossroads Center join the more than 55 PC and Macintosh computers already available to students across campus. Thirty units housed in the college computer lab are accessible 7 days a week, with extended hours at the end of each block and quarter.

Special programs: Prescott offers a student and faculty exchange with the School of Social Work at Bremen College, Germany. Participants can also make use of Bremen's links to other European colleges in the Netherlands, Sweden, Poland, and Latvia. For closer retreats, in cooperation with the Tonto National Forest, Prescott maintains for student and faculty study a small cabin and parcel of land in the mountainous desert region northeast of Phoenix. The college also owns property at Kino Bay, Mexico, which gives students an opportunity to study coastal and marine environments as well as different cultural perspectives. Students interested in education can observe and work as volunteers in the Skyview School, a nontraditional public K-8 school based upon Howard Gardner's Theory of Multiple Intelligences. An Eco League consortium of 6 environmentally like-minded colleges enables Prescott students to spend up to 2 nonsequential semesters at one of the other 5 campuses that range from Alaska Pacific University to the College of the Atlantic in Maine.

Campus life: No college housing is available, and students are on their own to find accommodations. There is a wide range in what students pay for lodging, with an estimated cost of $6200 for room and board over the 8-month academic year. Prescott has no fraternities or sororities and offers no intercollegiate sports; but student-generated soccer, basketball, volleyball, and softball games are popular, and their teams make regular appearances in the Prescott municipal leagues. Ultimate Frisbee also has many followers.

Weekends are rarely dull for Prescott students, since many courses have Saturday-Sunday field trips and most students are content to go skiing, climbing, biking, kayaking, or backpacking on their own. "Because we are surrounded by national forests," observes a sophomore, "it is (also) not uncommon to find a Prescott student sitting alone, reading a book in the back reaches of one of these forests." The student body is so small that "any party is almost anybody's party," says a junior, and students frequently stumble upon impromptu jamming/dancing sessions around town. Potlucks, drum circles, and poetry readings also are popular. Crime is minimal, other than incidents of people who are not students stealing mountain bikes left unlocked around campus.

It is the rare Prescott student who heads south to Phoenix, the nearest big city, to escape. Instead, students head to Joshua Tree or the Grand Canyon, just a 3-hour drive from Prescott, a town of 34,000, which *Arizona Highways* magazine has called "everybody's hometown."

Cost cutters: Fifty-six percent of the freshmen in the 2005–2006 school year received financial aid, all of that need-based. No data is available for continuing students. The average first-year award consisted of a $4627 need-based scholarship or grant and an average of $3347 in need-based self-help aid such as loans and jobs. The average financial indebtedness of a 2005 graduate totaled $18,235. Several scholarships also are available to students and are awarded based upon their academic performance, financial need, and sometimes their intended area of study. An extensive internship program includes some paid positions.

Rate of return: Sixty-eight percent of first-year students return for a second year. Twenty-three percent graduate in 4 years, 41% in 5 years, 46% within 6. Many students take time off to travel or pursue independent projects, interim activities that administrators encourage. Forty percent of recent graduates earned bachelor's degrees in environmental studies, 30% in integrative studies, and 23% in arts and letters.

Payoff: Approximately 60% of those who graduate begin work shortly after commencement, in teaching, counseling, or human services or with various outdoor-oriented organizations throughout the United States, among them the Forest Service, departments of Fish and Game, the National Park Service, and programs like Outward Bound. About half eventually go on to graduate or professional school.

Bottom line: Prescott offers the self-motivated student a chance to design his or her own curriculum, participate in the democratic workings of a college making a comeback, and spend as much time learning from the magnificent country of the Southwest as from books and lectures. "Although," cautions a third-year student, "I think it is to a student's advantage to have a lot of life experience before coming because of the nature of the school. Most students here do."

The University of Arizona

Tucson, Arizona 85721

Setting: Urban
Control: Public
Undergraduate enrollment: 11,490 men, 13,105 women
Graduate enrollment: 2933 men, 2969 women
Student/faculty ratio: 19:1
Freshman profile: 6% scored over 699 on SAT I verbal; 26% scored 600–699; 43% 500–599; 25% below 500. 7% scored over 699 on SAT I math; 29% scored 600–699; 42% 500–599; 22% below 500. 9% scored above 29 on the ACT; 42% scored 24–29; 42% 18–23; 7% below 18. 36% graduated in top tenth of high school class; 62% in upper fourth.

Faculty profile: 99% Ph.D.'s
Tuition and fees: $4498 in-state; $13,682 out-of-state
Room and board: $7460
Freshman financial aid: 35%; average scholarship or grant: $5488 need-based; $5021 non-need-based
Campus jobs: NA; average earnings: NA
Application deadline: Apr. 1
Financial aid deadline: Mar. 1
Admissions information: (520) 621-3237
e-mail: appinfo@arizona.edu
web site: www.arizona.edu

Stargazers don't have to be told about The University of Arizona at Tucson. On campus, the university boasts the highly respected Steward Observatory and Flandrau Planetarium with additional observatories on Mt. Bigelow to the north and Mt. Hopkins to the south, the famed Kitt Peak National Observatory to the west, and to the east on Mt. Graham, the world's most powerful optical telescope scheduled to become fully operational in fall 2006. Such a concentration of telescopic power pointed skyward easily makes Tucson the astronomy capital of the world, a fact that doesn't always dazzle the average college student. Instead, he or she is taken with a more earthly delight: the low in-state and out-of-state tuition for an education that in many areas rates a gold star.

Student body: "At UA, there is every kind of student for every kind of person," observes a Phoenix resident. About 30 percent of the undergraduates represent racial and ethnic minorities, or are foreign nationals, with in a recent year, 15% Hispanic students, 6% Asian-Americans, 3.5% foreign nationals, 3% African-Americans, and 2% Native Americans. (One wing of a residence hall is reserved for Native American students.) While two-thirds of the students call Arizona home, with a third of the rest generally from the West, that doesn't stop UA from boasting that it draws students from more different countries and territories (135) than any other university in the United States. With a student body so large and diverse, no single adjective describes any consistent majority. For every student who is politically involved, there is one who is apathetic. "Some care a lot about grades," notes a junior, "others about their parties on Friday nights." However, some broad outlines do emerge. Ninety percent attended public high schools. Academically, the university ranks on the whole as pretty average, with a fairly laid-back academic climate and highly social student body. But UA has its share of serious and superior students and not just in the sciences and technical fields. Over the past few years, UA honors students have been selected as prestigious Rhodes Scholars.

Academics: The University of Arizona, which was founded in 1885, awards degrees through the doctorate with 123 undergraduate majors offered in 13 schools and colleges. The academic year is divided into 2 semesters. Average class size for undergraduates can be as low as 20, although a popular course like Greek Mythology may enroll more than 500 students. However, large lectures such as this break into discussion sections of 18–22 students. Of the nearly 3250 class sections offered in a recent fall, about 230 had 100 or more students; more than a third of the classes, 1121, had 20 to 29 participants. Another 990 had fewer than 20. The smallest higher level courses usually enroll as few as 8, but tell that to some first-year students. "I dislike the 600+-person classroom," says a freshman prepharmacy major. "You feel like just a number and that they're trying to weed you out."

All students must fulfill general-education requirements that include courses in the traditional disciplines and that are common to all colleges. Only the level of math required depends upon the student's major and preparation prior to admission. A new home base for freshmen, the Integrated Learning Center, opened in spring 2002 *under* the university mall. The $20 million underground structure contains general education classrooms, lecture halls, and offices for advisors, tutors, and faculty as well as a light-filled atrium at its center to make it a cheery gathering place for first-year students. As additional help to newcomers, a Courses in Common program enables interested freshmen to take 3 general education courses as a cluster with the same group of 20 other first-year students.

The university is home to 1363 full-time instructional faculty members and 53 part-timers. No figure is available on the number who teach undergraduates; 31% of the faculty are women. One professor has won a Nobel Prize; two have been awarded a Pulitzer Prize. Faculty research is extensive and can make some professors less accessible than students would like. In fact, 42% of the introductory courses, and even some upper-level classes, students claim, have been taught by teaching assistants whose quality is mixed; some are great, others are very difficult to understand because of either a heavy foreign accent or ineffectual teaching style. But again, there are also professors who enjoy classroom teaching, many themselves graduates of the university who "understand and have insight into being a UA student," observes a freshman. A few professors have even been known to hold office hours on the veranda of a building to encourage students to stop by. Says a senior: "The teachers that actually want to *teach* are great. The problem is the teachers who care more about their research."

The space sciences, which include astronomy, lunar and planetary sciences, and aerospace engineering, have been Arizona's stars. The optical sciences program is 1 of 6 in the country, with superb faculty, state-of-the-art equipment, and a new library. Not far behind in the rankings are engineering, the physical sciences, and management information systems with its work in electronic decision making. The English department, in particular creative writing, earns accolades for its determination to ensure that even in the required, lower level courses every student is challenged to his or her full potential. Philosophy, anthropology, sociology, nursing, and architecture also rate an "A".

The social science and business programs, which have the largest enrollments on campus, incur student criticism mainly because of their size. The well-funded Eller College of Business and Public Administration tackles its high numbers with a "fantastic" advising program and excellent high-tech equipment. Students complain that the social sciences, on the other hand, tend to be underfunded and so are more apt to have larger class sizes and overworked instructors. The media arts and communication programs need better facilities and more helpful advising. Communication also lacks rigor, according to students. Programs in the College of Fine Arts also could use additional funding.

Facilities: Many of the university's undergraduates find the main library to be a frustrating place. Most of UA's collection of 4.9 million volumes, 6.0 million microforms, and nearly 27,000 current periodicals is housed in the main building. Still, says a freshman, "I have been able to actually find few of the books, articles, or journals the computer says are available." Scoffs a junior: "The library claims to have lots of books, but they are never in when you need them." The library's on-line electronic information system, named SABIO, a Spanish word meaning wise or learned one, offers access to the library's own holdings, wherever they are, as well as to local databases and Internet connections to hundreds of other library systems and thousands of databases around the world. As a study center, the library gets higher marks, growing noticeably quieter the higher one ascends among the 5 floors. In addition, UA has 6 other, more specialized libraries, including a science facility many undergraduates use.

Students have access to more than 2300 terminals located in approximately 10 labs around campus. The new Integrated Learning Center in the main library has 250 computers with high-speed Internet connections in its Information Commons. Still, says a management information systems major: "Demand far exceeds supply. Hours are extensive (18 hours daily), but lines are common." The university recommends that students in the College of Architecture have their own personal computers.

Special programs: The University of Arizona is 95% accessible to handicapped students, thanks to the vigilance and work of the Disability Resource Center. S.A.L.T., Strategic, Alternative Learning Techniques, provides exceptional support to those undergraduates with learning disabilities. Opportunities for off-campus internships, for exchanges at any of 170 U.S. college or university campuses, and for way-off study abroad are extensive.

Campus life: About 20% of UA undergraduates actually reside on the 357-acre campus, and many others cluster in apartments immediately off campus. Just 7% of the men and 11% of the women are members of the 25 national fraternities and 20 national sororities, but they exert influence far beyond their numbers. Independents, though in the majority, often feel left out of the weekend party scene. The nation's largest student-run carnival, Spring Fling, involves more than 7000 students annually. More than 280 student organizations with more than 10,000 members total are active on campus, with some of the more popular ones revolving around students' majors. Given UA's location in Tucson, a city of 800,000 people, students encounter some urban crime, which many students feel has increased in seriousness over the past couple of years. The student government runs a Safe Ride service to prevent assaults at night. Advises a Californian: "If you learn to not walk by yourself at night and be aware, you can avoid many situations."

Wildcats sports, played as part of the highly competitive NCAA Division I, are top dog at Arizona, with fall football games (and postgame parties), baseball, volleyball, and basketball among the biggest draws of the 8 men's and 10 women's varsity sports. For many fans, Arizona's basketball team *is* the university. The men's team has earned 20 consecutive NCAA tournament berths, the second longest streak in NCAA history. The team reached the Final Four in 1988, 1994, 1997, and 2001, and were champions in 1997. The women's softball team has won 6 national championships and played in the Softball College World Series for 16 consecutive seasons. Students not among the elite few percent sufficiently skilled to play intercollegiate athletics can participate in any of 27 men's and 26 women's intramural activities; 15% of the undergraduates join in. For those still not worn out, there are 36 club sports, among the most popular being rugby, volleyball, soccer, and lacrosse. An $11 million Student Recreation Center, created in response to student request, further increases the numbers.

Students in need of a weekend getaway usually "road trip" to Phoenix, 2 hours away, or Nogales, Mexico, between 1 and 2 hours. Any of the nearby mountain ranges offers quick respite from the heat and pace of school and are especially popular for winter skiing. The desert and canyons are also there to explore, and it doesn't hurt, boasts a state resident, that "we have awesome weather during the winter."

Cost cutters: Thirty-five percent of the freshmen and 52% of the continuing students received some form of financial aid in a recent school year. The average need-based scholarship or grant for freshmen equaled $5488; self-help aid such as loans and job earnings averaged $2781. Other non-need-based scholarships and awards averaged $5021. The average financial indebtedness of a recent graduate was $16,012.

The Associated Students of the University of Arizona works with the Board of Regents and state legislators to help keep tuition rates affordable. The university, in turn, is trying to recruit more top scholars and give them increased financial support, thanks to one of the nation's largest private-donor scholarship programs in a public university. As part of the program, high school seniors from Arizona who graduate in the top 5% of their class are given tuition waivers. Wildcat Excellence Awards for other high-achieving state residents pay $2000 to $6000; Arizona Excellence Awards for nonresidents pay

$2000 to $10,000. The extra funding for top scholars has paid off: 58 National Merit finalists were members of a recent fall freshman class. More than 360 recent freshmen graduated in the top 1% of their high school classes.

A cooperative education program is available to students in almost all majors.

Rate of return: Seventy-nine percent of entering freshmen return for the sophomore year; 31% earn bachelor's degrees in 4 years, 52% in 5 years, 57% in 6. A Finish in Four! plan outlines prescribed steps students can take to complete their degree requirements in 4 years.

Payoff: Fifteen percent of recent graduates earned bachelor's degrees in business and marketing. Eleven percent received degrees in history and the social sciences; another 10% earned degrees in communications and communication technologies. In recent years, just over a third of the graduates have gone on to pursue advanced degrees in graduate or professional school shortly after commencement. About 250 companies and organizations recruit on campus.

Bottom line: For some students, the University of Arizona is "what any state university would aspire to be: culturally diverse, socially open, athletically competitive, and academically reputable." For others, it is "good for big parties, but bad for big classes." At a university so large and diverse, it is up to the individual student to decide which niche works best.

Arkansas

Hendrix College

Conway, Arkansas 72032

Setting: Suburban
Control: Private (United Methodist)
Undergraduate enrollment: 441 men, 560 women
Graduate enrollment: 5 men, 3 women
Student/faculty ratio: 12:1
Freshman profile: 25% scored over 700 on SAT I verbal; 48% scored 600–700; 20% 500–599; 7% below 500. 14% scored over 700 on SAT I math; 45% scored 600–700; 33% 500–599; 8% below 500. 43% scored above 28 on the ACT; 17% scored 27–28; 28% 24–26; 10% 21–23; 2% below 21. 27% graduated in top tenth of high school class; 61% in upper fifth.

Faculty profile: 100% Ph.D.'s
Tuition and fees: $21,636
Room and board: $6010
Freshman financial aid: 97%; average scholarship or grant: $2527 need-based; $12,129 non-need-based
Campus jobs: 47%; average earnings: $1086/year
Application deadline: Rolling
Financial aid deadline: Feb. 15
Application information: (501) 450-1362; (800) 277-9017
e-mail: adm@hendrix.edu
web site: www.hendrix.edu

College mottoes are usually arcane sayings, scrolled in an ancient tongue, that look impressive on the college seal but carry little meaning. This is not so at Hendrix College in Conway, Arkansas, where its motto, "Unto the Whole Person," has become a watchword for providing balance in an otherwise hectic and demanding academic life. Hendrix's rigorous academics keep the intensity level high for bright freshmen who enter this college of 1001 undergraduates. Nutritional labeling in its dining hall encourages students to eat right and an expanded extracurricular fitness program helps them to become more physically active. "The potential opportunities for leadership and involvement abound," adds a senior, "and interaction with those around you is encouraged. It is as if the whole of campus life is designed around the liberal arts ideal of creating a whole, well-rounded person." Greek aside, some students think Hendrix's motto should be: "Work hard together, play hard together"—and do it for a whole lot less than at other highly competitive liberal arts colleges: about $27,600 in total costs for the 2005–2006 school year. Notes a satisfied sophomore: "When compared with other colleges nationally, Hendrix truly is a great value for the education you receive."

Student body: Hendrix students are not bashful when it comes to describing themselves. Notes a senior: "The student body is the 'cream of the crop,' Arkansas's best high school students." In fact, Hendrix, which received a chapter of the Phi Beta Kappa honor society in 1998, remains a well-kept secret known mainly to high achievers within the state: 55% are from Arkansas. Students presently come from 34 states and 4 foreign countries with a fifth of the out-of-staters coming from the Southwest. Nineteen percent of the enrollment is Methodist. Expanding racial and ethnic diversity is a constant priority, with 4% African-American, 3% Hispanic, 3% Asian-American, and 1% Native American. Fourteen students are foreign nationals. Students welcome the addition of people of all types to what some call "the hippie utopia of the Bible Belt." Observes an Arkansas resident: "Hendrix College students put the liberal in liberal arts." Adds another: "Diversity is celebrated here, whether it be political, religious, racial, or ethnic. . . . (And) while we are extremely competitive when it comes to class, we're a lot of fun when it's time to enjoy things." Some students even question whether "competitive" is the best word to describe the academic atmosphere. "Vigorous," and "motivating" is how one undergraduate describes it. Adds a freshman, "No one competes for the top grade; everyone works at it together."

Academics: Hendrix, founded in 1876, awards bachelor's degrees in 29 majors and a masters degree in accounting. The academic year follows a semester calendar. Average class size is 16 students, though a few popular classes each year, such as Organic Chemistry I, can rise to 65. Most freshman courses run closer to 30.

All first-year students begin their academic journey at Hendrix with 2 common courses, Journeys and Explorations: Liberal Arts for Life, which explore, using professors from many different departments, how different cultures and peoples have made sense of their own life journeys and how Hendrix students may successfully make the transition into college life. Students move on to a class, Challenges in the Contemporary World, that examines issues concerning the environment, economy, and social justice, to name a few. Also required are 7 additional courses in traditional academic disciplines. Freshmen entering in fall 2005 were the first students asked to complete an approved experience from at least 3 of 6 categories: artistic creativity, global awareness, professional and leadership development, service to the world, undergraduate research, and special projects. The Odyssey program, raves 1 student, is "a great opportunity to step outside of the academic bubble and become involved in real-world experiences."

The faculty numbers 107 members, all but 22 full-time. Sixty percent are men. Having dinner or playing cards at the home of a professor is nothing unusual at Hendrix; most students consider at least 1 or 2 faculty members to be close friends to whom they can turn for help with both academic and personal problems. Most professors enjoy the role and are more than willing to share their expertise in all areas. One student, who was reading *Henry V* in French, was overjoyed to have a professor she had never met come by and help translate a passage; as it turned out, the faculty member taught math!

It is a combination of brilliant and caring faculty, excellent facilities, and well-designed curricula that makes Hendrix's strongest departments as good as they are. Humanities majors join science majors in praising the school's biology and chemistry departments. Construction of a 30,000-square-foot addition to what was known as Reynolds Hall, home of the physical sciences, only enhanced a structure originally built on a foundation of advanced thinking. The original hall, built in 1931, came about when the voters of Arkansas outlawed the teaching of evolution in the state's public colleges and universities. In response, the then-president of Hendrix, John Hugh Reynolds, appealed for construction of a building in the state where science could be taught as science. The science program now enjoys a new facility for biology and psychology and new state-of-the-art labs for chemistry, computer science, mathematics, and physics. In 2003, a chemistry professor was named Outstanding Baccalaureate College Professor of the Year by two national education organizations.

In turn, science students rave about the faculty in the English department, who teach a rich variety of courses in British and American literature (with a strong component on southern writers) and encourage creative thinking and strong writing from their students. The business faculty is equally demanding and provides a curriculum geared toward preparing students for work as certified public accountants or for a master's program in business administration. The prelaw curriculum, centered around courses in history and political science, is also excellent, as are the programs in psychology, math, and physics. In history, students especially like the close look given to the social context of a time period as well as the actual events. Religion is admired for its 4 faculty members who all "excel at their special fields but complement each other wonderfully," says an interdisciplinary studies major.

The kinesiology program lacks the rigor some students desire and prepares majors better for coaching than for such fields as physical therapy. Computer science could use more courses for non-majors. Theater arts and the foreign language program, with majors in French, German, and Spanish, need a greater diversity of courses.

Facilities: Bailey Library, once an underground structure known for being "cold, dim, and intimidating," was transformed Cinderella-like in 1994 into an attractive 65,000-square-foot structure with room for 300,000 volumes and the latest in computerized research assistance. "It's the study and social center of campus," observes a junior. "If you need to find someone during the week, it's your best place to look." A special area with 18 study carrels is open around the clock. Current holdings exceed 218,000 volumes, with subscriptions to 9178 paper and electronic periodicals. Students still in need of a change of scene may opt to study in the comfortable surroundings of the Mills Social Science Center, named for former U.S. Congressman Wilbur D. Mills, a Hendrix graduate and one-time trustee. For additional sources, many head to the University of Central Arkansas across town, also accessible by computer.

The many students who bring their own laptops to campus enjoy wireless Internet access in the library and the student center as well as around several popular outdoor study spots. All students find the 39 PCs and Macs in the 24-hour lab attached to the library useful, especially those "who wait until the last minute to start writing that 20-page lab report," says an accounting major. Eighteen additional units are spread between 2 smaller labs.

Special programs: As part of a Hendrix-in-Oxford program, students can spend their junior or senior year studying with tutors at Oxford University in England. Hendrix-in-London allows students to spend spring semester at the University of London's Birkbeck College. An exchange at Karl-Franzens University in Graz, Austria, also is offered. Other exchange programs are available with more than 100 additional foreign universities on 6 continents through the International Student Exchange Program. Students wishing to specialize in engineering can participate in a 3-2 program with Columbia University in New York City, Washington University in St. Louis, or Vanderbilt University in Nashville and earn degrees from both that institution and Hendrix. Students can also spend a semester at American University in Washington, D.C.

Campus life: Eighty-five percent of Hendrix students live on the 38-acre main campus, which comes alive in the spring with flowering shrubs and other seasonal flowers. An additional 120-acre area containing most of the college's recreational facilities is located on the other side of U.S. Highway 64-65B, accessible via a pedestrian overpass. The bridge connects students with much of their stress-reduction program: the Mabee indoor activity center, which provides courts for all sports, an all-weather track, 5 outdoor tennis courts, and intramural playing fields. Although the school is located in a "dry" county with no local bars and has no fraternities, sororities, or football team, the college's social committee works doubletime sponsoring weekend movies, dances, comedians, coffeehouses, and concerts to keep students on campus. The residence halls also take turns hosting open events, and few bemoan the absence of a Greek system. Volunteer Action Center, which organizes community service in the area, is one of the most active student groups, along with the Multicultural Development Committee and the Young Democrats. Although the school maintains its ties to the Methodist church for historic and economic reasons, the relationship is nearly invisible around campus. "You'd never know Hendrix was Methodist unless you read the handbook," scoffs a recent graduate. Campus crime is limited, though keycard locks were added to every residence hall following the theft of several laptop computers.

Hendrix students are active in sports, with half of the men and the women involved in 20 intramural sports. Students find Hendrix basketball "a blast," thanks to enthusiastic fan support, with soccer and baseball also drawing a loyal following. Altogether, the college fields 8 varsity sports for men and 9 for women, all in NCAA Division III. Those who thrive on fresh air appreciate the Outdoor Activities and Recreation (OAR) organization, which makes the best of the college's location in the midst of the Ozarks, sponsoring backpacking, rock climbing and rappelling, windsurfing, trapshooting, and other leisure sports.

In the eyes of students, Conway (population 45,000) offers nothing but a dozen or so theaters and 1 putt-putt golf course. Those who desire more drive to the state capital, Little Rock, which is only 25 minutes away, and wet, or to the clubs on Beale Street in Memphis, Tennessee, 3 hours away.

Cost cutters: Tuition at Hendrix is low by national standards for selective colleges, thanks in part to a healthy endowment, about $149 million as of June 2005, church support, and the school's Arkansas setting. But while the price to attend Hendrix may seem reasonable to students in the rest of the country, "to us in Arkansas, Hendrix is anything but affordable," notes a state resident. About 96% of all freshmen and continuing students received financial aid in the 2005–2006 school year; for about 55% of both groups, aid was need-based. Need-based scholarships or grants for freshmen in fall 2005 averaged $2527; the average for need-based self-help aid, such as loans and jobs, was $3578. Other awards and scholarships for freshmen that were not need-based averaged $12,129. Academic Scholarships based on achievement generally range from $2000 to full tuition, fees, room and board, and are renewable for 4 years contingent upon satisfactory academic progress. To be considered, students should have a minimum 3.0 GPA and a score of at least 25 on the ACT or 1140 on the math and critical reading portions of the SAT. Almost 200 awards of varying amounts were awarded to freshmen in a recent year. Hays Memorial Scholarships, awarded to 4 entering students with a GPA of at least 3.6, 32 ACT, or 1410 SAT, cover tuition, room, board, and mandatory fees. Fifteen Leadership Scholars receive $1000 to $3500 annually. Alternative payment plans also are an option. The average debt of a 2005 graduate was $16,121.

Rate of return: Eighty-one percent of the freshmen return for the sophomore year. Fifty-five percent graduate in 4 years; 58% in 5 years; 61% in 6.

Payoff: In the 2005 graduating class, 16% earned degrees in psychology, 14% in biology, and 11% in history. Sixty percent generally go on within 2 years to professional or graduate school. Students seeking employment find jobs with many of the major accounting firms, which recruit heavily at Hendrix, as well as with large Arkansas companies such as Acxiom, Murphy Oil, Arkansas Freight Ways, and Tyson Foods. A number also take positions in the public school systems and hospitals throughout the region. More than 50 companies and other organizations recruited on campus in the 2004–2005 school year.

Bottom line: Hendrix is a college where everyone's voice can be heard. Notes an English major: "A hardworking student who is open-minded and enjoys diversity of opinion will benefit from and enjoy Hendrix the most. Professors here force you to question, but not necessarily to change, the traditional views of life."

Lyon College

Batesville, Arkansas 72503

Setting: Small town
Control: Private (Presbyterian)
Undergraduate enrollment: 229 men, 229 women
Graduate enrollment: None
Student/faculty ratio: 10:1
Freshman profile: 30% scored over 700 on SAT I verbal; 20% scored 600–700; 25% 500–599; 25% below 500; 0% scored over 700 on SAT I math; 45% scored 600–700; 40% 500–599; 15% below 500. 21% scored above 28 on the ACT; 17% scored 27–28; 34% 24–26; 24% 21–23; 5% below 21. 29% graduated in top tenth of high school class; 46% in upper fifth.

Faculty profile: 91% Ph.D.'s
Tuition and fees: $13,905
Room and board: $6085
Freshman financial aid: 100%; average scholarship or grant: $10,531 need-based; $11,096 non-need-based
Campus jobs: 14%; average earnings: $1625/year
Application deadline: Rolling
Financial aid deadline: Mar. 1
Admissions information: (870) 698-4250; (800) 423-2542
e-mail: admissions@lyon.edu
web site: www.lyon.edu

For most students enrolled in a 4-year college, the incentive to finish is a bachelor's degree and then a satisfying job or admission to graduate school. At Lyon College, formerly Arkansas College, renamed in 1994 to honor a long-serving chairman of the Board of Trustees, the ordinary incentive has been made a little sweeter. Thanks to a specially endowed Nichols Fellowship, students who have obtained junior status and are enrolled in good academic standing can spend about 2 weeks abroad in a study-travel course subsidized by the college. The travel typically takes place in the summer following the junior year after students have taken prerequisite courses the previous spring or beforehand. In the spring of 2006, qualified students could pick among 5 tantalizing courses each bearing just a $550–$650 fee. The experiences ranged from studying Dutch and Flemish art and architecture in Amsterdam and Brussels to exploring the language and culture of Japan through travels in Kyoto and Tokyo. Just over half, 53%, of the freshmen who start at Lyon go on to graduate in 4 years; 65% do so in 5 years. As a small campus in a small town in a dry county, Lyon often loses students to the larger and less expensive state universities. Administrators hope that bringing the world a bit closer to Batesville, at minimal additional charge, will keep more students there for the duration.

Student body: Eighty percent of all students are from Arkansas, with a total of 22 states and 14 foreign countries represented. The student body is 87% white Americans and 4% foreign nationals, with 5% African-Americans, 2% Hispanics and 1% each Native Americans and Asian-Americans. Although Lyon College has ties to the Presbyterian Church, only a small percentage are Presbyterian. The once largely conservative body has become more liberal in its thinking, though most members seem detached from current events. The majority were leaders in various activities in high school, and most see themselves as energetic members of a multi-talented and close-knit family. However, that closeness usually means that very little of a personal nature is private for long. Many are also driven to excel academically. Says a junior: "We strive for success while being able to keep an active social sense. One minute you can be playing intramural football, the next, discussing Aristotle while listening to bagpipes play in the background. Yes, that is Lyon College."

Academics: Lyon, which was founded in 1872, offers bachelor's degrees in about 2 dozen majors and combinations of professional concentrations and majors; students who wish also can design their own concentrations. The school year is divided into 2 semesters. Average class size is 12. Most lower-division classes hover around 25, although the core course Western Civilization can surpass 100. Along with fairly standard distribution requirements, all freshmen must take a 1-semester orientation course and sophomores must complete a 2-semester course sequence on the intellectual themes and important historical events of the Western tradition. Students also must demonstrate competency in English composition, college algebra, and a foreign language, and take 1 semester of physical education in each of their 4 years.

Forty-four of the 59 faculty members teach full-time; 23% of the total are women. Students find the close relationships with professors to be among the college's chief strengths. Says a sophomore: "The professors have a true 'open-door policy,' which allows you to get to know them as people, not just possessors of knowledge." By the same token, faculty members want to know more about students' personal lives to understand better what is affecting their academic performance. Many professors take roll or give daily reading quizzes and will call students who miss class without having notified them beforehand. Says a psychology major: "They motivate you to take risks that you normally would not have thought possible." In 12 of the past 17 years, Lyon faculty members have been named Arkansas Professor of the Year by the Council for the Advancement and Support of Education and the Carnegie Foundation for the Advancement of Teaching.

The sciences are among Lyon's best programs, strengthened by a directed research program that offers students hands-on experience as well as a chance to be published. One result of this intense preparation is that more than 90% of the students who apply to medical school or graduate programs in the sciences are accepted. Completion in 2003 of the 55,000-square-foot Church Derby Center for Mathematics and the Sciences has provided additional research and instructional labs to further expand learning opportunities for students. The humanities division, including programs in English, political science, history, and religion and philosophy, likewise draws applause for its range of course offerings, strong, diverse faculty, and emphasis on good writing. As one senior sums it up: "The reason political science, history, English, biology, and chemistry are all so good is, simply put, the faculty. They are excellent at relating to students, conveying complex information, and motivating students to do their best work." The much-acclaimed theater major can take a bow as well.

Spanish is the sole language major available; French is offered as a minor only. Says a junior: "We need more languages." Students have found some of the faculty in the business and economics division less engaged than their peers in other disciplines.

Facilities: Mabee-Simpson Library is an effective and pleasant study center, with comfortable furniture and plenty of private study rooms where students can "get away and get work done," says a political science major. Many also like recent additions to the collection that have raised the library's holdings past 199,000 volumes and 23,500 paper and electronic periodicals. "For a campus of this size," raves a sophomore, "the library far exceeds all possible expectations." Online research options and interlibrary loan help reduce the road trips students must make for extensive research projects. "The motto around the library," says a psychology major, "is: 'If we don't have it, we can get it for you.'"

More than 50 computers dedicated to student use are located in classrooms, residence hall lounges, the Union, the library, the new science building and other places. Access to the Internet is available from any residence-hall room as well as from numerous wired and wireless access points across campus. Most labs are open until midnight weekdays and longer during midterms and finals although many hard-working Lyon students wish the labs were open more hours. Says an English major, "There always is a computer available except for the middle of the night. If you call security, they will let you in, but it takes forever for them to get there."

Special programs: Traditional study-abroad programs are offered in addition to the Nichols Travel Fellowship courses. Lyon has exchange agreements with 2 universities in Northern Ireland and 1 in France, although study in other countries for a semester or year is possible. Joint engineering programs are available with the universities of Missouri at Rolla and Arkansas at Fayetteville.

Campus life: Seventy-six percent of the students live on the 136-acre campus in the foothills of the Ozark Mountains where campus crime is rare and the much respected student honor system keeps it even rarer. About a fourth, largely freshmen, leave for home on any given weekend. The Greeks and the Student Activities Council provide a wealth of weekend options and students soon learn to make their own fun. Says a junior: "Late night pranks, playing in the fountain, camping in the woods behind campus—I'll remember these long after any dance." The percentage of students pledging to 3 national fraternities and 2 national sororities has dropped over the past couple of years and now involves just 10% of the men and 13% of the women. The independent students find themselves welcome at most Greek functions as well as at the head of other campus organizations. Says an independent: "I'm dating the president of a sorority and I've been elected to offices and been appointed to positions all without Greek letters." Student involvement has been aided further by the Spragins House program, which since 1997 has grouped freshmen together in a cluster of residence halls that is overseen by a faculty member who lives in an adjacent campus residence. The house also encompasses extensive academic and cocurricular programming, which helps new students to get involved more immediately in campus life.

Basketball, baseball, and soccer games draw the best crowds of the 6 intercollegiate sports for men and 6 for women, played in NAIA competition. Soccer became a varsity sport for men in 2002 and for women in 2003. Half of the men and a third of the women are involved in the 14 intramural sports available to each sex.

Batesville (pop. 10,000) lacks many appealing places for students to hang out, although there are a few favored establishments. "Coming from a larger town," recalls a sophomore, "the thought of no mall was frightening. But I survived and have actually grown to like Batesville." For escape, students travel to Little Rock, 90 miles south, or Memphis, Tennessee, about 110 miles east. Students go hiking or caving in the beautiful Ozarks and canoe down the Buffalo River, often as part of outings with the Extreme Adventure Squad. Every April, thousands of people come to Lyon for the Arkansas Scottish Festival, where the college's own pipers, drummers, and Highland dancers perform.

Cost cutters: Tuition and fees account for about 30% of the cost of a Lyon College education, the rest made up largely by endowment and gifts. In addition, 100% of freshmen and 99.8% of continuing students were on some form of financial aid in the 2005–2006 school year; 63% of freshmen and 70% of continuing students were on need-based help. The average freshman award for a first-year student with need included a need-based scholarship or grant averaging $10,531 and need-based self-help aid such as loans and jobs averaging $4392. Non-need-based athletic scholarships for freshmen averaged $4957; other non-need-based scholarships and grants averaged $11,096. The average financial indebtedness of a 2005 graduate was $15,956. Lyon maintains an extensive academic scholarship program for which students are eligible regardless of their financial need. Each year 4 entering freshmen receive the Brown Scholarship, which covers full tuition, room, and board. First alternates for the Brown are awarded the Anderson Scholarship paying full tuition. Lyon Fellowships pay $10,000 to up to 8 members of the freshman class with a career interest in business, industry, or public service. Scholarships recently worth up to $7500 go to students with outstanding ability in art, music, theater, or Scottish Heritage. Scholarships recently paid $2000 to students who could contribute to the socioeconomic and cultural diversity of the college community. Other merit awards pay $6000, $8000, and $10,000 a year to students with exemplary records of achievement in high school. To be considered for many of the merit awards, students must have submitted all application materials by Jan. 15. A cooperative program also is available in every major.

Rate of return: Seventy-five percent of entering freshmen return for the sophomore year. Fifty-three percent graduate in 4 years; 65% in 5 years; 68% in 6.

Payoff: Among 2005 graduates, 20% earned degrees in biology, 17% in business administration and 15% in psychology. Fourteen percent of recent classes have gone on to various graduate and professional schools. Among the schools admitting Lyon grads, besides the University of Arkansas, have been Dartmouth, Duke, Yale, and the University of California, Berkeley. Of the vast majority who seek employment after graduation, most end up working for a variety of companies, primarily in the south-central region.

Bottom line: As a campus of fewer than 500 undergraduates in a town of just 10,000, Lyon College might appear at first to be too confining. Far from it. With excellent science and other academic programs that send alumni to some of the nation's best graduate schools, and opportunities for low-cost study and travel abroad, Lyon offers students who bring an open mind and good work ethic no limit to what they can experience.

California

California Polytechnic State University

San Luis Obispo, California 93407

Setting: Small city
Control: Public
Undergraduate enrollment: 9362 men, 7229 women
Graduate enrollment: 305 men, 331 women
Student/faculty ratio: 20:1
Freshman profile: 7% scored over 699 on SAT I verbal; 37% scored 600–699; 47% 500–599; 9% below 500; 15% scored over 699 on SAT I math; 50% scored 600–699; 31% 500–599; 4% below 500. 12% scored above 29 on the ACT; 62% scored 24–29; 26% 18–23, 0% below 18. 37% graduated in top tenth of high school class; 76% in upper fourth.

Faculty profile: 72% Ph.D.'s
Tuition and fees: $4245 in-state; $12,381 out-of-state
Room and board: $8145
Freshman financial aid: 31%; average scholarship or grant: $1459 need-based
Campus jobs: NA; average earnings: NA
Application deadline: Early decision: Oct. 31; regular: Nov. 30
Financial aid deadline: Mar. 1
Admissions information: (805) 756-2311
    e-mail: admprosp@calpoly.edu
    web site: www.calpoly.edu

Cal Poly got started after a penniless West Point dropout back in 1849 couldn't earn $8 a day because he didn't know how to drive a nail. "I could have told the man I talked to a great deal I had learned from books," the former West Pointer, Myron Angel, recalled, "but nothing about building a house." The result, more than 50 years later, was California Polytechnic State University in San Luis Obispo, a school where nail driving has been raised to an art form. Cal Poly's motto is simple and direct: "Learn by doing," and that's exactly what students do from the minute they step onto this branch campus of the California State University system. To get students "doing" as quickly as possible, high school seniors apply to a particular field of study so that instruction in the major can begin the first day of classes. The student is surrounded by every possible sort of equipment to make the hands-on experience as valuable as possible: architecture majors can test the strength of beams instead of just reading about their importance; agriculture students raise livestock on the campus farm or work in the dairy manufacturing plant; education majors teach school-age clients at a campus reading clinic; and accounting majors help to audit books.

Student body: Ninety-four percent of Cal Poly's undergraduates are from California with the rest in a recent year representing all but 2 states and 41 foreign countries. Hispanic and Asian-American students constitute the largest minority groups at 10% and 11% respectively, followed by African-Americans and Native Americans at about 1% each. Another 1% are foreign nationals. Ninety-one percent in a recent year were graduates of public high schools. Many undergraduates hold conservative political views, when they bother with politics at all. Students are very career-oriented, and the fast pace of the quarter system keeps the stress level fairly high as they work hard to keep up with assignments. Still, concludes a California senior: "The typical student takes his or her days in stride and remains down-to-earth and casual."

Academics: Cal Poly, founded in 1901, awards the bachelor's degree in 66 undergraduate majors plus the master's degree in 23 fields. The university is divided into 7 colleges. Most students take 3 quarters in a standard academic year, usually totaling 36 credits. Graduation credits vary by program requiring anywhere from 186 to 263 quarter units for a bachelor's degree. Many find themselves in courses with fewer than 30 classmates. In the first year, large lectures in such subjects as psychology can attract nearly 500. However, the required senior project enables each student to work closely with a faculty advisor.

The general education program required of all undergraduates draws courses from the areas of communication, science and mathematics, arts and humanities, society and the individual, and a technology elective. Students also must complete 24 units of interdisciplinary writing intensive courses.

Of the 1246 faculty members, 726 are full-time and all teach undergraduates. A third of the total pool are women. As a rule, no teaching assistants are used as instructors. For the most part, faculty win high marks for being knowledgeable as well as willing to help students outside the classroom.

According to students, engineering, agriculture, and architecture best exemplify the success of Cal Poly's "Learn by doing" philosophy. State-of-the-art lab facilities in the College of Engineering make possible imaginative student projects such as construction of a human-powered helicopter and solar car. To prepare tomorrow's agricultural specialists, the College of Agriculture offers work both inside in a new dairy science building and outside on a 5600-acre farm with beef and dairy cattle, horse, sheep, and swine, irrigated and nonirrigated fields for various crops, citrus groves, and complete processing units for dairy products, meat, fruit, and vegetables. Architecture students apply their knowledge in Design Village, where they compete in building 3-story structures that meet certain specifications, among them the requirement that students be able to live in their creations for the few days of the competition. One year, structures had to be built in the shape of fruits.

Although Cal Poly's College of Liberal Arts has developed slowly, students say it now offers excellent programs in journalism, political science, and the social sciences. But the school's emphasis clearly remains on more technical fields. Complains a social science major: "The liberal arts department has no building; engineering has over 5 with more under construction. There is no emphasis on liberal arts at all."

Facilities: The Robert E. Kennedy Library may appear ugly to some on the outside, but inside it generally has what students need amid its collection of 1.2 million volumes and 5400 on-line databases and other resources. The 5-story structure offers several large rooms equipped with chalkboards for group study as well as cubicles for more private preparation. Book and periodical searches are made easier with the Poly Cat computerized catalog system.

Even at a university as hands-on as Cal Poly, students complain that it is sometimes difficult to get time on a free computer. Though there are 1800 PCs and Macs located around campus, many computer labs are often reserved for classes, thus excluding other, sometimes desperate, students. On the other hand, many students benefit from the university's Computer-Aided Productivity Center, which provides support to academic programs in computer-aided drawing, design, and engineering analysis. The university strongly recommends that students have their own personal computers.

Special programs: As members of the California State University system, Cal Poly students can enroll for a full academic year at any of 34 foreign universities in 16 countries. Cal Poly's College of Liberal Arts sponsors a London study program to enrich the general-education requirements. Students in the colleges of Agriculture and Architecture and Environmental Design also may study in Australia.

Campus life: Nineteen percent of the undergraduates live on the 400-acre central campus, located south of the 5600-acre farm. Just 9% of the men and women belong to 10 national sororities and 23 national fraternities, which are known about campus for their TGIF Friday afternoon parties. The Interfraternity Council also offers an escort service from anywhere on campus to within a one-mile radius off campus, though incidents of crime are very low, students say. Students both in and out of Greek life generally spend Saturdays surfing or soaking up the sun at Pismo Beach, or hiking or biking in the open country around San Luis Obispo. The Ski Club, the Week of Welcome student-run orientation program, and professional groups such as the Society for the Advancement of Management are just a few of the 400 organizations open to undergraduates. Students average membership in 3 or more of these groups.

Football, basketball, baseball, and women's volleyball draw the biggest crowds among the 9 varsity sports for men and 10 for women, which all compete in NCAA Division I. (Football is I-AA.) A motto of "Enjoy by playing" takes hold for 14% of the students who participate in 320 teams in 14 intramural sports open to both men and women.

The start of every new year marks the day when Cal Poly students get to sit back and watch the rest of the nation admire their hard work and ingenuity. On January 1, Cal Poly students proudly show off the float which they, along with students from Cal Poly Pomona, designed, built, and decorated for the annual Tournament of Roses Parade. Though the Cal Poly float is the only one produced entirely by students, it has won awards for all but a handful of the past 50 years.

Students find San Luis Obispo's size and location particularly appealing. Its small-town environment (pop. 43,400) is not so large as to be distracting, yet the big cities of Los Angeles and San Francisco are a reachable 250 miles away for students in dire need of big-city stimulation.

Cost cutters: An estimated 31% of Cal Poly's freshmen and 35% of continuing students received financial aid in the 2004–2005 school year, the most recent year for which data was available. Virtually all of the aid was based, at least in part, on financial need. The average estimated freshman award included a $1459 need-based scholarship or grant and need-based self-help aid such as loans and jobs averaging $2731. Average debt of a 2005 graduate was $13,788. More than 1100 scholarships are awarded every year, generally to students with an overall GPA of at least 3.0. The Educational Equity Scholarship program helps defray educational costs to qualified minority and other underrepresented students. An extensive cooperative program also is available.

Rate of return: Ninety-one percent of the freshmen who enter return for the sophomore year. Twenty-one percent go on to graduate in 4 years, 56% in 5 years, 69% in 6.

Payoff: Among 2005 graduates, 20% majored in engineering, followed by 18% in business and marketing and 14.5% in agriculture. Two-thirds put their "learning by doing" to work full-time in the job market, bolstered by offers from 630 companies that interviewed students on campus during a recent school year. Graduates generally accept professional positions in a wide range of industries, including aerospace, electrical, retail, public accounting, finance, and printing and publishing firms. The median starting salary of recent graduates was $39,000. Most settle in the West. A fourth of the recent graduates went on to graduate or professional school within 6 months of commencement.

Bottom line: Cal Poly is for the student who knows exactly what he or she wants to study from the start of the freshman year and is prepared to work hard toward that goal, using both hands and head. But at the end of that road, assures a junior engineering major, "A B.S. from Cal Poly earns respect from prospective employers."

Thomas Aquinas College
Santa Paula, California 93060

Setting: Rural
Control: Private (Roman Catholic)
Undergraduate enrollment: 176 men, 183 women
Graduate enrollment: None
Student/faculty ratio: 12:1
Freshman profile: 40% scored over 700 on SAT I verbal; 48% scored 600–700; 11% 500–599; 1% below 500. 11% scored over 700 on SAT I math; 44% scored 600–700; 42% 500–599; 3% below 500. 37.5% scored over 28 on the ACT; 12.5% scored 27–28; 37.5% 24–26; 0% 21–23; 12.5% below 21. Class rank data: NA
Faculty profile: 62% Ph.D.'s

Tuition and fees: $18,600
Room and board: $5800
Freshman financial aid: 78%; average scholarship or grant: $10,157 need-based; $776 non-need-based
Campus jobs: 58%; average earnings: $3180/year
Application deadline: Rolling
Financial aid deadline: July 1
Admissions information: (805) 525-4417 ext. 361; (800) 634-9797
e-mail: admissions@thomasaquinas.edu
web site: www.thomasaquinas.edu

If you were to ask a student at Thomas Aquinas College why he or she came to a school of 359 undergraduates in rural southern California, you'd probably hear statements like the following: "I came for the Great Books program and for the trivium and quadrivium." "I was interested in discussion, rather than lecture-based classrooms." "I want to be a math teacher and learn math from its foundations." "I wanted a Catholic college with no apologies for being one." "I wanted to gain knowledge for its own sake, without focusing on grades and an eventual career."

If the picture that emerges is of a college worlds apart from the typical American university, say welcome to the new kid on the block, Thomas Aquinas College, named for the 13th century Italian saint and patron of all Catholic education. At Thomas Aquinas, instead of reading texts about what history's most influential thinkers said or did, students read the authors' own works. Instead of sitting passively in large lecture halls, students gather around tables to discuss under the guidance of a tutor what they have read. All students follow the same curriculum, which they must begin as freshmen regardless of what course level they may have achieved at other colleges. Students freely admit they have come to Thomas Aquinas to seek the truth, not a top-paying job or entré to the nation's top graduate schools. And for them, any college that strives to lead them to the truth for less than $25,000 a year, tuition, room, and board included, is a square deal even Euclid would find perfect.

Student body: All but 7% of Thomas Aquinas's students are Catholic, with 84% graduating from private or parochial schools. Thirty-six percent are from California, with the rest residents of 40 other states and 10 foreign countries. Foreign nationals account for 8% of the student body, with 7% Hispanics, and 3% Asian-Americans. One percent are Native American less than 1% African-American. Thomas Aquinas attracts students who are sincere, wholesome, inquisitive, and very earnest about their studies. "My fellow students are refreshing in that they take education seriously," says a Californian. "There is a strong camaraderie among students, a sense of higher purpose, as well as a lot of humor. We are politically and socially conservative, but not puritanical at all." Adds a junior: "Two qualities—joyfulness and intellectual zeal—characterize the students well." Most take their faith very seriously and enjoy the orthodox nature of the school. Says a senior: "Students support one another in their desire to live morally good lives, under the guidance of their Catholic faith…Here, peer pressure helps you live well." Though grades are given, there is little competition among students; instead, says a midwesterner, "the competition is between the class and the author as we struggle to understand him." It is even "something of an embarrassment," adds a westerner, "to be known to have looked at your grades, because this might indicate less than a truly philosophical disposition towards your education."

Academics: Thomas Aquinas, founded in 1971, offers 1 degree: a bachelor of arts in liberal arts. The academic year is divided into 2 semesters. Average class size is 17; the range never extends more than 3 or 4 students higher or lower.

At Thomas Aquinas, the core is the curriculum. Students learn traditional disciplines by reading, analyzing, and discussing the Great Books. Tutorials, laboratories, and seminars of 17 students provide opportunities for daily practice of skills such as inquiry and conversation and help students to recognize how various disciplines interrelate. Says a junior: "The program is very demanding and requires a lot of study and reading and most of all participation in the often lively classroom discussions where most of the learning at the school takes place." "Good student preparation is key," says another junior. "A discussion of a text that few of the students have read well," notes the student, "will obviously be inferior to one of a text that all have read with attention." The liberal arts are broken down into 7 components: grammar, rhetoric, and logic, known as the trivium, and geometry, arithmetic, astronomy, and music, called the quadrivium, terms students actually use. Each of these disciplines is included in the required language and logic and mathematic and music tutorials that start students off in the program. What is studied in the first year provides a foundation for coursework in the later years. Students take the mathematics tutorial all 4 years plus a philosophy tutorial for 3 years and a theology tutorial and experimental-science laboratory, both also for 4 years. Every student must pass an Algebra Enabling Exam before entering the junior year and, as a senior, must complete a thesis.

Like everything else at Thomas Aquinas, the faculty, who are known as tutors, is small but growing: 29 full-time members, compared with 15 just a few years ago and 5 part-time. All but 9% of the tutors are men. Instead of teaching a particular discipline, tutors, many of whom are graduates of the college, lead discussions across the board. "The true teachers are the great works themselves," observes a southerner. "The tutors are just guides in our coming to understand what the work is trying to teach us." Some tutors are more brilliant than others in their grasp of a difficult text; some newer members who are not alumni struggle to master new texts as well as to forget old teaching habits. As tutors, both the brilliant and the less so are careful not to give answers but rather to guide students to discover them. "They have the admirable attribute of not being overly attached to their own opinions," says a senior. "All of them have a desire to come to know about reality and often this entails admitting that someone else's opinion is better than theirs." Virtually all are revered and loved by their charges. Says a senior: "They encourage, guide, and inspire us and are true role-models living out the truths they believe." There is much casual interaction between students and faculty outside the tutorials. Students often eat lunch with their tutors, get to know their families, and spend Thanksgiving and Easter with them when the students can't get home. Concludes a sophomore: "Tutors are expected to perform the same general function as Socrates, and as a whole, I would say that they do this well."

Although technically, there are no departments or course-specific professors at Thomas Aquinas, students consider instruction in philosophy and theology to be the strongest. Greatness here lies in the quality of the tutors and the Great Books being read, ranging from Plato's *Apology* and *The Holy Bible* in the freshman year to Aristotle's *Metaphysics* and St. Thomas Aquinas's *On the Passion of Christ* as seniors. Students also rate mathematics highly because of the quality of the original texts and the emphasis on understanding concepts, not just memorizing formulas. Students note, however, that the coursework generally does not extend to the more advanced levels of mathematics found at other schools because instruction begins so far back at the discipline's foundations.

Even the greatest texts, however, cannot replace the highly technical equipment necessary to study science adequately at the start of the 21st century. A new science building, St. Albert the Great Hall, named for the church's patron saint of sciences, offers 5 labs and 4 classrooms that better enable students to reproduce many of the ground-breaking experiments of modern science. Foucault's Pendulum swings across the hall's 2-story atrium, putting everyone in the proper mood. By choice, Thomas Aquinas devotes less attention to history and the social sciences.

Facilities: St. Bernadine of Siena Library, which was completed in spring 1995, is the biggest and grandest building on campus, "everything a student could ask for," says a senior. Though its collection is small compared to that at other colleges, 58,000 volumes and subscriptions to 60 periodicals, students find that the curriculum is so focused on original texts, the demand for secondary-source materials is usually limited to those required for the senior thesis, for which the collection suffices. As a study center, marvels a junior, "the library is cathedral-like in its architecture and successfully raises the mind to ponder the higher things." The centerpiece of the structure is a carved Spanish ceiling from the 17th century that at the time of its construction was the largest of its kind in Spain. Once housed in the William Randolph Hearst estate, the ceiling was a gift to the college. Computerized research assistance enables students to access additional distinctive works such as St. Thomas's *Summa Theologica* and the entire Greek lexicon. On a less scholarly note, "they have a wide classical CD section and many CD players," adds a senior, "so that you can study to the masters while studying the masters."

The college offers 2 PCs for student use in one women's dorm and one men's dorm as well as 6 student computers in the library for e-mail and word processing, 3 of which have Internet access. Units in the library are available until 10 p.m. weeknights and until 5 p.m. on weekends and lines often form at the computers with Internet access. Many students have their own computers in their dorm rooms, which keeps demand lower than it might be, as does the curriculum. Notes an easterner, "As the emphasis at the college is on the Great Books, one is more liable to see a student with his or her nose in a book than with his or her face lit up by a computer screen."

Special programs: Twice a year, students complete something called a "Don Rag," in which they sit with all of their tutors and hear each tutor's observations on their individual progress.

Campus life: Nearly all of the students, 99%, live on the 170-acre campus and reside in 6 single-sex dormitories. Crime is not a problem: "Christian charity prevails," observes a sophomore. A 5-dollar bill can remain pinned to the lost-and-found bulletin board for days waiting for someone to claim it. The only potential problem comes from hikers along a nearby national forest path cutting through campus, although the college recently erected a gate at the school's entrance to discourage trespassing. Mass (in Latin) is offered 3 times daily and Rosary and Compline are said every day, but students are not required to attend. Still, the atmosphere on campus is deeply religious. Two chapters of the Legion of Mary involve students in spreading the Catholic faith off campus. The Polyphonic Choir is also very active. Thomas Aquinas has no separate student government; instead, student representatives serve as advisors to the administration.

"The typical weekend of a student always involves reading," observes an easterner, though most undergraduates find time to unwind between perusing pages for the upcoming week's seminars and tutorials. There are neither fraternities nor sororities, and most students start the weekend on Friday afternoons by gathering to play basketball, "the second most popular religion on campus," according to a junior. Intercollegiate sports are not offered, although college Crusaders soccer and softball clubs play other teams in the area. Of the 8 men's and 7 women's intramural sports, basketball, volleyball, and tennis are popular, as is the annual Turkey Bowl, a football game that pits underclassmen against upperclassmen. The school hosts 4 dances a year, "and for the most part," says a sophomore, "the students look forward to swing dancing and waltzing at these formal dances."

The college enforces "public displays of affection" rules and prohibits students from visiting classmates of the opposite sex in their dormitories. Students caught visiting usually are dismissed. Students describe the resulting male-female relationships as "respectful" and "fun, pure and good." During the week and at formal weekend dinners, dress codes are enforced for men and women.

The college's location at the foot of Topa Topa Mountain, 65 miles northwest of Los Angeles, enables students to head off for a head-clearing hike after a particularly intense discussion. "I like hiking up on the ranch above the school and climbing a tree to read my seminar readings," says an easterner. "It can be really peaceful." Hiking, fishing, horseback riding, and backpacking are available in the Los Padres National Forest, which borders the campus. On weekends, students escape to Ventura Beach, about 20 minutes away, for poetry readings, bonfires, or simply tossing friends into the water. Santa Barbara, an hour away, provides opportunities for shopping, bowling, or roller-skating.

Cost cutters: Seventy-eight percent of fall 2005 freshmen and 69% of continuing students received financial aid; for 75% of the freshmen and 63% of the continuing students, the aid was need-based. The average freshman award for the 2005–2006 school year included a need-based $10,157 scholarship or grant, $9806 in need-based self-help aid such as loans and jobs, and $776 in non-need-based awards and scholarships. The average financial indebtedness of 2005 graduates was $14,000. Special service scholarships employ students on campus for up to 13 hours a week over 35 weeks; in return, students receive $3180 in credit against their room and board. The college offers 3 tuition payment plans. Students not receiving a grant from the college or a Cal Grant, who pay for both semesters before August 1, receive a discount of $500. Those in a similar situation who pay for each semester by August 1 and December 1 receive a $300 discount. A 10-month installment plan also is provided.

Rate of return: Eighty-seven percent of the freshmen return for the sophomore year; 84% go on to graduate in 4 years.

Payoff: In a recent year, 15% of the graduates enrolled directly in graduate or professional schools. Within 5 years of graduating, a third of the students pursue advanced degrees in the arts and sciences. Another fifth head to law and medical schools. Among the graduate schools accepting Thomas Aquinas students in recent years are Brown, Columbia, Cornell, Harvard, and Princeton universities. About a fifth of the students take teaching jobs directly after graduation. Eleven percent of alumni have entered religious life.

Bottom line: Thomas Aquinas is a college that takes both the Catholic faith and the intellectual life very seriously, and expects its students to do the same. Advises one believer: "A prospective student doesn't have to worry about coming here with lots of facts and AP classes under his or her belt. The emphasis here is not on memorizing, but on understanding. Students must come with an openness to the truth and an eagerness for pursuing it. The most successful students here are not the ones who have had the most rigorous education before coming here, but are the ones who are careful and attentive thinkers."

University of California, Berkeley

Berkeley, California 94720

Setting: Urban
Control: Public
Undergraduate enrollment: 9989 men, 11,782 women
Graduate enrollment: 4463 men, 4061 women
Student/faculty ratio: 16:1
Freshman profile: 30% scored over 700 on SAT I verbal; 41% scored 600–700; 21% 500–599; 8% below 500; 46% scored over 700 on SAT I math; 35% scored 600–700; 15% 500–599; 4% below 500. 99% graduated in top tenth of high school class.
Faculty profile: 99% Ph.D.'s

Tuition and fees: $6512 in-state; $24,332 out-of-state
Room and board: $11,629
Freshman financial aid: 47%; average scholarship or grant: $11,096 need-based; $2393 non-need-based
Campus jobs: 27%; average earnings: $1936/year
Application deadline: Nov. 30
Financial aid deadline: Mar. 2
Admissions information: (510) 642-2316;
  e-mail: ouars@uclink.berkeley.edu
  web site: www.berkeley.edu

What prestigious West Coast university, in the words of an alumnus, has introductory lectures "the size of a large fishing village" and must have been the alma mater of the philosopher Nietzche because "alienation, facelessness, and anxiety are more intensely felt here than at any other college"? Despite this semiserious view from a former insider, nearly 36,800 high school seniors compete annually to be among the 3670 freshmen in Nietzche's fishing village, more formally known as the University of California, Berkeley. The lure of potentially rubbing elbows with the 7 Nobel Laureates on staff and sharing in the trickle-down from 32 graduate programs ranked among the top 10 in their fields has helped to make the undergraduate program at this university one of the most highly sought educational experiences for state residents and out-of-staters alike.

For Californians, who comprise 89% of the undergraduate student body, the deal is simply too good to pass up: a name equal to that of the East Coast Ivys for about a fifth of the tuition cost, just over $6500 in the 2005–2006 school year. However, graduates of California high schools must generally rank within the top 12.5% to be considered for admission. Out-of-staters, who recently paid just over $24,000 in tuition and fees, still three-fourths of that at prestigious private school counterparts, must rank within the top 4% of their high school classes. It's tough getting in, and for many, adjusting to life among the masses can be just as tough.

Student body: Berkeley is about as diverse as universities get. With 7% of the undergraduates not reporting their racial or ethnic origins, just 31% of the students are white Americans. Asian-Americans comprise 43%; Hispanics, 11%; African-American students, 4%; Native Americans, less than 1%; and foreign nationals, from 79 countries, 3%. Eighty-five percent of freshmen are graduates of public high schools. Undergraduates attend from all but 4 states. Within its ranks, the student body contains more than the usual share of politically active undergraduates concerned about social and world issues and about continuing the university's legendary tradition of student activism. Students use phrases such as "intellectually daring," "academically smug," and "having an 'anything goes' attitude," to describe themselves. For the most part, however, Berkeley students are motivated by the same concerns about their personal futures as are undergraduates at other colleges, though there are few outward signs of competition here, only a sense that everyone is silently working *very* hard. Students are independent and tend to go their separate ways: stories abound about high school classmates who come to Berkeley and don't bump into each other for a year.

Academics: UC Berkeley was the first member of the 10-campus University of California system when it opened its doors in 1868. Today, its programs, spread among 14 colleges and schools, offer nearly 300 areas of specialization through the doctorate, with more than 100 undergraduate majors alone based in 5 colleges and 2 schools. About 7000 courses are offered universitywide, ranging at the undergraduate level from classes in African-American studies and astrophysics to instruction in 70 different languages from Arabic to Tagalog. Berkeley is the only campus within the UC system to divide its courses by semester, and the range in class sizes is as wide as the span of the Bay Bridge. While upper-level seminars may have just 15 students, freshmen should brace themselves for economics and history lectures that have 900 notetakers. A Freshman Seminar Program, however, enables first-year students to meet in seminars of 15 to 25 participants with senior faculty. In a recent fall semester, 58% of the 3009 undergraduate class sections had fewer than 20 students. Fewer than 8% had more than 100 notetakers.

Berkeley students must meet the same requirements as other students within the UC system, basically proof of English proficiency and knowledge of American history and institutions. The Berkeley campus also instituted a special campuswide requirement of its own: passage of a course addressing theoretical and analytical issues that lead to a better understanding of race, culture, and ethnicity in American history and society. In addition, each college has its own set of general education requirements that cover the usual range of disciplines.

Berkeley boasts a star-studded faculty, currently including 7 Nobel Laureates (19 members all-time including recipients who have since died, retired, or moved on to other institutions after winning the award while at Berkeley), and 3 Pulitzer Prize winners (5 all-time), 130 members of the National Academy of Sciences, 85 members of the National Academy of Engineering, 28 MacArthur Fellows, and more Guggenheim Fellows and Presidential Young Investigators than at any other university in the country. Altogether, the faculty includes 1496 full-time members and 469 part-timers, all of whom teach undergraduates; 73% of the faculty are men. For the most part, students rave about the quality of the lectures, rich in creative thinking and well-reasoned ideas, that they pack the halls to hear. However, having such distinguished professors carries a price. Very often, faculty members, engrossed in important research or other academic matters, are too busy to meet one-on-one with students and may seem hurried and distracted throughout whatever office contact a student attempts to make. Shrugs one faculty fan: "You must have a TOUGH shell to succeed here." While graduate students help teach in many of the introductory courses, says a junior: "Often, they are just as brilliant as the faculty."

What some faculty may lack in personal attention and warmth, however, they compensate for in command of their subject matter. The sciences are particularly strong in distinguished faculty who, when they are not teaching, are expanding the frontiers of science in their research. The programs in business and engineering, especially electrical engineering and computer science, are highly competitive and impressively comprehensive in their course offerings. English is also a strong choice, with 9 of the 38 full professors in the department recently receiving the university's Distinguished Teaching Award, out of a total of nearly 150 recipients across 45 departments. Undergraduate courses offered in the Graduate School of Public Policy also win high marks.

Even the best programs, however, can be hurt by Berkeley's size and persistent budget crunch. English, for example, has very large classes, which can make learning less personal. Political science also needs smaller classes and more advisors. Some of the undergraduate science programs could use more updated equipment.

Facilities: It's hard to envision a book or periodical Berkeley doesn't have. Its collection includes nearly 9.8 million volumes, 79,390 current periodicals, 55 million manuscripts, 6.7 million microform items, 400,000 maps, and 121,000 sound and video recordings, all spread over 3 main facilities and 18 branch libraries plus other special libraries. If for some reason Berkeley doesn't immediately have what a student needs, Melvyl, the user-friendly computer program, puts the seeker in touch with the more than 20 million books available throughout the UC system. Students in need of human help have been discovering one of the earlier fallouts from the university's recent financial cutbacks: librarians are available for only limited hours; library hours in general have been shortened as well.

Students consider computers an integral part of life at Berkeley and report few frustrations finding a free unit. Fifteen general-access and instructional computer facilities around campus have about 600 PC, Macintosh, and Unix workstations. Additional labs are located in residence halls, libraries, and campus departments. The university strongly recommends that all students have personal computers.

Special programs: Berkeley students can study at any of 100 universities in 33 countries, including 15 centers established in the Pacific Rim over the last few years. Close-to-home exchanges are available with 7 colleges and universities, including Sonoma State and Mills College in Oakland; the politically inspired can spend a summer cross-country in Washington, D.C. To enhance the racial and ethnic climate on campus, Berkeley supports a program called Project DARE in which most entering students explore their experiences with people from different cultures and backgrounds. An Undergraduate Research Apprentice Program enables students to work one-on-one with faculty engaged in advanced research in the humanities and in the social, physical, and biological sciences.

Campus life: Berkeley's central campus covers 177 acres with additional land stretching over a total of 1232 acres overlooking San Francisco Bay. However, just a third of the undergraduates live on this vast spread. There are spaces for about 8,000 students in university-sponsored housing, and about twice as many students apply as these available spaces can accommodate, although the university guarantees spots to all freshmen submitting housing applications by the deadline. Most of the 14 local and 38 national fraternities and 7 local and 13 national sororities provide housing. A tenth of the men and women are Greek members. For those not living on campus or commuting from home, rents tend to be high. Campus residents have their own frustrations: homeless people sleeping on the campus and lack of available parking for cars as well as bicycles. Crime is considered a more serious problem off-campus than on.

There is clearly no typical weekend at Berkeley, with students dispersed among the 400+ organizations that cover a wide range of individual interests. Membership in the Berkeley College Republicans can be as high as in an animal rights group. Ethnic clubs, major-related associations, and journalistic endeavors all draw their share of participants. For the sports-minded, the campus has 4 gymnasiums, 4 swimming facilities, 2 weight rooms, squash, handball, racquetball, and tennis courts, a martial arts room, and two 400-meter tracks. Berkeley's PAC-10 varsity teams, the California Bears, have won conference and national championships throughout the 13 men's and 13 women's sports offered and helped to produce more than 100 Olympic contenders since 1912. If Berkeley were a country, it would have finished 18th in the medal count at the 2004 Summer Olympics in Athens, ahead of 179 other countries whose athletes competed at the games. The campus stadium, which seats 76,000, sells out every other year for the big game between Berkeley and archrival Stanford. Some 12,000 students also regularly participate in 14 intramural sports for each sex with thousands more taking the field and court in the 30 Division III intercollegiate club sports offered on campus.

The city of Berkeley has 103,000 people and enough local color to keep most students satisfied. For those who need a break, San Francisco is a popular destination.

Cost cutters: In the 2004–2005 school year, the most recent year for which data is available, 47% of first-time freshmen and 50% of continuing students received financial aid of some sort; 44% of all freshmen and 47% of all continuing students were on need-based aid. The average financial package for entering freshmen included a need-based scholarship or grant averaging $11,096 and need-based self-help aid such as loans and jobs averaging $5991. Non-need-based athletic scholarships for first-year students averaged $13,167; other non-need-based awards and scholarships averaged $2393. The average indebtedness of a recent graduate was $13,277. Freshmen can compete for Regents and Chancellor's scholarships, based on academic merit, completion of an essay and an interview with the faculty; these awards pay $1000 to students with no need and up to full fare for 4 years to undergraduates with financial need. Approximately 200 scholarships are granted yearly to both freshmen and entering advanced standing students. Alumni Leadership Scholarships for incoming freshmen are based on academic merit, recommendations, an essay, and an interview and cover from 1 to 4 years in varying amounts. Cooperative programs are offered in all majors. Close to 5000 students received work-study positions in a recent school year.

Rate of return: Despite the daunting size of classes and lack of personal attention that first year, 97% of entering freshmen return for the sophomore year. Sixty-one percent earn bachelor's degrees in 4 years; 84% within 5 years, 87% within 6.

Payoff: Molecular biology, political science, and economics were the top majors among recent graduates, each field claiming 8%, 7%, and 6% of the degrees respectively. Within 18 months of commencement, 17% of graduates in a recent year were enrolled in business school, 13% in law school, 11% each in medical school and programs in engineering and computer science, 10% in the arts and sciences, and 9% in education and counseling. Little wonder that national studies have found that more students who earn bachelor's degrees at Berkeley complete doctorates than graduates of any other university in the country. To recruit graduates for jobs, 625 companies and other organizations conducted interviews on the

Berkeley campus in a recent school year. This campus also boasts the largest number of Peace Corp volunteers among its alumni.

Bottom line: UC Berkeley can be a "shy person's nightmare," or the toughening environment that provides an independent, exploring mind with the raw materials to spin gold. The ingredients are here for an education of extraordinary breadth and quality, but students should not come expecting help to come to them, because they probably won't get it unless they seek it out.

University of California, Davis

Davis, California 95616

Setting: Suburban
Control: Public
Undergraduate enrollment: 10,112 men, 12,623 women
Graduate enrollment: 3301 men, 3601 women
Student/faculty ratio: 12:1
Freshman profile: SAT/ACT scores: NA. 95% graduated in top tenth of high school class.
Faculty profile: 98% Ph.D.'s
Tuition and fees: $8128.50 in-state; $25,948.50 out-of-state

Room and board: $10,791
Freshman financial aid: NA; average scholarship: NA
Campus jobs: NA; average earnings: NA
Application deadline: Nov. 30
Financial aid deadline: Mar. 2
Admissions information: (530) 752-2971
  e-mail: freshmanadmission@ucdavis.edu
  web site:www.ucdavis.edu

The University of California, Davis, just outside the state capital in Sacramento, started a century ago as a kind of agricultural substation for the Berkeley campus. But Davis is no cow college, though its nickname remains the "Cal Aggies." The agricultural college remains one of its strongest, with courses found few other places, and the program in veterinary medicine is among the best in the country, but a third of Davis graduates go on to pursue advanced degrees in the arts and sciences, business, law, and medicine. One in 4 eventually works in business; 1 in 7, in the health professions; 1 in 8, in science research. And just about nobody graduates from Davis without earning a bachelor's degree in bicycling: Davis (the city and the campus) has more bikes per capita than anywhere else in the nation, and students advise figuring bicycle maintenance costs into a budget. With Davis's costs, even for out-of-staters there's still plenty of room.

Student body: Ninety-six percent of Davis's students are from California, with 46 other states represented in a recent year; most of the nonresidents also are from the West. Ninety percent graduated from public high schools. The undergraduate student body is more diverse than most: in a recent year, 45% white American, 35% Asian-American, 10% Hispanic, 3% African-American, 1% Native American, and just over 1% foreign nationals from 113 foreign countries. (Five percent were of some other racial or ethnic origin or did not report.) A 40-foot long mural portraying the variety of cultures at UCD celebrates this diversity.

Davis undergraduates tend to be down-to-earth, fitness-oriented, and generally more liberal than their peers at other universities, but not uniformly so, says a junior. "You're exposed to many ways of thinking and different lifestyles." Most keep an eye toward enacting social change—as long as it doesn't interfere with their studies. Students in the biological and applied sciences, in particular, are intense about their work, although Davis's quiet, relaxed atmosphere can help soothe raw nerves. However, the campus continues to grow in enrollment, a condition most undergraduates don't relish.

Academics: UC Davis offers degrees through the doctorate with 103 undergraduate majors. The university is organized into 4 colleges and 5 professional schools, plus Graduate Studies. The academic year is divided into three 10-week quarters stretching from September to June. Required science and math classes range in size from 100 to 300 students, although an introductory nutrition lecture averages over 500 notetakers; some required humanities classes go as low as 20. Juniors and seniors can expect classes with 30–80 students, though some upper-level psychology and biological sciences classes may still enroll 150. Eight percent of all classes have 1 to 5 students.

Davis's general-education program is grouped around 3 main components: topical breadth, social-cultural diversity, and writing experience. Topical breadth is likewise divided into 3 broad academic areas, science and engineering, social sciences, and arts and humanities, and students must take 3 classes in each subject area that does not include the major. Under the heading of social-cultural diversity, students are required to take 1 course that involves such issues as race, ethnicity, social class, gender, sexuality, or religion. The writing component can be fulfilled with 3 courses that each require a minimum of 5 pages of writing.

A faculty recently numbering 1723 includes only 289 who work part-time. No breakdown is available on how many teach undergraduates. Nearly a third of the total pool are women. One member has won a Pulitzer Prize and several are in the National Academy of Sciences. Students consider the generally heavy research commitments of the faculty to be a double-edged sword. Sums up an English major: "Teachers' involvement in their fields makes them more aware of new developments and offers great opportunities for student assistance in these areas. But it can take away from their availability to students and their dedication to undergraduate education." On the plus side are outstanding teachers like the psychology professor who, every quarter, memorizes the names of all 125 students in his social psychology class. A $30,000 Prize for Undergraduate Teaching and Scholarly Achievement is but one program designed to encourage a stronger commitment to undergraduate instruction.

The biological sciences, which attract most premed students, are particularly competitive majors at UC Davis. The College of Biological Sciences offers 13 undergraduate majors spread across 247 courses. Specialties range from programs in genetics to exercise biology to plant biology. Construction of a new Sciences Laboratory Building with 34 classroom labs clustered by discipline was completed in January 2005. Professors in animal science in the College of Agricultural and Environmental Sciences work hard to help students achieve their goals and, in many cases, involve students in their research. Majors found in the College's Department of Land, Air, and Water Resources also are rewarding, with plenty of "hands on" work for students. Engineering benefits from heavy corporate support for equipment and for more advanced programs. The Women's Resource Center for Engineering is helping to widen the diversity of students in the field. A surprising standout among all the science-related fields is the studio art program, which features a world renowned faculty. Psychology, human development, political science, history, art history, English, and international relations also are considered strong, well-structured majors.

"The chemistry department needs help," says a chemical engineering major, who found a need for professors who explain complicated material more clearly and are more available to assist during office hours. Various ethnic studies programs such as Chicana/Chicano, African American and African, Native American, and Asian American studies all could use additional faculty and resources.

Facilities: A recently completed $22.8 million wing on Shields Main Library has almost doubled the size of the structure and made it a much roomier and, some say, more beautiful place to study. Shields and the more specialized libraries in law, medicine, the physical sciences, and the humanities together hold an impressive 3.3 million volumes and 4 million microform items, with subscriptions to more than 41,000 periodicals. The MELVYL computerized system helps students track down materials throughout the UC Davis libraries and the entire UC system, and on the Internet.

Personal computers are available in the residence halls and libraries, as well as in numerous other locations around campus, and can ordinarily be used from 8 a.m. until midnight on weekdays, with shorter hours on weekends. With the computer rooms often busy, a student who leaves his or her machine for more than 15 minutes may find he or she has been logged off and the unit given to someone else.

Special programs: Davis students can study abroad at more than 80 campuses in 32 countries. Special services are available to the handicapped through the university's Disability Resource Center. Internships with the state government are popular as Davis is only 15 miles west of Sacramento. A Davis in D.C. program also is offered.

Campus life: Just 19% of undergraduates—but about 90% of freshmen—reside on the 5980-acre campus, the UC system's largest, which includes a 125-acre arboretum and the university airport. Much of the peaceful atmosphere on the Davis campus is reflective of the surrounding community. Bicycles are everywhere (automobiles are banned from the inner campus), and the Styrofoam cup of coffee ubiquitous on most college campuses won't be found at Davis: the city and the campus banned the cups (not the coffee) because of the chlorofluorocarbons harmful to the ozone layer. While most hard-working students appreciate the quiet atmosphere, a noise ordinance in the city has made off-campus parties difficult, and the university has shut down campus parties at 12:30. Consequently, you won't find many wild Greek parties, though 9% of the men and women belong to the 28 national fraternities and 20 national sororities. The recently expanded and renovated Silo Student Union, originally a dairy barn constructed in the early 1900s, has been welcomed by students as a boost to campus social life.

Beginning in fall 2004, UC Davis started competing in the Big West Conference of NCAA Division I, though it formally does not make the switch until the 2007–2008 school year. The university moved from Division II where the Aggies football team had held the NCAA record for consecutive conference championships (20). Aggie football is but one of 12 men's and 14 women's varsity sports played, although the team probably generates the most excitement. Participation in intramural is high, with more than 13,000 students involved in 36 sports. Biking and jogging are favorite pastimes for the health-conscious student body as is a spin around the newly constructed outdoor roller hockey rink. "Almost everybody has a sport or work-out schedule," comments a Californian. With so much biking, bike theft has become the big crime on campus.

Two major campus festivities help to break up the routine. The annual Picnic Day open house draws as many as 70,000 people to the campus for activities that range from dachshund races and a dog Frisbee competition to musical and sports competitions. The 3-day Whole Earth Festival celebrates spiritual development and environmental innovations.

The general lack of nightlife around Davis (pop. 55,000), one of the last remaining college towns in California, sends students off for weekends in Sacramento, Lake Tahoe, or the San Francisco Bay area. Many go wine tasting through the Napa Valley, skiing in the Sierras, or even nightclub hopping in San Francisco.

Cost cutters: In a recent year, 64% of all UC Davis students received some form of financial aid. The average freshman award totaled $8000, with no breakdown available as to scholarships, grants, or self-help aid. The average financial indebtedness of recent graduates was $8300. In a recent year, Davis awarded $2.8 million in scholarships to undergraduates, including about 200 prestigious Regents Scholarships. Regents Scholarships, which generally go to students in the top 4% of their high school graduating class, recently paid an honorarium of $5855 to students without financial need. Students with need may receive a stipend up to the total cost of attendance for California students.

Rate of return: Ninety percent of entering freshmen return for the sophomore year. More than three-quarters of those who start eventually finish, although the time required is becoming longer. Just under a third, 32%, earn bachelor's degrees in the traditional 4 years, 69% in 5 years, and 78% in 6 years. A special Finish in Four! pilot program is designed to help undergraduates who wish to earn a bachelor's degree in 4 years.

Payoff: Psychology, agricultural business and management, and biological sciences were the 3 top majors among recent graduates, though no figures are available showing the percentage that specialized in each. The biological sciences are popular at all degree levels, with UC Davis awarding more bachelors and doctoral degrees in the field than any other U.S. college or university. Follow-up studies of earlier graduates show that two-thirds complete advanced degrees within 15 years of earning their bachelors' from Davis; more than half did their graduate work in education (21%), the health professions (19%), and the biological or physical sciences (16%). Three-quarters of all Davis graduates end up in jobs in business, the health professions, science and research, engineering, and education.

Bottom line: If you come to Davis, be prepared to study hard—and bring your bike.

University of California, Los Angeles

Los Angeles, California 90095

Setting: Urban
Control: Public
Undergraduate enrollment: 10,326 men, 13,524 women
Graduate enrollment: 5408 men, 5179 women
Student/faculty ratio: 18:1
Freshman profile: 18% scored over 700 on SAT I verbal; 44% scored 600–700; 30% 500–599; 8% below 500. 34% scored over 700 on SAT I math; 41% scored 600–700; 20% 500–599; 5% below 500. 29% scored above 29 on the ACT; 47% scored 24–29; 23% 18–23; 1% below 18. 97% graduated in top tenth of high school class.

Faculty profile: 98% Ph.D.'s
Tuition and fees: $7062 in-state; $24,882 out-of-state
Room and board: $10,619
Freshman financial aid: 57%; average scholarship or grant: $11,316 need-based; $6778 non-need-based
Campus jobs: NA; average earnings: NA
Application deadline: Nov. 30
Financial aid deadline: Mar. 2
Admissions information: (310) 825-3101
  e-mail: ugadm@saonet.ucla.edu
  web site: www.ucla.edu

In the alphabet soup of America's 4-year colleges and universities, few names stand out like U-C-L-A, the urban gem of the University of California system. The University of California branch campus in Los Angeles, founded in 1919, stands for an education rich in superlatives: one of the most diverse in terms of student body of any major research university, among the most varied in educational offerings with more than 3000 different undergraduate courses, and most likely to send large numbers of graduates on to higher education. More than a third of those who earned bachelor's degrees in a recent year opted to continue their education after graduating from UCLA: within that group, 20% headed for law school, 18% for higher degrees in the arts and sciences, 17% for medical school, and 8% to business school. For a student willing to risk becoming a number on an urban campus of over 35,000, the return is surely an education that is number 1 across the board.

Student body: Students proudly call their school "Diversity University," with little wonder. Thirty-four percent of the undergraduates are white Americans; 38% are Asian-American, 15% Hispanic, and 3% African-American, with less than 1% Native American, and 4% foreign nationals from 100 countries. About 5% chose not to report. Just over 20 years ago, only 14% of all undergraduates were ethnic minority students. Ninety-two percent are from California, with just over half from Los Angeles County, though every state in the United States has its share of Bruins on board.

The ethnic diversity of students, teamed with the broad range of political and social views present, makes for an unusually stimulating environment. Says a state resident: "I've been immersed in several cultures and experiences I never would have found in a smaller environment." Students on the south campus, where those majoring in the sciences hang out, tend to be more competitive than the north-campus disciples of the liberal arts and humanities. Still, wherever you look, the campus is generally filled with students who graduated in the top 10% of their high school classes. Eighty-one percent took their diplomas from public schools.

Academics: Students may earn bachelor's degrees in 126 different disciplines ranging from Afro-American studies to cybernetics. Master's degrees are offered in about 80 fields; doctoral and professional degrees, in close to 100. The College of Letters and Science and 4 of the 12 professional schools (the School of Engineering and Applied Science, the School of Theater, Film, and Television, the School of the Arts and Architecture, and the School of Nursing) offer major programs for undergraduates.

The academic year is divided into quarters, with most students taking 3 quarters yearly. Average class size for undergraduates is 62 in the lower division; 36, in the upper. General-education courses in the freshman year like Molecular, Cell and Developmental Biology enroll almost 500 students. Each of more than 180 classes in a recent year, ranging from Elementary Bambara to Advanced Biotechnology, enrolled a single student. Students learn to take in stride big-university hassles like large, impersonal lectures and the difficulty of getting into some classes. Advises a senior: "The easily discouraged and timid types may find some aspects of the university unpleasant. Someone shouldn't go here if he or she wants personal attention in all classes."

All students, except those in engineering, must earn a minimum of 180 units for a bachelor's degree. Engineering students need between 185 and 201, depending on the program. UCLA has no uniform core curriculum. The only universitywide requirements are 2: demonstrated proficiency in English composition, either by testing or coursework; and completion of a year's course in American history or government in high school with a grade of B or better, or taking 1 of a number of history, English, or political science courses at UCLA. General-education requirements vary by college or school. Review of the university's general education program several years ago resulted in the development of General Education Clusters. The clusters are year-long, team-taught, interdisciplinary courses for entering freshmen on such broad topics as the "Global Environment" and "The History of Social Thought." In a recent school year, 10 clusters involving 120 to 160 students each were offered, enrolling up to half of the entering freshmen class.

Full-time faculty number 1859, all of whom teach undergraduates. All 601 part-time members teach undergraduates as well. Sixty-eight percent of the faculty are men. UCLA faculty members have won Nobel Prizes in 1998, 1997, 1987, 1965, and 1960. The "publish or perish" mindset at UCLA holds benefits, as well as pitfalls, for students. Although the knowledge being taught is generally of the moment, some of the best researchers turn out to be the worst or least accessible teachers. "In the smaller departments, the faculty are extremely good," notes a major in Italian. "But in larger departments, classes are taught by teaching assistants, a lot of whom don't speak English clearly, and the professors are hard to reach because they are so involved in their research." Adds a political science major: "Quite often professors think only graduate students are serious, and sometimes undergraduates are robbed by the stereotype."

Among the most difficult programs, both to get into and to master, are communication studies, within the College of Letters and Science, engineering, in the School of Engineering and Applied Science, and film, in the School of Theater, Film, and Television. Communication studies is an interdisciplinary program, with specializations in mass communication and interpersonal communication, that draws upon courses in several fields, as well as the real-world media in the Los Angeles area. Both engineering and science majors in the College of Letters and Science boast Nobel-Prize winning professors and equipment as state-of-the-art as the state budget will allow. The highly selective film, television, and digital media program, known for its successful graduates, accepts only about 30 applicants a year into its upper-division coursework. A number of programs in the social sciences in the College of Letters and Science also make the grade. Highly qualified scholars distinguish the majors in history and geography. Political science draws affirmative votes for its expert faculty with broad experiences outside academia. The various ethnic studies programs, from Asian-American Studies to Chicana and Chicano Studies, feature knowledgeable, committed professors. Within the humanities, the English faculty is noted for its excellence and breadth of specialties from Medieval/Anglo Saxon/Celtic literature to Jewish and gender/sexuality studies.

Rather than weak departments, students complain of deficiencies found in even the best departments: overcrowded classrooms as enrollment swells and classroom capacities don't, as well as unavailability of courses when the student needs to take them. Undergraduates eager to study business won't find a management or finance major here; their best option is a major in business economics from the College of Letters and Science that offers management classes from the Anderson (Graduate) School of Management; a limited number of students also may earn a minor in accounting from the Anderson Graduate School, the only undergraduate program offered. Finally, there is the most oversubscribed, hard-to-get "class" students complain about most: a campus parking space in the city of freeways.

Facilities: The UCLA campus has 13 libraries, holding 8 million volumes, another 7 million microform items, and 78,000 periodicals. More than half the books are in the University Research Library, the 6-story graduate facility serving the social sciences and humanities. Powell, the main undergraduate library, contains more than 250,000 volumes and provides reading rooms. The remaining libraries hold specialized collections in subjects ranging from English culture of the 17th and 18th centuries to geology. Each library has its own personality and academic groupies. But among the 13, notes a city resident, "If you can't find something here, it doesn't exist."

Computers seem omnipresent around campus, but students say it never hurts to bring your own to avoid lines and other hassles. Widespread wireless access, from within most academic buildings to such popular outdoor venues as the Sculpture Garden, makes having a laptop especially attractive.

Special programs: The University of California's Education Abroad program enables UCLA students to study at 85 different campuses in 33 countries from Australia to Togo. Twenty to 30 students are selected each fall and spring to spend a quarter in Washington, D.C. A student research program enables undergraduates to work with senior faculty on research projects in a variety of departments within the College of Letters and Science, and in several of the professional schools. "It's an outstanding opportunity for undergraduates to gain research experience," observes a biochemistry major. "Many faculty give undergraduates in the program advanced responsibilities as well as recognition; I am listed as a coauthor of a paper just accepted for publication." The Division of Honors administers 3 scholarly journals: in literature, poetry, and the visual arts; in history, the humanities, and social sciences; and in the life sciences and physical sciences, each staffed entirely by undergraduates.

Campus life: A quarter of all undergraduates, and about half of the freshmen, live on the 419-acre campus located in the posh Westwood neighborhood of Los Angeles. Students accept the risk of theft and assaults as the price of attending college in an urban area, but say that vans and escorts and good lighting make traveling at night much safer.

The campus is fairly quiet on weekends, following Thursday "party nights" at the fraternities and sororities, which enroll 14% of the men and 11% of the women in 4 local and 23 national fraternities and 4 local and 14 national sororities. Many students go into Westwood for dinner and a movie, although neighborhood restaurants, like housing, tend to be pricey. To find their niche on the huge campus, students turn to 700 different clubs and organizations, built around ethnicity, academic majors, cultural talents, and sports. For the journalist, the Daily Bruin (circulation 22,000) is the fourth largest newspaper in Los Angeles. The music department has more than 20 performance groups. About 500 students, staff, and alumni take part every year in February's 26-hour Dance Marathon to raise funds for the Elizabeth Glaser Pediatric AIDS Foundation. The total raised each of the last couple of years: more than $200,000.

UCLA's overall performance in intercollegiate sports has long been impressive, with Pac-10 football and basketball drawing the biggest crowds of the 10 men's sports offered. UCLA teams have won more than 50 NCAA men's championships, the highest number in the nation, including at least 15 in tennis, 12 in volleyball, and 11 in basketball. The women's intercollegiate program is second in all-time women's NCAA titles, with 12 different sports available. Forty men's, women's, and coed intramural sports are provided for the vast majority of students who can't compete on an intercollegiate level. An estimated 75% of Bruins fans participate. Some 2000 students also have formed recreational clubs in more than 30 sports ranging from bowling and karate to lacrosse. Students can use structures built or remodeled for the 1984 Olympics.

The mountains and the beach are among the more popular escapes from the city campus. Those feeling lucky may strike out for Las Vegas, 283 miles away, or if not, stick closer to home and go to Santa Barbara (100 miles) or maybe Disneyland or Beverly Hills.

Cost cutters: Fifty-seven percent of the freshmen and 60% of the continuing students received some form of financial aid in the 2004–2005 school year, the most recent year for which data is available. Forty-eight percent of the freshmen and 51% of the continuing students received need-based aid. The average freshman award for a first-year student with financial need included a need-based scholarship or grant averaging $11,316 and need-based self-help aid such as loans and jobs averaging $4382. Non-need-based athletic scholarships for first-year students averaged $10,672; other non-need-based awards and scholarships averaged $6778. Average debt of a 2004 graduate was $13,894. Among merit awards, UCLA offers the 4-year Regents Scholarship, which pays a $5500 honorarium to recipients without financial need and the honorarium plus the amount of financial need for those who have it. Up to 100 awards are presented annually to entering freshmen and transfer students. Typically, the top 1.5% of the freshman applicant pool is invited to apply for the scholarship. University scholarships go to entering freshmen with a minimum 3.5 GPA who have financial need; these awards recently paid $500 to $2000 for one year only.

Rate of return: Ninety-seven percent of freshmen return for the sophomore year. Fifty-seven percent graduate in 4 years, 84% within 5 years; 87% in 6.

Payoff: Among 2005 graduates, the most popular majors were psychology and political science, each the choice of 9%, followed by sociology at 8%. Thirty-five percent of recent degree recipients enrolled in some kind of graduate or professional studies. Nearly 400 companies and organizations recruited on campus in a recent school year.

Bottom line: UCLA is big, but only as big as you let it be. For the student who is willing to pursue, but is not dependent on personal attention from professors, who gets involved in as many of the 700 clubs as suit his or her interests, and who enjoys "real-world" city living, UCLA is simply the Ultimate Choice in Limitless Academics.

University of California, San Diego
La Jolla, California 92093

Setting: Suburban
Control: Public
Undergraduate enrollment: 9733 men, 10,606 women
Graduate enrollment: 2134 men, 1425 women
Student/faculty ratio: 22:1
Freshman profile: 10% scored over 700 on SAT I verbal; 40% scored 600–700; 38% 500–599; 12% below 500. 26% scored over 700 on SAT I math; 48% scored 600–700; 24% 500–599; 2% below 500. 19% scored above 28 on the ACT; 33% scored 27–28; 20% 24–26; 25% 21–23; 3% below 21. 100% graduated in top tenth of high school class.
Faculty profile: 98% Ph.D.'s

Tuition and fees: $6681 in-state; $23,985 out-of-state
Room and board: $9421
Freshman financial aid: 50%; average scholarship or grant: $7196 need-based; $2586 non-need-based
Campus jobs: 25%; average earnings: $1878/year
Application deadline: Nov. 30
Financial aid deadline: Priority date: Mar. 2; regular: May 1
Admissions information: (858) 534-4831
  e-mail: admissionsinfo@ucsd.edu
  web site: www.admissions.ucsd.edu

At most major universities, students enroll in a particular college—Arts and Sciences, Engineering, or maybe Business Administration—because it has the specific major they want to pursue. At the University of California, San Diego, however, undergraduates pick 1 of 6 colleges because it offers the kind of academic environment in which they would like to study: lots of structured core requirements, an approach linking educational and career pursuits, or a global perspective. A student can study any major in any college, but graduates of the same major from different colleges will view the discipline a bit differently. In one area, though, they'll all agree: the price fits just about everyone, especially those lucky enough to live in California.

Student body: Not surprisingly, 95% of UCSD's students are from California, with most of the nonresidents coming from the Southwest. The undergraduate student body is comprised of 34% white American students, 41% Asian-American, 10% Hispanic, 1% each African-American and Native American, and 2% foreign nationals from 70 countries. There is no data on the remaining 11%. All but 12% graduated from public schools. Undergraduates are mixed politically between liberals and conservatives, Democrats and Republicans, though many generally are apathetic about voicing their political views. A majority opt for independent social activities and student club get-togethers over larger organized events. Without question, most of the students' focus is on academics, and they are very competitive in their studies. Says a communication major: "Getting an A- is not good enough for the average UCSD student. For most, studying and going to classes comes first." Still, there remains, in the words of one senior, something of a "laid-back beach attitude," instilled by the year-round sunny weather. For a majority, the secret to success at UCSD is not just knowing how to have a good time, but also knowing when to have one.

Academics: The San Diego campus, founded in 1960, offers degree programs through the doctorate. Undergraduates can pursue any of more than 130 majors. The academic year is divided into 10-week quarters in which students generally take 3 quarters of 4 courses each. Most freshman lectures have about 300 students, although once a week students meet in discussion groups of 15–20 students and a teaching assistant. From then on, the size of most upper-level courses depends largely on the major. Many science classes at the junior and senior levels enroll 200 or more. In other less popular majors, such as literature or classical studies, it is not uncommon to see as few as 10.

With so many large classes in a large university setting, San Diego's residential college system becomes all the more important. UCSD is divided into 6 colleges: Revelle, John Muir, Thurgood Marshall, Earl Warren, Eleanor Roosevelt, and its newest, Sixth College. All enroll about 3000 students, giving residents a small-college feel on a large campus. Students follow core requirements distinct to the educational philosophy of each school. At Revelle, students must complete a fairly structured set of traditional distributional requirements plus an area of focus noncontiguous to the major. John Muir College offers students more flexibility and specializes in year-long courses. Thurgood Marshall links coursework to developing students' skills as scholars and citizens; Warren, to the student's personal and career goals. Eleanor Roosevelt emphasizes interdisciplinary, cross-cultural studies and competency in a foreign language. Sixth explores the connections among culture, art, and technology. The college, which eventually will bear the name of a historical figure like the other colleges, enrolled its first students in fall 2002.

The total instructional faculty numbers 1149. Of that total, 965 are full-time faculty and 184 are part-time. All but 2% of the full-time faculty teaches undergraduates; no such breakdown is available for the part-time. Twenty-seven percent are women. Included among the faculty ranks are 5 Nobel Laureates, 5 recipients of the National Medal of Science, 1 winner of the Pulitzer Prize, a former astronaut, and 1 winner of the Fields Medal in mathematics, plus dozens of members of various national academies and societies. Relating to such a prestigious group of research-oriented professors is not always easy, although often less difficult than students expect. Notes a psychology major: "Some teachers try as hard as students to improve the quality and the number of student-faculty interactions." Many professors work to stay accessible by responding to student inquiries within a day or less and staying in touch outside of class via flexible office hours, e-mails, and "on occasion, personal beepers/home numbers," notes a senior.

The university's major strength is in the sciences, with the Division of Biological Sciences offering some of the most popular and most competitive majors. The biological sciences, plus physics, chemistry, computer science, engineering, psychology, and political science, are distinguished by outstanding faculty, well-designed curricula, and excellent equipment. Linguistics is also superb, with an extensive language lab, as is communication. The theater program draws its own applause, although some students feel the undergraduate major is often neglected in favor of the better known graduate program. Anthropology, in the words of a major, is "incredible."

Literature, as well as other majors in the humanities and some in the social sciences, tends to get less money and less attention than programs in the sciences. The visual arts could use more class offerings with a greater scope of media. Majors in some career fields that students look for, such as business, journalism, and nursing, are not offered. Business-oriented students generally seek degrees in economics or management science, although some wish there were more "real-world" emphasis. Economics and mathematics feature brilliant professors from many nations; still some undergraduates find their English difficult to understand. Says a senior: "Although the professors are world-renowned and come here to teach, the students are *very* demanding and very unforgiving when it comes to lectures." Mathematics professors, in particular, also do not seem to stay long before moving on to other jobs.

Facilities: No one can call Geisel Undergraduate Library named for Theodore Geisel, author of the fanciful Dr. Seuss books, "dull." Its 7-story, inverted pyramid design was described by one architectural critic as "hovering for all the world like an intelligence-stocked spaceship from a better planet." Adds a sophomore: "Its up-in-the-clouds feeling and beautiful views really put you in focus." To preserve the library's distinctive shape, an expansion was completed underground. Altogether, San Diego's extensive library system holds 2.6 million volumes, 2.9 million microform items, and subscriptions to 25,000 periodicals, spread over 10 buildings, including Geisel. Each building has its own study personality, with the small, intensely silent Biomedical Library rated most conducive to serious study and CLICS, the Center for Library and Institutional Computing Services, the most social. When students need help, they seek out MELVYL, the university's on-line computerized catalog with listings of holdings throughout the UC system.

Undergraduates have access to 1500 computers of various types across campus. Says a junior: "You can't go more than 100 feet without finding a computer available, both Macs and PCs." A majority of computer labs are open from 6 a.m. until midnight most days or around the clock at a number of sites. "The vast majority of students bring their own computers to campus," says a biology major, "so availability is plentiful if computers are required at anytime throughout the quarter." In fact, the university strongly recommends that all students have personal computers. A university-wide wireless Ethernet system makes laptop ownership all the more attractive.

Special programs: Student exchange programs are available with Dartmouth College in New Hampshire, and Spelman and Morehouse colleges in Atlanta. A semester in Washington, D.C. or London also is possible. The Education Abroad Program sends students to more than 30 nations, from Australia to West Africa. Each year, about 500 students participate in off-campus internships; others receive funding for undergraduate research through the Undergraduate Scholastic Grants Committee.

Campus life: Just over a third of the undergraduates (and 80% of freshmen) live on the rolling 1976-acre campus, which is perched on cliffs overlooking the Pacific Ocean. Housing availability varies among the 6 colleges. While cars are permitted on campus, free shuttle services, as well as bicycles and skateboards, are preferred, at least by the administration. Greek life is only mildly popular, although the black fraternities and sororities are more so; altogether, 10% of the men are members of 14 national fraternities, and 10% of the women join the 19 national sororities. Since there are no Greek houses on campus, parties are generally held elsewhere. The university hosts a quarterly festival, along with other frequent on-campus festivities, concerts, and social activities. Nevertheless, some students still complain of a lack of social interaction among undergraduates. Says a junior: "We are not a party school or a team-spirited school. We are, however, very focused on our studies."

Of the 400 student organizations and clubs, *Board@UCSD* bringing together surfers, skaters, and snowboarders, claims one of the largest memberships. For the cost conscious, a wide variety of student-run co-ops and enterprises sell goods for lower prices than other businesses on campus. A weekly Farmers Market has become immensely popular.

The UCSD Tritons compete in NCAA Division II. There is no football team, and few of the games played by any of the 12 men's and 12 women's intercollegiate teams have been well attended. As a result, Triton Tide spirit club works extra hard to increase student support. While teams in women's volleyball, tennis, soccer, and water polo and men's soccer and golf have captured national titles, the men's water polo team holds the most distinctive record: the l-o-n-g-est continuous match: 26 hours, good enough to make the Guinness world records. Intramural sports are enormously popular and involve 65% of the students in 27 men's and 23 women's sports, many of them played in "RIMAC," the 188,000-square-foot recreation, intramural, and athletic complex. Club sports also are popular, with the university surfing team the winner of numerous national club championships. The university also has been ranked by *Sports Illustrated* magazine as the "Best School for Surfing" in the nation. Notes a senior: "Participation rules over spectatorship here." One woman even jogged from 11 p.m. to midnight with a member of the campus escort service "when they were less busy and I had time," she added. Though students use the free service, campus crime is not considered much of a problem. The biggest crime on campus, warns a junior, "is the crime of opportunity, so if you leave your laptop unsupervised and your bike unlocked, it may not be there."

San Diego itself (the university is located just 12 miles north of downtown) offers Sea World, Balboa Park, and the world-famous San Diego Zoo, plus San Diego Chargers football and Padres baseball. There are more than 70 miles of beaches, and Tijuana, Mexico, is but a well-traveled half-hour's drive away.

Cost cutters: Fifty percent of all freshman and 46% of all continuing undergraduates received some form of financial aid. Aid was need-based for 47% of the freshmen and 42% of the continuing students. The average freshman award for the 2004–2005 school year, the most recent year for which data was available, included a need-based scholarship or grant averaging $7196 and need-based self-help aid such as loans and jobs averaging $5626. Other non-need-based awards and scholarships for first-year students averaged $2586. Average debt of a recent graduate was $13,808. While many scholarships are limited to residents of various California high schools and counties, several merit awards are not state-restricted. Among these are the renewable Regents Scholarships, which pay up to $2000 a year for 4 years to students without financial need; those with need receive a stipend to cover the difference between costs and their family contribution and other resources, excluding nonresident tuition. The Revelle and Chancellor's Scholarships, awarded to the most outstanding freshmen each fall, pay up to $5000 a year for 4 years. Off-campus rents rise with every foot of proximity to the beach, although apartments close to the school can be expensive as well.

Rate of return: Ninety-three percent of entering freshmen return for the sophomore year; 52% go on to earn their bachelor's degrees in 4 years; 88% do so in 5 years.

Payoff: Among recent graduates, 20% earned bachelor's degrees in engineering, 17% in biology, and 9% in economics. Thirty-three percent went on for advanced degrees, with medical school traditionally claiming the top spot among graduate programs. Usually, law school and advanced study in the humanities and social sciences also rank highly. After 5 years, just over 60% of former undergraduates have completed or are enrolled in an advanced degree program.

Six hundred companies, corporations, government agencies, and nonprofit organizations recruit on campus, enticing the remaining two-thirds of the graduating class to take jobs. Most graduates are employed in technical occupations such as engineering or computer science but also in life sciences, human services, and managerial, financial, and sales and marketing fields. Within 6 months of commencement, 97% of the new alums are either employed or enrolled in graduate programs.

Bottom line: "The academic atmosphere really is the clincher here," notes a senior at Eleanor Roosevelt College. "We are surrounded by incredible research facilities as well as an outstanding faculty. Having the 6 colleges allows a student to really benefit from a small community while attending a large university."

University of California, Santa Cruz

Santa Cruz, California 95064

Setting: Small town
Control: Public
Undergraduate enrollment: 6046 men, 7093 women
Graduate enrollment: 641 men, 663 women
Student/faculty ratio: 24:1
Freshman profile: 9% scored over 700 on SAT I verbal; 35% scored 600–700; 38% 500–599; 18% below 500. 8% scored over 700 on SAT I math; 38% scored 600–700; 40% 500–599; 14% below 500. 7% scored above 28 on the ACT; 0% scored 27–28; 48% 24–26; 38% 21–23; 6% below 21. 90% graduated in top tenth of high school class.

Faculty profile: 98% Ph.D.'s
Tuition and fees: $7603 in-state; $24,907 out-of-state
Room and board: $11,571
Freshman financial aid: NA; average scholarship: NA
Campus jobs: NA; average earnings: NA
Application deadline: Nov. 30
Financial aid deadline: Mar. 2
Admissions information: (831) 459-4008
  e-mail: admissions@ucsc.edu
  web site: www.admissions.ucsc.edu

Students enjoy the residential-college structure of a Yale University, the near perfect Ph.D. rating of an Ivy League faculty, the small class sizes of a traditional liberal arts college, and the written narrative evaluations of an avant-garde alternative school. And all this is contained within the structure of one of the most prestigious state university networks in the country. In short, the University of California, Santa Cruz offers the best of many academic worlds in a setting on the northern tip of Monterey Bay as laid back as Harvard Square is brisk. UC Santa Cruz, which turned 40 in 2005, operates on a residential-college system whereby students live, eat, socialize, and study together in 10 smaller colleges, each having 750 to 1550 students and 20 to 90 faculty fellows. Each college approaches the full range of academic disciplines from a slightly different perspective, as captured in the single, special core course all members of that college must take. Residents of a particular college, however, may pursue any major on campus and choose their courses from all that are offered at the 10 colleges. One procedure all students share is the method of grading. Instead of simply assigning every student only a letter grade, each professor also writes a narrative evaluation that describes the student's strengths and weaknesses in the course. On the negative side, just 48% of the entering freshmen stay on to earn bachelor's degrees in 4 years, and 68% do so within 6 years, but even these rates are 15 percentage points higher than in previous years. Advises a senior from the midwest: "Santa Cruz is for the student interested not only in the degree but also in learning."

Student body: Ninety-six percent of the undergraduates attracted to Santa Cruz are from California. Though all 50 states are represented, most out-of-staters come cross country from the northeast. Over a third are members of racial and ethnic minority groups, 19% Asian-Americans, 15% Hispanics, 3% African-Americans, and 1% Native Americans. One percent are foreign nationals from 22 countries. Eight of every 10 students graduated from a public high school. Students at Santa Cruz view themselves as intelligent, independent thinkers who are "aware" and are as concerned about what is happening across the globe as on their own campus. Some consider their classmates too "politically correct" in their thinking, but agree that, on the whole, they are more open minded and accepting of differences in ethnicity, race, and gender than students on most other campuses. Concludes a psychology major: "We are a creative, talented, enthusiastic, musically inclined, environmentally conscientious, surf-happy, hard-working, well-accomplished group of people"—no inferiority feeling there!

Academics: Santa Cruz awards the bachelor's degree in 60 majors, as well as other degrees through the doctorate. Like all UC schools except Berkeley, Santa Cruz follows the quarter system, with class sizes that average around 100 in introductory lectures, though some can reach 250, and that are broken down into discussion groups of about 20 students. That number shrinks to 25–60 in the junior and senior years. The residential college system is the soul of student learning at Santa Cruz, providing 10 very different perspectives on similar disciplines. For example, Cowell College, the oldest, which in a recent year still had 14 of its original faculty members, has long focused on study of the influence of Western civilization, with increasing emphasis on the sister theme of multiculturalism. Its faculty, though including professors in such fields as astronomy and chemistry, is concentrated largely in the humanities. Two of the newer colleges on campus, with the utilitarian names of College Eight and College Nine, follow themes of Environment and Society and International and Global Perspectives, respectively. College Ten, which opened in fall 2002, examines the theme of Social Justice and Community.

Along with the usual UC system course requirements in American history and institutions and English composition, there are general-education requirements that students in all 10 colleges must fulfill. These include 2 introductory courses from each of 3 areas—the humanities and arts, natural sciences and engineering, and social sciences, 1 more in-depth topical course from each of the same 3 areas, and 1 quantitative, 2 writing, 1 arts, and 1 ethnic/non-Western society course. In addition, each student must take a core course particular to his or her college, as well as fulfill any additional requirements of the college. Adlai E. Stevenson College, for example, requires freshmen to take a year-long class in Self and Society. Students at Kresge College simply need a fall-quarter course called Power and Representation. Students in all colleges must pass a comprehensive exam in their senior year.

Universitywide, Santa Cruz has 742 faculty members, 537 of whom are full-time and teach undergraduates. All 205 part-time faculty members also teach undergraduates. Forty-one percent are women. Students find the professors unusually committed to undergraduate teaching, quite accessible, and open to suggestions on ways their classes can be improved. (Just 1% of the introductory classes are taught by graduate assistants.) Says a sophomore: "I have admired my professors for their commitment not only to the subject matter but also for their commitment to being our teachers. They have not only been good teachers, but mentors also." Most encourage undergraduates to address them by their first names.

The sciences, in particular marine sciences and marine biology, are distinguished by excellent facilities and professors who remain student-oriented despite their individual research. The school's proximity to the ocean and to the wonderful Long Marine Laboratory enables undergraduates to participate in studies of dolphins, sea lions, and other marine mammals and of sea birds. Psychology is also a winner, recently boasting faculty with doctorates from Harvard, Stanford, and other top schools, and a clinical approach to the subject that students like. Indeed, so many students like psychology these days that classes are often overcrowded and sometimes hard to get. Politics, literature, economics, sociology, philosophy, computer engineering, and computer science earn high marks as well.

Faculty in chemistry, music, linguistics, and community studies tend to be more involved in research and, as a result, less inclined to deliver inspiring lectures and to work closely with students. The art department could use more studio space and additional teachers to provide more class sections, although the current professors are "great," says a major.

Facilities: If the McHenry (main) library and the new science library completed in 1991 were to receive only letter grades instead of narrative evaluations from student users, they would rate A's for their beauty and appealing study environments, and solid B's for research excellence. In these 2 larger facilities and the smaller library/study centers contained in the individual colleges, Santa Cruz has just over 1.5 million volumes and 22,000 paper and electronic periodicals. Students find the selection more than adequate for most lower-level research but less helpful for specialized upper-level projects. In those situations, students turn to MELVYL, the computerized catalog that tells them where materials are located not only among the libraries on campus but also throughout the entire UC system.

More than 280 Intel-based PCs, Macintoshes and Suns are located at 15 general-purpose computer labs around campus, in most of the colleges, in the libraries, and in the main computer/applied sciences building. Two labs are open 24 hours, most until midnight, but students still can expect short waits during peak hours. Busy—or lazy—students can save steps by checking online to see how many units are free in each of the labs across campus. The university strongly recommends that students have their own personal computers. For those that do, Internet access is available in all university-sponsored housing. Wireless access also is an option around campus.

Special programs: Students may spend a full academic year of 9–11 months at study-abroad programs in 27 countries or shorter terms at universities in 34 countries. Undergraduates in search of a different kind of cultural exchange can opt for an academic year at the University of New Hampshire or New Mexico. As part of a UC Santa Cruz in Washington, D.C. (UC-DC) program, upper-division students take classes from faculty members of 5 of the UC campuses and from visiting faculty from the Washington area. Engineering students may participate in a 3–2 program at UC Berkeley. Internships in all majors can be arranged, as well as extensive research opportunities at the Long Marine Laboratory, the Lick Observatory, Año Nuevo Island, the largest elephant seal rookery on the Pacific Coast, and other nearby centers. A Biological Sciences Resource Program provides extensive support services to ethnic minority students in the sciences.

Campus life: "Mellow but fun" is how students describe after-hours life at UC Santa Cruz. Just under half of the undergraduates, 45%, live in the 10 colleges, each as distinct architecturally as it is academically. Many of the buildings spread about the 2000-acre campus are designed to blend in with the surrounding flora. For those who prefer, a 42-space camper park on the north side of campus is available to students who own recreational vehicles (only in California!). Most on-campus social life revolves around independent activities or dinner and parties within the 10 colleges rather than campuswide. However, the recent addition of 4 national fraternities and 3 local and 3 national sororities has attracted some student interest, although still barely 1% participation. The California Public Interest Research Group and Amnesty International are 2 of the more active of the 100+ student organizations.

The campus maintains its own police and fire departments, and crime other than some bike theft is not considered much of a problem. Guards are posted at each campus entrance nightly from 8 p.m. until dawn. Car theft, especially, is a minor issue since the university requests that students not bring cars to campus because of restricted parking in the area. Students' biggest concern is the continued growth of the campus over the next few years.

Intercollegiate sports are not big in terms of student support (maybe it's hard to get fired up about a team nicknamed the Banana Slugs), although 15 sports for men and 17 for women are offered. There is no football, and all sports are played under NCAA Division III. Ten intramural sports for men and 11 for women also are fielded.

Hiking and surfing are quite popular because of Santa Cruz's proximity to the beach and various state parks. San Francisco is about 75 miles north, and San Jose about 35 miles northeast. The city of Santa Cruz (pop. 55,000), a well-known center for the arts, boasts many beautifully restored Victorian houses.

Cost cutters: No current figures are available to show the portion of first-year students who received financial aid, need-based or otherwise, in the 2005–2006 school year. Data shows, however, that 60% of the continuing students received some form of financial assistance. No figures are available to show the average amount of financial aid received, either as a scholarship or grant, need-based or not, or as self-help aid. Average debt of a recent graduate was $13,569. A number of scholarships, ranging from $250 a year to an amount that covers full financial need, are available to undergraduates. Campus Merit Scholarships range up to $2000 and cover a single year; students must reapply each year for these awards. Regents Scholarships are awarded for a full 4 years to entering freshmen with a minimum GPA of 3.7, based on academic excellence and promise. Recipients without need receive a $3000 honorarium, while other students get sums equal to their full in-state financial need. Deferred payment plans are available to students not receiving aid. A University Loan Program provides long-term loans with annual interest at 5%. Repayment begins 6 months after graduation or withdrawal from higher education.

Rate of return: Eighty-nine percent of entering freshmen return for the sophomore year. Forty-eight percent graduate in 4 years, up from 31% a few years ago. Sixty-eight percent finish within 6 years.

Payoff: Psychology was the most popular major for recent graduates, accounting for 15% of the degrees awarded. Biology and literature followed at 9% and 8% respectively. Less than a fifth of those who graduate go directly to graduate or professional schools, though over 50% eventually pursue advanced degrees. Popular career choices include law, management and administration, computer science, health sciences, advertising, financial services, psychology, and education and teaching. Four hundred twenty companies and organizations recruited on campus in a recent school year. Three alumni have won Pulitzer Prizes in the school's short 41-year history, in 1996, 1997, and 1999. The campus also ranks sixth among midsize colleges and universities in the number of alumni serving in the Peace Corps.

Bottom line: While Santa Cruz, with its 10 residential colleges, offers more general support to undergraduates than does the typical large state university, its narrative evaluation system favors students who are thinkers rather than memorizers, challengers rather than passive accepters, and self-starters eager to learn for the sake of learning. Concludes a recent graduate: "This is a school where people know how to think."

Westmont College

Santa Barbara, California 93108

Setting: Suburban
Control: Private (Evangelical Christian)
Undergraduate enrollment: 524 men, 830 women
Graduate enrollment: None
Student/faculty ratio: 16:1
Freshman profile: 17% scored over 700 on SAT I verbal; 43% scored 600–700; 34% 500–599; 6% below 500. 16% scored over 700 on SAT I math; 40% scored 600–700; 37% 500–599; 7% below 500. 23% scored above 28 on the ACT; 25% scored 27–28; 34% 24–26; 14% 21–23; 4% below 21. 50% graduated in top tenth of high school class; 70% in upper fifth.
Faculty profile: 95% Ph.D.'s

Tuition and fees: $27,806
Room and board: $8866
Freshman financial aid: 84%; average scholarship or grant: $12,837
Campus jobs: 47%; average earnings: $909/year
Application deadline: Early action: Nov. 1; regular: Feb. 15
Financial aid deadline: Mar. 2
Admissions information: (805) 565-6005; (800) 777-9011
e-mail: admissions@westmont.edu
web site: www.westmont.edu

If a student organization called Prayer Warriors sounds like a contradiction in terms, then you haven't heard of Westmont College in Santa Barbara, California. To a greater degree than many evangelical Christian colleges, Westmont manages to bridge the gap that usually separates the nondenominational Christian school from secular institutions. Although it prohibits the use or possession of alcohol or tobacco on college property, it does not extend these mandates to those of legal age off campus, an approach that students value. "Westmont encourages biblical standards and life-styles," notes a history major. "However, this is a college that encourages students to think things through for themselves and to be critical of their faith." The result is a campus where undergraduates "study" at the beach by day and go dancing after a Westmont Warriors basketball victory at night, much like students at other California colleges. But Westmont remains very much the campus where students minister to the needy in the inner city or around the world or gather quietly together in their Prayer Warriors group.

Student body: Sixty-eight percent of Westmont's students are from California, with the rest coming from 37 other states and 10 foreign countries. Twenty-one percent of the students are foreign nationals or members of racial and ethnic minority groups, with 11% Hispanic, 7% Asian-American, and 1% each Native American, African-American, and foreign national. Ninety-five percent of the students are Protestant; 30% graduated from private or parochial high schools. A senior from the Pacific Northwest describes undergraduates as "committed people, committed to Christ, academics, and friends." A sophomore sees them as "striving for excellence, not only academically but spiritually." Politically, students say a majority of their classmates are white, middle-class conservative Christians, although, observes a junior: "there has been a resurgence in the student body for social causes," among them the AIDS pandemic and malnutrition. Academically, students are described by a senior as "very astute and hardworking." Some students, however, according to a junior, "are consumed with a need to perform (for grades and GPAs) rather than to learn."

Academics: Westmont, which turns 70 in 2007, awards the bachelor's degree in 26 officially approved departmental and interdepartmental majors, and provides an option for students to devise their own concentrations. Students take courses divided between 2 semesters. The average class size is 20 students. Religious studies classes such as Life and Literature of the New Testament may reach 105, but more specialized, upper-level courses like physics can drop below 10.

Of the 124 semester units required for graduation, the college's general-education requirements include 20 semester units of Common Context courses, such as classes related to Biblical and Theological Canons, and 32 semester units of Common Inquiries courses in 8 categories, ranging from Reading Imaginative Literature to Exploring the Life Sciences. In addition, students must complete Common Skills courses in such areas as writing and quantitative and analytical reasoning, and additional courses related to Competent and Compassionate Action.

All faculty, trustees, and administrative staff annually reaffirm their belief in nine articles of faith that range from viewing the Bible as "God-breathed and true, without error in all that it teaches," to seeing the only hope of salvation from original sin to be through faith in Christ. Beyond such basic declarations of faith, the college leaves room for disagreement and discussion on more detailed areas of doctrine and theology. The faculty that results, which is split 87/48 between full-time and part-time members and is 69%

male, draws paeans of praise. "The professors are, for the majority, absolutely incredible," says a liberal studies major. "They teach and challenge us to think and to take time to evaluate and reflect and question what we are learning…. They take us out of our comfort zone."

Nowhere is this standard higher than in the religious studies department. Explains a major: "Its faculty continues to do independent research in their fields and have gained a reputation as some of the world's most renowned scholars. It is also a difficult track that takes no slackers." Professors in the history, English, political science, and philosophy departments draw similar high praise. "Passionate and engaging," raves an English major. Biology and chemistry offer top-notch facilities as well as close teacher-student relationships which combined, produce close to 90% placement in medical schools. Recalls a biology major: "The best experience to date was Star Trek and Pie Night with my organic chemistry professor. Where else can you get a lecture on addition reactions to benzene rings and great apple pie from the same guy?" Likewise, students in freshman-level chemistry were introduced to homemade pizza and liquid nitrogen ice cream by their professor.

Though faculty members have been added in the theater arts and art departments, many students still think these fields of study could be strengthened. The only foreign language majors offered are in French and Spanish but both programs remain small. French has had a single professor, Spanish, two professors and two adjuncts. Some students find the professors in the business/economics program to be very conservative and unwilling at times to acknowledge other points of view.

Facilities: The Roger John Voskuyl Library is fine for studying, with good lighting and plenty of tables, but small when it comes to research, providing more than 160,000 volumes and subscriptions to 3211 periodicals and newspapers. "Adequate but barely adequate," observes a senior. Undergraduates most appreciate the various on-line sources and ready access to materials through interlibrary loan. The library at UC-Santa Barbara "a researcher's dream," in the words of one user also is only about 20 minutes north. A Writer's Corner housed in the library provides tutors on call for every subject.

A full computer lab with 30 PCs and 47 Macintosh microcomputers is based in the library. However, the lab closes when the library does, at midnight, so many students say a personal computer is advisable for those who like to work later. The college strongly recommends that students have their own computers, which students say most do. High-speed Internet access is available in all dorms.

Special programs: Westmont students may spend a term on any of 12 campuses of other members of the Christian College Consortium or as part of 25 different programs, in any of several places in Europe, Latin America, East Asia, or the Holy Lands, or in Washington, D.C. or various states. Potters Clay is a well-attended mission to Ensenada, Mexico, held over spring break. A third of the students typically take part. The college's Leadership Development program engages participants in weekly seminars dealing with the foundations of leadership and helps them to develop leadership portfolios. A 3-2 engineering program is offered with Washington University in St. Louis, Boston University, and the University of Southern California. Individual students also have attended Stanford University and other campuses within the state university system.

Campus life: Eighty-five percent of Westmont students live on the 111-acre wooded campus located 90 miles north of Los Angeles in the foothills of the Santa Ynez Mountains. There are no fraternities or sororities, and residence halls provide much of the focus of student life, featuring events ranging from disco roller skating to nerd bowling. The activities culminate in the annual Spring Sing, in which each hall prepares a musical skit replete with costumes and props. About half the student body is involved in this event as are numerous professors. "It's fun to see them in another light," says a senior. Dances sponsored by the student government are well attended, as are "rerun" parties at which students dress up as their favorite characters from old television programs. Off-campus movies in Santa Barbara, volleyball, rollerblading, and barbecues on the beach, and dancing and hanging out at any of the local clubs or coffeehouses are all popular. Chapel attendance is required 3 times weekly, with 12 misses permitted each semester. Westmont Student Ministries, one of the largest student-run organizations, involves undergraduates in 20 different kinds of ministry, such as helping teenage mothers and the elderly both in the nearest neighborhoods and around the world. The gospel choir involves about 200 students "who desire to sing with soul," says an English major. Crime is rarely an issue on campus, in part because the security staff is very visible and the surrounding area displays "a real sense of neighborhood watch," notes a Californian. Petty theft is sometimes a problem, though, simply because students fail to lock their doors.

Sports are big on Westmont's campus, both to engage in and to watch. Six intercollegiate sports for men are played in NAIA competition, of which Warrior soccer and basketball draw the most fan support. Women's teams also are offered in 6 sports, with women's soccer, basketball, and volleyball garnering the most interest. Two-thirds of the men and women are involved in the 10 fall/6 spring intramural sports available to each, ranging from pickleball to flag football.

Hiking, mountain biking, and rock climbing in the mountains are popular getaways. Those in need of more urban diversion can head to Los Angeles, about 2 hours south.

Cost cutters: Eighty-four percent of the 2005–2006 first-year students and 85% of the continuing students received financial aid. Need-based aid went to 59% of the freshmen and 55% of the rest. The average first-year award for a recent year included $12,837 in scholarship or grant money. The average financial indebtedness of a 2005 graduate was $16,999. Top scholars without financial need are recognized and rewarded: the President's Scholarship pays $11,000, the Provost's Scholarship $9000, and the Dean's Scholarship, $7000, to students with high GPAs and SAT/ACT scores. Top students who apply for admission under the early-action plan can earn one of a handful of full tuition awards. Two-thirds of recent first-year students were scholarship recipients.

Rate of return: Ninety-one percent of the first-year students who enter return for the sophomore year. In the Class of 2005, 65% earned their bachelor's degrees in 4 years, 71% in 5 years; 72% in 6. Four percent graduated in just 3 years.

Payoff: The 3 most popular majors for 2005 graduates were communication studies and biology at 13% each, and English at 12%. Nearly two-thirds of Westmont graduates entered the work force soon after earning their degrees, many taking jobs with such firms as IBM, NCR, Burroughs, and Merrill Lynch. Most graduates stay in the West, many in California; some move to the Pacific Northwest, others to the Southwest. In recent years, about 60% of the graduates have pursued advanced studies either full-time or part-time, with the largest number headed for business school.

Bottom line: Says a recent graduate: "Westmont is a Christian college that offers a quality education that could compete with any top liberal arts program. It is a college where students can learn and at the same time, be valued." Those students not willing to be stretched academically as well as spiritually will miss out on much of what Westmont has to offer.

Colorado School of Mines

Golden, Colorado 80401

Setting: Small town
Control: Public
Undergraduate enrollment: 2278 men, 621 women
Graduate enrollment: 296 men, 111 women
Student/faculty ratio: 15:1
Freshman profile: 11% scored over 700 on SAT I verbal; 41% scored 600–700; 38% 500–599; 10% below 500. 25% scored over 700 on SAT I math; 56% scored 600–700; 17% 500–599; 2% below 500. 39% scored above 28 on the ACT; 22% scored 27–28; 27% 24–26; 11% 21–23. 1% below 21. 45% graduated in top tenth of high school class; 80% in upper fifth.

Faculty profile: 75% Ph.D.'s
Tuition and fees: $8143 in-state; $20,725 out-of-state
Room and board: $6750
Freshman financial aid: 85%; average scholarship or grant: NA
Campus jobs: 60%; average earnings: $750/year
Application deadline: June 1
Financial aid deadline: Mar. 1
Admissions information: (303) 273-3220; (888) 446-9489
e-mail: admit@mines.edu
web site: www.mines.edu

Students attending the Colorado School of Mines may have to complete "epics" in order to graduate, but you won't find them crafting their own versions of *The Iliad* or other such narrative poems. EPICS, which stands for Engineering Practices Introductory Course Sequence, involves freshmen and sophomores in 2 semesters of instruction in computer programming, decision making, graphics, map interpretation, technical writing, and oral communication. Students work together in teams of 4–6 to complete increasingly complex projects that reflect real world engineering problems where the data are imperfect and there is only a "best," not a perfect, solution. The final project involves an actual problem submitted by a university or corporate client and lasts a full semester. Past projects have included remedying a rock-fall hazard in the city of Plume with the U.S. Geologic Survey, designing a public park for Oak Creek, and fluorine extraction for Earth Sciences, Inc. And if the ups and downs of those projects aren't subjects for modern-day epics, what is?

Student body: Though the Colorado School of Mines, known simply as Mines, is a state-supported school, just 80% of its undergraduates are from Colorado; every other state also is represented. Over the last 5 years, Mines has grown more diversified, increasing its minority enrollment from 5% of the total population in 1987, to 16% in 2005. Of that percentage, 7% are Hispanic, 6% Asian-American, 2% African-American, and 1% Native American. An additional 3% are foreign national students from 52 countries. Ninety percent of the students attended public schools. Students are generally very conservative: "They don't like to make waves," says a Coloradan, although some do express their political views when an issue concerns international affairs in petroleum, mining, or engineering in general. There is a professional air about the group; few arrive in class wearing sweats or looking sloppy, and just about all are driven academically. Despite the competition for good grades (the higher the GPA, the better the starting salary), there is little rivalry among students. "The key here is survival (graduation)," says an easterner, "not what the person next to you got. Everyone looks out for him- or herself, but is also willing to help others. We're all in the same boat."

Academics: The School of Mines was first organized by an Episcopal bishop in 1869 to educate engineers to solve the state's mining problems; it was formally established by the then territorial legislature in 1874. CSM awards the bachelor of science degree in 7 programs in engineering plus chemistry, mathematics and computer science, economics and business, and physics, the master's in 13 fields, and the doctorate in 11. The academic program is divided into 2 semesters. The average undergraduate class size is 29. Some freshman classes, in topics such as environmental science, can top 200, but enrollment in upper-level courses can drop to 15 or even lower in some more specialized fields.

All freshmen take the same courses their first year. Along with the first term of the 2-term EPICS program, first-year students take courses ranging from Earth and Environmental Systems and Principles of Chemistry I and II to Physics I and Calculus I and II. Courses in the sophomore year are similar, but not identical, for all students. To satisfy requirements in the humanities and social sciences, students take courses with such names as Nature and Human Values, Principles of Economics, and Human Systems, plus a cluster of electives in these fields. A focus on job preparation begins in the early years as well. Recalls a fifth-year senior: "As early as your freshman year, students are already encouraged to have résumés, cover letters, and interviewing skills ready so that they may start hunting for summer jobs or co-ops."

The faculty consists of 400 members, 200 full-time, 200 part-time. All of the part-timers teach undergraduates as do 180 of the full-time members. Only 20% of the total pool are women. Professors are widely regarded as "excellent," with impressive knowledge in their respective fields thanks to years of practical experience in industry and extensive personal research projects. Most faculty do not let the research interfere with their accessibility to students, although some do. And while the majority "present the material well and want you to succeed," notes a sophomore, "some teachers staple 'drop slips' to tests and say, 'Get out while you can.'"

The combined result of rock-solid faculty and state-of-the-art equipment, much of it furnished by the industries the school serves, is a long list of strong majors. The programs in geological engineering, along with mining engineering (the school has its own 124-year-old mine), metallurgical and materials engineering, and petroleum engineering are especially challenging. Chemical engineering is thorough and tough in its coverage of both chemistry and engineering and has one of the top placement records for its graduates. Faculty in the smaller economics and business department are challenging but attentive.

The most popular degree program, general engineering, stresses the interrelated nature of electrical, civil, environmental, and mechanical engineering, while allowing students to specialize in 1 of the 4 components in their last 2 years. Unfortunately, neither the faculty size nor the equipment in electrical engineering has been able to keep pace with the rapidly growing student demand. Students also are divided over whether the legendary toughest program on campus, Physics II, is actually too tough. Some students contend that Physics I and II serve simply as "weed-out" classes and that professors fail to teach the material in a way that more students would understand.

Facilities: Arthur Lakes Library "is an excellent research and study area for engineering students," remarks a mechanical engineering major, "but it is terrible for anything else." And that suits the vast majority of Mines' engineering and science students just fine. Lakes houses 356,000 volumes and 2700 serial titles with hundreds of databases and e-journals. Its map collection, mostly of Colorado and the general mining and geological areas, is extensive at over 189,000 maps. Lakes also offers the computerized services of CARL (Colorado Alliance of Research Libraries) and puts students in touch with the more than 3 million entries held by Colorado's major research libraries.

Computers are a vital part of the Mines curriculum, incorporated into every class from design projects to writing programs. Altogether, several hundred PCs are readily available in every department, in residence halls, and at Mines' large computer center. Labs are open 7 a.m. to midnight weekdays, close earlier on Friday nights, and offer shorter hours on the weekends. Many buildings, but not all, have wireless access available for the many students who bring their own laptops.

Special programs: The McBride Honors Program in Public Affairs for Engineers provides 40 top freshmen with a series of interdisciplinary seminars in the liberal arts and social sciences, led by a faculty team of humanists, social and physical scientists, and engineers. McBride participants also must complete an internship during the summer after their junior year. Each engineering major is required to complete a 6-week summer field session that provides extensive practical experience. Opportunities for study abroad are available at more than 50 universities worldwide.

Campus life: Thirty percent of Mines undergraduates reside on the 373-acre campus, but more students than in previous years are staying on campus over the weekend. For many, the weekend begins with some free FAC (Friday Afternoon Club) entertainment, featuring a comedian, musician, or hypnotist. Attending an off-campus party or one hosted by the Greeks may follow. Nineteen percent of the men and women belong to 7 national fraternities and 3 national sororities; those numbers are about double the membership of a few years ago, and most say that the Greeks provide a much-needed social outlet as well as a support system during the 4 to 6 academically challenging years at Mines. Dating is somewhat awkward, given the nearly 4 to 1 male-female ratio, but relationships between the sexes are improving. Probably the most popular organizations on the academically intense campus are the professional societies, such as the Society of Petroleum Engineers, or the societies of women, African-American, and Hispanic engineers.

Mines fields 9 NCAA Division II sports for men and 7 for women, which together had one of their best all-around years in 2004–2005. The Orediggers football team went 8–0 and won the Rocky Mountain Athletic Conference for the first time since 1958. The soccer team went to the RMAC Tournament semifinals and for the first time in school history, both the men's and women's basketball teams qualified for the tournament in the same year. Seventy percent of the students get out on the field or court in intramurals, 20 sports for each sex. The school also broke ground on a new student recreation center in August 2005. On-your-own skiing, snowboarding, hiking, biking, and dancing are even more popular. Crime hasn't yet proved to be a problem on campus, in part because of its location in the quiet town of Golden (pop. 15,000), best known as the home of the Adolph Coors Company. Better lighting recently was installed and an escort service started to keep crime of low concern.

One of the more enduring Mines traditions involves making the world's oldest, and some say largest, electrically lighted school emblem, the "M," even bigger. Every year, each freshman is responsible for adding another 10-pound rock to the 104-by-107-foot structure, and first-year students paint the M (and themselves) during orientation. As a final tribute, seniors paint the M before D-parting. Mines students also recently built a new computer-automated and remote-controlled system for the "M" that incorporates 37 different animations of varying colors and shapes to mark school events and holidays, such as a jack-o-lantern in October.

Engineering Days, held every spring, constitute *the* social event of the year. The 3-day program, run by students, celebrates the history and traditions of the School of Mines and features, besides a prominent speaker, activities such as an ore-cart push to the state capitol in Denver, the oil-field olympics, contests in skills such as drilling, hand-spiking, and mucking, and a 4-wheel drive mud bog competition. When not pushing an ore cart, the 15-mile trip east to Denver is a journey frequently made by students in need of some urban excitement not available in Golden.

Cost cutters: In the 2005–2006 school year, 85% of both freshmen and continuing students received some form of financial aid; 74% were on need-based assistance. The average freshman award totaled $12,900, with no breakdown provided on the percentage that was scholarships or grants or self-help aid, such as loans or job earnings. The average financial indebtedness of a recent graduate was $17,500. Mines offers a number of scholarships based on academic merit or athletic ability without regard to financial need; some are funded by industries that the school serves. These awards range from $1000 for 1 year to full tuition for 4 years, with a large number available to out-of-staters and others restricted to Colorado residents. Cooperative programs are available in all majors. An alumni loan helps upperclassmen who have exhausted all other funding sources; the loans require repayment within 2 years of graduation.

Rate of return: Eighty-four percent of entering freshmen return for the sophomore year; 37% graduate in 4 years, 64% within 5, 67% within 6.

Payoff: General engineering, which includes the fields of civil, electrical, environmental, and mechanical engineering, was by far the most popular major for 2005 graduates: 42% of the class earned degrees in that area. Mathematics and computer science was the discipline of choice for 15% of the graduates. Chemical engineering claimed 10%. More than 90% of the graduates accepted engineering-related jobs, many with large oil and other resource companies such as Conoco, Exxon, Consolidation Coal, Shell, and Schlumberger throughout the United States and also worldwide. Twenty percent went on at least part-time for advanced degrees, the majority in engineering. Nearly 270 companies and other organizations recruited on campus in a recent school year.

Bottom line: Students have little doubt that their 4, 5, or 6 years of hard work at the Colorado School of Mines will pay off. With the average starting salary of all 2005 graduates standing at just over $50,000 and starting salaries for geophysical and petroleum engineers averaging more than $10,000 higher, a degree from Mines bears results.

United States Air Force Academy

Colorado Springs, Colorado 80840

Setting: Suburban
Control: Public
Undergraduate enrollment: 4000 men and women
Graduate enrollment: None
Student/faculty ratio: 8:1
Freshman profile: Middle 50% SAT I scores: 590–680 verbal; 620–700 math; 55% graduated in top tenth of high school class.
Faculty profile: 50% Ph.D.'s
Tuition and fees: No tuition; $2500 freshman fee

Room and board: No charge
Freshman financial aid: 100%; average scholarship or grant: NA
Campus jobs: None; average earnings: NA
Application deadline: Jan. 31
Financial aid deadline: NA
Admissions information: (719) 333-2520; (800) 443-9266
web site: www.usafa.edu

If you're a student who likes engineering with a touch of reveille, marching, soaring, and parachute jumping, all for a price tag as free as the wind, then the United States Air Force Academy may offer the baccalaureate program for you. But don't expect a free ride along with the cost-free tuition, room, and board. Although just 52 years old, the youngest of the nation's federally funded service academies matches its siblings push-up for push-up in academic, military, and athletic rigor. As at West Point and the Naval Academy, admission is highly selective: all applicants must have nominations to be considered, and those with letters from U.S. representatives, senators, or the Vice President have the best chance of getting in. Even then, only 15% of those who apply are admitted, based on their recommendations as well as top-notch academic and fitness records. Once in, first-year cadets unprepared for an education unlike anything experienced at a civilian college may find themselves free-falling right out the door.

Student body: The student body, known as the Cadet Wing, is predominantly white American, with 6% Hispanic, 6% African-American, 5% Asian-American, and 1% Native American in a recent school year. Another 1% were foreign nationals from 26 countries. For the most part, cadets are politically conservative, patriotic, highly intelligent, and extremely focused on the goal of becoming not just Air Force officers, but also the best from their class. Explains a first-class cadet (a senior): "The objective here is not to score high, but to score higher than everyone else. Cadets who score really high in academics are rewarded with additional privileges—another incentive to 'beat the mean score' of the class." As academically and athletically competitive as most cadets are, they also learn quickly that they must work together as a team and share a real spirit of camaraderie. As at all the service academies, students operate under an honor code that states, "We will not lie, steal, or cheat, or tolerate among us anyone who does."

Academics: The Air Force Academy offers only the bachelor of science degree in 32 fields. The academic year is divided into two 17-week semesters and a 10-week summer program. As a result, cadets receive only a 3-week summer holiday, spending the bulk of the summer in various leadership or military training programs, traveling to other Air Force bases around the world, or helping to train other cadets. Average class size is 17, although the largest core classes usually enroll 30 and the smallest upper-level courses just 7.

Each new class enters the academy in June and begins basic cadet training, an often-grueling introduction to military life. During this 5-week period, cadets have their hair cut to academy standards and may not smoke, have visitors, receive telephone calls, or leave the academy.

With the official start of the academic year, cadets begin work on the rigorous core requirements all must fulfill, mostly during their fourth-class (freshman) and third-class (sophomore) years. The 33-course core, which accounts for 65% of all academic requirements, is heavily science and mathematics oriented, and some cadets find the engineering requirements particularly difficult. Courses in language and expression, modern world and military history, American government, and geopolitics also are required. Cadets may then continue in a well-rounded basic academic program or specialize in 1 of the 32 majors offered.

There were 530 full-time faculty members in a recent school year, most of them Air Force officers, with a few from the other military branches. Civilian professors usually comprise a fourth of the faculty. Just 15% have been women in recent years. For the most part, cadets find the faculty extremely knowledgeable, professional, and practical. Some of their favorite instructors are ones who graduated from the academy themselves, because they understand the life of a cadet. The faculty's only downfall, according to one first-class cadet, "could be a difficulty in bringing their knowledge down to our level at times."

Although all of the engineering disciplines are strong and offer modern laboratory equipment, aeronautical engineering and astronautical engineering, the nation's only undergraduate degree program in pure space engineering since 1965, are the real heartstoppers. The astronautics laboratory includes both an airborne weapons simulator and a space-shuttle simulator; aeronautical has its own supersonic and subsonic wind tunnels and engine test cells. Mechanical engineering draws a 10-gun salute as well. The management major, which focuses on decision making, offers a strong alternative to engineering, with top-notch professors. The mathematical sciences major emphasizes quantitative problem solving and also rates a 10. The history department is distinguished by its excellent courses in military history. Political science, whose professors are more conservative than their peers at civilian universities, offers numerous research and leadership opportunities.

Majors in English and the humanities are smaller and often dismissed by the more technically oriented students as too "fuzzy." Scoffs one: "There is no great need for English majors in the Air Force." Foreign language study in 7 languages is available only as a minor.

Facilities: Compared to the state-of-the art laboratory equipment, the outstanding planetarium, which can duplicate the night sky at any location on earth, and the amazing athletic facilities, the academy library seems pretty basic. Cadets find its more than 700,000 volumes, 207,000 U.S. documents, and 2100 current periodical and newspaper subscriptions to be more than adequate to complete most research, although the hum of the air conditioner lulls many an exhausted cadet to sleep. In each of the last several years, more extensive computerized research aids have been installed and newly added wireless capability enables cadets to work on-line from any location in the building using a notebook computer.

Laptop computers are issued to all fourth-class cadets at the beginning of the year.

Special programs: Opportunities to travel are extensive. During their second-class summer, cadets participate in Operation Air Force, a 3-week worldwide program at an operational Air Force base to observe firsthand the duties of officers and enlisted personnel. Seven-to-10-day exchanges occur over spring break for select cadets to Air Force academies in 15 countries. During fall semester, small groups of second-class cadets can trade places with their peers at the U.S. Army, Navy, and Coast Guard academies, or at the Air Force Academies of France, Germany, Chile, Spain, and Canada. Parachute training is available to those who volunteer and meet stringent physical requirements. All jumps are free-fall solo.

Campus life: All cadets are required to live on the 18,000-acre campus. On weekdays, they typically rise at 6:00 a.m., have military training from 6:20 to 6:40, eat breakfast, beginning with formation, then attend classes from 7:30 a.m. until just before noon, when it is time for lunch, assembly, and parade, and then nearly 3 hours more of classes, military training, or study. Sports generally occupy cadets until dinner, served from 5 to 7 p.m., after which they study until taps at 11:30 and then collapse into bed.

Two to three Saturdays a month are spent on military training, including inspections and parades, which cadets of all classes must attend. These are usually completed by noon, after which cadets are free unless there is a home football game, which all must attend. Although free time and privileges during the week and on weekends increase as cadets approach their final year, even first-class cadets must carry out all scheduled military duties. Crime has not been a problem, although security has tightened around the campus following the September 11th attacks on the World Trade Center.

Cadets who are not playing 1 of the 17 men's or 10 women's NCAA Division I sports are required to play on a squadron intramural team 2 afternoons a week. Each of the academy's 36 squadrons participates in 13 team and individual sports, from basketball and cross country to wallyball and Ultimate Frisbee. Not surprisingly, the academy's athletic facilities are among the best in the nation. They include 3 full-sized gyms, an Olympic-sized swimming pool and a 40-yard pool, courts for squash, handball, tennis, volleyball, and basketball, 2 weight rooms, an ice rink, a basketball arena, a one-sixth-mile Tartan track and Astroturf field, 143 acres of outdoor playing fields, and two 18-hole championship golf courses. And that's not counting Falcon Stadium, built into the base of the Rampart mountain range, which seats 53,000 for football, soccer, and lacrosse games.

Students may choose among over 80 other extracurricular activities and clubs. Not surprisingly, 2 of the most admired clubs are the soaring team, where students teach others to fly in glider aircraft, and the jump team, whose job it is to teach others how to sky dive. Members of the popular Falconers Club train falcons and fly them during academy athletic events. Men outnumber women 5 to 1 at the academy, which has strained relationships between the sexes and recently focused attention on improving the culture and climate for female cadets following charges of sexual misconduct. When escape is possible (fourth-class cadets typically can leave campus only during 4 weekends a semester), many weary cadets flop down at the home of their sponsors, local families who serve as their homes away from home. Cadets lucky enough to have weekend passes enjoy hiking and skiing in Colorado's rugged Rocky Mountain setting.

Cost cutters: Although it costs Uncle Sam more than $280,000 to graduate 1 cadet from the academy, the cadet pays nothing, at least in money, beyond an initial fee recently set at $2500 when he or she enters. Tuition, room, board, and medical and dental care are free. All cadets also earn regular monthly pay, ($734 per month in a recent school year) which covers the costs of uniforms, books, a computer, and other supplies, with a modest amount left over for personal spending and a savings account. Those cadets unable to submit the full $2500 deposit receive a reduced monthly cash allotment until the deposit has been paid.

Rate of return: Eighty-two percent of the fourth-class students return for their third-class year; 71% graduate in 4 years; 77% in 5 years.

Payoff: Sixty percent of recent graduates earned degrees in 3 broad areas: 30% in engineering, which includes course work from 6 engineering fields; 19% in management; and 11% in the social sciences, which also covers 6 disciplines. All graduates accept commissions as second lieutenants and begin a 5-year active-duty commitment. About 55% of graduates have the opportunity to train as pilots, which incurs a 10-year active duty commitment upon completion of training. Many nonflying career posts in management, science and engineering, finance, intelligence, space and missile operations, logistics, and other areas also are available. Among recent graduates, 4% opted for graduate school in the arts and sciences, 3% for medical school, and approximately 2% pursued advanced degrees in engineering. Cadets interested in attending law school must first complete 2 years of active duty; Congress allows 25 active-duty Air Force officers a year to enter law school. Graduates of the academy also have distinguished themselves in the area of postgraduate scholarship. In the academy's 52-year history, 33 cadets have been selected as prestigious Rhodes Scholars.

Bottom line: Advises a first-class survivor: "It takes a special kind of person to endure 4 years at the Air Force Academy. He or she must be emotionally stable, athletic, self-disciplined, and honorable. Fourth-classmen (freshmen), especially, must be able to deal with many outside stresses while still upholding academic, athletic, and military standards. The 4 years spent here are continuously intense and pose by far the greatest challenge I could ever imagine at this point in my life."

University of Colorado at Boulder

Boulder, Colorado 80309

Setting: Suburban
Control: Public
Undergraduate enrollment: 12,381 men, 11,158 women
Graduate enrollment: 965 men, 908 women
Student/faculty ratio: 16:1
Freshman profile: 5% scored over 700 on SAT I verbal; 35% scored 600–700; 46% 500–599; 14% below 500. 7% scored over 700 on SAT I math; 44% scored 600–700; 39% 500–599; 10% below 500. 17% scored above 28 on the ACT; 17% scored 27–28; 33% 24–26; 24% 21–23; 19% below 21. 22% graduated in top tenth of high school class; 44% in upper fifth.

Faculty profile: 91% Ph.D.'s
Tuition and fees: $5372 in-state; $22,826 out-of-state
Room and board: $7980
Freshman financial aid: 81%; average scholarship or grant: $3635 need-based; $2793 non-need-based
Campus jobs: 24%; average earnings: $1806/year
Application deadline: Jan. 15
Financial aid deadline: Mar. 1
Admissions information: (303) 492-6301
    web site: www.colorado.edu

"How can anyone not love a great education in the perfect environment?" How, indeed, asks each new class of freshmen who flock to the University of Colorado at Boulder from every state in the union and from more than 100 foreign countries. "I came," expands one New Englander, "because the setting is beautiful, there is a lot of skiing, the university is less expensive than the other colleges I applied to, and it has an excellent molecular, cellular, and developmental biology program." While the scenery and the invigorating life-style may be the initial allure, the education proves energizing as well. Highly respected programs under faculty members who in many cases are nationally and internationally known justify on academic terms an education that can also be fairly inexpensive and fun.

Student body: Just over two-thirds of CU's undergraduates are from Colorado, with a third of the rest coming from other western states. Seventy-five percent in a recent year were graduates of public schools. Fifteen percent are from racial and ethnic minority groups, with 6% each Asian-American and Hispanic, 2% African-American, and 1% Native American. Another 1% are foreign national students. Students are open, friendly, generally liberal, and, regardless of their political stance, more likely to protest about various issues than their counterparts on other campuses. Says a senior: "Anti-abortion protests and 'Save the Wolves' campaigns can be seen on any given day across campus, showing the activist spirit that exists at CU." The range of academic levels and interests covers everyone from the highly motivated, serious student to the "complete ski bum." Students in engineering, business, and music tend to be the most competitive, as well as majors in the sciences and psychology within the College of Arts and Sciences.

Academics: The University of Colorado at Boulder, founded in 1876, offers about 85 majors at the bachelor's level, 70 at the master's level and 50 at the doctoral. The undergraduate program is spread among 5 colleges and 2 professional schools. The academic year is divided into 2 semesters. While freshmen should brace themselves for survey courses with nearly 500 classmates, (Principles of Microeconomics has had 486), language and writing programs may enroll as few as 15. Classes for juniors and seniors tend to have about 40 students, although some can go as high as 300.

Each of Colorado's colleges requires some course work in the arts and humanities, social sciences, and natural sciences, although the number of classes varies by program. A core curriculum in the College of Arts and Sciences, which enrolls about 70% of CU students, requires courses in 4 skill areas: foreign language, written communication, critical thinking, and quantitative reasoning and mathematical skills, plus

7 content areas. Students complain that the many requirements make it "nearly impossible" to graduate in 4 years, and fewer than 40% of entering freshmen do so.

All but 45 of the 1227 full-time faculty members teach undergraduates as do all but 18 of the 559 part-timers. Thirty-nine percent are women. Two faculty members won the 2001 Nobel Prize in physics. As a whole, the faculty cover the qualitative spectrum—the good, the bad, and the middle-of-the-road who are gifted researchers but "lack teaching skills or the motivation to improve as teachers," notes a senior. Students especially appreciate the many professors who let students share in their research efforts. Nearly a fifth of the introductory courses are taught by graduate students. "The biggest complaint with TAs," says a political science major, "is that in some disciplines like economics, engineering, and business, many TAs are foreign and accents make it difficult to understand and learn the material being taught."

The 11 degree programs in the College of Engineering and Applied Science provide some of the best equipment available anywhere, including outstanding wind tunnels in aerospace engineering sciences, a nuclear reactor, and an electron accelerator. More than a dozen astronauts are graduates of the school, and student-faculty research collaboration is fairly common. Special educational outreach programs such as Engineering for Developing Communities allows students to focus on creating and implementing sustainable technologies for developing communities around the world. The popular Leeds School of Business wins points for its executive-in-residence program that lets managers from the front lines share their perspectives in the classroom. The College of Music hits many a high note with its own library and research center, containing one of the largest collections of American music in the country, plus plenty of practice rooms, studios, and rehearsal halls that help polish more than 400 public concerts annually. The College of Arts and Sciences has its winning disciplines as well, in anthropology, molecular, cellular, and developmental biology, and psychology. The luster of the physics program, already bolstered by having 2 faculty members win the Nobel Prize in 2001, shines even brighter following presentation of the 2005 Nobel Prize in physics to a physicist who lectures in the physics department but mainly works as a fellow and senior researcher at an institute run jointly by CU Boulder and the National Institute of Standards and Technology.

Mathematics is considered by some students to be a weaker member of the College of Arts and Sciences and some programs in the College of Architecture and Planning have proved disappointing. The chief culprits are inadequate funding and teachers of lesser quality. And many undergraduates single out for criticism lower-division courses throughout the university. Too many, they say, are too big and have teachers who display little interest in their classes.

Facilities: The university's library system, consisting of a main library and 5 branches, holds 3.5 million volumes, 6.8 million microform items, and nearly 21,000 current periodicals. The central Norlin Library is a popular but noisy study spot; serious studiers can get work done if they steer clear of the common area on the second floor. The online system Chinook enables students to see what is available locally as well as at other area libraries. It also connects users to more than 400 electronic indexes, over 3000 full-text journals and magazines, and nearly 100 full-text newspapers. And, says a political science major, "there's plenty of friendly, underused library staff willing to help you search." Business students particularly treasure the William White Business Library, which subscribes to more than 1000 business journals in print and electronic format and contains over 60,000 monographs and bound volumes. Other branch libraries in earth sciences, engineering, math/physics, and music are located around campus. The Law School operates its own library.

More than 1200 Macs and Windows PCs are available at about 60 computing labs in academic buildings and residence halls. Many of the labs are open around the clock. Kiosks that enable students to check their e-mail also are scattered throughout campus. The university strongly recommends that students have their own personal computers.

Special programs: The Sewall and Farrand residential academic programs enable freshmen and sophomores, 330 at Sewall and 400 at Farrand, to take small classes in their dorms as well as to enjoy additional benefits of a "small college" setting while continuing to take other courses throughout the university. The Baker Residential Academic Program offers courses in the environmental sciences to 250 participants. Every year, the Undergraduate Research Opportunities Program sponsors approximately 100 students who wish to work jointly with a faculty member on a research or creative project. Students whose projects are approved receive up to $1200 in stipends or expense allowances to support their work; a limited number of $2400 fellowships are available for full-time summer research. The space track of the Colorado Space Grant Consortium involves undergraduates in building, flying, and operating space experiments, as well as in analyzing data from other research efforts. Over 60 study-abroad programs around the globe are offered for a semester, academic year, or summer; a fifth of the undergraduates take part.

Campus life: Less than a fourth of CU undergraduates (but all the freshmen) reside on the 600-acre campus perched at an altitude of 5400 feet, but life there is usually pretty active and exciting. Seven percent of the men are members of 1 local and 16 national fraternities; 8% of the women are members of 3 local and 13 national sororities. Though Greek parties are generally closed to nonmembers, there are plenty of activities for independents, with nearly 300 student groups to celebrate any academic, ethnic, extracurricular, or social event—even the end of the week, in the weekly FAC (Friday Afternoon Club), or the TNC (Thursday Night Club) for those who finish earlier. Based on its budget of $30 million, Colorado's student union is the largest student government in the nation. Boulder dance clubs are popular, as is just about anything associated with the outdoors, from cycling and skiing clubs to environmental organizations. The most common crimes on campus are bicycle and laptop thefts, although a variety of other criminal offenses do occur. The placement of emergency sirens throughout campus and stepped-up police patrols have helped thwart instances of more serious crimes.

The Golden Buffaloes—the "Buffs"—football team reigns during fall weekends on campus, and home games fill 52,000-seat Folsom Stadium. Fans also turn out to support less publicized efforts by the other 6 men's and 8 women's intercollegiate teams that compete in the Big 12 Conference of NCAA Division I. Intramurals in a recent year attracted 60% of the men and 40% of the women to 13 sports for each sex and 11 coed. Club sports in men's and women's ice hockey, rugby, and lacrosse as well as coed offerings in more unusual pastimes from fly fishing to rodeo and ice and speed skating, keep everyone active.

For those who need an urban escape, Denver is 30 miles southeast. When the snow flies, many students spend their weekends skiing or snowboarding at Vail and other resorts. Otherwise, year-round there's simply the great outdoors everywhere a student turns.

Cost cutters: For 81% of CU's freshmen and 69% of its continuing students, there was financial aid in the 2005–2006 school year. For 46% of the freshmen and 34% of the continuing students, the aid was need-based. The average freshman award for a first-year student with financial need included a need-based grant or scholarship averaging $3635 and need-based self-help aid such as loans and jobs averaging $4030. Non-need-based athletic scholarships for first-year students averaged $14,220. Other non-need-based awards and scholarships averaged $2793. The average indebtedness among just those 2005 graduates who borrowed was $17,225. Various grant and scholarship programs are available to students, some rewarding overall academic achievement, some focused on students planning to specialize in particular fields. Entering nonresident freshmen who graduated in the top fourth of their high school class are automatically considered for Chancellor's Achievement Scholarships that pay $5000 for each of the first 2 years and $2500 for each of the 2 remaining years of enrollment. More than 1900 such scholarships were awarded to freshmen in fall 2005. Each year, 50 Presidents Leadership Class scholars are admitted to a 4-year curriculum focusing on leadership development and receive a $1000-a-year merit-based award. First-year students displaying academic merit or promise may receive $2000 Norlin Scholarships that are renewable with continued participation in the Norlin Scholars Program. Six hundred part-time campus jobs, both on and off campus, are available to students who were not awarded work-study. A cooperative program is offered, primarily in business and engineering.

Rate of return: Eighty-three percent of entering freshmen return for the sophomore year. Just 38% graduate in 4 years; 61%, in 5 years; 66%, in 6 years.

Payoff: In the 2005 graduating class, 16% earned degrees in the social sciences, 15% in business/marketing, and 10% in communication and journalism. A quarter of CU graduates generally enroll in graduate or professional schools. Over 400 companies and organizations recruit on campus.

Bottom line: These words of a CU professor are often quoted around campus: "Do not let your studies get in the way of learning." University of Colorado students who use his advice wisely will find their eyes opened to the physical beauty and mental challenges of the world around them. Those who view his words as an excuse to ski, hike, and party at every available moment will wish they had let their studies "get in the way" a bit more.

University of Denver

Denver, Colorado 80208

Setting: Suburban
Control: Private
Undergraduate enrollment: 2119 men, 2364 women (full and part-time)
Graduate enrollment: 1389 men, 1765 women
Student/faculty ratio: 13:1
Freshman profile: Median SAT I scores: 580 verbal; 585 math; Median ACT composite: 26. 32% graduated in top tenth of high school class; 61% in upper fifth.
Faculty profile: 93% Ph.D.'s
Tuition and fees: $28,410

Room and board: $7965
Freshman financial aid: NA; average scholarship or grant: NA
Campus jobs: 26%; average earnings: $1400/year
Application deadline: Early action: Nov. 1; regular: Jan. 15
Financial aid deadline: Mar. 1 (priority)
Admissions information: (303) 871-2036;
  (800) 525-9495
  e-mail: admission@du.edu
  web site: www.du.edu

For true pioneers, doing something once is never enough, at least not in the case of John Evans, 19th century physician, builder of railroads, and founder of universities. In 1851, Evans, an educational zealot, founded Northwestern University in the community later named for him, Evanston, Illinois. Eleven years later, Evans was appointed governor of what was then the Colorado territory, and amid building railroads and helping to connect the wilds of Denver with the rest of the world, he founded Colorado Seminary in 1864. Better known since 1880 as the University of Denver, the school has maintained Evans's pioneering spirit. In 1929, DU developed one of the first collegiate programs devoted exclusively to international studies. Nine years later, the university instituted its common core curriculum, a series of interdisciplinary courses specially designed and taught by senior faculty, which became a model for others. In 1989, the university's academic advising system was ranked first in the nation among private colleges. In 2004, the university set its sights on expanding students' international experience, starting a program in which eligible juniors could study abroad for a quarter at no additional cost. With tuition and fees in 2005–2006 nearing $28,500, DU challenges the fiscal notion of a "best buy." But for the academic pioneer and the lover of the outdoors, solid learning in the "mile-high city" is worth discovering.

Student body: Just 44% of the students call Colorado home, with classmates drawn from all 49 remaining states and 94 foreign countries. The largest portion of the out-of-staters also come from the West. Hispanics at 6% and Asian-Americans at 4% constitute the largest racial and ethnic minority groups on campus. Three percent are African-American and 1% Native American. Nine percent are foreign nationals. Two-thirds in a recent year were public school graduates. Students describe themselves as politically liberal or conservative, depending on whom you talk to, outdoorsy, and sociable. "From hippie to high class to athletic," says a Californian. Academics are viewed as simply another part of an active collegiate life, with books often vying with mountain bikes and skis for student attention—and sometimes losing. Says an easterner: "A lot of students are very career-oriented, but many do not completely apply themselves and tend to be here for other reasons." Faculty would prefer "slightly more rigor," confides an administrator, and efforts have been under way to strengthen undergraduate programs.

Academics: Denver's academic offerings are broad for a school of fewer than 5000 full-time and part-time undergraduates. DU awards the bachelor's degree in 65 majors spread over 7 undergraduate schools and colleges. Graduate programs at the master's and doctoral levels are offered in 6 schools or divisions, including a College of Law.

The university follows the quarter system, with most students taking 3 of the 4 quarters, each of nearly 50 class days, in an academic year. Although the average class size is about 20 students, most freshmen will share courses with anywhere from 60 to nearly 200 classmates in some of the most popular sections of the mandatory core curriculum. The two-part core, which covers about 40% of the credits required to graduate, begins with various foundation courses in 7 basic subject areas ranging from creative expression to the natural sciences to English. An upper-level thematic core component consists of 3 courses each of which addresses a different theme, one, the theme of self and identities; a second, communities and environment, and a third, change and continuity. Students may choose from a variety of courses offered that represent each theme.

Just 40 of the 503 faculty members are part-time. A fourth of the 463 full-time faculty members teach at the graduate level only; two-thirds of the 40 part-time members do as well. Many of the undergraduate professors from departments as widespread as foreign languages and literature to English to biology boast degrees from the nation's top universities. Sixty-one percent are men. Students drawn to DU by the promise of close relationships with professors are not disappointed. Says a senior: "Professors attend campus social functions, hold study sessions in the pub, have small groups of students over for dinner, and do other things that make students here appreciate the fact that they attend a small university." Another much-appreciated detail: just 5% of the introductory courses are taught by graduate students.

Strong faculty, backed by a solid endowment and opportunities for out-of-classroom experiences in Denver, elevate programs in the Daniels College of Business to the top of students' academic picks. The faculty, says a business management major, are "incredible, with real-world experience combined with innovative ways to make it applicable and hands-on." Within the college, programs at the School of Hotel, Restaurant, and Tourism Management consistently rank among the top five of this type in the nation, and graduates of the School of Accountancy usually score well on the CPA exam. Among less career-oriented disciplines, psychology draws praise for its close-knit faculty and emphasis on student research. English, music, and political science also are considered noteworthy. Engineering majors find the professors very accessible and helpful, though like other technical majors at the university, the department is small and could use more funding.

Other smaller programs in the liberal arts, such as philosophy, religious studies, anthropology, and theater, are caught in the vicious cycle of limited funding, which supports fewer professors, who offer fewer classes, which attract fewer majors.

Facilities: For many students, Penrose is the library they love to hate. One complains, "Its system for shelving books was conceived in hell," although its periodical system was recently reconstructed, making access easier and more convenient to students. Another, who calls it "the worst place to study," simply heads for the Denver Public Library. But those engaged in research who find inadequate its 6000 current periodicals, and 2.7 million volumes of books, government documents, and other bound materials have only to call CARL for help. Through the library's computerized catalog, DU students have access to holdings of the Colorado Alliance of Research Libraries, which includes, among its 6 participants, the University of Colorado at Boulder and its 3.5 million volumes. Altogether, students have on-line access to several million additional publications, enough for just about any research project. Those with visions of food in their heads can sample the bounteous offerings of the Husted Collection, the largest collection of cookbooks at any U.S. university. The 8000 volumes explore 300 years of cooking and together are second only in size to the culinary holdings of the New York Public Library.

Since fall 1999, all first-year students have been required to bring a laptop computer to campus. Students can use their laptops just about anywhere, with more than 24,000 Internet connections located around campus, in the library, commons rooms, and every residence hall room. All buildings are wireless, too.

Special programs: Study abroad is offered in more than 45 countries through a variety of overseas programs. DU also runs its own fall quarter in London. The new Cherrington Global Scholars Program enables all juniors in good academic standing with a 3.0 GPA to study abroad for a quarter at no additional cost. Students may choose among DU programs across 6 continents. Back home, the university offers 2 integrated degree programs; one leads, over 5 years, to the baccalaureate degree and the master's in business administration, and the other teams the master's in business with a bachelor of science in either electrical or mechanical engineering, again in 5 years including 1 summer session. Another popular degree option is the business minor, which consists of 7 business courses that offer a general background in the field to students wishing to make their liberal arts major a bit more marketable. A minor in leadership also is an option; students who choose to take part in the Pioneer Leadership Program live for the first year in their own wing of a residence hall. A Partners in Scholarship program gives grants to students to conduct faculty-supervised research projects or to launch creative endeavors.

Campus life: Forty-three percent of the students reside on the 125-acre campus, which, being located in a residential neighborhood only 8 miles southeast of Denver's business district, faces its threat of robberies and car break-ins. However, the addition of more security personnel, as well as abundant emergency telephones and an escort service, makes students feel well protected. Says a senior: "I generally feel very safe, particularly because we are in the middle of a really nice, rather affluent neighborhood." For most undergraduates, the social life at DU revolves around 2 centers, the Greeks and the mountains. Thirteen percent of the men belong to 7 national fraternities; 12% of the women pledge to 5 national sororities. Independents say that the Greek system is the main social scene for all students, so there is little division on that score. Hockey games draw the biggest crowds among the 9 men's and 10 women's varsity sports, all played in Division I. More than 24 club sports and 16 intramural sports also attract good participation. "Recreation is big here," concludes a junior, and students have just the facility in which to prove it. The sports and wellness center that opened in 1998 provides an ice arena, community skating rink, gymnasium, multipurpose field house, an Olympic-sized swimming pool, exercise facilities, health clinic, yoga studio, tennis courts, and playing field, just about everything a recreation-loving student body could want.

Skiing, snowboarding, mountain biking, and hiking generally draw students off campus in all kinds of weather. About half the students and faculty turn out for Winter Carnival, an annual weekend of outdoor activities held at a major Colorado ski resort.

Cost cutters: About 53% of all DU undergraduates demonstrate financial need and receive some form of need-based assistance. No other figures are available to show the separate percentage of first-year students receiving aid nor the amount of the average scholarship or grant, or self-help assistance. The average total award to undergraduates who demonstrate need, which combines merit and need-based aid, is $23,078. DU offers about 500 merit awards each year, approximately 25% to incoming freshmen. Those first-year students who carried a 3.4 GPA with either a 24 or higher ACT or 1150 or higher SAT in math and critical reading are eligible to receive academic scholarships of between $4000 and 10,000. First-year students from the upper 5% of their high school graduating classes with even higher test scores and who show strong examples of leadership, community service, and extracurricular involvement are eligible for a limited number of full-tuition Alumni Scholarships. Two full-tuition scholarships for Native American students also are provided. Special awards in art, music, and theater are offered in varying amounts, up to full tuition in music.

Rate of return: Eighty-seven percent of first-time, full-time freshmen return for the sophomore year; 56% go on to graduate in 4 years; 68% in 5 years; 71% in 6.

Payoff: In a recent graduating class, 7.5% earned bachelor's degrees in communication; 7% specialized in biology, 6% in marketing. A third of the graduates typically enroll in graduate or professional school within 6 months of commencement, most seeking an MBA or other advanced business degree. Two-thirds find jobs within the same 6-month period. Says an administrator: "Major recruiters have been large corporations with Colorado ties: Coors, Gates Rubber, and oil companies. At present, most recruiters are Colorado-based, mid-sized employers such as Storage Technology and Boettcher & Co." One hundred sixty-five companies and organizations recruited on campus in a recent school year. Just over 90% of the graduates take positions within the state.

Bottom line: Says an accounting major from the midwest: "DU is a wonderfully relaxed yet academically inclined educational institution. Anyone with an interest in the outdoors will really love it here."

University of Northern Colorado

Greeley, Colorado 80639

Setting: Suburban
Control: Public
Undergraduate enrollment: 3817 men, 5868 women
Graduate enrollment: 295 men, 711 women
Student/faculty ratio: 23:1
Freshman profile: 2% scored over 700 on SAT I verbal; 18% scored 600–700; 47% 500–599; 33% below 500. 3% scored over 700 on SAT I math; 16% scored 600–700; 46% 500–599; 35% below 500. 4% scored above 28 on the ACT; 7% scored 27–28; 22% 24–26; 34% 21–23; 33% below 21. 23% graduated in top fifth of high school class; 47% in upper two-fifths.

Faculty profile: 77% Ph.D.'s
Tuition and fees: $3837 in-state; $12,381 out-of-state
Room and board: $6412
Freshman financial aid: 80%; average scholarship or grant: $3525 need-based
Campus jobs: 20%; average earnings: $1946/year
Application deadline: Aug. 1
Financial aid deadline: Mar. 1
Admissions information: (970) 351-2881; (888) 770-4UNC
e-mail: unc@mail.unco.edu
web site: www.unco.edu

An employer or graduate school admissions officer glancing through a typical college transcript thinks nothing of seeing codes like ECON 105, HIST 397, SPAN 202, or CHEM 321. But how about a course listed as MIND 181 or MIND 290? That could be a clue that some especially mind-stretching learning has been going on, which is exactly the case at the University of Northern Colorado, an hour north of Denver. The university's Life of the Mind project involves undergraduates in interdisciplinary courses that tackle broad intellectual concerns from the earliest examples of Western and Oriental thought to the most provocative twentieth century thinking. For example, MIND 181, the Great Traditions of Asia, discusses the Indian Hindu classic *The Upanishads*. These courses are offered as options within the regular Liberal Arts

Core program but are required for honors students. A public lecture series, linked to the Life of the Mind program, draws nationally known speakers to the campus.

Having celebrated its 115th birthday in 2005, UNC may be getting mind-blowing reviews from many of its honors students, but nationally it remains in the shadow of the bigger and better known University of Colorado and Colorado State. Among UNC students, programs specializing in business, education, music, and nursing tend to be rated among the best. The university's well-respected School of Music still makes UNC the only institution of higher education to have garnered a Grammy nomination, in 1985 in jazz. But for the price, about $19,000 for out-of-state tuition, fees, room, and board in 2005–2006, students in general are increasingly paying mind to what UNC has to offer.

Student body: The university very much remains a Colorado school, with 90% of all undergraduates from within state and half of the rest also from the region, although 46 states are represented. All but 8% are graduates of public high schools. Over a recent 7-year period, enrollment of racial and ethnic minority students rose by over 20%, although UNC is still not as diverse as many students and administrators would like. Fifteen percent are members of racial and ethnic minorities, including 8% Hispanic, 3% each Asian-American and African-American, and 1% Native American. One percent also are foreign nationals from 50 countries. Five cultural centers on campus serving Hispanic, African-American, Native American, Asian/Pacific-American, and international students, as well as a mentorship program that matches minority freshmen with upperclassmen, are helping to retain these students once they are admitted. Issues concerning diversity are about the only political or social concerns that prompt students to raise their voices. Overall, students find the mix at UNC to be low-key, friendly, and accepting. Notes a senior: "Nobody is very outrageous or extremely liberal. People who are comfortable being average are at home at UNC." On either side of the academic middle, though, are the competitive honors students and nursing and business majors, and those who are majoring in parties. But, cautions a junior, "those students coming here to party every night find their college career at UNC cut to a very short semester."

Academics: UNC awards degrees through the doctorate with 40 undergraduate degree programs spread among 5 recently reorganized colleges. The academic year is divided into 2 semesters. The average size of undergraduate classes ranges from 35 to 50 students. A freshman may well wind up in a biology lecture with 250 other students, but upper-level courses in his or her major may have fewer than 12.

Undergraduates who enter as of fall 2006 must meet the requirements of a new Liberal Arts Core. As part of the core, students must complete at least 40 hours distributed among such basic core courses as composition, math, arts and humanities, the social and behavioral sciences, and the physical and life sciences, plus at least 1 multicultural course and 1 international studies course. Several of the class options include courses from the Life of the Mind Project.

Of the university's 581 faculty members in a recent school year, 169 were part-time. Fifty percent of the full-time professors were women. All faculty taught undergraduates, though 17% of the introductory courses were taught by graduate students, some of whom get high marks from students. Others, recalls a senior, "were average at best." Undergraduates maintain that the number of good professors who display a personal interest in their students outweighs the portion who have trouble communicating with students and really don't care whether they do or not. "The best professors," says a senior, "are willing to give more than office hours in order to get to know their students. The bad professors couldn't care less about students and teaching is a chore they have to do in order to continue their research." A number of the "best" professors opt to live on campus in faculty housing, which further enhances relationships. Many professors also stay closely involved in the real world of work, serving as a practicing court justice, for example, or as a member of the Denver symphony.

Having faculty with feet firmly planted in both worlds keeps many of UNC's preprofessional programs strong. The Monfort College of Business offers the best of the old and the new: an experienced faculty and a high-tech academic program. The college also became in 2004 the first business school in the nation to win the Malcolm Baldrige National Quality Award, which recognizes business efficiency and competitiveness, from the U.S. Department of Commerce. The College of Education and Behavioral Sciences maintains, for many, a tradition of excellence that stretches back to the university's founding as a state normal school. Partner schools offer classes in kindergarten through twelfth grade, providing opportunities for hands-on experience. Students interested in elementary education major in a liberal arts emphasis in the Interdisciplinary Studies program that provides a broad background in mathematics, science, language arts, and history/social science. While some students find the education courses too easy and some faculty members not too skillful, others think professors do their best to stay on the cutting edge of the field and rate the program nothing less than "outstanding." Psychology, recently moved to the College of Education and Behavioral Sciences, also draws varied student reaction, with some majors finding the faculty a bit "unapproachable," and others valuing the variety of courses offered and the opportunities to gain clinical experience and to work with professors in their research. The School of Music in the College of Performing and Visual Arts is very selective, and well funded, with a dedicated faculty noted for providing students with many opportunities to perform. The theater arts program is considered first rate as well, though dance, offered only as a minor, has been hurt by recent budget cuts, and the excellent visual arts program, too, could use more funding. The School of Nursing in the College of Natural and Health Sciences is much admired for its 100% job placement rate. The college's program in speech-language pathology and audiology also is considered strong. In the College of Humanities and Social Sciences the philosophy department is especially responsive to students, offering a seminar every year at which students can evaluate the department and make suggestions of courses they would like to see offered. The Hispanic Studies department, which offers majors in Spanish and Mexican-American studies as well as bilingual and bicultural education endorsements, is also much admired by students.

Not all programs in the College of Humanities and Social Sciences fare as well, according to students. The modern language department has had to drop instruction in Chinese in response to budget cuts, leaving majors only in French and German, along with Spanish in the Hispanic Studies department and courses in Japanese. Some of the math professors in the College of Natural and Health Sciences are not as approachable or as good at transmitting their thoughts as peers in other disciplines.

Facilities: James A. Michener Library, named for the prize-winning author, a former student and faculty member at UNC, contains 1 million volumes and 2700 periodicals. Students find it roomy and conducive to study "except on Tuesday nights, when all the Greeks come," qualifies a junior. Students who choose may borrow a laptop from the library, or bring their own, and hide away in the many private areas offering wireless access. All of the books and periodicals, plus those at 6 other Colorado schools including the 2 larger state universities, are listed in a computerized catalog. Rounding out the selections are a music library with more than 72,000 scores and recordings and a library in the College of Education and Behavioral Sciences with some 27,000 volumes, largely for children and teenagers.

Most students value the 19 computer facilities which offer 565 largely Macintosh and IBM computers divided among 2 labs in the business college, 1 in the library, and 1 each in the main buildings for education, science, and journalism as well as in the student center and residence halls. All computers have Internet access. Many of the labs are closed at different times during weekdays for classes, a situation that tends to make the evening and weekend hours more crowded. Three labs are open around the clock, including a computer commons in the University Center, which students may access at any time with their identification card. Any student may reserve a computer ahead of time to insure that a unit will be available when he or she needs it.

Special programs: Through the National Student Exchange programs, students can study at more than 200 campuses throughout the United States. Opportunities for foreign study are available in England, Spain, France, Germany, Australia, and other countries. A semester at Oxford Polytechnic is popular as well.

Campus life: A third of UNC undergraduates including all freshmen reside on the 240-acre campus, which is divided into 2 distinct but adjacent parts: the central campus with older, ivy-covered buildings, and the west campus with modern, high-rise structures. Residence halls and classroom buildings are located on both. Weekends are divided by type as well, ranging from the very intense, where there seems to be nothing but nonstop partying, to those when just about everyone has left town. The Greeks sponsor some kind of event almost every weekend, usually including not just the 6% of the men and 4% of the women who are members of the 10 national fraternities and 8 national sororities but everyone else as well. Still, large numbers of Denver residents continue to make the hour's drive home and many winter weekends find students flocking to area ski resorts.

Students say UNC's move in fall 2003 to Division I from Division II in NCAA sports competition has drawn more fans to the sidelines. Football, which boasts a new stadium as well as 2 NCAA Division II National Championships, draws the best crowds among the 7 men's and 9 women's intercollegiate sports. Club hockey games are gaining attention as well. Twelve intramural sports for men and 11 for women also are an option. The annual UNC Jazz Festival gets everyone's heart pumping and feet moving in the spring.

Students find Greeley (pop. 77,000) to be as inexpensive for living as it is calm and peaceful. Vandalism, bike thefts, and car break-ins are the most frequent campus crimes. An increase in car break-ins during the 2005–2006 school year prompted stepped-up patrols and e-mails advising students how to take precautions to prevent thefts. An escort service until 2 a.m., well-placed emergency telephones, bike and car patrols and abundant lighting help students feel secure. Notes a westerner: "Police reports in the school newspaper make out the most troublesome 'crimes' to be very minor, such as getting a foot caught on a bunk bed or a random person driving through the parking lot."

Favorite travel destinations are the other members of the Colorado university system, located in Fort Collins, 30 minutes northwest, and Boulder, an hour southwest. Denver is an hour's drive south; the mountains are an hour and a half away.

Cost cutters: Eighty percent of freshmen and 74% of continuing students in the 2004–2005 school year, the most recent year for which data was available, received financial aid. For about 60% of both groups the aid was need-based. The average freshman award for a first-year student with financial need included a need-based scholarship or grant averaging $3818 and need-based self-help aid such as loans and jobs averaging $6921. Non-need-based athletic scholarships for first-year students averaged $5188. Non-need-based awards and scholarships averaged $2805. No figure is available on the average indebtedness of recent graduates. Trustees and Presidential scholarships pay $5000 and $1500 respectively to Colorado residents. Many resident freshmen receive the nonrenewable Provost's Scholarship, which pays $1000 to any incoming student who meets certain GPA and standardized test score criteria. Out-of-state students who meet similar criteria are automatically eligible for a $5000 National Undergraduate Scholarship. Performance awards in music, math/science, and athletics also are available.

Rate of return: Seventy-two percent of entering freshmen return for the sophomore year. Twenty-six percent go on to graduate in 4 years; 43% within 5 years; 47%, in 6 years.

Payoff: Among 2005 graduates, 24% earned bachelor's degrees in special education, 17% in sport and exercise science, and 15% in professional psychology. Just over 80% of UNC grads head immediately into the real world, taking jobs with school districts and social service agencies as well as major corporations like Hewlett-Packard and IBM. About 470 companies and organizations recruited on campus in the 2004–2005 school year. Twelve percent in a recent year pursued graduate study. Students typically settle in the Rocky Mountain region.

Bottom line: The University of Northern Colorado is little known outside the region, but for students willing to trade reputation for respectable programs in a number of fields, UNC is a reasonable choice. Advises a midwesterner: "High school students looking for a friendly atmosphere where you can get to know professors and faces on campus will do well here. Those interested in education, business, or theater will find great programs. Those looking for strong competition or anonymity, or strong school spirit and highly popular and successful college sports teams, may not like it as well."

Connecticut

United States Coast Guard Academy

New London, Connecticut 06320

Setting: Small town
Control: Public
Undergraduate enrollment: 752 men, 300 women
Graduate enrollment: None
Student/faculty ratio: 10:1
Freshman profile: 17% scored over 700 on SAT I verbal; 53% scored 600–700; 29% 500–599; 1% below 500. 20% scored over 700 on SAT I math; 70% scored 600–700; 10% 500–599; 0% below 500. 23% scored above 29 on the ACT; 63% scored 24–29; 14% 18–23; 0% below 18. 61% graduated in top tenth of high school class; 87% in upper fourth.

Faculty profile: 30% Ph.D.'s
Tuition and fees: No tuition; $3000 entrance fee
Room and board: No charge
Freshman financial aid: 100%; average scholarship or grant: N/App
Campus jobs: N/App; average earnings: N/App
Application deadline: Early action: Nov. 1; regular: Mar. 1
Financial aid deadline: N/App
Admissions information: (860) 444-8500; (800) 883-8724 e-mail: admissions@exmail.uscga.edu web site: www.cga.edu

Don't know your representative in Congress? (Maybe you're not even sure who he or she is.) Don't count the Vice President among your 500 closest friends? But you still think you'd like to attend one of the nation's 5 tuition-free service academies? Take heart. Although 4 of the 5 academies require that applicants be nominated by members of Congress or other high-ranking officials, the 130-year-old U.S. Coast Guard Academy does not. Instead, cadets are admitted according to a merit-based system that uses much the same criteria as civilian colleges. Prospective cadets are measured according to 2 main criteria: academic standing, which makes up 60% of the total score, and overall achievement based on an evaluation of a candidate's total file by a Cadet Candidate Evaluation Board. The board considers such factors as motivation, leadership, and personal perspective, as well as personal fitness, academics, and evaluations and recommendations. The screening is rigorous; the academy's acceptance rate, just 1 of every 3 applicants. Once in the door, cadets do as much marching and sprinting as they do studying. But the price tag is something any civilian can eagerly salute: no charge for tuition, room, or board; cadets pay only an initial $3000 fee—and agree to serve after graduation as officers in the U.S. Coast Guard for 5 years. Says a government major: "We wake up early and spend hours studying and marching because we look forward to the summer experiences and eventually graduating into the Coast Guard."

Student body: The corps of cadets in a recent year was 79% Caucasian-American, 7% Asian-American, 6% Hispanic, and 5% African-American, 1% Native American, and 2% foreign nationals from 14 countries. A fourth of the cadets typically come from the Northeast and Middle Atlantic states, although all 50 states are represented. Cadets are dedicated, with a sense of duty, well-rounded athletically as well as academically, and politically usually quite conservative. "Students tend to steer away from issues that challenge cultural norms or positions of authority," observes a senior, known as a first-class cadet. They also are determined to succeed, with good reason: a cadet's class rank determines where he or she will be assigned in the first job after graduation. Add to this incentive the fact that more than three-quarters of all cadets graduated in the top quarter of their high school class, and you have some of the nation's best competing to be the *very* best. Still, a genuine spirit of camaraderie seems to bind the cadets together, rather than letting the competition split them apart. "Life is tough here," says a first-class cadet, "and to make it through you really need to work together with your classmates." The honor concept, which states that a cadet "will not lie, cheat, steal, or attempt to deceive," further solidifies the bond. Because the academy is small, many cadets get to know members of other classes quite well and continue to see each other in the course of their Coast Guard careers. Says a second-class cadet: "Cadets are a closely bound group. Very rarely do cadets *not* spend time with other cadets."

Academics: The U.S. Coast Guard Academy offers bachelor of science degrees in 8 technical or professional areas: civil, electrical, mechanical, and naval architecture/marine engineering, marine and environmental science, operations research and computer analysis, government, and management. The academic year is technically divided into 2 semesters, although cadets spend most of their summers on training cruises aboard Coast Guard cutters or sailing the tall ship *Eagle* to exciting ports around the world, a duty most cadets don't mind. Says a first-class cadet: "Most of my friends from civilian colleges go home and cut grass while I am training for my job upon graduation." The first summer, known as swab summer, however, is far less glamorous, with fourth-class cadets (freshmen) becoming indoctrinated into military life. Especially here a 1-week cruise aboard the *Eagle* is a welcome break.

Class sizes usually range between 12 and 25 cadets, with classes in Biblical Literature recently enrolling just 4 and Introduction to Electrical Engineering topping out at 41. All cadets are required to complete a core of 25 courses that includes heavy doses of engineering and science, classes in the humanities, and professionally related courses in such areas as navigation, law, and officer duties. More than 70 of the 126 credits required for graduation are the same for all cadets, a lack of choice that some find constricting. All cadets also must pass intermediate and survival swimming.

All faculty members, 112 in a recent year, teach full-time, just 10% in a recent year were women, and as a group they reflect a mix of civilian and military backgrounds. Cadets find the faculty extremely bright and keenly interested in the subjects they are teaching. Because most members are commissioned officers at the academy on a 3-year term, not all are equally adept at getting their thoughts across in an understandable manner. However, the majority more than make up for any lack of teaching expertise with a commitment "to bend over backwards to help every student," says a first-class cadet. "Some even force extra help onto us." Those who are Coast Guard officers also understand the stresses and time constraints of being a cadet, "but the civilians bring us the outside world," adds a first-class cadet. The Coast Guard officers may be understanding but they are no less demanding. Says a first-class cadet: "They have huge expectations for us since we may someday be on the same ship or flying the same aircraft."

The academy has an excellent engineering program with technically advanced facilities, small classes under expert faculty (an associate professor of mechanical engineering was named the 2001 U.S. Professor of the Year for baccalaureate colleges), and real-life projects that often focus on current Coast Guard needs in ship design and construction. Cadets regularly use a radar trainer in their nautical science courses. The academy also has 1 of 6 ship's-bridge simulators in the nation; this consists of a 182-degree visual scene surrounding a life-size ship's bridge. The bridge gives cadets the chance to experience firsthand the challenge of handling a Coast Guard cutter in various kinds of wind and current conditions. Little wonder that the academy's marine engineering department won a nationwide ship-design contest in a recent school year!

However, not all disciplines encounter such smooth sailing. The marine and environmental science major gets by with more dated lab equipment, and its classes are more crowded than most. Its faculty, however, is excellent, in the words of a major, "always available for help and challenging students to think, design, and discover for themselves." Although cadets generally like the discussion-oriented government and management majors, they say the heavy emphasis on science and engineering makes it hard to concentrate on courses in these nontechnical areas. Government and management, however, have both become 2 of the 3 most popular disciplines in which cadets choose to specialize. Some cadets also would like to see instruction in foreign languages other than Spanish. "At least core courses in French and German should be offered," says a government major.

Facilities: "The library is my biggest complaint," observes an electrical engineering major, voicing the views of many. "The sources are outdated to the point where it's embarrassing." The collection of 150,000 volumes and 600 periodicals is heavy with government documents and technical materials although various computerized services make the materials easy to access. But cadets haven't far to go for more. Many simply use the Internet or trek across the street to the library at Connecticut College, which has 3 times as many volumes and much more variety. As a study center, the academy library usually is quiet, adds a government major "because not many students use it."

Each cadet is issued a PC notebook computer on entrance to the academy, and other computers with more advanced capabilities are located throughout the barracks, library, and academic buildings. All rooms are wired for Internet access, and there are many wireless areas around campus. Cadets' chief complaints in the 2005–2006 school year, according to a management major: "There are often problems with the Internet going down because of the number of cadets using it at the same time. There also are strict limitations on how much cadets can download from the Internet at one time."

Special programs: Cadets may spend the fall semester of their junior year at the U.S. Army, Navy, or Air Force Academy. They may also cross-register for classes at Connecticut College. The Academy Instruction Mission (AIM) program during the summer prior to a student's senior year in high school gives prospective cadets a taste of academy life. Typically, half of the graduates of the 1-week program earn appointments to the academy.

Campus life: All cadets are required to live on the 110-acre campus and to stay there, at least on weekdays; only first-class cadets may leave campus for a few hours on Wednesday evening. All cadets, except fourth-class members, are granted liberty on Friday afternoons. Says a second-class cadet: "Your time here as a freshman is controlled more than seniors. And you learn very fast what to do with free time." The cadets' lifestyle is very regimented: up at 6, with reveille, of course, followed by daily room inspection, personnel inspection, and breakfast. Morning classes run from 8 until lunch at noon; afternoon classes are held until 3:40. The hours between 4:00 and 6:15 are spent playing intramural or varsity sports, engaging in other extracurricular activities, or getting extra academic help. Then comes dinner, an optional meeting period between 7:30 and 8, and study until 10 o'clock, when taps sound, although cadets may continue to study until midnight. "The academics are tough," says a first-class cadet. "Add on sports, activities, and military requirements and duties, and there's not enough hours in the day." Leave and privileges are extended to cadets as they progress in years, but curfews are enforced. Saturday mornings are often filled with inspections, lectures, and other military obligations.

Every cadet is required to participate in intercompany and/or intercollegiate sports competition for 2 of 3 sports seasons. For those who don't play varsity football, attendance at all home games is mandatory, and other of the 12 men's, 9 women's, and 3 coed varsity sports played in NCAA Division III draw their own enthusiastic crowds. Sixty percent of the men and 74% of the women take part in 13 intramural sports offered for each sex. Many play a variety of club sports, with rugby a particular favorite. Confides a second-class cadet: "Practice is outside academy grounds so it is a good opportunity to get away from the academy."

The waterfront athletic facilities rank among the finest in the nation. The Rowing Center has a 16-person practice rowing tank. The Seamanship-Sailing Center has facilities to repair the academy's fleet of sailboats, which range in size from 14 to 28 feet. The Coast Guard sailing team competes around the world.

Musical groups like the Idlers, Ice Breakers, and Glee Club, as well as the Windjammers drum and bugle corps, are popular. Various engineering societies also have large memberships. Male-female relationships between cadets not from adjoining classes (for example, second class and first class) are discouraged. While drinking alcohol is allowed off campus, cadets are subject to mandatory random drug testing. Under the honor concept, cadets caught stealing are usually dismissed; crimes committed by outsiders are practically non-existent as well. "The academy is a fortress," says a third-class cadet. "I feel safe all the time."

Since only first-class cadets can have automobiles, most cadets must remain in New London (pop. 29,000), located 45 miles southeast of Hartford. Cadets without wheels who can leave campus generally go to their sponsor families, local residents who offer the weary cadets a haven for dinner and relaxation, or cross the road to events at Connecticut College. "There is one, and only one, important thing when it comes to weekend time at the academy," says a first-class cadet. "Get out of here." The best getaways for cadets with cars are major cities like New York, Boston, or Newport, Rhode Island. Weekend ski trips are popular among cadets with both cars and weekend passes, as are hiking, biking, rock climbing, and camping trips.

Cost cutters: Because cadets are considered military personnel rather than simply students, they receive a monthly stipend, recently about $730, while they are at the academy. This stipend helps cover the cost of books, uniforms, computer, and other incidental expenses. The federal government picks up the tab for all major charges such as tuition, room, board, and medical care. Each entering cadet need pay only a $3000 fee, which helps defray initial supply costs before the first paychecks come.

Rate of return: Seventy-nine percent of the cadets who enter the academy return for the second year. Sixty percent graduate in 4 years.

Payoff: About a fifth, 21%, of recent graduates earned bachelor's degrees in management. Nineteen percent majored in marine and environmental science; 17% in government. One hundred percent immediately fulfill their military obligation by serving at sea as junior officers in the U.S. Coast Guard for five years, the first 2 on a Coast Guard cutter. Assignments take them all over the United States, primarily along the coast, as well as to Europe, the Caribbean, and Japan, wherever they are called. Says a second-class cadet, "As can be witnessed in the wake of Hurricane Katrina, the United States Coast Guard has been absolutely phenomenal and in several years that will be me helping people." The Coast Guard also sends a considerable number of cadets to graduate school once they have completed their commitments.

Bottom line: The free education, although appealing, should not be the only reason to choose the Coast Guard Academy. "It is not free by any stretch of the imagination," says a government major. "You sacrifice parties and traditional college fun for service of your country." And that service quickly follows. Says a first-class cadet: "We graduate fleet ready—within 30 days of graduation you will be expected to put all your knowledge to the test when you report to your first unit. This is an awesome responsibility," and one prospective cadets need to keep uppermost in their choice to spend 4 years at the academy.

The University of Connecticut

Storrs, Connecticut 06269

Setting: Rural
Control: Public
Undergraduate enrollment: 7028 men, 7815 women
Graduate enrollment: 1817 men, 2133 women
Student/faculty ratio: 17:1
Freshman profile: 6% scored over 699 on SAT I verbal; 34% scored 600–699; 50% 500–599; 10% below 500. 9% scored over 699 on SAT I math; 41% scored 600–699; 42% 500–599; 8% below 500. 4% scored above 29 on the ACT; 54% scored 24–29; 34% 18–23; 4% below 18. 37% graduated in top tenth of high school class; 80% in upper fourth.

Faculty profile: 95% Ph.D.'s
Tuition and fees: $7912 in-state; $20,416 out-of-state
Room and board: $7848
Freshman financial aid: 93%; average scholarship or grant: $5473 need-based; $4867 non-need-based
Campus jobs: NA; average earnings: NA
Application deadline: Early action: Dec. 1; regular: Feb. 1
Financial aid deadline: Mar. 1
Admissions information: (860) 486-3137
e-mail: beahusky@uconnvm.uconn.edu
web site: www.uconn.edu

Almost since its founding as the Storrs Agricultural School in 1881, the University of Connecticut has been somewhat like the "Connecticut Yankee in King Arthur's Court." Like the character in Mark Twain's novel, the flagship campus of Connecticut's state university system has shared a table with many prestigious companions. Included are some of New England's most elite private institutions, among them Connecticut's own Yale University, alma mater of 70 college and university presidents, as well as U.S. presidents, including George W. Bush, his father George H. W. Bush, and Bill Clinton (a graduate of Yale Law School). But state residents and other students accustomed to looking only at New England's pricier, private options are finding a welcome surprise at the University of Connecticut. A 20-year $2.3 billion initiative known as 21st Century UConn has already meant more than 9 million square feet of new and renovated space on the University's main campus at Storrs as well as its other regional campuses, health center, and law school. New buildings have meant state-of-the-art equipment that has lured new faculty, who in turn have attracted bright, new students willing to give UConn a second look. They may expect just another large, impersonal state university, but many are discovering that a degree from UConn can "pack a punch" all its own.

Student body: The "jeans and sweatshirt" crowd at UConn is more diverse than it used to be. Though just 1% of the undergraduates in a recent year were foreign nationals from 53 countries, 6% were Asian-American, 5% African-American, and 5% Hispanic. In fall 2005, minority enrollment in the freshman class was 111% higher than the number enrolling in fall 1995; overall freshman enrollment was 61% higher than a decade earlier. The vast majority remain Yankee, 76% from Connecticut, with most of the rest also from the Northeast. Undergraduates come, however, from all 50 states. Students see themselves as down-to-earth members of the middle class. "Socially, UConn is very open," says a junior, "and it is easy for students to find their niche. Politically, UConn is open-minded and represents both liberal and conservative opinions." Academically, students sense that the quality of entering freshmen is higher than it was a few years ago, although the depth of competitiveness varies from department to department. Students in the drama, pharmacy, engineering, and biology programs tend to party less than their peers in other disciplines, but to earn A's and B's just about anywhere, a senior notes, "a student must work hard."

Academics: The University of Connecticut offers degrees through the doctorate with bachelor's degree programs available in 103 majors through 12 colleges and schools. The academic year is divided into 2 semesters. Class sizes range from about 300 students in the beginning years to fewer than 10 in the latter ones. Freshman English classes rarely have more than 25.

All new students must take courses from 8 academic fields in order to graduate. In 4 of the areas, students may choose from a select list of courses. In the areas of expository writing and culture and modern society, students must take specified courses as well as make choices. Some requirements in mathematics and foreign languages may be fulfilled by demonstrating a certain level of proficiency. As at many state universities, the core's main weakness is that some required courses are difficult to get. Students who want to fulfill some of their general education requirements in a more intimate setting can become part of the First Year Experience in which small groups of freshmen regularly meet in a seminar one hour per week and take the same cluster of theme-related courses with 25 other students with similar interests.

The UConn faculty in a recent year consisted of 842 full-time and 256 part-time members, all of whom taught undergraduates in varying degrees. About a third are women. Many students expecting no attention from faculty members are surprised to find professors as concerned as they are, with a range of quality tipping more toward the good than the average. Exclaims an out-of-stater: "In the 5 semesters I have attended UConn, I have encountered only 2 professors who I thought were poor teachers; for the most part, the rest were excellent." However, the large class sizes many students face in their early years do make it harder to establish close personal ties with faculty lecturers. More than a third, 36%, of the introductory courses in a recent year were taught at least in part by graduate students, making contact with full professors even more difficult for first-year and some upper-class students to achieve. Says a junior marketing major: "Most of my classes are taught by graduate students and although they are pretty good, I would rather know my professors."

The Schools of Engineering, Business, and Pharmacy, with its 6-year Ph.D. program, are among Connecticut's strongest, marked by superb faculties, modern facilities, and demanding curricula. Those who don't buckle down early in these majors often find themselves enrolled in other schools or colleges. English offers a wide variety of courses, and students say that many departments in the College of Liberal Arts and Sciences receive more support than their counterparts at other universities with strong professional schools. The Neag School of Education has undergone its own rebirth of new facilities and faculty since receiving a $21 million contribution to the school in 1999. Its 5-year Integrated Bachelor's/Masters Teacher Education Program continues to shape first-rate teachers who can "teach anywhere after graduation," notes a junior. The School of Fine Arts, particularly the general program in dramatic arts, gets good reviews, as do the School of Nursing, the program in nutritional sciences in the College of Agriculture and Natural Resources, and the program in biotechnology in the College of Liberal Arts and Sciences.

Communication sciences, in the College of Liberal Arts and Sciences, has had too many students for too few faculty members. And one junior targets her chief academic criticism at a nonacademic source: the Department of Residential Life. She observes: "The Department of Residential Life *needs* to start cutting down on parties and loud noise so that UConn can gain a reputation as a learning institution instead of a party school."

Facilities: Homer Babbidge Library, the largest public library in New England, has more than 2.4 million volumes, 2.6 million microform items, about 30,000 periodicals, and seats for 3000 readers. Students who find it intimidating at first gradually warm up to its advantages as "the" place on campus to study, although some find it a bit too social at night. A CD-ROM computer system helps reduce research time in fields ranging from agriculture and business to psychology. Departmental libraries also are available in music and pharmacy.

More than 1300 computer terminals are located around campus, in the computer center, the library, the various schools and colleges, and some residence halls. Every residence-hall room also has an Internet hookup for students who bring their own computers.

Special programs: Study-abroad programs for up to a year are available in 28 countries ranging from Austria and Costa Rica to the Netherlands and Japan.

Campus life: Three-quarters of UConn's undergraduates reside on the 4104 acres the university owns in and around Storrs (pop. 11,500), situated 25 miles east of Hartford. About 10% of the men and 7% of the women belong to 18 national fraternities and 9 national sororities (women can belong to fraternities here). Fraternity parties draw a large weekend crowd but otherwise students say the Greek influence is modest at best.

A decade ago, the university converted from a 5-day to a 7-day meal plan in an effort to keep more students around on the weekend. About 30% still go home, however, as working out, hanging out, partying, and playing loud music seem to be the primary weekend sources of entertainment. Campus crime is not regarded as much of a problem, but periodic "Stop the Prop" signs around campus attempt to dissuade students from propping open doors in the dormitories and thus inviting intruders. A student crime watch system called Husky Watch assists campus police in checking buildings, escorting students home at night, and other security measures.

Huskies basketball, both men's and women's, is huge. "It's one of the biggest things students here live for," says a junior. The 2003–2004 school year was especially successful with both the men's and women's basketball teams, perennial NCAA Division I favorites, winning the national championships, the women for the third straight year. The team also won the title in 2000. Varsity soccer Sundays are a must as well, especially since the men's team won the national championship in 2000. Attendance at football games, and other of the 10 men's and 12 women's intercollegiate sports, is less committed. Students field more than 850 teams in 28 intramural sports for each sex, ranging from ice hockey to inner-tube water polo. Individuals can compete in intramural jump rope or bike racing. With all those options in the recently improved program, nearly half the undergraduates end up participating. Practically every UConn student also seems to belong to the Ski Club, with the Crew Club popular as well.

Hartford, New Haven, and New London, the Connecticut triumverate, are all good in-state escapes. Boston and New York are farther away, but a lot more exciting. Students caution, however, that escape is difficult for those undergraduates who do not own cars.

Cost cutters: In a recent school year, 93% of the freshmen and 78% of continuing students received financial aid in the 2004–2005 school year, the most recent year for which data was available. About three-fourths of both groups were on need-based assistance. The average freshman aid package for a student with need consisted of a need-based scholarship or grant averaging $5473 and need-based self-help aid, such as loans and jobs, averaging $2925. Non-need-based athletic scholarships for first-year students averaged $10,603. Non-need-based awards and scholarships for first-year students averaged $4867. Average financial indebtedness of a recent graduate was $18,045. While many scholarships are designated for Connecticut residents only, options for non-residents have grown in recent years. Leadership Scholarships, valued at half to full tuition annually, reward entering freshmen who have demonstrated a commitment to multicultural diversity programs and initiatives through their leadership, special talents, and achievements. The Academic Excellence Scholarship, paying one-half tuition a year, goes to new students who ranked within the top 10% of their high school class and scored at least a 1350 on the SAT math and critical reading sections. Presidential Scholar Awards for valedictorians and salutatorians pay half tuition and are renewable over 4 years; recipients also get a one-time $2500 Undergraduate Research Fellowship for use during their 4 years at UConn. There are usually plenty of jobs around campus for undergraduates who want to work, regardless of financial need, through the university-funded Student Labor program. Cooperative programs and internships are available in a wide range of fields with companies as diverse as United Technologies and the insurance groups in Hartford.

Rate of return: Ninety-two percent of entering freshmen return for the sophomore year. Fifty percent graduate in 4 years, up from just 36% a few years earlier. Sixty-seven percent graduate in 5 years, and 72% complete their studies in 6 years. The graduation rate for minority students is 66% within 6 years following a first-year to second-year retention rate of 93%.

Payoff: Among recent graduates, undergraduates majoring in social sciences and history picked up 18% of the bachelor's degrees, followed by nearly 14% earning degrees in business/marketing, and 8% in liberal studies/general studies. Thirty-five percent opted to attend graduate or professional school within 6 months of leaving UConn; recent studies have found that about 60% earn advanced degrees at some point. About 80% take up job offers from the 200 companies and organizations that recruit on campus and enter the work force, many settling in the northeast.

Bottom line: Students who come to Connecticut to impress their friends should head south to Yale. Those who come with an eye toward saving several thousand dollars and who would relish personal attention, but won't wilt without it, should not only learn a lot but also have a good time doing it. "UConn can give a wonderful education and an all-around balanced life," says a physics major, "but the student must choose between grades and too much fun."

Delaware

University of Delaware

Newark, Delaware 19716

Setting: Small town
Control: Private/state-assisted
Undergraduate enrollment: 6266 men, 8633 women
Graduate enrollment: 1236 men, 1266 women
Student/faculty ratio: 13:1
Freshman profile: 7% scored over 700 on SAT I verbal; 35% scored 600–700; 45% 500–599; 13% below 500. 11% scored over 700 on SAT I math; 44% scored 600–700; 35% 500–599; 10% below 500. 21% scored above 28 on the ACT; 27% scored 27–28; 33% 24–26; 14% 21–23; 5% below 21. 35% graduated in top tenth of high school class; 69% in upper fifth.

Faculty profile: 75% Ph.D.'s
Tuition and fees: $7318 in-state; $17,474 out-of-state
Room and board: $6824
Freshman financial aid: 40%; average scholarship or grant: $6600 need-based; $4500 non-need-based
Campus jobs: 20%; average earnings: $1000/year
Application deadline: Early decision: Nov. 15; scholarship consideration: Jan. 15; regular: Feb. 15
Financial aid deadline: Mar. 15; Feb. 1 preferred
Admissions information: (302) 831-8123
e-mail: admissions@udel.edu
web site: www.udel.edu

In the world of higher education, where universities usually are divided between those that are publicly supported and those that are under private control, the 263-year-old University of Delaware in Newark is something of a hybrid. As a privately controlled university with state support, Delaware is also a quadruple header: a land-grant, sea-grant, space-grant, urban-grant institution, with major research commitments in all these areas. But undergraduate students are more impressed with what Delaware grants in the way of a low-cost, usable education. Remarks a New Yorker: "Between the classes, the diversity, and the city-like atmosphere (for a town of just over 30,000 people), I've learned more about life than I would have had I made another choice of college. This school opened my mind."

Student body: In a state like Delaware, which is second smallest in the union and 45th in terms of population, it's no surprise that just 41% of the undergraduates are in-state residents. Nearly all of the out-of-staters come from other, nearby middle Atlantic states though every state has students on campus. The student body is 86% Caucasian-American, 6% African-American, 3% Asian-American, and 4% Hispanic. About 1% are foreign national students from 100 countries. Seventy-nine percent of the students are graduates of public high schools. The vast majority are middle- to upper-middle-class suburbanites, politically inactive, socially very involved, and academically more interested than many care to let on. Notes an English major: "Although students seem to enjoy using their creativity academically, they do not seem to enjoy discussing it with their peers. There is a macho student image here." Those who care less about image, and more about studies, tend to be enrolled in engineering, business, nursing, and the sciences.

Academics: The University of Delaware offers degree programs through the doctorate, with over 100 undergraduate majors available in 6 colleges. The academic year is divided into 2 semesters plus a 5-week optional January term, which provides opportunity for in-depth course work, internships, and more than a dozen international programs. Average class size for undergraduates is close to 35, with courses like General Psychology enrolling 368 but a class in Chaucer attracting only a handful. Freshman English classes tend to top out at just 25 students, and a number of large lectures have discussion sections led by teaching assistants with 20–30 undergraduates. Altogether, about 80% of Delaware's classes enroll fewer than 50 students.

The only universitywide requirements are the course in freshman English and 1 of several approved 3-credit courses stressing multicultural, ethnic, and/or gender-related content. All degree programs require the completion of specific and/or elective courses in the humanities, social sciences, and natural sciences, although the number required in each field varies by college or discipline.

The faculty of 1370 members includes 244 part-timers. All teach undergraduates; less than 5% of introductory courses in a recent year were taught by graduate students. Thirty-nine percent of the total pool are women. States a senior: "Faculty here could be described as average: some are fantastic, others are terrible, but most are good. We have some really important researchers, scientists, poets, writers, and artists here, so that our faculty is diverse. However, faculty are not in touch with student life." There are those faculty members who make extra efforts to make sure students stay in touch with them. Recalls a junior: "One of my science professors had a hot line to call 48 hours before the final, with a promise to return your call within 2 hours."

All majors in the Alfred Lerner College of Business and Economics, economics, accounting, marketing, finance, management, management information systems, and operations management, are among Delaware's most difficult, but also the ones most in demand, largely because of their excellent teachers and well-structured curricula. Opportunities provided include a cooperative program, internships, winter sessions in London or Geneva, and minors in international business and business administration. The MBNA America Hall and Gore Hall provide blue-chip facilities to match the quality of instruction. Majors in the College of Engineering also are particularly intense, with state-of-the-art equipment, a great faculty, and important support from major corporations in the state, such as duPont, Astra-Zeneca, and Hercules. Chemistry benefits from facilities funded by duPont as well. Students in the much-admired program in hotel, restaurant, and institutional management, in the College of Human Services, Education, and Public Policy, (CHEP) test out their skills in the Vita Nova, an on-campus restaurant. The animal science program in the College of Agriculture and Natural Resources offers a rigorous preveterinary medicine program with first-rate facilities and faculty. The education programs in CHEP and the School of Nursing in the College of Health Sciences, as well as the English, biology, criminal justice, and geology programs in the College of Arts and Sciences, round out the A list.

Students say professors in the math department need to be more concerned with the "regular" student who is not a major. A number also speak limited English. Many of the foreign language instructors need to place more emphasis on having students speak the language.

Facilities: Morris Library, considered by students to be among the university's best features, has 3 million volumes, 3.4 million microform items, and 12,500 periodicals. The DELCAT computerized catalog plus a variety of other computerized information services provide access to more than 230 online databases and more than 34,000 electronic newspapers and journals. "The library is quiet enough and certainly comfortable enough," says a senior, "but many students prefer to study in Dougherty Lounge, an old church converted into a beautiful study lounge." But Morris does have its special benefits, the student continues, "more movies in the library collection than at Blockbuster Video!" Three branch libraries also located on campus contain materials in agriculture, chemistry, and physics; a fourth branch, containing materials on marine sciences, is located on the university campus in Lewes.

Twenty-eight general access and departmental computing sites around the campus with more than 900 PCs and Macs usually provide students ready access when they need it. Many labs are open until 2 a.m. All residence halls and many classrooms are equipped for connection to the Internet. Over 90% of all undergraduates bring their own computers to school. For times at the end of the semester when all known computers seem to be busy, students can refer to their computing site map, issued every semester, which tells them the location, hours of operation, and equipment available in every computer site. Students also may call a night in advance to reserve a computer for the following day. Wireless access is available in the library and many other sites around campus.

Special programs: Majors in engineering, and hotel, restaurant, and institutional management can take a fifth year to earn a Masters in Business Administration. A Washington semester is available through the political science department. Opportunities for study abroad are offered in 25 nations. In the Undergraduate Research Program, faculty members volunteer to accept undergraduates as their assistants or as junior members of their research teams; most students can earn academic credit for this experience. Special scholarships enable selected students to work on research in engineering, the sciences, and the humanities full time during the summer. More than 60% of undergraduates participate in research or independent study at some point before graduating.

Campus life: Fifty percent of the undergraduates live on Delaware's 1000 acres of red brick and white columns, although the university guarantees housing for all 4 years to those who want it. Fifteen percent of the men and women are members of 1 local and 17 national fraternities and 2 local and 14 national sororities. The Greeks are fairly exclusive about whom they invite to their parties, welcoming freshmen and sophomores by invitation only. By junior year, however, anyone is welcome. Bar hopping, dance clubs, theatrical productions, and parties of any and all sorts are popular alternatives. While freshmen are more apt to party early and often, sophomores tend to restrict their parties more to long weekends; in junior year, "the work kicks in and you go out once a week and party hard!" explains a senior. Over-21 seniors usually frequent the bars, as studies permit. Security measures are tight around campus and include emergency telephones, around-the-clock patrols, both escort and shuttle bus services, and keycard access to residence halls.

Delaware is NCAA Division I in all sports except football, where it is Division I AA, a fact that doesn't seem to bother the fans, who turn out in greater numbers for Fighting Blue Hen football games than for any other of the 11 men's and 12 women's varsity sports. The Fighting Blue Hens were the 2003 NCAA Division I-AA national champions. Basketball games also have been increasingly sold out following the Blue Hens recent back-to-back appearances in the NCAA tournament. Lacrosse games in the spring are the next biggest draw. Two-thirds of the men and one-third of the women prefer playing to watching and participate in 15 intramural sports for each sex.

Newark's prime location midway between Philadelphia and Baltimore sends students with cars off to major cities on the eastern seaboard. For those who don't want to stop in Baltimore, an hour away heading south, Washington, D.C., is just another hour further. Heading north, students reach Philadelphia in 50 minutes and New York City in 2 hours. The Delaware beaches also are a popular destination.

Cost cutters: Forty percent of Delaware's freshmen in the 2005–2006 school year received some financial aid, as did 38% of all continuing students. Thirty-one percent of the freshmen and 28% of the continuing students received need-based assistance. The average freshman award for a first-year student with financial need included a need-based scholarship or grant averaging $6600 and need-based self-help aid such as loans and jobs averaging $4750. The average non-need-based athletic scholarship for freshmen averaged $13,200. Other non-need-based awards and scholarships averaged $4500. The average 2005 graduate had debts of $15,200. Each year, between 10 and 12 Eugene duPont Memorial Distinguished Scholarships pay for tuition, fees, room, board, and a stipend to outstanding entering freshmen. About 100 outstanding prospects are invited to compete in March for these 4-year awards. Athletic, art, and music scholarships also are available. In a recent entering class, roughly a fourth of the students offered admission also were offered a scholarship based solely on academic merit. Most awards ranged in value from $2000 to $4000.

Rate of return: Eighty-nine percent of freshmen return for the sophomore year. Sixty-two percent graduate in 4 years; 75%, in 5 years; 76%, in 6 years.

Payoff: In the graduating class of 2005, majors in business and marketing claimed 17% of the degrees conferred, followed by majors in social sciences at 14% and education at 12%. Three-quarters of Delaware graduates traditionally take jobs immediately after commencement, many with major accounting firms, large corporations such as duPont and ICI, and banks throughout the middle Atlantic, the south, and the northeast. Five hundred companies and other organizations recruited on campus in a recent school year. A fifth of the degree recipients generally go to graduate school within 6 months of commencement.

Bottom line: Concludes a New Yorker: "The only students who don't succeed here are the party students who do no work and the close-minded students who are not prepared to be broadened by a large, diverse school. This university has a lot to offer. You just have to know how to get it."

Florida

Eckerd College

St. Petersburg, Florida 33711

Setting: Suburban
Control: Private (Presbyterian)
Undergraduate enrollment: 746 men, 1006 women
Graduate enrollment: None
Student/faculty ratio: 16:1
Freshman profile: 9% scored over 700 on SAT I verbal; 28% scored 600–700; 47% 500–599; 16% below 500. 5% scored over 700 on SAT I math; 29% scored 600–700; 46% 500–599; 20% below 500. 14% scored above 28 on the ACT; 17% scored 27–28; 31.5% 24–26; 24.5% 21–23; 14% below 21. 37% graduated in top fifth of high school class; 73% in upper two-fifths.

Faculty profile: 95% Ph.D.'s
Tuition and fees: $27,624
Room and board: $7868
Freshman financial aid: 90%; average scholarship or grant: $14,208 need-based; $9193 non-need-based
Campus jobs: NA; average earnings: NA
Application deadline: Apr. 1
Financial aid deadline: Mar. 15 (Scholarships: Feb. 15)
Admissions information: (727) 864-8331; (800) 456-9009
e-mail: martinle@eckerd.edu
web site: www.eckerd.edu

If prospective students look around the oceanside campus of Eckerd College in central Florida and see more than the usual share of gray hair, not to panic. It's not the upperclassmen, grown old prematurely from overrigorous academics. Nor, probably, the faculty, whose average age has been a comparatively young 47. Most likely, it's the 225 members of Eckerd's highly respected Academy of Senior Professionals, which brings retired leaders from various fields to campus to study, offer their perspectives, and generally interact with students. Prominent member-scholars have included the late author James Michener and John Hope Franklin, the noted African-American historian. Eckerd, only 45 years old in 2003 and the recent recipient of a chapter of Phi Beta Kappa, has a knack for being ahead of its time. The now widely accepted January term of intensive study was pioneered here. Eckerd's innovative autumn term brings freshmen to campus 3 weeks early to take 1 for-credit academic project from a mentor chosen earlier by the student. This approach enables freshmen to begin the first semester with 1 course already under their belts—and a good feeling about the good buy they found in sunny Florida.

Student body: About a third of Eckerd's students come from the Sunshine State. Every state plus 49 foreign countries were represented in a recent year, with a fifth of the out-of-staters coming from the Northeast. The student body is predominantly Caucasian-American with 4% Hispanic students, 3% African-American and 2% Asian-American students in a recent year. Eight percent were foreign nationals. A quarter of the students are Protestant, including 6% Presbyterian in a recent year, with 18% Catholic, 2% Jewish, and 7% of other faiths, including Muslim, Hindu, Buddhist, and Greek Orthodox. The rest claimed no religious affiliation or did not report any. Three-quarters typically are graduates of public high schools. Statistics aside, no single word or phrase truly captures the Eckerd student body. Though generally more liberal and environmentally and socially conscious than other college students, "the variety here," contends a New Englander, "ranges from Bible-quoting conservatives to jocks to more relaxed hippie types." While most students are academically adept and work hard for their grades, the college's sunny climate and oceanfront setting keep high-pressure academics in perspective. "Laid back" may imply too little personal effort, but the air is definitely casual. Students generally go barefoot, wear shorts to class, and call professors by their first names.

Academics: Eckerd, renamed in 1972 for a Florida civic and business leader, awards bachelor's degrees in about 40 disciplines organized into 5 interdisciplinary "collegia" instead of separate departments. The academic year is divided into 2 semesters plus Eckerd's baby, the January term, which allows students to study abroad or concentrate on 1 topic intensively at any of a variety of locales. Average class size for undergraduates is 20. Students meet their largest classes freshman year in lecture courses like Western Heritage in a Global Context, which involve the entire class of 400, breaking down into discussion groups of 20 led by their autumn-term mentors. Most introductory classes top out at 35, although a class in Russian history may have 50. Upperclass seminars often enroll just 10.

All freshmen must take a course in Western Heritage in a Global Context, where they read works such as *Hamlet* and *Candide*. In their sophomore and junior years, students take 4 courses chosen from offerings on 5 broad perspectives on human existence: aesthetic, global, environmental, scientific, and social relations. Seniors must take a course called Quest for Meaning, which includes community service. Writing is emphasized throughout the curriculum, with every student submitting a portfolio of his or her college work for review by the end of the second year. Students generally find the beginning and ending courses in Western Heritage and Quest for Meaning stronger than the perspectives courses in the middle. However, they complain that instruction by the mentors leading the smaller discussion groups is uneven in both quality and grading policies.

Full-time professors comprise about two-thirds of the Eckerd faculty, which recently totaled 148 members. Two-thirds of the full-time faculty are men. While some professors are not as skilled as others in getting their points across, just about all are praised for their willingness to act as true mentors and to work closely with students. "Every professor I have had at Eckerd knows my name and my strengths and weaknesses," says a marine biology major. "They have the ability to tailor what they teach to suit my needs." Many also share in the casual spirit on campus, joining their students in wearing shorts to class.

Marine science is easily Eckerd's star major, with the natural laboratories of Boca Ciega Bay and the Gulf of Mexico plus a superb curriculum guided and shaped by superb faculty members, among them one who is an expert on manatees and serves as chair of the National Marine Mammals Commission. A new marine science building and necropsy lab, where students can observe and learn from autopsies on marine mammals, have made the best even better. Other 5-star disciplines include international relations and international business, with their extensive opportunities for study abroad, as well as creative writing, environmental studies, psychology, and economics.

The math department needs better, more understanding teachers who can relate to students in introductory classes. Says a sophomore: "It is just hard for a Ph.D. in relativity to see calculus as difficult." Some students wish there were more extensive course offerings in theater, the visual arts, and instrumental music; visual arts could use better facilities.

Facilities: The new 400-seat Peter H. Armacost Library, named for the college's long-time recent president, officially opened in February 2005. The $15 million structure, with its striking 2-story glass wall that overlooks Chapel Pond, offers the latest in information technology plus space for 250,000 volumes. The collection, previously hampered by the size of the earlier structure, stands at about 114,000 volumes and 3009 periodicals. The new facility also offers 17 group study rooms.

Students have had few complaints about the 2 main computer labs and smaller labs in the dormitory complexes that altogether provide about 80 IBM and Macintosh microcomputers. The main labs generally are open until midnight; labs in the dorms, around the clock. The new Armacost Library also contains a 24-hour computer lab as well as a wireless network. The college strongly recommends that students have their own personal computers.

Special programs: About 60% of Eckerd students take advantage of the extensive opportunities for foreign study, including exchanges with universities in Europe, the Far East, and South America as well as a term at Eckerd's own study center in London. A Sea Semester allows students to spend half a term on shore at Woods Hole, Massachusetts, receiving instruction in oceanography, nautical science, and maritime studies, and the second half-term on the water, applying what they have learned. A Ford Apprentice Scholars program enables 20 juniors to participate in a 2-year program designed to encourage them to consider college and university teaching as a career. For prospective engineers, 3-2 programs are available with Washington University in St. Louis, the University of Miami, and Auburn and Columbia universities. Internships can be arranged in management and human development.

Campus life: Seventy-six percent of Eckerd students (plus pets, which students are allowed to keep in certain residence halls) reside on the 267-acre campus that stretches over 1.25 miles along Boca Ciega Bay and Frenchman's Creek. There are no fraternities or sororities, although the 8 residential complexes, each consisting of 4 houses with 34–36 students apiece, serve a similar social function, sponsoring theme parties and other social events. Says a student from the Rocky Mountain West: "The dorms have the best view of any dorms in the country. Looking over the Gulf of Mexico at a sunset is breathtaking!" The range of popular clubs extends from the *Triton* newspaper to the Earth Society, which promotes ecologically sound behavior on campus. Chapel attendance is not required, but many students enjoy attending religious services as well as musical and theatrical events in the unusual chapel-in-the-round located on an island in 1 of 3 small lakes on campus. Although crime has not been an issue, exterior residence hall doors are locked 24 hours a day and entry to the campus is limited to one main entrance staffed every evening and around the clock on weekends by campus security personnel. Only cars with Eckerd stickers or permission from Eckerd students are allowed entrance.

Five men's and 6 women's varsity teams compete as part of NCAA Division II athletics. Basketball and baseball draw the biggest crowds, with soccer the primary fall sport though some students are disappointed at the generally low turnout to cheer on the Tritons. Eighty percent of the men and two-thirds of the women find intramurals a better source of fun and competition between the various dormitories. Men's 2-on-2 beach volleyball contests are popular as well.

Eckerd's extensive waterfront program lets students take full advantage of the college's prime location. Available for student use is an extensive fleet of canoes, kayaks, sailboats, sailboards, and a Ski-Nautique power boat, as well as all the accoutrements for fishing, snorkeling, and water skiing. Triton teams compete in sailing and boardsailing. The program also has its serious side, featuring the Eckerd College Search and Rescue team, composed of volunteer students and alumni, who provide maritime search and rescue services to the Tampa Bay boating community.

While the Gulf beaches (3 miles away) are generally all the escape most students need, an even bigger leap from reality is available at Disney World in Orlando or Busch Gardens amusement park in Tampa.

Cost cutters: Ninety percent of all Eckerd freshmen and 92% of continuing students in the 2005–2006 school year received financial aid; for at least 55% of both groups, the aid was need-based. The average freshman award included a need-based scholarship or grant averaging $14,208 and need-based self-help aid such as loans and job earnings averaging $3528. Non-need-based athletic scholarships averaged $15,571; other non-need-based scholarships and awards averaged $9193. The average recent graduate had debts of $17,500. A wide range of merit-based scholarships are available. Eckerd's most prestigious awards, the Trustee, Presidential, and Dean's Scholarships, pay $25,000, $16,000, and $13,000, respectively, and are renewable. To be considered for these awards, students must be admitted by Feb. 15 and must have scored a minimum of 1300 on the math and critical reading portions of the SAT (or 29 ACT) and carried a 3.8 GPA. Honors Scholarships pay up to $10,000 a year and also are renewable. Other renewable scholarships, recognizing special talents in certain academic, athletic, and artistic fields, recently paid up to $5000 a year. Fifty Presbyterian students yearly can receive freshman awards of up to $7000, which also are renewable.

Rate of return: Eighty-four percent of freshmen return for the sophomore year. Sixty-four percent graduate in 4 years; 65%, in 5 years; 67% in 6 years.

Payoff: Thirteen percent of recent graduates earned bachelor's degrees in marine science; 11% in management; and another 11% in international business. Twenty-eight percent enrolled immediately in graduate or professional school. Two-thirds took jobs primarily in business, banking, and education, most opting to stay in the Southeast, regardless of their original home port. One hundred ten companies and organizations recruited on campus in a recent school year.

Bottom line: Students prepared to major in "beach studies and beer funneling" had best chug on past Eckerd. Advises a senior from up north: "Eckerd is for students who like to be challenged and get deeply involved in classes, extracurricular activities, and community life. A student seeking anonymity will not do well here since classes are small and discussion oriented and everyone knows everyone else. My only complaint has been not enough time to go to the beach!"

Florida Institute of Technology

Melbourne, Florida 32901

Setting: Small town
Control: Independent
Undergraduate enrollment: 1554 men, 710 women
Graduate enrollment: 355 men, 303 women
Student/faculty ratio: 13:1
Freshman profile: 8% scored over 700 on SAT I verbal; 32% scored 600–700; 42% 500–599; 18% below 500. 13% scored over 700 on SAT I math; 43% scored 600–700; 36% 500–599; 8% below 500. 27% scored above 28 on the ACT; 12% scored 27–28; 26% 24–26; 23% 21–23; 12% below 21. 27% graduated in top tenth of high school class; 56% in upper fifth.

Faculty profile: 90% Ph.D.'s
Tuition and fees: $25,150
Room and board: $6800
Freshman financial aid: 99%; average scholarship or grant: $14,504 need-based; $10,130 non-need-based
Campus jobs: 26%; average earnings: $1468/year
Application deadline: Rolling
Financial aid deadline: Mar. 15
Admissions information: (321) 674-8030; (800) 888-4348 e-mail: jmarino@fit.edu web site: www.fit.edu

Move over, Tang and Velcro. There's another name to add to the list of successful by-products of America's race into space. When, as early as 1958, scientists, engineers, and technicians were working by day at what is now Kennedy Space Center to put the first American on the moon, by night they were attending classes in Melbourne, 30 miles south, to keep abreast of the latest technological developments on Earth. The first man didn't land on the moon until 1969, but by then the scientists' school had already been given accreditation and a new name: Florida Institute of Technology. Today, the institute offers bachelor's degree programs in 57 majors, including unusual areas like ocean engineering and aviation computer science, but its price for a year's air and sea adventures remains rock-bottom. Tuition for engineering and science majors runs $25,150 for 12 to 19 hours; for all other majors, it is $2230 less. Add room and board of $6800, and the price still flies low compared to that at other engineering-oriented schools of its quality.

Student body: The combination of high tech, low costs, and a tropical campus on Florida's eastern coast sends a number of out-of-staters flying south. Just 31% of the undergraduates are from the Sunshine State, with students from 47 states and 79 foreign countries represented. Seventy-seven percent are graduates of public schools. The undergraduate student body is 7% Hispanic, 4% African-American, 3% Asian-American, and 1% Native American. Foreign nationals account for 15%. Says a student from the Pacific Northwest: "I enjoy how diverse our campus is, how we hear every major language, and some obscure dialects, spoken here. This diversity gives our students open minds and allows for a variety of opinions." Despite the popular image of engineering students as being rather intense and focused on their work, there are a number of surprisingly easy-going undergraduates at Florida Tech. Remarks a New Englander: "Students are here for 2 clear reasons: to bury themselves in their prospective majors and to soak up the Florida sun." As a result, many serious students make time to get their share of sea air come Friday through Sunday. But woe to those who spend too much time in the sun. Adds another New Englander: "The students who just come for the nice weather will not do well here because the courses are difficult and require studying." Only a small percentage take an equal interest in helping to run the school by participating in the student government, or student newspaper, or by working for political or social concerns off campus. But those who get involved relish the experience. Says a northerner: "From reggae jam sessions with the Caribbean Students Association to jungle clean-ups with our neo-hippie group SQUAMISH, there are endless opportunities to learn the ways of those different from you."

Academics: Along with its baccalaureate programs, Florida Tech offers master's degrees in 65 areas of study and doctoral degrees in 20 disciplines. Undergraduate programs are offered in the colleges of Engineering, Science, Psychology and Liberal Arts, Aeronautics, and Business. The academic year is divided into semesters. Average class size for undergraduates is 20. The largest classes, like general chemistry, enroll almost 70, while a course like Coastal Engineering Processes has just 2.

All students, regardless of major, must take math, science, computer science, social science, and composition courses plus 3 courses in humanities including Civilization I and II. Each major also has its own requirements and carefully outlines exactly which courses all students should complete at what time during their studies. Very few have room for electives.

The undergraduate faculty is divided between 166 full-time members and 55 part-timers. An additional 51 full-time members and 139 part-timers teach at the graduate level only. Eighty-two percent of the total are men. Despite the casual atmosphere present in most classroom discussions, students have great respect for their professors and the wide range of professional experience in industry, government, and academia that most bring to their teaching. A large majority are still very active in their fields, conducting research in areas as diverse as marine mammals and "smart skin," a covering being tested for use on airplanes to detect stresses and strains before they become dangerous. Students appreciate the fact that even the most brilliant professors of engineering or aviation never belittle or intimidate them as they wrestle with difficult material. Says a software engineering major: "I expected much less kindness from the faculty and never expected so much personal attention." However, undergraduates are less pleased with the quality of the graduate students being used in 5% of the introductory courses. "They're usually pretty good," says an aerospace engineering major, "but many need some help on how to deal with classes or maybe some specific teaching techniques!"

Although all of Florida Tech's engineering programs are excellent, those in ocean, computer, and aerospace engineering stand out as both unusual and especially demanding. The programs in oceanography and ocean engineering take advantage of the school's ideal location in frequent field and sea trips, using the school's own 60-foot research ship, the *Delphinus*. Computer engineering, in which students are taught to develop, test, and analyze systems for robotics and artificial intelligence, and aerospace engineering, where undergraduates learn to design vehicles for space travel, are as challenging as they sound. In the College of Science, majors in space sciences, and the biological sciences such as preprofessional marine biology, and aquaculture, a rare undergraduate program that studies finfish and shellfish culture, are outstanding. Says a marine biology major: "The department encourages undergraduate research and the faculty are very supportive and enthusiastic." Opportunities for research in both engineering and the life sciences became even more exciting with the recent opening of new, technologically advanced buildings for both fields. A new building with new teachers has helped to refuel the College of Aeronautics, which had experienced some unevenness in quality across its programs.

Still awaiting a similar boost, though not as likely to get it, are the programs in humanities in the College of Psychology and Liberal Arts and the College of Business, which traditionally have not been Florida Tech's strong points. The humanities and communications have low enrollment and a limited selection of courses although the number of full-time faculty with Ph.D.'s has increased. Psychology, students say, has an excellent graduate program but lacks rigor at the undergraduate level. Professors in the business college tend to emphasize theory over application and some fail to display much interest in their subject matter. The math faculty sometimes has difficulty explaining concepts clearly to students who are not majors in the field.

Facilities: Despite the fact that Evans Library was constructed only a decade or so ago, it seems older to the institute's technologically conscious students. Users find its collection of more than 419,000 volumes and government documents rather limited, even in technical materials, but especially in the humanities. The very good periodical collection consists of more than 17,000 paper and electronic journals. As a center for study, Evans is especially good for group work, offering numerous large rooms that can be reserved. The top 2 floors are "the quiet floors where no talking is allowed," says a sophomore.

For many, the best part of Evans Library is the computer center located in the library pavilion, which houses a large portion of the more than 250 workstations available in general public or department labs around campus. The engineering complex alone has at least 10 labs open to undergraduates. Students who need to work later than the lab hours can gain access using electronic keys around the clock. Wireless access also is available in most academic buildings and gathering areas and the majority of students who bring their own computers make use of it.

Special programs: Numerous internships with the National Aeronautics and Space Administration (NASA) and with private industries are available. Opportunities in undergraduate research are extensive in chemistry, oceanography, genetic engineering, and in the traditional engineering programs. The school's proximity to NASA also makes research available concerning space travel and the effects of launches on the area's environment. Study abroad is possible in Hungary, France, and Argentina, to name a few sites.

Campus life: Fifty-seven percent of the students live on the 130-acre campus, which features lush tropical gardens covering a fifth of the acreage and more than 200 species of palm trees. Campus-sponsored activities generally have a hard time competing with the local beaches and dance clubs. Just 15% of the men and women belong to 6 national fraternities and 3 national sororities; because their parties generally are open to everyone, and tend to rise and fall in popularity, independents view the Greeks as simply another club on campus. Some of the best parties are sponsored by the Caribbean Student Association, though lively parties in general are not hard to find. Around campus, bicycle theft is the worst problem, though security officers patrol in golf carts and on foot around the clock to prevent such incidents. Students hesitant about walking alone after dark also can call upon escorts in golf carts for a ride. The campus security office is located in the main women's residence hall for a bit of added protection. Students advise caution when traveling in the surrounding neighborhood.

Florida's technical students have proved to be athletes as well. The institute's soccer, basketball, and crew teams have each won national championships; in 2004–2005, the women's rowing team won the Sunshine State Conference Championship and advanced to the NCAA Division II Rowing Championships. In all, Florida Tech's men and women compete in 7 NCAA Division II sports for men and 8 for women. About half are involved in the 13 intramural activities available to each sex. Those not caring for organized sports go diving, sailing, or surfing on their own.

About a fourth of the student body leave Melbourne (pop. 66,000) to make regular pilgrimages to larger cities like Orlando, Tampa, and Daytona. When run-of-the-mill fun isn't enough, Disney World and Epcot Center are just 90 minutes away.

Cost cutters: All but 1% of the freshmen and 88% of continuing students received financial aid in the 2005–2006 school year. For 72% of the first-year students and 59% of the rest, the aid was based on need. The average freshman award for a first-year student with financial need included a need-based scholarship or grant averaging $14,504 and need-based self-help aid such as loans and jobs averaging $4854. Non-need-based athletic scholarships for first-year students averaged $11,728; other non-need-based awards and scholarships averaged $10,130. Average debt of a 2005 graduate was $24,234. Academic scholarships ranging in value from $5000 to $12,500 annually are available to incoming freshmen, especially those ranking in at least the top 10% of their high school classes and having high SAT or ACT scores. A cooperative program is available in all majors but is most popular with engineering students, especially those eager to work in the space industry. A number of installment-payment plans also are provided. Students majoring in aviation and taking flight courses can expect an additional cost for the first 2 years of $11,500 per year.

Rate of return: Seventy-nine percent of entering freshmen return for the sophomore year. Thirty-five percent earn bachelor's degrees in 4 years; 52% in 5 years; 54% in 6 years.

Payoff: In the 2005 graduating class, 10% of the degree recipients graduated with majors in computer engineering, 9% earned degrees in electrical engineering, and 8% in computer science. More than 60% accepted jobs immediately after graduation, most as engineers, scientists, or lab technicians at such firms as Harris Corporation, McDonnell Douglas, and Texas Instruments, or with the National Oceanic and Atmospheric Administration (NOAA) or NASA. The majority settled in Florida, California, and the northeast. About 100 companies and organizations recruited on campus. Almost 30% of the students pursued advanced degrees upon graduation.

Bottom line: Florida Institute of Technology makes good use of its location on the Atlantic Ocean near Kennedy Space Center to offer challenging programs in specialized areas of engineering, marine science, and aviation. How students use the miles of sunny, sandy beaches is up to them. As an administrator aptly put it, "Florida Tech is for serious-minded students who like to get their feet wet on the weekends and their hands dirty during the week!"

New College of Florida
Sarasota, Florida 34243

Setting: Suburban
Control: Public
Undergraduate enrollment: 266 men, 426 women
Graduate enrollment: None
Student/faculty ratio: 11:1
Freshman profile: 37% scored over 700 on SAT I verbal; 57% scored 600–700; 5% 500–599; 1% below 500. 18% scored over 700 on SAT I math; 53% scored 600–700; 28% 500–599; 1% below 500. 39% scored above 28 on the ACT; 27% scored 27–28; 26% 24–26; 8% 21–23; 0% below 21. 54% graduated in top tenth of high school class; 81% in upper fifth.

Faculty profile: 99% Ph.D.'s
Tuition and fees: $3679 in-state; $19,475 out-of-state
Room and board: $6330
Freshman financial aid: 88%; average scholarship or grant: $7556 need-based; $3600 non-need-based
Campus jobs: 4%; average earnings: $2049/year
Application deadline: May 1; priority date: Feb. 1
Financial aid deadline: Mar. 1
Admissions information: (941) 359-4472
  e-mail: admissions@ncf.edu
  web site: www.ncf.edu

To describe New College as simply the honors college of the State University System of Florida is like saying that steak tartare is raw beef: you lose a lot in the translation. Unlike most honors programs, New College is located on its own campus in Sarasota along the Gulf of Mexico. And that's not its only distinctive characteristic. New College is full of intellectual individuals: every student designs his or her own academic program with the guidance of a personally selected faculty sponsor. Written faculty evaluations are given instead of grades. New College itself, which was founded in 1960 as a private institution, emerged in 1975 as a marriage of 2 very distinct entities: the public state university system and the private New College Foundation, which enables students to obtain a very private college experience at a very public price. As one Florida resident once aptly put it: "New College: an Ivy League education for the price of a good stereo."

New College can charge its bright students so little (just under $3700 tuition and fees for Florida residents in 2005–2006 and not quite $19,500 for out-of-staters) in part because the New College Foundation maintains one of the highest endowments of any public college in the nation, about $39,000 per student in a recent year. Part of the endowment produces income also used for scholarships. Students value the intellectual freedom that the academic format makes possible. Says a philosophy major: "What I found most appealing as a prospective student, and what I find most appealing now as an established, third-year student, is the latitude and personal freedom students are given to pave their own path and to figure out where they are going...A class running 20 to 30 minutes overtime at New College is a common occurrence. Professors and students alike do not want to leave."

Student body: Eighty percent of New College's students are from Florida, with the rest representing 37 states plus the District of Columbia and 27 foreign countries. About 14% are members of racial and ethnic minorities, including 9% Hispanic, 3% Asian-American, and 2% African-American. Five percent are foreign nationals. Eighty-four percent are graduates of public high schools. New College students are generally liberal, with capital "L's" at both ends of the word. Describes a freshman: "We are accepting ... unbelievably creative ... inquisitive .... We are like something out of the sixties only we listen to music from the seventies." Students pride themselves on being open to any and all individual beliefs and lifestyles and tolerant of nearly all views (although conservatism does test their tolerance). Nevertheless, one graduate is a prominent Republican in the U.S. Congress, another has been Republican party chairman in New Hampshire, and a third ran for the U.S. Senate from Missouri on the Libertarian ticket. Concludes a junior: "Anyone who felt 'different' in high school will probably feel right at home here." Students are also very independent, intensely involved in their studies, and not afraid to take academic risks, in part because there is no grade point average to worry about. Because there are no grades, students compete within themselves, not with each other. Notes a senior: "When given the freedom, New College students tend to dive in head first. The challenge is always self-improvement and innovation, in whatever the field."

Academics: New College offers bachelor's degrees in more than 30 disciplines, and students can arrange interdisciplinary and special topic majors. The academic year is divided into 2 semesters plus a January term, which is set aside for independent study projects, 3 of which are required for graduation. Average class size for undergraduates is between 15 and 18 students. Tutorials with a single person are naturally the smallest. (Over 400 individual tutorials are taught each semester.) In a recent year, there were just 2 students in the smallest formal class, Historical Archaeology, and 52 in the largest course, Introduction to Psychology. If a class is getting too large, a professor may ask to see examples of students' work or limit the class to third- and fourth-year students.

The student-faculty academic contract is the backbone of New College's program. Each student designs with the faculty sponsor one written academic contract each semester that outlines what he or she will accomplish that term. Students must complete at least 7 semester contracts, plus the 3 independent projects done during the January terms. The contract must demonstrate breadth as well as depth in the student's choice of courses. To satisfy the breadth requirement, students must successfully complete by graduation 8 courses (from 111 options) that are designated to satisfy a Liberal Arts Curriculum, including at least 1 in the humanities, 1 in the natural sciences, and 1 in the social sciences. Sufficient courses related to an area of concentration satisfy the emphasis on depth. Seniors also must complete a thesis or project and defend it during an oral baccalaureate examination with a faculty committee.

Students select words such as "incredible," "inspired," and "passionate," to describe the 63-member faculty, all of whom are full time. Forty-seven percent are women. For the most part professors are intellectually stimulating, deeply engaged in their material, and very involved in students' lives. Especially popular are those who are open to student suggestions, willing to experiment with their classes, and not limited in their fields of discussions. One professor "may teach Greek," notes a humanities major, "but we sure learned a lot about etymology as well." Because most disciplines are small, with just 2 or 3 professors (sometimes only 1), it is crucial that students get along with their instructors, because there are limited alternatives in any one area.

Literature and psychology are among the largest programs, with more professors and a wider variety of courses. Psychology also has special computers for testing and experiments. Philosophy, history, religion, anthropology, sociology, and the natural sciences also are considered quite strong. New buildings that opened in 2001 and 2002 included a complex for the natural sciences and marine biology research center. Environmental studies benefits from Florida's natural resources.

German and Russian, economics, computer science and classics each need more professors, although those teaching are considered "first rate." In fact, says a philosophy major, "All departments are somewhat hamstrung by lack of faculty," which limits the number of courses and variety of perspectives that can be offered. The college's size also limits the range of departments.

Facilities: The Jane Bancroft Cook Library, completed in 1986, is large for just 692 students: almost 260,000 volumes and several thousand electronic and paper periodicals, but students find it a "sterile and cold" though quiet place to study. What New College doesn't have can usually be obtained on-line or on loan for 3 weeks from any other branch of the Florida university system. "The librarians are also incredibly nice, very helpful and accessible," says a public policy major. Every December, the staff hosts a holiday Wassail for the entire campus.

PCs are available in the library until 1 a.m. and in another lab on campus until 11 p.m. There also is an Apple lab, open all night, for those who prefer Macintosh computers—or need the extra work-time. All residence hall rooms also provide Internet connection, and many spots around campus offer wireless access.

Special programs: Opportunities for study abroad are available in 39 countries through the college's membership in the National Student Exchange, which also gives students access to programs at 150 universities in the U.S. and Canada. Students who choose may participate in programs through the School of International Training, the Council on International Educational Exchange, and other schools and organizations including the other institutions in the State University System of Florida.

Campus life: Seventy percent of New College's students reside on the 140-acre, bayfront campus, which offers a mix of modern dormitories designed by I.M. Pei, older historic buildings, such as the former home of circus great Charles Ringling, a new apartment-style residence hall that opened in 1998, and, adds a junior, "casually acquired, run-down places which are important to students." There are no fraternities or sororities, or intercollegiate or intramural sports, ("Having such institutions would be too 'conventional,'" says a junior) and popular clubs, which vary from year to year with student interests, range in seriousness from ones dedicated to recycling and gay rights to groups of students who gather simply to play silly games or eat ice cream. Favorites in the 2005–2006 school year included Nice RAK, Nice Random Acts of Kindness, that puts on various appreciation days and FMLA, known as Fem-Law, the Feminist Majority Leadership Alliance that promotes women's rights. A knitting and crochet club went by the name of Anarchy Death Sticks. Observes a senior: "Most clubs die rapid deaths after a year or two of prominence. But fear not, for as easy as it is for clubs to die, it is even easier to give birth to them." Pick-up games in basketball, Ultimate Frisbee, soccer, and softball usually keep the athletic crowd happy. Weekend "walls," which are largely impromptu parties held just about every Friday and Saturday night at Palm Court, the tiled courtyard between the 3 main dorms, are noted for their very loud music and lots of dancing. Well-liked campus police know all students by sight and are quick to spot outsiders. Crime generally is limited to thefts of bicycles and other personal items. U.S. Highway 41 splits the campus and women avoid walking alone along the road after dark. Extra lighting recently was added around campus to make everyone feel safer.

Tampa, the nearest big city, offers various alternative clubs and sporting events, though many students needing diversion simply seek out the closest beach.

Cost cutters: Eighty-eight percent of freshmen in the 2005–2006 school year received some form of financial aid; 84% of continuing and new transfer students did. Aid was need-based for 34% of the freshmen and 39% of the continuing and transfer students. The average award for first-year students with financial need included a need-based scholarship or grant averaging $7556 and need-based self-help aid such as loans and jobs averaging $2921. Other non-need-based awards for freshmen including scholarships and grants averaged $3600. Graduates in 2005 left with average debts of $15,045. All first-year students are eligible to receive 1 of 5 levels of scholarships, the amount based upon an institutional rating that takes into consideration a student's standardized test scores and weighted high school grade point average. The Presidential Scholar Award, for students who rate the highest, pays $2500 a year to state residents, and $11,000 a year to those from out of state. The other scholarships range in value from $500 to Floridians and $2000 to nonresidents to $2000 for in-state students and $8000 to those from outside.

Rate of return: Eighty-four percent of the freshmen who enter return for the sophomore year. Forty-nine percent graduate in 4 years; 65% in 5 years.

Payoff: Of the 2005 graduates, 7% majored in political science, and 5% each in psychology and humanities. Twenty percent of the students in a recent year went on to graduate or professional school. Within 5 years, 54% of the graduates from any one class are pursuing advanced degrees. As a result, New College has the sixth highest percentage of graduates going on to earn Ph.D.'s, ranking first in the social sciences and fifth in women earning Ph.D.'s in general and in the sciences. Sixty companies and other organizations recruited on campus in the 2004–2005 school year.

Bottom line: New College encourages students to be independent, experiment, study in depth, and work closely with faculty members. Not all students have the self-motivation, discipline, and confidence to succeed. "But if a structured university makes you feel like a brainless automaton, with your personality and drive capped, then come to New College," advises one who's glad he did.

University of North Florida

Jacksonville, Florida 32224

Setting: Urban
Control: Public
Undergraduate enrollment: 4014 men, 5510 women
Graduate enrollment: 180 men, 409 women
Student/faculty ratio: 22:1
Freshman profile: 3% scored over 700 on SAT I verbal; 38% scored 600–700; 52% 500–599; 7% below 500. 2% scored over 700 on SAT I math; 37% scored 600–700; 54% 500–599; 7% below 500. 2% scored above 28 on the ACT; 4% scored 27–28; 16% 24–26; 50% 21–23; 28% below 21. 45% graduated in top fifth of high school class; 77% in upper two-fifths.

Faculty profile: 95% Ph.D.'s
Tuition and fees: $3268 in-state; $14,911 out-of-state
Room and board: $6640
Freshman financial aid: 84%; average scholarship or grant: $2060 need-based; $2816 non-need-based
Campus jobs: 5%; average earnings: $6476/year
Application deadline: July 2
Financial aid deadline: Apr. 1
Admissions information: (904) 620-2624
e-mail: osprey@unf.edu
web site: www.unf.edu

When students at the University of North Florida boast about having "the best of both worlds," they're not just talking about being a state university with classes the size of those at a small college. North Florida is a young college in transition, which started in 1972 as a commuter school for juniors and seniors and admitted its first freshman class in 1984, each year enrolling more and more students of traditional college age. North Florida is also an urban university, with sleek, modern buildings and high-tech equipment, located within the boundaries of a 1300-acre campus that includes a wildlife sanctuary where deer, possums, raccoons, some small alligators, and even the school mascot, the osprey, flourish. There are 12 miles of nature trails open to the public plus glasslike lakes begging to be canoed. "I have come to appreciate UNF for its smaller size, its natural environment, and its dedication to academics," confides a sophomore who came "as a last resort" after being denied financial aid at her first-choice school. "Now I wouldn't be anyplace else!"

Student body: Eighty-four percent of North Florida's students are state residents, many drawn from the immediate northeast region. Though most out-of-staters also come from the South, 48 states and 111 foreign countries are represented. In a recent year, 92% were public-school graduates. Minority students account for 21% of the total, with 10% African-Americans, 6% Hispanics and 5% Asian-Americans. One percent are foreign nationals. Minority students also have gained visibility on the campus, accounting for more than a fifth of the UNF student senate members. With an average undergraduate age of 24 years, the student body tends to be split between 18- and 19-year-old freshmen and sophomores, many of whom become frustrated by a sense of apathy within the student body, and a larger number of older, nontraditional juniors and seniors who divide their time between classes at UNF and families and jobs off-campus. Politically, students are mostly conservative and generally focused on very clear academic and career goals. And while the natural surroundings give the campus a relaxed atmosphere, students say there is peer motivation to do well. Notes one upper-division student: "When I saw other students trying hard, my grade point average went from a 1.7 to a 3.1."

Academics: North Florida offers 50 undergraduate programs, 25 master's level programs, and 1 doctoral degree, in education. The university is divided into 5 colleges; its academic year into 2 semesters. Average class size for introductory courses is 38 though some lecture courses like the Legal Environment of Business can have 200 or so people. Most upper-level courses have about 30 students. The required core curriculum is fairly standard, covering 36 of the 120 credit hours needed to graduate and encompassing traditional areas from English composition to natural and social sciences to the humanities. In fall 1999, 100 first-year students took part in 4 freshman interest groups, which are learning clusters centered about an interdisciplinary theme. The pilot program was introduced as a way to make the general education program more interconnected and meaningful. A recent fall semester saw about 300 first-year students, a sixth of the class, involved in 11 freshman interest groups taught by 33 faculty members.

All but 57 of the 436 full-time faculty plus 227 of the 239 part-time members teach undergraduates. Just 1% of the introductory courses are taught by graduate students. Fifty-nine percent of the full-time faculty are men. Students generally find the faculty to be experienced in their fields, both within academia and in industry or other outside endeavors, and devoted to their students. Faculty quality varies widely, however. One senior has found her professors to be "outstanding" showing "care and concern for students as well as great teaching skills," while a junior observes that "some merely read or lecture from powerpoint presentations and don't get students interested or involved in class work."

The Coggin College of Business is lauded for its solid accounting program whose graduates have averaged more than twice the national passing rate on the CPA exam. Nursing students from the College of Health also boast a 93% passing rate on the state board exam and gain broad experience from the 14 major medical centers in the area. Says a major: "Every faculty member from the associate professors on up to the dean of the College of Health is visible, approachable, and understanding of the needs of the student as an individual." Both the business and health colleges also boast newly built structures featuring the latest in technology. The department of natural sciences in the College of Arts and Sciences benefits from having professors who believe in passing on "working knowledge," drawn from their own research experience as well as independent research projects that let students gain experience for themselves. Courses in such fields as chemistry and microbiology are taught by "brilliant yet understandable professors," continues the nursing major. A new Science and Engineering Building gives the same luster to student laboratory and research opportunities. The American music program, started in 1987, is gaining a national reputation, with students from across the nation coming to study under its premier faculty and many leaving with top honors from international competitions. The jazz studies program, in particular, is a winner, well noted for its jazz band and jazz combos that in recent years have received national recognition for musical excellence. A new fine arts center that opened in 2001 provides 29 classrooms and studios as well as additional rehearsal, practice, and performance areas for UNF's departments of Music and Communications and Visual Arts. Philosophy and psychology offer small classes with lots of interaction. History and political science feature excellent professors who always are willing to help.

Foreign language instruction is considered weak, largely because there are too few faculty members and the offerings are limited to a major in Spanish and a minor in French.

Special programs: Opportunities for study abroad and for internships with Jacksonville area businesses are available. A semester in Washington, D.C., also is an option.

Facilities: The 4-story Carpenter Library is a "terrific place to study and do research," says a senior, and it promises to become even better following expansion taking place during the 2005–2006 school year that will provide more space for computers and the print collection. The current collection stands at more than 746,000 volumes and about 3500 periodicals. Computerized research assistance is available, including a variety of databases and an on-line catalog that scans the local holdings as well as listings throughout the state university system. Private study carrels may be rented by the semester. Those needing a study break can head to an atrium on the first floor, now open 24 hours, thanks to the efforts of the student government. Hours for the rest of the library also were extended until 3 a.m, thanks to the student government's work, though the later hours are dependent upon having personnel provided by the student assembly available to work those extra hours.

Approximately 120 PCs are located in general purpose labs across campus. The main lab is open until 1 a.m. Students report few problems finding available units, even at finals time; if one of the more popular computer labs is full, others around campus generally are not. Only students in the building construction management program are required to provide their own personal computers. For those students who do bring their own units, wireless Internet access is available throughout most of the campus and in the residence halls.

Campus life: Sixteen percent of UNF's undergraduates reside on campus, which follows the model of a village green; most buildings are clustered together and connected by a 2-story covered pedestrian walkway, and all parking is contained along the periphery of the central area. Surrounding the center of activity are 850 acres of undeveloped land. While the residential population is low, it has increased steadily as younger students have enrolled and opted to live in the lakefront residence hall opened in 1989, in the newer blend of apartments and residence hall living built in 1998, or in the newest addition, a 500-bed residence hall, the first located outside the main campus core and near a recreation field. The Greek system has taken hold with about 6% of the men and women involved in 8 national fraternities and 7 national sororities. Two of the fraternities and 2 of the sororities are traditionally African-American Greek organizations. Nonmembers are welcome to attend most of the Greek parties, and many open get-togethers are offered with all resident students in mind. Jazz performed at the campus Boathouse Cafe is a special treat. Still, some undergraduates complain that while campus life is growing, too many "dead" weekends remain, with students who live close enough to go home doing so, despite the increase in campus programming. Says a Floridian: "The typical weekend consists of empty dorm rooms and empty parking lots." Security on the campus is considered good, and incidents of crime are low, though not nonexistent. Security cameras and numerous blue-light emergency phones throughout campus all keep incidents in check.

UNF's sports teams made the move to NCAA Division I in the 2005–2006 school year. Within Division II competition, UNF varsity teams had won national championships in men's golf and women's tennis. The baseball team also had been nationally ranked. There is no football among the 8 men's and 9 women's intercollegiate sports offered, although the Jacksonville Jaguars within the National Football League provide sufficient excitement. Students hope the move to Division I will raise school spirit and bring more students to university games. The range of intramural sports is more satisfying, with 12 offerings each for men and for women plus several popular club sports that attract 90% of the students. A new golf course on campus, part of a new golf management and learning center, was especially designed to serve as a model of environmentally sensitive golf facilities.

Because the UNF campus is just 10 minutes from the beach, the sea and sand are students' favorite sources of relaxation. The cities of Saint Augustine and Daytona Beach, as well as Disney World, also are frequent getaways.

Cost cutters: Eighty-four percent of all 2005 freshmen and 70% of all continuing students received financial aid. For 28% of the freshmen and 32% of the continuing students, the aid was need-based. The average freshman award for a first-year student with financial need included a need-based scholarship or grant averaging $2060 and need-based self-help aid such as loans and jobs averaging $2521. The average non-need-based athletic scholarship for a freshman was $4977; other non-need-based awards and scholarships for first-year students averaged $2816. The average indebtedness of a 2005 graduate was $16,708. Along with the usual array of federal programs, the school has offered a non-need-based work-study program, thanks in recent years to funding generated by the Florida state lottery. Out-of-state residents with special skills, high academic abilities, or other desirable qualities are encouraged to apply for a waiver of the out-of-state tuition. Various scholarship programs are available to assist top students, including the UNF Presidential (Guaranteed) Scholarships that pays $4000 a year over 4 years to selected students with an SAT combined math and critical reading score of 1300 or above or an ACT composite of 30. A $3000-a-year Presidential award requires slightly lower standardized test scores. The completed application packet must be on file by mid January to be considered for this award.

Rate of return: Seventy-five percent of entering freshmen return for the sophomore year. Twenty percent of the freshman starters graduate in 4 years, 46% in 5 years, 54% in 6 years. As a result, some students joke that UNF actually stands for U Never Finish. Two percent of entering freshmen don't just finish; they finish in 3 years or less.

Payoff: Ten percent of the 2005 graduates earned degrees in communications, 9% in business, and 7% in psychology. More than 280 companies recruited on campus in a recent school year, many from the Jacksonville metropolitan area.

Bottom line: A decade ago, an administrator cautioned that students seeking the features of more traditional campuses, such as numerous Greek organizations, lots of parties, and a homogeneous student body might not have their expectations met at UNF. Maybe it's time to look again, for while the student body remains diverse, North Florida's growing residential, social, athletic, and academic offerings are making this small university look more traditional every year.

Georgia

Agnes Scott College

Decatur, Georgia 30030

Setting: Urban
Control: Independent (Presbyterian)
Undergraduate enrollment: 877 women
Graduate enrollment: 3 men, 7 women
Student/faculty ratio: 10:1
Freshman profile: 22% scored over 700 on SAT I verbal; 44% scored 600–700; 30% 500–599; 4% below 500. 7% scored over 700 on SAT I math; 43% scored 600–700; 43% 500–599; 7% below 500. 26% scored above 28 on the ACT; 19% scored 27–28; 32% 24–26; 16% 21–23; 7% below 21. 27% graduated in top tenth of high school class; 60% in upper fifth.
Faculty profile: 100% Ph.D.'s

Tuition and fees: $23,570
Room and board: $8500
Freshman financial aid: 66%; average scholarship or grant: $17,390 need-based; $13,438 non-need-based
Campus jobs: NA; average earnings: NA
Application deadline: Early decision: Nov. 15; Scholarship decision: Jan. 1; regular: Mar. 1
Financial aid deadline: May 1 (Scholarships: Jan. 1, Priority: Feb. 15)
Admissions information: (404) 471-6285; (800) 868-8602
e-mail: admission@agnesscott.edu
web site: www.agnesscott.edu

For those who think a women's college with less than 900 undergraduates must offer too narrow an academic and social experience, a trip to Decatur, Georgia, 6 miles from downtown Atlanta, is in order. At Agnes Scott College, women serve in real leadership roles, holding down the college presidency and 60% of the faculty posts in recent years. Students themselves serve as voting members on faculty committees, including those concerned with academic standards and the college curriculum. Personally liberating is a student-run honor system that allows the young women to leave personal belongings unattended and take self-scheduled exams completely unmonitored. As part of the school's Global Awareness program, virtually every student, regardless of academic interest or financial situation, is urged to have some study-abroad experience in places as exotic as Turkey or Ghana. Observes a sophomore: "I am empowered, enlightened, and exposed to so many important and valuable lessons and ideas just by being here." The one-time seminary for girls, named for the mother of a major donor, may seem a bit pricey for a private college in the southeast, but compared with its academic peers around the nation, it's a winner.

Student body: Just over half, 51%, of Agnes Scott's students are from Georgia with 41 states plus the District of Columbia and U.S. Virgin Islands represented. Most of the nonresidents also are from the South. Seventy-one percent are graduates of public high schools. The student body is 19% African-American, 5% Asian-American, 3% Hispanic, and 2% bicultural. Eight percent are foreign nationals from 30 countries. Six percent are Presbyterian; an additional 30% are members of other Protestant denominations. Eighteen percent are Catholic, 2% Jewish, 37% members of other religious faiths, and 6% claim no religious affiliation. Agnes Scott is filled with intelligent, politically active young women from all political ideologies, and has more than its share of high achievers in academic as well as social areas. Notes one from the Southwest: "Most people here are very success oriented. Stress is everywhere. Academics are tough, and people are very competitive with themselves, not with each other." Because students are not working one against the other, a special bond links them with each other and with members of the supportive faculty.

Academics: Agnes Scott confers the bachelor of arts degree in 30 majors plus a master of arts in teaching secondary English. The academic year is composed of 2 semesters. The largest course enrolls just 40 people, with an average of 20 for entry-level courses. Fifty-six percent of all classes have 15 or fewer students.

Students must satisfy fairly standard distributional requirements of eight 1-semester courses in humanities and fine arts, natural science and mathematics, and social sciences in addition to classes in English composition, physical education, and a foreign language through the intermediate level. Also included are a first-year seminar, a second semester in science, and a course in social and cultural analysis.

Words like *exceptional, excellent, dedicated,* and *hard-working* keep cropping up in students' appraisals of the 110-member faculty, 29 of whom are part-time. (Just 3 of the part-time faculty teach at the graduate level only.) "They bring material to life," says a senior. It is not unusual to find students at professors' homes for dinners and parties, or for the faculty to attend various student functions. "They push us but they also help us," observes a junior. "All you have to do is ask."

The strongest departments according to students are biology and physics, English, political science, international relations, history, and psychology. The equipment in biology, chemistry and physics is excellent, with an electron microscope and a 30-inch reflecting telescope at the campus observatory, and students don't have to fight hundreds of other undergraduates or graduate students to use them. The observatory was renovated in 2001, including within its refurbished walls a new 70-seat planetarium; a new science center opened in 2003. English is one of the biggest departments and offers a breadth and depth of courses not found in some of the smaller departments. The emphasis on good writing is ever present, highlighted by an annual writers' festival that enables students to understand better how professional writers think and work. History, political science, and international relations feature challenging faculty; psychology demands numerous papers with presentations that prepare students for the real world. Students also value the rich course variety in the women's studies major; one-fourth of the college's faculty teaches courses cross-listed in the women's studies program.

The modern languages department, which offers majors in French, Spanish, and German studies, could use more upper-level classes as well as a broader scope in the range of languages offered. Classes in Japanese are offered for academic credit but do not constitute a major or a minor. Students with an interest in sociology or anthropology wish the department were bigger to allow for a major in each field instead of one combined. Dance, Africana studies, and environmental studies are offered as minors only.

Facilities: A newly expanded McCain Library opened in 2001, more than answering many student complaints about the earlier facility. "Beautiful and functional," says a history major. While the collection remains too small for some women's in-depth research tastes, with almost 222,000 volumes and 15,000 electronic and paper periodicals, the roomier interior study area is much more satisfying. More than 350 seats are wired for power and data, along with wireless connectivity throughout the building and outdoor reading terrace. Laptops are available for student use as are media carrels and sound-buffered group study rooms. Students can use GALILEO, an on-line database for periodicals, or borrow books or use periodicals from any of the 18 other members of the Atlanta Regional Consortium for Higher Education, giving them access to 12 million volumes. The facility also houses the Center for Writing and Speaking, which assists students with oral and written projects.

The college's Information Technology Services provides a computer network with 1 port for each student in residence hall rooms including cable TV and a telephone system. Students have access to more than 325 computers in public labs around campus, with 240 additional units housed in various classrooms. Several labs are open around the clock.

Special programs: The idea behind the Global Awareness program is to enable every Agnes Scott student to experience another culture as part of her college education. The student takes an interdisciplinary course on global issues in the fall and then, in January, travels in a group of 10–20, led by a faculty member, to the country she studied, living for 2–3 weeks of the month with a local family. In recent years, prices for undergraduates have averaged $1500 per person. In the spring semester, students follow up with an on-campus course that allows them to evaluate their experiences and complete independent projects. Thanks in large part to the program, nearly 40% of recent graduates have had an international educational experience. A Global Connections program provides an added component to regular academic courses, such as a class in Irish literature traveling to Ireland.

Right in the Atlanta area, there is the opportunity for internships at such institutions as the Centers for Disease Control and Prevention, the Cable News Network, the Federal Reserve Bank of Atlanta, and Coca-Cola. The Atlanta Semester combines internships with course work that examines the contributions of women leaders to social change. The Kaufman Internship Program for Women Entrepreneurs places Agnes Scott students as interns in women-owned businesses in the Atlanta area. Students can also cross-register for classes at any of 18 other area schools, such as Emory University, Georgia Tech, Morehouse, Spelman, or the University of Georgia. Academic exchanges for a semester or year are also possible with Mills College in Oakland, California, and with universities in Japan, Hong Kong, and Northern Ireland. A dual-degree program is offered in engineering with Georgia Tech and in art and architecture with Washington University in St. Louis. Young women with an interest in politics or public policy can spend a semester at American University in Washington, D.C., or participate in various workshops and seminars held in the nation's capital through the Public Leadership Education Network, a consortium of women's colleges. To assist students in making the transition to the world of work, the Year Five plan allows graduates to take classes where there is room free of charge for the year following graduation.

Campus life: Ninety-one percent of all traditional undergraduates live on the "new" 100-acre campus. Just over a decade ago, Agnes Scott celebrated her 100th birthday with a face-lift; 3 of the school's 6 dormitories were restored to their original Victorian elegance with period furnishings, some donated by alumnae, and chandeliers in the lobbies and parlors. Each Agnes Scott class has its inherited colors and a chosen mascot, and is paired with a sister class for competitions and activities. Many traditions, such as Black Cat, the culmination of first-year student orientation, revolve around the class system. There is little crime, given the school's location in a safe neighborhood near Atlanta, but security patrols are constant and escort services are available and used when students feel the need.

Ten percent of the women participate in the 6 intramural sports offered. A small portion also compete in 7 intercollegiate sports as part of NCAA Division III. Says a senior from the Midwest: "Our sports on campus don't draw a significant amount of attention but don't go unnoticed." Many Agnes Scott students look off campus for weekend activity, attending football and, to a lesser extent, basketball games at Georgia Tech. Fraternity parties at Georgia Tech, Emory, or Morehouse draw a crowd as well, and many men from surrounding colleges reciprocate by turning out for band parties at Agnes Scott. Says a senior: "Most students are not serious party types, but we do enjoy off-campus activities, most of them occurring at Georgia Tech." Student organizations ranging from Blackfriars, the oldest student theater troupe in Atlanta, to the Feminist Majority Leadership Alliance and the College Republicans are especially active.

Cost cutters: With an endowment of $282 million as of June 2005, Agnes Scott generally ranks among the top colleges and universities and second among women's colleges in resources per student. That circumstance assists in financial aid as well as support for programs and facilities. Sixty-six percent of entering freshmen and 62% of all continuing undergraduates in 2005–2006 received some form of financial aid. For all undergraduates given aid, the assistance was primarily need-based. The average freshman award for a first-year student with financial need included a need-based scholarship or grant averaging $17,390 and need-based self-help aid such as loans and jobs averaging $4496. Other non-need-based awards and scholarships for first-year students averaged $13,438. The average financial indebtedness of a recent graduate was $22,018. The Presidential Scholarship awards tuition, room, and board to the most outstanding applicants who rank in the top 2% of their high school class with a minimum 2190 combined SAT, 31 ACT, and GPA of at least 3.8. One Guizueta Foundation Scholarship, which also covers full tuition, room, and board, goes to a high-achieving high school leader, preferably Hispanic or Latina with financial need, who has a GPA of at least 3.5, a minimum combined SAT of 1920, and a 28 ACT. A wide range of other merit scholarships pays between $10,000 and $20,000 annually to students with competitive academic records. Music scholarships pay $1000 to $3000 a year; community service and leadership awards, $5000 annually. In one of the few outward signs of the college's Presbyterian heritage, $10,000 awards go to first-year students who are members of that church.

Rate of return: Eighty-four percent of entering freshmen return for the sophomore year. Sixty percent go on to graduate in 4 years, 63% within 5 years, 66% within 6.

Payoff: Over a third of the 2005 graduates earned degrees in 3 disciplines: 16% in psychology, 10% in international relations, and 9% in business/economics. Just over a fourth of the graduates immediately pursued advanced degrees. Those seeking employment find jobs mainly in financial fields, communications, and education throughout the Southeast. Many join up with employers with whom they logged summer or semester-long internships or in fields where they served as "externs" for a work week or participated in a shadow program for just an afternoon or day. Nearly 30 employers participated in the college's recruiting program in the 2004–2005 school year.

Bottom line: Notes an out-of-stater: "If you get involved—and there are more than enough ways to get involved, not to mention overinvolved—you will learn to be a leader. The Global Awareness program also has changed many people's lives, and everyone's perspective."

Berry College

Mount Berry, Georgia 30149

Setting: Rural
Control: Private
Undergraduate enrollment: 663 men, 1166 women
Graduate enrollment: 5 men, 12 women (90 part time)
Student/faculty ratio: 13:1
Freshman profile: 4% scored over 700 on SAT I verbal; 39% scored 600–700; 43% 500–599; 14% below 500. 4% scored over 700 on SAT I math; 32% scored 600–700; 50% 500–599; 14% below 500. 18% scored above 28 on the ACT; 20% scored 27–28; 29% 24–26; 26% 21–23; 7% below 21. 49% graduated in top fifth of high school class; 80% in upper two-fifths.

Faculty profile: 88% Ph.D.'s
Tuition and fees: $17,570
Room and board: $6772
Freshman financial aid: 99%; average scholarship or grant: $11,545 need-based; $15,303 non-need-based
Campus jobs: 69%; average earnings: $2592/year
Application deadline: Feb. 1
Financial aid deadline: Apr. 1
Admissions information: (706) 236-2215; (800) 237-7942 (800-BERRY-GA)
e-mail: admissions@berry.edu
web site: www.berry.edu

If you were to guess where the world's largest campus is located, what might you say? Texas, Brazil, China? Try Rome, Georgia, and the campus of 1850-student Berry College, which covers 28,000 acres. Tucked into the north Georgia mountain region, an hour from both Chattanooga and Atlanta, the campus includes forests, meadows, lakes and streams, and a working dairy farm that recently produced more milk per cow than any other dairy in Georgia. In addition to surrounding students with enchanting beauty, the campus also provides a way for students to earn precious tuition dollars by working on the farm, maintaining the expansive grounds, and generally keeping the college running. And that's after the college, founded in 1902, already has subsidized half the educational and general expenses for full-time students. In Berry's world, the mission is threefold: to educate the head through academics, the hands through work, and the heart through religion in life. But its expansive setting also gives the body plenty of room to run or take a rest when needed.

Student body: Eighty-five percent of Berry's students are from Georgia, with more than a third usually from the Atlanta area. A total of 33 states and 26 foreign countries have students on campus, though the majority of out-of-staters are from the Southeast. Eighty-nine percent in a recent year were from public schools. The student body is a lot less diverse than most members would like: 3% are African-American, 1.6% each Hispanic and Asian-American and less than 0.5% Native American. Not quite 2% are foreign nationals. Students tend to be fairly conservative in their political and religious beliefs. Although Berry is not affiliated with any particular religious denomination, it is Christian, and many students are involved in a dozen or so very active religion-in-life groups coordinated by the chaplain's office. Because the student body is so small, members say that those who differ from the majority, perhaps by being fundamentalist Christian or atheist or gay or politically extreme, tend to stand out more. However, students are especially friendly and generally quite accepting of any differences. Observes a senior: "While students usually fit into some defined group, most don't limit their friends in that way." Academically, the strong work ethic carries into the classroom and students strive for high grades that will get them good jobs after graduation although some students think their classmates could stand to be a little more challenged. Responds a junior: "We're good students who study hard but it's not our lives."

Academics: Berry offers bachelor's degrees in about 40 majors, master's degrees in business administration and education, and an education specialist degree. The academic year is divided into 2 semesters. Average class size for undergraduates is 20, although Principles of Biology enrolls about 70. Upper-division foreign language courses are among the smallest, with a half-dozen students, but most classes for juniors and seniors enroll from 15 to 30. Business, education, and psychology classes are sometimes crowded.

All students must take, in their first 2 years, 11 courses from a suggested list that covers all disciplines plus 2 electives and specified classes in English composition, speech, and physical education. In addition, as part of an emphasis on writing across the curriculum, every student must complete at least 2 writing-component courses in his or her major, 1 in the junior year and the other as a senior. The college also expects students as a graduation requirement to attend a minimum of 24 events in their 4-year career from a list of officially approved cultural offerings and pass a comprehensive exam or some other senior assessment in their major.

The total faculty numbers 189. All of the 130 full-time members and 59 part-timers teach undergraduates. Thirty-four percent of the faculty is female. The faculty includes many who are zealous about their subjects and the way they teach them, and others who are less excited, a difference that comes across in the quality of their classes. Says a senior: "The faculty here work hard at building a mentor-like relationship with their students." Students' biggest complaint is that faculty don't seem to stay around long enough, with those who don't gain tenure, including some popular teachers, leaving after only a few years.

Many students applaud the "hands-on" approach to learning emphasized in the business, education, and psychology programs and the dedication of their teachers. The Campbell School of Business, in particular, offers a well-funded program with plenty of opportunities for projects and real-world applications of material learned in the classroom. Education also gives students plenty of practical experience. Says an early childhood education major: "When Berry teachers enter the classroom, they are prepared to do a good job." Sociology and political science attract high caliber students and offer professors "who are demanding, encourage excellence in their students, and do not accept excuses!" The communication department gets the students' award for "most improved," with a 100% increase in the number of majors over a 6-year period. Faculty members have handled the growth well. They work cohesively as a team and remain open to student suggestions of how the program can be made even better.

Some programs, such as history and sociology and anthropology, have fewer professors than students would like, although they consider the ones in place to be very good. Foreign language lovers would like to see expanded course offerings for the 3 majors in French, Spanish, and German. Art and music could use better facilities.

Facilities: Memorial Library, with 200,000 volumes in book format and 528,000 in microfiche and nearly 1800 periodicals, was renovated a decade ago, improving Berry's study situation dramatically. "Its research facilities are very good for a small college," notes a communications major, "but by no means exceptional." Students in the natural sciences especially find the periodicals lacking; the collection is stronger for work in the social sciences. Some students travel to larger universities such as Emory, the University of Georgia, or Georgia Tech for additional materials. However, the college continues to put money into acquisitions and research technology, offering a computerized catalog, and numerous computers that access the Internet. The library also offers wireless connection to the Internet. Membership in GALILEO, the state of Georgia library network, gives students access to more than 64 databases and 2300 full-text periodicals.

Students have access to 4 general-use computer laboratories plus 2 smaller special-purpose labs, altogether containing more than 140 PC and Macintosh systems. Labs generally are open until 11 p.m. or midnight weekdays but are closed Saturdays and open for shortened hours on Sunday. Students would like to see longer hours on the weekends and during finals. "A 24-hour lab would be great," says a senior. The addition of Internet and E-mail access from the dorm rooms has encouraged more students to bring their own computers and has eliminated most waits in the labs.

Special programs: Berry offers a dual-degree program in engineering with Georgia Tech and Mercer University and in nursing with Emory University. The departments of foreign languages, English, and communications, plus the Campbell School of Business offer study abroad options in Europe during the summer; the art department offers an opportunity for travel abroad between the first and second semesters each year. Altogether, students may study abroad in more than 15 countries.

Campus life: Seventy-five percent of the students reside on the spacious campus, which includes a cluster of English Gothic buildings donated by Henry Ford. Though many of these are old and only recently had their heating and air conditioning systems overhauled, they add a special beauty and charm to the campus. In a recent year, about 30% of the faculty and staff also lived on campus, adding to the sense of community. Many undergraduates live within 2 hours of the college, and freshmen, in particular, tend to head home for the weekend, though students say the longer undergraduates remain on campus, the more things they find to do to keep them there once Friday classes end. Over the past few years, the student activities board has come up with assorted activities, such as mudwrestling, a tricycle race, and scavenger hunt, to capture students' imagination and convince them to stay. There are no fraternities or sororities to provide weekend parties, but groups of students get together to throw their own off campus at a local country club or civic center. The Baptist Student Union and Campus Outreach are among the more popular student organizations. Berry has rules concerning visitation hours in the men's and women's dorms, which some students don't like. Those who find these rules too restrictive can always speak up at the Berry Forum, held the first Tuesday of every month, where students can—and do—tell the administration their gripes. Campus security, however, is not one of the issues students complain about, as few consider crime much of a problem. As a deterrent, the campus is closed after dark, restricting access by outsiders, and doors to the women's dorms are locked at 6 p.m. Emergency phones have been added to the more isolated areas.

There is no football, but soccer is very popular, with spirited crowds at games for both the Vikings and the Lady Vikings, who, in 2003, held the record for most NAIA soccer victories at 290 wins. The college offers 8 intercollegiate sports for men and 8 for women. All but 10% of Berry students enjoy intramural sports, 16 for men, 15 for women. Many, such as flag football, swimming, and softball, are common to college competition; others, for example, pillo-polo, and water basketball, are special to Berry.

Atlanta, 1 hour south, and Chattanooga, an hour north, are popular weekend getaway spots, if climbing up one of Berry's mountains or over it to the reservoir won't satisfy.

Cost cutters: In the 2005–2006 school year, Berry students paid just 50% of the actual expenses for their education. In addition, all but 1% of the first-year and all but 3% of the continuing students received financial aid; about 55% of both groups were on need-based assistance. The average financial package for freshmen included a need-based scholarship or grant averaging $11,545 and need-based self-help aid such as loans and job averaging $3563. Non-need-based athletic scholarships averaged $7847; other non-need-based scholarships averaged $15,303. Average debt of a recent graduate, based on borrowing only from Berry College, was $12,592. A number of merit-based awards are available for top students: 10 Presidential Scholarships recently paid full tuition; Academic Scholarships were recently worth between $2480 and $10,210 to recipients who maintained GPAs of at least 3.0; departmental scholarships vary in amount. All are renewable over 4 years.

Berry's on-campus work program is available to all students regardless of need. At any one time, more than 70% are employed in more than 100 different jobs on campus; students may work from 10 to 20 hours a week, recently earning $775 to $1800 a semester. A cooperative education program also is available in more than a half-dozen majors from business administration and accounting to computer science and psychology.

Rate of return: Seventy-eight percent of the freshmen who enter return for the sophomore year. Fifty-one percent graduate in 4 years, 62% within 5 years.

Payoff: Thirteen percent of the 2005 graduates earned bachelor's degrees in psychology, 12% in business administration and management, and 9.5% in communication, journalism, and related programs. In recent years, a fourth of Berry graduates have gone on to pursue advanced degrees. Two-thirds use their work experience to help find jobs after graduation, many with major firms in the southeast, such as KPMG, Georgia Pacific, and State Farm Insurance, and in the numerous school systems in Georgia. Almost 140 companies and other organizations recruited on campus during a recent school year.

Bottom line: "The Berry community is generally intent on giving and getting a good education, devoted to work, and self-sufficient," says a southerner. "Those who have had everything handed to them may not succeed here. Students don't respect people who have too much money—and flaunt it."

Georgia Institute of Technology

Atlanta, Georgia 30332

Setting: Urban
Control: Public
Undergraduate enrollment: 7886 men, 3106 women
Graduate enrollment: 3201 men, 1186 women
Student/faculty ratio: 13:1
Freshman profile: 17% scored over 700 on SAT I verbal; 59% scored 600–700; 22% 500–599; 2% below 500. 37% scored over 700 on SAT I math; 56% scored 600–700; 6% 500–599; 1% below 500. 41% scored above 28 on the ACT; 23% scored 27–28; 29% 24–26; 6% 21–23; 1% below 21. Class rank data: NA

Faculty profile: 96% Ph.D.'s
Tuition and fees: $4648 in-state; $18,990 out-of-state
Room and board: $6802
Freshman financial aid: 84%; average scholarship or grant: $5195 need-based; $5064 non-need-based
Campus jobs: 2%; average earnings: $2400/year
Application deadline: Jan. 15
Financial aid deadline: Mar. 1
Admissions information: (404) 894-4154
  e-mail: admission@gatech.edu
  web site: www.gatech.edu

Apple Computer, G.E., Milliken, Northern Telecom/BNR, Shaw Industries… the names march through the alphabet, spelling out a list of some of the nation's best known and most powerful companies. Also spelled out are the names of major corporations whose current or recent chief executive officers or presidents are alumni of the Georgia Institute of Technology in Atlanta. The tuition at Georgia Tech is among the lowest in the nation at just over $4600 for state residents and less than $19,000 for out-of-staters, who comprise 30% of the undergraduate enrollment. "Even as an out-of-state student," says a senior from the Middle Atlantic region, "I saved a lot of money by choosing Georgia Tech over more pricey northeastern schools." It doesn't take a CEO to tell that the yield on a Georgia Tech investment can sometimes be very high.

Student body: As many places as Georgia Tech alumni end up going, there are just as many places that they come from, with 53 territories and states represented, along with 84 foreign countries. Nearly a third are members of racial or ethnic minority groups or foreign nationals, with 15% Asian-American, 7% African-American, 5% foreign national, and 4% Hispanic. Eighty-five percent in a recent year were public high school graduates. Students tend to be ambitious, bright (the average high school GPA of 2005 freshmen was 3.74), and hard-working, highly motivated, and very loyal to each other as well as to the school—qualities that help recent graduates in the job market. "Academics are by far the priority here and you can see that everywhere you turn," says an industrial engineering major. "People even study on their way to take a test." Once largely conservative, the campus, students say, is moving more toward the center in its political beliefs as the population becomes more diverse, and socially it can be as active as any other state school. Observes a junior from Georgia: "Many people outside of Tech perceive its students to be 'geeks' who are intelligent but do not have social skills. However, they are very wrong, as one visit to our campus would prove. People party here like crazy!"

Academics: Georgia Tech awards degrees in 32 bachelor's programs, 49 master's programs, and 28 doctoral programs. Reorganization of the institute's colleges a few years ago endeavored to broaden its offerings while maintaining its technical foundation. The present system includes 6 colleges, Engineering, Architecture, Computing, Sciences, Management and the Ivan Allen College of Liberal Arts, which offers degree programs in such fields as history, technology and society, public policy, and international affairs to name a few. Such majors are designed to attract students who have strong quantitative skills but may have previously avoided Tech because they did not want to become engineers.

The standard academic year is divided into semesters. Class sizes vary widely, from about 160 in a physics lecture to 30 in upper-level history and English courses. The big lectures, however, are broken into twice-weekly recitations of 25–35 students. Most upper-level engineering courses have between 30 and 80 participants.

Tech has general-education requirements that all undergraduates must fulfill. These include 12 hours of social sciences, science, mathematics, and technology, 9 in essential skills courses such as English composition and calculus, and 6 hours of humanities. Students also must take courses in U.S. and Georgia history and government plus a wellness course.

All but 27 of the 858 faculty members are full-time and all but 18% are men; in a recent year, 85 taught in the humanities and social sciences, still a small portion of the total but up from earlier years. "Full-time" at a school like Georgia Tech means "top of the crop" professors who divide their time between teaching and research, some tilting the balance one way, some the other. Observes an upperclassman: "Many professors are focused on their research and tend to see teaching as an afterthought. This does not make for an exciting classroom environment." To improve teaching, a Center for the Enhancement of Teaching and Learning offers training programs for graduate assistants who in a recent year taught 17% of the introductory classes, as well as consultation to faculty members on ways to improve teaching techniques.

It's no surprise that at Georgia Tech electrical, chemical, civil, and mechanical engineering and computer science have traditionally been the strong majors. Students in the College of Engineering thrive while working nearly nonstop to master a challenging curriculum under the tutelage of excellent instructors in some of the most advanced facilities in the nation. Unlike a lot of colleges, "the school takes a nice middle-of-the-road approach to the theory and the practical use," observes a major. But it is quite competitive, says an electrical engineering major, "as professors give tests so difficult that there is a substantial curve." Interest in computer engineering, aerospace engineering, and industrial and systems engineering, all especially strong programs, has increased. Among non-technical majors, top professors and curricula in the College of Management and in the Sam Nunn School of International Affairs in Ivan Allen College have gained respect, even among engineering students, who used to dismiss anything not engineering-related as a catchall for dropouts in their fields. It also is hard to dismiss the new Technology Square, a modern multi-building complex that opened in 2003 as the home of the College of Management.

Still, some of the reputational hierarchy remains at Tech, with all engineering majors at the top and all non-engineering majors below. Programs in the School of History, Technology, and Society are still evolving. Other of the liberal arts majors remain small with "limited class sizes and options," says a chemistry major.

Facilities: The Library and Information Center is enormous: 2.4 million volumes, 4.5 million microform items, 2 million technical reports from government- and industry-sponsored research and development, and more than 21,000 periodicals. "The library has any kind of technical periodical or book that a student could need," says a student in the College of Sciences, "but it lacks in the availability of fiction and popular periodicals." For those, students can run over to the library at Georgia State University or Emory University. Undergraduates rave about a highly advanced computerized research system, which quickly tells them where in the world, literally, the latest information can be found. GALILEO, a statewide database server, enables students to connect with more than 200 online databases that index thousands of periodicals and scholarly journals. As far as studying goes, the library is well laid out, with a "loud" side appointed with temporary wall partitions and tables for group studying, and a "quiet" side that provides more individual study carrels with a few tables interspersed. "During finals, everyone is in the library," says a junior.

All entering freshmen are required to own or lease a computer during their time at Georgia Tech. Each spring, accepted students are advised of the minimum platform and software requirements as well as purchasing and finance options. On campus, computers are just about everywhere—and do just about everything from exhaustive library searches to applying for housing and financial aid. Wireless access is available in the central part of campus, the various academic departments, and the library. Students also have access to 160 general-purpose computing workstations divided among 3 main labs. Labs in the library and the student center are open around the clock. Numerous other labs are located in the various schools but are specifically for their students.

Special programs: The International Intercultural Studies Program of the University of Georgia system allows students to spend summers or various portions of the academic year abroad in any of 29 countries; 350 Georgia Tech students participated in a recent year. Those preferring to stay closer to home cross-register for classes with other colleges and universities in the Atlanta area.

Campus life: Sixty-four percent of Georgia Tech's students reside on the 450-acre urban campus, whose mix of brick and concrete, with city skyscrapers towering above, may initially prove disappointing to students seeking a bit more green. Others, though, consider Tech quite green for an urban campus, and the severity softens even more when the dogwoods and azaleas bloom. While all students may attend the frequent weekend parties given by the 34 national fraternities and 1 local and 13 national sororities, to which more than a fifth of the men and women belong, many independents prefer to hop on city transit for a trip into downtown Atlanta. Tech's most prestigious club is easily ANAK, a group of campus leaders whose identities are secret until after they graduate and whose focus is to improve campus life and help the school. Because the campus has its own police department and has borders that set it off from the surrounding city, students say crime is kept to a minimum, though the usual big-city precautions are still necessary. Student foot patrols and a shuttle bus that runs until 2 a.m. also serve as deterrents.

Football fans won't be surprised at Georgia Tech's influence on the athletic field. The Heisman trophy was named for John Heisman, Georgia Tech's first full-time football coach. The Yellow Jackets have won several national championships and made more than 20 bowl-game appearances (with twice as many wins as losses)—not what a student might initially expect from an engineering school. Basketball is almost as popular, and the Ramblin' Wreck athletic club does its best to keep school spirit high at all sporting events. While only 5% of the students participate in any of Tech's 9 men's and 8 women's intercollegiate sports, 70% of the men but only 9% of the women engage in 20 intramural sports.

The students' biggest social gripe is the 5 to 2 male/female ratio, which can make on-campus relationships more frustrating than rewarding. Many men opt to date women from other, nearby colleges.

Cost cutters: Because of substantial state support plus an above-average endowment for a state school of more than $937 million as of June 2005, Georgia residents pay just a quarter of the total cost of their education. In the 2005–2006 school year, 84% of all Tech freshmen and 71% of continuing students received some form of financial aid; for about 40% of both groups the aid was need-based. The average freshman award for a first-year student with financial need included a need-based scholarship or grant averaging $5195 and need-based self-help aid such as loans and jobs averaging $3289. Non-need-based athletic scholarships for first-year students averaged $13,695; other non-need-based awards and scholarships averaged $5064. Average indebtedness of a 2005 graduate was $12,643. Each year, the President's Scholarship program offers from $2500 a year up to the full cost of education for about 110 in-state and out-of-state residents for 4 years. To be considered, students in a recent year needed to have SATs of at least 1350 for state residents or 1400 for out-of-staters. To qualify for consideration, students must apply for admission by October 31. State residents also benefit from the HOPE scholarship program, which enables high school graduates with GPAs of 3.0 to receive full tuition, and a $150 a term book allowance. More than one-third of Tech undergraduates participate in the institute's cooperative education program, with more than 600 companies and government agencies involved; opportunities also have been opening up for assignments overseas with firms in France, Germany, Japan, and other countries. In addition to gaining workplace experience that helps in getting better paying jobs after graduation, recent students earned $6000–$8000 a year, which can go toward current college expenses.

Rate of return: Ninety-two percent of the freshmen who enter return for the sophomore year; while just 29% graduate in 4 years, 67% do so in 5 years, and 76% in 6 years.

Payoff: Management was the major of choice for 14% of the 2005 bachelor's degree recipients, followed by majors in computer science at 12% and industrial engineering at 11%. The overwhelming majority of graduates hook immediately into the enormous Georgia Tech alumni network, taking jobs with firms all over the nation and the world. Among the largest employers of Georgia Tech grads have been the U.S. Air Force, IBM, and Georgia Tech itself (the current president is a Georgia Tech alum), with General Electric, Motorola, Schlumberger, and McDonnell Douglas among the nearly 600 companies and organizations that recruit on campus. Students state that a GPA of at least 3.0 plus extracurricular involvement can push starting incomes well into the $35,000–$45,000 bracket, and reality bears out their boast. Graduates in chemical engineering have led the way in recent years with an average starting salary of $43,000 annually. Tech also ranks first in the graduation of African-American engineers as well as first in graduating women engineers. Among recent graduates, a fifth opted to bypass the impressive starting salaries and pursue advanced degrees.

Bottom line: The student who has strong quantitative skills and can cope with pressure and intensity will be happiest at Georgia Tech. "It is the struggle that is important here," notes a northerner. "First off, you know that if you can make it through Tech, you can do anything. Secondly, employers seem to know that a Tech grad can handle anything, is dependable, and will get the job done." There also are Georgia Tech alumni in plenty of high and low places to help make sure the struggle is worthwhile.

Mercer University

Macon, Georgia 31207

Setting: Suburban
Control: Private (Baptist)
Undergraduate enrollment: 2371 men and women
Graduate enrollment: 715 men, 1029 women
Student/faculty ratio: 13:1
Freshman profile: 9% scored over 699 on SAT I verbal; 35% scored 600–699; 45% 500–599; 11% below 500. 7% scored over 699 on SAT I math; 43% scored 600–699; 44% 500–599; 6% below 500. 11% scored above 29 on the ACT; 44% scored 24–29; 43% 18–23; 2% below 18. 48% graduated in top tenth of high school class; 74% in upper fourth.
Faculty profile: 86% Ph.D.'s

Tuition and fees: $23,460
Room and board: $7413
Freshman financial aid: 93%; average scholarship or grant: $15,670 need-based; $17,027 non-need-based
Campus jobs: NA; average earnings: NA
Application deadline: Early action: Nov. 1; priority: Apr. 1; regular: July 1
Financial aid deadline: Apr. 1
Admissions information: (478) 301-2650; (800) 840-8577
e-mail: admissions@mercer.edu
web site: www.mercer.edu

Students tired of the ordinary approach to G.E. (general education), find challenge in the G.B. (Great Books) program at Mercer University in Macon, Georgia. One of 2 general-education tracks offered at this Baptist university, the Great Books curriculum consists of 8 courses that stretch from the freshman through the senior year. Starting with the classical culture courses, from Homer to Virgil, students read, write, and discuss their way through the 16th and 17th centuries with Shakespeare, Newton, and Galileo, straight on through the 19th-century English romantic poets and revolutionary realists, to the modern Age of Ambivalence with Dostoevsky and Freud. Those lured to Mercer by the Great Books program are not disappointed and end up finding a list of other great items for discussion at this small but comprehensive university.

Student body: Seventy-six percent of Mercer's undergraduates are from Georgia, with most of the rest also drawn from the South, although students recently attended from 38 states. African-Americans constitute the single largest minority group at 16%, followed by Asian-Americans at 5%, Hispanics at 2%, and Native Americans at less than 1%. Foreign nationals from 30 countries account for 2%. Forty-four percent of the students in a recent year were Baptist. Students find their classmates to be fairly conservative, determined to succeed, socially involved, sincere, and "well mannered, with plenty of southern hospitality," notes a Georgian. Adds a fellow Georgian, "The students at Mercer may not have been the valedictorians or salutatorians in high school, but they are the type who were involved in everything and still gave the vals and sals a run for their money!"

Academics: Mercer University, named for Jesse Mercer, a prominent Baptist clergyman, confers the bachelor's degree in more than 50 majors as well as master's degrees in church music and performance, education, business administration, and engineering, a specialist degree in education, and doctorates in medicine and law. At the Macon campus (Mercer also has a campus in Atlanta) are the College of Liberal Arts and the schools of business, engineering, and education, plus graduate schools of law and medicine. The Georgia Baptist College of Nursing merged with Mercer in 2001 and offers a baccalaureate program in nursing at the Atlanta campus. Graduate schools of pharmacy and theology also are based in Atlanta. Courses are split between fall and spring semesters, with an average class size of 25. The range goes as high as 50 in introductory economics and drops to 8 in the Great Books program.

All undergraduates in the College of Liberal Arts, whether they choose the Great Books program, which includes 24 hours of required course work, or the distributional track, which also covers 24, must demonstrate competency in a foreign language and take at least 1 laboratory science plus a non-laboratory course in scientific inquiry, a mathematics class, and a multidisciplinary senior seminar. All students begin with 2 semesters of a first-year seminar designed to build critical writing, reading, and thinking skills. The schools of business, engineering, and education require the same basic general-education plan, with slight modifications.

As part of an entire university faculty numbering 614, 345 teach full-time and 269 part-time. No breakdown is available on the portion that teaches at the graduate level only. Thirty-nine percent of the full-time faculty are women. For many students, the faculty is what makes Mercer the kind of personal university it is. Explains a marketing major: "They make you feel at home but also require you to *think* and use your brain to reach your highest potential. Nothing is ever spoon-fed here."

Various programs in the Eugene W. Stetson School of Business and Economics, as well as English, psychology, and the sciences in the College of Liberal Arts, are recognized by majors and nonmajors alike as among Mercer's best disciplines. The business school in a new building is solid and offers plenty of real-life experience and individual attention from faculty. Undergraduates especially like the innovative curriculum known as MAPS, Managed Academic Path to Success, which enables students to tailor their own approach to business rather than follow pre-set tracks in such fields as finance or management. All students take the same core of 12 business courses plus 4 courses to help them find and frame their specialty, then the personalization begins. Says a major: "It is still based in a traditional business discipline; however, students can add in classes from the education, engineering, or liberal arts schools to give their majors a different feel." Chemistry, biology, environmental science, and physics have reputations for being "tough but good," with excellent laboratory equipment. Some students, however, wish there were more support for struggling classmates in biology and chemistry. The presence of the medical school allows students to do research in the medical school library. The English faculty are especially likable and excellent in their teaching. In the School of Engineering, the biomedical engineering and technical communication majors are especially rigorous and demand total dedication from their students.

The program in communication and theater arts is considered too broad in its course offerings. Students want to be able to specialize in certain areas, although there are separate majors in journalism and media studies.

Facilities: Jack Tarver Library opened in 1989 offering twice as much space as the old facility, and generally has kept students satisfied ever since. The collection in the main 3-story structure includes about 200,000 volumes and more than 1000 periodicals. The law school and medical school holdings, which undergraduates may use, swell the total on campus to more than 418,000 volumes and about 5000 periodicals. Favorite features of the main library are the 24-hour study room and several computerized research features, including Galileo the on-line catalog to the state university system, several specialized CD-ROM databases, and the Internet. Students also can tap into the holdings of major libraries in Atlanta. As a special treat for English literature scholars, the library houses extensive collections of the works of Percy Bysshe Shelley and Robert Burns.

General-access labs in the library and Academic Resource Center and about a dozen departmental labs across campus provide about 200 computers for students to use. The 15-unit lab in the resource center is open around the clock. The university strongly recommends that students have their own personal computers, and a majority do.

Special programs: Study-abroad programs are available in a dozen countries from Australia to Morocco.

Campus life: Two-thirds of Mercer undergraduates live on the 130-acre Macon campus, which students describe as having a "very refined and rustic look." The college moved to this site in 1871, 38 years after its founding, and the campus includes some buildings from the early decades as well as fairly recent additions such as the library and the engineering and business schools. Macon (pop. 150,000) does have crime in the neighborhood surrounding the college, but students say the campus is well patrolled and well lit and surveillance cameras were recently installed. A 24-hour escort service also is available. Car break-ins are the most frequent problem.

Twenty-four percent of the men and 25% of the women belong to 9 national fraternities and 1 local and 7 national sororities, in which students have remained pretty much segregated by race. Greek activities dominate most weekends, and some independents attend, while others prefer to leave campus. About a third of the undergraduates, both Greeks and independents, participate in the 13 men's and women's intramural sports, which students say draw more fan support than the Bears varsity program. Without a football team, men's basketball is the best attended of the 7 men's and 8 women's intercollegiate sports played in NCAA Division I. A new 221,000-square-foot University Center opened in 2004 and provides a 3500-seat arena along with an indoor track, indoor pool, and weight room.

Because of Mercer's Baptist affiliation, there is definitely a religious influence on campus, which sometimes makes it difficult for liberal viewpoints to be heard. Chapel attendance is no longer required, but many students attend nonetheless. The Baptist Student Union is one of the most active organizations, although students say members of other faiths make their views known as well. The student chapter of Habitat for Humanity also is quite busy and recently completed construction on the area's first Habitat home.

Atlanta, a little over an hour away, is one of the more popular off-campus escapes.

Cost cutters: Ninety-three percent of Mercer freshmen and 87% of continuing students received financial aid in a recent school year; for 68% of the first-year students and 63% of the rest, the aid was need-based. The average freshman award for a first-year student with financial need included a need-based scholarship or grant averaging $15,670 and need-based self-help aid such as loans and jobs averaging $5773. The average non-need-based athletic award for first-year students was $13,651; other non-need-based awards and scholarships averaged $17,027. The average graduate had debts of $11,075. Some of the more lucrative, renewable, merit-based awards have included full-tuition Presidential Scholarships; Faculty Scholarships, recently paying $3000–$4000 per year; Faculty Grants, worth between $1250 and $3000 in a recent year, and General Scholarships, ranging recently from $500 to $2000. Cooperative programs are available in all majors, especially engineering.

Rate of return: Eighty percent of entering freshmen return for the sophomore year; 36% go on to graduate in 4 years, 51% within 5 years, 55% within 6.

Payoff: Twenty-two percent of the 2005 graduates earned degrees in business, 18% in engineering, and 10% in social sciences and history. In recent years, a third of Mercer graduates have gone on to pursue advanced degrees. The majority accept a wide range of jobs throughout the southeast, some taking positions with firms they worked for in cooperative programs. Nearly 170 companies and other organizations recruited on campus during a recent school year.

Bottom line: Mercer is small, southern, and Baptist but not extreme in any of these categories. Students graduating from small high schools tend to feel most comfortable, although freshmen looking forward to a strong athletic program will be disappointed. Says a senior: "Mercer gives you a degree in life, something that the prominent schools can't offer. They teach you to be a neighbor and citizen before they teach you to be a doctor or teacher."

Oglethorpe University

Atlanta, Georgia 30319

Setting: Suburban
Control: Independent
Undergraduate enrollment: 279 men, 505 women
Graduate enrollment: 5 men, 31 women
Student/faculty ratio: 13:1
Freshman profile: 10% scored over 700 on SAT I verbal; 26% scored 600–700; 41% 500–599; 23% below 500. 3% scored over 700 on SAT I math; 27% scored 600–700; 40% 500–599; 30% below 500. 15% scored above 28 on the ACT; 18% scored 27–28; 22% 24–26; 28% 21–23; 17% below 21; 27% graduated in top tenth of high school class; 57% in upper fourth.
Faculty profile: 96% Ph.D.'s

Tuition and fees: $22,300
Room and board: $8000
Freshman financial aid: 96%; average scholarship or grant: NA
Campus jobs: NA; average earnings: NA
Application deadline: Early action: Dec. 5; regular: Feb. 1 (priority)
Financial aid deadline: Apr. 1
Admissions information: (404) 364-8307; (800) 428-4484
e-mail: admission@oglethorpe.edu
web site: www.oglethorpe.edu

James Edward Oglethorpe established Georgia in 1733 as an American colony for debtors, an alternative to debtor's prison. In a similar manner, the university named after him, chartered 102 years later, helps to free students from the debts their peers at other colleges incur by offering one of the lowest small private-college tuitions in the nation: at $22,300 in the 2005–2006 school year, just 63% of the actual cost of the student's education, the balance coming from endowment, gifts, and other sources. In many ways, the campus is a throwback in time and place, with several of the buildings patterned after those of General Oglethorpe's alma mater, Corpus Christi College of Oxford University. Oglethorpe University may not be the Oxford of the South, but for the price it's an excellent imitation.

Student body: Oglethorpe's students are very Georgian and very southern. Sixty-two percent are from the Peach State, with most of the rest from the surrounding region. Altogether, students from 36 states and 21 foreign countries are present. About three-fourths are graduates of public high schools. Twenty-six percent are members of racial and ethnic minorities, 20% African-American, 3% Asian-American and 3% Hispanic. Four percent are foreign nationals. Students divide their classmates into all sorts of interesting subgroups that are distinct but open-minded toward others. Socially, there are the Greeks, the independents who live on campus, and the independents who live elsewhere. In terms of life-style, notes a sophomore southerner, "we have yuppies, hippies, wanna be's, frat rats, and bow girls." Philosophically, adds a senior, "on the largely nihilistic campus, there are Kantians and other moralists." In short, observes a senior: "this is an environment where you feel free to investigate and express who you are." The atmosphere also encourages students to learn from and help one another, which keeps outward academic competition to a minimum.

Academics: Oglethorpe offers the bachelor's degree in 28 fields plus an individually planned major, as well as a master's in education and in business. Classes follow the semester schedule. The average enrollment for undergraduates is 14, with a recent range from as few as 2 in advanced Japanese to 33 in some popular courses.

Oglethorpe's curriculum emphasizes the development of analytical, communication, and leadership skills, rather than just the acquisition of facts. Writing skills are taught in all disciplines. Oglethorpe has had a core curriculum for more than 50 years, making it one of the oldest core programs at a liberal arts college in the country. Its newest format, instituted in fall 1998, features 7 year-long interdisciplinary courses that students take throughout their 4 years at the university. The sequences feature the reading of a number of primary texts common to all the courses and extensive writing assignments. The courses range from the freshman-year Narrative of the Self to the senior level Science and Human Nature. Reflects a senior: "I find a lot of meaning in the classical philosophical texts we have read in the core. I feel confident that my professors are preparing me to think for myself and to make a living in the world while also living meaningfully." Additional classes are required in fine arts and either mathematics or a foreign language.

Fifty-seven of Oglethorpe's 125 faculty members are full-time; 32% are women. "The faculty is excellence 'at its best,' if such is possible," enthuses an English major. For many students, closeness to the faculty is the essence of their Oglethorpe experience. Says a junior: "Faculty members talk to you like you are their equal, not like you are inferior. In that respect, they also ask you to do the work that they know you are capable of doing." Faculty are evaluated by students every term on such areas as competence, ability to lead discussions, and student improvement in skills such as writing or thinking under the professor's tutelage. However, some students are less enamored with the adjunct members. "Some are good, some are lousy," says another English major. "Oglethorpe needs more quality, full-time faculty."

The sciences, English, business administration, and economics are considered by students to have the best faculties and most challenging curricula. The English professors are particularly energetic in their teaching and get very involved in students' lives; these close relationships have led to a high number of students being accepted to graduate programs in the field. Science professors provide a strong program, despite the twin problems of too much outdated lab equipment and too little space. Says a biology major: "The faculty are great teachers and provide a solid foundation for whatever you want to go into." Majors in philosophy, history, and politics also are assured of an outstanding education. Atlanta provides numerous opportunities for internships in business and many other fields; accounting majors in particular benefit from spring and fall receptions with members of the major accounting firms.

For some students, the smallness of the school means limited course offerings in even the best departments. For example, while the professors of sociology and philosophy are excellent, there have been only 2 and 3, respectively, limiting the diversity of courses and perspectives offered. Art and music also lack sufficient faculty; art needs better studios. The popular communication program needs additional faculty to handle student demand for its courses. Computer science alone is offered only as a minor, with 1 full-time professor, an ever-changing series of adjuncts, and little equipment. Students wish more foreign language options were available; the college offers majors in French and Spanish only, minors in those two fields plus Japanese and courses in German, Greek, and Latin.

Facilities: Designed as a model library for undergraduates, the 56,000-square-foot Philip Weltner Library opened in the fall of 1992. The building features the lighted tables, lancet windows, and elegance of an English college library updated with modern technology, 10 group study rooms, a 24-hour study area, a viewing room with state-of-the-art video and sound systems, and the Oglethorpe University Museum, which occupies the entire third floor. The bigger structure has already meant an additional 72,000 books, with nearly 152,000 volumes and 775 current periodicals now in the collection. Students find the holdings in psychology and medical research less strong than those in literature. For additional resources, students turn to the mammoth holdings of the Atlanta-Athens library consortium, available through interlibrary loan, on-line or a personal visit.

Several small labs, each with fewer than 20 computers, are available around campus. One lab is open around the clock. Says a senior, "Oglethorpe needs a bigger computer lab for busy times." Many students also have—and share—their own units. The school strongly recommends that students bring their own computers; PCs are recommended over Macs.

Special programs: Oglethorpe students can cross-register at any of 18 other Atlanta-area colleges. Those longing to study farther away can attend universities in Japan, France, The Netherlands, Germany, Russia, and Latin America. Three-two engineering programs are available with Georgia Tech, Auburn University, and the universities of Florida and Southern California. A joint program for undergraduates interested in the visual arts allows students to spend 2 years at Oglethorpe and 2 at the Atlanta College of Art. Internships are available in all majors. About 15 undergraduates a year are accepted into the Rich Foundation Urban Leadership Program designed to prepare Oglethorpe students to be leaders in the 21st century.

Campus life: Oglethorpe's 118-acre campus, 10 miles northeast of downtown Atlanta, is home to 56% of the full-time students, and 40% of those leave campus for the weekend. Most of the on-campus activity revolves around the 4 national fraternities and 3 national sororities, to which a third of the men and a fourth of the women belong. Prior to December 1993, all but 1 fraternity were accessible only by car. Now all the fraternities and sororities have new houses on campus in a Greek row, a move which has meant larger parties, open to everyone as always. Few university-sponsored events get much of a turnout, although student government has renewed its efforts to get more people involved. Because the entire campus is surrounded by fencing and is well patrolled every 15–30 minutes, students say city crime does not present much of a problem.

The Stormy Petrels do not draw many varsity sports fans, with basketball, baseball, and soccer getting the biggest crowds of the 7 men's and 7 women's teams in action in NCAA Division III. Six of every 10 men and 4 of every 10 women participate in the 12 intramural sports, half for each sex. In a takeoff on a Cambridge University tradition portrayed in the movie *Chariots of Fire,* Oglethorpe runners attempt to race around the university's academic quadrangle in the time between the first stroke of 12 on the bell tower and the final stroke.

Atlanta's clubs, restaurants, and sporting events provide much of the off-campus social life. There is also river rafting down the Chattahoochee River, Stone Mountain Park, and Six Flags amusement park. A city bus that stops directly in front of the campus and a rapid-transit train just a mile away make getaways easy.

Cost cutters: At least eight of every 10 undergraduates receive financial aid, 96% of the freshmen and 85% of all continuing students in the 2005–2006 academic year. Sixty-nine percent of the freshmen and 58% of the continuing students were on need-based assistance. No figure is available for freshman financial aid packages for the 2005–2006 school year. The average recent graduate left with debts of $16,250. Every year, 5 James Edward Oglethorpe Scholarships, which cover full tuition, room, and board and are renewable over 4 years, are awarded. Candidates must have high test scores and GPAs and a superior record of leadership in outside activities. Recipients are selected through an academic competition held on campus in the spring. Presidential Scholarships, requiring similar high test scores and GPA, pay $11,000 a year. Other Oglethorpe Scholars Awards pay from $4000 to $10,000 to students of superior academic achievement. A cooperative education program is offered in most majors, beginning in the sophomore year.

Rate of return: Eighty-one percent of all freshmen who enter return for the sophomore year. Fifty-three percent graduate in 4 years; 62%, in 5 years; 65% in 6.

Payoff: In a recent year, more than 40% of the students earned degrees in 3 academic areas: 18% in business administration, 13% in psychology, and 11% in communication and rhetoric. A third of Oglethorpe graduates pursue advanced degrees. Among the majority who enter the job market, most remain in the Atlanta area; many of the others accept jobs elsewhere in the southeast. A large number are employed by the major accounting firms and the Atlanta offices of major corporations such as Coca-Cola and IBM.

Bottom line: "Oglethorpe is best for students interested in intense work with faculty who will make them achieve," observes a midwesterner. "Students who do not know what they want will benefit from the core." Socially, the Greeks are most popular, but the eclectic student body should offer a niche to just about everyone.

The University of Georgia

Athens, Georgia 30602

Setting: Small city
Control: Public
Undergraduate enrollment: 9769 men, 12,846 women
Graduate enrollment: 1968 men, 2389 women
Student/faculty ratio: 18:1
Freshman profile: Median SAT I scores: 620 verbal; 620 math. 30% scored above 28 on the ACT; 22.5% scored 27–28; 11% 24–26; 4% 21–23; 3.5% below 21. 52% graduated in top tenth of high school class.
Faculty profile: 94% Ph.D.'s
Tuition and fees: $4628 in-state; $16,848 out-of-state

Room and board: $6376
Freshman financial aid: 94%; average scholarship or grant: $5768 need-based
Campus jobs: 2%; average earnings: $2632/year
Application deadline: Early action: Oct. 15; regular: Jan. 15
Financial aid deadline: Aug. 1 (Priority date: Mar. 1)
Admissions information: (706) 542-2112
e-mail: adm-info@uga.edu
web site: www.uga.edu

Which university was the first state-supported institution of higher education in the nation? Ask a Georgia Bulldog, and you'll probably hear "the University of Georgia." Ask a North Carolina Tarheel, and you'll get a different answer. It all depends on what you mean by "first." Although North Carolina's constitution first authorized the start of a state university in 1776, the legislature didn't get around to chartering it until 1789. By then, Georgia's General Assembly had already chartered its own university, 4 years before. From there, it's a matter of which school opened its doors first (North Carolina did), and in many ways Georgia has never caught up to its old rival in terms of national reputation for academic excellence. To make matters worse, Georgia has watched many of the state's brightest scholars choose its sister institution, Georgia Tech. But don't underestimate a Bulldog: more students are discovering a quality education at this university—at a chihuahua of a price. And alumni who remember the "party-school" days of the 1950s and 60s wonder whether they could gain admission alongside their children and grandchildren today. In the 2005–2006 school year, over half, 52%, of the entering freshmen were drawn from the top 10% of their high school graduating class.

Student body: Georgia prides itself on having students from almost every county in the state and every state in the nation. All but 15% of the undergraduates are from Georgia, with about 40% from the metropolitan Atlanta area. Most of the out-of-staters also come from the South. Minority enrollment stands at 11% with 5% African-American students, 4% Asian-Americans, and 2% Hispanics. Foreign nationals from 100 countries make up another 3% of the enrollment and further enrich the diversity. Eighty-seven percent in a recent year were graduates of public schools. While a large contingent of conservative, white students tend to predominate in the Greek system, all types appear at Georgia. Says a state resident: "There are liberals and conservatives, athletic fans and music fans, party animals and serious scholars. Because the university has such a wide range of majors, there are just as many different academic 'types.'" One "type" that students are seeing more of is those who find they must study harder to stay afloat, and really hit the books in order to excel. In fact, since 1996, the university has produced 4 prestigious Rhodes Scholars. "We're a lot more academically competitive than people think," adds a business major from the north, but there remain a number of easy majors that students "can party their way through," says a senior.

Academics: Georgia offers degrees through the doctorate in 12 schools and colleges, with more than 160 undergraduate programs. The academic year is divided into 2 semesters. A Maymester also is offered. Freshman classes can run from 20 to 300, while upper-division courses usually have fewer than 35. Honors classes range from 5–15 people.

All students must take 42 semester hours, about a third of the total required for graduation, in a Regents core curriculum. Students take classes in English and mathematics, and core courses in fine arts/humanities; science, mathematics, and technology; and social science as well as classes preparing them for entry into a major during their junior year. Also required are courses in environmental literacy and cultural diversity. Undergraduates must take in addition courses or pass examinations on the history and constitutions of the United States and Georgia.

The faculty who teach at Georgia is overwhelmingly full-time; in the 2005–2006 school year, only 447 of the 3361 faculty members worked part-time. No figure is available to show the portions that teach at the graduate level only. Thirty-six percent of the faculty is women. One faculty member, a professor of history and law, won the 1998 Pulitzer Prize for history. A quarter of the introductory courses in a recent year were taught by graduate students, reflecting a 10% drop from previous years. Some faculty members are clearly interested in research exclusively, and students would rather that they just forget teaching than alternate between research and instruction. But many undergraduates have found even professors in large classes to be receptive to students who take an interest in the subject matter. "Only 1 of my teachers in 5 terms hasn't gotten excited about the material and been willing to talk to me outside class," observes a philosophy major. "But I still learned a lot from that teacher."

A recently constructed $32 million biological sciences building has only enhanced Georgia's impressive genetics and biochemistry programs in the College of Arts and Sciences, providing a 5-star facility to match the faculty. Terry College of Business (especially its international business component) and the College of Journalism and Mass Communication, home of the Peabody Awards, are both considered tough and their facilities excellent. "If you can get into the journalism program," observes an admirer, "you'll get good, hands-on training that will lead to a great job." The College of Education draws praise for the extensive classroom experience it requires; Agriculture has "plentiful resources, small classes, and top-notch professors," says an environmental economics and management major.

Although the university offers bachelor of science degrees in agricultural and biological engineering, the mainstream engineering disciplines are left to Georgia Tech. Physics and foreign languages have reputations for being weak. Math is overcrowded and uses too many graduate students with poor English-speaking skills. However, the long-neglected art, music, and drama departments recently underwent a renaissance with the opening of the $35.7 million Performing and Visual Arts Complex.

Facilities: There are 3 major libraries on campus: the Main Library plus the science and law libraries, which among them house 4 million volumes, 6.5 million microfilm items, and more than 67,000 periodicals. The 258,000-square-foot Student Learning Center, located in the heart of campus, also is part library/part classroom building/part computer lab and offers 96 group study rooms and a wood-paneled reading room plus library staff to assist students in computerized research. While the 7-story Main Library can be intimidating at first, students say it becomes manageable thanks to computerized catalogs for both books and periodicals and extensive computerized databases. History and literature buffs will find some special treats: the original Confederate constitution, as well as the manuscripts and memorabilia of authors Erskine Caldwell and Margaret Mitchell.

Five hundred public access computers are located in the Student Learning Center. Computer labs also can be found in the main library and nearly 2 dozen other buildings across campus. Wireless Internet access is an option on most parts of the campus and in part of the downtown area. Most labs are open from

12 to 16 hours a day, but availability depends on how close the date is to the end of the term. Students' chief complaint has been that the only 24-hour computer labs are located in the dorms, though the Student Learning Center is open until 2 a.m. Sunday through Thursday.

Special programs: Opportunities for study abroad in 36 countries are provided by several academic departments, among them history and journalism, offering classes at Oxford in England as well as in countries such as Italy, Brazil, and France. More than 1400 Georgia undergraduates are involved in some form of international education each year. The Governor's Intern Program enables students to serve a full-time, 10-week internship in a state or local government agency; a Washington, D.C. semester is another alternative. An accelerated degree program that allows a student to earn both bachelor's and master's degrees in 5 years is an option in the School of Accounting. Cooperative programs with University Center institutions in Atlanta also are available.

Campus life: In a recent year, just a quarter of Georgia's undergraduates resided on the campus, whose north and south sections stretch over 605 acres. Most of the university's oldest structures, dating from 1806, are on the north half, with more modern structures, including most of the professional schools, going up on the south campus. Bus service helps students cover the miles more quickly. Large numbers reside off campus because of the affordability of local rents. Nearly a fifth of the men are members of 32 national fraternities; 24% of the women pledged to the 22 national sororities. Most fraternity parties are open to independents by invitation only, and many nonmembers think the Greek/non-Greek dichotomy detracts from campus unity. "Sometimes, non-Greek students are left out of activities," says one young woman. Music lifts the spirits of all souls, however, either on campus with the 407-member Redcoat Marching Band, or at well-known Athens nightclubs, which have given rise to such rock groups as R.E.M. and the B-52's. With the university police, the city police, and the state police patrolling the campus area and free escort vans, students say crime isn't much of a problem, though robberies do occur. Education about issues such as date rape and self-defense, as well as tightened dorm security, helps keep incidents low.

For students new to Georgia, the fall football season is "indescribable," with excited alumni as well as students packing the 92,746-seat stadium. "Football here is King," says a southerner, "and most students take advantage of tailgating, the game, and the after-game celebrations." Bulldogs basketball is a little less popular during the winter; baseball and tennis draw some crowds in the spring but generally lose out to the lure of the beaches. Altogether, 8 men's and 11 women's intercollegiate sports are played as part of NCAA Division I. Georgia athletic teams have won 24 national championships, 14 since 1999. In 2005, the women's gymnastics and swimming and diving teams and the men's golf team each claimed the national title in their sport. Nearly half the students participate in 28 men's and 27 women's intramural sports. The 425,000-square-foot Ramsey Student Center, cited by *Sports Illustrated* a few years ago as the best collegiate recreation/fitness center in the nation, rounds out the athletic offerings.

Although Athens itself (pop. 90,000) is a great college town, many students in need of a getaway go home or to Atlanta, an hour and a quarter away. Others prefer more natural escapes to the Georgia coast or the mountains of north Georgia.

Cost cutters: In the 2005–2006 school year, 94% of the freshmen and 77% of the continuing students received financial aid; between a fifth and a fourth was need-based. The average freshman award included a need-based scholarship or grant, averaging $5768; need-based self-help aid such as loans and job earnings averaged $2754. Non-need-based athletic scholarships averaged $8265. Of graduates who borrow, a typical graduate left with debts of $13,209. To attract top students, Georgia offers a number of renewable merit scholarships. The awards for state residents are on top of the popular HOPE, Helping Outstanding Pupils Educationally, state scholarship funded by the Georgia Lottery for Education that pays the full amount of mandatory fees in place during the 2003–2004 school year. Out-of-state recipients qualify for a Regents Waiver of the nonresident fees. Foundation Fellowships pay $14,000 a year, to superior out-of-state students and $9000 a year to top-flight in-state students who agree to participate in Georgia's highly acclaimed honors program. To be considered, students should have at least a 1400 critical reading and math SAT or a 31 ACT and a 3.7 GPA. Up to 25 Foundation Fellows are chosen each year. Special applications for the award are due by Nov. 15. Every student who is invited to interview for the Foundation Fellowship is assured of at least the Bernard Ramsey Honors Scholarship that pays $4500 to in-state students and $7000 to out-of-state students. Charter Scholarships recognize about 250 freshmen who have demonstrated outstanding achievement in academics, extracurricular activities, leadership, and service. The award provides $1000 a year to state residents, and $1000 annually to those who live out of state. Up to 10 renewable Vice-Presidential Scholarships, worth $1200, are awarded to other high-achieving students. Cooperative experiences can be arranged in any major.

Rate of return: Ninety-two percent of entering freshmen return for the sophomore year; 43% graduate in 4 years, 69% in 5 years, and 74% in 6 years.

Payoff: In a recent graduating class, the 3 top majors were psychology at just over 5%, and biology and political science at about 4.5% each. Nearly a fifth of Georgia's graduates go on immediately to graduate or professional schools. At least 60% take jobs with a wide range of companies throughout the southeast, among them Coca-Cola, Georgia Pacific, and Southern Bell. About 1400 companies and other organizations recruited on campus in a recent school year. About 40% of alumni settle in metropolitan Atlanta. Several graduates over the past 155 years also have settled in the governor's mansion. Since 1851, 25 governors have been graduates of the University of Georgia, including 7 of the last 9 state chief executives.

Bottom line: The University of Georgia is a big, high-spirited school, and extroverts generally have a happier and more successful time on campus than introverted types. But many more serious students are keeping Georgia "on their mind" when they're considering low-cost colleges with challenging academic programs.

Hawaii

Hawaii Pacific University

Honolulu, Hawaii 96813

Setting: Urban
Control: Private
Undergraduate enrollment: 1329 men, 2431 women
Graduate enrollment: 289 men, 329 women
Student/faculty ratio: 17:1
Freshman profile: 2% scored over 700 on SAT I verbal; 13% scored 600–700; 39% 500–599; 46% below 500. 1% scored over 700 on SAT I math; 17% scored 600–700; 37% 500–599; 45% below 500. 6% scored above 28 on the ACT; 5% scored 27–28; 31% 24–26; 24% 21–23; 34% below 21. 15% graduated in top tenth of high school class; 40% in upper fifth.

Faculty profile: 71% Ph.D.'s
Tuition and fees: $11,630
Room and board: $9450
Freshman financial aid: 80%; average scholarship or grant: $4066 need-based; $6115 non-need-based
Campus jobs: 6%; average earnings: $2443/year
Application deadline: Rolling
Financial aid deadline: Mar. 1
Admissions information: (808) 544-0238; (866) 225-5478
e-mail: admissions@hpu.edu
web site: www.hpu.edu

What snowbound high school senior hasn't fantasized about leaving the familiar behind and striking out for college on some tropical isle? Inexpensive such a choice is not, given the high cost of living in an island state like Hawaii and built-in extras like airplane flights to and from the mainland. If, however, you have a true entrepreneurial spirit and feel you were meant to study for finals on the beach at Waikiki, then say "Aloha" to Hawaii Pacific University, one of the best financial bets off the mainland at a total cost of just over $21,000 in the 2005–2006 school year. With no student housing on the original campus—a campus that consists of all or several floors of 8 high-rise buildings in downtown Honolulu—Hawaii Pacific for many years did not offer a traditional college experience. However, a merger in 1992 with the former Hawaii Loa College 8 miles away and connected by shuttle has provided an additional 135 acres in the green foothills of the Ko'olau Mountains, with plenty of room to roam and dorms for dozing. For those willing to overlook the lack of ivy in favor of no-frills academics, with a strong business orientation, a lei and lots of serious learning await.

Student body: Hawaii Pacific students rave about the diversity. The student body is 32% Caucasian-American, 21% foreign nationals, 38% Asian-American, 3% African-American, 4% Hispanic, and 1% Native American. Less than half, 48% of the undergraduates are from Hawaii, with half of the out-of-staters coming from the mainland west. All 50 states as well as 99 foreign countries are represented, including many island nations most Americans have never heard of. Undergraduates range in age from 17 to 50, with the average around 25. Three-fourths are graduates of public schools. For the most part, students are adventurous but serious about their studies, tending more toward the competitive than the laid-back end of the academic spectrum. Says a journalism major: "The undergraduates at our school all seem to know why they came here; (most) came for a specific reason with an intended major in mind." Many form study groups outside the classroom, where their varying racial, ethnic, and cultural perspectives provide an added dimension. "At HPU," says a New Englander, "expect to learn more about the world around you, its people and places, and how that affects things . . . Expect to be surprised!"

Academics: Hawaii Pacific—which just turned 40 in 2005 and is younger than some of its students—offers bachelor's degrees in over 50 largely business-related and liberal arts majors, although the merger added popular bachelor's degree programs in nursing and marine biology. Master's degrees in 11 fields also are available. The degree programs are well thought out, with a theme of entrepreneurship running through many of the offerings. The academic year is divided into 2 semesters plus a January term. Average undergraduate class size is 19, with the largest course, World Civilizations, sometimes getting as high as 48. Most classes top out at 30. Courses like a small business consulting seminar enroll 6–9 students.

General-education requirements account for about half of the 124 semester hours needed for graduation. The specific courses required cover a wide range of topics from World Civilizations I and II to Introduction to Computer Information Systems. Few students complain about these requirements, and most find them useful in broadening their education.

The total faculty numbers 624 with all but 28 of the 255 full-time members and all but 18 of the 369 part-timers teaching undergraduates. Forty-five percent of the faculty are women. Despite large numbers of part-time faculty members with professional commitments off campus, students say they like the faculty's real-world experience and close ties to industry and generally have no problem arranging to meet professors after hours. "They're not teaching from a book," says a transfer student. "They're teaching from their lives." A slightly older than usual student population also helps keep faculty members on their toes. Notes a senior from the Northeast: "The faculty respect the students and realize that they can possibly learn something from them." Professors also don't forget how far from home many students are. Says a junior from the Pacific Northwest: "Many have a big Thanksgiving dinner at their houses and they invite their students to come that aren't able to fly home for the short break." Students' chief complaints center on knowledgeable professors who have a hard time transmitting their knowledge clearly to undergraduates.

Many of Hawaii Pacific's top-rated programs are in its College of Business. The 5-star travel industry management program offers a bachelor's degree with at least 1½ years' experience in the Hawaiian travel industry; students intern at Hawaii's well-booked hotels and resorts. The accounting major has an especially good faculty and a program that adequately prepares students for the CPA exam. Management, international business, and business economics also benefit from faculty members who bring their life experiences and business connections as well as their academic expertise to the classroom. In the College of Natural Sciences, the marine biology and oceanography programs are naturals with an ideal climate, volcanic geology, coral reefs, and surrounding ocean available for study. Notes a senior: "The director of marine sciences is excited about what he does and makes every effort to guide the students." A recent affiliation with The Oceanic Institute, an applied research and education organization located on 56 acres on Oahu, is further expanding opportunities for advanced study in these fields. The communications program has grown steadily over the last few years, featuring new and varied courses and a knowledgable faculty always open to student input. Says a major: "The environment is filled with respect, compassion, and professionalism." International studies, says a major, "is made up of a great faculty who is involved in students' lives and activities and who comes from a diverse background."

With business and marine science programs clearly the university's strong suit, many majors in the College of Liberal Arts have suffered some neglect. Students say that the social sciences especially political science need more teachers; the psychology major could use a lab, too. Though enrollment in the humanities is low, students find the class discussions stimulating. Students with an interest in theater must design their own individualized major.

Facilities: Meader Library, housed over 4 floors in a downtown high-rise, and Atherton Library on the Hawaii Loa campus together provide a collection of 110,000 volumes and 167,000 paper and electronic periodicals. Computerized research assistance including a very good CD-ROM collection is available. However, Meader and Atherton libraries close earlier than most, at 8:30 p.m. every night except Friday and Saturday, when they close at 6 p.m. and 5 p.m. respectively. Atherton Library also is closed on Sunday. Students wanting longer hours usually end up at the central Hawaii State Public Library, just a few blocks away, or the University of Hawaii library at the Manoa campus, both of which are much bigger and open later.

An abundance of high-technology classrooms and laboratories became available to students in 2003 with the opening of the 4500-square-foot Frear Center. The Center houses nearly $2 million in new high-tech equipment, raising to about 400 the number of PCs available to students across the 2 campuses. Students still wish the labs were open longer hours, with most also closing before 9 p.m. The university strongly recommends that all students have personal computers. Wireless zones are located throughout both campuses.

Special programs: The college helps arrange paid internships for juniors and seniors in premanagerial or managerial positions at more than 90 local businesses and government agencies, ranging from Aloha Airlines to New York Life Insurance Company. A 3-2 engineering degree is an option with Washington University in St. Louis and the University of Southern California. Students may study abroad in 9 countries

Campus life: Hawaii Pacific operates 2 very different campuses as 1: the downtown, commuter campus with no residence halls of its own, and the suburban Hawaii Loa campus, just 15 minutes away, which is known as the windward campus because of its location on Oahu's windward side and has dormitories. Still, just 3% of the students live on campus, which means most look beyond collegiate borders for much of their fun. The downtown campus basically shuts down at night as far as student activity is concerned, with the exception of the frequent night classes offered. Certain campus basics, such as a cafeteria, a gymnasium, and a swimming pool, don't exist. There are no fraternities or sororities. Popular clubs among the 93 available are career- or culture-oriented; two examples are the Travel Industry Management Student Association and the United Samoan Organization. But students are not total grinds. "Some weekend activities that help students unwind are beach trips to swim, play volleyball, or surf and water sports such as kayaking or windsurfing," notes a Hawaiian Hoosier. Regularly scheduled dances, as well as an annual boat cruise, are especially popular. So are the nightclubs at Waikiki. Crime is not considered a problem in either of the campus areas though security guards patrol both. Some students are concerned about the number of homeless people who spend time around the downtown campus.

The Sea Warriors men's basketball team, and the women's volleyball team, are the best supported of the 5 men's and 5 women's intercollegiate sports offered under NCAA Division II competition. A Spirit Club helps to rally support for the teams. Sixteen intramural sports are available, 8 each for men and women, but only a tenth of the students participate. Because of year-round temperate weather—330 days of sunshine a year—students do a lot of hiking, biking, surfing, running, and just lying out in the sun, with or without a textbook.

Cost cutters: Tuition is kept low, thanks to support from the private sector, endowment funds, and grants. Eighty percent of the freshmen and 66% of continuing students in the 2005–2006 school year received financial aid; for 42% of the freshmen and 36% of the rest, the aid was need-based. The average financial award for a first-year student with financial need included a need-based scholarship or grant averaging $4066 and need-based self-help aid such as loans and jobs averaging $3678. The average non-need-based athletic scholarship for first-year students equaled $8577; other non-need-based awards and scholarships averaged $6115. The average financial indebtedness of a 2005 graduate totaled $19,750. While some merit awards, such as the 100% tuition waiver Presidential Scholarship, are restricted to Hawaii high school graduates, university merit scholarships are open to all students after they have completed 2 semesters of attendance. Other scholarships and tuition waivers are offered for participation in sports and other activities. High-achieving students who are graduates of U.S. high schools on the mainland are eligible for the Makana Scholarship that offers a 20% tuition waiver. To be considered, students should have GPAs of at least 3.5 and critical reading and math SAT/ACT scores of at least 1200/26. Eighty to 100% tuition waivers are available to students with demonstrated skill in cheerleading and dance performance. An extensive cooperative education program is available in all majors. Students can also save money by expediting the educational process, taking classes year-round, night and day, plus Saturdays. Says a journalism major: "You can tell your academic advisor how much time you want to take to graduate and he or she will put you on the appropriate degree plan." Although living in Honolulu can be expensive, many students cut costs by sharing apartments and food costs with others. And there's always the year-round balmy weather, which cuts back on expensive purchases of heavy clothing.

Rate of return: Sixty-six percent of freshmen return for the sophomore year; 25% go on to graduate in 4 years, 36% in 5 years, 40% in 6. Five percent take advantage of the chance to expedite their education and graduate in 3 years or less.

Payoff: Twelve percent of the 2005 graduates earned degrees in nursing and 6% each in justice administration and management. Many graduates take jobs in the travel industry with major hotel chains like Sheraton, Hilton, and Hyatt and with major airlines like Continental and Singapore. Others work with banks, accounting firms, and computer manufacturers in Hawaii, on the west coast, and in Asia. More than 130 companies and organizations recruited on campus in the 2004–2005 school year. A number combine graduate work with employment.

Bottom line: Students looking for a good party school won't find it at Hawaii Pacific University. But those seeking a largely career-oriented curriculum set in the booming Pacific basin with classmates from all different backgrounds, Hawaii Pacific can offer that, plus an ample dose of sand and sun. Observes a midwesterner: "Any student who wouldn't mind living in paradise would do well here."

Idaho

Albertson College of Idaho

Caldwell, Idaho 83605

Setting: Small town
Control: Independent
Undergraduate enrollment: 317 men, 444 women
Graduate enrollment: 4 men, 14 women
Student/faculty ratio: 12:1
Freshman profile: 14% scored over 700 on SAT I verbal; 35% scored 600–700; 35% 500–599; 16% below 500. 11% scored over 700 on SAT I math; 33% scored 600–700; 40% 500–599; 16% below 500. 24% scored above 28 on the ACT; 15% scored 27–28; 32% 24–26; 21% 21–23; 8% below 21. 34% graduated in top tenth of high school class; 60% in upper fifth.
Faculty profile: 86% Ph.D.'s

Tuition and fees: $15,765
Room and board: $5330
Freshman financial aid: 93%; average scholarship or grant: $3737 need-based; $4080 non-need-based
Campus jobs: 40%; average earnings: $775/year
Application deadline: Early action: Nov. 15; priority: Feb. 16; regular: June 1
Financial aid deadline: Feb. 15
Admissions information: (208) 459-5305; (800) AC-IDAHO (224-3246)
e-mail: admissions@albertson.edu
web site: www.albertson.edu

For years, the tiny College of Idaho in the Great Potato State suffered an identity crisis. Along with such life-threatening issues as declining enrollment, dwindling resources, and a faculty that had gone without pay raises for 3 years, there was the problem of being a small, private, liberal arts college with a name that suggested just another big public institution. Not anymore. In 1991, a hundred years after its founding, the former College of Idaho became Albertson College of Idaho, named for Joseph A. Albertson, owner of the nation's fourth largest grocery chain, who, along with other business leaders, helped reverse the fortunes of this once-failing college. Undergraduate enrollment now stands at nearly 800 full-time students, up from just 400 in 1980. An endowment approaching $44 million has increased almost 100-fold since bottoming out at a half-million dollars. Albertson, according to its students, is growing and meeting the mind-broadening curriculum challenges that high school graduates of the future will need. Warns a senior, a "tunnel-vision attitude is not very compatible with Albertson." Adds a sophomore: "Extracurricular involvement is expected."

Student body: Seventy-one percent of Albertson's undergraduates are residents of Idaho—"the smartest and most well-rounded students from high schools in the state," boasts a resident—with another 13% coming from Washington, Oregon, California, and Nevada. Most are the products of small to mid-sized towns in the region's rural areas. Altogether 29 states, up from 18 states just 4 years before, and 10 foreign countries are represented; 95% graduated from public schools. About 9% are members of racial and ethnic minority groups, including 5% Hispanics, 3% Asian-Americans, and less than 1% each African-Americans and Native Americans. Another 2% are foreign nationals. Students emphasize that their campus is not racially intolerant, just rather isolated. For the most part, the student body is characterized by a rugged individualism that lets each person be him- or herself, whoever that may be within a close and caring community. "This kind of supportive environment allowed me to expand and grow so much in the last year," says a sophomore. "Everyone is very down-to-earth, and studies are taken seriously." Not surprisingly, however, word of both good developments and bad travels quickly on the close-knit campus.

Academics: Albertson offers the bachelor's degree in 27 majors. A master of arts in teaching was introduced in 2002. The school year is divided into two 13-week semesters with a 6-week January term in the middle that allows students to travel or take innovative courses grouped around a theme. In a recent winter, the theme was "Global Interdependence." Faculty-led trips went to Australia, Thailand, Vietnam, Cambodia, and Laos as well as to Idaho's Sawtooth Valley. During the regular semester, class sizes range from almost 60 students in a music course to just 1 or 2 in some upper-level courses. The typical class enrolls about 15.

Albertson's Freshman Year Experience program was designed to help ease students' transition from high school to college. The experience, which divides first-year students into groups of 18, includes a two-semester writing course, a specialized curriculum, and a novel that students are assigned to read over the summer and be ready to discuss in fall classes. In a recent summer, all freshmen were sent copies of *The Things They Carried,* a novel about the Vietnam War by National Book Award winner Tim O'Brien. As a followup, O'Brien visited the campus in October to give workshops and lectures related to the work. In addition to the Freshman Year Experience, students must complete their choice of a certain number of courses spread over the traditional disciplines including a recently added cultural diversity requirement. Students with superior high school records, including a GPA of at least 3.75 and standardized test scores in the 90th percentile, may bypass these requirements and devise their own courses of study as Gipson Scholars.

The total faculty numbers 71 members with just 5 teaching part-time. Forty-two percent of the members are women. The faculty remain a bright spot. Teachers are in touch with their students, even knowing many by name who they have never had in class, and welcome requests for help, often outside scheduled office hours or without appointments. Observes an English major: "Faculty convey a sense of truly caring for the students, being both supportive and challenging at the same time." Many have been known to call students that don't show up for class and all serve a massive breakfast at midnight before final exams.

The college's premed program, especially the "incredibly rigorous" biology major, is considered superb, with a medical school acceptance rate of about 95%. History and music also shine thanks to exceptional teaching plus, for music, a new $6 million performing and fine arts center. History, says a senior, "has dynamic professors who are deeply connected to the student body and involved in campus life." The completion of a new building for business and international studies, also with funding from alumni Joe and Kathryn Albertson, along with strong ties to employers and alumni, make business a strong complement to Albertson's more traditional liberal arts offerings. The faculty members, says a major, "are always willing to give more help even when they don't have time."

As a result of the college's small size, course offerings in some fields can be slim. Although the departments of religion, philosophy, modern languages (majors in Spanish, minors in French and German), anthropology/sociology, theater, and art all have professors who are very good at what they teach, there are too few of them to offer sufficient variety in course selection. In chemistry and physics, a biology major notes, "the existing faculty members are tremendous in terms of the number of courses they teach each semester and the stamina they possess. But I fear that if no measures are taken to alleviate their course load, we will lose our current faculty due to burnout." Psychology faculty "are spread too thin," says a major, "with far too many advisees per professor. Students have to be more motivated than their professors to get stuff done."

Facilities: While Terteling Library is a roomy place to study, with many "quiet" areas, undergraduates find its sense of style lacking. Says a sophomore: "Our library as a physical place could use serious updates. Marcia Brady would feel right at home with the 70s decor." Students do like its "friendly-study atmosphere," says a junior, "including long check-out dates, allowing food," and knowledgeable and helpful staff members. Once the only library on campus, Terteling has been augmented by a second facility, the Kathryn Albertson Library in the recently constructed international center. Together, the two contain more than 183,000 volumes and subscriptions to 703 periodicals. With the aid of a computerized catalog, database searching, and interlibrary loan, students pursuing in-depth projects and papers divide their time between campus holdings, interlibrary loan, and the Internet.

A recently installed wireless network allows students to connect to the Internet from anywhere on campus. With about 250 computers around campus plus mini-labs in each residence hall, there are generally enough units available for student needs. (The college strongly recommends that all students have their own personal computers.) Labs in the libraries and main computer center close at 11 p.m., which many students find too early; the smaller clusters in the residence halls are open around-the-clock. "Getting on a computer isn't a problem," says a junior, "but finding a printer with paper at 3 a.m. during finals week can be tricky if you procrastinate."

Special programs: Off-campus experiences include worldwide study tours with department faculty in countries as diverse as Costa Rica and Kenya. New students who have demonstrated leadership potential in their academic and extracurricular activities are invited during spring semester of their freshman year to take part in a series of leadership workshops. Those who wish to continue and who qualify may participate in the program, offered as an interdisciplinary minor, during their junior and senior years. A 3–2 engineering program is offered with the University of Idaho, Boise State, and Columbia and Washington universities. A 3–2 program for a master of management degree is offered with Willamette University in Oregon. Joint admission programs also are offered for an MBA degree with Gonzaga University in Washington and with Boise State and in a master of accountancy degree with the University of Idaho. Internships are available in the state legislature in Boise or at the Smithsonian Institution in the nation's capital, with companies such as Union Pacific or in U.S. Senate offices, or in outdoor programs of Idaho outfitters and guides.

Campus life: A little over half, 52%, of Albertson's undergraduates including all freshmen and sophomores live on the 50-acre campus, which has experienced a building boom over the past decade. New structures include a performing and fine arts center, an international center, and a student activity center, as well as a $4.5 million renovation of all 5 residence halls, 2 new apartment-style dorms, complete renovation of the college's oldest building, and a new student union. Twelve percent of the men and 13% of the women belong to 3 national fraternities and 1 local and 3 national sororities. Because most of the Greek organizations do not have off-campus houses, students say there is little division between Greeks and independents. Popular clubs range from the Idaho Progressive Student Alliance that organizes demonstrations and seminars to promote diversity and tolerance to Campus Ministries that attracts about 75 students to its nondenominational Late Night Chapel on Tuesday nights at 9 p.m. in the Student Union. Says a senior: "Because the school is so small, organizations *want* you to help so it is very easy to get involved." Other than occasional auto break-ins, campus crime is not much of a problem. However, additional lighting and blue-light emergency phones were recently installed as an added precaution.

When winter comes, Albertson is an alpine skiers' paradise. The men's and women's ski teams have won more than 25 national championships in the last 24 years. For the recreational skier, 3 major resorts, including Sun Valley, are within a 3-hour drive of campus. When students aren't skiing, they're generally attending basketball games, being played in the new 3000-seat J. A. Albertson Activities Center. Here, too, the Coyotes men's basketball team has qualified for the national tournament at least 11 times in the past 20 years, winning the national championship in 1996. The women's basketball team was runner-up in 2001. The women's tennis team also has distinguished itself as 7-time champions among the 8 men's and 10 women's intercollegiate sports offered. Half of the men and women turn out for the 12 men's and 12 women's intramural programs. In any season the indoor climbing wall and Frisbee golf are hot!

For relaxation, students go to Lake Lowell, a large artificial lake outside of Caldwell, where they can swim, sail, hike, water ski, or just stare at the water. The more adventuresome head about 30 minutes in the opposite direction to take in some of the country's best white-water rafting. Shopping, dancing, or dinner in Boise, about 25 miles distant, also is popular. Caldwell itself (pop. 30,000) serves mainly as a takeoff point for biking, hiking, or other outdoor activities.

Cost cutters: Ninety-three percent of the 2005–2006 freshmen and 92% of the continuing students received financial aid. Eighty-nine percent of the freshmen and 83% of the rest received aid that was need-based. The average freshman award for a first-year student entering with need in fall 2005 included a need-based scholarship or grant averaging $3737 and need-based self-help aid such as loans and jobs averaging $3650. Non-need-based athletic scholarships for freshmen averaged $3415; other non-need-based awards and scholarships averaged $4080. Average debt of a 2005 graduate was $25,343. Albertson offers several merit-based awards of varying amounts. The Heritage Scholarship pays full tuition to freshmen based on a written essay and personal interview, plus the students' GPAs and SAT scores. Interested students are encouraged to apply by the early action deadline of Nov. 15. The award is renewable with a 3.5 GPA. Presidential and Trustee scholarships recently paid $6000 and $4000 a year, respectively, also based on grade point average and SAT scores. The low cost of living in Idaho helps reduce total expenses further.

Rate of return: Seventy-seven percent of entering freshmen return for the sophomore year. Forty-seven percent go on to graduate in 4 years; 56% finish in 5 years.

Payoff: More than a third of the 2005 graduates earned bachelor's degrees in 2 academic areas, 21 in business and 13% in history. Over the years, this tiny college also has produced 6 Rhodes Scholars. In a recent year, 14% of the graduating class pursued advanced degrees, many in medicine and law. Those who obtain jobs generally remain in the Northwest. About 20 companies and other organizations recruited on campus in a recent school year.

Bottom line: At a college the size of Albertson, a student can, in the course of 1 semester, be president of the Astronomy Club, act in a Shakespeare play, write for the school newspaper, and be involved in student government, all while researching a science project. And on a campus this small, everyone will know exactly how well he or she did in each pursuit!

University of Idaho

Moscow, Idaho 83844

Setting: Small town
Control: Public
Undergraduate enrollment: 4630 men, 3772 women
Graduate enrollment: 665 men, 536 women
Student/faculty ratio: 17:1
Freshman profile: 6% scored over 700 on SAT I verbal; 26% scored 600–700; 42% 500–599; 26% below 500. 6% scored over 700 on SAT I math; 26% scored 600–700; 43% 500–599; 25% below 500. 11% scored above 28 on the ACT; 9% scored 27–28; 23% 24–26; 26% 21–23; 31% below 21. 38% graduated in top fifth of high school class; 67% in upper two-fifths.

Faculty profile: 77% Ph.D.'s
Tuition and fees: $3968 in-state; $12,738 out-of-state
Room and board: $5342
Freshman financial aid: 57%; average scholarship or grant: $3263 need-based; $3286 non-need-based
Campus jobs: 50%; average earnings: NA
Application deadline: Aug. 1 (Priority date: Feb. 15)
Financial aid deadline: Feb. 15
Admissions information: (208) 885-6326; (888) 884-3246 (out-of-state)
email: finaid@uidaho.edu
web site: www.uidaho.edu

If the University of Idaho, with its 12,504 full- and part-time students, 586 faculty members, and 1500 other staff were a town, it would be the 13th largest city in the state. And what a city it would be. Down its center, leading to the Administration Building, would run "Hello Walk," so named because the president of the university during the 1920s used to greet students and faculty members with that salutation every morning on his way to work. Its athletic center would seat 17,000; its inhabitants include persons from 82 nations. Its cost of living and learning would be among the lowest for a university/town: just over $9000 for fees, room, and board for residents in the 2005–2006 school year and $18,080 in total costs for out-of-staters. At that rate, a year at the University of Idaho costs less for a nonresident than the resident fee charged at some major universities across the country. And as a bonus, students get 2 schools for the price of 1: with Washington State University in Pullman just 8 miles away, students can take any of more than 700 cooperative courses on either campus. As the townspeople of UI see it: why spend your undergraduate years anywhere else?

Student body: Seventy-five percent of the undergraduates at the University of Idaho are state residents, most from small, rural high schools. Nonresidents are drawn from all 49 other states, with the vast majority from the Northwest. Just 8% of the undergraduates are members of racial and ethnic minority groups; 4% are Hispanic, 2% Asian-American, and 1% each African-American and Native American/Eskimo. Three percent are foreign nationals from 82 foreign countries. All but 2% of the students are graduates of public high schools. Because the campus is somewhat remote, students bond together to create the "homey" feel of a close-knit family. Though a broad brush paints the undergraduates conservative, they are distinguished by a sense of individualism that residents say comes from being in Idaho. "U of I is where the 'radicals' or 'liberals' from conservative Idaho go to school," says a junior from the Pacific Northwest. "'Earthy' would be a good word to describe students. Birkenstocks, wool socks, earth tones, flannel, and beads reign supreme." Most are easygoing, intelligent, and friendly, working as hard as is needed but not to excess. Says a sophomore: "As far as academics go, the students range from the very devoted to the 'just having fun.'"

Academics: The university, which turned 115 in 2004, offers bachelor's degrees in more than 140 majors through 7 undergraduate colleges. Advanced degrees through the doctorate are also available in these 7 colleges plus the College of Law. The school year is divided into 2 semesters. The range in class sizes is wide, from 25 in English essay writing to about 270 in introductory biology, which includes 1 session each week in which students break into smaller discussion groups. All undergraduates, regardless of major, are required to complete general-education requirements in the traditional disciplines. A recently added core curriculum offers students the chance to replace some of their general education classes with more integrated courses, one in science as well as their choice of 1 of 9 interdisciplinary core discovery courses that fulfill requirements in the humanities and social sciences. Among the year-long freshman core classes offered in a recent fall were ones titled The New Wild West: People and Environment as well as Sex and Culture: Women and Men in the 21st Century.

Of the 586 faculty members on campus, 564 are full-time. All but 57 of the full-time members and all but 2 of the part-time teach undergraduates. Thirty-six percent of the total pool are women. Idaho has its share of intimidating and disinterested professors, and graduate students, many of whom tend to be easier on students than their mentors, teach 20% of the introductory courses. Still, many an undergraduate who came to Idaho expecting simply to be another number is surprised to find professors willing to respond to the needs of students who care about their education. "If you need help," says an American studies major, "the professors either take the time and help you themselves or give you several options in finding that help." Adds a music education major: "In the competitive majors, faculty like to push the students into doing more than they thought they could, and doing it better."

Among the university's strongest and most competitive programs, engineering, forestry, and agriculture get good funding and faculty, along with the other career-related fields of accounting and architecture. Engineering, in particular, has a great deal of teacher-student interaction and requires every senior to do a semester-long project that closely approximates a real-world situation. Says a journalism major: "One simple rule makes Idaho engineering the best: Idaho engineers get jobs." Test scores of Idaho students on the Fundamentals of Engineering Exam also average about 30 percentage points higher (93.7%) than the national average (60.9%). Various programs in the colleges of Natural Resourses, and Agricultural and Life Sciences benefit from the more than 11,000 acres of nearby farms and experimental forests owned by the university. As a result, observes an easterner: "Research and hands-on experience are a must." Geology and other disciplines in the College of Science offer first-rate curriculum, faculty, and facilities. The Lionel Hampton School of Music also boasts a curriculum that is focused yet flexible as well as strong loyalty from both students and faculty. Students in the College of Business and Economics particularly like the integrated core curriculum. The program combines many of the core business classes into a single year-long team-taught course that enables students to see how the various aspects of business, marketing, management, and finance fit together. "As good as it gets," boasts an admiring history major.

Some students wish the department of foreign languages and literature offered more majors than the 5 in French, German, Spanish, Latin and classical studies. Courses also have been offered over recent years in Chinese, Ancient Greek, Japanese, and Russian. The theater arts building needs repair; the dance program, which is in the College of Education, needs more attention. Says a junior: "We lack professors, lack professionals, and lack outside resources because of the small town." Math is among programs hurt by the number of teaching assistants who speak limited English. Observes a biology major: "There is a severe language barrier with many of the TAs in the chemistry/physics/math department." Her own department, the major continues, "is oversized and underfunded," which makes it hard for undergraduates to build personal relationships with the faculty, "who is great," the student adds.

Facilities: The bulk of the nearly 1.6 million volumes and 9183 current periodicals on campus is contained in University Library, with a separate law library holding materials most closely related to that field. After 2 years of construction, the main facility now offers 50% more floor space including a "quiet" floor and double the seating capacity (1100) plus additional room for more organized book storage. Students especially like the new rooms for individual and group study and the 24-hour lounge with food and drink plus the computerized catalog and data search system that help in research. Still, what materials cannot be found locally can often be acquired from nearby Washington State University, where the holdings more than double the resources available. A shuttle bus runs daily between the 2 facilities to pick up and return library materials.

More than 900 IBM and Macintosh computers are connected throughout 22 open-access labs across campus. A number of sites are open 23 hours a day, closed only between 2 a.m. and 3 a.m. All residence halls and Greek houses also have Internet access. Laptops are available for checkout at the library and Commons. And, the places students can go with their laptops! More than 40 locations, including the Commons, library, and student union offer wireless Internet connectivity.

Special programs: The university doubled the size of its honors program in 1988; a year later, Idaho produced 1 of 32 Rhodes Scholars in the nation. Study-abroad programs are available at 185 institutions in 50 countries; those eager to stay state-side can take courses at any of 150 other colleges and universities throughout the United States. Cross-registration for classes is also allowed over the western border at Washington State University and in-state at Idaho State.

Campus life: Forty-seven percent of Idaho's students live in residence halls, 4% in apartments, and 41% in Greek housing, all spread over 800 acres of campus in the rolling hill country known as the Palouse. Sixteen percent of the men are members of 19 nationally affiliated fraternities; 13% of the women belong to 9 national sororities. "Fraternities and sororities are big on campus," notes a senior, "and those students tend to be the 'social' people as well as the student leaders." Still, Greek parties are generally open to everyone, and there is little rancorous rivalry between residence halls and Greek houses. The fraternities provide an escort service to women who want it, and the library issues protective beepers to late-night studiers walking home alone. Such measures plus the addition of more lighting has given an extra measure of security to what students already considered a safe campus.

A third of all undergraduates participate in the 55 men's and/or women's intramural sports, ranging from flag football and softball to Frisbee golf and walleyball. The Kibbee-ASUI Activity Center (known as the Dome) hosts indoor football games, basketball games, track meets on a 300-meter indoor track, and rodeos. A new student recreation center, which opened in February 2002, features a 55-foot climbing wall inside a glass tower; it's considered to be the highest wall at any college or university in the nation. Vandals teams in NCAA Division I football, basketball (men's) and volleyball (women's) draw the best crowds among the 6 men's and 7 women's sports. Watching the Vandals Marching Band also is exciting.

It's a good thing there's so much to do in the scenic outdoors surrounding Moscow (pop. 21,300), because other than the university, a couple of malls, and a half dozen or so theaters, there's not much in the town. Instead, students look beyond to northern Idaho's wilderness, terrific for hunting, fishing, hiking, whitewater rafting, snowboarding, and cross-country and downhill skiing. The Sawtooth and Hells Canyon national recreation areas and the Snake, Clearwater, and Salmon rivers are a short drive away. The nearest big city is Spokane, Washington, 90 miles northwest.

Cost cutters: About 57% of both freshmen and continuing students received financial aid in the 2005–2006 school year. Just over 40% of both groups were on need-based assistance. The average freshman award for a student with financial need included a need-based scholarship or grant averaging $3263 and need-based self-help aid, such as loans and jobs, averaging $3564. Non-need-based athletic scholarships for first-year students averaged $12,442; other non-need-based awards and scholarships averaged $3286. The average financial indebtedness of 2005 graduates totaled $20,002. The Presidential Scholar Award worth $2500 goes to students with a GPA of 3.5 or higher and a minimum ACT of 30 or SAT math and critical reading score of 1340. UI Achievement Scholarships vary in amount according to students' GPA and class rank. Graduating seniors who ranked first in their class or had a 4.0 GPA receive $1500; those with a 3.8 to 3.99 GPA who were not ranked first receive $1000. Students who live in any of the 13 other states in the region that are part of the Western Undergraduate Exchange program may pay in-state tuition and fees plus 50% of that amount if they maintain at least a 3.3 GPA and minimum ACT score of 20, or combined critical reading and math SAT score of 950. Partial tuition waivers also are awarded to a limited number of high-achieving nonresidents from states not in the exchange region who have a 3.0 GPA and a 20 ACT or 950 SAT. Cooperative programs are available in most majors.

Rate of return: Eighty-two percent of the freshman class return for the sophomore year. Just 20% graduate in 4 years; 47%, in 5 years; 55%, in 6 years, reflecting an increase at every level over the last few years.

Payoff: Businss/marketing, claiming 13% of the 2005 graduates, was the largest field of study followed by education at 12%, and engineering at 9%. In recent years, a fifth of all graduates have gone immediately on to graduate or professional study. The vast majority take jobs in engineering, education, business, communications, agriculture, and forestry in the Sun Belt, California, and the Northwest. Every year, the University of Idaho co-sponsors a Career Expo with nearby Washington State University that attracts more than 175 companies offering students jobs, as well as opportunities for internships. One in 3 business, civic, and community leaders in Idaho is a University of Idaho graduate.

But then again, you never can tell what an Idaho graduate will go on to do. Philip Habib, a member of the class of 1942, worked as President Reagan's personal ambassador for 6 years in an effort to bring peace to the Middle East, the Philippines, and Central America. At Idaho he majored in forestry.

Bottom line: Idaho is pretty much your basic meat and potatoes campus, or maybe just the potatoes, since this is Idaho. Most find it to be a friendly, down-to-earth campus, where students who are a bit eccentric may have trouble finding many kindred souls, although they won't be shunned. Those who love the outdoors are happiest, but they have to spend their share of time indoors in classes and studying.

Augustana College

Rock Island, Illinois 61201

Setting: Suburban
Control: Private (Evangelical Lutheran)
Undergraduate enrollment: 987 men, 1376 women
Graduate enrollment: None
Student/faculty ratio: 13:1
Freshman profile: 33% scored above 28 on the ACT; 22% scored 27–28; 30% 24–26; 11% 21–23; 4% below 21. 29% graduated in top tenth of high school class; 55% in upper fifth.
Faculty profile: 96% Ph.D.'s
Tuition and fees: $23,457

Room and board: $6405
Freshman financial aid: 96%; average scholarship or grant: $12,816 need-based; $4241 non-need-based
Campus jobs: 68%; average earnings: $900/year
Application deadline: Rolling
Financial aid deadline: Apr. 5
Admissions information: (309) 794-7341; (800) 798-8100, ext. 7341
e-mail: admissions@augustana.edu
web site: www.augustana.edu

When students think of colleges and universities with winning football teams, names like Michigan, Notre Dame, and Southern California come to mind. But how about Augustana College, an Evangelical Lutheran school of 2360 students in Rock Island, Illinois, midway between Chicago and Des Moines, Iowa? Since the mid-eighties, the Augustana Vikings have been nationally ranked among NCAA Division III football teams, where membership means no athletic scholarships. The Vikings have won 4 national championships and been conference champions 19 times. As a college with 11 men's and 10 women's varsity teams, Augustana ranked fifth among all colleges and universities in the 2005–2006 school year for the number of student athletes recognized as Academic All American players. Augustana also ranks in the top 70 for the number of its graduates who go on to earn Ph.D.'s and among the top 50 liberal arts colleges in the sciences. Its applicants to medical school average a 90% acceptance rate; those to law and business schools, virtually 100%. Its campus boasts a chapter of Phi Beta Kappa, and only 5 schools in the nation, one of them being Harvard, have qualified for more National Debate Tournaments than Augustana. Clearly, Augustana isn't just making winning touchdowns on the football field; it's also scoring big in academics at a championship price of just under $30,000 for tuition, fees, room, and board in the 2005–2006 school year!

Student body: Eighty-eight percent of Augustana's students are from Illinois with nearly a fifth coming from the Quad Cities metropolitan area, which consists of Rock Island and of Moline and East Moline in Illinois, and across the Mississippi River, of Davenport and Bettendorf in Iowa. Twenty-eight states, most of them in the Midwest, are represented within the student body. About three-quarters of the students claim some church affiliation, with 22% Lutheran, 35% Catholic, and 17% members of other Protestant denominations. One percent are Jewish and 11% are members of some other faith. Minority enrollment has held steady over the past few years. Three percent of the students are Hispanic, 2% each African-American and Asian-American, and less than 1% Native American. Another 1% are foreign nationals from 24 countries. Students describe themselves as "genuine," "hardworking," "community oriented," and "religious," but say they are not overpowering in their faith or their practice of it. Students' political beliefs are temperate as well, ranging from conservative to moderately liberal. One area where students are not restrained is in staying active. Says a junior, "Augustana attracts natural leaders, people who are eager to get involved."

Academics: Augustana, which was founded by Swedish immigrants in 1860, awards the bachelor's degree in 43 majors. A number of students find it easy to double-major. The academic year is divided into 3 terms of 11 weeks each. The term system makes an already challenging academic environment seem more arduous. For freshmen and sophomores, average class size is between 20 and 30, though some introductory science lectures like Vertebrate Zoology have about 100. An upper-level political science class can have as few as 10 enrolled, several seminars have just 2.

As part of the college's general-education requirements, students must complete courses in college writing and research skills, religion, foreign language, cross-cultural perspective, and physical education, as well as 2 courses each from 6 Learning Perspectives that emphasize the intellectual connections among the various disciplines. These comprise perspectives on the past, the natural world, individuals and society, literature and texts, the arts, and human existence and values. The requirements fulfill about a third of the 123 credits needed for graduation.

The faculty numbers 145 full-time members and 78 part-time. Forty percent are women. The faculty puts an emphasis on knowing students' names and making them feel important. Because of the small size of the faculty, professors tend to be quite visible around campus, and the majority who are very good, as well as the few who are not, are well known to freshmen before the first term is completed.

Students hear little but good news about the faculty and tough curricula in the biology department. Hands-on experience is available to premed students at local hospitals. A $23 million building built in 1998 houses state-of-the-art laboratories and computer-supported classrooms for the biology, chemistry, and physics departments. English and history boast faculties with doctorates from some of the nation's best universities. Programs in speech communication, communication sciences and disorders (with its own on-campus diagnostic center), geology, psychology, and Spanish draw kudos from admiring students. Recent improvements in the teacher education curricula have provided majors with many more opportunities for valuable classroom experience in area schools. Two disciplines dear to Augustana's heritage, music and Scandinavian language and literature, also are considered winners.

Political science professors are well educated but students say some members lack effective teaching skills. Physics faculty members have sometimes seemed to be more interested in research than in teaching undergraduates. Anthropology is offered as a concentration within the sociology major.

Facilities: Ask students about the best building on campus and the majority will name "the library," followed by such adjectives as *excellent, awesome,* and *beautiful.* "I personally really like going to the library," says an elementary education major. The 5-story Thomas Tredway Library, completed in 1990, has private rooms for single as well as group study and seating for 630 people. Those who need a more social environment head to Java 101, the library's coffee house where they may sometimes find the college president holding open office hours. The holdings include more than 185,000 volumes and 1200 periodicals, which students generally find meet their research needs. "But the very best things," says a business administration major, "are the research librarians, who know everything."

Computer labs are available in the library and in the lobby of each residence hall, but most notably in the Olin Educational Technology Center, which opened in 1998 with open-access computer labs and work areas for students. The labs in the dorms, with 3–5 computers each, are open around the clock while those in the Olin building usually close at midnight but offer 24-hour access as each term's finals week approaches. Altogether, more than 1250 college-owned personal computers are available to students and faculty; residence hall rooms also have network jacks for student-owned computers. The college strongly recommends that students have their own personal computers. Wireless access is provided in selected buildings, such as the library and the first floor of the Olin center.

Special programs: About a third of Augustana's students participate in the college's off-campus programs, in which faculty members lead groups of undergraduates to 1 of 3 parts of the world to study and travel for 1 term. In fall 2006, for example, students and faculty were scheduled to travel to South America, studying art, political science, psychology, and biology. In fall 2004, the East Asian Term took students and faculty members to Japan, the Republic of China (Taiwan), and the People's Republic of China, including Hong Kong. The European term, taking place in London and the continent, was held in fall 2005. A wide variety of winter, spring, and summer programs and student exchanges also are offered in several countries throughout Europe, Asia, Africa, and Latin America. Full-time internships and "micro-internships" for 5 weeks full-time or 10 weeks part-time are options in most majors. Students interested in specializing in engineering, environmental management, forestry, landscape architecture, and occupational therapy can participate in cooperative degree programs with Duke, Iowa State, Northwestern, Purdue, and Washington universities plus the University of Illinois, Urbana-Champaign.

Campus life: Eighty-eight percent of the students live in residence halls, apartments, and houses spread over 115 hilly and wooded acres overlooking the Mississippi River. Most of the rest live in privately owned homes or apartments close to campus. Every weekend evening, the student-run programming board sponsors some kind of event open to the entire campus; likewise, at least 1 of the 7 local fraternities or 6 local sororities hosts an all-campus party on 1 weekend night. Just under a fifth of the men and a fourth of the women are members of the Greek organizations; those who are not find plenty of other outlets in the 110 campus groups available. Still, says a junior, "many independents interact with Greeks on many occasions." The 74-voice Augustana Choir has toured throughout Scandinavia and appeared in concerts at both Lincoln Center and Carnegie Hall in New York. Other, smaller groups focus on interests from biology to feeding the hungry. To discourage students from walking alone at night, an escort service picks them up anywhere on or off campus (within reasonable limits) and takes them anywhere on or off campus (same qualifiers) between the hours of 7 p.m. and 2 a.m. That service along with 24-hour desk security in the dorms makes students feel safe around campus. When an incident does occur, the college posts notices and sends out e-mails to all students informing them of the occurrence.

Needless to say, during the fall just about everyone turns out to watch Vikings football. Soccer and basketball games are nearly as popular, placing the 3 sports at the top of the 11 men's and 10 women's sports offered. A third of the men and a fifth of the women competed at the varsity level in a recent year. Intramurals in a range of activities from flag football to track bring out teams formed by Greeks, members of the residence halls, and other groups of students and faculty to compete for the coveted IM cup. Nearly half of the men and a fourth of the women take part in the 19 men's and 18 women's sports offered.

For diversion, the Quad-Cities area, which at more than 300,000 people is the largest metropolitan center between Chicago and Des Moines, offers shopping, walks along the Mississippi River, or the chance to try a little gambling at the riverboat casinos. Students who want to mingle with thousands of other kids their age travel to the University of Iowa or Western Illinois University.

Cost cutters: In the 2005–2006 school year, 96% of the freshmen and continuing students received financial aid. For at least 66% of all undergraduates, the aid was need-based. For first-year students with financial need, need-based scholarships or grants averaged $12,816 and need-based self-help aid such as loans and jobs averaged $3801. For students without financial need, non-need-based scholarships and other awards averaged $4241. The average 2005 graduate left with debts of $18,098. A variety of scholarships are available to top-ranked students. Presidential Scholarships pay from $10,000 a year to full tuition to top students. Dean's awards pay $7750 to $9000 a year; Founders pay $5000–$7500 annually. Music, art, and debate scholarships in amounts up to $2000 a year are available. Those who show promise as writers may receive $1000; in theater, up to $4000. Students who wish may pay their tuition in installments or make a single payment to cover 4 years of tuition, fees, room, and board at the rate in effect at the start of the freshman year.

Rate of return: Eighty-six percent of the entering freshmen return for the sophomore year. Seventy-one percent graduate in 4 years; 77% in 5 years.

Payoff: In the 2005 graduating class, 20% of the students earned degrees in business and marketing, 15% in biology, and 10% in social science. Thirty-four percent of the graduates pursue advanced degrees within 6 months of graduation, most in the arts and sciences. Altogether, the graduate school and job placement rate averages an excellent 95%, compared with a national average of 82%. Two hundred thirty-eight companies and organizations recruited on campus during a recent school year.

Bottom line: Augustana is a small school that will send a student out to see the world, as well as draw him or her into the active life of a small college community. Academic standards are high, but help is readily available to any student who asks. Says a senior: "Students can balance 3 classes a trimester, a sport, and a club or 2 with no problem because of the understanding of the professors, the coaches, and advisors. You can do it all—and trust me, I have!"

Blackburn College

Carlinville, Illinois 62626

Setting: Rural
Control: Private (Presbyterian)
Undergraduate enrollment: 590 men and women
Graduate enrollment: None
Student/faculty ratio: 16:1
Freshman profile: SAT/ACT scores: NA; Class rank data: NA
Faculty profile: 80% Ph.D.'s
Tuition and fees: $12,733
Room and board: $3895

Freshman financial aid: NA; average scholarship or grant: NA
Campus jobs: NA; average earnings: NA
Application deadline: July 31
Financial aid deadline: Apr. 1
Admissions information: (217) 854-3231, ext. 4293; (800) 233-3550
e-mail: admit@mail.blackburn.edu
web site: www.blackburn.edu

When a freshman enrolls as a resident student at Blackburn College in central Illinois, he or she agrees to contribute 10 hours of work per week in exchange for significantly reduced tuition and fees. But at Blackburn, responsibility doesn't end when the shift changes. Don't like the work assignment? Don't tell the college president. Complain to the student work committee, which makes all basic managerial decisions and oversees the entire program. Even the general managers are students. Don't like the look of the campus? Complain to the students who prune the hedges, maintain the buildings, and actually have helped build 9 of the 16 buildings, including recent additions to the gym and the library. Don't like the prices or the service at the bookstore? You got it: Even the bookstore is student managed and operated.

Founded in 1837 and named for the Reverend Gideon Blackburn, a Presbyterian minister and former president of Centre College in Kentucky, the college has been continuously governed by an independent board of trustees. The work program wasn't introduced until 1913, as a means of providing on-campus financial support to hard-pressed students. This program, the only one of its kind in the nation that is managed by students, has become Blackburn's most distinctive feature and the one that in recent years has drawn students from up to 20 states, in some years from as far away as California and New York, who are seeking a more affordable education and some real-world experience. Says a biology major: "Students start out at many basic jobs like cooking food or mopping floors, and through their years at Blackburn can work their way up to managing the dining hall. It's a great place to learn how the workplace really is: You start at the bottom and work your way up."

Student body: Eighty-five percent of Blackburn's students in a recent year were from Illinois, with most of the rest also from the Midwest. During a recent school year, 18 states had students on campus. All but 15% were graduates of public high schools. Eleven percent in a recent year were African-American, with 1% each Asian-American, Hispanic, and Native American. Eighteen foreign nationals from 9 countries rounded out the small population. The student group Cultural Expressions has worked to ensure that racial and ethnic concerns remain a top priority of the student councils and administrators, amid efforts to bring more minority students to campus. An Office of Inter-cultural Service recently was established to provide support to minority and international students. Given the need to balance studies and critical campus jobs, most students place "hard-working" at the top of their list of self-descriptive adjectives, along with "friendly," "honest," and "socially involved." While some students don't place an enormous emphasis on academics, those who do study hard find they can excel under the individual attention of professors.

Academics: Blackburn offers more than 25 fields of study, all culminating in a Bachelor of Arts degree. The academic year is divided into 2 semesters, with an average class size for undergraduates of 18. The largest courses, such as a section of general psychology, may enroll more than 40 notetakers. At the other extreme, a class in microbiology and immunology can have a single participant.

The general-education program requires course work in 2 areas. The first area, labeled Foundations of Learning, covers everything from classes in college-level writing to literature and science. The second component mandates that students take either 2 years of a foreign language or 18 hours of an approved concentration or minor, exploring relationships between different fields.

The faculty is small: recently 32 full-time members and 21 part-time. Thirty-five percent in a recent year were women. Students find most professors to be accomplished in their respective fields, open-minded, and helpful, occasionally too helpful. Notes a literature major: "Sometimes they are too concerned when you just want to be left alone." A number have less-than-inspiring teaching styles, relying too much on lecturing directly from the textbook.

The accounting major in the business and economics department and biology and chemistry are among the most competitive and challenging programs, with excellent faculty and good job and/or graduate school placement upon leaving. Other courses of study in business and political science also are well regarded and provide plenty of opportunity for leadership experience through the work program and elsewhere. Education students spend a lot of time in the local public schools, gaining valuable real-life experience, although some students think the college curriculum could be more rigorous. "The instructors," says a senior, "are goal-oriented and caring." The computer science major features "excellent teachers, small classes, and wonderful equipment," according to a senior specializing in the field.

Spanish is not just the only foreign-language major offered; it is the only foreign language offered, with the recent loss of instruction in French. Religious studies and philosophy are offered as minors only. Psychology, while popular, could use more professors to bring down class sizes and expand course offerings as well as more opportunities for experiential education. A recently added major in communications has been feeling the effects of too much student interest in its 4 tracks and needs more professors to keep pace.

Facilities: Student-built Lumpkin Library is limited in its offerings: just 80,000 volumes, many of which students consider outdated, and 79 serial subscriptions. An on-line catalog and a computerized index to additional periodicals and *The New York Times*, as well as other on-line resources assist in many research projects, with interlibrary loan providing materials Lumpkin lacks. A wing added by students has helped to provide more study space, and students hope that eventually more up-to-date resources will be purchased to stock it.

Just over 200 computers are available for general student use. Twenty microcomputers, including PCs and Macs, are located in the computer center with additional units in the library and in Hudson Hall, the main classroom building. For those students who wish to bring their own computers, which many do, all residence-hall rooms are wired for a fiber-optic computer network, including Internet access, as well as for cable TV.

Special programs: Blackburn offers a semester of study in Mexico, or Wales, or a term in the nation's capital either at the American University or as part of an internship and study program through the Washington Center. Prospective engineers can participate in a 3-2 program with Washington University in St. Louis. The Mueller Humanities Fellowship annually funds several self-enrichment projects proposed by students majoring in the humanities.

Campus life: Because of the cost-saving resident work program, three-quarters of Blackburn students call the 80-acre campus of gently rolling prairie both their home and their place of work. Campus dances help to compensate for the lack of any Greek life, but students say a number of residents simply leave campus when the weekends arrive. The opening of a new 24,000-square-foot student center in fall 2002 has helped convince more students to stay. The student-run security system keeps campus crime to a minimum.

Blackburn Beavers basketball, football, and soccer each draw their share of faithful fans among the 7 men's and 8 women's teams fielded under NCAA Division III. Thirty percent of the men and 20% of the women took part in a recent year. Nine intramural sports for men and the same number for women are options; 30% of the men and 40% of the women take part.

Carlinville (pop. 6000), in central Illinois, has Amtrak service, and many students travel within state to Springfield, 40 miles north, or across the border to St. Louis, Missouri, 60 miles southwest, for dinner, shopping, or a cultural event. A large number simply use their hours off to go home.

Cost cutters: The college's work program is two-dimensional, helping students to cut back on expenses while enabling the college to keep down operating costs by the vast use of student labor. Students' tuition discount increases as they advance in years and job responsibilities at the college. Freshmen, for example, recently saved $2307 from their year's work; sophomores saved $2650 a year, juniors and seniors, $3000. Altogether, 90% of all undergraduates received additional financial aid beyond the work program in a recent school year. About 80% in a recent year were on need-based aid. The average need-based gift aid for all undergraduates in a recent year was $7199. Average non-need-based gift aid was $4449; just 50 non-need-based awards were granted. Among recent graduates, the average financial indebtedness was $11,000. Top students also receive special help. Entering freshmen who graduated in the top 10% of their high school class with an ACT composite of 24 and a combined math and critical reading SAT of 1040 may be eligible for an Honor Scholarship worth half tuition and renewable up to 3 years if a satisfactory GPA is maintained. Honor Scholarship recipients may also apply for the Presidential Scholarship, which raises the Honor award to full tuition; 10 scholarships are awarded each year. Academic Achievement Scholarships pay one-fourth tuition to students drawn from the top half of their high school class with a GPA of at least 2.8 in college preparatory courses. Leadership Scholarships pay up to $1000. A cooperative education program also can be arranged.

Rate of return: Seventy percent of freshmen return for the sophomore year; 45% remain to graduate in 4 years; 47% in 5 years; 48% in 6.

Payoff: Among recent graduates, 30% of the class earned degrees in business, 27% in education, and 9% in biology. The vast majority of graduates remain in the midwest, continuing their management training with firms such as Claussen Pickle, Marriott, and Walgreens. Ten percent enroll in graduate or professional schools. The universities of Michigan and Minnesota and Washington University in St. Louis have all accepted a number of Blackburn graduates.

Bottom line: Blackburn's program teaches the willing student how to organize his or her time to allow for classes, studies, a job, and some fun. In an environment of about 600 undergraduates, however, students must want to work closely with their classmates, the faculty, and administrators; at Blackburn, there is no place to hide.

Bradley University

Peoria, Illinois 61625

Setting: Urban
Control: Independent
Undergraduate enrollment: 2263 men, 2792 women
Graduate enrollment: 96 men, 112 women
Student/faculty ratio: 14:1
Freshman profile: 4% scored over 700 on SAT I verbal; 30% scored 600–700; 41% 500–599; 25% below 500. 6% scored over 700 on SAT I math; 38% scored 600–700; 43% 500–599; 13% below 500. 17% scored above 28 on the ACT; 17% scored 27–28; 33% 24–26; 23% 21–23; 10% below 21. 30% graduated in top tenth of high school class; 50% in upper fifth.

Faculty profile: 85% Ph.D.'s
Tuition and fees: $18,830
Room and board: $6450
Freshman financial aid: 97%; average scholarship or grant: $11,162 need-based; $9626 non-need-based
Campus jobs: 26%; average earnings: $950/year
Application deadline: Rolling
Financial aid deadline: Mar. 1
Admissions information: (309) 677-1000; 800-447-6460
e-mail: admissions@bradley.edu
web site: www.bradley.edu

Bradley University has always adhered to the principle that a good education should be both classical and useful. Interested students need look no further than Bradley's present-day attitude toward learning and its roots as a school where 19th-century students would learn to do practical tasks for the modern world.

Lydia Moss Bradley, widow of Tobias Bradley, donated land as well as money for both buildings and yearly operating expenses to what opened in 1897 as Bradley Polytechnic Institute. The 150 students enrolled took classes in a wide range of fields, from watchmaking, food work, and sewing to Greek, mathematics, and physics. The fledgling institute even hosted an oratory contest.

Today, Bradley University offers undergraduate programs in more than 100 fields, many of which combine theory with useful application. In the popular Foster College of Business Administration, selected seniors use their knowledge to work on real-world problems with Illinois businesses and organizations; to date they have completed more than 1500 such projects since 1972. The present-day speech team recently became the 2005 National Champions. Since 1979, the team has won 115 individual national championships and 33 overall national titles. The campus environment remains one that would do the widow Bradley proud. Says a senior: "The biggest wave of excitement came when I realized how much of a difference one person could make at a school . . . Simply put, I can't imagine where I would be if I was at another school. Bradley allowed me to cultivate my character."

Student body: Illinois is home to 89% of the undergraduates, though students travel from 41 other states and 55 foreign countries to attend. A fourth in a recent year were graduates of private or parochial schools. Five percent of the undergraduates are African-American, 3% Asian-American and 2% Hispanic. Four percent are foreign nationals.

Undergraduates consider themselves to be friendly, motivated, opinionated, and involved, though as on many campuses, it sometimes seems that a minority are over-involved and a majority just want to have fun. Students describe their peers as fairly apolitical but more inclined to take part in community service projects and generally willing to study as much as is needed to succeed in their classes. Says a junior, "At times, Bradley seems like high school all over again—with all the drama, the cliques, the cliché parties—but overall it's an okay group of students who can do really amazing things if they're not too busy trying to look cool."

Academics: Bradley's 100+ undergraduate academic programs are spread among 5 colleges: the College of Liberal Arts and Sciences, the College of Education and Health Sciences, the College of Engineering and Technology, Foster College of Business Administration, and Slane College of Communications and Fine Arts. Fourteen graduate degrees in 31 academic areas also are awarded. Classes follow a semester calendar, with regular course offerings averaging 20 registrants, and the largest course, Economics 100, enrolling about 250.

In order to graduate, all students must complete 36 semester hours of general education courses in traditional fields. Included are courses in English composition, speech, and mathematics, Western and non-Western civilization, human values, fine arts, cultural diversity and social forces, and science.

Fifty-nine percent (326) of the 550-member faculty are full-time; a third are women. All members teach undergraduates. Students generally value their professors' expertise and commitment to helping the individual. Says a senior, "Bradley is a place where the faculty really make the university experience; the amount of attention, one-on-one instruction, all create an open, free atmosphere for learning." Undergraduates give more qualified praise to the adjunct faculty. Says a senior: "The part-time faculty are great sometimes and worthless other times."

Career-oriented fields of study command the most respect from students. The Foster College of Business Administration is considered strong because of its small student-teacher ratio, experienced faculty, and curriculum that exposes students to "real-world" problems. The College of Engineering and Technology benefits from brilliant faculty, superb technology, and excellent co-op and internship experiences with the hometown company Caterpillar Inc. The communications program within Slane College of Communications and Fine Arts also offers technologically advanced facilities and great professors. "It has definitely prepared me for my professional career," says a public relations major. Within the College of Liberal Arts and Sciences, the programs in political science, history, biology, and psychology all are considered strong with excellent faculty. The health science major features challenging classes taught by supportive faculty drawn from all 5 colleges and prepares students for a master's degree program in physical therapy or for entry-level jobs in the health care industry.

The education program in the College of Education and Health Sciences needs better communication among its faculty members so that students clearly understand what classes they should be taking. The art and theater programs in the Slane College of Communications and Fine Arts also need strengthening; art could use new equipment and more class options, the recently accredited theater department, more consistent faculty.

Facilities: Cullom-Davis Library, in the words of a political science major, "is one area in which we should do better." Continues the junior: "Although many students do utilize the library often, most would argue the material should be more in-depth and updated." The collection consists of about 542,000 volumes, 817,000 microform items, and 25,000 electronic and paper periodicals. Computerized research aids that connect Bradley with the holdings of 45 other academic libraries in Illinois, the Internet, and interlibrary loan, all help to compensate for Cullom-Davis's shortcomings. The library lets students check out laptops to assist them in their online research. As a study center, the facility sometimes proves so popular that it becomes noisy in all but the most out-of-the way places.

Approximately 80% of Bradley students bring their own computers to campus. For those who do not, there are approximately 900 units in public and academic labs available for student use. Many of the academic and other campus buildings offer wireless access to the Internet. Observes a senior: "Technology is ample, support services are strong, and there is never a problem finding a computer."

Special programs: Each year, 15 freshmen are designated as fellows through the Lewis J. Burger Center for Student Leadership and Public Service. Each fellow receives a $1000 scholarship renewable over 4 years, and in addition to regular course work agrees to complete specified activities and internships over 8 semesters. Internships are an important part of many students' education. Paid internships are available in all colleges; unpaid internships also are offered in communications, fine arts, and the liberal arts and sciences. Internships for the summer only are available in the College of Engineering and Technology. Opportunities for study abroad are offered in 30 countries; a semester in Washington, D.C. also is an option.

Campus life: Bradley means basketball for many students, in the words of 1 senior, as capacity crowds attest most winter weekends in Peoria's civic center. The men's and women's basketball programs along with men's soccer are the stars among the 6 varsity sports for men (no football) and 7 for women played in NCAA Division I. Half of the men and a fifth of the women take part in 24 intramural sports offered to each sex.

Bradley also means a lively Greek life to the 28% of the men and 25% of the women who pledge to the 16 national fraternities and 12 national sororities on campus. Many of these groups regularly hold date parties, formals, and exchanges. "Their status on campus is huge," says a sophomore. Independents find entertainment through other of the 220 clubs and organizations on campus, though many wish there were more campus-wide alternatives to the party scene. Continues the sophomore, "There is nothing that makes the school come together as one, and I wish that there were."

Within the past few years, Bradley has also come to mean an expanded campus of 75 acres with 4 new residential complexes featuring 4 bedroom suites. The new structures, which opened in fall 1999, marked the first phase of a 15-building student apartment community designed for juniors and seniors. Ninety-seven percent of Bradley's students live on campus, and most stay there once the weekend gets under way, although students from the suburbs of St. Louis and Chicago sometimes head for home.

Students find the campus itself to be secure, with student escorts available every evening from 8 p.m. to 1 a.m. (The university police provide an escort at other times.) Emergency telephones are located throughout the more brightly lit campus and police regularly patrol on bicycles. Some residence halls are locked around the clock; others are open only during daytime hours. Off campus, however, students report they must use extreme caution; in response to their concerns about walking to off-campus housing or apartment complexes, the university instituted a hot line to acquire an off-campus escort.

Peoria (pop. 183,000) does not provide much of a social outlet for college-aged students, although many favor the pubs, mall, and city parks. When students need to get away, they opt either to head for home or for a road trip to Chicago, 160 miles northeast, or to St. Louis or to Western Illinois or Illinois State universities.

Cost cutters: Students credit Bradley's extensive financial aid program with making the campus as economically diverse as it is. Giving support to the financial aid program is a strong endowment totaling over $190 million as of June 2005, up from $30 million in 1992. All but 3% of the 2005–2006 freshmen received some form of financial aid; 64% were on need-based assistance. All but 14% of the continuing students were given aid; for 56%, the aid was based on financial need. The average freshman award for first-year students with financial need included a need-based scholarship or grant averaging $11,162 and need-based self-help aid such as loans and jobs averaging $4431. Non-need-based athletic scholarships for first-year students averaged $13,101; other non-need-based awards and scholarships averaged $9626. Average debt for a 2005 graduate was $14,760. Bradley offers a wide range of merit scholarships. President's Scholarships pay $8500 to students who typically graduated in the top 5% of their high school class including valedictorians and who earned either a 1300 combined math and critical reading SAT or 29 ACT. Dean's Scholarships also pay $6000 a year to students who generally ranked in the top 10% of their graduating class and who scored at least 27 on the ACT or 1220 in math and critical reading on the SAT. University Scholarships pay $4000 for slightly lower achievement levels. Provost and Garrett awards pay $2000 to $4000 annually to African-American, Native American, Asian-American, and Hispanic students with demonstrated academic potential. Scholarships also are given for talent in athletics, theater, art, forensics, and music. Monthly installment and deferred payment plans are available. Co-op programs are offered in all majors.

Rate of return: Eighty-nine percent of the freshmen who enter return for the sophomore year. Sixty-two percent graduate in 4 years, 71% in 5 years.

Payoff: No single major captured a large portion of the 2005 graduates. Nearly 5.5% earned bachelor's degrees in elementary education; just over 4.5% received degrees in communications (advertising) and just under 4.5% earned degrees in psychology. More than three-quarters of the graduates turn their diplomas into paychecks, many with the 251 companies and organizations that recruited on campus in the 2004–2005 school year. Overall, less than a fifth of degree recipients pursue advanced degrees within 6 months of graduation. Thirty percent of the students with degrees in the liberal arts and sciences go on for graduate study. In the past 5 years, 82% of Bradley students applying to medical school have been accepted; acceptance to dental school and to graduate school in the natural sciences has rated 93% and 99% respectively.

Bottom line: Undergraduates consider Bradley to be the ideal size, providing the one-to-one attention of a small university but the opportunities and technology of a larger campus. "A high achiever and leader in high school would do well at Bradley," says a health science major. "The classes aren't easy and you must be dedicated to your studies in order to succeed. Teachers are always willing to help but they aren't going to hold your hand and walk you through each step."

Illinois College

Jacksonville, Illinois 62650

Setting: Small town
Control: Private (Presbyterian and United Church of Christ)
Undergraduate enrollment: 475 men, 534 women
Graduate enrollment: None
Student/faculty ratio: 14:1
Freshman profile: 6% scored over 700 on SAT I verbal; 35% scored 600–700; 47% 500–599; 12% below 500. 6% scored over 700 on SAT I math; 47% scored 600–700; 41% 500–599; 6% below 500. 11% scored above 28 on the ACT; 17% scored 27–28; 27% 24–26; 23% 21–23; 22% below 21. 23% graduated in top tenth of high school class; 43% in upper fifth.

Faculty profile: 83% Ph.D.'s
Tuition and fees: $15,500
Room and board: $6400
Freshman financial aid: 99%; average scholarship or grant: $10,757 need-based; $6575 non-need-based
Campus jobs: 56%; average earnings: $1034/year
Application deadline: Aug. 15
Financial aid deadline: May 1 (Priority: Mar. 1)
Admissions information: (217) 245-3030; (866) 464-5265
  web site: www.ic.edu

For a school founded in 1829 with an unmistakably midwestern name like Illinois College, the fledgling institution started out more New England than Harvard itself. Its first president, Edward Beecher, minister of the Park Street Church in Boston, was the brother of Protestant preacher Henry Ward Beecher and of Harriet Beecher Stowe, author of *Uncle Tom's Cabin*. Guest lecturers on campus included Ralph Waldo Emerson, Mark Twain, and Horace Greeley. A trace of those early years remains today in the college's 7 "literary societies," 4 for men, 3 for women, which began as centers for debate and criticism in the 1840s (Abraham Lincoln spoke on campus under sponsorship of a literary society) and still compete for trophies presented annually for literary excellence. But there is one topic of discussion to which the societies can find little opposition: Illinois's excellent tuition, room, and board, which totaled just $21,900 in the 2005–2006 school year.

The tuition debate just became even less arguable. As part of a new Illinois College Advantage Plan, getting under way with students entering in fall 2006, the new 2006 tuition rate of $17,100 is guaranteed to rise for all new students currently enrolled by only 4% a year throughout a student's 4 years on campus. That means tuition for students graduating in the Class of 2010 already know they will pay just $19,234 in tuition their senior year. That 2010 figure still is several thousand dollars less than the amount students currently pay at other small midwestern institutions with a chapter of Phi Beta Kappa.

Student body: Ninety-one percent of Illinois's students come from the state itself. Sixty-six percent of the remainder are also from the Midwest, with a total of 21 states and 14 foreign countries represented. Just 6% are members of racial and ethnic minority groups, with 3% African-American students, and 1% each Hispanic, Asian-American, and Native American. Twenty students are foreign nationals. Twenty-six percent are Catholic and 62%, Protestant; 9% are, like the college, affiliated with the Presbyterian Church or the United Church of Christ. Eleven percent claim no religious affiliation. Most students come from fairly small midwestern towns, and the atmosphere exudes "country comfort." Students are very congenial and mutually helpful when it comes to studying; while some strive for election to Phi Beta Kappa, others are more concerned about other pursuits. An administrator describes them as "good American, straight-arrow types," who tend to be family-oriented and conservative in their political and religious views, though few are vocal about expressing them. Some students wish their classmates were a bit less apathetic and more engaged in events on campus and in the world around them.

Academics: Illinois offers the bachelor's degree in 45 fields of study. Its academic year is divided into 2 semesters. Students can expect an average class size of 16, with courses like Introduction to Biology enrolling 45, and a class in French phonetics having just 1.

All students must fulfill basic general-education requirements that cover, on average, 2 semesters of coursework from each of the traditional disciplines. Students must also attend 30 convocations, which are weekly 1-hour presentations of general cultural interest. Few complain about the general course requirements, but students are divided over whether the convocations are a "waste of time or edifying."

Thirty-nine of Illinois's 111 faculty members are part-time. Forty-three percent of the total pool are women. Students find the majority of professors intellectually challenging and in love with teaching. Says a junior: "Most of my professors are excellent at teaching both inside the classroom and individually in their offices, over the phone, or even at the lunch table." Small class sizes enable faculty members to learn the names of all students, not just those majoring in the field, and allow them to spot and help students having trouble with the course content, "not to mention that if you miss class," says a sophomore, "don't be surprised if you receive a call from your professor!"

Political science boasts "vibrant professors with an honest love for their fields," notes an education major. Their peers in English, religion, and history also motivate students to think and discuss. Though classes in biology and chemistry are especially demanding, the faculty is generally there to help with problems and even to assist students in fulfilling their plans for jobs or advanced degrees after college. Research opportunities are numerous, says a major, and "several students over the course of a year often will have research published in a peer-reviewed magazine." Spring "breakaway" trips to the rain forests of Costa Rica and the Florida Keys in alternating years "give students an opportunity to experience first-hand what it means to be a biologist in the field, and more importantly, see the applications of their science out of the laboratory setting," says a third-year student. For those times when the lab is all there is, the Parker Science Building completed in December 2001 further expands student horizons on campus with such options as a rooftop observatory, a climate-controlled greenhouse with simulated rainforest and desert, and a laser light lab, among other research facilities. Chemistry and computer science, says a computer science major, "both have advanced technology that professors know how to use. The faculty also provides a foundation in theory and teaches necessary current skills."

The foreign language department offers majors only in French, German, and Spanish. Some students wish there were more professors and more courses. Students say the fine arts major that provides concentrations in art, theater, and music also offers fewer courses in theater and music than many undergraduates would like. The art department also lacks faculty and space. History, likewise, is a smaller department where students think a couple of additional faculty members (there are 3 plus a visiting instructor) and a wider array of courses would be helpful.

Facilities: Schewe Library's biggest drawback as a study center stems from the smallness of the college. Explains a senior: "You know too many people, and they always keep coming up and talking to you." As a research center, however, Schewe gets higher marks. Its collection of almost 167,000 volumes and 631 periodicals is adequate; and its on-line catalog is part of a statewide consortium that allows patrons to check out items at over 50 colleges and universities in state. The library also subscribes to many on-line databases that include thousands of additional full-text articles. An especially helpful reference librarian is much appreciated as well.

Six computer clusters and wireless laptop carts in the Kirby Learning Center, the Parker Science Center, and Baxter Hall house more than 120 IBM-compatible computers. Several labs are open 24 hours "allowing procrastinators a place to finish their papers at 3 in the morning," observes a senior. Students already working in a lab that closes earlier may stay until they are finished.

Special programs: An intercultural exchange program with Ritsumeikan University in Kyoto, Japan, brings 25 Japanese students to campus each spring for 5 weeks of study and sends Illinois College students to Kyoto for 5 weeks during the summer. The Breakaway Program enables juniors and seniors the chance to combine study and travel with faculty and small groups of students to a variety of locations around the globe. Previous destinations have ranged from a Civil Rights Tour of the South to a Literary Exploration of Australia and New Zealand. Eligible students may receive up to $750 from the College toward the trip. Those wanting a different experience closer to home can spend a term in Chicago or in Washington, D.C. Joint 3-2 programs are conducted in engineering with the University of Illinois and Washington University in St. Louis and in occupational therapy with Washington University. Internships are available in a wide range of majors.

Campus life: Although two-thirds of the students live on the 62-acre, colonial-style campus, a third of those may leave on the weekends, a fact that students consider one of the college's biggest social drawbacks. For the core of students who stay every weekend, monthly off-campus dances, Student Activities Board concerts and comedians, and sporting events are the main source of entertainment. In place of national social fraternities or sororities, the historic literary societies serve much the same function. These groups still engage in debates, extemporaneous speaking, and literary readings and criticism, but members are also likely to indulge in partying and other mainstream weekend social activities. Less than a sixth of the student body belong to these societies and some friction can emerge, especially during pledging. BASIC, which stands for Brothers and Sisters In Christ, is an especially popular group encouraging Christian discipleship.

Half of the men and a fifth of the women participate in the 9 men's and 8 women's intercollegiate sports played as part of NCAA Division III. Blueboys football and basketball generally draw the biggest crowds, though students attend the games as much to socialize as to watch. Five intramural sports for each sex also keep more than half of the men and a fourth of the women busy.

Jacksonville itself, a farming community (pop. 25,000), is best known as the "Ferris wheel and library-binding capital of the world," although neither boast carries much flair for college students. The rural environment does not produce much crime on campus, though a campus shuttle does transport students from the parking lot to their dorms. Periodic walk-arounds by students and administrators point out darker areas around campus that could use better lighting. Students sometimes travel to Springfield, the state capital, just 35 miles away; St. Louis, 90 miles south; Chicago, 250 miles distant; or home, wherever that may be.

Cost cutters: Illinois's healthy endowment of $123.5 million as of May 2005, which ranks in the top 10% of private colleges per capita, helps both to keep tuition low and to provide ample scholarship assistance. All but 1% of the freshmen and all but 3% of the continuing students in the 2005–2006 school year received some financial aid; at least 75% received need-based assistance. Sixty-eight percent of all students received an academic scholarship. The average financial award for a first-year student with financial need included a need-based scholarship or grant averaging $10,757 and need-based self-help aid such as loans and jobs averaging $4724. Other non-need-based awards and scholarships for freshmen averaged $6575. The average graduate left with $11,105 in debts. Five 4-year full-tuition William Jennings Bryan Scholarships are awarded in honor of the distinguished orator and member of the Class of 1860 who also belonged to a literary society. Edward Beecher and Jonathan Baldwin Turner Scholarships pay up to $6000 and up to $8000, respectively. Awards recognizing talent in music, art, and theater pay $500 to $2000. Many financial awards to upperclassmen are presented at the annual convocation banquet. Observes a senior: "With a good percentage of the students receiving awards and honors, other students may, and do, attend as a gesture of support." Many students in the 2005–2006 school year were concerned about recent cuts in student employment that limited both the number of jobs available to students and the number of hours they could work.

Rate of return: Seventy-four percent of freshmen return for the sophomore year. Forty-six percent go on to graduate in 4 years; 54%, in 5 years, 56% in 6.

Payoff: Seventeen percent of 2005 graduates earned bachelor's degrees in business administration, with another 14% receiving degrees in education and 12% in biology. A fifth of the graduates went on to pursue advanced degrees. The vast majority accepted positions, many in education and finance, primarily with firms in the Midwest. The college participates in consortium interviewing and job fairs that provide access to hundreds of employers each year.

Bottom line: Advises a senior: "The greatest asset Illinois College has to offer is its constant awareness of the individual. With a total population of about 1000, classroom sizes are ideal for one-on-one attention and assistance to students. Before coming here, I never gave much thought to pursuing an advanced degree. Thanks to information and encouragement from knowledgeable instructors and counselors, I am now anxious to further my education!"

Illinois Wesleyan University

Bloomington, Illinois 61702

Setting: Suburban
Control: Private
Undergraduate enrollment: 917 men, 1223 women
Graduate enrollment: None
Student/faculty ratio: 12:1
Freshman profile: 23% scored over 700 on SAT I verbal; 53% scored 600–700; 23% 500–599; 1% below 500. 24% scored over 700 on SAT I math; 49% scored 600–700; 25% 500–599; 2% below 500. 50% scored above 28 on the ACT; 24% scored 27–28; 20% 24–26; 6% 21–23; 0% below 21. 49% graduated in top tenth of high school class; 72% in upper fifth.

Faculty profile: 93% Ph.D.'s
Tuition and fees: $27,624
Room and board: $6426
Freshman financial aid: 89%; average scholarship or grant: $16,150 need-based; $10,216 non-need-based
Campus jobs: 45%; average earnings: $1853/year
Application deadline: Mar. 1
Financial aid deadline: Mar. 1
Admissions information: (309) 556-3031; (800) 332-2498
e-mail: iwuadmit@iwu.edu
web site: www.iwu.edu

In the revolution shaking up and sorting out America's colleges and universities, Illinois Wesleyan, the "Microuniversity," has been making its move. Whereas Illinois Wesleyan once contentedly billed itself as the Microuniversity of the Midwest, this university of nearly 2150 undergraduates has been striving to become the Microuniversity of the Nation. And it has a good shot at making it. Offering the size and personal attention found at most small liberal arts colleges plus professional schools in nursing, music, theater arts, and art, Illinois Wesleyan manages to fuse both worlds with ease. Students from 36 states and 15 foreign countries are attracted by the opportunity to explore diverse fields in depth—music and biology, physics and business administration. As a result, 15% of the multitalented student body in a recent year carried 2 or more majors. And the clincher that may indeed put Illinois Wesleyan on everybody's list of the best is its relatively "micro" tuition rate: just over $27,500 in the 2005–2006 school year, above average but offering, for the price, an academic package solidly above the field.

Student body: Eighty-four percent of Illinois Wesleyan's undergraduates are from in-state, with 69% of the rest from the Midwest. Fourteen percent in a recent year were graduates of private high schools. Students who are members of racial or ethnic minority groups account for just over 10% of the enrollment; 4% are African-American, 3% each Asian-American and Hispanic, and less than 0.5% Native American. Two percent are foreign nationals. For the most part, students focus on leading well-rounded lives, with an emphasis on learning as much outside the classroom as within. "A word that comes to mind is sleep-deprived," says a junior. "A large percentage of students are on the go all the time between studies, work, and extracurricular activities." Many are politically moderate, both Republicans and Democrats; the predominance of the College of Fine Arts, which enrolls 1 of every 6 students, gives the campus an added air of individualism. "The students," concludes a senior, "are very independent and represent every walk of life." They also know when to work together, pooling their efforts in study groups and class projects. Students in the natural sciences, music, and theater tend to be more competitive with one another.

Academics: Illinois Wesleyan, which celebrated its 155th birthday in 2005, awards the bachelor's degree in 35 majors through the colleges of Liberal Arts and Fine Arts and the School of Nursing. Students follow the semester schedule, with an optional May term devoted to intensive courses, travel, internships, or independent study. Freshmen and sophomores generally find classes of between 20 and 50 students; the largest class, General Biology, recently enrolled about 140. Most upper-level courses tend to have between 10 and 20 participants, with Language and Culture in Japan recently enrolling just 3. For freshmen entering the College of Liberal Arts, course work begins with various Gateway Colloquia, small discussion-oriented classes designed to develop students' proficiency in writing. One course unit apiece is required in 7 other areas, ranging from cultural and historical change to formal reasoning. Two course units are mandated in the natural sciences, the equivalent of 2 semesters of non-credit courses in physical education and 0 to 3 in a foreign language, as many as are needed to demonstrate proficiency. In either the general education program, major, or minor, each student must take a course concerning global diversity and 1 examining U.S. diversity, as well as 2 classes that are writing intensive. Students in the College of Fine Arts and the School of Nursing must fulfill similar requirements, with some variation by program.

The faculty consists of 161 full-time members, not including 22 coaches and librarians who also hold faculty rank, and 61 part-timers. Forty-two percent are women. "Professors truly attempt to get students to think and to critique," says a nursing student. "Sometimes they challenge your beliefs or make you defend your positions and they give examinations that require more than rote memorization." Students appreciate that faculty members stay active in scholarly research, publishing papers and performing, yet remain "not research-oriented but student-oriented," says a senior.

Biology is easily "the star of the school," according to a satisfied pre-med student, although other of the sciences—chemistry, physics, and psychology—also rate quite highly. A combination of in-depth coverage of material and extensive research opportunities translates into high placement of Illinois Wesleyan graduates in medical and graduate schools. The Center for Natural Science completed in 1995 makes available to advanced students such sophisticated equipment as a scanning electron microscope and a Fourier transform NMR. The School of Nursing gets students into the hospitals as early as their sophomore year and requires students to have detailed comprehension of such subjects as pharmacology, pathophysiology, and anatomy and physiology. Psychology offers internship opportunities for credit and expects majors to create and write their own theses, "a strength in applying to graduate programs," says a major. Music and theater arts both have excellent faculties and fine facilities. Accounting stresses communication almost as much as basic skills, which assists graduates in the job market; other business programs are equally satisfying, with excellent alumni support. Expanded course offerings—"rigorous but very worthwhile," says a major—and several dynamic young professors make political science a winner. English and history also are considered strong.

Several of the interdisciplinary majors, such as international studies and women's studies would benefit from more faculty and courses. Courses in the educational studies program could use more rigor. Students say that classes in the foreign language program sometimes seem designed more to fulfill general-education requirements than to provide for well-developed majors in French, German, and Spanish.

Facilities: Students enrolled in January 2002 became the first to enjoy the expansive learning environment provided by the new Ames Library. The $23 million structure, nearly triple the square footage previously available, offers room for 400,000 volumes across its 5 stories and seating for 500 plus at least 100 computer workstations. The university's collection currently stands at about 318,000 volumes and 1046 periodicals. Extensive computer technology is available, and students may check out laptop computers for use anywhere in the building. Library users especially like the way research materials are organized into scholarly workstations that consist of volumes related to a certain topic and a pod of 6 computers. Notes a biology and economics major: "When I do research, I can stay in that one area and find all the books and journals I need and then go to the computers that are 10 feet away. It's a pretty convenient way to arrange things."

The former library, Buck Memorial, became a campus computer center, large enough to accommodate more than 100 students at any one time and open from 8 a.m. until 11:30 p.m. Many night owls wish the hours were longer. Computers also are available in Ames Library (until 1:30 a.m.), the science center, and a few residence halls around the clock, providing about 400 Macintosh, Linux, and PC computers throughout the entire campus. About 80% of the students choose to bring their own computers to campus. For those who have laptops, wireless network access is available in both Ames Library and the student center.

Special programs: Undergraduates may study abroad in countries as far-flung as Singapore and Sweden through a variety of programs offered by various international institutes. Since fall 1997, a handful of students each year have had the chance to study at Pembroke College, Oxford University, England. The university also offers its own study-abroad semesters in London and Madrid. Cooperative programs in forestry and environmental studies with Duke University and in engineering with the University of Illinois and others also are available. Semesters spent in Washington, D.C., or at the United Nations, are options as well. Once a year, the John Wesley Powell Student Research Conference enables all undergraduates regardless of class level or academic interest who are pursuing individual research projects to present their projects in a public forum.

Campus life: Illinois Wesleyan prides itself on being a residential college, with 81% of its students living on the 80-acre campus, which extends about 1 city block in size. A typical weekend night might encompass students dropping by both hubs of Illinois Wesleyan's social life—a concert or movie at the new student center, a recently renovated 1920s-era gymnasium, followed by attendance at a fraternity party. A third of the men and a quarter of the women are members of 6 national fraternities and 1 local and 4 national sororities on campus.

For those who enjoy the fine arts, the excellent music and theater arts programs at Illinois Wesleyan keep the campus well stocked with almost nonstop performances by no less than 9 major music groups plus smaller ensembles, all of which are open to and often populated by nonmajors. An average of 10 exceptional theatrical productions also are given each year. The Blue Moon Coffeehouse features up-and-coming artists and draws 20% of the student body to its performances on many weekends. Between 100 and 150 students turn out Saturdays to help build homes with Habitat for Humanity. Crime is not considered much of a problem, although students appreciate such safety precautions as an emergency call station on each corner of the quad, an escort service, and locked residence halls after 10 p.m.

Sporting events really raise school spirit, especially play by the men's basketball team, back-to-back conference champions in 2002–2003 and 2003–2004, and Titans football, consistently ranked highly nationally. The women's softball team finished third in the nation in 2003. Illinois Wesleyan plays in NCAA Division III, which means no athletic scholarships and an emphasis on the student athlete in the 9 men's and 9 women's varsity sports offered. Fifty percent of the men and 10% of the women participate in the 9 intramural sports offered for each sex.

Bloomington is in the heart of central Illinois and has a combined population of 100,000 with its twin city, Normal. For those desiring a bigger metropolis, Chicago is a 2½-hour drive, St. Louis, 3 hours. Many students head to the big-school environment of Illinois State University for parties and relative anonymity among its 22,000 students.

Cost cutters: Eighty-nine percent of freshmen and 90% of continuing students received some form of financial aid in the 2005–2006 school year. For 54% of the freshmen and 52% of the rest, the aid was need-based. Grants or scholarships for freshmen that were need-based averaged $16,150. Need-based self-help aid in the form of loans and jobs averaged $5286. Other non-need-based scholarships and awards averaged $10,216. The average financial indebtedness of a 2005 graduate was $21,846. Alumni Scholarships recently paid $5000 to $15,700 to entering freshmen based on general academic performance, test scores, recommendations, and extracurricular involvement. Talent Awards for entering freshmen planning to major in art, music, music theater, and theater arts, recently ranged in value from $6400 to full tuition. As a relief to all, the university lets parents and students pay their bills on a monthly basis interest free without service charges.

Rate of return: Ninety-two percent of freshmen return for the sophomore year. Seventy-seven percent go on to graduate in 4 years, 81% in 5 years.

Payoff: Business administration, psychology, and biology were the top 3 majors of choice for 2005 graduates, claiming 20%, 10%, and 9% of the degrees respectively. A third of the graduates went directly to graduate or professional schools. The majority head immediately into the job market, becoming accountants, nurses, bankers, and teachers, and accepting posts with firms as varied as the major accounting firms, State Farm Insurance, and more than 50 hospitals. Most graduates remain in Illinois. Seventy-five companies recruit annually at the university.

Bottom line: Observes a sophomore: "I have found a place where I can achieve greatness on the football field (or on the stage) as well as in the classroom. The close-knit family aspect of Illinois Wesleyan only adds to its many strengths. I like the fact that I can go to class and know that my professor cares about me and the type of education that I will receive."

Knox College

Galesburg, Illinois 61401

Setting: Small town
Control: Independent
Undergraduate enrollment: 550 men, 651 women
Graduate enrollment: None
Student/faculty ratio: 12:1
Freshman profile: 29% scored over 700 on SAT I verbal; 42% scored 600–700; 22% 500–599; 7% below 500. 15% scored over 700 on SAT I math; 39% scored 600–700; 39% 500–599; 7% below 500. 44% scored above 28 on the ACT; 21% scored 27–28; 18% 24–26; 14% 21–23; 3% below 21. 32% graduated in top tenth of high school class; 61% in upper fifth.

Faculty profile: 94% Ph.D.'s
Tuition and fees: $26,090
Room and board: $6285
Freshman financial aid: 98%; average scholarship or grant: $16,591 need-based; $10,445 non-need-based
Campus jobs: 62%; average earnings: $1176/year
Application deadline: Early action: Dec. 1; regular: Feb. 1
Financial aid deadline: Feb. 15
Admissions information: (309) 341-7123;
(800) 678-KNOX
e-mail: admission@knox.edu
web site: www.knox.edu

Since its founding in 1837, Knox College has never shied away from free discussion. Its Old Main building was the site of the fifth debate between Abraham Lincoln and Stephen Douglas in 1858, and students can still sit in the chair Lincoln occupied. Samuel McClure, Knox class of 1882, was editor of the college's weekly newspaper *The Student,* before going on to become founder of *McClure's* magazine, which Theodore Roosevelt called the voice of "muckraking journalism." (Two dozen fellow Knox alums later joined the staff.) In its day, the college's interstate oratorical society, which lasted more than 100 years, was bigger than football is now and is reputed to have caused a few riots. While today's spirit of debate is hardly as raucous, students are no less engaged in lively communication. In fact, the entire freshman class learns just how to do so, jumping directly into a 1-term First-Year Preceptorial, which prompts students to think critically, debate intelligently, and collaborate constructively, all in the Knox tradition. "A commonly repeated phrase here is 'Freedom to flourish,'" says a senior, "and it is very fitting." Adds a junior: "If you are a student who has never thought outside the box, Knox will make you think outside the box."

Student body: The student body is more diverse than at many small midwestern colleges: 7% foreign nationals from 46 countries, 5% Asian-American, 4% each African-American and Hispanic and less than 1% Native American. Fifty-five percent are from Illinois, with half of the out-of-staters also from the Midwest and all but 4 states represented. Ninety-three percent are graduates of public schools. The smallness of the campus and the variety of things to do make it impossible to define students in terms of a single club, sport, or interest. Observes a sophomore: "There is a feeling of 'we-ness' that is easily recognizable here." While students detect a current of liberalism running through the student body, many find their classmates to be very open-minded and more conservative than they initially appear to be. But no attitude, idea, or activity is considered too unusual or unworthy of consideration. Says a Kansan: "People might not agree with your views, but they won't mind you expressing them." Environmental issues and matters of social equality grab their attention, and their voices, more quickly than do political concerns. An honor system further enhances the spirit of openness, with students taking unproctored exams anywhere in a given building. Many individuals thrive in the spirited atmosphere of questioning and exploring new ideas. Notes a classics major: "You get into debates constantly. These produce a very competitive atmosphere that can be overwhelming sometimes. But if you know your limits, it will be a fun experience."

Academics: Knox offers 34 majors leading to the bachelor's degree. The academic year is divided into three, 10-week terms, with students taking 3 courses in each term. There is an optional miniterm between Thanksgiving and Christmas. Average class size for undergraduates is 17, although some introductory biology courses have about 100. Widespread opportunities for independent study enable students to enroll in a course of 1, while many upper-level seminars have between 5 and 10 participants.

For the interdisciplinary First-Year Preceptorial, students meet initially in a large lecture and then break into groups of 16 for seminars under the guidance of faculty. The 1-term course explores personal identity through such readings in a recent year as Joseph Conrad's *Heart of Darkness* and works by Richard Dawkins, Chinese author Ding Ling, Chinua Achebe, and others. "The preceptorial prepares students for a liberal-arts education by opening up new ways of thinking," exclaims a foreign student. Otherwise, the core contains basic distributional requirements, demonstration of 6 key competencies such as writing and information literacy, and at least 1 experiential learning project before graduation.

Knox's 117-member faculty is predominantly full-time, with 22 part-timers. Forty-four percent of the members are women. Professors are passionate about their subject matter and though involved in their own research and writing, students find them very willing to collaborate on research projects, meet for lunch to discuss a recent lecture, or combine work and pleasure as a way to get to know each other better. Says a senior: "Most of the professors know their field *very well* yet treat the students as equals. They also are willing to allow students to move in new, non-traditional ways."

The English literature and creative writing programs are especially intense, with a talented and tough faculty. The literary magazine has won numerous national awards and graduates of the creative writing program boast a high acceptance rate into the widely respected University of Iowa Writer's Workshop. Biology and chemistry faculty members, award-winning teachers and researchers in their own right, are very involved in collaborative research projects with students. Excellent equipment, including electron microscopes, spectrometers, and chromatographs, enables students to participate in many highly advanced courses, such as Gene Expression, which provides hands-on experience with current techniques in molecular biology. The political science, psychology, and philosophy faculties also receive high marks for their teaching and easy one-on-one relationships with students. Political science offers excellent opportunities for internships.

The classics major, with 2 full-time classicists, and religious studies, offered only as an interdisciplinary minor with faculty drawn from other disciplines, are small and for this reason can offer only limited courses. Dance is offered as a minor only. Other more professionally oriented disciplines such as business and management and journalism also are offered just as minors.

Facilities: Seymour Library, which was totally renovated in 1991, is many a student's favorite place for relaxation and reflection, not to mention studying, with its wonderful oak paneling, wing chairs, fireplaces, leaded-glass windows, and rooms lined with books. Not too far away, in distance, at least, is the science library, which, notes a physics major, "still has the 1950s–60s look of efficiency over aesthetics." Together, the 2 facilities along with the music library house a collection that is substantial for a college of Knox's size: nearly 312,000 volumes and subscriptions to nearly 13,000 electronic and paper periodicals. A computerized catalog assists in finding materials on campus; the library also provides access through the Internet to collections at other institutions.

The entire Knox campus is wireless, and all living units and academic buildings have Internet connections. Students can work from any of 5 different networked computer labs equipped with more than 200 Power Macs and Pentium computers. The newest lab in the Student Union, with 50 units, is open around the clock. Other labs are open until midnight.

Special programs: Off-campus and study-abroad opportunities are extensive—more than 30 in number, and attract almost 50% of all Knox students. Three of the most popular programs are Knox's own, in Besançon, France, Barcelona, Spain and Buenos Aires, Argentina. Each year 15% of all seniors complete honors projects that are judged by panels of faculty, including examiners from major universities. Undergraduate research is encouraged in all areas, with more Knox students having their work selected for presentation at the National Conference on Undergraduate Research than do students from any of the Big Ten universities. More than 85% of Knox seniors will have completed a work of independent study or participated in a self-designed class before they graduate. For students interested in pursuing careers from engineering to architecture to law, there are numerous cooperative professional degree programs with universities ranging from Columbia in New York to Duke in North Carolina. Up to 10 freshmen a year are guaranteed admission to Rush Medical College in Chicago. Those considering careers in academia may aspire to be among the 20 Knox juniors participating in a Ford Foundation Research Fellowship Program that enables students to develop and carry through research, creative, and scholarly projects under the guidance of faculty mentors. A Peace Corps Preparatory Program provides interested juniors and seniors with a carefully outlined curriculum that includes classes in language, education, and international studies.

Campus life: On-campus housing is the way to live at Knox, with 95% of the students residing on the 82-acre campus, and generally loving it. Instead of sterile hallways lined by rooms, door after door, most accommodations feature suites, with a small group of double and single rooms gathered around a common living area. Theme houses, such as the jazz house, also are popular. Fraternity housing is an option for the 21% of the men who belong to the 4 national fraternities at Knox. Two national sororities, without housing, pledge 11% of the female students. Few of the Greek parties are closed, and even those that are closed remain open to "friends of the house." "Everyone has his or her favorite fraternity," notes a senior, "and none practices exclusion of all nonmembers." Students walking home after late parties can call on a campus escort service. Outside telephones around campus, improved lighting, and an enhanced security force generally make students feel safe. A campus club also distributes whistles to students to use in case of an emergency.

Weekends begin Friday afternoon, with readings by student and faculty members of the Caxton Club, the campus literary society. The Knox-Galesburg Symphony, which combines college and community players and was voted Illinois Orchestra of the Year in 1998, plays often. Many of the 100 student clubs encourage volunteerism at the college and in the community. A highlight of the academic year is the international fair that foreign students put on every January, which features the food, music, stories, and dances of their native countries and attracts hundreds of visitors.

The Knox Prairie Fire, as the intercollegiate teams are called, play in NCAA Division III, with 11 men's and 10 women's sports provided. Football in the Knox Bowl (an actual bowl, set into the ground) is perhaps the most popular sport, although women's volleyball and men's and women's basketball follow closely. Those not involved in intercollegiate competition turn out for the 4 coed intramural sports or the 5 club sports that range from fencing to men's and women's water polo. A new $2.4 million fitness center that opened in January 2006 keeps everyone in better shape.

Knox's home town of Galesburg (pop. 35,000), the birthplace of poet Carl Sandburg, is not far from the meandering Spoon River, immortalized in the anthology of poems by Knox alumnus Edgar Lee Masters. Lake Storey across town offers students an opportunity to shake the winter blahs and barbecue. Peoria and the Quad Cities are both 45 minutes away; Chicago, for those truly in need of a change of pace, is 200 miles distant. Many clubs sponsor trips to the Windy City.

Cost cutters: In the 2005–2006 school year, all but 2% of the freshmen and all but 3% of the continuing students received some form of financial aid. For 68% of both groups, the aid was need-based. The average freshman award for a first-year student with financial need included a need-based scholarship or grant averaging $16,591 and need-based self-help aid such as loans and jobs averaging $5950. Other non-need-based scholarships or awards for first-year students averaged $10,445. The average 2005 graduate owed $18,642. Altogether, about 90 scholarships, ranging in amount from $750 to full tuition, are awarded annually. Each year, renewable Lincoln Scholarships worth up to $15,000 a year are awarded to top students from around the country. Muelder Scholars, usually ranking in the top 5% of their high school classes, receive up to $10,000 annually; Scripps Scholars, drawn from the top 10%, get up to $7500 a year. First-year students with special ability in music, theater, dance, visual arts, and writing can receive renewable scholarships worth up to $3500 a year; freshmen who have been active in community service may receive a Social Concerns Scholarship of equal value.

Rate of return: Eighty-two percent of entering freshmen return for the sophomore year. Sixty-four percent graduate in 4 years; 70%, in 5 years.

Payoff: The largest number of 2005 graduates, 13%, majored in psychology; 9% each earned degrees in political science and in anthropology-sociology. Nearly 30% enrolled immediately in graduate or professional school, with the largest number pursuing advanced degrees in the arts and sciences. Knox ranks in the top 2% of all U.S. colleges and universities in percent of graduates who earn doctoral degrees. It ranks 11th in the percentage of graduates earning degrees in the natural sciences and mathematics. Those who entered the job market, many with the 100 or so companies and organizations that recruited on campus, took jobs with firms such as Aetna Insurance Co., Eli Lilly, Martin Marietta, Procter & Gamble, Smith Barney, and other, smaller businesses. Most took posts in the Chicago metropolitan area but large numbers moved to Indianapolis, Houston, Denver, and New York, and some even went abroad. Knox alumni clubs exist in both Tokyo and Kuala Lumpur. Knox ranks among the top fifty among all U.S. colleges in the number of alumni who are corporate executives.

Bottom line: "Knox provides a small-family atmosphere where the academic life becomes so intertwined with the social life that often they are the same," notes a westerner. "Students who are serious but don't want to live in the library or in front of a computer are perfect for Knox. Take 160+ years of pride and history, combined with modern facilities and attitudes, and you have one of the best places to spend 4 years of your life." Even Abraham Lincoln couldn't debate that.

Millikin University

Decatur, Illinois 62522

Setting: Suburban
Control: Private (Presbyterian)
Undergraduate enrollment: 2400 men and women
Graduate enrollment: NA
Student/faculty ratio: 13:1
Freshman profile: Average combined SAT I: 1100;
  Average ACT composite: 24; Class rank data: NA
Faculty profile: 84% Ph.D.'s
Tuition and fees: $21,216
Room and board: $6713

Freshman financial aid: NA; average scholarship or grant:
  NA
Campus jobs: NA; average earnings: NA
Application deadline: Rolling
Financial aid deadline: May 1
Admissions information: (217) 424-6210;
  (800) 373-7733
  e-mail: admis@mail.millikin.edu
  web site: www.millikin.edu

"Academic visionary" was probably among the few names, good and bad, that James Millikin *wasn't* called in a multifaceted life that spanned the turn of the century. In 1860, the man known as "Cattle King of the Prairie State" founded a bank in Decatur, Illinois, that grew to become the state's largest outside Chicago. Millikin's work in banking, real estate, and other industrial promotions in the burgeoning Decatur area made him its wealthiest citizen. Anxious to make a noble public gesture, Millikin offered $200,000 and land in the city if local citizens and the Presbyterian Church would invest an equal amount in the creation of a university. But herein lies the vision. What Millikin wanted was unique among schools at that time but increasingly mainstream for institutions of higher education in the 21st century. His legal stipulations were 2: that the new university embrace the "practical" side of learning along with the "literary and classical"; and that while religious in origin, it would not be narrowly "sectarian," and would remain open to all. The result was 1 of the nation's first small, comprehensive universities that, 105 years after its founding, has 3 professional schools and 1 for the liberal arts and sciences, programs in classical music that vie in excellence with those in accounting, and a comprehensive fee of under $28,000 in the 2005–2006 school year, which would make even Decatur's shrewdest investor smile.

Student body: Millikin's university remains best known within the Prairie State, with 85% of the enrollment from Illinois and most of the remaining 15% also from the Midwest, primarily Indiana and Missouri. There is a mix of students from the Chicago and St. Louis areas and from more rural areas of central Illinois. Nearly half of the undergraduates are first-generation college students, defined as children of parents who did not graduate from a 4-year college. A total of 33 states and 13 foreign countries were represented on campus in a recent year. Eighty-five percent of the students were graduates of public schools. While 53% of the students in a recent year were Protestant (just 3% were Presbyterian), 24% were Catholic, less than 1% Jewish, and 4% other denominations; 18% claimed no religious affiliation. Racially and ethnically, Millikin has become increasingly diverse, with 7% African-American students, 2% Hispanic, 1% Asian-American, and less than 1% each Native American and foreign national in a recent year. Like the founder, Millikin students are very "success-oriented." They pride themselves on being as well rounded socially as they are responsible academically, and display the same competitive edge in striving for student leadership positions as they do in their efforts in the classroom. Still, no one tries to get ahead at the expense of others, and nearly all, remarks a theater major, adhere to a general policy of "fitting in."

Academics: Millikin offers the bachelor's degree in more than 50 majors spread among 2 colleges—Arts and Sciences, and Fine Arts—and 2 schools—Business and Nursing. The university recently added a master's degree program in business administration. The academic year follows a 2-semester schedule. The class-size range is rather limited, stretching from a single student in senior research in chemistry to 70 in an astronomy class about the planets. Between 20 and 40 participants seems to be the norm for most freshmen and sophomore classes, while those in the latter years usually have between 5 and 20.

The Millikin Program of Student Learning has 2 components that every student must complete: sequential program elements and nonsequential ones. The sequential program includes courses in critical reading, writing, and research; U.S. and global studies; a university seminar taken during first semester freshman year; and a capstone seminar taken in the senior year. The nonsequential course work is drawn from classes in quantitative reasoning, natural science, fine arts and language/culture options. For the latter requirement, students choose 1 of the following 3 tracks: instruction in a second language; 3 courses in semiotic systems, such as computer languages, linguistics, or music theory; or 3 courses in history, social institutions, and cultures, preferably focusing on a single area of the world. Students also must complete an off-campus learning experience and, in consultation with their advisors, must develop a plan of study that includes cocurricular elements. Concludes a senior: "We are expected to take part, contribute, question, enlighten, and provoke."

In a recent year, 88 of the university's 242 faculty members were part-time. A third of the full-time faculty were women. Many students sum up the qualities of the faculty in a single word: friend. Notes a junior: "Faculty members are very supportive of their students. They help us struggle through the tougher classes and always pat us on the back when we have done well." At Christmas time, students may hear their favorite faculty members caroling outside the residence halls or Greek houses.

Undergraduates generally find strong programs spread among all 4 colleges and schools. One contender for best-all-around is the College of Fine Arts with well-executed programs in classical and commercial music (with a 24-track recording studio), theater, and art, especially its offerings in computer graphics. More than a quarter of all Millikin undergraduates study theater, art, or music. Music majors particularly appreciate the opportunities to perform, which are plentiful with 38 different groups available. In a business where placements often are hard to come by, the college also counts a number of successful actors, singers, dancers, and artists among its alumni. Says a theater major: "Graduates of the program can do more than just portray a convincing character. They can express themselves in writing, and be equally competent on the business side." In the College of Arts and Sciences, the English faculty earn points for emphasizing good writing and thoughtful discussions throughout their courses. Political science also involves students in lively class discussions. While business majors find their courses challenging, the Tabor School of Business enjoys a solid job placement record thanks, in part, to the emphasis on giving students real-life problems to tackle in groups. The School of Nursing, too, demands exceptional effort and dedication from its students, and returns that effort with preparation that leads to a 100% passing rate on certification exams and a 100% job placement rate as well. The teacher education program provides ample opportunities for students from their freshman year on to observe, intern, and teach in the classroom. Notes a junior: "Recently, I have had the opportunity to travel abroad and teach for a week in the Dominican Republic."

Language lovers may major only in Spanish with classes through the intermediate level offered in French and Italian. Religion also is a smaller program (no major offered) that serves students mainly at the introductory level; more challenging course work goes largely untapped. The psychology, sociology, and communication programs have been hampered by insufficient and/or outdated facilities.

Facilities: The strength of Staley Library as a research center lies primarily in what its extensive computerized catalog and databases can retrieve from more than 40 other academic institutions in Illinois plus other colleges around the country, rather than in what the facility provides on its own shelves. Students find the collection of 164,000 volumes and 919 current periodicals to be somewhat limited, though students have on-line access to the holdings of 50 academic libraries and more than 20,000 periodicals. More satisfactory is the breadth of academic needs addressed across the varied rooms of the structure. Over 5 floors, Staley contains a music library with 5000 recordings, a media center, language labs, a writing center, plenty of study space, and, for the late-night crowd, a 24-hour study room. But "because of the design of the building," says a senior, "sounds are amplified and travel quickly through the library, making it not a good place to study."

Millikin students have access to more than 500 IBM-compatible PCs and Macintosh computers divided primarily among 5 main computer labs. Three of the labs are open around the clock. There also are 24-hour labs in the residence halls.

Special programs: Study abroad through the Institute for the International Education of Students is available in 13 countries in 22 locations. Millikin has its own programs with Tunghai University in Taiwan and in Santo Domingo, the Dominican Republic plus its own semester in London. The business school has an exchange program in Paris. A semester in Washington, D.C. through American University, a term at the United Nations through Drew University, or an Urban Life Studies Center Semester in Chicago also is an option. Engineering students may take 3 years of courses at Millikin followed by 2 at Washington University in St. Louis, earning bachelor's degrees from both.

Campus life: Sixty percent of the university's students reside on the 75-acre campus. At Millikin, being Greek is not the litmus test of whether or not a student fits in, with just a fifth of the men and a fourth of the women recently accepting membership in 4 national fraternities and 4 national sororities. Independents usually rally together and have their own parties in designated houses off campus. One of the most visible of the 70+ student groups is the Millikin Marketing Association, which sells refreshments and college apparel at all home football and basketball games. The excellence of the College of Fine Arts also means a steady diet of recitals, concerts, and dramatic productions to complement regular University Center Board-sponsored events. Still, a number of undergraduates choose to leave campus for the weekend. While students generally feel secure on campus, occasional burglaries and muggings in the neighborhood nearby keep everyone cautious. Escort services, extra lighting, security phones, and keeping residence hall doors locked at all times help make students feel "safe as kittens," according to one male undergraduate.

Varsity athletics consists of 11 men's and 10 women's NCAA Division III teams. Football and men's and women's basketball and soccer are the biggest of the Big Blue sports. "Athletics flow through the vein of this campus," says a midwesterner. Sixty percent of the men and 40% of the women take part in the dozen or so intramural sports for each sex. In a recent 8-year period, only one other college-division team in the nation had more first-, second-, and third-team GTE Academic All-Americans.

Decatur (pop. 85,000) was once known as the Soybean Capital of the World, which today means beans to students more interested in livelier attractions. When the local parks and malls don't do the trick, students head out to visit thousands of other undergraduates at the University of Illinois, Illinois State, and Eastern Illinois University, each within an hour's drive of campus. Millikin is also within reach of several major cities: Chicago is 180 miles northeast, Indianapolis, 150 miles east; and St. Louis, 130 miles southwest.

Cost cutters: No data is available concerning Millikin's financial aid program in the 2005–2006 school year. However, in a recent year, 96% of the freshmen and 91% of continuing students received financial help; all but 4%–7% of both groups got need-based aid. No current figures are available to show the average amount of financial assistance given to freshmen as scholarships or self-help aid; there also is no data on the average size of student debt. Millikin need-based awards to Illinois residents recently ranged from $2000 to $8100 beyond that offered by an Illinois State Monetary Award. Awards to nonresidents may not exceed three-fourths of tuition. Millikin Merit Scholarships pay $5000 to $10,000 a year and are renewable. Service Learning Scholarships pay up to $2000 annually to students who plan to take part in the university's Service Learning Program.

Rate of return: Seventy-nine percent of the freshmen return for the sophomore year. Sixty percent graduate in 4 years; 61% within 6 years.

Payoff: More than a fifth of recent graduates earned bachelor's degrees in 3 fields: 9% in elementary education and 7% each in business administration and management and in music performance. Most students secure jobs in organizations such as the major accounting firms, major agribusiness companies, regional utilities, recording studios, public and private schools, and hospitals. More than 90 companies and organizations recruited on campus in a recent school year. Many accept posts in the Chicago or St. Louis area. Less than a fifth go directly to graduate or professional schools.

Bottom line: Millikin doesn't promise to make its graduates either "cattle kings" or the wealthiest citizens of any community. By following the founder's philosophy, if not his lifestyle, however, a well-rounded, well-grounded Millikin graduate will be ready if either opportunity comes his or her way. "Success," says a junior, "is inevitable."

Monmouth College

Monmouth, Illinois 61462

Setting: Small town
Control: Private (Presbyterian)
Undergraduate enrollment: 630 men, 710 women
Graduate enrollment: None
Student/faculty ratio: 14:1
Freshman profile: Middle 50% range of ACT composite scores: 21–26; Class rank data: NA
Faculty profile: 90% Ph.D.'s
Tuition and fees: $20,200
Room and board: $5750

Freshman financial aid: 98%; average scholarship or grant: $12,808 need-based
Campus jobs: 36%; average earnings: $900/year
Application deadline: Rolling
Financial aid deadline: May 1 (Priority date: Mar. 1)
Admissions information: (309) 457-2131;
  (800) 74-SCOTS (747-2687)
  e-mail: admit@monm.edu
  web site: www.monm.edu

Students who satisfactorily complete 4 years of courses at Monmouth College in the cornfields of Illinois don't just receive an ordinary bachelor's degree. Instead, they get what one history major calls "the clout of diversity," a degree that tells employers and graduate schools that they have taken thought-provoking courses in a wide range of subjects designed to make them valuable private citizens. The curriculum is well thought out: first-year students start with Introduction to the Liberal Arts, where they are pushed to think on the college level and to learn to express their thoughts both in speech and on paper. Four years later, seniors close their academic experience with a capstone course in Citizenship that takes an interdisciplinary approach to understanding important social issues. With 1340 undergraduates enrolled and 14 students to every faculty member, 90% of whom hold the highest degrees in their fields, students are guaranteed close contact with stimulating minds—and for a price the thrifty Scottish Presbyterians who founded the college in 1853 would still appreciate.

Student body: All but about a tenth of Monmouth's students are from Illinois, with 85% of the rest also midwesterners. A total of 23 states and 13 foreign countries have undergraduates on campus. Nine of every 10 students attended public schools. African-Americans constituted the largest group of minority students enrolled in a recent year, at 6%; Hispanics represented 3%, Asian-Americans, 1%, Native Americans, less than 1%. Two percent were foreign nationals. Monmouth students see themselves as fairly conservative, polite, sociable, and friendly, with a clear commitment to doing well academically, though not at the expense of disrupting the sense of community on campus. Says a junior: "We're people who just want a good education and a fun time getting it."

Academics: Monmouth awards the bachelor's degree in 26 majors under a semester calendar. Most classes contain from 12 to 16 students, though some introductory and business classes can reach 40 members. (General Botany has 50.) Juniors and seniors can expect several courses with fewer than 10 enrolled.

Monmouth's newly revamped general-education program accounts for 37 of the 124 credits required for graduation and is organized so that a student is enrolled in at least 1 component every year. The Introduction to Liberal Arts, taken freshman year, examines a single topic or theme from a variety of disciplinary perspectives. The course discussion draws on common readings and incorporates skills to be emphasized all 4 years across the curriculum: communication and quantitative reasoning. In the sophomore year, students focus on Global Perspectives in their coursework; in the junior year, an inward exploration of thoughts and feelings on the meaning and purpose of life through Reflections. Students also must take courses in the various academic disciplines as well as the final course in Citizenship.

The core, and other subjects, are enhanced by personal attention from the 93 full-time and 35 part-time faculty members. About half in a recent year were women. "They treat us as peers in a learning dialogue, rather than as robots taking notes," observes a sophomore. Adds a recent graduate: "They know what they are teaching, they believe in what they are teaching, and they believe in whom they are teaching."

Education wins student respect as a major that enables undergraduates in their freshman year to begin observing in the public-school classroom, serving as teachers' aides the following year. The sciences, especially chemistry, have excellent faculties and facilities. Students also rave about the biology department, which offers undergraduates the chance to perform independent projects using sophisticated lab equipment and various techniques. A field station on the Mississippi River and a prairie plot rich in native flora offer good ecological resources. English and history are the strongest of the humanities; English boasts a sufficient number of faculty to offer a variety of viewpoints. History offers its own brand of well-rounded "Renaissance men." Political economy and commerce also feature highly enthusiastic and dedicated faculty, along with a solid curriculum.

Sociology and anthropology, psychology, physics, and philosophy and religious studies are all hampered in the range of perspectives and courses they can offer because these departments have had fewer professors. French and Spanish, the only 2 modern languages offered as majors, need more courses at or above the 300 level.

Facilities: Students applaud the computerized catalog and extensive database searches available in Hewes Library, which offers a collection of 182,000 volumes and 547 periodicals. Though the size of the book holdings has grown dramatically over the last few years, students still find the resources lacking in up-to-date materials in the sciences. A row of small, private study rooms enables groups to meet without disturbing more solitary studiers. And when groups or individuals need a break, they can head to either the facility's latest art exhibit or the library café. Laptops also are available for checkout and use within the building.

The computer center, also housed in the library, plus 4 other labs around campus, make about 90 PCs available to students. The library center is open until midnight most of the time and until 2 a.m. during finals. One of the other labs is open 24 hours. All individual residence-hall rooms have been wired to the computer network for those students who bring their own personal computers.

Special programs: A program in the arts in London and Florence, an Urban Studies program in Chicago, offered by a consortium of colleges to which Monmouth belongs, and a semester in Washington, D.C., are especially popular. Opportunities to study in areas as far-off as Japan, India, and another dozen or so countries are available as well. Cooperative programs with Rush and Mennonite hospitals in nursing, and with Washington University, Case Western Reserve, and the University of Southern California in engineering are provided for those seeking degrees in these fields.

Campus life: Nearly all students, 97%, reside on the 70-acre campus, although a fair number who live within a 50-mile radius of the college go home for at least 1 day of the weekend. For those interested in being involved, there is much to keep a Monmouth student busy. About a fifth of the men and a fourth of the women are members of 3 national fraternities and 3 national sororities. The nation's first sorority, Pi Beta Phi, was founded at Monmouth, as was the third oldest, Kappa Kappa Gamma. Independent students say they sometimes feel left out of the social spin, though some fraternities do hold parties open to all. The college's own bagpipers and drummers help to preserve the school's Scottish heritage. "Here, everyone is Scottish," exclaims a sophomore. SOS, Students Organized for Service, is 1 of the most active groups. Crime is not considered to be a problem, though an escort service, new lights in the parking lots and streets, and emergency phones are available as precautions.

Fighting Scots athletics presents another popular option. About a third of the men and women participate in the 9 men's and 9 women's intercollegiate sports played in NCAA Division III. Football, men's basketball, and track draw the biggest fan support. Seventy percent of the men and 65% of the women take to the court or field in the 14 intramural sports offered to each sex. The new $22 million, 155,000-square-foot Huff Athletic Center significantly expanded the fitness options in fall 2003.

Monmouth itself is a pleasant, rural town of 9500 but students opt for shopping in Peoria or the Quad Cities of Moline and Rock Island in Illinois and Davenport and Bettendorf in Iowa, which are an hour away. Those wanting the really big city head for Chicago, 180 miles to the northeast. Others seek out the Mississippi River, just a half hour by car.

Cost cutters: All but 2% of the first-year and all but 6% of the continuing students received some form of financial aid in a recent school year. For 83% of all students, the aid was need-based. The average freshman award for a student with financial need in a recent year included a need-based grant or scholarship averaging $12,808 and need-based self-help aid such as loans and jobs averaging $4278. The average financial indebtedness of a recent graduate was $18,286. Academic merit scholarships ranging in value from $8000 to $9000 a year go to students with strong high school academic records. The amount of the award is determined by a student's performance on an essay and in an on-campus interview. Entering freshmen also may audition for awards in art, music, theater, or Latin, which pay $1000 to $3000. Bagpiping and Highland drumming scholarships may pay up to full tuition.

Rate of return: Eighty-one percent of freshmen return for the sophomore year. Fifty-five percent graduate in 4 years; 60% in 5 years, 62% in 6 years.

Payoff: Three fields of study accounted for 70% of the degrees awarded in a recent year: business at 29%, education at 25%, and communication/theater arts at 16%. In a recent year, nearly 30% immediately entered graduate or professional schools, about half studying business. The other graduates mostly took jobs in such fields as education, government, accounting, banking, business, sales, and communications. Nearly half signed up with firms in Illinois, many among the nearly 60 companies and organizations that recruited on campus in a recent school year.

Bottom line: Some top students find that Monmouth lacks the rigor of other more selective liberal arts colleges and can be easy to outgrow over the course of 4 years. However, none leave without having grown far beyond their freshman-year expectations. Because of Monmouth's emphasis on interdisciplinary education, says a senior from Illinois, "I have a very broad view of the world, along with a more detailed understanding and appreciation of others. My dynamic education has prepared me to deal with change, critical thinking, and problem solving."

North Central College

Naperville, Illinois 60566

Setting: Suburban
Control: Private (United Methodist)
Undergraduate enrollment: 784 men, 1126 women (223 part-time)
Graduate enrollment: 30 men, 29 women (280 part-time)
Student/faculty ratio: 14:1
Freshman profile: 5% scored over 700 on SAT I verbal; 35% scored 600–700; 44% 500–599; 16% below 500. 9% scored over 700 on SAT I math; 36% 600–700; 42% 500–599; 13% below 500. 17% scored above 28 on the ACT; 14% scored 27–28; 25% 24–26; 29% 21–23; 15% below 21. 21% graduated in top tenth of high school class; 40% in upper fifth.

Faculty profile: 86% Ph.D's.
Tuition and fees: $21,933
Room and board: $6993
Freshman financial aid: 94%; average scholarship or grant: NA
Campus jobs: 33%; average earnings: $1300/year
Application deadline: Rolling
Financial aid deadline: Sept. 1 (Scholarships: Feb. 1)
Admissions information: (630) 637-5800; (800) 411-1861
e-mail: admissions@noctrl.edu
web site: www.northcentralcollege.edu

The faculty is the heart of many a liberal arts college, and the 203-member teaching core at North Central College in the "Silicon Prairie" high-tech corridor west of metropolitan Chicago is no exception. Divided between full-time (111) and part-time (92) members, all but 12 of the part-time members are involved in teaching undergraduates. The two types of teachers, 45% of whom are women, bring a blend of academic theory and real-life experience to the classroom. While outside commitments sometimes keep some of the busy part-time faculty, many who have been with the college for years, off campus when some students need them, undergraduates practically are guaranteed to come to know at least a couple of their full-time professors very well. And it's not always the faculty-arranged internships or job contacts that career-minded students come to value most. Recalls this honors student: "I have been gently admonished more than once by more than 1 faculty member to take care of myself, get sleep, see the nurse, or take some time off if I have been working too hard. It is like having a bunch of parents around praising my successes, warning me when I'm slacking off, and making me see the other side when I get tunnel vision."

Student body: Ninety-two percent of North Central's students are from Illinois, with most of the rest from the surrounding region. Altogether, students come from 30 states and 24 foreign countries. Of the 12% who are members of racial and ethnic minority groups, 5% are Hispanic, 4% are African-American, and 3% are Asian-American. Less than 0.5% are Native American. About 1.5% also are foreign national. Though the college is affiliated with the United Methodist Church, only 8% of the undergraduates are church members. The largest portion, 26%, are Catholic. Students tend to be conservative in their thinking, reflecting the region from which most are drawn, yet open to exploration of other ideas and perspectives. Notes a student from the Far West: "Politically and academically, North Central students are typical midwesterners, diverse and industrious. Socially, the collective feeling on campus is one of an extended family." It has been difficult to extend that united feeling to the half of the student body who commute to campus, coming in for classes and leaving shortly afterwards. Efforts such as the Cardinals on Wheels commuter club have been made, however, to integrate these commuters more readily into the North Central family. (The large contingent of nontraditional, part-time students generally attend classes in the evenings or on weekends.) All in all, the students, whenever or however they study, maintain a healthy balance between academics and outside activities, with more competitive undergraduates in the honors program tilting the environment slightly to the academic side.

Academics: North Central which was founded in 1861 offers the bachelor's degree in more than 50 majors plus master's degrees in business administration, computer science, information systems, education, and the liberal arts. The academic year is divided into trimesters with students generally taking 3 courses every term. Because each 10-week term covers a semester's worth of information in every course, studying can become intense. To give students a breather, there is a month-long interim term between Thanksgiving and Christmas break for special projects and travel.

The average class size is around 21 students, with many introductory courses enrolling between 30 and 40 (the largest, Principles of Biology, has topped 45) and upper-level foreign language and natural science classes having fewer than 10. Classes for the most part are discussion-oriented.

A core curriculum that began with the freshmen who entered in fall 2000 requires that all students take 9 credit hours each of humanities and social sciences, 6.5 of life and physical sciences, 6 of English composition, and 3 each of speech communication and mathematics. In addition, all students must take seminars or classes that address the issues of religion and ethics, intercultural matters and leadership, ethics, and values. Each freshman also enrolls in FYI, Freshman Year Information, a 6-week, not for credit course designed to ease the transition from high school to college. Along with the regular major, a second major or a minor or some kind of foreign study, internship, or other off-campus experience is encouraged but not required to broaden the student's area of concentration.

North Central's business and computer science departments are especially strong, benefiting from the college's location in the high-tech corridor of Illinois. Notes an envious math major: "Not only does the college rely on the outside businesses for their expertise coming into the school, but also the students have innumerable internship and career possibilities." Much of the in-class work also involves actual case studies or company proposals. The English faculty are distinguished by the variety of their personalities and the diversity of their interests. The result is a curriculum that stretches from creative writing to adolescent literature to Literature and the Moral Life of Medicine. The political science major is noted for a team of professors who demand exactness in student assignments as well as regular class participation. "Biology professors," says a junior, "are very dedicated to and very good at preparing their students for graduate school." The education department combines practical experience with philosophical learning and guides students through all elements of teacher preparation, including job searches, résumé writing, and interviewing skills.

The small size of other academic areas has limited the breadth and depth of courses they can provide. Departments like mathematics, for example, have been able to offer some upper-level courses only every other year, so students must plan carefully. Regular foreign language majors are available in Spanish, French, German, and Japanese. Dance is offered as a minor only.

Facilities: "If North Central has one liability, it is the library," notes an English major. Students find the collection at Oesterle Library, almost 151,000 volumes and 603 periodicals, "meager" and "outdated," and unable to meet many of their research needs. On the brighter side, it does have numerous CD-ROM's, the Internet and numerous other computerized resources to assist students in determining what information they need; those materials not on campus or available on-line can usually be obtained through interlibrary loan or with a quick check at the nearby Naperville Public Library. As far as studying is concerned, Oesterle earns an "A" in quiet and comfort.

A total of 325 PCs are available from 7 a.m. to midnight in several computer labs and around the clock in the residence halls. All residence halls and other existing computer facilities are connected to the campus network and the Internet. The library, Boiler House Café, and the student center are all wireless as is the main spine of the campus and the areas outside of residence halls.

Special programs: North Central has exchange programs with Benedictine and Aurora universities. Farther afield, North Central offers extensive opportunities for study abroad. The Richter Fellowship program awards grants of up to $5000 to juniors and seniors proposing independent study programs in the United States or abroad; to be eligible, an upperclassman must have earned at least a B average in 3 courses closely related to the proposed field of study. In a recent school year, 37 undergraduates across all disciplines received grants totaling $50,000. A program in leadership, ethics, and values, open to all students and available as a minor, offers both introductory and advanced courses on the issue, noncredit workshops in which students can develop leadership skills, and modest grants to student groups for projects in the field. Participants also can take part in a dispute resolution program.

The city of Naperville (pop. 140,000) is a center of scientific research and development in the west Chicago suburban area, with firms like Amoco Research Center and AT&T Technologies providing ample opportunities for internships right in town or in Chicago, just 29 miles away. Physics students in particular enjoy the proximity of Argonne National and Fermi National Accelerator laboratories. A 3-2 program in engineering is offered with the universities of Illinois and Minnesota and with Marquette and Washington universities; a similar program in nursing is conducted with Rush University.

Campus life: About half, 48%, of North Central's students live on the 54-acre campus, bounded on all sides by the tree-lined, virtually crime-free residential streets of central Naperville. There are neither fraternities nor sororities, so residence halls are the focus of most weekend activity. One of every 5 students usually opts to go home or hop the train 3 blocks from campus to visit Chicago for the weekend. "It's hard to resist," admits a frequent visitor, although the Residence Life staff works to provide tempting activities on campus. Those with a love of the footlights can pool their talents with the faculty in a dramatic production put on every trimester or audition the first day of classes each fall for New Visions, the popular campus-ministry dramatic-musical touring company. The campus radio station, WONC, which broadcasts to more than 3.5 million potential listeners, boasts a staff of over 75, making it the largest club on campus; WONC is the winner of 20 Marconi college radio awards, more than any other college station.

The greatest number of students are involved in some kind of athletic competition. Just over a fourth of the men and a tenth of the women compete in the 10 men's and 9 women's intercollegiate sports. The Cardinals play as part of NCAA Division III; men's basketball and football and women's volleyball draw the biggest crowds although these are often mediocre at best. The cross country/track program is nationally ranked. The men's cross-country team won the national championship in 1999 and the men's outdoor track and field team won the national title in 2000. Half of the men and a third of the women blow off stress in the intramural program, which features 12 men's and 12 women's sports, including football for each, and special events such as golf tournaments and midnight bowling.

The Naperville Riverwalk, a 2-mile trail that runs along the DuPage River just a half mile from campus, is a popular place for walks, runs, or just hanging out.

Cost cutters: Ninety-four percent of the freshmen in the 2005–2006 school year, and 89% of the continuing students, received some form of financial aid; 68% of the freshmen and 65% of the continuing students were on need-based assistance. The average freshman award totaled $17,447, although no breakdown was provided on the portion that was a grant or scholarship or need-based self-help aid such as loans and job earnings. The average financial indebtedness of 2005 graduates was $14,608. Presidential Scholarships provide an initial award of $10,000 a year to high-achieving students who apply early. The awards are based on a combination of SAT/ACT test scores and a recalculated grade point average based on academic core courses. Scholarship recipients are invited to a campus program in November, January, or February to interview for the opportunity to increase the value of the scholarship to full tuition. Honor Scholarships, for slightly lower standardized test scores and grade point average, pay $5500 to $10,000. Science Scholarships pay $2000 to $4000. Awards for top students planning to study international business or international studies pay $1000 to $2000. Generous merit awards also are available in music, theater, forensics, art, and other fields. A 12-month plan makes tuition payments a bit easier to handle.

Rate of return: Of the freshmen who enter North Central, 79% return for the sophomore year; 55% go on to graduate in 4 years, 63% in 5 years.

Payoff: Degrees in business were the number-one choice of 2005 graduates, claiming 27%, followed by education at 15%, and social sciences at 10%. In recent years, two-thirds of the graduates have entered the job market, many taking positions with Fortune 500 companies in sales, accounting, and computer programming, primarily in the Chicago area or elsewhere in the midwest. A number of graduates also go into teaching. Of the fifth who pursue advanced degrees, most study in the arts and sciences.

Bottom line: "The holistic approach to education is evident here," observes a sophomore. "Any student who wants to develop his or her whole personality, not just the mind, should consider North Central."

Quincy University

Quincy, Illinois 62301

Setting: Small town
Control: Private (Roman Catholic)
Undergraduate enrollment: 407 men, 520 women
Graduate enrollment: 11 men, 17 women (256 part-time)
Student/faculty ratio: 17:1
Freshman profile: 3% scored above 28 on the ACT; 6% scored 27–28; 20% 24–26; 35% 21–23; 36% below 21. 23% graduated in top fifth of high school class; 51% in upper two-fifths.
Faculty profile: 83% Ph.D.'s
Tuition and fees: $18,330

Room and board: $6590
Freshman financial aid: 99%; average scholarship or grant: $2000 need-based; $6365 non-need-based
Campus jobs: 43%; average earnings: $1050/year
Application deadline: Rolling (Priority date: Dec. 15)
Financial aid deadline: Apr. 15 (Priority date: Feb. 15)
Admissions information: (217) 228-5210;
 (800) 688-4295
 e-mail: clynes@quincy.edu
 web site: www.quincy.edu

When the *Chicago Tribune* decided to look "where the books are" in the state of Illinois more than a decade ago, it found a treasure trove about as far cross-state as it could go: 280 miles southwest of Chicago in the Missouri border city of Quincy, home of what was then Quincy College, now Quincy University, a Roman Catholic school founded by the Franciscan Friars in 1860. While Quincy's collection then numbered well below the 202,000 volumes and 455 periodicals it boasts today for an enrollment of 930 full-time undergraduates, it was already among the 3 best-stocked libraries at 4-year in-state colleges. Today, the versatility of the Brenner Library spans the ages. Befitting a collection particularly strong in the humanities, it contains about 4000 rare books, including some from the 15th century. It also offers busy students the latest in 21st-century, time-saving computerized research aids. And if the *Tribune* were to write another article seeking "where the student-aid money is," it might just come back to Quincy. All but 1% of the entering freshmen and all but 5% of the continuing students received some form of financial aid in the 2005–2006 school year. For 4 of every 5 students, the aid was need-based. Altogether, the book/student-aid combo makes a pretty fair 21st-century deal.

Student body: Though students come from 26 states and 6 foreign countries to study at Quincy, 71% are from Illinois and 85% of the nonresidents are from the Midwest. Fifty-two percent are Catholic, with another 20% Protestant, 1% Jewish, 4% members of other faiths or unknown, and 21% claiming no religious affiliation. Just over half of the students, 52%, are graduates of private or parochial schools. Diversification of the student body racially and ethnically has occurred steadily over the last several years. Seven percent of the students are African-American, 3% Hispanic, and 1% each Asian-American and Native American. One percent are foreign nationals. On the whole, undergraduates see themselves as a close-knit, caring, casual, somewhat conservative body of people. Says a senior: "No one is really too opinionated, but no one is afraid to share his or her feelings or thoughts with you." Students study enough to stay on top of their academics, but rarely so much as to miss helping a friend or attending a good party. "Quincy has a very laid-back atmosphere and everyone pretty much gets along," says a sophomore. "But if students do not know when to study and when to have a good time, they are going to be out every night and end up flunking out of college."

Academics: Quincy offers bachelor's degrees in 33 majors plus master's degrees in business administration, theology, and education. An undergraduate who does not find a field that he or she would like to major in can design an individual "contract major" in consultation with faculty advisors and the academic dean. The academic year is divided into 2 semesters. Class sizes average about 20 students, stretching upward in the first 2 years to about 60 in Introduction to Psychology, and downward in the latter years, with only about 10 enrolled in many upper-division courses.

All undergraduates must complete a 48-hour general education program and 6 hours of theology/philosophy. All seniors must take a culminating seminar, practicum, or internship in the major field of study.

Fifty-four of Quincy's 127 faculty members are full-time, including a number of Franciscan friars. Seven of the part-time faculty teach at the graduate level only. Forty-three percent are women. Student-faculty relationships get off to a strong start under a freshman mentor program, in which 5–7 new students are assigned to a faculty member or administrator who helps ease their entrance into college. Relationships in the classroom are comfortable, with some teachers integrating student input into their lectures. Outside the classroom, it is not unusual to see faculty members visiting in the residence halls or chatting with students in their offices. And, cautions a senior, "If a faculty member doesn't see you in class for awhile, don't be surprised to receive a phone call from him or her!"

In particular, students like the approach of faculty in the business and history departments. The business professors "tell it like it is," drawing on their own personal experiences in the present-day world of work, and not just on what the books say. History is especially impressive, notes an elementary education major, "with its in-depth curriculum, outstanding teachers, and strong tutorial program." English, criminal justice, psychology, mathematics, and elementary education (with a very strong reading component) also offer well-constructed curricula of depth and breadth, and demanding professors who expect and give a lot. The small size of the biology department "leads to more hands-on and one-on-one instruction," observes a major. Challenging nursing classes are offered through nearby Blessing-Rieman College of Nursing.

There is no foreign language major, with beginning and intermediate-level courses only in Spanish. A minor in Spanish is offered, and a contract major in this language can be arranged. Degree programs in arts education, arts management, and studio art, in electrical and mechanical engineering, and in music and business studies are no longer available to students not enrolled as of the 2005–2006 school year.

Facilities: In Quincy's highly rated library, serious studiers head upstairs to the silent second floor, while those with other aims—to do research, study together, or simply socialize—congregate on the main floor. Some students wish the library stayed open later than 11 p.m. every night except Friday and Saturday, when it closes at 5 p.m.

Quincy is steadily working to upgrade its technology around campus. Students have access to 190 PCs spread among 9 computer labs. Many labs are open until 1 a.m. For added convenience, the college strongly recommends that students have their own PC-compatible personal computers on campus since network connections are available in all residence halls.

Special programs: Students wishing to gain a better understanding of the university's Franciscan heritage may participate in the 12-day Assisi Experience Program that enables students to journey to such sites in Italy as Assisi, Vatican City, and Rome. Through membership in the College Consortium for International Studies, Quincy students also may opt to participate in any of 40+ academic programs in 27 countries as well as special programs offered with Regent's College in London and with the Loyola University Rome Center. Closer to home a business certificate program enables students majoring in any of the traditional arts or sciences to complete concurrently 30 semester hours of specified course work in accounting, business, and economics.

Campus life: Seventy percent of the students reside on the 75-acre campus, spread over 3 sites along 18th Street in Quincy and connected by shuttle bus. As a security measure, roads intersecting the main campus have been closed off, a precaution that has made the campus feel not only more insulated but more unified as well. Quincy's first fraternity was added in the 1994–95 school year and attracts 4% of the men as members. The first sorority, which was organized during the 1997–98 school year, with a second added in 2000–2001, together include 11% of the women. While Greek activities are becoming more popular, many students still party at the senior houses or junior suites though increased efforts by Illinois State Police to cut down on underage drinking during fall 2005 have curbed some of the celebrating. Students over 21 typically hop off-campus for a night on the town. A number of students also simply leave campus for the weekend. There are regular daily Masses and a special Mass for students on Sunday nights; none is required, but many students attend.

Quincy fields 13 intercollegiate athletic teams, 7 for men, 6 for women, but here soccer reigns, with its own 2000-seat stadium. After 11 NAIA national championships, the Hawks men's soccer team now competes along with Quincy's other sports in NCAA Division II. Football returned to campus in 1986 after a 33-year absence and has gained in performance and enthusiasm; men's and women's basketball consistently draws big crowds. Sixty-two percent of the men and 40% of the women participate in the 22 intramural sports, split evenly between the 2 sexes. Faculty and administrators field their own teams. A new Health and Fitness Center that opened in spring 2002 provides sufficient court space and fitness equipment to keep everybody in shape.

In Quincy (pop. 50,000), students seeking a peaceful change of scenery need go only 18 blocks to find the Mississippi River. For a longer journey they can travel 17 miles downriver to Hannibal, the hometown of river chronicler Mark Twain; to St. Louis, 2 hours away; or even to Chicago, 4 ½ hours distant. Larger campuses, such as those of the universities of Illinois, Iowa, and Missouri, are within a 3-hour drive.

Cost cutters: Quincy has long found ways to make its private-school education more affordable. The contributed services of the Franciscan friars along with gift assistance have helped to keep down costs over the years and enabled Quincy to achieve its goal of meeting students' financial needs. As a result, 99% of the 2005–2006 freshmen and 95% of the continuing students received some aid; 82% of the freshmen and 89% of the continuing students were on need-based assistance. The average freshman award for a student with financial need included a need-based scholarship or grant averaging $2000 and need-based self-help aid such as loans and jobs averaging $4625. A non-need-based athletic scholarship for first-year students averaged $9400; other non-need-based awards and scholarships averaged $6365. Average debt of a 2005 graduate was $17,000. For high-scoring freshmen, a wide range of academic achievement scholarships are available. All students automatically are considered for merit awards, based on their standardized test scores and GPAs. The awards range in value from $1000 to $10,000. Art, music, and athletic awards also are available.

Rate of return: Sixty-nine percent of entering freshmen return for the sophomore year. Thirty-seven percent graduate in 4 years, 52% in 5 years, and 55% in 6 years.

Payoff: Elementary education was the top-choice major among 2005 graduates, comprising 14% of the class, followed by nursing at 13% and marketing at 7%. Twenty percent of 2004 graduates enrolled in graduate or professional school. Seventy-five percent accepted jobs soon after graduating, many as accountants with the major accounting firms, registered nurses in regional healthcare facilities, and teachers in public schools. Most stayed in the Midwest. Thirty-eight companies and organizations recruited on campus in the 2004–2005 school year.

Bottom line: Quincy is a family university: many students follow their parents, brothers, and sisters to the campus. Once there, they find themselves members of a supportive community where students enjoy close relationships with peers and professors. Says a senior, who entered 4 years before on academic probation: "Students here don't fall through the cracks!"

Shimer College

Waukegan, Illinois 60085

Setting: Suburban
Control: Private
Undergraduate enrollment: 52 men, 41 women
Graduate enrollment: None
Student/faculty ratio: 8:1
Freshman profile: SAT/ACT scores: NA; class rank data: NA
Faculty profile: 94% Ph.D.'s
Tuition and fees: $19,525
Room and board: $7000

Freshman financial aid: 90%; average scholarship or grant: $4000
Campus jobs: 55%; average earnings: $1800/year
Application deadline: July 31
Financial aid deadline: July 30 (Apr. 15 priority)
Admissions information: (847) 623-8400; (800) 215-7173
e-mail: info@shimer.edu
web site: www.shimer.edu

When students come to Shimer College from 14 states and 4 foreign countries, many are seeking a type of education and learning community most only dreamed existed. Few of the undergraduates were happy in the high school world of cliques, clubs, proms, homecoming, and athletic competition. Their minds felt limited by lectures and textbooks and in classmates interested more in the final grade than the substance of the subject. Enter Shimer College, with fewer than 100 full-time undergraduates, seminars with no more than 12 participants, assigned reading from original texts rather than textbooks, and faculty who serve as discussion leaders rather than lecturers. Says a satisfied senior: "We are a collection of lost souls who find each other here . . . I have been excited by the extent to which Shimer encourages intellectual freedom, fosters the continuation of the 'great conversation' and gives room for young adults to think, read, write, create, discuss, share, work, live, and love together in their trying search for knowledge. I am in no way disappointed." Notes another senior: "Shimer's pedagogical choice to facilitate learning through discussion rather than lecture has allowed me to grow into a more articulate and more thoughtful person." Adds a third senior: "Be prepared to be surprised."

Additional surprises may be in store for students following an announcement in January 2006 that Shimer will expand its operations to the main campus of Illinois Institute of Technology in Chicago beginning in fall 2006. While the college is expected to remain an independent institution and continue certain programs and services on the Waukegan campus, officials said the move would give Shimer students access to expanded facilities and services they had not had before, such as athletic facilities, health services, library services, and residential and dining options.

Student body: Shimer students see themselves as an eclectic group of individuals, for the most part quite liberal in their politics and committed to social change. Says a Westerner: "Democrats are generally considered corporate-friendly conservative by most Shimer students." Most are unpretentious, considerate, and casual but highly creative in their thinking. "There are no outsiders here," says a freshman. Continues the Westerner: "Rarely would students who associate themselves with pop culture have an interest in Shimer, but if they did, they would not be made to feel out of place here." Three-quarters of the undergraduates are from Illinois. Seventy-five percent are graduates of public schools. All but 12% of the undergraduates also are Caucasian-American, 5% are African-American, 2% Asian-American, and 1% Native American. Four percent are foreign nationals. The academic atmosphere, while communal rather than competitive, is nonetheless intense. "We are dedicated to learning and we do it together," says an Easterner. Cautions a freshman: "Discussion-based classes can be intimidating but they are full of respectful candor. The serious nature of Shimer's academics makes it equivalent to an Ivy but far less competitive, i.e., not at all." Adds a senior: "If you love to read and hate to be told what to think, you would fit in here perfectly."

Academics: When Shimer College first opened as a campus in Mount Carroll, Illinois, in 1853, its founders, Frances Wood Shimer and Cinderella Gregory, envisioned an environment in which students were admitted based on their capability, rather than their educational background. Nearly 100 years later, in 1950, the college adopted its distinctive curriculum that uses original sources and discussion-based classes, with a heavy reliance on the development of such skills as thought, speech, and writing. In 1978 the college reorganized under a new administration composed mostly of faculty and moved to Waukegan, 25 miles north of Chicago.

The required Shimer core curriculum consists of course sequences in 4 areas of study: the Humanities, levels 1–4; the Natural Sciences, levels 1–4; the Social Sciences, levels 1–4; and Integrative Studies, levels 1, 2, 5, and 6. Altogether, the core makes up 85 of the 125 semester hours needed to graduate with a bachelor of arts degree. All of the basic core courses, which are the first 2 levels of each of the 4 curriculum areas, are taken early in a student's academic program and consist of discussion-driven, faculty-led seminars averaging 7 participants, always drawing on original sources for the course content. In Humanities I, for example, concerning art and music, students read such texts as Plato's *Ion* and Copland's, *What to Listen for in Music*. In Integrative Studies II, the Nature and Creation of Mathematics, students read Euclid's *Elements*, Vol. 1, and Einstein's *Relativity*.

At the end of the basic core courses, students must take and pass a comprehensive examination demonstrating their skills in analysis, logic, and rhetoric before proceeding to a set of more advanced area core courses consisting of levels 3 and 4 in the humanities, natural sciences, and social sciences. At the end of this course work, students take an area comprehensive examination in their chosen major area of study, either the humanities, the natural sciences, or the social sciences. The majors never become more narrowly defined than that. A final level of the core curriculum, taken in a student's last full year of study, consists of Integrative Studies Levels 5 and 6, focused on the History and Philosophy of Western Civilization, stretching from the ancient world to the present. All students must also complete a senior thesis in their area of interest with an option to provide an oral defense. Observes a junior: "Our core curriculum means that every student takes the same 16 courses as every other student over the course of their stay at Shimer. This results in an academic conversation that never stops. Or rather, you will often hear Shimer students state explicitly that class will not be discussed for such-and-such an amount of time in this or that room." Undergraduates who wish also may request individual tutorials and electives enrolling up to 3 students in highly specialized subjects.

The success of the Shimer curriculum depends a great deal on the knowledge and skill of the faculty discussion leaders, who receive accolades ranging from "fantastic" to "brilliant." Fifteen of the faculty members are full-time; 3 are adjuncts; a fourth are women. Professors are regularly addressed by their first names. Says a humanities major: "By your second year, all faculty members are your friends and your mentors." Most administrators take courses or teach electives in areas where they have expertise. Says a major in the natural sciences and social sciences: "The faculty has a great respect for the intelligence and integrity of students, which results in a respectful, mutually encouraging environment for this dialogue community... The teacher (also) becomes a participant and is just as prone to flashes of inspiration and epiphany as students."

Because Shimer's academic program is not broken into specific departments, and because many professors guide seminars across several disciplines, students say it is hard to rate one broad area over another. A lack of up-to-date equipment for years had forced the natural sciences to focus more on theory than experimentation. That should change with Shimer's planned expansion to the Chicago campus of Illinois Institute of Technology. One benefit of the move would be to give students access to IIT's strong science and technological programs and equipment, something the Waukegan campus lacked.

Facilities: The move to IIT's Chicago campus should provide expanded library services to Shimer students, although as a humanities major noted: "Most papers at Shimer require that we not use outside sources, so the library is more for our own enjoyment." Heretofore, the strength of Shimer's library services was its professional librarian recently hired to assist students in their research through an on-campus "virtual library" being funded by a Department of Education Title III grant. Observes a senior: "The librarian is always ready and willing to assist with research needs, to the point of checking things out from local libraries for students and faculty." Shimer's own collection of 35,000 volumes was recently moved to a site on the Waukegan campus from its previous location at the Waukegan Public Library. The collection of the Illinois Institute of Technology consists of nearly 1 million largely technical items, although most Shimer students may never need the bulk of it.

Most students had found the main computer lab and the labs in the residence halls, all of which were open around the clock, generally sufficient to meet their needs. The Waukegan campus also offers wireless access throughout the buildings and grounds that students with laptops especially have enjoyed.

Special programs: Students who wish may study abroad at Oxford University in England. The Oxford program consists of Shimer core curriculum courses, taught by Shimer faculty, as well as 1-on-1 tutorials taught by Oxford tutors focusing on a specialized subject selected by each student. Internships in various fields can also be arranged.

Campus life: Fifty percent of Shimer's students have resided on the 3-acre Waukegan campus (most in dorm rooms that have their own bathrooms and kitchens), and 95% of the residents usually stuck around on the weekends to partake of all that makes Shimer's out-of-classroom life distinct. Poetry readings, community dinners, screenings of art and classic films, and impromptu discussions of various philosophical and ideological issues have all been staples of the Shimer weekend. Chess tournaments, informal boxing matches, and pick-up soccer games have proved popular as well. Not surprisingly, there are no intercollegiate or intramural sports, although the college provides a gymnasium for faculty and students to play basketball, volleyball, and other indoor sports. The college also had an arrangement in which students could use facilities at the local YMCA. Occasional theft from college offices has been about the only crime of note, although motion-sensitive lights and alarm systems have served as deterrents. Students also have made it a habit to walk in groups after dark or call friends with cars to taxi them between campus and locations off campus. "The neighborhood around Waukegan sometimes gets rough," says a Southerner, "but the city has been improving."

Major policy decisions concerning the college are made by the Assembly, the school's governing body, which is comprised of the wider Shimer College community. Each person, student, faculty member, or administrator has the same single vote, and nearly all committees are made up of faculty, administrators, and students.

The city of Chicago, an hour by train from Waukegan, and its suburbs have offered all the getaway most students needed.

Cost cutters: Ninety percent of all undergraduates received some form of financial aid in the 2005–2006 school year. All of the aid was based at least in part on financial need. The average scholarship or need-based grant totaled $4000; need-based self-help aid such as loans and job earnings averaged $2625. Among 2005 graduates, the average debt was $25,000. A number of scholarships and other forms of assistance are available. High school valedictorians and National Merit Finalists are considered for William Rainey Harper Scholarships that pay the full amount of tuition, books, and room for 4 years.

Rate of return: The humanities concentration was the most popular of the 3 major areas of study taken by members of the Class of 2005, claiming 55% of the graduates. Thirty-five percent earned degrees in the social sciences; 10% in the natural sciences.

Payoff: In recent years, 80% of the freshmen who entered Shimer returned for a second year. Fifty percent graduate in 4 years, 53% in 5 years, 58% in 6. A fifth of Shimer graduates go directly to graduate and professional schools. Shimer ranks first among liberal arts institutions and third among all U.S. colleges and universities (behind Cal Tech and Harvey Mudd College) in the percentage of graduates who go on to earn Ph.Ds. Nearly 23% of Shimer alumni are employed in education, from elementary schools through college. Seven percent are lawyers; 7% work in computer software. Others are employed in more than 40 sectors of the economy from consulting to philanthropy, from religious organizations to marketing.

Bottom line: Shimer is for students who found the typical high school lecture courses lacking and who are willing to delve through complex original texts and contribute to lively discussions on a wide range of subjects. Says a graduating senior: "I have gained as a writer and I have gained knowledge about things I never dreamed of knowing. My analytical skills, my comprehension, my communicative skills, my creativity, my ability to co-inquire with dignity and grace, all of these things have improved at Shimer." A senior-to-be put it more bluntly: "Shimer is for those who prefer digestion to regurgitation."

University of Illinois at Chicago

Chicago, Illinois 60680

Setting: Urban
Control: Public
Undergraduate enrollment: 6344 men, 7389 women
Graduate enrollment: 2909 men, 3572 women
Student/faculty ratio: 16:1
Freshman profile: 10% scored above 28 on the ACT; 10% scored 27–28; 26% 24–26; 27% 21–23; 27% below 21. 47% graduated in top fifth of high school class; 82% in upper two-fifths.
Faculty profile: 84% Ph.D.'s

Tuition and fees: $8302 in-state; $20,692 out-of-state
Room and board: $7954
Freshman financial aid: 57%; average scholarship or grant: $8860 need-based
Campus jobs: NA; average earnings: NA
Application deadline: Jan. 15
Financial aid deadline: Mar. 1
Admissions information: (312) 996-4350
  e-mail: uicadmit@uic.edu
  web site: www.uic.edu/depts/oar

In a city described by poet Carl Sandburg as "hog-butcher for the world," you don't expect a lot of TLC, especially at the University of Illinois at Chicago, which enrolls more than 13,700 full-time undergraduates, the vast majority of whom are commuters. Though life at UIC can be tough, with a lot of the bureaucratic red tape and fast-paced impersonality characteristic of large urban schools, Chicago's major public university has much to offer besides a great tuition rate. Its varied curriculum equals that of its better known, academically excellent sister in Urbana-Champaign; all but 16% of its faculty in a recent year held doctorates or terminal degrees in their fields; and despite its large and hurried population, the university makes decent attempts to provide a vigorous campus life. Over a recent 2-year period, 5 acres of concrete were torn out and replaced with grass and trees. Housing for 1000 additional students has been constructed since 2001. Observes a senior industrial design major: "It is incredible what you can learn going to a university with such a diversity of students in a big city like Chicago."

Student body: Racially and ethnically, UIC is extremely diverse. Less than half the undergraduates are Caucasian-American; 24% are Asian-American students, 17% Hispanic, 9% African-American, and 1% foreign nationals from 52 countries. Among the largest campus clubs are the associations of African-American, Latin, Asian, and Pakistani students. All but 3% of the students call Illinois home, with the vast majority coming from the Chicago metropolitan area. In fact, 1 of every 57 adult Chicagoans is a UIC graduate. With 42 states represented, a third of the out-of-staters are also drawn from the Midwest. In a recent year, less than half of the undergraduates were of traditional college age, with nearly a third between 23 and 27 years old. Seventy-nine percent attended public schools. A majority are first-generation college students from middle-class working families. Many know very little about college before entering and are mainly focused on getting good grades. "Since most undergraduates are commuters and there are few activities over the weekend, students tend to throw themselves into studying," observes a junior from the city. Competition in some of the sciences can, in fact, become quite cutthroat. With so many students moving on and off campus, it can be difficult to forge friendships, so undergraduates seek companionship in the clubs related to their racial or ethnic origins or professional interests.

Academics: UIC, which turned 60 in 2006, offers 88 undergraduate programs, 86 at the master's level, and 58 doctoral degree programs. Undergraduate studies are spread throughout 8 schools and colleges; the graduate-level medical and dental colleges and the School of Public Health also are part of UIC. The academic calendar follows a semester cycle. Entering freshmen can expect to share some general-education courses like Biology of Populations and Communities with 500 classmates, although even the largest lectures offer smaller discussion groups led by teaching assistants, and quite a few upper-level classes can be considerably smaller. Most courses average 30 to 70 students.

In addition to an English composition requirement and a class in cultural diversity, UIC students must complete a minimum of 6 semester hours each in the humanities, social sciences, and natural sciences, with another 6 in 1 or more of these 3 areas. While these are the basic requirements, some colleges stipulate a bit more and provide a list of approved courses that can be taken to satisfy these mandates.

The total university faculty recently included 1811 full-time and 757 part-time members. Among the full-time faculty, 965 taught undergraduates as did 222 of the part-time members. Sixty-four percent were men. Fourteen percent of the introductory courses in a recent year were taught, at least in part, by graduate students. For the most part, faculty members earn students' admiration and respect for their academic and professional accomplishments, though a number seem more involved in the status of their own research than the progress of their students. Says a computer engineering major: "Much of the faculty seems just to worry about giving out a grade and stuffing input into students' brains, but there are others who are highly stimulating and seem really to care about the students' education." An example of the latter is an energetic professor of physics, named the 1995 U.S. Professor of the Year by the Carnegie Foundation for the Advancement of Teaching.

The 3 professionally oriented colleges of Architecture and the Arts, Business Administration, and Engineering are distinguished by outstanding faculty with much experience outside the university and terrific equipment that seems to arrive in new batches on a regular basis. Architecture insists that students apply their book knowledge to real-life projects in the city. Programs in mathematics and the health sciences, influenced by the highly regarded College of Medicine, also are especially challenging. The department of philosophy has been ranked among the top 5 in the nation. Nursing and political science draw respect as well.

Students interested in journalism decry the lack of a journalism school, let alone a separate major, at a university located in the nation's third largest city. Music takes a back seat in the quality of its program and the students it attracts to the more established programs at nearby DePaul and Northwestern universities. English and psychology are among those disciplines that rely more heavily on graduate students, some good, some not so good, to teach lower-level classes.

Facilities: In addition to the main university library, which is named for former Chicago mayor Richard J. Daley, there are smaller ones for architecture and art, health sciences, mathematics, and science. Together, they hold nearly 2.3 million volumes and more than 39,000 periodicals, accessible to students through the Library User Information Service—LUIS, for short. Although students have few complaints about the extensive holdings, some feel frustrated in their search for materials, often running to a library that LUIS indicates has a particular volume only to find that it does not. The remodeled Daley library has become a much more appealing place to study, although noisy and crowded at times; when a student needs a change of scenery or some material UIC does not have, the Harold Washington city library is well worth a visit.

Computers, however, are one resource of which the university does not have enough, at least in the opinion of waiting students. Though 1100 workstations are located in about 15 laboratories in classroom buildings, libraries, and residence halls, students say only a few labs are open 24 hours a day and the number available is insufficient for a student body of UIC's size. A wireless network is available in public areas across campus. The university strongly recommends that students have personal computers.

Special programs: Undergraduates may study abroad as part of more than 60 programs in 30 countries. A Summer Bridge program, sponsored by the architectural college, helps minority students make a successful transition from high school to college by participating in a 6-week minisemester that combines instruction in various disciplines with orientation sessions in college-survival strategies, plus work experience in a Chicago-based architectural firm. A similar 13-week Freshman Success Seminar provides instruction in such skills as time and money management and understanding academic culture to new students university-wide. High school seniors who know what type of advanced study they want to pursue past their undergraduate years at UIC can look into Guaranteed Professional Program Admissions. This program guarantees a limited number of incoming freshmen a seat in the UIC professional or graduate program of their choice, provided they qualify upon completion of their bachelor's degree at UIC. Applicants should have a minimum ACT score of 28 or a minimum SAT math and critical reading score of 1240 and a high school class rank in the top 15% of their graduating class.

Campus life: UIC is very much Commuter U. Only 12% of all undergraduates live on the 240-acre campus, which is actually 2 clusters of buildings separated by a residential neighborhood. One cluster, where the College of Medicine and the medical center complex are located, has classrooms and labs largely related to the health sciences. The second, which is the general campus most undergraduates frequent, is still marked by notable amounts of "deathly" gray concrete, although the university's recent efforts to plant trees, grass, and flowers have made the environment look a bit brighter and greener. Because the campus is located in Chicago's near west side, just outside "the Loop," as the downtown area is called, security is usually tight and emergency phones are plentiful, though students say problems have been minor.

Since most commuting students participate in no weekend events, campus life after 5 on Friday pretty much depends on the enthusiasm of the few hardy souls left, who quickly develop a camaraderie with other residents. Interest in the 5 local and 6 national fraternities and 10 national sororities is small, just 10% of the undergraduates. In addition to some 220 registered student organizations, the university offers 2 student unions that are ranked third in the country in terms of size and facilities.

Resident students are also the primary backers of the 8 men's and 8 women's intercollegiate sports teams. The Flames, so called because the eastern edge of the campus is not far from where legend says Mrs. O'Leary's cow kicked over a lantern in 1871 and started the Great Chicago Fire, play in NCAA Division I. Basketball draws the most enthusiastic support, with a pep club called the Hoopers providing organized cheering. The 24-year-old Pavilion seats 12,000 and houses basketball and soccer games, concerts, convocations, and other events. Fifteen intramural sports are open to men, 14 to women.

Most weekends, UIC students in search of excitement catch the rapid transit to enjoy all that the Windy City has to offer.

Cost cutters: Fifty-seven percent of the first-year students and 67% of the rest received financial aid in the 2005–2006 school year. For 44% of the first-year students, the aid was need-based. No corresponding figure is available for the continuing students. The average freshman award for a student with financial need included a need-based scholarship or grant averaging $8860, and need-based self-help aid such as loans and job earnings averaging $3518. Non-need-based athletic scholarships averaged $11,117. The average 2005 graduate left with debts of $16,800. Tuition waivers are provided to needy undergraduates unable to qualify for grants from the state of Illinois. Along with scholarship monies awarded by the university and its various colleges, the Scholarship Association for UIC, a voluntary organization composed of faculty, staff, retirees, and friends of the university, provides about 100 awards to current UIC students. Cooperative programs are available in 5 colleges.

Rate of return: Seventy-seven percent of the freshmen return for the sophomore year. Twenty percent go on to graduate in 4 years; 42% in 5 years; 50% in 6. While figures remain low, graduation rates at all 3 levels are up at least 10% from 4 years before.

Payoff: Business and marketing at 20%, biological and life sciences at 11%, and engineering at 10% were the 3 most popular majors for 2005 graduates. Most alumni remain in the Chicago area, finding jobs in a wide range of fields. One hundred seventy-five companies and other organizations recruited on campus in the 2004–2005 school year. Of those who pursue advanced degrees (less than a fifth of the graduates in a recent year), many remain at UIC and enroll in the colleges of Medicine, Dentistry, or Pharmacy, or enter other highly sought graduate-level programs in the health sciences.

Bottom line: UIC is not for the faint-hearted nor for those seeking a school with lots of spirit (though the university does have its own fight song, entitled "Fire Up, Flames!"). Notes a senior from Chicago: "Students who are not motivated or who are easily frustrated or stressed should not come here. At UIC, a student is basically on his or her own and needs inner strength to succeed."

University of Illinois at Urbana-Champaign

Urbana, Illinois 61801

Setting: Small city
Control: Public
Undergraduate enrollment: 15,948 men, 13,957 women
Graduate enrollment: 4815 men, 9042 women
Student/faculty ratio: 12:1
Freshman profile: 14% scored over 700 on SAT I verbal; 42% scored 600–700; 33% 500–599; 11% below 500. 39% scored over 700 on SAT I math; 41% scored 600–700; 17% 500–599; 3% below 500. 33% scored above 28 on the ACT; 23% scored 27–28; 28% 24–26; 11% 21–23; 5% below 21. 47% graduated in top tenth of high school class; 76% in upper fifth.

Faculty profile: 88% Ph.D.'s
Tuition and fees: $8624 in-state; $22,710 out-of-state
Room and board: $7176
Freshman financial aid: 65%; average scholarship or grant: $3609 need-based; $1972 non-need-based
Campus jobs: 35%; average earnings: $1772/year
Application deadline: Priority: Nov. 15; regular: Jan. 2
Financial aid deadline: Mar. 15 (priority)
Admissions information: (217) 333-0302
e-mail: undergraduate@admissions.uiuc.edu
web site: www.uiuc.edu

If at first the idea of a school where 89% of the undergraduates come from a single state, and many of the rest are from the surrounding region, sounds a bit limited—well, there's nothing provincial about the University of Illinois at Urbana-Champaign. Although just 3300 of the university's 29,900 full-time undergraduates are from outside Illinois, and about 90% of these out-of-staters are midwesterners, the university boasts a reputation for academic excellence that stretches coast to coast and draws students from all 50 states and 121 foreign countries. Its library system has the fifth largest collection among universities in the United States behind Harvard, Yale and the universities of California at Berkeley and Los Angeles. Two professors were named Nobel Laureates, for medicine and physics, in 2003; distinguished alumni include 11 Nobel Laureates and 18 Pulitzer Prize winners. Its Greek system claims to be the biggest, the intramural sports program also one of the largest. There are more than 150 undergraduate programs of study and 1000 registered student organizations to fit just about any interest. For most of its 139 years, the university's first priority has been to serve the people of the state, and what it continues to serve them, as well as the few lucky nonresidents who get seats at the table, is one of the most varied educational dishes around. It is a school, in the words of a recent alumna, "that a high school senior should dream about attending. You cannot get a better education for the money."

Student body: Geographic homogeneity aside, most students consider their campus to be quite diverse. And while this university is much less so than its sister institution in Chicago, the composition has changed significantly over the past 15 years. Asian-American students account for 11% of the population, followed by African-American students at 7%, Hispanics at 6%, and Native Americans at less than 0.5%. Foreign students make up about 12% of the enrollment. In a recent year, 85% were graduates of public schools. As a whole, the group is fairly conservative (though liberals maintain there are sufficient "havens" in like-minded student clubs), and many find their initial fears of fitting into a campus of more than 40,000 undergraduate and graduate students and 7900 faculty and staff to be much worse than the actual experience. Observes a New Englander: "Going to a school with 40,000 students and not feeling like a number has been a positive experience. All extremes and everything in between can be found here." While the university atmosphere is rather competitive, given that 96% of the students graduated in the top two-fifths of their high school classes, majors in engineering and business rate highest on the intensity scale. By comparison, some liberal arts majors seem positively laid back; as a result there is a pretty healthy balance between hitting the books and tossing them aside.

Academics: The University of Illinois awards degrees through the doctorate with postbaccalaureate programs in more than 100 fields. Undergraduates can earn degrees through 8 colleges and one institute. Postgraduate programs only are offered through the colleges of Law, Medicine, and Veterinary Medicine, the schools of Social Work and Library and Information Science and the Institute of Labor and Industrial Relations. The academic year is divided into 2 semesters. Average class size for undergraduates varies by school. In the College of Fine and Applied Arts, for example, average class size can be 16; in the College of Business, 45. The introductory lectures that many freshmen take can soar past 750 students (Environmental Biology has had 752), although discussion sections generally have no more than 40. The big classes are what students swap war stories about, while the administration points out that 74% of all undergraduate classes in a recent year had fewer than 30 students and 44% peaked at 20. A Freshman Discovery Program provides courses of no more than 20 per class with tenure-track faculty to help foster greater interaction between first-year students and professors.

All students are required to fulfill at least 6 hours each in the arts and humanities, the social and behavioral sciences, and the natural sciences and technology, and to complete 4 hours of basic composition and either the third or fourth level (depending on the college) of a language other than the student's primary language. Students also must take another writing-intensive course, classes in quantitative reasoning, and 2 courses in Western/comparative cultures, and nonWestern/U.S. minority cultures. In addition, each college has its own set of core requirements.

Four hundred thirty of the 2701 faculty members teach part-time. All but 4 of the part-timers and 95% of the full-time faculty teach undergraduates. A third are women. Students come hoping to rub elbows with faculty on the cutting edge of research and publishing. Six of the 12 Nobel laureates who have served on the faculty received the Nobel Prize after leaving Illinois; one late professor emeritus was the only person ever to win the Nobel Prize in physics twice. Ten scientists received the National Medal of Science while on the faculty. With the vestiges of such brilliance in the air around them, many freshmen are taken aback by the limited student-faculty interaction that first year. Half of the introductory sections are taught by graduate students, many of whom students find easier to relate to, and others whose limited English skills make them difficult to understand.

Although in-depth contact in the early years usually still depends on the initiative of the individual student, the university has developed several programs that provide a setting for greater interaction. Along with the Freshman Discovery Program, 5 different living/learning centers provide enriched academic programs in the residence halls. The campus honor program, which admits 125 new freshmen annually, also helps to foster closer student-faculty relationships in small, intensive classes. There is something to be said, though, for the thrill of having award-winning professors at the helm of undergraduate lecture classes. Says a junior: "If we are not learning from a well-read book written directly by our professors, we are finding references to their work in the books we are reading." Once past the first year, many students find faculty members who are happy to meet with undergraduates and to share their expertise; others, unfortunately, are rarely available when students seek them out for help.

The College of Engineering, particularly the departments of electrical and computer engineering and computer science, boasts strong faculty with facilities to match, and extensive research opportunities for students. "Classes are quite hands-on," says an electrical engineering major. Faculty advising is well-structured and attentive, and student clubs associated with the college are extremely active and provide a strong sense of community. Graduates from these programs are known to command impressive starting salaries. Likewise, the College of Business, especially the accounting program, gives students a great return on their tuition investment. Admission into the College of Education is very selective and once accepted, says a major, students experience "a high level of commitment to excellence." Numerous programs in the College of Agricultural, Consumer, and Environmental Sciences, chemistry and psychology in the College of Liberal Arts and Sciences, and the bachelor's degree program in architecture in the College of Fine and Applied Arts, also are considered outstanding.

Other of the fine arts programs, as well as many of the humanities departments in the College of Liberal Arts and Sciences and the kinesiology and community health department in the College of Applied Life Studies, could use more funding. Students say more needs to be done to make many of the large programs in the College of Liberal Arts and Sciences more personal. Homework in some Spanish classes, for example, has been graded by a computer system. Says a sophomore: "I received no feedback on assignments and I struggled to improve. I also developed a discouraged attitude due to the lack of personal attention and feedback." Spanish, as well as Italian and Portuguese, sociology, and history, are among those disciplines that students have maintained could use additional faculty members.

Facilities: The University Library, with the main undergraduate and graduate structure and 41 departmental facilities around campus, holds more than 10 million volumes, 6 million tapes, records, slides, maps, and laser discs, and almost 90,000 current periodicals. A helpful staff and a finely tuned computer research system, along with a comfortable set of walking shoes, helps to make one of the largest public university library collections in the nation quite accessible to undergraduates. As for studying, one junior notes: "The libraries here are as different in atmosphere as the local bars: some are places for research, some for hard-core studying, and some for just basic socializing"—maybe even better than a bar. Grainger Engineering Library, which opened in 1994, is the largest engineering library in the country, and, says a political science major, "has some GREAT study areas. It is absolutely beautiful," as well as silent and technologically advanced. Some students, like this psychology major, find the main undergraduate library a bit dreary for studying because of its location, 2 stories underground. Explains the junior: "It's right next to the Morrow Plots, the world's oldest experimental cornfield. It's underground because they didn't want to throw shade on the corn. You can tell we go to school in central Illinois!"

At the research level, few universities can match Illinois's computer expertise. The university is home to the National Center for Supercomputing Applications where Mosaic™ web browsing software, which spawned exponential growth in the use of the World Wide Web, was first developed. In 1989 the university opened the Beckman Institute for Advanced Science and Technology, where interdisciplinary research is conducted on human and artificial intelligence. Though few undergraduates actually set foot in the institute, all point to it as an example of Illinois's academic stature.

More to the immediate benefit of undergraduates, an expenditure of about $4 million in recent years has made Illinois one of the most computer-accessible campuses around. More than 2300 computers are located in classrooms, general and departmental laboratories, and residence halls across campus. Sites generally are open until 2 a.m., with several available around the clock. All student dormitory rooms also are wired for computers, and numerous "e-mail only" kiosks around campus help to cut down on the number of lab computers being used solely for message-checking. Wireless access is available throughout the library, major populated areas in the student union, and many other buildings across campus. The university strongly recommends that undergraduates have their own personal computers.

Special programs: Study-abroad options in 58 countries abound for Illinois students of all interests. Architecture students can spend a year in France; programs in engineering are offered in nearly a dozen countries from Brazil to South Africa. Summer parliamentary and other political internships are an option in London. A term in Washington, D.C. is possible, too. Opportunities for leadership development are extensive in many academic departments.

Campus life: Just 18% of the Illinois students live in university residence halls on the 705-acre central campus, although all single undergraduates are required to live in some kind of university-certified housing until they turn 21 or have earned 30 semester hours of credit. Fraternity and sorority houses are popular options for the fifth of the men and women who go Greek. Greek life at Illinois claims to be the biggest system in the country with 56 national fraternities and 32 national sororities. Views about the Greeks are mixed among independents, some of whom find them elitist and feel left out of events as a result of their prominence, and others who find plenty to do without them. Many students dislike what 1 sophomore describes as a "clear division" between the 2 groups. Music lovers can participate in, or simply enjoy the performances of, about a dozen different choral groups, 3 concert bands plus the much-loved Marching Illini, 3 orchestras, 4 big-band jazz bands and seemingly countless small ensembles. The 1000 registered student organizations cover nearly every possible political, professional, ethnic, religious, and social interest imaginable. More than 1300 students are involved in various service projects through VIP, Volunteer Illini Projects. Armed robberies posed a problem at the start of a recent school year, but a variety of services were put in place to keep campus crime in check. Among them were a free Nite-ride service for those needing transportation anytime after dark, and a Whistle Stop program that provides whistles to women to help prevent assaults. One-touch emergency phones around campus and student security officers on bikes also make students feel safer.

Big Ten football, with its tailgating and pre- and postgame barbecues and parties, is probably the biggest NCAA Division I sport, played in a stadium that seats 69,000. Big Ten basketball games that fill 16,500 seats in Assembly Hall have seen fan support rise dramatically with their recent success in league play. In 2003, the men's team won its first Big Ten Title outright in 52 years. In 2005, the team won 37 games, an NCAA record for victories in a season, only to lose to the University of North Carolina in the Division I National Championship game. Men's teams are fielded in 9 other intercollegiate sports; women's teams in a total of 12, with women's volleyball the biggest attraction. Sixty-five percent of the men but just 17% of the women participate in one of the nation's largest intramural sports programs, offering 22 sports for men and for women. Not surprisingly, the intramural sports and recreation building is one of the most spacious of its kind in the world.

The adjoining cities of Champaign and Urbana have a combined population of 100,000. University-owned Allerton Park, located just 30 minutes from campus, offers a restful getaway spot neither too close nor too far away. Longer treks take students to Chicago, 140 miles north, or to St. Louis, Missouri, about 170 miles southwest. On-campus cultural escapes also are possible through Assembly Hall, which hosts concerts and Broadway productions as well as basketball games, the Krannert Art Museum, the Natural History Museum, and, as of fall 2002, the new Spurlock Museum, displaying artifacts from around the world and throughout history. Adds a student from the Southwest: "The vast cornfields are definitely not exciting, but their peaceful serenity is rather appealing when campus stress is high."

Cost cutters: In the 2005–2006 school year, 65% of the freshmen and 60% of the continuing students received financial aid. Thirty-eight percent of both groups were on need-based assistance. The average freshman award consisted of a $3609 need-based scholarship or grant, and $1781 in self-help aid such as loans and job earnings. The average non-need-based athletic scholarship averaged $8032; other non-need-based awards and scholarships averaged $1972. The average 2005 graduate left with debts of $15,536. In the past, there has not been much special scholarship help for out-of-staters trying to counter Illinois's rising nonresident tuition rates, although increased efforts to recruit and admit more out-of-state students are helping to bring more nonresident financial aid. Still, the majority of scholarship awards remain restricted to state residents and require both high scholastic achievement and financial need. University colleges and academic departments award most merit-based scholarships. A variety of work options from college work-study to extensive opportunities both on and off campus are available to students regardless of need and hometown. An installment payment plan also is offered. Students majoring in engineering or chemistry can participate in a cooperative education program. Tuition also is higher than the base rate for students with majors in various fields. Tuition in 2005–2006 was $3162 higher in engineering, $1264 higher in business, $2522 in chemistry and the biological sciences, and $532 in the fine and applied arts.

Rate of return: Ninety-three percent of all freshmen return for the sophomore year. Fifty-eight percent go on to graduate in 4 years; 78% graduate in 5 years; and 81% in 6 years.

Payoff: The 2 most popular majors for 2005 graduates were finance and psychology at about 6.5% each. Accounting followed at about 5%. Eighty-six percent of recent graduates found employment within 6 months of commencement, responding to the more than 4600 companies and organizations that recruited; half of them usually join an industrial or business firm, 25% a professional firm, and smaller percentages take posts with governmental agencies, health organizations, and educational institutions. Three-fourths remain in Illinois; the remainder scatter throughout the United States. Half of all seniors seeking employment have jobs before they graduate.

Most Illinois graduates don't stop with the bachelor's degree. In time, 43% of a graduating class will earn master's degrees in the arts and sciences, and another 42% will go to business, law, or medical school. Typically, more than 80% of the graduates who apply to law school are accepted, as are 65% of the medical school applicants.

Bottom line: Don't go to Illinois expecting to study at the feet of distinguished professors throughout the undergraduate years. Personal attention can be hard to come by, though outgoing people can usually find a way to get it. The University of Illinois at Urbana-Champaign is one of the few schools where a senior can say without exaggeration: "There are thousands of opportunities here for those who want to take advantage of them."

Wheaton College

Wheaton, Illinois 60187

Setting: Suburban
Control: Private (Evangelical Christian)
Undergraduate enrollment: 1140 men, 1202 women
Graduate enrollment: 112 men, 147 women
Student/faculty ratio: 12:1
Freshman profile: 42% scored over 699 on SAT I verbal; 42% scored 600–699; 15% 500–599; 1% below 500. 32% scored over 699 on SAT I math; 50% scored 600–699; 16% 500–599; 2% below 500. 46.4% scored 30–36 on the ACT; 47% scored 24–29; 6.4% scored 18–23; <1% scored below 18. 54% graduated in top tenth of high school class; 81% in upper fourth.
Faculty profile: 93% Ph.D.'s

Tuition and fees: $21,100
Room and board: $6660
Freshman financial aid: 49%; average scholarship or grant: $13,546 need-based; $3251 non-need-based
Campus jobs: NA; average earnings: NA
Application deadline: Early action: Nov. 1; regular: Jan. 15
Financial aid deadline: Feb. 15
Admissions information: (630) 752-5005; (800) 222-2419
e-mail: admissions@wheaton.edu
web site: www.wheaton.edu

For most bright high school graduates, the question of which college or university to attend usually centers on 1 chief concern, aside from the question of cost: which school is strongest academically. For high-achieving Evangelical Christian students, though, suitable choices are a bit harder to come by. While most are seeking a college or university that is academically challenging, they also want a school that not only respects but also enhances their Christian faith and way of living. Fear not. Those who seek can find what they're looking for at Wheaton College, a nondenominational, Evangelical Christian college just 25 miles west of Chicago. Over 90% of the faculty have doctorates; 5% of the fall 2005 freshman class were National Merit finalists, a number that year after year places Wheaton among the top 1% of U.S. colleges in the portion of its freshmen who are National Merit scholars. Notes a junior from the northeast: "Students here study hard and love what they learn. They talk about and evaluate the ideas that have been presented in class, in the media, and by peers and gained from their activities. It is a stimulating environment." And a total cost for tuition, fees, room, and board of $27,760 in the 2005–2006 school year is even more cause for rejoicing at what many consider the "flagship of Christian education."

Student body: The good news about Wheaton's value and values has spread to all 50 states, with just 28% of the undergraduates from Illinois. Increasing the racial and ethnic diversity has proved more difficult. Seven percent of the students are Asian-Americans, 3% Hispanics, 2% African-Americans, and nearly 1% foreign nationals from 40 countries. Less than 0.5% are Native Americans. But Wheaton generally has more than 160 MKs ("missionary kids") and other Americans who have lived overseas a number of years and bring multicultural perspectives to the campus. Sixty-seven percent of the students in a recent year were graduates of public schools; 29% graduated from private schools; and 4% were home-schooled. More than 30 Christian denominations are represented in the undergraduate student body. (A Christian commitment is necessary for admission.) Students are politically conservative (although a few "real radicals" keep things lively), clean-living, a bit naive, and conscientious about their schoolwork. One southerner finds her classmates "highly driven and motivated to do well. If you settle for mediocrity, you are in the minority." "Type A personality people," adds a junior. Spiritually, many newcomers, who associated Wheaton solely with Christian conservatism, find themselves challenged and often liberalized by the thoughtful debates and real-world mission experiences. Observes a Californian: "This is a Christian environment of intelligent Christians—not many 'Jesus freaks' here. While some do want to become missionaries or pastors, the majority want to live with the world but remember Christian ethics." Adds a midwesterner: "I have been pleased to find Wheaton to be much more open-minded politically and doctrinally than I expected."

Academics: Founded in 1860 and first headed by a former president of free-thinking Knox College, Wheaton has had but 7 presidents in its more than 130 years of history. The college offers bachelor's degrees in 40 majors, master's degrees in 17, and doctorates in clinical psychology and Biblical/theological studies. Students take courses divided into 2 semesters, with the average class enrolling 22 undergraduates. Freshmen shouldn't be surprised to find a World Civilization course enrolling 158 students, but as a junior points out, "One class of mine has 3 people, so we meet in the professor's office to discuss the readings over coffee."

Wheaton's very comprehensive general-education program covers 60 of the 124 credits required for graduation. Entering students begin with a 4-hour Freshman Block that includes classes in Theology of Culture,

Freshman Experience, and Foundations of Wellness. All of the traditional fields are well covered, demanding competency in Biblical content, a foreign language, mathematics, speech, and writing, as well as distributional studies in Faith and Reason, Society, Nature, and Literature and the Arts. The result is a well integrated program, and, says a senior: "One gets the sense that the courses required are all interrelated in terms of historic progression of thought."

The faculty consists of 191 full-time members and 96 part-time. Seventy-three percent of the faculty are men. All faculty members sign statements of faith affirming their allegiance to the basic Evangelical Christian tenets of the college; many begin classes with devotions, almost all with prayers. Unsigned but no less faithfully followed by the faculty is a commitment to see that their students are challenged yet helped whenever needed. "Professors don't just lecture and ask us to regurgitate the information," observes an education major. "They make us decide on our own what we believe and why." Adds a music major: "They know where to draw the line between mercy and justice." Students as well as faculty enjoy the "Dine with a Mind" program that encourages professor and student to meet one-on-one for breakfast or lunch and discuss academic as well as personal issues.

The list of Wheaton's academic strong points multiplies with each student polled. Philosophy, English, political science, international relations, psychology, and sociology are each marked by professors "who are knowledgeable yet likable and teach well while they inspire," according to a sociology major. Biblical and theological studies are strengthened by a diverse faculty teaching within a fairly conservative theological framework, with the support of excellent materials at the Billy Graham Center on campus and impressive guest speakers. Many students end up adding a minor in the field after being exposed to the department through their general education courses. Education majors analyze their performances before a classroom on videotape and must meet rigorous department standards for excellence. The natural sciences, particularly chemistry, provide committed instructors who demand much work from their students; as a result, about 80% of the Wheaton graduates who apply to medical school are accepted. While students find the labs excellent in their reinforcement of the lectures, some think the equipment needs to be upgraded. The Conservatory of Music is wonderful for students seeking a classical education in the field. Modern facilities in radio and television production, teamed with good opportunities for internships, ensure that the communications major also makes the topflight list.

Wheaton's academic shortcomings, according to students, generally occur because of limited funding or an insufficient number of professors in such subject areas as geology and foreign languages. Modern language majors are offered only in French, German, and Spanish. Art lacks funding for equipment and space and is among the areas students say is most affected by the college's Christian doctrines, restricting, for example, the study of nudes. "We're somewhat afraid of art at Wheaton," says a political science major.

Facilities: Buswell Memorial Library has most of the 343,000 volumes and 1500 paper periodicals (several thousand more are accessible on-line) available on campus; the Billy Graham Center Library, named for the Wheaton alum, has materials related to missions, evangelism, and revivals. A music collection of more than 5600 records, 3000 compact discs, and 11,600 scores also is housed at the main library. For most students, Buswell is both study hall and social hour, depending where they sit. Those who come to chat with their friends occupy the main lounge and pretend to read newspapers. Those in need of concentration head for the designated quiet floors, which, true to their name, are silent. A computerized catalog and numerous on-line searches help supplement a collection many students find outdated and lacking. Materials not housed locally can be obtained through interlibrary loan or by using cards and passes for the University of Chicago and other major libraries in the Chicago area.

The college's special collections, housed in the recently constructed Wade Center, are especially special. They include the books and papers of 7 British authors, among them J. R. R. Tolkien and C. S. Lewis; the Lewis memorabilia contain what many consider to be the magical wardrobe that inspired the children's book *The Lion, the Witch and the Wardrobe*; there also is the desk of J. R. R. Tolkien.

The main computer lab is located in Buswell Library; with 61 PCs and 5 Macs, "it is about 20% too small," observes one user. A smaller lab with 10 PCs and 4 Macs is located in the Billy Graham Center. Three to 6 PC's also are located in each of 5 residence halls. The lab in Buswell is open until midnight; in Billy Graham until 10 p.m., and in the dorms 24/7 except when they are closed as are all of the labs all day Sunday. Most students also have their own computers.

Special programs: In the spirit of Christian service, the college's human needs and global resources (HNGR) program offers a core of 5 courses available to all majors plus a 6-month internship in a developing country. In addition, the college conducts 9 of its own overseas programs in several countries in Europe, East Asia, Latin America, and the Middle East. Wheaton in the Holy Lands, for example, travels to the Middle East to study the Bible and religion. Wheaton's membership in the Christian College Consortium enables students to attend any of several other Christian colleges across the country. The college also operates educational and leadership training centers at its Black Hills Science Station in South Dakota and at Honey Rock Camp in the wilds of Wisconsin. Cross-registration is available with Illinois Institute of Technology. A 3-2 engineering degree also is offered with IIT as well as with University of Illinois and Case Western Reserve and Washington universities; one in nursing is conducted with Emory and Rush universities, the University of Rochester, and Goshen Nursing School in Indiana.

Campus life: Ninety percent of Wheaton's undergraduates live on the 80-acre campus, which is marked by lots of grass and red brick colonial buildings. There are no fraternities or sororities, and campus life is guided by the tenets of the college's recently revised Community Covenant, which in 2003 replaced a more stringent Statement of Responsibilities that had been last revised 3 decades before. The Covenant continues to forbid students while enrolled at Wheaton from using alcohol and tobacco in all settings, but for the first time allows dancing on campus as well as off (only square dancing had been permitted). The first campus swing dance was held in November 2003. As the new Covenant advises: "All members of the Wheaton College community will take care to avoid any entertainment or behavior, on or off campus, which may be immodest, sinfully erotic, or harmfully violent." Students generally have to find creative ways to spend their time. One popular event for freshmen and sophomores is "roulettes," in which roommates choose each other's dates as a surprise, and the entire dormitory floor goes out together. Students say some "undercover" partying with alcohol does occur; however, "breaking the pledge in any way is regarded as a breach of integrity by the student body," says a junior. Attendance at chapel is required. Incidents of crime, mainly thefts of bikes or bookbags, are few in number, though public safety officers recently stepped up patrols to keep unwanted trespassers off campus.

Community service plays a central role in campus life, and involves about half the student body. Every week, more than 600 students travel to Chicago to tutor children and visit nursing homes and mental institutions. A third of the undergraduates attend student-led meetings of World Christian Fellowship each Sunday to address global concerns and pray. During summer vacations and spring breaks, many participate in work or mission projects. Music is also a major pastime, with more than 300 students involved in 5 major vocal and instrumental groups.

Soccer, basketball, and football are the most popular of the 10 men's and 10 women's intercollegiate sports played under the no-scholarship rules of NCAA Division III. In recent years, the Wheaton Thunder, formerly known as the Crusaders, have won national championships in soccer and several top-10 finishes in swimming. Wheaton's tennis teams also have consistently won the conference title. Among club sports, ice hockey is enthusiastically followed, with excited Wheaton fans inclined to throw tennis balls at the opposing team whenever the Thunder score. Sixteen men's and 6 women's intramural sports also provide stress relief for 40% of the students.

Chicago, just a 30-minute train ride away, is easily the most frequent and exciting getaway, with as wide a range of plays, concerts, museums, and sporting events as a student could wish for.

Cost cutters: An endowment of about $294 million as of June 2005 helps Wheaton keep its tuition low. In addition to that support, 49% of all undergraduates in the 2005–2006 academic year received financial aid; 40% were on need-based assistance. The average need-based grant for a freshman totaled $13,546. Need-based self-help aid for a freshman averaged $4748; the average for non-need-based scholarship aid was $3251. The average financial indebtedness of 2005 graduates was $17,936. There are few awards not based on need, although President's Awards recently paid $1000 a year renewable over 4 years to students with a minimum GPA of 3.6, a 1400 critical reading and math SAT, and 32 ACT. Nearly 150 awards were made in a recent school year. James E. Burr Scholarships for underrepresented minorities recently paid $1000 to $4000 yearly. Special renewable music awards of $1000–$3000 also are available.

Rate of return: Of the freshmen who enter Wheaton, 95% return for the sophomore year. Seventy-seven percent graduate in 4 years; 85%, in 5 years.

Payoff: Among 2005 graduates, the 3 most popular majors were the social sciences at 15% and education and Biblical and theological studies at 9% each. About three-quarters of the students take jobs in business and education shortly after graduating, many with the nearly 200 companies and organizations that recruit on campus. Nearly half settle in the Midwest. Within 5 years of graduation, just over half have completed or are enrolled in an advanced degree program. In a recent national study conducted on liberal arts graduates pursuing doctoral degrees, Wheaton College ranked 9th among 925 institutions examined.

Bottom line: Notes an easterner: "Although the people who come here are committed to Jesus and Christian beliefs, Wheaton is no utopia, a fact that can be disillusioning to incoming students. The college is made up of real people who get stressed and give in to complaining at times. What is key here is a desire to rise above that level. We are being helped to achieve an outlook and understanding that will enable us to live our faith effectively in the modern, demanding world."

Indiana

Butler University

Indianapolis, Indiana 46208

Setting: Suburban
Control: Independent
Undergraduate enrollment: 1414 men, 2387 women
Graduate enrollment: 22 men, 36 women (447 part-time)
Student/faculty ratio: 12:1
Freshman profile: 8% scored over 700 on SAT I verbal; 37% scored 600–700; 48% 500–599; 7% below 500. 10% scored over 700 on SAT I math; 44% scored 600–700; 37% 500–599; 9% below 500. 32% scored above 28 on the ACT; 22% scored 27–28; 29% 24–26; 14% 21–23; 3% below 21. 43% graduated in top tenth of high school class; 68% in upper fifth.
Faculty profile: 85% Ph.D.'s

Tuition and fees: $23,774
Room and board: $8140
Freshman financial aid: 90%; average scholarship or grant: NA
Campus jobs: 25%; average earnings: $1200–$1500/year
Application deadline: Early admission: Dec. 1 and Feb. 1; regular: rolling
Financial aid deadline: Mar. 1
Admissions information: (317) 940-8100; (888) 940-8100
e-mail: admission@butler.edu
web site: www.butler.edu

About 130 years ago, Butler University was a college on the move, trying to escape the steady encroachment of the Indianapolis commercial district. Again, in the late 1920s, Butler found itself moving, this time to a wooded tract north of the city on the White River and the Inland Waterway Canal. Today, Butler, which turned 150 in 2005, is still on the move, though the White River remains the campus's westward border and the canal and its popular towpath continue to bisect the campus. Butler, say its proud students, is on the move upward, increasing its enrollment by more than 50% over a decade, renovating older structures, expanding its student center, adding living-learning centers, where faculty members or resident scholars live amid a cluster of students and building a new health and fitness facility scheduled to be open for the 2006–2007 school year. Its core curriculum, created in 1945, also has adapted to the changing times with its centerpiece interdisciplinary course aptly named Change and Tradition. At its heart, though, Butler's core remains what it always was: a way for all undergraduates, regardless of academic focus, to gain exposure to topics and issues outside their own range of experience and to learn to read and write better and think more critically so that they, like their university, can grow and successfully change with the times.

Student body: Butler remains very much a school of the Midwest. Though 43% of the undergraduates are not Hoosiers, with 46 states and 63 foreign countries represented, 90% of the out-of-staters hail from the surrounding area. Eighty-six percent are graduates of public schools. Ninety percent are white Americans, 3% each African-American and Hispanic, and 2% each Asian-American and foreign nationals. Students cite increased diversity, both in actual numbers of students and in heightened awareness of other cultures through courses and special programs, as another example of positive growth in recent years. In recognition of its efforts, the Black Student Union won the Lamp of Wisdom, Butler's highest award to a student organization for 3 years straight. "Most of the students can be described as preppy and well off financially," observes an easterner. "Politically, most are conservative, but more and more liberals are entering the school. Academically, students on the whole are competitive because of grade requirements for both majors and scholarships, but despite the emphasis on academics Butler is still a very social campus."

Academics: Butler offers the bachelor's degree in over 60 majors plus a master's degree in various fields, and a doctorate in pharmacy. Degree programs for undergraduates are spread among the 5 colleges of Liberal Arts and Sciences, Business Administration, Education, Fine Arts, and Pharmacy and Health Sciences. Classes are divided between 2 semesters, with the typical freshman class enrolling 32 students, upper-division classes dropping below 20, and some core courses exceeding 50. A biology class in immunology has had 110 enrolled.

As part of the Butler core curriculum, students must take specific courses in English, speech, physical education, and interdisciplinary studies, as well as distribution requirements in humanities, fine arts, social science, natural science, and quantitative and formal reasoning. The heart of Butler's core is its interdisciplinary Change and Tradition course, usually taken during the sophomore year, which focuses on a progression of Western and non-Western cultures ranging from 5th-century Athens to Traditional China to

Historic Nigeria. Undergraduates also must complete a computer literacy requirement and, in their junior or senior year, a writing-intensive requirement. Students find the wide-ranging core an excellent way to sample different disciplines before having to select a major at the end of the sophomore year.

Sixty-four percent of Butler's 434 faculty members are full-time, with a large number of part-time adjunct professors in music, pharmacy, and other professionally oriented fields. All but 26 of the 279 full-time members and all but 17 of the 155 part-timers teach undergraduates. Fifty-eight percent are men. Professors get high marks for competence and caring. "Most of them are true teachers as well as professors," observes a history major. More than a third of the faculty has been appointed since 1987, bringing new blood and fresh enthusiasm to many departments across campus.

Butler's preprofessional programs in pharmacy and business and the Jordan College of Fine Arts earn praise from both majors and admiring outsiders. Business benefits from proximity to internship and cooperative opportunities in Indianapolis. The 6-year Doctor of Pharmacy program boasts 100% job placement, with 96% of its graduates passing the state board exam on their first attempt. Fine arts majors rave about devoted faculty members and superb facilities; outstanding among them is Clowes Memorial Hall, a 2200-seat facility with a 90-foot stage. Broadway shows that come to Indianapolis perform at Clowes Hall, as "have I and other fine arts majors," explains a senior studying music theory and composition. The dance major is especially noteworthy.

Some programs within the liberal arts, such as history and geography, have fewer course offerings than students would like. Though students find the biology professors excellent, many think the laboratory equipment needs to be updated.

Facilities: Irwin Library, designed by world-renowned architect Minoru Yamasaki, blends Middle Eastern, Classical, Greek, Italian Gothic, and Japanese influences in a building that students regard as "the best place to study on campus." Most of the university's 309,500 volumes and 2126 periodicals are housed here. The Ruth Lilly Science Library holds materials in the fields of computer, physical, pharmaceutical and biological sciences, and is especially quiet for really serious study. The library system is computerized, and students have access to numerous assorted databases. However, science majors in particular find the journal selection lacking and head to the Indiana University Medical Library for assistance; other majors usually find what they need over the Internet or through interlibrary loan.

Sixteen main computer facilities, including 5 open around the clock, are available for student use. A couple are e-mail-only stations. Most labs contain between 18 and 30 Macintosh and Windows workstations. Though computer availability has increased over the years, the university still strongly recommends that students have their own personal computers and has provided network ports with Internet access in all residence-hall rooms for those students who do.

Special programs: In 1988, Butler welcomed to its campus the Institute for Study Abroad, a national organization that arranges foreign study at more than 90 different institutions of higher learning in Australia, the United Kingdom, New Zealand, Argentina, Mexico, Spain, Chile, Cuba, Costa Rica, and Ireland for 3500 students from more than 400 U.S. colleges and universities annually. The move enabled Butler students to receive individual help from institute counselors regarding study options in these countries. The university has also begun building its own exchange programs with other foreign universities, establishing a program with the University of Alcalá in Spain, among others. For those wishing to travel not quite so far, exchanges are available with 4 other institutions in the Indianapolis area through the Consortium for Urban Education. Other options include a joint program in engineering with Purdue University as well as cooperative programs in business administration. An Undergraduate Research Conference held annually on campus attracts over 500 students from 38 colleges and universities throughout the Midwest. A Butler Summer Institute awards students grants of $2000 plus housing while they work on summer research projects with faculty members.

Campus life: Although 56% of the undergraduates live on Butler's 290-acre campus, located just 5 miles from downtown Indianapolis, only half of them remain there on weekends. Since many come from nearby Ohio and Illinois, as well as other parts of Indiana, they are able to go home fairly frequently. Those who stay usually attend football and basketball games, and increasingly men's and women's soccer, as well as functions put on by Butler's 8 fraternities and 8 sororities. About a fourth of the men and women belong, but Greek parties are generally open to all. Every housing unit also sponsors an all-campus weekend. Housing units vary in type from freshman living-learning centers in which small groups of students share common courses and faculty mentors in residence to a coed apartment building for upperclassmen. Butler's Hampton House involves its members in year-long service projects and leadership experiences.

Many of the all-campus events not sponsored by the Greeks or dorms are run by a surprising source, the YMCA. This intercollegiate branch of the "Y," which is open to all men and women on campus, was founded at Butler in 1890. More than 115 years later, it continues to involve students in various community service projects. Although campus safety is a priority, with security lighting and safety call boxes available, students say vandalism and bicycle theft are really the only problems.

Butler's intercollegiate teams, 10 for men and 9 for women, don't just play in NCAA Division I; they win titles. Since 1997, teams in men's baseball, basketball, soccer, and cross-country and in women's cross-country have all won one or more conference titles. The men's basketball team concluded a record-breaking season in the 2001–2002 school year, making it to the quarterfinals in the National Invitation Tournament. The university's hockey club won the national championship in its conference in 2001. Ice hockey is one of 5 club sports provided. Twenty-three intramural sports are offered for men and for women in which 90% of the men and 54% of the women take part. Every spring, Butler hosts a 12-hour sporting contest that involves the entire campus.

Indianapolis offers many off-campus diversions to students, including 4 professional sports teams, the symphony, and an art museum within walking distance of campus. Broad Ripple, a kind of Bohemian village with shops, bars, and restaurants, is a popular place to hang out and people-watch. Butler's campus itself also offers avenues for mental and emotional escape, with the peaceful Holcomb Botanical Gardens and Norris Plaza, with its fountain, speaker's stone, and lush vegetation.

Cost cutters: All but 10% of the freshman and all but 14% of the continuing students received some form of financial assistance in the 2005–2006 school year. Forty-three percent of the freshmen and 45% of the continuing students were on need-based aid. No figures are available for the amount and types of aid entering freshmen received in fall 2005 or for the amount of average debt a 2005 graduate assumed. Freshman Academic Scholarships pay $5000 to $12,000 a year based on students' academic records, standardized test scores, and extracurricular commitments. They are renewable based on a student's grade point average. Families who wish can extend tuition payments over a 10-month period.

Rate of return: Eighty-seven percent of freshmen return for the sophomore year. Sixty-three percent graduate in 4 years; 69%, in 5 years, 72% in 6.

Payoff: Marketing and pharmacy were the top majors among 2005 graduates, accounting for 16% of all degrees each. Communications attracted 13%. In a recent year, a fifth of all graduates went directly to graduate or professional schools. The vast majority of graduates found jobs, many with such traditional employers of Butler graduates as Eli Lilly, Ernst and Young, PricewaterhouseCoopers, and Dow Phamaceuticals. About 300 companies and organizations recruited on campus in a recent school year.

Bottom line: "Butler is just the right size: big enough to offer many opportunities for students but not so big that people get lost," advises a senior. "Its location in Indianapolis, a medium-sized city, is perfect for finding internships and jobs."

DePauw University

Greencastle, Indiana 46135

Setting: Small town
Control: Private (United Methodist)
Undergraduate enrollment: 1071 men, 1270 women
Graduate enrollment: None
Student/faculty ratio: 10:1
Freshman profile: 13% scored over 700 on SAT I verbal; 41% scored 600–700; 41% 500–599; 5% below 500. 12% scored over 700 on SAT I math; 51% scored 600–700; 33% 500–599; 4% below 500. 32% scored above 28 on the ACT; 22% scored 27–28; 29% 24–26; 12% 21–23; 4% below 21. 48% graduated in top tenth of high school class; 78% in upper fifth.
Faculty profile: 99% Ph.D.'s

Tuition and fees: $26,470
Room and board: $7500
Freshman financial aid: 94%; average scholarship or grant: $9151 need-based; $9778 non-need-based
Campus jobs: 34%; average earnings: $630/year
Application deadline: Early notification: Nov. 1 and Dec. 1; regular: Feb. 15
Financial aid deadline: Feb. 15
Admissions information: (765) 658-4006; (800) 447-2495
e-mail: admissions@depauw.edu
web site: www.depauw.edu

DePauw is a school where students do their best to "do it all." About three-fourths are involved in fraternities and sororities, two-thirds participate in intramural sports, and many of the same go-getters help organize the Little 5 bicycle race while serving a shift at the campus radio station and holding down positions in student government. Three-quarters of all students study off campus for a winter term, semester, or year, and more than 1000 of the 2350 perform some form of community service in the Greencastle area.

Students admit there is pressure to get involved, balancing blue-chip academics with extracurricular commitments, but so effective has been the "do it all" approach that in a recent study Franklin and Marshall found DePauw to be eighth in the nation among private liberal arts colleges turning out top corporate leaders. Likewise, *Fortune* magazine ranked DePauw 11th among all colleges and universities based on the likelihood that DePauw graduates will become CEOs of American companies. Notes a junior from the east: "Graduates of DePauw can hope for high-paying jobs, maybe not immediately but further down the road. This university produces future leaders, and reputable employers know it!"

Student body: Fifty percent of DePauw's go-getters are Hoosiers, with most of the out-of-staters also from the Midwest. Altogether, students congregated in a recent year from 41 states and 19 foreign countries. Expanding racial and ethnic diversity continues to be a major focus of DePauw admissions. Five percent of undergraduates are African-American, 3% are Hispanic, 2% are Asian-American, 2% foreign nationals, 1% multiracial, and less than 1% are Native American. While integration of these students into campus life was once tougher than recruitment was, the establishment of an African-American fraternity, 2 African-American sororities and a Latino women's sorority has brought more minorities into Greek life. DePauw, along with a number of other small liberal arts colleges, has formed a partnership with the Posse Foundation located in New York City, to increase and enrich campus diversity further by recruiting students from the city's various cultures. Forty-five percent of the students in a recent year were Protestant (just 13% Methodist), 22% Catholic, with 1% Jewish, 1% other religions, 6% claiming no affiliation, and the rest with affiliation unknown. About 90% are graduates of public schools. Students tend to be conservative, some rather wealthy, with a definite DePauw "look" that, students say, can be achieved in 2 short semesters with the aid of an L. L. Bean catalog. (In this regard, they add, some liberal Democrats on campus manage to circulate "incognito" because they're dressed like the Republican majority!) The result is classmates who are preppier than their counterparts at other midwestern colleges and generally come off as self-confident, intelligent, and intent on succeeding. Says a senior: "Our undergraduates are driven students who expect a great deal out of themselves." Competition for top grades is high since most students are accustomed to receiving A's and B's, but, notes a Hoosier, "Students still feel comfortable studying together and exchanging ideas, with no fear of losing their academic standing because they shared too much with the next guy."

Academics: DePauw was founded in 1837 in Greencastle after residents had raised $25,000, a large sum in those days, to bring the Methodist college to the community. One hundred seventy years later, it still awards just a bachelor's degree in 44 majors. The academic year is divided into 2 semesters plus a January term. While average class size is 18, some freshman classes can have 30–40 enrolled with popular courses like World Geography hitting 45. A variety of seminars and more specialized upper-level courses have 10–15 students.

DePauw's program for first-year students is dubbed *depauw.year 1,* and involves entering freshmen in a wide range of in-and-out-of-class activities. The new students are enrolled in a topical seminar taught by a faculty member who also serves as their faculty mentor. In addition, first-year students are organized into mentor groups led by a student from the upper classes who coordinates discussions and social events and generally assists new students in their adjustment to the academic, residential, and social experience of college. Along with completion of the first-year program, all students must demonstrate proficiency in speech, writing, and quantitative thinking and must take courses from 6 broad subject areas, ranging from literature and the arts to social and behavioral sciences. In addition, every major requires completion of either a seminar, thesis, project, or comprehensive exam. During winter term, students participate in a common freshman experience on campus but as upperclassmen are free to choose internships, travel, or mission trips in which they perform some community service.

Forty-six of DePauw's 255 faculty members in a recent year were part-time; 42% were women. Students from a wide range of disciplines consider the faculty to be DePauw's greatest asset. Most are bright, as energetic as their charges, and seem to enjoy their time in class as much as their more personal contacts with students. "The classroom setting is somewhat informal," explains a sociology major. "Instead of a 50-minute lecture, most professors engage students in controversial debates or stimulating discussions."

Economics, in particular, boasts an incredible faculty, tough but dedicated to learning, who are supported by an impressive array of guest lecturers brought in by the university. Political science is equally well known for being intensely difficult but rewarding for those who make it, with plenty of opportunities for internships. Biology and chemistry are rigorous, with a new biological sciences building built in fall 1993, that provides state-of-the-art science research and learning facilities. The English literature major exposes students to a wide breadth of writers, while the writing major requires of its students all different kinds of original writing; history offers a similar variety of perspectives, from military to social to legal approaches. Another high note is the School of Music, which boasts many fine faculty members who work one-on-one with students and awards degrees in performance, music education, and music business. Communication majors rave about the Center for Contemporary Media, with facilities for print and radio and television production that they claim are better than those of the commercial TV studios in Indianapolis. Computer science, says a major, is simply "wonderful."

Though instruction is offered in 6 languages, French, German, Spanish, Chinese, Japanese, and Russian, with majors in the first 3, students have found the level of teaching to be more reflective of high school than of college. Others wish there were more course offerings in geology and geography.

Facilities: A $5 million renovation to the Roy O. West Library earns this comfortable study center an A+ from satisfied users. In fact, so many students now fill its expanded seating that it has become as well known for providing "face-time," that is, social interaction, as quiet time for study. The Prevo Library in the Science and Math Center is much smaller but also much more silent. Together, these 2 facilities, plus a smaller music library with recordings, contain about 284,000 volumes, 443,000 government documents, and more than 4000 current periodicals and newspapers on paper and electronically. Computerized databases assist in research, though for many in-depth projects such as senior theses students often make the 45-minute drive to Indiana University in Bloomington or to Purdue. Roy O. West Library is open until 2 a.m. Sundays through Thursdays and until 10 p.m. on the weekends. And best of all, adds a political science major, "the library has a coffee and smoothie shop, which is great for study cravings!"

All entering studare are required to purchase a laptop from the designated campus vendor for use during their time at DePauw. The policy is an extension of the direction most DePauw students already were moving on their own: recent studies showed that 90% of the undergraduates at DePauw already brought their own computers to campus, and half of them brought laptops. More than half of DePauw's classrooms are technologically capable, encouraging professors to incorporate use of the laptop into classroom instruction.

Special programs: DePauw's own overseas programs include semester studies of contemporary Eastern and Western Europe, based in Vienna, Austria, and Freiburg, Germany, as well as a Mediterranean Studies term in Athens. Students also may participate in a vast array of programs offered by other colleges. One of the most "transforming" experiences for many students is DePauw's own Winter Term in Service, which during January term sends students all over the world to perform some kind of service project in a developing country.

Prospective engineers can take 3 years at DePauw and 2 at Columbia, Case Western Reserve, or Washington University. A nursing program is offered with Rush University in Chicago. DePauw Fellows honors programs in management, media, interdisciplinary studies and science research are open to students in any major and focus on the individual specialty plus a semester-long paid internship in the field. A semester in Washington, D.C., also is an option.

Campus life: Ninety-eight percent of DePauw's students live on the 175-acre campus, replete with all the ivy-trimmed, brick buildings traditional-minded scholars dream about. Fraternities and sororities provide housing for about two-thirds of the residents. Three-quarters of the men and about 70% of the women belong to the 14 national fraternities and 11 national sororities, which have become the soul of social life at DePauw. Because the campus is so small, it is rare that an independent does not know someone at a Greek house, so he or she can usually get into any party; otherwise the Greek community has done little in the past to reach out to independents, some of whom admit to feeling "left out" at times. Members of an Independent Council, created in 1996 to increase social and leadership opportunities for independent students, have representation on the Student Congress. Greek and independent leaders also are working together to plan more all-campus social events that would include the entire student body. Students from all academic interests have found a second home at the Center for Contemporary Media, with many who have no career interests as journalists serving as disc jockeys and editors at the modern facilities. Crime at the houses, residence halls, and elsewhere on campus is generally low, although emergency security phones are scattered across campus in case they're needed.

About a fourth of the men and nearly a fifth of the women play NCAA Division III intercollegiate sports; 65% participate in 14 men's and 12 women's intramural offerings. Football is the biggest of the 11 men's and 10 women's varsity sports on campus, with almost nobody missing the Monon Bell game between DePauw and Wabash College, which has become the oldest continuous football rivalry west of the Alleghenies. Soccer and basketball evoke considerable student interest as do numerous club sports. Biking, in the land of the popular Little 5 bicycle race, is also big.

When students need a break from their heavy on-campus schedules, they can head in any direction: 45 minutes east to Indianapolis, 45 minutes south to Bloomington and Indiana University, 4 hours north to Chicago, and 4 hours west to St. Louis. Within closer range, "country runs" (by car) to a nearby lake or quarry are quite popular. The university's own 480-acre nature preserve offers trails for hiking, walking, and running and waters for canoeing. Greencastle itself, a picturesque farming community, has just 9000 residents, including those at the university. Cautions a sophomore: "Even to get to Wal-Mart, Taco Bell, or McDonald's, you need a car."

Cost cutters: DePauw's financial health is strong, with an endowment of $451.5 million as of June 2005. Ninety-four percent of all freshmen and 96% of continuing students received financial help in a recent school year; 56% of all freshmen and 51% of the continuing students were on need-based aid. The average freshman award for students with need included a need-based scholarship or grant averaging $9151 and need-based self-help aid such as loans and jobs averaging $4414. Other non-need-based scholarships and awards for first-year students averaged $9778. The average financial indebtedness of a recent graduate was $15,635. All admitted students with a 3.25 GPA are automatically considered for merit awards recently ranging from $3000 to $14,000. The amount of the award is determined by an academic index derived from the student's GPA, class rank, and standardized test scores. Merit awards, when combined with other special scholarships, are reduced to full tuition only. Other achievement awards for top-ranking students include Presidential Rector Scholarships, which can pay full tuition and replace merit awards; other Rector scholars can receive three-quarters tuition. A leadership and service award, the Holton Memorial Scholarship pays from $1000 up to full tuition to up to 50 students. Music Performance Awards can pay up to full tuition to outstanding performers in the vocal, instrumental, and composition fields. Science and Mathematics Scholarships of $1000 are added to merit awards for students selected through an on-campus competitive interview. A deferred payment plan provides for an initial outlay with the balance divided into 2 payments later in the semester.

Rate of return: Ninety percent of DePauw freshmen like the get-involved attitude and return for another year of it. Seventy-three percent graduate in 4 years; 78% in 5 years.

Payoff: Communication claimed the largest percentage of recent bachelor's degree recipients at 16%, followed by creative writing at 11%, and economics at 10%. About three-quarters of the graduates enter the work force shortly after finishing, many joining firms such as IBM, Eli Lilly, and General Electric. Fifty companies and organizations recruited on campus in a recent school year. The greatest numbers of graduates head to Chicago, Indianapolis, New York City, Washington, D.C., and San Francisco. Among recent graduates, a fifth went directly on to graduate or professional school. DePauw ranks 16th among the nation's undergraduate colleges as a baccalaureate source for Ph.D. degrees in all fields.

Bottom line: DePauw is a midwestern match for many more expensive, small, private East Coast colleges, though students must be prepared to welcome, or at least tolerate, a campus where Greek life has traditionally been strong, although social outlets for independents are increasing. There are plenty of academic, athletic, and social opportunities for student involvement and leadership but those who don't come with good time-management skills must either acquire them or miss out on a lot of what DePauw has to offer.

Earlham College
Richmond, Indiana 47374

Setting: Small city
Control: Private (Religious Society of Friends)
Undergraduate enrollment: 495 men, 683 women
Graduate enrollment: 28 men, 27 women
Student/faculty ratio: 12:1
Freshman profile: 27% scored over 700 on SAT I verbal; 40% scored 600–700; 24% 500–599; 9% below 500. 9% scored over 700 on SAT I math; 43% scored 600–700; 31% 500–599; 17% below 500. 20% scored above 29 on the ACT; 62% scored 24–29; 18% 18–23; 0% below 18. 30% graduated in top tenth of high school class; 53% in upper fifth.
Faculty profile: 97% Ph.D.'s

Tuition and fees: $27,684
Room and board: $5920
Freshman financial aid: 83%; average scholarship or grant: $12,422 need-based; $6150 non-need-based
Campus jobs: 50%; average earnings: $1120/year
Application deadline: Early decision: Dec. 1; early action: Jan. 1; regular: Feb. 15
Financial aid deadline: Mar. 1
Admissions information: (765) 983-1600;
  (800) 327-5426
  e-mail: admission@earlham.edu
  web site: www.earlham.edu

Outstanding courses in biology and English and thought-provoking programs in Japanese and peace and global studies have helped push Earlham College in eastern Indiana to the top of the academic roster. Yet it is other fundamental lessons transcending the curriculum that make Earlham one of the more unusual selective liberal art colleges. As students at a college founded in 1847 by Quakers who came to Indiana from the slave-holding South, Earlham undergraduates are taught to see themselves as part of a larger community that they have a responsibility to serve. Although the Quaker ideals of equality, simplicity, social justice, and nonviolence are as tough for a school like Earlham to put into practice as they are anywhere else, students value what their college is trying to do. "One of Earlham's more unique aspects is this community that it strives for and at a certain level maintains," observes an easterner. "Students actually try to attain academic integrity and honesty in an effort to live, learn, and work together and respect one another. All this is hardly perfected here, but these are the ideals and standards being sought."

Student body: Earlham draws students in search of these goals from 49 states and 51 foreign countries. Just a fourth of the undergraduates hail from Indiana and only a quarter of the out-of-staters are from other states in the Midwest. Two-thirds are graduates of public schools. Minority enrollment stands at 12%, with 7% African-American, 3% Hispanic, and 2% Asian-American. Seven percent are international students. Fourteen percent are Quakers. Says a Californian, "I am excited every day about spending time with people who grew up in different places and see the world in different ways than I do." All of the anti-establishment stereotypes can be found at Earlham, including students clad in Guatemalan garb and Bierkenstock sandals. "There are those who hang out at the food co-op and pick beans in El Salvador over Christmas break, but that isn't all that Earlham students do," explains one observer. "We also have a wide variety of athletes and student-government types." What generally unites such different kinds of people is commitment to the ideals that lured them to Earlham, which is often expressed by heavy involvement in politics and community service. About 450 students in an academic year volunteer in the Richmond community. Students may not appear to be competitive about grades, working cooperatively rather than against one another. (As the professors say, "Life is a group project.") But they are intense about their learning. Observes a junior: "Intellectual searching is encouraged through the accessibility of professors, opportunities for independent study, small classes, and extracurricular activities meant to enhance classroom learning. But often in the middle of a term everything comes down to stress, overload, and grades."

Academics: Earlham awards the bachelor's degree in 40 independent and interdisciplinary fields plus a masters of arts in teaching. The Earlham School of Religion, which is located on the campus, awards 3 graduate degrees, a Master of Divinity, a Master of Ministry, and a Master of Arts in religion. The academic year is divided into 2 semesters with an optional May term. The average class enrolls about 20 students. First-year students may encounter as many as 90 classmates in a Descriptive Astronomy lecture, but an upper-level seminar in various disciplines may have only 8 participants.

Earlham revised its general-education requirements in the 2002–2003 school year, with the intent to introduce students to different ways of knowing instead of specific topics of knowledge. The approach uses a variety of seminars and courses that focus on such skills as interpretation, comparative analysis and writing, abstract and quantitative reasoning, and scientific inquiry. Students also are expected to develop awareness of other cultures through class work examining domestic and international diversity as well as study of a foreign language. There also are requirements in the arts and in wellness.

Just 15 of Earlham's 108 faculty members are part-time. Forty-four percent are women. Professors are addressed by their first names and in most classes do not stand at the head of the class, in keeping with Quaker beliefs against hierarchy. Says a first-year student: "When I'm in class, I don't feel like I'm an 18-year-old college student being talked at by an unapproachable professor. I feel like I'm having a discussion with a colleague who happens to be quite advanced in the field we're discussing." Faculty are hired through an interview process that actively involves students and helps to bring to campus professors whose values and ideals most closely match Earlham's. "Professors here really respect the students and want to help them discover their academic potential," says a religion major. Some students describe this commitment to motivate students to do their best as "the doctrine of relentless pursuit."

Many of Earlham's strongest academic programs are a direct reflection of the college's ethical beliefs. Interdisciplinary programs in peace and global studies and human development and social relations are team-taught by faculty members from a variety of academic perspectives. Both majors require off-campus internships. The English literature faculty has a reputation for being both brilliant and demanding. Biology, 1 of Earlham's 2 largest departments, also boasts terrific professors—one member was the Carnegie Foundation's 2005 Indiana Professor of the Year—who work closely with students on independent research projects. The department offers an incredibly diverse curricula covering cell biology and pre-medical education as well as field biology, ecology, and even a program in tropical biology, which includes travel to Costa Rica, Amazonia, or the Galapagos Islands. The Japanese studies program demands competence in the Japanese language and strongly encourages its students to spend a year in Japan living with native families. Psychology requires all majors to design and run 3 or 4 independent experiments by the time they graduate. Philosophy, religion, politics, chemistry, sociology/anthropology, and music also win high marks.

Fine arts courses attract many more students than there are class sessions available. The departments of the fine arts division, which include art, music, and theater arts, also are not housed near each other on campus, which makes collaboration between faculty members more difficult. The business and non-profit management major, Earlham's version of a business administration program, was recently strengthened to raise it to the level of other programs, although students still say the quality of teaching could be improved.

Facilities: Earlham's 2 libraries together hold nearly 405,000 books and 2200 periodicals (plus 17,000 on-line), an ample collection for a student body of 1200. Most of the volumes are contained in the main Lilly Library, a place students find a bit too social in the evenings for concentrated study. (Wildman Science Library is a lot quieter.) In terms of research, though, "you couldn't find a better place than Lilly," notes a psychology major. Adds a double major in economics and politics: "The research librarians are excellent in helping us find what we want, even if we are not sure what we want!" The staff are known for the excellent courses they give to all students in the most effective use of the library resources, including the computerized catalog, various databases and the Internet. In 2001, Lilly Library received the Excellence in Academic Libraries Award from the Association of College and Research Libraries.

Eight public computing labs provide 133 Dell computers and 31 Macs for student use. One of the labs with 25 PCs and 6 Macs is open around the clock. There also are 12 other discipline-specific labs throughout the campus, providing an additional 72 computers. In addition, undergraduates with their own units, who represent 80% of the student body, can connect to the campus network from their residence hall rooms or via the wireless network from one of 40 points around campus. The computer center also lends computers to students to use outside the center for up to 3 days.

Special programs: Almost three-quarters of Earlham students participate in some significant off-campus experience; two-thirds are involved in study overseas. Many of Earlham's 24 programs, 14 of its own and 10 through the Great Lakes Colleges Association, immerse students in cultures and countries not always frequented by university overseas study programs, including programs in East Africa, India, and Northern Ireland. A semester also can be spent on the Mexico/U.S. border in El Paso and Ciudad Juarez and in Philadelphia, New York, or Chicago. A 3-2 program in engineering is offered with Case Western Reserve and Columbia universities, Rensselaer Polytechnic Institute, and the University of Rochester.

Campus life: Eighty-eight percent of Earlham students reside on the 800-acre campus, which consists of a 200-acre front campus, where the campus buildings are located, and a 600-acre back campus with woods, fields, and farmland. Many students choose to live in 30 small houses owned by the college; these include 4 language houses and "theme" houses, developed according to the interests of their residents. Included are a Peace House, a Service Learning House, and a Jewish Cultural Center, as well as African-American, Latino and Asian-American, and International Cultural Centers. There are no fraternities or sororities.

There is also no single center to the Earlham weekend social scene. The student activities board usually sponsors a "breadbox," or "cafe," with student performers or regional talent on Friday or Saturday night, plus events such as movies, lip synch competitions, and seasonal festivals. Some of Earlham's most active student organizations take a left-of-center slant, among them The Earlham Progressive Union and Amnesty International, which sets up tables every week for letter writing on behalf of prisoners in foreign countries. Say a first-year student: "Students at Earlham *do* things to make a difference in their areas of interest." The more traditional Earlham College Concert Choir and Chorale involves more than a quarter of the campus. Although crime is rare, extra lighting and an escort service to off-campus housing were added in response to student demand. Students are encouraged to walk in groups or in pairs when out at night, especially when off campus.

Earlham teams in football, basketball and soccer draw the most crowds of the 8 men's and 8 women's intercollegiate sports played in NCAA Division III. Thirty percent suit up for intercollegiate competition. Half take part in the 8 coed intramural sports. Club sports also are popular.

"A car is essential to happiness in Richmond," observes a transplant from New York State, who, along with most other students, finds little to do in the small city (pop. 40,000). With wheels, students head to Cincinnati, Indianapolis, and Dayton, 90 minutes away. Without them, walks in the back-campus woodlands or in the cemetery next door provide some mental escape.

Cost cutters: Earlham enjoys a large endowment for a small college: more than $378 million as of June 2005, which helps keep tuition low and financial aid reasonably high. Eighty-three percent of all freshmen and 85% of continuing students received some form of aid in the 2004–2005 school year, the most recent year for which data is available. Need-based assistance went to about 60% of all students. The average freshman award for first-year students with financial need included a need-based scholarship or grant averaging $12,422 and need-based self-help aid such as loans and jobs averaging $3905. Other non-need-based awards and scholarships for entering freshmen averaged $6150. The average 2005 graduate left with debts of $18,900. The college maintains a strong program of merit-based awards, including the Presidential Honors and Cunningham Cultural scholarships, which each pay $7000 and are renewable over 4 years. Two-thirds of Earlham's students participate in work-study.

Rate of return: Ninety percent of Earlham freshmen return for the sophomore year. Fifty-nine percent graduate in 4 years; 67%, in 5 years; 70% in 6.

Payoff: Eighteen percent of the 2005 graduates earned bachelor's degrees in the social sciences and history; 15% earned degrees in the biological and life sciences and 11% in interdisciplinary studies. More than 40% of recent graduates enrolled in graduate or professional school, most in the arts and sciences. Many of those who enter the work force take jobs in foreign service, teaching, management, or as lobbyists. "For many Earlham students," notes an education major, "the moral implications of their job are more important than the money they make." Eighty companies and organizations recruited on campus during a recent school year. Within 5 years of graduation, 73% of Earlham alumni decide to continue their schooling, with 35% pursuing degrees in the arts and sciences. A recent higher education study examining the percentage of graduates who go on to receive PhDs found Earlham ranked 26th of 1302 institutions of higher learning in the United States. When weighted by enrollment, Earlham ranked 8th in biology and the life sciences.

Bottom line: "Earlham is a place for the serious learner, someone who is concerned about the connections between academics and life," advises an English major. "Students who are unwilling to work hard and are irresponsible about how their choices affect the options available to others may not be happy here."

Goshen College

Goshen, Indiana 46526

Setting: Small city
Control: Private (Mennonite)
Undergraduate enrollment: 922 men and women (full- and part-time)
Graduate enrollment: None
Student/faculty ratio: 13:1
Freshman profile: Average combined math and verbal SAT I: 1167; average ACT: 25.8. 63% graduated in top fourth of high school class; 91% in upper half.
Faculty profile: 66% Ph.D.'s

Tuition and fees: $19,300
Room and board: $6450
Freshman financial aid: 99%; average scholarship or grant: $11,781 need-based; $10,167 non-need-based
Campus jobs: 52%; average earnings: $1470/year
Application deadline: Aug. 15
Financial aid deadline: Feb.15 (Priority: Feb. 1)
Admissions information: (574) 535-7535; (800) 348-7422
e-mail: admission@goshen.edu
web site: www.goshen.edu

For too many undergraduates, the general-education program is an ordeal to be endured in the first 2 years of college. These are the "good-for-you" courses that keep the focused student from plunging directly into his or her major. At their worst, they are large and superficial lecture classes that fail either to stimulate or to broaden. That's not the case, however, at Goshen College, a Mennonite school of fewer than 1000 full-time students in northern Indiana. As part of the general-education program, 80% of Goshen students leave their classrooms and spend 12 weeks living with families in countries such as Peru, Ethiopia, the Dominican Republic, Germany, the People's Republic of China, Indonesia, and Senegal. Traveling in groups of about 20 students with a faculty member, they spend 6 weeks studying the region through lectures and field trips and the remaining 6 weeks working in rural clinics, schools, and community development and mission projects. In the Study-Service Term, or SST, which is as much a part of general education at Goshen as 6 hours of humanities or natural science and mathematics, students learn by doing for others amid a language, history, and culture very different from their own. "Goshen stands out," observes a senior, "because of its integrity, ethics, and philosophy as written in its mission and carried out through programs such as SST. Goshen is not big, but it doesn't lack opportunities for students ready to take them on."

Student body: Just half of Goshen's students are from Indiana, with half of the rest also from the Midwest. Altogether, young people gather from 35 states and 40 foreign countries to study at Goshen. Eighty-three percent of the students in a recent year were white Americans and 4% were Hispanic with 3% African-American, 1% Asian-American, and 0.5% Native American. Nine percent were foreign nationals. Just over three-quarters of the students in a recent year came from public schools. About 55% of all students report being Mennonite or having Mennonite-related backgrounds, although 30 different Christian denominations are represented on campus as well as several world religions. Among the 195 freshmen who entered in fall 2005, 14 were National Merit finalists and 12 either valedictorians or salutatorians.

Students who seek out Goshen's brand of learning are as unusual as its programs. Considered politically liberal by some, Christian, and socially conscious, first-year students mingle with seniors as easily as with other new students. Many, though they come from different parts of the country, turn out to know the same people through national meetings of the Mennonite church, in which many have been active. Students work hard—"People here take what they're doing seriously," says a junior—but still consider themselves fun-loving. Although the strong presence of the Mennonite faith, with its emphasis on pacifism and the simple life and its bans on tobacco and alcohol, unites the campus on many issues, says a senior, "there is a real cross section of beliefs and opinions—which makes for good debate!"

Academics: Goshen, which celebrated its centennial year in 1994, awards the bachelor's degree in 33 fields. The academic year is divided into 2 15-week semesters in fall and spring plus a single 3½-week term in May. The standard general-education classes are among the largest on campus, with a course on Jesus and the Gospels enrolling almost 90. Most lower-level courses fall below 40 and upper-level ones have 20 or less. The off-campus experience offered by the Study-Service Term is easily the star of Goshen's general-education program, although the international education requirement can be completed on campus by those who prefer. To travel, students must demonstrate a certain level of language competency and, for a term in Peru or the Dominican Republic, pay the same semester fee, which includes transportation costs, as if they were staying on campus. Travel to other locales carries some additional costs. Altogether, the general-education program accounts for just over a third of the credits needed to graduate. Other on-campus components of the program include courses in all the major disciplines, including 9 hours in Bible, religion, and philosophy.

Fifty of Goshen's 122 faculty members in a recent year were part-time; not quite half are women and all are Christian, though not necessarily Mennonite. While students appreciate how well many professors lecture, they are more impressed with how well the faculty listen to them and their concerns. One-to-one mentoring is especially valued, although some students have thought the faculty could use some new members to provide added stimulation and hopefully more cultural diversity within their ranks.

English, science, and music emerge as leaders among Goshen's academic programs. English features excellent professors, including a poet in residence, as well as the Pinchpenny Press, which publishes small volumes of creative writing by students and faculty. Programs in the sciences, including one leading to a bachelor's degree in nursing, have been strengthened by the addition of a new building with modern equipment completed in 1992. Special research facilities include one of the nation's top labs for x-ray crystallography used by physics majors. Little wonder that in 2003, 100% of those physics students applying to graduate school (along with students in premed and social work) gained acceptance! Environmental science and biology students gain from Merry Lea Environmental Learning Center, 45 minutes south of Goshen, which serves as a 1150-acre living laboratory. The college also operates a facility in the Florida Keys for those interested in marine biology. The music program provides plenty of individual attention under excellent musicians "who could be anywhere but chose to be here," raves a major, as well as lots of opportunities to perform. Those opportunities became even better with the opening in fall 2002 of an $11 million performance and community music school, complete with 2 major performance halls, classroom and practice space, and an art gallery. Communication, with its well-respected student publications, and history, with the Mennonite Historical Library on campus, also get good reviews.

There is no major or minor in political science, just 6 classes in the field. A minor only is offered in global economics. Art and computer science could use better facilities.

Facilities: The Harold and Wilma Good Library lives up to its name—it is basically good, with sufficient resources to meet most students' research needs and a quiet atmosphere for study. The facility holds 120,000 volumes and 900 current periodicals, with an emphasis on peace studies. Database searching is available along with a computerized catalog. Students in need of more extensive materials can either use the Internet, the library's interlibrary loan system, which secures materials within a week, or go directly to the University of Notre Dame in South Bend, an hour away.

Five computer labs providing more than 70 PCs and Macs are open for student use; at least 2 are open around the clock. All dorm rooms are wired for access to the Internet.

Special programs: Students who wish to study off-campus outside the framework of the SST have alternative options in Europe and Latin America or at home in Chicago or Washington, D.C. May term courses also take students abroad to England, Spain, Italy, Ireland, and Guatemala. Students who prefer can spend a semester studying tropical agriculture at the University of Florida or focusing on environmental concerns in Mancelona, Michigan. A 3-2 degree in engineering is possible in conjunction with Case Western Reserve, the University of Illinois, and Washington University in St. Louis. Unlike at most colleges, the Goshen College honors program is open to any student who wishes to gain more extensive opportunities and greater challenge than can be found in the regular classes.

Campus life: Goshen (pop. 30,000), a community about 120 miles east of Chicago, doesn't have a lot to offer in the way of nearby urban diversion, so much of the college's weekend life revolves around campus events, of which there are many. "No matter how stupid, there is always *something* to take in on the weekends," says a junior. Movies, coffeehouses, talent shows, and sporting events keep most of the 69% who live on the 135-acre campus occupied. There are neither fraternities nor sororities, but most students find fellowship in such organizations as the Goshen Student Women's Association, the Black Student Union, the International Students Club, and Pax, a group that explores peace issues in the world. Chapels and convocations are held 2 times a week, and students are required to attend about half of the time. Though the Mennonite presence is strong, the issue of different faiths is handled "sensitively," says a junior. Crime, a rare occurrence to begin with, has been kept further in check by improved lighting.

Maple Leafs soccer and basketball games draw the biggest crowds among the 7 men's and 7 women's varsity sports played in NAIA competition. Nearly half of the men but fewer than a fifth of the women get involved in the 8 men's and 8 women's intramural sports. The club Frisbee football team is an all-time favorite source of competitive stress relief.

South Bend, home of the University of Notre Dame about an hour away, offers off-campus escape to those with cars. Closer by, the Merry Lea Environmental Center enables many students simply to "escape into nature."

Cost cutters: Ninety-nine percent of freshmen and continuing students in a recent year received financial aid. Seventy-five percent of the first-year students and 71% of the rest were on need-based assistance. The average freshman award for a student with financial need included a need-based scholarship or grant averaging $11,781 and need-based self-help aid such as loans and jobs averaging $4527. Non-need-based athletic scholarships for first-year students averaged $2400; other non-need-based awards and scholarships averaged $10,167. Average debt of a recent graduate was $15,689. Each year, 10 students receive President's Leadership Awards, good for up to $12,000. Candidates must meet 2 of the following criteria: be a National Merit Finalist, have ranked in the top 5% of their high school class, have a GPA of at least 3.8, or scored at least 1270 on the SAT math and critical reading portions or 29 on the ACT. National Merit Finalists who demonstrate need also are eligible for a scholarship of up to $2500; without need, $1000. Other merit scholarships pay up to $7000 as determined by looking at a student's GPA, SAT, or ACT scores, rank in class, financial need, and date of application. Other awards worth $1000 to $2500 go to African-American, Asian-American, Native American, and Hispanic students who ranked in the top half of their high school classes with GPAs of at least 2.5. Additional scholarships are awarded in athletics, business, communication, music, theater, and missionary interest.

In a recent year, 4 different payment plans were offered: full payment at each semester check-in, which earned a discount of $15; payment of $3000 at check-in with the balance to be paid within 30 days without interest; a monthly payment plan with no interest charges or fees other than an initial $70 payment; and other plans made by special arrangements.

Rate of return: Eighty percent of freshmen return for the sophomore year; 46% go on to graduate in 4 years; 65% in 5 years; 66% in 6 years.

Payoff: Ten percent of recent graduates earned degrees in organizational management followed by 8% in elementary education and 5% in nursing. About 30% of the men and women pursue advanced degrees within 6 months of graduation. Goshen recently ranked 36th among 500 colleges surveyed in the number of graduates who complete doctorates in education. The college also ranked in the top sixth among the nation's liberal arts colleges in the number of graduates who go on to earn Ph.D.s, according to a study completed by Franklin and Marshall College. Goshen graduates also are accepted in medical school at twice the national average, and accounting majors successfully complete the CPA exam on the first or second try 3 times the national rate. Many students enter service programs directly after college.

Bottom line: Advises a senior: "A student with curiosity, compassion, creativity, and interest in the world beyond him- or herself will go far here."

Hanover College

Hanover, Indiana 47243

Setting: Rural
Control: Private (Presbyterian)
Undergraduate enrollment: 438 men, 566 women
Graduate enrollment: None
Student/faculty ratio: 10:1
Freshman profile: 15% scored over 700 on SAT I verbal; 34% scored 600–700; 42% 500–599; 9% below 500. 8% scored over 700 on SAT I math; 43% scored 600–700; 42% 500–599; 7% below 500. 34% scored above 28 on the ACT; 14% scored 27–28; 25% 24–26; 25% 21–23; 2% below 21. 42% graduated in top tenth of high school class; 69% in upper fifth.
Faculty profile: 95% Ph.D.'s

Tuition and fees: $21,150
Room and board: $6500
Freshman financial aid: 80%; average scholarship or grant: $14,421 need-based; $14,452 non-need-based
Campus jobs: 27%; average earnings: $1300/year
Application deadline: Early action: Dec. 20 and Jan. 15; regular: Mar. 1
Financial aid deadline: Mar. 1
Admissions information: (812) 866-7022;
(800) 213-2178
e-mail: admission@hanover.edu
web site: www.hanover.edu

When students at Hanover College, located in the Hoosier Hills of southeastern Indiana, need faculty advice after hours, they don't have far to go. All but 6% of the 1004 full-time students live on the 630-acre campus, as do about a third of the faculty members and their families. Since Hanover's founding in 1827, the idea has been to create an academic community that encompasses much more than the hours spent in the classroom. A Principle-Based Code of Conduct, developed by students, faculty, alumni, parents, and staff in the 1998–99 school year, sets standards for such principles as the pursuit of academic excellence, respect for one another, and community responsibility. With just 8 of the 103 faculty members part-time (36% of the pool are women; 95% have the highest degrees in their fields), the core group maintains a strong commitment to the college and to campus life. "The Hanover faculty make Hanover what it is," says an Indiana native. "Because professors live on campus, you can call on them anytime and they all work to make students feel a part of the community that is Hanover." Adds a junior: "I've found much more community at Hanover than I could have hoped for. Students who are serious about learning, not just getting a diploma, will fit in well at Hanover."

Student body: Sixty-four percent of the community dwellers are Hoosiers; three-quarters of the rest also come from the Midwest, although 28 states and 17 foreign countries have residents on campus. Sixteen percent attended private high schools. Just 5% of the students are Presbyterian, with another 30% members of other Protestant denominations; 14% are Catholic and 1% members of other faiths. Fifrty percent claim no religious affiliation. Minority representation on campus is small, with 3% Asian-American, 2% African-American and 1% each Hispanic and Native American. Foreign nationals account for 5%. Undergraduates describe themselves as outgoing, genuine, and motivated. Students pride themselves on being open-minded, enabling those who tend to lean toward the liberal or conservative side of issues to find a willing forum for discussion, rather than frustration. Popular outlets for expression range from the College Republicans to People for Peace. "Overall, everyone is concerned with academics," says a senior. "Admittedly, some are more concerned than others." Many also tend to see academics primarily as a means to a good job, as evidenced by the 23% who graduate in business administration and elementary education.

Academics: Hanover awards the bachelor's degree in more than 30 majors. Students follow a calendar that contains 2 semesters followed by a May term that is open for travel, exchanges, and independent study. The largest class at Hanover, in Physical Geology, enrolls about 60; most introductory lecture classes tend to have about 50. After the first 2 years, courses pare down to 20 or fewer participants.

New liberal arts requirements went into effect in fall 2004. Students now begin their time at Hanover with an August Experience in which they gain an intense introduction to college-level modes of inquiry and end in their senior year with an integrative capstone course on Great Issues. In between, students take 1 or 2 courses in each of the following, Human Nature, the Great Works, the Examined Life, Modern Society, the Natural World, Other Cultures, Abstraction and Formal Reasoning, World Languages, and Health and Physical Education.

Among the traditional liberal arts disciplines, students find English, history, philosophy, theological studies, biology, art, and theater arts to be among the strongest majors, characterized by professors who have a passion for their field and for sharing it with students. "Each of these departments has professors who make students *want* to major in their area," says an English major who did. Productions of the theater department have earned distinction for their numerous appearances at the American College Theater Festival, held at the Kennedy Center in Washington, D.C. The philosophy major is small, though its faculty is surprisingly well rounded. Physics offers excellent computer facilities for the size of the school and program, though it could use a wider variety of courses. The biology, chemistry, and psychology faculty are talented and tough. Biology professors, in particular, notes a junior, "spend extra hours in the labs and in one-on-one meetings with students to make them feel more comfortable and better prepare them for the real world."

Sociology is considered less demanding than other majors, though its faculty is well respected among students; the elementary education and economics majors need more rigor as well. Some math professors have a hard time making complex concepts clear to students. Students observe that across the board, the small number of faculty on such a small campus means that students had better learn to get along with all their professors, because they likely will have them for several classes in their chosen major.

Facilities: The resources of Duggan Library are impressive for a school of Hanover's size but still small for a school of its academic expectations—about 223,000 bound volumes, 292,000 government documents, and 1667 periodical and newspaper subscriptions. Therefore, for many intensive projects students check online, head to Indiana University or the University of Louisville or wait for interlibrary loan. As far as being a place to study, Duggan has its spots to hide, though if they are taken, a student is likely to meet too many people he or she knows, and get a lot less accomplished!

Students have their choice of 2 main computer labs on campus stocked with IBMs and Macs. One lab in the library is open 24 hours, the other until 11 p.m. There also is a port in every dorm room.

Special programs: The Spring Term Consortium enables students to spend the merry month of May at any of 7 other colleges, among them Alma in Michigan, Transylvania in Kentucky, and Elmira in New York. Richter Grants provide funds for students to engage in individual research projects which are of particular interest to them. In a recent year, a Kansas native spent a summer riding the Trans-Siberian Railroad to study Russian culture. Others have gone to Australia to study koalas and to Europe to study concentration camps. The college also provides opportunities for study abroad through its curriculum, with classes in international business meeting in Western Europe and courses in sociology calling roll in China. It is not uncommon for political science students to study in Washington, D.C., while geology majors scramble around the Grand Canyon. The new Center for Business Preparation enables students to gain fundamental business knowledge and experience while majoring in a liberal arts discipline. Through curricular and cocurricular requirements, scholars apply business theories, explore careers, and network with alumni business leaders. Scholars also gain experience through a project-based internship, case research, and group consulting projects.

Campus life: In the close-knit Hanover community, whose red brick buildings overlook the Ohio River, the Greeks are the biggest thing around. Forty-two percent of the men and 59% of the women belong to 5 national fraternities and 4 national sororities, all of which have houses on campus. Even independents find themselves sometimes going to a fraternity house to party or just hang out. The Greeks, says a junior, "provide the social scene for a lot of people, (but) most weekends, students opt to stay in one night to get homework done and go out the other." Crime on the well-lit, isolated campus is barely a consideration. Says a junior from a large city: "Had I a Ferrari, I wouldn't be afraid to leave it running in front of the campus center while I went hiking!" The use of community bicycles around campus has helped cut down on bicycle thefts.

Football games, followed by basketball, boast the strongest fan support among the 8 men's and 8 women's sports played in NCAA Division III. "But the students support each other at most extracurricular activities," says a sophomore. "There are always fans at the events." Forty-five percent of the men and 35% of the women take part in intramural competition, 10 sports for men, 10 for women.

The town of Hanover is tiny, with just over 4000 people, so students look to neighboring Madison which is 3 times the population for shopping and restaurants. Only upperclassmen are allowed to have cars, however. Louisville is a popular day trip, just 45 miles south, while a 2-hour drive takes students to Cincinnati or Indianapolis.

Cost cutters: Hanover's endowment of about $142 million in June 2005 ranks in the top 10% in terms of funds per student. Eighty percent of the freshmen and 85% of the continuing students in the 2005–2006 school year received some form of financial aid. Virtually all of the freshmen and 72% of the continuing students were given need-based assistance. The average freshman award for a student with need included a need-based scholarship or grant averaging $14,421 and need-based self-help aid such as loans and jobs averaging $3478. Other non-need-based awards and scholarships averaged $14,452. The average debt of a 2005 graduate was $16,514. The Lilly Trustee Scholarship provides 3 awards paying $25,000 a year to the top applicants in the Scholarships for Merit Competition. Horner Scholarships pay $20,000 annually to 10 entering freshmen. Crowe/Long Scholarships pay $16,000 a year to 15 freshmen. Faculty Scholarships pay $1000 a year to 60 students. Pointe Scholarships pay $2000 to $6000 a year to students of under-represented ethnicities. To be considered for Scholarships for Merit, students typically have combined SAT critical reading and math scores of 1200 or above or an ACT composite of 27 and rank in the top 20% of their graduating class or achieve a 3.7 GPA. Students must apply to Hanover before January 15 to be considered. Other merit-based Academic scholarships pay $5000 to $14,000 a year.

Rate of return: Seventy-seven percent of entering freshmen return for the sophomore year. Sixty-eight percent graduate in 4 years; 69% in 5 years.

Payoff: Eleven percent of all 2005 graduates earned degrees in business administration; another 11% earned degrees in psychology; 9% specialized in biology. Just over 60% of the graduates leave Hanover for the work force, many accepting entry-level management and sales positions with firms in the Midwest and East. About 50 companies and organizations recruited on campus in the 2004–2005 school year. Almost 30% headed off to graduate or professional school. More than 60% of Hanover grads eventually pursue postgraduate or professional studies.

Bottom line: Students who come to Hanover have to want to be part of a close community in a rural environment. Says a city dweller: "It took some getting used to, yet this is a very comfortable atmosphere if you let it be. Hanover is academically far more difficult than I thought it would be, but faculty and students are, in general, helpful and supportive in the extreme!"

Indiana University Bloomington

Bloomington, Indiana 47405

Setting: Small town
Control: Public
Undergraduate enrollment: 13,452 men, 14,522 women
Graduate enrollment: 2756 men, 2741 women
Student/faculty ratio: 18:1
Freshman profile: 4% scored over 700 on SAT I verbal; 25% scored 600–700; 44% 500–599; 27% below 500. 5% scored over 700 on SAT I math; 29% scored 600–700; 43% 500–599; 23% below 500. 15% scored above 28 on the ACT; 14% scored 27–28; 29% 24–26; 24% 21–23; 18% below 21. 23% graduated in top tenth of high school class; 47% in upper fifth.

Faculty profile: 86% Ph.D.'s
Tuition and fees: $7112 in-state; $19,508 out-of-state
Room and board: $6244
Freshman financial aid: 42%; average scholarship or grant: $4964 need-based; $3721 non-need-based
Campus jobs: NA; average earnings: NA
Application deadline: Feb. 1 (priority)
Financial aid deadline: Mar. 1
Admissions information: (812) 855-0661
  e-mail: iuadmit@indiana.edu
  web site: www.iub.edu

Students surprised to find a cultural mecca in small-town Indiana obviously haven't tuned into Indiana University Bloomington. Indiana was founded in 1820 as a liberal arts institution, and it is the university's internationally recognized Jacobs School of Music that gives the campus a special resonance. Despite the fact that just 1600 of the 38,000 full- and part-time undergraduates and graduate students at IU are music majors, the education of all Indiana students is enriched by their presence. Everyday, somewhere on Indiana's bucolic campus, some kind of free musical performance can be found, and usually more than one since the school presents more than 1100 musical events annually. Monday night is jazz; Wednesday, the symphony, actually 1 of 5 symphony orchestras assembled by the school. Choral performances by groups as diverse as the Singing Hoosiers and the Pro Arte Singers, as well as operas performed by IU's own opera company, are as commonplace as movies on other campuses. And everything goes for a price that sets even the most off-key croaker singing—just over $25,700 for tuition, fees, room, and board for out-of-staters in the 2005–2006 school year and less than $13,500 for those happily humming Hoosiers.

Student body: Sixty-seven percent of Indiana's undergraduates are from in-state. Although half of the out-of-staters also come from the Midwest, every state is represented, along with 150 foreign countries. Observes a midwesterner: "I love that my school is so big that I can always meet someone new and they might be from a country that I've never heard of." Eighty-seven percent of the students in a recent year attended public schools. Ten percent of the student body are members of racial or ethnic minority groups, with 5% African-American, 3% Asian-American and 2% Hispanic. Four percent are foreign nationals. More than 30 multicultural organizations help these minority students to feel part of the IU campus.

Other students, many from smaller communities, who worry about being lost in Indiana's bigness, are quickly reassured by its small-town midwestern atmosphere. Undergraduates use terms like "open and friendly" and "spirited" to describe their classmates. Says a senior from Illinois: "The in-state students are a little conservative for my tastes but the school is almost a third out-of-state students!" Academically, each makes IU a little of what he or she wants it to be. Notes an east coast transplant: "This campus can be a party school *or* a study school, or even a combination, whichever the individual prefers." But, cautions a history major, "If you come for the parties, you may have a good time for a while but will quickly be gone."

Academics: IU Bloomington offers degrees through the doctorate, including an advanced degree from its highly respected School of Law, with more than 130 majors and 5000 courses leading to a bachelor's degree. Undergraduates may earn degrees from the College of Arts and Sciences plus 8 schools located on campus. The academic year is divided into 2 semesters. Indiana's largest classroom seats 415 students and is used by such lecture courses as Introductory Psychology. Nearly a fifth of all classes, usually those at the upper-division level, have fewer than 10 students. About two-fifths have less than 20. Regular course offerings average 35 enrollees.

Before undergraduates can enroll in any of Indiana's undergraduate schools except the Jacobs School of Music and honors students in the Kelley School of Business, they must take courses in areas such as writing, mathematics, foreign languages, culture studies, and traditional distributional requirements in IU's College of Arts and Sciences. Freshmen and sophomores also take intensive small classes known as Topics courses that stress writing, reasoning, and questioning skills. New students enrolled in Freshman Interest Groups take 2 or 3 of their first-semester courses together and live close to each other and to an upper-division peer instructor on campus. Undergraduates may enter different schools at different times; for example, students usually enter the schools of Journalism and Business in the sophomore year. Only in the School of Music are freshmen admitted directly into the professional institution though they still take general education courses in the College of Arts and Sciences. Many freshmen undecided about a major when they enter IU use the general-education courses to sample a wide range of subjects before choosing.

IU's faculty includes 1865 full-time members and 309 part-time. No figure is available for the portion of professors who teach at the graduate level only. A third of the full-time faculty are women. Three faculty members have received Nobel prizes; 1 has been awarded the Pulitzer Prize. Their résumés include advanced degrees from the nation's and world's premier institutions and real-life experience in the fields they teach. Students resigned to the prospect of no personal attention from professors in such a large setting are surprised to find a number of faculty members receptive to helping undergraduates. (IU also has a tradition of several top-level administrators teaching freshman classes.) Says a junior fine arts major: "If it is on the weekend, many are more than willing to meet you at a restaurant or coffee shop just to help you." Most faculty members, adds a telecommunications and philosophy major, "love to engage their students in debate and intellectual discussions, sometimes preferring the development of ideas over lesson plans." However, as wonderful as many faculty members turn out to be, the large number of graduate assistants who teach lower-division classes annoys many undergraduates. "Sometimes they are not very competent," laments a business major. But there are exceptions. Notes a journalism major, "One of my graduate assistants was one of the best teachers I've ever had, which dispels the myth that only full professors know how to be good teachers."

Not surprisingly, Indiana's Jacobs School of Music rates highly on student checklists for its first-rate facilities, personalized teaching from world-renowned instructors, and wide range of courses from majors in bassoon or violoncello to studies of early music before 1800 and electronic composing.

Admission to IU's Kelley School of Business, which ranks among the top 1% nationally, is limited to 1200 new students a year and is based largely on performance in 3 or more prerequisite math and business courses. Once admitted, students find the school's integrative core, consisting of general-education and basic business administration classes along with professional courses in 1 of 14 concentrations, to be a particularly demanding curriculum. They especially enjoy the case-study approach to teaching, which gives a real-life edge to their course work. Notes a finance and international business major: "The faculty provide great opportunities for internships and jobs. I had 7 offers for internships, one of which I accepted for full-time employment after completing the internship."

Classes in the School of Journalism are small and give professors plenty of opportunity to work closely with students to improve their writing; facilities for work in newspapers, magazines, radio, television, and photojournalism are up to date and cover just about every aspect of news gathering, production, and presentation. The already strong School of Education became even better after its move into a new building that incorporates state-of-the-art computer and video technology into its classrooms, laboratories, and library. In the College of Arts and Sciences, psychology, political science, telecommunications, and a wide range of foreign language classes from Arabic and Bambara to Turkish and Uzbek are noteworthy. Still, some students wish some of the classes placed more emphasis on conversation rather than written work. IU's Department of Central Eurasian Studies is the only one in the nation to study these cultures and languages. IU's chemistry program is the largest in the nation and offers first-rate facilities equaled at few other universities. Biology is considered "fantastic" as well. The fine arts program offers more than 25 different mediums for student focus.

Students caution that several majors in the College of Arts and Sciences, among them English, mathematics, philosophy and some lower-level science courses, use too few full professors in the classroom and rely too heavily on graduate assistants many of whom students find less than adequate to teach the course material. Students interested in engineering find no such major in Bloomington and head to Purdue.

Facilities: Students use words like "amazing" and "outstanding" to describe Indiana's collection of more than 6.7 million volumes, 5 million microform items, nearly 254,000 sound recordings, and more than 61,000 paper and electronic periodicals. A computerized catalog makes it possible to locate materials in either the Main Library, 15 departmental libraries, or 11 smaller libraries in the residence halls, as well as at IU libraries on other campuses. Materials housed at a different Indiana campus are delivered within 48 hours. Though several of the smaller libraries on campus provide quainter atmospheres for study, the "aesthetically basic" Herman B. Wells Library is where most undergraduates congregate. Upon entering, they may choose "sides" for study depending on how hard they need to do it: the 10 or so floors on the graduate side offer total silence for intense concentration; the 5 undergraduate floors are quiet but a bit more relaxed and open to socializing. The Cyber Café in the basement is great for study breaks but also provides computers along the walls for those who need to work while they eat. Twenty-four-hour floors are available for days when there's no time for breaks, even to sleep!

Indiana University is wireless—and "wired," with more than 1500 Macs and PCs spread among 100 or so computing labs in the library, the student union, academic buildings, and residence halls across campus. Computers in some residence halls, Wells Library, and the computer science department are open 24 hours, with most others accessible for extended times. More than half of all students also own a computer. Says a senior in the business school: "Every class I am taking this semester has a web page, and I download PowerPoint notes prior to each class, so I can follow along with lectures and class activities." The university strongly recommends that students have personal computers, although only computer science majors are required to have them.

Special programs: Study-abroad programs in more than 25 countries are available through IU's own college and schools, with additional options through other student exchange organizations. Business majors, for example, may spend a semester in Singapore or Santiago, Chile. Students in the School of Public and Environmental Affairs can spend a term in the Netherlands or as participants in the popular Washington Leadership program, in which they work and study in the nation's capital for a term.

Campus life: A junior science major describes IU campus life this way: "One of the most difficult aspects of going to Indiana University is actually getting to the act of studying. Each evening there are so many activities offered that a student can do too many things and forget that studying is vital as well." Forty-two percent of Indiana's undergraduates and 86% of all freshmen reside right where the action is: on the 1931-acre campus, which is marked by lots of trees and green spaces, a stream, and buildings of—what else—Indiana limestone. Another 15% live in Greek housing. Although just 16% of the men and 18% of the women are members of the 32 national fraternities and 23 national sororities, Greek members dominate most campus organizations and events; fraternity parties generally are limited to fellow Greeks. Observes a junior: "If less than 20% of the campus is Greek, that leaves more than 80% of the students that must find other ways to enjoy their weekends," which most readily do. Independents say that enough alternative activities are offered by 400 or so student organizations plus all those musicals, operas, concerts, and plays to keep nonmembers from feeling left out. Indiana Memorial Union, which boasts of being the largest student union in the world, has several restaurants and lounges, as well as a bowling alley and a 200-room hotel. Although incidents of crime on campus are few, IU devotes part of the first week of school to educating both men and women students about the dangers of rape, including date rape. Free buses discourage students from walking alone late at night; good lighting and emergency phones also are plentiful.

It comes as no surprise that among Big Ten athletic teams Indiana basketball rates 10+ for student popularity, with Hoosiers football and championship soccer only slightly further down the scale. "I was never much of an IU fan until I went to my first season of basketball games," says a junior. "Every student gets one courtside game and mine just happened to be against Michigan State when we won in the last 3 seconds of the game." In the exciting 2001–2002 season, Indiana lost to the University of Maryland in the final game of the NCAA Division I championship. But other sports inspire school spirit as well, and deservedly so. The 10 men's and 12 women's intercollegiate teams play as part of NCAA Division I, and altogether, have won about two dozen Division I titles and have produced more than 100 Olympic athletes. In a recent year, the swimming and diving team held the NCAA record for most consecutive titles in the sport, 6. Intramurals, with more than 27 sports for men and women, as well as 35 club sports, draw their share of enthusiastic athletes (in a recent year, 80% of the men, 20% of the women) not good enough for Big Ten play. The most exciting weekend of the year, by most students' reckoning, is the time of the Little 500, a bicycle version of the Indianapolis 500 car race. Preparation for the entirely student-run event begins a year in advance.

For escape on other weekends, Indianapolis, the home of the real Indy 500, is 45 minutes north and scenic Brown County and Lake Monroe are just 20 minutes south. Most students, however, just hang around the busy campus or Bloomington (pop. 65,000), a true college town.

Cost cutters: Forty-two percent of the first-year students received financial aid in the 2005–2006 school year; so did 37% of the continuing students. Need-based aid was granted to 27% of the first-year students and to 21% of the rest. The average freshman award for a student with financial need included a need-based scholarship or grant averaging $4964 and need-based self-help aid such as loans and jobs averaging $1788. Non-need-based athletic scholarships for first-year students averaged $15,450; other non-need-based awards and scholarships averaged $3721. Average debt for a 2005 graduate was $18,423. Resident and nonresident students with exceptional standardized test scores, class ranks, and grade point averages are eligible to receive $4000 Dean's Scholarships and $7000 Faculty Scholarships, respectively. High school valedictorians also receive $4000 awards for one year. The Wells Scholarship pays full tuition, fees, room and board, plus an overseas study opportunity to between 20 and 25 freshmen a year who rank among the best of the best. Cooperative programs are available in many schools, including those of business and journalism.

Rate of return: Eighty-seven percent of entering freshmen return for the sophomore year. Forty-six percent graduate in 4 years; 65%, in 5 years; 69%, in 6 years.

Payoff: In 2005, 20% received degrees in business/marketing; 16% in education and 10% in communications/journalism. Eleven hundred fifty companies and organizations recruited on campus in a recent school year; 23,000 interviews were conducted in business alone. In a recent year, a fifth enrolled in graduate school within 6 months of commencement. And job hunters can count on being aided by the 450,000 alumni located around the world.

Bottom line: Indiana University Bloomington provides the collegiate life many students dream of: big, beautiful campus, big-time sports, big social life, with an active Greek system. IU's price tag may fit that generic image, but name-brand professional schools turn what could be just "brand X" into "X-cellent."

Manchester College

North Manchester, Indiana 46962

Setting: Small town
Control: Private (Church of the Brethren)
Undergraduate enrollment: 1104 men and women
Graduate enrollment: NA
Student/faculty ratio: 16:1
Freshman profile: SAT/ACT scores: NA; class rank data: NA
Faculty profile: 92% Ph.D.'s
Tuition and fees: $19,360
Room and board: $6850

Freshman financial aid: 100%; average grant: $12,280; average scholarship: $8620
Campus jobs: 40%; average earnings: NA
Application deadline: Rolling
Financial aid deadline: Rolling (Scholarships: Mar. 1)
Admissions information: (260) 982-5055; (800) 852-3648
e-mail: admitinfo@manchester.edu
web site: www.manchester.edu

Among recent graduates of Manchester College in north central Indiana, nearly half the class majored in 2 career-oriented disciplines: business and marketing and education. Yet, according to students, not one of these popular majors had as much impact on the tenor and environment of the campus as one of the smallest yet strongest concentrations: peace studies. Manchester College's program in peace studies was the first such major established in the nation and remains a magnet for students from around the region who want to specialize in this field. Says a sociology major: "The peace studies program attracts a unique type of student to Manchester. These students usually bring an open and unassuming quality to campus life and discussion." Even students not majoring in the area become involved in peace issues, at the local, national and international levels. The Kenapocomoco Coalition, an informal group of students, faculty, and community members, sponsors weekly discussion groups and speakers from across the country and abroad to examine issues of peace, justice, and conscience. Much of the discussion is supplemented with opportunities for action. The combined influence of the peace studies program and the school's affiliation with the Church of the Brethren provides an environment in which even the most career-focused major is placed in a larger context of how it affects the community and world. Such lessons can be priceless, and for just $26,210 in tuition, fees, room, and board in the 2005–2006 school year, the price couldn't be more right.

Student body: All but 17% of Manchester's students in a recent year were from Indiana, and all but a small portion of that 17% also were from the Midwest. A total of 25 states and 30 foreign countries have residents on campus. Ninety-nine percent of the students are graduates of public schools. Eleven percent of the undergraduates are members of the Church of the Brethren. Another 50% belong to other Protestant denominations. African-Americans and Hispanics comprised the largest racial and ethnic minority groups, recently at 4% and 3% of enrollment respectively. Asian-Americans recently accounted for 1%. Foreign nationals comprised 5%. Manchester undergraduates tend to cover "every point on the political spectrum," says a senior, "radical leftists, moderates, conservative Republicans," and most find a forum in which they can be heard, and listened to as well. Students are hard-working and free-thinking, playful and compassionate toward each other as well as toward the social needs of the world. "Some students come mainly to play basketball or football," says a philosophy major. "A recent valedictorian went to Harvard Medical School. At Manchester, students can find people who are just like them, or better yet, find people with entirely different backgrounds and beliefs, which challenges their own stance on any issue." Concludes a sophomore: "Most are good people who care about the world around them."

Academics: Manchester, which turned 115 in 2004, awards the bachelor's degree in 45 majors plus master's degrees in accounting and in contemporary leadership. Classes follow a semester calendar, with a January term in the middle to provide time for internships, study and travel abroad, and concentrated classes on campus. The range of class sizes among 272 class sections recently offered extended to not quite 50 notetakers in 21 class sections to below 10 in 44. The greatest number of class sections, 84, contained between 20 and 29 students.

The general studies requirements focus on competency in basic skills and in mastery of specific subject matter from courses in Western Civilization and the Christian Tradition to the humanities, natural sciences, and social sciences. A required First-Year Colloquium involves freshmen in interdisciplinary courses that combine work in basic skills such as computer use, writing, listening, and speaking, with topics ranging from ethical issues to science to jazz. Three upper-level "connections" courses provide an interdisciplinary capstone to the general-education curriculum. Students also complete a requirement in Values, Ideas, and the Arts by attending a variety of convocations and programs.

Students use adjectives like "exceptional" and "dedicated" when describing the faculty, recently numbering 92 of whom 24 were part-time and 37% women. Says a senior: "The faculty teach in many styles from many perspectives and they 'challenge,' maybe an understatement, their students to be individuals, to explain their reasons for their beliefs, and to succeed." Students never doubt that the faculty want them to succeed and will meet with them wherever or whenever needed to help them reach their goals.

Manchester's strongest disciplines span the worlds of preprofessional majors and pure liberal arts. On the career-oriented side, the accounting program is considered very competitive and offers a semester-long internship off-campus that adds practical experience to the list of in-class abilities students acquire. Graduates recently boasted the highest passage rate in Indiana—twice the national average—on the first sitting at the CPA exam. The sociology and social work and education programs also are highly regarded. Notes an education major: "The education department is producing teachers with ability and conviction, due to intensive classroom observations in the local schools and great methodology training." Among the more traditional liberal arts, the religion and philosophy department is considered first-rate as are history and peace studies. Graduates in biology, chemistry, and bio-chemistry can anticipate an 89% acceptance rate to medical school, based on their solid preparation at Manchester.

Students say the modern languages could use more materials and professors; majors are offered in French, German, and Spanish. The art and music programs also need more staff and space, though brilliant faculty members maximize what they have. One of the college's 2 art professors was named the 2002 U.S. Professor of the Year for Baccalaureate Colleges by 2 national education organizations; the college's A Cappella choir performed at Carnegie Hall in 2001, will do so again in 2007, and performed at the Vatican in Rome in 2004. Theater arts is offered only as a concentration within a communication studies major. The communication studies major itself could use more modern equipment to better prepare those students interested in careers in broadcasting. In just about any program, notes a sophomore, "if classes are too easy, professors are more than willing to help you find outside projects to make them more challenging."

Facilities: Students looking for a quiet place to study head for the "fishbowl," the popular glass-enclosed study spot at the newly remodeled 3-story Funderburg Library. Those needing extended hours of silence find the perfect hideaway in the 24-hour study room. However, Funderburg can be frustrating when students need extensive research materials. Though its collection of 174,000 volumes has been placed on an online catalog, students complain that many of the sources date from the 1960s through the 1980s. The collection of 973 periodicals also falls short when researching unusual topics. Along with the Internet and numerous electronic databases, a statewide interlibrary loan program "probably the greatest aid," says a political science major, puts thousands of volumes within easy reach.

Computer labs in Clark Computer Center, the Administration Building, the Communication Center, the library, and residence halls fulfill most students' computer needs. "Most students have their own computers in their dorm rooms or houses," says a chemistry major, so lines and waits rarely occur. All residence-hall rooms are wired for Internet access.

Special programs: International study programs enable Manchester students to study in 12 countries ranging from Ecuador to Japan. During January term, more than a dozen Manchester professors usually offer courses which also involve travel outside the country. A cooperative program in nursing is available with Goshen College; an engineering degree done in conjunction with Washington University in St. Louis, Ohio State, or Purdue University also is an option.

Campus life: Nowhere is Manchester's sense of community stronger than in its five residence halls, where three-fourths of all undergraduates live. Together, neighbors on the various halls plan social gatherings and help to organize annual open houses which revolve around particular themes and engage students in friendly competition between floors. Since many of the residents live within 3 hours of campus, about half of the dorm dwellers often are homeward bound on any given weekend. Those who stay are usually too busy to notice the extra room. Groups like the Kenapocomoco Coalition, Amnesty International, Habitat for Humanity, and various organizations under campus ministry along with other clubs supplement the regular flow of movies, comedians, and dances provided. There are no Greek organizations. Crime also is of little concern. In a recent survey, 96% of Manchester students said they regarded the college's 124-acre wooded campus and its residence halls as safe and secure. Nevertheless, campus lighting recently was improved and emergency phones were installed to keep students feeling that way.

The recent success of Manchester's various sporting teams has spurred new excitement and interest around campus. Football, soccer, and basketball have traditionally drawn the biggest fan support among the 9 men's and 8 women's teams playing in NCAA Division III. Basketball games have sold out nearly every home game since the recent year when the men's team finished its season 31–1 and was runner-up in the Division III national tournament. The men's baseball team is a winner as well, competing in the NCAA tournament in the 2002–2003 school year. Not to be outdone, the women's tennis team completed a record 11–1 season in 2003–2004, with 4 players going undefeated in the regular season. A dozen intramural sports offer an especially favorite form of recreation, attracting nearly 90% of both men and women to the field or court.

Fort Wayne, 35 miles east, offers semiprofessional sports teams as well as a variety of entertainment not found in North Manchester (pop. 6000).

Cost cutters: In a recent school year, all freshmen and all but 4% of continuing students received some form of financial assistance, mostly based on financial need. The average award included a $12,280 need-based grant or $8620 scholarship. The average graduate left with debts of $13,461. Full tuition Honors Scholarships and Trustees Scholarships worth up to $13,000 are awarded annually. Presidential Scholarships worth up to $10,000 annually are awarded to first-time freshmen based on their high school academic records, test scores, high school class rank, outstanding leadership characteristics, and potential for achievement at the college. Dean's scholars can receive up to $9000 based on similar criteria. Director's Scholarships pay up to $7000. To be eligible for many of the most lucrative scholarships, students must have submitted their application for admission by Dec. 31. Tuition payments can be made in full, in 10 monthly installments, or carried over a longer period of time by special arrangement.

Rate of return: Seventy-five percent of the entering freshmen return for a second year. Forty-four percent go on to graduate in 4 years. Fifty percent earn degrees within 5 years.

Payoff: Twenty-eight percent of recent graduates earned degrees in business and marketing; 21% specialized in education and almost 8% each in communications, health professions and related sciences, and parks and recreation. Nearly a fourth of a recent class pursued advanced degrees within 6 months of commencement; just about all of the remaining three-fourths found employment within the same 6-month period. As part of an employment guarantee, Manchester graduates who have taken advantage of the college's services are still jobless 6 months after commencement can return to the college for additional undergraduate courses and career preparation for one year at no tuition charge. Only one graduate has taken the college up on the offer since 1995. Twenty-five companies and organizations recruited on campus in a recent school year.

Bottom line: Says a junior: "Manchester is a place for students who like the mainstream but it also offers outlets to high school students who for one reason or another may have found themselves on the fringes. All those who have conviction and are seeking a better world would find Manchester a great place to start. The opportunities are there to explore the world from many perspectives and to feel safe enough to test out ideas of one's own."

Purdue University

West Lafayette, Indiana 47907

Setting: Suburban
Control: Public
Undergraduate enrollment: 17,383 men, 11,813 women
Graduate enrollment: 3301 men, 2471 women
Student/faculty ratio: 15:1
Freshman profile: 4% scored over 700 on SAT I verbal; 22% scored 600–700; 47% 500–599; 27% below 500. 10% scored over 700 on SAT I math; 33% scored 600–700; 40% 500–599; 17% below 500. 20% scored above 28 on the ACT; 17% scored 27–28; 29% 24–26; 22% 21–23; 12% below 21. 27% graduated in top tenth of high school class; 50% graduated in upper fifth.

Faculty profile: 99% Ph.D.'s
Tuition and fees: $6458 in-state; $19,824 out-of-state
Room and board: $7000
Freshman financial aid: 44%; average scholarship or grant: $8946 need-based; $12,724 non-need-based
Campus jobs: 12%; average earnings: $859/year
Application deadline: Rolling except in nursing and flight technology (Nov. 15)
Financial aid deadline: Mar. 1 (priority)
Admissions information: (765) 494-1776
  e-mail: admissions@purdue.edu
  web site: www.purdue.edu

Which university has educated more engineers than any other university in the country? Alumni from which university include the first man and the last man on the moon? Which university established the first computer science department and pioneered the use of language laboratories, so prevalent in high schools and colleges today? If some game show hasn't considered starting a file of Purdue-nalia, it's missing out on a year's worth of brainteasers. Purdue University in northwestern Indiana is easily one of the most familiar names in higher education; students looking for the right stuff, may just find it here, at a very down-to-earth price.

Student body: Purdue's student body is about 75% white Americans, 5% Asian-Americans, 4% African-Americans, 3% Hispanics, and less than 1% Native Americans. Thirteen percent are foreign nationals from 126 countries. Indiana is home to 67% of the undergraduates, and though students come from all 50 states, the Midwest sends a larger share than other parts of the country. As a group, students bring with them strong doses of conservative values and a work ethic. As big as Purdue is, with nearly 39,000 full-time and part-time undergraduate and graduate students on the West Lafayette campus, the university is marked, according to those who attend it, by a general kindness among people and an atmosphere that accepts all types, of which there are many. "Because this school is so large," observes a student from Puerto Rico, "you learn to interact with all kinds of people from different backgrounds and nationalities." While the academic level ranges from highly competitive students in engineering and technology to more laid back liberal arts majors, those who want to excel can reach their goals with the help of extensive, free labs in many of the disciplines, complete with tutors to provide assistance. Says a senior: "The majority of undergraduates here are motivated, whether it is academically or socially; people here come to accomplish something and have set their minds to that."

Academics: Purdue, which was founded in 1869, offers degrees through the doctorate, with more than 500 undergraduate majors and specializations. Programs leading to a bachelor's degree are offered in 12 schools and colleges, with an academic year that is divided into semesters. The largest introductory courses, such as a management lecture, can have nearly 500 students in class, whereas some upper-level humanities courses have fewer than 12.

Purdue has no single set of general-education requirements. Mandated course work varies slightly among the 12 schools and colleges but usually includes classes in English, mathematics, science, computer science, and the social sciences.

The faculty consists of 1911 full-time members, all of whom teach undergraduates to some degree, and 313 part-time. No figure is available on the portion of part-time faculty who teach at the graduate level only. Seventy-one percent are men. Two faculty members have been awarded the Nobel Prize. Overall, the faculty earn grades of very good to outstanding, depending on the discipline. "More often than not," boasts a pharmacy student, "my professors use the textbooks that they wrote." As at most big-name universities, however, there are many frustrating exceptions, such as professors who clearly teach only because they must in order to do research. In a recent year, just under half of the introductory classes, 45%, were taught by graduate students, some of whom spoke broken English that students could not understand. Grumbles a health science major: "We have far too many graduate assistants and foreign teachers. Often I cannot understand my teachers regardless of how smart they are."

Purdue traditionally has been strong in the applied sciences, especially engineering, largely because of its highly respected faculty and excellent laboratory facilities. It has the highest enrollment of women engineering students in the country and was the founding campus of the National Society of Black Engineers. One of every 50 engineers in the nation has been educated at Purdue. First-year engineering students begin in the First-year Engineering Program, which requires courses in English and chemistry as well as calculus and computer programming. Only after completing their first year do students decide which of 13 areas to specialize in, ranging from aeronautical and astronautical engineering to nuclear engineering. The schools of Pharmacy and Nursing also are excellent; pharmacy students are allowed to sit for the state board exams immediately after graduation from the 6-year program including an apprenticeship period. In the College of Technology, electrical engineering technology is but one example of a program distinguished by rigorous yet dedicated faculty who are "committed to developing minds that can think," says a major. The aviation technology program, adds a major in this field, boasts "excellent facilities and great faculty who care about making their program the best." The payoff is great, as 90 to 100 percent of the program's graduates find employment, with starting averages among the highest for Purdue graduates. Students in the college's Organizational Leadership and Supervision (OLS) program consider it one of Purdue's "best-kept secrets," with professors who are "very friendly and always willing to meet with their students," according to a major. Undergraduates in more technical programs think OLS may have students who genuinely are interested in the field, but also others who view it as an easier avenue to a Purdue degree. The program in Hospitality and Tourism Management in the College of Consumer and Family Sciences and many programs in the colleges of Agriculture and Science rate highly as well.

The Krannert School of Management is respected by its majors for offering courses that prepare them for the real world of work, although some students outside the school think Purdue loses some of the best business students to the program at Indiana University. The College of Liberal Arts offers larger departments such as the psychological sciences and communication that are excellent, and smaller departments such as the visual and performing arts that hide in the shadow of the larger programs and, students say, need greater exposure. Again, in a university with such strong engineering and technology programs, liberal arts majors often face scrutiny from others regarding just how challenging their discipline is. Some majors in the College of Education are disappointed that there is not more opportunity for them to spend time in the classroom. The result, says a junior elementary education major, is graduates "feeling unprepared to teach."

Facilities: Undergraduates for the most part like Purdue's decentralized library system, which has 1 main library and 13 department-specific ones. Says a junior: "This is great because I can go to the chemistry library and not have to search through rows of math books to find what I want." All 14 libraries also are linked on a common web site so students can search from their residence hall or home and figure out which facility has what they are looking for. Altogether, the Purdue library system holds more than 2.4 million books, 3.2 million microform items, and 20,800 current periodicals. Materials not available on campus or via the Internet can be obtained through interlibrary loan. The libraries also get high marks as study centers. Says a junior: "They are an excellent place to study. I refuse to study at home."

Recognized among the nation's leaders in supercomputing applications, Purdue is computer friendly to undergraduates, too. "Awesome," is how one senior puts it. There are 5500 workstations located in 315 computer labs, about half of which are general labs, the others run by various departments. Some labs are open around the clock, others until 2 a.m. Computer screens in each lab show students where all labs with available computers are located on campus. Says one user: "If you are waiting in the lab, you can find the next closest on the screen and move there to avoid lines." There is also a lab in each residence hall and each room provides online access for student PCs. Ninety-seven percent of the buildings offer wireless access points, providing about 1275 access points around campus. Students, faculty, and staff certainly use the options provided to them: 1.1 million e-mail transmissions are completed daily.

Special programs: Purdue sponsors more than 200 study-abroad programs in 46 countries, some with other members of the Big Ten. Cross registration for classes also is an option at Purdue's regional campuses. For students willing to work double-time, a 3-plus-2 year, bachelor's/master's degree program is offered in management, enabling qualified students to earn bachelor's and master's degrees in 5 years.

Campus life: Thirty-six percent of Purdue's undergraduates reside on the 2307-acre largely traditional-looking, red brick campus. Seventeen percent of the men and women are members of 1 local and 49 national fraternities and 3 local and 26 national sororities, giving Purdue one of the largest Greek systems in the nation. Unfortunately, some undergraduates who don't pledge feel left out, especially because many opt not to attend the non-Greek events that are offered, considering them "un-cool." However, most eventually find companionship with students of like interests in at least 1 of the 730 student organizations available. There are also plenty of apartment and co-op parties. Although Purdue has no school of music, its 350-member All-American marching band is believed to be the largest in the world. Orville Redenbacher, the "Popcorn King" used to play the tuba in its ranks. Crime other than occasional bike theft is rare; 2 escort services help to keep other problems to a minimum. Purdue's yellow emergency call-box system is also thought to be the largest in the country.

Purdue, a member of the Big Ten, has always been a leader in big-college sports. Its gymnasium was the first university building in the United States erected solely to serve students' recreational needs, and the Recreational Sports Center still offers indoor facilities for everything from archery and badminton to gymnastics and track. Boilermaker football is the place for tailgating and cheering on Saturdays in the fall but come winter, basketball resumes its stance as king of the sports (this *is* Indiana), with the women recently making their third appearance in the NCAA Final Four. Together, the men's and women's basketball teams have won more Big Ten championships than any other school, 27 combined, 21 for the men alone. A total of 10 men's and 10 women's varsity sports are played as part of NCAA Division I. An extensive intramural program includes 26 sports that are open to both men and women plus one available just to men. Seventy percent of the men and 40% of the women take part. Students also can get involved in club sports in such traditional areas as rugby and lacrosse and more unusual pursuits such as canoeing, kayaking, and trap and skeet.

For racing buffs, big weekends don't come much bigger than that of the Grand Prix, a 50-mile go-kart race organized and run by undergraduates to generate scholarship funds. The twin cities of Lafayette and West Lafayette, with a combined population exceeding 70,000, are located 65 miles northwest of Indianapolis and 126 miles southwest of Chicago, making these 2 cities the natural getaway spots by car.

Cost cutters: Less than half, 44% of Purdue freshmen received financial aid in the 2005–2006 school year; 40% of continuing students did. For 36% of all undergraduates, the aid was need-based. The average need-based scholarship or grant for freshmen averaged $8946; need-based self-help aid, such as loans and job earnings, averaged $3208. Non-need-based scholarships for freshman athletes averaged $17,039. Other non-need-based awards and scholarships averaged $12,724. A typical 2005 graduate left with debts of $17,510. Academic Success Awards go to students earning at least a 1360 on the combined critical reading and math SAT or 31 on the ACT and ranking in the top 5% of their high school classes or with a 3.8 GPA. In-state residents who make the grade receive $2750 for the first year and $2550 for each of the next 3 years provided they maintain a 3.5 GPA; nonresidents receive $5250 the first year and an additional $2250 for each of the next 3 years, also dependent on a 3.5 GPA. Full-ride Beering Scholarships go to 2 to 10 of the top 80–100 high school seniors who have submitted their applications by the first week of December. To qualify for many of the most valuable awards, students should be sure to submit their applications by Dec.1 to be considered. Valedictorians receive scholarships worth $2250. Merit awards also are offered in each of Purdue's schools and colleges. Twelve cooperative houses, averaging 35 residents each, enable a student to reduce costs by working for 4–6 hours a week around the house he or she lives in. Yearly costs in the houses run from $2500 to $3200. Cooperative programs are offered in many disciplines, such as engineering, technology, management, agriculture, science, and consumer and family sciences. A budget payment plan allows students or their parents to spread out tuition, room, and board payments over 10 months.

Rate of return: Eighty-four percent of the freshmen return for the sophomore year. Thirty-six percent graduate in 4 years; 62%, within 5 years; 68% in 6 years.

Payoff: The 3 most popular majors for 2005 graduates were management at 7%, and mechanical engineering and psychology at 4% each. More than 60% of the grads in a recent year accepted jobs immediately after earning their degrees, many with some of the 550 companies and organizations that recruit on campus. Top employers of recent graduates have been IBM, McDonnell Douglas, General Motors, and Eli Lilly. Most graduates accept jobs in Indiana, Illinois, and California. A fifth enroll in graduate or professional school within a few months of commencement.

Bottom line: "Students who are responsible, are organized, and like to get involved in organizations will love Purdue, but should come with studying as their first priority," advises a management major. "Socially, there is always something to do here, and if you want to have a good time, you'll find it. But students need to know how to set priorities and make good choices."

Rose-Hulman Institute of Technology

Terre Haute, Indiana 47803

Setting: Suburban
Control: Private
Undergraduate enrollment: 1439 men, 326 women
Graduate enrollment: 33 men, 5 women
Student/faculty ratio: 12:1
Freshman profile: 13% scored over 700 on SAT I verbal; 52% scored 600–700; 33% 500–599; 2% below 500. 35% scored over 700 on SAT I math; 55% scored 600–700; 10% 500–599; 0% below 500. 56% scored above 28 on the ACT; 20% scored 27–28; 18% 24–26; 5% 21–23; 1% below 21. 62% graduated in top tenth of high school class; 87% in upper fifth.

Faculty profile: 100% Ph.D.'s
Tuition and fees: $27,138
Room and board: $7419
Freshman financial aid: 98%; average scholarship or grant: $15,271 need-based; $9127 non-need-based
Campus jobs: 56%; average earnings: $1569/year
Application deadline: Mar. 1
Financial aid deadline: Mar. 1
Admissions information: (812) 877-1511; (800) 248-7448
  e-mail: admis.ofc@rose-hulman.edu
  web site: www.rose-hulman.edu

Most students, as they head off to college, expect to pay for 4 or 5 years of tuition, room, board, books, and more than an occasional slice of pizza. At formerly all-male Rose-Hulman Institute of Technology in Terre Haute, Indiana, where the first class of women enrolled in the fall of 1995, students pay several thousand dollars less than their peers for 4 years of intensive math, science, and engineering. But undergraduates can expect to pay more in other ways. As an admissions officer once candidly admitted, Rose-Hulman students earn their degrees with "blood, sweat, and tears," a fact most undergraduates quickly learn. But the payback for those long days and late nights of studying often in cooperative groups is well worth the effort. For a recent graduating class, more than 475 recruiters came to campus and conducted at least a couple thousand interviews—with just 325 seniors, who received an average of 2 job offers apiece. The lowest offer had a starting salary of $38,000; the highest, $70,000; the average, $51,000. Current average starting salaries have risen slightly to an even more impressive $52,000. What the admissions officer should have said was "blood, sweat, tears, and cheers" for the bright financial future a degree from Rose-Hulman brings.

Student body: Forty-four percent of the students drawn to this rigorous education are from Indiana. Though all 50 states and 18 foreign countries are represented, the Midwest is also home to three-fourths of the rest, with many of the undergraduates coming from small towns in the region. Diversity is lacking at Rose-Hulman, where just 4% of the students are Asian-American, 3% African-American, and 1% Hispanic. However, every spring, current minority members do their part to increase the rolls by calling, writing, and visiting prospective minority students with an interest in engineering. Twenty-five of the students are foreign nationals. Eighty-two percent are graduates of public schools. Among the nearly 500 freshmen who enrolled in one recent fall, 24 earned a perfect 800 on the mathematics portion of the SAT I or a perfect 36 on the math portion of the ACT. Twenty percent of the fall 2005 entrants ranked first, second, or third in their high school graduating class. A fourth are first-generation college students. Students trust one another, and while serious about their studies, are not cutthroat. In fact, many undergraduates use words such as "focused," "intense," and "difficult" rather than "competitive" to describe the academic environment. Notes a chemical engineering major: "Professors encourage students to work together, as we will have to when we get jobs." The fact that most professors don't grade on a curve also helps to promote cooperation. Rose students span all stereotypes. Says a junior: "Trekkies, nerds, geeks, jocks, preps, normal guys, whatever," though most share well-defined career goals. Adds one woman: "The students are very open-minded to all opinions, and if not, they're very willing to debate the point!"

Academics: The college, founded in 1874 by pioneer industrialist and entrepreneur Chauncey Rose, was the first, in the 1880s, to grant a degree in chemical engineering. The Hulman name was added in 1971 to acknowledge the gifts of a Terre Haute family that transferred all the assets from its foundation to the institute. Rose-Hulman, as it was renamed, offers a bachelor's degree in 15 programs of study in engineering, mathematics, science, and economics plus a master of science degree in similar disciplines. The academic year is divided into quarters, with students taking 3 quarters in a September-to-June year. The average class size for undergraduates is 20. A course in Biomaterials—Prosthetic Devices is often the largest at 70 class members; genetic engineering is generally the smallest at 3.

The core curriculum is rigorous and prepares students for the engineering program ahead. All freshmen take the same courses, which include a course in College and Life Skills, a class in Rhetoric and Composition, a humanities elective, and 3 levels of calculus that are taught using a computer algebra system on laptop computers that all freshmen are required to purchase from the college. The process enables students to concentrate on creative problem solving, rather than manipulating formulas over and over again. One-fifth of all required coursework is in the humanities and social sciences.

The faculty is virtually all full-time with only 9 of the 157 members part-time. Eighteen percent are women. Unlike their counterparts at major research universities, Rose-Hulman faculty members are hired to teach undergraduates; job performance evaluations are based on effectiveness in the classroom, not on the number of papers published. There are no "weed-out" classes, and "their doors are always open for the student," says an electrical engineering major. "In fact, I have a professor who has stayed until 10 o'clock at night to help students before a test." Nonetheless, the faculty is known to expect a lot. Says a senior: "Although professors provide a lot of personal attention, they also allow for a lot of room for you to learn on your own. They challenge students daily and I believe are more in tune with the individual needs of the students."

The big three in engineering, electrical, mechanical, and chemical, serve over half the student body with "the ultimate" in equipment (the labs were recently renovated) and with faculty who have long-standing reputations for excellence in the classroom and in industry. Corporations also give the school a list of real-life projects for seniors to work on in these areas. Civil engineering draws similar kudos for its "outstanding staff with experience and teaching excellence," in the words of a satisfied major. Students also value the spirit of comradeship shared by majors and faculty alike. The math program boasts superb faculty who are as helpful as they are brilliant.

While courses in the humanities and social sciences provide a desirable counterbalance to the highly technical curriculum, students say many do not mesh well with the engineering disciplines and are viewed as less important. Some students would like more options in foreign language instruction, beyond coursework in German, Japanese, or Spanish, which leads to a minor in modern languages. The economics major, which many students add as a second major instead of on its own, also is not considered as well developed as other programs.

Facilities: Logan Library is small, with more than 79,000 volumes and 33,335 electronic and paper periodicals, but what it lacks in breadth of volumes it supplies in depth for technical resources. The LUIS computerized research system quickly tells students what materials are available on campus and which must be obtained from Indiana State University or St. Mary of the Woods College, also in Terre Haute, with which Rose-Hulman students have borrowing privileges. Students especially like Logan's numerous small, soundproof study rooms that are useful for either group work or silent study. But not all take full advantage of what Logan has to offer. Confesses a mechanical engineering major: "I personally hardly ever use the library. Most information I ever read is found on-line."

All freshmen are required to purchase a laptop computer that, including software and network card, costs approximately $3200. (The institute provides a financing plan to spread the cost over 4 years.) Students are connected directly to the campus network from each dorm room. Altogether, there are more than 8000 wired data ports and more than 40 wireless access points around campus.

Special programs: Rose-Hulman is the only college in the nation to offer a bachelor's degree in engineering or science combined with a Certificate of Proficiency in Technical Translation in German. Participants in this program are urged to spend a summer studying at an approved program for foreigners in Germany. Any student may study abroad at colleges in 8 countries, including Australia, Ireland, and Germany. Undergraduates wanting to experience a larger university may take classes at Indiana State, just 10 minutes and 10,000 additional students away. Entering freshmen with an exceptional aptitude for mathematics may participate in the Fast Track Calculus program, which enables 20 students to take computer-based calculus covering differential, integral, and multivariable calculus in just 5 weeks during the summer prior to enrollment. Those who finish begin their freshman-year as "mathematical sophomores."

An entrepreneur-in-residence program enables students and faculty to work closely with an entrepreneur, testing his or her ideas in the laboratory and helping to bring them to the attention of industry.

Campus life: Sixty percent of Rose-Hulman's students reside on the 200-acre campus, which features 2 lakes and rolling, wooded hills and meadows. Thirty-seven percent of the men are members of 8 national fraternities, which sponsor several parties over any given weekend. Forty-three percent of the women belong to 2 national sororities. "Fraternity/sorority life dominates the social scene," says a senior, but since the campus is small, most independents know someone in a fraternity and are included in its parties. The cafeteria has been closed on weekends, so students typically head out to eat, watch movies, and play putt-putt golf. Students give special credit to the resident assistants and sophomore advisors who live on each freshman floor and provide support, as well as organized activities such as parties, blood drives, and 'Hallympics.' Says a sophomore: "Rose-Hulman is made for students to excel yet it is also a place for them to live life." Undergraduates also give hope to younger students who struggle in class with the institute's highly successful Homework Hotline, a free math and science tutoring service for Indiana students in grades 6 through 12. From September through January in the 2005–2006 school year, Rose-Hulman tutors helped more than 26,300 callers to the toll-free hotline. Incidents of crime are few.

Twenty percent of the men work off stress by participating in at least 1 of 12 intercollegiate sports, competing in Division III of the NCAA. A fifth of the women take part in 11 varsity sports offered. The 80% who just watch turn out most often for Fighting Engineers football, men's basketball, women's volleyball and men's and women's soccer games. Ninety percent of the men and 50% of the women play the 14 men's and 14 women's intramural sports offered, with 75 intramural basketball teams alone hitting the court in a recent year.

For escape, about a quarter of the students go home, as Terre Haute's entertainment offerings are rather limited or head for parties at Indiana State. Several new hangouts opened by former Rose students are providing additional options. Students also road trip to Bloomington and Urbana, the homes of Indiana University and the University of Illinois, respectively, as well as to Indianapolis.

Cost cutters: Ninety-eight percent of all freshmen and continuing students in the 2005–2006 school year received some financial aid; 71% of the freshmen and 65% of the continuing students received need-based assistance. The average freshman award for first-year students with financial need included need-based scholarships or grants averaging $15,271 and need-based self-help aid such as loans and jobs averaging $10,582. Other non-need-based awards and scholarships for freshmen averaged $9127. The average 2005 graduate left with outstanding loans of $33,105. With the good job offers most alumni receive, few have problems with repayment; in fact, the loan default rate is just over 1%. Honor scholarships for students who rank in the top half of Rose-Hulman's freshman class recently ranged from $3000 to $18,000 a year. Presidents' Scholarships recently paid $18,000 to the top of the crop. Cooperative programs are available in several majors.

Rate of return: Ninety-two percent of entering freshmen return for the sophomore year. Seventy-four percent graduate in 4 years. Eighty-one percent finish in 5 years.

Payoff: Thirty-one percent of the 2005 class graduated with degrees in mechanical engineering, 15% in chemical engineering, and 14% in electrical engineering. Given the large number of recruiters and the high starting salaries offered, it is little wonder that the vast majority enter the job market directly after graduating, as production, design, project, aerospace, or other kinds of engineers or as management trainees. The top 20 corporate employers of Rose-Hulman graduates recently included General Electric, Eli Lilly, Marathon Oil, and Texas Instruments; a large number also are hired by the Naval Weapons Support Center. Nineteen percent of recent graduates resisted immediate affluence and went directly to graduate or professional school. In previous years, alumni have used their rigorous academic training to advance in law school at Indiana and St. Louis Universities, and in business school at the universities of Chicago and Pennsylvania. The acceptance rate to medical school has been 90% since 1975. "Versatility comes with a Rose degree," says a junior. "After 4 years, I want to be able to choose between a high-paying job, graduate school, or medical/law school."

Bottom line: Rose-Hulman is for men and women with aptitude in mathematics, chemistry, and physics who are interested in an engineering-intensive education. "The key to success here is motivation and willingness to work," says a mechanical engineering major. "If you can get into Rose, Rose makes sure every possibility is exhausted so you can become a qualified engineer."

Saint Joseph's College

Rensselaer, Indiana 47978

Setting: Small town
Control: Private (Roman Catholic)
Undergraduate enrollment: 336 men, 520 women
Graduate enrollment: NA
Student/faculty ratio: 15:1
Freshman profile: 1% scored over 700 on SAT I verbal; 13% scored 600–700; 37% 500–599; 49% below 500. 0% scored over 700 on SAT I math; 9% scored 600–700; 43% 500–599; 48% below 500. 2% scored above 28 on the ACT; 14% scored 27–28; 13% 24–26; 36% 21–23; 35% below 21. 30% graduated in top fifth of high school class; 61% in upper two-fifths.

Faculty profile: 79% Ph.D.'s.
Tuition and fees: $20,120
Room and board: $6480
Freshman financial aid: 97%; average scholarship or grant: $5367 need-based; $6233 non-need-based
Campus jobs: 33%; average earnings: $1500/year
Application deadline: Rolling
Financial aid deadline: Mar. 1
Admissions information: (219) 866-6170; (800) 447-8781
e-mail: admissions@saintjoe.edu
web site: www.saintjoe.edu

Several years ago, academic deans at colleges and universities throughout the United States were asked to name schools where general education programs were succeeding. The 2 most frequently cited universities were well known to most: Harvard University and the University of Chicago. The third- and fourth-choice schools, however, were unfamiliar to just about everyone except educators and the students most directly involved in their innovative programs: Alverno College in Milwaukee, Wisconsin, and Saint Joseph's College in northwest Indiana. The Core Curriculum at SJC, which involves professors from up to 10 different departments in its planning and execution, starts freshman year with a 1-semester look at The Contemporary Situation. It then retraces human development through 9 other courses ranging from The Roots of Western Civilization to the impact of influences such as the cosmic and biological sciences, Christianity, and contributions of other cultures. Students attend large lecture classes followed by smaller discussion groups that challenge their members to examine the issues. There's nothing stuffy or old-fashioned about this Core Curriculum. Students praise it for being interesting and regularly updated by faculty concerned to keep it current. The 2-semester session on Intercultural Studies includes performances of traditional dances and ceremonies and exhibits of representative paintings and sculpture from Africa, India, China, and Latin America. The Banet Core Education Center contains 2 lecture halls, one dedicated to the Core program, 10 classrooms primarily for Core discussion groups, a Core science lab, a computer classroom, and a Core planning office. Says a pre-engineering major: "This program graduates students who are masters of oral communication and writing skills." As an added bonus, because its structure stretches required classes over 4 years instead of concentrating them in a year or 2, career-minded students may plunge into the study of their majors as early as freshman year. Concludes this future engineer: "Saint Joseph's is a sleeper that can really surprise you."

Student body: Despite the strength of its Core program, the College remains little known outside Indiana; 71% of its students are from in-state with most of the rest also from the Midwest, though 19 states are represented. African-American and Hispanic students constitute the single largest minority groups, at 6%, and 3%, respectively. Students who are Asian-American and foreign nationals from 4 countries each make up 1% as well. Forty-six percent of the students are Catholic and 38% Protestant. A feeling of family unity pervades the small campus, at which everyone soon knows everybody else. Most undergraduates are politically conservative. Academically, students tend to be slightly above average; the extent to which they are willing to challenge themselves varies widely. As one student has noted, some in the upper 20% seem to study 24 hours a day, whereas others, on the lower end, appear to party just as much!

Academics: Saint Joseph's, which turned 110 in 2001, awards the bachelor's degree in 45 majors, with a master's degree in church music and liturgy. Most graduate students attend during the summer session. The regular academic year is divided into 2 semesters; an optional 5-week session, beginning in early May, features some unusual team-taught courses for credit on subjects that have ranged from the African novel to American presidential assassinations. During the regular school year, the average class enrolls 15 students, but no course ever gets very big. A mathematics course in real number systems can have nearly 60, while a class in quantitative analysis may enroll only 2.

Fifty-six faculty members teach full-time; 21 work at the college only part-time. Fifty-eight percent are men; some are members of the school's Catholic religious order, the Missionaries of the Precious Blood. Students drawn to SJC by the promise of close relationships with professors are not disappointed, and many share friendships outside the classroom. The concern most faculty members show in their preparation for classes extends to ensuring that their students do not fail, at least not from lack of help. "Students are challenged to be the best," observes a junior, "and professors try to keep any from falling through the cracks."

Saint Joseph's academic strengths cover both ends of the spectrum, from the popular business program, led by superb faculty who stay on top of their fields and expect students to do the same, to the ageless liberal-arts Core. Education also gets good grades and wins praise for sending its students into K-12 classrooms as early as freshman year and every year thereafter. The social sciences stay strong thanks to a faculty who work constantly to improve their courses. The criminal justice major features excellent professors with years in jobs related to the field. The communication department provides students with access to campus radio and television stations, and nursing majors work at St. Elizabeth Hospital in nearby Lafayette.

Students perceive various majors in the humanities, such as English, philosophy, history, and religion, have been hampered by losing professors to teach Core courses, thereby reducing the number of more advanced classes that can be offered to majors. Physics, once offered as a minor, is taught in only a handful of courses. There are no majors in individual foreign languages with minors in French, German, and Spanish the only language options.

Facilities: Robinson Memorial Library is small in both physical size and holdings, with 156,000 volumes and 399 periodicals; many of the materials also are too outdated to be of much use. Students who start early and have 2 weeks of waiting time can order materials through interlibrary loan from 80 other regional libraries; procrastinators can use information on-line or make the half-hour drive to Purdue University in West Lafayette. In most cases, computerized research assistance saves the day. Twenty-eight on-line databases are readily available to students as are the resources of 26 private Indiana colleges, through the school's membership in the Private Academic Library Network of Indiana. Recent remodeling of the structure has made it a more inviting place to study, although some students complain users talk too much.

About 70 computers, mainly PCs, are available for student use in 4 main centers on campus, as well as in a few of the dormitories. The centers generally are open from 8 a.m. to midnight Mondays through Thursdays, and shorter hours on the other days. Network access is available in dorm rooms for students who have their own computers. Wireless access also is available from various locations on campus, including the 2 main academic buildings.

Special programs: Students may spend the junior year or a semester abroad at one of SJC's extension campuses in locations such as England, France, Germany, Austria, the Netherlands, Spain, and Mexico. Internships in the nation's capital are offered through the Washington Center, as well as in all academic majors.

Campus life: Sixty-eight percent of the students reside on the 180-acre campus, but many leave on Friday or Saturday, in part to take a break from the "typical" Saint Joseph's weekend. There are no fraternities or sororities, so dormitories and individual floors within them generally fulfill the same social functions. The campus coffee house, known as Cup O' Joe, is a popular hangout. Though attendance at Mass is not required, many who are Catholic attend Mass offered over the weekend, and a number of Protestant students join in retreats and other religious activities. One of the most popular spring weekends, when students rarely leave, falls during the Little 500 event, fashioned after the Indy 500 race and featuring go-karts and a carnival atmosphere. Crime, outside of some vandalism, is not much of a problem as the campus is well patrolled—sometimes too well, students say, at least in the parking lots, where parking tickets are freely given.

Football, men's and women's basketball, and soccer are the most popular of the 9 men's and 9 women's varsity sports played under NCAA Division II. Almost half of the men and over a fourth of the women get involved in the 6 intramural sports offered to each.

The College's setting in the small town of Rensselaer (pop. 5500) is perhaps students' biggest disappointment, and many make the 30-minute drive to Purdue for big-campus excitement. Chicago is only 90 minutes away.

Cost cutters: In the 2005–2006 school year, 97% of freshmen and continuing students received financial aid; for 84% of the freshmen and 80% of the continuing students help was based on financial need. The average freshman award for a student with financial need included a need-based scholarship or grant averaging $5367 and need-based self-help aid such as loans and jobs averaging $1212. Non-need-based athletic scholarships averaged $2251; other non-need-based awards and scholarships averaged $6233. The average financial indebtedness of a 2005 graduate was $23,417. Presidential Scholarships pay full tuition for 3 students who meet 2 of the following criteria: an SAT critical reading and math score of at least 1100 or a 24+ ACT; class rank in the top 15% of the class or an adjusted GPA of 3.0. A completed application must be received before Jan. 1. Honors Scholarships pay up to $10,000 per year and Dean's awards pay up to $8000 yearly to students meeting similar standards. SJC Scholarships pay up to $6000 yearly to students who rank in the top 25% of their high school classes; Puma Scholarships pay up to $4000 to those drawn from the top 35%. Athletic and performance scholarships also are provided. Various work and payment plans are available, too.

Rate of return: Seventy-one percent of entering freshmen return for the sophomore year. Forty-nine percent graduate in 4 years; 54% in 5 years; 55% in 6.

Payoff: Having achieved the balance offered by the Core Curriculum, 20% of the 2005 graduates earned degrees in business with another 16% specializing in education and 7% in criminal justice. The vast majority of alumni take jobs shortly after leaving college, many with small- to medium-sized businesses and others with major firms located throughout the Midwest. Thirty-one companies and organizations recruited on campus in a recent school year. Less than a fifth of recent graduates pursued advanced degrees within 6 months of commencement.

Bottom line: At Saint Joseph's, no student graduates with a narrowly focused career orientation, thanks to the pervasive influence of the Core Curriculum. This is a small college, in a small town, so students seeking a diversity of classmates and of cultural opportunities may not find the stimuli they need. On the other hand, those in need of extra academic and personal attention are generally well satisfied. Notes a senior: "Because of all the support programs here, a student *cannot* fail unless he or she simply doesn't care and refuses to put forth any effort."

Saint Mary's College

Notre Dame, Indiana 46556

Setting: Suburban
Control: Private (Roman Catholic)
Undergraduate enrollment: 1366 women
Graduate enrollment: None
Student/faculty ratio: 10:1
Freshman profile: 6% scored over 700 on SAT I verbal; 32% scored 600–700; 47% 500–599; 15% below 500. 2% scored over 700 on SAT I math; 32% scored 600–700; 52% 500–599; 14% below 500. 12% scored above 28 on the ACT; 19% scored 27–28; 34% 24–26; 28% 21–23; 7% below 21. 34% graduated in top tenth of high school class; 70% in upper fourth.
Faculty profile: 77% Ph.D.'s

Tuition and fees: $24,358
Room and board: $8180
Freshman financial aid: 89%; average scholarship or grant: $9557 need-based; $4236 non-need-based
Campus jobs: 45%; average earnings: $1800/year
Application deadline: Early decision: Nov. 15; regular: Mar. 1
Financial aid deadline: Mar. 1
Admissions information: (574) 284-4587;
(800) 551-7621
e-mail: admission@saintmarys.edu
web site: www.saintmarys.edu

If there is a way for a young woman to be part of the Fighting Irish of Notre Dame without enrolling in introductory lectures that sometimes reach 300 students, having limited exposure to female professors, and paying an additional $7200 a year in tuition and fees, Saint Mary's College has figured it out. This women's college of about 1350 students has a well-integrated exchange program with its powerful neighbor across the street, which enables St. Mary's women to take courses or earn second majors at Notre Dame, share in activities ranging from the student newspaper to study-abroad programs, and get season tickets to Fighting Irish football games. Observes a satisfied southerner: "It is truly the best of both worlds here, and students have the choice of how they want to balance the 2 opportunities, equally or unequally."

Student body: That double world and other factors have drawn young women from 45 states and 9 foreign countries to mingle at St. Mary's. Only 30% of the students are Hoosiers; 69% of the rest traveled just short distances from the surrounding dozen midwestern states. Eighty-two percent of the women are Catholic, though students say they range from the devout to the nonpracticing, with just 14% Protestant, and 4% students of other faiths or no religious affiliation. Less than half of the students, 46%, are graduates of private or parochial schools. Attracting racial and ethnic minorities has been a problem for the school, though numbers have been improving with 4% Hispanic students, 2% Asian-American, and 1% each African-American, Native American, and foreign nationals. The admissions office remains committed to bringing in 20 new minority students each year, but as a senior from the Midwest questions, "How diverse is a small, Catholic, women's liberal arts college in northern Indiana ever going to be?" St. Mary's women are a spirited and involved group, and while "there's not much diversity," admits a junior, "there's much individuality." Students find a range of political leanings among their classmates often tied to their roots in either Democratic Chicago or more socially conservative midwestern families. But that's not always a guarantee of how students will react. Says a junior: "Our undergraduates are, for the most part, very independent, outspoken, focused on the future, and moderately religious." There also is a good-sized contingent of classmates considered to be fairly "preppy." Academics are taken seriously but are kept in balance with social activities. Says a sophomore, "It's understood you don't ask people about their grades unless they offer to tell you."

Academics: St. Mary's was founded in 1844 by 4 Sisters of the Holy Cross from France who came to join the Catholic brothers of the Holy Cross in their efforts to set up a college in northern Indiana, the future University of Notre Dame. After 11 years at a location a few miles away, St. Mary's moved to its present site opposite the then-all-male institution. While Notre Dame has gone on to provide advanced degrees through the doctorate, St. Mary's has limited its offerings to bachelor's degrees in over 30 majors. Average class size in the 2-semester calendar is about 15, but the largest classes, such as the Biology Lecture Series for prospective majors, can pack in about 90. And though theoretically the lower limit on class size is 15, a course in International Law may enroll as few as 2.

Students must demonstrate proficiency in a foreign language and in English composition, with an additional advanced composition course required in the major. Distributional requirements vary by major, but some combination of coursework in history, English literature, mathematics, the natural and social sciences, philosophy, and religious studies is mandated for most. "Tedious to complete but very beneficial to a student's mind," admits a nursing student. Women in all majors must pass a senior comprehensive that involves doing a project or a research paper or taking an oral or written exam.

Just under two-thirds, 63%, of the 198-member faculty teach full-time; 64% are women. All remain on full-time alert for students in academic trouble. Not only do students find it easy to contact professors outside the classroom, day or night, in their offices or homes, for extra help, but also professors may contact students who they think are not working up to ability. "Faculty for the most part are wonderful," says a senior. "They really try to work with students for the greatest academic growth possible."

Superb faculty of this variety help make the career-oriented departments of business, education, and nursing challenging and successful. The English department is split evenly between conservative and liberal professors, providing a strong variety of courses and diverse perspectives. The sciences are noted for both excellent faculty and facilities located in an expanded and renovated science teaching and research center. Psychology features faculty who hold students to rigorous academic standards. While the interdisciplinary program of humanistic studies is small, it has an endowed chair and good interplay of courses in literature, history, and philosophy that provide a broad view of cultural history. Professors in the women's studies program are admired, says a senior, "because they encourage free thinking outside the Catholic sphere."

Other small departments such as philosophy, sociology, social work and anthropology, and modern languages, which offers majors in French and Spanish, a minor in Italian, plus classes in German, could use more professors. There only is a minor in physics.

Facilities: The Cushwa-Leighton Library is a popular study center, in no small part because it offers private rooms for group study as well as plenty of couches and rocking chairs for those who like to be comfortable when they work. The facility houses about 228,000 volumes (with room for 250,000) and 634 current periodicals though some students complain of too much outdated material. Database searches are available and well used, and a computerized catalog links St. Mary's to the 3 million volumes and more than 17,000 current periodicals held by Notre Dame. A 24-hour study area with computers is located downstairs. The library is among the many buildings on campus connected by underground tunnels, making it easier to head for that rocking chair on a blustery South Bend night.

Most students have no excuse for saying they couldn't get access to a computer; the college's main 24-hour lab is connected to all but 1 student residence hall by the same tunnel system. Smaller satellite labs in various classroom buildings, the library, and residence halls complete the network. A total of about 200 PCs and Macs are available for student use. While the number of computers generally is sufficient, says a senior, "*many* times—too much so—the printers are broken or out of paper." The college strongly recommends that students have their own personal computers and all but a small percentage do. Wireless coverage also is available across campus.

Special programs: More than 25 years ago, St. Mary's established a campus in Rome, primarily to serve sophomores who have completed a year of college-level Italian. Programs set up since then provide similar experiences in Seville, Spain; Dijon, France; and Innsbruck, Austria. In addition, 20 students from St.

Mary's and Notre Dame can spend a year at St. Patrick's College in Maynooth, outside Dublin, Ireland. For those who can't decide where to study, a semester-around-the-world is offered in alternate years for 20 St. Mary's and Notre Dame students. The program includes 10 weeks of study in Cochin, India, plus travels in Eastern and Western Europe, and throughout the Far East. The cost of the program is equal to a semester's tuition, room, and board plus a surcharge determined primarily by the cost of transportation, which was $5300 in a recent school year. Back home, students may cross-register for courses at Notre Dame and at 5 other colleges in northern Indiana. A 3-2 engineering degree also is an option with Notre Dame. Student Independent Study and Research Awards enable 4 student-faculty partnerships to perform research and study over the summer; student participants in a recent year received a $3000 stipend plus housing. A Mentor Research Assistant Program, which involves 4 students each semester, is directed at women of color.

Campus life: Eighty-four percent of St. Mary's women live on the 275-acre campus, located along the Saint Joseph River. There are no sororities, and most women do their weekend partying at Notre Dame. One-to-one dating between students on the 2 campuses is common as well. Most of the 100 clubs available are cosponsored with the university, including the Notre Dame band, dramatic productions, and the daily student newspaper. Clubs related to students' majors are popular, as well as ones dedicated to developing good job skills, among them Toastmasters, the public speaking club, which recently had 3 separate groups in action. Right to Life also is quite active; many students also participate in programs put on by the college-sponsored Center for Women's Intercultural Leadership, which encourages study abroad and understanding of other cultures. While women say they feel very safe on campus, and crime is low, students are cautious about walking alone at night and use the escort service available. A key card also is required for entrance to all residence halls.

During football season, the big attraction is, of course, Fighting Irish football, and a person had better have a pretty good excuse not to attend. Along with the game, St. Mary's students enjoy tailgaters beforehand, as well as postgame parties. Back on their own side of the street, 8% of the women participate in the 8 varsity sports with teams known as the Belles offered as part of NCAA Division III. Sixty-one percent turn out for the 17-sport intramural program offered in cooperation with, you guessed it, Notre Dame. Club sports in crew, gymnastics, and fencing also have attracted much interest.

Since South Bend itself has little to offer culturally or socially to college students, many road trip 90 miles west to Chicago to sample all that their college town lacks. Weather permitting, the dunes along Lake Michigan are a favorite escape as well.

Cost cutters: The college's endowment fund (almost $102 million as of June 2005) and the contributed income of Catholic clergy help to keep down costs. Eighty-nine percent of fall 2005 freshmen received financial aid, as did 60% of continuing students. For at least three-quarters of both groups, the aid was based on financial need. The average freshman award for a student with financial need included a need-based scholarship or grant averaging $9557 and need-based self-help aid such as loans and jobs averaging $4236. Other non-need-based awards and scholarships averaged $8055. The average financial indebtedness of a 2005 graduate was $24,617. Presidential Scholarships, awarded to first-year students who ranked in the top 3% of their high school class, recently paid $9200 annually. Other competitive awards, based on academic achievement, ranged from $5000 to $6600. Holy Cross Grants paid $500 to $5500 to students of color according to financial need.

Rate of return: Eighty-seven percent of entering freshmen return for the sophomore year. Sixty-nine percent graduate in 4 years, with an additional 5% earning degrees within 5 years.

Payoff: In the 2005 graduating class, 15% earned bachelor's degrees in elementary education, 11% in communications, and 10% in business administration. More than three quarters of the graduates entered the job market soon after earning their degrees, many taking positions as account executives, auditors, or sales and marketing representatives with major corporations in cities like Chicago, New York, and Atlanta. Many accepted offers from 36 firms and organizations that recruited on campus. Among recent alumni, 45% reported being employed in business, industry, or government, 10% in nursing, and 18% in teaching. Twenty-one percent were enrolled in graduate or professional schools.

Bottom line: Easy entry into a good job or graduate school comes as no surprise to an English-humanistic studies major. "Graduates from St. Mary's have an edge in the job market because they are used to speaking and thinking quickly in small classes," she says. "They also leave with the confidence that they have been well prepared to solve problems, in the work force and in life."

Taylor University

Upland, Indiana 46989

Setting: Rural
Control: Private (Evangelical Christian)
Undergraduate enrollment: 805 men, 991 women
Graduate enrollment: 7 men, 6 women
Student/faculty ratio: 15:1
Freshman profile: 14% scored over 700 on SAT I verbal; 35% scored 600–700; 41% 500–599; 10% below 500. 16% scored over 700 on SAT I math; 39% scored 600–700; 34% 500–599; 11% below 500. 25% scored above 28 on the ACT; 37% scored 27–28; 26% 24–26; 16% 21–23; 9% below 21. 37% graduated in top tenth of high school class; 60% in upper fifth.
Faculty profile: 73% Ph.D.'s

Tuition and fees: $20,746
Room and board: $5630
Freshman financial aid: 89%; average scholarship or grant: $3343 need-based; $4566 non-need-based
Campus jobs: 28%; average earnings: $1135/year
Application deadline: Early decision: Nov. 1; regular: Jan. 15
Financial aid deadline: Mar. 10
Admissions information: (765) 998-5134; (800) 882-3456
e-mail: admissions_u@tayloru.edu
web site: www.tayloru.edu

As one of the oldest Evangelical Christian colleges in the country, Taylor University operates under a system that could be described as "Taylor trust." Unlike many Christian schools, which mandate that students attend a certain number of chapel services every week throughout their enrollment, Taylor *expects* its students to attend every Monday, Wednesday, and Friday but keeps no attendance records. As the Life Together Covenant signed by every student explains, "Rather than require attendance, we expect that individual honor and commitment to the Taylor University community will motivate us to attend chapel." Undergraduates appreciate the trust placed in them, finding, in the words of a recent graduate, that it "allows students to make their own decisions and become their own persons while still remaining in a spiritually encouraging atmosphere." The approach seems to work: about 90% of Taylor students attend chapel regularly, and all but 12% of the freshmen who enter this small university amid the cornfields of Indiana opt to return for a second year. For students who want an environment where being Christian is the "norm," Taylor provides a near-perfect fit.

Student body: A third of Taylor's students are from Indiana; 74% of the rest are from the Midwest, though all but 4 states have students in attendance. Foreign nationals from 22 countries make up 1% of the enrollment. Asian-Americans, Hispanics, and African-Americans each comprise 2%. One hundred percent are Protestant. Seventy-nine percent are graduates of public schools. Despite Taylor's firm religious foundation, students say there are few dogmatic people on campus and a wide range of views are accepted on matters considered to be "nonheretical." Still, observes a junior, "the Taylor atmosphere by no means stifles the natural course of exploration or changes in one's life but most students tend to stay within a conservative Christian comfort zone." Many are politically and globally aware and quite vocal about their viewpoints. Describes a senior from the East: "Students are basically friendly, all-American people whose spiritual backgrounds give them a real concern for others." Newcomers expecting to find a "stuffy and extremely conservative air," as one midwesterner did, are pleasantly surprised. Students are very social and "there is a balance of good clean fun and wholesome morals and values," she notes. The pre-med programs are especially competitive, though not cutthroat academically, and most students across the disciplines are motivated to do well. Says a junior: "Students tend to be focused and disciplined especially in planning for future careers."

Academics: Taylor, which was founded in 1846 and renamed in 1890 to honor a missionary evangelist, awards the bachelor's degree in 44 majors. Its academic year is divided into 2 semesters, with a 1-month January term. Most classes have about 25 students, with the New Student Orientation course clearly the largest, since it enrolls the entire first-year class as a way to create unity. Most other courses in the early years rarely exceed 60 participants, and most junior and senior classes enroll 20 students or less.

Taylor's general-education requirements reinforce its Christian foundation. Besides the orientation and senior seminars, all students must take Bible Literature I and II, Contemporary Christian Belief, and Historic Christian Belief, plus other courses covering the usual academic fields, including a cross-cultural course. Two of those courses, or additional ones, must have strong writing components and another 2 extensive work in public speaking. The required coursework covers nearly half of the 128 semester hours needed for a degree, making it difficult for some students with double majors to graduate on time.

The full-time faculty numbers 137, with 59 part-time members. Nine of the full-time members teach at the graduate level only. Twenty-six percent are women. The small campus and shared spiritual beliefs lead to strong bonds between students and teachers, most of whom live within walking distance of campus. Notes a communication studies major: "Often professors invite students over to their homes for study sessions or breakfast meetings. They invest in students outside of the classroom as well as within the discipline."

In many cases, the extra investment creates strong programs such as business, psychology, and computer science, where the firm but loving hand leads students directly into good jobs after graduation. Majors in computer science, for example, are required to pass a 3-part comprehensive exam, given during the junior and senior years, which includes written, oral, and programming components. The result: 100% job placement upon graduation. The elementary and Christian education programs, too, are noted for providing a caring approach to teaching and learning with plenty of real-life classroom experience. The biology major and the environmental science minor that can accompany any major are both noted for their individual attention and sound preparation for students applying to graduate or professional school. The Center for Environmental Studies offers top-flight equipment and laboratories. Professors in the departments of history, political science, and Biblical studies, Christian education, and philosophy are among "the most respected faculty members," says a communication major. Social work, with its challenging and extensive curriculum; psychology, with its "phenomenal" faculty; art, with its new Visual Arts Center; and music, with its high expectations of majors, also make students' 'A' list.

New faculty in the communication arts department, as well as new equipment, promise to provide a badly needed spark to the program. Sociology needs more than its current 2 professors, although the 2 offer extensive opportunities for hands-on research and "unique, life-changing experiences" in the program, adds a junior. The modern languages department offers majors only in French and Spanish; students wish there were less turnover among faculty members, a greater breadth of classes and more languages offered.

Facilities: For the most part, Taylor students love Zondervan Library, completed in 1986 and named for the cofounder of a Christian publishing company, and find it a quiet and effective place for serious study. Although it has 186,000 volumes, many of which students consider dated, and 13,000 paper and electronic current periodicals, students mainly rely on the Internet and other computerized resources for research. "For majors other than psychology or Bible our reference sections are lacking," says a junior. Students use the online catalog to search Zondervan's holdings as well as those at 25 other private college and seminary libraries within Indiana. The much larger library at Ball State University accessible with a Taylor student ID is only 20 minutes away for those who need additional resources in a hurry. A 24-hour study room is available when the library is closed.

"Computers and technology are one of Taylor's strong points," says a psychology major. Taylor boasts an 8:1 student-to-computer ratio, with computer terminals in each dormitory, and several academic buildings plus 2 general purpose labs. All buildings also are wireless. Students' biggest complaint is that the labs close too early for last-minute paper writers; 1 closes at midnight, the other at 11 p.m. The university strongly recommends that students bring their own computers, preferably PCs, which many do.

Special programs: Membership in the Christian College Consortium enables Taylor students to spend a term at any of 12 other Christian colleges across the country. Opportunities to travel abroad during interterm or a semester are available through various academic programs as well as on mission trips; countries include Israel, China, Kenya, Costa Rica, Egypt, Russia, and various European nations. An American Studies Program, based in Washington, D.C., gives students a chance to work as interns and participate in an academic seminar program for 3 or 4 months. A 3-2 engineering program is offered with any accredited engineering school. Taylor's own Natural Science Research Training Program encourages scholarly research and publication in professional journals by Taylor faculty and students.

Campus life: Ninety-seven percent of Taylor students reside on the 250-acre rural campus, which appears to some to be "in the middle of nowhere." (It is actually just 65 miles north of Indianapolis.) As this junior recalls: "Coming from the Chicagoland area and now entering the cornfields, I asked myself, 'What do people do here?'" Responds a senior: "Being in such a rural setting, students come up with random, creative forms of entertainment." There are neither fraternities nor sororities, so dormitory wings serve as the social focus for many weekend events. One popular mixer is the "pick-a-date" program, in which a person's roommate gets a date for him or her; that night the entire group go do something together. Sometimes these group dates can have more than 100 participants. Dorms are single-sex, with "open house" hours from 7 p.m. to midnight on Friday and Saturday nights. Every student is required to sign a Life Together Covenant that says he or she will not drink, smoke tobacco, use drugs, or dance (other than in university-sanctioned folk dances, at weddings, or as part of choreography in campus productions) either on or off campus. A student discipleship coordinator in each residence-hall wing develops small-group programs centered on Bible study and burden bearing and sharing. Taylor World Outreach coordinates ministry in the community and in local schools as well as overseas in various Lighthouse missions over the January term. In one recent Lighthouse trip to Ethiopia, students taught organic farming methods. Campus crime in this rural community is practically nonexistent. Says a junior: "As silly as this sounds, the biggest crime is 'bike borrowing' when someone will 'borrow' another person's bike without his or her permission."

A tenth of the students in a recent year participated in the 8 men's and 7 women's NAIA intercollegiate sports available. Most of those not playing turn out to cheer on the team, with Trojans football, soccer, and basketball and women's volleyball attracting the most support. All but 10% of the students get involved in the 28 men's and women's intramural sports, divided 14 for each. "Everyone plays intramural sports all year-round," exclaims a junior. Many form teams with neighbors from their residence-hall wings. Notes a senior: "Championship T-shirts are given to the winning teams and worn proudly around campus."

When Upland (pop. under 3500) begins to close in, students head out either north to Marion (pop. 36,000), 15 minutes away, or to Fort Wayne, an hour; or south to Muncie (pop. 77,000), 20 minutes away, or to Indianapolis, the biggest of all, a little over an hour's travel time.

Cost cutters: In the 2005–2006 school year, 89% of freshmen and 87% of continuing students received financial help to pay for college; 58% of the freshmen and 56% of the remaining students got need-based assistance. The average freshman award for a student with financial need included a need-based scholarship or grant averaging $3343 and need-based self-help aid such as loans and jobs averaging $2718. Non-need-based athletic scholarships for first-year students averaged $596; other non-need-based awards and scholarships averaged $4566. Average debts of a 2005 graduate totaled $17,910. In addition to providing need-based support, Taylor rewards academic excellence and Christian living; its renewable Christian Leadership Scholarships pay 25% of tuition. President's Scholarships pay 25% to 50% of tuition to students who carried a 3.5 GPA and earned scores of at least 1350 in math and critical reading on the SAT or 31 on the ACT; Dean's Scholarships pay 10% or 15% of tuition to students with SATs of at least 1200, ACTs of 27–29, and a 3.5 GPA. An Ethnic Student Scholarship pays 25% tuition to undergraduates who contribute to the university's cultural diversity. Opportunities for students to earn money range from various leadership and admission office stipends to opportunities to teach music to community children. A cooperative program in premedical technology is available.

Rate of return: Eighty-eight percent of entering freshmen return for the sophomore year. Seventy-two percent go on to graduate in 4 years; 76% in 5 years.

Payoff: Ten percent of the 2005 graduating class earned degrees in business, with another 7% specializing in psychology and 6% in education. Three-quarters of the graduates take jobs immediately, many with firms such as Prudential Financial, IBM, and Sohio Oil, plus other of the nearly 90 companies and organizations that recruit on campus. Most graduates settle in the Midwest, South, and East. Thirteen percent of recent graduates opted to continue their education within 6 months of earning their bachelor's degrees.

Bottom line: Advises a senior: "Taylor will definitely change the way a student thinks, as a Christian, about society. One learns to integrate faith and learning and apply it in one's daily living. Intelligent, persistent Christians do best here; a person who is not willing to give up things such as drinking, dancing, and smoking for 4 years at Taylor may not succeed."

University of Evansville

Evansville, Indiana 47722

Setting: Urban
Control: Private (United Methodist)
Undergraduate enrollment: 926 men, 1507 women
Graduate enrollment: 22 men, 34 women
Student/faculty ratio: 14:1
Freshman profile: 8% scored over 700 on SAT I verbal; 34% scored 600–700; 41% 500–599; 17% below 500. 7% scored over 700 on SAT I math; 35% scored 600–700; 38% 500–599; 20% below 500. 23% scored above 28 on the ACT; 14% scored 27–28; 25% 24–26; 24% 21–23; 14% below 21. 30% graduated in top tenth of high school class; 56% in upper fifth.

Faculty profile: 87% Ph.D.'s
Tuition and fees: $21,660
Room and board: $6660
Freshman financial aid: 99%; average scholarship or grant: $16,730 need-based
Campus jobs: 19%; average earnings: $1300/year
Application deadline: Early action: Dec. 1; regular, Feb. 1
Financial aid deadline: Mar. 1
Admissions information: (812) 488-2468; (800) 423-8633
e-mail: admission@evansville.edu
web site: www.evansville.edu

It used to be that Evansville, Indiana, was the cultural, industrial, and retail center for the 3 strongly similar cultures comprising the TriState region of southern Illinois, western Kentucky, and southern Indiana. Today, the University of Evansville is becoming a crossroads for a much wider band of cultures. Its student body from 41 states, although still drawing 60% of its members from Indiana and half of its nonresidents from the region, also attracts almost 120 undergraduates from 42 foreign countries. One of the largest and most active organizations on campus is the International Students Club, which counts Hoosiers as well as Hindis among its members. The academic centerpiece is the World Cultures Sequence within the university's core curriculum. This 2-semester course begins with a discussion of the ancient world, and concludes with the emergence of the modern world. Writing is emphasized, both in the study of significant texts from the periods and in the frequent preparation of papers by the students. Participants give World Cultures a 5-star rating, at a university more and more are finding to be a little United Nations on the banks of the Ohio. "Not everyone is best friends with everyone else," says a senior, "but we *all* respect each other."

Student body: Although the university's racial and ethnic diversity is increasing, the enrollment still strongly reflects the school's geographic location. Just 2% of the undergraduates are African-American and 1% each are Hispanic and Asian-American though 5% are foreign nationals. Twenty-one percent are Methodist, with another 44% from other Protestant denominations; 32% are Catholic. In a recent year, all but 6% attended public schools. Politically, there are enough students to debate both the conservative and liberal sides of issues, with a fairly solid chunk best described as "middle-of-the-road." Observes a sophomore: "We make every effort not to be cut off from the real world. As a whole, the student body is politically active, academically competitive, and socially liberal." Few see themselves as academic grinds, and most comment on their "well-rounded" peers who actively participate in campus organizations and recreational sports programs. Still, says a state resident, "There are very many challenging courses, and seeing that 1 in 7 students was a valedictorian, there are always those students who push you to do better—and the professors contribute to that drive as well."

Academics: The University of Evansville, which began in 1854 as Moores Hill Male and Female Collegiate Institute, has substantially broadened its offerings to encompass over 80 undergraduate majors spread across 4 schools and colleges plus master's degree programs in physical therapy, health services administration, public service administration, and electrical engineering and computer science. Classes are divided between 2 semesters, with the typical introductory lecture recently enrolling 25. Some freshman classes such as Fundamentals of Biology topped 60 in a recent year. Once students enter their majors, the average class size drops to 15 or 20, although courses in some popular fields remain larger.

The addition of the World Cultures Sequence to the university's core curriculum provided focus to what used to be basic general-education requirements. Under the present 41-hour program (out of 120 semester hours needed to graduate), students must take the 6-hour World Cultures component plus 32 hours distributed among a broad range of academic disciplines and 3 hours of a senior seminar that emphasizes independent scholarship and written and oral discourse. Every student must demonstrate first-year university-level competency in a foreign language and, at the end of the World Cultures sequence, must pass a writing proficiency exam in order to graduate.

Fifty-seven of the university's 234 faculty members are part-time. One third are women. Professors get high marks for their ability to use research to stay on top of their fields and to incorporate it into their teaching without letting it interfere with their accessibility to students. Most encourage students to visit their offices "to discuss papers or presentations but also life in general," says a junior, and are visible on campus at university activities and as advisors to student-led organizations. Thanks to the faculty, says an environmental administration major, "We are not just a university; we are a university community." However, as at all universities, there are some tenured professors who, says a psychology major, "are no longer challenged and therefore don't feel the need to challenge us."

Within Evansville's university community, 2 disciplines in particular stand out among their peers: physical therapy and theater. The 5-year physical therapy program is very selective in its admissions standards and very challenging to complete, combining a rigorous course of study with much hands-on experience. "The theater department is 'huge,'" says a creative writing major, "not really in size but in hipness, popularity, and presence." The theater program not only is widely respected and admired on campus, but also has gained national recognition through its award-winning performances at the American College Theater Festival. Other programs, which stand somewhat in the shadow of these 2 but also are considered stellar, are creative writing and psychology, with its emphasis on undergraduate research. Archaeology has its own Etruscan "dig site" outside Siena, Italy. Engineering, already an impressive major, became that much better with the opening in August 2001 of a 3-story addition to the Koch Center for Engineering and Science. The new addition and renovation of the older facility enables students to engage in more hands-on learning and collaborative, multidisciplinary projects, extending well beyond the standard format of professors lecturing and students taking notes. The business program draws applause for its innovative curriculum that combines hands-on training such as a required internship with fundamental coursework such as a 2-semester class titled "Experience in Entrepreneurship." Says a major: "The business program offers nothing but opportunities!"

The nursing program needs improvement; communications, more rigor. Language majors are available only in French, German, and Spanish, although minors are offered in Russian Studies, Latin American Studies, and Japanese Studies, as well as a minor in Classical Languages and classes in Italian, Greek, Hebrew, and Latin. Education majors would like to see more attention paid to courses for secondary school teachers.

Facilities: The university's 2 libraries, the Bower-Suhrheinrich and the Clifford Memorial, are actually a single joined facility with books primarily contained in 1 portion and study rooms mostly in the other. Because the library is such a popular place to study, some floors have actually been designated "social floors" in hopes of confining stage whispers to these levels. As far as research goes, students generally find the 286,000 volumes and 970 current periodicals to be adequate for research in lower-level classes, while the wide range of computerized research aids assist with the more advanced assignments.

There are 7 public computer labs, several departmental computer clusters, and a small computer lab in each residence hall. One lab is open from 6 a.m. until 2 a.m. "and in 3 years," says an interpersonal communications major, "I've never had to wait longer than 10 minutes for a computer." One hundred percent of the campus is networked; the library and most classroom buildings also allow wireless connectivity between laptop computers and the Internet. The university strongly recommends that all students have personal computers; students majoring in engineering and computer science are required to provide their own.

Special programs: Across the Atlantic, the University of Evansville owns Harlaxton College, a branch campus housed in a Victorian manor 1 hour by train from London, England. Approximately 30 courses are offered there each semester, from which students may choose 2 or 3 in addition to a required introductory course in British life and culture. Forty-four percent of the 2005 graduating class reported studying there or in other places around the world. Back on this side of the ocean, engineering students may participate in cooperative programs with various industries. Internships, though required in business programs, are encouraged in all fields of study.

Campus life: Students want to make one point clear: Evansville is no suitcase college, despite its location in an urban area and its proximity to many larger cities and students' homes. Seventy-one percent of the undergraduates live on the campus, which covers 6 city blocks in an upper-middle-class residential neighborhood; most of these residents spend their weekends right on campus. Greek life involves 22% of the men and 23% of the women as members of the 6 national fraternities and 4 national sororities. The sororities have no houses, but fraternity-house parties are popular with independents as well as members. The Student Activities Board regularly sponsors comedians, bands, and game nights. Vandalism and petty theft are the only crimes considered to be troublesome and these are minimal. Blue light poles with emergency phones and an escort service are readily available, just in case a student needs them.

Evansville fields competitive NCAA Division I teams in Purple Aces baseball, soccer, and basketball. Altogether, a total of 6 men's and 8 women's intercollegiate teams are offered. Twenty-seven intramural sports are also available to men and women, with 67% of the men and 42% of the women participating.

Because Evansville is located within 3 hours of a wide variety of very different cities—Nashville, Indianapolis, Cincinnati, Louisville, and St. Louis—when students want to get away, it's up to them where they'll choose to point their cars.

Cost cutters: Ninety-nine percent of 2005–2006 freshmen and 95% of all continuing students received financial aid. Seventy-one percent of freshmen and 69% of continuing students were given need-based assistance. The average freshman award for a student with need included a need-based scholarship or grant averaging $16,730 and need-based self-help aid such as loans and jobs averaging $3900. Non-need-based athletic scholarships for first-year students averaged $17,700. The average financial indebtedness of the 2005 graduate was $17,400. Trustee scholarships pay half, two-thirds, three-fourths, or full tuition to a limited number of Indiana high school valedictorians. Academic scholarships ranging in value from $4000 to $12,000 a year are awarded according to students' GPAs, difficulty of courses, and standardized test scores. Leadership Activity Awards pay $4500 a year; United Methodist scholarships, $4750 yearly.

Rate of return: Eighty-one percent of freshmen return for the sophomore year. Forty-five percent go on to graduate in 4 years; 59%, within 5 years.

Payoff: More than a third of the 2005 graduates earned degrees in 3 broad fields: 14% earned degrees in the health professions and related sciences; 12% in visual and performing arts; and 11% in business and marketing. More than three-quarters of Evansville graduates convert their degrees to jobs immediately, often with nationwide employers such as INTEL, Bristol Meyers-Squibb, GE, Ernst and Young, Whirlpool, and Toyota, as well as many local and regional companies, schools, and hospitals. One hundred twenty-nine companies and organizations recruited on campus during the 2004–2005 school year. Sixteen percent of the degree recipients go on to graduate school.

Bottom line: Adds a junior: "I want to emphasize the personal touch that students receive here. It is very hard to get lost in the shuffle. The professors are very competent and enthusiastic, and students can actively participate in class discussions. There also are more than 100 organizations to get involved in, and it is very easy to become an officer because there are not hundreds of members fighting for these posts."

Valparaiso University

Valparaiso, Indiana 46383

Setting: Small town
Control: Private (Lutheran)
Undergraduate enrollment: 1374 men, 1451 women
Graduate enrollment: 337 men, 349 women
Student/faculty ratio: 13:1
Freshman profile: SAT/ACT scores: NA; 54% graduated in top fifth of high school class; 77% in upper two-fifths.
Faculty profile: 88% Ph.D.'s
Tuition and fees: $22,750
Room and board: $6220

Freshman financial aid: 96%; average scholarship or grant: $13,799 need-based; $7145 non-need-based
Campus jobs: 40%; average earnings: $1000/year
Application deadline: Aug. 15
Financial aid deadline: Mar. 1 (Jan. 15 for academic scholarships)
Admissions information: (219) 464-5011;
(888) GO-VALPO
e-mail: undergrad.admissions@valpo.edu
web site: www.valpo.edu

The Chapel of the Resurrection at Valparaiso University in northwest Indiana may be the world's largest collegiate chapel, but it means a lot more than mere size to this 3850-student university. Sharing the center of the 310-acre campus with a new library and information center, the Chapel is a symbol of both the university's Christian beliefs and its indomitable spirit of survival. Twice since its founding in 1859, the university closed its doors, seemingly forever, once after the Civil War and again after going bankrupt after World War I. Valparaiso's more recent resurrection occurred in 1925, when the Lutheran University Association purchased the school. Today, as an independent university affiliated with congregations and members of the Lutheran Church, Valparaiso has emerged as a solid financial investment for the career-minded student who wants a bachelor's degree that will work for him or her. Says a civil engineering major: "This school has provided me with wings as well as landing gear. What more could a person ask for?"

Student body: Forty percent of Valpo's undergraduate student body is Lutheran, with Catholics comprising 21% and Protestants of other denominations 26%. Hoosiers make up 35% of the enrollment, with 86% of the out-of-staters coming from other states in the Great Lakes region. All but 2 states in the nation are represented. Eighty percent of the students are graduates of public schools. Valparaiso's enrollment remains predominantly white, though diversity is increasing. Foreign nationals from 45 countries account for 2% of the undergraduate student body. Another 4% are African-American, 3% Hispanic and 2% are Asian-American. Native Americans account for less than 1%. Students tend to be mostly conservative (although the liberal contingent has its say), with many who are caring and spiritual, albeit a bit sheltered, and active in promoting Christian ideals through community service projects. A number have siblings, parents, or other relatives who are Valparaiso graduates. While many find the academic climate to be quite challenging, others do not seem affected by it. "I don't think there's a lot of competition between students," observes a senior, "but at the same time students strive for success in the classroom."

Academics: Valparaiso grants bachelor's degrees in more than 70 majors with undergraduates taking courses in the colleges of Arts and Sciences, Business Administration, Engineering, and Nursing, as well as at Christ College, which houses the honors and humanities programs. The university also awards the master's degree and, from its School of Law, the J.D. degree. The academic year is divided into 2 semesters with an average class size for undergraduates of 20. The range normally falls between 10 and 85 students, although some specialized courses such as Advanced Japanese may enroll only 1 and Exploring Engineering may reach 115.

General-education requirements get off to a strong start, beginning with a required, 2-semester interdisciplinary class known as the Valpo Core. The 10-credit course, entitled the Human Experience, primarily involves faculty from the humanities, arts, and sciences but also includes professors from business, nursing, and engineering. Each semester's Core is divided into three 5-week topics, ranging in the first semester from Birth and Creation to Education-Coming of Age to the subject of Citizenship and Service. The texts used vary from Mary Shelley's *Frankenstein* to the Dalai Lama's *The Power of Compassion;* films range from *Gattaca* to *Casablanca*. In addition, students must take 12 credit hours of math or natural science, at least 3 each in English, theology, social analysis, U.S. diversity, and global diversity, and 1 of physical education. A special program of honors courses at Christ College replaces many of the regular general-education requirements.

All but 119 of the 364 faculty members are full-time and all but 29 of the 245 full-time members teach undergraduates. Twenty-two of the 119 part-time members teach at the graduate level only. There are no teaching assistants. Forty percent of the faculty are women. Students use adjectives like *hard-working, considerate,* and *enthusiastic* to describe their professors. About a fourth of the pool muster only a C average for their teaching abilities. However, the vast majority, notes a history major, "are good, caring people, who as teachers want you to learn, not just test well."

Christ College, the honors school, attracts many top students to the university with the promise of stimulating courses of fewer than a dozen participants to promote lively discussion. Christ College scholars also complete a traditional major in any of the other colleges. The College of Engineering is noted for being especially demanding with excellent equipment and extensive opportunities for cooperative work experience. The College of Business Administration uses the same combination of individual attention and practical training with a required internship to place well-prepared graduates in the job market. In the College of Arts and Sciences, chemistry and physics, international economics and cultural affairs, English, social work, music and music education, theology, and meteorology enjoy strong student support. Meteorology boasts its own storm-chase team that has over $12,000 worth of field instrumentation and computers for use when on the trail of a twister. As of spring 2006, Valpo also will have become the only exclusively undergraduate meteorology program in the nation with a Doppler radar system. The College of Nursing also commands respect, thanks, in part, to a new state-of-the-art Visual Nursing Learning Center that gives students hands-on learning in a simulated real-world setting with actual equipment and lifelike mannequins.

Smaller programs in the College of Arts and Sciences, among them, sociology and communication law have only 3 or 4 professors each, which can limit the number of perspectives and course offerings provided on the subject. The communications department as a whole, with majors in new media-journalism, public and corporate communication, public relations, and television-radio, as well as communication law, has become one of the university's fastest growing programs and needs more room to accommodate undergraduates. Students say the education department could use some livelier professors and a new building.

Facilities: The center of campus has gained another awe-inspiring structure alongside the Chapel of the Resurrection: the new Christopher Center for Library and Information Resources, which opened in fall 2004. The 115,000-square-foot structure features on its first floor a comfortable reading room overlooking Resurrection Meadow as well as a café, a 60-seat computer lab, media lab, and writing center. The remaining 3 floors house the automated book storage and retrieval system as well as extensive space for stacks of the university's general collection. The collection numbers 635,500 volumes, plus subscriptions to 25,500 paper and electronic periodicals. The on-line catalog provides access to materials at the Christopher Center as well as to an additional 146,000 volumes (and 3258 current periodicals) held at the library of the School of Law. Interlibrary loan also makes available material from the University of Notre Dame and Indiana University.

Valpo has 3 main computer centers, 1 on each end of campus and 1 at the center in the new Christopher Building, (plus 1 in the law school), which are open until midnight, longer as finals approach. Smaller labs with about a dozen PCs and Macintosh computers also are available around the clock in each residence hall. Other computers are scattered across campus, making a total of 820 computers in 63 laboratories and classrooms as part of a wired and partially wireless network. "Students rarely wait," says a senior, "since so many bring personal computers." Only engineering students are required to have personal computers, preferably the Pentium IV (2.4 GHz).

Special programs: Students may spend a semester at Valparaiso's study centers in Cambridge, England, or Reutlingen, Germany, or spend the same time or longer at other programs in Germany, Mexico, France, Japan, Spain, Greece, Namibia, or China. Engineering students can participate in a 5-year program that combines study in engineering and in German, study abroad, and a cooperative education placement in Germany. Students also can study closer to home in Chicago or Washington, D.C. Cross-registration is offered with Indiana University Northwest.

Campus life: Two-thirds of the undergraduates live on campus, primarily in coed or single-sex residence halls or the 8 fraternity houses; only seniors are permitted to live elsewhere. One senior man describes the after-hours life this way: "Socially, there is the Greek system and the Greek system, so there is very little to do on weekends if you are not Greek." Twenty-five percent of the men belong to 9 national fraternities; 18% of the women are members of 6 national sororities. Many parties are restricted to house members until 11 p.m., when independents and other Greeks can attend. Student programming offers movies, comedians, coffeehouses, a monthly dance club, and other attractions open to all.

Nineteen religious services a week, including daily chapel and Sunday worship, are offered at the Chapel of the Resurrection and at St. Theresa of Avila Catholic Student Center. Attendance is not required, but, observes a senior, "Sunday chapel is a must—almost a social event!" For the musically inclined, Valpo has 3 choirs, 2 bands, and a symphony. A new 240-seat recital hall and 300-seat theater with orchestra pit have further enhanced the weekend's cultural offerings. Occasional incidents of bike theft and vandalism to cars keep students and campus security alert, and emergency phones as well as an escort service are provided.

While Valparaiso offers a wide range of intercollegiate sports, 8 each for men and women through NCAA Division I (Division IAA in football), the turnout for Crusaders men's basketball and women's volleyball is largest in number, spirit, and decibel level. Half of both men and women engage in the 20 intramural sports provided to each sex. "There always are games going on," notes a senior.

The small town of Valparaiso (pop. 26,000) is located less than an hour from Chicago, which presents an easy and inviting getaway; for those without cars, the student union board sponsors bus trips into the city at least once a month. In warmer weather, Indiana Dunes National Lake Shore on Lake Michigan (just 20 minutes away) gives students a taste of sand and sun.

Cost cutters: The Lutheran Church helps to underwrite Valparaiso's current operations, and several endowed faculty positions and some endowed plant maintenance funds also serve to offset instructional and operational costs. In the 2005–2006 school year, 96% of Valparaiso freshmen and 93% of continuing students received financial aid; 71% of the freshmen and 68% of the continuing students got need-based help. The average freshman award for a student with financial need included a need-based scholarship or grant averaging $13,799 and need-based self-help aid such as loans and jobs averaging $4860. Non-need-based athletic scholarships for freshmen averaged $19,110; other non-need-based awards and scholarships averaged $7140. A typical 2005 graduate left with debts of $23,853. Valparaiso merit scholarships range from the Achievement, which pays $4000 to $5000 a year to the Founders, which pays full tuition, with 2 scholarships in between. Which award the student receives depends on such factors as his or her grade point average and standardized test scores. Dependents of professional Lutheran Church workers are eligible for Martin Luther Awards recently worth $4500. Cooperative programs are available to students majoring in various disciplines within each of the colleges, although students say opportunities seem most plentiful in the College of Engineering. Tuition payments may be made monthly, over 3 months each semester, or by credit card.

Rate of return: Eighty-six percent of the entering freshmen return for the sophomore year. Sixty-one percent graduate in 4 years; 72% in 5 years.

Payoff: Practical, career-oriented majors were the 2 top choices among 2005 graduates: 9% earned degrees in nursing and 6% in elementary education. Five percent each earned degrees in psychology and English. The vast majority plunged immediately into the world of work, accepting jobs with firms such as Abbott Laboratories, Cincinnati Bell, Motorola, and Procter & Gamble. Valparaiso annually provides the U.S. Air Force with more meteorology graduates than any other university nationwide. About 30 companies and organizations recruited on campus in the 2004–2005 school year. A fourth of the 2004 graduates opted instead to pursue advanced degrees, several at such universities as Northwestern, Stanford, and Johns Hopkins. Within 5 years, about 40% seek further study.

Bottom line: Valparaiso falls within the size range for colleges where students benefit from a close-knit community without knowing absolutely everything about each other. While the Lutheran influence is evident, primarily in a general air of caring and conservatism, few find the religious element intrusive—although it *is* hard to ignore the world's largest collegiate chapel set right in the middle of campus!

Wabash College
Crawfordsville, Indiana 47933

Setting: Small town
Control: Private
Undergraduate enrollment: 871 men
Graduate enrollment: None
Student/faculty ratio: 10:1
Freshman profile: 8% scored over 700 on SAT I verbal; 41% scored 600–700; 40% 500–599; 11% below 500. 12% scored over 700 on SAT I math; 45% scored 600–700; 33% 500–599; 10% below 500. 37% graduated in top tenth of high school class; 60% in upper fifth.
Faculty profile: 96% Ph.D.'s
Tuition and fees: $23,388

Room and board: $6728
Freshman financial aid: 72%; average scholarship or grant: $17,328 need-based
Campus jobs: 60%; average earnings: $1500/year
Application deadline: Early decision: Nov 15; regular: Feb. 1
Financial aid deadline: Mar. 1 (Priority date: Feb. 15)
Admissions information: (765) 361-6253; (800) 345-5385
e-mail: admissions@wabash.edu
web site: www.wabash.edu

The men of Wabash College have been asked a certain question so many times that they know it's coming even before it's asked: Why, in this age of coeducation, did they choose to attend a small college in a small town without any women? The answer, for many, seems as natural as the question: The education and the financial aid offered at this small, 175-year-old college are too good to overlook. Students enjoy close relationships with a superb faculty, all but 4% of whom have doctorates, a rigorous curriculum that emphasizes a strong liberal arts foundation as preparation for future professional programs, and a financial aid policy featuring tempting scholarships to top students. In addition, Wabash men obtain a baccalaureate degree that places approximately 75% of them in graduate or professional schools within 5 years of leaving the college. That ranks Wabash 16th among colleges and universities nationwide for the percentage of graduates ultimately receiving their Ph.D.'s (13%). Women can come later, the students say, and will have to, since the Wabash Board of Trustees voted in 1992 against admitting women—a change most faculty had supported but the Student Senate had rejected 22 to 1. In the eyes of most Wabash men, the educational opportunities of their all-male college are better left untouched.

Student body: Seventy-one percent of Wabash students are Hoosiers, with 70% of the rest hailing from the Midwest. A total of 30 states are represented. Though the student body remains heavily white, the founding of the Malcolm X Institute for Black Studies has helped attract more African-American students to campus. Fourteen percent of today's students are members of minority groups: 6% are African-American, 4% Hispanic, 3% Asian-American, and 1% Native American. Four percent are foreign nationals from 22 countries. Ninety-four percent are graduates of public schools. Students tend to be hard-working and goal-oriented; they "enjoy a good debate," as one political science major puts it. "There is a sense of pride, honor, camaraderie, and tradition at Wabash." Adds an English major: "It's a very intense place. People are very focused on their futures but also committed to enjoying themselves," within certain boundaries that is. The young men who come to Wabash learn to respect and follow one rule of conduct, known as the Gentleman's Rule: "A Wabash man will conduct himself, at all times, both on and off campus, as a gentleman and a responsible citizen." Observes a senior: "We are given a lot of freedom to grow up, make decisions for ourselves, and accept the consequences."

Academics: Wabash offers the bachelor's degree in 21 majors, with classes following a semester schedule. Like the school, classes tend to be small and personalized, with the largest introductory lecture in Chemistry I recently having 64 students. Most freshman classes settle between 20 and 30 with upper-level courses often topping out at 10. Six classes in a recent year had a single student.

Each student begins his studies at Wabash with a freshman tutorial of no more than 15 participants; topics have been as varied as "The Art of War" and "Painted Ladies: Greek Art and Myth." Sophomores follow up with 2 courses in cultures and traditions. Beyond demonstrating proficiency in English and a foreign language, students must also fulfill distributional requirements in language studies, literature and fine arts, behavioral science, natural science and mathematics, and history, philosophy, or religion. Study in the academic major culminates with both a written comprehensive examination and a senior oral exam. "I am not looking forward to these exams," notes a senior approaching D-day, "but I am proud that we have to take them."

The faculty lies at the heart of Wabash's success as a small liberal arts college. All but 2 of the 89 members are full-time; 19% are women. "The best part of being a student at Wabash is the opportunity to meet, talk to, and share ideas with the faculty, both in and out of class," raves a sophomore. "The faculty is always accessible, day and night, in their offices or at their homes. Such close interaction between teachers and students leads to lifelong friendships."

Students' picks for the strongest academic programs target nearly all departments. Classics, English, philosophy, religion, economics, and political science feature outstanding professors; biology and chemistry offer extremely challenging curricula, good facilities, and extensive opportunities for research. The theater major, though small, is both rigorous and rewarding.

Students are just as perceptive about Wabash's weaker spots. Physics has a reputation for having lesser professors and equipment. Music, too, needs better equipment. History could be made more rigorous. Mathematics needs more effective instruction. There are no majors in such career-focused fields as business and communication, although business is offered as a 6-course sequence of largely economics and accounting courses that can be combined with any major. Computer science is offered only as a minor.

Facilities: Recently renovated Lilly Library houses nearly 432,000 volumes and 4776 current periodicals, quite ample for a college of 871 students but not always adequate for the depth some research projects demand. The catalog and periodical listings are computerized and database searching and Internet access are available. When students want to peruse materials for themselves, the 14 libraries at Purdue University are just 30 minutes away.

More than 300 computers (primarily Dell Pentium computers) are available for student use for an average of 15 hours daily, in the library, the computer center, several classrooms, and in all departments. Some of the labs are open around the clock, and many fraternities also have their own "house" computers. All students also have Internet access from their rooms and a wireless network is available in most buildings.

Special programs: Opportunities for study abroad are available through the Great Lakes Colleges Association, of which Wabash is a member, plus a variety of independent programs in which Wabash students have had success in the past. The college also administers its own program at the University of Aberdeen in Scotland. Students may also take a semester to study the humanities at the Newberry Library in Los Angeles, the arts in New York, science at Oak Ridge, Tennessee, or politics in the nation's capital. A 3-2 engineering degree is offered with Columbia University in New York or Washington University in St. Louis. A 3-3 program in law also is an option at Columbia. Students interested in secondary education may participate in a Ninth Semester Teacher Education Program.

Campus life: The Greeks are big at Wabash, with 65% of the men pledging to 10 national fraternities. Weekend parties at the houses, with plenty of drinking, visits from area sororities, and bands almost every weekend, form the hub of social life on campus. About half the parties are open to independents who students say can sometimes feel left out on the Greek-dominated campus.

On nonparty weekends, the students, 91% of whom reside on the 55-acre campus, either stick around for a home basketball game or engage in their second favorite sport: road-tripping to visit friends at any of several larger universities within a 2-hour drive, Purdue, Indiana, DePauw, Butler, and the University of Illinois at Urbana-Champaign. Football also is big, especially the annual Monon Bell game between Wabash and DePauw University, the oldest continual small college football rivalry west of the Alleghenies. Altogether, there are 11 intercollegiate sports played in NCAA Division III and 23 intramural events.

Forty percent of the men play at the varsity level, 80% in intramurals. As popular as playing on the Little Giants teams is being a member of the cheering squad, the Sphinx Club, a prestigious group that promotes campus spirit, in part by leading the cheers at various sporting events, dressed in red and white striped overalls and white beanies. Members are usually the most popular and most athletic students on campus. The club also does philanthropic work in the community and is responsible for upholding the various much-loved college traditions, among them the Chapel Sing and other freshman class pledge events.

Crawfordsville (pop. 14,000) is located in farm fields 45 minutes northwest of Indianapolis. While it experiences little in the way of neighborhood crime, it also offers little in the way of diversion to students, although several nearby state parks are enjoyable.

Cost cutters: A solid financial aid program is one of the most effective enticements drawing students to Wabash, thanks in part to an endowment worth about $334 million in June 2005, which on a per student basis ranks in the top 30 among all colleges and universities. Seventy-two percent of the freshmen and 76% of all continuing students received aid in the 2005–2006 school year. Seventy-one percent of the freshmen and 70% of the other students got need-based assistance. The average freshman award for a student with financial need included a need-based scholarship or grant averaging $17,396 and need-based self-help aid such as loans and jobs averaging $4046. The average 2005 graduate left with debts of $17,328. Wabash also offers several hefty merit scholarships. Chief among them is the Lilly Award, covering full tuition, fees, room and board, which recognizes leadership activities and leadership potential and goes to a maximum of 10 men in each freshman class. Honor Scholarships are awarded to 30 men based on their performances on a written examination taken at the college; the awards pay up to $20,000 annually. Fine Arts Fellowships pay up to $12,500 annually to students in the visual arts, creative writing, music, and theater. President's Scholarships acknowledging outstanding achievement in high school pay up to $17,500 based on class rank and test scores. Concludes a junior: "I have never met anyone here who pays full tuition." Students not receiving need-based financial aid are eligible to pay 4 years' tuition up front. Monthly payment plans are available.

Rate of return: Eighty-nine percent of freshmen return for the sophomore year. Sixty-nine percent remain to graduate in 4 years; 72% in 5 years; 75% in 6. Beginning with the class of freshmen who entered in fall 1999, Wabash has guaranteed graduation within 4 years or the college assumes the cost of the extra tuition. The student is still responsible for room and board charges as well as other fees. To be eligible for the 4-year guarantee, the undergraduate must be a full-time student for 8 consecutive semesters, must complete 34 course credits with a cumulative GPA of at least 2.0, and must persist in the major first declared during his sophomore year. The student also is responsible for knowing graduation requirements and arranging his course schedule to complete them.

Payoff: English was the major of choice among 2005 graduates, accounting for 17% of the degrees, followed by history at 14%, and psychology at 11%. More than a third of the graduates enrolled in graduate or professional school. In recent years, students seeking jobs have tended to enter financial, sales, and manufacturing management positions with regional and national firms such as INB, Bank One, Edward D. Jones, Eli Lilly, and Aerotek. While nearly a third begin careers in business, almost a tenth work in government, social service, or teaching. Forty companies and organizations recruited on campus in the 2004–2005 school year.

Bottom line: Concludes a senior from the East: "Few students come to Wabash because it's an all-male college, but once you get here, you find yourself willing to fight to the death to keep it that way. The male camaraderie is overwhelming."

Iowa

Buena Vista University

Storm Lake, Iowa 50588

Setting: Small town
Control: Private (Presbyterian)
Undergraduate enrollment: 574 men, 624 women
Graduate enrollment: None (69 part-time)
Student/faculty ratio: 14:1
Freshman profile: 8% scored above 28 on the ACT; 5% scored 27–28; 23% 24–26; 29% 21–23; 35% below 21. 28% graduated in top fifth of high school class; 60% in upper two-fifths.
Faculty profile: 82% Ph.D.'s
Tuition and fees: $21,688

Room and board: $6054
Freshman financial aid: 99%; average scholarship or grant: NA
Campus jobs: 57%; average earnings: $787/year
Application deadline: Rolling
Financial aid deadline: June 1
Admissions information: (712) 749-2235; (800) 383-9600
e-mail: admissions@bvu.edu
web site: www.bvu.edu

Although Buena Vista University in Storm Lake, Iowa, was founded in 1891, in many ways its life didn't really begin until May of 1980, when the tiny college of fewer than 1000 students received an anonymous gift of $18 million. That gift, the stuff of which college fantasies are made, marked the start of Buena Vista's transformation from just another small liberal arts college in an out-of-the-way place into a serious contender for top students and first-rate faculty. Like any full-blooded American school, Buena Vista chose, as its first purchase with its newfound millions, a football stadium, constructed in the fall of 1980, followed by a 550-car parking lot in 1982, and ultimately the $10 million Harold Walter Siebens School of Business/Siebens Forum. The building was named for the heretofore anonymous donor, a Storm Lake native who had earned millions in oil and gas and decided to donate much of it to his father's alma mater, Buena Vista College. The rest was history. After the opening of the business school, a campuswide telecommunications system was installed, wiring all of the dorms for audio, visual, and computer-data reception and providing teleconferencing capabilities to link BV students with the world. In 1986, the former campus center became a communications center, housing sophisticated equipment for the college radio and television stations and the student newspaper. Two decades later, on a completely wireless campus where a notebook computer is provided for every student, undergraduates who otherwise might never have considered Buena Vista are drawn to its highly advanced structures in business and communications and the opportunities provided for real-world experience. In their eyes, Seibens's $18 million has been *very* well spent.

Student body: Still, most of BVU's student body continues to come from the surrounding geographical area. Seventy-eight percent are from Iowa, with all but a small portion of the rest from other midwestern states. Altogether, 16 states and 1 foreign country have students enrolled. All but 8% attended public schools. Six percent are Presbyterian, the rest mainly of other Protestant faiths or Catholic. Because most students are drawn from small towns in Iowa and the surrounding region, creating a racially and ethnically diverse campus has posed problems for administrators. The college has responded by stepping up recruitment of Asian students, with the largest numbers in recent years coming from Taiwan and Japan. Despite such efforts, Buena Vista remains predominantly white, with 2% Asian-American and 1% each African-American and Hispanic students. Although the student body is becoming less conservative and more aware of different cultures, the vast majority still have had limited experience with people unlike themselves and remain apathetic toward issues with little direct impact on their lives. Says a student from a large city in the Midwest: "I am disappointed by the lack of cultural awareness." As far as academics are concerned, a corporate communication major notes: "The old saying 'college is what you make of it' really applies here. Challenging courses are offered, but not everyone takes them."

Academics: Buena Vista, which became a university in 1995, offers bachelor's degrees in more than 40 majors and 15 preprofessional programs in 5 undergraduate schools. BVU also provides 1 graduate level program, a master of science in education. The academic year is divided into 2 semesters plus a January term, which students use to explore various interests on campus, with corporations, or in other countries. The average class size for undergraduates is 18. Most freshman and sophomore classes enroll from 30 to

60 students, while upper-level courses in chemistry and math, for example, can have 5–15. The ever-popular business major usually continues to have 40 students per class, even at the upper level.

All students must complete 30 hours of general-education distribution requirements and demonstrate competency in written communications and mathematics. A Freshman Seminar is required of all first-year students in the fall term. Along with their major, students must take 9 credit hours in each of 2 other disciplines, at least 3 of those 9 credits at the upper level; students who wish may opt to choose 1 minor field of study instead of the 2 areas of concentration. For a change of pace, all students must attend 8 cultural events or lectures every semester for at least 4 semesters, including at least 1 event each term sponsored by 3 different schools and 2 or more of the major all-campus convocations, concerts, and events. Students applaud the Academic and Cultural Events Series or ACES, as it is called, which in recent years has exposed undergraduates to such world-class speakers and performers as former British Prime Minister John Major in 2005, and in earlier years, former Israeli Prime Minister Shimon Peres, and violinist Itzhak Perlman.

Eighty-one of Buena Vista's 119 faculty members are full-time. Forty-four percent are women. On a scale of 1 to 10, with 10 being perfect, many give the faculty an 8, based primarily on their knowledge, friendliness, support to students, and genuine love of teaching that comes through in the classroom. "Their willingness to always be there for the student is important," says a finance major. The small minority who bring down the grade lack the necessary teaching know-how to get their knowledge across effectively and are sometimes close-minded to new ideas.

Business and mass communication, the main beneficiaries of the Siebens gift, are, in the eyes of students, clearly Buena Vista's best offerings. Both disciplines focus their courses on real-world issues and are rich in faculty with on-the-job experience and in top-of-the-line classroom materials. The business school/forum, which is built underground, includes a special resource room that lets students receive the latest market information from Wall Street and other sources, as well as several areas where teleconferencing is possible. Students like the case-study method used in instruction, as well as the internship experience required of all majors. The Lage Center for Communication enables students to use the latest equipment for work in radio, television, and print journalism, making hands-on experience possible on virtually a daily basis. Opportunities for internships also are plentiful. As a result, a student emerging with a major either in mass communication or in corporate communication has good entree into the job market.

Though overshadowed by these better funded programs, science and psychology also earn student respect for the excellence of their faculties who encourage students to develop their own ideas and push them to be their best. The opening of the $26 million Estelle Siebens Science Center in fall 2004 finally raised the quality of the science equipment to the level of the gifted faculty. The School of Education, too, would gain more applause, were it not for the other dominant programs. Fans say that the art major deserves to be named "best in show" for being "exceptional" despite having few faculty members and lesser facilities.

By contrast, other programs, such as philosophy and religion, social work, political science, history, foreign language, and theater have a harder time offering a variety of courses and varying perspectives because each has only two or three professors. The only foreign language major offered is in Spanish; minors are available in Japanese, Chinese, and German.

Facilities: As remarkable as students find the Siebens and Lage buildings, many used to consider Ballou Library to be just as remarkable—remarkably bad, in this case, but not anymore. A 49,000-square-foot addition to the library opened in early 1996, providing a new technology center as well as more attractive study space. The collection stands at 132,000 volumes with subscriptions to 675 periodicals, up from 475 a few years before. Recent remodeling of the main building has added better lighting and made the surroundings more comfortable for study though at times it can become too social for serious study. That's when users turn to the sound-proof study rooms on the bottom floor, or hide in various corners. An online catalog is helpful, as are assorted computerized search engines.

Fall 2000 marked the official start of the eBVyou program, designed to make Buena Vista a model wireless learning community. As part of the plan, all students are leased a notebook computer for use during their time on campus. Raves a senior: "Students always have access to their own computer and to the worldwide web. Moreover, laptops can be used for taking notes in class, viewing professors' slide shows, and even submitting homework and taking tests." The university will upgrade the units every 2 years and students who wish may purchase theirs at fair market value at the time of graduation.

Special programs: Prospective engineers can spend 3 years at Buena Vista and another 2 at Washington University in St. Louis, earning bachelor's degrees from both. A program with the University of Iowa College of Dentistry lets BVU students enter their first year of dentistry school after 3 years in Storm Lake. Students can work 6 months as English tutors at Taipei Language Institute in Taiwan, attend Hokusei Gakuen University in Sapporo, Japan, or take part in other programs in Australia or several European countries. As far as internships go, students say, "Just give faculty and administrators a name and a place, and they'll do their best to get you there." Business majors can spend an interim term in Florida, meeting in seminars with corporate leaders. After the freshman year any student may apply for a Rollins fellowship; 1 or 2 fellows each year receive stipends to be used for a self-developed life experience, research project, or special program that will enhance their leadership abilities and career potential.

Campus life: Eighty-eight percent of Buena Vista's students live on the 60-acre campus overlooking the 3200 acres of water known, of course, as Storm Lake. But most don't stick around for the lakefront view over the weekends. Without Greek organizations to turn to for regularly scheduled parties, many freshmen and sophomores head for home, while juniors and seniors go dancing at a local bar or take in a movie. This still happens despite the fact that the college is sponsoring more weekend entertainment such as bands, comedians, and casino nights. Large numbers of students participate in the college's media outlets, its radio station KBVC, its television station Innovation Video, which produces programming for the local cable outlets, and the college newspaper, *The Tack*. Altogether, about 50 clubs and organizations are available to students. Buena Vista is associated with the Presbyterian Church, but, as one junior remarked, "I know we're religiously affiliated, but I can't even tell you with what denomination." Crime, other than some vandalism to cars in the parking lot, has not been considered a problem. As a precaution, the university hired a full-time director of campus security and 2 part-time officers. Other recently added measures include the installation of more lighting around campus and emergency phones.

Intercollegiate sports remain the primary attraction at Buena Vista, and are drawing bigger crowds, with Beavers football, basketball, and women's volleyball ranking highest in spectator viewing. In addition to these sports, the college fields teams in 8 other men's sports and 8 other women's, all played under NCAA Division III. Total participation may exceed crowd support some nights, with 23% of the men and 11% of the women recently engaged in some varsity sport. Approximately 60% in a recent year were involved in the 10 men's and 10 women's intramural teams. Along with the offerings of a new recreation center that opened in 2001, the college maintains canoes and sailboats for use on Storm Lake and on river trips throughout the year.

The town of Storm Lake (pop. 10,000) offers little of interest to students other than some parks, restaurants, bars, and bowling alleys. Those not homeward bound sometimes make a longer trip for shopping in Sioux City, 65 miles west.

Cost cutters: Siebens's initial gift and subsequent donations from him and others have helped give Buena Vista a healthy endowment exceeding $114 million as of June 2005. One result has been more financial aid: 99% of fall 2005 freshmen and 98% of continuing students received financial assistance of some sort. At least 89% of both groups received need-based aid. The average package of financial aid given to freshmen in 2005 totaled $20,022; no breakdown is available on the portion that was grants, loans, or earnings from jobs. A typical graduate in 2005 left with debts of $26,759. A wide variety of merit scholarships are available, to first-year students. Three levels of Foundation Scholarships pay $6500, $7500, and $8500 annually, based on students' class rank, grade point average, and ACT scores. To earn other competitive awards, applicants must attend 1 of 2 Scholarship Recognition Days in early February or early March. The most prized awards available are the Trustee Scholarship, which pays full tuition to 5 freshmen who ranked in the top 5% of their high school class with a 3.85 GPA and 29 ACT, and a Multicultural Award that pays full tuition, room, and board to students of diverse backgrounds with strong academic and leadership qualities. A Dean's Fellowship pays $2000 plus a $1000 international travel stipend and a $500 domestic travel stipend, also based on GPA, class rank, and ACT scores. For all scholarships, students must meet 2 of the 3 criteria to be considered.

Rate of return: Of the freshmen who start at Buena Vista, 76% return for the sophomore year. Fifty-one percent graduate in 4 years; 60%, within 5 years; 62% within 6.

Payoff: Almost 30% of recent graduates earned degrees in 3 areas: 12% in education, 9% in management, and 8% in marketing. The majority take jobs immediately upon graduation with major firms such as Touche Ross, Georgia Pacific, Amoco, and IBM, as well as in journalism and teaching. Forty companies and organizations recruited on campus in a recent school year. Among recent graduates, 14% headed for graduate or professional schools.

Bottom line: Buena Vista's small size allows even the unsure student to gain self-confidence while using up-to-the-moment equipment not commonly found at schools of this type. While Buena Vista may give its students all they could dream of having professionally, the college lacks social diversity and a variety of after-hours activities. Notes a midwesterner: "I do not recommend Buena Vista to students coming from large high schools or from schools on either coast, or to those who are politically liberal. These students will tend to be bored, annoyed, or both."

Central College

Pella, Iowa 50219

Setting: Small town
Control: Private (Reformed Church in America)
Undergraduate enrollment: 702 men, 899 women
Graduate enrollment: None
Student/faculty ratio: 15:1
Freshman profile: 12% scored above 28 on the ACT; 11% scored 27–28; 26% 24–26; 30% 21–23; 21% below 21. 24% graduated in top tenth of high school class; 49% in upper fifth.
Faculty profile: 88% Ph.D.'s

Tuition and fees: $19,928
Room and board: $6846
Freshman financial aid: 100%; average scholarship or grant: $10,533 need-based; $2155 non-need-based
Campus jobs: 79%; average earnings: $713/year
Application deadline: Mar. 1
Financial aid deadline: Apr. 1
Admissions information: (641) 628-5285; (877) 462-3687
e-mail: admissions@central.edu
web site: www.central.edu

The term "go Dutch" means: (a) to cheer on a winning football team in Pella, Iowa; (b) to celebrate the 3-day Tulip Festival in Pella, Iowa; (c) to participate in an 8-country study-abroad program based in Pella, Iowa; (d) to attend a college in Pella, Iowa, and do all of the above at a price anyone can enjoy. If you guessed (d), you already have a sense of just what attending Central College in Pella, Iowa, can mean to a motivated student. Undergraduates say they are drawn to the 1600-student campus in south central Iowa by the school's winning academics *and* athletics. Another magnet is the 9 study-abroad programs, which nearly half of the student body take advantage of before graduating. Foreign language programs are offered in France, Spain, and Austria; English language programs, in England, Wales, the Netherlands, China, and Mexico. Internships at many of these outposts such as 5 months working with a member of the British Parliament while studying in London, are simply icing on the Dutch buttercake.

Student body: The home port of most students, however, remains Iowa, with 79% of the enrollment from in state. Most of the rest also come from the midwestern region, but 39 states and 17 foreign countries are represented. Just 10% of the students in most years are members of the school's denomination, with Methodists, Roman Catholics, and Lutherans accounting for the majority attending. All but 2% are graduates of public schools. Since so many students come from small towns in Iowa, a state with few racial and ethnic minorities, building diversity on campus has been a challenge. Foreign nationals and Hispanic students each represent 2% of the enrollment, followed by Asian-Americans, African-Americans, and Native Americans at 1% each. Aware that many of Central's majority students have had little contact with persons from other racial and ethnic groups, the college Coalition for a Multicultural Campus has promoted ways to improve integration, as well as come up with methods to attract more minorities to Central. While many students enter the college with a predominantly conservative outlook, juniors and seniors note that the study-abroad experience so many have, and bring back to classmates in Pella, raises the awareness of the undergraduates as a whole. Overall, students find the environment stimulating. Says a senior: "This campus stresses academics but also the need to be involved and have fun as part of your college experience."

Academics: Central, which turned 150 in 2003, awards the bachelor of arts degree in 36 majors. The college follows a semester schedule. The largest class, General Psychology, may approach 40 people, with the majority typically having between 25 and 30. Most upper-level students enjoy classes of just 10–20.

All students must complete 44 of the 120 semester hours needed to graduate in a core curriculum that consists of 3 broad areas entitled foundations, focus, and cultural awareness. Students also must take 21 semester hours in distribution requirements. In addition, each student must receive a communication skills endorsement from his or her major department before graduating.

The 139-member faculty (95 full-time, 36% women) is generally attentive to student concerns but has little tolerance for those not motivated to learn. Notes a junior: "While a student may not like all of his or her professors, very few faculty members are not respected for their ability to teach. And most students will find at least 1 professor who proves especially valuable to the success of their studies." Relationships between students, faculty, and administrators are close even outside the classroom. "Where else," asks a sophomore, "can you go on a double date with a dean!?"

Central's foreign language instruction is "la crème de la crème," with majors in French, German, and Spanish strengthened by the opportunities to study abroad and live amid native speakers for a year. But students need not wait until they are overseas for such immersion. Most of the upper-level professors on campus are themselves native speakers, and daily classes as well as labs provide much practice in speaking, as well as learning about the culture. Central is not a one-discipline school, though. Also on the winning list are programs in education, English, philosophy, religion, business, biology, chemistry, psychology, and political science, largely because of top-notch faculties and opportunities for practical, hands-on applications whenever possible.

Other programs, however, are hampered by insufficient support: sociology and anthropology would benefit from additional faculty to offer more variety in classes. Art has lacked adequate facilities but the number of majors keeps increasing.

Facilities: Most students consider Geisler Library to be a suitable place for study, with many individual study rooms, carrels, and worktables scattered about to satisfy all levels of concentration. The collection includes more than 229,000 volumes and 925 periodicals (plus another 12,000 electronic periodicals and newspapers), with additional material usually available within a few days from other Iowa libraries. Sometimes the college provides transportation to the University of Iowa library although a computerized catalog, numerous periodical search systems and the Internet have reduced the need for trips.

Few fault the number and location of computers on campus, with nearly 400 PC and Macintosh computers available to students in labs and classrooms plus another 194 units in the library and for special academic use. All residence-hall rooms have Internet connections, and more than 90% of Central students bring their own computers to campus to use them. During the 2005–2006 school year, the library and numerous other areas throughout campus were being added to a wireless network already present in the recently renovated science center.

Special programs: Many freshmen who choose Central are attracted by the opportunities to attend the college's programs on 9 permanent branch campuses in 8 countries around the world. Just over a tenth of the full-time students enrolled at Central spend the same semester at an overseas campus. Nearly 50% complete off-campus study before they graduate. Students conversant in French, German, or Spanish are encouraged to spend an entire academic year in Paris, Vienna, or Granada, respectively, although 1-semester options are also available. English language programs in London and Colchester (England), Bangor (Wales), and Leiden (The Netherlands) enable students to spend 1 or 2 semesters at any of these 4 programs or to combine a semester in one city with a second semester in another. English language program in Merida (Mexico) and Hangzhou (China) also are offered. Numerous opportunities are available to study stateside in Washington, D.C., or Chicago. Cooperative programs are offered in engineering and architecture with Washington University in St. Louis.

Campus life: Since 1974, most buildings on the Pella campus have been either constructed or substantially remodeled, resulting in a new fitness center (completed in 1999), a new student center (opened in 1990), and a new dining hall arranged like a European marketplace (1997) as well as 15 honor houses designed for upperclassmen and clustered together to form a cohesive village. Add a figure-8-shaped pond right in the middle of campus, and it's little wonder that 87% of the students choose to live on the 130-acre spread.

Just 12% of the men and 5% of the women belong to the 4 local fraternities and 3 local sororities at Central, so being a member or not being one has little effect on how involved a student chooses to be. Many underclassmen who live nearby have typically gone home for weekends although an increase in student programming has kept more around. One of the biggest events has been the annual Lip Sync musical pantomime contest, which involves about 90% of the student body as participants or spectators. The breadth of interest reflected in the 60 organizations registered on campus covers everything from the Career Development Society, open to students of all majors, to Students Concerned about the Environment (SCATE), and InterVarsity Christian Fellowship. Central's campus and Pella are considered "extremely safe and comfortable," says a student from Des Moines, although escort services and security patrols remain available.

Sporting events are popular, especially when the Dutch are hot. In recent years, Central teams have won 11 NCAA Division III championships in football and softball and women's track, cross country, and basketball. Football, however, is the most popular of the 10 men's and 9 women's teams supported, with students and parents turning out for the games. The team has won 26 Iowa Conference titles and has made 16 NCAA playoff appearances, the most in Division III. As of the 2005–2006 school year, the squad had not had a losing season since 1960. Half of the men and a fifth of the women belong to at least 1 varsity team. Sixty percent of the men and 40% of the women participate in the 12 men's and 12 women's intramural sports offered.

While many students enjoy Pella (pop. 10,000) as a livable community, a trip to Des Moines, just 45 miles northwest, usually adds some excitement. In warmer weather, many head to nearby Red Rock Lake for beach parties, waterskiing, or swimming or to the Bos Landen Golf Course in town, recently named the best in Iowa.

Cost cutters: Virtually all of the undergraduates in the 2005–2006 school year received financial aid; about 82% were on need-based assistance. The average freshman financial aid package for a student with financial need included need-based scholarships or grants averaging $10,533 and need-based self-help aid such as loans and job earnings averaging $2779. Other non-need-based awards and scholarships for first-year students averaged $2155. The average 2005 graduate left with debts of $19,851. The highest-paying scholarships are reserved annually for the most promising and academically gifted entering freshmen who typically boast a GPA of 3.75, an ACT of 28 (1230 critical reading and math SATs), or rank number one in their high school graduating classes. To be considered, they must have applied for admission by early January and participated in 1 of 2 special scholarship days in February. The Kuyper Scholarship pays full tuition; the Pella Rolscreen Fellowship pays $14,000. Presidential Scholarships pay up to $11,500 a year. Other academic awards pay up to half tuition.

Rate of return: Eighty percent of entering freshmen return for the sophomore year. Sixty-six percent graduate in 4 years.

Payoff: Among 2005 graduates, 13% earned degrees in business management, 12% in elementary education, and 11% in exercise science. Nine out of 10 graduates immediately accept full-time jobs, many with the Federal Deposit Insurance Corporation, Principal Financial Group, and Pella Corp., as well as with accounting firms and school systems throughout the Midwest. Eighty companies and organizations recruited on campus in a recent school year. Eighteen percent of recent graduates enrolled in graduate or professional schools at least part-time.

Bottom line: Central students are proud of who they are and what they can accomplish at their college. Notes a third-year student from an Iowa town of fewer than 2000 people: "I am a junior studying economics. I play varsity volleyball, will get to study in Wales next semester, and have made *great* friends. You *can* have it all at Central College."

Coe College

Cedar Rapids, Iowa 52402

Setting: Urban
Control: Private (Presbyterian)
Undergraduate enrollment: 1300 men and women
Graduate enrollment: NA
Student/faculty ratio: 13:1
Freshman profile: Average combined SAT I score: 1151; Average ACT composite score: 25. Class rank data: NA
Faculty profile: 95% Ph.D.'s
Tuition and fees: $23,930
Room and board: $6260

Freshman financial aid: 98%; average scholarship or grant: $14,657 need-based; $9396 non-need-based
Campus jobs: 43%; average earnings: $1400/year
Application deadline: Early action: Dec. 10; regular: Mar. 1
Financial aid deadline: Mar. 1
Admissions information: (319) 399-8500; (877) CALL-COE
e-mail: jsulliva@coe.edu
web site: www.coe.edu

Coe College in Cedar Rapids, Iowa, may have one of the shortest names in higher education, but that's about its only limited aspect. Though based in a city and state not widely recognized for their cosmopolitan flavor, Coe's enrollment of about 1300 undergraduates recently included 66 students from 16 foreign countries as well as residents of 34 states. Every fall, the college brings the opera to campus—again, not your typical campus cultural offering. And when it was time to renovate the main library several years ago, just any job wouldn't do. An architect from Chicago came on site to examine the situation, analyzing the way students studied, where they placed their books, how they sat, and how much light they liked, and incorporated these findings into the final design. The result is "a studier's dream," says a junior, a structure double its original size that seats 620 students over 4 floors, with a choice, on each level, of various types of tables, booths, lounging chairs, and private rooms. Little wonder students use adjectives like *perfect* and *user friendly* to describe it. Such overall care and attention have helped put Coe on the "short list" of high-quality liberal arts institutions—and all at a tuition rate that leaves this college standing tall.

Student body: About two-thirds of Coe's student body are from Iowa, with most of the out-of-staters also coming from the Midwest. Ninety percent attended public schools. While Coe has managed to attract a significant number of international students to diversify its largely midwestern student body, it has had a harder time bringing members of domestic minority groups to campus. In a recent school year, 2% of the enrollment were African-American, and less than 1% each Hispanic and Asian-American. An annual Prejudice Awareness Weekend helps to break down barriers that can hamper integration. The Coe "community," as students like to call it, is a mixture of Eastern Iowa conservative and solidly liberal viewpoints, encompassing those who want to change the world, and those content to let others handle the problems or just to let them be. "Because of our blend of personalities," a student from the Southwest observes, "Coe is not one-sided on any issue, other than academic excellence. When it comes to classwork, all Coe students agree that that is why they are here." Adds a business major: "Students who are not academically focused do not survive at Coe!"

Academics: Coe College was founded in 1851 and named for Daniel Coe, who gave a Presbyterian minister $5000 to start a college; 155 years later, that college awards the bachelor's degree in 41 majors and interdisciplinary programs plus a master of arts in teaching. Its academic year follows a 2-semester calendar. Average class size is small, about 16 students; an introductory biology class, however, may enroll almost 50. "But even in this large class," a sophomore notes, "the professor will stop for questions." An upper-level course in entomology may have only 3 participants.

Flexibility and choice highlight Coe's general-education requirements. Students begin their course of study with a first-year seminar drawn from several options covering different topics. Students in all sections write numerous papers and attend special cultural events. Some time during their 4 or 5 years of study, students must take 11 courses from 5 broad categories that comprise the liberal arts: the natural sciences, quantitative and behavioral analysis, creative expression and the fine arts, Western historical perspective, and diverse cultural perspectives. In addition, 4 writing-emphasis courses besides the first-year seminar are required but may be classes used to satisfy other general-education requirements. The final requirement, an academic practicum, mandates that students perform 5 hours of community service, attend 1 issue dinner, and participate in 3 small-group workshops, before they complete an internship, off-campus study, honors project, or some other kind of independent activity, typically in the junior or senior year.

When asked about the faculty, students disagree on which words best describe them: "topnotch" or "fantastic" or "the factor more than anything that keeps me coming back to Coe," according to a student who keeps returning from the Rocky Mountain region. Eighty of the 138 members are full-time; 42% of the total in a recent year were women. Students are won over by professors' ability to make them feel stimulated rather than intimidated by their knowledge. Many include interested students in their research and take them along to help present research projects at national conferences. One physics major went to England with other student researchers and 2 physics professors the summer after her freshman year. To encourage even greater student-faculty interaction, a program enables faculty members to take students to a community event and be reimbursed by the college. Says a senior: "They understand the big picture of our college life and understand that although we should be students first, we still have other responsibilities as well. We aren't only students to them, but we are recognized as athletes, singers, dancers, leaders, etc."

With a faculty of such wide-ranging talents spread across the curriculum, most students name their own specialities, plus others, as being among Coe's best. Biology boasts one of the largest staffs and most rigorous programs on campus and offers special equipment for a concentration in molecular biology. Chemistry and physics are marked by first-rate equipment and excellent professors as well, though students say some could be more helpful to classmates unfamiliar with hard sciences. The physics faculty includes a member recognized by the White House in 1999 and several more "exceptional" professors, according to one major. The psychology faculty, which features specialists in each of several areas from cognitive to abnormal to psychobiological psychology, require all seniors to take a comprehensive exam to graduate. The English and Rhetoric departments are noted for their writing workshops in journalism, poetry, and fiction, which challenge students to perform at a level equal to that found in graduate-school writing workshops. Says a participant: "Professors spend many hours working with students to improve them as writers, not just patch up their writing mistakes." Adds a senior: "The relationships that are developed by writing students and their professors are almost as priceless as the knowledge and skills they gain." Nursing students benefit from a close working arrangement with St. Luke Hospital across the street from the college. Business, says a psychology major, "challenges business majors who are looking for an 'easy' degree."

Professors of philosophy, religion, foreign languages, and theater, while excellent, are too few in number to provide the breadth of courses available in other bigger departments. Students in the music program would like to see expanded offerings in newer areas such as jazz and musical theater, rather than just the traditional classical/choral instruction.

Facilities: In keeping with its expansion, Stewart Memorial Library continues to add new acquisitions to Coe's already impressive collection of about 217,000 volumes and 1380 periodicals. The facility includes a computerized catalog plus 400 bibliographical databases. "If by the slightest chance Stewart cannot supply us with the materials needed," adds a psychology major, "the University of Iowa is a mere 20 minutes away." Many materials related to chemistry are kept in a separate departmental collection, with some 9000 audio/video tapes and compact discs housed in a music library. A world-class art collection helps students in need of a break pass the time viewing works by such artists as Grant Wood, Picasso, Matisse, and Toulouse Latrec.

More than 250 computers are available for student use in laboratories located in the computer center, library, classroom buildings, and residence halls. A couple of the labs are open around the clock. The most popular lab, with 60 units in the library, is open until midnight. While students admit there is a sufficient number of computers around campus, some would like to see more units in the library. Each student residence hall room also has a port for accessing the network at any hour, and many students bring their own computers to make use of these ports plus the wireless access available throughout much of the campus.

Special programs: Because Coe is 1 of 14 colleges grouped together as the Associated Colleges of the Midwest, students have a wide range of off-campus study options open to them. These vary from a term in Costa Rica doing tropical field research to one in Chicago studying urban life, as well as opportunities for travel to several European countries, India, Japan, and Hong Kong. Coe also has its own exchange programs in 8 countries including Thailand, South Korea, and Germany. A joint degree program is offered in architecture with Washington University. Students may cross-register for classes at Mount Mercy College and the University of Iowa. Coe also offers its own study terms in Washington, D.C., and New York City.

Campus life: All but 15% of Coe's students reside on the 53-acre campus called "Coe-topia" by outsiders because of its parklike setting in the heart of Cedar Rapids. As one junior from suburban Chicago notes, "When you are on the campus, you don't even remember the city exists," though it's there when students want to go to a museum or a concert at the civic center located just 5 blocks from campus. Greek life includes about a fourth of the men and a fifth of the women in 5 national fraternities and 3 national sororities. Little rivalry exists between students who belong and those who don't, and most Greek parties are open to all. Only one group has a house, and the others have specific wings in the residence halls. Each residence hall board of directors also plans extensive activities, such as dating games, roommate competitions, and Sunday suppers, to keep weekends lively for all. Among the 60 organizations available, the International Club attracts the most interest from both foreign national and American students, as well as hundreds more who attend the annual Cultural Show and banquet. The Coe Alliance promotes harmony among students of different sexual orientation. During the early fall and spring, most gather for Friday on the Quad, which features a picnic supper and a performance by a live band or DJ from 3 p.m. to 7 p.m. Because Coe is located in a city of 175,000 people, students use caution when walking in the neighborhood surrounding the campus. On the college grounds, crime is not much of a problem, and better lighting, security phones, escort services, and other safety measures help to keep it that way. The biggest problem has been with theft from cars in the campus parking lots.

Cheering on the Kohawks is a favorite weekend activity for many, with "verbal crowds," as one student terms the onlookers, appearing most often at football games. Altogether, Coe fields 11 men's and 10 women's varsity teams, which play as part of NCAA Division III. About a third of the men and a fifth of the women suit up to participate. Seventy-five percent of the men and 60% of the women turn out for 24 intramural sports. It seems, notes a junior, that "almost all of campus works out at least 3 times a week."

Students who need to get away and want more than Cedar Rapids can provide generally head to the University of Iowa to mingle with the thousands and attend a Big Ten sporting event.

Cost cutters: Ninety-eight percent of the freshmen and 95% of the continuing students received financial aid in a recent school year. Eighty percent of the first-year students and 79% of the rest received need-based assistance. The average freshman aid package included a need-based scholarship or grant averaging $14,657 and self-help aid such as loans and jobs averaging $5492. Other non-need-based awards and scholarships for first-year students averaged $9396. Debts for the average recent graduate totaled $22,157. All entering freshmen may compete for prestigious academic scholarships starting at $1000, in such fields as science, theater, art, music, business, nursing, foreign languages, and writing. Academic scholarships are available to students in amounts based on a combination of grade point average, ACT/SAT test scores, and class rank. Academic scholarships range in value from $8000 Dean's Scholarships to $20,000 Trustee Scholarships. Winners of the Trustee awards may be eligible for 1 of 3 full-tuition Williston Jones Scholarships. Students not qualifying for academic scholarships may receive Daniel Coe awards paying

$4000 to $7000 a year. A 10-month payment plan allows students or parents to stretch out their payments instead of making them at the start of each semester.

Rate of return: Eighty-one percent of the freshmen who start at Coe return for the sophomore year. Sixty-three percent graduate in 4 years; 69% in 5 years.

Payoff: Sixteen percent of recent graduates earned degrees in economics and business administration, followed by 7% in psychology and 5% in English. Just over a fourth of the graduates opted to pursue advanced degrees. Most of the graduates entered the job market immediately, many accepting posts with the 81 companies that recruited on campus in a recent school year.

Bottom line: Students from every state and all parts of the world who are open to the idea of attending an "urban" college in Cedar Rapids, Iowa, will be pleasantly surprised by the rich academic life and out-of-classroom experiences they can share with a faculty many students come to regard as mentors and friends. Notes a senior from Arizona who took the chance: "Anyone who would like to explore more than one area of life will be thrilled with the diverse education available at Coe."

Cornell College

Mount Vernon, Iowa 52314

Setting: Small town
Control: Independent (Methodist)
Undergraduate enrollment: 524 men, 642 women
Graduate enrollment: None
Student/faculty ratio: 11:1
Freshman profile: 17% scored over 700 on SAT I verbal; 49% scored 600–700; 29% 500–599; 5% below 500. 15% scored over 700 on SAT I math; 45% scored 600–700; 34% 500–599; 6% below 500. 30% scored above 28 on the ACT; 17% scored 27–28; 28% 24–26; 23% 21–23; 2% below 21. 20% graduated in top tenth of high school class; 45% in upper fifth.
Faculty profile: 91% Ph.D.'s

Tuition and fees: $23,680
Room and board: $6430
Freshman financial aid: 97%; average scholarship or grant: $16,745 need-based; $10,115 non-need-based
Campus jobs: 65%; average earnings: $1200/year
Application deadline: Early decision: Dec. 1; regular: Feb. 1
Financial aid deadline: Mar. 1
Admissions information: (319) 895-4215; (800) 747-1112
e-mail: admissions@cornellcollege.edu
web site: www.cornellcollege.edu/

You might think that sharing a name with a prestigious member of the Ivy League would cause a small college an identity crisis, but not Cornell College in Mount Vernon, Iowa. Students who go to middle America in search of *this* Cornell know exactly what they're looking for: the OCAAT program, the one-course-at-a-time approach to learning that distinguishes Cornell's 4-year baccalaureate program from most others. This approach, started in 1978, allows students to focus on a single class at a time, 5 days a week, 2–3 hours a day, for 3½ weeks. They then take a 4-day break and move on to another course for another 3½ weeks. Students take 8 courses over 8 months, with the ninth month available for another course at no tuition, a job or internship, a vacation, or a special project. The program allows students to become totally engrossed in topics they love, and to devote extra time to areas they find troublesome. The result is graduates who like what they've become. "Cornell has a good name," boasts a recent graduate. "It produces well-rounded nonprocrastinators who are adaptable to most tasks."

Student body: Cornell students come from 45 states to try the OCAAT program: fewer than a third, 30%, are from Iowa, though 74% of the out-of-staters also live somewhere in the Midwest. Eighty-nine percent are graduates of public schools. Foreign nationals from 16 countries constitute 3% of the enrollment. Hispanics make up 3%, African-Americans, 4%, Asian-Americans, 1%, and Native Americans, less than 1%. Three percent identify themselves as of multiple racial or ethnic origins or some other than the 4 categories listed. Forty-eight percent claim no religious affiliation; 9% are Methodist, 26% members of other Protestant denominations; 15% Catholic, 1% Jewish, and less than 1% members of other religious faiths. Students consider their classmates to be hard-working, caring, accepting of others, and fairly liberal-minded. Says a sophomore: "Politically, Cornell is diverse, although the majority of the student body probably leans left. Though there are fewer conservatives on campus, the Cornell Republicans are incredibly organized and visible on campus. Political debates and events at Cornell can get *quite* heated because of this." While the academic environment is not competitive *among* students, they do compete against themselves and against the clock to keep up with daily reading and other assignments. Observes a senior: "The atmosphere is pretty intense, as this calendar ensures that you do not loaf."

Academics: Cornell was founded in 1853 and renamed 4 years later for a prominent New Yorker and distant cousin of the man who endowed Cornell University; this Cornell, however, gave but a small contribution to "his" college and was, in fact, offended to have had the school renamed for him. The name stuck, and under it Cornell awards bachelor's degrees in more than 40 majors. Average class size hovers at 17, and all but a few courses are capped at 25. Larger lecture classes that exceed that number usually have 1 or 2 professors. Other courses, such as freshman English, have upper limits of 17.

Bachelor of arts students (there is no B.S.) must take courses in the traditional disciplines. Although highly writing intensive, the curriculum gives students their choice of classes within the various fields and sufficient flexibility to double-major if they wish. Cornell also offers a bachelor of special studies degree for which students design their own majors and need not fulfill the general requirements as well as a bachelor of music degree.

Ninety-four of Cornell's 109 faculty members are full-time. Fifty-two percent are men. Because faculty teach just 1 course at a time under the block plan, virtually all become as involved as their students in the classes. Students know that for these professors teaching ranks ahead of other duties. Says a biology major: "The professors are interested in making students work to find answers to their questions." Adds a biochemistry major: "Professors expect you to show up for class *every* day, and some will call and check up on you." Some students have less kind things to say about the part-time faculty. While praising the full-time members as "wonderful," this junior says many adjunct members are far less skilled at teaching everything in 3½ weeks. She notes: "By the time they are used to the block plan, the month is over and they haven't accomplished much."

As for Cornell's academic strong points, most students simply say, "Name any department," as each has its great professors and innovations. Indeed, students' picks of top departments just about cover the course catalog. From history to politics to psychology to biology, Cornell's best programs are those that make the most of the block plan. A recent graduate recalls: "Freed from 50-minute time segments, fascinating discussions are never cut off, classes can take field trips, and less review is necessary because, when studying a topic on a daily basis, the information is fresh in our minds." Because students and faculty have no competing academic interests during a block, professors eagerly take courses on the road. One student studied geology in the Bahamas; another, in the Rockies. Shakespeare comes alive in England, as does Spanish in Mexico. One-month internships in politics, especially during Presidential election years, are extremely valuable. The biology faculty earns bonus points from students for its support outside of the classroom as well as in. Says a major: "The faculty can always be seen at sporting events, theater productions, and art shows. The members want their students to be successful in the classroom but also provide numerous research opportunities." An attentive math faculty, too, says a major, "keeps tabs on conferences and undergraduate research opportunities, and provides means to attend them (car pools, mainly)."

Perceived weaknesses in some of Cornell's programs vary from student to student and are generally related to how easily information from a particular discipline can be assimilated in such a short period of time. While some students flourish, others flounder. For some, their downfall is math or science; for others, a foreign language or the language of music. While there is no major in communication studies, students would like to see more full-time faculty to handle increasing student interest in these courses; physical education classes tend to be "GPA boosters," which could stand more rigor.

Facilities: Cole Library, built in 1957, has undergone a series of facelifts, including major renovations in 1966 and 1995 and remodelings in 1987, 1988, and 1989, which finally have produced a facility students find "a fabulous place to study," in the words of one user, with room for resources to grow. Added amenities include a coffee shop and writing studio. Currently the collection of more than 177,000 volumes and 779 current periodicals is not as helpful for more advanced research projects as many students would like, but a trek to the University of Iowa libraries takes but 20 minutes. A computerized catalog, expanded database searching and the Internet are invaluable as the block plan adds urgency to any wait for materials from interlibrary loan. Helpful librarians who are experts in various subject areas also expedite the research process.

About 120 PCs are located in the library, the student commons, all academic buildings, and a few residence halls. Computers generally are available from 7 a.m. to 11 p.m. or midnight, for the first 3 weeks of the block and until 2 a.m. in one lab during finals, although students say they can easily obtain all-night passes from their professors for additional time. Access to E-mail, the Internet, and other services is available from every residence-hall room. The library and the Student Commons both offer wireless connectivity.

Special programs: Because of the nature of Cornell's academic calendar, many of the special internships and study-abroad programs offered at other schools are integrated here into the regular coursework. Study abroad options are available in 25 countries while internships include a stint at the Washington Center in the nation's capital. A 3-2 program in forestry and environmental management is offered with Duke

University. Similar arrangements are provided in natural resource management with the University of Michigan, in social services with the University of Chicago, and in engineering, and architecture (a 3-4 program) with Washington University in St. Louis. A 2-2 program is offered in nursing and allied health sciences with Rush University in Chicago. Because the block plan requires only 8 of 9 blocks a year, industrious students can finish in 3½ years.

Campus life: All but 10% of Cornell's students live on the 129-acre hilltop campus. The campus itself is listed as a Historic District on the National Register of Historic Places, so, as one student puts it, "state of the art, it is not." Renovation, however, has kept most buildings looking classic rather than decrepit and a new pedestrian mall lined with distinctive lighting and young maple trees further unifies the campus. In place of fraternities and sororities, the college has social groups, 8 for men and 7 for women, to which about 30% of the students belong, although they live in dormitories with nonmembers. No single 1 of the 76 clubs available dominates the campus, and many small groups involving fewer than a dozen students cover every interest from fencing to chemistry to politics. One of the larger groups known as Chess and Games attracts students interested in computers, video games, anime, and yes, chess. A very active Leadership and Service Office coordinates a wide range of outlets for student involvement; among the most popular is Lunch Buddies in which college students eat lunch and play at recess with local elementary school youngsters. Rams Leading Change, a leadership development program involves individuals in projects to improve campus and community life. "Block-plan dating" occurs as students change courses and meet new people every month. Crime, other than occasional instances of theft, is not considered to be much of a problem. "Because Cornell is such a safe campus," says an Iowan, "Campus Safety's duties are generally limited to issuing parking tickets."

A majority of students turn to varsity or intramural sports as a way to relieve stress in the intense OCAAT calendar. Almost 60% of the men and 50% of the women take part in athletics, many in the 10 men's and 9 women's intercollegiate sports offered under NCAA Division III; football, basketball, and soccer tend to attract the most spectators. Forty intramural sports are offered for men and women, 25 coed, ranging from standard fare such as basketball and bowling to the more offbeat euchre and watermelon seed spitting contests. Amid the older buildings, the Life Sports Center, built in 1986, as well as an all-new strength-training facility and all-weather 440 meter track, provide a welcome change.

Mount Vernon, described by some as a New England town set in eastern Iowa, can become too confining with just 3000 people, so students head elsewhere to catch city lights. Many travel to Cedar Rapids or Iowa City, home of the University of Iowa, each no more than a half hour away; school-sponsored transportation is available on some Saturdays. During the longer breaks of 4 days between blocks, students either stay on campus for special events such as Winter Weekend, or travel home, or, to larger, more distant cities, such as Chicago or Minneapolis.

Cost cutters: In the 2005–2006 school year, 97% of the freshmen and 96% of continuing students received financial aid; the help was need-based for 71% of the freshmen and 70% of the remaining undergraduates. The average freshman award for a student with financial need included a need-based scholarship or grant averaging $16,745 and need-based self-help aid such as loans and jobs averaging $3855. Other non-need-based awards and scholarships for freshmen averaged $10,115. Average debts for a 2005 graduate equaled $17,970. Freshmen with strong academic records are invited to apply for 1 of more than 100 scholarships. These include the William Fletcher King Scholarships, which pay $20,000 a year and go to 6 students. Finalists for the Fletcher award may receive Fellows Scholarships paying $17,500 a year to 8 students. Twenty Trustee Scholarships pay $15,000; President's and Dean's awards, to varying numbers of students, pay $12,500 and $10,000, respectively. Music and Theater scholarships pay $5000 to students with talent in those fields, who both interview and audition on campus; Buzza Scholarships pay $5000 annually to fine artists. Two deferred payment plans also are options.

Rate of return: Eighty-one percent of Cornell freshmen enjoy the OCAAT approach and return for a second year. Sixty-three percent graduate in 4 years; 65% in 5 years, 66% in 6.

Payoff: Psychology and economics and business were the leading fields of study for 2005 graduates, with 13% earning bachelor's degrees in these disciplines. History ranked third at 9.5%. In a recent class, just under two-thirds took jobs as teachers, business analysts, counselors, and management trainees, primarily in the Midwest and Southwest. In a recent year, nearly a third of the grads went on within 6 months of commencement to graduate or professional schools. More than 60% of Cornell alumni enter graduate programs in law, medicine, engineering, and other fields within 5 years of graduation.

Bottom line: Procrastinators, change your ways now, or choose a less intense environment. Successful Cornell students quickly learn to schedule less strenuous courses for times when their outside commitments, such as sports teams or dramatic productions, are heaviest. But most find the results worth the struggle. Concludes a junior: "Why wouldn't someone study 1 course and only 1 course at a time, given the chance? The depth we are able to achieve during each class is fantastic!"

Drake University

Des Moines, Iowa 50311

Setting: Suburban
Control: Private
Undergraduate enrollment: 1255 men, 1658 women
Graduate enrollment: 398 men, 606 women
Student/faculty ratio: 14.5:1
Freshman profile: 10% scored over 700 on SAT I verbal; 43% scored 600–700; 34% 500–599; 13% below 500. 14% scored over 700 on SAT I math; 37% scored 600–700; 32% 500–599; 17% below 500. 25% scored above 28 on the ACT; 32% scored 27–28; 21% 24–26; 18% 21–23; 4% below 21. 31% graduated in top tenth of high school class; 63% in upper fifth.

Faculty profile: 96% Ph.D.'s
Tuition and fees: $21,462
Room and board: $6170
Freshman financial aid: 98%; average scholarship or grant: $11,768 need-based; $9638 non-need-based
Campus jobs: 28%; average earnings: $1556/year
Application deadline: Mar. 1 (Pharmacy: Dec. 1)
Financial aid deadline: Mar. 1
Admissions information: (515) 271-3181; (800) 44-DRAKE
e-mail: admission@drake.edu
web site: www.choose.drake.edu

Drake University in Des Moines, Iowa, never goes by the acronym DU, but if it were looking for letters to go by, IU might be more appropriate. Not I as in Iowa, but I as in Internships, for that's what students who attend this university of 2900 full-time undergraduates in Iowa's capital and largest city get when they enroll. More than 70% of Drake's undergraduates have at least 1 internship before graduating. Journalism majors thrive in this city of 400,000, home to *The Des Moines Register* newspaper, the Meredith Corporation, a major magazine publisher, and several television stations, as well as the Iowa caucuses held every presidential election year. Students majoring in business, actuarial science, politics, pharmacy, education, and many other areas benefit from the school's prime locale and faculty connections. It doesn't hurt, either, that the Des Moines area counts among its residents and workers more than 12,000 Drake alumni, many of whom are corporate and civic leaders eager to offer an internship to a future alum. IU may never be imprinted on Drake University sweatshirts, but it's surely imprinted on the education most satisfied students receive.

Student body: Thirty percent of Drake's undergraduates hail from Iowa with all but 10 states having at least 1 resident on campus. However, 85% of the out-of-staters also come from the Midwest. All but 11% attended public schools. Undergraduates say that the student body is primarily upper middle class. "The majority are conservative," notes a midwesterner, "but there is enough diversity of opinion to make life interesting and expose students to new and challenging ideas." Some of these ideas come from the 5% who are foreign nationals from 53 countries and the 8% who are American members of racial and ethnic minority groups: 3% each Asian-American and African-American and 2% Hispanic. City slickers expecting a college "filled with farmers' children in the middle of nowhere" are pleasantly surprised to find classmates from big cities like Chicago, St. Louis, and Milwaukee, as well as bright, highly motivated, and involved rural dwellers. For the most part, all share the same inner drive to succeed. "Drake is very competitive, but just below the visible surface," a Minneapolis resident points out. "Most students come here from competitive backgrounds, in sports, academics, or debate, for example, so that competitiveness carries through into their activities at Drake." A Southerner calls them "very focused." A majority, adds a public relations major, "will leave Drake in 4 years with a direction and a job."

Academics: Drake, which was founded in 1881 and named for Union Army officer Gen. Francis Marion Drake, grants degrees through the doctorate, including a J.D. degree from its law school. Bachelor's degrees are awarded in more than 75 majors through 4 undergraduate schools and colleges. The College of Pharmacy and Health Sciences offers a 6-year Doctor of Pharmacy degree, including a 2-year pre-pharmacy program. The academic year is divided into 2 semesters. Undergraduates can expect an average class size of 25–40, though an introductory biology lecture may enroll 224. Most writing courses have 15–20 members; highly specialized courses can drop below 6.

The Drake Curriculum involves all members of the entering class in a variety of first-year seminars that emphasize communication skills and critical thinking. The general-education curriculum mandates coursework in 10 areas of inquiry: writing, critical thinking, artistic experience, historical consciousness, information literacy, international and multicultural understanding, life and physical science, values and ethics, and the engaged citizen. What courses each student takes to fill each of these mandates is up to him or her, in consultation with an advisor. A capstone experience for every undergraduate completes the curriculum.

The Drake faculty numbers 246 full-time members and 142 part-time. Forty-three of the full-time members and 57 of the part-time teach at the graduate level only. Forty-three percent of the total pool are women. Despite the presence of a number of graduate programs, no classes are taught by graduate students. Undergraduates praise the "student-focused faculty" as one senior puts it, for being there for them, a quality evident in the enthusiasm displayed in professors' teaching and the personal attention provided. While many conduct research, students say it does not interfere with their devotion to teaching. In fact, many professors involve undergraduates in their research projects. Says a junior: "They treat their students as professionals."

Some of the best can be found in Drake's most accomplished programs, among them business, pharmacy, journalism, and biology, which all give students a solid push into the world beyond graduation. The College of Business and Public Administration wins raves in part because of Aliber Hall, a relatively new building that includes 4 computer classrooms and laboratories, as well as for a faculty that constantly refines and upgrades its programs. The college's star is its major in actuarial science, one of a few in the nation; this prepares students for careers in the insurance industry, for which Des Moines is a leading center. Drake's 6-year pharmacy program leading to a doctorate in the College of Pharmacy and Health Sciences also is distinguished by outstanding faculty, research opportunities, and work in patient service and care. While there is much hard work, the rewards can be great; since 1984, every one of the program's graduates has obtained a job in the industry.

The journalism major in the School of Journalism and Mass Communication is a natural in Iowa's capital city. The faculty is dynamic, and the state-of-the-newsroom facilities include a computer writing and editing lab, a digital video editing system, and radio and television studios. Two of the 1991 Pulitzer Prize winners received their journalism education at Drake. The public-relations major, with its year-long campaign strategy program, is considered strong as well. In the College of Arts and Sciences, budding biologists, too, are offered plenty of hands-on experience. Philosophy, religion, English, politics, and rhetoric and communication studies also feature dedicated faculty who reach outside the campus to bring influential and thought-provoking speakers to students.

Drake no longer offers majors in foreign languages, an area that some students in previous years found lacking. Instead, students who wish to learn a language other than English can participate in DULAP, the Drake University Language Acquisition Program, in which groups of up to 4 students meet for small group practice sessions with a native speaker partner. Languages offered in the 2005–2006 school year were Arabic, (Mandarin) Chinese, French, German, Italian, Japanese, Kiswahili, Russian, and Spanish. Student support for the approach is mixed.

Facilities: One of the best features of the main Cowles Library, according to students, is sometimes not having to go there to work, since students with personal computers can search the library's holdings from their rooms without venturing outdoors. While many find the current collection of 15,000 paper and electronic periodicals and the extensive database searches to be especially helpful, others grumble that it is tough finding a book published since 1975 amid Drake's half million volumes. The collection also is stronger in some areas, such as English and political science, than others. Recent renovation has added storage space for additional volumes and improved facilities for government documents and serials. It also provided several small study rooms and refurbished the grand reading room. Still, says a biology major, "the library is consistently mocked as one of the best social opportunities on campus." Students needing a quieter environment seek refuge in the law school library amid its stacks of 250,000 volumes, or in the pharmacy college reading room, with another 2500 volumes and current issues of major pharmacy journals. There is also a well-stocked curriculum library in the School of Education.

Five computer labs around campus, in the library (open until 1 a.m.), student center, and various academic buildings, ensure that most students have ready access to a computer. Every residence hall room also has 2 Ethernet ports, 1 per student, that give students with their own computers high-speed connections to the campuswide network, Internet, and e-mail. The university strongly recommends that undergraduates have their own personal computers, and a majority do. During the 2005–2006 school year, the university was moving toward making the entire campus wireless.

Special programs: Drake students can study overseas for a semester or a year in 67 countries around the world, from Australia to Taiwan to Zimbabwe as well as more traditional European nations. Students who can't make up their minds where to go can take a semester at sea with stops in countries in Asia and around the Mediterranean Sea. A semester in Washington, D.C., also is possible. Both 2-2 and 3-2 engineering programs can be arranged with Washington University. A 3-3 program enables undergraduates in the College of Business and Public Administration, the School of Journalism and Mass Communication and the College of Arts and Sciences to complete both undergraduate and law degrees by enrolling for 3 years in each area.

Campus life: Drake's 120-acre campus is a mixture of traditional and modern architectural styles, with several buildings listed in the National Register of Historic Places and 16 designed in the 20 years after World War II by well-known architects such as Eliel and Eero Saarinen. Ninety percent of the undergraduates reside in campus housing, which includes fraternity and sorority houses. The Greek system is influential around campus and attracts about a fourth of the men and the women to 8 national fraternities and 4 national sororities. While the Greeks are popular, students say that little tension exists between Greeks and independents and few nonmembers lack places to go. Continues the senior: "There is always a crowd in the laundromat and area bars on Friday and Saturday nights." A new student-created and -operated coffee house Cool Beans @Drake attracts 70 to 100 students nightly.

One of Drake's most attractive features is the ability that students feel they have to change university policies and practices and to plan their own programming. The result is a strong student senate and an activities board that includes 300–400 members on its various committees. One hundred sixty student clubs including such diverse groups as the professional business fraternity and Rainbow Union also lend their voices. While crime *on* campus has not been a matter of great concern to students, a troubling crime rate *around* campus has kept security vigilant. The campus is well lit, with numerous emergency phones, strict policies for visitor entrance into dormitories, and a "Saferide" shuttle service that is free at night until 2 a.m.

Drake's varsity teams, which naturally were known as the Ducklings, Drakes, Ganders and even Tigers before becoming the Bulldogs, compete in 8 men's and 10 women's sports in NCAA Division I, with football playing in Division I-AA. Men's and women's basketball games are the most popular varsity sports. Sixty-five percent of the men and the women participate in the 24 intramural sports offered to each sex. Drake's biggest athletic event—or event of any kind, for that matter—is the 96-year-old Drake Relays, which attract some of the best track athletes in the world to campus the last weekend in April. The event is entirely student-run and involves a week of activities leading up to the races.

Although the Des Moines metropolitan area is large for Iowa, students like to road-trip to bigger cities, from Chicago and Omaha to Minneapolis and St. Louis. Many also find that the cultural offerings of Des Moines provide at least some escape for the mind.

Cost cutters: Ninety-eight percent of freshmen and 97% of continuing students in the 2005–2006 school year received financial assistance to attend Drake; for 66% of the first-year students and 63% of the rest, aid was need-based. The average freshman award for a student with financial need included a need-based scholarship or grant that averaged $11,768 and a need-based self-help component such as loans and jobs averaging $6238. Non-need-based athletic scholarships averaged $18,167. Other non-need-based awards and scholarships averaged $9638. Average debt for the 2005 graduate was $18,029. A vast array of merit- and need-based awards help make a tuition that many find "initially scary" more affordable. Alumni Scholarships pay full tuition, fees, room, and board to 6 students who ranked in the top 5% of their high school classes or who had a 3.75 GPA and at least a 29 ACT or 1270 math and critical reading SATs. Applications for the Alumni awards must be postmarked by January 20. Carpenter Scholarships pay full tuition to 10 Alumni Scholarship finalists. Presidential Scholarships are worth $5000 to $10,000 a year to students with qualifying test scores and GPAs. Cooperative experiences, as well as internships lasting a semester or summer, are provided in all majors. An 8-month installment payment plan rounds out the offerings.

Rate of return: Eighty-five percent of the freshmen return for the sophomore year. Sixty-two percent graduate in 4 years; 69% within 5 years.

Payoff: Seventeen percent of the 2005 graduates earned degrees in journalism and mass communications, 14% in marketing and management, and 7% in biology and biochemistry, cell, and molecular biology. The vast majority of Drake graduates go directly into the job market, most with businesses, others in teaching and government work, mainly in Iowa, Illinois, Missouri, Minnesota, Kansas, and Nebraska. Many graduates with business degrees stay in Des Moines and work in the insurance industry. Altogether, 40 companies and other organizations recruited on campus in the 2004–2005 school year. A fifth of recent graduates pursued advanced degrees, with the greatest number headed to graduate schools in the arts and sciences.

Bottom line: Drake is for doers, for those who enjoy the academic challenge more fully if it is surrounded by lots of opportunities to get involved in student clubs and to have some impact on the way the university is run. At Drake, a student can speak and feel quite assured that his or her voice will be heard.

Grinnell College

Grinnell, Iowa 50112

Setting: Small town
Control: Private
Undergraduate enrollment: 701 men, 845 women
Graduate enrollment: None
Student/faculty ratio: 11:1
Freshman profile: Median SAT combined score: 1390; median ACT composite score: 31. 73% graduated in top tenth of high school class; 93% in upper fourth.
Faculty profile: 96% Ph.D.'s
Tuition and fees: $27,504
Room and board: $7310

Freshman financial aid: 95%; average scholarship or grant: $18,952 need-based; $10,888 non-need-based
Campus jobs: NA; average earnings: NA
Application deadline: Early decision: Nov. 20; regular: Jan. 20
Financial aid deadline: Feb. 1
Admissions information: (641) 269-3600; (800) 247-0113
e-mail: askgrin@grinnell.edu
web site: www.grinnell.edu

Even the haziest of history students has heard the oft-quoted advice "Go west, young man," offered by Horace Greeley, 19th century social reformer, newspaper editor, and founder of the New York *Tribune*. But to whom did Greeley give this counsel? The recipient was Josiah Bushnell Grinnell, a clergyman who had lost his job after preaching an antislavery sermon to his Washington, D.C. congregation. Seeking a new post, Grinnell took Greeley's advice and left the East Coast for Iowa, where he founded the town of Grinnell in 1854 and gave land and buildings in 1859 to what was first Iowa College and ultimately Grinnell. Now, at the beginning of the 21st century, bright students from across the country continue to take Greeley's advice, but with a new twist. "Go west," has become "Go somewhere different," which is what more than half the undergraduates of Grinnell College do when they travel over 500 miles from their homes to attend a small liberal arts college in Iowa. Many are the same students who might typically be found at better known schools in the east. But what Grinnell may lack in general name recognition, it makes up for in academic quality. Repeated rankings of highly selective liberal arts colleges find Grinnell's name among the top 20 institutions, and generally for several thousand dollars less. And it continues to attract top scholars, in part because of its freedom from any general-education or core requirements outside of a single course and the mandates of the major. Although most students find themselves working harder than ever, they are free to explore any road of learning they choose, in the spirit of what going west has always meant.

Student body: Just 13% of Grinnell's students in a recent year were from Iowa, with less than half of the out-of-staters coming from the Midwest. All 50 states and 53 countries are represented. In keeping with the college's geographic diversity, its racial and ethnic makeup is more varied than that found at other small midwestern colleges of 1550 students. In a recent year, 4% each were Asian-American, Hispanic, and African-American, 1% Native American, and 10% foreign nationals. Over 80% of the enrollment usually are graduates of public schools. Undergraduates enjoy the lively student body that emerges. Says a junior: "Students here are liberal, bright, opinionated, and not afraid to tell you about it. They enjoy debate with just about anyone, which makes the classroom experience wonderfully engaging if not exhausting." "Grinnellians" says a senior, "are quirky, interesting people, people who you just know are going to do interesting and exciting things with their lives after they leave Grinnell." Many were not among the most popular students in high school and "for various reasons, stuck out," says a sophomore, "whether it was because of academic excellence, body piercings, orange hair, love of learning, whatever." Most are politically liberal ("Republican is almost a dirty word here," relates a southerner), and a favorite pick-up line, says a midwesterner, is "What's your cause?" One faux pax students do not commit is working against others to be the best. Says a senior: "It is self motivation not competition with others that drives students." Adds a junior: "There is not an emphasis on grades but there is huge emphasis on being creative, analytic, and eloquent."

Academics: Grinnell awards the bachelor's degree in 25 majors and 10 interdisciplinary concentrations, as well as in self-designed majors. In a recent year, 3% of the student body were enrolled in independent majors. Because there are no specific introductory courses that all students must take, there are few bulging lecture halls. The required tutorial for first-year students has no more than 13 participants; most other first-year classes enroll fewer than 30, and throughout the curriculum there are only 4 "large" lecture classes with between 40 and 60 students. Upper-level courses usually enroll between 9 and 13. A fourth of all classes have fewer than 10 students. The college follows a semester calendar.

The single course required of all Grinnell students is a 1-semester tutorial based on varying topics designed to sharpen writing, speaking, thinking, and research skills. The 33 tutorial subjects offered in a recent school year ranged from *Cartooning* to *Biotechnology: Bountiful Harvest or Bitter Harvest* to *Elvis Everywhere*. While students are not required to take a broad range of courses outside the major, academic advisors watch their charges' schedules carefully to encourage a well-rounded approach to learning. Eighty-five percent, for example, end up taking foreign language courses from elementary Latin to Chinese.

The Grinnell faculty are drawn from as many regions as the students, with a high percentage earning advanced degrees at premier institutions not only in the United States but also in England, Canada, Japan, and other nations. Forty-three of the 199 faculty members are part-time; 37% are women. All professors balance schedules of teaching with research in their respective fields, but rarely if ever, students claim, is research done at the expense of undergraduate learning. Professors expect a lot from students, in the way of class attendance, participation, and preparation, but they also give a lot in the classroom and outside. Says a history major: "Students are often pleasantly surprised the first time their professors invite them to have coffee at the campus forum or when their advisor is willing to talk about personal troubles over dinner at a quiet restaurant in town. Most students will remember with fondness the professors who held occasional classes at their homes, with fresh-baked cookies and a family pet to play with."

The opportunity for students to share in professors' research projects is one factor that makes Grinnell's programs in biology, chemistry, and physics so attractive, in addition to their excellent facilities and wide range of classes. Research is a degree requirement for all chemistry majors, for example, and one-fourth of the graduates end up coauthoring a published scientific paper based on their research at Grinnell. Anthropology, with excellent faculty whose specialities range from primatology to field methodology, also offers extensive opportunities for research. The modern foreign language program, with majors offered in Chinese, French, German, Russian, and Spanish plus classes in Japanese, is considered strong "because of the intensity and immersion of the programs," says a sophomore. English, history, and philosophy win honorable mention thanks to the "amazing faculty" in each. East Asian studies, mathematics, political science, economics, and Russian, Central, and Eastern European studies are considered strong as well, though some students would like to see more full-time faculty in the political science and economics departments.

Students wish the fine arts, though strengthened by construction of the new Bucksbaum Center for the Arts, would offer a more varied selection of courses.

Facilities: Burling Library, once cited by an architectural magazine as "the most comfortable library in the nation for a small liberal arts college," offers users a full range of noise levels over its 4 floors, from the very social first floor to the silent corners of the upper echelons "where it's considered blasphemy to breathe too loudly," says a sophomore. Students over the years have assigned names to various study spaces: "Mission Control" faces the "plank" or entrance ramp; undergraduates requiring full concentration for mental gymnastics head to the towers of carrels dubbed "the jungle gyms." Grinnell's collection is ample for a school of 1550 undergraduates: more than 503,000 volumes and 3032 current serials. Burling's human staff also wins praise for being "terrific at their jobs," applauds a senior. An expanded science library in the Noyce Science Center carries the latest major scientific periodicals for students with needs in those disciplines. When campus resources aren't enough, students simply go online. A music library within Burling has more than 29,000 audio and video tapes and CDs.

More than 400 networked computers are available exclusively for student use in residence halls and most academic buildings. The majority are accessible from 8 a.m. to 1 a.m. All college residences also have "port-per-pillow" network connections for students with their own computers. Since many students bring their own, there usually are plenty of campus computers to go around except for a "noticeable crunch," says a senior, at midterm and finals time. Wireless access points also are expanding across campus.

Special programs: More than 50% of Grinnell's students take part in 1 of 70 off-campus programs, including dozens offered in 32 countries. Every year, the college sponsors its own popular fall and spring terms in London. In the fall, the emphasis is on students utilizing London and Great Britain as a classroom, with course content changing from year to year according to the expertise of the Grinnell faculty who join the London staff for the semester. In spring, students spend part of their time abroad in an internship. A Grinnell-in-Washington, D.C. program also is an option. Cooperative programs are offered in architecture, business, law, and engineering with several notable institutions, including Cal Tech and Columbia. The 3-2 option in engineering available at many liberal arts colleges was actually originated by a Grinnell professor. Many courses above the introductory level offer a "plus-2" credit option for students who wish to do additional work such as extra reading or lab work.

Campus life: Nineteen of Grinnell's 69 buildings are residence halls, indicating the importance the college places on having a living and learning community. North Campus has 9 residence halls connected by a loggia that many of the men and women use for parking bicycles; South Campus has 6 halls, and the new East Campus that opened in fall 2003 has 4 that are linked in a similar manner. Seven college-owned houses adjacent to the 127-acre campus are used as theme houses or co-ops in which students plan and prepare their own meals. Fourteen percent of the students choose to live in apartments in town. Harris parties that vary in theme from a disco ball to Frank, a classy party in honor of Frank Sinatra, and activities held at the student center are the focus of much weekend life; the only Greek organization on campus is a Greek sight-reading group, just 1 of 170 or so clubs and activities that deal with topics from gay rights to community service. "No matter what the issue," observes a history major, "either we have a group or one can be started." The issue of crime on campus and in the surrounding area has begun attracting more student attention. "Grinnell is a small, quiet community, but a false sense of security is dangerous," advises 1 young woman, and precautions such as better lighting and an escort program have been adopted.

Sporting events generally attract decent crowds, composed mainly of friends out to support other friends, with the notable exception of the Grinnell men's basketball squad that packs Darby Gymnasium with fans eager to cheer the team's "run n'gun" style of play. The Pioneers won the Midwest Conference Championship in 2001 and 2003. Altogether, the college fields 10 men's and 10 women's teams that compete in NCAA Division III and involve 40% of the men and 25% of the women in their play. The intramural program attracts 40% of the undergraduates to the 11 men's and 11 women's sports offered.

The Grinnell Outdoor Recreation Program (GORP) sponsors more exotic forms of physical activity such as horseback riding, camping, rock climbing, and canoeing. Although the town of Grinnell (pop. 9100) has its share of attractive Victorian clapboard houses and broad streets, students head to the larger cities of Des Moines and Iowa City, an hour west and east, respectively, to enjoy a greater variety of shopping, restaurants, and clubs. For even more people and urban hustle, Minneapolis/St. Paul is 265 miles north, Kansas City, 250 miles south, Chicago, 280 miles east, and Omaha, 180 miles west. But some students find surprisingly little need to escape. Observes a freshman from the Pacific Northwest: "The classes and environment at the school outweigh the oddness of being in the middle of Iowa. And the cornfields are pretty."

Cost cutters: Grinnell's tuition and fees cover only 28% of the actual cost of a year's education (tuition at comparable colleges usually covers two-thirds). The difference is made up by gifts and private philanthropy, as well as income from a hefty endowment that totaled $1.4 billion in June 2005, a figure that puts Grinnell in the top 10 among all colleges and universities in endowment per student. More than $23 million of that endowment income and other sources goes toward providing financial aid. In the 2005–2006 school year, 95% of the freshmen and 86% of continuing students were given financial help; for 61% of the first-year students and 53% of the rest, the assistance was need-based. The average award to freshmen included need-based scholarships or grants averaging $18,952 and need-based self-help aid such as loans and jobs averaging $5074. Other non-need-based awards and scholarships for first-year students averaged $10,888. The average financial indebtedness of recent graduates was $16,818. Most aid is based on financial need, although the college does award a number of its own academic scholarships. The Grinnell Trustee Honor Scholarship pays $5000 to $15,000; various designated and endowed scholarships based on need and merit pay $600 to $10,000 a year. Each year, more than 650 students also have opportunities for campus employment. Parents of students who do not receive need-based aid can pay 4 to 8 semesters of tuition upfront at the rate in effect during the freshman year, thereby avoiding any future increases. A variety of loans offered by the college carry a low interest rate, recently 4%.

Rate of return: Ninety-two percent of Grinnell freshmen return for a second year. Eighty-three percent graduate in 4 years; 84%, in 5 years.

Payoff: In a recent graduating class, 11% majored in biology, 9% in English and 8% in sociology. Thirty percent of recent graduates pursued advanced degrees within 6 months of graduation. Generally, two-thirds go on to graduate or professional school either immediately after graduation or later in their careers; Grinnell ranks in the top 1% of colleges and universities whose graduates eventually earn Ph.D.'s. Fifty percent of recent graduates immediately entered the job market working in Iowa, throughout the rest of the United States, and abroad in a wide range of enterprises from large businesses to public and private education to the Peace Corps. More than 110 companies and organizations recruited on campus in a recent school year. A fifth of recent graduates reported being involved in internships, volunteer commitments, or working and studying part time.

Bottom line: "At Grinnell," says a senior, "students have the freedom to explore their own interests, develop their own plans of study outside the major, and not get bogged down in requirements or unchallenging courses. Financial aid is pretty strong, too, as the college tries to meet all of a student's need and is willing to listen to concerns about an award and make adjustments. In many different ways, Grinnell is a real community of support."

Loras College

Dubuque, Iowa 52004

Setting: Small city
Control: Private (Roman Catholic)
Undergraduate enrollment: 762 men, 750 women
Graduate enrollment: 5 men, 7 women (77 part-time)
Student/faculty ratio: 13:1
Freshman profile: 0% scored over 700 on SAT I verbal; 17% scored 600–700; 44% 500–599; 39% below 500. 0% scored over 700 on SAT math; 39% scored 600–700; 39% 500–599; 22% below 500. 6% scored above 28 on the ACT; 9% scored 27–28; 19% 24–26; 34% 21–23; 32% below 21. 27% graduated in top fifth of high school class; 53% in upper two fifths.

Faculty profile: 98% Ph.D.'s
Tuition and fees: $21,098
Room and board: $6095
Freshman financial aid: 99.7%; average scholarship or grant: $3356 need-based; $6195 non-need-based
Campus jobs: 35%; average earnings: $940/year
Application deadline: Rolling
Financial aid deadline: Apr. 15
Admissions information: (563) 588-7236; (800) 245-6727
e-mail: admissions@loras.edu
web site: www.loras.edu

What's in a name? For its first 100 years, Loras College in Dubuque, Iowa, wasn't quite sure. Although the Roman Catholic college had been founded by the Most Reverend Mathias Loras, the first bishop of Dubuque, in 1839, it functioned at various times under the names of 3 saints: St. Raphael, St. Bernard, and St. Joseph, and was also known as Dubuque and even Columbia College, before adopting the name of its founder during the centennial celebration. Today, the Loras name on a bachelor's degree signifies, students are convinced, a solid liberal arts education from a small and caring school. Placement records support that view. Nearly 90% of Loras graduates obtain jobs related to their majors. Within a year of graduation, 97% have found employment or are enrolled in graduate school. Loras may have taken a while to find a name, but the one the college settled on is certainly working for its satisfied alumni.

Student body: Because of Loras's location at the junction of 3 states, Iowa, Illinois, and Wisconsin, most students are drawn from this tristate region, providing a mixture of undergraduates from both the big cities of Illinois and the small towns of Iowa. Fifty-four percent are Iowans, with a total of 26 states and 7 foreign countries represented. Fifty-nine percent of the students are Catholic; 34% are graduates of private or parochial schools. Six percent of the enrollment are members of racial and ethnic minority groups or foreign nationals; foreign nationals account for 3%. African-Americans, Hispanics, and Asian-Americans each make up about 1%. Loras students tend to be friendly and easygoing, kind-hearted and accepting of others, and politically conscious but not especially active in working for change. A larger portion are committed to social service. Academically, notes a senior from an Illinois city, "We have students who excel academically and like Loras for the opportunity it offers, but we also have an equal, if not greater, number who are more laid back about their studies."

Academics: Loras awards the bachelor's degree in more than 40 undergraduate majors and 13 preprofessional areas of study plus a master of arts in some fields. Its academic year is divided into 2 semesters. While students in the first 2 years encounter classes of between 20 and 60 members (Introduction to Chemistry has had 69), courses at the junior and senior levels mostly have 5–20 participants.

A new general education program took hold with the Class of 2005. Students take 19 credits in foundational general education courses, classes in such areas as writing, mathematics, and public speaking; 2 mission courses in democracy and global diversity and in Catholic tradition, as well as 15–16 credits in advanced general education courses, including such topics as Humanity in the Physical Universe, Identity and Community, and Cultural Traditions Across Generations. Six credits in the advanced courses must be a thematic cluster of 2 related classes. In addition, all undergraduates must complete an electronic portfolio reflecting their ability to write and think as well-educated Loras graduates.

The college's full-time faculty numbers 111, with 30 part-timers, virtually all of whom serve as full-time friends and scholars. Sixty-five percent are men, a number of them priests. "Most of our professors can teach, not just lecture and test," stresses a history major. "While being caring and understanding, they push us hard so that we can achieve the challenges they put before us. They never let us feel completely satisfied; they make us want to know more." But most also can sense when help is needed. One student having trouble with some chemistry homework went to the professor at his office for help. Later that evening, the professor called the student at home to see how he was doing on the homework they had discussed. "Faculty have a genuine concern for students," says a senior.

Such dynamic faculty make the departments of biology, chemistry, physics, history, economics, and English, particularly the writing program, outstanding. Chemistry gets an added boost from the excellent lab equipment it offers to majors. Faculty in the highly popular accounting and business department are well qualified and up-to-date in their knowledge, while those in religious studies are highly respected scholars. Math professors take students who have "math phobia," says one former sufferer, "and go way beyond the call of duty to spend time with students outside of the classroom." The communication arts department, with majors in public address, journalism, media studies, and public relations, provides students with plenty of opportunities to gain real-world experience. "In 4 years, I have seen places only seen on CNN," says a journalism major. "The possibilities are endless for someone who works."

A shortage of faculty keep art, music, and classical studies from being as strong as other departments. Art purists will find a major only in integrated visual arts, which combines courses in studio art, graphic design, and interactive multimedia. The sole foreign language major offered is in Spanish with elective coursework occasionally offered in first-year French. A minor in classical studies offers courses in first and second-year Ancient Greek and Latin.

Facilities: The 90,000-square-foot Academic Resource Center that greeted student studiers in fall 2002 replaced the increasingly cramped and often noisy Wahlert Memorial Library, which had been built in 1960. The new structure, which devotes about 70% of its space to library functions, also contains writing and math labs, a tutorial center, 3 classrooms, and the Barnes and Noble College Bookstore, along with ample space for individual and group study. The college's book and serial collection, the third largest private collection in the state, consists of more than 347,000 volumes and 11,000 paper and electronic periodicals, also with computerized listings. Resources from the nearby University of Dubuque and Clarke College also are available to Loras students.

Loras joined the growing ranks of laptop campuses in fall 2001. All students receive an IBM Think Pad that they can use thanks to the campus's wireless access in all classrooms, the Academic Resource Center, and all campus-owned houses and common areas. The college also has one general-purpose lab open around the clock.

Special programs: Students at Loras can cross-register at the University of Dubuque and Clarke College at no additional cost. Nursing students can earn a cooperative bachelor of science degree with the University of Iowa. Loras undergraduates also can study abroad in England, Spain, and 7 other countries. Every year, Loras offers 9 service trips of its own to work with the hungry and homeless in areas ranging from Washington, D.C. and Appalachia, to Haiti and Honduras. A Learning Disabilities Program provides tutors to students with diagnosed learning disabilities for an additional fee.

Campus life: Sixty percent of the students reside on the 60-acre campus, which overlooks the Mississippi River from a setting atop the highest bluff in Dubuque. While many students leave campus on Friday afternoons to go home or visit friends at neighboring colleges, a greater portion are opting to stay behind. Those who do generally attend a movie, comedian, or band sponsored by the College Activities Board or head for a party off campus. There are no longer any fraternities, which had attracted just 2% of the men, and just 3% of the women belong to a single national sorority. Campus Ministry involves a number of students in support groups, well-attended retreat weekends, service trips, and Bible study. Although campus crime is not a serious problem, a 24-hour escort service is available to discourage students from walking alone at night.

A total of 21 varsity sports are offered, 11 for men, 10 for women, as part of NCAA Division III competition. DuHawks football and men's and women's basketball games are usually the best supported. Nearly half of the men and a fourth of the women competed at the varsity level in a recent year. Eighty percent of the students are involved in an extensive intramural program for both sexes. Skiing and skating also are popular in the frigid Dubuque winters.

Although Dubuque (pop. 62,300) offers enough urban entertainment for most undergraduates, Iowa City, home of the University of Iowa, remains a popular place to mingle with large numbers of other students. For hard-core city lovers, Chicago is a 3½ hour drive.

Cost cutters: All but 0.3% of freshmen in the 2005–2006 school year received financial aid, as did 98% of the continuing students. For 55% of the freshmen and 48% of the rest, the aid was need-based. The average freshman award for a student with financial need included a need-based scholarship or grant averaging $3356 and need-based self-help aid such as loans and jobs averaging $3599. Other non-need-based scholarships and awards averaged $6195. The average indebtedness of 2005 graduates was $17,190. Students with high ACT scores and impressive high school class ranks receive greater portions of their financial aid packages in the form of gifts. The prestigious Regent Scholarship provides 2 full-tuition awards and 5 awards worth $15,000 each to top students with at least a 3.5 GPA or who served as valedictorian and also had a 30 ACT or 1320 critical reading and math SAT score. Other levels of merit awards ranging from $5000 to $9000 a year depend on the student's grade point average and standardized test scores. Leadership Incentive Grants pay $1000 to $5000 a year.

Rate of return: Seventy-eight percent of the freshmen who enter return for the sophomore year. Fifty-five percent graduate in 4 years; 65% in 5 years; 66% in 6.

Payoff: In the 2005 graduating class, 32% earned bachelor's degrees in business, followed by 30% in education, and 9% in social science and history. Of the vast majority who enter the work force immediately, 86% in a recent class found jobs in the Midwest; 6% accepted employment in the South, and 5% traveled to jobs outside the United States. The remainder scattered throughout the rest of the nation. Most enter business and industry, working in accounting, finance, sales, marketing, and management with some of the 85 companies and organizations that recruited on campus in a recent school year. The fifth who in a recent year sought advanced degrees did so primarily in law and medicine.

Bottom line: Loras is a close-knit college that strives to balance the academic, social, cultural, and spiritual aspects of education. "If you're sincere about learning," advises a business/religious studies major, "and not just about what the textbooks have to offer but about what life can add as well, then Loras is for you."

Luther College
Decorah, Iowa 52101

Setting: Small town
Control: Private (Evangelical Lutheran)
Undergraduate enrollment: 1026 men, 1450 women
Graduate enrollment: None
Student/faculty ratio: 14:1
Freshman profile: 17% scored over 700 on SAT I verbal; 45% scored 600–700; 26% 500–599; 12% below 500. 16% scored over 700 on SAT I math; 47% scored 600–700; 30% 500–599; 7% below 500. 24% scored above 28 on the ACT; 19% scored 27–28; 25% 24–26; 21% 21–23; 11% below 21. 32% graduated in top tenth of high school class; 55% in upper fifth.
Faculty profile: 79% Ph.D.'s

Tuition and fees: $24,570
Room and board: $4230
Freshman financial aid: 99%; average scholarship or grant: $18,463 need-based; $8563 non-need-based
Campus jobs: 66%; average earnings: $897/year
Application deadline: None
Financial aid deadline: Mar. 1
Admissions information: (563) 387-1287;
(800) 458-8437
e-mail: admissions@luther.edu
web site: www.luther.edu

There couldn't have been a worse time for a new college to enroll its first freshmen in the hope of having a graduating class 4 years later. Though Luther College opened its doors on September 1, 1861, and conducted its first classes with 16 students, the Civil War, illness, and other disasters left no one to graduate in 1865. The first graduates received their diplomas the following year. Today's graduation rate is much better—in fact, quite good. Sixty-five percent of the students who begin at Luther receive bachelor's degrees 4 years later. Notes a state resident: "It's actually cheaper for me to go to Luther and graduate in 4 years than to go to a state school for 5 or 6 years," which is the amount of time it is taking more and more students to complete a baccalaureate degree. At Luther, where tuition, fees, room, and board totaled $28,800 in the 2005–2006 school year and 99% of all students received financial aid, the mathematical problem "(total cost – financial aid) × 4 years" isn't proving difficult at all.

Student body: Just over a third of Luther's students, 36%, are from Iowa; 90% of the out-of-staters are from the same region, with many in both sectors the products of small to mid-sized towns. Observes a city dweller: "There are a lot of people from small towns but no small minds." Altogether, 36 states and 25 foreign countries are represented. Foreign nationals comprise 3% of the student population, while members of domestic minority groups account for 4%, with 2% Asian-American and 1% each African-American and Hispanic students. Not quite half the undergraduates, 43%, are Lutheran; many are of Norwegian descent. Ninety percent attended public schools. Politically, students are "on the whole progressive," says a philosophy major, "but not incredibly liberal, with some really conservative people." According to an Iowa junior, the single best word with which to describe the 2550-member student body is *aware*. He explains: "Students are aware of who they are, where they are, and what they want to be. They are aware of the needs of others, as well as the needs of their own spiritual selves." Most also are very much aware of the importance of academics at Luther. Students concur that the majority are highly motivated, conscientious, and thorough where their studies are concerned. "At the same time," adds a fellow midwesterner, "it is never hard to find someone with some free time to socialize." Sometimes, as a biology major points out, the best times can come during study sessions at 3 o'clock in the morning.

Academics: Luther grants the bachelor's degree in more than 60 fields of study, ranging from biblical languages and Africana and Scandinavian studies to accounting, nursing, and computer science. The academic year is divided into 2 semesters plus a January term. During freshman year, students encounter a few introductory lectures with more than 200 enrolled (General Psychology has 240), though discussion sections usually have fewer than 25 participants. Most advanced courses rarely top 30.

All students must take a core program that begins with PAIDEIA (an ancient Greek term for education), which at Luther means a 2-term freshman studies course that combines English and history, followed by an interdisciplinary course taken sometime after the first year that focuses on the process of making ethical decisions. Because all undergraduates take PAIDEIA, many view the course as a "bonding experience" that unites entering first-year students to each other and to upper-level students, who took the course before them—and survived. "It's just so everywhere," grumbles a junior, who wishes it wasn't. Students must also take an assortment of classes in the traditional disciplines. Every senior ends the required course of study with a research paper or project in his or her major.

Sixty-four of Luther's 243 faculty members are part-time. Forty-three percent are women. As tough as student graders can be, most of those at Luther give their professors "solid A's." Explains a junior: "They care about their students, get to know them as individuals, and assist them in selecting and finding careers." Adds a senior: "They make learning interactive, which is much more successful than a simple lecture style." Many undergraduates are pleased by the quality of new faculty members being added, noting that they seem to have the same commitment to both the discipline and the eager disciples. Students also like the fact that they get to complete evaluations of their professors every term, and says a communication major, many faculty members "actually respond and act upon them."

The college's academic strengths are varied: biology, music, and nursing head many students' picks. The music program benefits from a virtuoso faculty plus the facilities of the Jenson Hall of Music, which has 3 recital/rehearsal halls, an organ studio, and 36 practice rooms. The long-time music professor who also directs the Nordic Choir is respected both on campus and throughout music circles. Nursing offers a strong clinical program in which students spend their junior year at the Mayo Clinic in Rochester, Minnesota, 70 miles north. Advanced equipment, such as electron microscopes, available in biology, enhanced by much personalized attention during labs, gives premed students an extensive background in research. "The professors," adds a major, "have high expectations and often test a lot of material at once. They do not back down from their standard of excellence." As a result, biology majors boast an acceptance rate into medical school almost twice that of the national average. No-nonsense preparation in the economics and business department, bolstered by the opening in fall 1995 of a new "high-tech" building, draws many corporations to campus with offers of impressive starting salaries. A highlight of the structure is the Round Table Room, an electronic decision-making facility. The religion department features faculty who enjoy promoting discussion, rather than just repeating known facts. The philosophy faculty likewise is "superb," says a major.

Smaller programs such as theater and dance, political science, health, and anthropology could use more faculty. The communication major lacks the technologically advanced equipment available in other programs. Russian studies is offered only as a minor though majors are available in French, German, and Spanish and in Scandinavian studies.

Facilities: Students find Preus Library to be a great place to study, with plenty of tables and carrels as well as rooms for both group and individual work. However, the collection of 339,000 volumes and 1612 periodicals (plus full-text on-line periodicals), draws mixed reviews. Some consider the holdings more than adequate, while others like this biology major qualify their praise: "For graduate-type research, one is likely to be frustrated by the inability to find all that one wants." Research help is provided by Preus' on-line catalog known as Magnus as well as numerous indices and databases.

The Franklin W. Olin Building for economics and business, math, and computer science is the place on campus to find computers after midnight, provided students are in the building before the stroke of 12. The three 24-hour labs in Olin plus several other labs around campus, open until midnight, with Windows-based and Macintosh computers generally satisfy students' computer needs. Students with their own personal computers also have Internet access from their dorm rooms. Wireless access is available in most of the major buildings around campus.

Special programs: Luther conducts its own year-long academic program in Nottingham, England, including field experience with various social service agencies in the city. A 1-semester experience in Malta is another option. Students may also spend a year or a semester at Lillehammer College or Telemark College in Norway or with programs in numerous other far-flung cities. Internships are available at the Iowa General Assembly or at the nation's capital as part of a semester program offered by American University. A 3-2 option in engineering is available with Washington University or the University of Minnesota; first-year students may also be guaranteed admission to the University of Iowa College of Dentistry after spending 3 years at Luther.

Campus life: Eighty-four percent of Luther's students reside on the 175-acre central campus, with the Upper Iowa River, where students can canoe or tube, flowing through its lower portion. (The college owns an additional 625 acres adjacent to the central campus that are used for farming, environmental research, and biological studies.) All but a small number of students spend their weekends at Luther. "Why leave?" asks a sophomore. "There is such a wide variety of activities available, such as movies, dances, or concerts, that it is hard to choose." Other popular attractions are Marty's Cyber Café, the on-campus coffeehouse, and a local bowling alley. Still, students describe weekend life as "mellow," rather than frenetic, with little pressure to do anything if one prefers to loaf. Fewer than 10% of the men and women are members of the 4 local fraternities and 4 local sororities, which plan weekly events for their members, though Greeks and independents mix quite freely. Seven very active choirs, especially the highly touted Nordic Choir, attract large numbers of student participants, and a full contingent of 1000 current undergraduates and alumni turn out to sing in the annual Messiah concert. Various service programs within Campus Ministry, as well as a number of "issue" organizations ranging from environmental to international concerns, draw their share of supporters. Opportunities for student worship, from daily chapel and Wednesday night Eucharist to Sunday traditional and contemporary worship services, are numerous for those who want it but not oppressive to those who don't. "Though the school's mission has a lot of Christian values within it," notes a junior, "I don't ever feel put upon to go to church or anything." Although crime is not considered much of a problem, dormitory entrances are locked from 10 p.m. until 8 a.m. and an escort service is available.

Intramurals are an especially popular way to unwind, with 60% of the men and 50% of the women trying their skill at the 45 sports offered to each sex. Ten men's and 9 women's intercollegiate teams compete in NCAA Division III. Norse soccer, both men's and women's, has joined football and basketball as a popular varsity sport, though, admits a foreign national, "I was a bit surprised that most sporting events are not heavily supported by students." Ultimate Frisbee is an extremely popular club sport.

The best getaway for many students is simply to hop on a bike and cycle through 1 of a half-dozen wonderful parks in the area or if the season is right, to ski at a run right off campus. Decorah (pop. 8500) is located 15 miles south of the Minnesota border, with Rochester and Cedar Rapids both 90-minute drives. The nearest city, Lacrosse, Wisconsin, is only 45 miles east.

Cost cutters: Support from the Evangelical Lutheran Church, a sturdy endowment of nearly $84 million as of June 2005, and other gifts help keep down tuition. In the 2005–2006 school year, 99% of all undergraduates received financial aid; at least 71% were on need-based assistance. The average first-year award for students with need included need-based scholarships and grants averaging $18,463 and need-based self-help aid such as loans and jobs averaging $5603. Non-need-based awards and scholarships for first-year students averaged $8563. A typical 2005 graduate left with debts of $18,504. The college awards 2 honor scholarships to its most impressive students. A Regent Scholar receives $7500 to $12,000 a year; a Presidential Scholar gets between $3500 and $7000 annually. Academic Achievement Awards pay $3000 a year. Semester, monthly, and deferred tuition-payment plans are available.

Rate of return: Eighty-five percent of the freshmen who enter return for the sophomore year. Sixty-five percent graduate in 4 years; 74%, in another year; 75% in 6.

Payoff: Biology at 10%, management at 9%, and psychology at 8% were the 3 largest disciplines among graduates in the 2005 class. About two-thirds accept jobs soon after finishing, many with major companies such as IBM, 3M, and the well-known accounting firms in cities throughout the Midwest. More than 190 companies and other organizations recruited on campus in a recent school year. Just over a fifth of the graduates immediately head off to graduate or professional schools.

Bottom line: "Luther," says a New Englander: "is the perfect place for the student that looks at the world and thinks, 'I want to help this place. I want to realize my purpose. I want to learn!'"

The University of Iowa

Iowa City, Iowa 52242

Setting: Small town
Control: Public
Undergraduate enrollment: 8485 men, 9709 women
Graduate enrollment: 2298 men, 2516 women
Student/faculty ratio: 11:1
Freshman profile: 12% scored over 700 on SAT I verbal; 36% scored 600–700; 36% 500–599; 16% below 500; 15% scored over 700 on SAT I math; 39% scored 600–700; 34% 500–599; 12% below 500. 13% scored above 28 on the ACT; 16% scored 27–28; 33% 24–26; 25% 21–23; 13% below 21. 23% graduated in top tenth of high school class; 43% in upper fifth.

Faculty profile: 97% Ph.D.'s
Tuition and fees: $5612 in-state; $16,998 out-of-state
Room and board: $6560
Freshman financial aid: 80%; average scholarship or grant: $2400 need-based; $2700 non-need-based
Campus jobs: 65%; average earnings: $2200/year
Application deadline: Apr. 1
Financial aid deadline: ASAP after Jan. 1
Admissions information: (319) 335-3847;
(800) 553-IOWA
e-mail: admission@uiowa.edu
web site: www.uiowa.edu

If a library is the heart of an educational system, then the University of Iowa is in no danger of cardiac arrest. In recent studies, Iowa's network of libraries has ranked 26th of 113 university research libraries in the United States and Canada in number of volumes held (4.5 million) and permanent staff (235), 37th in expenditures for library materials and 8th in satisfaction of lending requests from other libraries. The main library, 11 departmental libraries, and a law library together cover 11 acres of space, seat more than 7000 readers, and provide more than 70 miles of shelving for collections. While the system may seem intimidating at first, students soon learn their way around, discovering which environment is best for concentrated study (the law library), where they should go for an all-nighter (the 24-hour study floor in the Harding Health Center), and who or what knows where everything is located (InfoHawk, the on-line catalog). What most students know without asking, though, is that for an education as broad as the local cornfields, with kernels of knowledge just waiting to be picked, it's hard to beat The University of Iowa.

Student body: Sixty-nine percent of Iowa's undergraduates are home-grown, with the largest portion of out-of-staters also coming from the Midwest. The rest are residents of all but 1 of the remaining states and 59 foreign countries. Ninety-one percent attended public schools. Four percent of Iowa's undergraduates are Asian-Americans; about 2% each are African-Americans, Hispanics, and foreign nationals. One percent are Native Americans. Most Iowa students, many of whom were raised in small, homogeneous communities, are eager to enhance diversity and pride themselves on being more liberal than visitors anticipate. Boasts a senior: "Our campus has the reputation of being the most liberal place in Iowa," known, not so favorably by some residents of Des Moines, as the "People's Republic of Iowa." Observes an Iowan: "The interaction of students from Chicago's elite North Shore and Iowa's desolate Western towns truly makes The University of Iowa one of a kind." In a community of 18,000 full-time undergraduates, such a wide range of political views as well as academic abilities is the norm. Notes an accounting major: "Iowa has some of the best minds and most intelligent people in the country, as well as many students who struggle just to get by." The pace for all picked up several years ago when the university instituted a plus/minus grading system that encourages serious students as well as those in trouble to work for the extra few points that could make a difference. Overall, undergraduates describe the student body as "spirited," in its approach to sports, campus living, and academic achievement. "Grassroots politics is everywhere," says a southerner. "With all the student groups on campus, people are always organizing," which also helps to make the large campus feel much smaller and friendlier.

Academics: The University of Iowa, founded in 1847, awards degrees through the doctorate; the bachelor's is offered in more than 100 majors, over half of which are found in the College of Liberal Arts. Freshmen may enroll in either the liberal arts college or the College of Engineering. As sophomores or juniors, they can apply for admission to the colleges of Business Administration, Education, Nursing, and Pharmacy. A limited number of students also may earn bachelor's degrees in nuclear medicine technology and radiation sciences from the Carver College of Medicine. Graduate programs only are offered in the Graduate College and the colleges of Law, Dentistry, and Public Health. The academic year is divided into 2 semesters. The most popular courses, such as Elementary Psychology, can enroll nearly 800 students, while required freshman classes in rhetoric may have just 22. The huge introductory lectures break into weekly discussion groups of a couple dozen students working under a teaching assistant. Class sizes in a student's major may range from 10 to 80, depending on the program.

The university has general-education requirements that cover about a third of the credits needed for graduation. The basic program comprises students' choice of classes in rhetoric, historical perspectives, foreign language, interpretation of literature, humanities, natural sciences, quantitative or formal reasoning, and social sciences. In addition, undergraduates must select 2 courses from a list that includes cultural diversity, fine arts, foreign civilizations and culture, physical education, social science, humanities, or historical perspectives. Many students, especially those who enter Iowa with no idea of what major they want, enjoy browsing through the various disciplines. To make the general-education experience, with its large, impersonal introductory lectures less overwhelming and impersonal, Iowa has developed a voluntary program in which a group of freshmen may enroll in 3 "Courses in Common" their first semester. Students get to know each other, and because they feel part of a unified group, instead of solitary individuals, they begin to take a more active role in their learning. In a recent year, the program included more than 450 incoming freshmen, about 14% of the new class.

The university employs 1595 full-time faculty members and 98 part-time, all of whom teach undergraduates in varying degrees. Just over a quarter are women. Seventeen members (3 current) have won the Pulitzer Prize. One senior assesses the situation this way: "Some teachers are here to teach, and they are outstanding; they get into the class and make it interesting. Others are here to do research. Often they don't care about the students and teach straight out of the textbook." Students sense that these professors are being pulled away from something more important to teach their class. At the upper levels, some of that research emphasis provides opportunities for students to become involved in a professor's work. As proud as many students are of the volume of published material produced by the Iowa faculty, however, it can seem, remarks a senior, "as if the faculty I know is made up mostly of teaching assistants, not professors." But that isn't necessarily bad. "Some of the best classes I've had have been taught by TAs," says a pre-med student. The biggest problem with TAs tends to be the number who speak limited English.

Students love their nationally recognized English department. Iowa's status as the home of the first Writer's Workshop, founded in 1936, as well as of an International Writing Program, gives undergraduates at all levels the chance to work with prominent authors. Separate creative writing workshops also have an outstanding reputation; participants swear that one-time English haters will, at the very least, leave comfortable with the subject, and students who initially liked English will decide to major in it. Political science is a winner as well, marked by renowned faculty and excellent course offerings. Artistic disciplines such as dance, theater, art, and music also are highly rated (Iowa was the first university to accept creative work in these fields as theses for advanced degrees) and draw standing ovations for their excellent faculties and superb facilities. The College of Pharmacy is widely respected for being tough and boasts a 100% placement rate in the job market. The new building for the College of Business Administration has added finishing touches to a program whose improvement has been a university priority and that already attracts some of the best students and outstanding faculty who push them to do even better. The sciences, biology, chemistry, physics, and psychology are enhanced by the presence of Iowa's excellent medical school, hospitals, and clinics, although some majors say the equipment used by undergraduates should be updated. A new biology building has helped those majors, but "we need a new chemistry building," says one science major. They also warn newcomers of known "weed-out" courses at the lower levels of these competitive disciplines.

The colleges of Education and Engineering pale only because of the luster of these majors at the University of Northern Iowa and Iowa State, respectively. Still, many majors in these fields find their offerings "very comprehensive," and a new engineering building adds a "plus" to that program's already solid rating. The university also does not offer a number of other majors available at the Iowa State campus, such as programs in agriculture, veterinary medicine, forestry, architecture, and animal science.

Facilities: No other word but *big* describes Iowa's main library: 5 floors (the studying gets more serious as you go up; the second floor is for flirting; the fifth for graduate students), with most of the university's 4.5 million volumes, 7.1 million microform items, and over 50,000 current periodicals available electronically or on open stacks. An on-line catalog known as InfoHawk directs students to holdings in the main library as well as to those throughout most of the system. Seven-hundred fifty databases are accessible as well. Not surprisingly, students and faculty generally find what they want somewhere on campus. The dozen other departmental libraries provide more specialized periodicals plus smaller, more comfortable study areas. "And the librarians in each one are amazing at answering questions," says a junior studying health promotion. The Health Sciences Library in particular offers plenty of private carrels and a 24-hour study zone with couches for napping and vending machines for snacking.

There are 52 computer clusters and departmental labs on campus, with at least 2 open 24 hours a day. More than 1700 networked microcomputers are available to students and are used for just about everything at Iowa. Hookups to the computer network are available in each dorm room. Wireless networking is available at 40 campus locations.

Special programs: Iowa offers its own study-abroad programs in several countries, including a course in journalism taught in London and another in business and society conducted in Seville, Spain. Opportunities for foreign study provided by other organizations raise the total number of travel options to more than 45 countries. A semester in Washington, D.C., as well as a summer at Lakeside Laboratories, the university's biological field station in northwest Iowa, also is available. Cross registration for classes is offered with Iowa State and the University of Northern Iowa.

Campus life: Twenty-seven percent of Iowa's undergraduates reside on the 1900-acre campus, which runs along the banks of the Iowa River. A number of students enjoy living in Learning Communities in which students are grouped on a residence hall floor or over a few floors according to academic interests that range from health sciences to writing. Because the university butts up against Iowa City's downtown area, a large part of the weekend activity spills over into the approximately 20 bars, 20 restaurants, 6 movie theaters, and a mall, all within walking distance. The Greek system at Iowa is big but not dominating, with 7% of the men and 12% of the women belonging to 16 national fraternities and 13 national sororities. While Greek parties aren't open to the entire campus, few independents have reason to feel left out, given the choice of more than 400 other student groups to join. The Liberal Arts Students Association is the largest and sponsors a variety of programs from recycling drives to road races. Many also get involved in planning the annual Riverfest or the 30-hour dance marathon held every year to raise money for children with cancer. Students say university officials are sensitive to crime prevention and recently added blue light security phones as a precaution. SafeWalk and SafeRide programs are available and the student government distributes safety whistles. Within the dormitories, locked doors in the lobbies, locked bathrooms, and metal doors on rooms all serve as crime deterrents in an already low-crime community.

"Football is incredibly, or some would say obnoxiously, popular," says a Hawkeye fan. "The town is all but paralyzed with traffic during home games." Tailgating precedes the Big Ten conference games— "Nothing else like tailgating Hawkeye style!" says a sophomore—and (hopefully) victory celebrations follow; there's usually a party regardless of the score. Basketball and wrestling also draw healthy crowds among the 10 men's and 12 women's NCAA Division I sports played. Intramurals, with residence halls and Greek teams involved in the 29 men's and 29 women's sports offered, draw spirited involvement as well.

About the only reason Iowa students leave campus in significant numbers is to follow the football team to an away-from-home game. Otherwise, most find plenty to do in Iowa City, a pleasantly entertaining community of 90,000. For those times when a change of scenery is needed, rock climbing in the Wisconsin Dells, a ride on the Mississippi riverboats, or road trips to Cedar Rapids, about 20 miles north, Des Moines, 110 miles west, or even Chicago, 220 miles east, can be easily arranged.

Cost cutters: Tuition rates for students in the colleges of Business, Engineering, and Pharmacy are higher; in business in the 2005–2006 school year, rates were about $250 a year higher, in engineering, about $300, and in pharmacy, almost $11,000 a year more for out-of-state students, $7500 more for in-state. Eighty percent of Iowa's freshmen and 90% of continuing students received financial aid in the 2005–2006 school year. For about 40% of both groups, the aid was need-based. The average financial package to freshmen with need included an average need-based scholarship or grant of $2400 and average self-help aid such as loans and jobs of $2100. The average non-need-based athletic scholarship to first-year students was $9000; other non-need-based awards and scholarships averaged $2700. The average financial indebtedness of a 2005 graduate was $16,500. The university offers more than 350 scholarships to outstanding students based on financial need or merit or both. Twenty Presidential Scholarships pay $10,000 a year to top students; 350 applicants for the Presidential award, including the winners, receive $3000 Old Gold Scholarships. Fifty to 100 Opportunity at Iowa Scholarships pay $5000 a year. National Scholar Awards to top nonresident students pay $2650 annually. Cooperative programs are available in all majors, and a co-op office helps students find summer or annual internships that provide salary and academic credit.

Rate of return: Eighty-four percent of the entering freshmen return for the sophomore year. While just 38% graduate in 4 years, 62% do so in 5 years, and 66% in 6 years. A Four-Year Graduation Plan helps students who follow certain guidelines to graduate in 4 years. The 4-year graduation rate has risen 8% since the program first was offered in 1995.

Payoff: Communication studies at 7%, and English and psychology at 6% each accounted for the largest numbers of graduates in the 2005 graduating class. Most new alumni attend graduate or professional schools or find jobs with the 270 employers that recruit on campus; the university keeps no statistics.

Bottom line: Because of its widely respected writers' workshops and pioneering work in theater, art, dance, and music, the University of Iowa is a Big Ten school with a thriving intellectual-artistic air. Observes a senior: "If more students would see for themselves that we are not just a bunch of dumb midwestern hicks stuck out in the middle of a cornfield, they would realize that Iowa is the right choice. Not only do the excellent facilities and outstanding faculty make this university special, but also the diverse atmosphere provided by being in Iowa City creates an academic environment that just can't be found anywhere else."

Wartburg College
Waverly, Iowa 50677

Setting: Small town
Control: Private (Evangelical Lutheran)
Undergraduate enrollment: 823 men, 909 women
Graduate enrollment: None
Student/faculty ratio: 16:1
Freshman profile: 12% scored over 700 on SAT I verbal; 24% scored 600–700; 44% 500–599; 20% below 500. 16% scored over 700 on SAT I math; 36% scored 600–700; 28% 500–599; 20% below 500. 12% scored above 28 on the ACT; 13% scored 27–28: 24% 24–26; 28% 21–23; 23% below 21. 31% graduated in top tenth of high school class; 52% in upper fifth.
Faculty profile: 94% Ph.D.'s

Tuition and fees: $21,130
Room and board: $6185
Freshman financial aid: 99%; average scholarship or grant: $5581 need-based; $9252 non-need-based
Campus jobs: 65%; average earnings: $1138/year
Application deadline: Early action: Dec. 1; regular: Sept. 1
Financial aid deadline: Mar. 1 (priority)
Applications information: (319) 352-8264;
(800) 772-2085
e-mail: admissions@wartburg.edu
web site: www.wartburg.edu

For students not well versed in Lutheran Church history, Wartburg Castle, built in 1027 and located near Eisenach, Germany, was the place where Martin Luther took refuge during the Protestant Reformation. While there, Luther translated the New Testament into German, helping to unify the country and convert religion into the language of the people. For students not well versed in the lore of small liberal arts colleges, Wartburg College, which was founded in 1852 and named for the castle, has likewise distinguished itself as an educational institution affiliated with the Evangelical Lutheran Church where undergraduates can seek refuge from the world in a town of 10,000 residents, and yet be part of the world through extensive domestic and international travel experiences. A Venture Education program provides traditional classroom experiences in Australia and several European and Asian nations, while the Diers Program, a more individualized form of cross-cultural immersion, allows students to work with people in a vastly different culture, such as in Africa and the Navajo Nation, while maintaining an independent course of study at Wartburg. Students with musical talent can join the Wartburg Choir, Wind Ensemble, or Castle Singers, all of whom have performed stateside at Carnegie Hall, Walt Disney World, the Kennedy Center, and other locales, as well as touring throughout Europe and South Africa. Right on campus, the Institute for Leadership Education provides workshops, mentoring programs, and coursework, including an interdisciplinary minor in Leadership Certification, that encourage students to take risks and rise to their potential; Wartburg West allows students to study or participate in internships in Denver, Colorado. Says a junior: "Wartburg does a wonderful job of providing students with opportunities to develop themselves and face the world as prepared leaders and contributors." At Wartburg College, students enter as bright, unformed high school graduates and in 4 or 5 years are transformed into well-rounded citizens ready to lead and to serve.

Student body: Three-quarters of Wartburg's undergraduates are from Iowa, with all but 8% of the rest also from the Midwest. As a group, students come from 24 states and 37 foreign countries. Just 5% in a recent year attended private schools. African-American students constitute the single largest racial or ethnic minority group at 3% of enrollment; Asian-Americans and Hispanics each comprise 1%. Foreign nationals account for 5%. Campus forums on race and diversity-related topics, "have certainly opened my eyes," confesses a midwesterner and help to foster better relations between groups. A third of the students are Evangelical Lutheran, with another third members of other Protestant denominations and a fourth Catholic. The rest are of other faiths, such as Jewish, Buddhist, or Muslim, or claim no religious affiliation. Students describe themselves as rather traditional (some say conservative) in their values, friendly, hard-working, involved, and service-oriented. "The vast majority come from middle-sized communities in the Midwest that have an acute sense of what is morally correct," says an Iowan. "People at Wartburg respect one another." That sense of respect permeates their sense of academic fairplay. Notes a biology major: "Academically, there is competitiveness but also compassion. People are not going to step on you to better themselves; they would rather have you reach their level and see you have success with them." There also is a fair percentage of students who care less about academic success and "are more concerned with their social image and parties," observes another biology major.

Academics: Wartburg awards only the bachelor's degree in more than 50 majors. The academic year is divided into 2 semesters, with an additional May term in which students can enjoy more opportunities for international and multicultural travel or explore new topics on campus. The average class size is conducive to personalized learning: freshmen can expect to have maybe 2 large lecture classes of about 80 students though these courses break into discussion or laboratory sections of 15 to 20 people. The smallest course has 5 participants, though most upper-level courses have between 10 and 20 members enrolled.

All students are required to participate in the Wartburg Plan of Essential Education, which encompasses a third of the credits needed to graduate. The curriculum is integrative and designed to teach critical thinking skills, achieve college-level competencies in fundamental academic skills, connect the disciplines through interdisciplinary study, and integrate faith and learning with a special emphasis on values and ethics. Five course credits are required in verbal reasoning, mathematical reasoning, scientific reasoning, lifelong wellness, and intercultural understanding. Students also must take 4 interconnected courses in natural science (with lab), social science, and humanities/fine arts plus 5.5 to 6 course credits in integration-related courses, completing at least 2 courses in faith and reflection, 2 in interdisciplinary studies, and a final capstone course in the student's major during the senior year. The remaining two-thirds of the required academic credits are split relatively evenly between classes in each student's major and electives.

About 60% of Wartburg's 179 faculty members are full-time; 42% are women. Entering freshmen soon discover what comes first in the minds of the vast majority of professors—the students. Says a junior: "Professors challenge students to think critically and see things from new perspectives, and are available outside of office hours if needed by their students." While the full-time faculty are described as "topnotch," some of the adjunct and visiting professors are viewed as only "fair."

Wartburg's academic strengths span a diversity of disciplines, with students focusing their best picks on 3 programs: biology, music, and education. All of the health sciences, but especially biology, are noted for their "brilliant" but down-to-earth faculty, challenging courses, and consistently strong placement in medical and graduate schools. A newly renovated science center that opened in fall 2004 provides twice the space of the earlier facility. Although all of the music programs are strong, the music therapy major is especially noteworthy, not just at Wartburg, but throughout the region. Graduates of the program find ready placement in educational facilities, geriatric centers, and state and private institutions, where they work with children, adolescents, and adults. The education program maintains a strong tradition of using top-notch professors and a strong curriculum to train and inspire high-quality schoolteachers; well-planned placements in various school systems also give this program a grade of A+. Psychology, social work and math, computer science, political science, and physics are considered winners, too. Religion is viewed as being especially strong for those considering careers in the ministry. The communication arts program boasts top-of-the-line facilities including a television studio, and a faculty who is "especially caring and wants all students to achieve."

Community sociology, philosophy, French, and German have had just a single full-time professor, limiting the perspectives and personalities available to students. The theater program could use more resources and rigor. The fitness management and business administration majors carry a reputation for being less challenging programs.

Facilities: The Robert and Sally Vogel Library, named for a long-time Wartburg president and his wife, opened in fall 1999. Its 3 stories are organized with multiple uses in mind. The first floor is devoted to books, journals, and magazines, arranged on mechanical book stacks. It also houses an education lab. The second floor is for research, with 18 computers set aside for accessing the Internet, First Search, or other hightech aids, and more than 70 units for research, paper writing, and other purposes. The third floor, students' favorite, is for studying. "Whether it be small rooms with a table, chairs, and a white board, or a nice comfortable rocking chair in front of a window overlooking campus, the library has a study area for every type of studier out there," observes a biology major. Vogel houses about 147,000 volumes and 829 current periodicals, which are adequate for all but the most exhaustive research projects.

About 200 Apple Macintosh and PC-compatible microcomputers are spread among 10 different labs throughout campus. Most are open until 2 a.m., the lab in the library until midnight, with extended hours as finals week approaches. Says a senior: "I've made it through 3½ years here without a computer of my own and have never had a problem." Internet access is also available from every residence hall room for those students who do choose to bring their own computers and "an Internet plug everywhere you turn," says a math/computer science major.

Special programs: All together, Wartburg offers opportunities for study abroad in 21 countries; 44% of all students take part. An intercultural studies minor also is available. Along with the chance for an internship out west in Denver, those who prefer can head east to Washington, D.C. Joint degree programs are offered in engineering with the universities of Iowa and Illinois, with Iowa State and Washington universities, and with other universities in medical technology and occupational therapy. A deferred admittance program is an option with the University of Iowa College of Dentistry. Students with an interest in nursing can complete 2 years of appropriate courses at Wartburg and complete their clinical training at the University of Iowa College of Nursing. As an alternative, students may enroll directly in the Allen College B.S.N. program in Waterloo, Iowa, enabling them to complete their clinical work at Allen while taking their humanities and sciences classes at Wartburg.

Campus life: Seventy-nine percent of Wartburg's students live on the 118-acre campus, which is the focus for most weekday studying—and relaxing. Without fraternities and sororities, students turn to the extensive campus programming, such as comedians, movies, and performances by outside music groups as well as Wartburg's own, which is regularly provided. Campus Ministry involves students in non-mandatory worship services (they organize the popular Wednesday night Eucharist service) and off-campus retreats. The Student Health Awareness Committee holds 2 blood drives and a health fair every year, and generally keeps students advised of what's best for their physical, mental, and emotional well-being. Most students already enjoy peace of mind when it comes to concern about campus crime. Few consider crime, other than occasional car vandalism, much of a problem, either on campus or in Waverly. Precautions are taken, however, and include such security measures as using frequently changed combination locks on all residence hall doors after 11 p.m., and providing a student escort service.

Sporting events are well supported on campus, especially Knights football, in the new 5000-seat Walston-Hoover Stadium, and basketball games, which "are both huge," says a fan. All-weather FieldTurf, an artificial playing surface used by some NFL and Division I teams, replaced grass on the football field, which is surrounded by a new 8-lane all-weather track done in an eye-catching "Wartburg Orange." Wrestling also draws a good amount of attention among the 10 men's and 9 women's intercollegiate sports that compete in NCAA Division III. In a recent school year, the Knights won 9 conference championships and finished second in 4 sports. Forty percent of the men and 25% of the women take part in intercollegiate sports. More than half of the men and women turn out for intramural sports, 4 each for men and women, 6 coed.

When students need to wave good-bye to Waverly for awhile, most head for home or to the Waterloo-Cedar Falls metropolitan area, 15 miles south, which offers more options for shopping, entertainment, and eating out, as well as additional cultural and athletic events at the University of Northern Iowa. Des Moines is 2½ hours to the southwest, Minneapolis-St. Paul, 3½ hours north, and Chicago, about 6 hours east.

Cost cutters: All but 1% of the freshmen and continuing students received financial aid in the 2005–2006 school year; 73% of the freshmen and 69% of the remaining students were on need-based assistance. The average freshman award for a first-year student with financial need included a need-based scholarship or grant averaging $5581 and need-based self-help aid such as loans and job earnings averaging $3094. Other non-need-based awards and scholarships averaged $9252. The average financial indebtedness of a 2005 graduate was $13,506. Students who have a minimum ACT score of 28 or an SAT critical reading and math score of 1240 or ranked in the top 10% of their class or had a 3.85 GPA, are eligible for the Regents Scholarship, which pays $7500 to full tuition a year. Presidential Scholarships pay $4500 to $7500 yearly to students who scored a minimum of 25 on the ACT or 1140 on the SATs or ranked in the top 20% of their high school class or had a 3.5 GPA. A Meistersinger Music Scholarship pays up to $4000 a year, awarded on the basis of an audition.

Rate of return: Eighty-one percent of entering freshmen return for the sophomore year. Fifty-six percent go on to graduate in 4 years; 63% in 5 years; 68% within 6.

Payoff: Business administration was the major of choice for 20% of the 2005 graduating class, followed by majors in communication arts at 14% and biology at 11%. The majority of graduates take jobs within months of commencement; teaching, social work, and business are frequent career choices. Many students seek jobs in the Midwest and upper Midwest in various educational and social service settings, or in small to moderate-sized companies. More than 100 companies and organizations recruited on campus in the 2004–2005 school year. About a fifth of a recent class pursued advanced degrees, with medicine, physical therapy, and other health sciences among the primary interests for graduate and professional study.

Bottom line: Wartburg challenges students to look beyond the classroom walls to what they can offer their chosen profession, their family, and the world when they are finished. Says a sophomore: "I like who I am becoming, because of my experiences and education here."

Kansas

University of Kansas, Lawrence

Lawrence, Kansas 66045

Setting: Suburban
Control: Public
Undergraduate enrollment: 9133 men, 9554 women
Graduate enrollment: 1808 men, 2354 women (medical campus included)
Student/faculty ratio: 20:1
Freshman profile: 17% scored above 28 on the ACT; 13% scored 27–28; 28% 24–26; 27% 21–23; 15% below 21. 28% graduated in top tenth of high school class; 56% in upper fifth.
Faculty profile: 95% Ph.D.'s
Tuition and fees: $5413 in-state; $13,866 out-of-state

Room and board: $5502
Freshman financial aid: 47%; average scholarship or grant: $3752 need-based; $2538 non-need-based
Campus jobs: 18%; average earnings: $4160/year
Application deadline: Apr. 1 (Feb. 1 out-of-state applicants)
Financial aid deadline: Mar. 1 (Scholarships: Jan. 15)
Admissions information: (785) 864–3911; (888) 686-7323
e-mail: adm@ku.edu
web site: www.ku.edu

When John Winthrop, well-known Puritan and spoiler of good times, said, "Ye shall be like 'a city upon a hill,' serving as a model to others," he did not have the University of Kansas in mind. But on a hill amidst the plains of Middle America, "a mountain among flat lands," in the words of one student, the flagship University of Kansas, which turned 140 in 2006, most certainly draws bicoastal attention, offering a wealth of big-college experiences for a comparatively small price. Ten schools and 1 college that admit undergraduates issue nearly a dozen different baccalaureate degrees. Thirty foreign languages are regularly taught, from Arabic and Croatian to Swedish and Wolof, the dominant language of Senegal, with some Kiswahili, Slovene, Hausa, and a good share of Jayhawk basketballspeak thrown in. At this city on the hill, "basketball games are truly a religious experience," observes a state resident—not quite what John Winthrop had in mind.

Student body: With almost 19,000 full-time undergraduates and 4200 full-time graduate students, the University of Kansas is bigger than all but a half-dozen Kansas cities—and more racially diverse than most. The undergraduate student body is 82% white American, 3% foreign national from 113 countries, 4% Asian-American, 3% each African-American and Hispanic, and 1% Native American. The racial and ethnic origins of 4% are unknown. Seventy-three percent of the students are from Kansas, with two-thirds of the out-of-staters also from the Midwest, although all 50 states are represented. The majority of students are friendly, approachable, down to earth, and very proud of being Jayhawks. While freshmen tend to spend a lot of their first year socializing, sophomores and juniors devote more time to studying and to voicing their opinions on various political issues. "Seniors," says one, "are career-oriented and push toward those last high grades. They have very little spare time." Still, undergraduates span a wide range of academic abilities, from those who come for the parties and ballgames, to honors students from both in-state and out who could have gone to college anywhere. "If you can think of a political, academic, or social mindset," says a junior, "you can likely find one or two KU students who embrace that particular attitude or attitudes."

Academics: KU, as the university is familiarly known, awards degrees through the doctorate, with the College of Liberal Arts and Sciences and 10 professional schools offering undergraduate programs in more than 100 majors. Joint-degree programs give students the opportunity to combine degrees, such as one from the College of Liberal Arts and Sciences with one from the School of Business. KU's medical center campus is located in Kansas City. The academic year is divided into 2 semesters. While lower-level classes in English and mathematics rarely have more than 40 students, an introductory lecture in general psychology can enroll over 950. Such large lecture classes generally offer smaller discussion or lab sections of 15–30 participants led by graduate teaching assistants (TAs). Some upper-level engineering classes may have 50 in attendance, but most courses in other majors rarely exceed 30.

The College of Liberal Arts and Sciences, which enrolls the greatest number of undergraduates, requires candidates for the bachelor of arts degree to select courses from a variety of disciplines, including oral communication and logic, Western Civilization, non-Western culture, and a laboratory science. General-education requirements for the bachelor of science degree in the College of Liberal Arts and Sciences or in any of the 10 professional schools vary by school or program although all include English composition and literature.

The university employs 1185 full-time faculty and 127 part-timers. Of that group, only 24 of the full-time members and 3 of the part-time faculty teach at the graduate level only. Thirty-four percent are women. Eighteen percent of all undergraduate sections are taught by graduate students; undergraduates are most apt to encounter overworked TAs in the College of Liberal Arts and Sciences. "They can be good and they can be bad; it's pretty much luck of the draw," says a psychology major in the college. Notes a senior in engineering: "Excluding labs and discussion sections, I have had only 3 courses taught by graduate TAs, and all 3 were quite good. The faculty at KU can be very accessible and willing to visit with students at times other than their scheduled office hours." Participants in the college honors program, in particular, have good access to top professors.

The William Allen White School of Journalism and Mass Communications is well known for its high-quality faculty and hard-working students. Engineering, too, features a curriculum that is as rigorous as it is competitive, with an exceptional program in aircraft design that brings bright students together with internationally renowned professors. Facilities and faculty make the architecture program "simply fantastic." Other well-respected majors in the College of Liberal Arts and Sciences and the various schools include psychology, biology, theater, accounting and pharmacy, as well as Spanish, and Russian and East European studies. The business faculty, says an accounting major, "is very energetic, challenging, and always there to help out."

KU's physics department has had a poor reputation around campus, in part because of professors more interested in their research than teaching. A recent move to put better professors into lower-level classes has helped to improve the situation. Math, though, remains hampered by a heavy reliance on graduate teaching assistants. Newer majors, such as women's studies and African and African-American studies, are considered weaker because they receive less financial support than larger departments. Throughout the university, students say, academic advising is in need of improvement, although an advising support center provides some answers.

Facilities: KU's 10-story main Watson Library, along with 11 other, more specialized facilities, houses more than 4 million volumes, 4.1 million microform items, and almost 42,000 current periodicals. Despite its size, most students find Watson surprisingly easy to navigate, with rooms arranged for group study, individual study, silent study, and "social" study. The Anschutz Science Library provides space for a half-million volumes and gathers together in one spot all the science and technical materials. "The main floor of Anschutz gets noisy," says an environmental studies major, "but other floors provide a quiet and study-friendly atmosphere." The computerized research aids are considered more than adequate.

Computers seem to be everywhere around campus. Hundreds, in fact, are located in labs in the residence halls, in each professional school, in the libraries and in numerous other buildings. The main lab in Anschutz Library is open around the clock. Wireless zones are located just about everywhere as well.

Special programs: Study-abroad programs are available in more than 50 countries throughout Europe, Asia, and Latin America. A semester in Washington, D.C., also can be arranged.

Campus life: Just 18% of KU's undergraduates reside on the 1100-acre campus of white limestone buildings with red roofs. Outstanding students have the option of living in 1 of 9 scholarship halls, 5 for men and 4 for women. In each hall, about 50 students share cooking and housekeeping duties and, it is hoped, intellectual and social stimulation. A residence hall with a fine arts emphasis also is available.

Fourteen percent of the men and 17% of the women belong to 24 national fraternities and 17 national sororities respectively, making the KU Greek system among the biggest in the nation. Most of the fraternities and sororities maintain chapter houses near campus. Some rivalry exists between Greeks and independents; Greek parties are generally restricted to members and invited guests only. Jayhawks of diverse interests can choose among 400 student organizations on campus. As of 2005, KU debate teams had won the National Debate Tournament 4 times, more than any other school except Dartmouth College. Theft and vandalism are 2 of the most troublesome crimes at KU, though the addition of 25 security officers, as well as better lighting and more blue emergency phones throughout campus, has helped alleviate the problem. Special programs also are directed at freshmen "to warn them that this new home is not as safe as Mom's and Dad's house," says a senior.

KU basketball is always big, with tickets usually sold out before the school year begins. Football is only slightly less popular among the 7 men's and 11 women's intercollegiate sports played in NCAA Division I. The 241-member Marching Jayhawks also has its own enthusiastic fans and several years ago was named best collegiate marching band. About half of all undergraduates participate in the 20 intramural sports and 20+ club sports offered. Kansas Crew is a competitive rowing club in which membership carries a certain amount of prestige. Ultimate Frisbee and rugby also have become popular recreational pastimes.

Students can seek peace in the quiet wooded areas on campus or at Potter Lake, near Campanile Hill, site of the traditional graduation procession. Museums of art, natural history, classics, anthropology, entomology, and invertebrate paleontology all are located right on campus. Clinton Lake, a few miles away, offers beaches and barbecue spots. When Lawrence (pop. 80,000) becomes too familiar, Topeka, 20 miles west, and Kansas City, 40 miles east, are twice and three times bigger, respectively, and within easy reach.

Cost cutters: In the 2005–2006 school year, 47% of the freshmen and 46% of continuing students received financial help. For 36% of all undergraduates the aid was need-based. The average aid package for freshmen with need included a need-based scholarship or grant averaging $3752 and need-based self-help aid such as loans and jobs averaging $2720. Non-need-based athletic scholarships for first-year students averaged $12,057 and other non-need-based awards and scholarships averaged $2538. The average financial indebtedness of a 2005 graduate was $17,243. Although Kansas offers a number of scholarships, most are restricted to state residents and tend to be in amounts of $2500 or below. To be considered, students must have a cumulative GPA of at least 3.25 on a 4.0 scale and must have submitted their application for admission by Jan.15. National Merit finalists and semifinalists, valedictorians and salutatorians, top-ranked minority students and other high achievers are eligible for awards that pay $10,000 a year. Many complain that it is difficult for a nonathlete to get a no-need scholarship. Awards are presented for independent undergraduate research in all disciplines; approximately 10 awards of up to $250 each were available during a recent academic year, with up to 20 awards of $1000 each presented for summer research.

Rate of return: Eighty-three percent of the freshmen return for the sophomore year. Just 26% graduate in 4 years, though 51% do so in 5 years, and 57% graduate in six years.

Payoff: Three majors accounted for just over a fourth of the degrees awarded in the 2005 class: business at 11%, psychology at 8%, and journalism at 7%. Kansas graduates take jobs in a wide variety of fields, including teaching, accounting, entry-level management, and sales. About 500 companies and other organizations recruited on campus during the 2004–2005 school year. A fifth of recent graduates pursued advanced degrees.

Bottom line: Jayhawk basketball may be the biggest event on the University of Kansas campus, but at times freshmen will wonder whether their introductory lecture courses don't run a close second in terms of size. Although classes do get smaller, and undergraduates are remarkably helpful and friendly, "students who are ready to stand on their own do best here," advises a senior. "Those accustomed to a lot of teacher attention without investing any energy of their own in the dialogue will fall behind at KU. Here, responsibility for a student's education is placed squarely in his or her own hands."

Kentucky

Bellarmine University

Louisville, Kentucky 40205

Setting: Urban
Control: Private (Roman Catholic)
Undergraduate enrollment: 602 men, 1135 women
Graduate enrollment: 77 men, 143 women
Student/faculty ratio: 14:1
Freshman profile: 6% scored over 700 on SAT I verbal; 19% scored 600–700; 49% 500–599; 26% below 500. 3% scored over 700 on SAT I math; 28% scored 600–700; 49% 500–599; 20% below 500. 10% scored above 28 on the ACT; 12% scored 27–28; 27% 24–26; 31% 21–23; 20% below 21. 18% graduated in top tenth of high school class; 43% in upper fifth.
Faculty profile: 80% Ph.D.'s

Tuition and fees: $21,500
Room and board: $6150
Freshman financial aid: 100%; average scholarship or grant: $4550 need-based; $16,659 non-need-based
Campus jobs: 15%; average earnings: $1571/year
Application deadline: Early action: Nov. 1; regular: Feb. 1
Financial aid deadline: Mar. 1 (priority); scholarship deadline: Jan. 15
Admissions information: (502) 452-8131; (800) 274-4723
e-mail: admissions@bellarmine.edu
web site: www.bellarmine.edu

Louisville, Kentucky, is best known as the home of the Kentucky Derby horse race, the first leg of the Triple Crown, and Derbymania takes over every corner of the city the first week in May—every corner, that is, except one. At Bellarmine University, the first part of Derby week usually coincides with final exams which end the Thursday before the big race. But for those looking for a sure bet in the ranks of higher education, there may be no greater return on the money than that offered by this youthful Roman Catholic institution, which turned just 55 in 2005. Bellarmine remains pretty much a dark horse to handicappers outside the South; but with tuition, fees, room, and board totaling just over $27,600 in the 2005–2006 school year and 100% of its freshmen on some kind of financial aid, this small university in a big city wins the roses every time.

Student body: Bellarmine remains largely a Kentucky success story, with 78% of its students from in-state and the rest mostly midwesterners. A total of 32 states are represented. Forty-two percent are Catholic, and 44% are graduates of private or parochial schools. Students who are foreign nationals or members of racial or ethnic minority groups account for 9% of the total enrollment. Four percent of the students are African-American, with 2% Asian-American and 1% each Hispanic and Native American. There are 37 foreign nationals from 15 countries. Approximately a third of the undergraduates are traditional-age students who live on campus; about half are 18- to 22-year-old commuters, and the remaining portion are older commuters. Bellarmine students describe themselves as conscientious go-getters when it comes to studying or weekend partying but apathetic onlookers about most events outside the classroom. "Socially, students are very conservative," observes a Louisville native. "They *do not* deviate from the norm."

Academics: Bellarmine awards the bachelor's degree in more than 50 disciplines plus master's degrees in 6 fields and a doctorate in physical therapy. The school year is divided into 2 semesters. The biggest class at Bellarmine is a course in art history, which enrolls about 40 students. Most courses in the early years average no more than 25 members, while those for juniors and seniors run between 5 and 20.

A 49-hour core curriculum begins with a freshman seminar and a course in expository writing and ends with a senior seminar that explores such critical issues facing contemporary society as racism, economic and social justice, and environmental concerns. In between, students must complete coursework in the traditional academic fields, including 6 hours each in philosophy and theology and classes in the American and transcultural experience.

All but 7 of the 113 full-time faculty and all but 12 of the 121 part-timers teach undergraduates. Nearly half of the total pool are women. Students describe the faculty in superlatives, "the pride of our campus," raves a business administration major. "Our faculty is all about helping us succeed," says a senior. Throughout the disciplines, undergraduates value professors' active involvement with both students and the surrounding community, which keeps them current in their fields as well as flush with good contacts for student internships and permanent jobs. Students seeking more rigor in their academic coursework say faculty "will work with you to go above and beyond the minimum requirement so as to attain the level you want," notes a history major.

Such faculty traits are commonplace at the Rubel School of Business, and are one reason the school as a whole is so popular and graduates of its accounting program, in particular, perform highly on the CPA exams. The economics curriculum also is especially strenuous. English, philosophy, and history are noted for having excellent faculty and rigorous requirements. Education majors get a lot of experience in K–12 classrooms well before it is time to practice-teach; nursing school graduates usually excel on the national licensure exam. The already demanding biology program got an additional boost in 2003 with the opening of the 28,500-square-foot Norton Science Center, full of newly equipped science and research labs. Says a psychology major: "Due to the curriculum and the teachers in this major, it really allows only the elite of the major to succeed." The pre-physical therapy program, which leads to a bachelor of health sciences and later a doctorate in physical therapy, is excellent as well.

Political science, sociology, psychology, theology, physics, computer science, math, and foreign language instruction are limited by having too few faculty members and too few courses available to students. Observes a senior majoring in political science: "While I have enjoyed my experience in this department, I have had 4 different advisors since I have been here and there has never been any full-time professor who has stayed in the department." The communications major is considered too lenient and needs more space as well as more faculty. The art department, too, needs more space, resources, and equipment. Though there is no theater major, there still is an active program with 5–6 dramatic performances offered on campus each semester, and the option of an academic minor in theater. Some students find the music faculty to be too competitive with each other. "It is hard to enjoy or learn in an atmosphere like that," says a junior, "and it turns away a lot of students."

Facilities: The $10 million W. L. Lyons Brown Library opened on campus in January 1997, tripling the space available for research and study. Students appreciate the building's bright atmosphere, with plenty of rooms provided for group study as well as private concentrated work. "The study rooms are my favorite," notes a senior. "I can check out a laptop and hide in those." However, undergraduates still find the current collection of 117,000 volumes and 547 periodicals a bit slim and too heavy in older, dated materials. Comments an English major: "Excellent building—shame there are no useful books." Numerous databases in such fields as education, psychology, science, and literature as well as access to the Internet give many of these students a lift. Science majors go to the University of Louisville medical center.

Computing facilities are available around the clock in the library's 24-hour lounge, in Pasteur Hall, and in all of the residence halls and until midnight in other academic buildings. Residence-hall rooms are wired for Internet and campus network access.

Special programs: Students may cross-register for courses at "Kentuckiana Metroversity," the name given a group of other colleges and universities in Kentucky and southern Indiana. Study abroad is possible at over 100 universities in 58 countries. A summer biology program allows students to study marine life in the Bahamas. Internships in a wide range of majors from accounting and art to political science and psychology are available in the Louisville area. A Washington semester also is offered.

Campus life: Thirty-six percent of Bellarmine's students reside on the 135-acre campus located in a residential setting 10 minutes from downtown Louisville. The lack of a busy campus life, stemming from the large number of commuters, is one of students' chief complaints about the university. Though parties, dances, mixers, and other events can be found over any given weekend, many a dorm resident still picks up a friend from the residence halls and heads for home. "The idea that it is 'uncool' to go to a Bellarmine function has diminished to some extent," a senior notes, and upperclassmen are reporting a noticeable increase in attendance at various campus events. The recent opening of the 21,000-square-foot Campus Center offers numerous options for hanging out, among them a campus living room with big-screen TV and a view of the athletic fields and a multipurpose room perfect for movie viewing, small group performances, receptions, or meetings. A new 200-bed residence hall with a seminar room for classes and several recreation spaces also adds to the growing sense of community. FLOW, a new hip hop dance organization, has quickly become one of the most popular clubs on campus. There is just one social fraternity, and 1 social sorority, so only 2% of the men and women are Greeks. Occasional vandalism to cars and theft from dorm rooms and campus buildings are the most serious crimes on the campus, which is located in the secluded, residential Highlands neighborhood. A strict dorm visitation policy, surveillance cameras, and sufficient security staffers all have helped produce results. Students who don't feel safe walking after dark can call a security escort.

Two of the biggest weekend events, which even commuters come back to campus to watch, are basketball and, increasingly, soccer games, just 2 of 9 sports for men and 10 for women offered as part of NCAA Division II. A third of the men and a fourth of the women get involved in intramural softball and volleyball, both of which are coed, as well as in men's and women's basketball, men's flash ball, and various sports tournaments. A "team" of a very different sort, the university's mock trial team, earned its own distinctive laurels by winning the American Mock Trial Association's national championship in April 1999, beating teams from Stanford, Rhodes College, and other prestigious institutions.

For times when a trip home or a tour of Louisville's hot spots just won't do it, students head to Lexington, where the University of Kentucky is located, or gather in groups for a visit to Cincinnati, Ohio.

Cost cutters: One hundred percent of freshmen in the 2005–2006 school year and 97% of continuing students received some type of financial aid; for 43% of freshmen and 46% of continuing students the help was need-based. The average need-based grant for freshmen equaled $4550; need-based self-help aid such as loans and job earnings averaged $3898. Non-need-based athletic scholarships averaged $2186. The average for other non-need-based awards and scholarships was $16,659. A typical graduate left with debts of $12,263. Several years ago, the only full-tuition scholarships were for athletes, but no more. The Bellarmine Scholars Program pays full tuition over 4 years plus one summer study stipend to freshmen generally drawn from the top 5% of their high school class, with high standardized test scores who perform well on an essay and interview. Other merit awards recently paid from $1000 a year to $7000 annually, depending upon a student's GPA, class rank, and standardized test scores. Various tuition installment plans are provided.

Rate of return: Eighty-four percent of entering freshmen return for the sophomore year. Forty-six percent graduate in 4 years; 59%, in 5 years; 62%, in 6 years.

Payoff: More than a third of 2005 graduates earned bachelor's degrees in 3 professional fields: 21% in nursing, 10% in business, and 8% in liberal studies. Less than a fifth went directly to graduate or professional schools. The vast majority take jobs directly after graduation with accounting firms, hospitals, school systems, social service agencies, and various national, regional, and local businesses. Thirty-five companies and other organizations recruited on campus in a recent school year.

Bottom line: Bellarmine students have no perception that the university's size limits what they're learning today or where they'll be tomorrow. Notes a junior: "The small classes allow interaction with professors, and the small student body promotes formation of lasting friendships that are not possible at larger commuter universities."

Berea College

Berea, Kentucky 40404

Setting: Small town
Control: Private
Undergraduate enrollment: 617 men, 912 women
Graduate enrollment: None
Student/faculty ratio: 12:1
Freshman profile: 9% scored over 700 on SAT I verbal; 33% scored 600–700; 40% 500–599; 18% below 500. 5% scored over 700 on SAT I math; 27% scored 600–700; 48% 500–599; 28% below 500. 5% scored above 28 on the ACT; 9% scored 27–28; 29% 24–26; 35% 21–23; 22% below 21. 25% graduated in top tenth of high school class; 55% in upper fifth.

Faculty profile: 91% Ph.D.'s
Tuition and fees: No tuition; $516 fees
Room and board: $4980
Freshman financial aid: 100%; average scholarship or grant: $26,190 need-based
Campus jobs: 100%; average earnings: $2248/year
Application deadline: Rolling
Financial aid deadline: Apr. 1
Admissions information: (859) 985-3500;
(800) 326-5948
e-mail: jamie_ealy@berea.edu
web site: www.berea.edu

In the United States, where education is the ladder up which generations have climbed out of poverty, it is considered bad policy, almost unpatriotic, for a college to reject a qualified student simply because he or she is too poor to pay the tuition. Berea College in the Appalachian Region of Kentucky has given the old policy a new twist by rejecting candidates who can afford to pay their own way. Using fairly strict family income guidelines, Berea requires all students to have financial need in order to enter the college. Once there, students pay no tuition and, in the 2005–2006 school year, paid just under $5500 for room, board, and fees. Instead, they work 10 to 15 hours a week in various jobs around campus to pay their tuition as well as help to offset other costs. It's a deal many want but few get: just a fourth of those who seek admission to Berea are accepted.

Student body: Berea's enrollment is largely regional, by choice. In accordance with school policy, 80% of the students must be from the 8-state southern Appalachian region plus Kentucky. As a result, 36% of the 2005–2006 undergraduates were state residents, with mostly southerners among the 40 other states represented. All but 7% in a recent year attended public schools. Berea was founded in 1855 as the first interracial and coeducational college in the South and 150 years later, continues to mark steady increases in the racial and ethnic diversity of its student body. Nineteen percent are African-American, 2% Hispanic, and 1% each Asian-American and Native American. Seven percent are foreign nationals from 67 countries. Berea's enrollment of just over 1500 places students in a kind of "surrogate family" in which upper-classmen greet newcomers warmly and the college president knows many students by name. Although Berea is not affiliated with any specific religion, it has strong Christian roots, and many of the students are Christian, "as you can tell," says a freshman, "by the smile on their faces and the kind words they give to others." Students study a lot and are very concerned about getting good grades, but there is more cooperation than competition, with fellow undergraduates working as tutors, teaching and lab assistants, and peer counselors. "It is not possible to succeed at Berea without working hard," says a student from the northeast. "It is emphasized from the start that the student's first priority is to study."

Academics: Berea awards bachelor's degrees in 28 disciplines. The academic year is divided into 2 semesters plus a January term. Classes range in size from fewer than 6 in some upper-level courses to about 40 in Fundamentals of Nutrition, though most classes level out between 20 and 30.

As part of the 33 courses required for graduation (nursing students need 35) students have been required to take a sequence of required core classes beginning with "Stories: Encountering Others through Literature" and "U.S. Traditions: Texts of Freedom and Justice" in the freshman year and finishing with a senior seminar in "Christianity and Contemporary Culture." Also required have been courses in the natural and social sciences, quantitative reasoning, cultural studies, and lifetime wellness. But Berea expects more from its students than just specific coursework. Every term except the final 1 of the senior year, students have had to attend at least 7 convocation events, including lectures, symposia, and concerts of an intellectual, aesthetic, or religious nature. A revised general education program is to be implemented over the coming years; the program will have a continued emphasis on literacy but offer a different design.

All but 29 of the 159 faculty members are full-time; 41% of these full-time professors are women. Virtually all, too, are here because they believe in Berea's philosophy. Notes a family studies major: "Most faculty members are committed to the student. They expect quality work and, because of that, students perform better."

Berea's hands-on programs get the warmest applause from students. The nursing program is particularly demanding, with a tough faculty and curriculum and the benefits of a working hospital nearby. Chemistry and biology feature wonderful faculty who include students whenever possible in the teaching and learning process.

A minor only is offered in computer science, although interested students have designed their own independent majors in computer science and computer and information science. Majors in foreign language are limited to French, Spanish, German, and Classical Languages, but coursework has been available in Hebrew and sometimes in Japanese.

Facilities: The 3-story Hutchins Library contains almost 374,000 volumes (about 331,400 print volumes and 42,500 e-books) and 1508 periodicals. Recent remodeling has made the facility a more comfortable place to study, and a computerized catalog and several computerized indices to journal articles have increased the comfort level of research as well. A separate science library offers more specialized resources. Students in need of additional materials turn usually to interlibrary loan, although Eastern Kentucky University in Richmond is only 15 miles away, whenever a car is available.

For a $300 fee, Berea provides every student with a laptop computer. The fee goes toward helping to pay the cost of networking all residence hall rooms and classrooms and providing appropriate software and sufficient technical support. At the end of their third year, students exchange their laptops for a new model, which they can keep upon graduation. In addition, more than 150 networked microcomputers are available for student use: 70 in the college's 24-hour computer lab, recently added on to Hutchins Library, and the rest in various academic buildings and residence halls.

Special programs: During Berea's January term, students may enroll at a number of institutions, including Middlebury College in Vermont and Gustavus Adolphus College in Minnesota while paying room and board at Berea. Juniors may participate in a year-long exchange with Kansai Gaidai University in Osaka, Japan. Study abroad also can be arranged in numerous additional countries; 15% of all students spent time abroad in a recent school year. A 3-2 engineering program with the University of Kentucky or Washington University is available as well. Summer programs in most academic areas give students an opportunity to work full-time with professors engaged in research projects.

Campus life: Eighty-four percent of Berea's students reside on the 140-acre campus in the foothills of the Cumberland Mountains. Farmlands, including the experimental farms, piggery, and poultry farm, cover an additional 1200 acres. Part of the college's 7700-acre Fay Forest is reserved for the watershed that supplies the college and the town with water. The college also provides laundry service, printing, recreational facilities, and electricity for the community.

There are no fraternities or sororities, so weekend movies and dances are quite popular, as is open house in the single-sex dormitories. Students put their Christian faith into action through work with various service organizations, among them Students for Appalachia, which provides tutoring and outreach programs for the area. Berea's folk dance troupe, the Country Dancers, represents the college at festivals throughout the year. Since 1875, the entire campus has canceled classes 1 day each fall to celebrate Mountain Day, a time when students, faculty, and staff climb up the pinnacle in Fay Forest. When some undergraduates found the Berea campus a little too dark at night, better lighting was installed, and security officers took extra steps to make sure dormitory doors were not propped open for friends, thereby inviting other, unwelcome visitors.

Men's Mountaineers basketball is big at Berea. Men also compete in 4 other single-sex NAIA intercollegiate sports; there are women-only teams in 4 sports; and coed teams in swimming, golf, soccer, and cross country. A third of the men and 15% of the women in a recent year were involved in the 8 intramural sports available to each sex. Club sports also have gained in popularity.

Since Berea—the college, the town, and the surrounding county—is "dry," many students travel 15 miles north to the town of Richmond (pop. 22,000), which has bars. However, cars are viewed as a luxury (not necessary for travel around campus or to town), so only graduating seniors and nontraditional students are allowed to have them, which makes getting any distance away from campus particularly difficult.

Cost cutters: Berea's sizable endowment, $861 million as of June 2005, enables the school to hold true to its mission of educating only those who could not otherwise afford to attend college. Every student is guaranteed some way to pay for the true cost of one year at Berea, usually through federal and state grants, and private scholarship assistance averaging $26,190 for 2005–2006 freshmen, and $2800 in a recent year for his or her labor on campus. Any portion of the educational costs not covered by these outside funding sources is guaranteed by the college. In addition to the $2800 basic labor grant, all students are paid an hourly wage for 10–15 hours a week of work in the campus labor program. Specific jobs range from clerk to skilled computer programmer to director of an intramural athletic program. Students also run the Boone Tavern Hotel and Gift Shop, as well as the college farm. Thirty percent of the jobs are in academic areas, including the library and computer center, 20% in administrative offices, 10% in one of 5 craft areas, 10% in hotel management, and 10% in community service. Labor earnings beyond those of the basic $2800 grant can pay from 20% to 60% of the cost of room, board, and fees. The balance may come from the family and from the student's summer earnings. As a result, a recent graduate took home a diploma and just $7299 in debts.

Rate of return: Eighty-two percent of the freshmen who enter return for the sophomore year. Thirty-five percent go on to graduate in 4 years, 60% in 5 years, 62% in 6.

Payoff: Eleven percent of the 2005 graduates earned degrees in business administration, 9% in industrial technology management, and 8% in child and family studies. Seventy percent in a recent year accepted jobs immediately after graduation, many with major corporations such as IBM and Ashland Oil throughout the South and Southeast. Eighty to 100 companies and other organizations regularly recruit on campus. Other graduates go into teaching, nursing, and other service occupations. In a recent year, about 12% enrolled directly in graduate or professional schools. In a 56-year period, Berea produced more Ph.D.'s than any other 4-year college in its 9-state region.

Bottom line: "Berea is a small place with heart," observes a recent graduate. "A student with potential who was too shy or unaware of how to fulfill that potential in high school can fit in well here. A student who is used to getting everything and having it all will not."

Centre College

Danville, Kentucky 40422

Setting: Small town
Control: Private (Presbyterian)
Undergraduate enrollment: 509 men, 549 women
Graduate enrollment: None
Student/faculty ratio: 11:1
Freshman profile: 20% scored over 700 on SAT I verbal; 42% scored 600–700; 35% 500–599; 3% below 500. 12% scored over 700 on SAT I math; 44% scored 600–700; 35% 500–599; 9% below 500. 32% scored above 28 on the ACT; 20% scored 27–28; 33% 24–26; 13% 21–23; 2% below 21. 56% graduated in top tenth of high school class; 72% in upper fifth.

Faculty profile: 97% Ph.D.'s
Tuition and fees: $23,110
Room and board: $7700
Freshman financial aid: 90%; average scholarship or grant: NA
Campus jobs: 44%; average earnings: $1312/year
Application deadline: Feb. 1
Financial aid deadline: Feb. 15
Admissions information: (859) 238-5350; (800) 423-6236
e-mail: admission@centre.edu
web site: www.centre.edu

Among the Goliaths of American higher education, tiny Centre College in Kentucky's Bluegrass Country has always been the feisty David. With an enrollment of just over 1000, and a tuition that remains two-thirds the rates of other selective liberal arts colleges, Centre prefers to run with the big boys of academe. For much of the last 20 years, it has topped all colleges in the percentage of alumni who give money annually to their alma maters, and its endowment per student ranks among the top 100. It is one of the 3 smallest coeducational colleges in the nation to have a chapter of Phi Beta Kappa. The college also offers this commitment to all students who meet its academic and social expectations: completion of an internship, study abroad, and graduation in 4 years, or Centre provides the fifth year of study tuition free. Even Woodrow Wilson, then president of Princeton University, took note of the academic upstart in 1903 when he remarked: "There's a little college down in Kentucky which in 60 years graduated more men who have acquired prominence and fame than has Princeton in her 150 years." Beating Harvard 6-0 in a 1921 football game, often hailed as the greatest sports upset in the first half-century, only solidified Centre's indomitable spirit, and the winning formula C_6H_0 still mysteriously appears as graffiti on campus walls, a reminder never to count out this tiny titan.

Student body: Centre remains predominantly blue-grass rather than blue-blood, with 65% of its students from Kentucky. The largest group of out-of-staters comes from the South with a total of 38 states represented. Two-thirds of the students are graduates of public schools. Sixty-one percent are Protestant (10% Presbyterian) and 18% Catholic, with 1% each Jewish and members of other faiths. Nineteen percent claimed no religious affiliation. One of Centre's greatest weaknesses, in the eyes of socially conscious undergraduates, is its predominantly white student body, although the minority population has nearly doubled in the past few years. Three percent are Asian-American and 2% African-American. Sixteen students are foreign national from 7 countries. The freshman class that entered in fall 2005 contained one of the highest percentages of minority and international students in recent years, at 9%. Forty percent also were from outside Kentucky. Centre students tend to be politically moderate to conservative, highly motivated, intelligent, hard-working, and involved. Observes a sophomore: "Everyone is extremely involved, if not a leader in whatever activities he or she chooses to participate in." Because freshmen attracted to the college are used to being in the top slot, undergraduates are competitive, "but not in the traditional sense," continues the sophomore. "While students do wish to place above their classmates, it is less of a student-to-student competition and more of a personal competition. I would gladly encourage the person next to me in class to do well on an assignment but my first priority is to make sure that I meet my own personal standards."

Academics: Centre, which was founded by pioneer Presbyterians in 1819, offers bachelor's degrees in 25 majors, plus student-designed concentrations. The 4-1-4 calendar allows students to take 4 courses each in the 13-week fall and spring terms and 1 course in the winter term. Entering freshmen can expect an average class size of 17, rarely, if ever, over 30 (the largest class, Anthropology II, has 50), with classes naturally getting smaller as students progress to higher levels.

Entering students begin their general education coursework by demonstrating competency in 3 areas: expository writing, mathematics, and foreign language, either through coursework or test scores. Students also must show expertise beyond a basic level by taking a more advanced class in either foreign language, mathematics, or computer science. All undergraduates take a Freshman Studies course with no more than 14 classmates, plus 2 courses each in the humanities, society, science, and fundamental questions. Students must round out their Centre experience by attending a certain number of designated campus events every semester to earn 12 convocation credits a year.

The 88 full-time and 10 part-time faculty, 42% of whom are women, are highly rated by students as Renaissance men and women who are well-spoken and intelligent, and not just in their particular fields. Remarks a senior: "Their degrees and genuine interest in educating students make them not only wonderful teachers but also friends who visit and make house calls!" One student who overslept and failed to appear for a history final was surprised when his "house call" involved the professor and the entire class coming by to wake him up for the test! Adds a government major: "Overall, the faculty receives an A from me, although they rarely give As. Their experience and dedication blow me away time and time again."

Innovative professors who teach creatively with much enthusiasm help to make the humanities some of Centre's strongest disciplines. The English faculty win acclaim for their "sheer quality of instruction," with similar kudos going to peers in philosophy, religion ("phenomenal"), and classical studies. "Every professor that I have had in history and government has been incredible," adds an English major, while others say equally admiring words about the faculties and coursework in economics, international studies, and psychology. The winter-term Congressional Simulation in the government department is the talk of the campus. Mathematics and the life and physical sciences are not to be outdone, with reputations as the most strenuous courses of study but ones that impressively prepare their majors for medical or graduate schools. "Students are always involved in independent studies, internships, interviews, fellowships, scholarships, etc.," says a major in biochemistry and molecular biology. "The faculty inspire and encourage every chance they get." Olin Hall for the physical, mathematical, and computer sciences, which opened in 1988, is a superbly equipped facility for a school of 1000 undergraduates. In the art department, the glass-blowing program is exceptional. The music program, though small, boasts excellent professors, including Vince DiMartino, an internationally known trumpet player and teacher.

Still needing improvement, according to some students is the foreign language program, where some students say the emphasis on foreign language proficiency for a large number of students has meant less time for the faculty to provide extensive opportunities for in-depth study. Majors are available in French, Spanish, and German studies. Says a junior: "Centre has one of the best study-abroad programs, but its foreign language program is lacking." Students looking for more career-oriented majors such as nursing, communications or business and accounting will not find them offered here, but that doesn't deter resourceful Centre students. Reports one student who initially was disappointed to find no public relations or broadcast journalism major: "To fulfill my broadcast journalism desires, I helped start a Centre television station on campus."

Facilities: At a college so small, Doherty Library has its faults as a place for concentrated work because, in the words of a sophomore, "everyone knows everyone else so that very often the library becomes a place to gather socially, rather than to study." Recently completed renovation of the library has brought additional space for 80,000 volumes, greater technological offerings, and a bit more elbowroom. The current collection stands at almost 218,000 volumes and 2076 paper and electronic periodicals. Any materials the Centre library doesn't have, the staff works diligently to obtain through a speedy interlibrary loan program, or students head directly to the University of Kentucky library.

One hundred fifty PCs are networked and available in the residence halls, classroom buildings, and the library. Most labs are open around the clock, and students with their own personal computers have 24-hour access to the Internet and e-mail, as well as the library's databases. Wireless access is available in the library, dining hall, student center, and other areas.

Special programs: For many students, Centre's opportunities for study out of Danville are among its outstanding features with about 75% of all Centre undergraduates studying abroad at least once in their 4 years on campus. Centre has opened its own residential study programs in Merida, Mexico; London, England; and Strasbourg, France, and continues to offer summer study at Oxford through membership in the Associated Colleges of the South. Extensive travel/study programs examining everything from the art, music, and architecture of 4 major European cities to tropical ecology in the Galapagos Islands are led by Centre faculty during the winter term. Centre also participates in a 3-2 engineering program with the University of Kentucky and Vanderbilt, Columbia, and Washington universities.The John C. Young Scholars program enables selected seniors to engage in independent study and research. A semester of study in Washington, D.C. is an option through The American University.

Campus life: Ninety-five percent of Centre's students reside on the 115-acre campus, which includes 9 recently constructed Greek houses in Greek Park, which, in turn, adjoins a renovated hemp warehouse that has become the 3-story student center. Much of the weekend activity focuses on these new sites; all Greek parties are open to everyone, but when the student activities council sponsors an event at the warehouse, no Greek parties can take place. Fifty-eight percent of Centre's men and 65% of the women belong to 5 national fraternities and 4 national sororities. Says a senior: "Fraternities and sororities are very popular—but not exclusive. It's very common to see people from different Greek organizations hanging out together along with non-Greek students." A popular student group, known as CARE (Centre Action Reaches Everyone), provides tutoring and friendship to children, the elderly, and other needy people in the Danville area. The *Cento*, the student newspaper, and various Christian fellowship groups also draw a lot of student interest and participation. Though Danville (pop. 18,000) is a small town, students say the lack of serious crime is not taken for granted, and security measures such as a swipe card system for all dorm and classroom building doors and additional emergency phones serve as deterrents. With the police and fire stations just 2 blocks away, "This place is safer than Whoville," remarks a midwesterner.

When Centre students aren't studying or partying, they're usually involved in some athletic competition, either intercollegiate or intramural. Half of the men and women participate in the 9 varsity sports offered to men and 10 to women. The Colonels compete in NCAA Division III, with football and men's and women's soccer and basketball drawing the most fervent crowds. Such crowds include a fan fondly known as "Dead Fred," the portrait of a deceased alumnus who attends all football games with brothers from his old fraternity house. Eighty percent of the men and 70% of the women get involved in 15 intramural activities.

The impressive Norton Center for the Arts provides big-city entertainment, such as Harry Connick, Jr., Willie Nelson, and the Broadway musical *Cats* right on campus at no extra charge to students. For other big-city activities, students head 35 minutes northeast to Lexington, home of the University of Kentucky, or a bit over an hour northwest to Louisville.

Cost cutters: Centre's continued strong alumni giving (61% contribute) and its large endowment ($162 million as of June 2005) combine to help keep tuition low and financial aid acceptably high. Ninety percent of freshmen and continuing students in a recent school year received financial aid; 70% of the first-year students and 66% of the rest got need-based assistance. The average freshman award totaled $17,922, with no breakdown provided on the portion that was scholarship or grant monies or loans and job earnings. The average financial indebtedness of a recent graduate was $14,300. Centre offers renewable merit scholarships to more than 50% of each freshman class. Trustee Scholarships, which go to the most outstanding students, pay full costs of tuition, room, and board. President's Scholarships pay the cost of tuition; other awards start at $5000 a year. Fine Arts Scholarships pay $2500 and $5000 a year. For added help, Centre offers an interest-free 10-payment tuition plan.

Rate of return: Ninety percent of the freshmen who enter return for the sophomore year. Sixty-five percent graduate in 4 years; 77%, within 6 years.

Payoff: Forty-two percent of recent graduates earned degrees in history/social science, 15% in biology, and 11% in English. Just over a third opt to pursue advanced degrees within 6 months of graduation. Within 5 years of leaving Centre, three-fourths seek further study. In the last 40 years, Centre has graduated two-thirds of the state's Rhodes Scholars; in the last 10 years, the college has had 23 Fulbright winners. A majority of Centre graduates take jobs shortly after graduation, many with firms in the Southeast and Midwest.

Bottom line: Amid the rush toward vocationally oriented majors at other colleges, Centre holds firm to the traditional liberal arts. Notes a state resident: "Centre upholds the academic tradition of the northeast while providing the hospitality of the South in a beautiful campus environment." Good time-management and social skills are mandatory, though, on such a small campus where being involved is a way of life.

Georgetown College

Georgetown, Kentucky 40324

Setting: Suburban
Control: Private (Baptist)
Undergraduate enrollment: 586 men, 723 women
Graduate enrollment: 13 men, 33 women (441 part-time)
Student/faculty ratio: 12:1
Freshman profile: 10% scored above 28 on the ACT; 11% scored 27–28; 26% 24–26; 31% 21–23; 22% below 21. 27% graduated in top tenth of high school class; 49% in upper fifth.
Faculty profile: 86% Ph.D.'s
Tuition and fees: $19,170

Room and board: $5780
Freshman financial aid: 98%; average scholarship or grant: $14,359 need-based; $9139 non-need-based
Campus jobs: 40%; average earnings: $1200/year
Application deadline: Rolling (Early decision: Dec. 1; Recommended: Feb. 15)
Financial aid deadline: Mar. 1 (Priority: Feb. 1)
Admissions information: (502) 863-8009; (800) 788-9985
e-mail: admissions@georgetowncollege.edu
web site: www.georgetowncollege.edu

You won't find its basketball games on national television, its library contains only 152,500 volumes instead of 2.3 million, and the town for which it was named has just about as many people as attend the more prestigious university of the same name in the nation's capital. But for $25,000 including tuition, fees, room, and board, in the 2005–2006 school year, just over half the price of the other Georgetown, students at Georgetown College, a Baptist school in Georgetown, Kentucky, get a solid liberal arts education that has produced 34 college and university presidents, 5 Rhodes Scholars, a one-time advisor to a U.S. president, a U.S. congressman, and a proud claim: no Georgetown premed student has ever quit or flunked out of medical school. Notes a junior: "Georgetown makes its students feel that they are capable of achieving whatever they want"—and many do!

Student body: Regardless of what dreams Georgetown alumni go on to pursue, more than three-quarters, 84%, begin their quest as residents of Kentucky. Twenty-two other states mostly in the Midwest, are also represented. Ninety percent of the students attended public schools. Just 7% of the undergraduates are foreign nationals or members of racial or ethnic minority groups: 4% African-Americans, and 1% each foreign nationals from 8 countries, Asian-Americans and Hispanics. Students "range from the 4.0 bookworm to the every-weekend partyer," in the words of one observer, but as a whole are inclined to be politically conservative to moderate in their beliefs. Forty-two percent of the undergraduates are Baptist; 78% belong to some Protestant denomination, 12% are Catholic, 6% claim no religious affiliation, the rest, some other. Notes a sophomore: "I expected the school to be less progressive in its thinking because of the Baptist affiliation but am excited about the level of open-mindedness I have found. The Christian atmosphere also makes students more friendly and responsible." The result is an academic environment described by one senior as "relatively competitive," in which students readily balance their studies, social activities, and faith commitments.

Academics: Georgetown, founded in 1829, awards bachelor's degrees in 43 disciplines and the master's degree in education. Its academic year is divided into 2 semesters, plus a 3-week miniterm that follows each semester. The average class size is 18. Only 6% of classes have 30 or more students, and no more than one class each semester has more than 40. The average class size for first-year students is about 20; for seniors, about 10. Boasts a senior: "I have had 3 professors who have had their entire classes over for dinner!"

Fifty-six semester hours of general-education coursework is required, including classes from 7 areas: effective communication, Christian faith and values, cultural and aesthetic values, foreign language and culture, natural sciences, social sciences, and physical education. All students must also take comprehensive examinations, written, oral, or both, regardless of the major. Many find the general-education courses, which fulfill nearly half the 128 credits needed to graduate, to be harder than some classes for the major. "Our requirements are tough," says a junior, "and sometimes wake freshmen up to the fact that college is an academic place." Students also are required to attend before graduation 48 cocurricular events. They may choose among such events as lectures, concerts, forums, and worship services.

Georgetown's faculty consists of 109 full-time members and 72 part-timers. All teach undergraduates. Forty-three percent are women. Most professors manage to strike a good balance between being friendly with students and maintaining an air of respect and authority in the classroom, "a toughness, as scholars developing scholars," in the words of 1 senior. The results, in many cases, have proved exciting to students. Observes a music major: "I am not a morning person, but I got stuck with a 9 a.m. biology class.

This professor made the class worth getting up for. Now that's a great teacher!" Adds a psychology major, "The faculty is the reason a liberal arts education is so appealing."

Biology, chemistry, and environmental science are but 3 of Georgetown's excellent programs; majors face strenuous curricula that have gained a large number of their predecessors entrance to medical school and other graduate programs. Chemistry students are especially proud that 1 professor has written the organic and basic chemistry textbooks he uses in his classes—"an excellent opportunity to study with the author," says an American studies major. The religion department, says an English major, "is very open-minded and challenges students to explore their beliefs." English and history both feature a good variety of fine professors; English faculty members include an internationally recognized Renaissance scholar. Philosophy's top teachers attract competitive students "who encourage and strengthen each other," says a history major. Education is widely respected for giving students plenty of in-the-classroom experience as early as the freshman year. Psychology offers a wide variety of courses and knowledgeable faculty who use teaching approaches other than lectures to get students excited about the material.

Majors that students find to be weaker are generally those with too few faculty members to offer sufficient variety of courses and perspectives on a discipline. Included on this list are physics, art, theater, French, and German. The third foreign language major, Spanish, recently gained additional faculty members. The communications faculty is regarded by some students as being too lax and disorganized, which sometimes makes their classes seem unproductive and too broad in their scope. The interdisciplinary women's studies program, established in 2001, is offered only as a minor.

Facilities: Fall 1998 brought with it completion of the $12 million Anna Ashcraft Ensor Learning Resource Center, a much-awaited replacement for the dimly lit, oft-crowded former library. "An excellent place to study," says a senior. A "magnificent four-floor structure," raves a history major. Students hope an expansion of the book collection, standing at almost 164,000 volumes is next. While the paper selection of periodicals also is small at less than 750 subscriptions, the addition of electronic sources raises the total subscriptions to a more satisfactory 32,500. For those times when the extensive computerized research systems fail to provide what students need, Georgetown's on-line catalog also lists the holdings at the University of Kentucky, which is just 15 minutes away.

About 200 PCs are available in the library and departmental labs. Hours in the main labs are from 8 a.m. to midnight, weekdays. Undergraduates with their own computers may access the network from their dorm rooms.

Special programs: For students interested in spending all or part of the junior year abroad, Georgetown offers an exchange program with the University of Caen in France, and also participates in an assortment of other programs taking students to Vienna, Madrid, Paris, Nanjing, and Mexico, to name just a few sites. A program with Regent's Park College at the University of Oxford enables Georgetown students to participate in a year of study at Oxford or complete 1 of 2 six-year ministerial education programs, earning degrees from both institutions. A 3-2 engineering program is offered with the University of Kentucky and Washington University. A similar joint-study program for nursing students is available with the University of Kentucky. The Harper Gatton Leadership Medallion Program provides a 5-semester leadership development program for sophomores, juniors, and seniors who are interested in exploring issues of leadership and ethics. Through the program, participants network with campus and community leaders. In 2001, the college added a Center for Commerce, Language, and Culture. The program prepares undergraduates to enter the global business world by offering them a sound foundation in business and economic principles, fluency in a second language, and greater understanding of the culture behind the global market and business world.

Campus life: All but 7% of Georgetown's undergraduates live on the 104-acre campus, and more are staying there over the weekend, thanks to a concerted effort by both the administration and student government to provide more campus activities. Twenty-five percent of the men and 35% of the women belong to 1 local and 4 national fraternities and 4 national sororities. All have houses on "the quad," though many host Greek events that are open to independents. The Baptist Student Union and Habitat for Humanity are 2 of the most popular and active organizations. While chapel is not required, students may fulfill some of their cocurricular credits by attending worship services. A business fraternity also keeps quite busy and competes annually at the national level. Likewise, the Georgetown Varsity Academic Team won its fifth league championship in 8 years in 2003, its third consecutive title. (The team placed 2nd in 2004 and 3rd in 2005.) Campus traditions include exchanges of serenades between the men's and women's residence halls throughout the year, as well as an annual scholarship pageant in which women compete for the title "Miss Belle of the Blue." Campus crime is not a problem and is not likely to become one if administrators can prevent it; added security measures include more lighting and emergency phones, and, on the inside hallway doors of all dormitories, locks to which only floor residents have keys. Campus safety officers walk students to their dorms after dark.

Attending a Georgetown Tiger football game is always a big event, especially since the team is usually ranked in the top 10 of NAIA Division II competition and were national division champions in both 2001 and 2000. Men's basketball, soccer, and the nationally ranked women's volleyball team also draw crowds to their home games. Altogether, Georgetown fields 5 men's, 5 women's, and 3 coed varsity sports. Teams for intramural sports, 11 for men, 11 for women, represent various dormitories and dorm floors, faculty-staff combinations, and commuting students. Forty-three percent of the men and 15% of the women participate. The campus also is the site of the Cincinnati Bengals training camp.

Lexington, with terrific shopping, dance clubs, horse racing, and the goings-on of the University of Kentucky, is the nearest big city, just 12 miles south. Louisville is about 60 miles west; Cincinnati, nearly equidistant north. Around Georgetown (pop. 11,000) a popular spot for quiet reflection is a duck pond at the Kentucky Horse Farm, located a few minutes from campus.

Cost cutters: In the 2005–2006 school year, 98% of the freshmen and 97% of the continuing students received financial aid; for about 65% of all undergraduates, the aid was need-based. The average freshman award for first-year students with need included a need-based scholarship or grant averaging $14,359 and need-based self-help aid such as loans and jobs averaging $3652. Non-need-based athletic scholarships for first-year students averaged $5704; other non-need-based awards and scholarships averaged $9139. Average debt of a 2005 graduate was $15,081. Trustees Scholarships cover from $5000 up to full tuition, fees, room, and board for students with first-rate academics. Valedictorians can receive $9000 a year. The Pastors' Christian Leadership Scholarship, which is based on church and community service, provides 10 awards worth $2500, and another 80 awards worth $1000 each. Bagby "Scholarship-Loans" are provided with the understanding that recipients will pay them back when, and if, they can. On-campus work is readily available as is off-campus work in community service.

Rate of return: Eighty-five percent of Georgetown freshmen return for the sophomore year. Forty-six percent go on to graduate in 4 years, 59% in 5 years; 61% in 6. Some leave because they find the school too conservative, others, not as conservative as they would like.

Payoff: Sixteen percent of 2005 graduates earned bachelor's degrees in business, 10% each in communications arts and psychology. About half of all graduates go directly to graduate, law, or medical school at least part-time while working. The vast majority immediately enter the job market, most often in business, government, or education.

Bottom line: Georgetown offers little to students looking either for an "anything-goes" environment or for an ultraconservative Bible college. Says a recent graduate: "Students here are pushed to educate themselves, not fill a space. This college helped me to reach deep within myself and to find these abilities and energies I didn't even know I had."

Transylvania University

Lexington, Kentucky 40508

Setting: Urban
Control: Private (Disciples of Christ)
Undergraduate enrollment: 452 men, 683 women
Graduate enrollment: None
Student/faculty ratio: 14:1
Freshman profile: 15% scored over 700 on SAT I verbal; 35% scored 600–700; 35% 500–599; 15% below 500. 11% scored over 700 on SAT I math; 39% scored 600–700; 33% 500–599; 17% below 500. 29% scored above 28 on the ACT; 23% scored 27–28; 27% 24–26; 15% 21–23; 6% below 21. 50% graduated in top tenth of high school class; 76% in upper fifth.
Faculty profile: 97% Ph.D.'s

Tuition and fees: $19,650
Room and board: $6590
Freshman financial aid: 99%; average scholarship or grant: $12,719 need-based; $11,890 non-need-based
Campus jobs: 29%; average earnings: $1265/year
Application deadline: Early decision: Dec. 1; regular: Feb. 1
Financial aid deadline: Scholarships: Dec. 1 and Feb. 1; other: Mar. 1
Admissions information: (859) 233-8242; (800)TRANSY U (872-6798)
e-mail: admissions@transy.edu
web site: www.transy.edu

In introducing Transylvania University in Lexington, Kentucky, it may be easier to start with what this small college of about 1150 full-time students is not: it is not the alma mater of Count Dracula. Its name means "across the woods" in Latin and refers to the university's location in the vast settlement region called Transylvania by a pioneer land company whose chief scout was Daniel Boone. The university's prestigious alumni, dating back to its founding in 1780 as the first college west of the Allegheny Mountains, include Jefferson Davis, the president of the Confederacy; 2 U.S. vice presidents; 50 U.S. senators; and 36 governors—but no known vampires. The students of today are bright and energetic, and more so each year, as greater numbers of top high school seniors hear of and compete for prestigious full-tuition scholarships presented to each entering class. "If you come here, you can make great jokes about vampires and Dracula," acknowledges a student from neighboring Ohio, "but Transy is very challenging academically and students are competitive with each other."

Student body: The lure of these scholarships remains strongest in Transy's old Kentucky home, with 79% of the students in a recent year drawn from in-state. Mostt of the rest also are southerners, although 35 states and 1 foreign country have students on campus. Fifteen percent attended private or parochial schools. Minority enrollment at the university is low, with 2% each African-American and Asian-American students and 1% Hispanic. There was a single international student in the 2005-2006 school year. The Diversity Action Council helps to make the predominantly white student body more aware of minority undergraduates' concerns. Nine percent of the enrollment are members of the Christian Church (Disciples of Christ). Fifty percent are affiliated with other Protestant denominations; 18% are Catholic, 1% are Jewish, 1% are Mormon, Muslim, Orthodox, and Buddhist. The rest claim no religious affiliation. Students use words like *motivated* and *eclectic* to describe their classmates, with political viewpoints ranging from very conservative to "highly liberal." However, as 1 senior observes, "At Transy it's really easy to get lost in studying and all the other social aspects of school and just lose touch with what's going on in the world." Indeed, academics and involvement in after-class activities vie for students' attention. "Almost everyone is active in more than 2 or 3 organizations," notes another junior. "Many people strive for both high academic rank and social standing, which are the top priorities on campus."

Academics: Transylvania offers the bachelor's degree in 25 majors plus the option of a student-designed concentration. Coursework is divided between 2 semesters, followed by a May term. Students can expect to find an average class with 18 students, although the range can extend from 2 in classical mechanics to 36 in general chemistry. Most general-education courses enroll between 25 and 30 students.

Students begin their general-education coursework with a Foundations of the Liberal Arts program that emphasizes group discussion and analysis of seemingly unrelated reading material. Says a junior, "It challenges each student to think differently about the world around him or her." From that beginning, students take additional courses that include among them the study of Western and non-Western tradition, fine arts, foreign language, natural science, and mathematics and computer science. The program used to take up half of the courses required for graduation, but modified requirements enable students to have time to take a major and a minor or simply enjoy more electives. Most majors have capstone course requirements.

Fifteen of the 97 faculty members are part-time. Sixty-three percent are men. Some professors emerge as better teachers; others take more active parts in student activities. Most, however, make extra efforts to be accessible to students and try whenever possible to make coursework more meaningful by relating it to issues in the workplace and the world. Says a psychology major: "The professors understand that learning is facilitated not through monotony but innovation. They can be friends, advisors, or purely instructors as the individual student chooses."

The programs in accounting and business administration, especially the concentration in hospitality management, all housed in a new building, naturally benefit most from the real-world emphasis, as well as the latest in 21st-century instructional aids. Many classrooms have ceiling projectors that can show computer programs, Internet information, videos, and other information sources on a screen for the entire class to view. Other classrooms have computers at each desk so that an individual's work can be projected and discussed by the entire class. Chemistry and biology feature high-caliber faculties who expect students to understand their fields thoroughly before contemplating medical school. Such thorough preparation enables more than 90% of all students who apply to medical school to gain admission. Professors in history, economics, political science, psychology, and philosophy lend their varied experiences and perspectives to stimulating classroom discussions. Those students who opt to take their arguments to law school find an acceptance rate of close to 100%. Several faculty members in the English department have received the university's Bingham Award for excellent teachers; as individuals, says a major, "the professors have very different styles of teaching but all work together so well." Computer science is considered a winner also.

Anthropology, sociology, and foreign languages have been plagued by limited student interest and few resources. Anthropology became its own major separate from sociology in fall 2003, which students had hoped would mean steadily growing resources and student interest. Foreign language majors include French language and literature, Spanish language and literature, and teaching majors in these fields. German is offered only as a minor though a special major can be arranged. Religion and communication, the latter offered only as a minor, are 2 programs that could benefit from having more faculty members.

Though no fine arts program is especially large, drama majors are disappointed in the low number of professors (2) and limited variety of their classes; many of the college's productions, however, are excellent and gained an added flair after being staged in a new high-tech theater that opened in 1999.

Facilities: Transy's library complex is modern but small with just 120,000 volumes but 12,000 paper and electronic periodicals. Computerized research aids offer both book and periodical searches, some of which show the resources available at the University of Kentucky libraries. The university itself is but 5 minutes away by free Transy shuttle bus, making an on-site search for materials convenient as well. A tendency to socialize rather than study at the Transy facility can be avoided by hiding in the stacks or various study rooms.

Just over 260 PCs are available for student use in 8 laboratories spread among all academic buildings and residence halls. The labs in the dormitories are open around the clock. "You only have to wait if there is a paper due in the freshman English class," says a senior. Students also can access the campus network and Internet from their dorm rooms. The university strongly recommends that undergraduates bring their own computers, preferably a model that can run Windows XP; most of the students do. There also are 30 wireless access points around campus.

Special programs: Transylvania's membership in the Spring Term Consortium enables students to spend the month of May at other colleges across the country that have a 1-month year-end term. Other off-campus programs available for May, a summer, a semester, or a year are offered in Spain, England, and various other European centers, as well as in Mexico, in the nation's capital, and in the Kentucky legislature. A 3-2 engineering program is offered with the University of Kentucky and Washington and Vanderbilt universities.

Campus life: Seventy-six percent of Transy students reside on the 48-acre campus, located within a few blocks of downtown Lexington. Greek life is a high priority, with 50% of both the men and the women belonging to 4 national fraternities and 4 national sororities, none of which has separate houses but instead floors of the upper-class residence halls. Most leadership positions around campus are held by Greeks, a situation that contributes to a feeling among some independents of being left out. Those not involved in Greek life or invited as guests to the weekend parties are more likely to hang out with friends or head for home after Friday classes end, though more are finding reasons to stay on campus. "Something always seems to be going on," says a junior, "and if it is not, you can make something happen because you know everyone." Popular student groups include Alternative Spring Break, which organizes students to perform community service somewhere in the U.S. during spring vacation, and various Christian fellowship groups. Although the neighborhood surrounding Transy is not considered very safe, students say they feel secure, thanks to surveillance cameras, emergency telephones, 24-hour car, foot, and bicycle patrols by campus police, and security alarms in some residence halls. A neighborhood watch program also exists in the dormitories.

One in every 4 Transy students is a varsity athlete. Pioneer basketball is the most popular and most successful sport, with invitations to at least 16 NCAA/NAIA postseason tournaments. Transylvania recently began competing in NCAA Division III, after years of impressive play in NAIA competition. In a recent year, men's soccer, women's tennis, men's and women's basketball, and men's and women's swimming all earned NAIA playoff berths. In 1999, the women's soccer team was national runner-up, after compiling a 23-1 record. Despite the Pioneers' winning ways, students say that crowds for games other than basketball and women's soccer are rarely very large or very spirited with many Transy fans preferring to watch the bigger school sports at the University of Kentucky. A number also turn out to watch the men's intramural football games. Eighty percent of the men and 60% of the women participate in the 10 men's and 10 women's intramural sports offered. A new athletic and recreation center opened for spring 2002. A new field for women's soccer and softball opened in 1996; a new baseball field 10 minutes north of campus was dedicated in 2000.

A day watching the horses at Keeneland Race Track or simply driving through the local bluegrass horse country provides a good study break. Other students prefer hiking the Red River Gorge, about an hour southeast. Lexington (pop. 260,000) as home to the University of Kentucky offers its own share of cultural diversions, but many find Cincinnati, 80 miles north, and Louisville, 80 miles west, excellent changes of scenery.

Cost cutters: In the 2005–2006 school year, 99% of all freshman and 98% of continuing students received financial aid; about 60% of both groups received need-based assistance. The average freshman award for first-year students with financial need included a need-based scholarship or grant averaging $12,719 and need-based self-help aid such as loans and jobs averaging $4124. Other non-need-based awards and scholarships averaged $11,890. The average indebtedness of a 2005 graduate who received loans was

$15,673. The most highly coveted award at Transylvania is the William T. Young Scholarship, which pays full tuition and fees to a select group of freshmen every year, renewable over 4 years if a GPA of at least 3.5 is maintained. To be considered for the Young scholarship, students must apply for admission by Dec. 1. Those who are selected as Young finalists are required to complete an additional essay and attend an on-campus interview. Financial need is not a consideration for this award, which is based primarily on the student's academic record. W. T. Young finalists can receive $10,000 renewable President's Scholarships, also based on merit. Other merit-based awards pay $6000 to $8500 annually. The Bryden Scholarship program benefits students from southern Appalachia who show academic promise and have financial need. Concludes a senior: "The many scholarships make a Transylvania education very affordable." Ten-month and installment payment plans are available.

Rate of return: Eighty-nine percent of entering freshmen like what they find at Transylvania and return for a second year. Sixty-five percent graduate in 4 years; 70%, in 5 years.

Payoff: Seventeen percent of the 2005 graduating class earned degrees in business administration, followed by majors in biology at 13%, and psychology at 8%. About 40% enroll in graduate or professional schools. Most of the rest take jobs immediately upon graduation, many as computer programmers, auditors, and sales representatives with firms like Peat Marwick, Coopers & Lybrand, IBM, Humana, and Ferguson Enterprises. Most alumni settle in the South and Midwest.

Bottom line: While Transylvania will always evoke its share of ghoulish jokes, its educational offerings strike straight at the heart of undergraduate excellence. Notes a senior: "I have been excited by the dedication of the faculty and the intellectual stimulation of the classroom. One of the strong points of a liberal arts education is that it offers students the chance to explore a variety of different subjects, however, this can also be a weakness. I was introduced to ideas that I would have loved to explore more, but there just was not time."

Louisiana

Centenary College of Louisiana

Shreveport, Louisiana 71104

Setting: Urban
Control: Private (United Methodist)
Undergraduate enrollment: 334 men, 548 women
Graduate enrollment: 2 men, 11 women (127 part-time)
Student/faculty ratio: 12:1
Freshman profile: 11% scored over 700 on SAT I verbal; 37% scored 600–700; 30% 500–599; 22% below 500. 2% scored over 700 on SAT I math; 37% scored 600–700; 39% 500–599; 22% below 500. Median ACT composite: 25. 40% graduated in top tenth of high school class; 61% in upper fifth.
Faculty profile: 94% Ph.D.'s
Tuition and fees: $18,390

Room and board: $6370
Freshman financial aid: 98%; average scholarship or grant: $10,880 need-based; $9395 non-need-based
Campus jobs: 21%; average earnings: $1606/year
Application deadline: Early decision: Dec. 1; Early action: Jan. 15; regular: Feb. 15
Financial aid deadline: Feb. 15
Admissions information: (318) 869-5131; (800) 234-4440
e-mail: tcrowley@centenary.edu
web site: www.centenary.edu

At tiny Centenary College in Shreveport, Louisiana, "crowded" can mean a class pushing 30 or more students. The student/faculty ratio, already a low 12:1, drops below 8:1 when part-time faculty members are considered. With a full-time undergraduate student body of 882 members and fewer than 25 part-timers, Centenary may be smaller than many high schools in the United States—but it is big in some unexpected places. Centenary "plays" with the big boys, as its athletic teams compete in NCAA Division I, though, not surprisingly, the college is the smallest Division I school. As part of its graduation requirements, Centenary "thinks" big, expecting that each of its students will complete a community service project and participate in at least 1 experience of living and learning in another culture. But best of all, say students, Centenary views its undergraduates as individual members of a single, big family that requires plenty of attention. "Many people know me personally," says a sophomore, "the administration, staff, faculty, everybody, and that makes me feel good. This *is* my home away from home."

Student body: More than half of Centenary's students did not venture far from their real home to enroll: 62% are from Louisiana, with 92% of the out-of-staters also from the South. A total of 31 states and 13 foreign countries have students in attendance. Twenty-one percent are Methodist. Thirty-nine percent are members of other Protestant denominations; 20% are Catholic. Six percent are Unitarian and other faiths, 14% claim no religious affiliation. Seven percent are African-American, 4% Hispanic, 3% Asian-American, and 1% Native American. Foreign nationals comprise 2%. A fourth of the students in a recent year attended private or parochial schools. Students see themselves as more liberal-minded than conservative, determined, ambitious, and prepared to work hard, but not to the exclusion of all parties and fun, to achieve their academic and career goals. "This is definitely not a campus for people who stay to themselves," says a freshman. "Everyone here is very open and friendly."

Academics: Centenary, which was founded as the College of Louisiana in 1825, awards the bachelor's degree in 43 majors plus master's degrees in business administration and education. Its calendar follows a semester schedule, with a 3-week May module that begins at the end of the spring term. Most classes range between 10 and 15 students, with the largest class, in cell biology, enrolling about 50. "As a sophomore, I have a class with only 4 people," raves a southerner. "It's awesome."

The core curriculum, along with requiring students to experience different cultures at home or abroad and to donate their time to others, has subject-matter expectations as well. Undergraduates must take courses from the traditional academic areas as well as classes at the junior level that demonstrate proficiency in writing and speaking. Sophomores must participate in a program that helps them to choose a major and formulate some career decisions; seniors must take a seminar in the major they have chosen. All students also must attend 20 cultural events on the campus or in the community.

Centenary's faculty are instrumental in making the family feeling work, and most make it a point to know the names of all their students within the first few weeks of the semester. Seventy-two of the 122 faculty members are full-time. All of the full-time members teach undergraduates, as do 42 of the 50 part-timers.

Forty percent are women. Their grade from the students: an "A–"; the "A" for all their intelligence and encouragement; the "minus" for those few professors who could use more effective teaching methods.

Personal attention from professors has traditionally more than compensated for a lack of the most up-to-date facilities and equipment in some departments, although several renovation projects around campus have enabled faculty to become even more effective in their teaching. Biology and chemistry, for example, have long boasted medical school acceptance rates of 80%; recent remodeling of the science building has helped make the lab instruction even more rewarding. English (with its newly renovated building), physics, political science, religion, education, and business also are admired for having faculty who present a demanding curricula but are devoted to helping their students excel in it. Centenary was one of the first liberal arts colleges in the nation to offer an undergraduate degree in biophysics, and its tough curriculum, designed in consultation with major research universities and medical institutions around the country, shows it. Geology students benefit from the college's location in a geographic region whose economy is tied to oil and natural gas. Music boasts a superb choir and facilities to match, though some students say the program for stringed instruments needs to be made more rigorous. The Church Careers Institute, which prepares students for professional ministry, is the only such program offered at the undergraduate level.

Mathematics and computer science need both more up-to-date equipment and more and better professors. Computer science, a popular major at many schools, is offered only as a minor at Centenary. Other smaller departments such as psychology could also use more professors and greater diversity in course offerings.

Facilities: Magale Library is considered "passable" as a place to study and do research, although its collection of 180,000 volumes and 942 periodicals is healthy for a school of Centenary's size. "The atmosphere is quiet and relaxing and you will rarely be disturbed," says a biology major. Computerized resources include subscriptions to about 46,400 on-line full-text periodicals and 241 databases. Interlibrary loan further fills in the research gaps as does the Louisiana State University branch campus in Shreveport and the LSU Medical College, just a 5-minute drive.

Twenty-one fully networked computer labs give students access to some 300 computers throughout campus. Seven of the labs housing more than 130 units are based in Magale Library. Night owls and procrastinators wish the facilities were open past midnight though computers in the residence halls are available around the clock. The college strongly recommends that students have their own personal computers. Wireless access in the 2005–2006 school year was available in the library, in Jackson Hall, an academic building, and in the newly renovated student union.

Special programs: Through partnerships with other colleges, Centenary students can further broaden their experiences at any time of the year by participating during the summer in a British studies program at Oxford; taking a semester's instruction in classical studies in Rome; spending a year or a term in Denmark or a year at a university in France or Germany to name just a few options. Stateside, a semester in Washington, D.C., or at Oak Ridge National Laboratory in Tennessee also is possible. Dual degree programs in engineering are offered with 6 universities including Louisiana Tech, Washington, and Case Western Reserve universities. A 3-1 degree program in communications disorders is available with Louisiana State University Medical Center.

Campus life: All full-time students, except those who are married, living at home with their parents, or seniors 21 or over, are required to live in student housing as members of the Centenary family. The 65-acre campus, located 2 miles south of downtown Shreveport, boasts lush gardens and stately Georgian buildings. About a fifth of the residents leave for their real home when the weekend rolls around, while the rest divide their time between fraternity/sorority parties and sporting events. Twenty-three percent of the men and 26% of the women are members of 4 national fraternities and 2 national sororities. Independents usually have been invited to Greek parties, which has helped keep relations between the 2 groups close, although recent restrictions on Greek parties have limited attendance by non-members. The Baptist Collegiate Ministry and many of the science clubs are among the more active organizations. Crime, other than an occasional car theft, is not much of a problem on the well-patrolled campus, although students advise using caution when walking in the nearby neighborhoods.

Centenary fields 7 men's and 9 women's intercollegiate teams in NCAA Division I; basketball, soccer, and baseball are most popular with the fans. Sixty percent of the students take part in the 16 intramural sports open to each sex.

Shreveport, a city whose metropolitan area exceeds 300,000, is located 180 miles east of Dallas, Texas. Though the Shreveport area has many of the bars, dance clubs, restaurants, and malls that students enjoy, trips to Dallas, Houston, New Orleans, and Little Rock are easy to organize.

Cost cutters: Ninety-eight percent of freshmen and 96% of continuing students received financial aid in a recent school year. About 70% of all students received need-based assistance. The average freshman award for a student with need recently included a need-based scholarship or grant averaging $10,880 and need-based self-help aid such as loans and jobs averaging $3387. Non-need-based athletic scholarships for first-year students averaged $12,049; other non-need-based awards and scholarships averaged $9395. Non-need-based loans averaged $2502. Debts for a typical recent graduate were $15,300.

Nearly 300 different scholarships are available to students with outstanding academic potential and/or leadership skills. Nancy M. Christian Scholarships pay full tuition, fees, room and board to 5 outstanding first-year students. Every March, 40 candidates are invited to interview and compete for these awards, which are renewable; 1825 scholarships pay $10,000–$14,000 to 30 students who complete and submit a scholarship essay. Presidential, Dean's, and Trustee's scholarships, available to financial-aid applicants who also have shown outstanding academic achievement, pay $10,000, $7500, and $5000 respectively. Talent scholarships are offered in athletics, the performing arts, art, and in church careers. A monthly payment plan allows families to extend payments for annual tuition, room, board, and fees over a 10-month period. Families pay a one-time nonrefundable fee of $50 to participate.

Rate of return: Seventy-four percent of freshmen return for the sophomore year. Forty-two percent go on to graduate in 4 years, 54% in 5 years; 55% in 6.

Payoff: Fifteen percent of the 2005 graduates earned bachelor's degrees in business: 8% received degrees in biology, 6% in psychology. Just over a fourth of the graduates pursue advanced degrees within months of earning a bachelor's. Twenty percent in a recent year split evenly between study in business and the arts and sciences. Students pursuing advanced degrees in medicine are not the only ones with high acceptance rates. Ninety percent of the applicants to law school have been admitted to the institutions of their choice; 95% of those applying to preprofessional programs, such as graduate schools and physical therapy programs, also have gained acceptance. Many of those entering the work force accept jobs in teaching or counseling, in sales or other entry-level business positions throughout the South and Midwest. Outside the tri-state region of Texas, Arkansas, and Louisiana, students joke, they may have to tell people that it's Centenary College, not Seminary or Cemetery.

Bottom line: To succeed at Centenary, students must want to belong to a nurturing community that works to make its members feel important. Observes a junior: "Centenary's biggest asset is that everyone knows everyone. But its worst flaw is that everyone knows everyone." At Centenary, you can work and have fun, but you can't remain anonymous.

Maine

University of Maine

Orono, Maine 04469

Setting: Small town
Control: Public
Undergraduate enrollment: 3875 men, 3742 women
Graduate enrollment: 469 men, 701 women
Student/faculty ratio: 16:1
Freshman profile: 3% scored over 700 on SAT I verbal; 21% scored 600–700; 48% 500–599; 28% below 500. 5% scored over 700 on SAT I math; 22% scored 600–700; 46% 500–599; 27% below 500. 6% scored above 28 on the ACT; 11% scored 27–28; 25% 24–26; 28% 21–23; 30% below 21. 23% graduated in top tenth of high school class; 43% in upper fifth.

Faculty profile: 85% Ph.D.'s
Tuition and fees: $6910 in-state; $17,050 out-of-state
Room and board: $6732
Freshman financial aid: 82%; average scholarship or grant: $5880 need-based; $4126 non-need-based
Campus jobs: 25%; average earnings: $2000/year
Application deadline: Rolling
Financial aid deadline: Mar. 1
Admissions information: (207) 581–1561; (877) 486-2364
e-mail: um-admit@maine.edu
web site: www.umaine.edu

When students enroll at the University of Maine in Orono, they buy more than tuition, room, board, and books: they buy into a way of life. Orono (pop. 10,000) is located about halfway between the state's southern and northernmost borders, and 8 miles away from the third largest city, Bangor, which itself has only 36,000 residents. Administrators call the environment "vigorous." An Ohio native refers to it as cold. But if the weather's not always warm, students for the most part are. Adjectives like *relaxed, wholesome,* and *outdoorsy* are more prevalent here than *intense* or *pushy*. In short, if a student is willing to put up with the usual state-school bureaucracy and some large beginning classes, the University of Maine can prove a breath of fresh air.

Student body: UMaine consists primarily of Mainers, with 85% residents of the Pine Tree State. Seventy-six percent of the rest are also from the Northeast, although students come from 46 other states and 76 foreign countries to check out the "Downeast" way of life. Nontraditional students over the age of 24 make up about a fifth of the student body. Despite efforts to enhance diversity, UMaine remains predominantly white, with just 5% members of U.S. minority groups, including 2% Native American and 1% each Asian-American, African-American, and Hispanic. Two percent of the total enrollment are foreign nationals. Adding a special cultural flavor is the 20% of the student body who are Franco-American, an ethnic minority of French-Canadian and Acadian descent who account for approximately a third of the population of New England. The students who come to the university are "mostly from small Maine towns or those from other states who wanted to 'get away,'" says a New Yorker who did just that. Their politics, says a Mainer, reflect the full spectrum of views from "very liberal, modern-day 'hippies' to conservative 'Rush Limbaugh' types." Academically, the university does have disciplines, such as engineering and forestry, that are quite competitive, but on the whole, says a New Englander, "many appreciate the environment and the beauty of the land more than the textbooks." Adds a journalism major: "It makes for a relaxed learning environment where you can concentrate on what your strengths are and not worry about your neighbor's." "People," observes a freshman, "are not afraid to be who they are."

Academics: The precursor to the University of Maine opened in 1868 with 2 faculty members and 12 students studying agriculture and civil and mechanical engineering. The university today awards degrees through the doctorate, with 88 undergraduate majors spread among 5 colleges. The academic year is divided into 2 semesters. Classes for first-year students and sophomores tend to run from 75 to 150 students, although Introduction to Ocean Science can balloon to 352 in a large hall, with smaller lab sessions. Some upper-level engineering courses enroll fewer than a dozen; most courses for juniors and seniors have no more than 20.

All students, regardless of college, are required to meet general-education requirements that cover 6 broad areas. The mandates consist of 2 courses in the physical or biological sciences, 18 credits in Human Values and Social Context, 6 credits in mathematics, English 101 (college composition), plus 2 writing-intensive courses, a course in ethics, and a senior capstone experience in the major. In addition, students must fulfill course requirements particular to each college.

There are 496 full-time and 327 part-time faculty members. Forty percent are women. Six percent of the introductory courses are taught by graduate students. Faculty quality is mixed: "On this campus," says a senior, "there are faculty who teach and those who lecture to fill in time between periods of research. The teachers are easy to distinguish because of the genuine respect they show for the students, the school, and the area." Faculty are for the most part very easy to talk to, though their rigor also varies. Says a senior: "Some instructors are bleeding hearts and create grading systems impossible to flunk, while other instructors are drill sergeants in the classroom."

Nearly 140 years after the university's opening, Engineering remains its strongest and most competitive college, thanks to first-rate facilities and faculty, high standards, and hard-working students who meet them. Ingenious engineering students have won many national awards for their concrete canoe, concrete toboggan, and cardboard canoe races. Chemical engineering is particularly noteworthy, attracting strong financial support from the state's pulp and paper industry and providing numerous on-site opportunities for majors; students who prefer may earn a B.S. degree in pulp and paper technology. Says a chemical engineering major: "The curriculum is rigorous and the professors push students to the limit with challenging assignments. Along with these challenges, they offer all of the support needed for students to be successful. Numerous times, professors come at night to help students study for exams." The College of Natural Sciences, Forestry, and Agriculture features degree programs in forest resources, another field of study critical to the state's economic well-being. The college boasts some of the newest facilities on campus and offers a wide range of concentrations from forest operations science to wildlife ecology. The marine biology track in the college's School of Marine Sciences also earns student admiration, as do classes in the earth sciences. History, in the College of Liberal Arts and Sciences, is marked by a stellar faculty boasting degrees from many Ivy League universities as well as Cambridge University in England. The interdisciplinary minor in Canadian studies offers a greater number and wider range of courses in this area, more than 90, than are available at any other university in the nation. A recently added interdisciplinary major in New Media attracted 200 students in its first year; the program explores the systems, technologies, history, art, design and theory of information, artifacts and networks, drawing on the teaching talents of faculty from at least a half-dozen fields from graphic design and engineering to creative writing and journalism.

The College of Education and Human Development has drawn much student criticism for being less rigorous than other colleges. Programs in art, dance, and music in the College of Liberal Arts and Sciences get by with fewer professors and limited resources, though music majors think their "gifted" professors deserve an ovation for their masterful instruction. Though art and music continue as majors, there is only a minor in dance and a single faculty member. The struggling theater major also lacks funding and adequate facilities to serve talented students interested in this field.

Facilities: The Raymond H. Fogler Library, the state's largest, has more than 1 million volumes, a third of which are stored in an annex building, and subscribes to 3889 journals. Students turn to URSUS as their electronic guide for accessing all books, serials, and nonprint materials owned by Fogler and other libraries in the state university system, as well as electronic journals and assorted indexes and databases. What the library boasts in terms of research capabilities it sometimes lacks as a serious study center. However, when traffic patterns flow correctly, computer users and those wishing to talk while they "work" remain on the first floor; moderately serious studiers go up 1 level to the second floor, and those needing the most quiet surroundings head directly to the third floor.

Approximately 500 PCs and Macs are available in computer clusters throughout the campus. The largest clusters are located in the library where the cluster is open until midnight and in the student union, where computers are available until 3 a.m. All are open around the clock during finals week. All residential complexes also have been wired for computers in students' rooms. Short waits of no more than 5 to 10 minutes are possible. The addition of e-mail checking stations in the library and Memorial Union has freed the computer clusters for students involved in writing papers and other academic projects. All academic buildings and some administrative buildings have wireless access. Only the College of Education requires that all majors in education programs leading to teacher certification have a laptop computer and specific software.

Special programs: Opportunities to study abroad are offered in more than 40 countries from Australia to Turkey. The National Student Exchange Program also makes it possible for UMaine undergraduates to study for a semester or a year at any of more than 150 universities throughout the United States and its territories. A semester in Washington, D.C., is another option.

Campus life: Forty-three percent of UMaine students, mostly freshmen, reside on the 3300-acre spread, which a New Jersey senior describes as having "a special, small, faraway feel." No figures are available to show the percentage of men and women involved in the 1 local and 12 national fraternities and 6 national sororities, although in recent years fewer than 10% of the men and 5% of the women have been members. These groups draw a "mixed reception on campus," in the words of 1 senior, with some undergraduates feeling they keep too much to themselves, and others finding them a staple of both the campus party scene and of community outreach. Black Bear Volunteers, which organizes community service projects both on and off campus, is one of the largest and most influential student groups.

Not surprisingly, the outdoor way of life is big at UMaine. Of the 226 clubs and associations available to students, kayaking, hang gliding, and skiing all involve large numbers of undergraduates in programs they wouldn't find at a big-city school. White-water enthusiasts can find Class II and III white water within a half mile of campus. For those longing for a bit of culture, the Maine Center for the Performing Arts offers more than 40 live performances during the academic year, ranging from the Peking Acrobats to Yo-Yo Ma. Police patrol the roomy campus on mountain bikes and in cars. Crime other than some bike theft is not a problem on the small-town campus, though lighting has been improved and more call boxes have been added. A Campus Walking Companion program provides escorts nightly.

Football may be popular in the fall, but in winter and early spring watch out for the Black Bears ice hockey team, the 2-time NCAA Division I national champions in 1999 and 1993 and frequent Frozen Four participant who pack Alfond Sports Arena for every home game. "You're not anybody if you don't go to at least 1 hockey or women's basketball game," says a sophomore. When spring eventually arrives, always later than the calendar claims, baseball draws enthusiastic crowds as well. Altogether, 9 men's and 10 women's intercollegiate sports teams compete in NCAA Division I. (The football team is Division I-AA). Seventy percent of the students in a recent year took part in the 35 single-sex and 18 coed intramural and club sports available.

For escape, there's Acadia National Park to the southeast, with its rugged, rocky shore, and Baxter State Park to the north, which offers hiking and camping near Mount Katahdin. Shopping at L.L. Bean or other outlet stores in Freeport is also a welcome diversion. Boston is just 4 hours away.

Cost cutters: A historical commitment to make the university accessible to all Maine citizens has kept in-state tuition low. In the 2005–2006 school year, 82% of the freshmen and 83% of continuing students received financial aid; for 63% of both groups, the aid was need-based. The average award for first-year students with need consisted of need-based scholarships or grants averaging $5880 and need-based self-help aid such as loans and jobs averaging $4219. Non-need athletic scholarships averaged $14,845; other non-need-based awards and scholarships averaged $4126. A typical UMaine graduate had $20,930 in debts. For scholars who rank in the top 20% of their high school graduating class and have a minimum score of 1100 on the math and critical reading portions of the SAT, a wide range of merit-based scholarships are available. Seniors attending Maine high schools who ranked first or second in their class recently received full tuition to cover 8 semesters of study. Other awards, based on class rank, standardized test scores, and residency, recently ranged from $2000 to $7500 a year. No-need on-campus employment also is offered, including a work-merit program that in a recent year gave a maximum of $800 a semester to students with 3.2 GPAs to work in their major fields of study. A cooperative program is an option in more than 50 of the university's 91 majors.

Rate of return: Seventy-nine percent of the first-year students who enter UMaine return for the sophomore year. Thirty percent go on to graduate in 4 years; 51% do so in 5 years; 56% in 6.

Payoff: Thirteen percent of the 2005 graduates earned degrees in education, 12% followed in engineering, 11% in business. Twenty-four percent of the 2004 graduates went immediately to graduate or professional schools. Students seeking jobs are hired by firms primarily in the Northeast, such as International Paper, UNUM Life Insurance Co., Jackson Laboratories, and Measurex, as well as by municipal, state, and federal government agencies. Among the less traditional employers seeking out UMaine graduates are Wilderness Rafting Expeditions and Sugarloaf Ski Resort. One hundred seventy-eight companies and organizations recruited on campus in the 2004–2005 school year.

Bottom line: For out-of-staters, 4 or 5 years at the University of Maine can be like shifting down the gears on a high-speed engine. Notes a Boston area resident: "UMaine, like all schools, has its ups and downs, from classes to budgets to nightlife, but a student can learn a lot if he or she is active. School up here is more than exams and especially benefits someone who has an appreciation for the beauty and the opportunities of this area. No more city living for me!"

Maryland

Mount Saint Mary's University

Emmitsburg, Maryland 21727

Setting: Rural
Control: Private (Roman Catholic)
Undergraduate enrollment: 611 men, 874 women
Graduate enrollment: 178 men, 43 women
Student/faculty ratio: 15:1
Freshman profile: 2% scored over 700 on SAT I verbal; 25% scored 600–700; 49% 500–599; 24% below 500. 3% scored over 700 on SAT I math; 25% scored 600–700; 47% 500–599; 25% below 500. 40% graduated in top fifth of high school class; 68% in upper two-fifths.
Faculty profile: 89% Ph.D.'s

Tuition and fees: $22,900
Room and board: $8030
Freshman financial aid: 97%; average scholarship or grant: $4101 need-based; $9800 non-need-based
Campus jobs: 35%; average earnings: $1451/year
Application deadline: Mar. 1
Financial aid deadline: Mar. 15
Admissions information: (301) 447-5214; (800) 448-4347
e-mail: admissions@msmary.edu
web site: www.msmary.edu

At venerable Mount Saint Mary's, a nearly 200-year-old Catholic institution of 1485 full-time undergraduates in rural western Maryland, numbers tell only half of the school's impressive story. As is true at a growing number of "liberal arts" colleges across the nation, the most popular major is the decidedly un-liberal-arts discipline of business which attracted 31% of the 2005 graduates. But employers and graduate-school admission officers expecting to find just top-flight number-crunchers had better look beyond the bottom line. Mount Saint Mary's requires all students to complete a 4-year core curriculum that features interdisciplinary courses, team teaching, and extensive writing and thinking and accounts for 52–58 of the 120 credits needed for graduation. In a recent report by the National Endowment for the Humanities, the curriculum was praised as an example of what core curricula should be. The Association of American Colleges, which includes such prestigious institutions as Williams and Amherst, asked Mount Saint Mary's to serve as a mentor for other colleges and universities seeking to develop core programs. "This program has received national recognition and deserves it," says a graduate. "As a member of one of the first classes to complete the 4-year curriculum, I feel that it develops very well-rounded and knowledgeable individuals."

Student body: Sixty-one percent of those who attend The Mount are from Maryland. Most of the rest also come from the Middle Atlantic region, although a total of 27 states and 12 foreign countries are represented. Eighty-three percent of the undergraduates are Catholic, and 45% are graduates of private or parochial schools. Twelve percent of the students are foreign nationals or members of racial or ethnic minority groups: African-American students account for 7% of the enrollment; Hispanics, for 3%; Asian-Americans, 2%, and foreign nationals, 1%. Students as a whole are outgoing and enthusiastic about being part of The Mount family. Says a sophomore: "We are active in our school and help foster community among each other." Most undergraduates adhere to established religious and family values and are becoming more academically oriented as the school's reputation widens. The atmosphere, in the words of a senior, "is laid-back in social acceptance but can be fierce in studies. No one here wants to fail."

Academics: Mount Saint Mary's University, which was a college until 2004, awards the bachelor's degrees in 27 majors plus master's degrees in business administration, education, and theology. The academic year is divided into 2 semesters. Average class size for undergraduates is 20–25 students. The largest course, Introduction to Biology, attracts about 70 notetakers; a course in ecology enrolls only 6.

Freshmen begin The Mount's model core curriculum by taking a year-long seminar that emphasizes writing, speaking, and thinking skills, plus a course each term in European history paired with 1 in the literature or fine arts of the period being studied. Sophomores follow up with a 1-semester course on The West in the Modern World plus 2 philosophy courses. In the first 2 years, students also are expected to take mathematics, a foreign language, social science, and natural science. Juniors complete a 2-term course in the American experience, plus 2 courses in theology; seniors, a course in ethics and 1 in a non-Western culture. Majors in fields such as science and education that have many requirements in the disciplines can follow a modified sequence of core courses.

The faculty of 178 includes 95 full-time members and 83 part-time. All of the full-time and 61 of the part-time members teach undergraduates. Forty-one percent of the members are women. Faculty are admired for the intelligence and broad range of experience they bring to the classroom, as well as a willingness, demonstrated by most, to provide extra help to students in need. Observes a junior: "A professor will not think twice about clearing his or her desk to offer help, guidance, or a listening ear. That makes a difference!" Faculty members also are highly visible members of the Mount community outside of their offices, taking an active part in lectures, presentations, special dinners, and as advisors to numerous clubs.

The business major is the overwhelming favorite of students, in large part because of the quality of its experienced faculty and the breadth of its courses, from business law to environmental economics to entrepreneurship. Accounting is noted for its excellent placement record. Elementary education has a solid reputation for preparing knowledgeable teachers; students must apply for entrance to the program no later than the beginning of sophomore year. Though attracting fewer majors, history, political science, and international studies, English, sociology, psychology, theology, philosophy, and biology and chemistry all are cited for their "brilliant" and enthusiastic faculties.

There is no major or minor in physics. The rhetoric and communications department has made significant improvements in its program over the last few years but still needs better facilities and equipment. Says a senior: "The great thing about the Mount's programs is that faculty will do all that they can to improve and expand the majors; you get the sense that the teachers are on your side."

Facilities: Students are increasingly finding Phillips Library to be a quiet and comfortable place for study, as long as they avoid the first floor and head either 1 floor up or 1 floor down. Extra lucky users may find a private room for individual study, or one for a small group. (There also is a 24-hour quiet study hall in another building.) With a collection of just under 210,000 volumes and 935 periodicals, research, especially for newer books or materials in such areas as business, can be frustrating. Students reserve their praise for the computerized catalog and periodical searches, which most consider "great," and for resources in theology and philosophy, which are especially strong. Material that Phillips does not have can usually be found over the Internet, or from the resources of 3 other Maryland libraries with whom The Mount shares materials.

About 135 computers are available to students in 7 labs around campus. Six of the labs are for general student use. One lab is reserved for computer science majors. Labs usually close at midnight; however, a student already inside working on a project may stay all night if he or she wishes. Tech support also is available until midnight. The college strongly recommends that students purchase laptops through the college-buying program and make full use of the wireless campus.

Special programs: Mount Saint Mary's sponsors its own foreign study semesters in Ireland, England, Spain, Italy, and Costa Rica, which join Mount faculty with native professors in coursework directly related to each nation's history and culture. Opportunities for study abroad in numerous countries from Austria to Japan are made possible through the college's affiliations with various institutions. Internships can be arranged in most majors. A dual-degree program in nursing is offered with The Johns Hopkins University.

Campus life: Eighty-one percent of Mount Saint Mary's students reside on the 1400-acre campus, a collection of old stone buildings on the side of a mountain. There are no fraternities or sororities, although students looking for a party can generally find one at the campus apartments, which are occupied mostly by seniors. On nice afternoons, students gather at the covered bridge or at Twin Lakes. The number of campus-sponsored activities on the weekends has increased dramatically, including an alcohol-free sports lounge that was started by a group of students and an after-Mass social on Sundays. A new student center opened during the 2002–2003 school year. More than 70 clubs keep many students busy in areas fairly focused on their interests, such as the social dance club and Circle K. Though attendance at Mass is not required, many students attend the Sunday evening worship service. Campus Ministry also involves many students in service projects. Security officers maintain a high profile on campus to keep crime practically nonexistent. What crime exists usually involves minor damage in the residence hallways. Residence halls remain locked at all times and students must swipe their Mount cards to gain entrance.

Soccer and lacrosse, the official "team sport of Maryland," are becoming increasingly popular at the Mount and promise to become more so following construction of a new $3.5 million stadium and field that began in fall 2005. Altogether, the university offers 9 men's and 10 women's sports played as part of NCAA Division I. Mountaineers basketball attracts the largest crowds to men's and women's home games. Rugby is a "huge" club sport, which also draws many supporters to its Saturday afternoon matches. An extensive intramural program provides 20 sports for each sex, some of them coed.

Mount Saint Mary's is 2 miles from Emmitsburg (pop. 2300), which, while growing, still offers students little in the way of big-city entertainment. Instead, trips sponsored by student organizations to D.C., Baltimore, and New York are popular. The historic Gettysburg Battlefield is just 12 miles north. For relaxation close at hand, students walk or mountain bike to a place called "the cliffs" where the view is exhilarating; a visit to the Grotto of Lourdes further up the mountain from the college also is great for spiritual renewal.

Cost cutters: Ninety-seven percent of the freshmen and 92% of continuing students received financial aid in a recent school year. For 66% of all undergraduates, the aid was based on need. The average freshman award for students with need included a need-based scholarship or grant averaging $4101 and need-based self-help aid such as loans and jobs averaging $3958. The average non-need-based athletic scholarship for first-year students equaled $7554. Other non-need-based awards and scholarships averaged $9800. The average recent graduate left with $8553 in debts.

The university awards academic scholarships based upon such criteria as high school course selection, course achievement, class rank, standardized test scores, and involvement in extracurricular activities. Scholarships range from Mount Heritage Grants that pay $5000 annually to active students with B averages to Mount scholarships that pay $12,500 a year to A students with high test scores and recognized leadership in their high schools and communities. The Kuderer Scholarship provides full tuition to 3 entering freshmen with SAT math and critical reading scores of at least 1200 who also scored highly on a competitive exam given in January. A monthly installment plan is available.

Rate of return: Eighty-four percent of the freshmen who enter return for the sophomore year. Sixty-four percent graduate in 4 years; 68%, in 5 years.

Payoff: Business topped all majors among 2005 graduates at 31%, followed by elementary education at 11%, and sociology at 8%. The majority of newly minted alumni take jobs with such firms as Ernst & Whinney, IBM, Shearson Lehman Hutton, Deloitte and Touche, and USF&G, largely throughout the mid-Atlantic states. One hundred companies and other organizations recruited on campus in the 2004–2005 school year. Just over a fourth of the graduates entered graduate or professional schools within 6 months of commencement.

Bottom line: Students at Mount Saint Mary's know for whom their university is—and is not—right. As they see it, an "average Joe" possessing leadership potential can excel at The Mount. Says a junior: "Mount Saint Mary's is perfect for making close friendships, taking education seriously, and having the freedom to run or bike through the mountains."

St. Mary's College of Maryland

St. Mary's City, Maryland 20686

Setting: Rural
Control: Public
Undergraduate enrollment: 788 men, 1061 women
Graduate enrollment: None
Student/faculty ratio: 14:1
Freshman profile: 18% scored over 700 on SAT I verbal; 48% scored 600–700; 27% 500–599; 7% below 500. 6% scored above 700 on SAT I math; 51% scored 600–700; 36% 500–599; 7% below 500. 39% graduated in top tenth of high school class; 57% in upper fifth.
Faculty profile: 96% Ph.D.'s

Tuition and fees: $10,833 in-state; $19,710 out-of-state
Room and board: $8043
Freshman financial aid: 75%; average scholarship or grant: $1500 need-based; $2700 non-need-based
Campus jobs: 5%; average earnings: $1000/year
Application deadline: Early decision: Dec. 1; regular: Jan. 15
Financial aid deadline: Mar. 1
Admissions information: (240) 895-5000; (800) 492-7181
e-mail: admissions@smcm.edu
web site: www.smcm.edu

If the name St. Mary's College of Maryland brings to mind a small, private, Catholic-affiliated school for women, think again, because 3 of those 4 impressions are wrong. Small, yes, but this St. Mary's not only is coed, but also is a public institution and is named after St. Mary's City, site of the third oldest continuously inhabited English settlement in the New World. As a publically supported college, St. Mary's offers a comparatively low tuition to out-of-staters as well as Maryland residents. And in a nation where being state supported usually implies an enrollment of several thousand, St. Mary's has just 1849 full-time undergraduates and no graduate students. As 1 of 2 "public honors" colleges in the nation, it's the closest a student can come to a private-college feeling for a very public price.

Student body: All but 19% of St. Mary's students are Maryland residents, with most of the rest also from the Middle Atlantic region. Thirty-six states and 32 foreign countries have students on campus. Eighteen percent attended private or parochial schools; 19% are Catholic, 34% Protestant, 3% Jewish, 6% other faiths, and 38% claim no religious affiliation. Eighty-two percent of the enrollment is white American, 9% African-American, 4% Asian-American, and 4% Hispanic; 1% are foreign nationals. There also is a smattering of "feathered," representing the ducks and peacocks that make the campus their year-round home. St. Mary's students tend to be friendly and outgoing, with a comparatively liberal slant to their political views. "People here are very casual, and it's okay to be different," says a senior. Adds a freshman: "There are guys here with bright colored hair and others who wouldn't even cut their hair differently. It makes life on campus interesting at all times." While the academic air is fairly relaxed as well, recent media attention to the college has attracted an abundant applicant pool, 2200 applicants for 488 slots, meaning that admission officials can pick the best of the crop. One outcome is higher standards for performance on campus. Comments a senior: "Though students would like to remain laid-back, they are finding it harder to be that way."

Academics: St. Mary's, which started as a seminary for women in 1840 and has been a 4-year college only since 1967, awards the bachelor's degree in 21 disciplines. Its school year is divided into 2 semesters. Class sizes shrink with each progressive year, starting with an average of 40–50 freshmen in a course, though Principles of Biology may enroll 60. By sophomore year, the average has shrunk to 25–30 students, while classes for juniors and seniors have as few as 15.

All students must complete designated courses in each of 4 categories: Abilities and Competencies, which includes courses in writing, and foreign language; Heritage of the Modern World, with required classes in fine arts, history, and literature; Sciences in the Modern World, which offers a choice of courses in mathematics and the physical, biological, behavioral, and policy sciences; and Integration and Analysis, with a required course in Values Inquiry plus a senior seminar in the major field. Students' chief complaint about the program is that the rigor of classes varies greatly from "pitifully easy" to very difficult, depending on which professor is teaching a particular course.

St. Mary's has 129 full-time faculty members and 82 part-timers. Forty-six percent are women. Close friendships between students and faculty are commonplace, given the prevalence of small classes. "They're extremely accessible," says a biology major. "Sometimes they're almost too readily accessible. You just can't hide!" The days when less challenging faculty members team taught in order to go sailing on nice days are long gone.

Biology is the jewel in St. Mary's crown, given the college's riverfront setting close to Chesapeake Bay, which enables majors to specialize in the study of marine and aquatic life. Students can conduct data-gathering cruises abroad a research boat or examine flowing river water in an estuarine studies lab. Dry-land research is optimum as well in a newer science building containing 6 biology labs, 3 chemistry labs, and physics and geology labs, with extensive new equipment. Opportunities for student research are not limited, however, to the natural sciences: psychology students pursue various projects under the supervision of a creative faculty. History and anthropology/sociology majors also go beyond their textbooks to engage in first-hand archaeological and historical research in St. Mary's City. English, theater, philosophy, political science, mathematics, and music win kudos as well for the quality of their faculties and curricula.

There is only a general foreign language major, with concentrations offered in French, Spanish, and German. Chinese recently was added as another concentration within the major. Undergraduates wish even more opportunities for in-depth study were available especially in related fields such as Asian studies.

Facilities: A recent renovation of Baltimore Hall, St. Mary's library, combined with construction of a new addition, basically gave students a new library, twice the size of the old. While the overhaul enhanced the library's value as a comfortable study center, it also brought into focus the inadequacy of the modest collection of 158,000 volumes and 2100 periodicals Electronic access to another 21,100 periodicals has silenced most complaints in that department. Students also have access to holdings of the University of Maryland library system, which expands the collection considerably as well. The computerized catalog rates an A+, as do the more than 250 computer databases. Materials contained at the University of Maryland are available through interlibrary loan. Students embroiled in senior papers and other large research projects may travel on their own to Washington, D.C., 70 miles north.

Students have access to approximately 255 computers in general-purpose labs across campus. There also are several smart classrooms and discipline-specific labs. Some computer labs are open around the clock, provided the student enters the building before midnight. Labs in the residence halls also are open for 24 hours. Students are encouraged to own their own computers, which the vast majority does. For those with laptops, wireless access is available in all academic building areas.

Special programs: Study-abroad programs are available at the Centre for Medieval and Renaissance Studies in Oxford, England, as well as in various programs in France, Germany, Thailand, China, and West Africa. Internships in all fields are extensive, with placements available worldwide. The St. Mary's City Field School in Historical Archaeology enables students from various disciplines to take part in local digs. One or 2 St. Mary's students may study for a year at The Johns Hopkins University in Baltimore. Engineering students may participate in a 3-2 program with the University of Maryland at College Park. The Nitze Scholars Program, named for Paul Nitze, former ambassador and Secretary of the Navy, enables about 14 high achieving students in each entering class to complete an alternative, more integrated curriculum with an emphasis on leadership and service. Each scholar also receives $3000 a year, in addition to any other merit awards.

Campus life: Eighty-five percent of St. Mary's students reside on the 319-acre campus, located on a broad, baylike bend in St. Mary's River. The riverfront setting makes aquatic activities a major weekend attraction, with even landlubbers trying their hand at swimming, rowing, canoeing, kayaking, windsurfing, and sailing. There are no fraternities or sororities, and though the rural environment makes some students restless, most find their niche in at least 1 of 78 clubs and organizations. "I expected the school to be boring since it is so far away from any big city life," recalls a sophomore, "however, I was pleasantly surprised by the number of activities and clubs on campus to get involved in." Expanded weekend activities such as popular coffeehouses, a nightclub at the student union on alternate weekends, and excellent theater productions also have helped St. Mary's shed its bygone image as a "suitcase college." Notes a Baltimore resident: "Most students stay on campus now and *create* their own fun." On rare occasions, fun becomes vandalism, one of the few minor crimes, along with bike and book theft, that occur at St. Mary's. To ensure that crime stays at this low level, a Night Hawk Program uses students to patrol the campus on foot with flashlights and walkie-talkies until 2:30 a.m. to assist undergraduates who need escorts. Emergency phones are stationed around campus.

Seven men's and 8 women's intercollegiate sports compete in NCAA Division III, including coed sailing. Men's and women's basketball draw the largest crowds. The sailing team has won 10 National Intercollegiate Sailing Association championships. At least 30% engage in a 12-sport intramural program. Among club sports, men's rugby and Ultimate Frisbee have strong followings. (The rugby parties are an event unto themselves!)

Because most students live within 100 miles of campus, some get away by going home, though less often than in the past. St. Mary's City is in a rural area "stuck in the middle of nowhere," according to a city dweller, "which can be both good and bad." For times when St. Mary's feels bad, Washington, D.C. is just 90 minutes away by car and Baltimore, 95 miles north, is also less than a 2-hour drive.

Cost cutters: It's hard to believe that St. Mary's was almost closed by the state Commission on Higher Education in 1947 because of its isolation—and high cost per student. Today, it is Maryland's most selective public college and is on just about everybody's list of good buys. In the 2005–2006 school year, 75% of all freshmen and 71% of continuing students received financial aid; for 27% of freshmen and 40% of continuing students, the aid was need-based. The average freshman package for a student with need included a need-based scholarship or grant averaging $1500 and need-based self-help aid such as loans and jobs averaging $1000. Other non-need-based scholarships and awards averaged $2700. Seniors in the 2005 class departed with an average debt of $17,125. St. Mary's Academic Achievement Awards pay from $3000 up to an amount equal to in-state tuition and fees to students who have challenged themselves with a rigorous high school curriculum and ranked in the top 10% of their class or scored above 1300 on their math and critical reading SATs. Presidential Merit Awards recognize students with strong academic and extracurricular records with awards worth $500 to $3000 a year.

Rate of return: Eighty-nine percent of freshmen who enter St. Mary's return for the sophomore year. Seventy-two percent receive bachelor's degrees in 4 years; 75%, in 5 years.

Payoff: Psychology was the major of choice for 14% of the 2005 graduates, followed by economics at 12%, and political science at 11%. In a recent year, 35% enrolled in graduate or professional schools within a year of commencement, the vast majority pursuing advanced degrees in the arts and natural sciences. Sixty-eight companies and organizations recruited on campus in the 2004–2005 school year.

Bottom line: St. Mary's is small any way you look at it: small town, small college, small classes, small price tag—and sometimes *too* small in terms of ready-made action. But for those ready for such an environment, says a big-city senior, "It's hard not to know everyone or to be enlightened by what you learn. A degree from St. Mary's means more every year; you get a top-of-the-line education for a bargain-basement price."

United States Naval Academy

Annapolis, Maryland 21402

Setting: Small town
Control: Public
Undergraduate enrollment: 3600 men, 600 women
Graduate enrollment: None
Student/faculty ratio: 7:1
Freshman profile: 28% scored over 700 on SAT I verbal; 45% scored 600–700; 27% below 600. 34% scored over 700 on SAT I math; 53% scored 600–700; 13% below 600. 81.5% graduated in top fifth of high school class; 94.5% in upper two-fifths.
Faculty profile: 90% Ph.D.'s

Tuition and fees: No tuition; $2200 freshman fee
Average annual increase: N/App
Room and board: No charge
Freshman financial aid: N/App; average scholarship or grant: N/App
Campus jobs: N/App; average earnings: N/App
Application deadline: Nominations due by Jan. 31
Financial aid deadline: N/App
Admissions information: (410) 293-1858; (800) 638-9156
web site: www.usna.edu

A quick look at the curriculum and campus life of the U.S. Naval Academy reveals immediately that the academy is not for everyone. In exchange for tuition, fees, room, and board and medical and dental care paid by Uncle Sam, plus a monthly salary of $764 in the 2005–2006 school year, midshipmen take a core curriculum that includes coursework in calculus, electrical engineering, leadership, weapons systems, and naval science. New students report to duty the summer before they enter as freshmen and spend subsequent summers at sea or in training programs that cover everything from airborne warfare to tactical planning through computer war games. In exchange for their free schooling, graduates must fulfill a 5-year commitment to serve in the U.S. Navy or Marine Corps. Says a senior, or firstie in Navy lingo: "We are dedicated to both the country and the U.S. Navy for to be less would make it impossible to bear this place and its rules."

This is not just a school; it's a job where the employees are constantly challenged mentally, physically, and personally. Despite the rigorous program, more than 11,000 young men and women annually seek admission to the Naval Academy. To be considered, candidates must obtain nominations from such sources as members of Congress, the President, Vice President, or Navy or Marine Corps officers. The process starts early, and students are advised to apply for nominations during the spring of their junior year in high school, or as soon thereafter as possible. Only 1 in 3 applicants with an official nomination is accepted, and nearly all who get the good news decide to enroll.

Student body: The undergraduate student body is drawn from all 50 states, with each region equally represented. A third of those admitted in fall 2005 already had some college or post-high-school education; 91% were varsity athletes; 59%, members of the National Honor Society. Almost 6% were sons and daughters of alumni. In recent years, 80% of all midshipmen have been white Americans, 7% each Hispanic and African American, 5% Asian-American, and 1% each Native American and foreign nationals. (As many as 40 students each year are from designated countries, and are enrolled through the Secretary of the Navy.) Because of the comparatively small numbers of women and minorities, some members of these groups say they feel more closely scrutinized than their white, male counterparts and therefore are inclined to stick together. Midshipmen, as the students are called, tend to be quite conservative in their politics, very disciplined, intensely loyal, hard-working, and highly competitive. Notes a firstie: "Everything is competitive here because each class is ranked from top to bottom according to academics, physical abilities, and military performance." The resulting class rank determines what job a midshipman will get after graduation; those who are most successful are rewarded with the best assignments. Adds a fellow firstie: "Most people come here used to being the best. At the academy, many learn failure for the first time, and those who can pick themselves up when this occurs will succeed."

Academics: The academy, which was founded in 1845, offers a bachelor's degree in 19 disciplines: 7 in engineering, 8 in science, mathematics, and computer science, and 4 in the humanities and social sciences. The academic year is divided into 2 semesters with summer training required. The first year starts with plebe summer, when civilians are turned into midshipmen, being taught everything from how to salute to how to sail to how to fire small arms, all accomplished within a tight schedule of rigorous physical conditioning. Upperclassmen spend summers in various ways: at sea aboard fleet units visiting foreign ports, offshore under sail, at the academy, or at the sites of the 4 warfare specialities: naval aviation, Marine Corps, surface warfare, and submarine warfare.

During the standard academic year, classes generally enroll from 20 to 30 midshipmen. The largest course, usually a required chemistry lecture, may reach 60 but breaks into smaller lab sections of no more than 25; several upper-level courses may enroll only 10.

All undergraduates must follow a very demanding core curriculum that emphasizes professional military training, math, science, and engineering. Even majors in English or history must take 3 semesters of calculus, 1 of statistics, 2 each of electrical engineering and naval engineering, and 2 each of chemistry and of physics, among other courses; this program entitles every midshipman to graduate with a bachelor of science degree. Instruction in physical education also is required during all 4 years, and each semester students must pass examinations in applied strength, long-distance running, and obstacle course.

The 600 full-time faculty members, a fifth of whom are women, are split fairly evenly between civilian and military professors; the military officers, whom many midshipmen prefer as instructors, teach about half of all academic courses and also most of those that are professionally oriented. All faculty members are considered to be very knowledgeable, to be research and application oriented, and to make good use of the impressive 1:7 faculty-student ratio. Notes a systems engineering major: "I have always been treated with respect and compassion. The faculty understand that we are training to become junior officers and treat us accordingly."

Up-to-the-minute equipment in Rickover Hall, ranging from wind tunnels to towing tanks to a sub-critical nuclear reactor, helps to make engineering the highest ranking collection of majors among academic divisions. Each of the 7 branches—aerospace, ocean, naval architecture, mechanical, electrical, systems, and general—offers a first-rate faculty and plenty of personal attention. As the disciplines most prized and utilized by the Navy, these departments receive attention second to none. Chemistry also rates 5 stars.

By the same token, majors like English, history, economics, and political science are lowest in the pecking order, largely because the Navy does not emphasize their value. Says an oceanography major: "These majors are considered 'baggits' since they aren't related to math, science, or engineering." However, students who major in these disciplines rate their faculties very highly. Foreign language instruction, which leads to minors in Arabic, Chinese, French, German, Japanese, Russian, and Spanish, has suffered from neglect; math and mechanical engineering "could use an influx of new professors to help relate better to newer generations of students," says a systems engineering major.

Facilities: With 530,000 volumes and 2000 periodicals, Nimitz Library is strong in engineering and naval materials but weaker in nontechnical resources. Its catalog is computerized, and periodical searches are made easy with the help of several CD-ROM indexes. The library seats 1500, more than a third of the student body, and is known for being quiet. For additional resources, midshipmen head, when leave permits, to the University of Maryland or simply go on-line.

All plebes are required to purchase specified desktop microcomputers, which are kept in dorm rooms and hard-wired to the academy network. There also are special computer rooms in the dormitories, library, and all academic buildings.

Special programs: Firsties may study for a semester in Washington, D.C. Those named Trident Scholars may spend the final year in independent research. Midshipmen who complete all Naval Academy requirements early may begin work toward a master's degree at a nearby institution such as Georgetown or The Johns Hopkins University.

Campus life: The academy campus, known as the Yard, is located on 338 acres between the south bank of the Severn River and historic Annapolis, Maryland's state capital. John Paul Jones, the Revolutionary War naval hero, is buried beneath the academy chapel. All undergraduates live on the Yard in a single dormitory, and getting off campus is basically a function of the greater privileges that come with each subsequent year. Plebes, for example, can leave the academy only on Saturday afternoons and evenings, but must remain in Annapolis and in uniform. Firsties are free to go into town wearing civilian clothes all day Saturday, Sunday morning and afternoon, and every afternoon after classes and may also leave the campus for as many weekends as they wish, except when they have military obligations. Most midshipmen leave for the maximum time allowed. Dating between midshipmen is discouraged, according to students, and most see men or women who do not attend the academy. Alcohol is prohibited on the Yard but not off, and midshipmen must refrain from drugs during their leisure hours. As naval officers, they are subject to random drug testing and are expelled if they test positive. Crime is not an issue on campus as all gates are guarded by Marines and all midshipmen who adhere to a strict honor code are also on watch rotations in the dormitory. Notes a firstie: "I feel confident leaving my room door wide open 24 hours a day."

During plebe year, a typical weekday begins at 5:30 a.m. with a personal fitness workout and breakfast, followed by four 1-hour classes between 8 and noon, formation for lunch at 12:10, the meal at 12:20, 2 more classes until 3, and then athletics and extracurricular activities; drill and parade occur twice weekly in the fall and spring. Mandatory study time for plebes is from 8:30 until 11:00 p.m. An additional period from 7 to 8:30 p.m. is available for extracurricular activities or study.

Sports are a vital component of Navy life. All midshipmen are required to participate in athletics, either intercollegiate or intramural, and those not playing must attend home football games. The academy participates in 20 NCAA Division I men's and 9 Division I women's intercollegiate sports in which a third of the men and half of the women take part. Twenty-five intramural and club sports involve everyone. Lacrosse, water polo, basketball, and wrestling are especially popular. The rugby club also is nationally ranked. As part of its extensive athletic facilities, the academy offers a fleet of more than 150 sailing craft, a world-class swimming and diving tower, and a championship golf course. A midshipman who still has energy to spare can participate in various service, musical, or religious clubs, SCUBA and parachute clubs, or a flying club with instructors to help the student earn a private pilot's license.

As restricted as plebes' time is away from the Yard, each finds a dose of TLC, a Saturday night dinner, and a homey place to relax with a local family that serves as a sponsor for the midshipman during his or her years at the academy. Once past the first year, however, most midshipmen opt to leave Annapolis whenever possible, many traveling to Washington, D.C. or Baltimore, each a half-hour's drive away. However, all but firsties must park their cars at least 2 miles outside the academy grounds, so that getting to the car can be the longest part of the journey.

Cost cutters: Before entering the academy, each midshipman must pay an entrance deposit of $2200 as a contribution toward the cost of uniforms and supplies, including a personal computer. To help defray first-year costs not covered by the deposit, such as those for books and laundry service, the federal government advances an interest-free loan ($1500 in a recent year) to entering midshipmen. This loan—and hardship loans for those unable to come up with the entrance deposit—are repaid through monthly deductions over 4 years from the midshipman's pay of $764 a month. "None of this means that a Naval Academy education is free," emphasizes a second class midshipman. "Prospective candidates should understand that the academy requires a great deal of time, effort, and commitment." Adds a third class midshipman: "I pay—with restricted freedom."

Rate of return: Eighty-nine percent of plebes return for the sophomore year. Seventy-six percent graduate in 4 years.

Payoff: In a recent graduating class, the 3 most popular majors for midshipmen were political science at 16% and economics and systems engineering at about 10% each. All graduates are commissioned as ensigns in the U.S. Navy or second lieutenants in the U.S. Marine Corps and must serve at least 5 years. A small percentage go on to medical school or graduate school in the arts and sciences. In 2005, the academy led all U.S. colleges and universities in the number of students named Rhodes Scholars—4 of the 32 selected. The academy had 3 in 2004. Most midshipmen consider their degrees marketable far beyond the naval services. Observes an aerospace engineering major: "Civilian employers know that we have invaluable management experience and are responsible and trustworthy." More astronauts, 54, have graduated from the Naval Academy than from any other institution in the nation.

Bottom line: While the Naval Academy provides a superb education, especially in engineering, usable just about anywhere, a prospective student must keep in mind that the academy is not just another technically oriented school. Advises a firstie: "A lot is expected here besides academics. There are several other obligations: lectures, sports, meetings, various training activities, and drills. And every student must remember: he or she comes here to get a commission in the Navy or Marine Corps."

Massachusetts

Assumption College

Worcester, Massachusetts 01609

Setting: Suburban
Control: Private (Roman Catholic)
Undergraduate enrollment: 839 men, 1256 women
Graduate enrollment: 14 men, 84 women
Student/faculty ratio: 16:1
Freshman profile: 2% scored over 700 on SAT I verbal; 19% scored 600–700; 52% 500–599; 27% below 500. 1% scored over 700 on SAT I math; 22% scored 600–700; 50% 500–599; 27% below 500. 1% scored above 28 on the ACT; 5% scored 27–28; 16% 24–26; 38% 21–23; 40% below 21. 27% graduated in top fifth of high school class; 66% in upper two-fifths.

Faculty profile: 94% Ph.D's.
Tuition and fees: $24,095
Room and board: $8780
Freshman financial aid: 93%; average scholarship or grant: $7706 need-based; $9708 non-need-based
Campus jobs: 33%; average earnings: $800/year
Application deadline: Early decision: Nov. 15; regular: Feb. 15
Financial aid deadline: Feb. 1
Admissions information: (508) 767-7285; (888) 882-7786
e-mail: admiss@assumption.edu
web site: www.assumption.edu

Fewer than 10 of every 100 Assumption College undergraduates actually specializes in social and rehabilitation services, the college's well-respected major designed to prepare students for careers in a wide range of "helping professions." But most of that 100 benefit from Assumption's own helping profession: providing an undergraduate education that embraces each student like a family member and makes sure every one receives whatever help is needed to earn a bachelor's degree. Thanks to this approach, two-thirds of entering freshmen graduate in 4 years. Assumption, in the words of a New Englander, "gives students many of the safeties of home with all the independence of college. On the campus, a student is surrounded by friends and faculty who care, yet still is on his or her own to make decisions arising in every-day life or related to a career."

Student body: Sixty-eight percent of Assumption's undergraduates are from Massachusetts, with all but 4% of the nonresidents also from the Northeast, primarily New England. A total of 24 states are represented. Thirty-two percent of the students attended private or parochial schools. Eighty-three percent are Catholic. Less than 6% are members of racial and ethnic minority groups; 2% are Hispanic, 2% Asian-American, 1% African-American, and less than 1% Native American. Five students are foreign nationals. Various recruiting efforts are targeting local Hispanics and overseas populations in an effort to widen the college's diversity. Assumption students tend to be conservative in their thoughts, dress (Abercrombie and Gap), and politics, and many have led rather sheltered lives, at least before entering college. Still, this conservatism doesn't manage to suppress a curiosity about different outlooks and experiences and a zest for life, and most students have little problem dividing their time between the library and the dance floor. Undergraduates relish the sense of community and school spirit that is contagious to newcomers. Less contagious is the individual commitment to academics. Notes a senior: "One can choose to excel and there is enough support within the school to do so easily. One also can coast through the school but his or her grades will demonstrate the commitment."

Academics: Assumption was founded in 1904 by the Augustinians of the Assumption, a religious order of men then conducting schools primarily in France and Belgium. Until the late 1940s, the college's curriculum was bilingual and the enrollment predominantly Franco-American. Today, Assumption confers the bachelor's degree in 35 fields and a master's degree in business administration, counseling psychology, rehabilitation counseling, school counseling and special education. (Students can earn a 5-year bachelor's/master's degree in all but counseling psychology.) The 2-semester calendar features classes with an average of 23 undergraduates. Freshmen will rarely find more than 30 students enrolled in any one class, with the exception of Concepts in Biology, which approaches 50 notetakers. The general education curriculum, where some of the larger classes are found, covers areas from philosophy and theology to laboratory science and humanities. Students' chief complaints center on the 2 courses required in philosophy plus 2 in theology, which many consider 1 course too many for those not interested in these fields.

The faculty of 215 members includes 133 full-time professors and 82 part-time, all of whom teach undergraduates. Sixty percent are men. Although the vast majority of professors are lay men and women, several priests and sisters are included in the ranks. Professors are viewed as devoted to their students and willing to "do anything within reach" to help them attain whatever goals they have set. Says a senior: "There are a few 'pure' academics, but most have real-world experience that they expertly weave into their lessons. Many of the most experienced faculty members also teach introductory classes each and every semester."

In the college's highly touted social and rehabilitation services department, such faculty members bring valuable clinical experience to the classroom. Students share in this experience not only through lectures but also through wonderful internship opportunities. The accounting program is especially competitive, with excellent instructors in most of the business-related programs. Elementary education, which requires its students to major in a liberal arts or science discipline, also is first rate. Among less career-oriented disciplines, English, history, theology, philosophy, sociology, politics, and psychology each offers its own brand of first-rate faculty members committed to the field and the students. The opening of a new science center in 2003 has energized Assumption students interested in the natural sciences. The facility features 5 multiuse class-rooms, 10 teaching laboratories, and 7 labs dedicated to faculty and student research. Says a senior: "The new laboratories and classrooms have made the study of the natural sciences much more exciting for students here."

Music is not offered as a regular major, although students with an interest in the field can develop a special major or earn a minor. There also is a minor in theater and television arts; students complain that the program could use a performance center. "The theater 'workshop' used to be a garage," notes a political science major. "The stage is about 25 feet by 10 feet. And there is no 'backstage.' We change and put on makeup in a hallway used by graduate students and teachers at night." Physics is not offered as a major or a minor.

Facilities: Assumption's 3-story d'Alzon Library is the talk of the campus: but not inside the building. As a popular study center completed in 1988, it offers lots of comfortable chairs and several quiet study rooms and cubicles. As a research center, it houses almost 220,000 volumes and 1902 periodicals although much of the book collection consists of older volumes, including an outstanding collection of French books and manuscripts. Students also have access to the diverse collections of 12 other colleges and universities in the Worcester area. Users find the computerized catalog and databases extremely useful in their search. "The one *major* problem with the library," says a senior, "is the lack of computers. There are only 7 or 8 computers in the entire building."

A new Information Technology Center that opened in 2002 provides more than 150 computers in public-access labs and classrooms. Additional units are available in other classroom buildings. Computers usually can be accessed until midnight most nights and later during exam periods. Ninety-two percent of Assumption students bring their own computers to campus.

Special programs: Students may take classes at any of 12 other Worcester area schools, among them College of the Holy Cross and Worcester Polytechnic Institute. Area attractions, such as Old Sturbridge Village, provide additional curriculum enrichment. A joint degree in engineering is offered with Worcester Polytechnic Institute. Internships in Washington, D.C., as well as in Worcester, are popular, too. A partnership with Columbia University provides students an opportunity to work at Biosphere II in Arizona. Although the college does not offer its own international exchange programs, it encourages students to study abroad.

Campus life: Assumption guarantees student housing for all 4 years, and all but 11% of the undergraduates accept the offer. A popular option is the 160-bed, Living-Learning Center that includes classroom space, faculty apartments, and a computer lab, along with 4-person suites for students. Campus life is important to Assumption students, and most remain on the 175-acre campus for the weekend, taking part in popular all-campus events, such as concerts, comedians, and lip-sync contests. The Reach Out Center, which involves more than 800 students annually in volunteer work throughout the community, and Campus Ministry, which offers students candlelight prayers, dinners, and retreats as well as a popular mission to Mexico, are 2 of the most active campus organizations. The student newspaper, *Le Provocateur*, also has a dedicated following. Since Assumption has no fraternities or sororities, underclassmen sometimes visit the fraternities down the street at Worcester Polytech; upperclassmen either hang out at the campus pub, or sponsor their own apartment parties. Damage to dormitories, usually a result of parties that have grown too wild, is probably the worst crime on campus, according to students. To keep incidents of crime low, dormitory doors are locked at 8 p.m., doors to dorm floors are locked at 11 p.m., and every visitor through the single guarded gate must have a guest pass signed by a student.

There's no doubt about the most popular varsity sport on campus—Greyhound basketball, especially since the team has won the NCAA Division II, Northeast 10 Conference championship 3 times in recent years. Football, soccer, hockey, and baseball draw their share of enthusiastic fans as well. Altogether, the college sponsors 11 intercollegiate sports for men and 10 for women. Three-quarters of the men and women participate in 16 intramural sports for each sex. The ski club attracts a lot of winter enthusiasts to its weekly trips in season.

Just 3 miles from campus is downtown Worcester, which, as the state's second largest city (pop. 176,000), usually presents enough cultural and social attractions to keep most students right in town. Those wanting something even bigger drive to Boston, Providence, or Hartford each an easy hour away. For quieter moments, the campus duck pond is a favorite retreat.

Cost cutters: Ninety-three percent of Assumption's freshmen and 92% of continuing students in the 2005–2006 school year received financial aid; for 64% of first-year students and 67% of the rest, the aid was tied to need. The average freshman award for a first-year student with financial need included a need-based scholarship or grant averaging $7706 and need-based self-help aid such as loans and jobs averaging $3577. The average non-need-based athletic scholarship for first-year students averaged $33,588. Other non-need-based awards or scholarships averaged $9708. The average financial indebtedness of a 2005 graduate was $20,356. Scholarships are presented to students on the basis of scholastic achievement, standardized test scores, character, and leadership potential, with the amount of the award, which can range up to full tuition, determined by financial need. A Presidential Merit Award provides up to $16,000 based on a combination of high school class rank, GPA, and SAT scores. Aquinas, Milleret, and Lyceum awards pay $13,000, $11,000, and $9000 a year, respectively.

Rate of return: Eighty-four percent of entering freshmen return for the sophomore year. Sixty-eight percent graduate in 4 years; 70%, in 5 years; 71% in 6.

Payoff: Twelve percent of the 2005 graduates earned degrees in psychology. Ten percent specialized in English, 8% in management. Three-quarters of the graduates convert their degrees almost immediately into positions in the job market, most remaining in the Northeast and taking positions with many of the 70 companies and organizations that have typically recruited on campus. While two-thirds of the new employees join the private sector, another fifth enter the fields of education and human services. Twenty-three percent of recent graduates headed immediately to graduate school.

Bottom line: A recent graduate offers this recommendation: "The graduating high school senior who is a little intimidated by the thought of leaving home and is unsure of his or her career path, but is serious about growing emotionally and spiritually, as well as academically, will find Assumption an extended family."

Franklin W. Olin
College of Engineering

Needham, Massachusetts 02492

Setting: Suburban
Control: Independent
Undergraduate enrollment: 163 men, 123 women
Graduate enrollment: None
Student/faculty ratio: 9:1
Freshman profile: SAT/ACT scores: NA; class rank data: NA
Faculty profile: NA
Tuition and fees: None; $150 student-activity fee
Room and board: $10,870

Freshman financial aid: 100%; average scholarship or grant: $30,600 to all students
Campus jobs: NA
Application deadline: Jan. 6
Financial aid deadline: NA
Admissions information: (781) 292-2222; (781) 292-2300
e-mail: info@olin.edu
web site: www.olin.edu

Many students select a particular college or university in order to be part of a tradition of learning that stretches back for generations. Students who decide to attend Franklin W. Olin College of Engineering in a suburb of Boston make their choice for a very different reason: to be part of the creation and shaping of a new learning tradition. Olin College admitted its first class of students in fall of 2002, and students from as far as away as Idaho and as near as other Massachusetts towns could not resist being part of the creative process. "We were going to be the pioneers," recalls a senior from North Carolina, "the first to attend and mold a brand-new institution." Continues a junior from Texas: "I wanted to study engineering with a more hands-on approach. I knew I would prefer a smaller school with a more family-like atmosphere and I didn't want to lose arts, humanities, and social sciences just because I was studying engineering." Adds another senior: "Having a say in what happened to me over the next four years was an opportunity I couldn't pass up."

What also was difficult for many to pass up was the price: a scholarship equal to the price of tuition, estimated at $30,600 in the 2005–2006 school year, which stretched over 4 years, would approach $130,000. With an emphasis on engineering that is project-based and interdisciplinary, with emphasis on business and entrepreneurship as well as the arts, humanities, and social sciences, Olin College makes learning a tradition that students are delighted to pass along.

Student body: Olin may be an engineering school but students pride themselves on not being stereotypical, one-dimensional engineers. Says a senior from the West: "Everyone here was very accomplished academically in high school but Olin people have many passions outside of science. There are artists, musicians, athletes, actors, jugglers, writers, etc. The Olin ideal, in a way, is about finding diverse interests." The small student body is certainly geographically diverse. Students come from all but 4 states, with the largest numbers in 2005–2006 from California (47), Texas (23), and Massachusetts (21). Sixteen percent of the students are members of minority groups, with no breakdown available as to their individual race or ethnicity. While the workload is rigorous, students describe themselves as "intense" rather than competitive. Says an electrical and computer engineering major: "The classes here are challenging enough without the added stress and worry of having to compete with others." Professors encourage group work in many areas. Continues the student: "When requested by faculty, students will work individually, but otherwise, the environment fosters communication and peer instruction." Politically, students see themselves as a mixture of liberals and conservatives, socially, generally fun-filled and a bit "goofy."

Academics: Olin College was the final and largest legacy of the F. W. Olin Foundation, which over 7 decades donated more than $800 million, largely in the bricks and mortar construction of 78 buildings bearing the Olin name on 58 college and university campuses. In 1997, the foundation decided to use the last of its assets to construct its biggest structure: Franklin W. Olin College of Engineering. As the college's name implies, Olin offers bachelor's degree programs in engineering only, with majors in electrical and computer engineering, mechanical engineering, and general engineering. The general engineering program offers concentrations in bioengineering, materials science, computing, systems, and an individually designed major. Class sizes typically range from 5 to 40 students, with most generally around 20.

Students are introduced to Olin's projects-based, interdisciplinary approach to engineering in the first semester of their freshman year when they take the first of 2 Integrated Course Blocks. The blocks are team-taught examinations of engineering, math, and science. In the first year, students also take a course in engineering design, in science, either biology or material science, an Arts/Humanities/Social Sciences (AHS) Foundations course, plus a course in business and entrepreneurship. In the sophomore and junior years, students take an increasing number of engineering courses but still some AHS or entrepreneurship classes. While the college offers its own AHS classes, students are free to sample the wider variety of courses at nearby Babson and Wellesley colleges and Brandeis University. Students take the entrepreneurship courses at Babson.

The final year largely revolves around a year-long Senior Consulting Program for Engineering (SCOPE) project on which 4 to 8 students typically work together plus an independent self-study related to the SCOPE project. Students tend to like the approach. Says a mechanical engineering major: "It is wonderful when physics and math are taught together freshman year, and the electrical and mechanical aspects of engineering are brought together in a Principles of Engineering course."

The full-time faculty numbers 32, twice the number on campus when the college opened in 2002. Forty-one percent are women. The faculty, according to students, are gifted in their fields, committed to making a difference in how engineering is taught, and willing to be as supportive to the students as possible—whatever the hour. Notes an electrical and computer engineering major: "I get replies to homework questions by e-mail at 2 a.m., extra office hours on weekends, and I've held meetings with some faculty members for committee work around midnight in pajamas. They are brilliant and excited to share their knowledge." There are no graduate students, so no TAs, only NINJAs, which stands for Need Information Now? Just Ask. The NINJAs are other students who tutor first-year students in their classes, and says a junior, "are very appreciated and heavily used."

Students find the 3 main engineering disciplines offered, electrical and computer, mechanical, and general, to be of consistently high quality. "Olin doesn't have departments," observes a mechanical engineering major, "which emphasizes one of the best aspects of the curriculum: different areas and ideas being synthesized." Across the board, on such a newly built campus, the equipment in the classrooms, laboratories, and project rooms is state of the art.

In each area, majors wish there could be a few more course offerings. Observes a general engineering major: "Some courses are offered every semester, while other more specialized courses are sometimes offered every other year." Because the school and its programs are still evolving, professors are open to student input on possible improvements, which they readily give. Continues the student: "Things are new so we constantly try new things and then evaluate what worked and what didn't."

Facilities: Olin's library may be small by the usual standards but students find it, in the words of 1 senior: "a great place to buckle down to get work done, to take exams, or to meet a friend to work on homework together." The 2-story facility contained in the 76,000-square-foot Olin Center currently houses just 1500 reference volumes, 100 current periodical titles on display shelves, and 20,000 volumes on lower levels. The library eventually will hold 45,000 print volumes, though students seem content with the extensive computerized research aids already available. The holdings naturally are strongest in science and engineering, though students may borrow materials in the humanities from nearby Wellesley College. But the amount of nontechnical material has been growing, thanks to something called the community collection. Explains a Texan: "Each entering student is allowed to recommend one book that they think Olin should have, and it is purchased and marked as a community collection book." The library, which seats 91 in 5 group study rooms as well as study carrels, also is open around the clock. "With 24-hour access," says a mechanical engineering major, "there is almost always someone in the library."

Every student is required to purchase a laptop computer from the school at an estimated cost of $2500 over 2 years. For larger projects, the Information Technology Space, also located in the Olin Center, provides a 24-hour computer lab. Says a mechanical engineering major: "It is mostly used for 3-D modeling of large assemblies and video/sound editing. During midterm and finals weeks, our computer lab is more crowded because it has a 42-inch poster printer that everyone likes to use for projects but everyone seems to be able to print their posters." Additional computers are located in the library and the science building, also accessible around the clock. The campus is equipped with plenty of Ethernet ports and there is wireless access in every building.

Special programs: Olin College extends its idea of connectedness to areas outside the classroom, getting faculty and staff involved as leaders in various cocurricular groups, giving students transcript acknowledgment for various cocurricular offerings, and encouraging individual projects known as "passionate pursuits." Toward this end, Olin College offers direct study abroad exchanges with selected institutions around the world; a third of the junior class took part in the 2004–2005 school year. Just over half of all students took part in independent study and research projects. Cross-registration for classes is offered with Babson College, Wellesley College, and Brandeis University. A fast-track master's degree in Management with a specialization in Technical Entrepreneurship is available with Babson College.

Campus life: Olin's campus consists of 5 of the 8 structures scheduled to be built on 75 acres of land outside Boston in Needham. The buildings are an academic center, a campus center, the Olin Center with the library and computer technology space, and 2 residence halls providing housing for 354 students. The college shares a recreation/athletic complex, theater, chapel, and health center with Babson College next door. But if the campus structures are lacking, the accompanying student life isn't. Despite the fact that the college offers no varsity sports or Greek life, students find some kind of activity, a dance, film, or the occasional big party, to break up the mounds of weekend homework. Exclaims a senior: "Our student activities committee is wicked active as are our clubs." The most popular clubs aren't the discipline-related organizations one might expect. Undergraduates' choices range from SERV, Support, Encourage, and Recognize Volunteers, that involves 60% of the students in some form of community service to FWOP, the Franklin W. Olin Players who put on at least 1 theatrical performance each term, to Open, an organization that works to raise awareness of and openness toward all lifestyles and sexual orientations. A student honor code provides a level of trust among students that many find freeing in terms of taking unproctored exams and leaving laptops and bags lying around. "Our biggest problem," says a junior, "is forgetting that some parts of our campus are open to people who are not members of the Olin community and therefore not necessarily willing to follow our values of respect for others." Blue light phones, security cameras, and a 24-hour police force provide an extra measure of security. All buildings are locked after business hours and students have card access.

Though there are no varsity sports, students can usually find a pick-up Ultimate Frisbee or soccer match on Saturday or the weekly Sunday morning football game. "Church, football, homework, and the Simpsons are probably tied for most popular Sunday activities," says a Virginian.

Boston or Cambridge, a half-hour drive or hour subway ride, or the neighboring campuses of Babson and Wellesley colleges, tend to be the most popular destinations for off-campus escapes. Surfing in Providence, Rhode Island, skiing or snowboarding in Maine, New Hampshire, or Vermont, or clubbing in Montreal occasionally take students further away.

Cost cutters: Every student receives a scholarship equal in amount to tuition. Students whose financial need is greater than the tuition rate may receive scholarship aid to cover at least part of the room and board. While no percentage is available to show the portion of students receiving aid on top of the tuition scholarship, the final grant of the F. W. Olin Foundation before it closed its doors in 2004 was a $30 million donation toward scholarships and a gift-matching program.

Rate of return: Thus far, 99% of entering freshmen have returned for their sophomore year. With the first class graduating in spring 2006, no figures were yet available on the percent of that original class to earn bachelor's degrees. Majors among the 27-member Class of 2006 were divided as follows: 49% in general engineering, 27% in electrical and computer engineering, and 24% in mechanical engineering. Within general engineering, the largest number of students specialized in systems engineering, followed by bio-engineering.

Payoff: Predicted an administrator in advance of Olin's first-ever commencement: "We expect our graduates to be admitted to the finest graduate schools and to obtain jobs, primarily in engineering but in every profession."

Bottom line: Advises a junior: "The student who would benefit most from 4 years at Olin is a student who is willing to work hard, enjoys working with other people, loves to learn, and seeks out opportunities for growth, who likes synthesizing ideas, and who has enthusiasm." It also is important to be committed to the field of engineering but not to the exclusion of other disciplines and extracurricular passions.

Gordon College

Wenham, Massachusetts 01984

Setting: Small town
Control: Private (Nondenominational Christian)
Undergraduate enrollment: 558 men, 1029 women
Graduate enrollment: none full-time (55 part-time)
Student/faculty ratio: 17:1
Freshman profile: 11% scored over 700 on SAT I verbal; 48% scored 600–700; 33% 500–599; 8% below 500. 7% scored over 700 on SAT I math; 49% scored 600–700; 34% 500–599; 10% below 500. 24% graduated in top tenth of high school class; 43% in upper fifth.
Faculty profile: 71% Ph.D.'s
Tuition and fees: $22,924

Room and board: $6270
Freshman financial aid: 50%; average scholarship or grant: $10,938 need-based
Campus jobs: NA; average earnings: NA
Application deadline: Early decision: Nov. 15; regular: Mar. 1
Financial aid deadline: Mar. 1
Admissions information: (978) 867-4217; (866) 464-6736
e-mail: nancy.mering@gordon.edu
web site: www.gordon.edu

Amid New England's plethora of 4-year colleges and universities, public and private, with and without religious affiliation, it is hard to be unique. But as Gordon College, located 25 miles from Boston on the scenic north shore, moves well into its second century of existence, it can lay claim to being the only nondenominational Christian liberal arts college in the region. Its mission is twofold: to challenge students academically with a rigorous curriculum that invites exploration of diverse viewpoints, and to test and stretch students' religious faith in an environment that balances campus rules with freedom to make choices. Its motto, Freedom Within a Framework of Faith, isn't just words, says a freshman. "Because it is a Christian college, I've actually been surprised by the open atmosphere of questioning one's faith and searching for truth." To earn such freedom, every applicant to Gordon is required to write a statement of faith; every student must attend chapel twice weekly and refrain from using alcohol, tobacco, or drugs on campus or at college-related events elsewhere. (Dancing, however, is not prohibited nor is there a dress code or curfew as is found at many other Christian colleges.) As a result, graduates emerge with a stronger faith in God, in Gordon, and in the good life for which their education has prepared them.

Student body: As the only nondenominational Christian College in New England, Gordon attracts most of its students from the region. Although just over a fourth are from Massachusetts, more than half of the out-of-staters are also from the Northeast. However, students come from all but 5 states and a total of 24 foreign countries. Hispanics, Asian-Americans, and African-Americans, who each account for 2% of Gordon's enrollment, constitute the largest racial and ethnic minority groups on campus. Native Americans follow at 1%. Foreign nationals make up 3%. Because 93% of the students are Protestant, many of them evangelical, and 3% are Catholic, with only 4% of no religious denomination, undergraduates as well as faculty and staff share a Christian perspective that creates a strong community bond. Notes a student from Missouri: "The caring and friendliness of all people from the custodians to the president make an incredible impact on students." Students see their campus as a mixture of Republicans and Democrats, more conservative than liberal but challenging to all points of view. A student from the Pacific Northwest observes: "This school is not for the . . . closed-minded conservative Christian but don't think that the liberal mindset won't have its challenges." In students' quest for meaning in their lives and in their learning, the majority concurs about being serious about their studies, working hard, and encouraging others in their efforts. Affirms a junior: "I have been excited to see students take both their studies and their faith seriously."

Academics: Although Gordon was founded as a Christian college in 1889, it did not develop a liberal arts curriculum until almost 40 years later. Its enrollment underwent significant expansion in 1985, when Gordon merged with Barrington College in Rhode Island, a school that shared a similar history. Today, Gordon offers its nearly 1600 full-time undergraduates majors in 36 fields leading to a bachelor's degree; the college offers master's degrees in education, teacher and music education. Classes follow a semester calendar with sizes that in the early years may range from 35 to as high as 170 in a visual arts class, Arts in Concert, but usually drop to between 8 and 25 in a student's major. Nearly 60% of the classes have 20 or fewer students; in a recent year, only 30 of the nearly 600 courses offered had more than 50 enrolled.

Gordon's core curriculum begins with a year-long first-year seminar that probes fundamental issues in the liberal arts and in character development. One of the favorite first-year courses is La Vida Wilderness Expeditions, a 12-day experience in the Adirondacks that includes backpacking, a ropes course, rock climbing, and group problem-solving, among other physical, mental, and spiritual challenges. (For those who prefer, a less strenuous 7-week outdoor activity course may be substituted for La Vida.) Overall, the core courses fall into 2 categories: Introduction to Christianity and the Liberal Arts, which includes the first-year seminar and La Vida as well as classes in the Old and New Testaments, a foreign language, writing, and physical education, and distribution requirements, which cover the traditional disciplines.

Gordon's faculty numbers 93 full-time and 72 part-time members; more than a fourth, 29%, of the full-time faculty are women. Students value professors' commitment to being Christian mentors as well as scholars. Observes a senior: "They present their material both objectively and through a Christian world view. However, they don't spoon feed! My professors have found a healthy balance between nurturing and challenging me." Adds a sophomore: "They are scholars of their particular subject or discipline but their hearts are for the students."

The college's academic strongholds range from the sacred to the secular. The major in Biblical and theological studies is well constructed and features several prominent scholars, including one who has helped translate the Bible and a second who created a 2-part television series for PBS on the Jewish and Christian faiths. Sociology too is distinguished by impressive faculty that includes a leading authority on Christian social action toward the poor. Biology is especially rigorous, and successful graduates of the program have been admitted to many prestigious medical schools, such as those at Harvard and the University of Pennsylvania. The concentration in marine biology benefits from Gordon's proximity to the ocean, a little over 2 miles away. The music curriculum shines with the presence of a full-scale orchestra headed by a Grammy-nominated conductor, who " *pulls* talent out of people and helps them refine it," according to a music fan, plus an artist-in-residence in piano. Says a junior: "Music is embraced with excellent professors who stress their love for music through a rigorous program that builds students into musicians." The 6-year-old Phillips Music Center provides state-of-the-art electronics, an intimate recital hall, and an instrument repair shop. The programs in early childhood, elementary, and special education, psychology, and economics, business, and accounting are considered strong as well.

Communication arts and theater arts are smaller majors. Says a major in English and communications: "They are excellent but need to grow and provide a wider variety of classes and professors." Physics, too, is small but what it lacks in providing interaction with lots of other majors, it more than offers in first-rate teaching and successful graduates in nationally recognized labs and graduate schools.

Facilities: Jenks Learning Resource Center is considered by most students to be Gordon's outstanding building, offering areas designated for serious study as well as rooms for quiet discussion. The cozy structure, says a sophomore, "makes huddling up in a corner somewhere to study almost enjoyable." Studiers who demand pin-drop silence often head to Goddard Library of nearby Gordon-Conwell Theological Seminary in Hamilton. Students find Jenks's collection of more than 191,000 volumes and 510 periodicals to be adequate for most research projects. Various periodical databases also enable students to search through over 5000 periodicals, 3000 of which are available full text on-line. A computerized catalog makes it possible to search for materials locally as well as at other libraries in the Boston area through NOBLE, the North of Boston Library Exchange.

Two PC labs and 1 Mac lab are available for general student use. Labs usually are open until midnight. A series of kiosks across campus also enable students to check their e-mail, without tying up units in the labs. All told, about 125 computers are available for student use. Availability tends to be adequate, except during finals when waits are even then only about 5 minutes. Several wireless points are available around campus for those students with laptops.

Special programs: Gordon offers a vast array of off-campus programs both at home and abroad. As part of the college's own programs or others provided by its membership in various consortia, Gordon students may study at Daystar University College in Kenya, at Aix-en-Province, France, or in Orvieto, Italy, among other places. Undergraduates with an interest in marine biology have the opportunity to study at many sites in a variety of climates. Above water, students may cross-register for courses with 11 other 2- and 4-year colleges and universities in the area. Those with career interests in engineering may participate in a 3-2 program with the University of Massachusetts at Lowell; others preferring the allied health field may complete 2 years at Gordon and then transfer to Thomas Jefferson College of Allied Health Science in Philadelphia. A semester in Washington, D.C., San Francisco, or Hollywood also is an option.

Campus life: All but 12% choose to live in what many consider an "ideal" setting. The 440-acre campus boasts its own lake with a sand beach, miles of hiking, mountain biking, and cross-country skiing trails, and several ponds for canoeing. In addition, it is situated just 5 minutes from the ocean, 30 minutes from Boston, and 90 minutes from the ski slopes. It is little wonder, then, that few students miss having fraternities or sororities; instead, they busy themselves in some physical activity on campus or explore the immediate environs. The Summer Missions Program that involves students in short-term mission trips around the world, and the Lynn Initiative, which engages undergraduates in service projects in the city of Lynn are popular organizations around campus. Attendance at chapel is required twice a week, with 10 absences permitted each semester. Most students also attend the popular student-led worship service on Sunday evening, which is known as Catacombs. Many students enjoy the roominess and atmosphere provided by the recently constructed chapel, which seats about 1500 and is one of the largest traditional New England-style chapels in the region. Campus crime is not much of a problem, though residence halls are locked around the clock, security cameras have been installed, and an escort service is available as a precaution.

Students support their athletic teams, the Fighting Scots, throughout the various seasons, with men's Saturday-afternoon soccer and lacrosse matches as well as basketball drawing the most spirited crowds. However, intercollegiate options for women slightly outweigh those for men, 9 sports to 8, all played under NCAA Division III. An active intramural program involves 60% of the men and 40% of the women in 15 sports for both.

The town of Wenham is located just north of Salem of "witch trials" fame and near other small, historical towns that offer intriguing sites for an afternoon's exploration. The cultural and athletic excitement of Boston is reachable in a half hour by car or an hour by commuter rail. Vermont, New Hampshire, and Maine are colorful havens for escape in the fall.

Cost cutters: About a third of tuition and fees is returned to students in the form of financial aid, which in the 2005–2006 school year provided assistance to 50% of freshmen and 52% of continuing students. Aid was need-based for 43% of the freshmen and 46% of the continuing students. The average freshman award included a need-based scholarship or grant averaging $10,938, and an average of $4140 in self-help aid such as loans and jobs. The average debt of a recent graduate was $7413. Competitive scholarships to top-ranking students include A.J. Gordon Scholarships, which pay $12,000 a year to 30–35 students on the basis of academic excellence, promise of achievement and leadership, and performance in an interview. Students who rank in the top 10% of their high school graduating class with combined SATs in math and critical reading of 1300 or higher should request the application. To be considered, candidates must complete the admission process by December 1. Competition dates are in February. Dean's, Challenge, and Discipleship awards worth $2000 to $8000 go to entering freshmen based on their previous academic records. Presidential Scholarships of $1000 to $2000 a year are awarded to Christian high school graduates in the top of their classes. Cooperative programs are encouraged in all majors.

Rate of return: Eighty-eight percent of entering freshmen return for the sophomore year. Fifty-three percent stay on to graduate in 4 years, 66% within 5 years; 68% within 6.

Payoff: Education was the most popular major among 2005 graduates, claiming 13% of the class; 12% earned degrees in English, 10% in social sciences. Gordon's most recent survey of graduates found that 65% were employed full-time in their fields of interest; 14% were working full-time outside their chosen field; 13% were in graduate school full-time and 5% were employed part-time and in graduate school part-time. The remainder fell into other categories, but less than 1% of the graduates were unemployed 2 years after graduating.

Bottom line: Gordon offers a strong, academically based Christian community to students who are seeking intellectual as well as spiritual stimulation. Says a New Englander: "It's a Christian college that is not afraid to be human; it holds true to Biblical teaching while at the same time teaching you to be a critical thinker." The physical senses also are sure to get a lift from the college's prime location near the Atlantic Ocean and the city of Boston.

Northeastern University

Boston, Massachusetts 02115

Setting: Urban
Control: Independent
Undergraduate enrollment: 7209 men, 7521 women
Graduate enrollment: 1309 men, 1572 women
Student/faculty ratio: 16:1
Freshman profile: 10% scored over 699 on SAT I verbal; 48% scored 600–699; 34% 500–599; 8% below 500. 14% scored over 699 on SAT I math; 55% scored 600–699; 26% 500–599; 5% below 500. 15% scored 30–36 on the ACT; 69% scored 24–29; 14% 18–23; 2% below 18. 36% graduated in top tenth of high school class; 73% in upper fourth.

Faculty profile: 88% Ph.D.'s
Tuition and fees: $28,792
Room and board: $10,550
Freshman financial aid: 91%; average scholarship or grant: $13,524 need-based; $13,352 non-need-based
Campus jobs: NA; average earnings: NA
Application deadline: Early action: Nov. 15; regular: Jan. 15
Financial aid deadline: Feb. 15
Admissions information: (617) 373-2200
  e-mail: admissions@neu.edu
  web site: www.northeastern.edu

Amid the complexities of higher education, it's still the ABCs that lure students to Northeastern University: an Amazing Array of courses, its Back-Bay Boston location, and its Comprehensive Cooperative education plan. The 5-year, year-round cooperative program enables students to alternate months of classes with months of work experience with any of more than 2000 employers in New England, elsewhere in the United States, or overseas. According to participants, the program lets a student graduate "with a resumé and not just a diploma." In addition, undergraduates earn, on average, $12,500 per year while on the job and pay only for the terms they're taking classes. The dollars earned help make attending school in Boston, one of the most appealing but most costly collegiate locales, a much more affordable endeavor. Add a curriculum with more than 80 undergraduate majors from accounting to linguistics and psychology, and Northeastern is a university very much in D-mand.

Student body: Thirty-four percent of Northeastern students come from Massachusetts. In fact, it has been said that 1 out of every 5 Bay Staters chooses Northeastern for his or her college education. Another third of the student body hails from the mid-Atlantic states, and the final third from all of the remaining states. Sixty-four percent of the undergraduate student body are white American, 7% Asian-American, 6% African-American, 5% Hispanic, and less than 0.5% Native American. Five percent are foreign nationals, recently from 125 countries. The racial and ethnic origins of 12% are not known. Students who seek out Northeastern are usually self-motivated, hard working, and more mature than their counterparts on campuses without regular involvement in the world of work. Many students who did not enjoy learning in high school find themselves turned on by Northeastern's practical approach to education. However, those undergraduates excited by Northeastern's academic offerings sometimes get frustrated by the number of unmotivated students who remain apathetic to schoolwork as well as to political and social issues.

Academics: Northeastern, which was founded by the Boston YMCA in 1898 as the Evening Institute for Young Men, awards degrees through the doctorate, with undergraduate majors offered in 80+ fields through 6 undergraduate colleges. A limited number of highly qualified freshmen are admitted to a bachelor's/juris doctor degree program that continues the cooperative education approach through law school. In 2003, Northeastern switched from the quarter system to a semester plan, consisting of 15-week terms in the fall and spring and two 7½-week half sessions during the summer. Co-ops run 6 months and alternate with a full semester of coursework. Students earn a bachelor's degree in 5 years instead of 4. All students except those in the College of Arts and Sciences are required to participate in the cooperative plan. Although most arts and sciences students choose the cooperative option, the college offers a full-time academic program that can be completed in the standard 4 years. A 4-year plan in which majors take fewer terms of cooperative education is available also in the colleges of Engineering, Business Administration, and Computer and Information Science.

Freshmen can expect most of the required courses in each college to enroll as many as 150–200 students. The largest class, Foundations of Psychology, recently had 250. Most upper-level sessions have 20–40; popular majors in business and criminal justice tend to have a few more than 40, while engineering classes beyond the first year usually enroll fewer than 20. Eighty-one percent of Northeastern's class sections have fewer than 39 students; 40% have 10 to 19.

Students spend all of the first year on campus taking liberal arts and general-education courses that are required before they can accept their first job assignments. As a result, freshmen pay higher tuition than upperclassmen who spend less time in the classroom. Each school or college sets its own core curriculum mandates, but all demand that students complete a freshman English course and an upper-division writing requirement. Every student also must complete a diversity requirement, either coursework or an appropriate program, a recent addition that was initiated by the student government association. Students majoring in engineering, nursing, and pharmacy have the most requirements; those specializing in business and criminal justice have slightly fewer.

Northeastern's faculty numbers 1257 in all, with 853 full-time and 404 part-time. Forty-two percent of the total pool are women. While many professors are superb and eager to share their knowledge with students at any time of the day or night, the university has its share of poor instructors, as well as teaching assistants who speak little English. Complains a finance major: "Research is a big factor toward tenure here, and some students feel that the faculty aren't 'student friendly.'"

The names of Northeastern's strongest majors read like a list of professions, rather than subjects. Business (especially international business), engineering, computer science, and criminal justice, plus nursing, and pharmacy, each feature faculty members who are active in their fields and offer programs that incorporate knowledge from the worksite into classroom instruction. The physical therapy and athletic training programs in the Bouvé College of Health Sciences are winners, as is the recently strengthened School of Journalism, a unit of the College of Arts and Sciences. Physics, history, and political science also are noted for their excellent faculty and variety of courses.

Many liberal arts disciplines have traditionally received less attention and financial support than the career-oriented areas; the results are fewer good professors and more limited cooperative opportunities. Majors such as philosophy and cultural anthropology do not benefit as well from the "learn-by-doing" approach. Communication studies bears a reputation for being easy, which attracts more students less inclined to do the assignments and frustrates those students with a genuine interest in the field. Says one major: "It's hard for professors to exhibit their more passionate side when the students sitting in front of them don't even have the decency to read the assignment . . . The program has the faculty that could make it a very competitive and coveted program on campus. When the department raises its standards, the program will only improve."

Facilities: Snell Library, which opened in the spring of 1990, is physically the largest and, some claim, the most technologically advanced academic library in Boston. It seats 2800 people over its 5 levels and 240,000 square feet and provides ample space as well for the collection that numbers 968,000 volumes (with room for 1.5 million), 2.3 million microform items, and nearly 7400 periodicals. Its catalog and circulation system are computerized, and a 17-station CD-ROM optical disk network enables students to search any of numerous databases. About 500 of the study carrels located throughout the library are linked to the university's academic computing network, so that users who wish may bring their laptops for hookup. For the few times when Snell does not have everything a student researcher needs, the Boston Public Library is but a 10-minute walk away. Students can use their Northeastern ID to take out books from other Boston libraries.

More than 1000 computer workstations are available for student use across campus. InfoCommons, the campus's newest round-the-clock high-tech lab, offers more than 100 PCs and Mac computers loaded with the latest software for design, engineering, business, and computer science majors. Each of the 6 undergraduate colleges also has at least 1 lab for its own students, which supplement general-use labs across campus. Printers represent the key remaining problem. Notes a junior: "When it gets busy, it can take up to 20 minutes for something to print at the common print station. During midterm or finals week it can sometimes take up to 35 or 40 minutes as the station usually is understaffed." Wireless access is available in common areas across campus, including Snell Library, the InfoCommons, Curry Student Center, the cyber cafes, the Marino Recreation Center, and many of the outdoor quads.

Special programs: Placements for work-abroad programs are offered in such countries as the United Kingdom, Ireland, Australia, Israel, France, and Spain. Study abroad programs are offered in many of these same countries and others throughout the world. Cross-registration is available locally with the New England Conservatory of Music and Hebrew College. A program called Northeastern University Progress in Minority Engineering (NUPRIME) works to increase the number of African-Americans, Puerto Ricans, Hispanic-Americans, and Native Americans in the university's engineering programs by providing academic and financial support. The School of General Studies enables new students whose credentials do not predict success in traditional first-year programs to get special help in basic skills such as reading comprehension, writing, and mathematics.

Campus life: On-campus housing is guaranteed for freshmen and sophomores, and two-thirds of Northeastern's undergraduates reside in residence units adjacent to and on the 67-acre campus. The campus abuts the Museum of Fine Arts and is within walking distance of Symphony Hall, Faneuil Hall, and much-revered Fenway Park. On-campus housing options have grown significantly over the last 5 years, bringing the total number of beds to just over 6900. A number are included in the new Behrakis Health Sciences complex, which was completed in fall 2002 and includes dorms along with high-tech labs, classroom space, and parking. Weekend social events on campus tend to pale in comparison with what Boston can offer, leaving school spirit practically nonexistent. A new on-campus nightclub "afterHOURS" is helping to add some life to campus nightlife. Still, says a junior, "it is hard to be involved in campus groups here because many of the performance groups are poorly subscribed and don't usually draw crowds for their performances." Four percent of the men and the women are members of 10 national fraternities and 8 national sororities; though Greek houses are located off campus, a number of resident students regularly make the trek to attend their parties. Because of the university's location right in the city's Back-Bay section, students are alert to the ever-present threat of violent crime. However, undergraduates say that most incidents can be avoided if students remain aware of their urban surroundings and use proper caution in their after-hours activities. With an increase in the number of students living on campus has come stepped-up campus security. Guards are stationed at all hours on all 3 of the overpasses over the train tracks. An escort service is available around the clock, police officers patrol the campus on mountain bikes, and most residence halls have proctors stationed at the doors to check who enters. Theft is the biggest problem. Notes a journalism major: "Students leave items unattended in the library or leave their doors unlocked in the dormitory, and things get ripped off." Security cameras recently were installed in the library to help curb theft of personal items.

In a recent year, half the men and women took part in 14 intramural and 8 club sports. Among the 9 men's and 10 women's NCAA Division I sports offered, ice hockey, with teams for both men and women, and basketball draw the most fan support; football, played in Division I-AA, attracts slightly smaller crowds. Though many teams from ice hockey to crew have won national championships, students rarely have any problem getting in to watch the competitions. The $12 million, 81,000-square-foot Marino Recreation Center, completed in fall 1996, draws its own strong following. The downhill skiers and outing clubs are among the most popular student groups.

Students have only to step off campus to get away from university life, both in distance and in time, as they visit Boston's historical landmarks along the Freedom Trail. Within walking distance of Northeastern are a half dozen of the more than 60 colleges and universities in the Boston area, among them the Massachusetts Institute of Technology and Boston University. Weekend trips to Cape Cod or Martha's Vineyard, skiing in New Hampshire, and shopping at L. L. Bean or other Maine outlet stores provide more distant escapes.

Cost cutters: Ninety-one percent of the freshmen and 78% of continuing students in the 2005–2006 school year received some form of financial aid. For 62% of the freshmen and 60% of the continuing students, the aid was need-based. The average freshman award for a fall 2005 student with need included a need-based scholarship or grant averaging $13,524 and need-based self-help aid such as loans and jobs averaging $4435. Non-need-based athletic scholarships for first-year students averaged $20,628; other non-need-based awards and scholarships averaged $13,352. Average indebtedness of a recent graduate was $14,811. More than 190 academic scholarships are available to top students. The Carl S. Ell Scholarship pays full tuition, room, and board to entering freshmen in the top 1% of first-year applicants. Ralph L. Bunche Scholarships pay full tuition, room, and board and Reggie Lewis Memorial Scholarships pay full tuition to freshman applicants in the top 2% of the applicant pool. Deans' Awards pay up to $15,000 a year, and Excellence and Achievement Awards up to $12,000 annually to students within the top 25% of freshmen applicants. The Boston housing market ranks among the most expensive in the country, so those planning to live off campus should budget accordingly.

Rate of return: Ninety percent of entering freshmen return for the sophomore year. Fifty-four percent graduate in 5 years; 61% in 6 years.

Payoff: Nearly half of the 2005 graduates earned bachelor's degrees in 3 disciplines: 28% in business/marketing; 11% in engineering and 8% in health sciences. Ninety-five percent convert their work experience into permanent jobs after graduation; more than 70% end up signing on with firms where they held cooperative positions. Seventy-eight percent settle in New England; most of the rest join firms in the mid-Atlantic states. Eighteen percent begin working at least part time toward advanced degrees.

Bottom line: Here's what a recent graduate says: "A good prospect for Northeastern is a kid who did okay academically in high school but preferred working at an after-school or weekend job, is mature, and can take care of him- or herself. There is plenty of opportunity here for eggheads, bookworms, and rich kids who are going into their dads' businesses, but they'd be better off at Boston University or Harvard."

Stonehill College

Easton, Massachusetts 02357

Setting: Suburban
Control: Private (Roman Catholic)
Undergraduate enrollment: 925 men, 1335 women
Graduate enrollment: 4 men, 3 women
Student/faculty ratio: 17:1
Freshman profile: 4% scored above 700 on SAT I verbal; 45% scored 600–700; 46% 500–599; 5% below 500. 5% scored above 700 on SAT I math; 50% scored 600–700; 40% 500–599; 5% below 500. 9% scored above 28 on the ACT; 19% scored 27–28; 46% 24–26; 18% 21–23; 8% below 21. 48% graduated in top tenth of high school class; 79% in upper fifth.

Faculty profile: 85% Ph.D.'s
Tuition and fees: $25,540
Room and board: $10,564
Freshman financial aid: 91%; average scholarship or grant: $7019 need-based; $6355 non-need-based
Campus jobs: 31%; average earnings: $876/year
Application deadline: Early decision: Nov. 1; regular: Jan. 15.
Financial aid deadline: Feb. 1
Admissions information: (508) 565-1373
e-mail: admissions@stonehill.edu
web site: www.stonehill.edu

At most colleges today, a student can count on gaining some practical and relevant work experience at a nearby company or government agency. At Stonehill in Easton, Massachusetts, a Catholic college 22 miles south of Boston, the opportunities don't stop in this country or on this side of the Atlantic. A student of any major with a GPA of 3.0 or better may spend 15 weeks, $4^{1}/_{2}$ days a week, during the spring term of the junior year or the fall of the senior year completing an internship at any of a wide range of organizations in London, Paris, Geneva, Dublin, or Zaragoza, Spain. Work opportunities are available in diverse fields. While the experience is priceless, the tuition for the semester abroad also is definitely something to write home about: the same as for Stonehill on campus, which, at less than $26,000 in the 2005–2006 school year, is one of the better buys for a school in the Boston area.

Student body: The student body at Stonehill is rather homogeneous, a quality many undergraduates have been working hard to change. Sixty percent are from Massachusetts, with two-thirds of the out-of-staters also from the Northeast. A total of 28 states and 9 foreign countries are represented. Minority enrollment has increased from a low of 1.3% in fall 1991 to 10% in fall 2005, with the percentage of African-Americans, Hispanics, and Asian-Americans standing at 3% each with 1% foreign nationals. The steady increase has come through the work of an Intercultural Affairs Committee and its establishment of various campus support groups, among them Diversity on Campus, the Fear No People Committee, the Stonehill International Club, and the Cultural Committee of the Stonehill Government Association. Sixty-seven percent are Roman Catholic, 10% are Protestant, 4% are Greek Orthodox and other faiths, 1% Jewish, and the rest claim no religious affiliation. Thirty-three percent are graduates of private or parochial schools. "Many," adds a Massachusetts senior, "seem to be from small, if not private, high schools where values and academics were highly emphasized." Students use words like *open-minded, friendly, hard working,* and *fun-loving* to describe their classmates; though most are rather apathetic about politics and social issues when they arrive on campus, a number change that stance as they become more involved in community-service and other organizations. Many carry a reputation for being party people. Notes an international student: "Students have a good social sense, party and have fun, and still are able to take and do their work seriously, which is pretty impressive."

Academics: The college's earliest years were spent as Our Lady of Holy Cross Seminary, which was established in 1934 to train men for the priesthood. The institution became a 4-year college for men in 1948, enrolling the first women 3 years later. Until 1972, the college was run by the Eastern Province of the Congregation of Holy Cross but now is led by a predominantly lay board of trustees and functions as an independent institution in the Catholic tradition, awarding the bachelor's degree in 30 disciplines and a master's in accountancy degree program. The academic year is divided into 2 semesters. Average class size for undergraduates is 20, although the largest course, Biological Principles, enrolls 50.

As part of Stonehill's 4-year Cornerstone Program, first-year students begin with 2 sets of linked courses in the humanities (philosophy/religious studies and English/history), 2 foreign language courses, and a 1-hour Cultural Encounters seminar. In the second year, students participate in a learning community that consists of another 2 linked courses and an integrative seminar; in their third year, they take a moral reasoning course; in the fourth, a capstone requirement, usually met within the major field of study. Students also are required to take courses in natural scientific inquiry, social scientific inquiry, and statistical reasoning.

Just over half, 53%, of the 253 faculty members are full-time; 38% of the faculty are women. Students generally find the professors to be "great," involved in their subject matter, helpful and sincere in their desire to challenge and help students. Says a sophomore: "All of the professors I have had promote discussion and require hard work to pass, not to mention get a good grade." In addition to the regular interchange that occurs in classes, special programs like directed study enable students to work side by side with members of the faculty and administration in areas not covered by the ordinary courses. And on such a closeknit campus, students never know where they will encounter professors outside of class. Says a senior: "Many members of the faculty eat meals in the student dining commons; there are several who would prefer to join a table of students rather than their peers. My friends and I have learned that we cannot skip our morning class and expect to eat in the commons—we're bound to run into our professors there!"

The department of business administration has one of the most rigorous programs on campus, integrating the study of business and the liberal arts. A business major must complete 14 business core courses (in addition to the cornerstone core) as a foundation for 6–7 other courses in the area of concentration, such as international business, finance, marketing, management, or accounting. Students find the curricula in biology, chemistry, computer science, health-care administration, and political science to be equally demanding. Psychology has top-notch professors, a new lab, plus a newsletter to keep its students informed of psychology-related events on campus. The English faculty "are great," boasts a major, "and not afraid to go against standard canon." Those expecting the religious studies faculty to confine their curriculum to Catholicism "couldn't be further from the truth," advises a political science major. "The professors are particularly challenging and the courses offered are wide-ranging and interesting." Education also has professors who "push hard so that you can become a good teacher," says a major.

Students wishing to pursue extensive study in foreign languages are disappointed to find French and Spanish the only majors possible, with German offered just as a minor. Adds a senior biology major: "I know a few students who because they want to study a different language, like Russian or Chinese, go to neighboring colleges to study the language that they want there." Theater arts, too, is offered only as a minor as are art history, physics, and journalism.

Facilities: The MacPhaidin Library, which opened in fall 1998, is "incredible," in the words of 1 user. "It is open and airy, never hard to find a seat, and a quiet place to study." The facility offers extensive on-line resources, among them, the library's catalog, journal indexes, and access to more than 1000 full-text electronic journals. A research cluster of networked computers with Internet access, a computer classroom for research instruction, network connections at all tables, and individual seats as well as wireless access also are available. The library's own collection stands at more than 205,000 volumes and 2210 periodicals. Students turn to interlibrary loan for additional materials. Observes a junior: "I personally have never left the library having not accomplished and exceeded the goals I had going in."

Twelve computer labs are scattered across campus with more than 300 desktop and laptop computers connected to the Internet through a wired and wireless network. Notes a senior: "Within the campus, there is always at least one computer lab open at every point of the night." Wireless access is available throughout the campus and in all residence halls. More than 98% of all first-year students in the 2005–2006 school year brought a computer to campus; 90% of the units were laptops.

Special programs: Students at Stonehill may take courses at any of 8 other area schools, 3 of which are 2-year colleges. Further afield, students typically spend a semester or 2 in more than 100 study abroad programs worldwide. Students may also participate in a semester-long internship in New York City or Washington, D.C. There also are extensive opportunities for field studies in a wide range of majors and places. Selected students who have completed their first, second, or third year at Stonehill are eligible for the SURE program, which stands for Stonehill Undergraduate Research Experience and provides an opportunity for high achievers in all disciplines to participate in research projects with faculty members. SURE scholars receive a stipend totalling $2800 for an 8-week or $3500 for a 10-week summer stay. A 3-2 program in computer engineering is offered with the University of Notre Dame.

Campus life: Eighty-nine percent of the students live on the 375-acre campus, which residents describe as "typically New England," especially in the fall. Special-interest housing is available to those students with a concern for such issues as social justice, community service, the environment, and other topics students wish to explore. Most enjoy the fact that there are no fraternities or sororities, which they feel would disrupt the spirit of campus unity. More than 300 students participate in an extensive community outreach program known as "Into the Streets" in which they work with disadvantaged and special needs youth, the homeless, and the elderly. A number also put in a shift at the campus's 24-hour radio station WSHL, which is noted for its progressive music programming. Student social space known as "The Hill," complete with coffee shop and snack bar grill, pool tables, a fireplace, dance floor, and state-of-the-art audio and visual technology gives students nightly entertainment alternatives. After-hours admission to the campus is monitored by a roadblock that allows only weekend guests who have been invited by a student and who register to enter. Students also are held responsible for the behavior of their weekend guests.

Sixteen percent of all students take part in the 9 men's and 11 women's intercollegiate sports played in NCAA Division II. Basketball, baseball, women's lacrosse (the 2005 National Champions), and football games attract many spectators. The opening of a new football stadium in fall 2005, along with a new team name, the Skyhawks, has bolstered attendance at Saturday games. Twenty-two intramural sports involve at least 75% of the students. Club sports, too, are popular.

Boston, just 22 miles north, is the easiest getaway a student can make, although some prefer the 45-minute trip to Cape Cod, Newport, or Providence, R.I. The college makes escaping to Boston a bit easier with a free shuttle bus service operating over 40 hours a week from Tuesday through Sunday to the MBTA Red Line, area malls, and cinemas. Stonehill students also are given free admission to Boston's Museum of Fine Arts.

Cost cutters: Ninety-one percent of the 2005–2006 freshmen and 90% of continuing students received financial aid; for 63% of the freshmen and 62% of the others, the aid was need-based. The average freshman package for a first-year student with financial need included a need-based scholarship or grant averaging $7019 and need-based self-help aid such as loans and jobs averaging $6997. The average non-need-based athletic scholarship for freshmen was $8168; other non-need-based awards and scholarships averaged $6355. The average debt of a 2005 graduate was $17,390. Each year, the college awards several merit-based scholarships ranging in value from $2500 upward. Among the more prestigious are the Novak-Templeton Scholarship, which pays $7500 to half tuition based on outstanding scholarship and cocurricular contributions, Honors Scholarships, which pay $6000 to half tuition to students who are on average in the top 3% of their high school class with competitive test scores and significant cocurricular involvement, and the Presidential Scholarship, paying $4000 to half tuition, to those who ranked usually in the top tenth of their high school class with similarly impressive test scores and high school coursework. Most scholarships, however, are awarded based upon both merit and financial need. Tuition discounts may be available to families with more than 1 child enrolled at Stonehill.

Rate of return: Ninety percent of the students who enter as freshmen return for the sophomore year. Eighty-one percent go on to graduate in 4 years; 83% in 5 years; 85% in 6.

Payoff: Majors in business claimed the largest number of 2005 graduates at 25%, followed by education at nearly 8% and communication at just over 6%. Many Stonehill grads accept jobs in accounting, business, education, and health care, primarily with firms in Massachusetts but also in other parts of New England and around the country. Seventy-five companies and organizations recruited on campus in the 2004–2005 school year. Sixteen percent of recent alumni pursued advanced degrees.

Bottom line: Stonehill provides a small-college/small-town environment for students who want a supportive, familial community, albeit a bit homogenous, that also offers easy access to the bigness, bustle, and diversity of Boston. At Stonehill, says a New Englander, "a student can make a difference. In fact, it is not unusual for a junior or even a sophomore to head a group or organization. All he or she has to do is join, and participate. Here, any student can be someone."

Suffolk University

Boston, Massachusetts 02108

Setting: Urban
Control: Independent
Undergraduate enrollment: 1645 men, 2325 women
Graduate enrollment: 149 men, 262 women (1173 part-time)
Student/faculty ratio: 14:1
Freshman profile: 2% scored over 700 on SAT I verbal; 15% scored 600–700; 44% 500–599; 39% below 500. 0% scored over 700 on SAT I math; 13% scored 600–700; 45% 500–599; 42% below 500. 1% scored over 28 on the ACT; 7% scored 27–28; 18% 24–26; 36% 21–23; 38% below 21. 24% graduated in top fifth of high school class; 54% in upper two-fifths.

Faculty profile: 92% Ph.D.'s
Tuition and fees: $21,220
Room and board: $11,940
Freshman financial aid: 79%; average scholarship or grant: $6685 need-based; $5552 non-need-based
Campus jobs: 20%; average earnings: $1500/year
Application deadline: Mar. 1
Financial aid deadline: Mar. 1
Admissions information: (617) 573-8460;
(800) 6 SUFFOL
e-mail: admission@suffolk.edu
web site: www.suffolk.edu

Suffolk University in Boston is clear proof that you can't judge a college by its address. Suffolk is located on Beacon Hill, an area of the city settled by the upper-class and oh-so-haughty Boston Brahmins, that still smacks of yesteryear with its maze of cobblestone streets, red-brick sidewalks, and 18th- and 19th-century townhouses and mansions. But Suffolk's up-scale address is about its only blue-blooded distinction. The university draws its roots from the Suffolk Law School, founded in 1906 as a place where persons previously denied access to the legal profession because of social class, religion, or income were welcome to attend. The College of Arts and Sciences came into being in 1934 and offered one of the first programs in the nation whereby a student could earn a bachelor of arts degree entirely through evening study. With the addition of the School of Management in 1937, Suffolk assumed its present position as the university of Boston's working class, set in Brahmin territory. Eighty-three percent of its students are commuters, many with middle-class economic backgrounds. While remaining true to its egalitarian roots, with a tuition rate two-thirds that of more prestigious Boston-area schools, Suffolk is set apart from the majority of urban commuter institutions in that it remains small, with just under 4000 full-time undergraduates, is attentive in its teaching, and has been nationally recognized for its efforts to retain and graduate, not just admit, all kinds of students. Notes a sophomore: "Students are wanted here, and plenty of people make sure the individual knows that. It is a school that gives a very personalized education." Quips a senior: "It's the only place on Beacon Hill where everybody knows your name!"

Student body: Given Suffolk's dedication to serving commuter students, it is not surprising that 67% of its undergraduate enrollment is from Massachusetts, with 71% of the out-of-staters also coming from the Northeast. Students are present, however, from 39 states and 56 foreign countries. Sixty-nine percent are graduates of public schools. Just under 15% are members of racial and ethnic minority groups, including 7% Asian-Americans, 4% Hispanics, 3% African-Americans, and less than 0.5% Native Americans. Ten percent of the undergraduates are foreign nationals. Says a student from Germany: "Suffolk University prides itself on having a large population of international students who enjoy sharing their cultures and languages with others." *Hard-working* tops the list of adjectives students use to describe their peers. Though many must juggle courses, jobs and/or families, most are energetic and enthusiastic about being college students and are eager to meet newcomers on campus. "Because Suffolk is primarily a commuter school, I thought it would be hard to get to know people," observes a junior. "Fortunately, I have made many friends, including 3 close ones whom I know I will have for the rest of my life." Most undergraduates are up on current events and, as time permits, are politically active, especially given that the Massachusetts State House is next door. Because many students are paying for all or at least part of their educations, they generally take academics seriously. By the same token, however, because jobs and/or families often cut into study time, most are happy simply to do the best they can.

Academics: Suffolk awards the bachelor's degree in 70 majors, as well as a full range of masters' degrees, a doctorate in clinical psychology, and the juris doctor degree at Suffolk Law School. In 1996 Suffolk acquired the New England School of Art and Design and integrated its courses in graphic and interior design and fine arts into the curriculum. Classes follow a semester schedule and are known for being small in size and personal in attention. Notes a junior: "Here a student can ask questions in class rather than wait for small study groups with graduate students." In a recent school year, the largest class was Business Finance with just over 50 students enrolled. Typically, classes enroll less than 25 students with some upper-level courses having 15 or fewer.

General-education requirements differ between the College of Arts and Sciences, the Frank Sawyer School of Management, and the New England School of Art and Design at Suffolk, and also vary according to the degree program being pursued. Even in the School of Management, however, students must take at least 44 semester hours of liberal arts classes out of the 122 hours needed to graduate, including a course in cultural diversity.

Just over 60% of the 716-member faculty is part-time. All but 12 of the 280 full-time members teach undergraduates; all but 7 of the 436 part-time members do so as well. Forty-two percent of the pool are women. A large percentage also are foreign born. Says a junior: "This shows diversity, cultured backgrounds, and knowledge of the world." Students generally praise professors for being well versed in their subject matter and sensitive to the special circumstances of commuter students. Most will make time to see undergraduates even when the professor's schedule, or that of the student, seems hopelessly overloaded. One senior recalls how, as a freshman carrying a C+ average in Spanish at mid-term, her professor called *her* at home to make sure the student was aware that there were tutors available to help her. Observes a senior: "Many professors are adjuncts and work in the field they teach, making them fresh and exciting, bringing real world examples into the class to complement the assigned text." There is a minority of professors, however, many of whom teach courses at other universities or have those other "real world" jobs, who "really have no time for the students," says a psychology major.

Several disciplines in the College of Arts and Sciences and most programs in the School of Management stand out as Suffolk's strongest academic offerings. Government, sociology, communications, and journalism lead the way in terms of knowledgeable, helpful professors and opportunities for internships. Notes a government major: "Being right across from the State House not only gives you an academic viewpoint but also a practical one, and it is relatively easy to come by internships not only in Boston but in Washington, D.C. as well." History and English also are considered excellent. In the School of Management, majors in accounting, marketing, international business, and management, in particular, gain from having dedicated faculties many of whom are still active as consultants and solid up-to-date curricula.

Smaller departments such as those for modern languages and philosophy have more limited course offerings. French, for example, "has very few classes to offer after the basic level," says a senior with a minor in the field. Theater could use more faculty and more classes. Students say the natural and physical sciences also have not been as well developed as the social sciences and lack depth for those who wish to major in these fields. Some strengthening of these fields has come from a recent cooperative agreement with Massachusetts General Hospital that has led to new majors in radiation biology and medical biophysics. Says a junior: "Suffolk has some excellent professors in the natural sciences; however, the labs and lab equipment must be modernized." Mathematics needs more professors who can speak English clearly and communicate better with students.

Facilities: Few undergraduates had bad things to say about the old Mildred Sawyer Library, which occupied space 6 stories underground. Nearly everyone, though, eagerly awaited the opening in spring 2006 of the new Mildred F. Sawyer Library, covering 42,000 square feet and 3 stories above ground. The new space, twice the size of the old, is completely wireless with additional state-of-the-art technology—"a real treat," raves a media studies major. Most seating also is located next to the structure's many windows with views of Tremont and Beacon streets and the historic Granary Burial Ground. Together, Sawyer Library, plus the law school and design school libraries, house over 300,000 volumes and subscribe to more than 15,000 electronic and paper periodicals. The facilities have been known as quiet places to get a lot accomplished, so many commuters do their studying on campus, rather than closer to home. Students with Suffolk ID cards also can access any of 13 other libraries in the Fenway Library Consortium, including the Boston Public Library, and their 2.6 million volumes.

The School of Management houses about 100 Dell and Compaq computers; additional IBM-compatible and Macintosh units are located in the liberal arts college and in the residence halls. The New England School of Art and Design also has 4 computer labs, 3 with Macintosh computers and 1 with IBM PC-compatibles. A student generally can find a free unit when he or she needs it.

Special programs: Opportunities for study abroad are available in 31 countries, including Suffolk's own campuses in Madrid, Spain and Dakar, Senegal. Special grants funded by alumni pay transportation costs to various study abroad destinations, Ireland among them. Full-time internships also are popular in several nations as diverse as Ecuador and England. A special InterFuture program invites high-ranking juniors to prepare an intercultural, independent study project over an 8-month period and then carry out the research at home and abroad, both in a North Atlantic nation and in a developing country. Part-time internships with government offices in Boston or full-time experience in Washington, D.C. also can be arranged. Students with math and critical reading combined SAT scores of 1100 or above and class rank in the upper 20% are eligible to apply for a combined 5-year bachelor's-masters degree program in business administration. A limited number of high-achieving students may take part in combined bachelor's and law-degree programs. Suffolk also owns and operates a marine biology station at Cobscook Bay in Maine. Students may cross-register for classes at Emerson College.

Campus life: In reality, no students reside at Suffolk's 2-acre campus on Beacon Hill, although more than 600 undergraduates live in apartments, residence halls, and guest houses within walking distance of Suffolk. That includes the 345-bed residence hall across from Boston Common, which since its opening in August 2003 has become a favorite hang-out where freshmen can get to know one another better. "Suffolk is an urban campus," observes a junior: "We have no quad, unless you count Boston Common; we have no flashy buildings, unless you count the State House (next door)." Since few upperclassmen return to campus over the weekend, other than to put in time at the library or attend a campus play or sporting event, 90 minutes every Tuesday and Thursday have been set aside for student activities. Well over 800 students use that time to participate in some 75 extracurricular clubs. Those who don't belong to an organized group can always pop into a Friday afternoon theme party, enjoy lunchtime entertainment, or take part in periodic ethnic and cultural festivities. One national fraternity and 1 local sorority attract just over 1% of the student population. The 7-year-old Student Performing Arts Program already is center stage with popular theatrical offerings ranging from an a cappella group to a children's theater troupe. The community service group SOULS, Suffolk's Organization for Uplifting Lives through Service, involves many students in performing their own good works in the city. Crime is not a prime topic of concern around campus, although students have learned to use common sense at night and lock doors and not leave purses or other belongings unattended in campus buildings. Remarks a senior: "We benefit from the strong and varying law enforcement presence: we are located next to the State House with capital police, the Federal Building with state troopers, Boston Municipal Court with the Boston and Suffolk County police department, and Boston Common with park rangers. In addition to all the above, there is our own Suffolk Campus PD." Escorts also are provided to the residence hall, train stations, and parking garages.

Suffolk fields 7 intercollegiate sports for men and 6 for women, played under NCAA Division III. Men's and women's basketball and men's hockey and soccer draw the largest numbers of fans, though most students prefer to root for the Red Sox, Bruins, or Celtics. A fifth of the men and over 5% of the women turn out for the 1 woman's and 2 men's intramural sports offered. "Also, roller-blading along the Charles River is a great way to clear your mind," says a junior.

For most students, their primary physical activity is juggling responsibilities and commuting back and forth from home. For these students, their number one campus escape also is home or the sights and sounds of Boston. "If you're at a loss of what to do on the weekend," says a transfer student from New Hampshire, "you're not trying."

Cost cutters: Seventy-nine percent of 2005–2006 freshmen and 73% of continuing students received financial aid; for 68% of the freshmen and 56% of the rest, the assistance was need-based. The average freshman award for a first-year student with need included a need-based scholarship or grant averaging $6685 and need-based self-help aid such as loans and jobs averaging $5068. Other non-need-based awards and scholarships for freshmen averaged $5552. A recent Suffolk graduate typically left with $19,102 in debts. Suffolk provides several innovative options in the area of merit-based financial aid. Each year, 254 awards of between $1000 and $1500 are presented to students based on financial need and academic merit. Although these awards known as President's Incentive Loans/Grants are made as loans for which a student must sign a promissory note with the university, each student who graduates has his or her "loan" automatically forgiven and converted to a grant that need not be repaid. A student who withdraws, transfers from Suffolk, or fails to maintain satisfactory academic progress, however, must repay the loan with interest. Trustees' Ambassador Scholarships worth $4000 go to 20 undergraduates on the basis of academic performance and ability to present a positive image of Suffolk to prospective students and parents. In return for the funds, students work 10 hours a week helping admissions and financial aid officers recruit talented students. Under a similar setup, students can receive $4000 for working in orientation or scheduling or as tutors at the learning center. Entering freshmen who graduated in the top 10% of their high school class and achieved a GPA of at least 3.5 and a combined math and critical reading SAT of 1250 or above are automatically considered for a wide range of merit scholarships. The Dean's Scholarship ranges in value from $500 to $5000. Students who are a direct descendant of a Boston firefighter may qualify for a Vendome Scholarship that pays one third of tuition costs. More traditional merit-based Fulham, Chase, and Corcoran scholarships paid $3300 in a recent year to high achievers. A cooperative education program is an option in every major; more than 200 students participate. And there's an extra benefit for being a good student at Suffolk. A Grandfathered Tuition Plan for Meritorious Students absolves undergraduates with a minimum cumulative GPA of 3.6 from yearly tuition increases.

Rate of return: Seventy-five percent of entering freshmen return for the sophomore year. Thirty-five percent graduate in 4 years; 52% do so within 5 years; 56% in 6 years.

Payoff: Communications topped all majors among 2005 graduates, claiming nearly 16% of the class; sociology majors followed at 10%, management at 9%. In a recent class, 85% of the graduates found jobs within 6 months of getting their diplomas, primarily with firms in New England, and 28% entered graduate study, full- or part-time. More than 40 companies and organizations recruited on campus in the 2004–2005 school year.

Bottom line: Suffolk is a small, private, largely commuter university that, according to students, doesn't feel like the typical, impersonal, too-busy-to-care urban school. "This school brought me out of my shell," notes a sophomore. "Suffolk has many *nice* people who really care about the student on many levels."

Michigan

Albion College

Albion, Michigan 49224

Setting: Small town
Control: Private (United Methodist)
Undergraduate enrollment: 845 men, 1096 women
Graduate enrollment: None
Student/faculty ratio: 13:1
Freshman profile: 8% scored over 699 on SAT I verbal; 39.5% scored 600–699; 34% 500–599; 18.5% below 500. 10.5% scored over 699 on SAT I math; 52.5% scored 600–699; 30% 500–599; 7% below 500. 9% scored above 29 on the ACT; 53% scored 24–29; 36% 18–23; 2% below 18. 30% graduated in top tenth of high school class; 64% in upper fourth.

Faculty profile: 91% Ph.D.'s
Tuition and fees: $24,296
Room and board: $6928
Freshman financial aid: 97%; average scholarship or grant: $17,560 need-based; $12,346 non-need-based
Campus jobs: NA; average earnings: NA
Application deadline: Early action: Dec. 1; Regular: Mar.1
Financial aid deadline: Mar. 1
Admissions information: (517) 629-0321; (800) 858-6770
e-mail: admissions@albion.edu
web site: www.albion.edu

Top students in search of a well-balanced liberal arts education that doesn't neglect the practical side of life need look no further: Albion College, the first private college in Michigan to have a chapter of Phi Beta Kappa, is out front again in the growing areas of management, public service, and leadership. The Gerstacker Liberal Arts Institute for Professional Management, founded in 1973, combines a major in economics and management with courses in business ethics, writing, and public speaking, 2 semester-long internships, and a summer session—all within a 4-year period. The Gerald R. Ford Institute for Public Service, so named because the former President launched the program in 1977, supplements various majors with coursework in government, economics, history, and ethics, along with at least 1 semester-long internship in government-related institutions ranging from the White House news office to the Michigan Legislature. The latest addition, the Sleight Leadership Program, offers a similar sampling of courses and outside experiences to help produce future leaders. Such programs draw to Albion many top scholars who otherwise might have chosen other strong liberal arts colleges. But when they leave 4 or 5 years later, many rave as much about the overall curriculum, the interaction with scholarly faculty, and the general respect that their degree commands from both job recruiters and graduate school admissions officers as about these specialized offerings.

Student body: Michigan is home base for 90% of Albion's students, with other midwesterners accounting for most of the remaining 10% plus students in a recent year from 28 other states. Eighty-four percent in a recent year were graduates of public schools. Minority enrollment is small with African-American students at 4% comprising the largest racial and ethnic group on campus. Asian-Americans account for 2.5%, Hispanics and Native Americans, less than 1% each. Fifteen students in the 2005–2006 school year were foreign nationals. Umbrella, the governing body of Albion's diverse multicultural groups, raises awareness of the needs and concerns of various underrepresented populations on campus. Twelve percent of the total enrollment in a recent year were Methodist; 28%, Catholic. Twenty-six percent claimed no religious affiliation. Most students come from moderately conservative, upper-middle-class families and are preppy and very academically motivated. That feeling intensifies the longer a student resides on campus. "By the time I was a senior," reports one student, "I was spending 8–10 hours a day studying." While not everyone is as conscientious, there is an academically competitive, though never cutthroat, atmosphere. Emphasis is not one-sided, however—students get as involved in their extracurricular lives as they do their scholarly ones. The word, says a sophomore, is "overcommitted."

Academics: Albion, founded in 1835, offers bachelor's degrees in 27 disciplines. The academic year is divided into 2 semesters. Freshmen will generally encounter classes of between 15 and 35 students; juniors and seniors will usually find 5–15. There are exceptions at both ends, however, with a biology course in organismal function topping out at about 70 members in the lecture and a course in chemical thermodynamics and kinetics having only 2 participants.

All students are required to fulfill courses in 7 core areas: 2 units each in natural sciences and mathematics, social sciences, and humanities, and 1 each in fine arts, environmental studies, gender studies, global studies, and ethnicity studies. Students also take a first-year seminar that in a recent school year explored topics ranging from Genes and Society to Religion and the Arts. In addition, all freshmen must demonstrate competency in 5 modes of inquiry that include such areas as historical and cultural analysis and scientific analysis.

The faculty includes 139 full-time members and 36 part-time. Forty-one percent of the total pool are women. The vast majority of professors earn a triple E rating, which stands for "excellent, excellent, excellent." A number serve as faculty advisors to many of the 120 campus clubs and organizations or in community groups, yet they generally find extra time to help a student. Observes a freshman: "The 'open door' policy is great. At any time my professors are willing to talk with me about papers, my future, or the noon faculty basketball game." Many also encourage students to get more actively involved in their own learning. Says a senior: "The ownership I have taken over my own education is the most beneficial thing that Albion has given me."

Faculty members who make time for students to perform hands-on research have helped push biology and chemistry to the forefront of Albion's academic offerings. Biology students, in particular, are inspired by the great enthusiasm that faculty members show for their subject matter as well as the opportunity to work with first-rate equipment. Altogether, science students leave Albion well prepared: 95% of those with GPAs of 3.4 or higher who applied to medical school in recent years have been admitted. A new science complex with 4 stories of laboratory space as well as a 7000-square-foot atrium and greenhouse was expected to open in fall 2006. The facility will for the first time house all 5 of Albion's science departments under a single large roof.

The excellent Gerstacker program and a winning prelaw concentration of courses in political science, psychology, history, and philosophy also win students' highest approval ratings. Philosophy, political science, psychology, history, geology, and English each feature dedicated faculty who continuously challenge students to examine and re-examine their viewpoints. A newer program in athletic training already shows promise with its "amazing" team of instructors.

The foreign language department, with majors in French, German, and Spanish, would be enhanced by having more variety and rigor in its course offerings. The speech communication major needs more faculty to keep pace with growing numbers of students.

Facilities: The old and the new meet at Albion's library, where an enclosed walkway connects Stockwell Memorial Library, built in 1938, with Mudd Learning Center, completed in 1980; the two offer a combined collection of more than 355,000 volumes plus 900 periodicals with another 700 available as electronic subscriptions. Extensive computerized research aids ranging from a computerized catalog to numerous databases enable students to get their work done more efficiently. Researchers in need of materials not immediately available at Albion can go on-line or take a van that runs at least once a week to the University of Michigan or wait for sources to arrive via interlibrary loan. As a place to study, the library gets a grade of "soothing," with its supply of alcoves and rooms offering privacy and solitude.

More than 500 computers are available on campus for student use. Suites of microcomputers, including Macintoshes and Windows PCs, are located in all buildings and residence halls on campus. Residence-hall rooms are Internet-accessible to those who bring their own computers. (The college strongly recommends that students have their own units.) One lab on campus is open around the clock; most others until 1 a.m. A majority of the campus is wireless.

Special programs: Study-abroad opportunities are available in 19 countries from Mexico to India. Students may also participate in domestic off-campus programs in Philadelphia, New York, and Oak Ridge, Tennessee. Internships in education are offered at the Bank Street College of Education in New York City. Three-two engineering programs are available with Columbia, Case Western, and Michigan Tech universities, as well as the University of Michigan. Cooperative degree programs in other fields also are offered.

Campus life: All but 12% of the students live on the 225-acre campus, which boasts its share of ivy-covered buildings grouped around a central quad. Greek life is a primary focus of weekend activities, with a third of the men and women belonging to Albion's 6 national fraternities and 6 national sororities. There's usually a party at 1 of the fraternities on both nights of the weekend, and most guest lists include independents as well as other Greeks. Only fraternities offer housing to their members; sorority sisters may gather at special lodges for meetings and other social functions but live in the residence halls. Students say life on campus has gotten better for all undergraduates with construction of the Kellogg Center, a 24-hour student union offering lecture and entertainment halls and other activity-oriented facilities. The center also houses the Student Volunteer Bureau, which coordinates various community service projects in which more than half the students participate. The Department of Campus Safety, which is staffed by 32 student officers and 18 student dispatchers, provides escorts for students at night, and, says a midwesterner, "employs more staff than my high school had teachers, making everyone feel safe." Just to be sure, student senate members and the Dean of Students take an annual walk together to determine what areas of campus may need better lighting.

The NCAA Division III football team, winner of the 1994 national title, draws the biggest crowds to its games of the 9 varsity sports for men, although interest in Britons basketball has grown considerably. Nine varsity sports also are available to women. Sixty percent of the men and half of the women engage in the 19 men's and 18 women's intramurals provided, some of which are coed. Lacrosse is a popular club sport. The beautiful Albion countryside also is good for walking, running, biking, or rollerblading.

When the town of Albion (pop. 10,000) begins to feel too isolated, students head off to larger universities like Michigan State, the University of Michigan, or Western Michigan, each within a 45-minute drive. Detroit is 90 miles east; Chicago, 175 miles west. Adjacent to campus is a 135-acre nature center on the bucolic banks of the Kalamazoo River, which is just right for relaxing and reading Thoreau or Whitman.

Cost cutters: Ninety-seven percent of Albion's freshmen and continuing students in the 2005–2006 school year received financial aid; for 60% of all students, the aid was need-based. The average need-based grant for freshmen totaled $17,560; the average non-need-based scholarship was $12,346. Average debt for a 2005 graduate was $23,010. Four-year academic scholarships extending in value up to $12,500 are available to excellent students who graduate with high standardized test scores and GPAs of at least 3.2. Trustees Scholarships pay up to $14,000 a year to those who scored the highest on the ACT (30+), the SATs math and critical reading (1300+), and had a GPA of at least 3.9. The highest achievers among these scholars are considered for Distinguished Albion Scholarships that pay 72% to full tuition annually. Candidates must take part in an on-campus competition in mid February. Various tuition payment plans also are offered.

Rate of return: Eighty-six percent of the freshmen who enter return for the sophomore year. Sixty-seven percent graduate in 4 years, 72% within 5 years.

Payoff: Twenty percent of the 2005 graduates earned bachelor's degrees in the social sciences, 11% in psychology, and 9% in the biological sciences, with nearly 9% each in the physical sciences and visual and performing arts. Typically, about two-thirds of the graduates accept jobs shortly, many in accounting, banking, sales, teaching, communications, and human services, primarily in the Midwest and East. Two hundred and five companies and organizations recruited on campus during a recent school year. Within 10 years of graduating, about 70% of Albion alumni are involved again in higher education, as many as 20% in graduate school in the arts and sciences and at least 15% in business school.

Bottom line: Albion is a college that is ALIVE, in the words of a satisfied senior, with opportunities for Academics, Leadership, Involvement, and Volunteerism for Everyone. "A student can dive in and sample a wide variety of these things," the Michigan resident continues. "Anyone with a propensity for a well-rounded life will love it here."

Alma College

Alma, Michigan 48801

Setting: Small town
Control: Private (Presbyterian)
Undergraduate enrollment: 517 men, 725 women
Graduate enrollment: None
Student/faculty ratio: 13:1
Freshman profile: 22% scored over 700 on SAT I verbal; 26% scored 600–700; 35% 500–599; 17% below 500. 15% scored over 700 on SAT I math; 39% scored 600–700; 22% 500–599; 22% below 500. 14% scored above 28 on the ACT; 14% scored 27–28; 28% 24–26; 25% 21–23; 19% below 21. 40% graduated in top tenth of high school class; 53% in upper fifth.

Faculty profile: 88% Ph.D.'s
Tuition and fees: $21,134
Room and board: $7410
Freshman financial aid: 99%; average scholarship or grant: $18,976 need-based; $2998 non-need-based
Campus jobs: 36%; average earnings: $800/year
Application deadline: Rolling
Financial aid deadline: Mar. 1
Admissions information: (989) 463-7139; (800) 321-ALMA
e-mail: admissions@alma.edu
web site: www.alma.edu

Students expect major universities like Johns Hopkins and the University of California, Davis, to turn out impressive numbers of graduates in the life sciences. But how about Alma College in rural central Michigan, a school of 1250 undergraduates and no graduate programs? Although business was the major of choice for 1 in 6 Alma graduates in the Class of 2005, biology ranked second, claiming 1 of every 7 graduates, and that figure doesn't include the smaller number who specialize in biochemistry. From year to year, the percentage of biology majors ranges from about 10% to as high as 20% of degree recipients, usually placing among the 3 most popular fields of study.

Though Alma's national reputation in the sciences may be limited, students know a strong program when they see it. All biology professors carry the highest degrees in their field, and the college recently spent more than $10 million expanding and updating the science facilities, which include a human cadaver lab. Boasts an admiring computer science major: "We now have equipment that, within the state, only the University of Michigan and Michigan State can duplicate—and Alma students get to use it as undergraduates." Even without the latest additions, Alma's emphasis on involving students in research has brought results: over the past dozen years, 90% of all Alma graduates who applied to medical schools have been admitted, compared to just over 50% nationally. Alma College may not be the best known name in scientific circles, but its personalized program is a sure prescription for success.

Student body: Although Alma has been striving to attract more students from outside the state's borders, 94% of the enrollment comes from Michigan, with all but 2% of the nonresidents also midwesterners. Altogether, 21 states and 9 foreign countries are represented. Ninety-three percent of the students attended public schools. Nine percent of the undergraduates are members of Alma's religious denomination, Presbyterian. Protestants of other denominations account for 24%; Catholics, 22%; and persons of more than 15 other faiths and denominations, 14%. The remaining 30% claim no affiliation. Minority students make up about 6% of the enrollment, with 2% Hispanics, 2% African-Americans, and 1% each Asian-Americans and Native Americans. One percent of the students are foreign nationals. Undergraduates tend to be politically conservative, a reflection, many say, of the small towns and small-town values a majority have grown up with. Students say that an increasing liberal contingent helps "to shake things up a bit," though both ends of the spectrum agree that Alma is an academic school where hard work is the prevailing philosophy. Notes a sophomore: "Having so many high school valedictorians, graduate-school hopefuls, and med school want-to-be's makes for a lot of competition," though even Alma, adds a junior, has "our fair share of slackers."

Academics: Alma, which turned 120 in 2006, offers bachelor's degrees in 28 majors. The academic year is divided into 2 semesters, ending with a May term that allows students to study a subject in depth on the home campus, on another campus, in a foreign country, or on the job. Although an introductory psychology class can enroll almost 70, most freshman-level courses have far fewer, between 20 and 30 students. Classes for juniors and seniors rarely have more than 20 participants, and a course in advanced German may have just 1.

All undergraduates must demonstrate proficiency in computation, a foreign language, and composition, and must take at least 4 "quill" courses that require significant writing, plus complete 48 credits in arts and humanities, social sciences, and natural sciences. One faculty member refers to the program as "WAC, SAC, and TAC": writing across the curriculum, speaking across the curriculum, and thinking across the curriculum.

Eighty-two of the 119 faculty members are full-time. Thirty-eight percent are women. The best professors draw on rich academic and practical backgrounds to relate their subjects to a broader context. It's the personal interaction, however, that wins with students. Says a junior: "At Alma, it is not uncommon to call a professor in the late evening to clarify a question for an assignment or in preparation for an exam. Many science professors also come in on Sundays to work in the labs with students." Faculty also participate in many of the same cultural and recreational activities as students. Adds another junior: "If one were trying to avoid his or her professors, it would be virtually impossible to do here."

Alma's strongest academic programs are clearly the sciences and business and international business administration. The business programs feature professors with strong backgrounds in the field plus excellent job placement records. An interdepartmental major in international business administration requires extensive foreign language ability and participation in courses on multinational issues that help prepare students for careers with firms in France, Germany, Japan, Spain, or Latin America. History provides excellent opportunities for scholarly research and publication and has helped to send more than 90% of Alma's prelaw students on to law school over the past dozen years. Political science, long highly regarded around campus for its diverse and challenging faculty, has also impressed crowds in the Big Apple. For 9 of the last 10 years, the college's Model United Nations team has won top honors at the New York conference, which draws teams from 245 colleges and universities in the United States and from 18 foreign countries. The popular major in exercise and health science offers great opportunities for students to perform research with professors and gain hands-on experience themselves.

More faculty are needed in smaller departments such as economics, computer science, sociology and anthropology, and physics. Though students consider the existing foreign language program, with majors in French, Spanish, and German, to be excellent, some wish there were majors or minors in additional languages.

Facilities: For most students, Monteith Library is *the* place to study on campus—"the hot spot for learning," says a senior—and it usually manages to accommodate both the students who are willing to mix a little socializing with their studying and their counterparts, who head directly to the designated quiet area to be free from any distraction. The collection of 266,500 volumes and 1583 periodicals seems to satisfy most students' basic research needs. The opening in 1996 of an 8000-square-foot wing provided additional shelf space for up to 80,000 volumes, 26 student study carrels with plug-in connections to the Internet, 3 group-study rooms, and a computerized classroom with 25 workstations. The entire library also offers wireless Internet access. Items not available locally are easily obtained through interlibrary loan with more than 20 other libraries or online.

The college computer system makes available 266 computers and workstations throughout the campus. Computers located in the academic buildings are available until midnight; during midterms and finals, until 2 a.m. Computers in the dorms are accessible anytime. The college strongly recommends that students bring their own computers. Wireless access is available in the college's small housing units and in several academic buildings besides the library.

Special programs: Students may cross-register for the 1-month spring term at 6 other campuses that follow the same 4-4-1 schedule. The May term also provides numerous opportunities to take Alma courses overseas; recent classes were conducted in Peru, Poland, England, and China. Alma also offers its own study-abroad programs for a semester or a year in Mexico and 4 European countries, with its program in Paris the largest offered by any U.S. college or university. Three-two programs in engineering are available with the University of Michigan and with Michigan Technological University. Spending a semester in Washington, D.C., at American University, at the Urban Life Center in Chicago, or in the Philadelphia Center Internship Program also is an option.

Campus life: Eighty-three percent of the undergraduates reside on the 125-acre campus located 5 minutes from downtown Alma, the heart of this community of 9000 residents. Weekend activities for students have grown considerably over the last several years but many students from the surrounding area still opt to go home or to neighboring universities once Friday classes are finished. Seventeen percent of the men and 26% of the women are members of 1 local and 4 national fraternities and 1 local and 4 national sororities. Students report no schism between Greeks and independents, and most fraternity parties are open to nonmembers by invitation. The Union Board regularly schedules dances with live bands, comedians, and musical performers for everyone to enjoy. More than 30% of Alma's students perform with 1 or more of the college's musical ensembles, which include jazz and Scottish kiltie bands. The college dance company performs to standing-room-only audiences during its 3 performances each term. Although campus crime is practically nonexistent, residence halls are locked at night and security officers patrol campus 24 hours a day to keep the situation that way.

Involvement in athletics is high at both the intercollegiate and the intramural level. More than a third of the men and women test their talents in 9 men's and 9 women's varsity sports, played in NCAA Division III. Although many of the women's teams, such as basketball, have achieved better records, it's the men's teams, for example, football, basketball, and baseball, that draw the bigger crowds. About half of the men and a fourth of the women turn out for 10 intramural sports, including flag football, racquetball, and wallyball. Alma's athletics-minded students welcomed the opening in September 2001 of the Alan J. Stone Center for Recreation, built at the request of students and named after the college's eleventh president who served from 1988 to 2000. The 53,000-square-foot facility houses 4 courts with lines for tennis, basketball, and volleyball, including one court for in-line hockey and indoor soccer. There is also a suspended 3-lane track, fitness room, and climbing wall.

The town of Alma, 50 miles north of Lansing, the state capital, offers 1 movie theater and 2 bowling alleys for student entertainment. The most popular bars are in the bowling alleys. Many students road-trip to East Lansing and Mount Pleasant to mix with their counterparts from Michigan State and Central Michigan universities, respectively.

Cost cutters: In the 2005–2006 school year, 99% of freshmen and continuing students received financial aid; for about 75% of both groups, the aid was need-based. The average freshman award for a student with need included a need-based scholarship or grant averaging $18,976 and need-based self-help aid such as loans and jobs averaging $5000. Other non-need-based awards and scholarships averaged $2998. A 2005 Alma graduate typically left with $18,947 in debts. Renewable scholarships based on a student's high school grade point average and standardized test scores achievement, include the Trustee Honors and Presidential scholarships that pay $12,000 and $11,000, respectively, and Tartan and Dean's Awards worth $4000, $7000, and $10,000 apiece. Performance and religious leadership awards pay up to $1000. A variety of payment plans are available.

Rate of return: Eighty percent of the freshmen return for the sophomore year. Fifty-two percent graduate in 4 years; 69%, in 5 years; 71% in 6.

Payoff: In the 2005 graduating class, 17% earned degrees in business administration, followed by 14% in biology and 12% in exercise and health science. Three-quarters of Alma graduates usually proceed directly into the job market, most accepting positions in the 4-state region of Michigan, Illinois, Indiana, and Ohio. A study of a recent graduating class found 33% employed in professional, technical, or managerial positions, 13% in sales and marketing, and 12% in education with another 12% in the military and other occupations. Within 6 months of commencement, a fourth are enrolled in graduate or professional school. Within 5 to 10 years of earning their bachelor's degrees, 70% of Alma graduates have been or are involved in some kind of advanced study.

Bottom line: Alma meets and exceeds all of the standard "rates" that characterize a high-quality educational institution: a decent tuition rate, a solid graduation rate, an impressive student-acceptance rate into graduate and professional schools, and a steady rate of work for eager participants. But undergraduates stress that Alma also boasts a very high "student happiness" rate, which makes all the other measures worth that much more.

Calvin College

Grand Rapids, Michigan 49546

Setting: Suburban
Control: Private (Christian Reformed Church)
Undergraduate enrollment: 1818 men, 2150 women
Graduate enrollment: 2 men, 2 women (48 part-time)
Student/faculty ratio: 12:1
Freshman profile: 16% scored over 700 on SAT I verbal; 38% scored 600–700; 34% 500–599; 12% below 500. 17% scored over 700 on SAT I math; 41% scored 600–700; 33% 500–599; 9% below 500. 24% scored above 28 on the ACT; 21% scored 27–28; 26% 24–26; 20% 21–23; 9% below 21. 47% graduated in top fifth of high school class; 72% in upper two-fifths.

Faculty profile: 82% Ph.D.'s
Tuition and fees: $19,150
Room and board: $6585
Freshman financial aid: 92%; average scholarship or grant: $9325 need-based; $4115 non-need-based
Campus jobs: 45%; average earnings: $1200/year
Application deadline: Aug. 15
Financial aid deadline: Aug. 1 (Priority date: Feb. 15)
Admissions information: (616) 526-6106;
(800) 688-0122
e-mail: admissions@calvin.edu
web site: www.calvin.edu

To most of today's high school students, many with a tenuous grasp of history, let alone theological history, the name Calvin College brings to mind something about the Protestant Reformation, the Puritans, a literal interpretation of the Bible, and strict rules regarding clean living, something many teenagers want nothing to do with. But to those familiar with Calvin College, a school of about 4000 undergraduates affiliated with the Christian Reformed Church, the name brings to mind a place where students feel loved, guided, and challenged. Observes an easterner: "They teach and practice responsible freedom, meaning that they trust you to make the right choices, but if you start to screw up too much there is a support system to put you back on track." At just under $26,000 for tuition, fees, room, and board in the 2005–2006 school year, that's a price even John Calvin himself would not want to reform.

Student body: Forty-nine percent of Calvin's undergraduates are members of the Christian Reformed Church, which traces its roots to Dutch settlers in the nineteenth century who came to western Michigan in their search for freedom from the established church of The Netherlands. Because the roots of the church are here, students of this faith from 49 states and 45 countries seek out Calvin College. However, the majority of undergraduates, 52%, are from the college's and church's home state of Michigan, and a fifth of the out-of-staters also are from the Midwest. Fifty-eight percent of the undergraduates are graduates of private or parochial schools. All but 4% are Protestant, mostly from other evangelical Protestant churches, and none are Jewish, with 1% Catholic and the rest split between members of other religions, those who claimed no affiliation and those who gave no information. The racial and ethnic makeup of the student body reflects the strong Dutch heritage of both the college and the church. Eighty-seven percent of the students are white Americans and 3% Asian-Americans, with 1% each African-Americans and Hispanics and less than 1% Native Americans. Foreign nationals account for 7%. Students describe themselves as "moderately conservative" for the most part, more conservative than students found on most secular campuses, but more liberal than those found at many other Christian colleges. Many enter "kind of clueless," says a senior, about what is happening beyond their protected collegiate environment but are open to learning. Says an accounting major: "Students explore many political, academic, and social issues with great vigor and enthusiasm. They particularly deal with issues of faith and why they believe what they do." Students tend to be outgoing and friendly but still attentive to their studies, though just *how* attentive can vary depending on the major. "Most students are diligent without being obsessive," says a senior. "Cutthroat competition and studious social outcasts are rarities."

Academics: Calvin, which was founded in 1876 as a college and seminary, awards the bachelor's degree in more than 40 majors plus a master's degree in education. Classes follow the semester calendar, including a 1-course interim term in January. Students in their first 2 years find all but the largest lecture courses range from 20 to 30 participants, declining to below 20 in the latter 2 years. The largest course, Introduction to Cell Biology and Genetics, enrolls about 60; the smallest, a modern physics laboratory, 2.

Calvin's core curriculum, entitled "An Engagement in God's World," is central to each student's collegiate experience. Both course content and student learning are guided by and centered around 4 components: the core gateway, which includes a course in Developing a Christian Mind; core competencies, in such skills as writing, research, fitness, and foreign language; core studies in the traditional disciplines; and a core capstone that consists of integrative studies courses typically taken in the junior or senior year.

To teach at Calvin, faculty members, who number 309 full-time, 89 part-time, and 70% men, must subscribe to the creeds of the Christian Reformed Church and agree to work in their teaching and personal relations to reflect "the Lordship of Christ and the authority of the Word of God." The end result, for most students, is a faculty dedicated to making their charges grow and excel academically as well as spiritually. "They are excited to share their subject area as well as their faith," says a sophomore.

Though the approach to academics at Calvin is distinctly Christian, students' list of best majors, which bears a strong career focus, could be found at any secular campus. Education, engineering, and nursing top the ranks, thanks largely to a winning combination of "incredible" faculty and plenty of work in real-life situations. Engineering, and other of the sciences, also benefit from first-rate laboratory equipment; physics students in particular work closely with professors in their research and sometimes get publishing credit with them. An $18 million, 70,000-square-foot hall of science with 30 well-equipped labs for biology, biotechnology, chemistry, and biochemistry and a nearby engineering building with 2 design centers offer space for in-depth research and design work. The education department is quite competitive, with well-developed teacher aide and student teaching programs. Students must apply to gain admittance to the program. Nursing students gain valuable clinical experience at Spectrum Health hospitals and in community-based agencies as well as special experience in mental health nursing at Pine Rest Christian Hospital. Among less professionally focused majors, a philosophy major boasts: "The philosophy department is outstanding, and the history and English departments aren't far behind."

Too many professors in the religion and theology department, say students, are ordained pastors who have the real-life experience but lack sufficient knowledge about how to relay it meaningfully. The geology and political science programs are small and in need of expansion. The mathematics department could use more challenge; Spanish, French, and German, more native speakers. Art, says a major, is in need of a new home. "It's stuck in the basement of our main building," says this senior. "In my opinion, an art department should have windows in it, but ours does not."

Facilities: The 5-story Hekman Library, located in the center of campus, offers holdings that are extensive for a college of 4000: 480,000 volumes, and 15,000 paper and electronic periodicals. Its resources are fully computerized and usually adequate to meet the needs of most users. The second floor houses materials related to the origins and leaders of the Christian Reformed Church; the fourth floor contains one of the most extensive collections of books and articles on John Calvin and Calvinism available anywhere. The library seats about a third of the student body, primarily at individual study carrels and at tables where studiers are meant to be seen, and not heard. The biggest complaint students have is that the building is closed on Sundays.

An expansive computer facility on the first floor of the library houses more than 250 PC and Macintosh computers for student use. There also are 3 Pentium PC labs and 2 other Mac labs, plus smaller computer classrooms and labs spread among the different academic buildings, residence halls, and on-campus apartments. Altogether, more than 800 units are available. Students have few complaints about computer availability during the term, other than the all-day Sunday closing of the main lab "rather inconvenient," says a junior, but finals time can bring waits of 15 to 20 minutes. A senior notes that students needing computers receive a pager "to tell them when a computer is ready so it is possible to go study while they are waiting."

Special programs: Calvin students may study abroad in 16 countries throughout Latin America, Europe, Africa, or Asia or spend a semester on this continent in Washington, D.C., in Los Angeles studying film, in Chicago, Oregon, or at the Au Sable Institute of Environmental Studies in northern Michigan. A 3-2 program in occupational therapy is offered with Washington University in St. Louis.

Campus life: Just over half of all undergraduates, 58%, reside on Calvin's 390-acre campus, located just 7 miles southeast of downtown Grand Rapids; all first-year and sophomore students under the age of 21 not living at home are required to stay in the residence halls. There are no fraternities or sororities, and no parties on campus, so students generally go off campus to party or engage in a variety of alternative activities provided, such as hayrides, dances, bowling, plays, and movies. Say a senior: "Students are lively, and there is an emphasis on going out and trying new things." The Dance Guild is among the most active of the 40 student organizations. More than half the students also are regularly involved as volunteers in a wide range of local projects. Chapel service is held weekdays at 10 a.m.; though attendance is encouraged, it is not mandatory. Residence-hall doors are locked around the clock and students can gain entrance only with the use of their IDs. A vehicle patrol and escort service also give support around the college grounds. Students, as a rule, are regularly cautioned not to walk, run, or bike alone, especially at night, though most say they generally feel very secure on campus.

The Calvin Knights basketball team, the 1992 NCAA Division III champs, draws a spirited crowd to its Saturday games. Men's soccer and ice hockey, a club sport, too, are popular. Not to be outdone, the Calvin women's cross-country team took home the national championship trophy in 1998 and 1999. Altogether, Calvin fields 8 intercollegiate sports for men and 9 for women. A fourth of the men but fewer than a fifth of the women take part in the 18 intramural sports provided for men and 14 for women.

The Grand Rapids metropolitan area (pop. 600,000) offers much of what restless students are looking for in the way of first-run movies, malls, coffee bars, and restaurants. Chicago, which offers even more, is about 3 1/2 hours away. Those preferring a more peaceful refuge need go no further than the woods, ponds, and wetlands of the college's 90-acre ecosystem preserve.

Cost cutters: Ninety-two percent of the freshmen and 90% of continuing students received financial aid in the 2005–2006 school year. For 62% of both groups, the aid was based on need. The average freshman award for a first-year student with financial need included a need-based scholarship or grant averaging $9325 and need-based self-help such as loans and jobs averaging $5100. Other non-need-based awards and scholarships for freshmen averaged $4115. An average 2005 graduate left with debts of $18,000. More than 400 scholarships are awarded annually to first-year students and more than 800 to those returning. About 80 Trustee Scholarships worth $10,000 a year are awarded to students admitted by Feb. 1 who rank within the top 3% of freshmen admitted to the college. Other awards based on grade point average, standardized test scores, and students' performance on an essay range from the $1000 Knollcrest to the $6000 Presidential Scholarship with three levels of scholarships in between. Mosaic Awards pay $6000 a year to students with excellent academic records whose ethnic, cultural, and/or socioeconomic backgrounds would create a more diverse student body. Multicultural Awards of $3000 each go to prospective North American ethnic minority students. Denominational grants pay $750 to $1250.

Rate of return: Eighty-eight percent of freshmen return for the sophomore year. Fifty-six percent graduate in 4 years; 72% do so in 5 years, 74% in 6.

Payoff: Business, elementary education, and English were the most popular majors among 2005 graduates, claiming 10%, 8% and 7% respectively of the degrees awarded. Nearly a fifth of recent graduates have pursued advanced degrees within months of commencement at Calvin. Among a recent study of 925 private colleges, Calvin ranked 15th in the number of students going on to earn a Ph.D. Nearly 300 companies and organizations recruited on campus in the 2004–2005 school year. Fifty-five percent of Calvin graduates work in the nonprofit sector.

Bottom line: Calvin College provides a liberal arts education in the reformed Christian tradition, and students must be comfortable with both parts of that statement in order to succeed here. Students who have been raised in the Christian Reformed Church or who accept its religious beliefs will appreciate most the fine education and moral and spiritual support the faculty and other students have to offer. Those attracted simply by Calvin's size, location, and low tuition without the religious connection could feel out of place.

Hope College

Holland, Michigan 49423

Setting: Medium-sized city
Control: Private (Reformed Church in America)
Undergraduate enrollment: 1174 men, 1855 women
Graduate enrollment: None
Student/faculty ratio: 14:1
Freshman profile: 20% scored over 700 on SAT I verbal; 37% scored 600–700; 36% 500–599; 7% below 500. 20% scored over 700 on SAT I math; 40% scored 600–700; 34% 500–599; 6% below 500. 28% scored above 28 on the ACT; 18% scored 27–28; 28% 24–26; 19% 21–23; 7% below 21. 34% graduated in top tenth of high school class; 54% in upper fifth.

Faculty profile: 77% Ph.D.'s
Tuition and fees: $21,540
Room and board: $6668
Freshman financial aid: 96%; average scholarship or grant: 13,809 need-based; $6616 non-need-based
Campus jobs: 40%; average earnings: $1515/year
Application deadline: Rolling
Financial aid deadline: Mar. 1 (Feb. 15 priority)
Admissions information: (616) 395-7850; (800) 968-7850
e-mail: admissions@hope.edu
web site: www.hope.edu

Every now and then, a freshman comes to Hope College with little hope—and becomes a believer in him- or herself. "I came to Hope as a last resort," recalls a recent graduate. "It was the only school that would accept me. I was a marginal student at best, but Hope motivated and nurtured me, and made it possible for me to enter law school"—and not just any law school, but the prestigious Northwestern University School of Law. "Although I wouldn't call the competition for grades intense or the classes frustratingly difficult, I would stack the education provided here against that obtained at any other school," he continues. "Hope is always there for its students." And it stands by at a price that lets an undergraduate save thousands of dollars toward the cost of an advanced degree at whatever prestigious graduate school a Hope education makes possible.

Student body: Although Hope's encouraging message attracts students from 42 states and 32 foreign countries, 72% of the undergraduates come from Michigan, and most nonresidents, too, are midwesterners. Eighty-six percent are graduates of public schools. A lack of diversity, according to students, is among Hope's greatest shortcomings, but efforts are being made to widen the school's economic, racial, and ethnic composition. At present, students come predominantly from white, upper-middle-class families. Enrollment is 92% white American, with 2% each foreign national, Asian-American, African-American, and Hispanic. Members of the Reformed Church in America account for 19% of the enrollment; most of the rest are also Protestant, with 11% Catholic, 22% other faiths, and just 1% who claim no affiliation. Although Hope's Christian foundation is an integral part of its learning environment, students expecting a campus full of "Bible bangers" are quickly set straight. Students are concerned and caring, rather than evangelical, in their faith. A member of a rival college refers to Hope undergraduates as "happy, smiley students," who often appear sheltered from outside political or social issues. However, according to an out-of-the-mainstream senior, there is a subset of "artistic, weird, and unique types who paint, write, and discuss philosophy, who care about issues and speak out." Students' prevailing sense of community extends to their attitude about academics. Says a senior: "While competitive and serious, students help each other out, encouraging and offering assistance when necessary. Hope students care about others, invest in their community, get involved and think deeply and seriously about issues of life, faith, and intellect."

Academics: Hope, which was founded by Dutch pioneers in 1866 and still has students of Dutch heritage, awards bachelor's degrees in 83 majors. The academic year is divided into 2 semesters, with 4-week May, June, and July terms available for intensive off- or on-campus study. Average class size is 25, with Ecology and Evolutionary Biology sometimes enrolling past 70 and a number of upper-level courses only 6.

Hope's general-education program, covering 56 of the 126 hours needed to graduate, begins with a first-year seminar, a class in expository writing, and a course in health dynamics. Students also must complete the second semester of a foreign language, 10 hours in mathematics and natural sciences, 6 hours each in religious studies, the social sciences, and the arts, 8 hours in cultural heritage, a course in cultural diversity, and a senior seminar.

Thirty-two percent of the 316 faculty members are part-time. Forty-one percent are women. Students spare no superlatives when describing their professors, with "outstanding," yet "down to earth," covering the scope of their assets. Drawn from about 110 different colleges and universities, most faculty have converged at Hope because they enjoy interacting with students, and it shows. Class over dinner or dessert at a professor's home is not uncommon. Remarks a senior: "Our faculty care about the growth of students, as intellects, as personalities, and as human beings." Regular student evaluations ensure that weaker professors are closely scrutinized and are let go if they do not improve. Most evaluations find only winners. Since the year 2000,

3 professors of physics, biology, and chemistry have all been nationally recognized for their contributions to research in their fields and for involving so many undergraduates in their work.

Such "fantastic" faculty and excellent facilities contained in a new $38 million science center distinguish biology, chemistry, and psychology above all other fields at Hope. Adds a chemistry major: "Professors are available to help students often. There isn't a 'weed out' mentality among the faculty regarding the students." Here, research is something faculty members do with students, not closeted by themselves. Recalls a junior chemistry major: "I was planning to get involved in research my sophomore year at the earliest. But 2 *days* after I stepped on campus, I was asked to join a project." And, notes an admiring history major, "These projects include more than simply cleaning out beakers but also working on the hypothesis, design, and implementation of a project." Little wonder, that every year Hope ranks among the top 10 private schools in its support of students for funded research in the sciences. Research stipends further enable selected biology and chemistry students to pursue full-time projects during the summer.

Each year, 30–35 psychology students also are involved in independent study projects, many making use of Hope's excellent new laboratories. Again, the emphasis has reaped rewards as, over the last 20 years, Hope's psychology department has ranked at the top for producing first-, second-, and third-place winners in a national psychology student research competition. Though less renowned than the sciences, English, religion, political science, education, history, physics, and dance also are rigorous and well respected. The theater and art programs are both very supportive of student creativity; the theater faculty is especially talented and professional in their work.

Students complain that some of the computer science professors too often talk over their heads. Philosophy also needs more professors who can communicate effectively with students.

Facilities: Van Wylen Library, completed in 1988, is "the perfect place to study," according to a senior. The 5-level library was designed with students in mind, with space for group as well as private study, plus food and drink and tables for eating and socializing at the Cup and Chaucer in the lobby. Most find that the collection of almost 362,000 volumes and 8500 current periodicals, plus about 11,000 recordings in a branch library at the Nykerk Hall of Music, satisfies the majority of research needs. A computerized catalog plus extensive search capabilities makes the process very efficient. The Western Theological Seminary Library, a block away, provides resources Van Wylen lacks; its collection also is accessible by computer.

Nearly 100% of Hope students surveyed in 2005 owned their own computers; almost two-thirds owned laptops. Students unsure about bringing their own computers to campus can try out the more than 200 largely Windows-based computers available in 18 general-use labs. Additional computers in department-specific labs bring the total available to over 300. Many locations around campus also are wireless.

Special programs: Hope students can take advantage of many off-campus study programs, as far away as Hong Kong or Israel, among the 57 countries where study is possible, or as near as Chicago or Washington, D.C. The most popular option by far is Hope's own Vienna Summer School, in which 50–70 students live with Austrian families and study a wide range of courses from business to literature and music. For more than 20 years, Hope has shared an exchange program with its Japanese sister school, Meiji Gakuin near Tokyo, under which Hope students study in Japan for 6 weeks in May and June, and Japanese students come to Hope during September.

Campus life: Eighty-one percent of Hope students live on the 120-acre campus, which is centered around the "Pine Grove," a wooded area where the original buildings were constructed more than a century ago. Just 6% of the men and 15% of the women belong to 5 local fraternities and 6 local sororities, which sponsor many weekend parties. Upperclassmen who live off campus and often are fraternity members as well also hold parties in their rented houses. Traditional events are big for independents and Greeks alike, among them a tug-of-war pitting freshmen against sophomores in a pull across the Black River, and NyKerk, a song, oration, and drama contest between women from the 2 lower classes. Just about every weekend, there is a wealth of comedians, singers, movies, and special events planned, so it was no surprise to students in 2004, as well as in 2002 that Hope's student activities program was recognized with the "Excellence in Programming" award for colleges in the Mid-America region.

Anywhere from 50 to 100 students take part in the Fellowship of Christian Athletes, which is not restricted to the sports-minded. An Environmental Issues group keeps earthly matters at the fore and, starting another Hope tradition, sponsors an annual Earth Day concert in the Pine Grove. The radio station and literary magazine also have strong followings. Chapel is held Monday, Wednesday, and Friday mornings during community hour, and though attendance is not required, over a third of the students consistently take part. "Hope," says a senior, "is a 24-hour safe zone," in part, because security measures on campus are strictly enforced. All dormitories have key-card security systems, all room doors are self-closing and self-locking, and emergency phones are well positioned around campus. An escort van also is available from 6 p.m. to 2 a.m. nightly, though students are more apt to use it to avoid cold weather than for concerns about their safety.

Flying Dutchmen football, basketball, soccer, and volleyball are the most enthusiastically supported of the 9 men's and 9 women's NCAA Division III sports on campus. In the 2004–2005 school year, Hope athletes competed in NCAA post-season competition in 10 of the 18 college-sponsored sports, tying the school record. In 2002–2003, the men's soccer team advanced to the regional finals while the women's basketball team advanced to the quarterfinals. The club sports of hockey, lacrosse and Ultimate Frisbee have their own strong followings. Seventy-three percent of the men but just 28% of the women participate in more than a dozen intramural sports, from badminton to volleyball.

In warm weather, most students escape to the beach on the shores of Lake Michigan, just 5 miles away. Because the Holland area (pop. 90,000) lacks the dance clubs and varied restaurants of a bigger city, most undergrads seeking these diversions head for the Grand Rapids metropolitan area (pop. 600,000), 26 miles northeast. Those in need of an even larger urban area head to Chicago and Detroit, each at least 3 hours away.

Cost cutters: Ninety-six percent of freshmen and 89% of continuing students in the 2005–2006 school year received financial aid; for 60% of the freshmen and 57% of the rest the aid was need-based. The average freshman award for a first-year student with financial need included a need-based scholarship or grant averaging $13,809 and need-based self-help aid such as jobs and loans averaging $3917. Other non-need-based awards and scholarships for freshmen averaged $6616. For 2005 graduates, the average financial indebtedness was $16,618. To attract and recognize students with superior academic records, the college offers various merit-based scholarships. Among them are the $17,000 Trustees Scholarships, which go to 20 of the highest achievers; $6500 to $14,000 Presidential Scholarships; $5000 to $6000 Distinguished Scholar Awards; $3000 to $4500 Alumni Honors Scholarships; and $2500 Distinguished Artist scholarships. High school valedictorians who are not selected to receive any of the other merit-based awards may be given $5000 Valedictorian Scholarships.

Rate of return: Eighty-nine percent of freshmen return for the sophomore year. Sixty-four percent graduate in 4 years; 74%, in 5 years, 75% in 6.

Payoff: Management was the major of choice for 12% of the 2005 graduates, followed by psychology at 11%. Seven percent earned degrees in the English/language arts composite major designed for future teachers. About a quarter of a recent class went on to pursue advanced degrees. Almost two-thirds accepted jobs shortly after graduation with major corporations throughout the nation. Nearly 40 companies and organizations recruited on campus in the 2004–2005 school year. In a study of 914 institutions, Hope ranked in the top 4% in the nation in producing future Ph.D. holders in the sciences between 1920 and 1990. The department of chemistry was in the top 1%.

Bottom line: Advises Hope's happy law-school student: "Hope provides an education that is as good as or better than that found at many schools with much more familiar names. And this college does it without all the pressure found at those other schools."

Kalamazoo College

Kalamazoo, Michigan 49006

Setting: Suburban
Control: Independent
Undergraduate enrollment: 1546 men, 717 women
Graduate enrollment: None
Student/faculty ratio: 12:1
Freshman profile: 26% scored over 700 on SAT I verbal; 60% scored 600–700; 13% 500–599; 1% below 500. 26% scored over 700 on SAT I math; 51% scored 600–700; 22% 500–599; 1% below 500. 30% scored above 28 on the ACT; 0% scored 27–28; 60% 24–26; 10% 21–23. 43% graduated in top tenth of high school class; 77% in upper fifth.
Faculty profile: 92% Ph.D.'s

Tuition and fees: $25,734 (year on campus)
Room and board: $6708
Freshman financial aid: 98%; average scholarship or grant: $9180
Campus jobs: NA; average earnings: NA
Application deadline: Early decision: Nov. 15; regular: Feb. 15
Financial aid deadline: Feb. 15
Admissions information: (616) 337-7166; (800) 253-3602
e-mail: admissions@kzoo.edu
web site: www.kzoo.edu

There's Special K cereal to eat, a 14K ring to wear, a 10K race to run—and, to round things out, the K-plan to study under at Kalamazoo College in western Michigan. At Kalamazoo, undergraduates combine a strong program in the liberal arts and sciences with 3 different types of off-campus experiences: an optional career-development internship, the opportunity for college-subsidized foreign study in sites from Senegal to Spain, and a required senior individualized project. In the course of 4 years under the K-plan, it is not unusual for a student to have undertaken a 3-month internship at the Art Institute of Chicago, lived and studied in France for 6 months, and created and completed a 3-month project of his or her own design. With tuition, fees, room, and board of almost $32,500 for 3 quarters spent on campus in the 2005–2006 school year (adjustments are made for time spent abroad, in internships, or engaged in senior projects), Kalamazoo is not among the cheapest best buys around. But for a program that offers a world of classroom learning, on-the-job experience, life in a foreign culture, and independent study, there's not much a K-plan education leaves out.

Student body: Although the college in recent years has stepped up efforts to bring more out-of-state and nonwhite students to campus, Kalamazoo, in the words of 1 of the few easterners on campus, still has "too many white students from Michigan." Seventy-six percent of the college's enrollment in a recent year were state residents, with other midwesterners making up most of the rest. A total of 38 states and 14 foreign countries have students on campus. Fifteen percent in a recent year were graduates of private or parochial schools. Nine percent were members of U.S. racial and ethnic minority groups: 4% Asian-Americans; 2% each African-Americans and Hispanics and 1% Native Americans. Foreign nationals recently accounted for another 2%. Students describe Kalamazoo as "a campus of achievers," of "individual thinkers," "an upbeat, positive place, where people feel good about the work they are doing." Although students cover the political spectrum, the majority are more liberal and better informed about world events than their counterparts on many other campuses and can be quite passionate about their areas of study. Observes a senior: "We are hard-working, hard-playing, type A, with a general scorn of slackers, lazy people, Rush Limbaugh, and people who don't recycle." Liberal-minded students generally may carry the numbers but there are enough thoughtful and vocal conservative thinkers, says a sophomore, "to make for a comfortable as well as stimulating political culture." Students tend to be individualistic and independent in their relationships and work, but never ruthless. "The environment is intense but not too competitive," states a chemistry major. "Learning is emphasized as much as grades, and students are very willing to help others learn."

Academics: Kalamazoo, which was founded by American Baptists in 1833 but is independent today, awards the bachelor of arts degree in 27 disciplines. The academic year is divided into quarters. Typically, freshmen take courses on campus during fall, winter, and spring quarters and an internship during the summer. Sophomores may also take 3 quarters of classes and an internship during summer or study abroad for spring quarter. Juniors may spend fall and winter quarters abroad and 1 quarter on campus or take all 3 quarters overseas. Seniors complete their individualized projects during 1 quarter, with classes the remaining quarters. Students generally encounter classes of about 20. Introductory courses in psychology and chemistry are the biggest, enrolling 90 at times, although seminars are held to about 8.

While participation in the foreign study and career-development programs is optional, though elected by at least 80% of the undergraduates, every student must complete the senior individualized project, which the student designs independently under the supervision of a faculty advisor. Examples are creative work in the arts, laboratory or field research, theses, student teaching, and internships. During their time on campus, undergraduates also must attend at least 25 lectures, plays, or concerts offered as part of the Liberal Arts Colloquium, plus fulfill distribution requirements in traditional academic fields. Each student must pass a comprehensive examination in the major and complete a portfolio, done for some students as an interactive personal Web site, which reflects the individual's overall educational experience. The K-plan is demanding, but satisfying, says a sophomore: "It isn't so much that these things are available but that the college is committed to supporting the student through all of these programs. The emphasis here is to be yourself, explore yourself, expand yourself."

The college has 103 full-time faculty members; no figure is available for the number who teach part-time, though in previous years it has been fewer than a dozen. Nearly half, 48%, in a recent year were women. "We also have a good cultural mix of teachers," says a sophomore. At Kalamazoo, the classroom is but 1 of several academic and social gathering places in which students and professors are encouraged to become better acquainted and to exchange ideas. Remarks a senior: "The faculty are approachable, not just voices echoing through a lecture hall." Adds a junior: "Most are very excited about their subjects and are eager to pass their knowledge along to the student." They range, concludes a senior: "from excellent to incredible."

The faculties in biology and chemistry are particularly demanding, and the variety of courses they offer is very rich. The sciences have benefited from a close working relationship with local corporations such as Pharmacia-Upjohn and AM Todd, plus the facilities of the recently constructed $10 million science center. Psychology features terrific opportunities for hands-on experience plus a faculty that is "supportive as well as motivating," says a major. The English faculty are exceptional and are noted for teaching the most advanced and progressive theories of literary criticism. For a small school, Kalamazoo offers instruction in an impressive array of 7 foreign languages: Latin, Ancient Greek, French, German, Spanish, Chinese, and Japanese. However, majors are available only in French, German, and Spanish. Anthropology, sociology and religion draw kudos as well.

Student criticisms are few. The minor in international commerce, the concentration in women's studies, and the fine arts majors in art, art history, music, and theater arts all could use additional courses, according to students. The education department was being phased out in the 2005–2006 school year.

Facilities: The new Upjohn Library Commons building opened to eager students in January 2006. The new facility is 72% bigger than the old with an additional 37,450 feet for study and shelving. The extra space provides more room for books enabling the collection to grow to 500,000 from its recent holdings of 350,000 volumes. Current periodical holdings stand at 1250. An on-line catalog and various computerized databases provide research assistance to the holdings at Upjohn as well as those at the libraries of Western Michigan University (which is 10 minutes away), the University of Michigan, and Michigan State. Students enter the new library through a glass atrium; a favorite feature already is the new second-floor Reading Room outfitted with fireplaces, comfortable seating, and plenty of natural light. Also high on the list are the "Book Club" coffee shop and the computer stations dotting every floor with wireless and network ports.

About 130 PCs and Macintosh computers are available for student use, though 10 are restricted to physics students. One of the 6 labs on campus is open around the clock, with hours at the others increasing as the workload does, usually reaching 24 near finals week. All residence-hall rooms are wired for access to the computer network; the college recommends that students make use of this and bring their own computers to campus, which most do. Wireless access also was expanding during the 2005–2006 school year.

Special programs: Kalamazoo's career-development program enables students to integrate classroom study with "real-world" internship experience at more than 2100 sites in the United States, Europe, Asia, and Africa. Eighty percent take part. No tuition is charged for participation in the program, and no academic credit is given. About 75% of students doing internships receive a salary, stipend, or other subsidy. Students usually complete the internship in the summer following the freshman or sophomore year. Over the last 40 years, over 80% of Kalamazoo's undergraduates have studied in a foreign country. Programs lasting 3 and 6 months operated in Ecuador, France, Germany, Great Britain, China, and Kenya. A 9-month program only has been offered in Senegal; 3 months or shorter in Spain. Students also have studied in Russia, Japan, Greece, The Netherlands, and many other countries through approved programs. Other available off-campus experiences range from a fine arts program in New York City to a science term at the Oak Ridge National Laboratory in Tennessee. A 3-2 engineering plan is offered with the University of Michigan or Washington University. Cross registration also is an option with Western Michigan University.

Campus life: Seventy-five percent of Kalamazoo students live on the 60-acre hilltop campus, although with the variety of off-campus programs, seldom is everybody there at any one time. There are no fraternities or sororities, and most weekends are spent either at all-campus parties in dormitory lounges, which are held a few times every quarter, or at smaller gatherings in the dorms. Says a sophomore: "'I have too much to do,' is always an accepted excuse around here." The quadrangle at the heart of the campus, known as the Quad, is a focal point for some of the crazier doings. Says a junior: "Students have been known to streak the Quad, slide the Quad on trays when there is snow, and write messages with chalk on the sidewalk." Some of the most popular organizations on campus represent students' eclectic interests, from the InterVarsity Christian Fellowship to groups supporting women's, gay, and environmental causes. The College Democrats and College Republicans are always sponsoring spirited debates and thought-provoking speakers, even during nonelection years. The Frelon Dance Company involves about 100 students in its popular annual spring show and periodic workshops. Though crime is not considered a serious problem, the campus has instituted electronic key cards for entering residence halls around the clock and classroom buildings after 6 p.m., emergency telephones across campus, additional lighting, escort services, and a 24-hour patrol. "Campus crime is trivial," says a sophomore. "Hooliganism is the largest concern."

More than a fourth of the men and nearly a quarter of the women play as Hornets on the 8 men's and 8 women's varsity teams. The college has had NCAA Division III tournament finalists in both men's and women's tennis and soccer, women's volleyball, and men's swimming. Basketball is very popular, and the recent football teams have been the best in 30 years. The campus tennis facilities are especially fine, as they serve as the site of the U.S. Tennis Association Junior National Tournament. A fifth of both the men and the women are involved in the 12 men's and 11 women's intramural events.

Kalamazoo itself is a pleasant city with a metropolitan population exceeding 225,000 including about 30,000 college students from Kalamazoo College and Western Michigan University. Nevertheless, road tripping to Chicago, 2½ hours away, is popular. East Lansing and Ann Arbor, homes of Michigan State and the University of Michigan, respectively, are each less than 2 hours away. The beach on Lake Michigan at South Haven is a 30-minute drive.

Cost cutters: Tuition and fees cover about two-thirds of the cost of Kalamazoo's program, with the remainder made up from endowment, gifts to the college, and the annual fund. In a recent school year, 98% of freshmen and 96% of continuing students received financial assistance; for 46% of both groups the aid was need-based. The average freshman award in a recent year consisted of a $9180 scholarship or grant, with the full package totaling $17,130. Average debt of a recent graduate was $17,400. Kalamazoo offers competitive scholarships in math/science, foreign languages, history/social sciences, writing, music performance, art and photography, and theater, which pay $2000, renewable over 4 years. Scholarship exams are offered in late January and February; students must have applied for admission by Jan. 15 to be eligible. Kalamazoo College Honors Awards pay from $3000 to $13,000, also renewable over 4 years. Some career internships and senior projects may involve salaries or stipends, although both may also have additional costs. Monthly tuition payment plans are available.

Rate of return: Eighty-eight percent of entering freshmen return for the sophomore year. Sixty-five percent graduate in 4 years; 71% do so in 5 years, 73% in 6 years.

Payoff: Fourteen percent of recent graduates earned bachelor's degrees in economics. Another 14% specialized in English and 12% in biology. Many graduates take jobs immediately, a number with the U.S. government or companies such as Pharmacia-Upjohn, Kellogg, and the major accounting firms throughout the country. Boasts a senior: "Kalamazoo grads stand out from the crowd not just because we're from an excellent school but because we have more to offer an employer in the way of experience." Among recent graduates, 30% immediately pursued advanced degrees. Within 5 years of commencement, about 85% of Kalamazoo alumni enroll in advanced study, 40% in the arts and sciences, 20% in business, and 16% in medicine.

Bottom line: Advises a recent graduate: "Students need to enjoy taking risks, expect a lot from themselves and others, and be willing to work under intense stress to survive happily here. K's education definitely prepares us for the rigors of grad school, and the career-development and senior projects introduce us to the real world."

Kettering University
Flint, Michigan 48504

Setting: Suburban
Control: Private
Undergraduate enrollment: 2008 men, 368 women
Graduate enrollment: 4 men, 2 women (513 part-time)
Student/faculty ratio: 18:1
Freshman profile: 10% scored over 700 on SAT I verbal; 34% scored 600–700; 46% 500–599; 10% below 500. 23% scored over 700 on SAT I math; 56% scored 600–700; 20% 500–599; 1% below 500. 23% scored above 28 on the ACT; 24% scored 27–28; 29% 24–26; 20% 21–23; 4% below 21. 30% graduated in top tenth of high school class; 52% in upper fifth.

Faculty profile: 93% Ph.D.'s
Tuition and fees: $23,898
Room and board: $5440
Freshman financial aid: 90%; average scholarship or grant: $3992 need-based; $3723 non-need-based
Campus jobs: 13%; average earnings: $754/year
Application deadline: Rolling
Financial aid deadline: Feb. 14
Admissions information: (810) 762-7865; (800) 955-4464
  e-mail: admissions@kettering.edu
  web site: www.kettering.edu

At most colleges and universities, it is expected, or at least hoped, that a student will get a good job after graduation. At Kettering University, known as GMI Engineering & Management Institute until January 1998 and run by General Motors from its founding in 1919 until 1982, many students have jobs *before* they are enrolled. As part of Kettering's 4½-year cooperative education program, each student admitted to Kettering is assigned to a staff co-operative education manager and begins his or her search for a prospective employer as soon as the student makes a commitment to attend the university. The majority of students get a job with one of the 700 potential co-op employers by the end of their first school term. Students alternate 11 weeks of classroom work with 12 or 13 weeks of paid on-the-job experience in automotive, aerospace, chemical, biomedical, or computer industries, to name just a few. Students typically stay with the same employer over their time at Kettering, gaining a depth and range of experiences and positions of increasing responsibility. With employers in 43 states, the majority of students are able to live at home during their co-op terms. Over their college years, Kettering students typically earn $40,000 to more than $65,000 through co-op. Such impressive earnings make the 2005–2006 total costs of almost $29,400 look a lot less formidable!

Student body: Sixty-three percent of Kettering's undergraduates are from Michigan, though students travel from all 49 other states and 24 foreign countries to earn while they learn. Eighty percent of the out-of-staters, however, are from the Midwest. All but 15% of the students are graduates of public high schools. Kettering is more diverse than many other private institutions: 7% of its undergraduates are African-American and 5% are Asian American, 2% each foreign national and Hispanic, and 1% Native American. However, students wish there were more diversity, especially in the balance of the sexes. Observes a sophomore: "Our diversity, unfortunately, looks exactly like upper management in any large corporation." Men currently outnumber women by a ratio of over 5:1, although groups of female students have been working to recruit more young women to Kettering and, once on campus, connect them with same-sex faculty members.

Among both sexes, students expecting to find a campus filled with "nerdy" people are pleasantly surprised to find a wide variety of bright, motivated people who study hard but not to the exclusion of all else. Still, students in general are intense, conservative, largely young Republicans, who are quite career-oriented and driven to succeed. "Students here are very future-minded," says a mechanical engineering major. "They carry planners and seem to look like executives." They also are apt to be found studying, and doing other things, a lot harder than most did in high school. Notes a second-year student: "Students are usually fiercely competitive academically, and that same competition permeates through all other activities, especially intramural sports and Greek cup competitions." Nevertheless, the saying at Kettering is "cooperate to graduate," despite professors' propensity to grade on a curve, "which means that you're ultimately competing with your classmates for a grade," observes a senior. "What's interesting," he continues, "is that while it's competitive within the classroom, many informal study groups will form throughout the term, so in reality everyone helps everyone out."

Academics: The university was renamed for the late Charles F. Kettering, long-time vice president of research and development for General Motors, whose inventions range from the electric starter for automobiles to freon for air conditioning and refrigeration to an incubator for premature infants. Kettering University offers a bachelor's degree in 4 areas of engineering, in management, in computer science, applied physics, applied mathematics, chemistry, biochemistry, and environmental chemistry; it also awards several master's degrees. The academic year is divided into 2 semesters. Each semester, in turn, is divided into two terms that consist of 11 weeks in the classroom, and 12 to 13 weeks of co-op experience in industry. Average class size is 25 students, although first-year courses such as a lecture in manufacturing processes can enroll 58. Several upper-level courses may enroll just 6.

The 4½ to 5-year curriculum is highly structured with specific courses required in most of the fields that include 32 hours of liberal studies and 40 hours of math and science courses for math/science/engineering majors. Nonetheless, many students still are able to elect concentrations within their majors, complete a minor or a dual major, or even spend a semester abroad at selected universities with whom Kettering has found equivalent classes. Every student must also develop and complete a senior thesis project typically on a topic that tackles a real world problem for their co-op employer; students receive two thesis advisors, one assigned by the school and a second by their employer. During a recent school year, 72 of the senior thesis projects generated more than $70 million in potential savings for the employers. Some students have even earned patents for their thesis projects.

All 140 full-time and 17 part-time faculty members teach undergraduates, with their foremost priority being teaching, rather than their own research. Eighty percent are men. Graduate students teach 1% of the introductory courses. The students, because of their own work experience, are able to keep an already strong faculty on their toes. Notes a recent graduate in management: "Professors must be aware of 'real world' examples, or they will be rejected by students." Students also appreciate when faculty members understand their time pressures and go out of their way to provide extra study sessions and to tutor outside of class. Adds another management major: "Most professors understand the intensity here and are willing to work around other classes to insure that we don't have too many projects, papers, tests, or exams due in a limited time period. Professors want to see their students succeed and foster that belief." At the traditional midnight breakfast during finals week, faculty and staff even serve the students! Students' chief complaints center on the number of faculty members whose limited English speaking skills make them difficult to understand.

Industrial engineering and mechanical engineering boast "incredibly good" faculty and extensive labs and equipment for student use in computer-aided design and management. The new C.S. Mott Engineering and Science Center, which opened in 2003, contains a GM/PACE e-design and e-manufacturing studio, an engine test center, biomedical labs and SAE (Society of Automotive Engineers) student vehicle project labs. Electrical engineering runs a close third in quality of faculty and equipment. Although engineering students look at management students as "having it easy," majors find the classes challenging and the professors still very in touch with industry. Students also feel that the intermittent work experience gives them an edge in the job market when competing with the numerous management majors graduating from other more traditional colleges and universities.

The Department of Liberal Studies, whose programs students say are least emphasized by the school, offers minors only in 4 fields: economics, history, literature, and international studies. "The Science and Math Department exists mainly to support the various engineering curricula," says a mechanical engineering major; as a result, stand-alone majors in applied mathematics, applied physics, computer science, and 3 branches of chemistry could use more investment from the university.

Facilities: The library, located on the second floor of the Academic Building, is especially compact, just 128,500 volumes and 550 periodicals, and weighted heavily toward materials for engineering students with little for management majors. Research materials that students can check out are not always as up to date as students would like, although the reference materials kept on hold tend to be very recent and useful. On-line services help out with periodical research and a computerized catalog checks the listings at other libraries in the area. The library also recently became the home of the archives of the Society of Automotive Engineers, which includes in its collection more than 396,000 patents dating from 1796 to 1999.

Students have access around the clock to more than 350 workstations, networked PCs and CAD (computer-aided design) workstations; and users report encountering few difficulties finding a free computer when needed. Most students also have their own units, which the university strongly recommends.

Special programs: High-ability students may enroll directly in the Master of Science in Engineering program and substitute completion of a master's thesis for the undergraduate thesis requirement. International exchange programs enable students to study in England, Germany, and Scotland.

Campus life: Twenty-six percent of the undergraduates live on the 85-acre campus that consists of 10 main buildings. A 4-story residence hall houses all unmarried first-year students as well as some upperclassmen, as space permits. (Most upperclassmen live in campus apartments, Greek housing or apartments or private homes near campus.) Most of the main structures are connected by underground tunnels that afford convenience and protection from inclement weather, as well as any need to walk outside after dark. Since the course load each term is heavy, students must spend a lot of time studying over the weekend to keep up. However, the vast majority still make time for partying. Forty percent of the men and 35% of the women are members of a lively Greek system consisting of 13 national fraternities and 6 national sororities. Most Greek events are open to independents as well as members. The Outdoors Club, the Firebirds Car Club, for car enthusiasts, and the Society of Automotive Engineers are 3 of the most active organizations. For all students, the problem of crime in Flint (pop. 150,000) is a serious one. Students worry about break-ins at homes they rent just off campus and fear having their cars stolen or vandalized. To help resolve the problem, the university recently hired 2 Flint police officers as well as additional security guards to patrol not only the campus and parking lots, but also the area around homes near campus where many upperclassmen live. The lots themselves also have been improved with better lighting and surveillance cameras.

Given the constantly shifting student body, there are no intercollegiate sports but involvement in intramurals is wildly successful. Fifty-two percent of the men and women take part in the 22 intramural sports for men and women, "a good way to escape from studying," says a sophomore. The ice hockey and soccer clubs also are quite popular.

Flint, located 60 miles north of Detroit, has little to offer in the way of off-campus diversion, so students who live within a few hours of campus often seek relief in a home-cooked meal at home. Those who reside further away may travel to northern Michigan, Detroit, or the university cities of Lansing and Ann Arbor.

Cost cutters: Ninety percent of the freshmen and 85% of the continuing students received financial help in the 2005–2006 school year. For 74% of the first-year students and 62% of the rest, the aid was need-based. The average first-year award included a need-based scholarship or grant averaging $3992 and need-based self-help aid such as jobs and loans averaging $3723. Other non-need-based awards and scholarships averaged $8718. Students also are eligible for various merit scholarships that range from $5000 to $10,000 annually based on grade point averages and standardized test scores. While cooperative education does help to pay the bills, students caution that tuition payments must stretch over 5 years, instead of 4, and off-campus work does have its own special costs, among them suitable clothing, transportation, and living expenses if the job site, one of more than 800 possible locations, is not near a student's home. However, placements are made within a student's local area whenever possible. Average debt of a recent graduate was $30,903; still, the university boasts a virtual zero default rate on student loans of its alumni, thanks in large part to the good-paying jobs they receive with their diplomas. A 10-month payment plan, possible with a nonrefundable annual $40 participation fee, helps many families with current tuition payments.

Rate of return: Eighty-eight percent of first-year students return for a second year. Fifty-two percent graduate within 5 years; 61%, within 6 years.

Payoff: Not quite half of the 2005 graduates, 48%, earned bachelor's degrees in mechanical engineering; 13% followed with degrees in electrical engineering and 5% in industrial engineering. Typically, over 90% of Kettering graduates secure full-time professional positions by or shortly after graduation and 70% are offered full-time positions by their co-op employers, such firms as Sun Microsystems, Ford, Chrysler, and GM, UPS, United Technologies, TRW, GE, and Rockwell International. Most boast average starting salaries of more than $45,000. (Among graduates surveyed between July 2004 and June 2005, the average starting salary ranged from a low of $32,000 to a high of $63,616.) A fifth seek advanced degrees, most in business sciences, or engineering and a majority do so on a part-time basis while working, often with their employers paying for tuition. Fifteen percent of Kettering's alumni, more than 1700 graduates, have held the positions of CEO, president, owner, board chair, or vice president of their companies. The pull-tab on aluminum cans, the port-a-potty, and the skin graft machine were all invented by Kettering graduates.

Bottom line: Students who make it at Kettering don't expect to get a job or admission into graduate or professional school; they expect to get a *good* job or admission into a *top* school. For those graduates who have worked hard both on the job and in the classroom, that's a goal implicit in the small type on the diploma. Affirms a mechanical engineering major: "This school teaches students the essentials of the real world. Students who want the 'normal' college experience with football games, and so on, will be unhappy here."

University of Michigan

Ann Arbor, Michigan 48109

Setting: Small city
Control: Public
Undergraduate enrollment: 12,074 men, 12,372 women
Graduate enrollment: 6891 men, 5731 women
Student/faculty ratio: NA
Freshman profile: 26% scored over 700 on SAT I verbal; 47% scored 600–700; 24% 500–599; 3% below 500. 44% scored over 700 on SAT I math; 42% scored 600–700; 12% 500–599; 2% below 500. 88% graduated in top tenth of high school class.
Faculty profile: 91% Ph.D.'s

Tuition and fees: $9213 in-state; $27,601 out-of-state
Room and board: $7374
Freshman financial aid: 73%; average scholarship or grant: $7813 need-based; $4081 non-need-based
Campus jobs: NA; average earnings: NA
Application deadline: Feb. 1
Financial aid deadline: Sept. 30
Admissions information: (734) 764-7433
  e-mail: ugadmiss@umich.edu
  web site: www.admissions.umich.edu

The Michigan fight song, "Hail to the Victors," may be best known for its efforts to cheer on the football squad during frequent Bowl appearances, but its message applies also to just about any student who emerges with a bachelor's degree from 1 of the nation's biggest but most respected public universities. With almost 3000 faculty members scattered across 19 schools and colleges, more than 40,900 different courses open to undergraduates, and 7.9 million bound volumes in its 24 libraries, Michigan presents a formidable challenge to the unsuspecting freshman. Nevertheless, students determined to cut through the big-school bureaucracy and large introductory lectures to earn that victory degree will eventually enjoy their reward: fighting off the thousand-plus employers who recruit these highly prized Michigan grads.

Student body: The university's enrollment of state residents is low compared to the numbers at other publically supported institutions, with 69% Michiganders. Three-fourths of the nonresidents are also from the Midwest, with students present from every state and 90 foreign countries. Almost a third are foreign nationals (5%) or members of racial and ethnic minority groups, among them 13% Asian-Americans, 8% African-Americans, and 5% Hispanics. At Michigan, undergraduates cover all political and social extremes from the stereotypical all-American fraternity or sorority house member to the activist with a radical agenda to change the status quo. Somewhere, there seems to be a group for everyone among Michigan's 900+ student activities and organizations, though on a campus of this size it often takes some determined looking to find the right niche. While Michigan has its share of parties, especially around football season, it is clearly no party school, and most undergraduates find it quite challenging. Notes a freshman: "Competition is intense here and people study hard, concentrating on getting good grades."

Academics: Michigan, founded in 1817, awards degrees through the doctorate. Undergraduate majors in more than 200 fields are offered in 11 of the 19 professional schools and colleges. The academic year is divided into trimesters. Freshmen who take courses in introductory anthropology or sociology will find themselves sharing a lecture hall with about 500 classmates, though discussion groups involve between

20 and 40 participants. In contrast, a student taking introductory Latin or Greek may be enrolled in a class of just 15.

Many undergraduates find Michigan's Residential College an attractive alternative to the numbers game. The college, which is part of the 18,000-student College of Literature, Science, and the Arts, (LSA) enables more than 900 honors students to live together in the RC for the first 2 years, taking half of their courses in the larger university setting and the rest in RC classes of no more than 40 people. The college offers multidisciplinary concentrations in the humanities, natural sciences, and social sciences, as well as courses in fine arts, music, and foreign languages. Another living-learning community called the Lloyd Hall Scholars Program also is available for first- and second-year students and specializes in small seminars, experimental minicourses, opportunities for independent study, and a special class on leadership and service learning, as well as reserved spaces in sections of the LSA introductory and sophomore-level courses taught elsewhere on campus. Approximately 350 first-year students are admitted to the program annually, more than 60% from out-of-state.

Each of Michigan's schools and colleges has its own course requirements, most of which allow students lots of flexibility in their choices. LSA, for example, requires proficiency in quantitative reasoning and a foreign language; coursework in the humanities, social sciences, and natural sciences; completion of 2 writing courses, an introductory composition course and a junior-level one; and any 1 of several courses dealing with racial or ethnic intolerance.

Michigan's total faculty recently numbered 2936 members, 2347 full-time and 589 part-time. Just over a third of the full-time and just over a fourth of the part-time faculty members typically teach at the graduate level only. Thirty-eight percent of the total pool were women. Three faculty members have won a Pulitzer Prize; 1, a Nobel Prize. More than 800 teach in the liberal arts college. Many students complain that professors are more interested in their research and in securing grants to fund it than in their undergraduates, who usually wind up in the hands of teaching assistants of varying abilities. However, there are professors across the campus whose stunning lectures and determination to interact with students, at least as upperclassmen, make their departments winners.

English in the LSA has an excellent faculty noted for its special efforts to establish personal contact with undergraduates. The social sciences, such as psychology, sociology, history, and political science, are considered particularly strong. The Stephen M. Ross School of Business and the College of Engineering, 2 of the most competitive divisions, are awash in state-of-the-art facilities and equipment and in professors who are tops in their fields. Students in the School of Natural Resources especially like the way many of their professors encourage undergraduates to become more active participants in the learning process.

Communication studies and the geological sciences in the LSA have been weakened by a draining of funds from their departments. Students charge that because of the language requirement in the LSA many foreign language departments funnel their money into introductory-level courses, leaving limited options for more advanced students. Like everything else, though, the language offerings at Michigan are enormous, recently including, for example, classes in Armenian, Punjabi, and Tagalog, as well as concentrations in Persian, Greek, Hebrew, and Turkish.

More serious than complaints targeted at specific programs, however, are charges leveled by many undergraduates at a general academic environment. Students say that many lower-division classes, especially in the mammoth College of Literature, Science, and the Arts, are "huge and impersonal, the climate is uncaring, and there is almost no student-teacher contact, and little attempt to achieve it." Most academic counseling also gets thumbs-down.

Facilities: With more than 7.9 million volumes, 8.2 million microform items, and subscriptions to 67,554 periodicals, Michigan's 24 libraries usually have whatever resource an undergraduate needs... somewhere. A computerized catalog known as MIRLYN enables students to find material located anywhere on campus with a few strokes of the keyboard, a tremendous step-saver on a campus where the libraries are so spread out. More than 500 permanent staff members also are available to help point the way. Two main libraries, the undergraduate (known as Ugli) and the graduate, hold the bulk of the collection and offer study environments students either love or hate.

Wireless access is available just about everywhere on campus, in the libraries, classroom buildings, laboratories, office buildings and student unions. The university also provides an interactive map to help students identify where wireless access is available. In addition, 17 general-use computing sites across campus, in classroom buildings and libraries, plus another 15 in residence halls, give undergraduates access to 2500 workstations including Macintosh, Dell, and other computers. An additional 550 workstations are available around-the-clock in the 250,000-square-foot Media Union. Business Administration and Engineering provide workstations for their students only. Computers located in the residence halls are open around the clock and all residence hall rooms are wired for Internet connectivity. Many of the other labs are open until 2 a.m.

Special programs: Michigan students can participate in English-language study-abroad programs in such European countries as England, Ireland, and Italy, as well as in programs where knowledge of languages as diverse as Japanese and Swedish is required. A domestic exchange with historically black Morehouse College in Atlanta is available to architecture and urban planning students. More general cross registration is available with other Big Ten institutions and the University of Chicago. A Washington semester also is an option. The Undergraduate Research Opportunity Program offers first- and second-year students the chance to work 6–10 hours a week for an entire academic year on in-depth projects in most academic disciplines.

Campus life: Thirty-seven percent of Michigan's undergraduates live on the campus, which covers some 3177 acres. Though the Greeks are very active, hosting parties every weekend as well as a number of community fundraisers, they are still far from dominant on the varied Michigan social scene. Twelve percent of the men belong to 1 local and 30 national fraternities; the local group allows women to be members. Fifteen percent of the women pledge to 22 national sororities. Other popular student organizations among the more than 900 offered include the College Republicans and Democrats, various "cause" groups involved in environmental and social work, and the *Michigan Daily* newspaper. Bike theft is generally the most common crime on campus; some students say even this could be reduced with better lighting. A Nite Owl Bus Service and officer bike patrols offer added protection.

There's rarely a problem filling Michigan's 107,501-seat stadium during football season, especially at the big game against Ohio State. Wolverines basketball is a major draw as well. Altogether, Michigan fields 12 men's and 13 women's intercollegiate sports, played in NCAA Division I. Twenty-five intramural sports are offered for each sex; 59% of the men but only 12% of the women took part in a recent year.

One of the more serene escapes is the Arb, an arboretum near campus that provides lots of wide-open spaces for walking or tossing a Frisbee. Ann Arbor (pop. 100,000) is a near perfect college town for wandering and browsing through bookstores, although students with cars sometimes make the 50-mile drive to Detroit for museums or clubs.

Cost cutters: Seventy-three percent of recent freshmen and 63% of continuing students received financial aid; aid was need-based for 50% of the freshmen and 44% of those continuing. The average freshman award for a student with need included a need-based scholarship or grant averaging $7813 and need-based self-help aid such as loans and jobs averaging $5588. Non-need-based athletic scholarships for first-year students averaged $22,690; other non-need-based awards and scholarships averaged $4081. A recent graduate left with average debts of $21,326. Many merit-based awards are restricted to Michigan residents. Those available to out-of-staters generally extend in amount up to $10,000 a year. Annual tuition varies according to the college in which a student is enrolled and according to whether the student is a freshman or sophomore or an upperclassman. In the College of Literature, Science and the Arts, which enrolls most undergraduates, entering freshmen from Michigan paid $9024 in tuition minus fees in the 2005–2006 school year; juniors and seniors from Michigan paid $10,194. Nonresident freshmen and sophomores paid $27,412; nonresident upperclassmen paid $29,350. Rates for certain professional schools such as engineering and kinesiology were $160–$1740 higher; for other undergraduate programs, such as education, nursing, and music, tuition and fees were about $100 lower. A co-operative program is available in engineering. Jobs are widely available both on campus and off.

Rate of return: Ninety-six percent of freshmen return for the sophomore year. Sixty-two percent graduate in 4 years; 80%, in 5 years; 82% in 6. The 4- and 5-year completion rates are among the highest for large state-supported universities and exceed the rates at many small liberal arts colleges.

Payoff: Twenty-one percent of the 2005 Michigan graduates earned bachelor's degrees in engineering; 11% specialized in psychology, 6% in business. Thirty percent of recent graduates entered graduate or professional schools. More than half found employment within 6 months of commencement. More than a thousand companies and organizations recruited on campus in the 2004–2005 school year.

Bottom line: The University of Michigan offers just about anything a student could want in the way of courses, majors, and extracurricular activities. And while it is often hard for undergraduates to make personal contact with faculty members, professors have no problem identifying students who mistake Michigan for a party school. For these misguided souls, the oft-repeated Michigan chant, "Go blue!," will signify a sorrowful parting of the ways and at least a temporary reassignment to the "home" team.

Minnesota

Augsburg College

Minneapolis, Minnesota 55454

Setting: Urban
Control: Private (Evangelical Lutheran)
Undergraduate enrollment: 1008 men, 1234 women
Graduate enrollment: 158 men, 271 women
Student/faculty ratio: 15:1
Freshman profile: 5% scored over 700 on SAT I verbal; 35% scored 600–700; 42% 500–599; 18% below 500. 5% scored over 700 on SAT I math; 25% scored 600–700; 55% 500–599; 15% below 500. 9% scored above 28 on the ACT; 11% scored 27–28; 29% 24–26; 25% 21–23; 26% below 21. 32% graduated in top fifth of high school class; 58% in upper two-fifths.

Faculty profile: 79% Ph.D.'s
Tuition and fees: $21,960
Room and board: $6340
Freshman financial aid: 89%; average scholarship or grant: $11,308 need-based; $1631 non-need-based
Campus jobs: 44%; average earnings: $1710/year
Application deadline: Early advantage: Dec. 15; regular: May 1
Financial aid deadline: Apr. 15
Admissions information: (612) 330-1001; (800) 788-5678 e-mail: carrollc@augsburg.edu web site: www.augsburg.edu

Racial and ethnic diversity isn't always easy to achieve at colleges in Minnesota, where the population is more than 95% white. But around the Twin Cities, diversity is spelled A-U-G-S-B-U-R-G, the name of a Lutheran college of some 2250 undergraduates that has made serving students of all colors, ethnicities, and special needs a top priority. While most of the student body are white Americans, largely of Scandinavian heritage, 2% are foreign nationals from 31 countries, 5% are African-American, 3% are Asian American, and 1% each are Native American and Hispanic. The college's program for Native Americans boasts the highest retention rate in the state: 80–85%. Its excellent system of tunnels, skyways, and elevators, which connects 10 major buildings, makes the campus very accessible to the physically disabled as well as the meteorologically timid. The Center for Learning and Adaptive Student Services (CLASS) and the Access Center, located in new and expanded facilities, also have been recognized nationally as leaders in the field of educating students with learning and physical disabilities. For those who seek personal attention from professors, there are small classes, rarely exceeding 30, while for big-city lovers Minneapolis and St. Paul offer a full range of cultural and recreational attractions. About the only student who wouldn't enjoy Augsburg is one who feels uncomfortable with different kinds of people and ways of learning, and as far as undergraduates are concerned, he or she can change that attitude—or go elsewhere.

Student body: If any common trait links Augsburg students, it can be described in the words of this Minnesota native: on this campus "overall, people are down to earth—no false pretensions. You can find almost any type of person you want here, but that much they have in common." Another commonality is the state of origin, with 89% of the students from Minnesota, reflecting a mix of rural and urban backgrounds, and 93% of the out-of-staters also from the Midwest. Thirty-nine states have students on campus. Twenty-one percent of the undergraduates are Lutheran; 16% are Catholic. Eighteen percent claim no religious affiliation. Other than small percentages of students who are Jewish, Buddhist, Orthodox, Hindu, or Muslim, most of the rest are members of other Protestant denominations. Over 90% in a recent year were graduates of public schools. With Augsburg's comparatively wide mix of racial and ethnic backgrounds, the atmosphere about campus is accepting and adaptable. Politically, most students hold moderate to liberal viewpoints and are described as being "people-conscious," an attitude expressed through work both to alleviate world hunger and (closer to home) to feed the needy of the Twin Cities. Notes a St. Paul resident: "People at Augsburg really care about their community and strive to make it better." When it comes to books and courses, a senior notes, "The students aren't terribly academic, but most are willing to work."

Academics: Augsburg, founded in 1869 and named for Augsburg, Germany, site of the confession of faith by Lutherans, offers a bachelor's degree in more than 50 majors in the day program and 12 in a Weekend College aimed at nontraditional adult students. In addition, Augsburg offers master's degree programs in 6 fields. The academic year is divided into 2 semesters plus a January term. Undergraduates find classes from 15–30 students on average. Comments a physics major: "The class sizes are good because you can speak your mind instead of just listening to the teacher lecture." Astronomy enrolls the most at about 50, while an upper-level history or philosophy seminar often has fewer than 6.

Entering freshmen begin their college work with a fall seminar, part of an extended orientation program known as the First Year Experience. The general-education program is based on developing students' perspectives and skills. Throughout their 4 years, undergraduates take courses cutting across a wide range of disciplines that approach the world from 8 different viewpoints: the Western heritage, human identity, aesthetics, the social world, the natural world, intercultural awareness, and (reflecting perspectives of Augsburg itself) the city and Christian faith. Students also are evaluated on their entry-level skills in areas such as reading, writing, critical thinking, mathematics, and word processing and must take coursework where needed to enhance their abilities.

The faculty is composed of 156 full-time members plus 133 part-timers, many of whom teach in the Weekend College. Fifty percent are women. While there are some professors whose lectures fail to make their subjects sufficiently clear, the majority give solid performances in the classroom and, more importantly, follow up with encores in their offices or wherever and whenever students need extra help. Says a junior: "They have a fire for the subject matter and are genuinely interested in the learning student."

Two of Augsburg's strongest programs—social work and education—best express the college's people-approach to education. Both disciplines are well known about campus for their superior faculties and excellent opportunities for hands-on work in the inner city. Because the social work program is accredited, students pursuing graduate studies in the field can save as much as a year of advanced work, compared to students coming from other programs. Communication studies, too, offers "incredible internship opportunities in major-market television, radio, newspapers, and film as well as superior facilities," says a major. History, political science, sociology, religion, computer science, and English also earn high marks. Music features a large staff and good facilities, although some students wish the curriculum included more courses in jazz and non-Western music. The program in physics provides excellent research opportunities funded by NASA and linked with NASA satellites. The rigorous physician's assistant program receives hundreds of applications for 28 new-student slots each year. And little wonder: All members of 5 consecutive recent graduating classes earned 100% passing rates on the national board of examination.

Business administration, which includes specializations in finance, management, and international business, is energized by strong interest from students, but some nonmajors think the program is not sufficiently challenging. Some students have found members of the economics faculty difficult to understand. The French major lacks courses; mathematics, too, has had limited offerings. Biology could use more space and funding. Construction of a new science center and renovation of the Science Hall are included as part of the current capital campaign.

Facilities: The James G. Lindell Family Library, which opened in September 1997, is "nice, big, and beautiful," raves a junior. Its collection, however, is not so glowing, according to students, with just over 182,000 volumes and 686 periodicals that together sometimes pose a problem to students engaged in intensive research. Here, the Lindell Family librarians' never-say-quit attitude helps out. In most cases, relief is available on-line or just 2 blocks away at the gargantuan University of Minnesota main library, with some 6 million volumes and more than 38,000 periodicals. Students also have access to the holdings of the College of St. Catherine, Bethel, Corcordia, and Macalester colleges, the University of St. Thomas, and Hamline University. The computerized research assistance that hooks students into all these outside resources plus the twice daily courier service that delivers the materials are much appreciated and much used step-savers. There also are small music and physics libraries on campus, too.

Students have access to over 210 on-campus computer systems in 10 labs and classrooms. Laptops also are available for checkout at the library. Students' chief complaint is that the labs aren't open long enough; one lab is open around the clock, most others until 11 p.m. Wireless access is available in the library and student center.

Special programs: Augsburg's Center for Global Education offers 5 semester-long, living and learning experiences in Cuernavaca, Mexico, with travel to Central America, and from Namibia to South Africa, all for the same price as tuition, room, and board at the Twin Cities campus, plus air fare. Each of the programs focuses on a different social issue such as women and development from both Latin American and South African perspectives, sustainable development and social change, and multicultural societies in transition. Other semester-abroad programs also are offered world-wide. Those preferring to stay closer to home may cross-register at all-female College of St. Catherine, the University of St. Thomas, Macalester College, and Hamline University, each located across the Mississippi River in St. Paul. A 4-year program in social work, sociology, or psychology with a speciality in chemical dependency is available with a downtown community college. Three-two engineering programs are offered with the University of Minnesota, Michigan Technological University in Houghton, and Washington University in St. Louis.

Campus life: Fifty-five percent of the undergraduates live on the 23-acre city campus, based just blocks away from the Minneapolis theater district and bordered on the south by Interstate 94. There are no fraternities or sororities, and a new residence hall recently replaced 22 campus-owned houses that were the sites of many weekend parties. The Augsburg choir; the LINK, a student-coordinated community service organization; MPIRG, a public interest research group; and other organizations serving the college's multiracial, ethnic, and special-needs communities garner some of the most enthusiastic student support. In keeping with the college's Lutheran tradition, a 20-minute chapel is held 5 days a week; though attendance is optional, almost all offices are closed and no classes are held during that time. Because Augsburg is located in a relatively high crime area in the city, students are continually reminded to call the escort service, rather than walk alone at night, and generally to use caution off campus. However, students report feeling safe on campus because of the strong emphasis on crime prevention.

One area where Augsburg does not shine, students say, is in its weak support of athletic events on campus. None of the 9 men's and 9 women's NCAA Division III sporting events is overwhelmingly popular; basketball, wrestling, and men's and women's ice hockey attract the biggest crowds, with the 10-year-old women's intercollegiate ice hockey team drawing greater interest each year. A fourth of the undergraduates take part in 4 coed intramural sports. An ice arena with 2 rinks is available for hockey, recreational skating, and broomball. A dome covering the Astro-turf football and soccer fields lets students run, walk, golf, or play a number of sports indoors during the chilly winters.

The theater district nearby, with its spicy mixture of plays and ethnic restaurants, provides much of the students' off-campus entertainment—along with the larger cultural and sporting events at the Minneapolis Metrodome, just a mile away. Those tiring of city life simply head for 1 of the 10,000 lakes for which the state is famous. America's largest shopping mall, the Mall of America, is also only about 20 minutes away.

Cost cutters: In the 2005–2006 school year, 89% of freshmen and 75% of continuing students received some kind of financial assistance; 77% of the freshmen and 64% of the rest were on need-based aid. The average freshman award included need-based scholarships or grants averaging $11,308. No figure was available for the portion that was self-help aid such as loans and jobs earnings. Other non-need-based scholarships and awards for first-year students averaged $1631. A typical 2005 graduate left with debts of $24,546. The President's Scholarship pays from $13,000 to full tuition to 14 first-year students who had a GPA of at least 3.7 and a 27 or higher on the ACT (or 1210 critical reading and math SAT); 3 of the 14 recipients receive full-tuition awards. Students must complete a separate application by Feb. 1 and agree to live on campus and participate in the college's honors program. The Regent Scholar program recently paid $3000 to $9000 based on GPA and standardized test scores. Ethnic Leadership and Performing Arts scholarships each pay $2500 a year. The college offers a cooperative program in every major, plus other kinds of internships for varying lengths throughout the year, in large and small, for-profit and nonprofit, institutions. Two different payment plans allow families to distribute costs more evenly.

Rate of return: Eighty percent of entering freshmen return for the sophomore year. Thirty-eight percent graduate in 4 years, 53% in 5 years, and 55% in 6 years.

Payoff: Just over a fifth of the 2005 graduates earned degrees in 3 career-directed fields: 10% in business/management and 6% each in elementary education and accounting. Three-fourths took jobs immediately after graduating, most in the upper Midwest, at firms like West Publishing, 3M, and Norwest Banks, and as teachers in public and private schools in the Minneapolis-St. Paul area. More than 60 companies and organizations recruited on campus in the 2004–2005 school year. A fourth of recent graduates went directly to graduate or professional schools; 40% eventually pursue advanced study.

Bottom line: Augsburg's greatest strength is its acceptance of personal differences, and the college expects as much from its students. Notes a recent graduate: "Augsburg offers cultural awareness, personal growth, and the benefits of the Twin Cities in addition to its academics. An extreme overachiever or intensely academic person, however, probably would not benefit from Augsburg."

College of Saint Benedict

St. Joseph, Minnesota 56374

Setting: Small town
Control: Private (Catholic—Benedictine)
Undergraduate enrollment: 1993 women
Graduate enrollment: None
Student/faculty ratio: 13:1
Freshman profile: 4% scored over 700 on SAT I verbal; 39% scored 600–700; 39% 500–599; 18% below 500. 6% scored over 700 on SAT I math; 35% scored 600–700; 44% 500–599; 15% below 500. 17% scored above 28 on the ACT; 14% scored 27–28; 36% 24–26; 25% 21–23; 8% below 21. 36% graduated in top tenth of high school class; 70% in upper fifth.

Faculty profile: 80% Ph.D.'s
Tuition and fees: $23,454
Room and board: $6637
Freshman financial aid: 97%; average scholarship or grant: $14,435 need-based; $9605 non-need-based
Campus jobs: 45%; average earnings: $2100/year
Application deadline: Rolling (Early action: Dec. 1, priority date: Jan. 15)
Financial aid deadline: Mar. 15
Admissions information: (320) 363-2196; (800) 544-1489
e-mail: admissions@csbsju.edu
web site: www.csbsju.edu

Young women who attend the College of Saint Benedict in central Minnesota are really getting the benefits of 2 colleges: one all-female, one all-male. The College of Saint Benedict, located in the tiny community of St. Joseph, is run by the world's largest convent of Benedictine nuns. Four miles west is Saint John's University, run by the largest abbey of Benedictine monks. While each campus maintains its separate residential community, the two single-sex institutions encourage cross registration for classes, even using the same registrar's office, provide computerized research assistance that lists the resources of both libraries, and requires their students to complete the same core curriculum and major-program requirements to graduate. The result is like a chemistry experiment in which neither of the two ingredients really blends with the other but rather maintains its own special properties, with combined action only at certain critical junctures. But in this case, when the 2 elements meet, say students from the cooperating colleges, it's clearly a match made not in the test tube, but in heaven.

Student body: Eighty-three percent of Saint Ben's students are from Minnesota, including a mixture of women from small towns and from the suburbs of Minneapolis/St. Paul. Nearly all of the non-Minnesotans are from the surrounding geographic region. There are undergraduates, however, from 31 states and 23 foreign countries. Though 67% of the women are Catholic, with the rest mainly Protestant, only 23% attended private or parochial schools. The enrollment includes 4% who are foreign nationals, many from the college's extension program in the Bahamas, 2% Asian-American, and 1% each Hispanic and African-American. Most women attracted to Saint Benedict's are creative, involved, and open-minded. Observes a student from the Pacific Northwest: "The most active group of students on campus is a liberal, contemplative, adventurous bunch. There's a fairly large group who take a more passive, politically conservative role, but the verbalized and visible student opinion is one concerned with social justice and environmentalism," which students say is very much influenced by the Benedictine emphasis on respect for nature and neighbors. While the majority maintain a good balance between their academic and social lives, they still take their studies quite seriously. Continues the student: "Students value learning and worry about tests and stay up all night writing papers. This isn't a lax environment but it's definitely aimed more toward community learning, not competition."

Academics: Saint Ben's, founded in 1887, grants the bachelor's degree in 40 disciplines. Courses are divided between 2 semesters. While the required first-year symposium has no more than 16 students, an introductory biology lecture may exceed 40. Most classes, however, average around 22.

The joint core curriculum involves "Bennies and Johnnie," as they are called, in a 4-year exploration of the human condition through a series of cross-disciplinary, and "flagged" courses that stress skills, such as writing and quantitative reasoning, as well as gender and global issues. In the freshman symposium with which undergraduates begin their course of study, 8 men, and 8 women, and 1 professor work together for 2 semesters to build writing, speaking, thinking, and interpersonal communication skills. The disciplinary courses run the gamut from fine arts and humanities to mathematics and the natural and social sciences. In addition, each student must demonstrate proficiency in mathematics and a foreign language and complete a senior values seminar. Most women view the curriculum as being "strict" but "invaluable." "When it comes to an area a student is not majoring in," says a senior, "those classes can be quite challenging."

All but 22 of the 170 faculty members are full-time, 56% are women, about 20% are Benedictine nuns, and all are 100% approachable. Most professors enjoy give-and-take in the classroom and openly admit when they are wrong or do not know the answer. "The professors are generally excellent at encouraging and facilitating discussions that teach independent thinking," says a sophomore. "Most of them really make you want to learn," remarks a senior. The fact that Benedictine sisters live on every dormitory floor makes the out-of-classroom faculty-student bonds even stronger.

Saint Ben's students consider the professional program in nursing, as well as coursework in the sciences and fine arts, to be among the strongest majors offered. Nursing is noted for its rigor and extensive opportunities for hands-on experience, including a chance to spend a semester studying and working in Port Elizabeth, South Africa. Boasts a senior: "Most of our nursing students will have a position secured by January of their senior year." For fine arts majors, there is no more inspirational place to work than the magnificent Benedicta Arts Center on campus. Biology and chemistry majors thrive in the 14-year-old science center complete with modern labs and equipment. English, theology, psychology, economics, and nutrition science also make the grade-A list. The peace studies program is a source of pride for majors and non-majors alike who admire the passionate and scholarly faculty and fascinating courses that students apply to campus life.

Social work is a small department that lacks the variety of professors found in other areas. The communication and management departments are understaffed, making it difficult, students say, to get the classes they need and limiting the variety of offerings. Both fields also carry a reputation for being "easy" majors in need of more hands-on, technologically advanced alternatives to lecture classes.

Facilities: The real strength of Clemens Library is its very personal, user-friendly environment. Opened in 1986, the facility is decorated in warm, relaxing colors and offers chairs for every study posture with terrific views of the outdoors. Some students find the atmosphere a bit too relaxing and conversation-inducing, but users in search of quiet have learned to head to the back of the library and stay away from the buzzing front end. Those needing more silent surroundings generally go to Alcuin Library at Saint John's University, a much less hectic and "colder" facility, according to some. A psychology-theology major puts it this way: "St. Ben's is great for group studying and light research while St. John's is great for burying yourself in a dark corner to study or do research for hours with no distraction." Clemens contains about a third of the 716,000 volumes and 2000 paper periodical subscriptions held jointly by the 2 colleges. (More than 12,000 additional periodicals are available electronically.) Besides having access to the resources of Alcuin, students can receive information through MINITEX, an interlibrary exchange program hooked into the collection of the University of Minnesota and other libraries in the upper Midwest. St. Cloud State Library is also 15 minutes away.

Students usually find a sufficient number of computers available around the clock in the residence halls and campus apartments, and until 2 a.m. in the other labs around campus. All residence-hall rooms and apartments also have been wired for computer hookups.

Special Programs: A double-degree program is offered in engineering with the University of Minnesota. Study abroad for a semester is an option in 13 countries, from China to Chile. Half of all Saint Ben/Saint John students study abroad. Students may gain a different kind of experience as summer research fellows through the departments of biology, chemistry, math, psychology, and nutrition, as well as through the honors program. Faculty members work with students on research projects that usually are student-centered and may culminate in a paper that is presented at a national conference.

Campus Life: Eighty-two percent of Saint Ben women reside on the rather contemporary campus spread over 315 acres. While the college has its own student government, campus newspaper, and campus ministry program (but no sororities), it shares many extracurricular activities with the brother school including just hanging out at Brother Willie's Pub on St. John's campus. A Joint Events Council made up of students from each college plans social, cultural, and recreational events for the 2 student bodies. Dances are popular, with live bands almost once a week, swing dance nights once or twice a month, and a night club with dancing on Friday and Saturday nights. The prestigious Forum debate society attracts 100 top students from both campuses, with other students joining major-related clubs and service organizations, most notably Volunteers in Service to Others (VISTO). The regularly scheduled Bennie Bus makes trips to Saint John's fairly easy, and some students say they value their relationship with the men more since members of the opposite sex are not present all the time. Though incidents of crime are few, cross-campus escorts are provided and any incidents that occur are well publicized to alert other students. Residence halls are locked around the clock, and visitors must be escorted into the buildings. Emergency phones are available throughout campus.

Saint Ben's women like the way the college promotes women's athletics, such as adding women's ice hockey as a varsity sport. A tenth of the students in a recent year suited up for the 11 NCAA Division III intercollegiate teams; 70% take part in 10 to 15 intramural and 21 club sports, including lacrosse. Saint John's football, basketball, and hockey games are big social events, but the Saint Ben's Blazers basketball, soccer, and lacrosse teams draw enthusiastic crowds as well. Rollerblading and cross-country skiing on some 30 miles of groomed trails are popular personal sports, as are weekend canoe and hiking trips with the Outdoor Leadership Center (OLC).

To get away, Saint Ben's students generally take the "shopping bus" to St. Cloud (metropolitan pop. 185,000), which makes the 10-mile trip east 3 times daily, or head 4 miles west for a walk in the woods on Saint John's campus. Says a Minnesotan: "When my friends and I need to go 'off campus,' we rent sleeping bags from the OLC and go camping on 3200 acres of forests and lakes." The Twin Cities, about 90 miles southeast, provide the major urban escape.

Cost cutters: Ninety-seven percent of freshmen and 95% of continuing students in 2005–2006 received financial aid; for 68% and 66% respectively, the help was need-based. The average freshman award consisted of a need-based scholarship or grant averaging $14,435 and need-based self-help aid such as loans and jobs averaging $6021. Other non-need-based awards and scholarships for first-year students averaged $9605. The average Saint Ben's graduate left with debts of $24,764. Regents/Trustees Scholarships pay $12,500 to women with GPAs of at least 3.6, 1980 combined SATs or ACTs of at least 30; Presidents Scholarships range from $7000 to $10,5000 to those with a GPA of 3.6 who have demonstrated leadership and service, and Dean's Scholarships of $3000 to $6500 go to those with a minimum 3.3 GPA and similar achievements. Women must apply for admission by Jan. 15. No-need awards in art, music, and theater paying up to $2000 a year are available to students who have excelled in these fields. Diversity Leadership Scholarships pay up to $5000 annually.

Rate of Return: Eighty-eight percent of the women return for a second year. Seventy-six percent graduate in 4 years; 81%, in 5 years, 82% in 6.

Payoff: Psychology was the major of choice for 11% of 2005 graduates. Ten percent each specialized in communication and biology. Eighty percent use their degrees for immediate entry into fields such as teaching, nursing, accounting, retailing, and financial accounting throughout the upper Midwest. More than 100 companies recruited on campus in 2004–2005. Among recent graduates, less than 20% sought advanced degrees.

Bottom Line: The College of Saint Benedict provides opportunities for young women to live separately from men and attain leadership positions in their own campus organizations while still participating in coed classes and joint social activities. At Saint Ben's, the emphasis is on individual academic, personal, and spiritual growth. Advises an English major: "Students who don't value the pursuit of knowledge or who are only after grades, or who want lots of lecture and regurgitation wouldn't do well here. To be successful at St. Ben's, students have to participate in class discussions, think on their own, come to class, and see education in a noncompetitive way." Those who love nature thrive best, as there are few urban stimuli close at hand.

College of St. Catherine

St. Paul, Minnesota 55105

Setting: Urban
Control: Private (Roman Catholic)
Undergraduate enrollment: 11 men, 2351 women
Graduate enrollment: 82 men, 625 women
Student/faculty ratio: 11:1
Freshman profile: 14% scored over 699 on SAT I verbal; 30% scored 600–699; 38% 500–599; 18% below 500. 8% scored over 699 on SAT I math; 30% scored 600–699; 38% 500–599; 22% below 500. 9% scored above 29 on the ACT; 52% scored 24–29, 38% 18–23; 1% below 18. 34% graduated in top tenth of high school class; 75% in upper fourth.

Faculty profile: NA
Tuition and fees: $21,385
Room and board: $6120
Freshman financial aid: 90%; average scholarship or grant: $7991 need-based; $17,660 non-need-based
Campus jobs: NA; average earnings: NA
Application deadline: Rolling
Financial aid deadline: Apr. 15
Admissions information: (651) 690-8850; (800) 656-5283
e-mail: admissions@stkate.edu
web site: www.stkate.edu

At a time when many women's colleges across the nation are losing enrollment and weighing whether or not to go coed, one Catholic women's college, based in the heart of the country, just seems to keep getting stronger. The College of St. Catherine, run by the Sisters of St. Joseph of Carondelet, is the largest Catholic women's college in the country, with about 2350 full-time undergraduates; almost 1250 part-timers, many of whom attend in the evenings or every other weekend; and about 1300 full- and part-time graduate students. The combined total of just over 4900 makes St. Kate's the largest private women's college in the United States just ahead of the grande dame of eastern schools, Smith College in Northampton, Massachusetts, which has a larger full-time undergraduate enrollment (about 2500) but smaller part-time and graduate-level programs. Though very different schools, Smith and St. Kate's each represent the best in strong women's colleges. In the past decade, St. Catherine's has boasted among its students Rhodes, Fulbright, Truman, and Goldwater Foundation scholarship winners. Noted a recent graduate: "Of 24 Ramsey County District Court judges (recently) on the bench, 5 were women. Of these 5, 4 were graduates of the College of St. Catherine. This statistic is not just a coincidence. This college develops leaders."

Student body: St. Catherine's remains largely a favorite of the local population. Ninety percent of the undergraduates are from Minnesota. Half of the remaining students are also from the Midwest, with women recently from 29 states and 30 foreign countries present. Fifty percent are Catholic. Fifteen percent of the undergraduates are 25 or older; the average age of all full-time undergraduates is 21 years, both statements showing the large number of women who transfer to St. Kate's after unsuccessful starts at other colleges or after a few years out of school. St. Catherine is also varied racially and ethnically. Just below a fifth of the students are members of U.S. racial and ethnic minority groups, including 8% African-Americans, 7% Asian-Amerians, 3% Hispanics, and about 0.5% Native Americans. Foreign national students comprise 2%. Though men may enroll in courses at the weekend college and earn credit, a man may not receive a bachelor's degree from St. Catherine's. Women are usually impressed by the quality of classmates they meet, finding a majority to be ambitious, hard-working, self-confident, and friendly. "Women on the go," observes a sophomore. Most are politically and socially aware, a trait highly valued around campus. Close friendships develop easily. The academic atmosphere is challenging but nurturing, rather than stressful; and because undergraduates are not graded on a curve, they can concentrate on their own mastery of subject matter, rather than worrying about how their grades compare with those of their classmates.

Academics: St. Catherine's, which turned 100 in 2005, confers the bachelor's degree in about 40 disciplines plus master's and doctoral degrees. The school year is divided into 2 semesters plus a January term that gives students a chance to explore new topics through independent study, study abroad, internships, or courses at other universities. Average class size for undergraduates is 13, but the range extends from as high as 78 in an introductory nursing course to 30 in many core classes to 3 in some upper-level science courses.

A core curriculum instituted in fall 1995 retains many traditional distributional requirements, including at least 2 courses in philosophy and theology, but it starts and finishes with 2 classes that excite many students. Freshmen take a multidisciplinary course, the Reflective Woman, in which students develop communication and critical thinking skills while discussing important intellectual and everyday issues. Attention also is given to setting goals and career development. As juniors or seniors, students conclude the core requirements with a multidisciplinary seminar entitled the Global Search for Justice. Several versions of the course are offered every term, with each examining the condition of justice experienced by people in a different culture or geographic region outside of Europe and North America. Students also must demonstrate proficiency in writing and computer literacy to graduate.

Seventy-nine percent of both the 246 full-time faculty and 237 part-time members are women, a statistic whose significance is not lost on the many undergraduate women seeking positive role models. More importantly, most professors are rarely too busy to meet with students outside of class and to remain attentive to their concerns. Says a senior: "The faculty care about the students and are open to helping them achieve their dreams."

The "people professions" of nursing, occupational therapy, and education are St. Catherine's strong points. These areas feature excellent, involved faculties as well as ample opportunities for students to gain practical experience. Occupational therapy, a dual bachelors/masters program, requires all majors to complete 2 fieldwork placements of 3 months each. Psychology, philosophy (featuring a faculty member who dressed as Descartes for a lecture), social work, sociology, and English also earn students' respect. Smaller departments such as theater, art, French, and Spanish are big in the individual attention they offer.

Some of St. Catherine's primary weaknesses lie in majors it does not offer, such as foreign languages beyond French and Spanish, computer science (offered only as a minor), or journalism. However, 30 additional majors, including German, Norwegian, and Russian as well as computer science and journalism, can be pursued at the University of St. Thomas, Augsburg or Macalester college, or Hamline University. Together, these 4 colleges plus St. Catherine's share cross registration as members of the Associated

Colleges of the Twin Cities (ACTC). Among majors St. Kate's does offer, political science needs more faculty, more choice in courses, and more focused standards; history and international relations also could use more faculty.

Facilities: When undergraduates in the Twin Cities are looking for a serious place to study, most come to the library at St. Kate's, which, according to students, has a reputation for being quiet. When it comes time for St. Kate women to do in-depth research, however, many of them look outward to the other area libraries. In fact, most view St. Kate's holdings of almost 391,000 volumes and 2166 periodicals as just part of the more than 1 million volumes and 5000 periodicals readily available through the other ACTC libraries. College buses run hourly to facilitate library service between the participating campuses, and computer linkages tell students what materials are available where. If none of the 4 other private-college libraries has what is needed, usually the source can be obtained from the University of Minnesota in Minneapolis.

More than 350 PCs are located in 3 large computer centers as well as in every residence hall. One of the main labs is open around the clock, as are all those in the residence halls. The college also offers a laptop leasing program, "complete with financial aid," says a senior.

Special programs: St. Catherine's students may take 1 class a semester at any of the other ACTC colleges or spend up to a year at any of 12 other colleges sponsored by the Sisters of St. Joseph, ranging from Chestnut Hill College in Philadelphia to Mount St. Mary's in Los Angeles. Both full-year and semester programs of study in 7 European countries plus Australia, Korea, Japan, and Colombia are available. Study in Mexico, France, and England during the January term also is offered. Other educational opportunities range from programs in city arts or metro-urban studies, based right in the Twin Cities, to Latin American studies, based in Bogota, Colombia. Dual-degree programs in engineering are available with Washington University in St. Louis and the University of Minnesota in Minneapolis and in pre-forestry and environmental studies with Duke.

Campus life: Thirty-seven percent of St. Kate's students plus a family of ducks on the local Dew Drop Pond reside on the 110-acre wooded campus a few minutes from the cultural center of the Twin Cities. Because students at St. Catherine's interact so closely with those from the 4 other local, coed colleges, the school's single-sex status does not leave women socially isolated. During a typical semester, about 600 men and women students from other colleges take courses at St. Kate's and many others come to use its quiet library and other facilities. Although crime is not a problem, an escort service is provided on a 24-hour basis and is widely used. Students also are kept advised of any crimes on campus, in the surrounding area, or at neighboring schools.

Most campus life centers around cultural, sporting, and social events in the Twin Cities and at other nearby colleges. There are 2 local sororities that anyone who wishes may join, but more students turn out for clubs in their majors or get involved in peace and social justice work. An organization gaining membership and attention has been Women Helping Women, a group through which St. Catherine students work with a homeless shelter in downtown Minneapolis; students provide child care for the homeless children on the weekends and raise funds for the shelter. Sports traditionally have not been big on campus, though the new fitness facility that opened a few years ago has begun to spur more athletic action. Five percent participate in the 9 intercollegiate sports played in NCAA Division III. Just 7% are active in 8 intramural sports.

When students need to get away from campus, many take a walk along the Mississippi River, just a few blocks from St. Catherine's, or head for home, which for many is within a 200-mile radius of the Twin Cities.

Cost cutters: St. Catherine's low tuition stems in part from the contributed services of the Sisters of St. Joseph. Ninety percent of freshmen and 83% of continuing students in the 2005–2006 school year received financial aid; for 72% of the freshmen and 69% of the rest, the assistance was need-based. The average freshman award included a need-based scholarship or grant averaging $7991 and need-based self-help aid, such as loans and jobs, averaging $5308. The average non-need-based scholarship equaled $17,660. Average financial indebtedness totaled $27,519 for 2005 graduates. St. Catherine of Alexandria Scholarships paying $3500 to $8000 in a recent year are awarded annually on the basis of a competitive written essay and personal interview; students qualify through test scores or class rank. Other merit awards recently recognized valedictorians with $10,000 and one student with extraordinary artistic or musical talent with full tuition and fees for 4 years. Presidential Scholarships recently paid $9500 a year for 4 years. To qualify students should have high school class rank in the top 15% and either an ACT composite of 26 or higher, or combined SAT math and critical reading scores of at least 1200. Two payment plans are provided.

Rate of return: Eighty-one percent of the freshmen return for their sophomore year. Forty percent go on to graduate in 4 years; 55% in 5 years, 58% in 6.

Payoff: Among recent degree recipients, nursing led all other majors, with 17% of the class, followed by occupational therapy at 10%, and elementary education at 9%. Less than 15% of St. Kate alumni pursue graduate studies, with the largest numbers seeking advanced degrees in education, English, library science, and nursing. Ninety percent enter the job market soon after graduation, primarily in medical and human service fields, communications, business, and education. Major firms such as 3M, Honeywell, Pillsbury, and Abbott Northwestern Hospital have been regular employers. Most graduates remain in Minnesota, with others moving to California, Wisconsin, and Illinois.

Bottom line: The College of St. Catherine works best for students who are open to the opportunities a women's college can offer. Remarks a sophomore: "This is a great college experience for women who aspire to be leaders and who want to make a difference. Excellence with ethics is the goal here."

Concordia College
Moorhead, Minnesota 56562

Setting: Urban
Control: Private (Evangelical Lutheran)
Undergraduate enrollment: 1029 men, 1735 women
Graduate enrollment: 5 men and women
Student/faculty ratio: 14:1
Freshman profile: 11% scored over 700 on SAT I verbal; 29% scored 600–700; 39% 500–599; 21% below 500. 15% scored over 700 on SAT I math; 19% scored 600–700; 43% 500–599; 23% below 500. 11% scored above 28 on the ACT; 13% scored 27–28; 29% 24–26; 28% 21–23; 19% below 21. 30% graduated in top tenth of high school class; 51% in upper fifth.

Faculty profile: 67% Ph.D.'s
Tuition and fees: $19,520
Room and board: $4990
Freshman financial aid: 95%; average scholarship or grant: $4998 need-based; $8160 non-need-based
Campus jobs: NA; average earnings: NA
Application deadline: Rolling
Financial aid deadline: None
Admissions information: (218) 299-3004; (800) 699-9897
e-mail: admissions@cord.edu
web site: www.concordiacollege.edu

While most colleges offer some kind of program for study abroad to its students, Concordia College, a Lutheran school in western Minnesota, offers a World Discovery Program that begins more than a half semester before a student's departure and continues for a half semester after his or her arrival home. The intent of the program is to make each student's time abroad a "once in a lifetime" experience. Faculty begin by helping the student select a program most appropriate to his or her educational goals. Then, in the semester prior to travel, the student takes an orientation seminar designed to familiarize him or her to life in another culture. Upon returning to Concordia, the experienced traveler takes a reentry seminar together with other returning students, helping all to assess, reflect, and learn from their individual experiences abroad. Whether the trip itself is for a semester or a year, whether the student speaks Russian, Swahili, or English only, the World Discovery Program is a round-trip ticket to terrific travel. And Concordia, which makes it all possible, says a Spanish major, "can best be described as a supportive family."

Student body: Two-thirds of Concordia's students are Minnesotans. The remainder are mainly other midwesterners, although students arrive from 35 states and 33 foreign countries. All but 4% are graduates of public schools. Just over half, 55% of all students are Lutheran; 22% are members of other Protestant denominations, 16% are Catholic, and 7% claim no religious affiliation. Concordia's student body is predominantly white, mostly of Scandinavian heritage. Asian-Americans make up 2% of the enrollment; African-Americans and Hispanics each comprise 1%. Foreign nationals account for another 5%. While Concordia undergraduates are generally more conservative in their political thinking and dress than students at other private colleges in the state, they are not reserved in their enthusiasm for life. Most are outgoing, open-minded, involved, informed, down to earth, and full of vitality. Concordia students have a name for classmates who are especially friendly, even to strangers: "happy Cobbers."

While most Cobbers find the coursework challenging, a senior observer recently broke down the intensity meter as follows: 30% laid back, 40% concerned, and 30% competitive academically. Overall, however, there is positive peer pressure that often causes the laid-back 30% to push a little harder than they had anticipated. Concedes a junior: "In high school, I was not motivated by the achievements of other students; here I am. But it's not so much competition as a realization that I can do better."

Academics: Concordia, which turned 115 in 2006, confers the bachelor of arts degree in 78 majors, including 18 honors majors and 12 preprofessional programs, a bachelor of music degree, and a master's degree in nursing. The academic calendar consists of 2 semesters, which end in early May to make way for the optional May Seminars Abroad in which approximately 200 undergraduates travel in groups of about 15 with faculty in their academic areas of interest. Average class size for undergraduates is 22. Highly specialized courses such as studio art may enroll as few as 4 students, while a biology lecture may reach 60. Most students, however, rarely encounter classes with more than 30.

All students are required to take a 7-part core curriculum that begins with Principia, a 1-semester freshman-year discussion of timeless issues; continues with Discourse, 2 courses to promote clear written and oral expression and critical thinking skills; and ends with Integration, classes that show juniors and seniors how 2 or more disciplines interrelate. Throughout the process, students also must fulfill distributional requirements that cut across all fields, plus 2 classes in physical education and 2 in religion, and demonstrate proficiency in mathematics, usually by testing or coursework.

Concordia's faculty numbers 263, including 43 part-timers. Almost half are women. While some members, in the view of students, are ready for retirement, the vast majority are viewed as inspiring, thought-provoking, and eager to help. Explains a sophomore: "Professors are dedicated to excellence yet take the time to get to know each student." There also is mutual respect between teacher and student as well as high expectations. Says a junior: "They are excited about what they teach and expect you to be the same." Most also make it a point to be involved in campus and community activities and don't confine their teaching to the syllabus. Says a senior: "Class discussions are encouraged and current events are incorporated into classes, not strictly textbook material. They make us think!"

The most respected professors are scattered across widely divergent fields, such as modern foreign languages, music, biology, elementary education, and religion. Concordia offers majors in French, German, Spanish, Russian studies and Scandinavian studies; a minor is available in Norwegian, and there is instruction also in Chinese, Japanese, Biblical Greek, and Hebrew. Language students frequently serve as counselors at weekend programs at Concordia Language Villages in Bemidji. The sciences and music are particularly demanding majors at Concordia and leave little room for students to take courses outside the field. Biology is distinguished by professors "willing to go the extra distance for students," and by a variety of rigorous labs, cooperatives, and internships that result in an excellent placement record for graduates in medical and dental schools. Says a major: "(Having) human cadavers in upper-level anatomy classes is a rare undergraduate opportunity—but extremely beneficial!" Music combines talented professors with ample opportunities for students to perform. Mathematics, chemistry, and computer science feature demanding classes and a faculty "who have a genuine desire to help," observes a mathematics major. Elementary education provides a good balance between theoretical knowledge and practical experience, with a total immersion that many majors find "intense." Religion is characterized by well-trained faculty who offer both liberal and conservative approaches to eternal problems. Other winners include English, history, and international education.

Other departments have a way to go to make the A list. Business education suffers from a lack of student interest. Students find other secondary education programs to be less helpful than they had hoped. Notes a senior hoping to teach at the secondary-school level: "I do not feel that I am prepared for the real world of teaching. The classes were full of busy work with pointless assignments." Home economics has sought a new life and mission as the department of family and nutrition science, but students say classes are still too easy and professors guide majors too much in their coursework. Art, classical studies, and philosophy are small departments with limited course offerings but excellent faculty.

Facilities: For most research projects, Concordia students view Ylvisaker Library not just as a single facility with more than 300,000 volumes and 1500 periodicals, but rather as 1 unit of a triumvirate that makes available about 1.25 million volumes and 5000 periodicals. Through what is known as the Tri-College University program, involving Concordia along with Minnesota State University, Moorhead and North Dakota State University, all within a 3-mile radius of each other, students of each college may use the library resources of the others. They may either go in person to visit the libraries via a twice-daily shuttle bus, or check by computer to see whether the materials are available and, if they are, have them delivered on the bus. For information not contained in any of these libraries, an on-line catalog also lists the holdings of more than 30 other regional college and university libraries; these sources can be obtained through interlibrary loan. Ylvisaker is strongest in materials related to religion and music, weakest in business journals. As a study center, Ylvisaker is such a popular place to study, "our second home," says a junior, it can become a bit noisy.

Seven main computer labs on campus, plus smaller ones in all residence halls, house about 350 computers, mainly IBM PCs, all of which have Internet access. Computers in the library are available until midnight; those in the residence halls, around the clock, most of the rest, until between 11 p.m. and 2 a.m. Lines only usually appear, says an accounting major, on "Sunday nights after a weekend of procrastination."

Special programs: Students can participate in 30-day biology field studies in areas such as Mexico, the Caribbean, and Hawaii or join an archaeological dig in Israel where one student recently unearthed a cache of 99 gold coins. For language students in Spanish, French, and Norwegian, for-credit practicums are available in which undergraduates live and work with selected families in countries where these languages are spoken, in exchange for room and board. An off-campus program in urban studies is offered in Chicago, and another in national government and politics is conducted in Washington, D.C. Cross registration for no more than 1 course a semester is available at Minnesota State University, Moorhead or North Dakota State University in Fargo. A 4-year program in engineering can be obtained through joint study at Concordia and North Dakota State; a 3-2 program is available with Washington University in St. Louis and the University of Minnesota.

Campus life: Concordia is owned and operated by the northern Minnesota, North Dakota, and Montana congregations of the Evangelical Lutheran Church in America and reflects that affiliation in its conservative living arrangements. All Concordia freshmen and sophomores are required to live on the 120-acre campus in single-sex housing and must comply with restrictions on visitations by members of the opposite sex. While disgruntled undergraduates maintain that the strict intervisitation policy inhibits natural male-female relationships, most tolerate the rules as "simply an inconvenience" that fails to ruin an otherwise wonderful sense of community on campus. Upperclassmen may live in college-owned apartments or off campus.

There are no fraternities or sororities, and students simply put their energies in other activities. Nearly one third of the undergraduates are involved in 1 or more of 16 music ensembles that recently included 2 handbell choirs, a marimba choir and jazz ensembles, as well as the famed Concordia Choir, College Orchestra, and College Band, which perform throughout the United States and Europe. More than 300 undergraduates are involved in theater productions as well as a large number in Campus Service Commission, a service organization. Although attendance at Wednesday night communion service is not required, "it is very popular, almost a social event," observes a junior. Sunday Night at East, a weekly contemporary worship service, also attracts a large crowd. Students concerned about walking alone around campus after dark can call Safe Walk for an escort between 9:30 p.m. and 2 a.m. Most undergraduates consider the campus and surrounding area to be very safe, although they appreciate recently improved outdoor lighting.

Football and women's basketball, both of which have won national championships, as well as men's basketball, draw the biggest crowds of the 10 men's and 10 women's intercollegiate sports played in NCAA Division III. Intramurals are competitive as well; in a recent school year, 275 students and faculty vied for the highly prized T-shirts awarded to winners in each of the 8 intramural events.

For a big weekend, students travel to Minneapolis/St. Paul, 240 miles southeast, or to Winnipeg, Manitoba, Canada, 210 miles north. The communities of Moorhead, Minnesota, and Fargo, North Dakota, separated by the Red River of the North, together have nearly 175,000 residents. The Moorhead shopping and business district is within walking distance of campus, and bus service is free.

Cost cutters: Concordia is able to keep its costs $3000–$5000 lower than those of other Evangelical Lutheran Church in America and Minnesota private colleges, thanks to a sturdy endowment and to donations recently averaging $5.5 million annually. In a recent school year, 95% of all first-year students and 78% of all remaining students received some form of financial aid; for 57% of the first-year students and 53% of the rest, the aid was need-based. The average freshman award for a student with financial need in a recent year included a need-based scholarship or grant averaging $4998 and need-based self-help aid such as loans and jobs averaging $4612. Other non-need-based awards and scholarships for first-year students averaged $8160. An average graduate left with $18,135 in debts. The Presidential Distinction Scholarship is the college's top award, with $50,000 awarded over 4 years. The scholarship is given to 50 first-year students. In addition, hundreds of first-year students receive merit awards ranging from $4000 to $10,000 a year. Performing Arts Scholarships acknowledge talent in theater performance and production, forensics, debate, and music and pay $10,000 over 4 years. Almost every major provides for a cooperative education placement or internship.

Rate of return: Eighty-one percent of the freshmen who enter return for the sophomore year. Sixty-two percent graduate in 4 years; 69%, in 5 years.

Payoff: Sixteen percent of recent graduates earned degrees in business, with 14% graduating in foreign languages and 11% in English. Three-fourths of Concordia graduates take jobs immediately upon graduation, most as teachers or in management, finance, or marketing positions with firms based in the midwest and Great Lakes region. Eighty-six companies and organizations recruited on campus in a recent school year. A fourth of the graduates enrolled directly in graduate or professional schools. Within 5 years of graduation, approximately 40% pursue advanced degrees.

Bottom line: Just over 100 years ago, Concordia's purpose was "to influence the affairs of the world by sending into society thoughtful and informed men and women dedicated to the Christian life." Newly into its second century, Concordia graduates head out into the world conversant in many native tongues, well versed in the liberal arts and a professional discipline, and eager to give that "happy Cobber" greeting to everyone they meet. Cynics need not apply here.

Gustavus Adolphus College

St. Peter, Minnesota 56082

Setting: Small town
Control: Private (Evangelical Lutheran)
Undergraduate enrollment: 1095 men, 1451 women
Graduate enrollment: None
Student/faculty ratio: 13:1
Freshman profile: 18% scored over 700 on SAT I verbal; 47% scored 600–700; 29% 500–599; 6% below 500. 14% scored over 700 on SAT I math; 46% scored 600–700; 33% 500–599; 7% below 500. 24% scored above 28 on the ACT; 18% scored 27–28; 28% 24–26; 22% 21–23; 18% below 21. 41% graduated in top tenth of high school class; 63% in upper fifth.
Faculty profile: 94% Ph.D.'s

Tuition and fees: $24,865
Room and board: $6055
Freshman financial aid: 93%; average scholarship or grant: $13,311 need-based
Campus jobs: 66%; average earnings: $1600/year
Application deadline: Rolling; regular: Apr. 1 (Priority date: Dec. 1)
Financial aid deadline: Apr. 1 (Scholarships: Mar. 1; Priority date: Dec. 1)
Admissions information: (507) 933-7676; (800) GUSTAVU(S)
e-mail: admission@gustavus.edu
web site: www.gustavus.edu

As college costs at private schools across the nation continue to outpace inflation, Gustavus Adolphus College, located 65 miles southwest of Minneapolis, has found a way to give a price break to its continuing students—the Guaranteed Cost Plan. For a 1-time premium of $600 payable in the fall of the first year, students' annual increases for tuition, room, and board are limited to 3.9% during their enrollment at the college. This option enables students and their parents not only to plan better financially for the years ahead, but also to save what could be a few thousand dollars over the 4 years until graduation. Students who chose not to enroll in the plan when they entered as freshmen in the fall of 2002 paid $30,555 in tuition (not including fees), room, and board for the 2005–2006 school year; those who joined the plan in 2002 paid just $27,846 for the year (again, not considering mandatory fees). About 75% of the students participate in the program. In the words of a former student who already had a sister at Gustavus and a brother at a major private university when she enrolled as a freshman, "My parents were quite thrilled with the plan: they were going to be saving money without having to compromise on the quality of education that I would receive."

Student body: Seventy-seven percent of Gustavus students are from Minnesota. Just 8% of the out-of-staters are from outside the Midwest, with undergraduates coming from 40 states and 19 foreign countries. Just 7% attended private or parochial schools. Twelve of the 705-member fall 2005 freshman class were National Merit finalists; 62 freshmen were valedictorians. "As a Swedish Lutheran college in the rural Midwest, diversity comes hard," notes a state resident, and statistics bear out this statement. Just 4% of the enrollment are Asian-American and 1% each Hispanic and African-American, with another 2% foreign nationals. Observes a sophomore: "While we may have a low percentage of racial and ethnic diversity, we have a very high percentage of diverse thoughts, which enrich everyone's educational experience." Fifty-three percent are Lutheran, with a definite "Gustie" type: blond-haired, blue-eyed, Scandinavian, open, friendly, intelligent, and moderately conservative (some say moderately liberal) in dress and actions. Observes a senior: "Students know about the 'causes' and may believe in them but hold back on acting for fear of being labeled as radicals." While Gusties are very social and involved in extracurricular learning, they put pressure on themselves to succeed in the classroom as well. Notes a recent graduate: "Next to the common cold in the spring, consciousness of academic performance is the most contagious disease on campus." Students point out, however, that few classmates compare grades. The environment, says a political science major, is "competitive but not cutthroat," and most students enjoy working together in study groups.

Academics: Gustavus Adolphus, which was founded in 1862 and acquired its present name 14 years later to honor the 17th-century Swedish King Gustav Adolf II, offers the bachelor of arts degree in 74 majors. The school year is 2 semesters plus a January term. Average class size is 15. A general biology lecture attracts the largest number, at almost 90, but labs have only 24 students a section. Other freshman-year classes have enrollment caps, such as 16 for First Term Seminar. Senior seminars in virtually all majors enroll no more than 10.

Entering freshmen may choose between 2 core curricula. Under Curriculum I, students select courses from 6 broad subject areas ranging from the arts to human behavior and social institutions. Everyone must begin with a First Term Seminar involving groups of 16 students in critical thinking and an exploration of values. Two courses in a foreign language or culture (including 1 in a non-Western culture) or 1 course plus a semester of study abroad also must be taken.

Undergraduates opting for Curriculum II study the same subject areas but do so in a predesigned program of 12 sequential, interdisciplinary courses, highlighted by field trips and retreats. Courses in the first year include, for example, Historical Perspective and The Individual and Morality, followed in other years by The Literary Experience, The Individual and Society, and The Natural World. Two foreign language courses and a class in quantitative reasoning also are required. Participation in Curriculum II is limited to 60 students in each entering class; while coursework is more time-consuming and difficult to combine with certain majors, most students find they learn to relate diverse topics better, thereby facilitating all their learning. Advises a junior: "You can't go wrong with either approach, but students are clamoring to get involved in Curriculum II." Regardless of which core they take, all undergraduates must also complete 3 courses from at least 2 different departments that require a substantial amount of writing.

The Gustavus faculty of 244 members includes 57 part-timers; 40% are women. "Trying to name the top 10 professors over campus would be nearly impossible because they are all so good," remarks an English major. Though most faculty members have impressive academic and career credentials, just about all treat students as colleagues; even professors who are revered as "geniuses" are approachable to undergraduates. Stories of their teaching exploits are legion; among the best known are the biology professor who knew the name of each of the 70 participants in his lecture class by the end of the first week, and the history professor who dresses up as characters from American history and has the class ask him appropriate questions. Amiable doesn't mean easy, though. Notes a senior: "The professors are very challenging and expect hard work and dedication to their classes in order to receive good grades."

The Gustavus science programs earn respect from majors and nonmajors alike for their 5-star facilities, including an automated DNA sequencer, and faculties. Biology, says a political science major, features "a near-perfect mix of notable scholarship and top-notch teaching." Chemistry, with its emphasis on student research, has produced more American Chemical Society majors than its counterpart in any other liberal arts college in the Midwest. A highly enthusiastic and committed faculty in physics, plus a new building, enables students to enjoy an excellent track record of placements in graduate school. The rigorous environmental studies program offers extensive opportunities for "great research, study abroad, and faculty interaction," says a major. Math professors are known for being willing "to meet with you outside of office hours as many times as you need to grasp a concept," says a major. Classics professors earn a rating of "tough but excellent"; those in history are admired for their intellectual breadth and devotion to student research and discussions; the English faculty, too, says a major, "are incredibly well-rounded in their fields of interest and are warm and caring as well as brilliant." Political science is considered by this major to be "very well organized and challenging," with members of the faculty who push students to understand all sides of an issue. The programs in music, theater, and education are equally impressive. Entrance into the small but winning athletic training program is highly competitive.

The geography department is small and has not only limited course offerings but minimal requirements, according to students. While psychology is very popular and offers wonderful opportunities for hands-on experience, students say classes can run large because of an insufficient number of faculty. The communication studies program is stronger in courses on rhetoric than on broadcasting. It also could use more faculty members to handle heavy student demand for its courses. The foreign languages department, with majors in French, German, Spanish, and Russian and Japanese Studies, also could use more faculty. Students, however, especially enjoy those professors who are native speakers and love the variety of unusual classes offered, from sign language to Sanskrit. Some students would like to see more ethnic studies programs, such as African-American studies, added to the interdisciplinary offerings already available in Latin American, Latino and Caribbean studies, and Scandinavian studies.

Facilities: The Folke Bernadotte Memorial Library holds just over 294,000 volumes and 999 periodicals, a collection that students consider more than adequate for their research needs. Moreover, for many users, getting to these materials and others is a "joy," thanks to a computerized catalog system and MINITEX, a statewide interloan system that provides access to millions of volumes at the University of Minnesota and elsewhere. Says a political science major: "It is very easy to conduct a very large research project, and never leave the Gustavus campus." Bernadotte also offers late hours, until 1 a.m. Sundays through

Thursdays, and a wide range of study options among its 1200+ seats. Says a junior: "You can find the perfect environment to fit your needs, whether that be complete silence or small distractions and a little noise."

Computer labs containing approximately 400 units are located in every residence hall and in every academic building. Most labs are open until 10 p.m. weekdays and during the day on weekends although about 2 weeks before finals, most stay open until at least 3 a.m. Individual rooms in all residence halls are wired for access to the Internet and labs in the residence halls are open around the clock. Students say getting a free computer is rarely a problem since so many students have their own, which the college strongly recommends. All residence halls and most academic buildings also have wireless capacity.

Special programs: Half of the students participate in an international study experience in nearly 40 sites spread among 22 countries. The college has its own exchange or residential programs in Sweden, Japan, India, Australia, Malaysia, The Netherlands, and Scotland. General cross-registration for courses is available at Minnesota State University, Mankato, just 15 minutes away; for more specialized study, undergraduates may participate in cooperative degree programs in nursing with St. Olaf College and in engineering with the University of Minnesota and Minnesota State University, Mankato. A semester in Washington, D.C. also can be arranged. Opportunities for undergraduate research are extensive; in a recent 3-year period, Gustavus Adolphus boasted the third largest group of students presenting papers at the National Conference for Undergraduate Research. A Center for Vocational Reflection sponsors seminars, retreats, and other activities that encourage students to reflect more deeply about concerns for the welfare of communities in which they live and to consider such areas as political involvement and community service.

Campus life: Eighty percent of the Gusties live on the 340-acre hilltop campus, which is divided informally into north and south sides. The north side tends to house the livelier, more outgoing, party-loving crowd; the south, the quieter, more achievement-oriented students. A fifth of the men and 17% of the women are members of the 6 local fraternities and 1 national and 4 local sororities, though involvement holds no special social status around campus. Notes a sophomore: "The only benefit would be that you hear about parties before the rest of the campus!" Dancing in the Dive, a 19-year-old "dry" campus bar-cum lounge-cum study room, is a popular activity. For the melodically inclined, there are 24 musical ensembles, such as the Gustavus and Adolphus bands and the Lucia Singers; about a third of the student body participates. MAGIC, a student-led community service organization that stands for Meaningful Activities for Gusties in the Community, also draws a large portion of undergraduates, as does the weekly student-led worship service Proclaim. Says a Southerner who left her "warm winters" to head north, "This place doesn't die on the weekend; it gets more exciting!" Although students consider crime almost nonexistent, to control a slight rise in thefts a few years ago the dormitories are locked 24 hours a day, open only to residents with keys. Blue emergency lights are prevalent around campus. "Security escorts are available," says a westerner, "however, most students who use this service just want a warm ride to their residence halls on cold winter nights."

A fourth of the men and women participate in the 12 men's and 13 women's NCAA Division III intercollegiate sports offered. Men's football, basketball, and men's and women's hockey and soccer games typically draw the biggest crowds. The men's soccer team was the runner-up in the 2005–2006 Division III national championship game. Eighty percent of the men and 70% of the women turn out for 17 men's and 10 women's intramural activities.

The community of St. Peter (pop. 9000) can be rather confining, and students sometimes flee to the Twin Cities of Minneapolis and St. Paul, which are, at most, $1^1/_2$ hours away. The shuttle Gus Bus travels to the Mall of America on weekends. Mankato (pop. 40,000) is just a 15-minute trip. Others opt to relax by walking through the peaceful 135-acre campus arboretum.

Cost cutters: The Guaranteed Cost Plan is just 1 program that makes Gustavus Adolphus an even better buy than its comparatively low comprehensive fee indicates. In the 2005–2006 school year, 93% of freshmen and 92% of continuing students received some kind of financial aid; 68% of freshmen and 65% of the remaining students had need-based assistance. The average freshman award for a first-year student with financial need included a need-based scholarship or grant averaging $13,311 and need-based self-help aid such as loans and jobs averaging $5200. An average 2005 graduate left owing $17,900. Students who rank at or near the top of their high school class with at least a 30 ACT or 1320 critical reading and math SAT are eligible for President's Scholarships that pay $8000 to $12,500 annually. Students must complete a separate application and participate in a scholarship competition in late February or early March. Dean's Scholarships, also based on academic achievement, test scores, and GPA, pay up to $7000 a year. Students who have demonstrated a commitment to community service can receive $500 to $1500 Norelius Service Awards. Andrew Thorson Scholarships recently paid up to $3000 to needy students from towns of less than 2000 residents or who graduated from high school classes of fewer than 100 in rural areas. The Paul L. Rucker Scholarship pays up to $5000 annually to students who bring cultural diversity to campus. The Jussi

Bjorling Music Scholarship, named for the famous Swedish tenor, awards $1000 to $4000 a year to students with outstanding musical ability. Students with talent in theater and dance may receive awards ranging from $500 to $2000 annually.

A cooperative education program provides internships, paid and unpaid, in many majors; more than 50% of the students participate. Most academic departments also choose upperclass students as assistants. And graduates don't forget their alma mater: Gustavus Adolphus ranks among the top 1% of all colleges in the nation in the percentage of alumni who contribute to their school, thereby helping to keep costs down for future classes.

Rate of return: Eighty-nine percent of freshmen return for the sophomore year. Seventy-nine percent graduate in 4 years; 82%, in 5 years.

Payoff: Of the 2005 graduates, 11.5% earned degrees in communication studies, 10% in psychology, and 7% in biology. A third of the new alums continue their studies in graduate or professional schools, 20% in the arts and sciences, and the rest in business, law, and medicine. Two-thirds jump into the job market right after graduation, working mainly in the Midwest as accountants and auditors, marketing and sales representatives, and teachers. Seventy-five percent ultimately attend graduate or professional school.

Bottom line: Gustavus Adolphus is a college where students refuse to stay in any single academic cubby hole. Many science majors take up music; a number of business majors participate in intercollegiate sports. Notes a senior: "Gustavus is academically challenging without being impossible. Its main focus is personal learning, not weeding out poorer students. Here, one's values and beliefs are constantly but constructively challenged."

Hamline University

St. Paul, Minnesota 55104

Setting: Urban
Control: Private (United Methodist)
Undergraduate enrollment: 1890 men and women
Graduate enrollment: 2650 men and women
Student/faculty ratio: 14:1
Freshman profile: Median SAT I scores: 598 Verbal; 589 Math; Median ACT composite: 24. 26% graduated in top tenth of high school class; 54% in upper quarter.
Faculty profile: 99% Ph.D.'s
Tuition and fees: $23,130

Room and board: $6680
Freshman financial aid: 71%; average scholarship or grant: $14,783 need-based; $4552 non-need-based
Campus jobs: 60%; average earnings: $2100/year
Application deadline: Early action: Dec. 1; regular: May 1
Financial aid deadline: Mar. 15
Admissions information: (651) 523-2207; (800) 753-9753
   e-mail: cla-admis@hamline.edu
   web site: www.hamline.edu

What does the typical student want from a college education? For the majority, the answer is a good job in the field of his or her choice, or maybe entry into a top-ranked graduate school that will lead to an even better job. Hamline University in St. Paul, Minnesota has taken what students *want* from college and what they *should have* from college and come up with the Hamline Plan. The plan's 11 goals, which include items like communicating effectively in writing, in speaking, and on the computer, reasoning logically, and working independently, determine what kinds of courses all students must take to graduate. For most students, the end result is very much what they want—and get from Hamline. One recent graduate enrolled for postgraduate work at Stanford, after turning down M.I.T., Harvard, and Caltech. For other students, the lifelong skills are just as impressive. Notes a senior: "My bachelor's degree has given me critical thinking skills, compassion for oppressed people and outrage at institutionalized discrimination, the ability to be creative and resourceful, and knowledge of where to find needed information." In today's world, attributes like those are priceless—and obtainable at Hamline for just under $30,000 in the 2005–2006 school year.

Student body: Minnesotans are the prime beneficiaries of the Hamline Plan, with 66% of the undergraduates from in-state. Though most of the out-of-staters are also midwesterners, students come from 28 states and 30 foreign countries. Three-fourths typically are graduates of public schools. Eight percent are Methodist. Six percent of the undergraduates are Asian-American; 4% African-American, 2% Hispanic, less than 1% Native American, 3% each biracial/multiracial and foreign nationals. Hamline students pride themselves on representing a multitude of backgrounds and interests, but, for the most part, resist the tendency to form cliques. Notes a senior: "Some are highly political, some are highly close-minded, some are athletes, some are rebellious. Some are vocal; others are far too intelligent for this institution." Liberal thinkers tend to outnumber those who are more conservative. Notes a junior: "I feel very out-numbered as a Republican but I can (still) have great conversations with people about in-depth entertaining subjects." Academically, students report fewer parties during the week and plenty of classes that are intense and in which members really challenge each other. That said, however, Hamline students refuse to be overfocused on a single area and become as involved, and sometimes overinvolved, in extracurricular activities as possible.

Academics: The university, which became Minnesota's first college in 1854, was named for a Methodist bishop who gave the founding gift of $25,000. More than 150 years, 49 buildings, and millions of dollars in giving later, Hamline awards bachelor's degrees in 38 fields, and master's degrees and doctorates in several fields, including a J.D. degree from its law school. The academic year is divided into 2 semesters plus a January term. Average class size for undergraduates is 20 students. The largest introductory lectures in political science or psychology generally enroll 40–60; advanced foreign language courses may have just 5.

The 11-point Hamline Plan begins with a first-year seminar, designed to develop students' understanding of the liberal arts. New students are enrolled in groups of 16, each led by a faculty member who serves as mentor and advisor. Students choose their seminars by topics, which include a surprising mix of interdisciplinary topics and teachers, for example, "Fact and Fiction in the 21st Century," taught by a chemistry professor. All freshmen must take an introductory writing course plus 1 writing-intensive course in each of the remaining 3 years in areas ranging from biology to philosophy. Other highlights include 2 speaking-intensive courses and 1 computer-intensive course (a recent seminar on Emily Dickinson fulfilled this requirement), as well as distributional requirements, an internship or a seminar on career areas, and an independent project. Many of the requirements can be filled within a student's major.

One hundred thirteen of the 176 full-time faculty members and 111 of the 436 part-timers teach undergraduates. Half are women. On the whole, students rate their professors as 9 on a scale of 1 to 10, leaving room for the occasional bad teacher, although most students say they rarely encounter a teacher who does not reach them somehow. Remarks a political science major: "The faculty includes a lot of young people with plenty of energy. There are some professors who continually challenge themselves and read new material for a course at the same time the students do." Adds a westerner: "Professors are always willing to talk, advise, or share a cup of coffee."

All of the sciences—biology, chemistry, and physics—are top of the line, with emphasis on small classes and "real" research using the most advanced equipment that enables many undergraduates to publish their findings in refereed journals. Not to be outdone, an English major boasts: "I can't imagine a more complete English department than Hamline's. The professors work with the student and exact from him or her a level of achievement not reached at many other schools." Anthropology boasts 7 full-time faculty members, each with a different area of expertise. Psychology, sociology, philosophy, communication studies, management and economics, religion, and global studies also draw high approval ratings. The legal studies program benefits from having the law school and library, which is open to all undergraduates, on campus, though students complain it sometimes is difficult to meet with the numerous adjunct professors after class. The criminal justice and forensic sciences program gains from the working knowledge of faculty experienced in these fields. Education requires extensive practical experience in local classrooms, many located in an elementary school across the street.

History needs more faculty and a wider variety of course offerings. Art has great professors but lacks adequate facilities. The majors in French, Spanish, and German need more faculty; music and theater need a wider variety of class offerings. Computer science, offered only as a minor, could use more than the single professor, who also teaches math classes. Students say some mathematics faculty members find it difficult to work with students who are nonmajors in their fields.

Facilities: The holdings of the undergraduate Bush Library are small for a university: 140,000 volumes and 900 periodicals, although that figure more than doubles when subscriptions to 226,000 volumes and microfiche equivalents and more than 2600 periodicals at the law school library are added. Bush also has almost 15,000 electronic reference sources and aggregator database sources. Still, students complain mightily about the qualty of materials available at Bush. Says a junior: "Research is frustrating—often articles or books needed are not to be found, or they are at the other colleges in our consortium. Most periodicals are also severely outdated—or nonexistent." A savior to many is the on-line computerized research system that links Hamline with the resources of 7 other private colleges in the Twin Cities; a daily courier is available to retrieve needed materials. The online service also links the state library network to Hamline, making available the vast resources of the University of Minnesota. As a study area, Bush gets a gold star for adaptability: each of the 4 floors has a different personality, from laid-back to super intense. Some greater degree of quiet usually is mandated on 1 of the 4 floors, and those needing larger spaces of total silence can study at the newer but smaller Hamline Law Library.

Undergraduates have access to 360 PCs housed in 6 computing labs across campus. The main lab is open until midnight, though students would like to see it accessible around the clock. All residence-hall rooms are connected to the campus computer network. The university strongly recommends that students have personal computers. Wireless access is available in all classrooms, libraries, and residence housing.

Special programs: Hamline students may participate in more than 60 academic disciplines, as well as the library service and social events, at the College of St. Catherine, the University of St. Thomas, and Macalester and Augsburg colleges, all accessible by free shuttle bus. A special 3-3 program enables a Hamline student interested in law school to earn a bachelor of arts and a law degree at the university in 6 years. Off campus 3-2 programs are available in engineering and occupational therapy with Washington University in St. Louis and in engineering with the University of Minnesota. A wide range of options for foreign study in 45 countries are offered, from January term trips to Peru and Ireland to semesters in Germany and Senegal. Students may also spend a term studying the arts in New York or politics in Washington, D.C. or attending Clark Atlanta University, a predominantly black college in Georgia.

Campus life: A little less than half, 43%, of the undergraduates reside on Hamline's 60-acre campus, set in a residential neighborhood midway between the downtown sections of St. Paul and Minneapolis. Dances and off-campus parties constitute much of the weekend activity; there is also an eclectic mix of activities sponsored by various members of the 80 campus groups, from Pride Black Student Alliance to Community to Community, a community service group. The Greeks have become negligible players at Hamline. Just 5% of the women belong to Hamline's 1 local sorority. Hamline's single national fraternity, which had enrolled just 10% of the men, no longer exists on campus. About a third of the students go home on any given weekend. Despite Hamline's location in the heart of the Twin Cities, students say that by using proper caution they generally feel very safe on campus, although there has been a problem with cars being broken into in the campus parking lots. Security phones and security officers on patrol are within quick reach, and a 24-hour escort service is available to discourage walking alone late at night. Surveillance cameras also have been added to the parking lots.

Sports generally draw student support more enthusiastically on the field or court than in the stands. A third of Hamline's men and women play on 9 men's and 10 women's NCAA Division III teams. Fighting Pipers football and men's basketball games had been the only sports that gained even limited student spectator attention until women's volleyball, basketball, and gymnastics began to surge in popularity and fan support. The women's gymnastics team responded, winning the National Collegiate Gymnastics Association Division III title in March 2000. Still, crowds for most school sporting events remain small. Instead, students opt to do for themselves: 70% of the men and 65% of the women get involved in the 8 men's, 10 women's, and 10 coed intramural sports available. Hamline was the site of the first collegiate basketball game in the nation, and some undergraduates have long maintained that the facilities hadn't improved much since then. (Norton Field House was built in 1937; the stadium, in 1921.) The opening of the Lloyd W.D. Walker Fieldhouse in 1998 provided long-awaited new fitness and training facilities for both varsity and intramural athletics. In 2004, the multipurpose Klas Center and football stadium were added.

To satisfy an appetite for big-time athletics, many students drive or take the bus into either St. Paul or Minneapolis to see games by the Twin Cities' professional sports teams, as well as to attend concerts or plays, often at discounted prices. Lake Como and its year-round zoo offer relaxing diversion as well.

Cost cutters: In a recent school year, 71% of the freshmen and 70% of the continuing students received financial assistance; for most of those students, the aid was need-based. The average freshman award for a student with need included a need-based scholarship or grant averaging $14,783 and need-based self-help aid such as loans and jobs averaging $1738. Non-need-based awards and scholarships averaged $4552. The average financial indebtedness of a recent graduate was $21,156. The Presidential Scholarship pays from $6000 up to full tuition, to at least 20 new high academic achievers annually and is renewable. To be considered for the full-tuition award, students must apply by Jan. 20. Other merit awards recognizing strong achievement records include Honors Scholarships, paying $4000 to $8000 a year and Trustee Scholarships, paying $3000 to $6500. A number of scholarships recently worth $3000 also are available to students who excel in specific academic and creative fields. Internships are available in virtually all academic departments; in more than two-thirds, students are paid for their efforts. A budget plan enables students to spread tuition payments over 10 months.

Rate of return: Eighty-four percent of the freshmen return for the sophomore year. Sixty-one percent graduate in 4 years; 64%, in 5 years; 67% in 6. A Four-Year Graduation Assurance Program guarantees that all classes required to graduate and adequate academic counseling will be available to insure graduation in 4 years or Hamline will pay the fifth year of tuition!

Payoff: A fourth of all recent graduates earned degrees in 3 disciplines: 14% in psychology, 12% in management, and 10% in English. The vast majority of Hamline graduates enter the job market soon after commencement, most settling in the Twin Cities metropolitan area, others moving elsewhere in the Midwest or branching out to either of the 2 coasts. Just over a third of recent degree recipients enrolled directly in graduate or professional schools, many part-time while working.

Bottom line: Hamline is a school that focuses on what a student can become, rather than on what he or she has been in the past, and provides all the ingredients for success. Notes a Minnesota resident: "The curriculum is strong across the board, campus organizations are plentiful, and the Twin Cities environment allows access to several places for entertainment. Most graduates from Hamline eventually become very successful. This college is a gold mine that few know about." That isn't true anymore.

Macalester College

St. Paul, Minnesota 55105

Setting: Urban
Control: Private (Presbyterian)
Undergraduate enrollment: 766 men, 1061 women
Graduate enrollment: None
Student/faculty ratio: 12:1
Freshman profile: 50% scored over 700 on SAT I verbal; 35% scored 600–700; 12% 500–599; 3% below 500. 37% scored over 700 on SAT I math; 51% scored 600–700; 12% 500–599; 0% below 500. 56% scored above 28 on the ACT; 41% scored 27–28; 0% 24–26; 3% 21–23; 0% below 21. 65% graduated in top tenth of high school class; 88% in upper fifth.

Faculty profile: 95% Ph.D.'s
Tuition and fees: $28,642
Room and board: $7858
Freshman financial aid: 77%; average scholarship or grant: $19,090 need-based
Campus jobs: 65%; average earnings: $1500/year
Application deadline: Early decision: Nov. 15 and Jan. 3; regular: Jan. 15
Financial aid deadline: Feb. 8
Admissions information: (651) 696-6357; (800) 231-7974
  e-mail: admissions@macalester.edu
  web site: www.macalester.edu

Macalester College is a school that emphasizes the "liberal" in the liberal arts. Around the Twin Cities, its increasingly traditional student body used to be known as those "flaming liberals down the street," spoken not without a touch of envy. Its curriculum remains rich in the traditional liberal arts, with no majors in such career-oriented fields as accounting or business administration. Macalester also has kept very loose distributional requirements: just 8 semester hours in the social sciences, 8 in the natural sciences and mathematics, and 12 in the humanities and fine arts. Mac students generally find they can fulfill these almost by accident. New requirements emphasizing writing and quantitative thinking are scheduled to begin for students entering in fall 2007. Students also must complete a small class with their advisor in the first semester of their freshman year and a semester class each concerning international diversity and domestic diversity, plus demonstrate proficiency in a second language equal to 4 semesters of college study. The focus on broadening understanding about different cultures reflects more than restricts the preferences of many students, as more than 50% study overseas as part of their Macalester experience. Twelve percent are foreign nationals from 80 countries, another 16% are members of U.S. racial and ethnic minority groups. Undergraduates speak of Macalester in the same breath as such elite colleges as Bard, Sarah Lawrence, Reed, and Oberlin, whose higher costs and generally lower percentages of students on financial aid make Macalester's $36,500 price tag, with 3 of every 4 undergraduates on aid in the 2005–2006 school year, seem more affordable—in a liberal sort of way. "The 'myth' of the liberal arts education is a reality here," says a senior. "At Macalester, students study what interests them most, not what is a 'marketable' major for the new century."

Student body: Macalester draws its students from all 50 states. A fourth are from Minnesota; a third of the out-of-staters, from elsewhere in the Midwest. Seventy-one percent are graduates of public schools. Because of a long-standing commitment to make Macalester as racially, ethnically, and internationally diverse as possible, the college makeup is very varied for its location. "This campus is not UCLA by any means," says a midwesterner, "but there is a minority and international student presence, although most of us wish it were greater." Asian-Americans account for 7%; African-Americans 4%; Hispanics 4%; and Native Americans, 1% of the total enrollment. Students see themselves as liberal-minded and socially conscious, almost to the point of viewing some stands on controversial issues as "the Macalester thing to do." Just how much students *do* about their positions varies greatly with each individual. Says a senior: "Frequently there are on-and-off campus Mac-organized protests for what the primarily liberal student body sees as 'just' causes." Nonconformism also is worn like a badge of honor at Macalester. Notes a sophomore: "A student can be as odd as he or she wishes, and no one attacks or publicly criticizes. There also is no set social structure with popular people at the top and 'geeks' at the bottom." Academically, as well as socially, the climate is mellow, or appears so on the surface. "Macalester is filled with lazy intellectuals, although some are merely creating the impression of not working hard," says an easterner. Most students prefer sitting around over coffee discussing issues in a thoughtful manner rather than comparing test results. Notes a New Englander: "Even though everyone is so smart and they have done so many amazing things in their lives thus far, they are modest and would prefer to talk about how they can help the community now." As far as grades, "It's not too difficult to obtain a B," says a physics major, "but very tough to get a 4.0."

Academics: Macalester, founded in 1855, awards the bachelor's degree in 25 departmental and 10 interdepartmental concentrations. The academic year is divided into 2 semesters plus a January term. Average class size for freshmen and sophomores generally runs from 20 to 30, although a course in Principles of Art can enroll 82. Juniors and seniors usually find classes of no more than 20, and specialized upper-level courses, such as Advanced Inorganic Chemistry, may have only 1.

Although the curriculum is unusually broad, with 700+ courses, students have complained that its depth in certain specialized concentrations, such as Russian, Central, and East European studies, was not nearly as great as its breadth. However, the college is midway through the hiring of 28 additional faculty members, designed both to reduce the student-faculty ratio to 10-to-1 and add depth to those curriculum areas where it is needed. Most students love the freedom the still minimal general-education requirements allow, but some acknowledge that it is possible to graduate with glaring omissions or imbalances in coursework, such as 2 math courses but no laboratory science.

Macalester has 151 full-time faculty members plus 72 part-timers "always game for a rousing debate," says a senior. Forty-eight percent are women. A fifth are U.S. and international faculty of color. Macalester students are tough on their professors, respecting their solid academic credentials (many boast degrees from Ivy League institutions) but criticizing some for failing to keep up in research or for having too "midwestern" a view of the world. On the other hand, reflects a psychology major, "professors a student doesn't even know will go out of their way to help, as faculty in every science department did with my honors projects, even though I had not taken classes in their fields." Their passion for sharing their knowledge is contagious. Notes a sophomore: "There have been a few classes that I can't wait to go to. I hurry to class and sit in the front row." Adds a senior: "I have been pushed academically to levels I never imagined, which is a good feeling."

The social sciences rank among Macalester's strongest disciplines. A 5-star history department features a faculty as balanced and committed to students as it is knowledgeable. International studies thrives under renowned and challenging professors as well as the campus's own lively multicultural climate. A student double-majoring in international studies and political science says both departments feature "two factors that make a department great: intellectually challenging professors and innovative and challenging ideas." Stimulating professors make economics, classics, and anthropology with its opportunities for fieldwork at the undergraduate level very popular. Observes an anthropology major: "There also is a big emphasis on doing projects that will help people. In my intro anthropology class, we made a book in English and Mongolian and sent it to Mongolia." Geography and psychology likewise team terrific teaching with multiple opportunities for undergraduates to gain hands-on experience. Many think the programs in the natural sciences rival the best found anywhere, with top-notch, dedicated biology and chemistry teachers and excellent support programs and equipment. A $20 million expansion and renovation of the science facilities completed in 1997 has further enhanced opportunities for student-faculty collaboration. The physics and astronomy department is a winner as well. The faculty in Hispanic and Latin American studies includes excellent teachers who are a lot of fun, but students wish there were more of them. The distinctive Humanities, Media and Cultural Studies program provides, in the words of one student, "critical theory and media analysis generally seen in grad school," although some students looking for more hands-on journalism courses are disappointed. "All the humanities are great," concludes an English major.

The fine arts area is one where students find need for improvement. The visual arts department lacks classroom and studio space. The dance program, part of a combined major with theater, could be improved by offering more variety in the kinds of dance instruction offered. The educational studies department is small, and students say too often overlooked, offering an academic minor with 5 faculty members, 1 full-time. The linguistics program also is small with just 2 full-time faculty members.

Facilities: The library, which opened in 1988, is "a big, brand-new, $15 million living room," raves a recent graduate, with abundant resources for a college of Macalester's size: over 455,000 volumes and 2647 periodicals. Still, some science and prelaw students, as well as seniors doing in-depth projects in other fields, find they must spend large amounts of time on-line or at the University of Minnesota, where additional material is available. A computerized catalog provides information on resources at all of the local libraries to which Macalester students have access. Each computer station also has a printer so that students can have records of their references. The library contains seating for every study need, including group study rooms, single, private student "offices," plenty of carrels, and overstuffed chairs in hidden nooks, which are great for naps.

Five public access labs are open to students, 3 of them making computers available to students around the clock. Says a senior: "There should probably be one more 24-hour lab but that's only needed for peak cramming times like finals and midterms." Every residence hall is networked with one data outlet per pillow and most students bring their own computers. Laptops with wireless network access also are available for loan in the library and in the campus center. Wireless access is available in most academic buildings. The college strongly recommends that all students have personal computers.

Special programs: Macalester students can take courses at 4 other local colleges—Augsburg, the College of St. Catherine, Hamline University, and the University of St. Thomas—and can participate in a variety of study-away programs well outside the Twin Cities area. More than 24 overseas programs have been approved for Macalester credit, ranging from a semester or year at the American University in Cairo to a term or year at the University of Stirling in Scotland. Nearly 200 students annually receive academic credit for internships locally, nationally, and overseas. Cooperative degree programs in engineering, nursing, and architecture are offered with several major universities in the Midwest.

Campus life: Seventy percent of Macalester's students reside on the 53-acre campus, located just 4 miles west of downtown St. Paul. The college has neither fraternities nor sororities, a situation in which many undergraduates take pride. Recalls a senior: "My freshman year we did have a mock fraternity called 'Phi Beta Booty,' which was pretty amusing since it mostly consisted of guys dressed up in sheets for about a week." Nonetheless, Macalester's weekend parties are well known around the other Twin Cities campuses. Macalester also supports its own very active music scene, not even counting the free bagpiping lessons that are offered. "I know of at least 10 different bands that play in dorm basements or at the off-campus homes of juniors or seniors," says a senior. "The fact that almost all of the parties are open to everyone makes for a pleasant 'scene.'" Those not into partying or music often go to 1 of several local coffee shops for discussion, or turn talk into action with 70 student organizations, from MACTION, a community service group that involves a fifth of the students in weekly volunteer work, to MPIRG, which emphasizes environmental activism, to various support groups for African-American, gay, and women's rights. Although Macalester is related to the Presbyterian Church, it emphasizes a pluralistic view in regard to religion, including a Hebrew House for Jewish students who keep kosher and a chapel used by Muslims for Friday prayers and by Quakers for Sunday morning meetings.

Despite Macalester's proximity to downtown St. Paul, crime usually is limited to thefts of laundry, bikes, and the occasional wallet. Theft of laptops has increased as more students have them and leave them unguarded. However, infrequent assaults remind students to be cautious when walking alone on campus or in the surrounding area. To keep assaults and thefts in check, the security force has been beefed up, hours for the escort service have been extended, and more educational efforts have been instituted.

Other than the occasional toss of a Frisbee, no sporting event commands much attention, though the Scots soccer games, both men's and women's, attract enthusiastic crowds. Despite the generally low fan support, 25% of the men and 20% of the women turn out to play the 10 men's and 11 women's NCAA Division III sports fielded. A fourth of the undergraduates go out for the 20 men's and 20 women's intramural sports, ranging from softball to broomball, which is a brand of ice hockey played without skates and with a broom and rubber ball. About 10% play a club sport, with rugby the college star.

The Twin Cities offer a wealth of theaters, art museums, and film societies, as well as plenty of dance clubs and ethnic restaurants. "The scene is incredible," says an Easterner, "and students take full advantage of it." A scenic overlook of the Mississippi River, a little more than a mile away, provides another kind of breather from campus life. Students caution, however, that the river walk and most other outdoor activities are usually more enjoyable when undergraduates can't see their breath. Remarks an easterner: "There is a unique temperature here that only the people in Antarctica would understand." On the days when zero degree Fahrenheit seems warm, most students end up studying or hanging out with friends indoors—unless, of course, it's time for the annual Grand Avenue snowball fight, an event not to be missed regardless of the chill.

Cost cutters: Seventy-seven percent of the freshmen and 74% of the other undergraduates in the 2005–2006 school year received financial help to pay for Macalester. For 71% of the freshmen and 68% of the continuing students, the aid was need-based. The average freshman award for a student with need included a need-based scholarship or grant averaging $19,090 and need-based self-help aid such as loans and jobs averaging $4772. An average 2005 graduate had $15,000 in debts. DeWitt Wallace Distinguished Scholarships go to students who are National Merit semifinalists, commended students, or finalists and range from a minimum of $3000 upward, depending on need. The 2005 freshman class included 51 National Merit scholars. DeWitt Wallace Scholarships also worth $3000 go to middle-income students with solid academic records who need financial assistance. Catharine Lealtad Scholarships for high-achieving African-American, Hispanic, and Native American students are worth a minimum of $3000, which can be increased according to financial need. National Presbyterian Scholarships recently paid up to $1400 a year, also depending on need.

Rate of return: Ninety-two percent of Macalester freshmen return for the sophomore year. Eighty-two percent go on to graduate in 4 years; 84%, in 5 years.

Payoff: In the 2005 graduating class, economics at 11%, political science at 8%, and psychology at 7% claimed the largest numbers of degree recipients. About 30% of Macalester graduates pursue advanced degrees shortly after leaving; nearly 60% earn advanced degrees within 6 years of graduation. Two-thirds earn doctorates; a third, professional degrees. Since 1967, Macalester has had 11 students who were named Rhodes Scholars, including a senior from Jamaica who was awarded the honor in the 2005–2006 school year. Thirty percent of new alums take their first jobs in business; 20%, in social service, foreign service, and government work. More than 50 companies and organizations recruited on campus in a recent year.

Bottom line: Macalester provides a traditional liberal arts experience that the traditional and less-than-traditional student will find liberating. Says a New Englander: " Macalester offers such a unique combination of personal attention, intellect, activism, internationalism, and multiculturalism that I wouldn't want to go anywhere else."

Saint John's University

Collegeville, Minnesota 56321

Setting: Rural
Control: Private (Catholic—Benedictine)
Undergraduate enrollment: 1845 men
Graduate enrollment: 25 men, 12 women
Student/faculty ratio: 13:1
Freshman profile: 13% scored over 700 on SAT I verbal; 36% scored 600–700; 39% 500–599; 12% below 500. 9% scored over 700 on SAT I math; 51% scored 600–700; 26% 500–599; 14% below 500. 19% scored above 28 on the ACT; 18% scored 27–28; 31% 24–26; 25% 21–23; 7% below 21. 42% graduated in top fifth of high school class; 77% in upper two-fifths.

Faculty profile: 88% Ph.D.'s
Tuition and fees: $23,474
Room and board: $6275
Freshman financial aid: 96%; average scholarship or grant: $14,142 need-based; $8584 non-need-based
Campus jobs: 63%; average earnings: $2100/year
Application deadline: Rolling (Priority: Dec. 1)
Financial aid deadline: Priority: Mar. 15
Admissions information: (320) 363-2196;
(800) 544-1489
e-mail: admissions@csbsju.edu
web site: www.csbsju.edu

When students from the University of St. Thomas in Minneapolis chant, "Go back to the woods," at the big football game against rival Saint John's University, everyone knows exactly what the fans are yelling about. Saint John's is located on 2450 scenic acres of woodlands in rural central Minnesota. Founded by Benedictine monks in 1857, the university remains under the sponsorship of Saint John's Abbey, the largest Benedictine monastery in the world. The relationship between monks and students is close, with monks living in student residences in the college's own incorporated community, known naturally as Collegeville. While Saint John's is all male in its residential setting, its academic program is very much coed. In an unusual arrangement, the university shares a common academic calendar and core curriculum, a combined library and academic computing system, and a single registrar's office that offers cross registration for classes with all-female College of Saint Benedict, located just 4 miles away in St. Joseph. A free and frequent shuttle bus links the 2 campuses. Saint John's may indeed be part of a monastery in the woods, but monastic living is not included in the deal.

Student body: Eighty-two percent of Saint John's students are from Minnesota, with most of the rest also from the Midwest. Undergraduates are drawn, however, from 36 states and 24 foreign countries. Sixty-seven percent of the young men are Catholic; 23% Protestant and 2% of some other faith; 22% are graduates of private or parochial schools. Four percent of the students are members of minority groups: 2% Asian-American, 1% Hispanic, and 1% African-American. Four percent are foreign nationals. The atmosphere at Saint John's is warm and friendly, with students helping one another to study and to survive personal crises. A recent study found the graduates to be nearly evenly split among those with liberal viewpoints, those taking middle-of-the-road positions, and those holding conservative opinions. "Somewhat conservative in dress, somewhat liberal in thought," says a junior. Eccentrics are few, and most students settle easily into the peaceful rural setting, which helps to keep academics in perspective. Notes a senior: "The atmosphere is quite competitive academically; however, stress is virtually nonexistent. The faculty, monks, staff, and students all foster a low-stress environment, and their efforts work."

Academics: The university offers a bachelor's degree in 40 fields and a master's degree in 4 through its School of Theology, which is open to women. Courses are divided between 2 semesters. An average class for underclassmen enrolls about 30 students, with some introductory lecture courses having 60. The freshman symposium is limited to 16, and most other upper-division classes range from 10 to 25.

Students at Saint John's and Saint Ben's share the same core curriculum, which explores, from a variety of perspectives, the question of what it means to be human. The program begins and ends with cross-disciplinary courses at the freshman and senior levels. A 2-term freshman symposium gives students their choice of topics through which they develop skills in thinking and interpersonal communication. From that foundation, students take traditional courses from various fields as well as "flagged courses" that focus on writing, discussion, gender and global perspectives, and quantitative reasoning. In addition, undergraduates must demonstrate competency in foreign language and mathematics, and finish with a senior "capstone" class in which 20 participants analyze ethical dimensions of contemporary life. Many of the men grumble that the core is too rigid, and that, while it introduces them to disciplines they might otherwise never have taken, it makes it very hard for students in some single majors or, especially, double majors to graduate in 4 years.

Saint John's full-time faculty numbers 176 with 29 part-time members. About a fifth of the faculty members are Benedictine monks, with another 29% women. Students praise the professors, particularly the monks, for the respect they show to students and for the kindness that motivates most of their actions. "There is a deep connection to the students," says a sophomore. Lunch with a professor is nothing special in terms of how often it occurs but usually is noteworthy for the quality of conversation enjoyed at both ends of the table.

Programs in political science, biology, chemistry, history, philosophy, classics, and English are each distinguished by superb teachers who double as enthusiastic learners. For biology in particular, the surrounding campus provides a wonderful natural laboratory, with access to wetlands and forest, matched indoors by equally fine, modern equipment in a recently renovated building. The resources of the university's monastic library, which has preserved on film handwritten manuscripts from throughout Europe and Asia, make history a choice major although some students wish there were more variety in the classes offered. The theology department is sound, and its offerings pale only in comparison to Saint John's exceptional graduate-level program. Accounting, economics, education, and nursing all boast experienced and knowledgeable professors who help turn out successful, employable graduates.

Management remains St. John's most popular major; however, the popularity of the program has strained faculty resources, limiting the number and variety of class sections offered. Students in other fields also maintain it has a reputation for being "easy" and needs to adopt more rigor to attract higher quality students. Communication also could also use more challenge and more faculty to accommodate growing student interest. Sociology and social work could use more professors. Foreign language instruction has been hampered by faculty having to concentrate most of their efforts on classes students take merely to fulfill core requirements rather than on more advanced classes for undergraduates with a love of the field.

Facilities: The joint holdings of the libraries at Saint John's and Saint Ben's are substantial, 716,000 volumes and 14,863 current periodicals (more than 12,000 electronic), with about 70% of the collection housed at Saint John's Alcuin Library. Its holdings are particularly strong in history, theology, philosophy, and classical literature, although sparse in materials in all fields published since 1980. A computer catalog links the 2 facilities, enabling students to research the collections of both from either. Students also have access to the resources of the University of Minnesota and other libraries in the upper Midwest. As a building, Alcuin is 3 levels with a basement known as the "dungeon" that demands silent individual study.

Many find the overall study environment to be "gray and imposing," rather than comfortable, but that atmosphere does tend to make study time more efficient in order to get out as quickly as possible.

Computers in 2 large labs on St. John's campus, both open until 2 a.m., plus units in the various academic departments, satisfy most students' high-tech needs. Additional computer labs with 3 to 4 units are located on each residence-hall floor. The availability of computers is so sufficient, says a senior, "I did not buy a computer any of my 4 years here, just used the ones provided. They're new and up to date." For those students who do bring computers, all student rooms have been wired for access to the campus computer network.

Special programs: Together with Saint Benedict's, Saint John's sponsors international studies programs in 13 countries; half of the St. Ben's and St. John's student body participates. A 5-year dual-degree program is offered in engineering with the University of Minnesota. Students also may serve as summer research fellows through the departments of biology, chemistry, math, psychology, and nutrition, and through the honors program. The fellowships are generally for 400 hours (10 weeks of 40 hours per week), involve faculty members working with students on largely student-centered research projects, and often culminate in the student presenting a paper for a national conference.

Campus life: Eighty-two percent of the men reside on the serene, woodsy campus, which includes Lake Sagatagan on its grounds. There are no social fraternities, but a single service fraternity shared with the women of Saint Ben's enrolls about 150 members, with others joining the Catholic Knights of Columbus. Says a sophomore: "One idea or belief that permeates the campus is a commitment to social justice." VISTO (Volunteers in Service to Others) and SIFE (Students in Free Enterprise) attract many students, as does the campus radio station, where the highly successful Minnesota Public Radio was founded in 1967. Brother Willie's Pub is a popular dance spot attracting students from both campuses most weekends. An increase in thefts on campus in recent years has prompted more men than in the past to start locking their doors. Concern about assaults, primarily against women visiting the campus, has raised student awareness about the need to be more cautious and has resulted in tighter security measures such as better lighting, more frequent security patrols, and more emergency telephones. However, actual incidents of crime are so few, says a sophomore, "that monthly reports are in single digits."

A third of the men are involved in a highly competitive NCAA Division III intercollegiate sports program. Hockey, basketball, and especially stadium-packing football, the 2003 Division III national champions, engage the most attention of the 12 varsity sports played. The football squad also holds the record for the most victories in NCAA Division III history, winning 526 games, losing 217, and tying 24 in 95 seasons. Says a junior: "Football games might as well be mandatory because everyone goes." All but 10% of the students participate in a 10 to 15 sport intramural program, many coed, and 21 club sports. With over 100 members per semester, Saint John's rowing club has one of the highest club memberships on campus, including both men and women, and has won several national competitions. Being a member of the rugby club also carries some prestige. Without leaving the expansive college grounds, students can enjoy hiking the numerous woodland trails or fishing, swimming, canoeing, rowing, or wind sailing in Lake Sagatagan.

St. Cloud (metropolitan pop. 185,000), 10 minutes away, is the nearest big city. For more distant escape, students head south to Minneapolis/St. Paul, a little over an hour away, where a number of them reside. Naturally, a lot of weekend traffic heads to St. Joseph and the women of Saint Ben's.

Cost cutters: Saint John's is able to hold down costs in part because the 40+ monastic members of the faculty and staff return 55% of their salaries to the university. In the 2005–2006 school year, 96% of the freshmen and 93% of continuing students received financial help to pay for college; the aid was need-based for 61% of the first-year students and 58% of the rest. The average freshman package consisted of a need-based scholarship or grant averaging $14,142, and need-based self-help aid such as loans and jobs averaging $4993. Other non-need-based awards and scholarships for first-year students averaged $8584. The average 2005 graduate had debts of $24,663. A wide range of merit scholarships are available, including Regents/Trustees Scholarships that pay $12,500 to applicants with GPAs of at least 3.6, combined SATs of 1980, and ACTs of at least 30; Presidential Scholarships, awarded to freshmen with GPAs of at least 3.60 who have demonstrated leadership and service, that pay $7000 to $10,500, and Dean's Scholarships worth $3000 to $6500 for freshmen with similar achievements who carried slightly lower GPAs of 3.3 or above. Diversity Leadership Scholarships pay up to $5000 a year. Two separate monthly payment plans are available.

Rate of return: Eighty-eight percent of the freshmen return for the sophomore year. Seventy-four percent graduate in 4 years; 81%, in 5 years; 82% in 6.

Payoff: Sixteen percent of the 2005 graduating class earned bachelor's degrees in business and management, with 10% majoring in biology and 9% each in political science and economics. Three-quarters of the graduates generally move directly into the work force in fields such as accounting, retailing, consulting, and professional sales in technical, industrial, and medical fields, or as management trainees, with firms throughout the upper Midwest. More than 100 companies and other organizations recruited on campus in the 2004–2005 school year. Just over a fifth of the recent grads enrolled in graduate or professional schools.

Bottom line: The Saint John's experience will be most special to young men who don't mind living in a male-only environment that provides regular interaction with women, who enjoy a peaceful if somewhat sheltered rural setting, and who appreciate the opportunity to share in the lives of the Benedictine monks who are everpresent as teachers, counselors, and friends. Remarks a junior: "Saint John's stresses the education of the mind *and* the soul."

Saint Olaf College

Northfield, Minnesota 55057

Setting: Small town
Control: Private (Evangelical Lutheran)
Undergraduate enrollment: 1256 men, 1749 women
Graduate enrollment: None
Student/faculty ratio: 15:1
Freshman profile: 30% scored over 700 on SAT I verbal; 42% scored 600–700; 24% 500–599; 4% below 500. 24% scored over 700 on SAT I math; 44% scored 600–700; 27% 500–599; 5% below 500. 28% scored above 29 on the ACT; 56% scored 24–29; 14% 18–23; 2% below 18. 49% graduated in top tenth of high school class; 71% in upper fifth.

Faculty profile: 93% Ph.D.'s
Tuition and fees: $26,500
Room and board: $6300
Freshman financial aid: 79%; average scholarship or grant: $15,105 need-based
Campus jobs: 61%; average earnings: $1151/year
Application deadline: Early action: Nov. 15; regular: rolling (Feb. 1 preferred)
Financial aid deadline: Feb. 1 (Priority date: Dec. 1)
Admissions information: (507) 646-3025; (800) 800-3025
e-mail: admissions@stolaf.edu
web site: www.stolaf.edu

Saint Olaf College in southeastern Minnesota gives fresh meaning to the term *global awareness*. In the school's Global Semester, students travel around the world for 1-month stays each in Egypt, India, Hong Kong, and Thailand, with shorter visits to Switzerland, Nepal, and China. Under the supervision of a Saint Olaf faculty member, undergraduates take 5 courses, 1 in each of the 4 countries, covering subjects from one nation's history to another's religion, plus a fifth course in global issues. Saint Olaf also offers a similar semester in the Middle East, with a 5-course program based in Turkey, Egypt, Greece, and Morocco, and a semester in Asia, which includes courses in China, Thailand, and Vietnam.

All told, Saint Olaf (named after Norway's patron saint, who ruled as King Olaf II almost 1000 years ago) offers more than 60 programs in every continent except Antarctica, with as much diversity in length of study, number of students, and type of accommodations as can be found anywhere. If the students, known as Oles (pronounced "oh-lees"), are a fairly homogenous mix when they enter college, the foreign and domestic travel experience that 75% of them gain by the time they graduate certainly broadens their perspectives.

Student body: Over half of all Oles, 57%, begin their journey as Minnesotans, with three-fourths of the out-of-staters also from the Midwest. All but 2 states plus 20 foreign countries have students at Saint Olaf. Fourteen percent are graduates of private or parochial schools; 1% has been home-schooled. A third of the undergraduates are Lutherans with another third members of other Protestant denominations, 13% Catholic, less than 1% Jewish, 18% other faiths, and 2% claiming no religious affiliation. First-generation college students account for nearly 13% of each incoming class. Each year, the largely white, blonde, and blue-eyed Scandinavian enrollment at Saint Olaf becomes more racially and ethnically diverse, although it still remains predominantly white. About 4.5% of the students are Asian-American, 1.5% each Hispanic and African-American and 1% foreign nationals. Less than 1% are Native American. Oles of all colors and ethnic origins are known for being highly motivated and industrious, well aware of the world outside Northfield, socially conservative but moderate to liberal in their political views. "Some people call us 'radical moderates,'" remarks a senior, "but that's because most of us are used to seeing both sides of every issue and understanding different perspectives." The word *wholesome* also has been used to describe the student body, though even Saint Olaf, says a senior, has its share of "socially intense athletes who also are very intellectual, nonsocial geeks, as well as students who are out to make a statement." But, as the student continues, none of these smaller groups and the wholesome majority ever have problems interacting. Despite the fact that nearly half of the freshmen graduated in the top tenth of their high school classes and nearly all (91%) ranked in the upper two-fifths, St. Olaf maintains a casual and friendly social and academic climate without the intense competition found at other equally selective schools. However, the academic schedule is fast-paced, and, confesses a junior, "I'd be very surprised if there was a student here who at least once a semester hasn't felt completely overwhelmed with papers, tests, and extracurricular activities."

Academics: Saint Olaf offers the Bachelor of Arts degree in 40 major areas with 20 concentrations and the Bachelor of Music degree in 4 areas. The school year is divided into 2 semesters plus a January term. Eighty-four percent of all classes have fewer than 29 students, with freshmen mostly encountering classes of 25–35 participants. A Principles of Psychology lecture may top 60 beginning students, but more specialized upper-level courses in all disciplines may have fewer than 10 enrolled.

Saint Olaf's curriculum begins with a first-year seminar that introduces undergraduates to the liberal arts, plus coursework or demonstrated proficiency in writing, mathematical reasoning, oral communication, physical activity, and intermediate-level fluency in a foreign language. The core centers on 2 requirements in each of 6 areas of exploration: Western culture, cultural diversity, the Bible and theology, arts and literature, natural science, and human behavior and society. Some courses may fulfill more than 1 requirement. Along with their majors, which all include a writing component, students must also complete an upper-level course addressing ethical issues and norms of justice guiding moral reasoning.

Forty-five percent of Saint Olaf's 196 full-time and 135 part-time faculty members are women. Of the 135 part-time members, more than 20 are music adjuncts. Most of the instructional faculty hold advanced degrees from the nation's top universities and are experts in their respective fields. To most undergraduates, however, they are kind and giving people as well as first-rate teachers. Notes a sophomore: "They are very open to differing opinions and willing to discuss issues, either personal or class-related, with students." Adds a junior: "They make me think, they make me laugh, they keep me engaged."

Years of excellence in music and the sciences have drawn the best faculty and students to Saint Olaf. The music program inspires awe with a demanding and respected curriculum that offers majors in performance, music education, church music, and theory-composition. The chemistry facilities are "fantastic," and student researchers put them to the test in such fields as spectrophotometry, nuclear magnetic resonance, and X-ray crystallography. The large math faculty is excellent even in entry-level classes; several professors have written the textbooks they use that employ a creative yet practical approach to the subject. English, studio art, biology, sociology, psychology, and China and Asian studies are all characterized by strong faculty who push students to meet their high expectations and motivate them with creative programs. Religion and philosophy feature some of the nation's best thinkers as faculty in these disciplines; the religion department also claims to be the largest and to offer the broadest array of courses of any liberal arts college in the nation. And, befitting a college named after Norway's patron saint, a distinctive major in Norwegian offers classes from the beginning level through Advanced Conversation and Composition plus courses, both in the language and in translation, in Norwegian literature and culture.

The majors in family studies and social work need more professors to provide both smaller class sizes and a wider selection of courses being offered. A newer major in computer science, just added in the 2002–2003 school year, needs time to develop.

Facilities: Saint Olaf offers its 3000 undergraduates the use of 2 impressive libraries in the college's best-known fields, science and music; a facility that specializes in collections of the Danish philosopher Soren Kierkegaard; plus the all-encompassing Rolvaag Memorial Library, "an oasis of quiet and solitude," says an English and political science major. Together, the 4 libraries house about 707,000 volumes, 2538 periodicals, and more than 275,000 non-book items, including CDs, videos, sound recordings, and software. To supplement Saint Olaf's ample holdings, computerized research aids link students with resources at Carleton College, across the river in Northfield, the University of Minnesota, and more than 40 other libraries in the region. In students' experience, there is rarely a book or article that cannot be obtained in just a couple of days. And yet, given all of the computerized and spatial amenities, as an economics major notes, "Our biggest library bonus has to be our phenomenal reference staff. If patience is a virtue, they all are going to library heaven."

Saint Olaf has 54 computer classrooms. Students also have access to more than 800 laptop and UNIX-based workstations in various public and department labs on campus. Computer labs can be found in every residence hall and academic building. "I am entirely dependent on the labs," says a sociology and English major, "and I have never found them to be inconvenient." However, 96% of the students are less dependent and bring a computer with them to campus, although a majority surveyed still report using the campus labs. Those with laptops, including three-fourths of the fall 2005 freshmen, can connect to the campus wireless network that extends to some residence halls, the library and student commons and numerous academic buildings.

Special programs: Students at Saint Olaf may propose self-designed, integrative majors through the Center for Integrative Studies. The individualized majors may combine diverse methods and styles of learning along with varying subject matter and resources from both on and off campus. As an added component, each major must contain an electronic web portfolio that demonstrates meaningful connections among the various parts of the major. A Great Conversation program offers first-year students and sophomores the opportunity to fulfill 8 graduation requirements by taking an integrated sequence of 5 courses over 2 years in classes of 19 students each that read, discuss, and write about the great texts of Western civilization from antiquity through the present. An undergraduate with advanced foreign language skills may either read, for courses such as history, economics, or religion, texts that are written in a language other than English or enroll in total immersion courses in which all of the coursework for these disciplines is conducted in a foreign language. St. Olaf students who don't find all that they want on campus, or in the extensive programs overseas, can cross the river to take courses at prestigious Carleton College. A prelaw accelerated program is offered in conjunction with Columbia University, as well as a 3–2 option in engineering with Washington University. A term in the other Washington, the nation's capital, also is popular.

Campus life: The fact that 96% of all Oles live on the 300-acre hilltop campus helps to create a strong sense of community, felt by most undergraduates. There is always a smorgasbord of dances, bands, movies, political speakers, and sporting events to keep residents entertained. The 175,000-square foot Buntrock Commons, which opened in fall 1999 and may be the largest commons at a small private college, offers a surround-sound theater and alcohol-free nightclub, along with numerous eating areas, lounges, and conference rooms to help house all these activities, or provide a place for Oles to just hang out. There are no fraternities or sororities. Instead, social groupings are organized around Saint Olaf's 117 student clubs and organizations, with music, music, music drawing a third of the students to the college's 23 music organizations. The elite of this group are the internationally acclaimed St. Olaf Choir, Band, and Orchestra, which go on at least one major tour within the United States each year and perform internationally every few years. Each ensemble is open to budding biologists and mathematicians as well as to music majors. The Saint Olaf Choir recently completed a concert tour of France, Austria, Germany, and the Czech Republic; the Saint Olaf Band toured in England, Ireland, Northern Ireland, Scotland, and Wales.

Saint Olaf is a trusting community where undergraduates carry a small card provided by the student government that encourages, among other qualities, "respect for the dignity of others" and "honesty in all aspects of life." Students' reliance on the good intentions of their peers is evidenced by the pile of expensive jackets and book bags left outside the cafeteria during meals—which usually are still there afterward. While most view the Northfield community as a remarkably safe place to reside, those who feel less sure can call upon the safety transport service to drive them after dark. Students also need a key card to enter residence halls after midnight.

Athletic events at Saint Olaf draw respectable crowds, generally not because students love the sport being played but rather to show support for classmates out on the field or court. Though crowds are rarely overwhelming, football, soccer, and basketball draw the most fans. Thirty percent of the men and 17% of the women participate in the 14 men's and 13 women's intercollegiate sports played in NCAA Division III. Seventy percent of the men and 60% of the women recently turned out for a 32-sport intramural program, 16 for each sex. Those preferring less structured recreation can turn to the 95,000-square-foot Tostrud Center, which was dedicated in September 2002 and includes along with tennis, volleyball, and basketball courts, a free weight room, climbing wall, Nordic ski room, and elevated and 6-lane tracks.

For undergraduates who find the town of Northfield (pop. 16,500) less than stimulating, a bus service run jointly with Carleton College provides a lifeline to the Twin Cities, 35 miles north, 3 Fridays through Sundays. When a more natural escape is preferred, there's always a walk through "Norway Valley," a wooded ravine near campus.

Cost cutters: Seventy-nine percent of the entering freshmen and 73% of continuing students in the 2005–2006 school year received some form of financial aid. Sixty-two percent of all undergraduates received aid based on financial need. The average freshman award consisted of a need-based scholarship or grant worth $15,105, and need-based self-help aid such as loans and jobs averaging $5572. The average debt for 2005 graduates was $19,410. An expanded merit scholarship program makes awards (renewable for all 4 years) to incoming first-year students. Buntrock Academic Scholarships pay $7500 to $11,000;

the Award for Service Leadership in Community and Church pays $4000. Music scholarships pay $1500 to $6000 yearly. The best students among those with need usually get the most attractive financial-aid packages, with more grants and fewer loans. Saint Olaf scholarships pay up to full tuition and fees to those with demonstrated need and high academic performance. A good work-study program is available to all students who wish to work.

Rate of return: Ninety-two percent of Saint Olaf freshmen return for the sophomore year. Seventy-eight percent graduate in 4 years; 83%, in 5 years; 84% in 6.

Payoff: Among 2005 graduates, 10% earned degrees in English, 9% in psychology, and 8% in biology. More than a fourth of recent classes have enrolled directly in graduate or professional schools. More than 50% accept jobs shortly after graduation in a variety of fields that put their liberal-arts backgrounds to the test, many with firms throughout the Midwest, such as Target Corp., Cargill, General Mills, St. Paul Companies, and CSC, as well as with nonprofit and service organizations. More than 100 companies and other organizations recruited on campus in the 2004–2005 school year.

Bottom line: Concludes an out-of-stater: "I would recommend Saint Olaf enthusiastically to any high school student motivated enough to work hard, flexible enough to try new things, open enough to accept differences and adversity, confident enough to think independently, and genuinely excited about education. While few Oles embody all these characteristics, most embody some."

University of Minnesota, Morris

Morris, Minnesota 56267

Setting: Small town
Control: Public
Undergraduate enrollment: 722 men, 1121 women
Graduate enrollment: None
Student/faculty ratio: 13:1
Freshman profile: 15% scored over 700 on SAT I verbal; 35% scored 600–700; 35% 500–599; 15% below 500. 13% scored over 700 on SAT I math; 40% scored 600–700; 35% 500–599; 12% below 500. 14% scored above 28 on the ACT; 15% scored 27–28; 36% 24–26; 25% 21–23; 10% below 21. 35% graduated in top tenth of high school class; 59% in upper fifth.

Faculty profile: 97% Ph.D.'s
Tuition and fees: $9722 in-state; $9722 out-of-state
Room and board: $5750
Freshman financial aid: 61%; average scholarship or grant: $5669 need-based; $2719 non-need-based
Campus jobs: 53%; average earnings: $1065/year
Application deadline: Early action: Dec. 1; regular: Feb. 1
Financial aid deadline: Mar. 1
Admissions information: (320) 589-6035; (888) UMM-EDUC
e-mail: admissions@morris.umn.edu;
web site: www.morris.umn.edu

If the University of Minnesota, Morris, were to place a classified ad, it might read like this: "**Wanted**: *Students in the top 10% of their high school graduating classes, National Merit Scholarship finalists, or Native Americans. In return for enrollment at small public liberal arts university in west-central Minnesota, each high-ranking student will automatically be granted at least $1500 for 1 year's attendance. Freshmen graduating in the top 5% of their high school classes will receive $2000. All National Merit finalists who choose UMM as their first-choice school and all qualified Native Americans pay no tuition. Students who are not Minnesota residents pay the same as state residents. Students who accept must not be concerned about academic prestige and must like small-town/small-campus atmosphere.*"

For the bright undergraduate who doesn't mind constantly explaining that he or she does not study at the mammoth Twin Cities campus of the University of Minnesota across state, there are few financial deals better than that offered at the university's Morris campus. In the 2005–2006 school year, in-staters paid just $9722 in tuition and fees; out-of-staters paid the same. The idea, according to university officials, is that, as a national liberal arts college UMM should make its high-quality education affordable to students from across the country, not just in Minnesota. From this baseline, the heavy discounting begins, such as granting $1500 to all recent graduates in the top 10% of their high school classes and $2000 to those in the top 5%. All told, at least 60% of both freshmen and continuing students in the 2005–2006 school year received some financial aid beyond that already given by the low tuition charged. While extremely gifted students may find UMM outside the honors program less challenging than they had hoped, the vast majority of solid achievers will like the education their low tuition brings.

Student body: Eighty-six percent of Morris's students are Minnesotans. Most of the rest, from 26 additional states, also call the Midwest home. Ninety-five percent attended public schools. In part because of its offer of free tuition to qualified Native Americans, a carryover from UMM's early days as an American Indian boarding school, a comparatively high 8% of the undergraduate enrollment are Native Americans. Three percent of the student body are Asian-American and 2% each African-American and Hispanic. Twenty-three foreign nationals from 14 countries are present. The mix of students on such a small, rural campus, says a midwesterner, "has opened my eyes to the diversity of the world." Students 24 years of age and older comprised about 8% of the population in a recent year. Undergraduates, some of them first-generation college students, are largely unpretentious and politically active. Says a senior: "Students here are not afraid to deal with issues." Just over a quarter of the in-state students are from the Twin Cities metropolitan area; most of the rest of the state residents are from rural communities. Students of color are mostly recruited from larger cities in Illinois, New Orleans and the Twin Cities. American Indian students are recruited from throughout Minnesota, South Dakota, and beyond. UMM exudes an informal, friendly air in which students, faculty, and administrators address each other by their first names. But don't mistake the students as academically lax. Says a sophomore: "Most students who excelled in high school find themselves surrounded by students who are just as smart as they are. The competition is not detrimental, though. Students who know more about something are always willing to share, so everyone has a sense of equality." Many also find that it is not difficult to be conscientious students at rural UMM because there are few distractions in the area.

Academics: Morris, which turned 45 in 2004, offers 30 different majors plus 6 preprofessional programs. As a public liberal arts college within the University of Minnesota system, UMM grants no advanced degrees. The academic year is divided into 2 semesters with a May term. Average class size is 18. Environmental Geology usually draws about 300 to its popular spring lecture course, but the classes most students encounter in their first 2 years have from 20 to 70 members. In the latter years, many classes in a student's major will have only a dozen or so participants, though courses in management economics and psychology will continue to attract more.

In addition to the 40 semester credits required in a student's major, all undergraduates must take 60 semester credits of general-education coursework. Included are a wide range of courses that cover all skills, from writing to speaking to computing, and all fields, from history to different cultures, to the arts and the natural world. A required First-Year Seminar is designed to help students to think critically and assess the quality of diverse sources of information.

UMM's faculty consists of 145 full-time members, with just 4 part-time. Forty-two percent of the pool are women. Most professors are regarded as extremely knowledgeable in their fields, though there are some, say students, who may have become too accustomed to teaching material in the same way year after year. Many undergraduates are especially enthusiastic about a growing base of exciting, younger teachers, some of whom turn out to play Friday afternoon basketball games with students. Says an economics/management major: "It is relatively easy to create a good relationship with a faculty member that will blossom into a research opportunity." But young and old faculty members alike, observes a junior, "show a genuine concern for the students, and that's the most important thing!"

Departments strong in faculty and curriculum include psychology, elementary and secondary education, English, history, computer science, political science, and geology. Psychology majors must do their own research projects, which students maintain are of graduate-school quality. Political science professors keep active in grass-roots politics and community polling and happily help arrange internships for students. The sciences have been revitalized since the opening in fall 2000 of a new laboratory and classroom wing. The science faculty is considered "hard working, dedicated, and caring," says a chemistry major. The economics/management program is known for its solid track record of placing graduates in good jobs from which they rapidly advance.

The theater department has 3 excellent faculty members, says a major, but only 3. They juggle classes and put together a major production every semester. As a result, says the student, "They have to stagger their courses, offering some only every other year or when feasible." Mathematics needs better quality professors who understand how to teach students as well as they do the subject matter. A newer major in women's studies needs more time to develop. Foreign language lovers would like to see more faculty and more offerings than majors in French, German, and Spanish.

Facilities: Briggs Library is a good place to study and to socialize, depending on where a student sits. While talking is permitted on the busy first floor, each level higher becomes progressively quieter until total silence is demanded on the fourth floor. In terms of research, however, it is less easy to find what is needed. The collection holds just over 197,000 volumes, too many of which were published before 1960, according to students, and 13,000 periodicals, 12,200 of which are available on-line. However, on-line computer searches of the massive holdings at the University of Minnesota Twin Cities campus and delivery of the needed materials have proved a lifesaver for many a research project. Since Briggs is considered *the* place to study but seats less than a third of the enrollment, students grumble that seating is sometimes hard to find. "Considering the library hasn't been renovated in over 10 years, there is room for improvement," says a senior. Students do like the fact that the structure became wireless in fall 2005.

The student center, science center, and several other academic buildings and residence halls also provide wireless access. Students who prefer to use the university's computers will find about 125 Windows and Macintosh computers spread among 6 labs. Two are open around the clock. ResNet is available in all dorm rooms. Students also can access the supercomputers on the Twin Cities campus of the University of Minnesota and around the nation.

Special programs: UMM students may participate in all study-abroad programs offered by other colleges of the University of Minnesota system, as well as by Morris itself and by other institutions. Nearly half of all graduating seniors leave UMM having had some kind of international experience. One overseas option gaining in popularity is the English Language Teaching Assistant Program, which enables students of any major to spend a term in a foreign country helping to teach English. Extensive off-campus internship experiences also can be arranged. Back on campus, students may collaborate with faculty on research as part of the Undergraduate Research Opportunities Program, which provides financial stipends and/or expense allowances to undergraduates for research, scholarly, or creative projects done in partnership with a faculty member. A program for advanced students called Morris Academic Partners pays $2000 to juniors involved in an academic or research experience with a faculty member that enhances their intellectual competence and their interest in graduate or professional school. Morris Administrative Internships pay $2000 to students to assist administrators in program initiatives. A Minority Mentorship Program pays up to $1000 to minority students working closely with a faculty member in an educationally meaningful experience. Concludes a global business major: "The vast number of opportunities for academic enhancement, including study abroad, honors, service learning, and undergraduate research, have been a benefit to me and many of my peers."

Campus life: Sixty percent of the UMM undergraduates live on campus, which is located on 130 acres of rolling prairie along the Pomme de Terre River in west-central Minnesota. Ninety-five percent of first-year students live in campus residence hall communities. Eighty-two percent of all undergraduates opt to stay busy while on campus by participating in a club, organization, or committee. Movies, dances, house parties, and other forms of entertainment are generally available over the weekend to keep most undergraduates occupied. The expanded student center with a dance club provides a satisfying campus hangout. The Swing Dancing Club attracts as many as 150 people at its regularly scheduled teaching sessions. The Black Student Union, Diversity Peer Educators, and E-Quality, which addresses issues concerning gay, lesbian, bisexual, and transgender people, are 3 of the most active groups on campus, providing plenty of speakers and other forums open to campus and community members. Crime is not something most undergraduates spend much time worrying about. "Students laugh when campus security or local police publish the list of crimes," says a senior. "Usually there are at most a few thefts and about 450 parking violations." A slight increase in incidents produced a security task force concerned with researching new security measures; the number of call boxes and lights around campus were increased as a result. As follow-up, each fall the vice chancellor and sergeant in charge of campus police join student leaders in search of areas that may need additional lighting or other improvements.

UMM's sports program made the transition during the 2003–2004 school year from NCAA Division II to Division III. It also changed the makeup of its 6 varsity sports for men and 10 for women. The 2003–2004 school year was the final season for men's and women's wrestling; women's swimming was added in the 2004–2005 school year. Women's soccer recently was voted the most exciting team to watch although volleyball and men's basketball also tend to draw a crowd "due to the chance that they might win a game," says a junior. Intramurals draw more spirited involvement, with 70% of the men and 56% of the women turning out for the 12 men's and 12 women's sports offered. The judo, karate, and saddle clubs and outdoor center all have enthusiastic followings, as does the new $5 million Regional Fitness Center, complete with indoor track, heated pool, basketball courts, and a cardiovascular fitness room.

There isn't much to the town of Morris (pop. 5000). As a result, those who opt to leave make the 45-minute trip northeast to Alexandria (pop. 9000), or the 3-hour drive east to the Twin Cities. Observes one city girl: "I have gotten used to the inconvenience of a small town, but never expected how great it would feel to lie out in the middle of a field with a group of friends staring at the amazing stars."

Cost cutters: Sixty-one percent of all freshmen and 74% of continuing students received financial aid in the 2005–2006 school year; 59% of the freshmen and 61% of the rest were on need-based assistance. The average freshman award for a student with need included a need-based scholarship or grant averaging $5669 and need-based self-help aid such as loans and jobs averaging $4853. Other non-need-based awards and scholarships averaged $2719. The average 2005 graduate left with debts of $15,194. In addition to UMM's generous scholarships based on high school class rank, President's Distinguished Student Scholar Program awards are worth up to $3000 a year, renewable over 4 years, and go to minority students with superior academic records, high test scores, and leadership abilities.

Rate of return: Eighty-two percent of entering freshmen return for the sophomore year. Just 44%, however, go on to graduate in 4 years; 60%, in 5 years; 67% in 6. Some starters who choose to specialize in more technically oriented fields, as well as others who tire of the small-town environment, transfer to the larger Twin Cities campus.

Payoff: Among 2005 UMM graduates, a third earned degrees in 3 fields: 12% each in biology and English and 10% in elementary education. Over a quarter of the class enrolled directly in graduate or professional schools. Forty-five percent do so within 3 years of graduation. The vast majority of graduates enter the work force soon after commencement in business, education, government, and various nonprofit organizations. Most students take entry-level jobs as management trainees, sales and marketing representatives, computer programmers, underwriters, scientists, teachers, public administrators, and social workers. Just over 70 companies and other organizations recruited on campus in a recent school year.

Bottom line: Students who seek a personally supportive environment that doesn't put much strain on the pocketbook may well find what they are looking for at the University of Minnesota, Morris. But what this small campus provides in informal student-faculty relationships and strong academic programs, it lacks in a well-known name that status-conscious students can display on their sweatshirts. Concludes a satisfied senior: "It feels just like a private school, but it costs so much less."

Mississippi

Millsaps College

Jackson, Mississippi 39210

Setting: Urban
Control: Private (United Methodist)
Undergraduate enrollment: 526 men, 513 women
Graduate enrollment: 15 men, 14 women
Student/faculty ratio: 12:1
Freshman profile: 14% scored over 700 on SAT I verbal; 42% scored 600–700; 33% 500–599; 11% below 500. 9% scored over 700 on SAT I math; 35% scored 600–700; 41% 500–599; 15% below 500. 33% scored above 28 on the ACT; 20% scored 27–28; 19% 24–26; 19% 21–23; 9% below 21. 26% graduated in top tenth of high school class; 56% in upper fifth.
Faculty profile: 97% Ph.D.'s

Tuition and fees: $20,690
Room and board: $7566
Freshman financial aid: 97%; average scholarship or grant: $7354 need-based, $10,758 non-need-based
Campus jobs: 50%; average earnings: $1029/year
Application deadline: Early action: Dec. 1; regular: Feb. 1
Financial aid deadline: Mar. 1
Admissions information: (601) 974-1050; (800) 352-1050
e-mail: admissions@millsaps.edu
web site: www.millsaps.edu

When Major Reuben Webster Millsaps and other Methodist leaders donated funds 116 years ago to found a "Christian college for young men" on the outskirts of Mississippi's state capital of Jackson, their largesse seemed large indeed. The 2-building college with 149 students and 5 instructors enjoyed an endowment of $70,432. Today, $70,000 can't buy 2 years of liberal arts education at most of the most selective colleges in the nation, but it buys much more at Millsaps. For just over $28,000 in tuition, fees, room, and board in the 2005–2006 school year, students can "buy" a liberal arts education at a school whose reputation has begun to extend beyond the Southeast. One reason is surely Millsaps's lower cost, compared with that of other selective colleges across the nation. Then, too, the installation in 1989 of a campus chapter of Phi Beta Kappa, the nation's oldest honor society, served to corroborate all the good things students and administrators had been saying for years.

Student body: Forty-nine percent of Millsaps students still come from Mississippi, with 95% of the non-residents also from the South. A total of 32 states and 15 foreign countries have undergraduates on campus. A third are graduates of private or parochial schools. Nineteen percent are Methodist, with another 33% members of other Protestant denominations, 17% Catholic, 1% Jewish, and the rest belonging to other faiths or claiming no religious affiliation. African-American students account for 12% of the enrollment; Asian-Americans 3.5%; Hispanics, 1.5%. Foreign nationals comprise less than 1%. Undergraduates run the gamut from "rather sheltered, upper-class graduates of private schools who are given everything they want from their parents, to very hard-working students who do everything they can to pay for a Millsaps education," observes a Mississippi sophomore. However, students on all rungs of the economic ladder, and of liberal as well as conservative bents, agree on the importance of academics at Millsaps, though most attain a healthy balance between studying, activities and partying. Says a senior: "Most of us are over-achievers interested in being involved on campus and succeeding academically." Competition for good grades is felt more at the group than the individual level, with fraternities and sororities competing very hard against one another to achieve the highest GPA.

Academics: Millsaps offers the bachelor's degree in 28 disciplines plus interdisciplinary studies. Master's degrees in liberal studies, accountancy, and business administration also are awarded. The academic year is divided into 2 semesters. Average class size runs from 15 to 20, with the largest class, U.S. History to 1877, enrolling about 40, but some courses for juniors and seniors having fewer than a half dozen.

All undergraduates must take 10 core courses extending from the humanities to the natural and behavioral sciences; however, students may select 1 of 2 different routes to fulfill the humanities mandate. In one option, students take 4 multidisciplinary topics courses on the ancient world, the premodern world, the modern world, and the contemporary world. Under the second plan, freshmen begin a 4-course Heritage Program that includes course work in Western civilization, art, religion, philosophy, music, and English. Participants in the Heritage program extol the way it "effectively pulls history together into an understandable whole." Adds a mathematics major: "The interdisciplinary nature of our core prepares students for the interdisciplinary nature of the real world." Both routes begin with a class, Introduction to Liberal Studies, and end the senior year with Reflections on the same.

Each student must also demonstrate proficiency in writing by submitting a portfolio of papers by the end of the sophomore year. Says a junior: "After leaving Millsaps, you can write a 7-page paper in 40 minutes to an hour." Seniors end their course of study with comprehensive exams, part written, part oral, in their major fields.

The faculty numbers 92 full-time and 5 part-time members. Women account for 44% of the ranks. The majority earn considerable student admiration for competence in their respective fields and unselfishness in giving out-of-classroom time to undergraduates. Says a senior: "Most are very interactive with students and do not try to separate themselves. In classes that are not viewed as 'exact' sciences, the faculty does well in presenting ideas instead of pushing them on students." Adds a junior: "On a scale of 1 to 10, our faculty rates a 15 . . . They try to help us learn beyond the basics and to think for ourselves."

The English faculty are "extraordinary," according to majors and nonmajors alike, because they emphasize writing, group thought, and varying types of learning. Biology and chemistry, which have long had top-of-the-line professors, have equipment and facilities to match in the Olin Hall of Science, dedicated in 1988. The well-respected Else School of Management offers a variety of tough courses and a faculty who assist students in finding internships and jobs. Geology, with concentrations in classical and environmental geology, and history are excellent as well. Programs as diverse as religious studies and art share a common quality, says a fine arts major. "They encourage students to think outside the box."

Political science, psychology, and physics are examples of departments with just a handful of faculty members, who, though excellent, cannot provide the diversity of courses and perspectives many students would like. Classes also are larger and sometimes offered only in alternate years or occasionally. The major in theater lacks sufficient funding and faculty. Students wish more faculty were available to teach courses in French and German. (Spanish also is offered as a major.) Several courses in all 3 majors also are offered only in alternate years or on demand.

Facilities: The Millsaps-Wilson Library houses a collection of 193,000 volumes and 10,500 online and paper periodicals. Because the structure is small, seating just 350 students, it is sometimes hard to break away from other students, so that socializing becomes a problem. At the other extreme, students complain about humming, not from classmates but from overhead fluorescent lights, which, too, "can be rather irritating when one is trying to study," says a biology major. A computerized catalog and on-line databases make research far less trying. For additional resources, students find that the Eudora Welty Library, the Jackson public library, and the University of Mississippi Medical Center Library directly across the street serve as good complements to what also is available through the Internet and interlibrary loan.

There are 120 PCs located in 9 academic labs. The majority are available from 7:30 a.m. to almost midnight (units in the library are available until 2 a.m.), which some students think is not long enough. But most acknowledge that the quality of computers has increased greatly in just the last few years. The college strongly recommends that students bring their own personal computers, preferably Dell; the college offers discounts on all Dell models to students, faculty, and staff. All residence halls and fraternity houses are Internet-accessible with 2 ports per room. Wireless network access is available in the library, the College Center, the central outdoor areas, and the top two floors of Murrah Hall, which houses the business school, in the first phase of a project that will cover the entire campus.

Special programs: Undergraduates with an interest in the classics may take advantage of special programs in Rome or Athens. Millsaps also conducts its own 2- to 6-week summer programs in London, Munich, and Florence, Nice, and Paris, and in Ghana, Yucatan, and Costa Rica. Semester options are available within the United States in the nation's capital or working in the Mississippi State legislature. A program funded by the Ford Foundation enables 12 students a year who are considering careers as college professors to work closely with faculty mentors in their areas of academic interest. Those planning to become engineers can participate in joint programs at Auburn, Columbia, Vanderbilt, and Washington universities. A 3-2 master's program in business administration is available right on campus.

Campus life: Eighty-one percent of Millsaps students reside on the 100-acre campus, which withstood Hurricane Katrina's high winds with minimal damage. Just over half of the men and women choose to unwind as members of 6 national fraternities and 6 national sororities, which sponsor many campus functions. In addition to Greek events, there are many all-campus parties. On weekends when no major events are planned, however, about a fourth of the resident students leave. The campus ministry team involves between 70 and 80 students and staff in planning the weekly chapel services (which are optional), as well as service projects and faculty-student forums on various issues. While students insist that Millsaps has been comparatively safe for an urban campus, security measures are prevalent, among them, good lighting, emergency telephones, card access to buildings, and closing of the entrance gates to campus from 5 p.m. to 5 a.m. Security officers are to remain stationed at the gates during the daylight hours. Students still advise not walking alone across campus after dark.

Seven varsity sports for men and 7 for women are played in NCAA Division III. Other than football, no sporting event is well attended, and several underclassmen report being disappointed by the lack of school spirit. Two-thirds of the men and a fifth of the women participate in 20 intramural sports for each sex.

When students need to flee, they pay a visit to nearby Ross Barnett Reservoir. Most find that Jackson (pop. 425,000), which also is the state capital, has enough about town to keep them occupied. In fact, says an out-of-stater, "Jackson has grown to be one of my favorite places."

Cost cutters: The tuition charged at Millsaps covers approximately 56% of the cost of education, the balance being met by income from endowment, which totaled $88 million as of June 2005, and by gifts. In the 2005–2006 school year, 97% of the freshmen and 94% of the continuing students received financial help; 60% of all first-year students and 57% of the rest were allotted aid based on need. The average freshman award included a need-based scholarship or grant averaging $7354 and need-based self-help aid such as loans and jobs averaging $4825. Other non-need-based awards and scholarships averaged $10,758. An average graduate left with debts totaling $22,285. High-achieving students are eligible for a variety of merit-based scholarships. They include Presidential Scholarships that pay $12,000 to $25,000 a year; the Second Century scholarships worth up to $12,000 annually; and Millsaps Awards, paying up to $11,000 a year. To be considered for the Presidential and Second Century awards, students must have their applications postmarked by Dec. 1. United Methodist Scholarships recently paid $500 to $1500; Jonathan Sweat Music Scholarships cover $2000 to $10,000 annually. Various no-fee payment plans also are available.

Rate of return: Eighty-three percent of freshmen return for the sophomore year. Sixty-three percent graduate in 4 years, 69% in 5, 71% in 6.

Payoff: In the 2005 graduating class, 14% earned degrees in psychology, 13% in business administration, and 8% in biology. Half of the graduates typically pursue advanced degrees. The rest took jobs immediately upon graduation, many as management trainees and in sales and service positions with leading firms such as United Financial, Blue Cross/Blue Shield, and Deposit Guaranty National Bank throughout the Southeast and Midwest. Although just 60 companies and organizations recruited on campus in a recent school year, 160 companies requested resumés from graduating seniors.

Bottom line: Millsaps is a college for high school graduates serious about learning and about having a full social life. Cautions a senior, "A student who wishes to passively subsist for 4 years would probably be frustrated at Millsaps because most of our students are passionate about their education and their involvement. Millsaps has a very nurturing environment that lets students develop to their full potential."

Missouri

College of the Ozarks

Point Lookout, Missouri 65726

Setting: Small town
Control: Private (Presbyterian)
Undergraduate enrollment: 585 men, 719 women
Graduate enrollment: None
Student/faculty ratio: 16:1
Freshman profile: 4% scored above 28 on the ACT; 5% scored 27–28; 18% 24–26; 33% 21–23; 40% below 21. 33% graduated in top fifth of high school class; 61% in upper two-fifths.
Faculty profile: 58% Ph.D.'s
Tuition and fees: $330

Room and board: $3800
Freshman financial aid: 100%; average scholarship or grant: $12,161 need-based
Campus jobs: 100%; average earnings: $2884/year
Application deadline: Mar. 15 (Priority date: Feb. 15)
Financial aid deadline: Mar. 15 (Priority date: Feb. 15)
Admissions information: (417) 334-6411 ext. 4219; (800) 222-0525
e-mail: admiss4@cofo.edu
web site: www.cofo.edu

At most colleges, students expect to receive letter grades for their performance in subjects such as English, biology, or business administration. But at College of the Ozarks, 40 miles south of Springfield, Missouri, students also earn grades for their performance at various work assignments around campus. The grade reflects each student's level of cooperation, interest and enthusiasm, initiative and responsibility, attendance and punctuality, care of college equipment, and quality of work on the job. A student who receives a grade below C or below average is given 1 term to improve or face dismissal from the work program. An F usually means immediate dismissal from the program. If assigning letter grades to campus work seems a bit extreme, it should be realized that an Ozarks work assignment isn't just any after-hours job. In exchange for working 15 hours a week during each 16-week semester, plus two 40-hour weeks during school vacations, all full-time students at College of the Ozarks receive free tuition and pay only for room and board, books, personal expenses, and a $330 fee. Full room and board scholarships are available to qualified students who work 12 40-hour weeks on campus during the summer. College of the Ozarks, which refers to itself as Hard Work U, demands much from its students in the way of job performance as well as adherence to campus rules and participation in religious services, but in return it makes possible for many a college education that would be unaffordable elsewhere. Says a junior: "With C of O's student work program, students can graduate very near to debt free, which is an amazing opportunity."

Student body: Sixty-two percent of the students are from Missouri; the rest represent 39 other states, with three fourths of them coming from the Midwest. Preference for admission is given to students from the Ozarks region, defined as the mostly rural and mountainous area encompassing southern Missouri and northern Arkansas, with a small portion of Kansas, Illinois, and Oklahoma. Just 4% represent racial and ethnic minorities: about 1% each African-American, Hispanic, and Native American, and 0.5% Asian-American. Two percent are foreign nationals from 15 different countries. Seventy-four percent of the students are Protestant and 6% Catholic; the rest claim no religious affiliation. Eighty-five percent graduated from public schools. According to C of O guidelines, a family of 2 with 1 student in college has to have an adjusted gross income no greater than $37,000; the income of a family of 4 with 1 in college should not exceed $48,000. C of O students, says a junior, "were not raised in an atmosphere of give, give, give. Instead, it was work, work, work."

While students at College of the Ozarks consider themselves to be conservative with "a few rebels and liberals," undergraduates say that the college is even more conservative than many of them are. A number complain of what they see as too many rules that come with their free education, for example, no one of the opposite sex allowed in single-sex housing, no alcohol, and a weeknight curfew of 1 a.m. "Those rules become the tuition for the students," says a senior. However, those who come prepared for a lot of rules often find the environment less confining than they had expected, and find support in closeknit relationships with one another. And the number of C of O wannabe's remains hefty, with 2137 students applying for 254 fall 2005 freshmen slots. Says a student from the area: "Since we are required to work for our education, most appreciate the education more."

Academics: College of the Ozarks, which was founded in 1906 and known as School of the Ozarks until 1990, awards the bachelor's degree in 34 fields. Classes follow the semester calendar, with the largest lectures rarely exceeding 50 students (though Citizenship and Lifetime Wellness can have almost 90) and most upper-level courses enrolling no more than 20. Every undergraduate must complete a 2-part general-education program that includes specific courses in English, speech, religion, history and political science, math, and swimming and fitness, as well as the student's choices among suggested courses in arts and letters, social science, and physical science. A course common to all new students entitled Citizenship and Lifestyle Wellness is team-taught by members of the military science and athletic departments. The course is designed to reinforce the college's 5-fold mission, which is to emphasize academic, vocational, spiritual, patriotic, and cultural growth. The general-education program entails 55–56 of the 124 credit hours required for graduation.

Seventy-one of the college's 115 faculty members are full-time; 44, part-time. Twenty-seven percent are women. For many students, their professors are the best part of their college experience. Most show their deep concern for the students and work closely with them. "Some classes totally 'bond'," says a sophomore, "when a group of students get a great teacher and love the subject." Students say a number of new, younger faculty members also has enhanced the learning environment. "Even the very few professors I have not liked," says a sophomore, "have been willing to give their time to help me understand concepts and showed they care."

Professors in the departments of education, computer sciences, philosophy and religion, psychology, and business administration who work 1-on-1 with their students make these departments especially strong. The history faculty "are good, well-educated teachers to whom we can relate and who truly teach us," praises a junior. The music department, which offers emphases in general music and music ministry and secondary teacher certification in choral and instrumental music, draws accolades as well. Says a sophomore: "A high academic standard with quality staff makes obtaining a music degree challenging but well worth the effort." The agriculture program, with farms for hands-on learning is especially distinctive. While students find the biology professors excellent, many say that budget constraints making facilities outdated keep the department from reaching its full potential. The English faculty, says a junior, "seem excited about what they are teaching and make it fun to learn."

Some students express disappointment at the quality of instruction in the mass communication department and say funding for better equipment, such as updating the editing suites and adding a television station, is greatly needed. Complains a student specializing in public relations: "The books used are at least 8 years old. This doesn't help much considering the speed of technology in this field." The only language major is in Spanish with minors only in German and French. Students in the family and consumer sciences program wish it were shown more respect around campus and had a greater variety of professors in some concentrations.

Facilities: Lyons Memorial Library houses nearly 121,500 volumes and 6952 electronic and paper periodicals. Students find the holdings adequate for most of their research needs; interlibrary loan and sometimes occasional trips to Southwest Missouri State University in Springfield, 45 minutes away, are required for more extensive projects. Various computerized research tools have made searches easier and more productive as has the on-line catalog and Internet. As far as studying, the atmosphere generally is quiet if a bit sterile and, says a senior, "study tables placed next to large windows provide a good view of the lake and valley." The library closes at 10 p.m. Sundays through Thursdays, at 5 p.m. Fridays and Saturdays.

Students find the 136 computers available in laboratories around campus fall short of their ever-increasing needs. Many users also wish more labs were open past 10 o'clock on weeknights. (One general-purpose lab is open around the clock.) The bigger labs also tend to be closed from Friday night through Sunday afternoon. Says a business and speech major: "This is a *huge* inconvenience to students and myself. We never have to wait in line; you just can't work in the labs on the weekend, which is the only free time we have at C of O!" At least 1 or 2 computers providing 24-hour access to the Internet were recently added to the lounges of each residence hall. Internet access also is available from individual dorm rooms.

Special programs: The study-abroad program was suspended during the 2005–2006 school year. Engineering students can participate in a 3–2 program with the engineering school of their choice.

Campus life: Two-thirds of the undergraduates live on campus in single-sex housing. (Student members of the volunteer fire department live in the campus fire station.) To cope with school regulations, says this volunteer, "We unwind by getting off campus." Many students leave the scenic 1000-acre spread overlooking Table Rock and Taneycomo lakes to party off campus, go home, hike, fish, go next door to Branson with its shopping, theme parks, and shows, or travel to Springfield, the nearest "little big city," with 133,000 people. A number also hold additional jobs off-campus, many in Branson, during the weekend. With neither fraternities nor sororities on campus, men's varsity basketball games are about the biggest all-campus draw, with the campus hosting the NAIA national basketball tournament from the 1999 through the 2007 school years. Men's baseball and women's basketball and volleyball comprise the 3 other inter-collegiate sports played under NAIA rules. The student-administered intramural program involves 30% of the men and 12% of the women in 24 intramural sports split evenly between the sexes. Clubs such as S.I.F.E., Students in Free Enterprise; community-service programs; and various Christian fellowship groups, such as the Baptist Student Union, attract the most interest from students.

Residential students with fewer than 91 semester hours are required to attend 7 chapels and 7 convo-cations a semester. Students may choose from a wide variety of convocations offered in several different content areas. Crime on campus is virtually nonexistent. The campus gates are locked at 1 a.m. and campus security patrols around the clock. Students also must be in their dorms by 1.

Cost cutters: In accordance with the college's founding philosophy, 100% of the students are on financial aid. The cost to College of the Ozarks to provide an education is approximately $15,400 a year for each student. In effect, some students may receive that amount in a scholarship or other form of financial aid derived from earnings from the school's endowment, worth $296.5 million as of May 2005, operation of the mandatory work program, various federal, state, or private grants or gifts for which a needy undergraduate is eligible, or other sources. The resulting aid package for a first-year student with financial need was a need-based scholarship or grant averaging $12,161 and need-based self-help aid such as loans and jobs averaging $2884. Non-need-based athletic scholarships for freshmen averaged $2662. Students work at a wide range of campus jobs extending from the commonplace to the more unusual: computer programmer, printer, campus motel manager, day-care attendant, weaver, library attendant, and maker of C of O jellies and fruitcakes. To help defray the cost of room and board, books, and other items, top-ranked students can receive additional scholarship moneys based on their financial need, ACT scores, high school grades, and activities. A major result of this well-supported education is that the average financial indebtedness of recent graduates was just $4079—a fraction of that at most other colleges.

Rate of return: Seventy-six percent of freshmen return for the sophomore year. Twenty-one percent graduate in 4 years; 39% in 5 years; 44% in 6 years.

Payoff: Nineteen percent of the 2005 graduates earned bachelor's degrees in education, 15% in business and 8% in psychology. The vast majority of the graduates use their work experience on campus to enter the job market within 6 months of commencement. Eleven percent of a recent class went on to pursue advanced degrees.

Bottom line: While College of the Ozarks offers what is substantially a free or, in terms of room and board, books, and personal expenses, an extremely low-cost, education, students say that they "pay" in other ways, such as in their adherence to campus rules. Says a senior: "This is a work-study school: If you don't want to work, you don't get to study, and vice versa. You get an education, practical job skills, and little or no debt upon completion. These plusses far outweigh any rules that some equate with minuses."

Drury University
Springfield, Missouri 65802

Setting: Urban
Control: Private (United Church of Christ and Disciples of Christ)
Undergraduate enrollment: 669 men, 872 women
Graduate enrollment: 57 men, 174 women (164 part-time)
Student/faculty ratio: 13:1
Freshman profile: 7% scored over 700 on SAT I verbal; 36% scored 600–700; 38% 500–599; 19% below 500. 10% scored over 700 on SAT I math; 33% scored 600–700; 44% 500–599; 13% below 500. 23% scored above 28 on the ACT; 13% scored 27–28; 29% 24–26; 24% 21–23; 11% below 21. 29% graduated in top tenth of high school class; 61% in upper fifth.

Faculty profile: 88% Ph.D.'s
Tuition and fees: $14,687
Room and board: $5430
Freshman financial aid: 92%; average scholarship or grant: $6102 need-based; $3962 non-need-based
Campus jobs: 43%; average earnings: $2250/year
Application deadline: Aug. 1
Financial aid deadline: Mar. 15
Admissions information: (417) 873-7205;
(800) 922-2274
e-mail: druryad@drury.edu
web site: www.drury.edu

Drury University may be a smaller largely liberal arts institution in southwestern Missouri with just over 1500 full-time students in its traditional day program, a full-time faculty numbering 123, and a campus covering 60 or so acres, but these small numbers haven't stopped this school from thinking big. Drury's newest venture, entitled Global Perspectives 21, is designed to prepare students more adequately for the 21st century. The program, which got underway in fall 1995, focuses on the global environment, its challenges, and opportunities—no easy endeavor. Its own institutional goals are no less ambitious: to be nothing short of the "Harvard of the Ozarks." Those who snicker clearly don't know Drury. In July 1991, the college's School of Architecture was granted full accreditation by the National Architectural Accrediting Board, the first such stamp of approval given to a program at an independent liberal arts college. Standards in its teacher education program are among the most rigorous in Missouri, and nearly all the students who apply to medical or law schools are admitted. One good feature not gaining dramatically in stature is Drury's rates for tuition, room, and board: just over $20,000 in the 2005–2006 school year.

Student body: Eighty-one percent of the students are from Missouri, many from the surrounding Ozark area. Though 85% of the out-of-staters also are from the region, undergraduates from 34 states and 22 foreign countries are in attendance. All but 15% are graduates of public high schools. Just 5% in a recent year were members of the United Church of Christ and the Disciples of Christ; 64% were members of other Protestant denominations. Members of U.S. minority groups and international students account for 9% of the enrollment. Foreign nationals make up 4%, Asian-Americans 2%, and Hispanics, African-Americans, and Native Americans about 1% each. Students are known for being "armed with a smile," and generally conservative in their outlook with pockets of more liberal thinkers. There is a mixture of rather well-to-do students from larger cities and scholarship students from smaller towns. Most are goal-oriented, but not all are equally determined in their work. Notes a senior: "Some students strive for outstanding academic success and usually are enrolled in the honors program. But there are many who just want to graduate without much effort."

Academics: Drury, which was founded in 1873 and was known as Drury College until a few years ago, awards bachelor's degrees in 63 majors plus master's degrees in criminology, criminal justice, communication, business administration, and education. The academic year is divided into 2 semesters with optional January and May terms that are set aside for special projects. Average class size for freshmen is 26, with the largest classes, such as the lecture in Science and Inquiry, enrolling nearly 100. Juniors and seniors often encounter fewer than 20 in their classes, with more specialized higher-level courses, such as Probability and Statistics, enrolling only 4. Upper-level business and communications classes are most crowded but rarely top 30.

As part of the Global Perspectives 21 program, undergraduates begin their studies with "Alpha Seminar: The American Experience," a writing-intensive course designed to help students develop skills for success in college. Students follow with courses that revolve around 2 themes: global studies and scientific perspectives. The global studies courses examine Western cultures, minorities and indigenous cultures, values inquiry, and creativity. Mathematics, scientific inquiry and research, human behavior, political science and economics, and health and well-being make up scientific perspectives. Students completing the Global Perspectives 21 Program, which accounts for almost half of the 124 semester hours needed to graduate (170 hours in architecture; 150 in accounting), earn a minor in global studies.

The Drury faculty includes 123 full-time and 62 part-time members; 40% are women. On such a small campus, which prides itself on providing personal relationships, the slogan, according to a recent graduate, is "You can't hide from your professors, and they can't hide from you." Many even take attendance in class. Their backgrounds are diverse; included are former business owners, experienced researchers, and long-time teachers. In quality the faculty range from intelligent and exciting to those members "who have stopped teaching and started lecturing from the book and focusing on their own research," observes a senior.

In the past few years, the Hammons School of Architecture has emerged as the site of Drury's landmark discipline, thanks largely to construction of the 5-star building in 1990 and national accreditation of its 5-year baccalaureate program, which followed a year later. Professors in the Breech School of Business stay current by going back into the "real" world every 3–5 years to gain practical experience. Says a business administration major: "This keeps the faculty up to date, so they don't have to depend on the *Wall Street Journal* and textbooks to know what's going on." Students themselves stay challenged both inside the classroom and outside as part of the active SIFE (Students in Free Enterprise) team, which won the world championship in Mainz, Germany, in October 2003 for the second time in 3 years. The Drury team was first runner-up behind the team from the University of Zimbabwe in 2005. And while science majors boast a 95% acceptance rate into medical schools (many graduates attend Saint Louis University with which Drury has an admission agreement), students say the credit is due to extremely helpful faculty members, since adequate laboratory equipment has been sorely lacking.

Though the communication majors in advertising, integrated media, public relations, and speech communication benefit from their own new building, erected in 1989, undergraduates find some of the classes and professors insufficiently challenging. Foreign language instruction, too, lacks enough diversity in its courses as well as enough faculty. Course offerings in the social sciences also are rather limited. Political science and history, in particular, need less faculty turnover and more vigor and innovation in their teaching. The mathematics department is marked by too many "confused" students who fail to understand what some of the professors are trying to teach.

Facilities: The opening of the highly computerized Olin Library in the fall of 1992 marked a turning point in Drury study and research. Its light and airy atmosphere makes it "very conducive to thinking" in the words of a prelaw student, unless the Greeks are having their study hall hours "when it's a big social scene," remarks a junior. As a research center, an English major notes, "it is good at finding *where* in Springfield the information can be found." Students find Olin's own holdings, which stand at 178,000 volumes and 868 periodicals, inadequate for many research projects, though the on-line catalog and various computerized research aids can often help point to the needed materials at either the Springfield public library, 4 blocks away, or to the library at Southwest Missouri State University, a mile away.

Three hundred eighty-nine computers are available to students around the clock in several technology centers across campus. All university-owned computers are connected to the Internet; network ports are available in student housing (1 port per occupant) as well as in many common areas such as classrooms and the library. Eighty percent of the campus including some outdoor areas and all academic buildings also provides wireless network access.

Special programs: Drury juniors and seniors can spend a semester at Regents College in London, mixing with students from 40 other nations; the only extra cost is airfare. The Drury Center in Volos, Greece, presents another possibility for living and learning abroad. Undergraduates also may study in Spain, Germany, Denmark, and Australia, and several other countries or spend a semester in Washington, D.C. (Forty percent of Drury students end up studying abroad.) Closer to home, 2 students a year are invited to study the environment, public policy, astronomy, and more at Biosphere 2 in Arizona. Three-two programs in engineering are available with Washington University and the University of Missouri. An international management program allows students to spend 3½ years at Drury and 1 year at the American Graduate School for International Management in Arizona, better known as Thunderbird, and to earn a bachelor's degree from Drury and a master's from Thunderbird. For students interested in going on to study medicine, Drury has partnerships with the Kirksville College of Osteopathic Medicine, St. Louis University School of Medicine, and the University of Missouri School of Medicine. Leadership Drury is a 4-year program that develops leadership qualities though lectures, group activities, and rope courses in which students climb up, over, and through challenging obstacle courses made from ropes; the courses encourage risk-taking in a safe environment and help build self-esteem.

Campus life: Fifty-two percent of the undergraduates reside on Drury's campus, which is centered around Drury Lane, in the middle of Springfield in the heart of the Ozark Mountains. Some students find Greek life more influential than they had expected. Thirty-two percent of the men and 24% of the women are members of 4 national fraternities (with new houses) and 4 national sororities, which control most of the Drury social life with parties open to members and independents alike. School-sponsored dances, while offered, tend to be less popular. Many residents end up leaving on Saturdays, although fewer than in the past, thanks to an increase in campus programming other than dances. Most "crime" consists of minor incidents committed by neighborhood kids: air being let out of tires, for example, or broken windows with an occasional car break-in. Nonetheless, because Drury is located in an area where the potential for more serious crime exists, campus security patrols around the clock and more lighting and security cameras have been added.

Drury's nationally ranked basketball team brings out the most fans, with the swimming and soccer teams not far behind. Altogether, Drury fields 7 intercollegiate sports for men and 7 for women in NCAA Division II competition. Half of both the men and the women get involved in the 6 intramural sports offered for each sex.

When life at Drury gets dreary, students road-trip to the nearest bigger cities: St. Louis, Kansas City, or Tulsa, Oklahoma, each about 3 hours away. Springfield (pop. 150,000) is located amid the Ozarks, which afford plenty of opportunities for hiking, canoeing, fishing, swimming, waterskiing, or simple exploration.

Cost cutters: Ninety-two percent of entering freshmen in the 2005–2006 school year and 89% of the continuing students received financial assistance of some sort; for 91% of the freshmen and 86% of continuing students, the aid was need-based. The average freshman award for a student with need included a need-based scholarship or grant averaging $6102 and need-based self-help aid such as loans and jobs averaging $4096. The average non-need-based scholarship for a freshman athlete was $6287; other non-need-based awards and scholarships averaged $3962. A 2005 graduate owed, on average, $15,450. For the brightest undergraduates, Drury offers scholarships based on academic achievement: Trustee Scholarships cover 4 years' tuition, fees, room and board for 10 students who scored a 29 or higher on the ACT or at least 1920 on the SAT and held a GPA of 3.5 or higher and performed well on a campus interview. Ten finalists in the Trustee competition who did not receive a scholarship can win a Presidential Award of $10,000; Academic Honor Scholarships pay $500 to $5000 to additional high achievers. The amount paid varies according to the standardized test score and high school grade point average. Students who ranked in the top 2% of their graduating class, valedictorians, and salutatorians, receive $1000. And Drury agrees to match dollar for dollar, up to $500, a limited number of selected scholarships made by outside agencies, not including the federal or state government.

Rate of return: Seventy-eight percent of the freshmen who enter return for the sophomore year. Forty-seven percent graduate in 4 years; 63% in 5 years.

Payoff: Over 40% of the 2005 graduates earned bachelor's degrees in 3 fields: 18% in business administration, 13% in biology, and 10% in communication. A third of the new graduates enroll in graduate or professional schools. In a recent period, nearly 90% of the applicants for advanced work in business, psychology, and law were accepted. Of the 60% who took jobs shortly after graduation, about half went into private industry, primarily with firms in the Midwest. Private companies that have hired Drury graduates include Mercke, Bank of America, and State Farm Insurance. Other alumni work for government and non-profit agencies such as the Missouri State Auditors and for various health-care centers, or enter public school teaching. Fifteen companies and organizations recruited on campus in the 2004–2005 school year.

Bottom line: For students unsure about making the major step up to college, Drury provides a personal atmosphere and a closeness with professors that combine to make learning comfortable, but not without challenge. Says a senior: "This school gives opportunity to hard-working, determined students."

Rockhurst University

Kansas City, Missouri 64110

Setting: Urban
Control: Private (Roman Catholic-Jesuit)
Undergraduate enrollment: 564 men, 697 women
Graduate enrollment: 114 men, 203 women
Student/faculty ratio: 11:1
Freshman profile: 1% scored over 700 on SAT I verbal; 44% scored 600–700; 41% 500–599; 14% below 500. 4% scored over 700 on SAT I math; 41% scored 600–700; 43% 500–599; 12% below 500. 20% scored above 28 on the ACT; 15% scored 27–28; 26% 24–26; 25% 21–23; 14% below 21. 25% graduated in top tenth of high school class; 57% in upper fifth.

Faculty profile: 84% Ph.D.'s
Tuition and fees: $19,540
Room and board: $5900
Freshman financial aid: 93%; average scholarship or grant: $4946 need-based; $9202 non-need-based
Campus jobs: 22%; average earnings: $1500/year
Application deadline: Early decision: May 1; regular: June 30
Financial aid deadline: June 1 (Priority date: Mar. 1)
Admissions information: (816) 501-4100; (800) 842-6776 e-mail: admission@rockhurst.edu web site: www.rockhurst.edu

A half-dozen times throughout the academic year, Rockhurst students stop studying for the next exam in accounting or writing a last-minute paper in English to get involved in discussions of broad and timely topics. As part of the university's Visiting Scholars Series, noted philosophers, theologians, and leaders in a wide range of other fields, from poet Robert Frost in 1959 to the 1980 Nobel Peace Prize winner and Argentine human rights advocate Adolfo Perez Esquival in 2003, present lectures to the community, often followed the next day by informal colloquia with students or visits to individual classrooms for further discussion. Many classes drop what they have been studying to center their coursework around the topic of an approaching speaker. The series is designed to enrich the intellectual and cultural climate on a campus where many students come to college from small towns and suburban communities throughout the Midwest or commute from their homes near Kansas City, dropping in for classes and then heading out again. It is just one approach by which Rockhurst, one of the nation's 28 Jesuit colleges and universities, exposes students to worlds bigger than their own and to ideas that most have never before considered.

Student body: Sixty percent of Rockhurst's undergraduates are from Missouri; most of the rest are from the surrounding region, with a total of 30 states and 10 foreign countries represented. Sixteen percent of the undergraduate enrollment are members of U.S. minority groups, 7% African-Americans, 5% Hispanics, 3% Asian-Americans, and 1% Native Americans. Seventeen students are foreign nationals. Sixty-four percent of the undergraduates are Catholic; 46% are from private or parochial high schools. Undergraduates are for the most part conservative, although about a fourth are quite liberal in their thinking, and a growing number from both ends of the spectrum are described as being "vocal, rebellious, and caring on certain issues," such as health care, and peace and justice. If the outward look tends toward the preppy, the inward academic drive is much harder to label. Says a chemistry major: "There are very social people who go out every night and then there are the studious people who rarely go out," and of course, the grand middle who do some of both. Observes a math and English major: "I find that most students work hard to do well academically but they are motivated by personal dreams and Rockhurst professors, not competition with others."

Academics: Rockhurst, founded in 1910, awards the bachelor's degree in 40 fields, the master's in 6, and a doctorate in physical therapy. The academic year is divided into 2 semesters. Most classes for freshmen and sophomores have 20–35 students, but enrollment shrinks to between 10 and 20 in the latter years. While many required courses in the health-care fields have 40 participants, some upper-level language courses proceed with as few as 5.

The rigorous Rockhurst core is yet another way by which this Jesuit university seeks to broaden students' career-oriented focus. The core is organized around the 7 classical modes of inquiry: artistic, historical, literary, philosophical, theological, and the scientific, which includes both relational inquiry in the social sciences and causal in the natural sciences. Students must also demonstrate proficiency in oral and written communication and in mathematics. The program fills about 2 years of coursework, and students credit the core with providing a "foundation of knowledge" upon which everything that follows seems to make more sense.

All but 16 of Rockhurst's 129 full-time faculty members teach undergraduates, as do all but 15 of the 91 part-timers. Forty-three percent of the total pool are women. Students value the real-life experience most lay professors bring to the classroom; the head of the Global Studies Department worked for the CIA for several years; the chair of the chemistry department worked in industry. But their talents don't stop there. Observes a senior: "The faculty not only teach us, but they prepare us by challenging us mentally to step out of our comfort zones. They mentor us and always are willing to assist us both inside and outside the classroom setting." Adds a junior: "They reflect the mission and values of our university."

The business program, in particular, features excellent instructors in a case-study approach to learning that majors maintain will provide a grade A education "if," in the words of an accounting student, "we survive it." The allied health fields at Rockhurst are also impressive with rigorous programs in nursing, physical therapy, occupational therapy, and communication sciences and disorders. Chemistry and biology majors get a strong start with the Freshmen in Science Program which provides a network of support in that first critical year; faculty get to know students by name, help them with registration, and organize various activities for them throughout the year. The premed program also is noteworthy and sends a number of students to Georgetown, Creighton, and St. Louis University medical schools, many with an early guarantee of admission. A science building, constructed in 1996, has brought more modern facilities. Psychology benefits from having professors who, says a major, "are very willing to meet with students and spend one-on-one time explaining concepts, going over papers or exams, and just helping out in general." The American Humanics certificate program, which prepares students for work in human service organizations, philosophy, and political science, where the professors engage students in simulations of significant events, are winners as well.

Students wish more options for study were available in the arts. Art, theater, and music are offered as minors only, with fewer faculty and course offerings—"*No* band or orchestra classes at all," observes a marketing major—for those students who might enjoy these subjects as complements to their career-oriented majors. "If the Department of Communication and Fine Arts had more support," notes an accounting major, "it could change many lives." Sociology needs more than the 2 professors it currently has. The program in foreign languages and literature could use more variety; majors in French and Spanish only are offered as well as a minor in German.

Facilities: Students with a lot to do head immediately to Greenlease Library's top floor, which is reserved for quiet study only. Says a political science major: "The only sounds are those of a chair being scraped against the tile floor or of a person walking by." For research, most find Greenlease and its collection of 375,000 volumes and 6000 electronic and paper periodicals suffices, though for more extensive projects, students either go on-line, use interlibrary loan, or cross the street to the general and law libraries of the local University of Missouri campus or walk 2 blocks west to the Linda Hall Library of Science and

Technology. Greenlease Library recently became a consortium member of the MOBIUS system that facilitates rapid interlibrary loan from participating libraries across the state; the move makes available 17 million different titles from consortium members. Other alternatives for finding information include the various branches of the Kansas City public library or the Truman and Eisenhower presidential libraries.

Students have access to 500 microcomputers spread among computer laboratories, classrooms, the library, and residence halls. Some labs remain open until midnight with 3 available around the clock. Most students also bring their own computers to connect to the Internet from their dorm rooms. The entire campus also is wireless, a boon to those with laptops.

Special programs: Full-time Rockhurst students may take 1 course each semester at other Kansas City area schools. Study abroad for a year or a term is offered in 4 countries in Europe, in China, and in Mexico. Three-two engineering programs are offered with the University of Missouri, Rolla and Columbia, the University of Detroit-Mercy, and Marquette University. A congressional internship in Washington, D.C. also is an option, as is a term at Fordham University in New York.

Campus life: Sixty-one percent of the students, mainly freshmen and sophomores, live on the 55-acre campus, with most upperclassmen living in townhouses on campus or in the surrounding neighborhood. For a majority of undergraduates, fraternities have become the "lifeline" of the school. Just 7% of the students are involved with the 4 national fraternities, 2 national sororities, and the university's own pseudosorority, the Rockhurst Organization of Collegiate Women. Membership in the university's coed service fraternity is popular as well. In 1996 an on-campus pub was added, giving all students, regardless of Greek membership, a place to study, grab a bite, and generally hang out. Further renovation of the Rock Room student union over the last 2 years also has given students a small-stage space for concerts and speakers, a big screen TV, and comfortable furniture in which to sip coffee from the Daily Perks and hang out. While being Greek still carries some cachet on campus, the Center for Service Learning involves a vast array of students in volunteer work in Kansas City, in other states, and beyond the U.S. borders. Students build a service transcript while at Rockhurst and receive a copy upon graduation. Because of Rockhurst's urban location, the threat of crime is a concern, and students quickly learn to be street smart. Notes an out-of-stater: "If students never walk alone, always lock their cars, and always lock their rooms, they generally have no problem." Most undergraduates consider the campus security force to be first-rate and extremely available, especially with the steady addition of numerous security measures such as security personnel patrols, surveillance cameras and emergency phones throughout campus, and most recently, increased lighting in the parking lots and along campus walkways. Says a sophomore: "Once you live on campus, you realize how secluded it is and you actually feel very safe." Students advise using special caution when spending time in the surrounding neighborhood.

About a tenth of the men and women play on the 5 men's and 5 women's NCAA Division II varsity teams. Women's and men's soccer, which is nationally ranked, draw the most (some say the only) enthusiastic attention from spectators, although the recent start-up of a spirit club and pep squad has helped raise the overall level of enthusiasm. Basketball and women's volleyball, which also is consistently nationally ranked, attract smaller crowds and the new baseball field is expected to increase the number of fairer-weather fans. Two-thirds of the men and a third of the women take part in 12 intramural sports for men and women throughout the year. New workout space, dubbed the Student Body by students, with $60,000 worth of cardiovascular and weight-training equipment also is getting a lot of use.

For most students, getting away just means taking advantage of all that Kansas City has to offer, from riding the trolley to attending the symphony to taking in a Kansas City Royals or Chiefs game. When neither the campus nor Kansas City has what a student needs or wants, there is always home, or the home of a friend who lives within driving distance.

Cost cutters: In the 2005–2006 school year, 93% of the freshmen and 85% of the other undergraduates received financial aid of some sort. Seventy-six percent of the freshmen and 67% of the remaining students were provided with need-based assistance. Observes one aid recipient: "If you want to come to Rockhurst, they will find a way for you." The average freshman award for a student with need included a need-based scholarship or grant averaging $4946 and need-based self-help aid such as loans and jobs averaging $3129. Non-need-based athletic scholarships for first-year students averaged $10,242; other non-need-based awards and scholarships averaged $9202. Average debt of a 2005 graduate was $14,556. Renewable academic merit scholarships range from the $5500 Community Scholarship to the full tuition Trustees' Scholarships. Presentation of these 2 awards, and the 5 scholarship levels in between, are based on students' class rank, grade point average, and standardized test scores. The Finucane Service Award pays $1500; athletic awards, from $500 to full rides. Any family may participate in payment plans covering 3 installments a semester or 10 monthly installments. Cooperative programs are available.

Rate of return: Eighty-nine percent of freshmen return for the sophomore year. Fifty-one percent graduate in 4 years, 63% within 5 years, 66% in 6 years.

Payoff: In the class of 2005, just over a third, 35%, of the graduates earned bachelor's degrees in business, followed by 21% in nursing/health professions and 13% in psychology. Two-thirds of Rockhurst graduates enter the job market soon after commencement, many accepting positions in management, accounting, physical therapy, and nursing, most frequently in the Midwest. More than 60 companies and organizations recruited on campus in the 2004–2005 school year. Large numbers settle in the Kansas City area and work for companies such as Hallmark Cards, AT&T, Sprint or MCI, the Research Medical Center, and Hoechst Marion Roussel. Over a fourth head directly to graduate or professional school, most in the arts and sciences.

Bottom line: Rockhurst is a small, caring campus in the heart of a big city that offers strong academic and professional programs built on the foundation of the Jesuit adherence to the liberal arts. "As limited as Rockhurst is in its size," says a senior, "it provides opportunities to succeed and grow that no large university could ever match."

Saint Louis University

St. Louis, Missouri 63103

Setting: Urban
Control: Private (Roman Catholic-Jesuit)
Undergraduate enrollment: 2952 men, 3865 women
Graduate enrollment: 1258 men, 1665 women
Student/faculty ratio: 12:1
Freshman profile: 9% scored over 700 on SAT I verbal; 44% scored 600–700; 39% 500–599; 8% below 500. 14% scored over 700 on SAT I math; 43% scored 600–699; 34% 500–599; 9% below 500. 19% scored above 28 on the ACT; 18% scored 27–28; 38% 24–26; 18% 21–23; 7% below 21. 36% graduated in top tenth of high school class; 57% in upper fifth.
Faculty profile: 95% Ph.D.'s

Tuition and fees: $24,958
Room and board: $8200
Freshman financial aid: 99%; average scholarship or grant: $12,644 need-based; $22,568 non-need-based
Campus jobs: 18%; average earnings: $1663/year
Application deadline: Physical therapy freshmen: Dec. 15; physical therapy and occupational therapy transfer students: Feb. 15; regular: Aug. 1
Financial aid deadline: Mar. 1 (Dec. 1 preferred for scholarships)
Admissions information: (314) 977-2500; (800) SLU-FORU
e-mail: admitme@slu.edu
web site: www.slu.edu

When top high school seniors with plans to attend medical or law school gain admittance to Saint Louis University in Missouri, they may also have assured themselves admission to the university's postgraduate professional programs. Under special School of Law and School of Medicine Scholars programs, a beginning freshman with an excellent high school record may enroll in a special prelaw or premedical course of study. If he or she maintains a cumulative GPA of 3.40 or higher for the first 2 years, SLU's medical or law school may grant conditional acceptance. Though students are notified of their acceptance before starting the junior year, they must maintain a cumulative GPA of 3.40 and take the required standardized exams to ensure admission upon completion of the bachelor's degree requirements. The concept attracts excellent undergraduates who might not normally consider SLU and adds just one more touch of excellence to this Jesuit university's already strong reputation in preprofessional fields.

Student body: Fifty-four percent of SLU's undergraduates are from in-state, with 72% of the rest also midwesterners. All but 4 states plus 55 foreign countries have residents on campus. Forty-two percent are Catholic. Half the enrollment in a recent year attended public schools. Undergraduates enjoy a variety of races and cultures on their campus. Nine percent are African-American, 5% are Asian-Americans, 3% foreign nationals, 3% Hispanics, 2% foreign nationals, and less than 1% Native Americans. Most undergraduates consider themselves friendly and accepting, conservative to moderate in their political thinking, and enthusiastic about involvement in community service. "We are concerned with the affairs and well-being of the community," says a sophomore. But for nearly all students, the first priority is studies. Remarks a junior: "Many of us are working our way through school and know what we are here for. This is not to say that we do not have fun. But most of us are committed and believe in succeeding."

Academics: Saint Louis University was founded in 1818, making it one of the oldest schools west of the Mississippi. The university awards degrees through the doctorate, with undergraduate programs on the main campus and nearby medical campus offered in more than 185 majors through 9 colleges and schools. The university's Parks College offers undergraduate programs in aviation science, various fields of engineering, and computer science. The school year is split into 2 semesters. Most lower-division courses enroll between 20 and 35 students, although Psychology 101 can have over 300 notetakers. As a student becomes more advanced in his or her major, class sizes drop to between 5 and 25.

Each of SLU's colleges and schools has its own general education requirements, most of which contain the trademark Jesuit emphasis on courses in philosophy and theology. A new core curriculum in the College of Arts and Sciences requires that students take courses from 11 subject areas: English, foreign language, cultural diversity, fine and performing arts, literature, science, math, world history, philosophy, theology, and social sciences. Many students find the emphasis on philosophy and theology particularly enriching, so much so, that more courses in these fields have been added in several of the divisions.

The total faculty at Saint Louis University consists of 1127 full-time and 2083 part-time members; most, however, teach at the graduate level only. In the 2005–2006 school year, only 507 of the full-time faculty and 394 of the part-time taught undergraduates. Thirty-seven percent of the faculty are women. Graduate students in a recent year taught just 7% of the introductory courses; students find the majority to be quite knowledgeable and say they relate easily to undergraduates. Likewise many of the professors, especially the Jesuit priests on staff, establish an immediate rapport with their students. Remarks a philosophy major: "I have had professors who have gone out of their way to sit down and spend extra time on a problem, as well as professors whom I have invited out to dinner or lunch." Faculty-affiliates assigned to each residence hall can even be found cooking for students or attending programs with them. Research is a vital part of faculty members' out-of-classroom hours and is incorporated into their teaching. There are some professors, however, whom students find too intelligent and removed from students.

The health-related sciences offer some of the university's most challenging professors and coursework, as well as proximity to the vast equipment and other resources of the SLU School of Medicine. Sharing the spotlight are the rigorous 5½-year physical therapy program in the Edward and Margaret Doisy College of Health Sciences (named for the late SLU faculty member who won the Nobel Prize in Medicine in 1943 and his spouse) and the premed majors in biology and chemistry in the College of Arts and Sciences. Notes an admiring nonmajor: "These disciplines require undivided attention from the student. One cannot participate in either of these programs half-heartedly, as they have very strict standards." Most other programs in the College of Health Sciences, especially the nursing program, also require adherence to rigorous course schedules that include much clinical experience—and great job placement when it's all over. The John Cook School of Business offers "a wide range of core business classes that make us well-rounded business majors when we graduate," observes a marketing major. Psychology, meteorology, philosophy, theological studies, and English, particularly in the upper-division courses, also feature "superb" faculty within the College of Arts and Sciences. Students of meteorology can hone their skills as interns at the National Weather Service, at any of the 4 commercial television stations, or at the many radio stations in the area. The prelaw program is another winner.

Other disciplines within the arts and sciences, such as the fine and performing arts, have been weakened by inadequate resources. The choir rehearsal room, for example, was converted several years ago into another financial aid office. Students interested in studying such languages as Chinese and Japanese must go to other local universities for classes; modern language majors are available in French, German, Spanish, and Russian studies, with classes also offered in Hindi, Portuguese, and Italian. Professors of mathematics seem less able than their peers in other disciplines to get across their subject matter clearly. Students seeking to specialize in advertising or broadcast journalism are disappointed to find only 2 broad tracks offered in the communication major: 1 in Communication Professions, which prepares students for careers in journalism, public relations, advertising, organizational communication, and political communication, and a second in Communication Technology, which prepares students for careers that rely on new computer technologies, such as multimedia design, publication design, and instructional technology.

Facilities: As its name suggests, Pius XII Memorial Library is a great place to study if someone needs absolute quiet, although "social" floors and rooms for group study also are available. Altogether, Pius XII and the other more specialized divinity, law, and Medical Center libraries maintain collections of more than 1.9 million titles, 2.6 million microform units, and 15,597 periodicals; some undergraduates even turn to these more specialized graduate-level libraries for their most concentrated study. A wealth of computerized research aids are available to students, such as MERLIN, the on-line catalog and numerous CD-ROM databases. What SLU doesn't have can usually be obtained through interlibrary loan or from the nearby Washington University and University of Missouri libraries.

More than 1200 PCs are available for student use at several centers around campus, including several specialized labs in various schools and colleges. Undergraduates' chief complaint is that most computers are not available past midnight, the time when, for some students, serious working hours are just beginning. The university strongly recommends that students have personal computers. Wireless access is available in some sections of the campus.

Special programs: A campus of Saint Louis University in Madrid, Spain, enrolls both Spanish and American students, with large numbers concentrating their studies in a business certificate program, social work, or bilingual education. Other year-long programs are offered in Lyons, France, in Baden-Württenberg, Germany and in Belgium. Homebound engineering students can participate in a 3-2 program with nearby Washington University or cross-register for other courses at Washington University or the University of Missouri at St. Louis.

Campus life: Student interest in residing on the university's urban campus has grown steadily over the years, with 43% of all students and 85% of all first-year students choosing to live on the 244-acre campus in midtown St. Louis. Students discover a strong sense of community there, enhanced by the school's Jesuit roots and its determination to be part of, rather than apart from, the urban neighborhood where it is located. In that effort, a large number of students live out the Jesuit mission of serving others and do an average of 50,000 hours of volunteer work annually in the local community. That environment also keeps students constantly aware of the potential for violent crime in their urban surroundings, although students maintain they feel quite safe within campus boundaries. A free 24-hour escort service is available, more foot and bike patrols and blue light phones have been added, and much effort is expended to educate students on how to live in an urban area. Notes a local resident: "If you utilize the buddy system and common sense there is very little threat of harm."

Greek life grows stronger every year, with 12 national fraternities and 6 national sororities enrolling nearly a fifth of the men and almost a fourth of the women as members. Many students welcome the increased interest in the Greeks and their parties as yet another sign of a thriving campus social life that will convince more undergraduates, both Greeks and independents, to stay once the weekend arrives. The Greeks also contribute about a third of the 50,000 community service hours logged by students. To enhance the campus environment further, the university has added a pond and "contemplative park." Says a senior: "Reading a book on a bench at the beautiful dolphin pond and fountain relaxes the most stressed-out person."

Sporting events also keep many residents as well as commuters on campus either to watch or to participate. Billikens basketball brings out the greatest number of fans; attendance at games consistently ranks in the top 20 nationally. Fan support at men's soccer games has ranked in the top 3 nationally for the past several years, many enjoying the new natural grass soccer facility that opened in 1999. These are but 2 of 7 NCAA Division I sports provided for men; there are 9 for women. Sixty percent of the men and 40% of the women students turn out for an intramural program that consists of about 20 sports for each sex. The Simon Recreation Center was recently named one of the 20 top facilities in North America and can accommodate every type of sport or fitness enthusiast.

For most undergraduates, the city of St. Louis, with everything from the zoo to Gateway Arch to the Landing, a collection of downtown bars and dance clubs, provides sufficient off-campus adventure. Recent campus expansion places the university next to Grand Center, St. Louis' arts district and cultural center.

Cost cutters: In the 2005–2006 school year, all but 1% of the freshmen and continuing students received some form of financial aid; aid was need-based for 51% of the freshmen and 61% of the rest. The average award for first-year students with financial need included a need-based scholarship or grant averaging $12,644 and need-based self-help aid such as loans and jobs averaging $8941. Other non-need-based awards and scholarships for freshmen averaged $22,568. Debts of $18,164 were the average among 2005 graduates. Forty percent of the new freshmen receive university-funded scholarships for academic merit. Presidential Scholarships pay full tuition over 4 years to 30 entering freshmen typically in the top 3% of admitted students who have a minimum 3.8 GPA and a minimum 30 ACT or 1320 SAT in math and critical reading. Ignatian, University, Dean's and Provost scholarships pay $4500 to $13,000 a year based on similar criteria. Other scholarships are awarded to qualified students based on community service, leadership, and talent in the fine and performing arts and in athletics. A cooperative program in business is available, and work-study jobs are plentiful on campus.

Rate of return: Eighty-six percent of the entering freshmen return for the sophomore year. Sixty-one percent graduate in 4 years; 74% in 5 years, 75% in 6.

Payoff: Biology at 7% was the top major among 2005 degree recipients followed by business administration and nursing at 6% each. Thirty percent of recent graduates went on to professional or graduate schools immediately after earning their bachelor's degrees. The remainder took jobs nationwide in such fields as accounting, aviation, marketing, education, social work, nursing, and physical therapy. Many remain in the St. Louis area, working for local hospitals or companies such as Boeing, Anheuser-Busch, Monsanto, and Citicorp. Opportunities for employment are strong: St. Louis recently ranked fifth among cities as the home base of Fortune 100 companies and sixth as the headquarters of Fortune 500 firms. More than 270 companies and other organizations recruited graduates in the 2004–2005 school year.

Bottom line: Saint Louis University is an urban research university that refuses to act like one, caring for each individual as a total person and drawing its undergraduates into the life of the surrounding community—and not just for internships and job contacts. Notes a philosophy major: "The Jesuit tradition of educating the whole person has worked for me, and I'm sure it can for any other student."

Truman State University

Kirksville, Missouri 63501

Setting: Small town
Control: Public
Undergraduate enrollment: 2281 men, 3175 women
Graduate enrollment: 59 men, 128 women
Student/faculty ratio: 15:1
Freshman profile: 16% scored over 700 on SAT I verbal; 50% scored 600–700; 29% 500–599; 5% below 500. 12% scored over 700 on SAT I math; 48% scored 600–700; 33% 500–599; 7% below 500. 38% scored above 28 on the ACT; 22% scored 27–28; 27% 24–26; 12% 21–23; 1% below 21. 48% graduated in top tenth of high school class; 73% in upper fifth.
Faculty profile: 83% Ph.D.'s

Tuition and fees: $5862 in-state; $10,042 out-of-state
Room and board: $5380
Freshman financial aid: 98%; average scholarship or grant: $3188 need-based; $3326 non-need-based
Campus jobs: 21%; average earnings: $1696/year
Application deadline: Early action: Nov. 15; regular: Mar. 1
Financial aid deadline: Apr. 1
Admissions information: (660) 785-4114; (800) 892-7792 in-state
e-mail: admissions@truman.edu
web site: www.truman.edu

While it is not unusual for a normal school to grow from a teachers college into a regional state university, there's nothing "normal" about the transformation at Truman State University, known prior to 1996 as Northeast Missouri State. This former state teachers college didn't stop at becoming a regional university; it went on to gain status as a nationally recognized leader in curriculum innovation and one of the best educational values in the nation. The extra "value" behind Truman derives from its value-added model of assessment, a method of determining how much students have learned after they've entered college and to what extent various parts of the curriculum are enhancing their knowledge. Through periodic testing of undergraduates throughout their 4 years on campus, the university can determine how much knowledge they have acquired in particular subjects, pinpointing areas where they, as well as the curriculum, may need help. As a result, students don't just pay fewer dollars in tuition when they go in (only $5862 for state residents and $10,042 for out-of-staters during the 2005–2006 school year); the university makes sure they have received full value for their dollars by the time they come out.

Student body: Seventy-three percent of the undergraduates are from Missouri, with most out-of-staters from Illinois and Iowa. Altogether, the enrollment represents 40 states and 46 foreign countries. A fifth of the students attended private or parochial schools. Foreign national students comprise 5% of the enrollment, African-Americans 4%, Asian-Americans and Hispanics, 2% each and Native Americans, 1%. While most students are conservative, more undergraduates seem to be moving toward the center, and even a bit to the left, in their political thinking. Still, a majority, whatever their philosophies, generally keep their viewpoints to themselves and are described by classmates as being "not very politically active," or even "apathetic." As the university's visibility has increased, so has the quality of students, changing the reasons most attend. "Whereas in the past," observes a recent graduate, "students seemed more concerned with the parties—and the price—now more undergraduates seem to have chosen the university for its academic reputation." Students see themselves as *friendly* and *outgoing* but *goal-oriented* and *serious* about their assignments. Says a junior: "Students here know that studying is a necessity. It's not uncool to be studying until 9 or 10 p.m. on weekends before you go out to relax." The result is an environment on Monday mornings that is decidedly competitive. Says a senior: "There is a competitiveness in each of us; even if we do not show it, everyone knows it exists. We have all achieved a lot to be accepted to this school and want to be known as being brilliant."

Academics: Truman, which was founded in 1867 and has been officially designated as Missouri's public liberal arts and sciences university, offers bachelor's degrees in 43 majors in 7 academic divisions, as well as master's degrees in 8 fields. The academic year is divided into 2 semesters. Average class size for undergraduates is about 24 students, with upper-level classes averaging 15. Freshmen will encounter an English composition class with a maximum of 24 students, but also some introductory courses, such as Lifetime Health and Fitness that can have 94 enrolled. About 130 lower-division and 220 upper-division courses enroll fewer than 10.

All students must complete 63 hours of coursework in the liberal arts, equal to about 2 years of their degree requirements. Up to 16 of these hours are required in such skill areas as written and oral communication, mathematics and statistics, computer literacy, and personal well-being. (Students have opportunities on campus to test out of several of these courses.) An additional 23 hours must be drawn from the scientific, historical, social scientific, philosophical/religious, aesthetic, and mathematical modes of inquiry. Up to 15 hours more come from an extended freshman program, a junior interdisciplinary writing-enhanced seminar, a course providing intercultural perspectives, and elementary proficiency in 1 foreign language. Students earning bachelors of arts, fine arts, and music degrees must attain intermediate proficiency in a language. Those earning bachelor of science and bachelor of science in nursing degrees need additional classes in science, mathematics, statistics, computer science, and social science or logic. A minimum of 2 writing-enhanced courses are mandated for students with majors in the liberal studies program. All students end their studies with a "capstone" or culminating experience in their majors.

The school's famed assessment program utilizes standardized tests and other yardsticks to determine what concepts students have or have not grasped and what skills the curriculum has overlooked. Surveys administered annually to sophomores and juniors, as well as ones given to graduating seniors and alumni, also provide insights into the university's performance.

The total Truman faculty numbers 378. All but 7 of the 353 full-time members teach undergraduates, as do 7 of the 25 part-timers. Thirty-nine percent of the faculty are women. One percent of the introductory classes is taught by graduate students, although one junior notes, "because it is so difficult to get a position, all of them are very gifted teachers." Although Truman has its share of boring know-it-alls, undergraduates find most faculty members to be very student-oriented in their attitudes toward learning and eager to get involved in outside activities such as intramurals. Notes a biology major: "Student-teacher relationships here are excellent, and the faculty, most of whom are highly intelligent and motivated, really seem to stoke a student's ambition to learn and excel."

Among Truman's well-regarded programs, the division of business and accountancy clearly produces results. Thanks to strong faculty, curriculum, and advising, the division has produced graduates who are partners in all the major accounting firms and, since 1982, has pushed Truman into the ranks of the top 10 schools nationwide (number 4 in the nation in 2002) for the number of students attaining first-time passage on the CPA exam. The English faculty and writing labs are also tops, and students often see how their end-of-term surveys are used to bring about changes. Biology thrives on faculty who put a lot into their teaching, rigorous requirements, and a "fantastic" amount of undergraduate research. Students have gained even more opportunities for collaborative research following the completion in fall 2005 of expansion and renovation of Truman's science facility. The renovations, which doubled the size of the original facility, have provided additional classroom and laboratory space for biology, chemistry, physics, and agriculture as well as new laboratory spaces for work in advanced cellular/molecular biology and biochemistry. Political science wins votes for its dedicated, challenging faculty; nursing also is in A-1 shape. Other outstanding programs include Russian, art history, psychology, history, and communication disorders.

Students wish the math and computer science programs were more innovative in their curricula and teaching techniques. Says an English major: "The mathematics faculty sometimes has trouble relating to the average students and only wants to teach the gifted math students. Yet all students are required to take math classes and some have extremely difficult times not because the material is too hard but because the teachers don't explain it well enough." There is also no undergraduate education major at this former teachers college. A student who wants to teach must earn a bachelor's degree in a specific subject and then complete an extensive on-site internship and course requirements for a master's degree in education—an approach widely applauded by educators nationwide.

Facilities: It's not unusual to hear students exclaim "I love our library!" when asked about Pickler Memorial Library. Notes a senior: "I have never seen a cooler library…it is so aesthetically pleasing. When it was rebuilt (in the early 90s), they incorporated a lot of natural lighting with windows along the whole outside and the ceiling." Users hope the collection continues to expand beyond its current holdings of 460,000 volumes and 3396 periodicals. Access to the collection, books, periodicals, and newspapers is computerized with extensive database searches available. When it becomes too loud in the main part of the library for concentrated study, students can move upstairs to one of the private cubicles set around the perimeter of the second and third floors. The library's hours, open until 1 a.m., also "accommodate the procrastinator in every college student," says a communication major though the hours were cut back a few years ago from a more preferable 2 a.m. closing.

More than 400 general-use computers are located in 89 labs and classrooms in the library and student union, most academic buildings, and residence halls. Twenty-four-hour access is provided in the residence halls and, until 1 a.m. in the academic buildings and library. Observes a sophomore: "The labs do get busy during finals, especially in the library, but you can go elsewhere on campus." The campus was scheduled to be entirely wireless by the end of the 2005–2006 school year.

Special programs: Truman participates in study abroad programs in about 50 countries. Excellent opportunities for internships are available in Washington, D.C. and in Jefferson City, the state capital; bright Truman students are especially popular with state senators and representatives. A 3-2 engineering program is offered with the University of Missouri Rolla.

Campus life: Just over half of the university's undergraduates, 51%, live on the 140-acre campus, most in 8 residential colleges where students and faculty live, eat, work, and socialize together. Liberal studies courses are offered within the halls, and professional and upperclass student advisors in each college help guide students in course selections and career choices.

Thirty-one percent of the men and 22% of the women are members of 18 national fraternities and 1 local and 10 national sororities. While the Greeks host their mixers, independents feel far from left out and sponsor their own residence or campus-wide parties. Students say, however, it is harder for men to socialize without fraternities than it is for independent women and many of the most visible students on campus are Greek. Delta Sigma Pi, the coed national business fraternity, is extremely popular and an 8-time winner of the title of outstanding chapter in the nation. The coed service fraternity Alpha Phi Omega also is especially active around campus and in the community. Notes a senior: "We were all overachievers in high school and are trying to do the same thing here." Although students regard Truman as a "low-crime college," measures such as lighting along walkways, an escort service, blue emergency lights and phones, and extensive educational programming about rape prevention for both sexes have been taken to keep it that way.

Football and basketball draw the most spectators among the 11 men's and 10 women's intercollegiate sports played in NCAA Division II. Swimming has gained more attention since the women's team has won the Division II national championship for 5 consecutive years. Seventy-four percent of the men and 40% of the women take part in the intramural program, which offers 21 sports to each sex. A new student recreation center opened in August 1997, in response to a student referendum calling for a new general use athletic facility. Students also were involved in all aspects of planning for the structure.

Ten to 20 percent of the resident students go home every weekend, or travel in groups to a friend's house, another city, or another college. For many, the small-town atmosphere of Kirksville (pop. 17,000), 200 miles north of St. Louis, can get a little dull. During warmer weather, students escape to Thousand Hills State Park. Columbia, homebase of the University of Missouri, is approximately 1½ hours away.

Cost cutters: In the 2005–2006 school year, 98% of the freshmen and 92% of the continuing students received financial assistance; just 32% of the freshmen and 30% of the rest were given help based on financial need. The average freshman award for a student with need included a need-based scholarship or grant averaging $3188 and need-based self-help aid such as loans and jobs averaging $2875. Non-need-based scholarships for freshman athletes averaged $3523; other non-need-based awards and scholarships averaged $3326. A typical 2005 graduate left with a diploma and $16,546 in debts. Several merit awards are available for high-achieving entering freshmen: 12 renewable General John J. Pershing Scholarships, named for the distinguished alumnus, cover amounts up to full tuition, room, and board plus a summer or semester of study abroad. President's Honorary Scholarships recently ranged in value from $750 to $1500 and also go to students with strong high school records. Combined Ability Scholarships pay from $1000 to $2000 depending upon the combined percentile of an entering student's high school class rank and standardized test scores. Other renewable scholarships include Truman Leadership Scholarships, covering amounts up to full tuition, room, and board for Missouri students with outstanding leadership experience in high school, and Undergraduate Research Scholarships, which provide grants for undergraduate research beginning in the freshman year. Scholarships may be renewed if the student maintains a 3.25 grade point average; however, in return for full renewal, the recipient must work in a service project for the university for 5 hours a week. Those who prefer not to work may renew one-half of their scholarships in exchange for no service obligation. To be eligible for many of the competitive scholarships, students must have been accepted for admission to Truman by Jan. 15.

Rate of return: Eighty-six percent of the freshmen who enter return for the sophomore year. Forty-one percent graduate in 4 years; 62% do so in 5 years; 66% in 6.

Payoff: Fourteen percent of the 2005 graduates earned degrees in business administration, followed by 10% in biology and 9% in psychology. Forty-five percent of recent classes have gone directly to professional or graduate schools, including such top names as Yale, Stanford, and Harvard; over half have studied in the arts and sciences. Most of the rest are employed by business and industry, many with firms throughout the Midwest, such as the major accounting firms, McDonnell Douglas, and Hallmark, Inc.

Bottom line: Students, faculty, and staff take pride in the national reputation being earned by their state university. "The sense that we are getting better and better pervades the campus," says a St. Louis resident. "This is a 'people place' where a student won't ever feel like a number. It is tough and an undergraduate has to work hard, but the excellent quality and the friendliness of the faculty make our university a rewarding place to be."

University of Missouri, Columbia

Columbia, Missouri 65211

Setting: Small city
Control: Public
Undergraduate enrollment: 9631 men, 10,348 women
Graduate enrollment: 1213 men, 1444 women
Student/faculty ratio: 17:1
Freshman profile: 22% scored above 28 on the ACT; 18% scored 27–28; 30% 24–26; 24% 21–23; 6% below 21. 24% graduated in top tenth of high school class; 48% in upper fifth.
Faculty profile: 92% Ph.D.'s
Tuition and fees: $6960 in-state; $16,085 out-of-state

Room and board: $6540
Freshman financial aid: 44%; average scholarship or grant: $6110 need-based
Campus jobs: 6%; average earnings: NA
Application deadline: May 1
Financial aid deadline: Mar. 1
Admissions information: (573) 882-7786; (800) 225-6075 in Missouri and Illinois
email: MU4U@missouri.edu
web site: www.missouri.edu

It's not just media hype to call the University of Missouri School of Journalism a world leader in the field. Before the journalism school's founding at Mizzou in 1908, there was no other formal university program for educating students in the truthful and trenchant use of the pen. Today, the school's offerings extend well beyond basic print journalism, with undergraduate sequences in advertising, magazine writing, photojournalism, convergence journalism, and radio-television. Students divide their time among extensive liberal arts courses (they enter the school as juniors), journalism courses, and meeting daily deadlines at the *Columbia Missourian* newspaper, KBIA-FM public radio, or KOMU-TV, the only university-owned commercial TV station in the U.S. With professional centers for Freedom of Information, Science Journalism, and Investigative Reporting, among others based at the school and a recently constructed building that houses the newspaper offices, classrooms, state-of-the-art multimedia and graphics labs, and other facilities, it's little wonder that students call their program "the best in the world."

Student body: Mizzou is very much a school of Missouri residents, with 81% coming from in-state. Most of the out-of-staters simply cross the borders from Kansas and Illinois, although students from all 50 states and 101 foreign countries are present. African-American students account for 5% of the undergraduate enrollment, along with 5% of the students who are foreign nationals, 3% who are Asian-American, 2% Hispanic, and 1% Native American. While enrollment of African-American students has increased by 42% since 1992, their return rate for sophomore year, almost 86%, is slightly higher than the campus-wide rate of 84%. Construction of a $2.4 million home for the university's Black Culture Center also has assisted in recruitment efforts. Though a majority of students hold midwestern values and are moderate to conservative in their thinking, liberals find a home, albeit small, in the campus's very vocal minority. Undergraduates are generally very involved in their out-of-the-classroom lives, and students describe the academic climate as "what you make of it," with plenty of opportunity for competition in certain schools and an equal amount of diversion for those who are more socially minded. However, students caution that those who cling to the "party school" reputation Mizzou once held may find themselves out in a semester or 2.

Academics: Mizzou, founded in 1839, offers degrees through the doctorate in 20 schools and colleges; 10 of them provide 88 areas of undergraduate study. Top-ranked high school seniors are eligible for honors preprofessional programs that guarantee a spot in one of the university's highly competitive professional schools. Students who meet the individual school's entrance qualifications for its preprofessional program and maintain an outstanding grade point average as an undergraduate will be automatically admitted to the School of Law, School of Medicine, and College of Veterinary Medicine, as well as to highly competitive undergraduate programs at the Sinclair School of Nursing and the School of Journalism. Mizzou is one of only 6 universities in the country with medicine, veterinary medicine, and law schools all on one campus. Undergraduate classes are divided between 2 semesters, and usually are experienced first by freshmen as either lecture sessions that range from 150 to 400 participants or required English and math courses that are kept to 20 or 25. Freshman Interest Groups let groups of about 20 first-year students who are interested in the same field of study live together in the same residence hall and take classes together the first term as a way to bond and give each other academic and social support. Students who participated in each of the 90+ FIGs recently underway at Mizzou were enrolled together in 3 core courses focused on a specific major, career, or theme. First-year and returning students also may take part in one of 21 Sponsored Learning Communities that focus on a specific major, interest area, or other common interest and offer study groups, computer labs, and other special features to the participants. Honors seminars involve just 8 participants, although most upperclassmen find their courses generally enroll around 50, depending on the major.

An 8-component general education program is being phased gradually into the university curriculum. Since 1993, all entering students have had to take freshman English plus 2 additional writing-intensive courses, demonstrate competency in college algebra and take 1 additional course in developing math and reasoning skills, plus complete a state-mandated course in American history or political science. As part of more recent mandates, students must demonstrate computer and information proficiency, complete 27 hours of coursework divided evenly among 3 content areas, social and behavioral sciences, physical and biological sciences, (including one lab course), and humanities and fine arts, and undergo a capstone experience in the major. An undergraduate seminar, emphasizing critical thinking and oral and written communication, still remains to be implemented.

The Missouri faculty is overwhelmingly full-time, with just 109 part-timers amid the 1364 faculty members. All faculty teach undergraduates. Thirty-two percent of the total are women. While some professors rate more highly as researchers than as teachers, according to students, a number emerge as quite open-minded and willing to help students who display an interest in their classes. Says a senior: "Some faculty members are very passionate about their fields but could be more passionate about the students. Others have great reputations and rapport among students and are also challenging." Students' chief complaint about the teaching assistants is the number, especially in math and engineering, whose English is difficult to understand.

Though Missouri's journalism program may be best known and held in the highest esteem by students of all majors, other fields of study also are well regarded. The College of Agriculture, Food and Natural Resources is noted for its grade A research equipment and well-designed programs, most notably in hotel and restaurant management and in food science. Many students like to combine the strengths of 2 outstanding programs by majoring in, for example, agricultural journalism. In the College of Arts and Science, English and history are cited for having excellent faculty and engaging courses. Psychology, chemistry, and the biological sciences offer extensive opportunities for undergraduate research. The physical and occupational therapy programs in the School of Health Professions are first-rate, as is the School of Accountancy, with its advisory board composed of representatives from the major accounting firms, in the College of Business. Accountancy recently became an integrated 5-year program in which students earn both bachelor's and master's degrees at the end. The College of Human Environmental Sciences, with majors in such fields as social work and family studies, offers plenty of close student-faculty interaction and a 400-hour internship that thoroughly prepares students for postgraduate careers.

The School of Fine Arts, in the College of Arts and Sciences, needs more up-to-date facilities that will support the strong talent among faculty and students. Says a fine-arts proponent: "Most recently, fine arts enthusiasts protested when plans for a new fine arts center, which is needed, were scrapped in favor of a parking garage." Plans yet again to construct a new fine arts center are contained in the university's current capital campaign. Other programs in the College of Arts and Sciences are criticized for the lack of advising they provide to students. Says a social work major: "There are not enough advisors and they don't have the opportunity to spend quality time with the students to devise an adequate academic plan." The opening in summer 2001 of Mizzou's new Student Success Center places the office of Advising Services in the same location as the Career Center and Academic Retention Services to make all support services more accessible to students. More advisers also have been hired.

Facilities: The main Ellis Library offers students both a quiet, relaxing place to study and a comprehensive research facility containing most of the university's 3.25 million volumes, 6.9 million microform items, and 26,886 periodicals. (The rest is spread among 7 branch libraries.) "We have an incredible amount of resources," observes a senior. "The most difficult part sometimes is finding where things are." MERLIN, the computerized catalog, helps to navigate and links Mizzou with resources at the university's 3 other branch campuses and with Saint Louis University. Two hundred electronic databases connect to students with a wide range of periodical articles. Renovation of the main-floor reference area during the summer of 2004 created a much-used Information Commons. Says a management major: "The new Information Commons has become a popular place to study and the addition of more Ethernet ports and wireless access throughout Ellis has made accessing such online resources as electronic reserves and online journals even easier."

Fourteen general-access computing labs and a dozen classroom sites contain more than 1000 workstations equipped with Macintosh and Linux computers, scanners, and color printers. One general use lab is open until 4 a.m., others until 1 a.m. or 2. Many labs stay open for 24 hours during finals although the student government during the 2005–2006 school year was weighing support for a lab to be open around the clock throughout the semester. In addition, 12 residence halls provide access to additional workstations. Residence halls are wired for in-room Ethernet access. A majority of the campus is wireless.

Special programs: Undergraduates may take courses at any of 3 private Missouri colleges and 1 smaller public university for the same rate they pay at Mizzou. For those longing to get further away, students may travel to any of 2000 programs in 27 countries. In a recent school year, more than 500 Mizzou students studied abroad. Internships are readily available in most majors, especially political science, as is a semester in the nation's capital. The university's increasingly popular service learning program involves at least 10% of Mizzou undergraduates in about 85 courses that include community service as part of their course content. A number of programs also are available to fund research by undergraduates in the physical sciences, social sciences, and other fields.

Campus life: Less than half, 42%, of the university's undergraduates reside on the 1358-acre campus which is distinguished by its historic quadrangle rimmed by red brick buildings and 6 freestanding Ionic columns in the middle, all that remains of a structure that burned in 1892. "Socially, the campus revels in its traditions," says a junior, "and most of the biggest events are related to tradition and expansions thereon." Going Greek is especially big, with about 20% of the men and 25% of the women belonging to 32 national fraternities and 25 national sororities. Greek members exert more influence on university life than their weekend parties indicate; they have held approximately 80% of the leadership positions on campus. Unless independent undergraduates choose to attend Greek parties or hook into other of the 442 recognized organizations on campus, those under the age of 21 sometimes find their social lives rather curtailed. While movies are a fairly common diversion on most campuses, students here boast that their films committee is one of the best in the country, and the featured flicks bear out this claim. The university has undertaken a number of educational efforts directed at making students more aware of campus safety. Recent emphasis has been placed on informing students about rape, advising women about what precautionary measures to take and what to do if such a crime occurs. A system of emergency telephones and "lightways," which are brightly lit sidewalks patrolled by ROTC cadets, helps to make undergraduates feel safer as does Students Walking Students, an escort system. An on-call shuttle service also runs from 6 p.m. until 2:30 a.m. As added insurance, campus police keep officers on bike patrol around the clock.

On most fall and winter weekends, attendance at Big Twelve Conference football and basketball games is a "must," usually followed, win or lose, by a social stop at a fraternity or residence hall party. Homecoming, which got its start as a national collegiate tradition at Mizzou in 1911, is not surprisingly one of the big campus events. Other of the 8 men's and 10 women's intercollegiate sports played in NCAA Division I draw smaller crowds. About half the students find release in the 26 different intramural sports available. Eight co-rec sports also are popular. In 2005, *Sports Illustrated on Campus* named the Mizzou Student Recreation Complex as the Number 1 college recreation facility in the country. Its amenities include a 50-meter competitive pool and diving well and a new climbing and bouldering wall.

When there is no major sporting event to attend or intramural game to play, many students slip away to lovely Lake of the Ozarks in south Missouri or to Kansas City or St. Louis, each about 2 hours away. The wineries in Rocheport or Herman, Missouri, also are popular getaways.

Cost cutters: Forty-four percent of the entering freshmen and 42% of continuing students in the 2005–2006 school year received some financial aid. The aid was need-based for 39% of the first-year students and

36% of the rest. The average freshman package in the 2005–2006 school year included a need-based scholarship or grant averaging $6110 and need-based self-help aid such as loans and jobs averaging $3939. Non-need-based athletic scholarships for first-year students averaged $9023. Average debt of a 2005 graduate was $17,907. A number of Mizzou's scholarships are available through the individual schools and colleges. Most other awards are restricted to state residents. Curators Scholars Awards pay $3500 a year to state residents drawn from the top 5% of their high school class with ACT composites of 28 or SAT math and critical reading scores of at least 1240; Mark Twain Nonresident Scholarships pay $4000 or $5500 to nonresident students with ACTs of 27 or above or SATs of at least 1200, ranking in the top fourth of their high-school class. Students majoring in 33 disciplines, including all of those offered in engineering as well as some in business, journalism, agriculture, and the arts and sciences, may take part in cooperative programs.

Rate of return: Eighty-four percent of entering freshmen return for the sophomore year. Thirty-seven percent go on to graduate in 4 years; 63%, in 5 years; 67%, in 6 years.

Payoff: Business at not quite 17%, journalism at 9.5%, and sociology at 9% were the top majors among 2005 graduates. Three-quarters of Mizzou graduates usually enter the job market immediately after earning their degrees, many with major firms like Upjohn, Procter and Gamble, and Marriott. Most stay in Missouri, although graduates of the renowned School of Journalism can end up anywhere around the world. Fifteen hundred companies or other organizations recruited on campus in the 2004–2005 school year. No figures are available on the portion of students who pursue advanced degrees.

Bottom line: Observes a marketing major: "Students who can adjust to being part of a large environment and not always having 1-on-1 attention succeed best at Mizzou. This is a school that will either prepare a student for the future or show him or her how to get on track elsewhere. Either way, no one leaves Mizzou without *some* kind of education."

University of Missouri, Rolla

Rolla, Missouri 65409

Setting: Small town
Control: Public
Undergraduate enrollment: 4250 men and women (full- and part-time)
Graduate enrollment: 1300 men and women
Student/faculty ratio: 14:1
Freshman profile: Middle 50% range SAT I verbal and math: 1140–1350; Middle 50% range ACT: 25–30. 40% graduated in top tenth of high school class; 61% in upper fifth.
Faculty profile: 99% Ph.D.'s

Tuition and fees: $7492 in-state; $17,502 out-of-state
Room and board: $5840
Freshman financial aid: 92%; average scholarship or grant: NA
Campus jobs: 38%; average earnings: $1080/year
Application deadline: July 1
Financial aid deadline: Nov. 1 (priority scholarship); Feb. 1 (regular scholarships); Mar. 1 (other aid)
Admissions information: (573) 341-4164; (800) 522-0938
e-mail: admissions@umr.edu
web site: www.umr.edu

A favorite mathematical formula at the University of Missouri, Rolla, the predominantly engineering campus of the state university system, is one that students won't find in any textbook but is held dear nonetheless: 3.0 GPA = 47K. Translated into words, it means that a student who graduates from the well-respected Rolla campus with a grade point average of 3.0 or higher is almost certain to be offered the average starting salary of at least $47,000. That's not a bad return on a tuition in the 2005–2006 school year of not quite $7500 for in-state residents and about $17,500 for out-of-staters.

Student body: State residents take full advantage of Rolla's formula for success, with 75% of the undergraduates from Missouri. Nearly 90% of the rest also are midwesterners, although a total of 43 states and 34 nations recently had residents on campus. Eighty-five percent are graduates of public schools. African-Americans recently accounted for 5% of the undergraduate population, followed by foreign nationals at 3%, Pacific Islanders at 3%, Hispanics at 2%, and Native Americans at 1%. Students tend to be very conservative ("the majority are Republican and white," says a senior), but they rarely get involved in social or political issues, preferring to focus most intently on individual career goals. Classmates use words like *determined, conscientious, apolitical,* and *hard-working* to describe themselves. Says a state resident: "I was expecting a lot of 'nerdy' people who were all study and no fun, but I found UMR to be full of intelligent people who know how to have fun, too!" Adds a senior: "Thankfully, there are no pocket protectors on campus." Though A's are hard to come by, students still strive for them, and the pursuit often becomes quite stressful. Many form study groups to help each other prepare for exams. Socially, undergraduates find the campus divided between those who get overinvolved in activities and academics, and those who concentrate solely on their studies. The result is graduates who leave Rolla with 2 very different views of campus life.

Academics: UMR, founded in 1870, offers degrees through the doctorate. Bachelor's degrees are awarded in 25 majors, most of them math and science oriented, with concentrations in a dozen different kinds of engineering. The academic year is divided into 2 semesters. For freshmen and sophomores, the average lecture enrolls 100–130 students (the largest, Engineering Physics, has about 150) with recitation groups of about 25 each. Upper-level lecture courses have around 30, with recitations of about 20.

General-education requirements vary by major, although all engineering students must take plenty of math and science plus a certain number of courses in the humanities and social sciences, as specified by the Accreditation Board for Engineering and Technology. Students complain that, while the same books are used and the same material is covered in these required classes, the great disparity in the quality of teachers heading the various course sections affects the workload and the grades assigned. A special advising program acquaints first-year engineering students with the opportunities available in each of the different fields of engineering before they choose specific majors. Only after completing 2 or 3 semesters of specified courses does a student decide in which engineering specialty he or she would like to concentrate.

All but 29 of the 304 full-time faculty and all but 18 of the 88 part-time faculty members taught undergraduates in a recent year. Just 14% of the faculty were women. Graduate students in a recent year, taught 25% of the introductory courses, mainly the introductory lab courses and some recitations. Student council members closely monitor the TAs for their English proficiency and quality of instruction. Undergraduates may anonymously complete a form over the Internet concerning any TA with a language proficiency problem so that the complaint can be addressed without repercussions for the student. Undergraduates find most of the regular faculty members to be extremely knowledgeable and generally helpful, though some, in the words of an engineering management major, tend to be "excellent researchers but poor teachers," who sometimes, have trouble communicating their ideas clearly to undergraduates. Others speak limited English that is difficult to understand. The fact that the total university enrollment numbers only 5600 makes it easier for undergraduates to have close working relationships with professors, especially the many who genuinely want their students to succeed. "Most are willing to take time for students out of class," say a chemical engineering major. "They put students before their research."

At UMR, an engineering student can't go wrong with any of the choices offered. Mechanical, civil, and electrical engineering are the largest departments with superb faculty and labs. Renovation and expansion of the existing mechanical engineering building began in fall 2005. The heart of the new Mechanical and Aerospace Engineering Complex, when completed, will be a Product Innovation and Creativity Center, which will enable students to learn leadership, teamwork, and communication skills while working on real-world, hands-on projects. The chemical engineering curriculum is particularly challenging. Students specializing in any of the smaller departments in the School of Materials, Energy, and Earth Resources, among them ceramic engineering and nuclear engineering, are treated to wonderful individual attention from faculty members. Nuclear engineering benefits from having its own nuclear reactor and a student-faculty ratio of less than 10 to 1. Students say, however, that the basic undergraduate labs in some areas could use upgrading. Engineering is not Rolla's only strong point; majors in biological sciences and chemistry provide rigorous alternatives with challenging courses and extensive opportunities for research. The math and physics departments "are excellent," notes a nuclear engineering major, "as they create the understanding and logical thinking in their classes needed for the rest of a student's engineering career." The history department also has a reputation for being "one of the best in the region," boasts a physics major.

With so much equipment, attention, and money focused on engineering and the other math- and science-related disciplines, it is not surprising that most other areas in the humanities and social sciences garner the lowest respect from students and the least amount of additional funding. Such "back-burner" majors include English, philosophy, and psychology. Some students think that the freshman engineering program could use better advising, especially for undecided engineering majors.

Facilities: When looking for students on the Rolla campus, one of the first places to search is the Curtis Laws Wilson Library, where undergraduates spend much of their time. The collection consists of 435,000 volumes and 1580 periodicals; and while it is generally adequate in materials related to science and technology. The resources available in nontechnical disciplines are far less satisfactory. For English or history papers, students often borrow materials from or simply go to the university campus in Columbia or St. Louis. A computerized catalog tells which materials are located locally or are available at the other university campuses. Numerous electronic journals and other resources of the Internet are available and well used. Students may check out laptops, and Ethernet hookups are available at all study tables. Many students wish the library were open around the clock to match the lengthy hours most of them study.

Undergraduates have access to about 650 networked IBM PC and Apple Macintosh microcomputers available at 38 Computer Learning Centers. Also available are about 100 various UNIX workstations. Many of the sites are open around the clock. Much of the campus also has gone wireless so students with their own laptops can use them just about anywhere. Says a sophomore: "Finding a computer to use is a non-issue."

Special programs: UMR offers a semester in London in cooperation with 6 other Missouri universities; other opportunities for study abroad are available in 20 countries. Internships are possible at the state legislature and with various engineering and science companies. The Opportunities for Undergraduate Research (OURE) Program lets students do research with a faculty advisor for 1 school year; the university funds the project and recently paid the student a $1000 stipend. About 100 projects were awarded in a recent school year.

Campus life: Just over half of UMR's undergraduates, 58%, reside on the 284-acre campus, which has at its northwest edge a partial reconstruction of Stonehenge as a tribute to man's technical and humanistic potential. Since about 40% of the enrollment are from the St. Louis area, many make the 90-mile drive home for the weekend. Fraternity and sorority events are popular. A fourth of the men are members of 20 national fraternities; a quarter of the women belong to 1 local and 5 national sororities. Some independents complain that Greeks "do their best to exclude non-Greeks"; as a result, those not involved in alternative parties or other activities join the traffic leaving town. Both sides, however, usually find themselves doing more than their share of weekend homework. The St. Patrick's Day celebration is the largest event on campus, with a parade and contests between organizations to honor the patron saint of engineering. The St. Pat's committee involves students year-round in planning the annual festivities, insuring that everyone has a green sweatshirt and other memorabilia before the big day arrives. The solar car student design team draws enthusiastic supporters on campus as well as across the nation following its victories in 2004 in the Formula Sun Grand Prix (completing a record-breaking 444 laps or 932.4 miles) and in 2003 in the American Solar Challenge (beating 19 other cars traveling Route 66 from Chicago to Los Angeles). Other design teams tackle such competitive projects as a radio-controlled airplane, concrete canoe, and a solar house. Crime is not a problem with ample emergency lights and phones around campus. The student council does a "lighting walk" several times a year with faculty and physical plant workers to insure that no areas are considered too dark and unsafe. Two alcohol-related deaths a few years ago have since led to an increase in alcohol awareness programs.

Miners basketball and football draw the most spectators of the 7 men's and 5 women's varsity sports played in NCAA Division II, but even those crowds are not always large. Intramural sports are especially popular: three-quarters of the men and a quarter of the women form teams representing the residence halls, Greeks, and special groups and compete in 19 sports for men and women. The club sports of rugby, water polo, and tae kwon do have especially strong followings.

Rolla (pop. 16,100) is located in the Ozark region, 90 miles southwest of St. Louis, and is considered by many to be an inexpensive but sometimes boring place in which to live. Those who don't go home or to St. Louis or Columbia sometimes take student-organized "float" trips down a nearby river or go camping, hiking, biking, or fishing. "Pretty much anywhere out of Rolla is an escape," says a Rolla resident.

Cost cutters: In a recent school year, 92% of the freshmen and 84% of the continuing students received financial aid. For 50% of all undergraduates the assistance was based on need. The average aid package totaled $9321, with no breakdown provided on the portion that was scholarships or grants or need-based self-help aid such as loans and jobs. A typical recent graduate left with $16,850 in debts. A number of merit awards are restricted to Missouri residents, among them the lucrative Chancellor's Scholarship that recently paid $12,000 in combination with other scholarships and grants to students who ranked in the top tenth of their high school class with an ACT score of 30 or higher. Excellence, Trustees, and Missouri Miner Scholarships pay varying amounts to high-ability nonresidents based on their standardized test scores, high school class rank and GPA. The priority deadline for consideration is Dec. 1. An installment plan allows students to pay fees in 5 segments each semester. Rolla's cooperative program is available to majors in engineering, computer science, geology, mathematics, physics, the social sciences, and the humanities.

Rate of return: Eighty-three percent of the freshmen return for the sophomore year. Just 14% graduate in 4 years, while 43% do so in 5 years, and 57% in 6 years.

Payoff: In a recent graduating class, 17% earned bachelor's degrees in mechanical engineering, 10.5% in civil engineering, and 10% in electrical engineering. Seventeen percent in a recent year went on immediately to pursue advanced degrees in engineering. The vast majority took jobs; for engineering majors the fields of work ranged from patent and trademark work to missile systems to consulting or design. Among the more than 500 companies and other organizations that recruit on campus and ultimately hire many Rolla graduates are IBM, Ford Motor, and du Pont, largely in the Midwest.

Bottom line: Being bright at UMR isn't enough, advises a recent graduate: "Students expecting to get by on past accomplishments or intelligence alone will not do well here—at least until they realize they need to study."

William Jewell College
Liberty, Missouri 64068

Setting: Suburban
Control: Private (Baptist)
Undergraduate enrollment: 529 men, 756 women
Graduate enrollment: None
Student/faculty ratio: 17:1
Freshman profile: Middle 50% ACT scores: 23–28. 30% graduated in top tenth of high school class; 60% in upper fourth.
Faculty profile: 65% Ph.D.'s
Tuition and fees: $18,500
Room and board: $5350

Freshman financial aid: 56%; average scholarship or grant: $12,773 need-based
Campus jobs: NA; average earnings: NA
Application deadline: Early decision: Nov. 15; regular: Aug. 15
Financial aid deadline: Mar. 1
Admissions information: (816) 781-7700, ext. 5137; (800) 753-7009
e-mail: admission@william.jewell.edu
web site: www.jewell.edu

When top students go to William Jewell College in Liberty, Missouri, they get a touch of elite Oxford and Cambridge universities at a price fit for a commoner. As part of the college's Oxbridge Alternative honors program, 10–20 freshmen and sophomores each year begin studies toward their major subject areas utilizing the one-to-one tutorial mode of instruction made famous at these British institutions. Oxbridge students spend all or part of the junior year at Oxford or Cambridge and take comprehensive examinations at the end of the senior year. Students not enrolled in the Oxbridge program who meet entrance requirements also may study at these prestigious universities. Altogether, Oxbridge and its offshoots attract high achievers to William Jewell, and the entire college benefits as a result.

Student body: Missouri is home to 75% of William Jewell students, with undergraduates present from 28 states, mainly in the Midwest, and 12 foreign countries. Ninety percent attended public schools. Thirty percent of the undergraduates are Baptist, with another 45% belonging to other Protestant denominations. Twenty percent are Catholic, and 5% claim another or no religious affiliation. African-Americans account for 4% of the enrollment, and there are 2% Hispanics and 1% each Asian-Americans and Native Americans. Thirteen students in the 2005–2006 school year were foreign nationals. Students are mainly conservative to moderate in their political views, ambitious, and hard-working, though a wide range of academic aptitude and effort are represented. Observes a midwesterner: "There is not a particularly high level of overt political or social awareness, but a handful of outspoken students cause there to be an increasing amount of discussion and action." Many are concerned about attaining good grades, though are usually friendly and supportive in their pursuit. Notes an Oxbridge participant: "The atmosphere at Jewell is fairly competitive in the junior and senior years, but the pressure is certainly not as intense in the first 2 years." The typical Jewell student also is involved in several different extracurricular activities.

Academics: The college was founded in 1849 as an all-male school to honor Dr. William Jewell, a frontier statesman and physician. Coed since 1921, it offers bachelor's degrees in 34 majors. However, students can design their own concentrations, a privilege that, say many who have done so, "allows for creativity and self-fulfillment." The academic year is divided into 2 semesters. Most classes for entering freshmen enroll between 20 and 35 people. The largest class, Cell and Molecular Biology has 39; Intermediate Greek has 1.

Students must complete a 3-level general-education program that draws heavily on interdisciplinary learning. Says a senior: "The things I have learned within this program have changed and challenged me academically, spiritually, and politically." In Level 1, students complete coursework in oral and written communication, math model building and statistics, and physical education and must demonstrate proficiency in a foreign language. All freshmen also must take a 4-hour humanities-based course entitled The

Responsible Self that probes what it means to be responsible from several cultural and ideological perspectives. As part of the Level II mandates, students must take 1 interdisciplinary course from 3 of 4 academic areas, the humanities, religion, the natural sciences, and social sciences, not including the area containing the student's major. Students may choose from a handful of humanities courses that deal with Cultures and Traditions; from religion courses studying the Sacred and the Secular; from natural sciences courses examining Science, Technology, and the Human Experience, and social science courses discussing Power and Justice in Society. Level III involves a capstone course focusing on issues of public concern and a college theme.

The faculty include 76 full-time members and 59 part-timers. Forty-nine percent are women. Although many of the college's best professors from various disciplines participate in the Oxbridge program, faculty members in the regular curriculum receive rave reviews as well from their students. Most score as high for their academic and teaching expertise as for their willingness to help students outside of class. Relates a sophomore: "I had a couple of professors e-mail me this summer to check up on me and offer advice about things to be considering in the next 3 years."

Among the traditional departments, English and music are noted for their strong faculties and high expectations for majors. Nursing offers a practical and innovative curriculum that consistently enables 100% of its graduates to pass the national licensure examination on the first try. Biology, biochemistry, and chemisty also feature a fine faculty, challenging curriculum with opportunities for intensive independent research, and great facilities. The programs in political science and international relations combine distinguished faculty with excellent opportunities for student internships.

The psychology program does not demand as much of its students as other disciplines do; many majors view it as a springboard to graduate school and not "the real thing" in itself. Business, too, carries a reputation for being a "fall-back" major for undergraduates not wishing to work harder in other programs. The foreign language department needs more professors of higher quality; majors are offered in French and Spanish and a minor in Japanese area studies. Art is among those smaller programs limited by having only 3 full-time professors. There is no sociology major.

Facilities: The Charles F. Curry Library is primarily a good place to study while it continues to build up its research collection, currently about 271,000 volumes and 780 periodicals. "We don't have many scientific journals, which is frustrating for me personally," says an Oxbridge molecular biology major. "However, we have a very helpful staff and an excellent interlibrary loan system with other colleges." An on-line catalog connects Curry with the holdings of 40 other Kansas City area libraries; extensive computerized databases and the Internet also help fill most students' research needs. Students head directly to Curry's second floor to avoid the socializing sometimes found on the lower levels. "Quiet, and wireless Internet . . . what more could you want?" asks an organizational communication major. Actually, respond some classmates, open hours past midnight would be helpful.

Undergraduates say lines are few for the 120 or so IBM and Apple PCs housed in the library and elsewhere. Most labs are open until at least 11 p.m. an hour that, again, many students find too early. The college strongly recommends that students have personal computers, and there are Internet hookups in every room. "Now that wireless is more widespread," says a senior; "you really can get on the network nearly anytime anywhere."

Special programs: Overseas study opportunities are available for as little as a few weeks to a full year in 30+ locations countries in Africa, Asia, Australia, Latin America, and Europe. Domestic off-campus programs are available at the United Nations, in Washington, D.C., or in Kansas City. A 3-2 engineering program is offered in conjunction with Washington or Columbia university or with the University of Missouri at Columbia or the University of Kansas. A 3-2 program in occupational therapy also is available with Washington University, as is one in forestry and environmental management with Duke. The 2-year Pryor Leadership Studies Program enables participants to learn and improve their leadership skills through placement in different environments ranging from an introductory seminar to an Outward Bound Experience to internships in vocational and volunteer settings.

Campus life: Not quite two-thirds of the students live on the 200-acre hilltop campus, whose red brick buildings with white columns are visible from all sides. On most weekends, students either head for home or hole up in the library for some extra work. On-campus study breaks are provided by the 3 national fraternities and 4 national sororities, to which a third of the men and women belong. Greek parties keep students, both members and nonmembers, around on big weekends, and relations between Greeks and independents are generally friendly. Also of great interest is the Harriman Arts program, which has attracted performers such as Luciano Pavarotti, Leontyne Price, and Itzhak Perlman, to Kansas City's Music Hall and Folly Theater at no cost to students. Christian Student Ministries is an especially popular student organization that puts on worship jam, a contemporary worship service, every Thursday night and oversees various religious groups, among them Alpha Omega, a Christian women's society. Unity Association focuses on increasing student diversity and understanding on campus. Campus crime generally is restricted to occasional car break-ins in the parking lot.

Cardinals football and basketball, 2 of 9 intercollegiate sports for men, also do their part to keep students on campus and out of the library. The men's sports, along with 9 for women, are played as part of NAIA competition. Fifty percent of the men turn out for 12 intramural sports; there are also 12 sports for women; 40% participate.

For escape, Kansas City is 20 minutes away. Students often take advantage of the close proximity to attend Royals baseball or Chiefs football games. Around Liberty (pop. 20,000), Taco Bell is usually packed at about 10 p.m. "Another late-night escape spot is Perkins restaurant," adds a senior, "but this is for serious study."

Cost cutters: Fifty-six percent of the freshmen and 57% of the continuing students received financial aid in the 2005–2006 school year; for all but about 7% of the recipients in both groups, the aid was need-based. The average need-based freshman aid package included a need-based scholarship or grant averaging $12,773 and need-based self-help aid averaging $4780. Graduating seniors in 2005 left with average debts of $17,133. Academic Scholarships, based on high school class rank within the top 30% and an ACT score of at least 23 pay $2000 to $8000 for each school year. The best and brightest who participate in Scholar Recognition Days may be eligible for one of 20 Jewell Scholarships that pay $9000 to full tuition. Twenty Oxbridge Honors Scholarships pay $9000 to high-ranking program participants. Other awards in the fields of music, athletics, journalism, art, and electronic media, debate, theater and church-related vocations also are available in varying amounts.

Rate of return: Eighty-one percent of the freshmen return for the sophomore year. Fifty-six percent graduate within 6 years.

Payoff: Twenty-five percent of the 2005 graduates earned degrees in business, 18% in health professions and related sciences and 9% in psychology. In a recent year, a third enrolled directly in graduate school. Many of the graduates seeking employment find jobs in the Kansas City area.

Bottom line: In both its Oxbridge and interdisciplinary general-education programs, William Jewell offers unusual opportunities for a hard-working student who enjoys studying and learning, not just working for a grade. In the words of a recent graduate, "Jewell has much to offer an exploring mind."

Montana

Carroll College

Helena, Montana 59625

Setting: Small town
Control: Private (Roman Catholic)
Undergraduate enrollment: 550 men, 733 women
Graduate enrollment: None
Student/faculty ratio: 14:1
Freshman profile: 3% scored over 700 on SAT I verbal; 22% scored 600–700; 45% 500–599; 30% below 500. 1% scored over 700 on SAT I math; 27% scored 600–700; 44% 500–599; 28% below 500. 7% scored above 28 on the ACT; 9% scored 27–28; 36% 24–26; 25% 21–23; 23% below 21. 37% graduated in top fifth of high school class; 69% in upper two-fifths.

Faculty profile: 70% Ph.D.'s
Tuition and fees: $17,078
Room and board: $6246
Freshman financial aid: 71%; average scholarship or grant: NA
Campus jobs: NA; average earnings: NA
Application deadline: June 1
Financial aid deadline: Mar. 1
Admissions information: (406) 447-4384; (800) 992-3648
e-mail: enroll@carroll.edu
web site: www.carroll.edu

When recent graduates of Carroll College in Helena, the state capital of Montana, talk about the "blast," they're usually not referring to the biggest party on campus. Very early on the morning of February 2, 1989, a runaway train collided with 2 tanker cars filled with hydrogen peroxide, causing an explosion that rocked the 180-year-old campus, injuring no one but blowing out all the windows in the main women's dormitory, knocking out power throughout campus—and the town—and causing damage of some sort to each of the 11 buildings at the college. All this would have been bad enough at high noon in the middle of summer, but it happened shortly before 5 a.m. on a morning when the thermometer read 34 degrees below zero but the temperature felt like 60 below with the wind. Town-gown relationships were put to their severest test: by noon, all 1200 students had been evacuated from the campus and placed in residents' homes. Once students were allowed to return to campus, they tallied their losses of ruined clothes and stereo systems and lived, in some cases, 3 to a room until the buildings could be repaired. "We have a very strong sense of community here, which was put to the test during the train explosion," recalls a recent graduate. "It was exciting to see us come together. I cannot stress enough the faculty-student and student-student closeness here." To which a member of the Class of 2007 adds: "Carroll is just one big happy family."

Student body: Just under two-thirds of the Carroll "family" are from Montana, with most of the other members also from the Northwest. However, a total of 30 states and 11 foreign countries have students on campus. Sixty-seven percent of the undergraduates are Catholic; 19% attended private or parochial schools. Foreign nationals, many from countries in the Pacific Rim, account for 2% of the student body. Hispanics, Native Americans, African-Americans, and Asian-Americans each comprise about 1%. Politically, there is a mix of Democrats and Republicans, though few are vocal about their preference. Carroll students are described as genuine, friendly, outgoing, and helpful to classmates in need. "Academically, we're full of study bugs," exclaims a junior, but most manage to keep up in their studies and also maintain a steady balance of social and athletic activities.

Academics: Carroll awards the bachelor's degree in 40 fields. Courses are divided between 2 semesters. An average class for freshmen enrolls about 20, though a history course, Montana and the West, has 66. The range in most upper-level classes is from 10 to 20 participants; Engineering Statistics has just 2.

All students are required to complete a core curriculum that begins with an Alpha Seminar that introduces all first-year students to the practices and values of a Catholic liberal arts education. The course emphasizes such vital skills as critical reading, writing, and discussion. Other components of the core include specific classes in theological foundations, college composition, and basic communication as well as students' choice of courses in 8 areas of knowledge. Students also must complete courses or experiences that explore the issues of global diversity and national diversity.

Fifty-three of the 135 faculty members are part-time; 38% are women. About a fourth of the faculty earned their bachelor's degrees at Carroll. Like their students, the professors seem to have attained a comfortable balance in their jobs, in this case between being tough and challenging undergraduates to do better, and being understanding and available at any time for individual help. "At Carroll," observes an out-of-stater, "the learning relationship is enhanced by the friendly respect involved." Adds a theology major, "I often go hiking with one of my professors, and another invites his classes over for homemade hot fudge sundaes!"

Biology is perhaps Carroll's most competitive major, with high standards, excellent professors, and numerous opportunities for student research. Facilities include a general laboratory and 3 advanced labs, an animal room, radio biology equipment, and a greenhouse. Thanks in part to the research-intensive approach to learning, 100% of one recent year's graduates who applied to medical school were admitted. Majors in chemistry and psychology are considered challenging and excellent as well; the new Mary Alice Fortin Science Center, housing 4 instructional chemistry labs and 2 instrumentation rooms, opened in 2000. Nursing is rigorous, too; 95% to 100% of its graduates consistently pass their national exams on the first try. Students rate the history faculty as brilliant, giving especially high marks to the seminar in which participants research, write, and evaluate major papers based on primary and secondary sources. The elementary education and public relations majors and the mathematics program, which provides a superb foundation for later studies in engineering, also are viewed as winners. For most engineering specialties, students take their first 3 years at Carroll as a mathematics major and then take 2 additional years at an affiliate university with an engineering program. However, Carroll has its own accredited civil engineering major that benefited in 2003 from a new 4290-square-foot laboratory with facilities for materials testing and for hydraulics and fluid mechanics experiments.

Though students find the few philosophy and theology professors to be excellent, more are needed so that additional courses can be offered every year instead of in alternate years; political science is understaffed, but first-rate as well. Within the fine arts, only a major in theater, a minor in music performance, and courses in visual art are offered and all 3 areas need additional space and faculty. Additional professors also are needed in the foreign language program; majors are offered only in French and Spanish with few classes in each. Students wish the environmental studies major had more of its own courses and did not rely so much on classes drawn from other departments.

Facilities: Student satisfaction with Corette Library depends on 2 factors: where the user sits, and what he or she is researching. "Finding your spot isn't too tough," says a senior. An undergraduate who studies in a quiet corner or closed conference room usually can get a lot accomplished, while those left to sit in the middle sections appear stuck "in a meeting place or social hour," says a sophomore. Though Corette's overall collection of 89,000 volumes and 504 periodicals is small and outdated in many fields, students researching topics in the natural sciences are more likely to find sufficient materials, while those needing information in the social sciences usually go on-line. The state and city/county libraries also are located in Helena. Database searches and electronic access to almost 10,000 full-text journals plus a computerized catalog make basic research a lot easier.

About 100 computers are available for student use around campus. The main computer lab, located in the science building, is open until midnight. All of the dormitories have their own smaller 24-hour labs. All residence hall rooms also are wired for access to the campus network. Wireless access is available on campus as well.

Special programs: Foreign study through the College Consortium for International Studies is possible in over two dozen countries for anywhere from 2 weeks during the summer to a full academic year. Study abroad is required for all French and Spanish majors. Three-two engineering programs are offered with Columbia, Gonzaga, and Montana State universities, with the universities of Notre Dame and Southern California, and with Montana Tech of the University of Montana.

Campus life: Fifty-four percent of Carroll's undergraduates, and 95% of all freshmen, live on the 64-acre campus. There are no fraternities or sororities, and residents usually turn out in large numbers for regularly scheduled dances, plays, movies, and other activities organized to keep them on campus. Carroll's Catholic foundation and relationship with the diocese of Helena are integral, though not controlling, aspects of the college. About 60% of the undergraduates regularly attend Mass, and a twice yearly weekend retreat draws about 150 participants. Community service involves about a third of the student body in work with various non-profit organizations. Crime is not much of a problem, although the women's dormitory is locked and closely monitored, with rules regarding times that men can be in the building. Additional lighting and security recently was added around campus. The city of Helena itself (pop. 24,000) has a low crime rate. Notes a student from a much larger Northwest city: "People leave their car running when they go into a store and it is always there when they get back."

Carroll students are good talkers. The Talking Saints Forensics team consistently ranks first in the Northwest, and in 2005 ranked fourth nationally among more than 200 colleges and universities of all sizes in the nation in parliamentary debate. (The team won the national championship in 1999.) Students aren't bad on the playing field, either. Fall weekends, everybody turns out to cheer for the Fighting Saints football team, which plays in the NAIA Frontier Conference and has been national champion from 2002 through 2005. Football, basketball, and swimming are the only 3 varsity sports for men, along with 5 sports for women, basketball, swimming, and volleyball, plus golf and soccer. Seventy percent of the men and half of the women participate in 10 men's, women's, and coed intramural sports, with increasing numbers every year enjoying the remodeled physical education building that emerged from the blast of '89. New athletic fields and a 4000-seat soccer-football stadium complete the package.

In fall and spring, students head for nearby Canyon Ferry and Spring Meadow lakes or take energizing bike rides or hikes into the mountains. Weekend float trips also are popular, as are skiing and snowboarding in winter. Glacier and Yellowstone national parks are each within a 3-hour drive of Helena. The capital city has little to offer on its own in the way of exciting nightlife.

Cost cutters: In the 2005–2006 school year, 71% of the freshmen and 68% of the continuing students received financial help. For about 60% of both groups, the aid was need-based. The average freshman award totaled $14,377, with no breakdown provided on the portion that was scholarships or grants, need-based or not, or need-based self-help aid such as loans and jobs. A typical 2005 graduate left with debts of $22,868. The Presidential Scholarship pays $8500 a year to new freshmen based on their GPAs and standardized test scores. Other merit awards pay $3500, $5000, and $7000 annually. Forensic/debate, athletic, and activity scholarships cover from a quarter to full tuition, renewable over 4 years. Cooperative programs are available to juniors and seniors in any academic major.

Rate of return: Seventy-nine percent of the freshmen who enter return for the sophomore year. Forty-three percent graduate in 4 years; 56% in 5 years, 57% in 6.

Payoff: Nearly half of the 2005 graduates earned bachelor's degrees in 3 majors, 21% in business, 14% in elementary education, and 10% in biology. In a recent year, 30% went directly on to graduate or professional schools. Two-thirds accepted employment with firms such as IBM, Microsoft, and Qwest Communication, and with various school districts and hospitals throughout the Northwest and Midwest. Ninety-five companies and organizations recruited on campus in a recent school year.

Bottom line: Sophisticated "high rollers" will not be happy at Carroll, where students relish a fairly simple life of studying, partying, and frequent forays into the mountains for hiking, biking, skiing, or snowboarding. Though Helena offers little in the way of big city glitter, true gold is found in the close relationships students form with faculty and with each other on campus.

Montana Tech
of the University of Montana

Butte, Montana 59701

Setting: Small city
Control: Public
Undergraduate enrollment: 1026 men, 684 women
Graduate enrollment: 23 men, 20 women
Student/faculty ratio: 17:1
Freshman profile: 2% scored over 700 on SAT I verbal; 24% scored 600–700; 40% 500–599; 34% below 500. 3% scored over 700 on SAT I math; 32% scored 600–700; 39% 500–599; 26% below 500. 0% scored above 28 on the ACT; 25% scored 27–28; 13% 24–26; 37% 21–23; 25% below 21. 35% graduated in top fifth of high school class; 66% in upper two-fifths.
Faculty profile: 75% Ph.D.'s

Tuition and fees: $5078 in-state; $14,070 out-of-state
Room and board: $5356
Freshman financial aid: 80%; average scholarship: $2000 need-based; $2000 non-need-based
Campus jobs: 23%; average earnings: $1800/year
Application deadline: Early decision: Feb. 1; regular: rolling
Financial aid deadline: Mar. 1 (Scholarships: Feb. 1)
Admissions information: (406) 496-4632; (800) 445-TECH
e-mail: admissions@mtech.edu
web site: www.mtech.edu

It used to be known as the college with the long, long name, Montana College of Mineral Science and Technology. In 1994, its new name became simply Montana Tech of the University of Montana, renamed in a reorganization of the state university system. The college was founded in 1893 on "the richest hill on earth," so called because of Butte's bulging veins of copper, zinc, manganese, and other mineral deposits. But today's students don't need blue blood or the Midas touch to enroll in this engineering school. For just under $20,000 in tuition, fees, room, and board for out-of-staters in the 2005–2006 school year, students at Montana Tech can choose from a mother lode of mineral- and energy-related engineering disciplines, and as Tech grads be appraised as the richest ore today's employers could ever want to mine.

Student body: Eighty-six percent of Montana Tech's students are from in-state, with the remaining 14% from 36 states and 16 foreign countries. Ninety percent graduated from public high schools. Two percent of the enrollment are foreign nationals, with 2% each Hispanic and Native American and 1% each African-American and Asian-American. Tech's nontraditional older students tend to be more liberal than their younger, more conservative classmates, many of whom are from small, rural communities, farms, and ranches. Although students are by and large logical in their thinking and focused on their careers, there are few hard-driving pursuers of the 4.0. Instead, students are openly friendly and casual and work together on difficult projects. "The majority of the students at Tech do everything 'all out,'" says a general engineering major. "Not only do students here work and study hard but they also play hard."

Academics: Montana Tech offers 29 undergraduate majors, 12 of them in engineering, and 9 master's degree programs. Half the undergraduates major in some field of engineering, half in the arts and sciences. Students take courses divided into 2 semesters, with the average class having about 21 members.

In an effort to make all Tech students better rounded, courses in communications, humanities, mathematical sciences, physical and life sciences, and social sciences are mandated. Students also must take 2 designated writing courses at the 3000 or 4000 level. Engineering students must, in addition, satisfy very detailed requirements within their individual majors. The end result for many, students say, is that there is little time to take a class simply for enjoyment.

Forty-three of the 150 faculty members are part-time. Eighty-one percent are men. Graduate students teach no courses. Most students are on a first-name basis with professors and find them easy to talk to, although not always easy to understand. A few in some disciplines are "so brilliant," say students, that they have difficulty explaining complex issues so that they are clear to undergraduates. A majority bring to the classroom a plethora of real-life experience gained while working in industry, and they continue to consult with outside businesses to stay current. Across the board, concludes a senior, "The faculty want every student to succeed and will work with him or her well beyond the call of duty." And it's not just Montana Tech students who have noticed. Within a recent 6-year period, the Carnegie Foundation for the Advancement of Teaching has chosen a Montana Tech professor as the state's professor of the year for 4 of those years.

The fields of engineering upon which Montana Tech built its reputation, petroleum, mining, and metallurgical-mineral processing, as well as newer offerings in such areas as environmental and software engineering, remain its strongest offerings with solid-gold faculty and rigorous curricula. Tech's enrollment in mining engineering and petroleum engineering are among the largest in the nation, and through advanced computer applications students can do computer-assisted mine planning and valuation. The $5.5 million building used for many of the metallurgical-mineral processing classes is rated "outstanding." Geological and geophysical engineering have superb instructors and state-of-the-art equipment, plus a natural laboratory in Butte and southwest Montana. Environmental engineering benefits from "exceptional" professors and extensive field trips to industrial operations. Likewise, petroleum engineering majors team classroom study with work in the natural field laboratories of Montana, adjacent oil-producing states, and the provinces of Canada, and in recent years have enjoyed frequent campus visits by recruiting companies. The popular general engineering program, which provides students flexibility to specialize in civil, mechanical, electrical, or welding engineering, or in another area of the student's choice, provides the breadth of classes and faculty expertise that enable students to tailor their degree programs.

Tech's College of Humanities, Social Sciences, and Information Technology, which offers degree options in business and information technology, information technology and design, liberal studies, and professional and technical communications is considered by some students, especially those in Tech's hard-core engineering disciplines, to have less challenging courses. Observes a business major: "The liberal studies department is almost out of place with its unconventional nature and placement among scientists."

Facilities: The library collection is small, about 167,000 volumes (though nearly 260,000 microform items) and 394 periodicals. The collection is rich in sources related to science, mathematics, geology, and their practical applications to engineering, especially all aspects of mining engineering. It is meager, however, in materials pertaining to the humanities and business. On-line and CD-ROM access to bibliographic databases is helpful; the brief hours, 7:30 a.m. until 10 p.m., are not. Students generally find the facility to be quiet and conducive to study.

More than 500 networked PCs are readily available at 9 labs around campus, with almost no wait ever necessary. Students also can have 24-hour-a-day access simply by "calling security to be let into the lab of their choice," says a sophomore. Hookups for student-owned PCs are provided in residence halls. As of fall 2005, the school had 3 wireless "hotspot" buildings but hoped to have wireless access in all buildings by fall 2006.

Special programs: A student/faculty exchange program is offered in petroleum and environmental engineering with the People's Republic of China and in mining engineering with Peru. Students also may cross-register for classes at Montana State University, the University of Montana, and Flathead Valley Community College.

Campus life: Just 13% of Montana Tech's students live on the 56-acre campus, located on the southern bench of Big Butte, from which the city takes its name. There are no fraternities or sororities, and a typical weekend revolves around socializing with friends at house parties or dances at uptown bars. Those who love the outdoors, however, are usually more than satisfied to go skiing, fishing, hiking, biking, rock climbing, or hunting within a few miles of campus. "You can't beat the location for outdoor activities," enthuses a junior from the Pacific Northwest. In fact, the opening day of hunting season rates right along with homecoming and St. Patrick's Day in Butte as a major annual event. Popular organizations on campus are the societies of Petroleum, Mining, and Geologic Engineers, Club Met, which promotes metallurgical and minerals processing engineering, and the Environmental Engineering, Ski, Fly-fishing, and International clubs; many hold meetings and activities during the week to encourage the large commuter population to participate. Occasional car break-ins have been the most serious crime on campus, although for the most part, students find crime to be "nonexistent."

The Tech Orediggers take part in 3 sports for men: football, basketball, and golf, and 3 for women: volleyball, golf, and basketball, in NAIA Division I. Football games draw the largest crowds. Sixteen percent of the men and 5% of the women take part in the 10 men's and 10 women's intramurals provided.

Butte (pop. 38,000) is a mining boom town that remains one of Montana's most colorful cities. It is located within an easy drive of some of the state's most spectacular scenery, at Glacier and Yellowstone national parks and the Pintlar and Bob Marshall wilderness areas. The surrounding mountain ranges, all part of the Continental Divide, offer plenty of places for quiet reflection.

Cost cutters: Eighty percent of the freshmen and continuing students received financial aid in the 2005–2006 school year; virtually all aid was need-based. The average freshman award for an entering student with need included a need-based scholarship or grant averaging $2000 and need-based self help aid such as loans and jobs averaging $4000. Non-need-based athletic scholarships for first-year students averaged $3236; other non-need-based awards and scholarships averaged $2000. The average graduate left with $11,500 in debts. Approximately one-third of any given freshman class shares more than 150 scholarship awards worth more than $1 million. A number of scholarships are available to both residents and nonresidents. The Freshman Challenge Scholarship, for example, recently paid $500 to $2000 to between 25 and 50 residents and nonresidents. The Freshman Academic Scholarship paid $500 to $1000 to 8–16 new students. Nonresidents who graduated in the top third of their high school class and carried GPAs of at least 3.20 and an ACT of 25 or higher or combined SATs of at least 1140 are eligible for Chancellor's Scholarships recently worth $2000. A number of awards for study in specific fields of engineering also are available. Cooperative programs are offered in most engineering majors, occupational safety and health, and computer science.

Rate of return: Sixty-one percent of the freshmen who enter return for the sophomore year. Forty percent graduate in 4 years; another 20%, in 5 years; and an additional 7%, in 6 years.

Payoff: Nearly half of the 2005 graduates earned bachelor's degrees in 3 fields: 17% in general engineering, 14% in petroleum engineering, and 12% in business and information technology. The vast majority of students take jobs immediately upon graduating, in computer science and engineering science with firms like Boeing, and in environmental engineering with companies like Arco, throughout the Northwest and West and in Texas. More than 150 companies and organizations recruited on campus in the 2004–2005 school year. A tenth of the graduates generally pursue advanced degrees in petroleum, mining, and minerals engineering, computer science, and geology. About 3% in recent years have gone on to business school.

Bottom line: Montana Tech takes high school graduates with a strong background in math and science and routinely turns them into highly sought engineers and other experts in mineral- and energy-related fields. Most of the engineering programs place 100% of their graduates, with an average annual salary of over $48,000. "The richest hill on earth" lives up to its name, "the best education for the money," concludes an out-of-stater.

The University of Montana

Missoula, Montana 59812

Setting: Small city
Control: Public
Undergraduate enrollment: 4470 men, 5150 women
Graduate enrollment: 569 men, 705 women
Student/faculty ratio: 20:1
Freshman profile: SAT/ACT scores: NA. 17% graduated in top tenth of high school class; 41% in upper fourth.
Faculty profile: 86% Ph.D.'s
Tuition and fees: $4944 in-state; $13,932 out-of-state

Room and board: $5658
Freshman financial aid: 79%; average scholarship or grant: $3069 need-based; $3000 non-need-based
Campus jobs: NA; average earnings: NA
Application deadline: Rolling (Priority: Mar. 1)
Financial aid deadline: Mar. 1
Admissions information: (406) 243-6266; (800) 462-8636
e-mail: admiss@umontana.edu
web site: www.umt.edu

Students who come to The University of Montana in Missoula are drawn as much by what can go on outside the classroom as what happens within. Outside, the attractions are readily apparent: breathtaking views of the snow-capped Rockies under Montana's ever-changing Big Sky. The campus is nestled in a beautiful valley that exudes healthful living and is within easy biking distance of one of the nation's largest wilderness areas. But Montana's wonders don't stop at the building's doors. Inside this small state university of just over 13,500 full- and part-time students is an emphasis on undergraduate teaching that brings astonishing results: the university has produced 28 Rhodes Scholars, a record that recently placed Montana 5th among U.S. public institutions and 17th among all colleges and universities nationwide in the number of students who receive these prestigious scholarships to Oxford. And all this comes at a price for in-staters and out-of-staters that is anything but sky high—about $10,600 for tuition, fees, room, and board for residents and just under $20,000 for nonresidents during the 2005–2006 school year.

Student body: About 70% of the undergraduates are from Montana, "and the remaining 30% wish they were," says an administrator, with most of the wannabe's coming from other northwestern states. All 50 states send students to the campus, though, as did 67 foreign countries in a recent year. All but a fifth generally are graduates of public high schools. Minority and foreign national students in a recent year comprised 7% of the enrollment, more than halfway to the university's goal of having its minority student body reflect the state's minority population of 10%. Four percent of the enrollment was Native Americans. One percent each was African-American, Asian-American, and Hispanic. The fact that at least a quarter of the students are typically older than 25 adds a real-life dimension to many classroom discussions. Notes a Montanan: "There are many neo-hippies and granolas, cowboys, loggers, yuppies, and nontraditional students." Undergraduates in general are easygoing and very accepting of personal differences. Observes a sophomore: "We are liberal (for the most part), well informed, socially, politically, and environmentally aware, and friendly." While there is respect for the 4.0 scholars, the general air about campus is fairly laid-back, with upper-level students more interested in discussing issues with the faculty than studying to get straight A's. Says a senior: "Students are outspoken in all their opinions. That makes for entertaining classes and social atmospheres. They keep everyone on their toes."

Academics: The University of Montana, which turned 110 in 2003, offers bachelor's degrees in about 50 majors plus master's degrees in nearly as many fields. Doctorates are awarded in 10 disciplines, including a juris doctor degree from the law school. Undergraduate programs are administered in the College of Arts and Sciences and 6 professional schools. High-ranking students from all subject areas can also take courses through the Davidson Honors College. The university follows a semester calendar. Most classes in the first 2 years have from 20 to 40 students; the largest classes, such as introductory history lectures, may enroll over 200. Many upper-level courses have as few as 10 participants.

General-education requirements are twofold. All students must demonstrate proficiency in such skills as writing, mathematics, and foreign languages or symbolic systems, for example, computer science or music. All juniors must complete a writing exam. Students must also take credits in an academic spectrum ranging from the expressive arts and ethical and human values to the natural and social sciences. Depending on high school preparation, the requirements can represent 25%–30% of the total credits needed for graduation.

The full-time faculty numbers 579 with 223 part-time members. No figure is available to show the portion that teaches at the graduate level only. Two percent of the introductory courses in a recent year were taught by graduate students, "some very good and some very bad," notes a junior. Women recently comprised a third of the total faculty pool. Students seem to genuinely like and admire most of their professors, who, in turn, demonstrate great concern for the success of their students. Notes a music major: "Many teachers are attracted to the way of life available here, so we get a better faculty than we normally would, based just on salaries." Adds a journalism major: "The professors put their hearts and souls into teaching at this university, and it shows."

Montana's business program is housed in a newer building with "remarkable" technology in the classrooms; all its programs are considered strong, especially accounting, which in a recent year, boasted the highest first-time passing rate in the nation on the Uniform Certified Public Accountant Examination. Students of drama and dance enjoy the benefits of a modern facility with 5-star equipment, which they have shared with students from the radio-television department of the School of Journalism. The journalism school gains much of its strength from its own dedicated faculty with strong professional backgrounds and a curriculum that has deep roots in the liberal arts: just one-fourth of the coursework is taken in the journalism school, with most classes in traditional areas such as history, literature, and psychology. Students must apply to be admitted to the journalism school in their junior year and must have already taken at least 3 semesters of preprofessional courses. The approach bears impressive results: 8 graduates of the UM Journalism School have won Pulitzer Prizes. A new building for the School of Journalism, scheduled to open in spring 2007, will bring the print and broadcast journalism departments under the same roof. Montana's traditionally strong forestry program enables students to gain invaluable field experience by spending a spring term at Forest Resources Camp in the university's 29,000-acre Lubrecht Experimental Forest. Wildlife biology majors also benefit from extensive fieldwork opportunities nearby. The 5-year pharmacy and physical therapy programs win respect, as does economics, especially its "cutting edge" classes in environmental economics. The foreign language department boasts top-flight computer-assisted learning aids and instruction in 8 languages, including Arabic and Persian; communication studies is noted for its highly skilled faculty and use of real-life cases in its coursework. Psychology, sociology, anthropology, and music are considered winners as well.

The School of Education has been overwhelmed by the large number of majors in this field, and the faculty, although strong, has been spread too thin to give students the kind of individual attention and advising that many need. A number of the science labs lack up-to-date equipment, but in these disciplines, too, students consider the faculty very good. Math has had too many teaching assistants who speak little or no English. Some students think too many members of the philosophy faculty "are more interested in their own philosophy rather than the philosophies of the world."

Facilities: Students are basically satisfied with the Maureen and Mike Mansfield Library, named for the late former U.S. senator from Montana and his wife, which holds most of the university's collection of 1 million volumes, nearly 2 million microform items, and 4700 periodicals. Specialized materials in law are housed at the law school. Though much of the book collection is considered "fairly old and out of date," students find the computerized cataloging system to be advanced, and the periodical collection to be more satisfactory, with easy computerized access to numerous databases in diverse fields, from education to wildlife management. Wireless Internet is available in the library as well. Since the library is usually quiet, many students do their serious studying there.

Six large general-use computer labs in the library, student center, and fine arts and liberal arts buildings, supplied with IBM PCs and Apples, make technology readily accessible to students. With closings before midnight, labs are not open as late into the evening as some users would like. A handful of computers also are located in each residence hall and are open around the clock. The university strongly recommends that students have personal computers. Wireless access is available in the library, the University Center, and several academic buildings.

Special programs: Montana students can attend any of 128 institutions across the United States for up to a year through the National Student Exchange. Student exchanges also are offered internationally with universities in Japan, China, Denmark, and New Zealand, or undergraduates may participate in Montana's own annual study-abroad programs in Europe, as well as semiannual trips to Japan and Russia and occasionally to China and South America. Internships are available at companies throughout Montana, as well as at the state capital in Helena. Cross registration for courses is possible with either of the university's affiliated campuses, Western Montana College in Dillon or Montana Tech in Butte.

Campus life: Just a fourth of the university's undergraduates reside on the 220-acre campus at the base of Mount Sentinel, which is frequented by grazing horses, deer, and an occasional mountain lion. Hiking up to the giant white M set on the mountain slope is a favorite mind-clearing and leg-stretching activity for the health-conscious students; the more daring hang-glide from Mount Sentinel's top. Greek life is moderately popular, with 10% of the men and 8% of the women members of 6 national fraternities and 4 national sororities in a recent year. Most undergraduates view these organizations as "simply one facet of our student body." Other students turn to the various musical groups or departmental associations, such as the Ad Club or the Foresters Club, noted for its wildly popular annual ball. Bike theft is the most common crime on campus, given the abundance of cyclists. Measures such as additional lighting along walkways, emergency telephones scattered around campus, and peepholes in the dormitory doors have been taken to ensure personal safety. There is also an escort system.

Montana students are very sports oriented. Seventy percent of the men and more than half of the women get involved in more than 30 intramural sports. Even larger numbers devote their extra hours to hiking, mountain biking, skiing, snowboarding, camping, rafting, kayaking, or hunting, in season. Of the 6 men's and 8 women's intercollegiate sports, Grizzly football (NCAA Division I-AA) and Grizzly basketball and Lady Griz basketball, both NCAA Division I, draw the biggest crowds and Lady Griz games are often sold out. "Football is huge here," says a Montanan, "and it's not unusual to find every seat filled in 23,088-seat Washington-Grizzly stadium." The football team won the national championship in the 2001–2002 school year; the Lazy Griz basketball team were Big Sky conference champs in 2004. In March 2006, the Griz basketball team advanced to the second round of the NCAA tournament, marking its first victory in the opening round since 1975. The Lady Griz soccer team also attracts steadily increasing crowds to its games. Observes a junior: "Griz fans range from the university students to Missoula residents to little kids decked out in Griz paraphernalia." The quintessential Griz fan, Monte, the mascot, was named the 2002 Capital One National Mascot of the Year. Sports clubs in rugby, rodeo, fencing, judo, and volleyball also are popular.

Since Missoula (pop. 90,000 including the surrounding Missoula Valley) is the biggest city in western Montana, students desiring greater urban excitement must head out of state: 200 miles west to Spokane, or even 250 miles further west to Seattle. Though Missoula offers a fairly active nightlife, most student escapes represent a search for a different type of wildlife; the most frequent destination is the nearest of 4 wilderness areas, known as the Rattlesnake and one of the nation's largest, just 1½ miles from campus. Glacier National Park is about 4 hours away; Yellowstone, closer to 5 hours. Mental escape is available every spring through award-winning nature films from around the world presented at the International Wildlife Film Festival held in Missoula.

Cost cutters: Montana's out-of-state tuition is not much more than the in-state rate charged at some other state universities, a lure that draws adventuresome freshmen to the northern Rockies. Seventy-nine percent of the freshmen and 83% of the continuing students received financial aid in a recent school year. Virtually all of the aid in both groups was need-based. The average freshman award for a student with need included a need-based scholarship or grant averaging $3069 and need-based self-help aid, such as loans and jobs, averaging $3961. Non-need-based athletic scholarships for first-year students averaged $2297; other non-need-based awards and scholarships averaged $3000. The average recent graduate left with debts of $15,700. The Presidential Leadership Scholarship pays either $8800 or $11,300 to up to 15 students who had a GPA of at least 3.80, and scored at least 28 on the ACT or 1260 on the math and critical reading portions of the SAT. One-year freshman scholarships are worth up to $1200 to students drawn from the upper fourth of their high school graduating class, with a GPA of 3.40 or higher and an ACT composite of at least 24 or SAT of at least 1890. Annual departmental and athletic awards vary in type and amount. Work opportunities are usually plentiful, with cooperative education programs available in most majors. A tuition installment pay plan also is an option.

Rate of return: Seventy-eight percent of the entering freshmen return for the sophomore year. Just 27% graduate in 4 years; 29% in 5 years; 57% within 6.

Payoff: Among recent graduates, business, education, and forestry were the 3 most popular majors, claiming 17%, 11%, and 9% respectively, of the bachelor's degrees awarded. A survey of recent bachelor's degree recipients found that nearly a quarter pursued advanced degrees after leaving the university; the largest numbers typically study business or the arts and sciences. Eighty-three percent were employed in their academic fields or in activities of their choice. Fifty-eight percent had found jobs in Montana. More than 75 companies and organizations recruited on the Montana campus during a recent school year.

Bottom line: Montana is a great deal for residents of Big Sky country, and also quite appealing to out-of-staters who yearn to study in wide-open spaces. In many liberal arts and professional fields, the University of Montana offers grade A academics and a quality of life that many find "laid back yet exciting." But be prepared: Many students who come to Montana end up wanting to stay there and have even been known to try to convince their parents to move there as well!

Nebraska

Creighton University

Omaha, Nebraska 68178

Setting: Urban
Control: Private (Roman Catholic-Jesuit)
Undergraduate enrollment: 1526 men, 2205 women
Graduate enrollment: 1105 men, 1256 women
Student/faculty ratio: 14:1
Freshman profile: 8% scored over 700 on SAT I verbal; 44% scored 600–700; 37% 500–599; 11% below 500. 11% scored over 700 on SAT I math; 47% scored 600–700; 33% 500–599; 9% below 500. 25% scored above 28 on the ACT; 20% scored 27–28; 29% 24–26; 19% 21–23; 7% below 21. 40% graduated in top tenth of high school class; 65% in upper fifth.

Faculty profile: 85% Ph.D.'s
Tuition and fees: $22,378
Room and board: $7540
Freshman financial aid: 86%; average scholarship or grant: $15,096 need-based; $8752 non-need-based
Campus jobs: 52%; average earnings: $1493/year
Application deadline: Aug. 1
Financial aid deadline: Apr. 1 (Scholarships: Jan. 1)
Admissions information: (402) 280-2703; (800) 282-5835
e-mail: admissions@creighton.edu
web site: www.creighton.edu

For some high school students, acceptance into the undergraduate college of their choice is not enough. Before they have cracked open their first book, they are already worried about where they'll be going to medical school or law school, and what their chances of admission will be. For this kind of student, and many others, Creighton University, Nebraska's Jesuit institution, is especially attractive. In addition to its undergraduate college of about 3700 full-time students, Creighton has highly respected schools of Medicine, Law, Dentistry, and Pharmacy and Health Professions. Although each of these professional programs receives many more applications than there are spaces available, they all give special consideration to Creighton undergraduates. The law school even allows some students in the College of Business Administration to earn both a bachelor's and a juris doctor degree in 6 years. It's just another way that the Jesuit-based Creighton education opens many doors, near at hand and far away, to its successful graduates. Says a senior biology-theology major: "I am prepared to succeed in the working world, while making decisions for the betterment of others."

Student body: Less than half of Creighton's undergraduates, 45%, are from Nebraska. Seventy percent of the rest also are midwesterners, although students congregate from 49 states and 40 foreign countries. Enrollment is tipped slightly in favor of graduates of public high schools (63%) over parochial or private ones (37%). Sixty-one percent of the undergraduates in a recent year were Catholic. Domestic minority and international students comprise 18% of the total, with almost 9% Asian-Americans, 3% each African-Americans and Hispanics, 2% foreign nationals, and 1% Native Americans. Students see themselves as moderate to conservative, caring, quite academically inclined, and highly self-motivated. An average grade is not sufficient for many, especially majors in the sciences and nursing and those hoping to gain admittance to medical, law, or dental school. "This intent," says a sophomore, "forces many more students to be competitive in the classroom." However, even the most serious students value Creighton's sense of family unity too much to disrupt it with hypercompetitive behavior. "Students are social-minded and know how to have fun," says a biology major, "but we also are responsible and realize that academics must have the 'front seat.'"

Academics: Creighton, founded in 1878, awards degrees through the doctorate. Bachelor's degrees can be pursued in more than 50 majors through the colleges of Arts and Sciences and Business Administration, as well as the School of Nursing. Creighton operates on a 2-semester calendar. Most classes in the first 2 years have from 20 to 30 students, although the largest survey courses in biology, psychology, and history enroll between 90 and 150. Juniors and seniors can expect most courses to range from a low of 8 to a high of 35.

Both undergraduate colleges and the School of Nursing have their own general-education requirements. The core curriculum in the College of Arts and Sciences addresses fundamental concepts, values, and methods of scholarly inquiry and intellectual debate. The core covers 18 hours each of courses in theology, philosophy, and ethics, and in culture, ideas, and civilizations; 7 hours in natural science, and 6 in social and behavioral sciences. Students also must take 12–15 hours in such skills as college writing, mathematics, foreign language, and communication or studio/performing arts and complete 4 writing-intensive courses. Says a classical civilizations major: "The core curriculum is rigorous but helps create a well-rounded student who is capable of thinking independently." The core curriculum in the School of Nursing has the same subject categories but different hour requirements; the business core is different overall.

Sixty-seven Jesuit priests reside on campus and teach classes in various departments, serving as a vital component of the 649-member faculty. A total of 475 faculty are full-time; of that number, 271 teach undergraduates only, although some of the others do teach some classes below the graduate level. Of the 174 part-time members, 112 teach undergraduates on a regular basis. Forty-three percent of the total pool are women. Most professors, though there are exceptions, are known for being eager to help students anytime, despite commitments to research and publications. Because faculty are so willing to assist, students find that coursework becomes challenging but not impossible and that going to class is a relatively pleasant experience. Says a senior: "These professors are helping me become a good person, not just a good student." Students' chief complaints focus on the quality of some of the adjuncts. Says a marketing major: "You will find these individuals filling the holes in all of the departments, and hole-fillers are about the only thing they are. I have suffered through several classes with adjuncts and been thoroughly disappointed. But keep in mind that I feel the majority of faculty is awesome. They have challenged my potential in class and shown their array of academic expertise."

The combination of demanding curricula and extraordinarily helpful faculty makes biology and chemistry in the College of Arts and Sciences and the Nursing Program 3 of the toughest and most respected majors on campus. Not far behind is political science (taken by many prelaw students), which, according to a major, features "a collection of diverse, impressive faculty who really focus hard on individual students. They help you plan years of your life, not just your college career." Theology, likewise, features professors "who really show a love for theology and pass this love onto their students," notes a sophomore. "In addition, the credentials they have are second to none." History, philosophy, atmospheric sciences, journalism, and psychology also are marked by great professors dedicated to excellence.

Some business majors find their program "unsatisfying," with too few courses offered in each major area, little variety, and too much focus on the basics of the field. "Many of the teachers," says a finance major, "have grown into old habits and refuse to change with the changing student faces." The accounting major is considered by some to be the strongest business offering; the program in management information systems, among the weakest. Says a management information systems major: "There just aren't enough qualified professors." Physics lacks sufficient faculty with a caring attitude and up-to-date equipment. The computer science faculty, several of whom are foreign, often are difficult to understand and sometimes "teach" by repeating word for word what is in the textbook.

Facilities: Creighton's 3 libraries house more than 854,000 volumes and over 23,000 paper and electronic periodicals; Reinert Alumni Memorial Library, the main undergraduate facility, holds more than half of this collection. The rest is divided between libraries at the law school and the health sciences center. When undergraduates need to concentrate, they usually head to the graduate libraries, as Reinert Alumni often is abuzz with students socializing. "The (main) library is the social hub of our campus," says a senior. "If you need to find someone, you go to the library." Student chatter isn't the only deterrent to concentrated study at Reinert Alumni; frustrated users also complain about dim lighting. Most users find both the computerized catalog listing book holdings at all 3 libraries and the database searches especially helpful. For additional assistance, the library is hooked into the local University of Nebraska campus.

More than 500 personal computers are available for student use in various labs throughout campus. The university strongly recommends that all students have personal computers; first-year pharmacy students are required to have their own units. Students especially like the wireless network pervasive throughout campus that enables them to go on-line in the library, student center, coffee shop, or outside.

Special programs: Undergraduates may study abroad in 41 countries. Creighton has its own semester abroad program in the Dominican Republic and an affiliate program at the University of Limerick in Ireland. Opportunities also can be arranged in Washington, D.C. An accelerated program in nursing enables those with a college degree to obtain a nursing degree in 1 year.

Campus life: Fifty-nine percent of the undergraduates reside on campus; all unmarried freshmen and sophomores from out of town are required to do so. The grounds are pleasant, covering 28 square blocks on the northwest edge of downtown Omaha, and are traversed by cobblestone paths and feature a huge water fountain. The university president can often be found sitting outside St. John's Church in the center of campus, chatting with students and listening to their concerns. Greek life is popular, involving a fifth of the men and just over a fourth of the women as members of 5 national fraternities and 6 national sororities. However, independents say little social significance is attached to going Greek, and most find plenty of alternative parties and activities to keep busy. Student groups from the Gay Straight Alliance to the African American and Native American student associations are quite active and visible around campus.

Skutt Student Center, constructed in 1987, and the adjoining Kiewit Physical Fitness Center, a block long and as wide as a football field, are favorite after-hours hangouts. Many attend Candlelight Mass on Sunday nights, although participation is neither required nor expected, and a number look forward to periodic weekend retreats sponsored by Campus Ministry and the Center for Service and Justice. Community service, sometimes for an afternoon in Omaha or occasionally for more extended time in such far-off places as the Dominican Republic, is vital to many. Notes a Nebraskan: "Many students keep service as a focal point in their lives here."

Creighton's urban setting keeps both the university's public safety officers and the students vigilant to the potential for violent crime. Breaking into cars has to date been the most serious offense, but students are constantly urged to walk with others off campus, to lock their car doors, and to keep valuables out of sight. Emergency phones recently were installed in the parking lots and around campus. A shuttle service is provided until 3 a.m. to and from campus for undergraduates living in Greek housing or other areas heavily populated by students. Strict visitation hours also are observed in the dormitories, where doors are locked at 7 p.m. Students also must swipe ID cards to enter academic buildings after 7 p.m.

NCAA Division I soccer, basketball, and baseball are biggest among the 6 men's and 8 women's intercollegiate sports teams. The men's soccer team, which draws enthusiastic fans to its weekday as well as weekend games, lost in the 2005 NCAA quarterfinals match, their fourth quarterfinal match in the last 6 seasons. More than 14,000 turned out in February 2004 to watch an opponent finally break the basketball team's 28-game home winning streak by 1 point. And baseball fans not only can root for the Blue Jays but also for other teams that gather for the College World Series, which the university hosts each June. Says a junior: "Spirituality is constantly very strong here but the excitement of Division I NCAA sporting events is also emphasized." Two-thirds of the men and 40% of the women take part in the approximately 20 intramural sports provided for each sex.

Of course, Omaha (pop. 353,000, with about 775,000 in the greater metropolitan area) is considered THE place for a great steak. On weekends, many students go downtown to the "Old Market" shops, which are within walking distance of Creighton. Road tripping to Kansas City, about 3½ hours south, also is popular.

Cost cutters: An endowment that has more than tripled since 1991 and stood at more than $239.5 million as of June 2005 has helped both to hold down costs and to provide additional financial support to students. Eighty-six percent of the freshmen and 67% of the returning students in the 2005–2006 school year received financial aid; for 59% of the freshmen and 41% of the continuing students, the help was need-based. The average freshman award consisted of need-based scholarships or grants averaging $15,096 and need-based self-help aid such as loans and jobs averaging $5188. Non-need-based athletic scholarships for first-year students averaged $18,577; other non-need-based scholarships or awards averaged $8752. Debts of the typical 2005 graduate totaled $26,013. A wide range of university-sponsored scholarships are available for top students, including 20 Presidential Scholarships, which pay three-quarters of the tuition. Other academic scholarships based on a student's grade point average and standardized test scores pay $4000 to $8000 a year. The Scott Scholarship pays full tuition to students enrolling in the College of Business Administration; to be considered, students should have a 3.9 GPA and either a 31 ACT or 1360 combined math and critical reading SATs.

Rate of return: Eighty-seven percent of entering freshmen return for the sophomore year. Sixty-three percent graduate in 4 years; 73%, in 5 years; 75%, in 6 years.

Payoff: Twenty-six percent of the 2005 graduates earned bachelor's degrees in health professions and related sciences, followed by another 21% in business/marketing, and 8% in biological/life sciences. Thirty-nine percent went immediately on to graduate or professional schools. The rest of the grads accepted jobs primarily in Nebraska, Colorado, Iowa, Minnesota, Illinois, and Missouri. About 200 firms, including such major corporations as Eli Lilly, US West Communication, and Union Pacific Railroad, interview yearly or post job notices on the Creighton campus.

Bottom line: Students with an eye toward graduate or professional school have much to gain at Creighton University. But so do other undergraduates seeking a challenging curriculum and a caring community bonded by the Jesuit respect for the individual. Notes a senior: "The sense of values and tradition makes Creighton a very comfortable place in which to learn and grow. It is big enough to offer individuals a wide variety of opportunities, but small enough so that everyone can be involved."

Hastings College

Hastings, Nebraska 68901

Setting: Rural
Control: Private (Presbyterian)
Undergraduate enrollment: 574 men, 547 women
Graduate enrollment: 12 men, 20 women
Student/faculty ratio: 14:1
Freshman profile: 16% scored over 700 on SAT I verbal; 28% scored 600–700; 43% 500–599; 13% below 500. 19% scored over 700 on SAT I math; 26% scored 600–700; 36% 500–599; 19% below 500. 15% scored above 28 on the ACT; 19% scored 27–28; 28% 24–26; 27% 21–23; 11% below 21. 55% graduated in top fifth of high school class; 88% in upper two fifths.

Faculty profile: 71% Ph.D.'s
Tuition and fees: $17,268
Room and board: $4950
Freshman financial aid: 99%; average scholarship or grant: $9643 need-based
Campus jobs: 37%; average earnings: $775/year
Application deadline: Aug. 1
Financial aid deadline: May 1
Admissions information: (402) 461-7403; (800) 532-7642
e-mail: mmolliconi@hastings.edu
web site: www.hastings.edu

When students at Hastings College in rural southeastern Nebraska offer adjectives to describe themselves, their choices are simple: *friendly, positive, sincere, involved, hard-working.* Make that *Hard-working,* with a capital *H.* While not as aggressive or outwardly competitive as students at more intense, better known schools, Hastings undergraduates take their studies very seriously and work hard toward their academic and professional goals. No wonder, then, that a student finishing in the middle of a recent graduating class carried a grade point average of 3.3984. The GPA required to graduate summa cum laude, in the top 3%, was 3.9774. Since 1980, Hastings has produced 10 of the prestigious Harry S. Truman Scholars; this designation is awarded annually to 1 student from each state who is preparing for careers in public service. "This college really expects a lot from you," observes a junior. "Trust me—you'll learn the true meaning of study once you arrive"—and what true value from a dollar can be, thanks to total costs of under $23,000 in the 2005–2006 school year.

Student body: About three-fourths of Hastings students are from Nebraska; most of the out-of-staters also are from the Midwest. Altogether, students gather from 23 states and 5 foreign countries. Thirty-eight percent of the students are Protestant (8% Presbyterian) and 22% are Catholic. Eighty-eight percent are graduates of public high schools. Just 5% are members of racial or ethnic minority groups: about 2.5% African-American, 1.5% Hispanic, and less than 1% each Asian-American and Native American. Fifteen international students attend as well. The Multicultural Student Union works to make students of different racial and ethnic backgrounds feel that they are an integral part of the campus community. "We're a reasonably diverse group in terms of interest," says a senior. "Whatever your interests may be, you can always find people who share the same passions."

Academics: Hastings, which was founded in 1882, offers the bachelor's degree in 61 majors in 31 areas of study plus a master of arts in teaching. The calendar is divided into 2 semesters with a 3-week interim term in January that allows students either to take an unusual course on campus or to get involved in an off-campus experience. During the regular semester, class sizes generally range between 20 and 30, with the largest lecture course, Human Anatomy and Physiology, recently enrolling about 45. Upper-level courses often have no more than 10 participants.

An undergraduate has 2 options in planning his or her course of study: the Liberal Arts Program and a self-designed approach. Hastings' Personalized Program enables students to design their own courses of study, after finishing 2 semesters at the school, with the guidance and approval of a faculty committee. Generally, just 10–15 students follow this path. The vast majority take the Liberal Arts Program, which requires coursework from 9 focus areas: student services (2 hours), computer tools (2 hours), health/wellness (2 hours), foreign language (6–8 hours), social science (6 hours), fine arts (4 hours), mathematics/science (7–9 hours), communication (5–7 hours), and the humanities (16 hours). In most areas, students may choose from various courses within each field. Says an English major: "Our strong core curriculum is responsible for breeding respect for academic studies beyond one's major, for extracurricular activities beyond one's talents, and for people whose backgrounds are different from one's own."

Few students have complaints about the other "core" at Hastings: its team of dedicated and demanding faculty members. Seventy-nine of the college's 121 faculty members are full-time; the remaining 42, part-time. Thirty-three percent are women. Students see nothing part-time about the expectations faculty have of students. "The faculty here really push their students to be the best," notes a double major. "They will not accept poor performance. If someone is in danger of failing a course, the professor usually meets with the person individually and takes time to find a way for improvement." Faculty members also sponsor many student clubs and organizations. Says a junior: "The faculty perform so well because they are progressive active learners themselves." The one bad side effect of such heavy involvement both in and out of the classroom, students say, is occasional faculty burnout around April.

Communication arts, business, and the sciences rank among Hastings' strongest academic programs. Students majoring in any of the programs within the Communication Arts/Business and Economics Department (CABE) take a special core of courses along with the liberal arts core. Communication majors receive hands-on training at the student-run radio and television stations, housed in the Gray Center for Communication Arts, which was dedicated by President Reagan in 1988. Students especially enjoy working on the award-winning "Bronco News Now," a student-run news program. Business, says a major, boasts "new classrooms with new technology, as well as professors with real-world experience." Biology, chemistry, physics, and mathematics professors are highly experienced and demanding. Plans to construct a new science building should answer growing student concern about outdated labs and equipment. Music offers wonderful practice rooms, each graced by a Steinway piano, and an excellent faculty. English features energetic and knowledgeable professors "who relate well and interact with students in a way to make each feel special," says an English major. Psychology and history boast similarly inspiring faculty. The art department, with its distinctive glass-blowing program, also draws praise from students, as does the education major, known for its emphasis on giving students field experience starting in their first year.

Other programs are hurt by their small size. The foreign language division offers majors only in Spanish and German, with just 2 full-time professors. The political science program, with a single full-time professor and two professors emeriti in the 2005–2006 school year, needs additional faculty members. The religion department needs to be housed in a single structure to better serve increasing student interest in its courses. The programs in sociology and theater arts also are small.

Facilities: Although Hastings has many impressive buildings, Perkins Library is not on the distinguished list. The facility, named for the inventor of Kool-Aid who lived in Hastings, is quiet with plenty of spots for secluded study but houses just 140,000 volumes and 935 periodicals. Additional computers, on-line databases, and an on-line catalog that connects students to resources at 10 other schools have helped alleviate most shortcomings. Along with the technological improvements, students especially like the overstuffed chairs and the free coffee and free water available.

Computer access is more satisfying, with more than 150 PCs and nearly 30 Macs available to students in numerous buildings across campus. The 2 main labs are open from 6 a.m. until 2 a.m., and a small lab in the student union never closes. There also are limited wireless spots located around campus that can handle approximately 100 users at one time.

Special programs: Opportunities for foreign study are increasing at Hastings. Student-faculty exchange programs exist with institutions in 7 countries, compared with just 3 a few years ago. As a result, students may study in Russia, Spain, The Netherlands, England, Germany, Northern Ireland, or Thailand. Hastings teams up to offer 3-2 engineering programs with Columbia and Washington universities and Georgia Institute of Technology, and 3-2 occupational therapy programs with Boston and Washington universities. A new Values and Vocation Program, funded by the Lilly Endowment, encourages students to think deeply about the ethical and spiritual dimensions of work and to consider careers of service to others.

Campus life: As a small college in a rural town of 24,000, 150 miles west of Omaha, Hastings relies heavily on the energy and involvement of its students for campus life. Three-quarters of the undergraduates live on the 109-acre campus, which, says a junior, "looks like a college should look." Six apartment buildings added since 2004, house nearly 300 upperclassmen. While a number of students still leave on any given weekend, more and more are finding or creating their own entertainment on campus. Notes a sophomore: "This college encourages student involvement, and it is not hard to keep very busy."

Bronco games, primarily football, basketball, and volleyball, played under NAIA Division II, draw good crowds. Women's basketball is a real crowd pleaser, especially following its back-to-back national championships in 2002 and 2003. Nearly half of the men and a third of the women participate in the 9 sports for each sex. Intramurals are especially big, with 93% of the men and 66% of the women taking part in the 9 men's and 9 women's sports and games offered, in everything from football to billiards to chess.

The 4 fraternities and 4 sororities at Hastings are local and involve just a fifth of the men and 30% of the women with no houses, "which does not create strong factions in our college community," says a senior. Peer Educators build awareness about AIDS, alcohol, acquaintance rape, and other serious issues. Ignite, a new campus group that combined three earlier campus ministries, attracts 50 to 100 students to its meetings and sponsors a number of campus events. The Artist Lecture Series Student Symposium Committee draws speakers, some nationally known, to campus to address a selected topic, most recently, Terrorism: Complexities, Controversy, Consequences." A student-run, nondenominational worship service is held every Wednesday morning, during which time no classes or other activities can be held, although attendance is not required. Crime, other than occasional tire slashings and petty theft, is not a problem. Nonetheless, residence halls are locked around the clock and dark areas along campus walkways and parking lots recently received new lighting.

Although some students make the drive to Lincoln to watch Nebraska football games, or to Omaha or Denver for more urban action, others in need of an off-campus getaway settle for nearby Heartwell Park or the larger community of Grand Island (pop. 33,000), just 15 minutes away.

Cost cutters: All but 1% of Hastings freshmen and all but 2% of continuing students received some form of financial aid in the 2005–2006 school year. For 79% of the first-year students and 71% of the rest the aid was need-based. The average freshman award included need-based scholarships or grants averaging $9643 and need-based self-help aid such as loans and jobs averaging $3868. Non-need-based athletic scholarships for first-year students averaged $4957. The average financial indebtedness of a 2005 graduate was $14,598. Many students are pleased with the aid available. Says an out-of-stater: "Because financial aid was so strong, I was able to bring down the cost of Hastings to what in-state tuition would have been for me at my state school."

The college uses just over a third of its tuition dollars, 36%, to fund various need-based grants and academic and special-skills scholarships. The Walter Scott Scholarship provides 3 full tuition awards. Students of superior academic achievement and strong leadership potential who compete for the Scott award are also considered for the Trustee's Scholarship valued at $10,000 a year, the President's Scholarship paying $8000 annually and the Pro Rege Scholarship that pays $6000 yearly. To be considered for the Scott scholarship, students must rank in the top fifth of their high school class, have an ACT composite of 26 or SAT combined math and critical reading score of at least 1170, and strong evidence of leadership in school and community activities. Other academic scholarships in varying amounts are awarded to students who graduated in the top third of their high school class or had a combined math and critical reading SAT score of 1050 or ACT composite of 23. Three additional full-tuition awards, the Kessler Scholarship, go to students of similar superior academic achievement who have outstanding potential for Christian leadership. Any student can choose to pay by 1 of 3 different plans including a 12-month installment plan in which payments begin in August and include a service charge of 1%.

Rate of return: Despite hefty financial aid, financial problems remain the chief reason why students leave Hastings early, as any of 6 public institutions in Nebraska can be attended for approximately half the tuition charged at Hastings. As a result, just 78% of all freshmen return for the sophomore year. Fifty-one percent graduate in 4 years; 61% in 5 years.

Payoff: Among 2005 graduates, 23% majored in education, 19% in business administration, and 13% in biology. Among recent alumni, not quite a fifth went on to pursue advanced degrees. Many business graduates found jobs with Coopers & Lybrand, State Farm Insurance, Norwest Financial, and the FDIC. Education majors usually prefer to stay and teach in Nebraska, although recent graduates have accepted jobs in Denver, Las Vegas, El Paso, and even Manchester, New Hampshire.

Bottom line: Advises a senior: "Students who come here must be able to adjust to a small campus 'family,' since everyone knows everyone else by the end of the school year. Hastings is best for the student who is outgoing, willing to participate in lots of campus organizations, and ready to study hard."

Nebraska Wesleyan University

Lincoln, Nebraska 68504

Setting: Suburban
Control: Private (United Methodist)
Undergraduate enrollment: 705 men, 901 women
Graduate enrollment: 0 men, 7 women (167 part-time)
Student/faculty ratio: 13:1
Freshman profile: 12% scored above 28 on the ACT; 12% scored 27–28; 28% 24–26; 29% 21–23; 19% below 21. 21% graduated in top tenth of high school class; 48% in upper fifth.
Faculty profile: 89% Ph.D.'s
Tuition and fees: $18,400

Room and board: $5015
Freshman financial aid: 97%; average scholarship or grant: $6806 need-based; $2098 non-need-based
Campus jobs: 25%; average earnings: $1300/year
Application deadline: Early decision: Nov 15; regular: May 1
Financial aid deadline: Aug. 15
Admissions information: (402) 465-2218; (800) 541-3818
e-mail: admissions@nebrwesleyan.edu
web site: www.nebrwesleyan.edu

Before prospective employers even begin to ask graduates of Nebraska Wesleyan University where they went to school, the alumni like to interject: "No, not the school with the football team—Lincoln's *other* university." Standing in the enormous shadow of the University of Nebraska at Lincoln, located just 4 miles away, might prove daunting to a less confident small school, but Nebraska Wesleyan knows what it is—and isn't. Though the university resumed offering masters degrees in fall 2001, after a 61-year hiatus, this small university of just over 1600 students continues to act as an intimate undergraduate college that offers its students opportunities for personal growth and leadership. In 2005, a Nebraska Wesleyan senior was named one of 32 Rhodes Scholars in the U.S, an award many consider to be one of the nation's most prestigious scholarships, which enables the recipient to study at Oxford University in England. Members of the United Methodist Church still sit on the college's governing board, and the church provides financial support for the religious life program. But, as an English major once said, "Our roots may go back to John Wesley, but education, not religion, is the primary concern here."

Student body: Ninety-two percent of the university's students are from the Cornhusker state. A majority of the out-of-staters also are Midwesterners, with residents of 25 states and 11 foreign countries on campus. A fifth of the undergraduates are Methodist, with nearly 40% members of other Protestant denominations and 23% Catholic. Four percent belong to various U.S. racial and ethnic minority groups, with 2% Hispanic and 1% each Asian-American and African-American. There are also 16 international students. Though organizations like the Rainbow Club work to bring minority and majority students closer together, increasing diversity is difficult. Notes a senior: "One must keep in mind that Nebraska itself (home to over 90% of the students) is not markedly diverse." Many of the undergraduates are from rural communities, are politically conservative ("but want to be more liberal in their thinking," says a Nebraskan), and value hard work and independence. "The average student is well read, opinionated, and fairly competitive," says a senior. "Who wins what award, sport, or activity is very important here." On the whole, the campus is very Nebraskan: friendly, warm, and down to earth. In the words of a state resident, "There is eye contact at Wesleyan."

Academics: Nebraska Wesleyan, founded in 1887, offers the bachelor's degree in 48 departmental and interdisciplinary majors. Master's of Science degrees in nursing and in forensic science were recently added to the undergraduate offerings. The school year is divided into 2 semesters and a January term. Most classes enroll between 20 and 30 students. Courses such as Introductory Biology are the largest with 160, although labs hold no more than 25. Some foreign language courses enroll as few as 3.

The general education curriculum, "Preparing for Global Citizenship," begins with a 9-hour first-year experience, plus courses of between 3 and 13 hours in such fields as global perspectives, Western intellectual and religious traditions, U.S. culture and society, fine arts, and scientific inquiry. Students find especially valuable the courses that expose them to issues of diversity in American culture and the world; many find the health and wellness requirement least helpful. Undergraduates also must complete a senior comprehensive, which can be either successful completion of a comprehensive exam in the major, a thesis or independent study, or a performance or internship appropriate to the major field of study.

The faculty is split between 102 full-time and 123 part-time members. All but one member of the full-time faculty teaches at the undergraduate level; all but 8 of the part-time do. Fifty-two percent are women. In a recent national study, Nebraska Wesleyan faculty members ranked in the top 10 among professors from 140 liberal arts colleges in terms of morale and satisfaction, a finding of no surprise to students who refer to many of their contented professors as "mentors." Observes a math and music major: "Professors recognize you even if they have never had you in class. And professors that have had you continue to be a part of your life academically and socially, inviting you to dinner or out for breakfast or coffee. That is just the best!" Adds a senior: "The faculty understands how important it is to make connections beyond standing up in front of the class every day."

Psychology offers an exciting program, best known on campus and off as the sponsor of the annual Xtreme Rat Challenge, known for nearly 30 years as the Rat Olympics until officials of the U.S. Olympic Committee threatened to sue the university in 2003 if it didn't change the name. The department also hosts a huge Psych Fair held every other year for state high school students. Facilities are excellent, too, including a sleep chamber, sensory deprivation equipment, and learning and motivation labs, part of the 3000 square feet of undergraduate lab space provided. "Business," boasts a major, "has a good faculty full of street-smart, not just book-smart, professors." Math has gained a reputation as a "progressive program," working to incorporate computers into the curriculum and experimenting with new teaching styles. The biology, chemistry, and physics departments feature outstanding faculty and curricula; grant money has helped upgrade the equipment. "While these classes are some of the most difficult," observes a history major, "the students that do complete these majors are much more likely to go to medical school." Political science, history, and English also are winners.

The communication and theater arts program has grown substantially in recent years and offers a hardworking faculty eager to work with students plus such extracurricular assets as an excellent theater with the largest costume library in the region and a successful forensics team. Says a communication major: "We also have a 'communication lunch' every Friday where we get together and discuss upcoming events or what is going on around campus." The music department likewise has claimed major improvements, adding new instruments, computers, and synthesizers, while maintaining a strong vocal music program. More faculty and resources for teaching foreign languages are needed; majors are offered in French, German, and Spanish plus a minor in Japanese. Religion is an example of a small major in which students often end up taking several courses from the same professor.

Facilities: Cochrane-Woods Library is changing with the times. No longer limited by its healthy collection of more than 207,000 volumes and 708 periodicals, the library offers a computerized catalog, an excellent web-based journal system, and networking with a consortium of 10 Nebraska colleges that share an automated library system. Undergraduates may also travel across town to use their student cards at the University of Nebraska libraries. As a study center, Cochrane-Woods rates an "XQ" for "extremely quiet."

One of the best features of the library is its computer facilities with IBM and Macintosh labs. In addition to the center at Cochrane-Woods, which keeps the same hours as the library, PCs are located in 35 different labs, 11 of them general use, spread across each of the Greek houses, in every dorm and academic department, and in the administration building. Altogether, the labs provide a total of 343 microcomputers, all of which are networked and were recently upgraded. Seven labs in residence halls and at least 1 general lab are open 24 hours. Concludes a senior: "The technology here is top-notch."

Special programs: Through university membership in the International Student Exchange Program, undergraduates may enroll in about 100 institutions located in 35 countries, from Argentina to Wales. Nebraska Wesleyan also has its own exchange agreement with Kwansei Gakuin University in Japan and offers a faculty-led program in Mexico. A student-teaching abroad program enables education majors to practice-teach in Australia, New Zealand, England, Ireland, Scotland, Wales, Germany, Taiwan, or India. Undergraduates with an interest in political affairs can spend a semester on Capitol Hill. The city of Lincoln, the state capital, also provides opportunities for internships in state government, national business, and banking. A 3-2 engineering program is offered with Columbia University in New York, Washington University in St. Louis, or the University of Nebraska across town.

Campus life: About 40% of the students reside in dormitories on the 50-acre campus, with another 20% living in fraternities and sororities; a majority of the 2 groups stay put on weekends though a number do head for nearby homes. With the University of Nebraska in town, "there's always something to do in Lincoln," observes a resident, and many find plenty to do right on campus. Almost a fourth of the men and women are members of 1 local and 3 national fraternities and 2 local and 2 national sororities. The fact that most functions remain open to nonmembers helps to boost interaction between Greeks and independents. Says a senior: "It is not a big deal to join a fraternity or sorority. Even if you do join one, you will end up hanging out with the same people anyway." There also is academic pride in being Greek here, as the grade point average of the fraternity and sorority chapters have been higher than the general campus average. The Global Service Learning Program, as well as various student government bodies and undergraduate positions on university committees and advisory groups such as the boards of Governors and Trustees, give students input on issues close to campus and farther afield. Says a student representative to the Board of Governors: "I actually hold a full voting position and have a full say in what happens in the meetings. The student voice at Nebraska Wesleyan is highly valued and appreciated." Undergraduates also serve as members of Campus Watch, teams of students who escort classmates at night. Over the last few years, a 24-hour security guard service, improved lighting, locks on dorm doors around the clock, and new security phones across campus have helped to keep Nebraska Wesleyan relatively crime-free.

Participation in intercollegiate sports is big: about two-fifths of the men and a fifth of the women compete on the 8 men's and 8 women's intercollegiate teams, as part of NCAA Division III and NAIA Division II. Men's basketball has been the big winner in recent years, with several regional and national NCAA standings that have meant sold-out home games. The football team attracts good crowds as well, and women's volleyball, soccer, and basketball have started drawing bigger crowds. Seventy-five percent of the men and 25% of the women participate on the 10 men's and 10 women's intramural teams, some of which are coed. In recent years, the college has gained several new recreational facilities, including a $9 million health and fitness center, football stadium, baseball field, all-weather track, and tennis courts.

Though Lincoln, as the state's second largest city (pop. 200,000) and home of the University of Nebraska's flagship campus, offers much in the way of local entertainment, trips to Omaha, 50 miles east, to Kansas City, and to the Colorado ski slopes are common getaways.

Cost cutters: As a student said: "Wesleyan has a scholarship for everyone"—or just about. Ninety-seven percent of the freshmen and 95% of the other undergraduates in the 2005–2006 school year received financial aid; about 70% of the undergraduates were on need-based assistance. The average freshman award for a student with financial need included a need-based scholarship or grant averaging $6806 and need-based self-help aid such as loans and jobs averaging $2370. Other non-need-based awards and scholarships averaged $2098. An average 2005 graduate who borrowed left with debts of $17,100. The Board of Governors Scholar Award pays $10,000 a year to students who scored 32 or higher on the ACT or 1410 or above on the combined math and critical reading portions of the SAT. Wesleyan Scholar Awards at $8500 a year, Trustees Scholarships at $7000 annually, President's Scholarships at $5500, and Recognition Scholarships at $4000 all reward strong standardized test scores and class rank. Talent scholarships are offered in art, music, and speech and theater. A monthly payment plan and deferred tuition loan also are options.

Rate of return: In 1986, just 70% of Nebraska Wesleyan's freshmen returned for the sophomore year. With better academic advising and an early-alert system to detect potential dropouts, the percentage of freshmen who come back for a second year has increased to 82%. Fifty-six percent go on to graduate in 4 years, 67% in 5 years, and 68% within 6.

Payoff: In the 2005 graduating class, 17% of the students majored in business administration, followed by 13.5% in education and 10% in nursing. Nearly 30% of the degree recipients proceed directly to graduate or professional schools. Two-thirds of the graduates seek higher degrees within 5 years of commencement. Those headed for the workplace tend to settle in the Midwest, taking jobs in business, social services, education, and government. More than 80 companies and organizations recruited on campus in the 2004–2005 school year.

Bottom line: Concludes a recent graduate: "At Nebraska Wesleyan, I was taught to deal with situations and problems in a general sense and am now able to put a number of sources to work for me to resolve them. And so, when I am asked, 'What can you do?' I can proudly respond, 'What have you got to offer?'"

Nevada

University of Nevada, Reno

Reno, Nevada 89557

Setting: Urban
Control: Public
Undergraduate enrollment: 4600 men, 5657 women
Graduate enrollment: 490 men, 611 women
Student/faculty ratio: 19:1
Freshman profile: 2% scored over 700 on SAT I verbal; 18% scored 600–700; 44% 500–599; 36% below 500. 2% scored over 700 on SAT I math; 22% scored 600–700; 44% 500–599; 32% below 500. 2% scored above 28 on the ACT; 8% scored 27–28; 27% 24–26; 32% 21–23; 31% below 21. Class rank data: NA
Faculty profile: 88% Ph.D.'s

Tuition and fees: $3270 in-state; $12,737 out-of-state
Room and board: $8885
Freshman financial aid: 29%; average scholarship or grant: $2805 need-based; $2797 non-need-based
Campus jobs: NA; average earnings: NA
Application deadline: Early action: Nov. 15; regular: Mar. 1
Financial aid deadline: None (Priority date: Feb. 1)
Admissions information: (775) 784-4700 x opt 1; (866) 2NEVADA
e-mail: asknevada@unr.edu
web site: www.unr.edu

Odds are that high school students don't immediately think "Nevada" when they're contemplating educational bargains. Nevada is a place where most people go to win big, and generally end up losing a lot. But amongst the slot machines and roulette wheels near the state's western border with California, the University of Nevada branch at Reno is getting winning reviews from students who expected only to come out even in an academic sense. Those who thought, "All the good students go to California," are finding that undergraduates from 49 states and 74 foreign countries have been seeking degrees in some of UNR's best-known fields, such as mining, engineering, and anthropology, or pursuing an unusual minor in Basque studies. "Partiers die here," warns a Wisconsin resident, "because the casinos are open 24 hours." But, for total costs of just $12,155 in-state and $21,622 out-of-state in the 2005–2006 school year, students with good study habits and clear goals who are willing to apply themselves may win the educational jackpot. Observes a westerner: "Reno allows students to advance at their own pace, and the small classes and faculty interest make everyone feel important."

Student body: Though some students travel from great distances to try their academic luck in Reno, 82% of the undergraduates are state residents and 63% of the rest are also westerners. Hispanics account for the largest contingent of minority students at 7%; Asian-Americans make up 6%; African-Americans, 2%, and Native Americans, 1%. Foreign nationals comprise 4%. UNR's greatest diversity comes from the maturity of its undergraduates, whose average age is 22. While the average age of freshmen is a fairly typical 18, the average age shows a steady rise through the classes, with juniors averaging 25 years and seniors, 28. Partly because of the range of ages, the student body is more varied than that at more traditional state universities, including older students carrying full-time jobs as well as classes, more youthful members of the very active Greek organizations, students who commute from their parents' homes, and the minority, just 14%, who live on campus. Says a senior: "It's not so much a question of what students are like here but more of what a student would like to find. Students here cover everything." Such a large number of commuters, however, means a dearth of school spirit, outside of the Greeks. And while undergraduates are not apathetic about their studies, there is little noticeable drive to excel. Notes a junior, "Students here know when it is time to let their hair down, and when it is time to put their noses in the books."

Academics: The university, founded in 1874, offers bachelor's, master's, and doctorate degrees. More than 70 undergraduate majors are available through 7 colleges and 3 schools. The academic year is divided into 2 semesters. Classes for freshmen can range from Elementary French with 20 students at most to Survey of American Constitutional History, which recently enrolled 300. Classes for juniors and seniors have 10–40 participants, although courses in fields such as English and political science are sometimes larger.

Regardless of major, every student has to complete a university core curriculum that gives a choice of courses in mathematics, natural sciences, social sciences, and fine arts. Every freshman is placed in 1 of 3 levels of a first-year writing course, depending on his or her ACT or SAT score. Everyone also takes the same 3 required classes in Core Humanities but concludes his or her coursework in the senior year with

2 capstone courses related to the major. The core covers up to 36 of the 124 or more semester credits required for graduation.

The total faculty numbers 909 full-time members and 90 part-time. Of the 909 full-time faculty members, 560 teach undergraduates, as do 42 of the 90 part-timers. Thirty-seven percent of the full-time faculty are women. Five faculty members have won Pulitzer Prizes. The faculty vary in quality from the enlightened and enthusiastic to the disinterested and dull; but, whatever their merit, a majority tend to be available when students need them. Most, say undergraduates, are easy to approach with questions and seem to enjoy sharing their knowledge as well as their time. Graduate students teach 8% of the introductory courses. Their quality varies as much as that of the professors, from those "who are great if not better than the professors," according to one sophomore to others "who are very well educated and teach well but who don't speak English well enough (for us) to understand them," according to another.

The College of Engineering, with majors in civil, electrical, and mechanical engineering, and the mining-related programs in the College of Science both offer excellent faculties, up-to-date equipment, and ample resources, largely because of the importance of these fields to the state. The College of Science features 2 recently constructed, 60,000-square-foot buildings that house undergraduate and advanced laboratories equipped with sophisticated instrumentation for the study of mining, chemical, and metallurgical engineering, and geological sciences. The program in logistics management in the College of Business Administration was the first of its kind on the West coast and still holds a primary place, according to satisfied majors. Journalism students point with pride to their headliner faculty and demanding curriculum. The speech pathology and audiology department in the School of Medicine offers a clinic at which undergraduates gain first-hand experience. The College of Agriculture, Biotechnology and Natural Resources provides excellent training facilities, with several farms and other stations. In the College of Liberal Arts, anthropology is a winner, given the university's location in the Great Basin, as are chemistry, biochemistry, mathematics, physics, and geography in the College of Science. "The sciences offer excellent professors and tutoring programs," says a biochemistry major. "Professors and staff are very willing to help answer any questions."

Students say that programs related to the fine arts, such as art, music, and theater, have less support on campus and more limited course offerings. Education majors complain that their college is often disorganized, sometimes no longer offering courses that prospective teachers are required to take or giving conflicting information to advisees. Only French, German, and Spanish are offered as foreign-language majors, although minors are available in Basque, Italian, Latin American, and Japanese studies and courses in Russian, classical Greek, and Latin. Students say better advising and more challenging coursework is needed in many of the social sciences in the College of Liberal Arts, as well as in some of the larger programs in the College of Business Administration.

Facilities: Groundbreaking for a new 295,000-square-foot Knowledge Center took place in September 2005. The Knowledge Center, which is expected to open in 2007, will replace the current main Noble Getchell Library with a technologically advanced facility. The current Getchell Library and 5 branch facilities hold nearly 1.1 million volumes, 3.4 million microform items, and 15,900 paper and electronic periodicals. The 5 branches house materials related to engineering, life and health sciences, medicine, mines, and physical sciences. Undergraduates generally find Getchell to be too noisy for concentrated study, though the smaller facilities "are excellent for studying," says a sophomore. "Very quiet and empty." WolfPAC, the computerized catalog, provides access to most of the university's holdings through terminals around campus. More than 100 electronic databases, as well as access to the Internet, provide additional support. Also located on the UNR campus is the 70,000-volume law library of the National Judicial College, an affiliate of the American Bar Association.

More than 1000 computers are spread among just about every academic building and residence hall. Waiting has occurred most frequently at the computer lab on the lower level of the main library. Wireless service for students with laptops is available in 32 campus buildings and in 4 outdoor areas.

Special programs: Through the National Student Exchange, undergraduates may study at any of more than 120 colleges and universities across the United States while paying tuition, room, and board at Reno rates. A consortium including Reno and 16 other universities enables students to study on 7 European campuses, 2 Latin American campuses, and campuses in Australia, New Zealand, China, Israel, and Thailand. Reno's proximity to the state capital in Carson City expands internship possibilities in political science and related fields.

Campus life: The predominantly commuter campus, spread over 290 acres just north of Reno's business district, has an eastern look with its ivy-covered red brick and white pillars. However, the low-key lifestyle is very western. Just 7% of the men and 6% of the women are members of 2 local and 11 national social fraternities and 4 national sororities. For many, the Greeks represent the primary extracurricular life, and nonmembers like to get on their guest lists for parties. "Because so much of the student body is apathetic," notes a senior, "the Greeks control everything, which is good if you are Greek." In an effort to increase the alternative entertainment for all, a creative programming group called Flipside, started by the student government, has added comedy clubs, music groups, and other events, helping to triple the number of on-campus activities. To further enhance campus life, a new student union, adjacent to the new Knowledge Center, also was under construction in the 2005–2006 school year with opening scheduled for fall 2007. Despite the campus' proximity to downtown Reno, an increase in police patrols and lighting and a reliable escort service keep crime at a distance. Petty theft and instances of students driving under the influence of alcohol are the primary incidents.

Even commuters have a way of coming back for Wolf Pack football, the biggest of Reno's 7 men's and 8 women's sporting events which are played in NCAA Division I. Tailgaters and all-day parties, again sponsored mainly by the Greeks, are part of the frenzy of home games, heightened whenever the team ranks highly in its division. Basketball also is big, as is the "Blue Crew," who turns out to raise school spirit and support for all Wolf Pack teams. Two-thirds of the undergraduates engage in 14 men's and 11 women's intramural sports. Skiing, snowboarding, hiking, and biking are favorite independent forms of recreation.

The Reno-Sparks area (pop. 290,000) is ideally situated for easy getaways to scenic Lake Tahoe, just 30 miles west, during the spring and fall; to nearby ski resorts, such as Squaw Valley, during the winter months; and to San Francisco, 250 miles west, for a weekend anytime.

Cost cutters: Twenty-nine percent of the freshmen in the 2005–2006 school year and 32% of the continuing students received some form of financial aid; aid was need-based for 15% of the first-year students and 22% of the rest. The average aid package for a first-year student with need included a need-based scholarship or grant averaging $2805 and need-based self-help aid such as loans and jobs averaging $2718. The average non-need-based athletic scholarship for freshmen totaled $10,950; other non-need-based awards and scholarships averaged $2797. The average debt of a 2005 graduate was $16,273. High-achieving state residents benefit most from scholarship funding. President's Scholarships paying $4000 annually are available to 25 Nevada residents with ACT composite scores of at least 31 or SAT combined math and critical reading scores of 1380 and minimum GPAs of 3.5. The Governor Guinn Millennium Scholarship pays $80 a credit hour ($960 maximum per semester) to state high school graduates with 3.25 GPAs and required high school courses. Most other scholarships range from $500 to $2500. The University also awards a number of out-of-state tuition grants-in-aid that recently were worth $1250 a semester and are based upon academic proficiency and the rendering of a special service to the university. Cooperative programs are available in engineering.

Rate of return: Seventy-five percent of the entering freshmen return for the sophomore year compared with just below 60% a decade ago. Nevertheless, just 15% graduate in 4 years, 39% in 5 years, and 47% in 6 years. While low, these figures are 4 to 6 percentage points higher at each level than a couple of years before.

Payoff: Among 2005 graduates, 7% earned bachelor's degrees in general studies, 5% in elementry education, and 5% in psychology. In a recent year two-thirds of the graduates accepted jobs immediately in areas such as management and teaching, primarily in the West. A third attended graduate school, either full- or part-time, in the arts and sciences. Within 5 years of earning their bachelor's degrees from Reno, 60% of the graduates go on to advanced study.

Bottom line: The University of Nevada, Reno is a place where serious students can get a good education, and those who are socially inclined can have fun and perhaps pick up a degree sometime over the next 6 years or so. For undergraduates seeking a more traditional campus life, going Greek is the best buffer against the apathy of a largely commuter campus.

New Hampshire

University of New Hampshire

Durham, New Hampshire 03824

Setting: Small town
Control: Public
Undergraduate enrollment: 4677 men, 6131 women
Graduate enrollment: 467 men, 770 women
Student/faculty ratio: 14:1
Freshman profile: 3% scored over 700 on SAT I verbal; 25% scored 600–700; 51% 500–599; 21% below 500. 4% scored over 700 on SAT I math; 29% scored 600–700; 49% 500–599; 18% below 500. 20% graduated in top tenth of high school class; 47% in upper fifth.
Faculty profile: 91% Ph.D.'s
Tuition and fees: $9778 in-state; $21,498 out-of-state

Room and board: $7032
Freshman financial aid: 84%; average scholarship or grant: $2708 in-state $8650 out-of-state need-based; $4164 in-state $28,462 out-of-state non-need-based
Campus jobs: 34%; average earnings: $1763/year
Application deadline: Early action: Dec. 1; regular: Feb. 1
Financial aid deadline: Mar. 1
Admissions information: (603) 862-1360
e-mail: admissions@unh.edu
web site: www.unh.edu

The University of New Hampshire may have opened in Hanover in 1866 as part of Dartmouth College, but it long ago came into its own as a major research university where undergraduates find themselves at the center of academic life. The 200-acre campus, described as "expansive, green, and quiet," is divided by College Brook flowing through the middle and is dotted with 80 kinds of trees and 75 different types of wildflowers. At the edge of campus are 260 acres known as College Woods, where students hike, jog, or cross-country ski along 5 miles of paths, depending on the season and the depth of snow. Also surrounding the campus is another 2400 acres of university-owned fields, farms, and woodlands. Boston is but an hour away, and the White Mountains just 30 minutes more; beach-lovers can be at the ocean in as little as 15 minutes. But the tranquil surroundings are only part of UNH's amenities. Notes an engineering major: "It offers a private-school atmosphere with the breadth of a large university." Adds a communication and theater major: "UNH has an unbelievably friendly environment where the students are constantly interacting with each other and with the faculty." Even better, it does all that at a shrewd educational bargain any Yankee-minded out-of-stater would love.

Student body: Fifty-seven percent of UNH students are from in-state, with 77% of the rest also from the Northeast. However, undergraduates travel from 44 states and 26 foreign countries to attend. Three-quarters of the students graduated from public secondary schools. Asian-Americans and Hispanics each account for 2% of the enrollment; African-Americans comprise 1%. Foreign nationals also make up 1%. Though the total is small, it nonetheless reflects a steady increase in the number of minorities over the last few years. Students are casual and down to earth, energetic and "active, active, active," observes a senior. "Having too much to do is never enough on this campus." Politically, students are not as conservative as many classmates expected them to be. One New Yorker described the student body as being "on the conservatively liberal side and enveloped with middle-class attitudes." Although few actively participate in rallies or political debates, a Yankee streak of independence engages many in self-initiated activities, mostly outdoors. The academic climate, observes a junior, "ranges from committed to distracted." What newcomers may interpret as an intense rush to class in the chilly winter months usually slows to a more amiable pace once spring arrives. "Students get friendlier as the weather warms up," observes a Bay Stater.

Academics: UNH offers degrees through the doctorate, with 100 majors and 2000 courses offered at the baccalaureate level alone. Undergraduates are concentrated in 6 colleges and schools. The academic year is divided into 2 semesters. Freshmen can anticipate 2 classes of approximately 200 people each in most required survey courses and others of between 15 and 30 students. (First-year English classes are limited to 25.) By junior year, classes within the major rarely exceed 50 and generally range from 25 to 30.

All students must take first-year courses in writing and quantitative reasoning, 3 courses in biological science, physical science, or technology, and 1 course each in historical perspective, foreign culture, fine arts, social science, and philosophy, literature, and ideas. Seven of the required courses must be "writing intensive," including the freshman year course in composition, an upper level course, and 1 course in the major. First-year students also can choose from dozens of small "inquiry seminars." Taught by top faculty, inquiry seminars offer interdisciplinary study of such topics as global warming, civil rights, and risk taking, and satisfy general education requirements. Undergraduates generally value the breadth of topics to which they are introduced yet complain that, because most of the survey classes are so large, it is impossible to acquire more than a superficial grasp of the material. Some of the more popular courses also can be difficult to get.

The full-time faculty numbers 574 with 77 part-timers. All but 71 of the 574 full-time members teach undergraduates; all but 3 of the 77 part-timers do. Thirty-eight percent of the faculty are women. Just 2% of the introductory courses are taught by graduate students. For a major research university where professors have gained national and international recognition, students find most of the faculty to be down to earth and dedicated and, says a senior, "not only available but also encouraging and enthusiastic. They don't just teach their material; they inspire students through it." One professor of Shakespeare, for example, took students during after-class hours to see performances of the Bard's plays in Portland, Maine, and in Boston. Intensive faculty research generally is conducted during sabbatical leaves, so as not to interfere with classroom work.

English in the College of Liberal Arts emerges as one of UNH's most respected disciplines. Classes in the department are kept small, and undergraduates have easy access to some of the university's most distinguished yet approachable professors; 2 are nationally recognized experts in teaching writing, and others have won numerous fellowships and awards for their work. A Pulitzer prize-winning poet teaches many poetry classes each semester. Professors in the English/journalism program insure that "students do not just learn and understand." says a major, "They *do* and understand." History isn't to be outdone in the awards department: in a recent 5-year span, 6 faculty members in the department received national book awards for works dealing with subjects from African-American sailors to religion in Roman Egypt. Theater gets an ovation as well from its students. The College of Engineering and Physical Sciences garners student votes for being demanding and competitive in virtually all disciplines. The Whittemore School of Business and Economics is widely respected around campus. The hotel administration program, in particular, stresses practical experience, gained largely through operating the food and lodging operations at the school's own on-campus learning laboratory, the New England Center Hotel and Conference Center. Revamping of the business administration program has produced cutting-edge options in such fields as entrepreneurial venture creation, international business and economics, and information systems. The undergraduate program in marine and freshwater biology in the College of Life Sciences and Agriculture gets high marks for its extensive laboratories and the opportunity to live and study during the summers at Shoals Marine Laboratory on Appledore Island, one of the Isles of Shoals. "We have awesome programs involving off-campus research," raves a marine biology major. "I was excited to get an opportunity to work in a lab on urchins." Nursing, in the School of Health and Human Services, is hard to get into but is extremely rewarding in job preparation for those who make the grade. The health management and policy program also is highly regarded and very personal in its approach to learning.

For a music major with hopes of a performing career, the offerings are considered good but not outstanding. Sociology is considered an easy major that is chosen by students who have no interest in other areas, which hurts those undergraduates with a serious interest in the subject.

Facilities: Dimond Library, situated in the center of campus, is a place both to meet friends and to study in silence, if a student finds the right spot. The structure offers 3 reading rooms with soaring ceilings, skylights, 125 computer workstations linked to worldwide electronic databases, and over 200 desks wired for laptop computers. "The Dimond Library is one of the most beautiful places on our campus," says a sophomore, "and it is a great place to get work done." Dimond holds most of the university's 1.8 million volumes, 3 million microform items, and 34,000 periodicals (both paper and electronic). Specialized collections in chemistry, engineering and mathematics, the biological sciences, and physics are housed in 4 branch facilities. The listing of books, periodicals, and newspapers is all on-line, as are holdings at other area libraries. UNH membership in the elite Boston Library Consortium gives students around-the-clock access to a combined collection of more than 31 million volumes through interlibrary loan on-line or on-site visits to the member libraries.

Seven clusters around campus make available more than 300 computers. Two of the clusters are open around the clock. Notes a senior: "At midterm and finals weeks, the clusters are crowded but not so crowded that you don't get your turn in a timely manner." ResNet provides every student in all residence halls a high speed connection to the Internet. Wireless access is available at many spots around campus.

Special programs: The university sponsors an exchange program in which students spend the junior or senior year at any of 18 English- or French-speaking universities in the province of Quebec, Canada or at any of 11 institutions in Nova Scotia. Study also is available in Dijon, Brest, and Grenoble, France; Granada, Spain; Budapest, Hungary; London and Cambridge, England, and other cities around the world. Within New Hampshire, cross-registration for courses is offered with 11 other public and private colleges. More distant domestic exchanges are available with more than 170 other state institutions through the National Student Exchange. Various research opportunities programs offer undergraduates a chance to collaborate with faculty members on research projects in various fields and provide grants and/or work-study funds for the research undertaken. A hundred students received salaries and stipends from funded research in a recent year. The International Research Opportunities Program enables UNH students to work for at least 9 weeks during the summer after junior year with foreign research partners of UNH faculty.

Campus life: Over half, 57%, of the undergraduates reside on campus, with most splitting their week-end activities between on-campus events and day trips for hiking, biking, or skiing in the surrounding countryside. In fact, the Ski Club and the Outing Club, which owns 3 lodges in the White Mountains used as weekend retreats, are the most active and popular student groups. More than 200 other organizations popular with undergraduates range from the Diversity Support Coalition to Theatre Sports, a local take on the improvisational comedy show, "Whose Line Is It Anyway?" One local and 8 national fraternities and 5 national sororities involve 4% of the men and 5% of the women as members, "less than the intra-mural sport broomball," observes a senior. While the Greeks provide much of the social activity on campus, students say they do not dominate and there is no pressure to become involved in order to be socially accepted or find fun things to do. More weekend events in the student union, which has a new entertainment center with a stage and dance floor and 2 movie theaters are drawing larger crowds. Programs such as SafeWalk, an escort program, a campus shuttle, and SafeRide, a service that provides transportation for drivers or passengers of drivers who have had too much to drink, are available. However, notes a junior, "usually friends make an effort to walk each other around at night, so the other services are not used by a majority." Dorms also are locked around the clock.

Of the 10 men's and 14 women's intercollegiate teams that play in NCAA Division I, men's and women's ice hockey reign as king and queen, as the case may be, with football (played in Division I-AA) a strong second, and gymnastics also drawing impressive crowds. A recreation and sports complex completed in fall 1995 provides seating for more than 6000 fans at hockey and basketball games, along with extensive facilities for individual workouts. Many students participate in 12 intramural sports open to men, 13 to women, 12 coed; most of the rest get some kind of exercise on their own.

The small size of Durham (pop. 10,000) makes the historic seaport city of Portsmouth, about 3 times as large with several shopping malls and dance clubs, a popular getaway less than 15 miles east. Boston, the mountains, the beach, and L. L. Bean also are great, nearby escapes.

Cost cutters: Eighty-four percent of the freshmen and 76% of continuing students in the 2004–2005 school year, the most recent year for which data is available, received some form of financial aid. For about 60% of both groups, the aid was need-based. The average freshman award for an out-of-state student with need included a need-based scholarship or grant averaging $8650 and need-based self-help aid such as loans and jobs averaging $6625. Non-need-based athletic scholarships for out-of-state first-year students averaged $27,250; other non-need-based awards and scholarships for freshmen entering from out-of-state averaged $28,462. First-year students from in state, who pay considerably less than nonresidents in tuition, also received a lower amount of aid in all categories. Need-based grants for in-state freshmen averaged $2708; self-help aid, $2163; athletic scholarships, $7381, and non-need-based scholarships, $4164. A typical 2005 graduate left with $21,459 in debts. A number of merit scholarships carry 2 levels of pay-ment, one for in-state students, a second for out-of-state. The Presidential Scholarship, for example, pays $4000 in-state and $9000 out-of-state to students drawn from the top 10% of their high school graduating class with an ACT score of at least 30 and SAT combined critical reading and math score of 1300 or higher. For slightly lower class rank and test scores, the Dean's Scholarship pays $1000 to in-state students and $6000 to out-of-staters; the Director's Scholarship pays $3000 to nonresidents. The highest paying scholarship, the Governor's Success award, is restricted to in-state residents and pays $10,000 a year to students who ranked in the top 2% to 3% of their high school class with combined critical read-ing and math SATs of 1300 or above and an ACT of at least 30. Recipients must participate in the hon-ors program. A single Tyco Scholarship pays full tuition, fees, room, and board plus $2000 a year in funds for research or travel to an outstanding student admitted to the College of Engineering and Physical Sciences. Cooperative education is available in 25 majors. An accelerated program permits a fast learner to register for up to 20 credits per semester, 4 credits above the normal load, without additional cost and to earn a bachelor's degree in 3 years. Students majoring in engineering and computer science paid an additional $370 for the 2005–2006 school year. Business majors paid an extra $480.

Rate of return: Eighty-six percent of entering freshmen return for the sophomore year. Forty-four percent graduate in 4 years; 68%, in 5 years; 71% in 6.

Payoff: Majors in business administration at 10% accounted for the largest number of 2005 graduates followed by psychology at 8% and English at 6%. Most alumni find employment with firms throughout New England and the Northeast; more than 250 companies or organizations recruited in the 2004–2005 school year. Law school is the principal professional school of interest.

Bottom line: As at any major research university, undergraduates must have good study habits and some self-initiative to survive. Given those abilities, however, students in many majors will find faculty eager to help them succeed. Someone who loves the outdoors and frosty New England winters, "who despises free time and likes to be involved in a wide range of activities will love it here," says a senior who does.

The College of New Jersey

Ewing, New Jersey 08628

Setting: Suburban
Control: Public
Undergraduate enrollment: 2432 men, 3293 women
Graduate enrollment: 25 men, 105 women
Student/faculty ratio: 17:1
Freshman profile: 14% scored above 700 on SAT I verbal; 53% scored 600–700; 25% 500–599; 8% below 500. 23% scored above 700 on SAT I math; 54% scored 600–700; 18% 500–599; 5% below 500. 68% graduated in top tenth of high school class; 90% in upper fifth.
Faculty profile: 90% Ph.D.'s
Tuition and fees: $9857 in-state; $15,120 out-of-state

Room and board: $8458
Freshman financial aid: 78%; average scholarship or grant: $12,033 need-based; $7267 non-need-based
Campus jobs: 33%; average earnings: $1764/year
Application deadline: Early decision: Nov. 15; regular: Feb. 15
Financial aid deadline: Mar. 1
Admissions information: (609) 771-2131; (800) 624-0967, out-of-state; (800) 345-0967 in-state
e-mail: admiss@tcnj.edu
web site: www.tcnj.edu

What 4-year college in the Garden State recently accepted just 45% of the applicants who wanted to enroll, boasts a freshman class in which all but 10% of the students graduated in the top fifth of their high school classes, and in the past 2½ decades has earned more athletic championships than any other college not offering athletic scholarships? If you guessed Princeton University, New Jersey's premier institution of higher learning, look about 8 miles southwest and more than $15,000 cheaper. At first glance, The College of New Jersey, known until 1996 as Trenton State College, a former teachers college, may seem like Princeton's poor relation, but out-of-staters are learning what New Jersey residents have known for several years now: The College of New Jersey offers a blue-ribbon liberal arts education for a down-home price.

Student body: New Jersey is home to 95% of TCNJ's undergraduates, with classmates drawn from just 5 other states and 15 foreign countries. A third of the students are graduates of private or parochial schools. Minority students account for 19% of the enrollment, including 6% who are African-American, 7% who are Hispanic, 5% Asian-American and 1% Native American. One percent are foreign nationals. While TCNJ undergraduates are not as diverse in terms of ethnicity, color, age, or geography as those at some other New Jersey colleges, the students still see themselves as a varied group. Remarks a state resident: "We range from radicals to ultraconservatives, from 'artsy' to preppy, from jocks to philosophy buffs." Many within the ranks wish their classmates were less politically apathetic and more willing to take a stand, on either side, of issues. Instead, students focus more on academics, although the atmosphere is described as "friendly and comfortable," rather than intense, and undergraduates work to maintain excellence in their extracurricular lives as well as their scholarly pursuits. Says a sophomore: "Our student body is intelligent without being academically obsessed and can have fun but maintain a solid GPA."

Academics: The College of New Jersey, chartered as the New Jersey Normal School in 1855 and the oldest of the state's public colleges, awards the bachelor's degree in more than 50 majors and master's degrees in 18 disciplines. Programs are spread among the 7 schools of Art, Media and Music, Culture and Society, and Science, Business, Education, Engineering, and Nursing, with about half the undergraduates majoring in the arts and sciences. The academic year is divided into 2 semesters. Average class size for undergraduates is 30 for the freshman and sophomore years and 20 for the last 2 years. Foundations of Art recently enrolled 60. At the other extreme, a course in the writing of W.E.B. DuBois enrolled just 4.

The College of New Jersey unveiled in fall 2004 its new Liberal Learning program that accounts for approximately one-third of the courses undergraduates need to graduate. The cornerstone of the new program is a required 15-person First Seminar that introduces students to the "habits of the mind and the methodologies of research." The emphasis is on making students active contributors to their own learning rather than passive recipients of others' knowledge. Students' residence assignments also are based upon their choice of First Seminar topic, designed to enhance the opportunities for student engagement. Other requirements include courses that deal with civic responsibilities and that focus on such subject areas as the arts and humanities, social sciences, natural sciences, and quantitative reasoning.

The faculty numbers 331 full-time and 354 part-time members; 47% of the total are women. All of the full-time faculty members and 291 of the part-time teach undergraduates. Though no classes are taught by graduate assistants, some students complain of too many adjunct professors, some of whom "aren't always of the best quality," according to a junior. Like most colleges, TCNJ has its share of "awful" teachers who, regardless of their brilliance, seem incapable of explaining material clearly to students. However, most faculty members do get their points across and are motivated by love of their subject matter and "a genuine love for teaching," enthuses a history major. "Professors generally will extend office hours at a moment's notice. They want you to know that they are people as well as professors." In 2 consecutive years, a professor of English and journalism and a professor of nursing were named New Jersey Professor of the Year by CASE, the Council for the Advancement and Support of Education.

TCNJ provides the latest scientific equipment for biology majors, including transmission and scanning electron microscopes; their users include some of the college's most eager students and well-qualified professors who pass along their enthusiasm for the subject. Helping the process along is a new biology building completed in June 2000 as part of a new $55 million state-of-the-art science complex. The overall complex, completed in fall 2002, houses the biology, chemistry, mathematics, and physics departments. The various business and education programs are for the most part thorough and give undergraduates a good mix of theory and practical experience. Business students gained an additional boost with a new building that opened in fall 1999. However, at this former teachers college, students specializing in elementary education must also complete a major in either the School of Art, Media and Music, of Culture and Society, or of Science, leaving very little room for electives. English earns acclaim for its well-taught concentrations in journalism and professional writing, English liberal arts, and secondary education. In 1996, a new home for the School of Nursing opened, featuring a state-of-the-art clinical learning lab that simulates both pediatric and adult hospital settings.

Spanish is the only foreign language major, though minors exist in French, German, Italian, and Spanish. Criminology and Justice Studies has too few courses other than those related to corrections; however, to fill the gaps, students may take a combined BS/MA Law and Justice program with Rutgers University, in which students complete 3 years at TCNJ followed by 18 months at Rutgers. Physics is limited in its course offerings. Political science could use more professors, though the ones it has are excellent, and a greater variety of classes. Communication studies, too, could use more diverse courses; computer science could use a core of teachers who stay longer and are easier to understand. Art needs better facilities.

Facilities: A new library greeted students when they arrived in fall 2005 and it's "great for everything," says a senior. "The new model creates a number of environments for many activities," including individual and group study and relaxing—or refueling with caffeine—in a café on the first level. Though the collection is large in number with 572,600 volumes and over 19,000 paper and electronic periodicals, students say many of the books are "antiquated" and sources in some subject areas are lacking. Electronic databases and a computerized catalog are both great timesavers. What still brings a smile to most undergraduates is the team of professional librarians who "are wonderful and get excited about helping students," says a history major. The staff is larger than that found at many other schools, with an expert available in nearly every discipline, so undergraduates are rarely stymied in their searches. Materials the library does not have usually can be easily obtained from the state library in Trenton, or from Princeton University.

Approximately 580 networked PCs and workstations are available for student use in 30 labs around campus, including 1 in each residence hall. Lab hours vary, with many closing as early as 11 p.m. and a few open as late as 2 a.m. The lab in the student center is open around the clock at finals time. Says a senior: "Finals week and midterms are usually those times when waits become an issue, but not a large one. Students can always find another lab within a short distance if they are not able to wait." All residence-hall rooms are wired to the campus computer system, offering full access to the Internet. The college strongly recommends that students have their own personal computers. Most of TCNJ's campus was wireless as of the 2005–2006 school year, with plans already in place for connecting the remaining areas.

Special programs: Study abroad, supervised by the Office of Global Programs, is available for a semester or a year in programs sponsored by the International Student Exchange throughout Africa, Asia, Australia, Canada, Europe, and Latin America. The college has its own exchange agreements with schools in 4 countries. Similar exchanges can be made within the United States at any of 155 participating colleges and universities in 47 states, the U.S. Virgin Islands, Guam, and Puerto Rico, through the National Student Exchange. Prospective physicians may be admitted as freshmen to both TCNJ and New Jersey Medical School; they spend the first 3 years at The College of New Jersey, and provided they maintain a 3.2 GPA each semester at TCNJ, they complete the last 4 at the medical school campus in Newark earning both B.S. and M.D. degrees. A similar program with the SUNY College of Optometry in New York City offers a 7-year combined B.S.-O.D. (optometric doctor) degree. Internships are numerous with the major accounting firms, various agencies of state government, and the media. Cross-registration is available through the New Jersey Marine Sciences Consortium.

Campus life: Sixty-one percent of TCNJ's 5725 full-time undergraduates reside at the college, with another 1200 living in housing nearby. The campus in suburban Trenton, which covers 289 tree-lined and landscaped acres and is bordered by 2 lakes, is not what many people envision when they think "central New Jersey." Twelve percent of the men belong to 2 local and 9 national fraternities; 14% of the women pledge to 14 national sororities. Although these groups are quite active on campus, students feel little pressure to join in order to have a good social life and many Greeks are friends with independents, and vice versa. Still, TCNJ carries the image of a "suitcase college." Though more undergraduates stay for the weekends than leave, in the words of a senior, "the goal of many on-campus students is to go off-campus." Lion's Pride and Athletic Spirit programs work to motivate students to attend on-campus events. The most troublesome crimes are car theft and theft of personal property caused primarily by students' failure to lock their doors. A student patrol unit helps keep watch over campus at night, and security staff go on duty at 8 p.m. at each dormitory to ensure that only residents, or guests signed in by residents, enter. Students advise caution, however, when walking off campus in various sections of Trenton.

Sixteen percent of the men and 8% of the women participate in 11 men's and 10 women's intercollegiate sports; 60% of the men and 40% of the women engage in the 9 men's, 9 women's, and 8 coed intramural activities. Fourteen sports clubs also are available. The College of New Jersey offers one of the top NCAA Division III (nonscholarship) athletic programs in the nation, with 36 national championships and 29 runners-up awards since the 1978–79 school year, the most of any of the nation's 396 Division III colleges and universities. During one recent school year, 17 Lion teams appeared in NCAA Division III championship competition. Says a senior member of the softball team: "The athletic program here is second to none. There is no better place for an athlete." Football is the most popular spectator sport.

Home, Princeton, and Washington Crossing Historic Park are quick getaways for most students. However, Philadelphia is only a 20-minute train ride away, and the beach only an hour's trip.

Cost cutters: Seventy-eight percent of the 2005–2006 freshmen received financial assistance, as did 69% of the continuing students. About a third of all students were on need-based aid. The average freshman package for a student with financial need included a need-based scholarship or grant averaging $12,033 and need-based self-help aid such as loans and jobs averaging $2906. Other non-need-based awards and scholarships for first-year students averaged $7267. Average indebtedness of a 2005 graduate totaled $18,524. TCNJ's merit-based scholarship program offers New Jersey high school graduates between $2500 and full tuition, fees, room and board for 4 years based upon a combination of SAT scores and class rank. Out-of-state students also are eligible for between $2000 and full tuition, fees, room, and board per year also based on test scores and class rank. Scholarship recipients also receive a laptop computer.

Rate of return: Ninety-five percent of the freshmen who enter return for the sophomore year. Sixty-one percent graduate in 4 years; 79%, in 5 years; 81% in 6.

Payoff: In the Class of 2005, 14% earned degrees in business administration, 11% in psychology, and 9% in elementary and early childhood education. In a recent class, 13% of the graduates continued on immediately to graduate or professional school. The majority took jobs, mainly in the Middle-Atlantic region and northeast corridor, with such companies as AT&T, Prudential, Pillsbury, and the major accounting firms. Eight hundred companies and organizations recruited on campus in the 2004–2005 school year.

Bottom line: The College of New Jersey may never outrank Princeton in the Garden State, but satisfied students are convinced they're getting much more than a garden-variety education for their tuition dollars. Here's some sound advice to prospective freshmen: Leave at home any preconceptions of what attending a public college in New Jersey will be like and, adds a junior, "Come with academics on your mind."

Rutgers, The State University of New Jersey, New Brunswick/Piscataway Campus

New Brunswick, New Jersey 08903

Setting: Suburban
Control: Public
Undergraduate enrollment: 11,920 men, 12,322 women
Graduate enrollment: 1419 men, 2059 women
Student/faculty ratio: 16:1
Freshman profile: 9% scored over 700 on SAT I verbal; 38% scored 600–700; 44% 500–599; 9% below 500. 19% scored over 700 on SAT I math; 44% scored 600–700; 32% 500–599; 5% below 500. 69% graduated in top fifth of high school class; 95% in upper two-fifths.

Faculty profile: 98% Ph.D.'s
Tuition and fees: $9557 in-state; $17,156 out-of-state
Room and board: $8578
Freshman financial aid: 51%; average scholarship or grant: $8379 need-based; $5641 non-need-based
Campus jobs: NA; average earnings: NA
Application deadline: Rolling
Financial aid deadline: None (Priority: Mar. 15)
Admissions information: (732) 932-1766
  web site: www.admissions.rutgers.edu

It wasn't much fun to be a student at Queens College, the predecessor of Rutgers University, in the early days after its founding in 1766. For one thing, recreation was forbidden on Sundays, and students were confined to their rooms except to attend church services, clad in black academic robes. The Rutgers of today is much more relaxed with a typical weekend filled with social and sporting events. The only confinement is self-imposed library duty, to keep pace with Rutgers' challenging academic programs. Over the years, Rutgers University, especially its largest and oldest undergraduate division Rutgers College as well as all-female Douglass College, has become an increasingly selective and popular public institution, attracting many middle-class students of Ivy League quality who are unable to attend these costly schools. "I came here with low expectations," says a senior forced to turn down admission to both Columbia and the University of Pennsylvania because his family could not afford them. "Now, however, I feel that my education has been just as academically challenging as it would have been at one of the Ivys. Rutgers offers a nonelitist and yet intellectually stimulating education at a comparatively reasonable price."

Student body: Students find their classmates diverse in every sense of the word, except geographically: 91% are New Jersey residents. Most of the out-of-staters also are from the surrounding Middle Atlantic region, though undergraduates attend from 19 states and recently 51 foreign countries. More than a third are members of racial and ethnic minority groups: 17% Asian-Americans, 7% Hispanics, and 7% African-Americans. Two percent are foreign nationals. Notes a state resident: "We have more Antonios and Mohammeds than Muffies and Buffies." Efforts continually are underway by both the administration and student organizations to increase integration. Says a freshman: "Rutgers teaches a lesson about diversity that no student ever forgets." While the university has a strong contingent of liberal thinkers, students say a number of conservative Rutgers Republicans make their presence known. Observes a sophomore: "Politically the spectrum of beliefs ranges from anarchist to staunch conservative." The range of academic abilities and motivation is wide as well, encompassing "many honor students as well as others who have never received an A," observes a junior.

Academics: Rutgers University awards degrees through the doctorate, with bachelor's degrees in more than 70 disciplines. Students at the New Brunswick/Piscataway campus enroll in 1 of 4 liberal arts colleges, Rutgers, Douglass, Livingston, or University (the adult evening) college, or in 1 of 8 professional schools. Classes are spread across 4 locales connected by shuttle bus in the New Brunswick/Piscataway area. The university follows a 2-semester calendar. Classes are frequently big, with the largest introductory science lectures enrolling 400 students, and many freshman classes having around 200. Some view these courses simply as "weed out" sessions to discourage less capable students from pursuing majors in those fields. Upper-level courses range from 15 to 75, with honors and senior seminars generally having 15–20 participants. While students are drawn by the wide variety of courses offered, they acknowledge that the tradeoff is usually a lack of personal attention, at least in the early years. "No one explicitly tells a student what to take," notes a biological sciences major, "and lack of advice can pose a problem for someone who has trouble making decisions." Students say funding cuts also have resulted in fewer classes being offered each semester, and many more people in those sessions that are available.

All students must take liberal arts core requirements that include 12 credits each of humanities, social sciences, math and science, and 6 credits of English composition. Other requirements vary according to the individual college or professional school.

The 1535 full-time faculty members all teach undergraduates in varying degree, as do 662 of the 680 part-time members. Just over a third of the total pool are women. Students are for the most part delighted with the number of exceptional professors they discover (1 faculty member has been awarded the Nobel Prize; 2 a Pulitzer) but caution that many seem to emerge as individuals only when an undergraduate has reached upper-level courses in his or her major. Even then, in some of the more popular classes, it may be up to the student to take the initiative to develop a relationship. Remarks a senior: "Students who have difficulty making an effort to meet professors may graduate not knowing any of them. There are ample opportunities for undergraduates to become personally acquainted with their professors, but students must be willing to make the effort." Not all faculty members, however, seem open to such involvement. Says a sophomore: "There are many wonderful professors who are willing to put in the time to help if the students are. There are also professors who find it pleasurable to intimidate students out of wanting to work their best."

Graduate assistants in recent years have taught 33% of the introductory courses, mainly recitations, and, observes a senior: "I have had some excellent grad students who are far better teachers than some Ph.D.'s." Others, however, complain about having teaching assistants of poorer quality, many of whom speak broken English, who are used—some say overused—in a variety of departments. Many students worry that a recent emphasis on expanding Rutgers' research role is increasing the number of professors who forsake the undergraduate classroom for the privacy of their labs or writing sanctuaries.

Many bright students with an interest in politics seek out Rutgers because of the Eagleton Institute of Politics, which allows 20–25 juniors annually to take coursework there in American politics and public policy. The history, women's and gender studies, and English departments emerge as winners, thanks to teaching that is considered "uncommonly good." The life sciences and psychology are well funded, as shown by their excellent laboratory equipment and top-notch faculties. Offerings in the life sciences recently were expanded to include majors in biological sciences, cell biology and neuroscience, genetics, and molecular biology and biochemistry. Juniors and seniors who have performed well academically and who have an interest in pursuing independent research can find abundant opportunities in the labs of faculty in the university's many research centers and institutes as well as in the Robert Wood Johnson Medical School. Majors who desire more interaction with faculty members find an avenue via groups such as the Biology Club, which offers forums where professors discuss the classes they will be teaching the next semester or the research they are conducting. The physics department also is smaller and ensures plenty of faculty attention in the classroom as well as opportunities for research. Art history, American studies, anthropology, classics, communication, and philosophy "a powerhouse," in the words of 1 major, are highly regarded as well. All of the foreign language majors, in Chinese, French, German, Italian, Portuguese, Russian, and Spanish, are intense, with excellent classroom instruction.

Although the chemistry department generally is impressive, its introductory classes are a nightmare for many first-year students because they are huge and are led by teaching assistants who are difficult to understand. "You have to teach yourself the course," exclaims a political science major. Students in some lower-level mathematics classes also report that "unless you are very talented in math and are interested in pursuing math, science, or engineering as a career, the 2 professors I had couldn't care less," recalls a classics major. The program in Administration of Justice is considered strong in terms of internships and field placements but the courses tend to overlap and lack substance and many are taught at night by adjunct faculty. Economics could use a more energized faculty, fewer graduate assistants, and smaller classes.

Facilities: Alexander Library and the Library of Science and Medicine contain the bulk of the university's 3.4 million volumes, 4.6 million microform items, and 20,800 periodicals, newspapers, and government documents. The recent expansion and renovation of Alexander Library increased total available space by a third and seating capacity by 400 spaces. At peak times, 1200 students can find seats in the much improved environment, which also offers more hookups for computers. The total collection, spread throughout 13 New Brunswick area libraries plus 6 in Camden and Newark, usually meets most undergraduates' research needs; the computerized card catalog, known as IRIS, and extensive databases like Med-line and PSYCHLIT also help navigate what many consider a "humongous" system. "The librarians are unusually helpful," says an economics major, "although the computer system can sometimes be confusing."

Computers, like everything else at Rutgers, are spread among the 4 locales that make up the New Brunswick/Piscataway campus; several of the centers are open around the clock and a majority are open until midnight or later. The longest waits occur during midterms and finals when the labs are crowded and a number of students are trying to print papers. "The labs at Douglass (College) are always quiet and don't have a wait," observes a senior.

Special programs: Four dual-degree programs are available: a 5-year B.A./M.B.A. program with the Graduate School of Management, a 5-year B.A./B.S. program with the College of Engineering, a 5-year teacher certification program through the Graduate School of Education, and an 8-year B.A./M.D. program with the University of Medicine and Dentistry of New Jersey. Under special circumstances, undergraduates may cross-register for classes at Princeton University. Students who prefer may spend the junior year at any of more than 80 state colleges and universities across the United States for the same rate as they pay at Rutgers. A semester in Washington, D.C. is available through the political science department and the Eagleton Institute of Politics. Foreign study is offered in 8 countries in Europe plus Kenya, Namibia, South Africa, India, Israel, and Mexico, and in Costa Rica during the summer.

Campus life: Just under half (49%) of Rutgers students live in residence halls, apartments, and suite-style housing and theme houses divided among the College Avenue campus and the campuses of Douglass and Livingston colleges in New Brunswick and the Busch campus in nearby Piscataway. Many women consider the Douglass College campus to be the most beautiful, "providing a quiet and peaceful haven for de-stressing," in the words of a resident.

Because many students leave for the weekend, most social activity begins on Thursday nights and is largely focused on the College Avenue campus. About 9% of the men and 5% of the women join the 27 national fraternities or 15 national sororities. Although many students enjoy attending Greek parties, students say that being a member is not a prerequisite for a satisfying social life. Partying at off-campus apartments is a popular alternative, and more students are turning up for comedy nights and concerts, as well as such one-of-a-kind events as the Bugs Bunny Film Festival. Many students invest their energy and hours on the *Daily Targum*, which claims to be the oldest independent college newspaper. Adds a junior: "During the fall and spring, there is seldom a day when a student can walk down the street or into the dining hall without encountering some organization attempting to recruit members, educate students on a certain issue, or fund-raise for charity."

One of the least popular, but most necessary, pastimes is riding (and often waiting for) the frequently crowded buses that connect the various university campuses. The password is "Be patient." Another is "Be careful," as crime is a problem in the downtown areas of New Brunswick. To keep crime off campus and to restrict access to residence halls, key cards instead of regular keys are issued to students, and from 9 p.m. until 3 a.m. security officers or students are posted at the main doors to screen all visitors. A "green lantern" security patrol and escort service and emergency phones also are provided. Between the hours of 2 a.m. and 6:45 a.m., when the intercampus bus system is not running, students who need transportation from one campus to another may call the university police and a service shuttle called the Knight Mover, which provides door-to-door service free of charge.

Men's and women's basketball draws the most "die-hard" fans of the 15 men's and 15 women's intercollegiate sports played in NCAA Division I. However, a winning soccer team and the football team's recent entrance into the Big East Conference have brought more attention to these other arenas. The first collegiate football game was actually played at Rutgers in 1869, when the team beat Princeton. Participation in intramural sports, 28 each for men and women in a recent year, also is popular.

"New Brunswick may not be the most desirable place to live," says a New Jersey resident, "but it is well situated, with a train station right on campus." As a result, trips to New York, a 40-minute ride, and Philadelphia, about 2 hours away, are quite manageable. In the spring, the Jersey shore is a favorite destination; in winter, the Pocono Mountains for skiing and snowboarding.

Cost cutters: Fifty-one percent of the freshmen and 50% of continuing students received financial aid in the 2005–2006 school year. Thirty-two percent of the freshmen and 33% of the rest were on need-based assistance. The average freshman award included a need-based scholarship or grant averaging $8379 and need-based self-help aid such as loans and jobs averaging $3810. The average non-need-based athletic scholarship presented to a first-year student totaled $6365; other non-need-based awards and scholarships averaged $5641. A recent graduate left with debts of $15,362. Students are eligible for a wide range of university scholarships, including the James Dickson Carr Scholarships recently worth up to $10,000 awarded to minority students and the Outstanding Scholarship Recruitment Program for high-achieving New Jersey residents with awards ranging from $2500 to $7500 a year, the amount determined by SAT scores and class rank. The Rutgers National Scholarship for students who live outside New Jersey recently paid $5000 a year to students with combined SAT math and critical reading scores of at least 1250 or an ACT of 28 or higher who ranked within the top tenth of their high school class. Prospective students must submit their applications for admission by Dec.1 to be considered. The 4 liberal arts colleges and the 8 professional schools also offer their own individual scholarships. New Jersey residents majoring in programs at Cook College, where the Department of Agriculture, Food, and Resource Economics is based, or in the School of Engineering or School of Pharmacy paid $811 a year more in tuition in the 2005–2006 school year; non-residents in these programs paid an additional $1639 in tuition for the year. Students report that bureaucracy is as difficult to deal with in the financial aid and business offices as it is anywhere else across the 4 campuses.

Rate of return: Eighty-nine percent of first-year students return for the sophomore year. Forty-six percent graduate in 4 years; 66%, in 5 years; 71%, in 6 years.

Payoff: Twenty percent of the 2005 graduates earned bachelor's degrees in social sciences. Ten percent received degrees in psychology, 8% in the biological and life sciences. Over 20% fulfilled double majors of some kind. Most Rutgers College alumni enter the job market mainly in fields such as banking and finance, pharmaceuticals, retail, education, telecommunications, and utilities. About 500 companies recruited on the New Brunswick/Piscataway campus in a recent school year. Between 15% and 30% opt to pursue advanced degrees.

Bottom line: At its best, Rutgers offers academic programs that can compete on equal terms with those from the Ivy League, in a much more racially, ethnically, economically, and politically diverse setting. However, undergraduates must be open-minded as well as determined to succeed. Advises a senior: "Although there are support systems here and people to go to for every question, it is at first often difficult to find these outlets. Prospective students should realize that they are for the most part on their own, and should be ready to take responsibility for their actions."

New Mexico

New Mexico Institute of Mining and Technology

Socorro, New Mexico 87801

Setting: Small town
Control: Public
Undergraduate enrollment: 826 men, 297 women
Graduate enrollment: 155 men, 85 women
Student/faculty ratio: 9:1
Freshman profile: 17% scored over 700 on the SAT I verbal; 48% scored 600–700; 25% 500–599; 5% below 500; 20% scored over 700 on SAT I math; 44% scored 600–700; 31% 500–599; 5% below 500. 17% scored above 29 on the ACT; 60% scored 24–29; 22% 18–23; 1% below 18. 41% graduated in top tenth of high school class; 71% in upper fourth.

Faculty profile: 86% Ph.D.'s
Tuition and fees: $3644 in-state; $10,463 out-of-state
Room and board: $4866
Freshman financial aid: 87%; average scholarship or grant: NA
Campus jobs: NA; average earnings: NA
Application deadline: Aug. 1
Financial aid deadline: June 1 (Priority date: Mar. 1)
Admissions information: (505) 835-5424; (800) 428-8324 (TECH)
e-mail: admission@admin.nmt.edu
web site: www.nmt.edu

If geology is your thing, there are few better places to study at a more down-to-earth price than New Mexico Institute of Mining and Technology in the sunny Rio Grande Valley south of Albuquerque. At this publicly supported institution, where 86% of the undergraduates are from in-state, the combined tuition, room, and board were just over $15,000 for out-of-staters in the 2005–2006 school year and just over $8500 for lucky residents. Because Tech is small, with just 1100 full-time undergraduates, students often join faculty members in stimulating research projects at unusual facilities. Where some schools have fountains or statues, New Mexico Tech has its own mountain, Socorro Peak, 7243 feet above sea level, located west of the campus quadrangle and containing a mine used for seismic studies. Less than an hour away is Langmuir Laboratory for Atmospheric Research, built by New Mexico Tech, which provides opportunities to study thunderclouds, lightning, and precipitation up close. If the low fees and unusually laid-back atmosphere for a high-tech school don't give students a jolt, a stormy night at Langmuir Lab surely will!

Student body: Though most undergraduates come from the Southwest, students are enrolled from 50 states and 38 foreign countries. All but 13% in a recent year were graduates of public schools. Three percent of the students are foreign nationals. Over a fourth are members of racial and ethnic minority groups, largely Hispanics, who comprise 20% of total enrollment. Native Americans account for 3%, Asian Americans for 3%, and African-Americans for 1%. To help increase its diversity, the school hosts summer programs for Native Americans and other minorities in fields such as mineral engineering and science to encourage these students to study more math and science. Most Tech undergraduates are conservative, though not very vocal, about their politics, and are devout science-fiction fans. Observes a New Englander: "Students here are fiercely independent and don't like being told what to do. They also enjoy pulling pranks and criticizing the administration." While the academic atmosphere is noticeably more relaxed than at other topflight technology institutes, students know when to work, and work hard, though they rarely compete against one another. Continues the easterner: "The curriculum is too difficult to make competition anything but a waste of energy. Anyone showing a strong drive to beat out others will likely end up with few friends." Concludes a recent graduate: "Students work hard but they work together."

Academics: New Mexico Tech, which celebrated its 115th birthday in 2004, offers degrees through the doctorate. A bachelor of science is awarded in more than 20 fields, plus a bachelor's degree in general studies. The academic year is divided into 2 semesters. Freshmen will encounter some classes with 20 members and others, such as a general chemistry lecture, 5 times as large. Most upper-division courses have from 5 to 30 participants, with the average size being 15.

All students must earn at least 130 credit hours to graduate, of which 42 are in basic science, including 10 hours of physics and 8 each of calculus, chemistry, and biology, geology, or engineering.

Coursework in written and spoken English, the social sciences, literature, philosophy, and the arts also is required, as is a senior seminar or senior design project.

The faculty consists of 125 full-time members and 22 part-time. Five members of the full-time faculty but no part-time members teach at the graduate level only. Twenty-three percent are women. Despite their expertise, these professors are far from aloof and many make time to join students for various social activities. "It's all very personal," says a psychology major. "We know our professors, where they live and what projects they are working on. They're approachable while still being prominent in their fields." Twelve percent of the introductory courses are taught by graduate students.

The departments of earth and environmental science and physics make excellent use of the school's prime natural location and extensive area research facilities such as Langmuir Lab and the Joint Observatory for Cometary Research. Their faculties also are happy to draw students into their broad range of research projects. The astrophysics option, in particular, benefits from the college's nearness to the Very Large Array radio telescope and from "New Mexico's climate, elevation, and latitude, which are conducive to radio astronomy," says a recent graduate. "And the professors are wonderful teachers." A working experimental underground mine and a rock mechanics lab make the majors in mineral and environmental engineering particularly strong. The demanding materials engineering program gives students opportunities to join faculty in study at the Energetic Materials Research and Testing Center. Electrical engineering comes alive with a team of energetic professors, while the major in petroleum engineering carries its own spark of intensity. Despite the school's technological emphasis, a well-respected program in technical communication, one of a few offered in the Southwest, includes good doses of history and literature from a great faculty. Biology features well-rounded faculties who provide students with plenty of opportunities to assist them in research in immunology, genetics, and other fields.

A major in management, recently added to prepare students for careers in high-technology industries, has worked to integrate itself successfully into Tech's science and engineering focus. Likewise, a newer major in information technology brings together coursework in computer science, management, and engineering. The chemistry faculty maintains a reputation for displaying little interest in teaching. And if for some reason a student should want to major in English, history, political science, or another liberal arts discipline—well, too bad, there's no such program.

Facilities: The recent opening of Joseph R. Skeen Library has dramatically improved the study environment for hard-working Tech students. The 54,000-square-foot, 3-level facility is much bigger, brighter, and more comfortable than the old building, although silent studiers wish quiet hours were more rigorously enforced. Its collection of almost 322,000 volumes and 884 periodicals is weighted heavily toward materials on petroleum and mining engineering but is improving its offerings in such areas as the arts and history. The catalog is computerized with "wonderful" search engines; more than 50 FirstSearch databases are available. For additional materials, students go to the University of New Mexico in Albuquerque, 75 miles north.

Not surprisingly, computers are used extensively throughout the curriculum. About 250 Linux, Windows, and SUN workstations are located in the campus computer center, (open until midnight most nights); there also are PC labs with about 60 machines and an Apple lab with 10 Macintosh systems. The college strongly recommends that undergraduates bring their own computers, which they can use to access the campus network from their dorm rooms.

Special programs: Students may cross-register for courses at New Mexico State, the University of New Mexico, and the Los Alamos National Labs. Internships are available in the technical communication major and several others. Students in any major can work toward certification as secondary school teachers and may observe and teach in the Socorro public school system.

Campus life: Forty-four percent of the undergraduates live on the 320-acre campus, which adjoins an additional 20,000 acres used for experimental activities. Though many find the expansive grounds with their buildings of Spanish hacienda-style architecture a pleasant environment, the campus is located "in the middle of nowhere," complains an easterner. There are no fraternities, sororities, or intercollegiate sports, although a 9-sport intramural program for men and for women and such popular club sports as rugby, soccer, and tournament racquetball and squash keep many students occupied. On some days, it's even possible to find a game of cricket! Says a state resident: "We are doers, rather than watchers." Undergraduates have their share of eclectic interests, reflected in such popular clubs as the Society for Creative Anachronism, in which students relive medieval customs and combat. Watching Star Trek also is a favorite pastime. Crime is minimal, mainly car vandalism and some burglary.

Albuquerque is the closest city with opportunities for dining, dancing, and shopping not available in Socorro (pop. 9000). The nearby Magdalena Mountains and Box Canyon offer plentiful opportunities for hiking, camping, mountain biking, and rock climbing, which is very popular.

Cost cutters: In a recent school year, 87% of the freshmen and 91% of the continuing students received financial aid. Need-based aid went to 40% of the first-year students and 63% of the rest. No figures are available to show the amount of aid to first-year students that was need-based grants or merit-based scholarships, or self-help aid such as loans and job earnings. The average debt of a recent graduate was $14,000. Generally a GPA of 3.0 and an ACT score of at least 23 or combined math and critical reading SAT of 1050 or above qualify a student for scholarship consideration. The Gold Scholarship pays $6000 to students with a 3.5 GPA who are National Merit Finalists; Silver Scholars can receive $5000 a year for having GPAs of 3.5 and ACTs of 30 or SATs of 1320. The Presidential Scholarship pays $4000 a year for slightly lower grades and test scores; the Copper Scholarship, $2000 a year and the Bronze, $1000 based on similar criteria. Both work-study and part-time jobs are available in research or other academic pursuits. Cooperative education programs are offered in computer science and all engineering majors.

Rate of return: Sixty-eight percent of the freshmen return for the sophomore year. Thirty-three percent graduate in 5 years; 40% in 6 years.

Payoff: The major in electrical engineering claimed 16% of the 2005 graduating class; 10% each majored in math and computer science, and almost 10% in physics. About a third of graduates go on to graduate or professional school, most pursuing advanced degrees in the arts and sciences. Alumni attend such impressive universities as Stanford and Harvard Medical School and the universities of Illinois, Iowa, and Washington. Those seeking employment are generally placed with little problem in positions throughout the United States and internationally. A third remain in New Mexico. ARCO, Conoco, Unocal, Hewlett-Packard, the U.S. Department of Energy, and the Environmental Protection Agency have all been recent employers of Tech grads. The average starting salary of a 2004 graduate with a B.S. in engineering was $54,800.

Bottom line: A southwesterner offers the following advice to prospective undergraduates at New Mexico Tech: "If you're committed to your studies and can find ways to entertain yourself, you will succeed at Tech. But be prepared to live differently! While the academic offerings are exciting, Tech is not a liberal arts school and those who believe in being aware and involved may not like what they perceive as apathy among the students."

New York

Canisius College

Buffalo, New York 14208

Setting: Urban
Control: Private (Roman Catholic-Jesuit)
Undergraduate enrollment: 1431 men, 1879 women
Graduate enrollment: 260 men, 431 women
Student/faculty ratio: 16:1
Freshman profile: 3% scored over 700 on SAT I verbal; 24% scored 600–700; 50% 500–599; 23% below 500. 4% scored over 700 on SAT I math; 27% scored 600–700; 50% 500–599; 19% below 500. 11% scored above 28 on the ACT; 12% scored 27–28; 25% 24–26; 33% 21–23; 19% below 21. 18% graduated in top tenth of high school class; 43% in upper fifth.
Faculty profile: 94% Ph.D.'s

Tuition and fees: $23,297
Room and board: $8960
Freshman financial aid: 98%; average scholarship or grant: $5348 need-based; $10,155 non-need-based
Campus jobs: 19%; average earnings: $1458/year
Application deadline: May 1
Financial aid deadline: Feb. 15
Admissions information: (716) 888-2200; (800) 843-1517
e-mail: admissions@canisius.edu
web site: www.canisius.edu

To call Canisius College, a Jesuit school in western New York, the second choice of many top students is like saying that someone settled on a Chevy Camaro instead of a Porsche. The difference in quality is not nearly as great as the difference in price. Recalls a recent graduate: "Canisius is often the second choice of students who are accepted to such schools as Cornell, Georgetown, Notre Dame, and Syracuse universities but can't afford the tuition there. As a result the atmosphere here is moderately to highly competitive." At a total cost of just over $32,000 in the 2005–2006 school year, Canisius shaves about $10,000 off the fees charged at students' first-choice schools—and awards financial aid to 9 of every 10 undergraduates besides. Continues this satisfied alumnus: "Canisius has placed students in some of the best graduate schools: Harvard Law, Notre Dame, and the Columbia School of Journalism, to name a few. It is definitely one of the best buys available."

Student body: Nevertheless, Canisius remains little known to students outside New York State. Eighty-eight percent of the undergraduates are state residents, with most of the others from the Northeast as well. A total of 32 states and 14 foreign countries have students enrolled. In a recent year, two-thirds were Catholic; nearly a third had attended private or parochial schools. Minority and foreign students represent almost 16% of the enrollment. Six percent of the undergraduates are African-American, 2% Hispanic, and 1% Asian-American. Six percent are foreign nationals. Students describe themselves as hard-working, and sometimes passionate about their politics. Says a junior: "There's a great amount of both Democrats and Republicans. Although friendly, sometimes these two groups can get very intense about their particular views and discussions can become heated. However, in many ways, people's passions about their political views help them to strive academically. Although there are some apathetic students, most people really intertwine their passions and interests with their academic course load." Most know what they want from their educations and their lives, and despite a challenging academic environment, a majority maintain a good balance between their studies and their extracurricular lives, with few individuals excelling in one area at the expense of the other.

Academics: Canisius, founded by German Jesuits in 1870 and named for the 16th-century Dutch scholar St. Peter Canisius, awards the bachelor's degree in about 50 majors and master's degrees in 15 fields. The regular academic year is divided into 2 semesters. Class size for freshmen usually ranges from 24 to 26 students, although Evolution, Ecology, and Population Biology recently enrolled about 60. Upper-level classes in the major can be as small as 7–10 and usually no more than 20.

In keeping with the emphasis on liberal education so characteristic of Jesuit institutions, all Canisius students must complete a 54-hour program of humanistic studies that covers nearly half of the 120 credits needed to graduate. Four specific general-studies courses, 2 in literature and composition and 1 each in religious studies and philosophy, are required of all freshmen and sophomores. Students also have their choices of 2 area-studies courses in 7 of 8 traditional fields, excluding the field of the major.

The faculty is divided 217 to 279 between full-time and part-time members. All but 12 of the full-time faculty teach undergraduates. No figure is available to show the portion of part-time faculty who do. Thirty-two percent are women. The full-time faculty in particular bring varied academic backgrounds to their classrooms; members hold degrees from more than 100 different universities including 24 degrees from Europe, 16 from Canada, 9 from Asia/Pacific, and 2 from South America. Newer faculty members continue the best traditions laid down by older ones. Says a senior: "Our faculty is devoted to its students. The faculty members are friends, mentors, role models, confidants, advisors, and cheerleaders." Adds a junior: "I genuinely know that all of my teachers not only know *who* I am but also care about my success in their class and about my overall academic and personal success."

Any of the 9 programs in the Richard Wehle School of Business gets a triple A rating from students, thanks to blue-chip faculty who provide plenty of personal attention. Accounting, in particular, is noted for having one of the highest first-time passing rates in the country on the CPA exam. In 2002, Canisius ranked among the top 5 colleges and universities in the country. Two graduates in the Class of 2002 also earned the top 2 highest composite scores on the November 2002 New York State CPA exam. Business students can also complete internships, some of them paid, with a wide range of national companies. Numerous programs in the School of Education and Human Services, most notably the major in athletic training, also are viewed as first-rate courses of study that bear results. Within the College of Arts and Sciences, chemistry, biochemistry, and biology boast superb equipment for use in student research and dedicated faculties to match. Says a biology major: "Sometimes, students are sent to (research) conferences where they are the only undergrads and they do very well, sometimes even placing above graduate students." English and political science are regarded as being strong majors as well.

Students in the communication studies program, which recently added a new degree program in digital media arts, enjoy the benefit of having new technology and "always available" professors and generally have few problems finding jobs upon graduation. However, the program carries a reputation among some students for being easy. The fine arts could use better facilities and more attention from the administration, students say. Observes a senior: "The fine arts and art history need more support to help complement the strong business/science departments. The arts need more full-time faculty, better funding, and more recognition for the work faculty members currently are doing to improve their departments." A new major in music was added in 2003, joining an existing major in art history. Courses only still remain for students interested in the field of studio art.

Facilities: The expanded and modernized Andrew L. Bouwhuis Library, which students consider "truly magnificent," holds over 336,000 volumes, with room for more than 750,000, and not quite 17,000 paper and electronic periodicals. For most undergraduates, Bouwhuis has become *the* place to study during weekdays and even on weekends. The library lends laptops for use in the building over a wireless network enabling more students to make use of the extensive electronic resources. Students who need additional resources jump on the subway that runs near campus and head to the State University of New York at Buffalo or the county library. But that's rarely the case, says a junior: "Students from the University at Buffalo Medical School come here because our library is better than theirs."

More than 490 computers are housed in 30 laboratories open various hours for student use across campus. These include 5 Internet Plazas stocked with about 40 computers where students can check their e-mail or access web sites, 7 general purpose labs with almost 200 units, and 4 residence hall computer labs with 30+ computers plus a variety of department and special purpose computer labs. While even the 24-hour labs tend to be more crowded around finals time, students say waits rarely last more than 5 minutes. The college strongly recommends that students bring their own personal computers.

Special programs: The Canisius Earning Excellence Program, known as CEEP, enables students to work with faculty or off-campus supervisors in intellectually stimulating research projects. Notes an athletic training major: "Through CEEP, I have done independent research with the physics department and now I am doing research through the University at Buffalo Medical School." Any student may cross register for 1 course per semester at any of 14 other institutions in the region. Cooperative programs also are available with the Fashion Institute of Technology in New York City and the State University of New York College of Environmental Science and Forestry in Syracuse. Qualified sophomores may apply to the SUNY Buffalo Medical or Dental School or to the SUNY Health Science Center College of Medicine at Syracuse for a guarantee of admission after their graduation from Canisius. A 7-year joint degree program also is available with the SUNY Buffalo Dental School, the Ohio and New York colleges of Podiatric Medicine, and the SUNY College of Optometry. A 3-2 program in engineering is an option with the University of Detroit Mercy. Study abroad is offered in 10 countries from Germany to Australia. A semester in Washington, D.C. can be arranged by the political science department.

Campus life: Forty-two percent of Canisius undergraduates reside on the 36-acre campus, rimmed on all sides by urban neighborhoods. Most campus buildings are connected by underground or overhead walkways, a lifesaver in the infamous Buffalo winters. Just 1% of the men and women belong to 1 national fraternity and 1 national sorority, which are minor social forces. "House" parties hosted by students who live off campus, not necessarily Greek, are much more popular sources of weekend fun, and Java Jams are known to draw a crowd on Thursday nights as a way to involve commuters who tend not to be around campus on the weekends. For more cultural sustenance, many attend the performances of the Buffalo Philharmonic held on campus or are active in such groups as the German Club, which organizes Oktoberfest. The Residence Hall Association and the Commuter Student Association both plan numerous activities to keep their respective populations, and others, involved in campus life. The Jesuit influence is pervasive, though not oppressive, and many students regularly participate in the Sunday candlelight service. Says a junior: "Canisius is a welcoming place that allows people to live out their faith, no matter what it may be." Crime on campus, despite the college's urban location and some muggings and robberies in the surrounding neighborhood, is not a serious problem. A shuttle bus daily conveys students until 2 a.m. to their cars in the parking lots, or safety officers escort them to the dorms. Says a student from Buffalo: "I always see public safety officers around campus either walking or driving." Three-quarters of the college's resident housing contain swipe-card access. Off-campus housing owned by the college is equipped with alarm systems.

Basketball is the chief crowd pleaser among the 8 men's and 8 women's intercollegiate sports whose teams compete in NCAA Division I. Football, track, tennis and the rifle team were all dropped as intercollegiate sports as of fall 2003. Reaction to the cuts has been mixed, says a senior, since few sports, other than men's and women's basketball, garner much student support. (In 1995, the Golden Griffins men's basketball team competed in the NIT [National Invitation Tournament] Final Four playoffs at Madison Square Garden.) Just 11% of the men and 8% of the women turn out for 12 intramural sports available to each sex, many of them coed. Though part of an urban campus, the Demske Sports Complex, which is completely covered with AstroTurf and fully lit, offers space for team and intramural play in soccer, lacrosse, baseball, and softball. Professional sporting events like Buffalo Bills football and Buffalo Sabre hockey games draw a number of students, many on college-sponsored trips.

To take a break from the urban surroundings, many undergraduates bicycle, run, or just relax in nearby Delaware Park. Warm weather also attracts many to Buffalo's renovated waterfront. Niagara Falls is 20 miles away; Toronto, a 2-hour drive.

Cost cutters: In the 2005–2006 school year, 98% of the freshmen and 95% of the returning students received some form of financial aid. Eighty percent of the freshmen and 76% of the continuing students were on need-based assistance. For first-year students, the average need-based scholarship or grant totaled $5348; need-based self-help aid, such as loans and jobs, averaged $4601; non-need-based athletic scholarships averaged $14,132 and other non-need-based awards and scholarships averaged $10,155. The average debt of a 2005 graduate was $21,801. Presidential Scholarships pay $21,500 per year to a limited number of high-achieving freshmen who in a recent year had a 97% high school average and SATs of 1300 or an ACT composite score of 30, plus satisfactory performance on a personal interview. As many as 75 Ignatian Scholarships pay $16,000 annually to incoming freshmen with a slightly lower grade point average and test scores. Students must have applications for admission postmarked by Nov. 15 to be considered for the Presidential and Ignatian awards. In addition, Canisius awards to incoming freshmen annually an unlimited number of other renewable scholarships, which pay between $6500 and $12,000 a year and are based on standardized test scores and high school records. The Martin Luther King Scholarship program rewards academically talented and needy minority students with from $5900 to $20,000. Students may pay tuition in 3 monthly installments each semester.

Rate of return: Eighty-four percent of the freshmen return for the sophomore year. Fifty-one percent graduate in 4 years; 66% within 5 years.

Payoff: Ten percent of the 2005 graduates earned bachelor's degrees in education, followed by 9% in communication studies and 7% each in psychology and management. A quarter of each graduating class typically pursues advanced degrees within 6 months of Commencement. Over the last 5 years, 90% of pre-law students have been accepted into professional schools. In 2002 and 2003, 100% of pre-med students were accepted into professional schools. Those graduates not immediately continuing their education take jobs in fields such as banking, teaching, accounting, computer programming, and marketing, primarily in New York, Pennsylvania, and Ohio. Major employers have included Verizon, National Fuel

Gas, PricewaterhouseCoopers, Fisher-Price, General Motors, General Electric, and Merrill Lynch. About 30 companies and organizations recruited on campus in the 2004–2005 school year.

Bottom line: Observes a recent graduate: "Canisius is big enough for a student to preserve some distance from others but not so big that he or she is swallowed up by the masses. Personalized attention, concerned professors, and high job (and graduate school) placement all make this college special."

City University of New York/ Hunter College

New York, New York 10021

Setting: Urban
Control: Public
Undergraduate enrollment: 3271 men, 7135 women (5225 part-time)
Graduate enrollment: 185 men, 826 women (4201 part-time)
Student/faculty ratio: 17:1
Freshman profile: SAT/ACT scores: NA. Class rank data: NA
Faculty profile: 85% Ph.D.'s
Tuition and fees: $4319 in-state; $11,147 out-of-state

Room and board: $3726 (Room only)
Freshman financial aid: 73%; average scholarship or grant: NA
Campus jobs: 25%; average earnings: NA
Application deadline: Jan. 15 for freshmen; Mar. 1 for transfers
Financial aid deadline: May 1
Admissions information: (212) 772-4490; (800) 772-4000
e-mail: admissions@hunter.cuny.edu
web site: www.hunter.cuny.edu

There is nothing half-hearted about Hunter College, the former women's college and normal school located in the heart of Manhattan. One recent graduate from the Bronx described it as "offering an educational experience that culturally and politically is more different, more diverse, and more radical than what most mainstream or Ivy League colleges provide." Although located on New York's posh upper East Side, Hunter is very much a working-class college, with an energy that makes the campus sizzle. Its curriculum is rich in traditional subjects like English and political science, as well as in programs, such as women's studies and Latin American and Caribbean studies, that are targeted at the interests of its special populations, many of whom are the children of immigrants and the first in their families to attend college. The student body is highly stratified, starting with competitive honors undergraduates at the top and working down to remedial students at the bottom, with every ability level in between. Clearly Hunter is not the hometown educational experience middle America is known for providing. But when did anyone mistake the Big Apple for just another slice of apple pie?

Student body: Seventy-five percent of the undergraduates at Hunter College are from New York City. Another 10% are from other parts of New York State. Four percent are from other states, 6% are from other countries, and the rest have origins unknown. In a recent year, the other states numbered 35 and the other countries, 149. Thirty-six percent of the undergraduates are white American; 22% are Hispanic; 16%, African-American; 21%, Asian-American and less than 0.5% Native American. Though the college has been coed since 1964, women still outnumber men by a greater than 2-to-1 margin. Forty-five percent of the degree-seekers are older than 22. Hunter students, most of whom are liberal Democrats, are very politically aware and enjoy engaging in a free-flowing exchange of ideas concerning everything from social justice to budget cuts. In their words, their antennae are raised to "learn every minute, every day"; and although all but a tiny fraction commute to and from school, many enjoy using their extracurricular time to organize clubs, edit journals, and participate in student government. Bright scholarship students who wish they could have afforded a private college in Manhattan, such as Columbia or New York University, are thrilled by the stimulating environment. "I thought I would be the only intelligent student on campus but was proved dead wrong," recalls a graduate of the city's famed Stuyvesant High School. "Students here know that they don't have an Ivy League name to drop at interviews, so they have to compensate by getting good grades."

Academics: Hunter, founded as Normal College for training teachers in 1870, confers the bachelor's degree in about 50 departmental majors plus 10 interdisciplinary areas. Master's degrees can be earned in more than 40 fields, and bachelor's/master's programs in 9 areas let high achievers complete both degrees in a shortened period of time. Hunter follows the 2-semester calendar. Class sizes vary widely, but are more often bigger than smaller, and classes of 50 for juniors and seniors are not uncommon. "Courses generally are overcrowded but not unbearable," observes a junior. "Picture the Rose Bowl."

All but honors students must complete coursework in English composition, the humanities, science and mathematics and the social sciences. Every undergraduate also must fulfill a pluralism and diversity requirement by taking 1 course from each of 4 areas: the culture or political/economic systems of Africa, Asia, or the indigenous peoples of the Americas; the contributions and perspectives of Africans, Asians, Latinos, or Native Americans in the United States; the perspectives and concerns of women and/or issues of gender/sexual orientation; and major issues—artistic, literary, practical, or theoretical—reflected in the intellectual traditions of Europe. Altogether, the distribution requirements cover about a third of the 120 credits needed to graduate; students seeking a bachelor of arts or fine arts degree also must take a foreign language; those earning a bachelor of science typically take more math and science but no foreign language.

Part-time faculty outweigh full-time at Hunter in terms of numbers, with 642 full-time members and 792 part-timers. They represent "all political stripes," as one admirer boasts. Most receive high praise for remaining professionally active, many drawn to Hunter by the stimulating environment of New York City, and yet profoundly interested in their students' progress and well-being. While they vary greatly in teaching effectiveness and instructional styles, they usually try hard to remain accessible though some, maintains a sophomore, "only care about publishing." Since the average student is not assigned to a counselor or faculty advisor, it is up to the undergraduate to seek help if needed. However, one transfer from an Ivy League university was delighted to find faculty as helpful as they are. Says the senior: "Professors at Hunter are often willing to dedicate a surprising amount of time to individual instruction, especially considering the size of the student body."

Students rank English as the most exciting program on campus. At varying times, its faculty has sparkled with such renowned writers as Philip Roth, as a visiting professor, and Louise DeSalvo, and provides a full range of approaches to literature from the traditional to the modern. Political science and history also have their shares of impressive names on staff, many of whom commute back and forth between commitments at Hunter and at NYU or Columbia. However, some describe the political science professors as "disinterested." The music faculty are wonderful as well, "dedicated and talented," says a major, "You can learn a lot by their teaching but also by their example." The program in physical therapy is well respected and highly competitive, accepting 1 of every 8 applicants annually; nursing and other health sciences are similarly tough. Geography majors enjoy the use of advanced technology for cartography. Religion is a small gem of a department with "a talented and dedicated faculty, a wide variety of courses, and a lot of flexibility in program planning," says a major. Education, physical education, and urban studies also win gold stars.

Sociology and psychology are both large and impersonal departments. "There are some great professors," says a major, "but it is unlikely that you will get much contact with them outside of class without a lot of effort." Computer science has the potential to be strong but has been hampered by too few dollars. The ethnic programs in Africana, Puerto Rican-Latino and Latin American and Caribbean studies also are underfunded and understaffed. Students want more variety of courses in the Romance Languages—French, Italian, Portuguese, and Spanish.

Facilities: Students have generally given 9-story Wexler Library an A+ for its wonderful study environment, but found its collection and research capability to be worth no higher than a B. That grade has been coming up, though, thanks to technological improvements over the past several years. Beginning with the Hunter Navigator, a computer program available on every floor, students can easily find out where everything is located, from the databases to the restrooms. LEXIS/NEXIS, which scans all major newspapers, and Ethnic Newswatch, which provides full-text access to ethnic and minority newspapers and magazines, are but 2 of 450 databases recently available. An Internet lab provides about 10 workstations. Interlibrary loan and document delivery services also have been extended, which helps to boost the quality of Wexler's collection of 735,000 volumes, many which students consider outdated, 1.2 million microform items, and 2300 periodicals. A lifesaver for many is the renowned New York Public Library at Fifth Avenue and 42nd Street. Branch facilities also are located at the School of Social Work and the health science center.

The Instructional Computing Services center houses the bulk of computers for students on campus with more than 110 units in 9 labs. Computers also are available in the main library and several other buildings though more are needed. The ICS lab is open until 10 p.m., Monday through Thursday, and until 6 p.m. the remaining days.

Special programs: Students seeking different academic experiences may enjoy the amenities of a small, private college at Marymount Manhattan or can acquire insights into East European Jewish life and culture by taking courses at the YIVO Institute of Jewish Research. Those eager to get farther away may take any of several 4-week, 2-course programs offered in January and during the summer months, enabling a student in a recent year to study Spanish in Madrid and Argentina, Italian literature in Florence, film in London and Edinburgh, social work in Mexico, Jewish social studies in Israel, and English literature in Paris. The college also offers its own exchanges with Queen Mary College at the University of London and with any of Deakin University's 3 campuses in Australia. Hunter also participates in the National Student Exchange, enabling undergraduates to attend any of about 170 public colleges or universities in the United States. General cross-registration for courses can be arranged with all CUNY campuses. The Public Service Scholar Program, a full-year program designed to encourage top students to enter public service, combines seminars on issues of public concern with internships in government. Other internships are easily obtainable in various city institutions such as the Museum of the City of New York, the Asia Society, the National Broadcasting Company, or *The New York Times*. Concludes a junior: "Here a student has the chance to gain experiences unparalleled anywhere else."

Campus life: One percent of Hunter's undergraduates live on campus, but not on the main campus, whose 4 buildings, located at 68th Street and Lexington Avenue, are interconnected by skybridges towering above Manhattan's Upper East Side. Hunter's single dormitory, housing 646, is located at the college's Brookdale campus, on 25th Street and 1st Avenue, where the nursing and health sciences schools are located. Although students say the social life of the dorm is active, it remains as disjointed as activities on the main campus and involves a lot of informal "hanging out" in cafes and hole-in-the-wall bars. Most organized events revolve around membership in ethnic clubs, such as the Caribbean Students Union, one of the largest and most active, and in clubs reflecting students' academic interests. There usually is at least 1 school-sponsored dance every weekend. Crime is an issue to which most students living in New York have grown accustomed; they say it is not especially bad around campus, thanks in part to surveillance cameras and a 24-hour foot patrol.

"Sports and fraternities at Hunter are a joke," says a dorm resident, with interest in the minimal Greek life holding at 2%. For the athletically inclined, Hunter fields 9 men's and 11 women's intercollegiate teams in NCAA Division III, with men's basketball drawing the largest crowds. The college also offers intramurals.

For most off-campus socializing, students find that the galleries in Soho and just about anything in Greenwich Village fit their interests and pocketbooks more closely than the surrounding Upper East Side.

Cost cutters: In a recent school year, 73% of the freshmen and 70% of the undergraduates received financial aid. No figures are available on the average amount awarded to freshmen as scholarships or grants, loans, or work contracts. Tuition awards based on academic merit include the Scholars Award, which recently paid $2200 a year for 4 years and guaranteed housing at the Hunter College residence hall. Eligible freshmen must have achieved a 90% or better high school average and at least 1200 combined math and critical reading SAT plus complete an essay and interview.

Rate of return: Eighty-one percent of the freshmen return for a second year. Just 36% graduate within 6 years, a reflection, in part, of Hunter's largely older, very busy student body, a number of whom drop out and later re-enroll or because of commitments to work and/or family, take longer to graduate.

Payoff: In a recent graduating class, 15% earned degrees in psychology and 10% each in sociology and English. Most graduates take jobs in social services, finance, publishing, and other media outlets; a majority stay in the New York area. Recent employers of Hunter grads have included Random House, Coopers and Lybrand, Memorial Sloan-Kettering Cancer Center, WNYW/Fox, the New York Urban League, and Planned Parenthood. Those who pursue advanced degrees do so mainly in social work, law, and the arts and sciences.

Bottom line: Mature, self-reliant undergraduates who are culturally and politically active and who appreciate diversity in all areas, including their courses of study, are happiest at Hunter. Warns a recent graduate: "Students who just want to make money regardless of other considerations shouldn't come here, although the school would probably do them good!"

The Cooper Union for the Advancement of Science and Art

New York, New York 10003

Setting: Urban
Control: Private
Undergraduate enrollment: 593 men, 326 women
Graduate enrollment: 28 men, 3 women
Student/faculty ratio: 17:1
Freshman profile: 30% scored over 700 on SAT I verbal; 50% scored 600–700; 16% 500–599; 4% below 500. 58% scored over 700 on SAT I math; 25% scored 600–700; 12% 500–599; 5% below 500. 85% graduated in top tenth of high school class; 95% in upper two-fifths.
Faculty profile: 82% Ph.D.'s
Tuition and fees: Full-tuition scholarship; $1450 fee

Room and board: $11,000 (room only)
Freshman financial aid: 100%; average scholarship or grant: $2680 need-based
Campus jobs: 44%; average earnings: $1126/year
Application deadline: Early decision for art and engineering: Dec.1; regular for architecture: Jan. 1; for art: Jan. 10; for engineering: Feb. 1
Financial aid deadline: Apr. 15
Admissions information: (212) 353-4120
e-mail: admissions@cooper.edu
web site: www.cooper.edu

Peter Cooper may have built America's first commercial steam locomotive in 1830, but he never went to college. He may have helped Cyrus Field lay the first transatlantic telegraph cable, but he didn't know how to spell. These shortcomings didn't stop Cooper from running for President at age 85 on the Greenback ticket, but they did prompt him to start The Cooper Union for the Advancement of Science and Art so that other young talents might not suffer from the same lack of formal education. Nearly 150 years after Cooper Union opened in 1859, the college still fulfills its founder's purpose: to provide an education to undergraduates who deserve but cannot afford one. How it accomplishes this feat has changed somewhat since fall 1996. Previously, Cooper Union used to charge no tuition, only required fees and room costs. Now, the college provides each student with a full-tuition scholarship, supplementing what undergraduates receive from federal and state aid with funds from its own coffers. The end result is the same: students pay no tuition. Undergraduates specializing in just 3 disciplines—art, architecture, and engineering—say there is nothing like the Cooper experience at any other U.S. college, especially for just $1450 a year in fees plus housing costs. In one freshman-level guided design class, engineering majors prepared a 2-inch-thick report on how to solve the gridlock problem in New York City. Architecture students routinely use the Big Apple as an urban laboratory; art majors work under some of the most creative and world-renowned names in the field. But while the faculty and coursework may rival those of other world-class institutions, Cooper Union remains an enigma to many—except the privileged few hundred students each year whose talent and hard work gain them access to one of the last great deals in Manhattan.

Student body: Sixty percent of Cooper Union's undergraduates are from the Empire State with most of the out-of-staters also from the Northeast and Middle Atlantic regions. Students from 40 states and 14 foreign countries are present. A fourth are graduates of private or parochial schools. The student body is a mix of ages, races, cultures, and personal histories. Half are white; 25% are Asian-American, with 9% Hispanic, and 5% African-American. Ten percent are foreign nationals. Undergraduates, many of whom worked after high school or attended college elsewhere, generally arrive already confident of their abilities and committed to clear professional goals. If not, they're in for some disappointment, since Cooper Union offers no general liberal arts program for a student who decides against majoring in any of its 3 fields. Students in each area have their own natural style. The engineers, who number about 500, tend to be incredibly bright and career oriented but more conservative and "Joe College" than the others. A majority of the 150 architecture students are older and consequently more socially and emotionally mature. Although students in all 3 disciplines are independent-minded, the 250 studying art tend to be the most individualistic free-thinkers ("eccentric," in the words of one major) and spend less time with each other than their counterparts in other fields. The school is extremely competitive, an outcome, in part, of having so many bright and creative people in such intense surroundings, and students think nothing of working throughout the weekends on routine projects, not just those due near the end of a term. "School is basically the only thing on the minds of most Cooper students," observes a sophomore. "A typical weekend is: Friday night, work; Saturday, work; Saturday night, work; Sunday, work, and pray that you've worked enough!"

Academics: Cooper Union awards the Bachelor of Architecture, Bachelor of Fine Arts, and a Bachelor of Engineering in 5 fields of engineering, including interdisciplinary studies plus a master's in engineering. A new focus of the engineering program encourages students to design their own individual courses in multidisciplinary aspects of engineering, enabling students to customize their degree emphasis. The architecture program takes at least 5 years to complete. The academic year is divided into 2 semesters. Small classes are standard fare at Cooper Union, even in the freshman year. No course has been known to exceed 50 students, (Computer Architecture has had 50) and many art majors routinely enjoy classes of 15. Engineering management has only 4. Independent projects also are plentiful.

All students in the first 2 years take a sequence of required courses in humanities and social sciences. The first year is devoted to language and literature; the second, to modern world history. Beyond these classes, each discipline has its own additional mandates in the humanities, social sciences, math, and natural sciences, as well as rigorous requirements in its special field. Majors in architecture must complete a thesis; those in art and engineering, a senior project. There is little time just to take an elective a student would like to pursue.

The faculty is predominantly part-time: 53 full-time members versus 191 part-timers, many of whom are working professionals who teach primarily art and architecture. Twenty-six percent are women. At times, the large number of world-renowned professionals on staff, many of whom have worldwide egos to match, can interfere with the quality of teaching. By and large, however, the faculty's depth of knowledge and passion for their fields inspire in students the same high standards of love, labor, and commitment. One junior's assessment: "Collectively brilliant."

Students across the board in art, architecture, and engineering consider their educations to be of 5-star quality. The facilities provided within each field are extensive. For example, resources available to art students extend from well-equipped black and white and color darkrooms to a full-floor sculpture shop with materials for work in wood, clay, metal, and plaster, plus a bronze casting foundry. Students in the Irwin S. Chanin School of Architecture are most impressed by the 5 levels of required classes in design that are expansive in their scope, from discussion of poetry and theory to materials and construction. As far as engineering is concerned, an electrical engineering major points out: "Cooper does not cut corners where it counts, which is why the junior and senior engineering labs are so well equipped!" In chemical engineering, for example, students work with such analytical instruments as infrared spectrometers and high-powered liquid chromatographers, "about which most undergraduates only read," says a major. Construction of a new home for the Albert Nerken School of Engineering, and other Cooper Union offices, was expected to get under way sometime in 2006. The proposed 9-story, almost 200,000-square-foot structure is bold in its design, conceived as a "vertical campus" organized around a central atrium that is spanned at various levels by sky bridges—sure to make even the most jaded New Yorker want to take a peek inside.

Most complaints center on the general-studies coursework surrounding the 3 main disciplines. Cooper Union's independent students wish the humanities department was more open to creative thought, though many consider that deficiency an outgrowth of the program's limited course offerings. Foreign language classes are considered rather weak, largely because they are elementary and intermediate levels mostly, taught using tutorial cassettes along with native speakers. In a recent spring semester, the only courses offered were in elementary French, German, and Japanese, intermediate French and Japanese, and advanced Japanese. The physics department lacks organization, inspiring presentation of subject matter, and a cohesive, personable faculty. It is the only engineering class held in a lecture hall. And some students simply wish there were more interdisciplinary classes relating to the 3 subject areas.

Facilities: Amid a wealth of well-equipped facilities, Cooper Union's library falls short. Students have come to accept the fact that the collection of 100,000 volumes is generally dated (though students value the really old books published 150 years ago) and contains little beyond materials about (you guessed it) art, architecture, and engineering. The 350 periodicals are deemed inadequate as well. However, students find salvation in regular access to the Bobst Library at nearby New York University, as well as at the Parsons School of Design and The New School for Social Research. An on-line catalog connects users to materials housed at these other campuses. A CD-ROM periodical catalog helps immensely in tracking scientific journals. An Electronic Resource Center provides additional access to a variety of CD-ROM and Web-based databases. Says an electrical engineering major: "The Internet has taken over the role of the library for the most part, at least in my major." As a study center, Cooper's library provides a quiet, comfortable setting for reading, lounging, and sleeping.

The walk-in computer center, which is housed in the Engineering Building, contains more than 100 PCs. A computer studio in the School of Art contains 40 Macintosh workstations. Normal open hours for both centers are until 10 p.m. Monday through Saturday but extend to around-the-clock during finals. The senior electrical engineering labs have additional IBM computers and the art and architecture schools also have very advanced computers for graphic arts and other needs. The one residence hall has a handful of IBMs and 4 Macs, which always are available 24 hours a day.

Special programs: The School of Art enables undergraduates to study abroad in 9 countries; majors selected by a faculty jury may spend a semester at any of 10 other art schools along the east coast. Architecture students also are encouraged to interrupt their studies for a year to gain some outside experience, either foreign or domestic. Engineering students may opt for independent study at any of several British universities, including Kings and Imperial colleges; several summer research opportunities are offered in a half dozen countries. All students may cross-register for courses at the New School for Social Research in New York.

Campus life: Cooper Union's first student residence, located directly across the street, opened in fall 1992 and houses 183 first-year students. Residents find it "a great place to live," safe and clean with spacious rooms, kitchenettes, and great views. The rest of the campus consists of 4 buildings on Manhattan's lower East Side, and most students still commute from apartments in the neighborhood or from their homes in the other boroughs. A fifth of the engineering majors are members of 2 national fraternities; a tenth belong to 1 local sorority. All students are welcome at the Greek parties, though it is mainly other engineering students who attend. Many functions are held during the work week to accommodate commuters, although the tempo of weekend life on campus in general has picked up since the residence hall was built. Most undergraduates get involved in professional associations or the racial, ethnic, or religious groups most reflective of their special interests. The Chinese Students Association is one of the largest. Students from all areas with an interest in music come together in Pro Musica, a group that performs 3 concerts a semester, 1 classical, 1 jazz, and 1 rock/everything else. Few, however, rely solely on the local offerings for entertainment. For the most part, says a southerner, "a typical weekend is just about anything you want it to be, as New York City has practically everything to offer." Although the big city also offers its share of crime, to which Cooper Union is not immune, full-time security posted at the doors of all buildings keeps most incidents in and around campus confined to theft of school supplies and personal belongings. The school also gives mandatory seminars during orientation on living safely in the city. Says a senior from the West, not just the West Side: "How safe people actually feel is pretty much a measure of their relative paranoia, since crime against students is relatively unheard of."

About 40% of the men and 30% of the women take part in the 12 intramural sports available to each sex. As part of a limited intercollegiate sports program, with 5 sports for men and 2 for women, teams compete with squads from other schools, although Cooper Union belongs to no formal athletic association. Despite that, the tennis team recently won the metropolitan championship.

Escape from the stress of coursework is relatively easy for students willing to tear themselves away. Options include a walk around the block (you never know what you'll see or experience in Manhattan) or a subway ride to another borough. The Rollerblading Club provides a chance for students to skate together all over Manhattan. Students in need of a longer getaway seek the nearest mountains or the beaches of New Jersey or Long Island.

Cost cutters: A healthy endowment, which totaled $163 million as of a recent year, and a tough determination to keep the school assessible to all deserving students, regardless of income, make Cooper Union a dream come true for many. The commitment to providing a full-tuition scholarship equal in the 2005–5006 school year to $27,500, and charging just a $1450 fee extends for the length of any student's stay, including the longer period for engineering majors who wish to pursue a master's degree. In addition to the full-tuition scholarship that everyone gets, a third of freshmen and continuing students in the 2005–2006 school year received additional financial aid to help pay living costs, which in New York City can be staggering. Off-campus apartments are very expensive, and supplies for art and architecture classes are costly as well. The average financial package to fall 2005 freshmen included a $2680 need-based scholarship or grant and $2515 in need-based self-help aid, such as loans and jobs. The average financial indebtedness of a recent graduate was $11,617.

Rate of return: Ninety-seven percent of all freshmen who enter Cooper Union return for the sophomore year. In recent years, however, graduation rates have differed among the 3 schools. In the School of Art, 80% of the freshmen earn bachelor's degrees within 5 years; in the School of Engineering, 84% of the majors graduate within a 5-year period. Sixty-one percent of those enrolled in the rigorous School of Architecture emerge with bachelor's degrees within 6 years, which usually includes a year's outside experience.

Payoff: In the Class of 2005, fine arts majors accounted for 30% of the graduates, followed by majors in electrical engineering at 15% and architecture at 14%. About 60% of the engineering alumni pursue graduate work in fields as wide-ranging as law, medicine, and business, along with various engineering specialties. A smaller number of architecture students pursue advanced study, while many find jobs in the firms of adjunct faculty members. Graphic designers join a variety of New York publishing, advertising, and design firms. Fine art graduates often team up with working artists, find jobs in printmaking, litho shops, and museums, or teach in private schools. One hundred ten companies and organizations recruited on campus in the 2004–2005 school year.

Bottom line: Cooper Union expects much hard work and dedication from students in each of the 3 professional schools. In fact, some undergraduates who enroll directly after high school find that the academic rigors, teamed with the challenges of living in New York City, make the transition to college difficult. Nevertheless, students who feel ready for such an experience should go for it, advises a southerner who did. "You don't have to be a genius or a cold, indifferent intellectual to attend," says this student. "What you must have is simple passion for your subject and confidence in yourself and your work—and then be willing to work hard."

Elmira College

Elmira, New York 14901

Setting: Suburban
Control: Private
Undergraduate enrollment: 364 men, 819 women
Graduate enrollment: 20 men, 35 women (314 part-time)
Student/faculty ratio: 12:1
Freshman profile: 4% scored over 700 on SAT I verbal; 22% scored 600–700; 51% 500–599; 23% below 500. 4% scored over 700 on SAT I math; 20% scored 600–700; 51% 500–599; 25% below 500. 7% scored above 28 on the ACT; 20% scored 27–28; 42% 24–26; 29% 21–23; 2% below 21. 34% graduated in top tenth of high school class; 70% in upper fifth.
Faculty profile: 100% Ph.D.'s

Tuition and fees: $28,500
Room and board: $8700
Freshman financial aid: 82%; average scholarship or grant: $16,130 need-based
Campus jobs: 50%; average earnings: $1000/year
Application deadline: Early decision: Nov. 15 and Jan. 15; regular: Mar. 15
Financial aid deadline: Mar. 15 (Priority: Feb. 15)
Admissions information: (607) 735-1724;
  (800) 935-6472
  e-mail: admissions@elmira.edu
  web site: www.elmira.edu

Mark Twain called the farm 3 miles outside Elmira, New York, "Rest-and-be-thankful," although he rarely did either during the 20-odd summers he spent there visiting relatives of his wife, a native Elmiran. During sojourns at the farm, Twain worked on several books simultaneously, among them *Tom Sawyer* and *The Adventures of Huckleberry Finn.* The farm is now the site of the Elmira College Center for Mark Twain Studies, and the author's octagonal study, in which he was so prolific, is located on the campus. Since Twain's death, the lazy spirit of old "Rest-and-be-thankful" has brought no more relaxation to the 1180 full-time undergraduates who attend this independent college than it did to the famous author. Who can rest at a college where the general degree requirements consist of: a 2-term freshman studies program; coursework in various skills and subject areas; mandatory internships and community service; a performing arts appreciation requirement that brings more than 40 events to campus each year; and an unwritten pledge to learn the alma mater and other college songs that are sung at virtually every campus event? Indeed, undergraduates may not find their 4 years at Elmira restful, but after having spent a relatively less expensive $37,200 for tuition, room, and board in the 2005–2006 school year at this lesser known Phi Beta Kappa institution, an Elmira alumnus ends up with much to be thankful for.

Student body: Just under half, 46%, of Elmira's students are from New York State. Just over half of the rest also are northeasterners, with the total enrollment converging from 35 states and 23 foreign countries. Forty-one percent are graduates of private or parochial schools. Foreign nationals account for 6% of the enrollment, just above the combined total of all other racial and ethnic groups: 2% African-American and 1% each Hispanic, Asian-American, and Native American. Students describe the majority as conservative and resistant to changes off campus as well as on; in other words, most feel comfortable with Elmira's heavy emphasis on campus tradition, evident in everything from the purple and gold freshmen beanies to the snowblowers and lawn mowers painted in school colors. "Those with radical beliefs stand out," says a sophomore, "and often face resistance to accomplishing their goals." Known for being exceptionally friendly and helpful to one another, Elmira students also used to be fairly laid back. In recent years, however, the number who reach for a beer more often than a book has diminished as more valedictorians and salutatorians, who make up 13% of the enrollment, and other high-ranking high school graduates have been lured to campus with impressive scholarships. The addition of more "vals and sals," as they are called, has made classes more challenging, though some high-achieving students still wish there were more rigor. Says a valedictorian: "There is a core of students who are academically competitive, and the rest just seem to get by. For many, academic success is secondary to involvement and participation in clubs and organizations." Adds a senior: "Social activity is almost essential for acceptance here. People want to know you."

Academics: Elmira was founded in 1855 as the first women's college in the nation that boasted courses and degree requirements equal to those in place for men; it became coed in 1969. The college awards the bachelor's degree in 38 majors plus a master's in education. Its calendar, described as following a 4-4-1 schedule, encompasses 2 terms of 12 weeks each, followed by a 6-week leg known as Term III in which students can travel or take 1 or 2 classes on campus, and, they confide, generally have more fun. For the most part, freshmen can expect classes of 25–30 students; throughout the 4 years the extremes will rarely stretch above 40 (though a course in business law may hit 55) or dip to as few as 4.

General-education requirements include a mix of basic coursework and not-so-basic field experience. Students must take classes in skills such as writing, distribution requirements, and 2 first-year interdisciplinary courses When World Collide and Order and Chaos that introduce students to the history of ideas in the Western tradition. Freshmen and sophomores must attend at least 16 performing arts events a year and write about their experience for credit. Elmira also requires real-life experience, acquired through both a career-related internship and 60 hours of community service. Participants donate their time, more than 300,000 hours over 25 years, to organizations ranging from a local big brother/big sister agency to the area chapter of the Red Cross. One international business major put on a baseball clinic for young children through the YMCA.

Elmira's faculty consists of 82 full-time members and 17 part-timers. Nearly 43% are women. Each year, a faculty and a staff member are selected as advisors to the entering class and become their "patron saints" throughout the years. Close student-faculty relationships also are encouraged through such campus traditions as the midnight breakfast, which faculty and staff prepare on the eve of fall final exams, to the annual holiday banquet, where a student signs up to sit with the professor or administrator of his or her choice, who carves the turkey and serves each undergraduate. For the most part, students find the faculty to be warm, intelligent, and sincerely interested in their work and their charges. "On a scale from 1 to 10," raves a senior, "the faculty quality rates a 9.5!" Some members, the 0.5, have difficulty simplifying complicated material for undergraduates.

English literature, history, and business administration, especially the international business concentration, are among the departments rich in inspiring faculty. The English faculty in particular is varied in age, personal teaching styles, and academic specialties in both English and American literature. Students in the speech and hearing program gain valuable experience by running a clinic that serves both the campus and the local community. Education students spend 6 weeks of the freshman year getting in-classroom experience and then have it "better in the Bahamas" or in Scotland, where they can teach during Term III. "Learning is unavoidable," says an elementary education major, although some students think more full-time experienced faculty members are needed to keep the program strong. International business majors share similar opportunities for relevant internships; one major worked at a resort in the Bahamas over the summer, others in Germany, Canada, and Latin America. Nursing majors enjoy the benefits of 2 hospitals nearby, with steadily increasing experience in them each successive year.

The human services department needs additional faculty members. Says a major: "Human services literally has 2 people who teach all of the classes. This is good because you can build a strong bond with your professor but it would be nice to see what other viewpoints are out there." Other social science disciplines, such as criminal justice, sociology, and anthropology, would likewise benefit from additional faculty as well as professors who stay longer. Just French and Spanish are available as foreign language majors with very few courses offered in each area especially at the higher levels. Opportunity for independent study, however, is available in a wide range of languages not typically found at a small-college setting. The options recently included Arabic, Chinese, Modern Greek, Hebrew, Hindi, Japanese, Russian, Korean, Swahili, and Classical Greek. The programs in theater, art, and music are small as well, though theater is considered quite dynamic despite its size. Art and music, especially instrumental music, have facilities that students have found insufficient to meet their needs. While a number of majors do have limited course offerings, motivated students find the faculty willing and even eager to sponsor independent studies and other supplemental learning experiences. "Don't complain, initiate," advises a psychology major.

Facilities: *Quiet* and *spacious* are 2 adjectives students use most of the time to describe the Gannett-Tripp Library—except during finals week, when the GTL becomes noisier as some students go there to socialize while the dormitories enforce around-the-clock quiet hours. For a college of just 1180 full-time undergraduates, the facility houses 389,000 volumes and 1859 periodicals. Students complain that, although the quality of materials has been steadily improving in recent years, too many materials remain too dated to be of use. The online periodical databases most often please research-focused students. More to students' liking, the library offers a wide variety of study options, from soundproof rooms for group projects to lounges for relaxing. An extensive array of user-friendly Internet-connected computers dominate the ground floor. The second floor contains the Mark Twain collection, featuring not only written materials for use by students and visiting scholars but also the marble floor and wooden ceilings that once graced a local saloon frequented by Twain.

The Nathenson Computer Center, which opened on the terrace level of the library in fall 2002, has satisfied most students' computer needs. Altogether, about 100 networked PCs are available. Units in the Nathenson center are open until midnight on weeknights, the same hours as the library. Many students also have their own computers and make use of the high-speed Internet access from their dorm rooms. The college strongly recommends that students have their own computers.

Special programs: During the 6-week Term III, students may attend courses at other colleges that follow a similar calendar, such as Alma in Michigan or Hanover in Indiana, or study marine biology, Caribbean botany, archaeological research, or other subjects at a field station on San Salvador Island in the Bahamas. Credit for classwork in England or Italy also is an option. The highly competitive Junior Year Abroad program allows third-year students to spend a year or a term at a university in another country, with England, France, Japan, and Australia offering some of the more popular stays. Internships are available in Washington, D.C. A 3-2 program in chemical engineering is offered with Clarkson University. A cooperative program between Elmira and the schools of business at Alfred and Clarkson universities enable students to earn a bachelor's degree from Elmira in 4 years and one year later, a master's in business administration.

Campus life: As all undergraduates except adult students or residents commuting from their homes are required to live at the college, 92% of the student body call the 50-acre campus home. Without fraternities or sororities, events such as dances, bands, magicians, and comedians are usually scheduled to keep the campus from becoming too quiet. Permits regulating times, attendance, and the serving of alcohol are required for all parties held in the college apartments so many students choose to gather at local bars. Popular college groups range from the Outing Club to Students in Free Enterprise to Christian Fellowship to College Republicans. Traditions are an integral part of life at Elmira. In preparation for the Mountain Day held each fall, the college fire truck picks up students and takes them to the front steps of the President's Home, where they sing such traditional songs as the alma mater. This ritual is repeated for several nights until the president finally agrees to cancel classes and grant a free day of picnics and volleyball on the lawn. The college president boats across the college's pond as part of the "You Gotta Regatta" race. Being relatively crime free is another tradition the college hopes to maintain. A few troubling assaults upon students off campus by local residents a few years ago convinced students to start walking in groups or drive in the surrounding neighborhood, but for the most part, notes a junior, "Stealing a sweatshirt from the laundry room is the most drastic thing that happens." Nonetheless, new lighting has been installed throughout campus, dorms are locked around the clock, requiring students to use keys for entry at all times, and a student escort service is available to walk undergraduates anywhere on campus after dark. Emergency call boxes, shaded purple, naturally, also are prevalent.

The Soaring Eagles men's and women's hockey teams bring out most of the campus to their games. The women are 2-time national champions, in 2002 and 2003. The men advanced to the semifinals in 2006, their first appearance since 1993. Soccer, basketball, and lacrosse competitions also draw fans. In fact, most teams can count on enthusiastic cheering and singing by the Extreme Eagles spirit club. Forty percent of the men and 35% of the women are players as well as fans, being part of the 6 men's and 10 women's intercollegiate teams that compete in NCAA Division III. Eighty percent of the men and 70% of the women participate in the extensive intramural program, 21 sports open to each sex. The ski club, which organizes numerous day and evening trips to area mountains, attracts its own large following. Likewise, the Orchesis dance club, which puts on two well-attended performances each year, involves 100 or so students of all skill levels. The athletic center, with a hockey rink and four indoor tennis courts, is located 9 miles from campus. When it's time to wind down, the Clarke Health Center offers a relaxation room equipped with a large tub for bubble baths, various flavored teas, and relaxing music.

Elmira (pop. 36,000), a quiet community 90 miles southwest of Syracuse in the Finger Lakes region, offers excitement of an unusual sort. Harris Hill, a popular picnic spot, also is home to the National Soaring Museum, which houses the largest collection of classic and contemporary sailplanes in the world. The hill's soaring field is still used for national soaring contests and demonstration rides. The city of Corning, 20 minutes away, features the Steuben glass museum; Ithaca, home of Cornell University, is about twice as far; Syracuse is about two hours away.

Cost cutters: Eighty-two percent of the freshmen and 80% of the continuing students in the 2005–2006 academic year received some sort of financial aid; for 81% of the freshmen and 77% of the rest, the assistance was need-based. The average award for a freshman with financial need included a need-based scholarship or grant averaging $16,130 and need-based self-help aid such as loans and scholarships averaging $5292. The average 2005 graduate left with debts of $19,875. Approximately 60% of the undergraduates in a recent school year received honor scholarships, ranging in amounts from $4000 to full tuition. Included are such awards for academic honor or outstanding leadership activities as the Valedictorian Scholarship, which usually pays full tuition; the Salutatorian, covering 75% of tuition; and the Trustee, Mark Twain, Presidential, Founder, and Iris Leadership (named for the college flower), worth $15,000, $12,000, $10,000, $7000, and $4000 a year, respectively. The AXCEL program offers freshmen with high school GPAs of 3.50 or better a chance to save money by graduating in 3 years, instead of 4. Course-load limits vary based on college GPA.

Rate of return: Eighty-four percent of freshmen return for the sophomore year. Sixty-eight percent graduate in 4 years.

Payoff: More than 40% of 2005 graduates earned bachelor's degrees in 3 disciplines: 24% in business, 10% in education, and 8% in psychology. Forty-five percent of the new alumni went on directly for advanced degrees, the largest number in the arts and sciences and in business. The remaining graduates, who took jobs, entered fields such as accounting, sales, management, and teaching; most stayed in New York or moved elsewhere in the Northeast or to the South. Sixty companies and organizations recruited on campus in a recent school year.

Bottom line: Because Elmira is small and close-knit, students are looking for classmates who will also value the qualities of college life they hold dear: personal attention from faculty, easy relationships with friends, and the wealth of traditions so important here. Advises a senior: "Friendship and campus involvement are very important here and it is expected that you participate in school activities."

Hofstra University

Hempstead, New York 11549

Setting: Suburban
Control: Private
Undergraduate enrollment: 3702 men, 4329 women
Graduate enrollment: 832 men, 1268 women
Student/faculty ratio: 19:1
Freshman profile: 2% scored over 700 on SAT I verbal; 34% scored 600–700; 54% 500–599; 10% below 500. 3% scored over 700 on SAT I math; 38% scored 600–700; 52% 500–599; 7% below 500. 11% scored above 28 on the ACT; 11% scored 27–28; 28% 24–26; 29% 21–23; 21% below 21. 24% graduated in top tenth of high school class; 46% in upper fifth.
Faculty profile: 91% Ph.D.'s

Tuition and fees: $23,130
Room and board: $9500
Freshman financial aid: 90%; average scholarship or grant: $10,100 need-based; $9800 non-need-based
Campus jobs: 35%; average earnings: $1520/year
Application deadline: Early action: Nov. 15; regular: rolling (Dec. 31 priority)
Financial aid deadline: Feb. 15
Admissions information: (516) 463-6700; (800) HOFSTRA
e-mail: hofstra@hofstra.edu
web site: www.hofstra.edu

Hofstra University may be named for a Long Island lumberman who donated his estate for the campus, but to Hofstra students the name has come to symbolize "variety." With more than 2000 undergraduate courses ranging from African Humanism to Working Capital Management, Hofstra offers something for the most eclectic learner. More than 130 undergraduate majors are provided in the extensive College of Liberal Arts and Sciences and schools of Business, Communication, and Education and Allied Human Services, as well as in New College, a liberal arts school that specializes in interdisciplinary courses and freer modes of learning. A recently established Honors College and concentrations in Latin American and Caribbean Studies and Middle Eastern and Central Asian Studies have further expanded student options. And it doesn't hurt that the tree-lined campus is less than an hour's train ride from New York City. Academically, Hofstra has much to offer the energetic undergraduate who wants a more relaxed setting than can be found at more prestigious private universities. And the price for tuition, fees, room, and board, just under $33,000 in the 2005–2006 school year, is sure to reduce the stress level of many an ambitious scholar. Little wonder that 35% of the new students enrolling at Hofstra every year have come there after completing previous college study elsewhere.

Student body: Seventy percent of Hofstra students are New Yorkers, mostly from Long Island. Eighty-four percent of the out-of-staters also are from the Middle Atlantic region, with 45 states and 48 foreign countries having students on campus. African-Americans comprise 9% of the undergraduate enrollment, Hispanics 8%, and Asian-Americans 5%. Two percent are international students. Says a New Yorker: "The majority of students are very open with their differences, which enriches the educational experience." Although undergraduates are competitive and self-reliant, they are not uncooperative or unfriendly. Nevertheless, some out-of-staters complain of encountering a materialistic, "me first" attitude in some students from the surrounding area. Appearances are important, and rarely will someone attend classes in sweatpants. Says a New Yorker: "Everyone gets decked out in expensive-looking outfits—no matter what class they are going to!" While a majority are serious about their studies, many, observes a senior, are more socially inclined and "don't get or give all that they could academically from this school."

Academics: Hofstra, founded in 1935, confers degrees through the doctorate, including the juris doctor degree from its School of Law. Classes follow a semester calendar with a 3-week January interterm and 2 summer sessions. Despite the university's size, undergraduate classes average 22–28 students, though introductory business courses can enroll 70. New College classes generally have 16–18 participants. Students voice fewer complaints about class size than they do about availability, and enrollment caps on core classes are often waived to enable seniors to complete graduation requirements.

Students earning a bachelor of arts degree must complete a core program that includes courses in "appreciation and analysis" and "creative participation" in the humanities, in social and behavioral sciences and history and philosophy in the social sciences, and in the natural sciences and mathematics/computer science. Students also must place out of or study a foreign language and take classes that examine a non-European culture. Requirements for the bachelor of science, business administration, fine arts, and engineering degrees feature variations on this approach.

Part-time faculty who teach undergraduates outnumber full-time members who do, 573 to 430, out of a total pool of 719 part-time and 527 full-time. However, more than half, 60%, of the undergraduate teaching hours are taught by full-time faculty. Forty-six percent of the faculty members are women. One current faculty member has won a Pulitzer Prize; a second, a MacArthur Fellowship. The faculty are as varied in talents, abilities, and interest levels as the students. While most departments contain a select group of excellent professors who are both intelligent and accessible, students warn of others who, in the words of a senior, are "disinterested, uncaring, and unencouraging." Many find the faculty to be helpful, though sometimes they can be hard to find. Adds another senior: "The bad thing about some faculty is that you have to track them down for help. The good thing is that once you do track them down, they get on top of your issue."

In the Zarb School of Business majors in finance and in management draw especially high ratings, although all 8 concentrations offer in-depth and varied courses and solid faculty. Honors students in accounting can participate in internships with the major national and local accounting firms. Marketing majors often can intern at the offices of 2 major professional sports teams in the area: the New York Islanders hockey team and the New York Jets football team. The School of Communications offers facilities students find competitive with industry standards in television, radio, and film, including closed-circuit cable channels available on campus, audio and television news feeds, and a digital radio station. Drama in the College of Liberal Arts and Sciences also gets rave reviews, especially the working professionals who often make guest appearances as instructors. Other liberal arts programs in the winner's circle are psychology, sociology, philosophy, English, especially the creative writing component, history, computer science, and political science. New College students generally rave about the quality of "creative, unusual classes" in their program, says a member, with "lots of writing and discussion. Where else could I take a whole class on my favorite author, Richard Wright?"

Some students would like to see the dance program strengthened to meet the more rigorous standards for a bachelor's of fine arts degree. The BFA at Hofstra is offered only in theater arts. A new major in computer engineering was recently added. Previously, those interested in computer engineering earned a bachelor of science in electrical engineering with a computer option.

Facilities: Hofstra's collection, located in the main Axinn Library and the law library, consists of 1.2 million volumes and 9070 periodicals. The LEXICAT on-line catalog for books, periodicals, and other documents helps students keep up with new additions, about 15,000 volumes annually, although the materials are not organized as well as users would like. Some undergraduates find the 11-story Axinn Library spacious but impersonal; others consider the environment especially conducive to getting work done. "I like the tenth floor to study," says a junior, "because the view of Long Island is excellent up there!" For many dedicated studiers, midnight closing on weeknights is too early, although during midterms and finals, Axinn

Library is open around the clock. A 24-hour study room, café, and computer lab were scheduled to open in the 2005–2006 school year.

About 1600 PC, Macintosh, and UNIX workstations are available to students in the various labs and classrooms across campus. One lab is open around the clock. All resident students have Internet and e-mail access from their dorm rooms. In addition, several buildings also provide wireless access to the network. The university strongly recommends that undergraduates have personal computers. IBM or Macintosh laptops are recommended in certain majors.

Special programs: January and summer study-abroad options are available in any of 19 countries or at a marine biology laboratory in Jamaica. A semester in the nation's capital or in the New York State Assembly can be arranged through Hofstra's political science department. First-Year Program enrolls groups of 35 students in course clusters made up of 3 thematically linked subjects. This interdisciplinary approach to learning also enables new students to feel part of a smaller academic and social community and helps to ease the transition from high school to college.

Campus life: Forty-nine percent of the undergraduates live on Hofstra's 240-acre campus *cum* registered arboretum, located just 25 miles east of New York City. Although a number of residents leave when classes are over, some kind of social event usually keeps a core of students on campus over the weekend. Greek life is especially popular, especially among resident students, although only 6% of the men and 7% of the women actually belong to the 15 national fraternities and 3 local and 11 national sororities. Because there are no Greek houses, parties are held at Hofstra USA, a well-liked on-campus club, or at bars just off campus. One of the biggest of the 150 student groups is the Organization of Commuter Students, which keeps nonresidents tied into campus life. The university drama and music departments stage a popular Shakespeare Festival each spring, rivaled in spirit only by the annual student-run production of the Spectrum Players, a group founded by director-graduate Francis Ford Coppola when he was a Hofstra student. Six student publications ranging from *The Chronicle* newspaper to a humor magazine, *Nonsense*, are produced. Hillel, an organization for Jewish students, also brings speakers and programs to campus.

Most crime occurs in the campus parking lots and involves vandalism and thefts. To respond, public safety officers have increased their patrols; security around the residence halls also has been increased. A student ID is required to enter. Hofstra buses and public-safety escorts eliminate any need to walk alone at night. Says a junior: "I feel safe at my school at all times."

Football and basketball are the most popular of the 9 men's and 9 women's varsity sports played in NCAA Division I (football is I-AA) and provide as good a workout for those on the field as for members of the Spirit Support Teams. Twenty-five percent of the men and 12% of the women take part in the 7 men's and 7 women's intramural sports provided.

Hofstra's proximity to New York City, without the latter's hassles and expenses, means that a lot of students head to the Big Apple for a kind of excitement not found in suburban Hempstead (pop. 40,000). The south shore beaches are just 15 minutes away.

Cost cutters: In the 2005–2006 school year, 90% of the freshmen and 82% of continuing students received financial assistance. For 62% of the first year students and 58% of the rest, the aid was need-based. The average freshman award for a student with need included a need-based scholarship or grant averaging $10,100 and need-based self-help aid such as loans and jobs averaging $3425. Non-need-based athletic scholarships for first-year students averaged $24,525; other non-need-based awards and scholarships averaged $9800. The average 2005 graduate left with debts of $20,500. A limited number of full-tuition Distinguished Scholar Awards are presented annually to students with outstanding academic records, regardless of need. Phi Beta Kappa Scholarships pay at least $3500 a year to valedictorians. All students with outstanding academic credentials may receive merit scholarships worth up to a maximum covering full tuition.

Rate of return: Seventy-eight percent of entering freshmen return for the sophomore year. Thirty-six percent graduate in 4 years; 52% within 5 years, 55% within 6.

Payoff: Psychology claimed 12% of the 2005 graduates, followed by marketing at 9%, and education at 8%. In a recent year, a fifth of the class went immediately on to business school, with 13% heading off to study the arts and sciences, law, or medicine. Nearly half of all Hofstra graduates pursue advanced degrees within 5 years of commencement. Three-quarters enter the job market directly, many in accounting, computer-related, and teaching positions throughout the Northeast. Nearly 400 companies and other organizations recruited on campus in the 2004–2005 school year.

Bottom line: Self-disciplined self-starters with some idea of what they're looking for will fare best when confronted with Hofstra's vast array of academic goodies. This university can provide much, but how much is accepted depends mainly on the determination of the individual student.

Houghton College

Houghton, New York 14744

Setting: Rural
Control: Private (Wesleyan)
Undergraduate enrollment: 444 men, 893 women
Graduate enrollment: 4 men, 2 women
Student/faculty ratio: 14:1
Freshman profile: 14% scored over 700 on SAT I verbal; 34% scored 600–700; 39% 500–599; 13% below 500. 7% scored over 700 on SAT I math; 36% scored 600–700; 38% 500–599; 19% below 500. 22% scored above 28 on the ACT; 17% scored 27–28; 29% 24–26; 23% 21–23; 9% below 21. 32% graduated in top tenth of high school class; 57% in upper fifth.

Faculty profile: 84% Ph.D.'s
Tuition and fees: $19,420
Room and board: $6560
Freshman financial aid: 97%; average scholarship or grant: $10,214 need-based; $7303 non-need-based
Campus jobs: 47%; average earnings: $658/year
Application deadline: Rolling
Financial aid deadline: Mar. 1
Admissions information: (585) 567-9353; (800) 777-2556
e-mail: admission@houghton.edu
web site: www.houghton.edu

When freshmen enter Houghton College, a Christian college owned by the Wesleyan Church in rural western New York, they don't just sign up for courses in English, math, and science. They also sign a statement acknowledging "Responsibilities of Community Life," regarding such behaviors as drinking, gambling, and social dancing. Undergraduates begin each term with Christian Life Emphasis Week, in which a well-known Christian speaker or evangelist comes to campus for a series of meetings. Throughout the term, all students must attend a 40-minute chapel service 3 times a week; students are allowed to miss up to a third of the services each semester. It is clear that Houghton, known to many as "the Harvard of Christian colleges," is not the right choice for every bright high school graduate. But for a student prepared to make the commitment, there's a whole lot of learning to be had. "At Houghton," says a southerner, "they want you to develop your mind on your own; they aren't going to imprint a certain view on you. Any academically and spiritually focused student who is outgoing or active would do well here."

Student body: Sixty percent of the undergraduates are from New York, with 57% of the rest also from the Northeast. Altogether, students come from 37 states and 19 foreign countries. Thirty percent are graduates of private or parochial schools. Although only 17% are members of the Wesleyan Church of America, Houghton students generally come from conservative, evangelical, Protestant backgrounds. Still, one senior was surprised to discover that "all Christians do not agree on certain political and social agendas." Foreign nationals account for 3% of the student body, and there are 3% African-Americans, 2% Asian-Americans, and 1% each Hispanics and Native Americans. Also present are a number of "third-culture kids," students who are American but, as the sons and daughters of missionaries, have spent most of their lives overseas. Undergraduates describe themselves as intense, eager, friendly, and service oriented, with a senior providing this overview: "It is a solidly Republican student body, and Right to Life is a strong position around campus. Students here are not risk takers and tend to follow trends rather than to create them. They also are studious and industrious." Undergraduates view high grades as the key to future success, and it is not uncommon to see students attending social events with books or notes in hand. Says a sophomore: "There's usually a slight bit of uptightness, a seriousness about being scholars."

Academics: Houghton, founded in 1883, awards the bachelor's degree in 35 majors and masters degrees in music. The school year is divided into 2 semesters plus a May term, which offers 3- and 4-week courses on campus, plus opportunities to travel abroad and to do internships before full-time summer employment. Average class size is 17. The largest courses, such as Calculus I, enroll about 85 students. Specialized upper-level classes in, say, New Testament Greek, are as small as 3. "'Crowded' here is 40 students," recalls a recent grad.

The general-education requirements known as integrative studies are extensive and account for 54 of the 125 credits needed to graduate. Says an elementary education major: "So much of our emphasis is on gaining a larger perspective of the *whole* before we learn the specifics of our major." The coursework covers all traditional disciplines from English (writing, literature, and speech) to a lab science to Christian theology. A First Year Introduction, or FYI, required of all entering students, combines large-group presentations on such subjects as the meaning of liberal arts and life and career planning with small-group interaction and discussion, often led by upperclass peers.

All of the college's administrators, staff, and faculty, who number 83 full-time and 30 part-time members, are required to be committed evangelical Christians and must sign a Statement of Faith and adhere to the same Responsibilities of Community Life as the students. Twenty-two percent are women. For the most part, faculty are committed both to teaching and to their students, with whom they arrange frequent contact outside the classroom by, for example, eating in the dining hall and attending undergraduate variety shows; one professor gave a final exam at his house. Notes a junior: "The faculty seem to realize their God-given 'calling' to educate 'scholar-servants.'" The few "bad" teachers tend to be boring rather than uncaring or incompetent. Says an English major: "Students would have to work very hard *not* to have a personal relationship with at least 1 professor."

Biology is known for being exceptionally rigorous, and most of those who make it through the program are admitted to the medical schools of their choice. Observes a business major: "The standards are very high and quite inflexible. Many of those who start out as biology majors turn to other disciplines because of the difficulty." Music has long been one of Houghton's high notes, with demanding coursework and a new Center for the Arts completed in 1999. For those up to the challenge, the music faculty are superb, and the range of specialties and courses offered, from performance to church music to composition, is grand on anyone's scale. Majors in religion, Bible, and educational ministries draw on the expertise of outstanding professors and the overall environment of the college; psychology, English, history, philosophy, education, and communications also benefit from having faculty with diverse academic interests but a common belief in helping students. The major in studio art is considered quite rigorous. The college also offers a distinctive equestrian studies option within the recreation and leisure studies major.

Sociology has just 3 full-time professors and is hampered by Houghton's rural location, which makes field experience especially elusive. Business is equally hurt by the isolation from major cities. Foreign language majors are limited to French and Spanish, and students wish more emphasis were placed on speaking and translating and less on memorizing for tests. The programs in outdoor and therapeutic recreation and in computer science are understaffed and could use more up-to-date equipment.

Facilities: The Willard J. Houghton Library is a good place to study, students agree—"if you don't mind hard wooden chairs," adds a sophomore. The good news is there also are numerous individual desks with Internet hook-ups. Its collection of just over 237,000 volumes with access to 4090 periodicals, in the minds of many users, is "adequate" to meet the academic demands of the college; students think too many of the books are outdated. The college makes an effort to compensate by providing ready interlibrary loan and an excellent computer catalog known as GRACE, and database searching system. The library is closed for study on Sundays. There also is a separate music library.

The college issues laptop computers included in tuition to all entering freshmen and other new students for use during their time at Houghton. Every residence hall room has 1 port per pillow available for the units. Students gain ownership of these computers upon graduation. While many students like the program, others consider the laptops inadequate and the computer network slow. Says an English major: "I'd rather they just lower tuition and let us bring our own computers." All students also have access to 2 computer labs housing about 50 PCs, which are open from 6 a.m. to midnight, 6 days a week, and also to a smaller lab of about a dozen PCs available around the clock. Many areas across campus are wireless.

Special programs: Houghton students can take classes at any of 12 other western New York schools, including 3 branches of the state university system. They also may spend a semester at any of a dozen other Christian colleges across the country, from Westmont College in California to Gordon College in Massachusetts; off-campus learning opportunities through the Christian College Consortium may send students to Washington, D.C., Los Angeles, Latin America, or even to Oxford. Study abroad is available in 25 countries spread among Europe, Asia, Latin America, and Africa. First Year Honors and Houghton-in-England programs both involve 2 semesters in London. Houghton in Tanzania provides students an opportunity to study anthropology, history, animal ethology, and other subjects, and includes visits to the Maasai and other tribes. Houghton in Australia and Houghton in Adirondack Park programs as well as an extension program in Ashland, Oregon, also are available. A 3–2 engineering degree with Clarkson and Washington universities also is an option.

Campus life: Eighty percent of the undergraduates reside on Houghton's very rural, rather isolated campus covering 1300 acres 60 miles southeast of Buffalo. The college maintains a second campus in West Seneca, a suburb of Buffalo; the 2 locations are connected by a 2-way interactive audio-video link, enabling courses to be taught with students and faculty at both ends of the linkage. Students from the Houghton campus stay at the sister campus when doing internships in the city.

There are no fraternities or sororities, and students pride themselves on finding creative ways to make their own fun. Opportunities for Christian service are endless in organizations such as Allegany County Outreach, a kind of big brother/big sister group that works with needy local children, and World Missions Fellowship, which builds awareness about missions around the globe. Mandatory chapel takes on various guises, such as music by student groups, personal testimony from faculty and/or students, off-campus speakers, Biblical exposition, and discussion of current events. Crime is not a major concern on a campus where, according to a state resident, "people leave doors unlocked and cars open and running, yet few instances of crime occur. We are a trusting campus and thus far have been lucky." To make sure the luck doesn't run out, the student senate set up a student security system, including an escort program, to encourage undergraduates to play a role in their own protection.

"Soccer draws crowds," says a junior, attracting the largest group of fans of the 4 men's and 6 women's intercollegiate sports played in NAIA competition. Eighty percent take part in the intramural program, 8 sports for men, 6 for women. A confidence-building ropes course is taught in the physical education curriculum and also is offered as a prefreshman experience. Horse lovers have an indoor riding ring and a place to board their mounts. The expansive campus also has room for its own intermediate downhill ski slope with rope tows and 8 miles of cleared and marked cross country trails.

While Houghton's isolation serves to build a close-knit, extended family whose members rely upon one another for companionship and fun, students say that an occasional getaway from the college and town of 1600 is mandatory lest undergraduates become "over-Houghtonized." Escape isn't easy without a car, however, as Buffalo and Rochester are both about an hour away. Trips to Letchworth State Park and Niagara Falls are popular. Most students settle for an excursion to the nearest mall and movie theater, 35 miles away.

Cost cutters: In the 2005–2006 school year, 97% of the freshmen and 98% of the continuing students received financial aid. Seventy-nine percent of the freshmen and 80% of the rest were on need-based assistance. The average freshman award for a student with need included a need-based scholarship or grant averaging $10,214 and need-based self-help aid such as loans and jobs averaging $5078. Non-need-based athletic scholarships for first-year students averaged $7177; other non-need-based awards and scholarships averaged $7303. A typical 2005 graduate left with debts of $16,028. Houghton Excellence Scholarships paying $1250–$7500 are awarded to students who earn combined math and critical reading SAT scores of at least 1200 (26 ACT) or rank in the top 15% of their high school classes. Three top incoming students, with strong recommendations from their pastors, combined SAT scores of at least 1300 (or 29 ACT), and high school class rank in the top tenth, may receive Houghton Heritage Scholarships, which pay $12,500 annually. Special grants are available for children of ministers and missionaries. A student who is a member of a Wesleyan Church may be eligible for a $1000 grant.

Rate of return: Eighty-five percent of the freshmen who enter return for the sophomore year. Fifty-six percent graduate in 4 years; 65%, in 5 years.

Payoff: A third of the 2005 graduates earned degrees in 3 areas: 11% in childhood education, 11% in business administration, and 11% in psychology. Most graduates enter the job market shortly after commencement, a majority going into teaching, business, public relations/communications, and research, largely in the Northeast and Middle Atlantic states. More than 30 companies and organizations recruited on campus in the 2004–2005 school year. More than a fourth enter full-time Christian service as ministers or missionaries. Among 2004 grads, 36% went on to graduate or professional schools.

Bottom line: Advises an administrator: "The high school student considering Houghton should be seeking a traditional residential college experience and should be interested in making a strong commitment to both academic excellence and his or her faith in God. Houghton does not compromise on either standard."

Ithaca College
Ithaca, New York 14850

Setting: Small town
Control: Private
Undergraduate enrollment: 2657 men, 3304 women
Graduate enrollment: 74 men, 217 women
Student/faculty ratio: 12:1
Freshman profile: 7% scored over 700 on SAT I verbal; 39% scored 600–700; 45% 500–599; 9% below 500. 6% scored over 700 on SAT I math; 41% scored 600–700; 46% 500–599; 7% below 500. 29% graduated in top tenth of high school class; 54% in upper fifth.
Faculty profile: 90% Ph.D.'s
Tuition and fees: $25,194

Room and board: $9950
Freshman financial aid: 86%; average scholarship or grant: $14,710 need-based; $8411 non-need-based
Campus jobs: 42%; average earnings: $2200/year
Application deadline: Early decision: Nov. 1; regular: Feb. 1
Financial aid deadline: Feb. 1
Admissions information: (607) 274-3124; (800) 429-4274
e-mail: admission@ithaca.edu
web site: www.ithaca.edu

Ithaca College may have started life in 1892 as a conservatory of music, but just over a century later it is surely no "Johnny one-note." Ithaca now offers 94 majors in 5 schools; 2 of its most highly respected programs, in addition to music, are physical therapy and communications. These 3 programs have earned reputations within their fields for producing "career winners," to use the words of a recent graduate. And even though a student's major may not be any of these concentrations, he or she is free to take courses in all of the 5 schools, so that singing psychologists and accountants with a flair for dramatic script-working turn out to be just typical Ithaca students.

Student body: Forty-six percent of Ithaca's undergraduates are from in-state. Nearly three-fourths of the out-of-staters are from the Middle Atlantic region as well, although students are present from all but 3 states and from 70 foreign countries. Twelve percent are graduates of private or parochial schools. The college remains predominantly white, with about 3% each Hispanics, Asian-Americans, and African-Americans, 2% foreign nationals and less than 1% Native Americans. While Ithaca lacks racial and ethnic diversity, its student body is mixed in other ways, as described by a senior: "You can be a hippie or a prep; dye your hair purple or keep it natural; chat on your cell phone or sit on a lawn and watch the lake…gay or straight, black or white, it's all cool." Since many students are opinionated, the philosophical diversity often makes for lively interaction. "We're a melting pot of thought and activity," says a junior. "From the polemicists to the apathetic, everyone has a chance to be heard." Most undergraduates, however, share along with their open-mindness, a common pragmatism and interest in achieving a career goal. Students majoring in music, physical therapy, or communications are apt to be more competitive than their peers from other departments. There is also, says students, a good number of active partiers whose love of fun "if not balanced properly with class work will create problems," notes a business administration major.

Academics: Ithaca offers bachelor's-degree programs in 5 schools and 1 interdisciplinary division, master's-degree programs in 3 schools and a doctorate in one school. The college observes a 2-semester calendar. Classes average between 15 and 30 students. Introductory courses, as in psychology, however, may enroll as many as 100, while departmental seminars often have as few as 5. Each of the 5 schools prescribes a different core curriculum that generally balances liberal arts and professional courses. The general education program in the School of Humanities and Sciences, for example, explores the formation, function, and meaning of human communities through coursework ranging from mathematics and formal reasoning to examinations of values, beliefs and behaviors.

Ithaca's faculty numbers 616, of whom 441 are full-time and 175 part-time. Forty-five percent are women. Graduate students teach 6 percent of the introductory classes. In a few professors, students detect a certain "stuck-in-the-mud quality" induced by teaching the same course in the same way for too long. For every lethargic teacher, however, there are generally many more brilliant and inspiring ones who give 110% to their students. Notes a first-semester senior: "I can honestly say that I have had only 1 poor professor in my 7 semesters here." Underclassmen quickly find many faculty members as personal as they are professional. Notes a sophomore: "Each student is assigned a specific advisor, but I always feel like I have about 15 because each time I run into a professor I have had in class, he or she always checks up on me to make sure things are going all right."

Internships are frequent in the 5-star schools of Communications, Music, and Health Sciences and Human Performance. In the communications program, even freshmen get first-hand experience running radio and television stations that broadcast to the local community. The building for the Roy H. Park School of Communications, which was completed in 1989, offers state-of-the-art equipment to satisfy each of the 6 majors offered in the field, from cinema and photography to television-radio, as well as regular journalism. Experienced faculty with great connections to the working world, as well as strong alumni contacts, provide additional chances for hands-on experience. Across country, the college's James B. Pendleton Center located midway between Hollywood and Burbank enables students to complete semester internships in the Los Angeles film, television, and recording industries. Ithaca's music school supplies its own comprehensive programs in music education, jazz studies, composition, and sound recording technology, just to name a few, plus 24 performing ensembles and various other performance options that include opportunities for local, national, and international tours. Competition within the programs is intense, but faculty members are as friendly as they are virtuoso in their fields. The 6-year, B.S./D.P.T. physical therapy program in the School of Health Sciences and Human Performance is also a standout and very demanding. Students are admitted to the program in the freshman year and study for the first 3 years on the Ithaca campus. Following the junior year, students receive training at the University of Rochester Medical Center and Strong Memorial Hospital in Rochester. After 6 years, participants earn a bachelor's degree in clinical health studies and a professional doctorate in physical therapy. The undergraduate programs in speech-language pathology and audiology and athletic training/exercise science also deftly combines challenging coursework with clinical practicum experience during the junior and senior years. The Center for Health Sciences, which opened in 1999, features innovative learning laboratories that incorporate the latest computer-assisted multimedia instructional technologies and a modern wellness clinic that provides hands-on opportunities for applying techniques to prevent diseases.

In addition to Ithaca's 3 best-known programs, a science building with outstanding equipment and first-rate faculty eager to provide extensive opportunities for undergraduate research have pushed biology, chemistry, and biochemistry within the School of Humanities and Sciences to the "A" list in academics as well. Though smaller numbers of students usually major in these lesser known disciplines, their graduates routinely are accepted for advanced study at such prestigious schools as Caltech and MIT. Says a satisfied major: "Even though high school guidance counselors don't know a lot about Ithaca's chemistry program, the top graduate schools do." Students like the student-faculty research team program used in psychology. The theater arts program, especially the musical theater major, also is very competitive but rewarding to those involved. History is considered a "gem," says a major, "a small department with faculty who cares about knowing and challenging students." The major in writing offers an eclectic breadth of courses ranging from classes in persuasive argument and autobiography to humorous writing and writing about sports.

Other programs in the School of Humanities and Sciences have fewer courses and less energetic faculty than their counterparts in the professional schools. The foreign languages program offers a more limited range and number of classes than many students would like. The art program, too, needs special attention: its classrooms lack adequate studios and supplies and are housed in the basement of the Athletic Fieldhouse, far from the other, more centrally located academic buildings. The business school recently received accreditation and plans to construct a new environmentally friendly building, but still faces some student criticism of faculty members whose English is hard to understand. Asks a major, "How is one supposed to learn when they can't understand the lecture coming from the professor?"

Facilities: Ithaca's library offers 355,000 volumes and 2500 periodicals, though most students turn to the facility's extensive computerized research aids for finding most of their sources. Says a recreation major: "While I don't remember ever having seen a book less than 10 years old, I can usually find all my information on computer or in journals." Additional information is only a 10-minute bus ride away at the massive Cornell University library system with its 7.1 million volumes and 65,000 periodicals. As a study center, the 5-story Ithaca library is satisfying—above the first 2 floors, that is, where most socializing is done. "The higher up you get, the quieter it is," says a junior. Music students, in particular, find ample resources on campus; Pulitzer-Prize-winning composer Karel Husa designated the library as the repository for all his recordings and music scores. Television-radio majors, and others, especially enjoy access to the Rod Serling archives, including scripts from his Twilight Zone television series.

Approximately 640 microcomputers, mainly Windows and Macintoshes, are located in about 30 labs across campus. Most computer rooms are open until 11 p.m. normally and until 1 a.m. during finals week though 2 centers are accessible 24 hours a day. "And there are Internet hookups everywhere imaginable for laptops," says a sophomore, as well as Internet kiosks located throughout campus for checking e-mail.

Special programs: Ithaca maintains its own extension campus in London, where students may continue their studies for a semester or a year in liberal arts, business, communications, theater arts, or music. The college also participates in exchange programs with colleges in Spain, Scotland, Australia, Singapore, Japan, and the Czech Republic. A variety of other foreign study experiences are available through such affiliated agencies as the School for International Training or the Institute for the International Education of Students. Students may take courses not taught at Ithaca at Cornell University or Wells College and pay no additional charge. A semester in Washington, D.C., also can be arranged. A 3-2 engineering program is offered jointly with Cornell, Rensselaer Polytechnic Institute, Clarkson University, or the State University of New York, Binghamton. A 4-1 M.B.A. program with the American Graduate School of International Management (Thunderbird), Clarkson, or Rochester Institute of Technology; 3-1 optometry programs with Pennsylvania College of Optometry and SUNY College of Optometry and a 1-semester program in marine biology with the Duke University Marine Laboratory also are options. First-year students who enter Ithaca unsure of what to study especially like the Exploratory Program in the School of Humanities and Sciences, which teams students with experienced academic advisors to help them select courses from the liberal arts and preprofessional curricula throughout the various schools before declaring a major.

Campus life: Seventy percent of Ithaca's students live on the 757-acre hilltop campus overlooking Cayuga Lake, a location physically relaxing but a bit snowy and chilly during the winter. Though the college itself is over a century old, the structures were built in the 1960s and onward, so the look is more modern. There are no social fraternities, only 3 national music fraternities and 1 social service sorority. For majors and nonmajors alike the campus radio and television stations are popular, with 200 students working at the 2 radio stations, and 200 to 250 each semester at the television station. Most students find some area of interest in the more than 160 clubs available. Concludes a senior: "Most everyone ends up doing something that he or she loves." Concerts and recitals sponsored by the music school, especially Ithacapella, the men's a capella singing group, as well as the theater arts department's productions, also provide a steady source of worthy entertainment. Monthly free IC After Dark events, with such themes as "Urban Cowboy" and "Haunted Hospital," also attract a following. Undergraduates generally feel very safe on the Ithaca campus. Says a sophomore: "Because Ithaca is located on a very steep hill, a mile from downtown, the only people who cause problems are fellow students." And even those problems are rarely alarming. A recent public safety log included such incidents as a student handing out unauthorized flyers, a bus causing damage to flowers, a student fainting and a found cell phone. Student Auxiliary Safety Patrols and more than 50 blue light emergency phones located around campus provide an extra measure of comfort.

Ithaca teams have claimed 3 NCAA Division III championships in football and wrestling, 2 each in baseball and women's soccer, and 1 each in field hockey, softball, women's crew, and gymnastics. Bomber squads also have produced individual national titlists in gymnastics, swimming, and wrestling. Altogether, the college fields 11 varsity sports for men and 12 for women, and though many attract large crowds, football is the centerpiece and remains "*the* place to be on fall Saturdays," says a junior. "And if you miss the Cortaga Jug Game, our annual match-up against hated rival Cortland State, you are considered a traitor!" Thirty-two percent of the men and 17% of the women take part in an extensive intramural program, 27 sports for each sex.

After the long, often harsh Ithaca winters, spring is fabulous, the outdoors beckons, and students make frequent trips to the waterfalls and gorges for which the area is known. Nearby Buttermilk Falls State Park is a favorite hangout, as is the downtown commons area. For indoor recreation, parties at Cornell University are popular.

Cost cutters: Eighty-six percent of the freshmen and 85% of continuing students received financial assistance in the 2005–2006 school year. For 74% of the freshmen and 68% of the remaining undergraduates, the aid was need-based. In an average freshman award, need-based scholarships or grants averaged $14,710, need-based self-help aid in the form of loans and jobs averaged $8133, and non-need-based awards and scholarships averaged $8411. Ithaca has a 2-tiered financial aid program through which approximately the top 25% of entering students receive annual renewable President's or Dean's merit scholarships, which range in value from $7000 to $13,000 or from $3000 to $7000, respectively. Students who demonstrate need can receive up to $10,000 in a need-based Access Grant annually. The Ithaca Leadership Scholarship pays $7000 to accepted applicants with a demonstrated record of leadership and above-average academic performance. The Premier Talent Scholarship pays up to $13,000 to music and theater majors with exceptional artistic, theatrical, technological, or managerial talent. Up to 20 outstanding high school seniors with an interest in communications are eligible to receive prestigious Park Scholar Awards that pay full costs of attendance, including 4 years of tuition, room, board, books, personal expenses, and a one-time computer purchase allowance of $2500. Fifteen exceptional entering students from ethnic or racial backgrounds that historically have been underrepresented in higher education are eligible to become Martin Luther King Jr. Scholars. Scholars receive up to full tuition in aid, with a minimum merit-based scholarship of $15,000. Applications to be considered for either the Park or Martin Luther King Jr. Scholars programs are due Dec. 15. Dana student work Internships provide highly qualified undergraduates with educationally relevant internships during the academic year or the summer; awards range from $3025 during the school year to $4375 for full-time summer work.

Rate of return: Eighty-six percent of entering freshmen return for the sophomore year. Seventy percent graduate in 4 years; 72%, in 5 years.

Payoff: In the 2005 graduating class, 10% majored in television-radio, 10% in business administration, and 5% in music. A third of recent graduates pursued advanced degrees within a year of commencement, 30% in the arts, sciences, and education, and 1% each in law and business. The vast majority, however, became employees of television networks, hospitals, and firms such as Xerox and IBM. About 120 companies and other organizations recruited on campus in the 2004–2005 school year.

Bottom line: The student who generally knows what career he or she would like to pursue is best served by Ithaca College, although the Exploratory Program helps give undecided undergraduates a boost. Ithaca, says a computer science major, offers a "2-sided education: theory in the classroom and an opportunity to gain experience through internships and other venues. The only type of student who would not succeed here is one who cannot manage his or her time and make choices. There are many choices that must be made, but help is available when the student asks for it."

Le Moyne College

Syracuse, New York 13214

Setting: Suburban
Control: Private (Roman Catholic-Jesuit)
Undergraduate enrollment: 915 men, 1403 women
Graduate enrollment: 39 men, 94 women (658 part-time)
Student/faculty ratio: 15:1
Freshman profile: 2% scored over 700 on SAT I verbal; 25% scored 600–700; 50% 500–599; 23% below 500. 2% scored over 700 on SAT I math; 31% scored 600–700; 51% 500–599; 16% below 500. 8% scored above 28 on the ACT; 10% scored 27–28; 31% 24–26; 34% 21–23; 17% below 21. 23% graduated in top tenth of high school class; 43% in upper fifth.

Faculty profile: 92% Ph.D.'s
Tuition and fees: $21,280
Room and board: $8290
Freshman financial aid: 92%; average scholarship or grant: $14,765 need-based; $9133 non-need-based
Campus jobs: 38%; average earnings: $1037/year
Application deadline: Early decision: Dec. 1; regular: Feb. 1
Financial aid deadline: Feb. 1
Admissions information: (315) 445-4300; (800) 333-4733
e-mail: admissions@lemoyne.edu
web site: www.lemoyne.edu

A school year at Le Moyne College in Syracuse, New York, isn't different from the preceding year only because it has a new class of freshmen, a few new faculty faces, or maybe a new building. It usually has a new issue. In a recent school year, for example, classes in a wide range of disciplines, public lectures, and panel discussions were devoted to examining the issue "On the Edge: In Search of Values for the New Millennium." In another year, campus discussion centered around a similar theme: "Values 2000: The Student Connection." The focus reflects a faculty-initiated Values Program, designed to make contemporary issues of human importance more pertinent to students. In recent school years, the campus topics have been wide-ranging, involving students in the discussion of such important issues as Science, Technology, and Values, Families and Public Policy, and Economic Justice. During the summer, faculty from as many as 14 departments discuss ways in which the upcoming issue can be integrated throughout the curriculum. In the fall, a student values committee sponsors its own relevant campuswide events. As a result of the project, visitors to this Jesuit campus, which turned 60 in 2006, are as likely to find students debating government policies on welfare or child care as discussing the last accounting test or recent victory by the Dolphin baseball team.

Student body: All but 7% of Le Moyne's students are from New York State, with undergraduates coming from a total of 24 states, mostly in the Northeast, and 4 foreign countries. Forty-five percent are Catholic; 18% are graduates of private or parochial schools. African Americans and Hispanics each comprise 4% of the enrollment, Asian-Americans 2%, and Native Americans 1%. Foreign nationals also account for 1%. The organization Pride in Our Work, Ethnicity, and Race (POWER, for short) brings multicultural issues before the rest of the student body by planning events for Latino and Black History months and inviting speakers to discuss such issues as racism and social discrimination. Students describe classmates as caring, family-oriented, somewhat sheltered, fairly conservative, helpful, and hard-working, qualities that carry over into the study habits of a majority. Says a sophomore: "There are definitely partiers who don't seem to care, but there is also a core of highly committed and motivated students." Most students also do their best to stay busy. Says a junior: "Le Moyne focuses on educating the 'whole person' in the Jesuit tradition, so we have students who are *very* involved whether it be academically, athletically, politically, or in leadership roles."

Academics: Le Moyne, named for the first Jesuit missionary who came to the central New York Iroquois Nation, confers the bachelor's degree in more than 40 majors plus masters degrees in business administration, education, and physician assistant studies. The academic year is divided into 2 semesters. An average class size of 22–25 varies from 2 in several courses to almost 80 in a class like Cell and Molecular Biology.

Students consider the core curriculum to be among Le Moyne's strong points, both in its subject matter and its approach, which develops students' problem-solving, critical thinking, and communication skills. The heart of the core is a 12-course, 4-year humanities sequence that features coursework in the foundations of Western culture including issues concerning the roles of women and minorities as well as discussions of literary, philosophical, and religious perspectives on the human situation. Courses in the natural and social sciences also are required.

All but 1 of the 154 full-time professors and all but 27 of the 170 part-time members teach undergraduates; 42% of the pool are women. As a body, the faculty emphasizes teaching, and professors pride themselves on being readily accessible to ensure that their instruction takes hold. "They care," says a midwesterner, "and they never hesitate to show students that they do, both inside and outside the classroom." One English major remains close friends with a business professor he met on a school-sponsored trip to build homes for Habitat for Humanity. A history student recalls a history professor who spent "a half-hour talking to me about career choices," the junior notes, "and I've never had him as a professor!" Student concern centers most on the adjunct faculty, whose numbers have grown. Says a political science major: "While these adjuncts are okay, they are not as high quality as the full-time professors and are much more limited in their availability."

Each year, graduates in Le Moyne's strong accounting major show how well respected that program is by getting good jobs. Other programs in the Division of Management also feature tough and well-connected faculty who help turn out successful graduates. Industrial relations, for example, has a strong internship program and a working faculty willing to let students accompany them on various mediation and arbitration assignments. Biology boasts excellent professors and first-rate facilities in a recently renovated building; special research laboratories house 2 electron microscopes available to students. Psychology offers students great opportunities to conduct research and experiments with professors. Philosophy and religious studies each offer a rich variety of courses, ranging from a philosophy class on questioning the existence of God to a religion seminar in Christianity and slavery. History, says an English major, has "incredible lecturers and professors," though some students question the quality of the part-time faculty who teach some of the introductory courses. Political science and English also garner respect, although some conservative students wish there were more professors from their side of the political spectrum. Adds a happy English major: "My professors have made learning relevant to our modern world and are adept at using technology to invite discussion boards outside of class."

Foreign languages with majors only in French and Spanish have few full-time professors and limited class offerings. The physics and computer science programs need more staff and better facilities. Education, a traditionally strong program at Le Moyne, consistently needs more funding to keep pace with the increasing mandates of the New York State Education Department. Visual arts and music are offered only as minors, although theater arts recently was expanded to a major from a minor.

Facilities: Noreen Reale Falcone Library, which contains more than 251,000 volumes and 35,500 paper and electronic periodicals, is an open, airy building with plenty of couches, cubicles, and individual and group study rooms. Concentrated work is best done during the day because the library becomes more of a social meeting place during the evening hours. A computerized catalog and assorted databases assist in research projects and on those rare instances when Falcone fails to satisfy, students usually find the answer through interlibrary loan or at nearby Bird Library at Syracuse University, with its collection of more than 2 million volumes and 10,000 periodicals.

About 325 PCs and Macs are available in public and departmental laboratories, all recently updated and connected to the campus-wide network. All dorm rooms also have access to the Internet. Labs in the science center, library, and main academic complex are open during normal building hours. Lab hours recently were shortened to 10 p.m. in some buildings because of a problem with late-night computer theft; labs in the library remain open until midnight. Wireless access is available throughout most of the campus, including all academic areas.

Special programs: Le Moyne offers its own study abroad programs at Essex University and the University of Leicester in England, the University of Stirling in Scotland, and in the Dominican Republic. Semester or year-long study within the United States is an option at Virginia Polytechnic Institute, at about 60 colleges and universities in New York State, or in Washington, D.C. for a semester. Joint 3-2 programs in engineering are offered with Clarkson University, the University of Detroit-Mercy, and Manhattan College. Three-4 programs are provided with the SUNY Buffalo School of Dental Medicine, New York College of Podiatric Medicine, and the Pennsylvania College of Optometry. Highly qualified students may apply for acceptance to the SUNY at Syracuse medical school at the end of the sophomore year and receive a guarantee of admission after graduation from Le Moyne. Similar assurance can be arranged with the SUNY at Buffalo medical and dental schools.

Campus life: Two-thirds of Le Moyne's undergraduates live on the 151-acre campus, known as "the Heights" because it overlooks the city of Syracuse. There are no fraternities or sororities, so students generally turn out for parties at the townhouses or for the dances, comedians, movies, or coffee-house performances that are regularly scheduled for the weekend. Community service is a vital part of campus life; Mass, though not required, is generally well attended. Many Jesuits serve as residence hall counselors who offer both formal and informal academic and social counseling. All dormitories have number keypads so that only undergraduates who know the 4-digit code, which changes every 2 weeks, can gain entry; visitors must be signed in. Says a junior "If you stand in the same place for 5 minutes, you will see one of our security officers drive by." Peer escort and nightly shuttle services also are available. As a result of these measures and others, most students say they feel secure on campus though they stress that caution should be used when walking off campus.

Nearly a fifth of the men and a tenth of the women play on 8 intercollegiate teams for each sex. The college's NCAA Division I men's baseball team in 2003 earned its first Division I tournament appearance since 1989 and its first league crown since 1998. All other sports are played in NCAA Division II, with basketball and lacrosse attracting the largest crowds. In 2005, the men's soccer team, also a campus favorite, earned its first NCAA tournament berth since 1977. About half the students participate in the intramural program, consisting of 9 men's and 8 women's sports.

When it's time to get away, the Emmaus retreat program on Cazenovia Lake draws a large number of participants. The ever-active Outing Club also does its part, sponsoring numerous trips to enjoy skiing, whitewater rafting, camping, and other outdoor activities. In quieter moments, students enjoy picnics and swimming at Green Lake; there also are lively parties at Syracuse University for the less quiet times. The city of Syracuse offers the Carousel Shopping Mall and other diversions.

Cost cutters: In the 2004–2005 school year, the most recent year for which data is available, 92% of freshmen and continuing students received financial aid; for about 82% of all students, the help was need-based. The average freshman award included need-based scholarships or grants averaging $14,765 and need-based self-help aid such as loans and jobs averaging $3968. The average non-need-based athletic scholarship for first-year students totaled $7088. Other non-need-based awards and scholarships averaged $9133. A typical recent graduate left with debts of $19,137. The Presidential Scholarship provides awards worth $17,500 annually to students who graduated among the top of their high school classes with high SAT and ACT scores. An Ignatian Scholarship worth $13,000 may be offered to students with similar scholastic records from Jesuit high schools. Dean's Scholarships pay $13,000; Leader Scholar awards provide $5500 minimum. Loyola and Community Scholarships pay $13,000 and $7500 respectively to members of underrepresented ethnic populations.

Rate of return: Among enrolling freshmen, 87% return the following year. Sixty-one percent go on to graduate in 4 years; 71% in 5 years; 74% in 6.

Payoff: Business claimed 22% of the 2005 graduates, followed by psychology majors at 17%, and English at 10%. A third of recent alumni went to graduate school within a year of earning their bachelor's degrees. Sixty-one percent took jobs primarily in New York State and the Northeast with the major accounting firms, IBM, Aetna, and other large corporations. About 80 companies and organizations recruited on campus in a recent school year.

Bottom line: For students unsure of what they want to major in, Le Moyne is a good choice thanks to a caring faculty willing to provide plenty of help and advice. Remarks a junior: "Although Le Moyne is young and therefore not very well known, its alumni have shown what a degree from this college can do—anything! Its well-rounded curriculum opens many doors."

Marist College

Poughkeepsie, New York 12601

Setting: Suburban
Control: Independent
Undergraduate enrollment: 1843 men, 2570 women
Graduate enrollment: 62 men, 105 women (681 part-time)
Student/faculty ratio: 22:1
Freshman profile: 4% scored over 700 on SAT I verbal; 36% scored 600–700; 50% 500–599; 10% below 500. 7% scored over 700 on SAT I math; 43% scored 600–700; 45% 500–599; 5% below 500. 16% scored above 28 on the ACT; 17% scored 27–28; 44% 24–26; 16% 21–23; 7% below 21. 21% graduated in top tenth of high school class; 55% in upper fifth.

Faculty profile: 82% Ph.D.'s
Tuition and fees: $21,202
Room and board: $9364
Freshman financial aid: 90%; average scholarship or grant: $5746 need-based
Campus jobs: 23%; average earnings: $1724/year
Application deadline: Early decision: Nov. 15; early action: Dec. 1; regular: Feb. 15
Financial aid deadline: Feb. 15
Admissions information: (845) 575-3226; (800) 436-5483
e-mail: admissions@marist.edu
web site: www.marist.edu

Historically, Marist College traces its roots to the Catholic religious teaching order of the Marist Brothers, who opened their first training center in the United States on the east bank of the Hudson River in 1905. Over the years, the novitiate changed with the times, eventually becoming a college for laypersons, with ownership passing from the Marist Order to an independent board of trustees. Today, Marist brothers remain on campus as some of the best-loved faculty members, but the college is in secular partnership with a new order having the initials I-B-M. In 1988, Marist and the giant computer corporation began a 5-year, $16 million joint study to explore how computer technology could be made more user-friendly in the future. This collaboration, which has continued since 1993 in several smaller projects, dramatically transformed the campus originally built by the labor of Marist brothers. As part of the project, a powerful 3090 mainframe computer, since upgraded 5 times, was networked to all parts of the college, from the classrooms to the labs to the dormitories. The current mainframe, a new Z Series 900, is of a power more apt to be found at a major research university than a college of 5750 undergraduate and graduate students. The result is a 21st-century campus with 7608 network ports, 42 "smart" classrooms (three-quarters of all classrooms on campus), and 25 computer labs. The library alone, which opened in 2000, claims to have more ports per student than any other library in the world. "Technology," says a junior, "is ingrained in the learning process at Marist College." And while the original Roman Catholic teaching brothers could never have envisioned the technology their campus would hold, 100 years later, the "learning process" remains a Marist labor of love.

Student body: Marist's Catholic tradition remains strong, with about 60% of its undergraduates in a recent year members of the Catholic faith. Six percent of the students are Hispanic, 4% African-American, 2% Asian-American and less than 1% Native American; another 1% are foreign nationals from 10 countries. Sixty percent of the undergraduates are from New York State; all but 10% come from the Northeast, though 36 states are represented. Seventy percent are graduates of public schools. Students view classmates as politically conservative, academically middle-of-the-road, and socially very involved in activities both on campus and in the community. Students have been described, notes one senior, as "walking straight out of the Abercrombie and Fitch catalogues," sometimes with little understanding of individuals who challenge traditional viewpoints. While some are drawn by Marist's values-oriented education, others are motivated more by a desire for success in their postgraduation careers. In general, however, students find classmates helpful and supportive of one another.

Academics: Marist offers the bachelor's degree in 30 majors, including a bachelor of professional studies in fashion design and in fashion merchandising. There are master's degree programs in 10 fields. The academic year is divided into 2 semesters, with a 3-week intercession in January, during which students can attend classes on an accelerated basis. During regular terms, the average class size for freshmen tops out at about 35, with upper-level courses usually dropping to between 10 and 20.

The core/liberal studies program at Marist builds upon a theme of understanding one's values system. Each student takes 3 foundation courses in the freshman year, philosophy, Themes in Modern History, and writing, a course in ethics in the junior or senior year, plus distribution requirements from the various academic fields. A "capping experience" in the student's major is mandatory for all bachelor's degree candidates except those pursuing the professional studies degree.

Of the 617 faculty who teach at all levels at Marist, 204 are full-time and teach undergraduates; 23 of the 413 part-time members teach at the graduate level only. Forty-three percent are women. Students find the overall quality rather mixed, with the Marist brothers ranking among the best teachers and numerous adjunct professors rating high on professional expertise and low on ability to transfer their knowledge to students. Faculty for the most part are considered helpful, accessible, and eager to foster in-class discourse and debate. "If students prove the professor wrong, all the better!" says a transfer student.

High-tech facilities, along with capable professors, characterize Marist's strongest programs. The Lowell Thomas Communications Center, which opened in 1987 with 2 television studios, 2 broadcast production studios, and computerized print journalism rooms, has helped make communications one of Marist's most popular majors, although some consider it overrated. Students like having professors with lots of real-life experience, and their connections help open up internship opportunities in the Big Apple, less than 2 hours away. Political science, too, provides plenty of opportunities for internships in Albany, New York City, and Washington, D.C., and for experience in studying voter behavior with the Marist Institute for Public Opinion. The Dyson Center, completed in 1990, is home to the well-regarded business and psychology programs, which involve students in computer-based simulations and computer-assisted group learning and problem solving. The program for psychology majors seeking special education certification is especially "intense." Not surprisingly, computer science is enhanced by Marist's partnership with IBM. Computer-science majors in a recent class enjoyed 100% job placement. The program in fashion design also draws rave reviews because of a demanding department head and plenty of opportunities for students to work with big-name designers in New York City.

The math, foreign language, and fine arts departments fall short of student expectations. Language majors are available only in French and Spanish, although courses are offered in Arabic, Chinese, English as a Second Language, German, Italian, and Japanese. Fine arts majors are offered in studio art and art history; music may be pursued as a minor. The science department also is smaller, and while solid, could use some additional support.

Facilities: The opening in January 2000 of the 83,000-square-foot James A. Cannavino Library drew enthusiastic praise from undergraduates. Remarked a sophomore: "Our new library offers students the opportunity to enhance their learning, create exceptional reports, and enjoy the best of the facilities offered on campus. It's more than a library; it's the future get-away spot." And so it has become. The 3-story structure, which tripled the size of the former library, overlooks the campus green and the Hudson River. It seats 860 students in a variety of individual and collaborative study areas. Network connections located throughout the building, providing at least 1 per seat as well as laptops that can be checked out from the circulation desk, provide access to digitized and on-line information available both in the library and on the Internet and World Wide Web. Cannavino's holdings remain small—just over 183,500 volumes and 252,000 microform items, though more than 18,000 periodicals can be reviewed electronically. The third floor houses various academic support facilities such as a writing center and multimedia classrooms. A 2-story atrium entrance and lobby offer an even greater support to serious studiers: a coffee bar.

The joint project with IBM has ensured that computers are plentiful around campus. Overall, there are 5 main areas on campus with 37 labs and clusters, 2 labs open around the clock, that provide more than 550 terminals. From each dorm room students with PCs can connect to the library and its consortia partners in the mid-Hudson and New York City areas, as well as to e-mail, topic-specific electronic conferences, the Internet and Internet 2. Students also may access Marist's wireless network from their residence halls, the library, dining room, lounges, and laundry rooms. The college strongly recommends that students have personal computers.

Special programs: Undergraduates may study abroad in 32 countries in Europe, Africa, Latin and Central America, and the Far East. Internships in a wide variety of majors are available with more than 1100 organizations, mainly in New York City, Albany and the mid-Hudson region but also throughout the U.S. and abroad.

Campus life: Seventy-three percent of Marist's students reside on the 150-acre campus, with more than 400 new housing units, including townhouses for 144 students opening their doors in the last few years. Priority points, awarded for qualities such as student involvement and grades, help determine where undergraduates will live—in the dormitories, in on-campus apartments, or in townhouses. Despite the allure of New York City and Albany, most students find enough campus activities, comedians, coffeehouses, casino nights, to keep them busy for the weekend. Greek life is small but fairly popular, with 1% of the men and 6% of the women belonging to 3 national fraternities and 4 sororities, 3 national and 1 local. Red Fox intercollegiate sports are also popular, and not just to watch, as part of NCAA Division I play. About 40% of the men and women participate in the 11 men's and 12 women's events, which range from basketball and hockey, which draw the biggest crowds, to men's and women's crew. The intramural program, with 4 coed sports, is especially active, involving about 1600 students. In the cultural arena, the Marist College Council on Theatre Arts is a favorite, producing several plays a year, some of them written by students and now appearing in the new 350-seat Nelly Goletti Theater located in the new $27 million student center. The TGIF comedy club also attracts a crowd to the center on Friday nights. The debate team is top-ranked in national competitions. With a highway and the Hudson River as boundaries and 24-hour security patrols, as well as dorm monitors at night and a student-run escort service, safety on campus is not much of a problem.

Students who want to get away but are unwilling to travel 1–2 hours to New York City or Albany find plenty to do around Poughkeepsie (pop. 30,000). Continuing north on Route 9, undergraduates can take in the stunning Vanderbilt mansion and grounds or Franklin Roosevelt's Hyde Park home. For quiet reflection, the banks of the Hudson River right on campus are ideal.

Cost cutters: Ninety percent of the freshmen in the 2005–2006 school year and 86% of the continuing students received some form of financial aid. Sixty-one percent of the freshmen and 57% of the rest were on need-based assistance. The average award for a first-year student with financial need included a need-based scholarship or grant averaging $10,971 and need-based self-help aid such as loans and jobs averaging $4954. Non-need-based athletic scholarships for freshmen averaged $7769. The average financial indebtedness of a 2005 graduate was $20,618. A new student with a good academic record may qualify for a Marist or Presidential Scholarship, on a 4-year renewable basis. The awards range from $8000 to

$12,000. Cooperative education programs are offered in computer science, computer information systems, business, and fashion design and merchandising.

Rate of return: Ninety percent of freshmen return for the sophomore year. Sixty-eight percent go on to graduate in 4 years; 76%, in 5 years.

Payoff: Twenty-one percent of the 2005 graduates earned degrees in business followed by 17% in communications, and 13% in psychology. Three-fourths of new alumni exchange their degrees for jobs, many with the 200 companies and organizations that recruit on campus. Firms that have hired Marist graduates include CBS-TV, PricewaterhouseCoopers, IBM, the New York Stock Exchange, and McGraw-Hill Publishing. Just over a fourth opt to continue their studies immediately, most in the arts and sciences. Recent graduates have gained admission to such premier universities as Stanford, Georgetown, McGill, and Oxford.

Bottom line: Says a senior: "The Marist-IBM joint study makes Marist one of the best places to go for computer studies. This college stays current with the times. Many teachers are not just academics: they often have businesses, have just retired, or teach because they like to. Because of its location on the Hudson, Marist is also a very nice place to be."

Rochester Institute of Technology

Rochester, New York 14623

Setting: Suburban
Control: Private
Undergraduate enrollment: 7986 men, 3454 women
Graduate enrollment: 650 men, 467 women
Student/faculty ratio: 13:1
Freshman profile: 9% scored over 700 on SAT I verbal; 37% scored 600–700; 44% 500–599; 10% below 500. 15% scored over 700 on SAT I math; 49% scored 600–700; 32% 500–599; 4% below 500. 24% scored above 28 on the ACT; 20% scored 27–28; 28% 24–26; 18% 21–23; 10% below 21. 30% graduated in top tenth of high school class; 50% in upper fifth.

Faculty profile: 85% Ph.D.'s
Tuition and fees: $23,619
Room and board: $8451
Freshman financial aid: 85%; average scholarship or grant: NA
Campus jobs: 50%; average earnings: $1800/year
Application deadline: Early decision: Dec. 1; regular: rolling
Financial aid deadline: Mar. 1
Admissions information: (585) 475-6631
  e-mail: admissions@rit.edu
  web site: www.rit.edu

Rochester Institute of Technology offers majors in economics, accounting, and biology, but for many students it's not the ordinary disciplines but the extraordinary ones that draw them to this campus of nearly 11,500 full-time undergraduates. Among the 200 different concentrations offered are microelectronic engineering and imaging science, each the first program of its kind in the country, as well as new media publishing and packaging science, available at few other colleges. The excellent cooperative education program, required in most majors, has placed marketing majors at ESPN in Manhattan and photography students at NASA, developing photos of Neptune. In sum, RIT is Rich In Treasures, at a price that, with the help of cooperative earnings, doesn't send most students or their families to the poorhouse.

Student body: Fifty-five percent of RIT undergraduates are from New York State, although students come from all 50 states and 80 foreign countries. Eighty-five percent are graduates of public schools. Asian-American students constitute the largest minority group on campus, at 7%. African-Americans and foreign nationals account for 5% of the enrollment; Hispanics, 4%; Native Americans, 1%. A student once described RIT's diversity in different terms, as including everything from "digit heads to frat boys," although a majority are politically and socially conservative. The presence on campus of the National Technical Institute for the Deaf adds approximately 1100 hearing-impaired students to the enrollment. A third of the undergraduates are transfer students from 2-year and other 4-year institutions. The atmosphere on campus is intense, driven both by a fast-moving quarter system and by the individual efforts of undergraduates to excel in their fields and attain good-paying jobs during school and upon graduation. "Students here are serious about their educations," observes a new media publishing major. "No matter where you go on campus you will find them talking about academics. Around here, class doesn't end once you leave the classroom."

Academics: RIT, founded in 1829, confers degrees through the doctorate in its 8 colleges, including the Institute for the Deaf. The school follows the quarter system, with students not in a cooperative education program attending classes for 3 terms during a regular academic year. Upperclassmen participating in a co-op program spend a 12- or 13-week quarter on campus, followed by 12 or 13 weeks in the workplace, and alternate periods of study and employment for either 1 year or 2, depending on the major. (Some find the pace so stressful they take off a quarter.) The cooperative education program is the fourth oldest and one of the largest in the nation, placing more than 3000 students each year in positions with any of 1300 employers, from Bausch & Lomb to Xerox. At least 80% of RIT's 200 undergraduate programs require some cooperative experience or offer it as an option. During the quarters spent on campus, most technical classes in the first 2 years range in size from 20 to 30 people; nontechnical classes have 25–35. Introductory lectures in chemistry and biology may approach 100. In the junior and senior years, classes in technical subjects drop to between 10 and 20 participants, while those in nontechnical areas decrease less. Opportunities for independent study also are available.

Each school or college requires students to take 36 quarter credit hours, 20% of the 180 hours needed to graduate, in the liberal arts. Although the mix of courses varies by program, most mandate 6 foundation courses in the humanities and social sciences, a disciplinary or interdisciplinary concentration of 3 advanced courses, 3 advanced electives, specific courses in writing and literature and physical education and a liberal arts senior seminar and project. Students earning a bachelor of science degree must also take an additional 20 quarter credit hours in math and science.

Two-thirds of the 1364 faculty are full-time; a third of the total pool are women. All but 23 of the 902 full-time faculty and all but 62 of the 462 part-time members teach undergraduates. Their qualities span the full range from brilliant to dull, accessible to aloof. Virtually all, however, are current in their specialties and provide instruction that incorporates the latest developments in their respective fields, as well as their personal professional experiences.

All 6 schools within the highly respected College of Imaging Arts and Sciences are winners. The college's School of Photographic Arts and Sciences offers 7 concentrations, from photojournalism to biomedical photographic communications, supported by 50 studios and more than 100 color and black-and-white darkrooms with modern equipment provided by Eastman Kodak, the hometown company. The School of Print Media also benefits from generous donations of equipment from industry. The School of Art, School of Design and School for American Crafts are equally distinctive and well supplied. The college's School of Film and Animation has grown from a small department to a school that has produced Academy Award-winning work. In the College of Science, the Chester F. Carlson Center for Imaging Science offers one of the few comprehensive facilities as well as the only undergraduate and graduate curricula devoted to the study of the formation, recording, manipulation, and perception of images such as those used in medical diagnostics. Students also find the department of biological sciences in the College of Science to be rigorous but rewarding.

All programs in the Kate Gleason College of Engineering thrive on state-of-the-art equipment, and the major in microelectronic engineering boasts its own fully functional computer-chip manufacturing facility right on campus. The mandatory cooperative experience, making all majors in the college 5-year programs, keeps students abreast of the latest developments in the workplace. The recently established Golisano College of Computing and Information Technology features very large and comprehensive programs in these 2 rapidly changing fields and also in software engineering. Students in the college also may pursue a new bachelor's degree program of advanced studies in network infrastructure, wireless communications, systems and security. The College of Business offers numerous opportunities for students to mix with faculty and alumni.

Other sciences, for example, chemistry and physics, offer excellent courses for students planning to major in these fields. However, classes directed at nonmajors are less impressive. Recalls a biology major: "After the attention I got in the physics department as a potential major, I feel gypped taking the courses for nonmajors. Whereas, before, the teacher was enthusiastic, in this case, the teacher didn't care enough even to read our lab reports. Majors, especially where labs are concerned, receive much better attention." The College of Liberal Arts, offering majors in advertising and public relations, criminal justice, economics, international studies, professional and technical communication, psychology and public policy, likewise has coursework many students find less challenging. Notes a computer science major: "Professors in this college seem to feel that students take their courses simply to fill electives, and they convey that attitude in their teaching."

Facilities: Recent renovation of Wallace Library doubled the physical size of the building and made it, in the words of one user, "a more soothing place to study." Its collection consists of 407,000 volumes and 2500 paper periodicals. Einstein, the computerized catalog, makes it easy for undergraduates to locate reference materials and request those needed for a project. For times when Einstein cannot find a critical mass on campus, students can turn to Connect New York, which puts them in touch with the resources of 10 other colleges and universities in the state.

Seventeen computer centers and labs on campus are available for student use and house more than 600 PCs. Students also can, and many do, link their own PCs to the Internet from individual dormitory rooms or off-campus locations. While most labs are open until at least 11 p.m., laptops are available in the library's After Hours Room around the clock. Wireless access also is available on campus.

Special programs: Students can take courses at nearby colleges in the Rochester area. Study-abroad programs are offered in 15 countries, including affiliations with universities in England, Japan, and Scandinavia.

Campus life: Sixty-one percent of RIT's full-time students live on the modern, 1300-acre campus, completed in 1968. Freshmen and sophomores reside in dormitories with their own recreation rooms, while juniors and seniors settle into 1 of the largest university-operated apartment systems in the country. Sixteen national fraternities enroll 5% of the men as members; 5% of the women pledge to 9 national sororities. Undergraduates say that the Greeks party largely among their members and invited guests, so their influence over the campus social life as a whole is small. Most of RIT's career-oriented students prefer to mix business with pleasure by socializing in the wide range of clubs related to academic majors. Vandalism and petty theft are the worst campus crimes, and even they occur infrequently. Dorms are kept locked around the clock to curb the number of incidents.

Although RIT offers strong NCAA Division III programs in men's soccer and lacrosse and women's tennis and volleyball, these pale in comparison to the major winter madness, men's ice hockey which is Division I. Altogether, RIT fields 12 men's and 12 women's intercollegiate teams. Nine thousand men and women participate in the 30 intramural programs open to both sexes.

Rochester, the third largest city in New York, earns high marks as a cultural and social attraction, with the college providing free bus service to malls, theaters, and clubs. That old-standby, Niagara Falls, is 90 minutes away. Toronto, a 3-hour drive, provides another excellent weekend getaway, though the nature trails in the woods next to the dormitories offer a closer and a cost-free way to unwind.

Cost cutters: In the 2005–2006 school year, 85% of freshmen and 75% of continuing students received financial aid; all but 10% in each group received need-based assistance. An average freshman award totaled $17,500, although no breakdown exists for the portion that was need-based or merit-based scholarships or grants or self-help aid such as loans and jobs. No figures on student debt are available. High school seniors may be eligible for Presidential Scholarships that pay $3000 to $10,000 a year dependent on a student's standardized test scores and class rank. More than 550 Presidential awards were made in a recent school year. Approximately 200 outstanding transfer students are eligible for Trustee Scholarships valued at $4500 to $6000 a year. The cooperative program helps students both to save money and to pay for college costs, as undergraduates are not charged tuition while on co-op assignments. In a recent year, a junior or senior working in the field of environmental management earned from $3975 to $7450 in a 13-week work assignment of 40 hours per week. A classmate working in the field of microelectronic engineering earned $6100 to $13,800. The fact that many of the cooperative programs are on a 5-year schedule allows parents to spread payments for 4 years of tuition over an extra year.

Rate of return: Eighty-eight percent of freshmen return for a second year. Sixty-two percent graduate within 6 years.

Payoff: In the 2005 graduating class, 13% earned degrees in engineering, 13% in information technology, and 9% in photography. Ninety percent of RIT's graduates take jobs immediately, many with such firms nationwide as Eastman Kodak, IBM, Xerox, Bausch and Lomb, and Marriott. Six hundred companies recruit on campus. At least 50% of the graduates begin their careers working full-time for one of their co-op employers. The few who seek advanced degrees do so in science, engineering, medicine, law, and business.

Bottom line: A student who comes to Rochester Institute of Technology should have an idea of the subject area in which he or she wishes to concentrate. But once that decision is made, the opportunities for enrichment are enormous for undergraduates who can keep up with the program. "This school is by no means easy," concludes a junior, "but it has a way of paying off," and not just at the end.

St. Bonaventure University

St. Bonaventure, New York 14778

Setting: Small town
Control: Private (Roman Catholic)
Undergraduate enrollment: 1078 men, 1122 women
Graduate enrollment: 84 men, 181 women
Student/faculty ratio: 17:1
Freshman profile: Average combined SAT I score: 1060; Class rank data: NA
Faculty profile: 85% Ph.D.'s
Tuition and fees: $21,775
Room and board: $7335

Freshman financial aid: 93%; average scholarship or grant: $10,928 need-based; $7042 non-need-based
Campus jobs: NA; average earnings: NA
Application deadline: Apr. 1
Financial aid deadline: Feb. 1
Admissions information: (716) 375-2400; (800) 462-5050
e-mail: admissions@sbu.edu
web site: www.sbu.edu

When students at St. Bonaventure University, the nation's first Franciscan university, are asked to name their institution's best programs, the list invariably includes majors in elementary education, journalism/communication, and accounting. But there is a hidden major that all graduates carry as well: thinking. It is hard not to be forced into contemplation on St. Bonaventure's serene 500-acre campus, where brown-robed Franciscan friars stroll against a backdrop of the Allegheny mountains. In addition, just 40 miles off campus the Mt. Irenaeus mountain retreat provides a setting even more conducive to personal reflection as well as quiet friendship. At Bona's, as the college is called, students find themselves learning to think critically and to examine a world beyond themselves. "At St. Bonaventure," a student has said, "we are thinkers, communicators—and smilers."

Student body: Seventy-six percent of St. Bonaventure's students in a recent year were from New York State, with most of the rest from New Jersey, Pennsylvania, Ohio, Massachusetts, and Connecticut. Altogether, undergraduates come from 34 states and 7 foreign countries. Forty-two percent in a recent year were graduates of private or parochial schools. African-American students recently accounted for 2% of the student body, and there were 1% each Hispanic, Asian-American, and Native American students. Another 2% were foreign nationals. Undergraduates tend to be warm, hard-working, thoughtful, and competitive, but not to the extent of compromising their ethics and values. Students credit the school's Franciscan tradition for creating a familial atmosphere of respect and consideration for others. That attitude carries over not only into the way students treat one another but also into the involvement of many in various social action programs as well as active social lives. "Most take their academics seriously," says a junior, "but they also take their social lives seriously, too."

Academics: St. Bonaventure, founded in 1858, offers the bachelor's degree in 33 disciplines plus master's programs in 22 fields. Classes in the 2-semester year average 22 students; the range extends from 4 in some upper-level courses to 45 for various introductory lectures.

Thinking is a cornerstone of St. Bonaventure's recently adopted core curriculum, housed in Clare College, named for a 13th-century noblewoman of Assisi who was inspired by St. Francis. The curriculum, which covers 36 of the 120 credits required for graduation, was designed to involve all students in a common set of courses that reflect the university's mission and Catholic identity. First-year students begin with a seminar titled The Intellectual Journey, that draws on the writings of St. Bonaventure, St. Francis, St. Clare, Plato, Homer, Dante, and others, and in a 2-semester course in Composition and Critical Thinking. Most of the other core area courses are interdisciplinary, such as Inquiry in the Natural World, which draws on physics, chemistry, and biology, as well as a class in Art and Literature. Students complete the curriculum with a senior-year capstone course University Forum, designed to apply the skills, knowledge, and insights from the core-area courses to contemporary social issues.

The faculty in a recent year numbered 148 full-time members, all but 28 of whom taught undergraduates. Fifty-five of the 65 part-time faculty members did so as well. Eighty percent of the total pool are men, several of them Franciscan friars. One percent of the introductory courses in a recent year were taught by graduate students. Though Bona's has its share of professors who put in their required class time but offer little outside, the vast majority do their best to make students feel comfortable about asking for academic help or personal advice anytime. These professors, says a psychology major, "are not just our advisors or instructors: they are our friends." A number have degrees from the university, a bond that enhances their commitment to the students and the school.

Accounting and journalism/mass communication rank as 2 of the university's strongest and most popular offerings. Their professors boast real-world experience, which is reflected in the curricula and the excitement of their teaching. Strong alumni networks in each of these areas help in the job search after graduation. The facilities are especially good at the Russell J. Jandoli School of Journalism and Mass Communication, a far cry from the days in 1947 when Professor Jandoli could not find enough typewriters for the new journalism department he had proposed starting. Today's facilities include a new television studio, a radio station that is consistently ranked among the top 5 college stations, and 2 Apple Macintosh desktop publishing labs that help students fine-tune their writing skills. Five graduates of the journalism program have gone on to win Pulitzer Prizes. Education is another popular concentration with faculty noted for their dedication and willingness to help. Psychology and English also are considered solid majors.

While students praise the quality of the science professors, some say the lab facilities must be upgraded to make majors more competitive, especially if they are preparing for medical school. The theology major remains small but hopes to attract more students to its curriculum, after recently being reinstated as a major following elimination of the major program a couple of years before. Students sense that the history department has been shrinking and could use more courses.

Facilities: As far as thinking spots around campus go, Friedsam Memorial Library offers nooks and crannies for the diligent hunter, although most of the main areas are too noisy for concentrated study. As a source for research, the collection of about 250,000 volumes and 1500 periodical subscriptions is stronger than it used to be, and a computerized catalog, and computers with periodical databases assist in the research process, though students say more terminals are needed. Despite these modern improvements, one of the library's chief treasures is among its most dated: the oldest Bible in America.

Five labs with about 130 computers, mainly Windows but also Macs, are open to students. The lab in Friedsam Library, with 56 PCs, is open until midnight. Units in 2 of the other 4 labs are available until 11 p.m. Students have full Internet access and few complaints.

Special programs: Study-abroad opportunities are available for a semester or a year through 25 colleges in 18 countries. Shorter sessions are conducted in Quebec and Puebla, Mexico, with a special 6-week summer program available at Oxford University. A semester in the nation's capital is offered through American University. As part of a 2-2 engineering program, students divide their 4 years between St. Bonaventure and the University of Detroit-Mercy; a 3-2 engineering option is available with Clarkson University.

Campus life: Three-fourths of all St. Bonaventure students live on the scenic campus, which for some is idyllic, but for others is a bit too isolated from major city centers. Without social fraternities or sororities, most weekend celebrating starts with happy hour at the campus Rathskeller and continues with students boarding the Bona bus to off-campus house parties in nearby Allegany, New York. Campus dances are held generally twice a semester; about once a term, a concert with name performers attracts 3500–4000 persons. A well-organized University Ministries program involves a number of students in community service projects. Eighty percent of all students are involved in some kind of service organization, either through the office of student life or University Ministries. In March 2006, more than 200 students joined faculty and other volunteers in spending spring midterm break helping victims of Hurricane Katrina along the Gulf Coast. Campus crime is confined largely to occasional car vandalism. As a deterrent, video cameras have been installed overlooking the campus parking lots. Security monitors are present in every building from 11 p.m. until 7 a.m. As a rule, students say they feel safe walking across campus at night.

Among the 7 men's and 7 women's NCAA Division I sports played, Bonnies basketball has scored highest in school spirit and often in the final outcome against formidable opponents such as Notre Dame and Indiana. (Former NBA All-Star Bob Lanier is a 1970 graduate.) Though the student body is small compared to that at rival schools, the noise and cheers generated are often equal in decibel level to those heard at bigger universities. Varsity soccer and women's lacrosse and the rugby club draw their share of enthusiastic support as well. Sixty percent of the men and 30% of the women recently took part in the 10 men's and 9 women's intramural sports available. Competition is keen between various housing groups for the president's club awarded at year's end to the team with the most points. During winter weekends, many students hit the ski slopes of southwestern New York, just 20 minutes away.

Buffalo, 70 miles northwest, is the nearest big city where students can do some shopping or watch a Bills game. Trips to Toronto also are popular, though many undergraduates simply head to the Mt. Irenaeus retreat for some hiking or cross-country skiing, contemplation, prayer, and a home-cooked meal.

Cost cutters: Ninety-three percent of the freshmen and 75% of continuing students in a recent school year received some form of financial aid. For all but a few percent of both groups, the aid was need-based. The average freshman award for a student with need included a need-based scholarship or grant averaging $10,928 and need-based self-help aid such as loans and jobs averaging $4219. Non-need-based athletic scholarships averaged $11,292; other non-need-based awards and scholarships averaged $7042. A typical graduate left with debts of $9500. The university's own scholarship/grant fund receives a welcome boost from the contributed services of many of the Franciscan priests and brothers on campus who donate part of their salaries to help deserving students. Students ranking in the top 5% of their class, with combined math and critical reading SATs of 1300 (29 ACT) are considered for a Presidential Scholarship paying $16,500 annually. Other merit scholarships and awards range from $7300 to $13,000.

Rate of return: Eighty-four percent of freshmen return for the sophomore year. Fifty-nine percent graduate in 4 years; 67%, within 5 years; 71%, in 6.

Payoff: The 3 most popular majors for a recent graduating class were elementary education at 12%, accounting at 11%, and marketing at 9%. Three-fourths of the graduates immediately enter the work force as accountants, systems analysts, programmers, and teachers, as well as in other positions, primarily in the Middle Atlantic region and New England. About 70 companies and organizations recruited on campus in a recent school year. About a fourth pursue advanced degrees shortly after commencement.

Bottom line: According to Bona's students, any high school graduate of average or better ability who is willing to work hard and does not need the excitement of a big city to have fun is an excellent candidate for St. Bonaventure. However, entrants are advised to check their "attitudes" at the door. Notes a senior: "Bona's is a special place if students open their eyes, minds, and hearts to the experience."

State University of New York at Geneseo

Geneseo, New York 14454

Setting: Small town
Control: Public
Undergraduate enrollment: 2103 men, 3075 women
Graduate enrollment: 5 men, 63 women (111 part-time)
Student/faculty ratio: 21:1
Freshman profile: 14% scored over 700 on SAT I verbal; 65% scored 600–700; 20% 500–599; 1% below 500. 16% scored over 700 on SAT I math; 71% scored 600–700; 13% 500–599; 0% below 500. 23% scored above 28 on the ACT; 47% scored 27–28; 25% 24–26; 2% 21–23; 3% below 21. 46% graduated in top tenth of high school class; 83% in upper fifth.

Faculty profile: 84% Ph.D.'s
Tuition and fees: $5520 in-state; $11,780 out-of-state
Room and board: $7390
Freshman financial aid: 64%; average scholarship or grant: $2509 need-based; $700 non-need-based
Campus jobs: 22%; average earnings: $2500/year
Application deadline: Early decision: Nov. 15; regular: Jan. 15
Financial aid deadline: Feb. 15
Admissions information: (585) 245-5571; (866) 245-5211
  e-mail: admissions@geneseo.edu
  web site: www.geneseo.edu

If there is any of that highly valued academic ivy climbing the walls of the 64-campus State University of New York, more than a fair share has settled along the beautiful Genesee Valley, at the SUNY branch campus at Geneseo. Here is a college where all but 17% of the 2005 freshmen ranked in the top 20% of their high school graduating classes. The students who apply to Geneseo also seek admission to other small, selective colleges, only they happen to be private and generally cost several thousand dollars more. For most applicants, Geneseo is no "backup" choice, and for good reason. For total costs of just under $13,000 in-state and just over $19,000 out-of-state during the 2005–2006 school year, undergraduates get personal attention from teaching-oriented professors, friendly classmates who are competitive without being cutthroat, a championship ice hockey team, and some of the most gorgeous sunsets in the nation. At Geneseo, some of the best things in life *are* free, and most of the others don't cost that much, either.

Student body: All but 4% of Geneseo's undergraduates are New Yorkers, with students on campus from a total of 22 states and 49 foreign countries. Less than a fifth are graduates of private or parochial schools. Asian-Americans comprise the largest number of minority students at 5%, Hispanics account for 3%, and African-Americans for 2%. Native Americans comprise less than 1% while foreign nationals represent 2%. Geneseo students are mainly liberal in their political views, and the vast majority are interested in academic achievement. "There are no dummies here," observes a senior. In fact, the undergraduates seem to grow smarter each year as the SATs and GPAs rise with each new entering class. And what does that do to the competitive edge on campus? Notes a junior: "As the standards of incoming freshmen increase, the professors become more demanding and raise their expectations based on those figures. Students, in turn, demand more of themselves and provide a greater challenge to their peers." The spiraling expectations, however, have not yet proceeded to the point where students are totally devoted to their schoolwork. As a sophomore member of the spiral notes: "We are very concerned with our GPAs but also concerned about having a good time on the weekends!" Adds a sophomore: "Geneseo takes pride in its clubs and organizations, community service, and athletics (so) students should want to give a lot to the campus and community."

Academics: Geneseo, which opened its doors as a normal school to train teachers in 1871, now awards bachelor's degrees in 48 majors, plus master's degrees. The academic year is divided into 2 semesters. Average class size in the first 2 years is between 30 and 40, though a Human Biology lecture averages around 150. Upper-level classes in a student's major generally have between 20 and 35 participants.

Students must take 2 courses each from the humanities, social sciences, natural science, and fine arts, and 1 course each in non-Western tradition, critical writing and reading, numeric and symbolic reasoning and U.S. history. In all but the humanities, there is a wide variety of courses from which to fulfill the requirements. The mandatory Western Humanities I and II sequence uses literature, history, and philosophy to examine the major Western value systems in place before the year 1600 in the first section and after 1600 in the second. Some undergraduates find the humanities core overambitious in its coverage, though others call it "a real strong point." Adds a communication major: "Geneseo offers a broad liberal arts education along with specific majors so students should be aware of that aspect."

The faculty includes 242 full-time members and 88 part-timers, all of whom teach undergraduates. Forty-one percent are women. A senior gives this appraisal: "Most of the professors are very nice people and are accommodating to the students. Some are excellent teachers; some are not. But most do know the students by name, and that's great."

While most students come to Geneseo for its small size and liberal arts environment, many find the college's professional programs to be its largest and some say strongest offerings. The schools of Business and Education are respected for turning out graduates prepared to face all challenges in their respective fields. In business, for example, every upper-level course demands a paper and presentation, "a useful tool for building communication skills," says an economics major in the school. Faculty also are very attentive advisors in helping students select appropriate careers and graduate schools. In education, much of the emphasis is on teaching in the multicultural classroom. In the highly regarded speech pathology and audiology department, many majors as early as their sophomore year are working with clients at the school's speech clinic. Within the liberal arts, the English department has experienced a growth in majors over the last 5 years, thanks in part to an enthusiastic faculty. New, young professors in sociology have added vibrancy to this discipline also. The new $50 million Center for Excellence in Science scheduled to open in fall 2006 will only enhance the already plentiful research opportunities available to undergraduates. The physics department boasts an impressive record in sending students to graduate school; its personalized approach to learning even extends way out of the classroom to an annual department camping trip. Geography's renown extends beyond its own departmental borders with a much-respected faculty and friendly atmosphere.

Students enjoy the extensive opportunities for hands-on experience in the communication department but wish the facilities could be more up-to-date. The foreign language program is small, with majors only in French and Spanish, and students say the variety of courses within each concentration is limited. Religious studies and dance are offered only as minors.

Facilities: Geneseo has 1 library, Milne, "the center of our community," notes a junior, that provides more than 665,000 volumes and 3645 periodicals including electronic titles. Of special note is a gold-star curriculum resources collection that contains some 10,000 media and nonmedia instructional curricula and other materials related to elementary, secondary, and special education. Students generally find Milne a satisfactory place to study except during Greek pledging when the pledge classes have study hours and often become noisy. Milne Library closes at 1 a.m.

All but 1% of Geneseo students bring their own computers with them. The 1% who doesn't has access to almost 900 computers located in all academic buildings and residence halls. The campus network offers wireless service partially in all buildings; full coverage is available in more than half the structures.

Special programs: The SUNY system sponsors approximately 90 study-abroad programs; a Washington, D.C. semester also is an option. A 3-2 M.B.A. program is available with Rochester Institute of Technology, Pace University, SUNY Buffalo, or Syracuse; a 3-2 program in engineering can be arranged with any of 9 different institutions. Other 7-year programs combining bachelor's and advanced degree work in dentistry, optometry, and osteopathic medicine are available. Students may cross-register for courses at other, more expensive Rochester area institutions without paying an additional fee.

Campus life: Fifty-six percent of the undergraduates reside on Geneseo's tranquil 220 acres. Since no campus building can be more than 4 stories high, the breathtaking views of sunrises and sunsets are certain to remain unobstructed. The hilly campus also makes it easier for freshmen to avoid those 10 extra pounds that often creep on the first year. Ten percent of the men are members of 7 local and 3 national fraternities; 12% of the women belong to 7 local and 6 national sororities. The Greeks are highly visible around campus, and often party with each other but also sponsor many open events. There also are enough campuswide activities, including Geneseo Late Knight, which offers entertainment every Friday and Saturday night from 10 p.m. to 2 a.m., and nearby nightclubs with bands and dancing, to keep nonmembers busy. The Big Brother-Big Sister program, the campus radio and television stations, and 160 other student groups also draw participants from both areas. Although crime is not much of a problem, 2 security vehicles patrol campus around the clock, and a late-night shuttle service known as Student Association Funded Escort (SAFE) tries to make students aware that crimes can happen even in a rural locale like Geneseo. Says a senior: "Often our biggest crime is people playing in the fountain on Main Street."

The Ice Knights hockey team and Blue Knights and Lady Knights basketball teams have been ranked in the top 5 in the nation over the past several years and top all of the 7 other men's and 11 other women's intercollegiate sports played in NCAA Division III. Half the students engage in 26 intramural sports offered for each sex including such rarities as underwater-snorkel-hockey. Men's and women's rugby and crew are 2 of the most popular club sports.

Geneseo (pop. 7000) is a charming college town with a main street drawn from another century. Favorite road trips take students to Rochester, 30 miles north (also accessible by a free shuttle bus every weekend), a bit further to Buffalo or Toronto, or, more frequently, just 5 minutes away to Letchworth State Park, site of "the Grand Canyon of the East."

Cost cutters: In the 2005–2006 school year, 64% of freshmen and 65% of continuing students received financial aid. For most of both groups, the aid was based on need. The average freshman award for a student with need included a need-based scholarship or grant averaging $2509 and need-based self-help aid such as loans and jobs averaging $3510. Other non-need-based awards and scholarships averaged $700. Debt of graduates in the Class of 2005 averaged $15,800. The Geneseo Foundation awards more than one-half million dollars in scholarships annually to new and continuing students. Three 4-year full-tuition Presidential Merit Scholarships are awarded to the most outstanding students. Twelve foundation Honors Scholarships worth $1400 go to freshmen enrolled in the college honors program and are renewable to those who remain in the program. Jobs on and off campus usually are provided to everybody who wants to work.

Rate of return: Ninety percent of entering freshmen return for the sophomore year. Sixty-three percent graduate in 4 years; 78%, in 5 years, 79% in 6.

Payoff: The three top majors for 2005 graduates were education at 20%, business administration at 10%, and psychology at 9%. Nearly half of the graduates took jobs immediately. Forty-six companies and organizations recruited on campus in the 2004–2005 school year. Just over 40% of a recent class continued their education in graduate or professional schools.

Bottom line: SUNY College at Geneseo is more like an expensive, selective private college than a low-cost public institution—until the tuition comes due, that is. Unlike many of its private cousins, Geneseo lacks both a geographically diverse student body and national name recognition, though the college's proud graduates intend to take care of the latter deficiency. Notes one: "Personally, I plan to include several articles about Geneseo whenever I send out my résumé."

State University of New York at Potsdam

Potsdam, New York 13676

Setting: Rural
Control: Public
Undergraduate enrollment: 1466 men, 1999 women
Graduate enrollment: 140 men, 368 women
Student/faculty ratio: 14:1
Freshman profile: 3% scored over 700 on SAT I verbal; 19% scored 600–700; 39% 500–599; 39% below 500. 3% scored over 700 on SAT I math; 16% scored 600–700; 42% 500–599; 39% below 500. 10% scored above 28 on the ACT; 11% scored 27–28; 20% 24–26; 11% 21–23; 48% below 21. 17% graduated in upper fifth of high school class; 38% in upper two-fifths.
Faculty profile: 79% Ph.D.'s

Tuition and fees: $5289 in-state; $11,549 out-of-state
Room and board: $7670
Freshman financial aid: 87%; average scholarship or grant: $4985 need-based; $2278 non-need-based
Campus jobs: NA; average earnings: $1200/year
Application deadline: Rolling
Financial aid deadline: Rolling (Priority date: Jan. 1)
Admissions information: (315) 267-2180;
(877) 768-7326 (in-state)
e-mail: admissions@potsdam.edu
web site: www.potsdam.edu

Like many colleges and universities across the country, Potsdam College, a school of about 3500 undergraduates in the State University of New York system, raised its general-education requirements a few years ago. And like many other institutions concerned about graduating a generation of "tongue-tied" Americans, Potsdam mandated that each student be able to demonstrate proficiency in a foreign language. Over the years, however, this college had already gained a national reputation for graduating scholars fluent in 2 languages not found in any Berlitz curriculum: the languages of music and mathematics. The internationally known Crane School of Music at Potsdam is the oldest and largest undergraduate music education school in the U.S., with 90% of its 500 majors studying music education and all music majors involved in performance. Likewise, the college's mathematics major has gained a reputation as one of the best small-college programs in the nation and is used frequently as a model of how mathematics should be taught. Either of these prestigious offerings may be the *pièce de résistance* for a college shopper seeking a main meal of music or mathematics, but just about any student interested in attending a homey campus that regularly dishes up 1-to-1 relationships with professors will savor what Potsdam has to offer.

Student body: Though Potsdam's name may be well known in some circles, its general appeal remains regional; just 6% of the undergraduates are from outside New York State, with 66% of the nonresidents also from the Northeast. Altogether, 26 states and 23 foreign countries have students in attendance. All but 2% of the undergraduates in a recent year attended public schools. The student body is predominantly white, with African-Americans, Hispanics and Native Americans each comprising 2%, and Asian-Americans, 1% of the total enrollment. Foreign nationals account for 3%. In terms of letter grades, students rate themselves as F, in this case, for fun-loving and friendly. "'Average' is probably the best word to describe us," says a junior. "We have average involvement in student government, average in classes, average in a social sense. There are few extremists at Potsdam." But that doesn't mean students are predictably the same. Says a senior: "The students here range from artsy eccentric people to preppy know-it-alls. The majority, however, are down to earth, fun-loving, and usually pretty smart." Academically, most strive to get As and Bs, though the general air is rather laid back except in mathematics and the music school, where students tend to be more competitive. For the most part, says a music education major, "We are challenged as much as we want to be."

Academics: SUNY Potsdam traces its roots to the founding in 1816 of St. Lawrence Academy by early settlers in northern New York. The former academy became a normal school in 1869 and joined the state university system in 1948. The college awards the bachelor's degree in more than 40 undergraduate majors plus a master's degree in English, mathematics, music, and education, including special education. The academic calendar is divided by semesters. Most classes in the first 2 years average 30–40 students, except some introductory courses which can enroll as many as 150. Most classes in the upper years have from 5 to 25 participants.

The general-education requirements begin with a freshman-year experience consisting of 2 courses in writing and thinking and in speaking, reasoning, and research and 1 in statistical analysis or problem solving. Students follow up with another writing-intensive course and a second that is speaking-intensive. Distributional requirements are categorized according to various "modes of inquiry," ranging from a course in cross-cultural perspective to classes in historical investigation and social analysis. Foreign language and physical education requirements round out the program. Fifty freshmen who prefer can fulfill more than a third of their general-education requirements in an Adirondacks Environmental Studies Semester that offers 5 team-taught courses using the park region as case study material.

The 366-member Potsdam faculty is about 70% full-time, with 111 part-time professors. All faculty members teach undergraduates. Forty-six percent are women. Undergraduates describe the faculty as "very student-oriented," though the quality is uneven. Observes a psychology major: "There are some older professors who really should retire because they lack the knowledge and enthusiasm to teach college students. However, the younger faculty here are very, very good at what they do."

Not surprisingly, students from all majors rate music and mathematics as Potsdam's most prized programs. Mathematics professors give students large amounts of personal attention in a well-designed curriculum. A 4-year B.A.-M.A. program also is an option for those seeking additional challenge. Music features superb professors, drawn from such highly respected schools as Eastman, Julliard, and Indiana University, "who will go out of their way to help you succeed," says a major. The school also offers a full ensemble of wonderful facilities and equipment. Included are more than 1200 band and orchestra instruments (not including 155 pianos, most of them Steinways, including 5 Concert Grand pianos), 1 digital and 2 analog synthesizer studios, and a newly renovated 1209-seat concert hall that is so acoustically well balanced that architects and music educators from around the world come to study it. Twenty-first-century instruction is provided in a high-technology classroom that offers a wide range of professional music composition software and hardware and Power Macintosh computers. Many students team a specialty in math or music with additional studies in Potsdam's excellent School of Education and Professional Studies. In fact, half of the music teachers in New York's public schools are Potsdam graduates. Political science also is a winner with "down-to-earth" and challenging faculty members. Psychology offers diverse course offerings and excellent research opportunities for majors. English, says a major, has "amazing and knowledgeable professors that really care."

While Potsdam may excel in the languages of math and music, in more traditional foreign tongues its offerings are slim with majors available only in French and Spanish. However, it is the only U.S. higher education institution to offer Mohawk language courses as part of its modern languages curriculum. Smaller departments, such as modern languages and physics, present special dilemmas to students. Notes a French major: "The small amount of faculty can make you feel uneasy in a class if you don't like the professor. There is no choice in who you can take classes with."

Facilities: Between the main Crumb Library and a music library, the college's collection consists of more than 408,000 volumes and 933 periodicals. The recently renovated Crumb is a popular place to study with "plenty of quiet corners," says a psychology major. However, undergraduates reserve most of their complaints for the research process. Observes a sophomore: "The library is good for studying and that's about it. For research, it is very poorly organized and difficult to use." Some relief is provided by an online catalog that links Potsdam with 4 other college libraries in the area. Students also can electronically access numerous indexes, abstracts and full-text databases as well as the Internet from any workstation on the campus network. The music library contains 16,000 books, 24,000 music scores, 16,000 sound recordings, and tapes of performances at Crane dating back to the late 1940s. The library's audio facilities include 7 listening rooms and 30 listening carrels.

Approximately 515 Macintosh and Windows-based PCs are available for student use. Computer labs are located in all residence halls, Crumb Library, and other academic buildings, with several open 24 hours a day. Individual residence hall rooms also are wired for the campus network, including access to the Internet. Thirty wireless hot spots exist on campus as well.

Special programs: Undergraduates may study abroad in England, Germany, Australia, or Mexico, plus other countries by request. Education majors may student-teach in Newcastle, England. The National Student Exchange lets students study at a wide range of public colleges and universities across the United States. In the local area, cross-registration is offered with Clarkson and St. Lawrence universities and SUNY Canton College of Technology. A 3-2 program in engineering and a 4-1 program leading to a master of business administration also are options at Clarkson; a 3-2 engineering program alone is available at SUNY Binghamton. A 3-4 program is offered with the SUNY College of Optometry in New York City. Internships are possible with the state government in Albany or with various agencies in New York City.

Campus life: Fifty-two percent of Potsdam's undergraduates reside on the 240-acre campus. Greek life is a popular, though decreasingly predominant component of campus social life, with 2 national and 4 local fraternities and 1 national and 7 local sororities. Many independents as well as the 4% of the men and 6% of the women who are members turn out for Greek parties, held on campus, off campus, and sometimes downtown. Other major sources of entertainment include the Crane School of Music, which offers more than 300 concerts and recitals put on by its own students and faculty as well as guest performers, and Hurley's, a nonalcoholic student nightclub. Says a mathematics major: "The Crane School adds a wonderful atmosphere here, providing concerts nightly." Crime is not a serious problem; security measures such as CEASE, Campus Escort Association for Safety and Education, and a late-night bus funded by SUNY Potsdam and Clarkson University help to keep students safe. Says a sophomore, "I don't think you can be outside and not see a blue light phone more than 50 feet away."

Of the 7 men's, 10 women's, and 2 coed intercollegiate sports played in NCAA Division III, Bears ice hockey and men's and women's basketball, soccer, and lacrosse are the big draws, with the Crane Pep Band providing musical support. The men's basketball team holds the division's all-time record for most consecutive games won—a 60-game winning streak. Among the 9 men's, 8 women's, and 6 coed intramural sports, broomball, which is like ice hockey but is played with a broom and sneakers, is the most popular. About 40% of the men and 23% of the women participate in the intramural program. Rugby is an especially active club sport for both sexes.

Potsdam (pop. 10,000) is located 140 miles northeast of Syracuse. The Canadian cities of Ottawa and Montreal are 70 and 80 miles distant, respectively. During the winter months, skiing at Whiteface Mountain in Lake Placid, site of the 1980 Winter Olympics, is a great way to forget the cold and the classroom, just 90 miles distant. Opportunities for sailing, canoeing, mountaineering, and other recreational activities are available at the college's Star Lake campus in the Adirondack wilderness.

Cost cutters: Eighty-seven percent of freshmen and 83% of continuing students in the 2005–2006 school year received financial aid. For 67% of the first-year students and 76% of the rest, the assistance was need-based. The average freshman award for a student with need included a need-based scholarship or grant averaging $4985 and need-based self-help aid such as loans and jobs averaging $8009. Other non-need-based awards and scholarships for first-year students averaged $2278. The average financial indebtedness of a 2005 graduate was $16,117. Most aid, according to students, comes in the form of Potsdam's low, state-supported tuition rate. A series of awards in the Adirondack Scholars program take their name from the mountain range near Potsdam and are awarded based on a combination of standardized test scores and grade point averages. An Adirondack Summit Scholar, for example, received $4575 annually in a recent year for a combined math and critical reading SAT of at least 1400, an ACT of at least 32, and a GPA of between 95 and 100. The same test scores with a GPA of between 90 and 94 provided a High Peaks award worth $4075. The Mt. Emmons Scholarship, recognizing the most difficult peak in the Adirondacks, pays in-state tuition and fees and provides a waiver of room and board charges and a $500 book stipend to 5 first-year students with SAT math and critical reading scores of at least 1300, an ACT composite of 29, and a GPA of at least 92. Adirondack Navigator awards recently paid $500 to $2000 annually. The Crane School of Music also awards scholarships based on individual performances as judged in an entrance audition. The Potsdam Auxiliary and College Educational Services, Inc., a not-for-profit corporation that operates the school's dining services, bookstore, and other facilities, also makes available 160 awards to students.

Rate of return: Seventy-six percent of the freshmen return for the sophomore year. Twenty-five percent graduate in 4 years; 43%, in 5 years; 46%, in 6 years.

Payoff: Twelve percent of the 2005 graduates earned bachelor's degrees in childhood education, 11% in music education and 9% in psychology. In a recent class, the majority of graduates converted their diplomas into dollars from the workplace; 34% pursued advanced degrees. More than 40 companies and organizations recruited on campus in a recent school year.

Bottom line: Undergraduates seeking a student-centered education that's gentle on the pocketbook will find that SUNY at Potsdam fits the bill. For those with an interest in majoring in mathematics or music, there isn't a better buy for the money.

State University of New York— Binghamton University

Binghamton, New York 13902

Setting: Suburban
Control: Public
Undergraduate enrollment: 5584 men, 5150 women
Graduate enrollment: 843 men, 776 women
Student/faculty ratio: 20:1
Freshman profile: 12% scored over 700 on SAT I verbal; 49% scored 600–700; 34% 500–599; 5% below 500. 24% scored over 700 on SAT I math; 56% scored 600–700; 19% 500–599; 1% below 500. 30% scored above 28 on the ACT; 29% scored 27–28; 26% 24–26; 12% 21–23; 3% below 21. 78% graduated in top fifth of high school class; 97% in upper two-fifths.

Faculty profile: 93% Ph.D.'s
Tuition and fees: $5838 in-state; $12,098 out-of-state
Room and board: $8150
Freshman financial aid: 80%; average scholarship or grant: $4061 need-based; $11,049 non-need-based
Campus jobs: 13%; average earnings: $1200/year
Application deadline: Early action: Nov. 1; regular: Feb. 15
Financial aid deadline: Mar. 1
Admissions information: (607) 777-2171
e-mail: admit@binghamton.edu
web site: www.binghamton.edu

As a graduate of the prestigious Bronx High School of Science in New York City, the young man was looking for a solid liberal arts education. He chose a university where the English department ranks among the nation's best and where the real-life lessons in economics can't be beat: the State University of New York campus at Binghamton near the border with eastern Pennsylvania, where in-staters paid less than $14,000 for tuition, room, and board in the 2005–2006 school year, and out-of-staters paid just over $20,000. Now an alumnus who was the only B.A. hired by a major publisher among MBAs from Yale, Harvard, and Chicago, the Binghamton University graduate boasts: "I obviously think that a bachelor's from Binghamton, if handled properly, can be equal, if not superior, to any degree from any other university in America. For about what a student spends a year on candy, movies, pizza, beer, and lots of other little extras combined, a state resident can attend Binghamton University. If it sounds too cheap, it's because of a flaw in the imperfect market of education. Jump on it while you can."

Student body: To date, much of the jumping has come from state residents, with 92% of Binghamton's undergraduates from New York, many from Long Island; the rest hail from 37 other states, mainly in the Northeast, and 66 foreign countries. Eighty-seven percent are graduates of public high schools. Twenty-nine percent of the students are Catholic; 22% are Jewish, and 19% Protestant. Twenty-four percent claimed no religious affiliation. Asian-Americans constitute the largest minority group on campus, at 18%, followed by Hispanics at 7%, African-Americans at 6%, and foreign nationals at 8%. "We're a pretty diverse bunch ethnically, which is cool," says a state resident, "but that can be problematic—or at least interesting—at times," though students say members of the various ethnic groups tend to stick together. Binghamton students are for the most part down to earth and politically and socially aware. "Political awareness/activity is not campus-wide," says a junior, "but a healthy percentage of the student body participates." Undergraduates also are academically quite bright, with all but a fifth drawn from the upper 20% of their high school graduating classes. Says a junior: "Students here have a drive to improve their academic and social skills and they do not rely on the school's reputation to deliver jobs or graduate school acceptances. While students study and are highly competitive in class, they also are social." "Very well rounded," observes a human development major. Students caution, however, that undergraduates cannot always count on faculty to push them to excel and must often rely on their own inner motivation to succeed.

Academics: Binghamton University, which turns 60 in 2006, awards bachelor's degrees in 61 majors, plus a large number of master's degrees and doctorates. Its undergraduate program is divided among Harpur College of Arts and Sciences, the original component of the university, and 4 professional schools of Management, Nursing, Engineering and Applied Science, and Education and Human Development, which offers masters-level programs only in education but undergraduate as well as graduate programs in the human development division. First-year lectures may feature 300 to 450 note takers (Introductory Psychology recently counted 444) and a professor with a microphone, though discussion sections generally enroll no more than 30. Juniors and seniors usually encounter fewer than 50 in most of their courses, and several classes with about 20, but many students still find classes in general to be larger than they would like.

All freshmen are required to take university-wide, general-education courses over their first 2 years divided among 5 categories ranging from creating a global vision to aesthetics and humanities to natural sciences, social sciences, and mathematics. In addition, each of the 5 undergraduate divisions has its own course requirements.

A recent hiring initiative is helping to increase faculty numbers by 20% following several years of state budget cuts that produced larger class sizes and greater reliance on graduate teaching assistants in some academic areas. The number of full-time faculty stands at 537, up 33 members from the 2003–2004 school year; the number of part-time faculty is up to 232 from 204 just 2 years before. Graduate students teach 16% of the introductory courses, already down 2% from fall 2003 levels. "Some of my best teachers have been grad students," says a history major, "but some of my worst, too." Thirty-six percent of the faculty are women. One faculty member who teaches sociology and history won the Pulitzer Prize for general nonfiction in 2001. All teach undergraduates, though many do so in varying degrees, depending on their research loads. Undergraduates often are surprised to find professors reasonably accessible, though it is up to the individual student to take the initiative. While some faculty members use the same teaching format they have for years, a majority, says a junior, are "excellent, highly regarded in their field, well researched, and heavily published."

Many of Binghamton's liberal arts programs rate an A+ from students. Political science features some "superstar" faculty and a terrific variety of courses, as does the excellent English department. "The English classes are great," says an anthropology major. "The anthropology classes also are good, with small classes and experienced professors." Almost all the science departments earn a grade of "good to excellent," says a biology major, "because of their faculty, teaching assistants, and modern outlook and equipment." Other students grumble, however, that some individual faculty members care more about research than teaching. The cinema department offers an "avant-garde, cutting edge" program. The theater department features experienced and talented faculty members who make each student feel like a star when it comes to dispensing personalized instruction. The Russian language program, though small, also features helpful, approachable professors and intriguing courses.

The professional schools are considered strong as well. Management offers many challenging programs, among them a well-designed accounting major, and numerous opportunities for internships. Raves an accounting major, "The School of Management does a really great job networking with alumni to find students jobs; many times even by the beginning of senior year students know they have a job after graduation." Engineering students receive plenty of individual attention. "You see and talk to your professors often," says a mechanical engineering major. Nursing earns high marks from both students and the State Board of Nursing. In a recent year, nursing graduates from Binghamton had a nearly perfect pass rate—98.8%—on the state board examination, the highest rate both within the SUNY system and of any baccalaureate program in-state. Human development majors in the School of Education and Human Development find the school's excellent advising system especially helpful.

For many students, psychology, despite its impressive variety of courses and extensive research opportunities, has come to epitomize some of the least likable qualities of the university. Many psychology classes are big and rely heavily on teaching assistants. Says a major: "It is difficult to achieve interaction with the faculty." In response to such complaints, the university's Center for Learning and Teaching has been working with faculty to help them make the switch from reliance on a lecture format to more active learning. In the meantime, beyond such general complaints as too many, too large introductory-level classes, and too many teaching assistants, undergraduates find a need for math professors with better teaching and English speaking skills who are more available to help students; and more faculty and variety of courses in some of the newer, less popular disciplines.

Facilities: The Binghamton library system consists of 5 facilities, 2.3 million volumes, 1.9 million microform items, and 36,500 electronic and paper periodicals. Students primarily divide their time among the Glenn Bartle Library, which holds most of the books in the humanities and social sciences but usually is noisy because of its sheer size; the science library, known for its pin-drop silence for serious concentration; and the fine arts library, which also attracts many Bartle refugees. Two smaller libraries in 2 residential colleges complete the network. A computerized catalog and CD-ROM technology help students find what they need. Says a senior: "If students can't find something they need, they either didn't look hard enough, didn't take enough time to look, or need something really obscure." For those occasions, a bus shuttles students to the libraries of Cornell University on Saturdays.

Ninety-nine percent of Binghamton's students bring a computer to campus (10% bring more than one!) and connect to the Internet. (Wireless access is provided in the dining areas of all residence halls, throughout one complete residence hall community, throughout most academic buildings, and in the university union and library.) For the 1% who do not, about 600 computers in public labs known as Pods are available in the library, in 5 academic buildings, and in 3 residence hall complexes. One lab is open around the clock; many close at 2 a.m., though a majority extends to 24 hours around finals time.

Special programs: The university offers foreign-study programs in 7 European countries plus other countries ranging from Australia and Belize to Morocco and Senegal. In addition, Binghamton students may participate in more than 100 overseas programs sponsored by the state university system. Internships with nonprofit agencies in Washington, D.C., and in the state capital of Albany can be arranged through the political science department. By planning carefully, students can combine bachelor's degrees in the liberal arts with master's degrees in any of the professional disciplines in one 5-year program.

Campus life: Fifty-eight percent of the full-time undergraduates reside on the 887-acre campus; a number live in residential colleges that provide added opportunities for students to interact with faculty members. All freshmen are required to live on campus. The annual residence hall competition and special events in the residential colleges are especially spirited and well attended as are the Late Nite Binghamton programs for night owls. Late Nite activities such as movies, poker nights, and bowling average just over 2000 students every weekend. Eight percent of the men and 9% of the women are members of 1 local and 19 national fraternities and 15 national sororities. Many underclassmen frequent the Greek parties off campus, though those who are not members rarely feel they are missing something. Says a senior: "Fraternities and sororities are a presence, not a necessity." The Black Student Union, Jewish Student Union (Hillel), and other racial and ethnic social groups also provide much social programming while working to raise awareness about other cultures. The *Pipe Dream*, the biweekly student newspaper, is regarded as quite influential in shaping student opinion. Campus crime, other than petty larceny and vandalism, is not considered much of a problem; residence halls require the use of a keycard for entry at all times. Three of 4 entrances to campus are closed from midnight to 6 a.m. and the fourth is guarded.

Basketball is the biggest, some say the only, draw among the 11 men's and 10 women's intercollegiate sports played in NCAA Division I. The new $33.1 million Events Center that opened in 2004 has made room for 6000 screaming fans to attend the America East men's games and helped raise school spirit in the process. Participation in intramural action draws enthusiasm as well, with half of the men and a third of the women taking part in the 20 sports offered for men, and 18 for women. Co-rec football is especially popular, with many in the dormitories, both men and women, competing.

For students who want to compare notes with other undergraduates, Cornell and Syracuse universities are each about an hour away. New York City and Philadelphia are both about a 3½ hour drive. The closest retreat is as near as the southern end of campus, which is covered by a 190-acre forest and a wetland nature preserve, with footpaths, a scenic pond, and indigenous beavers.

Cost cutters: Eighty percent of the first-year students and 68% of the rest received some form of financial aid in the 2005–2006 school year, all but 1% based at least in part on need. The average for need-based scholarships or grants among freshmen was $4061; need-based self-help aid such as loans and jobs averaged $3810. The average for non-need-based athletic scholarships among freshmen was $8208; other non-need-based scholarships and awards averaged $11,049. Average debt of a 2005 graduate was $15,041. Awards based on academic excellence include the Presidential Scholarship, which in a recent year paid $3400 annually over 4 years to 30 top students. A university job locator helps students find work in area businesses.

Rate of return: Ninety percent of freshmen return for the sophomore year. Sixty-seven percent go on to graduate in 4 years, 78% in 5 years; 79% within 6.

Payoff: Management, psychology, and English were the most popular majors among 2005 graduates, claiming 10% each. About 60% of the members of a recent graduating class took jobs, mainly in nursing, accounting, engineering (with such firms as IBM and GE, and with the federal government), management training (with Macy's, for example), finance, and banking. Most stayed in the Northeast, although a number accepted posts nationwide. About 120 companies and organizations recruited on campus in the 2004–2005 school year. Thirty-eight percent of recent graduates decided to attend graduate or professional school.

Bottom line: The ambitious student who is willing to become his or her own advocate in the educational process does best at Binghamton University. From there, a student is limited only by his or her own aspirations and work ethic. Advises a senior: "A high school student who is involved with a lot of extracurricular activities while maintaining a good GPA will benefit from this university. A person with straight As but nothing else will not take advantage of this school and will probably be bored with it. A student who does decently in high school without a good work ethic will most definitely suffer while here."

State University of New York, College of Environmental Science and Forestry

Syracuse, New York 13210

Setting: Urban
Control: Public
Undergraduate enrollment: 1460 men and women
Graduate enrollment: 300 men and women
Student/faculty ratio: 12:1
Freshman profile: SAT/ACT scores: NA. Class rank data: NA
Faculty profile: 80% Ph.D.'s
Tuition and fees: $5194 in-state; $11,454 out-of-state
Room and board: $10,180

Freshman financial aid: 80%; average scholarship or grant: $1400 need-based; $4350 non-need-based
Campus jobs: 45%; average earnings: $1200/year
Application deadline: Early decision: Nov. 15; regular: Mar. 1
Financial aid deadline: Mar. 1
Admissions information: (315) 470-6600; (800) 777-7373
e-mail: esfinfo@esf.edu
web site: www.esf.edu

Half a century before Earth Day became a national celebration, and before *being Green* meant anything other than wearing a shamrock on St. Patrick's Day, the State University of New York campus in Syracuse was already offering a course of study devoted to solving problems in forestry and the environment. Since its founding in 1911 as the New York State College of Forestry at Syracuse University, the present-day SUNY College of Environmental Science and Forestry has held fast to the 2 components of its birth name that still make it distinct: its focus on the environment through 10 primary academic areas, and its cooperative relationship with neighboring private Syracuse University, where students regularly attend classes or fraternity parties, borrow books from its extensive libraries, and cheer on the Orangemen during the NCAA Division I basketball playoffs. But ESF, as the campus is known to students, remains a branch of the State University of New York, with all that means in terms of lower tuition and fees, less than $5200 for state residents and just under $11,500 for out-of-staters in the 2005–2006 school year. As a close-knit campus of 1460 undergraduates, mainly transfer students, with only 228 freshmen enrolled in a recent fall, ESF prepares students for leadership roles in solving problems related to the natural world. Says a sophomore, "If you can get in, and you love the environment, ESF is the best place you could possibly be."

Student body: Students' chief complaint about ESF is that it has long been overshadowed by its powerhouse neighbor in terms of national acclaim, a fact reflected in the limited geographic area from which students are drawn. All but 9% of the undergraduates in a recent year were residents of New York State, with the remaining students coming from 24 other states and 9 foreign countries. Eighty-five percent are graduates of public schools. About 30% of the undergraduates in a recent year were 24 years of age or older. Two percent of the undergraduates each were African-American and Asian-American, and 1% each Hispanic and Native American. Seven percent were foreign nationals. Though in their outward appearance students for the most part defy the stereotypical image of environmentalists, most are indeed quite liberal-minded, down-to-earth, and genuinely concerned about environmental issues. "Activism is important to many," says a New Yorker. Because of the small size of the student body and the focus of the curriculum, students bond easily with one another, in both their classroom work and out of classroom activities. "Many of us like field work and would rather be outdoors," says a former New York City resident, which the hands-on approach to learning makes frequently possible. Adds a sophomore: "Students here have a sense of what they want and where they want to go."

Academics: ESF awards the bachelor's degree in more than 30 majors covering 10 broad academic areas: chemistry, environmental and forest biology, environmental studies, environmental resources and forest engineering, landscape architecture, paper science and engineering, forest resources management, and construction management and wood products engineering. Master's and doctoral degrees are awarded in 6 program areas. The college follows a semester calendar. Though the size of an entering freshman class is generally 230 or below, students should brace themselves for some lecture classes in the early years with 300 seatmates since some of these introductory courses are taken at neighboring Syracuse. An ecology lecture at ESF recently topped out at 125. As students begin to specialize in their junior and senior years, the courses more typically range between 6 and 30, depending on the major field of study.

No single set of course requirements cuts across all major fields of study, though courses in chemistry, English, mathematics, and botany can be found in each. Most majors also require a certain number of hours of humanities and/or social sciences. Students in all majors except landscape architecture must have 120 credits to graduate; landscape architecture, a 5-year program, requires 160.

Close relationships with faculty members enhance the connectedness students feel to the school. The faculty recently consisted of 122 full-time members and 3 part-time. Eighty-two percent were men. Just 1% of the introductory classes typically are taught by graduate students. "Many professors are involved in research and are very passionate about the classes they teach," says an environmental and forest biology major. "It doesn't take much to get them talking about their work. And they often involve students in their research projects, which allows us to gain some very valuable lab and field experience." A number take their obligation to get to know students very seriously. Recalls a senior: "I have had professors that actually took pictures of students—before class to learn their names better—to connect the name with the face." A small portion of the faculty are interested in research exclusively, adds a landscape architecture senior, "and could care less about students."

Because the scope of majors offered is so tightly focused and limited in range, students are for the most part quite satisfied with the quality of all programs offered. Environmental and Forest Biology, like so many of ESF's programs, features prominent researchers who work on the cutting edge of technology with regard to the environment, and yet are happy to share their expertise with undergraduates. Opportunities for hands-on experience at the college's 7 other campuses and several field stations covering 25,000 acres mainly in the Adirondack region are extensive and a regular part of the curriculum. Students' only concern is that the major is so popular (nearly 40% graduated with degrees in the field in a recent year) that some undergraduates could use more personal support than is readily available. One of the more unusual programs is paper science and engineering, which has its own experimental pulp and paper mill to give students a first-hand feel for the paper-making process. The 5-year landscape architecture program is quite intense for majors and features professors who are recognized nationwide for their scholarship and knowledge. Chemistry boasts rigorous standards and top-of-the-line equipment, following construction of a new building in 1996.

Students' criticisms of programs are minor. Some wish more were being done to help graduates in the forest resources management program find jobs; others would like to see more law and political science classes in the environmental policy option. The major in environmental studies could be better organized and use more attentive advisors. New majors recently were added in 9 disciplines ranging from aquatic and fisheries science to biotechnology and wildlife science. All classes in such subjects as English and the humanities must be taken at Syracuse.

Facilities: F. Franklin Moon Library is like the college, small but tightly focused. Its holdings include more than 130,300 volumes and 2000 current periodicals, predominantly related to the forestry, environmental science, and landscape architecture programs of the college. Students in search of materials not available at Moon can either scan via computer or by a short stroll the more than 2.8 million volumes, 3.6 million microform items, and 18,850 periodical subscriptions at the 6 libraries of neighboring Syracuse. Students also may access the SUNY Health Science Center libraries. Moon's own environment is considered quiet and usually conducive to study; it seats 400.

As with most other resources, ESF students have access to computers on both their own campus and that of Syracuse. A number of public clusters of computers on the ESF campus, 3 new in 2001, 1 open 24 hours, as well as more than a dozen clusters on the Syracuse campus, provide students access to Windows and Macintosh computers and SUN workstations, as well as UNIX systems. All dormitories are wired for direct access to the campus network and Internet from personal computers in student rooms.

Special programs: In addition to cross-registering for regular classes at Syracuse, ESF students in certain majors can take special coursework to expand their science-oriented degrees. Majors in chemistry and environmental and forest biology can prepare for provisional New York State teacher certification by taking classes at the Syracuse School of Education. Landscape architecture students are required to spend 1 semester off-campus in a self-designed and student-budgeted program; many use this time to study abroad. Other students who wish to study overseas may do so through programs at Syracuse University. The majors in forest resources management and in environmental and forest biology require summer field experience as part of their regular coursework; costs for the 7-week summer session in forest resources management recently were $2150; the environmental and forest biology program at Cranberry Lake Biological Station in the Adirondacks recently cost about $385 a week, plus travel and personal expenses.

Campus life: There are no residence halls on the 12-acre ESF campus, so students who want to live on campus actually room and board at neighboring Syracuse. Fifty percent of the undergraduates opt to live next door. Once there, students divide their weekend time between the ever-present rush of events provided at Syracuse University, and the various ESF-oriented clubs back home. Students can indulge their love of the outdoors through the popular Bob Marshall Club, which enables students to go hiking, camping, spelunking, canoeing, and climbing in the Adirondack Mountains. The Student Environmental Action Coalition gets undergraduates involved in raising environmental awareness through such events as potlucks, lectures, rallies, and demonstrations. The Wildlife Society also is quite visible, as is the Baobab Society that raises cultural awareness. One Friday a month, a different club or organization sponsors a campus-wide social gathering. Just 3% of the students are involved in the Greek life at Syracuse, which recently encompassed 20 national fraternities and 20 national sororities. Crime is pretty much a non-issue on ESF's campus, though blue emergency lights and public safety officers, trained at the state police academy, are omnipresent. Students are more concerned about crime off campus in the surrounding neighborhood. "The best idea is to never walk alone," says a junior.

ESF has no NCAA intercollegiate sports of its own and students are not allowed to participate in the Division I teams at Syracuse, so students take up the cheer of the Orangemen, most ardently during football, basketball, and lacrosse seasons. Students are welcome to participate in the 30-sport intramural program going on next door. Just 10% do so. "The only sport that we have that we can say is purely ours," says a landscape architecture major, "is the woodsmen's team through the Forestry Club." The club, which has been around since the college's founding as a forestry school, engages students in competitions throughout the Northeast and in Canada, testing their skills in traditional lumberjacking activities, such as the pulp toss, horizontal chop, and pole climb.

For escape, students with a taste for urban exploration get lost in all that the city of Syracuse (pop. 750,000 in the greater metropolitan area) has to offer. Others head with a group of friends into the Adirondacks.

Cost cutters: Eighty percent of the freshmen and 85% of the continuing students in a recent school year received financial assistance; for virtually all of the freshmen, and all but 5% of the remaining recipients, the aid was need-based. The average freshman award for a student with need included a need-based scholarship or grant averaging $1400 and need-based self-help aid such as loans and jobs averaging $4125. Other non-need-based awards and scholarships for first-year students averaged $4350. Typical debt of a recent graduate was $18,800. Although more scholarship funds are available to needy state residents than to nonresidents, a number of scholarships from private sources are available. Scholarships from the Syracuse Pulp and Paper Foundation range from partial tuition to the full amount of in-state tuition and are available to nonresidents as well. A cooperative program is offered in paper science and engineering.

Rate of return: All but 3% of the entering freshmen continue into the sophomore year. Forty-seven percent go on to graduate in 4 years; 68% do so in 5 years; 69% in 6.

Payoff: Thirty-eight percent of recent graduates earned bachelor's degrees in environmental and forest biology; 19% specialized in environmental studies; 9% in forest resources management. A majority of the graduates take their environmental know-how into the private or public sector for immediate employment, usually within New York State or throughout the Northeast. Between a fifth and a fourth of each graduating class pursue advanced degrees, primarily in fields related to the student's undergraduate major, although a small percentage go on to law, medical, or business schools.

Bottom line: For students who not only love the environment but are committed to learning how to preserve it through a highly specialized and challenging curricula with plenty of hands-on experience, the answer may be SUNY-ESF. The ingredients for success, say students, are a heart devoted to environmental issues, a head committed to studying difficult science-based courses, and hands, and feet, willing to do the work.

State University of New York
University at Albany

Albany, New York 12222

Setting: Suburban
Control: Public
Undergraduate enrollment: 5570 men, 5641 women
Graduate enrollment: 887 men, 1357 women
Student/faculty ratio: 19:1
Freshman profile: 3% scored over 700 on SAT I verbal; 24% scored 600–700; 61% 500–599; 12% below 500. 3% scored over 700 on SAT I math; 35% scored 600–700; 58% 500–599; 4% below 500. 36% graduated in top fifth of high school class; 75% in upper two-fifths.
Faculty profile: 97% Ph.D.'s

Tuition and fees: $5810 in-state; $11,760 out-of-state
Room and board: $8050
Freshman financial aid: 65%; average scholarship or grant: $4728 need-based
Campus jobs: 25%; average earnings: NA
Application deadline: Early action: Nov. 15; regular: Mar. 1
Financial aid deadline: Apr. 15
Admissions information: (518) 442-5435
e-mail: ugadmissions@albany.edu
web site: www.albany.edu

Here's a definition, coined by students at the State University of New York University at Albany, that the critical reading portion of the SATs as well as dictionaries of standard English missed in their latest editions: *podiating:* hanging out at a podium, most specifically, the podium or raised platform of academic buildings that surrounds the fountain on the uptown campus of the University at Albany. The popular podium is the centerpiece of the Albany campus and connects under a single, continuous roof 13 of the chief academic buildings, including classrooms and laboratories, the main library, performing arts center, and campus center, in a rectangle surrounding the fountain several steps down below where students enjoy sunbathing and other leisurely pursuits. As long as it's not February or March, when the podium becomes a wind tunnel and students are likely to freeze if they podiate too long, visitors to campus may well find undergraduates both podiating and radiating: satisfaction, that is, with all the money they're saving by attending a payer-friendly research university.

Student body: Ninety-four percent of UAlbany's undergraduates are from the Empire State, with the remainder from 36 other states, many in the Northeast, and 51 foreign countries. Efforts to make the racial and ethnic makeup of the student body more reflective of that in the state have begun to show results. Eight percent of the undergraduates are African-American, 6% Asian-American, 7% Hispanic, 1% Native American, and 2% foreign national. Although the campus has its share of apathetic students, a significant number are socially and politically aware, though not always active. The potential for protest rises, however, when SUNY funding is under debate in the state legislature. The student body includes many undergraduates who either could not afford to attend or were rejected for admission by Ivy League or comparable private institutions. The result is a student body in which bright, ambitious, and academically competitive undergraduates predominate. Warns a recent graduate: "If you are laid back, this place will crush you."

Academics: The University at Albany, which turned 160 in 2004, confers degrees through the doctorate. In addition to offering bachelor's degrees in 54 majors, the university also has 31 programs leading to joint bachelor's-master's degrees in 5 years. Undergraduate programs on the main campus are offered through the College of Arts and Sciences, plus the schools of Business and Education. On a separate downtown campus, connected to the main campus by shuttle bus, is the Nelson Rockefeller College of Public Affairs and Policy, the schools of Criminal Justice and Social Welfare and the new College of Computing and Information, which was created in 2005. The academic year is divided into 2 semesters, with the range in class sizes nothing short of tremendous. Freshmen may encounter 1 of the 3 largest lectures with 500 students, although an occasional seminar may have only 20; class sizes for juniors and seniors range from 10 to 70.

The general education program all undergraduates must complete draws coursework from 3 broad areas: disciplinary perspectives, cultural and historical perspectives, and communication and reasoning competencies. The area of disciplinary perspectives includes courses in the arts and humanities and the natural and social sciences. Coursework in cultural and historical perspectives draws on categories grouped as U.S. history, Europe, beyond Europe, global and cross-cultural studies, and U.S. diversity and pluralism. Within communication and reasoning competencies are classes in information literacy, oral discourse and writing, math and statistics, and a foreign language.

The university's 1161-member faculty consists of 631 full-time members and 530 part-time. All but 53 of the full-time members and all but 46 of the part-timers teach undergraduates. Forty percent are women. Two members have been awarded Pulitzer Prizes. Students have few complaints about the faculty when they're in the classroom, praising their expertise, teaching style, and enthusiasm for their subject matter. It's what does or does not happen outside class that is the focus of most concern. Notes a business administration major: "The faculty can be very cooperative at times and simply unavailable at others. Their heavy research schedules demand much of their time, so that teaching assistants, graduate students and/or adjunct faculty often must take the place of professors. Usually this substitution takes the form of providing extra help that students need or teaching the class in the professor's absence." Some of the graduate students, adds a mathematics major, "actually care more for the students than the professors do." Such faculty inaccessibility generally occurs in the lower-level courses; many professors welcome visits during office hours once a student has declared a major and has demonstrated initiative and interest in his or her coursework.

Not surprisingly for a school in a major state capital, one of the top-rated departments is the undergraduate political science program in the Nelson Rockefeller College of Public Affairs and Policy. "It's a challenge," says a major, "but it has a wicked supportive staff that will always help you out." Classroom theories and lectures come to life with the wide range of internships, fellowships, and part-time jobs available in the state assembly or senate or in state agencies. Undergraduate offerings in the School of Criminal Justice are considered excellent as well. The programs in the School of Business are among Albany's most competitive; entrance into the school during the junior year depends on a student's adjusted grade point average in a prescribed series of courses taken during the first 2 years. As a result, the upperclassmen enrolled are some of the university's best. The faculty, too, according to students, are largely "young, bright, and ambitious, just like their students." Accounting is particularly noteworthy: in a recent year the department had the highest passing rate in the nation for students taking the CPA examination; other years it has consistently placed within the top 5.

In the College of Arts and Sciences, the atmospheric science program, with sophisticated weather data systems, encourages undergraduates to participate in weather research. Biology, too, involves undergraduates in research projects. English boasts Pulitzer Prize-winning novelist William Kennedy as a member of its faculty. Students also praise the Arts and Sciences programs in geology, physics, foreign languages, urban planning, East Asian studies, and sociology, as well as the program in social work in the School of Social Welfare.

While undergraduates find little to fault in the quality of the psychology professors, some say this discipline attracts many students who enter because they do not know what else to study or because they do not have the GPAs required for more rigorous programs, such as business. As a result, observes a social welfare major, "the department has minimal expectations of its students and repeats basic course material from one class to the next." More advisors for majors are needed as well. Communications and economics also tend to attract students who are less motivated to learn. The math faculty, says a major, "should have the desire to teach instead of just focusing on research." The Advisement Services Center, designed to help advise students, primarily freshmen and others who have not yet declared their majors, is criticized for giving unclear and sometimes erroneous information.

Facilities: The Science Library which opened in 1999 includes space for the science, math, and technology collection on 3 of its 5 floors, as well as more than 500 seats for individual and group study. Having a new home for the science collection made room for an additional 600 seats in the 4-story general-purpose University Library, which used to house the science collection. Together, the 3 structures—the Science Library and University Library located on the main campus, as well as the Thomas E. Dewey Graduate Library for Public Affairs and Policy located downtown, which mainly has material related to criminal justice, public affairs, and social welfare—house more than 2 million volumes and 38,859 paper and electronic periodicals. While adequate places to study, although the University Library can get a bit noisy, their chief strength is as research facilities. Computerized aids include an on-line catalog, as well as extensive CD-ROM databases covering periodical literature in the natural sciences, social sciences, and humanities. Additional electronic services are contained in the science library. Materials not contained in the university libraries can sometimes be found at the New York State Library, also in Albany, although often, as a junior notes, "If the information isn't in our library, you probably won't find it since our libraries are the ones everybody comes to."

Five hundred plus computer terminals and microcomputers are available for student use in both academic buildings and residence halls. The largest clusters are located in 2 "user rooms" in the lecture center area of the podium; 1 of the rooms is open 24 hours. High-speed Internet connections are available in dorm rooms and wireless connections exist in several locations.

Special programs: Thousands of internship opportunities are available in the state legislature and other state agencies. The School of Social Welfare coordinates an extensive community service program in which more than 1000 students earn academic credit by working in over 300 nonprofit schools, organizations, and agencies. Students can cross register for courses at several neighboring institutions. A 3-2 engineering program is available at Rensselaer Polytechnic Institute or Clarkson University or with 2 SUNY branch campuses. Study-abroad programs exist at more than 20 universities in over 50 countries around the world including places as diverse as Russia, Israel, China, and Brazil.

Campus life: Fifty-four percent of the University at Albany's students live on the 515-acre main campus. Two percent of the men and 5% of the women are members of 1 local and 10 national fraternities and 3 local and 15 national sororities. Although the membership percentages are low, students say the Greek influence provides a sense of belonging and fellowship in the sometimes impersonal environment on campus. All told, about 160 social, cultural, recreational, and academic groups provide niches for students seeking companions of like interests. One of the most widely respected is the student-operated Five Quad Volunteer Ambulance Service. Minor burglaries and vandalism are the most prevalent crimes on campus. A "Don't Walk Alone" escort program designed to discourage students from going out by themselves after dark, a whistle-watch program which distributes free whistles for use in emergencies, as well as blue light emergency phones across campus, help to deter more serious crimes.

Interest in the University at Albany's 8 men's and 11 women's intercollegiate teams, especially football, has grown since the university's move to Division I from Division II. Great Danes basketball attracts the largest crowds. The 13 men's and 9 women's intramural teams draw interest from 50% of the students and offer different divisions for varying levels of expertise.

After a grueling New York winter, spring in Albany is particularly welcome; then, as an English major once said, "the fountains, trees, and grass overtake the cement." The long-awaited Rites of Spring also are a time for celebration, with an annual ceremony to mark the day when the campus water fountains are turned on. Other festivities in recent years have placed UAlbany in the Guinness Book of World Records for having the largest games of musical chairs, Simon Says, and Twister. During the winter months, getting away means skiing in New York or Vermont. Any time of year, New York City, 150 miles away, Boston, 165 miles, and Montreal, 164 miles, are favorite travel destinations.

Cost cutters: In the 2005–2006 school year, 65% of the freshmen and 62% of the continuing students received financial aid. Fifty-four percent of the students in both groups were on need-based assistance. The average freshman award for a first-year student with need included a need-based scholarship or grant averaging $4728 and need-based self-help aid such as loans and job earnings averaging $3999. Non-need-based athletic awards for first-year students averaged $12,862. The average debt of a 2005 graduate was $16,700. In addition to state and federal aid, the university offers several scholarships based on academic performance, including Presidential Scholarships and University Scholars Achievement Awards for out-of-state students, and, for minority students, Frederick Douglas Scholarships. Scholarship amounts vary according to the individual although Presidential Scholarships can pay as much as $2500 to in-state students and as much as $6000 to out-of-state students. Various tuition payment programs also are available. The tradeoffs for these programs, as well as for the low state-supported tuition, students say, are a financial aid bureaucracy and periods of uncertainty and stress every time a new state budget must be approved.

Rate of return: Eighty-five percent of entering freshmen return for the sophomore year. Fifty-two percent graduate in 4 years and 60% in 5 years, with an additional 3% earning degrees in a sixth year.

Payoff: Of 2005 graduates, 14% earned degrees in psychology, 14% in business, and 10% in English. A third of the new alumni went directly to graduate or professional schools. One hundred and eighty companies and other organizations recruited on campus in the 2004–2005 school year.

Bottom line: SUNY, Albany, undergraduates agree, is particularly attractive to the student who is independent and responsible, enjoys a big college experience, and plans to be among the third who go on to higher levels of education. Observes a New Yorker: "Because the school is not nearly as famous or as prestigious as Harvard or Notre Dame, the Albany name alone will not get me far. But the strong program I received here will eventually pay off."

United States Merchant Marine Academy

Kings Point, New York 11024

Setting: Suburban
Control: Public
Undergraduate enrollment: 889 men, 132 women
Graduate enrollment: None
Student/faculty ratio: 12:1
Freshman profile: 14% scored over 700 on SAT I verbal; 37% scored 600–700; 46% 500–599; 3% below 500. 9% scored over 700 on SAT I math; 58% scored 600–700; 33% 500–599; 0% below 500. 16% scored above 28 on the ACT; 47% scored 27–28; 37% 24–26; 0% below 24. 38% graduated in top fifth of high school class; 80% in upper two-fifths.

Faculty profile: 40% Ph.D.'s
Tuition and fees: No tuition; fees: $6516 (freshmen only)
Room and board: No charge
Freshman financial aid: 33%; average scholarship or grant: $2375 need-based; $967 non-need-based
Campus jobs: N/App; average earnings: N/App
Application deadline: Regular Mar. 1
Financial aid deadline: May (Priority: Mar. 1)
Admissions information: (516) 773-5391; (866) 546-4778
e-mail: admissions@usmma.edu
web site: www.usmma.edu

Prospective freshmen often worry that a big college will set them adrift during their 4 years on campus. But how about a school with just over 1000 students that puts the whole class out to sea for a year, does so while charging no tuition, room, or board and only limited fees, and provides a monthly paycheck of about $735 during the year afloat?

Welcome aboard the United States Merchant Marine Academy, where students get their sea legs while preparing for careers in the maritime industry and the armed forces of the United States. Like students at the other federal service academies, midshipmen here pay no tuition, room, or board; they are responsible only for initial fees that, in the 2005–2006 school year, ranged from a freshman outlay of $6516 to cover the purchase of a personal notebook computer plus other incidentals to about one-fourth to half that figure in subsequent years. Unlike students at the other academies, though, merchant marine midshipmen are paid only for the time spent at sea instead of for all 4 years, and they agree upon graduation to serve for 6 years in the merchant marine plus 8 years concurrently as ensigns in the U.S. Naval or Coast Guard Reserve. Although the Merchant Marine Academy has more restrictions on campus life than most civilian colleges, students find it less regimented than West Point. And while the academics are highly demanding, given that 4 years of coursework must be jammed into 3 years (with only a month off in the summer) in order to make time for a year at sea, most midshipmen wouldn't trade their education for a more traditional collegiate experience. Says a first-class (senior) survivor: "I think I am much better prepared to enter the 'real world' than my friends at other colleges. The system here is not always fun—in fact, it rarely is. But it works."

Student body: Almost 1650 high school seniors applied for 285 slots in the fall 2005 plebe or freshman class. (Candidates must be nominated by a member of Congress or another nominating authority, though not the president or vice-president, as is the practice at some of the other service academies.) Midshipmen represent 48 states plus 2 foreign countries. Four percent are Asian-American, 3% Hispanic, and 2% each foreign nationals and African-American. Seventy-two percent are graduates of public schools. The midshipmen tend to be politically and socially conservative, with such adjectives as *disciplined, dedicated, motivated,* and *proud* used most often to describe them. Though a majority were accustomed to being at the head of the pack in high school, they soon learn the importance of teamwork. Notes a second-class midshipman: "Friendships developed here are very special because you cannot make it through the academy without each other."

Academics: The Merchant Marine Academy was founded by an Act of Congress in 1936 after a disastrous fire aboard a passenger ship killed 134 people and convinced the federal government that officers in the merchant marine need rigorous, standardized training. Today's academy offers the bachelor's degree in just 6 majors: marine engineering, marine engineering systems, marine transportation, logistics and intermodal transportation, maritime operations and technology, and marine engineering and shipyard management. As an administrator has stated, "This is not a place to come to in search of a major." The school year is divided into 3 trimesters that run from the last week in July until the end of June, a very long 11 months. Classes rarely exceed 30 members, and they can drop as low as 6 in a subject like higher-level physics. Most courses enroll between 15 and 25.

The freshman or plebe year is particularly tough. It starts with a 2-week indoctrination program in early July that opens with reveille at 5 a.m. and morning calisthenics 10 minutes later, followed by, among other mandated activities, 7 hour-long periods of regimental training and at least an hour of intramurals until dinner begins at 6:10 p.m. One in 10 plebes voluntarily leaves the academy before the "indoc" period is over. Once those 2 weeks are completed, however, the first quarter lightens a wee bit: plebes get to sleep an hour later. However, throughout that first year, they have to balance a heavy load of 7 required classes each trimester with regimental duties.

All midshipmen must complete a rigorous core curriculum that includes 6 courses in the humanities plus courses in calculus, physics, and chemistry. Courses in physical education and ship's medicine, in naval science and in leadership and ethics also are mandatory. With at-sea training occupying half of the sophomore and junior years, there is little time for electives until senior year, and even then the space is scarce.

The faculty consists of 87 full-time members and no part-time. Just 10% are women. The faculty are noted for being knowledgeable and very experienced in their fields of expertise. A majority are dynamic instructors. But most also are known as tough and sometimes merciless graders; according to one midshipman, "Many professors have no qualms about failing two-thirds of the class." Problems occur, he continues, "when the professors have trouble coming down to the midshipmen's level—the faculty are *too* smart."

The academy's technical education is clearly its strong point, with state-of-the-art equipment supporting the 2 basic disciplines: marine engineering, which prepares midshipmen for careers as engineering officers, and marine transportation, which trains them to be deck officers. Navigation, electronics, and radar laboratories as well as steam, diesel engine, and jet turbine labs, provide "incredible tools for learning," says a marine transportation major. Midshipmen rave most about the Computer Aided Operational Research Facility (CAORF), which has a complete bridge simulator that allows students specializing in marine transportation to practice making traffic and voyage planning decisions under various kinds of open sea and harbor conditions.

There's little quarrel where the weak spot is: the humanities department. Midshipmen say, however, that its shortcomings lie, not in the quality of teaching, but rather in the limited emphasis the academy places on this field and the little time that students can devote to exploring it.

Facilities: Bland Memorial Library is known as a silent place where students can accomplish a lot; however, because midshipmen are required to wear uniforms there, most simply stay in the barracks to study since quiet hours are observed there as well. Bland's holdings of 182,000 volumes and 955 periodicals contain one of the nation's most complete collections of maritime-related materials, including a database specifically for this topic. The library also has access to over 450 databases in science, technology, the social sciences, and the humanities. For additional information, midshipmen simply take a short walk to the Great Neck Public Library.

Every plebe is required to purchase a personal notebook computer when he or she enters. Hookups in the barracks enable midshipmen to access the main database and to communicate via e-mail. There also are 5 laboratories housing about 200 computers. At least 1 classroom and the library have wireless access.

Special programs: For nearly every midshipman, the year spent at sea is more than worth the academic pressure endured during his or her time on land. The months afloat enable students to put into practice the theories and skills learned in the classroom and also expose them to foreign countries and cultures most had only dreamed about seeing. "During my sea-year," remarks a southerner, "I sailed around the world and visited more than 15 countries on 5 continents. I also sailed on a Russian square-rigger." Other special opportunities open to midshipmen include various internship and work-study programs in U.S. shipping companies.

Unlike students at the other service academies, who do not engage in combat if war breaks out while they are in school, midshipmen at the Merchant Marine Academy can see wartime duty as part of their training at sea. During the Persian Gulf War, midshipmen were involved in the massive sealift of military supplies to the Middle East; during World War II, 142 midshipmen were killed in the line of duty. They also see important peacetime duty, such as the humanitarian sealift to Somalia in Operation Restore Hope.

Campus life: The 82-acre academy campus, which is the required home port of all midshipmen, is located on the former estate of Walter P. Chrysler, the auto magnate, along the north shore of Long Island. Campus life revolves around 2 traditions: the honor concept, which states that "a midshipman will not lie, cheat, or steal," and the class system of privileges and obligations, which gives first classmen the most privileges and plebes the most obligations. Saturday mornings are reserved for regimental parades and inspections, but the rest of the weekend includes liberty and recreation for all but plebes, who may not leave campus for the first 8 weeks. They gradually "earn" liberty if their regiment performs up to snuff—or if they cheer loudly enough at Saturday football games. Liberty passes may be given for special occasions. Each regiment also sets up its own special events, such as a cadet ball at the Waldorf Astoria Hotel in New York City.

The academy maintains strict rules over student behavior. Midshipmen who are of legal age are free to drink alcohol off academy grounds but not in the barracks or anywhere but the academy pub. Drug use is strictly forbidden, and Naval Reserve status requires that all students submit to random drug testing. A 7:1 male to female ratio makes dating between students difficult; and, midshipmen say, a strict sexual misconduct policy renders relationships even harder to maintain. Because of the honor code and the fact that midshipmen run a 24-hour watch over the campus, crime is not a problem.

The academy fields 14 varsity teams for men and 5 for women in NCAA Division III. The academy cut its men's water polo and volleyball and coed rifle programs at the end of the 2002–2003 school year. Attendance at football games is mandatory, and many students enjoy playing or watching lacrosse, rugby, and baseball on their own. Nearly 25% of the midshipmen participate in at least 1 of the academy's extensive waterfront groups and activities, which include crew and sailing teams and a power squadron for recreational boating. Companies and battalions compete in an intense intramural program.

When midshipmen have weekend leave, the lights of the Big Apple sparkle brightly just 20 miles away. Organized trips through the Arts and World Affairs Program enable students to see Broadway shows and other cultural events at a discount. In the winter, many ski in upstate New York or Vermont.

Cost cutters: Each midshipman is on full scholarship and receives about $735 a month for the 10 months spent at sea on American flag ships. The freshman initiation fee covers such first-of-the-year expenses as calculators and PCs, student activity fees, and personal service fees for items like laundry, barber, and tailoring charges. Since the academy provides no direct financial aid other than free tuition, room, and board, midshipmen needing help to pay the up-front costs are urged to apply early for various government loans. Among 2005–2006 freshmen, average need-based self-help aid including loans totaled $5334. A third of the 2005–2006 plebes received some form of financial aid beyond the free tuition. Need-based scholarships or grants, such as Pell grants from the federal government, averaged $2375; other non-need-based awards and scholarships, generally from such outside sources as the Lions Club or NAACP, averaged $967. Average indebtedness of a 2005 graduate was $9221.

Rate of return: Ninety-two percent of the plebes return for the third-class year. Forty-five percent graduate in 4 years; 82% in 5 years.

Payoff: Among 2005 graduates, 34% earned bachelor's degrees in logistics and intermodal transportation, 29% in marine engineering systems and 15% in marine engineering and shipyard management. In recent years, 40% have accepted maritime positions at sea, 37% took maritime positions ashore, 20% entered active military duty, and 1% pursued advanced degrees. Two percent entered other fields.

In exchange for their virtually free education, midshipmen agree to serve concurrently for 8 years in the Naval Reserve and 6 years in the maritime industry. Midshipmen must complete the U.S. Coast Guard exam to qualify as third assistant engineers or third mates. Academy graduates go on to serve in all capacities in the maritime industry: as ship officers, steamship company executives, and admiralty lawyers, as ship builders and repairers, as oceanographers, and as career officers in the U.S. Armed Forces. A recent survey by Standard and Poors found that the U.S. Merchant Marine Academy ranked 18th among 550 colleges and universities in producing top executives of major corporations.

Bottom line: Putting in 4 years at the U.S. Merchant Marine Academy is a tough way to earn a bachelor's degree. Notes a second classman: "Because we spend a year at sea, we must accomplish in 3 years the requirements of a 4-year B.S. degree. In addition, we voluntarily subject ourselves to the discipline of a federal academy. To those who can meet the challenge, though, the rewards are bountiful."

United States Military Academy

West Point, New York 10996

Setting: Small town
Control: Public
Undergraduate enrollment: 3400 men, 600 women
Graduate enrollment: None
Student/faculty ratio: 8:1
Freshman profile: 20% scored over 699 on SAT I verbal; 46% scored 600–699; 31% 500–599; 3% below 500. 25% scored over 699 on SAT I math; 52% scored 600–699; 23% 500–599; 0% below 500. 72% graduated in top fifth of high school class; 93% in upper two-fifths.
Faculty profile: 39% Ph.D.'s

Tuition and fees: No tuition; freshman fee: $2400–$3000
Room and board: No charge
Freshman financial aid: N/App; average scholarship: N/App
Campus jobs: N/App; average earnings: N/App
Application deadline: Early action: Oct. 25; regular: Mar. 20
Financial aid deadline: N/App
Admissions information: (845) 938-4041
 e-mail: admissions@usma.edu
 web site: www.usma.edu

When a college catalog, which usually can be counted on to paint the brighter side of the baccalaureate years, highlights a Chinese proverb, "The more you sweat in peace, the less you bleed in war," better brace yourself for a rigorous 4 years on campus. Even then, a sojourn at the United States Military Academy will turn out to be a difficult way to earn free tuition, room, and board and a commission as a second lieutenant of the regular Army, along with a bachelor of science degree. Founded as a place to produce home-trained officers, the Military Academy opened on Independence Day, 1802, with 10 cadets and the prospect of an alumni network that would eventually include most leaders in U.S. military history, among them Ulysses S. Grant, Robert E. Lee, Dwight D. Eisenhower, Omar Bradley, Douglas MacArthur, and Norman Schwarzkopf. As grueling as the 4 years can be, with an additional 5 years of active military duty required upon graduation, 10 times as many high school graduates apply as there are available slots, and about 70% of those who are accepted decide to enroll and join the impressive chain of command.

Student body: Cadets come from every state in the nation and include only those who pass rigorous academic, physical, and medical tests and are nominated by an authorized source, such as a senator, a representative, or the vice-president. Eighty-one percent in a recent year, were graduates of public schools. Seven percent of the cadets were African-American, 5% each Asian-American and Hispanic, and 1% each Native American and foreign nationals from 19 countries. Women generally comprise about 15% of the enrollment. Over the years, acceptance of women by some male cadets has been grudging at best and, according to a report released in 2005 by the U.S. Department of Defense, hostile at worst. Nevertheless, during the 1989–90 school year a woman became the first captain in charge of the Corps of Cadets in academy history. With the graduating class of 1995, a woman graduated first in her class, ranking number 1 academically, militarily, and in physical training.

Cadets describe themselves as extremely intelligent (7% of the Class of 2008 were high school valedictorians), politically conservative, athletic, very hardworking—and driven. In fact, internal motivation is viewed, in the words of one cadet, as "a prerequisite to survival, not just success." Although cadets quickly develop a strong loyalty to one another, an edge of individual competitiveness continues to exist, since the army branch and the post that a cadet receives after graduation depend upon his or her class rank. Notes a third-class (sophomore) cadet: "Minimum standards must be maintained to stay here, but simply meeting them is discouraged. Cadets are expected to do their best in everything." Still, "Cooperate and Graduate" is a common saying at the academy, and cadets quickly learn that teamwork is important not only to surviving but to succeeding in such a physically, emotionally, and intellectually challenging environment. All also are firmly bound by the honor code, which states: "A cadet will not lie, cheat, or steal nor tolerate those who do." For this group of students, love of honor, service to country, and a desire to become leaders are much more than mere concepts.

Academics: West Point offers bachelor's degrees in 25 fields of study and 22 optional majors, the latter available to a cadet who wishes to examine a discipline in greater depth than is provided by the broader fields of study. The academic year is technically divided into 2 semesters with a 2-week January intersession, although cadets also train during the summer. In particular, the summer before classes begin for first-time cadets, known as plebes, is spent in 6 weeks of very tough basic training. Advises a survivor: "You will be humbled by the experience as you learn to live under a program designed to make you perform under stress, while providing the upper classes with opportunities to develop as leaders." Changes to the program, now called the Cadet Leader Development System, formerly known as the fourth-class system, have emphasized upperclassmen's use of positive leadership techniques rather than verbal abuse. One result has been a drop in the number of freshmen leaving the academy during those first 6 weeks: 1 summer after the changes were instituted, attrition was cut in half, from 10% to 5%. Other summers, spent in military field training and leadership training at posts around the nation and the world, give cadets the chance, as one put it, "to fire rifles and machine guns, drive tanks, ride in helicopters, and parachute."

Average class size is 15, with the largest courses enrolling fewer than 20 and the smallest electives, just 5. Every cadet is required to take 31 core courses that, in addition to the field of study or optional major, constitute his or her "professional major." The course of study is divided between 15 required courses in math, science, and engineering, and 16 in the humanities and public affairs, plus 4 short, intense courses in military science and 4 year-long sessions of physical education. Electives are chosen from 1 of the 25 fields of study, which mandate 9 courses, or any of the 22 optional majors, which require 10–13. A cadet who chooses to complete an optional major must also do a senior thesis or design project. More than 75% of the Corps of Cadets elect to major.

In a recent year, there were 577 faculty members, all full-time. Twelve percent were women. Most of the faculty tend to be U.S. Army officers, rather than academics, who consider it their duty to instruct cadets. Though many are West Point alumni and understand what cadets are going through, the realization does not make them any softer. "They expect high levels of performance," says a plebe. However, help is available whenever a student needs it. Remarks a cadet: "We get more one-on-one instruction than you could imagine." Adds a second-class cadet: "They are available nearly 24 hours a day to help us."

West Point's engineering departments are superb and offer cadets regular access to the latest technology government funding can buy. Students consider the faculty in the social sciences department, which includes courses in political science and economics, to be "unparalleled" for the professional experiences they bring to the classroom. Many come to West Point after having worked in such organizations as the Pentagon, State Department, or the United Nations. For many cadets, it is nothing short of "dumbfounding" to hear professors speak about world leaders as acquaintances with whom they have worked. The programs in 7 languages—Arabic, Chinese, French, German, Portuguese, Russian, and Spanish—also earn high marks, as does the department of behavioral sciences and leadership, which is big on practical advice. History and mathematics round out the "A" list.

Cadets say the course offerings of the department of law are too limited to provide adequate preparation for law school. Others find that the premed programs also fall short, in part, because the laboratory equipment needs updating. English simply suffocates under the cadet's heavy workload. As a mechanical engineering major stated, "The environment at West Point does not provide the time or the atmosphere for the quiet reflection required to appreciate literature."

Facilities: The library contains more than 600,000 volumes and 1500 periodicals; its strengths lie chiefly in the areas of military history and government documents. Though the library is typically quiet and offers 4 stories of space in which to read and carry on research, most cadets prefer to study in the barracks and access the computerized catalog with their personal computers, rather than don a uniform and study in the library. Some liken the library's atmosphere to that of a museum, with its numerous works of art and display cases.

All cadets are required to purchase personal computers when they enter West Point; the PCs enable students to communicate via e-mail worldwide, access databases, get grades and counseling reports, and submit completed homework assignments. West Point also offers a wireless network on campus.

Special programs: For those seeking a change of scenery but not necessarily a break from their rigorous regime, West Point permits 18 cadets to spend the first semester of their junior year at the Naval, Air Force, or Coast Guard Academy. In the summers preceding the junior and senior years, 3 weeks of participation in educational experiences include but are not limited to Operations Crossroads Africa, immersion language training in various foreign countries, medical internships, and workfellow positions with federal and Department of Defense agencies.

Campus life: The Military Academy campus covers more than 16,000 acres in Orange County, New York, 56 miles north of New York City. Although all students are required to reside on campus, large numbers leave on weekends whenever they can. Weekend leave is awarded, as are most privileges, according to seniority and military performance. Freshmen (plebes), for example, can leave the academy for only 2 weekends in addition to the Christmas holidays and on authorized trips. Recalls a recent graduate: "The activities on post, such as Saturday hops, are pretty boring, so the rule is, if you can get a weekend pass—take it!" With New York City just an hour away, few cadets have to be told more than once. Without a pass, the weekend offers an opportunity to sleep past 6 a.m. on Sunday morning and to spend some time at the nearby home of a family sponsor, who serves as a cadet's "home away from home" during his or her time at West Point.

As at the other service academies, students are given random urinalysis tests to spot drug usage; those testing positive may be required to leave. Crime is not among the various issues cadets must worry about. The honor code prevents trouble from starting inside the academy, and military police guards at the gates discourage it from entering from the outside.

Intercollegiate football is THE fall sport, preceded the night before by a spirited dinner and rallies and observed the day of the event by tailgating before and after the game. Notes a plebe: "Almost all cadets go because it is an occasion to unwind and be crazy." Basketball, gymnastics, hockey, and other of the 15 intercollegiate sports for men and 9 for women, most of which compete in the Patriot League, draw smaller though still exuberant crowds. As a third-class cadet observes: "Sporting events as a whole are extremely popular, and the spectator is considered as important as the participant in terms of spirit and motivation." A fifth of the men and a third of the women compete at the varsity level. The Black Knights women's basketball team competed for the first time in the NCAA Division I tournament in March 2006.

Thanks to former West Point Superintendent Douglas MacArthur, who first stressed the slogan "Every cadet an athlete, every athlete challenged," all cadets must participate in 1 intramural sport per semester. Eighteen sports for men and 14 for women recently were available. For those who long for a break from the physical, the well-known Cadet Glee Club, Tactics Club, and Model UN provide popular alternatives.

Cost cutters: At West Point, Uncle Sam pays for everything (and gets back full value). Cadets are paid an annual salary of $9173, much of which goes for the mandatory personal computer, uniforms, books, laundry, haircuts, and like items. Financial help is available to students unable to pay the initial fee which ranged in the 2005–2006 school year between $2400 and $3000.

Rate of return: Ninety-two percent of the plebes who remain after basic training return to become third-class cadets. In spite of the demanding schedule, an impressive 81% continue on to graduate in 4 years.

Payoff: For a recent graduating class, engineering was the most popular area of study claiming 36% of the cadets, followed by the behavioral sciences at 15%, and history at 8%. All but 2% of the graduates began immediately to serve their 5-year commitment as Army officers. The remaining 2% entered medical school. Since 1923, 77 West Point graduates have been named Rhodes Scholars and have attended Oxford University while on active duty, making the academy the nation's fourth highest source of these prestigious scholars. Two cadets were selected for 2004; 1 for 2005. Virtually all West Point graduates who remain on active duty for 20 years obtain an advanced degree.

Bottom line: For those who survive, the West Point experience represents 4 years of personal accomplishment, sacrifice, and deep pride. Concludes a second-class cadet: "This school helps you learn about yourself because it is in times of stress that you really tap into your potential. As a result of this experience, when you graduate you can't help but feel more confident about yourself and what you can do."

Webb Institute

Glen Cove, New York 11542

Setting: Suburban
Control: Private
Undergraduate enrollment: 64 men, 16 women
Graduate enrollment: None
Student/faculty ratio: 10:1
Freshman profile: 35% scored over 700 on SAT I verbal; 60% scored 600–700; 5% 500–599; 0% below 500. 70% scored over 700 on SAT I math; 30% scored 600–700; 0% below 600. 67% graduated in top tenth of high school class; 100% in upper fifth.
Faculty profile: 50% Ph.D.'s

Tuition and fees: None
Room and board: $8340
Freshman financial aid: 35%; average scholarship or grant: NA
Campus jobs: NA; average earnings: NA
Application deadline: Early decision: Oct. 15; regular: Feb. 15
Financial aid deadline: July 1
Admissions information: (516) 671–2213
  e-mail: admissions@webb-institute.edu
  web site: www.webb-institute.edu

There is an undergraduate enrollment of 80, with just 10 students to every full-time faculty member, and no tuition or fees. But if you have to ask what naval architecture or marine engineering is, then this highly specialized school on Long Island, 30 miles outside New York City, is not for you. In fact, Webb Institute is only for students who are sure that they want to be either naval architects or marine engineers. There is just one curriculum leading to a single degree, a bachelor of science in naval architecture and marine engineering, so if neither of these disciplines turns out to be your thing, you have no choice but to jump ship. "Webb is not for just anybody," says a senior, "but for the right person it's perfect."

When William H. Webb, the foremost shipbuilder in New York City in the middle of the 19th century, founded in 1889 the institute that bears his name, he wanted to establish a school that would train people to design the increasingly sophisticated ships that already had replaced the traditional wooden structures. Until Webb's death in 1899, he assumed all operating expenses of the college. Today, endowment income, together with gifts from foundations, corporations, alumni, and other individuals, largely defrays operating costs; students pay only for room, board, books, and supplies. "A person graduates having already designed an entire ship by him- or herself," says a junior. "But he or she best be prepared to work for that tuition-and-fee-free education."

Student body: Just 14% of Webb's students are from New York though the total range of states represented, at 22, is impressive considering the small size of the student body. Thirty percent of the students are graduates of private or parochial high schools. Two Hispanic students, 1 African-American, and 1 Asian-American were enrolled in the 2005–2006 school year. As fewer than 30 freshmen are admitted each year, competition for the few spaces is fierce; for the 2005 fall freshman class, 110 high school seniors applied, 33 were accepted, and 22 decided to enroll.

Students fearful of finding a group of nerds who are smart but totally introverted are delighted to discover many sociable and outgoing classmates. "I expected the student body to be like a dysfunctional family because of its size and the closeness, and it is," says a student from the Pacific Northwest. "But the camaraderie is astounding and the people here are great. There is not one person here that does not work hard and everyone cares about each other's well-being. I have never met a better group of people in my life." *Intense*—some would even say *tense*—is the adjective that best describes the students and the curriculum. Notes a sophomore: "We always have work due and can expect at least 7 hours of homework a night. At Webb, if you fail you are not asked to come back, so there is pressure to stay on top of things to do well." The students, all of whom are bright, also learn to help one another in their coursework. Says a senior: "Students push their own limits rather than competing with each other; many students will drop everything to 'help out a shipmate.'" given the college's small size, students also soon know one another's business and check up on each other during particularly stressful times. However, if a freshman doesn't hit it off with members of his or her class, the circle of alternative friends is rather limited.

Academics: The school year at Webb is divided into 2 semesters, separated by an 8-week winter work term. Because all undergraduates are pursuing the same bachelor's degree, they take the same sequence of demanding courses in each of their 4 years. Even then, class size is 25 tops and decreases in subsequent years as some students leave Webb for programs better suited to their needs. Individual attention is prevalent, though the senior thesis presents the greatest opportunity for independent study. The single curriculum is built largely on no-nonsense courses like calculus, physics, chemistry, and engineering with an emphasis on creative problem-solving. "The program is wonderful if you want to be a naval architect or marine engineer," remarks a recent graduate. "Pointless if not." The workload is heavy with students accumulating 146 credits over 4 years and covering what is a 2-semester course at some schools in 1 term at Webb.

Students praise the faculty, which numbers 8 full-time professors, 7 part-time, and no women, for their past or present experience with the maritime industry and their willingness to share it with undergraduates. Though there is an occasional condescending professor, most are very dedicated to the students and work closely on an equal footing with them to do what they can to help them succeed. "Some are not great teachers," notes a senior, "but almost all of them are brilliant and have something very usable to convey."

Students find the naval architecture and engineering portions of the program to be of equal excellence and rigor. The much-used marine engineering and mechanical laboratory includes a turbocharged diesel engine, and a turbogenerator. There is also a material science laboratory equipped for the microscopic examination, heat treatment, and physical testing of metals. A recent push to make capital improvements in all laboratories, including the 93-foot towing tank for testing boat and ship models, has helped to quiet earlier student concerns about aging equipment.

As is true at many technical schools, Webb's offerings in the liberal arts are deficient. Quips a recent grad: "The humanities department makes a valiant attempt to educate Webb students into becoming people, as opposed to just engineers, but it works on only 1 person out of 5!" Adjunct faculty primarily are brought in to teach these subjects.

Facilities: The Livingston Library is small and functional, recently offering just 51,000 volumes and 271 current periodicals, with both types of sources related primarily to the institute's 2 fields of concentration.

For detailed information on other subjects, students must look elsewhere. However, the on-line catalog and database searching assist tremendously in research. The library's range may be limited, but its hours are not: users may work there around the clock in any kind of weather since the library is attached to the building that houses students.

All students are issued a laptop for their use while enrolled at Webb. Laptops connect to the network that provides access to e-mail and the Internet using a wireless connection. In addition, 9 PCs are available in labs 24 hours a day, 7 days a week.

Special programs: All undergraduates spend January and February of every school year working in marine-related industry for pay. Freshmen are hired as helpers in shipyards, sophomores serve as cadets in the engine rooms of commercial vessels, and juniors and seniors work in professional capacities as design, research, or marine engineers in government or private industry. Work opportunities take students from San Francisco and the Mediterranean to Japan, The Netherlands, and Australia. Undergraduates earn each employer's going rate, and the money helps to pay for their room, board, books, and supplies at Webb, plus they gain experience that helps them get higher paying jobs immediately upon graduation.

Campus life: Webb is located on a turn-of-the-century estate situated on Long Island's north shore. It has its own beach and boathouse with 26 acres of green lawn and 6 academic buildings. All students reside in the estate mansion, and social life is pretty much centered around the campus. There are no local hangouts except the basement-level pub where students can play pool and darts and no fraternities or sororities. Clubs vary from year to year according to student interests, with the Webb Family Singers, known fondly as the Woofs, involving students, faculty, and staff, a perennial favorite. The Solar Splash team designs and builds an entry for an annual intercollegiate solar-powered boat competition, placing third in 2004. Observes a senior: "I expected school to be a lot less fun than it has turned out to be." The student body is largely self-governing through the Student Organization, to which all undergraduates belong. That group, along with the Student Court, sets policies and implements standards governing everything from dormitory life to athletic and social activities. For many undergraduates, the honor code, which covers both academic and social behavior, is one of Webb's best features. Observes a junior: "The result is a campus atmosphere that is very responsible and professional as well as trusting and safe." The isolation of the school, teamed with the honor code, creates an environment in which crime is not a consideration. Adds a sophomore: "A bigger problem is (us) leaving things around the school and forgetting where we left them."

Despite the institute's academic intensity, or perhaps because of it, most students opt to loosen up by playing on the 6 intercollegiate and 2 intramural sports teams. Observes a senior: "Anyone who wants to play is welcomed—there are no cuts—and the goal is to have fun." The varsity basketball, soccer, and sailing teams and intramural floor hockey are most popular. The Student Organization sponsors a whitewater rafting trip in the fall and a skiing trip in the winter. Using the institute's fleet of boats to sail on Long Island Sound also is a favorite activity.

When students need to get away from Webb or from Glen Cove (pop. 27,000), they take the train into New York City, although, says a westerner, "Webb is difficult to escape from because its location is an escape of sorts in itself."

Cost cutters: Each year, Webb agrees to pay 4 years' full tuition for all entering freshmen. In the 2005–2006 school year, 35% of the first-year students and 15% of the rest received additional financial aid to help cover the cost of room, board, books, and supplies, such as calculators and drafting equipment. The average freshman award totaled $2626, with no breakdown presented on the amount that was a scholarship or grant or self-help aid such as loans and job earnings. The average 2005 graduate left with debts of $11,612. To help hold down costs on campus, students volunteer to assist without pay in the maintenance and upkeep of the several labs, the shops, the libraries, the computer center, and other facilities as part of the "Beaver Day" work program.

Rate of return: Ninety-six percent of the freshmen who enter return for the sophomore year. All but 12% graduate in 4 years.

Payoff: After earning their degrees in naval architecture and marine engineering, a third of the recent graduates continued on to graduate school in engineering. The two-thirds who entered the job market work as naval architects with the U.S. Navy or Coast Guard, the pleasure craft industry, yacht designers, and research firms. Nine companies and organizations recruited on campus in a recent school year. Webb's overall graduation placement rate is 100% annually.

Bottom line: Webb Institute may be tuition-free, but it can impose other costs in terms of a limited social life and seemingly endless workload that some students may not be willing to bear. Advises a junior: "For the student who has a specific engineering career in mind and who has no aversion to hard work and sleepless nights, Webb is a fantastic opportunity."

North Carolina

Appalachian State University

Boone, North Carolina 28608

Setting: Small town
Control: Public
Undergraduate enrollment: 6117 men, 5866 women
Graduate enrollment: 262 men, 431 women
Student/faculty ratio: 19:1
Freshman profile: Average combined SAT I score: 1130. Class rank data: NA
Faculty profile: 90% Ph.D.'s
Tuition and fees: $3436 in-state; $13,178 out-of-state
Room and board: $4658

Freshman financial aid: 45%; average scholarship or grant: $4165 need-based; $2289 non-need-based
Campus jobs: NA; average earnings: NA
Application deadline: Rolling
Financial aid deadline: Priority date: Mar. 15 (Scholarships: Dec. 5)
Admissions information: (828) 262-2120
e-mail admissions@appstate.edu
web site: www.appstate.edu

When students at Appalachian State University in Boone, North Carolina, describe the strengths of their academic institution, many name qualities not commonly associated with a public institution: a strong liberal arts program, small classes, professors' dedication to classroom teaching. But the lists also include a number of fringe benefits that make Appalachian even more special to those enrolled. For example, one history major includes "Appalachian's outdoor programs, no noise pollution, pretty fall colors, and clean air." A Florida student highlights "all aspects of mountain life." A former New Yorker was delighted to find "plenty of snow" in Boone. Appalachian State, a former teachers college close to the borders of Virginia and Tennessee, is beginning to gain recognition beyond its corner of North Carolina as a mid-sized public institution where the quality of life outside the classroom is matched only by the quality of instruction within, and for a price for out-of-staters just half that at better known, private colleges. "When I first came here, I had every intention of transferring to a bigger and supposedly better school," says a Florida junior, "but now I wouldn't even think of it. Appalachian State is a great place to live and learn."

Student body: About 90% percent of Appalachian State's students are from the Tarheel state, with most of the out-of-staters also hailing from the South. Altogether, students in a recent year came from 45 states and 54 foreign countries. Ninety-seven percent attended public high schools. Just 6% of the students are members of racial/ethnic minority groups: 4% are African-American, about 1% each Hispanic and Asian-American, and still smaller percentages Native American and foreign national. Although the minority population is small, it is quite visible, with African-American students serving in recent years as either vice president or president of the Student Government Association. Whatever is lacking in racial, ethnic, and cultural diversity, students say, is compensated for in the range of life-styles and political and social perspectives, from "save-the-earth granolas" to future young executives. Notes a senior: "Students feel very comfortable in expressing themselves on this campus. They stand up for their views and beliefs but are also sensitive to each other's wants and needs." As the university becomes increasingly popular within the state, competition is picking up in many academic majors. Still, the outdoor orientation of most students keeps the intensity level low. Says a Georgian: "No matter how stressed you may be, you are in such an awesome setting that you cannot help but stay calm and serene."

Academics: Appalachian State, which turned 100 in 1999, awards the bachelor's degree in 91 majors through the colleges of Arts and Sciences, Business, Education, and Fine and Applied Arts plus the School of Music. Master's degrees are awarded in more than 80 programs. Students follow a semester calendar. Entry-level classes for freshmen range anywhere from 20 to 100 students, with a course like Introduction to Biology enrolling between 80 and 100. Once a student has chosen his or her major, classes tend to drop to 20 or fewer, although communications and business classes remain generally larger.

All students must fulfill general-education requirements that comprise approximately one-third of the total credits needed to graduate. Requirements range from 12 semester hours each in humanities and social sciences to 8 hours in natural sciences. In addition, students must complete a number of specially designated courses throughout the curriculum that emphasize particular skills, such as writing, speaking, and computational skills, and knowledge, such as multicultural and cross-disciplinary issues. The Watauga College Residential Program enables freshmen and sophomores to take interdisciplinary courses in English, history, the humanities, and the social sciences to complete the general-education requirements in these fields. Students participating in the program live together in 1 residence hall to enhance integration of the academic program with students' personal and social development.

Appalachian's faculty recently numbered 674 full-time and 272 part-time members (45% of the total pool were women); and while their abilities range from the inspirational to the deadly dull, "on the whole, they are pretty responsive to students' needs," says an education major. "The most positive aspect of this university is that the faculty's mission is to be outstanding teachers rather than researchers." In keeping with that mission, the Hubbard Center for Faculty and Staff Support on campus helps professors to design and redesign courses, experiment with new instructional materials and techniques, and analyze teaching for improvement. In a recent school year, when budget cuts forced reduction in the number of faculty, administrators with teaching experience took the helm of several freshman classes to preserve the university's emphasis on classroom teaching and small class size. Graduate students teach just 1% of the introductory courses.

The colleges of business and education offer 2 of the university's strongest programs, according to students. Construction of a new business building has helped to attract more and better instructors, enhancing an already challenging curriculum. The accounting program in particular is considered blue-chip, with good reason: accounting majors in 2003 scored the highest pass rate in the nation on all 4 parts of the national CPA exam, the last year when students were required to take all 4 parts at one sitting. The College of Education, with its roots in Appalachian's early history as a normal school to train teachers, enjoys good professors and a high job-placement rate. Among the liberal arts, political science, criminal justice, history, and English shine, with excellent professors and well-designed curricula. Communications is a winner, too. The School of Music offers a wide variety of top-quality programs in music education, music therapy, music industry studies, and music performance, with concentrations in sacred music, composition and theory, voice, and instrument. A new recording studio recently was constructed.

The Department of Foreign Languages and Literature offers extensive classes in Japanese, German, French, Spanish, Latin, Chinese, and Russian, but majors only in French and Spanish.

Facilities: The eagerly anticipated opening of the new 210,000-square-foot Carol Grotnes Belk Library and Information Commons in 2005 more than met student expectations. Says a senior: "I'm still getting acquainted with the setup, however, from my initial experience; there are hundreds of study places, nooks, and rooms. It is a very quiet building so the studying I have done in the library has been productive." When production takes longer, Belk offers a 24-hour cyber café. The collection, which stands at 544,000 volumes and about 4800 periodicals, is aided by the extensive access to more than 500 electronic databases and 35,000 electronic periodicals plus the ever-trusty ABC Express Plan. Explains a senior: "When you are looking up a book (on the computerized catalog) you are looking through the libraries of UNC (Asheville), Appalachian State (Boone), and Western Carolina University (Cullowhee). If we do not have the book you need, you can have it within 24 hours at no charge to you."

The new library and information commons also has more than 200 computer stations, adding to the number of units already contained in the more than 30 other labs spread among the 4 colleges, residence halls, and the student union. More than 750 IBM-compatible and Macintosh computers are available to students; the main lab in the student union is open around the clock. "Sufficient? Yes!" says a marketing major.

Special programs: Cross-registration for courses is possible with Auburn and Wake Forest universities and with the University of North Carolina, Greensboro. Opportunities for study abroad are offered at more than 100 sites in Europe, Asia, Central America, and South America. A 3-2 degree program in engineering is available at Auburn University in Alabama and Clemson in South Carolina. ASU also maintains 2 campuses away from Boone for experiential studies. The New York Loft, begun in 1974, offers living space for 22 people in the Gramercy Park district of Manhattan. Appalachian House, a satellite campus in Washington, D.C., which opened in 1977, is located on North Carolina Avenue near Dupont Circle.

Campus life: As noted before, much of the extracurricular life of Appalachian State derives from its setting in the beautiful Blue Ridge of the Appalachian Mountains. Just over a third of all undergraduates, 38%, live on the 250-acre main campus with 80% of that number remaining for any given weekend.

Mountaineer football, the only varsity sport played in NCAA Division I-AA rather than Division I-A, attracts big weekend crowds, drawing 17,000 people for home games. Basketball and baseball are the second and third most popular crowd pleasers among the 11 men's and 11 women's varsity sports. More than three-quarters of the student body take part in one or more areas of the university recreation program, which includes 19 competitive club sports, 6 men's, 4 women's, and 9 co-ed. Seemingly nonstop intramural activities also are offered each year, as well as over 100 outdoor recreation trips. Whitewater rafting, rock climbing, and caving are the 3 most popular offerings.

Greek life is a significant part of student life, though it attracts only 5% of the men and women as members of its 13 national fraternities and 9 national sororities. Says a junior: "The system here is big enough to have constant activities but not so large that you feel like you *must* be a part of it to fit in." Two of the fraternities and 2 of the sororities are historically African-American. Legends, a student-run nightclub, can hold 1200 people for dances and live entertainment. Altogether, more than 200 student clubs and organizations attract approximately 70% of the undergraduates as members. The campus is well lit and supplied with emergency call boxes, a police bike patrol and van service, though crime is not regarded as much of a problem. Recalls a senior: "The most troublesome crimes while I have been here were a bear gaining access to our gym and some alcohol/drug citations."

"To escape from campus life," prescribes a junior, "just drive a few minutes and you can be in an isolated location in the mountains. There are many campsites, mountains to ski (or snowboard), trails to hike, cliffs to climb, caves to explore, rivers to raft, and anything else that brings out the Daniel Boone in you." Those who still find the town of Boone (pop. 14,900) too confining head to the larger city of Charlotte or Greensboro.

Cost cutters: Forty percent of all freshmen and continuing students received some form of financial aid in a recent school year. For about 30% of the first-year students and 35% of the rest, the aid was need-based. The average freshman award for a student with need included a need-based scholarship or grant averaging $4165 and need-based self-help aid such as loans and jobs averaging $2716. Other non-need-based awards and scholarships for first-year students averaged $2289. The average financial indebtedness of a recent graduates was $14,482. In addition to federal and state aid programs, ASU provides a number of merit-based scholarships. Among the most prestigious is the Chancellor's Scholarship, which pays $4500 to up to 25 high-ranking freshmen in all majors; Academic Honors Scholarships pay $500 to $1000. A number of awards pay $1000 to $2500 to students according to their planned field of study. The W.H. Plemmons Leader Fellows Program recognizes students who have demonstrated leadership in their community with scholarships worth $1500. Applications for many merit-based scholarships carry a deadline of early December so incoming students are encouraged to obtain scholarship information early. A textbook rental program uses undergraduate student fees to lend each student the main textbook used in every course they are taking and "saves students from spending hundreds of dollars on books each semester," raves a senior.

Rate of return: Eighty-five percent of freshmen return for the sophomore year. Thirty percent go on to graduate in 4 years, 55% within 5 years, the third highest rate among all UNC institutions. Sixty percent earn their degrees within 6 years.

Payoff: The 3 most popular majors among recent graduates were elementary education at 8%, information technology at 6%, and management at 5%. About 15% of recent grads went on to pursue advanced degrees. Many graduates go on to jobs in computer science, accounting, and management. About 250 companies recruited on campus in a recent school year. Recent employers of graduates have included the DeKalb County Schools, DuPont, E. & J. Gallo Winery, Kellogg's, the Peace Corps, USA Today, Volvo, and Xerox Corporation.

Bottom line: Observes a junior English major: "When I was in high school, I did about average and was not involved with anything. At ASU I do fairly well to above average in some classes and am very much involved in school activities. If you think you can apply yourself and if you enjoy friendly people and a natural setting, then this is the best choice of colleges. But," he adds, "you'd better like snow and cold in winter!"

Elon University

Elon, North Carolina 27244

Setting: Suburban
Control: Private (United Church of Christ)
Undergraduate enrollment: 1801 men, 2806 women
Graduate enrollment: 43 men, 86 women
Student/faculty ratio: 17:1
Freshman profile: 6% scored over 700 on SAT I verbal; 46% scored 600–700; 42% 500–599; 6% below 500. 7% scored over 700 on SAT I math; 54% scored 600–700; 35% 500–599; 4% below 500. 25% graduated in top tenth of high school class; 57% in upper fifth.
Faculty profile: 83% Ph.D.'s
Tuition and fees: $18,949

Room and board: $6422
Freshman financial aid: 77%; average scholarship or grant: $3656 need-based; $2665 non-need-based
Campus jobs: 25%; average earnings: $1200/year
Application deadline: Early decision: Nov. 1; Early action: Nov. 10; regular: Jan. 10
Financial aid deadline: Feb. 15 (priority)
Admissions information: (336) 278-3566; (800) 334-8448
e-mail: admissions@elon.edu
web site: www.elon.edu

If colleges earned ratings like motels and restaurants, Elon University, a private institution of 4600 full-time undergraduates in the heart of North Carolina's Piedmont, would surely gain a quintuple A rating. The first two A's would be for the Active Academics that encourage students to get out of the classroom and travel abroad, help out in the community, or work in a company. The next 2 A's would represent the caring Attention of professors in class and their ready Availability after hours, often joining students in their out-of-classroom endeavors. The final A, and the most important for many middle-class students today, would stand for Affordability. With tuition, fees, room, and board at less than $25,500 in the 2005–2006 school year, that alone makes all the other qualities that much more Amazing.

Student body: Only 32% of Elon's undergraduates are North Carolina residents; the largest group of out-of-staters, another 32%, are from Virginia, Maryland, New Jersey, and Pennsylvania. Students attend from 44 states and 41 other countries. African-American students comprise the single largest minority group on campus at 6% of enrollment; Hispanics, Asian-Americans and foreign nationals each constitute 2%. Seventy-nine percent of the students graduated from public schools. Just 2% are members of the United Church of Christ, with which the college remains affiliated. Students drawn to Elon are looking for the full college experience and eagerly become involved in, and often aspire to lead, as many organizations as their study schedules will allow. Few are overtly political, "upper middle-class moderate liberals," observes a southerner. "Preppy" sums up the majority in a single word. "Close your eyes," says a New Englander, "and think of the typical khaki-pants-blue shirt-and-flip-flops-wearing frat boy, and the black-pants-and-pea-coat-wearing sorority girl, and you have pictured the typical Elon student." The overall environment, says a Pennsylvanian, "is very positive. People just seem happy!" They also seem smarter and more competitive, in the words of a recent graduate: "The sophomores and freshmen had higher grades and test scores than my class did to gain admission to the school and they have continued the drive toward academic excellence." But to date, the enhanced competitiveness has not become cutthroat. Adds a junior: "Friends congratulate you and bake you cakes or cookies when you get inducted into an honor society. It's a big deal that's joyful."

Academics: Elon, which turned 115 in 2004, awards the bachelor's degree in 48 majors, master's degrees in business administration and education and doctorates in physical therapy and law. Students follow a 2-semester calendar with a 1-month January term in the middle. Classes range in size from a high of 63 in Topics in Biology to a single student in private music lessons. However, first-year students will mainly find themselves in classes of 20–25 that drop to between 10 and 20 in the junior and senior years. Only 8 of the nearly 950 classes offered each semester have more than 40 students.

All students must complete a general studies program that contains 4 components: a first-year seminar based on the theme The Global Experience, which helps students learn to think and write clearly and critically; an experiential learning requirement for which undergraduates do either an internship, study abroad, perform some community service, do undergraduate research, or assume a leadership role; a liberal studies area in which students complete coursework in 4 traditional areas; and an interdisciplinary seminar that enables upperclassmen to explore subjects from multiple perspectives. Together, the 4 components complete 58 of the 132 hours needed to graduate. In addition, all seniors take a comprehensive exam in the major.

The faculty, says a senior, "are what keeps me coming back each year." The 370-member faculty consists of 279 full-time members and 91 part-time, marking an increase of 69 full-time positions in the past 5 years. All teach undergraduates. Forty-five percent are women. Students especially like the diverse teaching styles many professors use to engage undergraduates in the classroom and encourage them to apply what they have learned in the surrounding community. "They are very down-to-earth," says a senior. "You also get to know a lot of them outside the classroom working with other organizations." A number also encourage students "to work in teams in class to simulate real-world problem solving," says a senior.

That kind of real-life application is what makes many of Elon's programs winners to the students who take them. Majors as diverse as political science, sports medicine, and education all involve students in real-life applications of classroom learning. Such opportunities for the majors in journalism and communications (with emphases in broadcast and new media, corporate, and cinema) have been further enhanced by a $3.4 million renovation of the communications building that produced 2 new television studios, digital audio and video capabilities, and new computer labs and multimedia classrooms. The tangible benefit for students has been the opportunity to produce 5 different television programs—a news show, two sports shows, a game show, and musical-coffeehouse entertainment show—plus their own movies.

The opening of the $17 million McMichael Science Center in 1999 likewise increased the chances for biology and chemistry majors to work on semester and year-long research projects. Psychology also involves undergraduates in varied research opportunities; business administration majors profit from the expertise of professors, some of whom worked in major corporations before teaching. A new business center, scheduled to open in fall 2006, further brings the real world to campus with a financial center that offers real-time data from Wall Street and other global financial markets. The Love School of Business itself gained accreditation in 2004. The leisure and sport management, and physical education majors also are well respected for their curricula. The exclusive music theater major accepts just 16 students a year by audition and provides a showstopping rigor and depth of classes in music, acting, and dance.

Elon's weaker offerings tend to be ones where student interest has dwindled along with the size of the faculty and course offerings. Religious studies is small with a more limited program than other majors. Foreign language majors are offered only in French and Spanish; however, 3 levels of instruction are available in German, Greek, Japanese, Chinese, and Italian. History's faculty members are considered "outstanding," though some students wish more in-depth courses were offered in the wide range of specialties taught.

Facilities: Students in the 1999–2000 school year enthusiastically greeted the opening of the new Carol Grotnes Belk Library, which incorporates a traditional library setting with 21st-century electronic media. About 200 computers are available in a structure more than double the size of the earlier facility, including laptops with wireless capabilities that gives users access to hundreds of libraries, thousands of full-text journals, and a wealth of resources from the Internet. The library's own holdings of more than 250,000 volumes still prove frustrating for some students conducting upper-level research, although the on-line catalog lists holdings at 5 Piedmont-area libraries, including Duke and the Chapel Hill campus of the University of North Carolina. Users have less problem with the 24,500 periodicals available in print or on-line. The library is open 24 hours Sunday through Thursday and, notes a senior, "is amazingly populated with students for almost all 24 of the hours." Belk's effectiveness as a study center depends on whether talkative students head to any of the 22 group study rooms.

Students have access to more than 620 computer workstations spread among 20 labs across campus. Most are open until 1 a.m with one open around the clock, though students may use their ID cards to gain access to the buildings and computer labs at any time. All residence-hall rooms are wired for access to the campus network and Internet. The university strongly recommends that students bring their own personal computers to Elon, preferably an IBM-compatible or Macintosh.

Special programs: Sixty-three percent of Elon graduates have spent time studying abroad, placing Elon first among comparable institutions for the percentage of undergraduates who study overseas. Many attend universities in more than 20 countries with which the college has affiliations. More than half the faculty have led students in international travel and study. As part of the university's emphasis on experiential learning, undergraduates are offered an Elon Experiences Transcript, which documents students' involvement in leadership development, service learning, international and multicultural exposure, and internship/co-op and undergraduate research experiences. Seventy-eight percent of the students complete an internship and 32% hold at least one key leadership position before graduating. Recalls a senior history major: "After my internship in a British hospital, I am fully prepared to enter the medical field." The Isabella Cannon Leadership Program offers undergraduates the chance to study and practice the elements that make effective leaders. A 3–2 engineering degree is offered with North Carolina State,

Columbia, Washington, and North Carolina A & T State universities and with Virginia Tech and Georgia Tech. Students also may cross-register for classes with 7 other universities and colleges in North Carolina.

Campus life: Elon's 575-acre campus still is rich in the majestic white oaks from which the university's name, the Hebrew word for oak, was taken. For many students, their first glimpse of the red brick buildings with stately white columns, green lawns, and oaks is what convinces them to give Elon a try. All freshmen and sophomores not living with their parents are required to live on campus; 57% of the total enrollment end up making the campus their home. Elon's classic collegiate look is matched only by its classic collegiate weekends. "A typical weekend," says a southerner, "would include parties galore, Greek happenings, and involvement in community service." Greek life is popular, with 26% of the men and 43% of the women pledged to 11 national fraternities and 11 national sororities. Many independents join the Greeks in their revelry or form their own parties in apartments and houses close to campus. For some students, however, Greek life simply becomes "overwhelming," in the words of one senior. Another popular spot to hang out is Moseley Center, the 74,000-square-foot student activities center. Nearly 90% of Elon's undergraduates devote some of their time out of the classroom to community service; Habitat for Humanity is a popular choice for many students, who have pledged to build 1 house each year. WSOE radio, the *Pendulum* student newspaper, and ESTV, the student-run television station, also draw their own share of eager workers, including many first-year students. Few incidents of crime occur, although such precautionary measures as card swipes for dorm entrance, an escort service, safe rides, and emergency telephones are already in place.

If it's autumn, it must be Elon football, among the most popular of the 7 men's and 9 women's sports played in NCAA Division I; football is 1-AA. The 5-year-old 8250-seat Rhodes Stadium has attracted larger crowds to kickoff. Basketball also draws a large faithful following. Lacrosse and rugby are popular club sports; Elon offers 20 club sports and 20 intramural activities.

When students want to swap stories with other undergraduates, they haven't far to go. The University of North Carolina campuses at Greensboro and Chapel Hill and Duke University are all within a 30-minute drive. The community of Elon borders Burlington, a town of 50,000; Greensboro is 20 minutes away. The mountains and beach are both 3 to 4 hours' distant.

Cost cutters: Seventy-seven percent of the freshmen and 72% of the continuing students received some form of financial aid in the 2005–2006 school year; for 35% of all freshmen and 33% of all continuing students, the aid was based on need. The average award for a first-year student with financial need consisted of a need-based scholarship or grant averaging $3656 and need-based self-help aid such as loans and jobs averaging $3043. Non-need-based athletic scholarships for first-year students averaged $10,507; other non-need-based awards and scholarships averaged $2665. Average debt of a 2005 graduate was $21,667. The Elon University Fellows Program offers talented students scholarships worth $2000 to $6000 annually plus $750 in a study/travel grant along with internships, faculty mentoring, and special courses. These go to top students in the honors and leadership programs and in the arts and sciences, business, and journalism and communications. Presidential Scholarships award from $1000 to $3750 a year, engineering program scholarships pay $3000 annually, performing arts scholarships cover from $500 to $6000 annually, and music scholarships range in amount from $500 to $5000 a year. Only state residents may be considered for prestigious North Carolina Teaching Fellows awards, which pay at least $13,000 a year and provide air fare for a semester in London. Likewise, 8 Watson Scholarships are awarded each year to North Carolina high school graduates who have a strong academic record and a high financial need, providing those students with full tuition, room, and board or the student's full financial need. A 10-month tuition payment plan is available.

Rate of return: Eighty-nine percent of all freshmen enjoy their Elon experience and return for the sophomore year. Sixty-six percent go on to graduate in 4 years, 72% in 5 years; 76% in 6.

Payoff: Business was the major of choice for 19% of the 2005 graduates; journalism and communications followed at 17%; education and psychology, at 6% each. About 80% of Elon's alumni seek jobs shortly after graduating, many with the more than 500 companies that list jobs with the Career Center. A number stay in North Carolina or return to their home states. Approximately 25% pursue advanced degrees within 2 years of graduation; about 15% go directly to graduate school upon receiving their bachelors degrees.

Bottom line: "Elon tries very hard to make you burst out of your bubble and begin to have a worldview of things," says a junior. "Students also should want to be involved in many aspects of campus life and to be interested in leadership positions. If you don't want to get involved, Elon isn't the place for you."

Guilford College

Greensboro, North Carolina 27410

Setting: Suburban
Control: Private (Religious Society of Friends)
Undergraduate enrollment: 886 men, 1365 women
Graduate enrollment: None
Student/faculty ratio: 19:1
Freshman profile: 10% scored over 700 on SAT I verbal; 34% scored 600–700; 36% 500–599; 20% below 500. 4% scored over 700 on SAT I math; 31% scored 600–700; 43% 500–599; 22% below 500. 6% scored above 28 on the ACT; 10% scored 27–28; 28% 24–26; 31% 21–23; 25% below 21. 32% graduated in top fifth of high school class; 51% in upper two-fifths.
Faculty profile: 60% Ph.D.'s

Tuition and fees: $21,640
Room and board: $6530
Freshman financial aid: 92%; average scholarship or grant: $6173 need-based; $5965 non-need-based
Campus jobs: 32%; average earnings: $787/year
Application deadline: Early action: Jan. 15; regular: Feb. 15
Financial aid deadline: Mar. 1
Admissions information: (336) 316-2100; (800) 992-7759
e-mail: admission@guilford.edu
web site: www.guilford.edu

Certain qualities immediately evident at Guilford College in Greensboro, North Carolina, indicate that this is not the typical small, southern school. Guilford's history as the third oldest coeducational institution in the nation gives it a tradition of equality of the sexes not always found in the land of southern belles. Its ties to the Religious Society of Friends perpetuate an atmosphere of casualness and openness, where students call faculty by their first names and the college government operates on the principle of Quaker consensus, stressing tolerance and support for dissenting views. And, since its founding in 1837, Guilford has held fast to the Quaker emphasis on simplicity: nothing less than a solid liberal arts education at a simply decent price.

Student body: Just over two-thirds of the undergraduates are state residents. A total of 46 states and 15 foreign countries have students on campus, although half the out-of-staters are from the Middle Atlantic states. Two-thirds are graduates of public high schools. African-American students constitute the single largest racial or ethnic minority group on campus at 23%, followed by Hispanics at 2% and Asian-Americans and Native Americans at 1% each. Foreign nationals make up 1% as well. Though only 9% of the students are Quaker, a majority reflect the sect's qualities of open-mindedness, social consciousness, and concern for community. "While most fall slightly to the liberal side of issues," a northeasterner says, "all students are opinionated, involved, open, and friendly. Everyone wants to explore all sides of an issue if possible and is encouraged to do so." In such a process, however, competition against classmates is kept in check with an emphasis on teamwork. Students in many majors find it's "not too hard to get a B," observes a junior, "but an A often requires truly exceptional effort."

Academics: Guilford awards the bachelor's degree in 40 majors and 8 interdisciplinary concentrations. The academic year is divided into 2 semesters of 4 courses each, most enrolling between 15 and 20 students. The largest classes never get very big, with 49 in such popular courses as General Psychology. An upper-level sculpture class may have as few as 3.

Guilford's curriculum was restructured recently into 5 tiers composed of foundations, explorations, the major, concentration, and capstone. Each student normally completes 12 general education requirements consisting of the foundations, explorations, and capstone, plus 8 courses for the major and 4 for the concentration. The 4 foundations courses include a first-year experience seminar, a course in college reading and writing, and 1 course each in historical perspectives and foreign language. Explorations entails a course each in 4 of 5 areas—arts, business and policy studies, humanities, natural science and mathematics, and social science, excluding the major field of study. It also includes a course in intercultural issues, social justice/environmental responsibility, and U.S. diversity. The capstone represents an interdisciplinary studies course taken during the final 2 semesters at Guilford.

Guilford has 120 full-time and 77 part-time faculty members who display a diversity of outlooks, eccentricities, and teaching styles. Just under a fifth of the faculty and administrative staff are Quakers. Almost half, 46%, are women. Many undergraduates are surprised initially by the "exceptional" quality of most teachers at a college of Guilford's small size and budget. "What makes them good teachers is that so many are such good people," says a sophomore. "As a student, you feel as though they are on your side. They are friendly, often eccentric, and always eager to reach out to students in as well as out of the classroom." Professors also are encouraged to experiment with different methods of teaching, which keeps the learning lively. Students' complaints center on a small number of older professors with one-track minds.

The list of Guilford's strongest departments could fill half a blue book. For starters, the faculties in English, religious studies, psychology, economics, history, and political science earn high marks for their devotion to teaching and the depth and breadth of perspectives they provide, though psychology could use more faculty and structure. "Philosophy and religious studies," says an underclassman undecided about a major, "will make you exercise your mind in ways you never thought you could." Physics offers superb faculty and equipment and excellent students, placing Guilford among the top 3 public or private institutions in the state in the number of graduates in the field. Strong programs in women's studies, African American studies, education studies, justice and policy studies, foreign languages, sociology, biology, chemistry, and geology also draw applause.

Students say the math department tends to "scare away students" because professors have a hard time teaching lower-level courses clearly and with an interest in the undergraduates. Music lacks sufficient facilities.

Facilities: Expansion of Hege Library, which increased the space by 50%, moved this building from the minus column to the plus side of student ratings. The size of the collection improved to 254,000 volumes and 7380 paper and electronic periodicals and the creation of a brighter, roomier study environment and the addition of an art gallery to soothe stressed minds all draw rave reviews. Still, says a senior, "every tree, couch, and alcove serves someone as a favorite study place." An automated catalog ties into the catalogs of 15 other area campuses. For a first-hand look, though, students either walk across the street to check out the holdings of the Greensboro Public Library or visit the local branch campus of the University of North Carolina. The much larger libraries at Duke and UNC-Chapel Hill also are within easy reach. Hege is open until 2 a.m. Sunday through Thursday.

Two hundred seventy-five terminals and PCs are available around campus; the two labs in Bauman Telecommunications Center with 50 computers each are reachable 24 hours a day every day. Student-owned PCs in the dormitories also can be hooked into the system, providing access to the library catalog and the Internet, among other things. The new Frank Family Science Center also provides complete network access in all classrooms, an auditorium, and observatory. Areas with wireless access include the library, some classrooms, some residence halls, and community centers, including the popular Founders Hall terrace.

Special programs: Cross-registration for courses is available with 7 other institutions in the Greensboro area. Just over a third of Guilford's recent graduating classes have studied overseas in Mexico, England, Italy, France, Germany, China, Japan, and Ghana. Semester internships are available in Washington, D.C. and New York City. About 100 students a year take advantage of internships in the Greensboro area. Cooperative or dual degree programs are offered in forestry and environmental studies with Duke and in physician assistant training at Wake Forest University.

Campus life: Seventy-five percent of the students reside on the 340-acre, heavily wooded campus in northwest Greensboro. Students generally don't mind the lack of fraternities or sororities, and instead turn out for campuswide dances on the quad and regular coffeehouses featuring student and guest talent. Many undergraduates take part in student government, excited by the equal voice students are given in the college decision-making process. A large number of students also become active in Project Community, a group that coordinates volunteer efforts in community service. Guilford undergraduates, faculty, and staff log about 50,000 hours of community service in the area annually. HOME of Guilford involves many in hands-on work to fix and repair homes of low-income families in the Greensboro area. Although crime other than minor theft is not a problem, the college has improved its lighting around campus, recently installed "smart card" access to all residence halls, and added Greensboro police to campus patrol, along with student security and the bike patrol already doing duty. A "whistle-defense program" provides each student with a whistle to blow in case of trouble; other students or staff hearing the whistle are instructed to run to provide help.

Although the sports program is low-key, students do get involved in all levels of competition. Eight men's and 8 women's teams compete in NCAA Division III. Varsity football, basketball, soccer, and lacrosse draw the largest crowds, though none are very large. Thirty-nine percent of the men and 19% of the women are involved in the 4 intramural sports open to each sex. The rugby club also is a favorite, as is the Bio-hazard Ultimate Frisbee team.

As a city of 234,000, Greensboro is not particularly stifling. But students yearning to breathe free can easily escape eastward to the beach or westward to the mountains when they've had enough of suburban attractions. Winston-Salem also offers a change of scenery just 20 minutes away.

Cost cutters: Ninety-two percent of the freshmen and continuing students received financial aid in the 2005–2006 school year; for 62% of the freshmen and 58% of the other undergraduates, the assistance was need-based. The average freshman award for a student with need included a need-based scholarship or grant averaging $6173 and need-based-self-help aid such as loans and jobs averaging $5578. Other non-need-based awards and scholarships for first-year students averaged $5965. The financial debts of a typical recent graduate were $17,800. Entering students who have displayed academic potential and leadership skills in high school may receive one of three levels of scholarships paying $4000, $6500, or $10,000 annually. Recipients of awards at the 2 upper levels may also receive Honors Scholarships paying $2500. The Bonner Scholars Program supports 20 first-year students drawn from the top 40% of their high school classes who qualify for a high-level of financial assistance by replacing the work-study component of their financial-aid package with a scholarship. In exchange for the scholarship, students participate in a variety of tutoring and other community service programs that must include summer program options. Mary Hobbs Hall, a cooperative dormitory, enables its 55 women residents to reduce their housing costs slightly by doing chores for an average of 20 minutes a day. Students who wish to be considered for scholarships should apply for admission by Jan. 1.

Rate of return: Seventy-two percent of the freshmen return for the sophomore year. Fifty-five percent graduate in 4 years; 67%, in 5 years; 68%, in 6 years.

Payoff: Business management, claiming 13% of the 2005 graduates, was the most popular major, followed by psychology at 11% and criminal justice at 8%. Most Guilford grads immediately enter the job market, many accepting jobs in the Southeast, Northeast, and Middle Atlantic regions in fields such as accounting, education, social services, and management. Ciba-Geigy, AT&T, Jefferson Pilot, and banks and other corporations in the state's Research Triangle have hired a number of new alumni in recent years. Nearly 120 companies and other organizations recruited on campus in the 2004–2005 school year. Among recent graduates, about a fourth pursued advanced degrees within 6 months of commencement.

Bottom line: At Guilford, the Friends' philosophy is a way of life, expressed in the casualness of the teachers, the lack of student competitiveness, the emphasis on global awareness, and the peaceful acceptance of people as they are. "The environment offered is one of acceptance, growth, and reflection found in few other places," says a senior. "Guilford has hung on to its humane, knowledgeable, and ethical principles." And its students are the beneficiaries.

University of North Carolina at Asheville

Asheville, North Carolina 28804

Setting: Suburban
Control: Public
Undergraduate enrollment: 1179 men, 1641 women
Graduate enrollment: 1 man, 4 women (32 part-time)
Student/faculty ratio: 14:1
Freshman profile: 13% scored over 700 on SAT I verbal; 39% scored 600–700; 35% 500–599; 13% below 500. 6% scored over 700 on SAT I math; 38% scored 600–700; 46% 500–599; 10% below 500. 16% scored above 28 on the ACT; 11% scored 27–28; 32% 24–26; 26% 21–23; 15% below 21. 25% graduated in top tenth of high school class; 55% in upper fifth.
Faculty profile: 84% Ph.D.'s

Tuition and fees: $3525 in-state; $13,325 out-of-state
Room and board: $5712
Freshman financial aid: 62%; average scholarship or grant: $2776 need-based; $3209 non-need-based
Campus jobs: 20%; average earnings: $1531/year
Application deadline: Early action: Nov. 28; regular: Mar. 1
Financial aid deadline: Mar. 1 (Some scholarships: Dec. 1)
Admissions information: (828) 251-6481; (800) 531-9842
e-mail: admissions@unca.edu
web site: www.unca.edu/admissions

When most students think of attending the University of North Carolina, they automatically envision the Chapel Hill campus, with its 16,000 undergraduates, more than 70 majors, active Greek life, and electrifying Tar Heel basketball and football. But those seeking a smaller but no less satisfying environment are not out of luck. Nestled between the Blue Ridge and Smoky Mountains, 130 miles west of Charlotte, is the liberal arts jewel of the University of North Carolina system, its campus in Asheville. The only designated undergraduate liberal arts university within the 16-branch UNC system, it is but one of a handful of public liberal arts universities in the nation. With about 30 undergraduate majors and no class with more than 100 students, UNC Asheville manages to surprise even those who come thinking they know what they will find. Recalls a sophomore: "I expected UNCA to be a good school, but not this good! The faculty and fellow students are what make this place special." Adds a westerner: "I wanted a cheap small school in the mountains and I found that here. I also was excited to find the high standard for academic achievement." At total costs in the 2005–2006 school year of just $9200 for in-state residents and just over $19,000 for out-of-staters, UNC Asheville is a liberal arts gem many students find they can afford.

Student body: To date, all but 14% of the undergraduates attracted by what Asheville has to offer have been North Carolina residents. The largest contingent of nonresidents also comes from the South, although students attend from a total of 44 states and 21 foreign countries. Eighty-five percent are graduates of public high schools. Some students are disappointed by the lack of racial and ethnic diversity they find when they arrive: just 2.5% of the undergraduates are African-American, about 1.5% each are Hispanic and Asian-American, and less than 0.5% are Native American. Foreign nationals constitute 1%. However, students find the backgrounds and lifestyles of their classmates to be more varied and, for the most part, the undergraduates are open to change and tolerant of the differences of others. Observes a state resident: "In one class, I will meet students from all parts of the country, will have at least one international student, and will experience a wide range of political and religious beliefs." The political climate may represent a mixture of Republicans and Democrats, but few are passionate about their causes. Intellectually, the air is friendly and laid-back, though students say that stems not from easy course loads but rather from classmates individually doing what they can to achieve and not worrying about the other guy. Observes a junior: "Most students who do not want to study hard drop out soon."

Academics: UNCA awards the bachelor's degree in about 30 majors as well as a Master of Liberal Arts degree. The school year is divided into semesters. Students who come to Asheville in search of smaller classes find just that. Average class sizes range from just over 30 in biology and 26 in psychology to 11 in classics and 12 in music. In fact, among the 734 class sections offered, none has had more than 100 students. In a recent year, only 8 had between 50 and 99 enrolled; only 7, between 40 and 49. Over a third of all sections had between 10 and 19 participants.

A 4-course humanities sequence is the heart of Asheville's general education curriculum. Students generally take 1 humanities class in each of their 4 undergraduate years; the classes cover The Ancient World, The Medieval and Renaissance World, The Modern World: Mid-17th to Mid-20th Century, and the Individual in the Contemporary World. The courses examine the progress of civilization in the Western world as well as parallel developments in Africa, Asia, and Latin America. In addition, students make their choice of classes from traditional disciplines in the arts and sciences. A course in library research and a senior capstone experience consisting of undergraduate research, an exam, or a seminar also are required. Through the requirements, says a junior, "students are exposed to different academic areas, making stronger students who can make connections between science and history, journalism and psychology, math and music, etc." The general education requirements comprise at most 56 credits of the 120 needed to graduate; the number depends on how many credits students can fill by proficiency exam.

The Asheville faculty numbers 309 with 199 full-time members and 110 part-time. All teach undergraduates. Women comprise 40% of the total pool. One faculty member in the Mass Communication Department won the Pulitzer Prize in 1979 for her reporting on the Synanon cult. Many faculty members draw a rating from students of "excellent" or "superb." Says a junior: "The professors make efforts to really know their students. True, some are better professors than others, but most bad experiences stem from adjuncts and not the permanent faculty."

Students praise academic offerings across the breadth of UNCA's curriculum. Outstanding professors are a hallmark of the psychology department; extensive opportunities for hands-on work and internships distinguish the programs in atmospheric sciences and environmental studies. The National Climatic Data Center, located in Asheville, serves as an excellent resource for atmospheric sciences students. Environmental studies majors can complete their required internship at a wide range of federal, state, local, and private agencies located in Western North Carolina. History, says a major, "is very 'clubby' and the professors make you feel important as a part of their 'family.'" The education program, which requires that students major in another subject area, the mass communication department, the multimedia arts and sciences major, management, and the concentrations in literature and creative writing in the literature and language department also are considered first rate.

As at many campuses, the programs in music, art, and foreign languages tend to lack the resources and staff of other bigger departments. However, students interested in these fields will find dedicated faculty as well as majors in French, German, and Spanish and majors in art, drama, and music. Minors are offered in art history and dance. Women's studies recently was expanded to a major from a minor and students say the program still needs a few more courses to reach its full potential. A general problem for many students is the number of departments that can only offer some courses during odd or even numbered years because of too few professors.

Facilities: Ramsey Library and Media Center is center stage on the campus quadrangle. It offers a quiet air for those students interested in serious study; for those more intent on daydreaming, there is a breathtaking view of Mount Pisgah to the Southwest. Undergraduates engaged in long-term research can arrange to have a private study room for the academic year. Users find the collection of more than 262,000 volumes, 862,000 microforms, and 4810 current paper and electronic periodicals to be acceptable. The ABC (Asheville, Boone, Cullowhee) Loan Express also helps fill the gaps with its on-line list of materials housed at Appalachian State University (in Boone) and Western Carolina University (in Cullowhee) that students can receive in about a day. "I've never actually not been able to find what I was looking for," remarks a psychology major.

More than 375 PCs and Macs are housed in a half dozen or so general purpose and departmental labs as well as in the library and residence halls. All dorms also have a network port for each student with a PC. Students wish some of the labs would open earlier than 8 a.m. and stay open later than 11 p.m. "There is not a line until finals," says a junior, "which is murder because the printers take weeks to refill with ink and the dorm computers break often." Wireless access is available in the library, student center, and a few classrooms.

Special programs: The Undergraduate Research Program provides opportunities for students to work closely with faculty on research projects in any discipline. The program provides grants both for academic-year and summer research as well as for research-related travel. For other kinds of travel, students may take advantage of academic exchange opportunities in England, France, Germany, Finland, Australia, Ecuador, and Mexico. Summer courses in such areas as literature, art, political science, and history are offered at St. Benet's Hall, Oxford University. Co-operative degree programs are an option in nursing, forestry, and textile chemistry. A joint engineering degree is obtainable with North Carolina State University. Asheville students also may enroll for classes at Mars Hill and Warren Wilson colleges.

Campus life: Just a third of Asheville undergraduates live on the 265-acre campus and not quite half of them opt to travel home many a weekend. Students left on campus when Friday nights arrive view the weekends as a generally quiet time to relax and hang out with friends, so many don't miss the frenetic life of nonstop Greek parties and big-time sports. Only 3% of the men and 2% of the women are members of 3 national fraternities and 2 national sororities. While larger numbers attend their parties, more students tend to take in the comedians, solo artists, and speakers that frequently come to call, courtesy of the energetic student-run Underdog Productions. Campus crime is not considered much of a problem. The chief crimes, say students, are under-age drinking and illegal parking. As insurance, all residence-hall doors except the main ones are locked at 8 p.m. A resident assistant checks in residents and visitors between 8 p.m. and 5 a.m.

For some sports fans, their initial disappointment in Asheville campus life is the lack of a football team. Seven other sports for men and 7 for women compete in NCAA Division I. In 2003, the men's basketball team won the Big South Conference, advancing to the NCAA Tournament for the first time in the school's 76-year history. Basketball continues to draw the most fans, with soccer not far behind, though more students are inclined to hit the court or playing field themselves in the 15-sport intramural program or to take part in frequent adventure trips sponsored by UNCA's Outdoors Education Program. Pisgah National Forest, the Blue Ridge Parkway, and Great Smoky Mountains National Park all are favorite escapes, though students say a car is "essential" to getting wherever off campus they'd like to go, unless, of course, it's to downtown Asheville (pop. 70,000), which is just a 15-minute walk, "and a separate world from campus," observes a junior. Students especially appreciate the city's vibrant, lively local arts and music scene.

Cost cutters: Sixty-two percent of the first-year students and 58% of the rest received some kind of financial assistance in the 2005–2006 school year. Aid was need-based for 36% of the first-year students and 41% of the rest. The average freshman award for a student with need in the 2005–2006 school year included a need-based scholarship or grant averaging $2776 and need-based self-help aid such as loans and jobs averaging $2741. Non-need-based athletic scholarships for first-year students averaged $5167; other non-need-based awards and scholarships averaged $3209. Average debt of a 2005 graduate was $15,309. The University Laurels Program provides merit awards ranging in value from $1000 to full tuition and fees to students who have demonstrated high academic and/or artistic achievement. To be considered, students should be in the top tenth of their high school class with SAT critical reading and math scores of 1250 or higher (or a 28 ACT) and a minimum grade point average of 3.5 on a 4-point scale. Students must also participate in a Laurels Interview Day.

Rate of return: Seventy-six percent of entering freshmen return for the sophomore year. Thirty-three percent go on to graduate in 4 years, 50% in 5 years, and 54% in 6 years.

Payoff: Thirteen percent of the 2005 graduates earned bachelor's degrees in psychology, followed by 11% in management and 9% in literature. About a fifth decide to attend graduate or professional school, either full-time or part-time. All but a small percentage jump directly into the workforce, many with the 150 companies and organizations that typically recruit on campus.

Bottom line: The University of North Carolina at Asheville offers a low-key but academically challenging curricula for students who love the outdoors and don't need a busy campus weekend life to be happy. Notes a junior who traveled across country to live life in Asheville: "I love it here because the classes are never too crowded, the professors are passionate about the curriculum, and the social life is diverse."

University of North Carolina at Chapel Hill

Chapel Hill, North Carolina 27599

Setting: Small city
Control: Public
Undergraduate enrollment: 6589 men, 9322 women
Graduate enrollment: 2883 men, 3647 women
Student/faculty ratio: 14:1
Freshman profile: 24.5% scored over 699 on SAT I verbal; 50.5% scored 600–699; 22% 500–599; 3% below 500. 29% scored over 699 on SAT I math; 53% scored 600–699; 16% 500–599; 2% below 500. 34% scored above 29 on the ACT; 51.5% scored 24–29; 14.5% 18–23; 74% graduated in top tenth of high school class; 95% in upper fourth.

Faculty profile: 90% Ph.D.'s
Tuition and fees: $4613 in-state; $18,411 out-of-state
Room and board: $6516
Freshman financial aid: 60%; average scholarship or grant: $5524 need-based; $4740 non-need-based
Campus jobs: NA; average earnings: NA
Application deadline: Early notification: Nov. 1; regular: Jan. 15
Financial aid deadline: Mar. 1
Admissions information: (919) 966-3621
e-mail: uadm@email.unc.edu
web site: www.unc.edu

While the rest of the nation was celebrating the birth of independence in 1776, North Carolina was already taking steps to become a leader in public higher education. The state constitution, enacted the same year, authorized establishment of the University of North Carolina; however, the American Revolution, among other events, intervened, so that the university did not open its doors until 1795. Even then, Chapel Hill was the first state university to hold classes and has been a leader ever since; it is on just about everybody's list of the top major universities in the country. Only a third of the students who seek admission are accepted, placing Chapel Hill among the nation's most selective colleges. Fifty-five percent of those who are admitted decide to attend. And UNC is a good buy in anybody's book. For residents, it is hard to beat $11,129 for tuition, fees, room, and board in the 2005–2006 school year; out-of-staters paid $24,927. Since its founding more than 2 centuries ago, boasts a senior, "this school has maintained its high level of academic excellence while keeping its price tag very affordable. That record, combined with the beauty of the campus, located in 'the southern part of heaven,' sold me the minute I got my letter of acceptance."

Student body: Eighty-three percent of Chapel Hill "buyers" are from North Carolina, with the rest of the undergraduates recently coming from the other 49 states and 105 foreign countries. Nonresidents as a rule must have better academic records than residents to be competitive for admissions. For example, a North Carolina resident recently needed a combined SAT average of 1100 in math and critical reading to be considered; a nonresident, usually a combined score above 1300. Such a difference in standards has created some divisions between native Carolinians and others on the otherwise friendly campus, with out-of-staters describing themselves as "sort of elitist." Eighty-four percent of the total pool attended public high schools. Enrollment has been predominantly white, with 11% of the undergraduates being African-American, 6% Asian-American, 3% Hispanic, and almost 1% Native American. About 1% are foreign nationals. On a campus of about 16,000 full-time undergraduates, it is hard to find adjectives that fit the entire group. However, academically *top-notch,* politically *aware,* and socially *laid-back* are good for starters. Notes a state resident: "Certainly there are times of great stress such as exams, but generally we are comfortable living the southern way. Even the northerners learn quickly!"

Academics: UNC-Chapel Hill offers 71 baccalaureate, 110 master's, and 77 doctoral programs, as well as professional degrees in dentistry, medicine, pharmacy, and law. Undergraduate programs are housed in the General College, the College of Arts and Sciences, and 8 professional schools. The academic year is divided into 2 semesters. Average class size for undergraduates is about 60; the largest lectures in such fields as chemistry, economics, and history enroll about 350 with discussion groups of around 40. Honors courses and special seminars often have fewer than 10 students, though upper-level courses still can range from 20 to 60.

Before branching into separate disciplines, all students must first fulfill new general education requirements in the university's General College. The new curriculum divides requirements into Foundations, Approaches, and Connections. The Foundations include 17 hours of coursework in such skills as English composition and rhetoric, foreign language, quantitative reasoning, and lifetime fitness. The 25 hours in Approaches draw on classes from 3 broad areas, the physical and life sciences, the social and behavioral sciences, and the humanities and fine arts. To fulfill mandates of the final area, Connections, students must be sure that courses in the preceding sections cover each of the following: a communication intensive course, a quantitative intensive course, 1 course each in U.S. Diversity, the North Atlantic World, Beyond the North Atlantic World, the World Before 1750, and Global Issues, plus some kind of experiential education. Students earning an A.B. degree in the College of Arts and Sciences must complete an additional 9 hours of coursework. Students who wish may participate in the First Year Seminar Program, which gives entering freshmen their choice of more than 300 courses from 38 different university departments and schools. Each seminar enrolls up to 20 students. The seminars, which cover subject matter from the humanities to the sciences and are led by senior faculty, are designed to integrate first-year students more successfully into the intellectual life of the campus. The seminars emphasize critical thinking, writing, and oral communication, skills not always stressed by the large introductory lectures.

Most of the 1382 full-time and 115 part-time faculty members (38% of whom are women) get high grades from undergraduates. While many professors are praised for being "congenial" and quite willing to interact with students who are intellectually curious, a number of the most brilliant scholars are simply too busy with research to be accessible. "Ego-centered, unconcerned professors do pop up, especially in introductory courses," says a sophomore. Adds a senior: "It is possible to go through Carolina without having a single full professor." As a rule, graduate assistants teach lower-level classes in foreign languages and English composition and handle discussion groups in the large lecture courses. Altogether, 45% of the introductory courses have been taught, at least in part, by graduate students. Says a junior: "The grad student TA's are often just as exceptional as the most concerned professors."

Several disciplines in the College of Arts and Sciences get the nod from students. Chemistry, a popular major taken as preparation for medical school, has excellent professors and superb undergraduate lab facilities. Biology, too, is noted for good teaching. English is particularly strong, with many prize-winning professors and an "outstanding emphasis on southern literature." The creative writing program is among the best as well. History has small classes and "brilliant" professors; philosophy and Slavic Languages and Literature have their own exceptional faculty and courses. The School of Pharmacy is quite competitive, with teachers who make an effort to know their students. Entrance into the Kenan-Flagler Business School is both highly sought and tough to obtain at the end of the sophomore year. A new high-tech building makes this popular major even more impressive. The School of Journalism and Mass Communication also is excellent, with a strong national reputation, though students say the faculty has not been as good in radio, television, and motion pictures as in other concentrations. Alumni connections for internships and jobs are extensive and impressive: 26 Carolina journalism students and faculty members have won Pulitzer prizes.

In the College of Arts and Sciences, mathematics has suffered from too many instructors who either are inexperienced, difficult to understand, or are teaching only until they complete their dissertations for advanced degrees. The physics and astronomy department has been heavily research oriented, and both mathematics and physics have taken backseats to the programs offered in those disciplines at North Carolina State. While political science has had stellar professors, students rarely have gotten to see them, as many courses have been large in size and taught by less inspiring graduate students.

Facilities: Chapel Hill's library system is among the best in the Southeast, with more than 5.6 million volumes, 4.7 million microform items, and over 42,000 multicultural periodicals. Although it is sometimes as easy to get a date as a book at the 3-story Robert B. House Undergraduate Library, most serious students prefer to study in Walter Royal Davis, the 7-story main library with its 3000 seats and 7 miles of books. Notes a recent graduate: "I have gone there and taken my shoes off to walk because the squeaking of sneakers against tile is too loud." Books at both main libraries and 12 smaller departmental and school libraries are listed in the university's on-line catalog, which is linked to the libraries at Duke, NC

State, and North Carolina Central University. Numerous database searches also are available. For times when reading or researching doesn't head the list of student priorities, the House Undergraduate Library offers a wonderful nonprint section; teachers sometimes show classroom-related movies there, and students can watch a current favorite on a study break.

All first-year students are required to have laptop computers. They may either bring their own units, provided they meet proper specifications, or must choose from 2 purchase options from the university. Qualified students receive special loans or grants to assist with the purchase. "The campus is entirely wireless," remarks a junior, "which means I can access the Internet as I sit on the grass on the main quad with my back against a tree." Undergraduates also have had access to 840 computers in 19 central computer laboratories with laser printers.

Special programs: Undergraduates interested in studying abroad have their choice of more than 230 programs in 64 countries. A fifth of Chapel Hill's undergraduates study outside the U.S. Students designated as prestigious Morehead Scholars have their full expenses for 4 years covered and are provided extensive opportunities for summer internships, as well as international travel and study. Robertson Scholars may spend a semester in residence at rival Duke University. Other students also may participate in joint programs with Duke and North Carolina State universities.

Campus life: Forty-two percent of the undergraduates reside on the 729-acre plot of "southern heaven." Partying, according to students, is the number one leisure activity, and most residents stick around weekends to take part in the goings-on. However, the Greeks, who reside off-campus, host most of their parties on Thursday nights, so that those who absolutely have to get away on Friday can still take in a party or 2. Fall celebrations surrounding Tar Heel football are legendary, with plenty of pregame tailgating and postgame parties held at Little Frat Court, 3 fraternity houses located in a horseshoe. About 11% of the men and the women are members of 29 national fraternities and 20 national sororities including 1 Native American sorority. While their numbers appear small, students say the Greek influence is large and that it is impossible to win the student body president election without winning the Greek vote. Consequently, most student government offices are held by Greeks, which does draw some resentment from non-Greeks. Independents who choose to attend are welcome at the frat row revelry, as well as at most other Greek parties, though some prefer to unwind elsewhere, usually at the numerous bars, restaurants, and coffeeshops that line Franklin Street along the university border.

For students who are socially aware as well as social, the Campus Y, no longer affiliated with the national YMCA, serves as the umbrella organization for 30 different subcommittees aiding such groups as the homeless, the illiterate, and the handicapped, as well as tackling environmental concerns and other issues. The Black Student Movement also is quite active and influential. Crime has not been a pressing issue at the university, thanks to a student police force, a university force, and a safe ride service that help to keep problems under control. Better lighting and more emergency phones recently were added as extra insurance.

Undergraduates consider men's basketball "the unifying force on campus that draws together students, faculty, staff, and town residents more than anything else," says a fan. For years, it has been the greatest source of athletic pride among the 12 intercollegiate teams for men and 14 for women. However, football has increased both its victories and its fan support, while women's soccer has won 18 national championships since 1981. About half the students take part in the 40 intramural sports open to men and women. Some 25 sports clubs also draw substantial participation from faculty as well as students.

Most undergraduates find Chapel Hill (pop. 36,000), 25 miles from Raleigh, to be "the consummate college town." For escape, Atlanta to the south and Washington, D.C., to the north are within striking distance. In good weather, students flock to in-state beaches as well as to those in South Carolina and Florida. The mountains of North Carolina, Tennessee, and West Virginia are also popular destinations for hiking and skiing.

Cost cutters: Fifty-five percent of the freshmen and 46% of the returning students were given financial help in a recent school year. About 33% of both groups were on need-based aid. The average freshman package included a need-based scholarship or grant averaging $8158 and need-based self-help aid such as loans and jobs averaging $2296. Since 2004, the university has eliminated loans as part of the aid package for low-income freshmen as long as the student works on campus 10 to 12 hours a week. Other non-need-based awards and scholarships for freshmen in a recent year averaged $4170. The average non-need-based award for a freshman athlete averaged $11,648. Average debt of a recent graduate was $13,801. More than 150 scholarships are awarded each year to entering classes. The most competitive scholarship available is the Carolina Scholars Award that pays $7500 annually to students who are North Carolina residents and an amount equal to tuition, fees, room, and board to nonresidents. William Richardson Davie Awards pay $5000 to in-state students and an amount equal to tuition, fees, room, and board to out-of-staters who demonstrate leadership abilities as well as academic achievement; the scholarships are renewable. In 2005, the Board of Trustees approved devoting all proceeds from the sale of trademark-licensed university products, such as T-shirts and caps with the Tar Heel logo, toward scholarships. The action created 59 new merit-based scholarships, 53 to state residents.

Rate of return: Ninety-six percent of entering freshmen return for the sophomore year. Sixty-seven percent graduate in 4 years; 79% within 5 years.

Payoff: In the class of 2005, journalism & mass communications and social sciences & history claimed 16.5% and 13.5% of the graduates, respectively. Almost 11% earned degrees in business and marketing. Just over a fourth of the new alumni from a recent class went directly to graduate or professional schools, many gaining acceptance to some of the top schools in the nation. Chapel Hill boasts the 2nd largest number of undergraduates designated Rhodes Scholars among public universities, 39 since 1902. Graduates seeking employment readily find jobs on the East Coast, primarily the southeastern states, in such fields as sales, management, teaching, journalism, pharmacy, health care, law, and research. More than 160 companies and organizations recruited on campus in a recent school year.

Bottom line: Top students who come to the nation's oldest public university must be prepared both to forgo a lot of personal attention, at least in the first 2 years, and to deal with an academic environment in which most of their classmates also were the best and the brightest in their high schools. Having accepted those 2 conditions, a satisfied senior says, "I extend the challenge to anyone to find a better-rounded school."

Warren Wilson College

Asheville, North Carolina 28815

Setting: Small town
Control: Private (Presbyterian)
Undergraduate enrollment: 322 men, 498 women
Graduate enrollment: 21 men, 48 women
Student/faculty ratio: 13:1
Freshman profile: 20% scored over 700 on SAT I verbal; 39% scored 600–700; 36% 500–599; 5% below 500. 4% scored over 700 on SAT I math; 37% scored 600–700; 41% 500–599; 18% below 500. 23% graduated in top fifth of high school class; 79% in upper two-fifths.
Faculty profile: 92% Ph.D.'s
Tuition and fees: $18,916

Room and board: $5466
Freshman financial aid: 95%; average scholarship or grant: $9045 need-based; $3178 non-need-based
Campus jobs: 89%; average earnings: $2472/year
Application deadline: Early decision: Nov. 15; regular: Mar. 15
Financial aid deadline: Apr. 1 (Scholarships: Feb. 28)
Admissions information: (828) 771-2073; (800) 934-3536
e-mail: rickb@warren-wilson.edu
web site: www.warren-wilson.edu

If Warren Wilson College had a motto, it might be "Work for yourselves, work for others," which is exactly what the 820 undergraduates enrolled at this woodsy North Carolina campus do. To pay about half of the cost of room and board, or about $2400 of the total costs, all resident students are required to work 15 hours a week as part of 111 work crews that do everything from tend the farm's pigs to fix the plumbing to staff the computer labs. In addition, students must perform 100 hours of service to others before graduation, ranging from volunteering at a shelter for the homeless in Asheville to helping build a new school in Sri Lanka. The program not only makes college possible for those students who otherwise could not afford it but also teaches all undergraduates to accept responsibility, make decisions, and work shoulder to shoulder with people of different ages, interests, income levels, races, ethnic origins, and nationalities. "Warren Wilson," says a senior, "provides an atmosphere that inspires individuals to try things they never did before and supports them during the process."

Student body: Just 16% of the Warren Wilson workers are from North Carolina. Though 40% of the rest are from the region, the work force includes members from 44 states and 8 nations. Foreign nationals account for the largest racial/ethnic group on campus, about 4% of the total enrollment. African-American students constitute 2%; Hispanics, Asian-Americans and Native Americans, each about 1%. Twelve percent of all undergraduates are Presbyterian; 50% claim no religious affiliation. Seventy-four percent are graduates of public schools. The students who seek out Warren Wilson's communal work environment in the Blue Ridge Mountains are already more environmentally and socially aware than undergraduates at more traditional colleges. To newcomers, it seems as though the 60's sense of peace and harmony never left this campus. "Most students really want to make a difference in the surrounding communities and the world," explains a senior, and students say that those who do not arrive with a compatible spirit either transfer or graduate with a changed perspective. "Acceptance and tolerance are the way here," says a non-traditional student. The college has its share of "Trustafarians," as one student calls them, students who come from wealthy backgrounds and don't need to work hard but do, and also those of a more hypocritical bent, in the words of another student, who "preach against consumerism and capitalism while they wear Chaco's and drink from their Nalgenes." Still, to dismiss the undergraduates merely as 21st-century hippies is misguided. Observes a sophomore: "This school is filled with passionate, hard-working individuals. We mow the lawns, we wash the dishes, we deliver the mail, we fix the toilets, we milk the cows. We are Warren Wilson." Although students must manage their time well to balance all these commitments, few become outwardly frenzied and the overall atmosphere is fairly laid back. Notes a southerner: "We have a running joke about there being 'Warren Wilson time,' which runs about 5 or 10 minutes off schedule—and sometimes much more." Students here would rather enjoy a good debate about issues than compare GPAs. Concedes a junior: "I would prefer a stronger academic atmosphere, but we don't have enough time to be great workers, social changers, and hard-core studiers."

Academics: Warren Wilson was founded by the Presbyterian church in 1894 as the Asheville Farm School for mountain boys and has been a 4-year college only since 1967. It awards the bachelor's degree in 46 majors and concentrations plus a master's of fine arts in creative writing. The academic year is divided into 2 semesters. Each semester consists of two 8-week terms. Term and semester courses may be taken simultaneously. Few regular classes are ever larger than 30 students, though introductory chemistry has 35, and many classes have fewer than 5 registrants.

Warren Wilson's general education program starts with a first-year seminar involving students in groups of 10–15 where they learn strategies for learning, problem solving, and research, centered around a different topic in each seminar. Students must also take 2 courses in composition plus liberal arts courses in language and global issues, history or political science, mathematics, philosophy and religion, literature, natural science, social science, and artistic expression. The general education program covers up to 44 of the 128 credit hours required for graduation.

"The faculty is the best part of this school," enthuses a junior, expressing the view of many. That 5-star faculty includes 62 full-time professors and 13 part-timers plus an additional 22 part-time members in the master's of fine arts program. Nearly half are women. About a third of the faculty and staff live on campus, which, combined with the low student/faculty ratio, offers plenty of opportunity for individual attention and often friendship with professors. Says a human-studies major: "I can talk to them like peers and respect them like prophets." Though students say some faculty members do not push undergraduates as much as they could, there is no questioning professors' allegiance to their charges, the school, and its values. Says a senior: "The faculty manage to reach out from their excellent academic backgrounds to be creative, sympathetic mentors who get personally involved in students' academic development, and sometimes their personal development." The college offers its professors extended contracts but no tenure.

The work crews are a major element in some of the college's strongest academic programs. Students in the college's preveterinary program, most of whom major in biology or chemistry, can get hands-on experience at the school's student-run beef and pig farm: delivering animals, giving shots, administering medicines, and operating. Every major in the natural sciences, which include biology as well as environmental sciences, also is required to do an original research project, which is presented to his or her peers in a seminar. A recently completed science center has elevated the program yet another notch.

The environmental studies program is enriched by the personal interest of faculty and students and near-perfect natural surroundings for exploration. Environmental studies majors help develop programs for the college and western North Carolina, and work with the local community on land use and economic and energy issues. A natural resources team learns and implements forest management practices on the college's woodland acres. English faculty members are admired as "incredible communicators, inspirers, and teachers" who offer a workload that is "challenging and stimulating," according to a biology major. The social work and outdoor leadership programs are enhanced by the college's focus and location, although some students think not all of the outdoor leadership majors take the coursework as seriously as they could. The business and economics major recently was reorganized to focus on sustainable economic development, international business, entrepreneurship, and nonprofit management.

Majors in creative writing, sociology/anthropology, and philosophy were added in 2002. Still, a number of disciplines are offered only as minors; these include Appalachian studies, intercultural studies, Latin American studies, music, physics, theater, and computer science. Coursework is offered in French and

Spanish, with a minor in modern language available. Political science and history, teamed together as a major, each lack sufficient faculty. Concludes a senior: "Our school is so small, 1 or 2 people can be responsible for half the offerings of a given major."

Facilities: The recently expanded and renovated Shelley Mueller Pew Learning Center and Martha Ellison Library together have 107,700 volumes and 11,000 paper and electronic periodicals. What the collection lacks usually can be obtained in person or through interlibrary loan from one of the 12 member libraries of the Mountain College Library Network (MCLN) or from a branch library of the University of North Carolina system. "Most of the librarians are extremely helpful," says a junior. "When you go to a school this tiny you can't really expect to have a university-quality library system." The library catalog is automated as part of a 6-college regional consortium, consisting of 5 other members of the MCLN. As a study center, Ellison Library rates much higher, offering plenty of light, quiet, and open space to make a pleasant work environment. The library couches, says a frequent user, are "great for in-between-class napping." A study room is open around the clock though the rest of the library closes at 10:30 p.m. weeknights. During exam periods, the library stays open later—and serves tea.

PCs are located in one 30-seat lab and in 4 smaller teaching labs. The main lab, says a junior, "is open from 8:30 p.m. to 11 p.m., which is not always adequate because you can't work before an 8 a.m. class and long projects usually last past 11 p.m." Hours are extended during testing periods. Adds another junior: "The computers do not always function properly and are in many ways outdated. They are sufficient for writing papers, though." E-mail and Internet access is available to students from their dorm rooms and computer labs. The college strongly recommends that students have their own personal computers. There also is wireless access in 3 dorms, the library, and one of the computer labs.

Special programs: A newer program of the college, Warren Wilson WorldWide, enables each student to work, serve, and learn abroad or in a cross-cultural environment. Field experiences in North America, Latin America, Africa, Asia, and Europe help students understand how academics, work, and service can apply to the global community. In a program entitled "Discovery through Wilderness," students examine environmental issues in a geographical area that is largely wilderness; previous sites have been in Nova Scotia, the Caribbean, and the Pacific Northwest. Cross-registration is offered with the University of North Carolina at Asheville and Mars Hill College. Joint degree programs are available in engineering with Washington University in St. Louis, and in forestry and environmental management with Duke University.

Campus life: All but 13% of the students reside on the 1132-acre campus, located in the Swannanoa Valley in the Blue Ridge Mountains; the campus includes a 300-acre farm, about 600 acres of forest, and 25 miles of hiking trails. Although the campus is somewhat isolated, its locale suits just fine those with a love of the outdoors and lots of imagination. Popular wooded hangouts are Dogwood Ridge and the Riverbend, where the 2 big social events of each term, the opening No Brown Shoes party and the closing "Bubba" party, are held. There are neither fraternities nor sororities, but students gather for room parties or potluck suppers, as well as coffeehouses showcasing student talent at the Sage Café. Poetry readings, contra dances, movie nights, and theme parties can be found on any given weekend. Undergraduates also play very active roles in the college's governance though not as much as some students would like to see. Other students become involved in various social activist groups, among them the School of the Americas Watch, which works both legislatively and physically to close the SOA. Bicycle theft is the biggest crime. Emergency phones and brighter lighting recently were installed at isolated spots around campus and a third full-time security officer was added. Still, notes an easterner: "Usually the most excitement the night watch crew gets is when a cow gets loose."

Participation, rather than serious competition, is stressed in the 6 men's and 6 women's varsity sports played in the NSCAA, National Small College Athletic Association. In recent years, however, some of the teams have become more competitive; for example, the women's soccer team played in the NSCAA title game in 1998, the women's cross-country team won the national championship in 2000 and the college's mountain bike team took home the silver medal in the 2005–2006 national competition. The college's white-water program is ranked among the best in the nation. Men's and women's soccer and basketball are the favorite sports to watch. Five intramural sports for each sex also are offered. The biggest club on campus is the outing club, which sponsors trips for rock climbing, biking, kayaking, backpacking, and canoeing.

For students who need some urban diversion, downtown Asheville is but 15 minutes away, and many students ride the Asheville transit bus that runs through campus several times daily. However, most who want to escape books and labs find they can simply camp somewhere on the spacious school grounds and feel many miles away.

Cost cutters: In the 2005–2006 school year, 95% of the freshmen and 80% of the continuing students received financial help, over and beyond help from the required campus work program. Sixty-four percent of the freshmen and 56% of the rest were on need-based aid. The average award for a first-year student with financial need included a need-based scholarship or grant averaging $9045 and need-based self-help aid such as loans and jobs averaging $3224. Other non-need-based awards and scholarships averaged $3178; loans and work opportunities not based on financial need averaged $2983. Average debt of 2005 graduates was $16,211. Renewable Academic Honor Scholarships ranging in amount from $1000 to $5000 go to freshmen with scholastic merit. Valedictorian and Salutatorian Awards pay $4000 a year to students who graduated first or second in a high school class of more than 50; scholarships are automatically given to the first 10 qualified students who are accepted. Work Scholarships and Service Leadership Scholarships each pay $1500 to 2 students who bring specially needed work skills or demonstrated exceptional leadership service to their communities.

Rate of return: Sixty-six percent of the freshmen who enter return for the sophomore year. No current information on graduate rates is available, although in a recent year, just 32% graduated in 4 years; 37% in 5 years.

Payoff: In the 2005 graduating class, 16% earned bachelor's degrees in environmental studies, 12% in biology, and 6% in psychology. Forty companies and organizations recruited on campus in the 2004–2005 school year. A recent survey of Warren Wilson alumni found 17% enrolled in graduate school, 17% employed as teachers, 14% in social work, 12% working as artists, 10% in higher education, and 10% in science. The remaining 20% were split between those working as managers (6%), lawyers (4%), traveling (4%), and doing something else (6%).

Bottom line: An undergraduate once equated being at Warren Wilson with living in the real world: "You acquire knowledge, you go to work, you interact with people, you learn from experience, and you grow up. Only here, the weak get stronger and the stronger excel."

North Dakota State University

Fargo, North Dakota 58105

Setting: Urban
Control: Public
Undergraduate enrollment: 5177 men, 4233 women
Graduate enrollment: 279 men, 205 women
Student/faculty ratio: 19:1
Freshman profile: 7% scored above 29 on the ACT; 37% scored 24–29; 50% 18–23; 6% below 18. 18% graduated in top tenth of high school class; 43% in upper fourth.
Faculty profile: 91% Ph.D.'s
Tuition and fees: $5309 in-state; $5705 MN residents; $12,590 other out-of-state

Room and board: $5130
Freshman financial aid: 69%; average scholarship or grant: $3154 need-based; $1598 non-need-based
Campus jobs: 20%; average earnings: $885/year
Application deadline: Aug. 15
Financial aid deadline: Aug. 15 (Priority date: Mar. 15)
Admissions information: (701) 231-8643;
(800) 488-NDSU
e-mail: ndsu.admission@ndsu.edu
web site: www.ndsu.edu

When one of the largest student organizations is Saddle and Sirloin, which promotes the livestock industry, and the campus is home to the Bison sports teams, you know you're not talking about an East Coast Ivy. North Dakota State University, which turned 115 in 2005, remains about as rugged Midwest as they come. Though its academic offerings and research have become much more global in vision over the years, especially since the opening of its research and technology park, NDSU continues to draw strength from its roots as a college of agriculture and mechanical arts. Agriculture, now the smallest area of study, still offers its share of innovative programs in microbiology and food science, as well as more traditional majors in horticulture and forestry and agricultural economics. More than 97% of College of Agriculture, Food Systems, and Natural Resources graduates are employed within 3 months after they finish college. In some programs, opportunities exceed graduates by a ratio of 3-to-1. In-state and out-of-state tuition plus living costs are among the lowest charged anywhere in the nation, which is why more students from 36 states and 62 foreign countries decide to make NDSU the New Destination for Savvy Undergraduates.

Student body: Just over half of NDSU's undergraduates, 55%, are state residents followed by a large percentage of fellow midwesterners, many from just across the border in Minnesota. Ninety-three percent in a recent year were graduates of public schools. Just over 5% of the undergraduates are members of domestic minority groups or foreign nationals, with about 1.5% African-Americans, and 1% each Asian-Americans, Native Americans, and foreign nationals. Hispanics make up 0.5% of enrollment. Undergraduates represent a mix of backgrounds from rural areas and larger urban centers like the Twin Cities and are noted for being sincere, friendly, conservative but open-minded, and down to earth—"very real people," says a midwesterner. Adds a Minnesotan: "Students come from graduating classes of 5 to 600, so the backgrounds differ." Most students possess a serious work ethic, a reflection, in part, of the number who balance full courseloads with regular responsibilities on the family farm or elsewhere. Just over a tenth of the undergraduates are 25 or older. Despite commitments on and off campus, there always is time for socializing. For many, says a junior, "the attitude is that academics are essential, but they are not the only thing that matters."

Academics: Attending North Dakota State wasn't always the respected family tradition that it is today in many communities. In fact, when the city fathers of Fargo first proposed designating a square mile of the Red River Valley for an agricultural college, many local residents thought the city should have held out for "something big" such as the state penitentiary. Today, NDSU has gained respect, acreage, students, and academic programs, awarding degrees through the doctorate and offering 105 undergraduate majors in 8 colleges. The university follows a semester calendar. Class sizes range from small to very large, with freshman English courses restricted to 23 participants and general geology lectures enrolling 480. Classes for juniors and seniors generally have 15–50 participants; two-thirds of NDSU class sections have fewer than 30 students.

All students are required to complete a general education program consisting of 10 credits of course-work in science and technology including a lab course; 9 credits in writing, reading, and public speaking; 6 each in humanities and fine arts and in social and behavioral sciences; 3 in quantitative reasoning, a 2-credit course in wellness, and a 1-credit first-year experience course. Somewhere within these 36 credits students must have classes dealing with cultural diversity, global perspectives, and computer usage.

There are 525 full-time faculty members and 91 part-timers. No figures are available to show the portion who teach at the graduate level only though in a recent year, all but about 30 full-time members and all but 8 part-time taught undergraduates. Thirty percent are women. In the last few years, 20% of the introductory classes have been taught by graduate students who also assist with labs. Some undergraduates are concerned about the increased reliance on graduate teaching assistants, who used to teach just 7% of the courses. English, speech, and other first-year classes have seen the greatest increase. "Grad students can often be on a power trip or not care at all," says a sophomore, "but most of the grad student teachers I've had were pretty decent." Adds another sophomore: "It's hit or miss." High quality is more certain with the faculty. Most professors at NDSU are as down-to-earth, friendly, and approachable as their students. In the architecture department, for example, everyone is on a first-name basis. Some faculty are more involved in their research than others, though most "take the time to get to know the students and take time to help if needed whenever," says a senior. Still, most students are concerned about the low salaries paid to NDSU professors, a factor in the departure of some well-liked and excellent teachers.

Programs throughout the career-related colleges of Agriculture, Food Systems, and Natural Resources, Engineering and Architecture, Human Development and Education, and Pharmacy are among the most popular and most competitive on campus. The professors are tops in their fields, the equipment is top of the line, and these disciplines receive top dollar to keep them the university's strong points. Graduates in these disciplines usually have few problems in finding good jobs. Graduates of the dietetics program in the College of Human Development and Education boast a 100% employment rate. Chemistry and other science programs in the College of Science and Mathematics also are first-rate. Majors say the College of Business Administration and the accounting major specifically have improved both their coursework and teaching staff as part of an effort to gain accreditation, which the college did, though some students think the college needs to move into a larger building and offer more class sections.

For the most part, students conclude that courses in the College of Arts, Humanities and Social Sciences tend to be more impersonal and less respected than those in the professional fields. Language lovers wish that languages other than French and Spanish were offered as majors though NDSU students may also study German and Arabic on campus and Chinese, Japanese, Norwegian, and Russian at nearby Minnesota State University–Moorhead and Concordia University in Minnesota.

Facilities: NDSU's library system is composed of the main library plus departmental facilities in architecture, chemistry, and pharmacy, which together hold 785,000 volumes and 5090 periodicals. When students can't find what they want on campus, they can scan NDSU's on-line catalog system and check out the holdings at Minnesota State University-Moorhead and Concordia College in Moorhead, Minnesota, just across the river. If they find what they need, they can request the needed sources without even leaving the home library. Materials are delivered twice daily on a shuttle from the other schools. The 3-million-record catalog database also lists the holdings of other colleges and state universities in Minnesota. A wide assortment of databases in various subjects further expands the research options.

Computer clusters, including 9 for microcomputers, are located in each of the colleges and many residence halls; several are open for 24 hours. The main computer facility, the Industrial Agriculture and Communications Center, houses about 500 units and is open around the clock. "Computers are widespread and available," says a mass communication major, "but the printing is *horrible*." Students in the architecture and the landscape architecture programs are required to have personal computers at the sophomore level. All residence halls have in-room Internet access.

Special programs: As part of the Tri-College Consortium, North Dakota State students can take courses at Minnesota State University–Moorhead or Concordia College without additional charge. NDSU also has exchange programs farther afield, in Australia, Mexico, The Netherlands, and numerous other countries.

Campus life: Although 30% of the undergraduates reside on the 258-acre campus, many who live within driving distance are gone once the last weekly class is finished. Among those who stay and get involved on campus are the Greeks, who constitute just a small percentage of the men and women but still run most of the campus organizations. The Greek community includes 10 national fraternities and 5 national sororities, most of which share a friendly relationship with the rest of the campus. In spite of Greek influence, independents who wish to become leaders can easily do so, with more than 200 campus clubs and organizations covering all ranges of interests. In addition to the popular Saddle and Sirloin Club, whose annual livestock show and rodeos draw a good crowd, the Blue Key National Honor Fraternity and various departmental groups have devoted memberships. Vandalism and theft of items from unlocked residence-hall rooms and cars are considered the most prevalent crimes on campus. The student government sponsors an escort service, and residence halls are locked around the clock.

If anything can keep homebound students on campus, it's Bison football, one of 8 men's and 8 women's sports that made the move in the 2004–2005 school year from NCAA Division II to Division I. As part of Division II, the male Bison brought home several football and wrestling national championships, and the women produced several national championships in volleyball and basketball. But it's football the fans stampede to watch in the 20,000-seat FargoDome on campus. Following football season, students celebrate the return of the winning hockey club program, which recently was reinstated after being cut. For those who'd rather play than watch, an intramural program provides 5 men's and 6 women's sports that are fairly traditional, as well as a 6-sport coed program that includes turkey trot, curling, and something called "almost anything goes." Two-thirds of the men and a third of the women take part.

For those times on campus when it seems as though almost nothing goes, students head for various lake resorts in Minnesota or visit friends at nearby Minnesota State, Moorhead and Concordia College.

Cost cutters: In a recent school year, 69% of the freshmen and 67% of the remaining undergraduates received financial aid. For 52% of the freshmen and 58% of the rest, the assistance was based on need. The average freshman award for a student with need included a need-based scholarship or grant averaging $3154 and need-based self-help aid such as loans and jobs averaging $3591. Non-need-based athletic scholarships for first-year students averaged $4897; other non-need-based awards and scholarships averaged $1598. The average financial indebtedness of a recent graduate was $23,197. Academic scholarships from $300 to $3000 are awarded to freshmen and other students on the basis of academic achievement, extracurricular participation, and financial need. Incoming freshmen with an ACT composite score of 24 or higher (or a 1090 math and critical reading SAT) and a cumulative GPA of at least 3.5 are encouraged to apply. Minnesota residents qualify for reduced tuition rates; students from 20 other western and midwestern states and Canadian provinces also may qualify for lower charges. Cooperative education programs are available in most majors; NDSU ranks in the top 5% in the country for placement of co-op students.

Rate of return: Seventy-seven percent of the freshmen return for the sophomore year. Nineteen percent go on to graduate in 4 years, 46% in 5 years, and 55% in 6 years.

Payoff: True to the university's practical origins, most North Dakota State graduates major in career-related disciplines. Sixteen percent of the 2005 graduates earned degrees in engineering; 15% graduated in business; 11% in health and related sciences. Not surprisingly, the vast majority of new alumni head for jobs directly related to their majors. Almost 100 companies and organizations recruited on campus in a recent school year. Those who seek advanced degrees, not quite a fifth in recent years, generally have good prospects. Among NDSU zoology graduates in a recent class, 78% of those who applied to medical school were accepted, compared with a national average of 40%.

Bottom line: North Dakota State is a big, friendly, rather relaxed campus where students can specialize in some of the most traditional majors as well as some of the most advanced. Advises a junior: "A student who enjoys a challenge, who would like to get involved and make a difference, and who wants to keep the good old-fashioned values while experiencing technology and innovation should attend NDSU."

Bluffton University

Bluffton, Ohio 45817

Setting: Small town
Control: Private (Mennonite)
Undergraduate enrollment: 427 men, 578 women
Graduate enrollment: 51 men, 58 women
Student/faculty ratio: 16
Freshman profile: 3% scored over 700 on SAT I verbal; 14% scored 600–700; 46% 500–599; 37% below 500. 3% scored over 700 on SAT I math; 24% scored 600–700; 32% 500–599; 41% below 500. 3% scored above 28 on the ACT; 10% scored 27–28; 33% 24–26; 30% 21–23; 24% below 21. 39% graduated in top fifth of high school class; 75% in upper two-fifths.

Faculty profile: 70% Ph.D.'s
Tuition and fees: $19,428
Room and board: $6682
Freshman financial aid: 100%; average scholarship or grant: $12,061 need-based; $8061 non-need-based
Campus jobs: 66%; average earnings: $1052/year
Application deadline: May 31
Financial aid deadline: May 1 (priority)
Admissions information: (419) 358-3257; (800) 488-3257
e-mail: admissions@bluffton.edu
web site: www.bluffton.edu

When students at Bluffton University, a small Mennonite school in northwestern Ohio, start talking about "Tuition Equalization," they're not discussing a new mathematical equation. The term is short for the Tuition Equalization Scholarship Program, a concept that enables many entering freshmen to receive aid that is equal to the difference between tuition at Bluffton and the average tuition at selected 4-year public institutions in Ohio. For qualified students entering for the 2006–2007 school year, the award is worth $9758 in aid from the college, including a state grant if an Ohio resident, additional college funds if not, and earnings from a campus job. Recipients don't have to repay the funds. In addition, Tuition Equalization recipients are guaranteed that 100% of their demonstrated need will be met from a variety of college, state, and federal sources. To qualify, a student must have at least a 23 ACT or 1050 combined critical reading and math SAT score and either a GPA of 3.0 out of a possible 4.0 or a rank in the top 25% of his or her graduating class. The aid is renewable if the student maintains a 2.5 GPA. Bluffton, with its enrollment of just over 1000 full-time undergraduates and rules against using alcohol or tobacco on campus, bears little resemblance to the typical public university. But for qualified students interested in this type of program, few deals beat this very special kind of private education for a very public price.

Student body: Just 14% of Bluffton's students are from outside Ohio, most coming from other midwestern states. A total of 21 states and 15 foreign countries are represented. African-Americans constitute the largest minority at 5% followed by Hispanics, Asian-Americans and foreign nationals all at 1% each. Sixty-three percent of the students are Protestant; 20% of them are Mennonite. Sixteen percent are Catholic. Twenty-one percent are Muslim, Hindu, or Buddhist. Ninety-five percent attended public schools and many are from small high schools in small towns. Most students are the products of "sheltered middle-class America," observes a senior, and are warm and caring toward one another. Adds another senior: "It is generally a wholesome population, with an abundance of 'small-town idealists' and future elementary school teacher types." Students pride themselves on being open-minded and willing to learn about convictions different from their own. "Bluffton," says a junior, "is a community of respect where I am treated as an honorable human being." Many also keep aware of social and political issues. While there are undergraduates who drink and smoke on campus regardless of the rules, most respect authority and the Christian principles behind the mandates. Students work hard but do not compete against one another in their studies. Adds a sophomore: "Students are dedicated but not obsessed academically. They are searching to find fun in the midst of studying."

Academics: Bluffton, which was founded in 1899, awards a bachelor's degree in 39 majors plus master's degrees in education, business administration, and organizational management. The academic year is divided into semesters. Classes, like the college, are small, with the average introductory lecture rarely topping 35, though Principles of Macroeconomics has hit 48, and most regular course offerings staying below 25.

The Liberal Arts and Sciences Program spreads required courses throughout a student's four years, beginning with a first-year seminar and classes in English, math, and science and concluding with a senior-year course on Christian Values in a Global Community. Classes in the middle years include work in the humanities, theology, and a cross-cultural internship or similar service experience. In 2005, more than 150 students traveled to locales as varied as China, Italy, New York, and San Antonio as part of their cross-cultural experience during the summer preceding their senior year. The 15 courses cover about a third of the hours needed to graduate.

Sixty-four of Bluffton's 115 faculty members are full-time. Sixty percent are men. While students rate the academic quality of the faculty as above average, they go off the charts in regard to teachers' willingness to help students with both personal and classroom problems. Says a senior: "I feel as though I can go to any one of my professors and find a listening ear and a willing helper."

Experienced professors and solid curricula are the keys to Bluffton's 2 largest and, some say, strongest departments: business and education. The programs they offer provide a wide variety of courses. Education puts students into the classroom the first semester of their first year and keeps them there much of the time in their final 2 years. Business graduates find that many of the projects they worked on as undergraduates are just what employers are expecting from them as employees. The sciences, though a smaller department without the technology of bigger schools, provide plenty of faculty-student interaction, a rigorous courseload (organic chemistry covers close to 21 chapters in 10 weeks), and nearly 100% placement into graduate studies.

Computer science needs another professor as well as more rigorous, focused coursework that better prepares graduates for the workplace. Spanish is the only foreign language offered as a major with a single professor and one instructor. There also is no major available in political science, theater, or philosophy. The communication major could use more modern equipment at the campus newspaper and radio station to give students more effective hands-on experience.

Facilities: Musselman Library, with its 166,000 volumes and 5525 electronic and paper periodicals, is small and limited in its physical resources. Students very often rely on OhioLINK, which gives students access to more than 31 million library items located at more than 75 college and university libraries in-state. OPAL, which stands for Ohio Private Academic Librairies, connects students with the resources of other private libraries around the state. As a study center, Musselman is much more satisfactory—generally very quiet, sometimes too quiet! The reading room, extols a senior, is "very 'Harvard-like.'" The Lion and the Lamb Peace Arts Center has materials devoted to peace and conflict resolution.

The hub of Bluffton's computer network is the Technology Center, with more than 40 computers,. The center is open from 8 a.m. to midnight weekdays with reduced hours on the weekends, longer during finals. The science, business, mathematics, music, and education departments also have 3 to 5 computers each for use by their respective majors. Mini-labs in the dorms, holding from 3 to 8 computers each, are open around the clock. Each residence hall room also has 2 data ports offering 24-hour on-line network service to students who bring their own computers. Wireless networks are available in major buildings.

Special programs: Students may spend 14 weeks learning at Magee College of the University of Ulster in Londonderry, Northern Ireland, in order to understand better the complexities of the conflict in Northern Ireland. Every other year, students may opt to study Polish history and language at the University of Marie Curie Sklodowska in Lublin, Poland. Bluffton's Pathways to Mission and Vocation program provides opportunities, including scholarship funding, for students to learn more about careers in pastoral ministry and public service. A semester in Washington, D.C., the Los Angeles Film Studies Center, the Middle East, Russia, China, or Oxford University is offered through the Council for Christian Colleges and Universities, of which Bluffton is a member. Internships can be arranged for business, social work, recreation, and education majors, with a cooperative program also possible for business students.

Campus life: Seventy-five percent of the full-time undergraduates live on the Bluffton campus; the only students allowed to live elsewhere are those who are married or commuting from home. Just half of the resident students stay around on the weekend, with many others heading for home or to bigger cities. Although Bluffton is a campus on which the rules of behavior are clearly defined, students find the environment far from restrictive. Along with campus prohibitions on drinking alcohol, taking drugs, swearing, gambling, promiscuity, and smoking tobacco is one that bars self-selective fraternities and sororities. Students insist they don't miss these groups, and focus instead on the activities coordinated by various residence halls. The Marbeck Center Board also sponsors free activities such as hayrides, bowling, and dances. BASIC (Brothers and Sisters in Christ) is one of the most popular organizations involving more than a third of the residents; it brings together students of all denominations in groups of 10 to 14 who wish to share problems, discuss issues, and participate in programs centered around Christ. PALS, which stands for Peer Awareness Leaders, also is active presenting programs that encourage healthy lifestyles. Chapel is held weekly with about 250 students present, though attendance is not required. The Mennonite influence is felt primarily through basic premises of peace making, service to others, and emphasis on the simple life, reflected in campus programs and faculty and student lifestyles. Crime is not a problem; students regularly leave jackets and bookbags unattended in the student center during meals, confident that they will find them there when they return. Self-locking doors accessible only by key cards recently were installed at all residence halls for added safety. Security guards are available to escort concerned students after dark.

The 2000 conference championship Beavers football team is the star sport in terms of fan support, although men's and women's basketball and soccer, baseball, softball, and women's volleyball also have strong followings. Seven varsity sports are fielded for men, 7 for women, played under NCAA Division III; the men's and women's golf teams were cut in 2004. Fourteen intramural sports are split 50-50 between events for men and women. Half of the men and a fifth of the women took part in a recent year.

Bluffton (pop. 3600), located 75 miles north of Dayton, is midway between Lima and Findlay, each about 15 miles away, so going to someplace bigger is not very hard. Adjacent to the 65-acre wooded campus is a 130-acre outdoor educational center known as Swinging Bridge Nature Preserve, which is owned by the college and offers extensive nature trails and an 8-acre lake.

Cost cutters: All of the full-time freshmen and continuing students received some form of financial assistance in the 2005–2006 school year. For 88% of the freshmen and 71% of the continuing students, the aid was need-based. The average financial aid package for freshmen with need consisted of $12,869 in need-based grants or scholarships and $4945 in need-based self-help aid such as loans and jobs. Other non-need-based awards and scholarships averaged $8061. Average debt of a 2005 graduate was $20,039. Along with the Tuition Equalization Scholarship Program, Bluffton offers several additional merit-based awards. Students with at least a 3.75 GPA and 27 ACT or 1220 combined critical reading and math SAT score can receive $2000 on top of their Tuition Equalization award as part of an Academic Distinction Scholarship. An Academic Distinction Scholarship, to those with a 3.5 GPA and a 25 ACT or 1040 SAT, brings recipients an extra $1000. Any candidate for either the Academic Merit or Academic Honors Scholarship may be 1 of 2 freshmen selected through a day-long scholarship competition in January to receive the full-tuition Presidential Scholarship. Up to 10 new students from backgrounds that are underrepresented at Bluffton are guaranteed $3000 up to full tuition in aid. Leadership/Service Grants are worth $3500. The Learn and Earn program provides work assignments to students who wish to work; undergraduates can earn $1350 to $1700 for 8 to 10 hours of work weekly. Approximately 60% of the students take part.

Rate of return: Seventy-five percent of entering freshmen return for the sophomore year. Forty-nine percent go on to graduate in 4 years; 57%, in 5 years.

Payoff: The 3 most popular majors for 2005 graduates were the career-focused disciplines of organizational management at 25%, early childhood education at 11%, and business administration at 7%. Some graduates go into voluntary service, many take jobs as teachers, and still others work at various companies in Ohio. Two hundred companies and organizations recruited on campus in the 2004–2005 school year. Within 10 years of graduation, 30–40% of the alumni go on to pursue advanced degrees, though less than 10% do so immediately after graduation.

Bottom line: Bluffton University, concludes a junior, is a place where students are taught to "open our minds to seeing the world from different angles; to take service seriously; to take respect seriously; to pay attention to faith in our daily lives, and to use it in our careers."

Capital University

Columbus, Ohio 43209

Setting: Suburban
Control: Private (Evangelical Lutheran)
Undergraduate enrollment: 818 men, 1335 women
Graduate enrollment: 356 men, 312 women
Student/faculty ratio: 10:1
Freshman profile: 4% scored over 700 on SAT I verbal; 24% scored 600–700; 42% 500–599; 30% below 500. 5% scored over 700 on SAT I math; 22% scored 600–700; 45% 500–599; 28% below 500. 9% scored above 28 on the ACT; 10% scored 27–28; 24% 24–26; 31% 21–23; 26% below 21. 28% graduated in top tenth of high school class; 42% in upper fifth.

Faculty profile: 80% Ph.D.'s
Tuition and fees: $24,300 (first year)
Room and board: $6344
Freshman financial aid: 88%; average scholarship or grant: NA
Campus jobs: NA; average earnings: NA
Application deadline: Apr. 15
Financial aid deadline: Apr. 1
Admissions information: (614) 236-6101; (800) 289-6289
e-mail: admissions@capital.edu
web site: www.capital.edu

Capital University and The Ohio State University are both doctorate-granting institutions in Ohio's capital city of Columbus, but otherwise, few universities could be more dissimilar. Capital is Lutheran and small, with just under 2200 full-time undergraduates. Ohio State is a classic public university, enrolling 15 times as many full-time undergraduates as Capital. Ohio State has very loose general-education requirements; Capital's highly structured core includes 12 courses or goals everyone must fulfill. And whereas a weekend never passes at Ohio State without several parties or sporting events, a typical Saturday and Sunday at Capital are relatively quiet with limited partying other than for major events like homecoming. When it comes to price, however, Capital's is bigger, although the differential is not as great as it initially appears. In the 2005–2006 school year, state residents paid about $15,000 and nonresidents about $26,500 in total costs to attend Ohio State, compared with $30,644 for everything at Capital. In the 2005–2006 school year, Capital also charged more for first-year students than for upperclassmen. While freshmen paid $24,300 in tuition and fees, sophomores paid $23,800, and juniors and seniors, $22,800. Many Capital students also find that the financial aid available to 88% of all freshmen closes the price gap even more. Notes a midwesterner: "The cost of Capital with financial aid is comparable to that of a state school without aid"—which makes this smaller, private college a capital choice, so to speak, for the student who doesn't want to risk being lost in a crowd.

Student body: Ninety-three percent of Capital's students are from Ohio with about half of the remaining 7% from other midwestern states. Twenty-four states and 11 foreign countries have undergraduates on campus. Ninety-seven percent in a recent year attended public schools. African-American students account for 14% of the total undergraduate student body; Hispanics, Asian-Americans, and international students each make up less than 1%. Thirteen percent of the students are Lutheran. The bulk of the students are middle class and conservative, "with a few token radicals to keep things interesting," says a junior. "People are able to be individuals here, but can be frowned upon by the preppy-dressed majority." The general academic climate is fairly relaxed and friendly. Nursing and music majors are more likely to run into competition, though most students concentrate on keeping up their own grades and ignore everyone else's.

Academics: Capital, founded in 1830, awards the bachelor's degree in more than 60 majors through the College of Arts and Sciences, Conservatory of Music, and the 3 Schools of Nursing, Management, and Education, Professional Studies, and Social Work. Master's degrees are offered in various fields of business, music education, and nursing plus a juris doctor in the law school. Capital follows a 2-semester schedule. Classes average between 20 and 40 students, although, adds a sophomore, "I've already had classes as small as 6 and as large as 70." The biggest courses are generally introductory biology lectures.

Capital's core curriculum prescribes 5 specific courses or goals in the freshman year, 5 in the sophomore year, and 1 each in the junior and senior years that every student must take. The courses cover all traditional disciplines and range from Cultural Diversity in American Society to Ethical Issues and Contemporary Religious Conviction.

The faculty consists of 201 full-time and 198 part-time members; 45% in a recent year were women. No current figures are available to show the portion who teach at the graduate level only. Professors are noted for their personal approach to teaching and active involvement in campus activities. While a minority fail to challenge students sufficiently, most urge students not only to stay on top of the material in their particular courses but to keep on learning wherever possible. "Many see Capital as a starting point, not an ending," says a senior. "They encourage outside learning and are willing to help students clarify their opinions by discussing various points with them. These professors are real."

Capital's best academic offerings are in the School of Nursing and Conservatory of Music, both of which combine hard-working students and experienced faculty in a 7:1 student/teacher ratio. Education is also very demanding and gives prospective teachers plenty of early field experience. History and political science majors benefit from being located in the Columbus area, where numerous opportunities for internships in state government and various lobbying groups exist. Students in English relish a dedicated faculty and, says a major, an "open, creative kind of learning that is dependent upon student input."

Majors in leadership and management, accounting, marketing and financial economics in the recently established School of Management, which was created to meet the needs of the large number of business majors who attend Capital, are steadily becoming among the university's strongest. Foreign language lovers, however, still find few options, with majors only in French and Spanish and a minor in German. The behavioral sciences department with majors in psychology, sociology, and criminology could use more professors; in addition, the curricula has tended to be repetitive and less challenging at the upper levels. The math and computer science department could use more technologically advanced equipment. Though students like the professional writing concentration within the English major, many wish there were more courses and more full-time professors. The theater studies faculty is strong but the facilities and resources have been less so.

Facilities: Capital's Blackmore Library holds 300,000 volumes and 5765 paper and electronic periodicals. The OhioLINK computer network also makes available the catalogs and materials contained within about 30 other college and university libraries within the state. On rare occasions, students simply head directly to the Ohio State or local public libraries, or, to forget the research process entirely, to the art gallery on Blackmore's fourth floor. As a study center, the library rates a "Q" for quiet. A 24-hour study room enables students to meet and work in groups at any hour of the day or night.

Most students use the 30 Mac and 30 Windows computers in the basement of the library that are available until 11 p.m. weekdays. Hours are extended until 2 a.m. during finals. Terminals in the science-math building plus satellite labs in the campus center and each residence hall also are available to undergraduates. Wireless access is an option on all 4 floors of Blackmore Library and at the campus Crusader Club.

Special programs: Students may enroll in courses at 5 other Columbus-area institutions, including Ohio State and Otterbein College or spend a semester in Washington, D.C. A dual-degree program in engineering is offered with Washington University in St. Louis and with Case Western Reserve. Students may study abroad in 21 countries throughout Europe, Asia, Africa, and South America. Music majors may spend a fall at Kodály Institute in Hungary.

Campus life: Forty-eight percent of the undergraduates live on the 48-acre campus in the suburb of Bexley, 3 miles from downtown Columbus. Says a state resident: "I enjoy the opportunities of a big city with the feel of a small town." Though 2 national and 3 local fraternities and 3 national and 4 local sororities attracted just a fourth of the men and women as members in a recent school year, Greek influence over the campus social life has been relatively strong since it has been concentrated on those students who don't go home for the weekend. For independents who stay, and aren't interested in Greek parties, downtown Columbus and the Ohio State area offer a wide variety of entertainment alternatives. Music lovers can count on students from the conservatory to present a concert or recital nearly every weekend. For those interested in a good argument, the intercollegiate debate team consistently ranks in the top 25 in the nation and placed second in the National Championships in the year 2000. Crime is not a serious problem on the campus itself, with most incidents of vandalism confined to the university parking lots. Says a senior: "The biggest crime we have on this campus is parking in the wrong lots and receiving parking tickets from the city of Bexley for parking on the city streets for too long." Around-the-clock security patrols and escorts help keep the situation that way. Students warn, however, that walking alone at night just a few blocks away from campus can mean trouble.

Eight men's and 8 women's teams compete in NCAA Division III. Crusader basketball, both men's and women's, football, and women's soccer games draw the most spirited crowds, especially the Lady Crusader basketball team who are 2-time national champions. Nine intramural sports also are available for those men and women who wish to get involved. All sports got a boost with the opening in August 2001 of the 126,000-square-foot Capital Center. The all-purpose facility provides a 2100-seat arena for intercollegiate basketball and volleyball games, a 2500-seat stadium for intercollegiate football and soccer games and track, plus a field house for intramural and recreational activities and fitness equipment for the individual trainee.

When students need to get away, those who can go home do so; others head either to Ohio State or to the varied cultural attractions of the capital city.

Cost cutters: In the 2005–2006 school year, 88% of the first-year students and 82% of the rest were given assistance. No figure is available to show the percentage of students receiving aid that was need-based. The average freshman award totaled $15,250, although no breakdown was provided showing the portion that was scholarship, need-based, or merit, or self-help aid such as loans and job earnings. The average 2005 graduate left with debts of $25,171. Collegiate Fellowships, awarded on the basis of academic merit and an on-campus interview, pay up to full tuition. Brookman Fellowships pay up to full tuition to high-achieving entering freshmen who plan to major in mathematics or computer science. Presidential Scholarships in varying amounts go to top students planning majors in a wide range of fields except music. Cooperative programs also are available. Concludes a junior: "The school really tries to give students a chance to come here."

Rate of return: Seventy-nine percent of freshmen return for the sophomore year. Forty-eight percent graduate after 4 years; 57% within 5 years; 59% within 6.

Payoff: In a recent year, 13% of the graduates earned bachelor's degrees in multi-disciplinary fields, followed by majors in business at 11%, and social work, at 10%. Most Capital graduates trade their diplomas for full-time jobs, primarily in the Midwest, in industry, schools, hospital systems, and accounting firms. Many take jobs with the approximately 30 companies and organizations that recruited on campus during their senior year. Just over a fifth pursue advanced degrees shortly after commencement.

Bottom line: Advises a recent graduate: "Our entire campus would fit in the South Quad at Ohio State, but it is the people here who make the school."

Franciscan University of Steubenville

Steubenville, Ohio 43952

Setting: Small town
Control: Private (Roman Catholic)
Undergraduate enrollment: 1818 men and women
Graduate enrollment: NA
Student/faculty ratio: 15:1
Freshman profile: SAT/ACT scores: NA; class rank data: NA
Faculty profile: 73% Ph.D.'s
Tuition and fees: $17,500
Room and board: $5950

Freshman financial aid: 92%; average scholarship or grant: $7190 need-based
Campus jobs: 50%; average earnings: $1000/year
Application deadline: June 30
Financial aid deadline: Apr. 15
Admissions information: (740) 283-6226, ext 1220; (800) 783-6220
e-mail: admissions@franciscan.edu
web site: www.franciscan.edu

For the first several decades of its existence, the official name of Franciscan University of Steubenville was simply the College of Steubenville. This was like calling potato salad simply "salad": when the ingredient that gave the school its distinct flavor was not mentioned, it seemed just another garden-variety institution. While many students are drawn to Franciscan's excellent psychology and nursing programs, it is the spiritual climate that sets the institution apart, not just from universities as a whole, but from most other Catholic universities as well. A recent graduate calls it the "most faith-filled Catholic school in the nation." Others refer to it as a "center for Christian renewal." Notes a junior: "Our faith permeates every aspect of campus life; it is our identity and the reason most students come here. Although there is no mandatory attendance at any religious service, there is much to attend"—and most do. Undergraduates warn that students who are not Catholic (96% are) or as "faith-filled" may feel a bit out of place, though never rejected, and some who are not Catholic when they arrive like what they see and choose to convert. In any case, a price for tuition, room, and board of $23,450 in the 2005–2006 school year surely brings a sense of fulfillment to all in attendance who trusted—and now see for themselves—that such educational bargains do exist.

Student body: About a fourth of the university's undergraduates are from Ohio. Other students from the Midwest comprise the largest contingent of out-of-staters, though students are attracted to the university from every state and 17 foreign countries. Forty-one percent in a recent year were graduates of private or parochial schools. Hispanics and foreign nationals recently constituted the largest racial and ethnic groups at 4% and 3%, respectively. Asian-Americans followed at 2%, African-Americans and Native Americans at less than 1% each. Students attracted to Franciscan University are deeply conservative with regard to political, moral, and spiritual values, and many are very active in the pro-life movement. "Having all students who share the same views, for the most part, does not exactly create a challenging atmosphere where the individual has the opportunity to see the world from different perspectives," acknowledges a senior, "but the overall atmosphere that is created by this deep understanding that each student has with each other and the fellowship and community is certainly one that makes the school what it is and its benefits are truly unparalleled." Students are committed to their relationships with each other and to God, and increasingly over the last few years, to their studies. Says a senior: "There is a spirit in the student body that encourages rigorous academics."

Academics: Franciscan University, which turned 60 in 2006, offers bachelor's degrees in 34 majors and 7 master's degree programs. The undergraduate-level theology program is considered to be the largest in the country. Students follow a 2-semester system. In the first 2 years most classes enroll from 15 to 50 participants; the largest, Christian Moral Principles has 51. Courses in the latter 2 years generally range from 10 to 20, though some classes taught by especially inspiring professors may have many more.

Core curriculum requirements include 15 credits each in communications and humanities and 6 credits each in social science, theology, and natural science. While the specific theology core requirements are minimal, and many students wish there were more, most disciplines throughout the curriculum are examined first in an academic context, and second in a context of Christian values, so that theology is ever-present in the classroom and is a popular choice for a second major.

The university's faculty in a recent year was divided nearly evenly between 105 full-time faculty members and 101 part-time. No figures are available to show the number who taught undergraduates, though in previous years only a handful of the full-time members and less than a dozen of the part-time taught at the graduate level only. About a third of all faculty members are women. Although there are a few brilliant stars, most professors represent the full range of teaching abilities found at other less spiritually driven schools. However, with even the dullest lecturer the emphasis is 2-fold: to teach students the course material and to guide them spiritually, both in what they say in class and in how they act outside the classroom. Says a senior: "The faculty not only teach their subjects but they themselves lead a moral life, which comes across in their classes." The spiritual context for whatever subject they teach is ever-present as well. Says a biology major: "It is amazing to be sitting in a math or psychology class halfway through the period and the teacher stops everything because we forgot to open the class in prayer. Or when sitting in a developmental anatomy class, the professor is referencing the Holy Spirit as having something to do with the development of a chick embryo."

Disciplines concerned with healing the mind, soul, and body—psychology, theology, and nursing—are the university's 3 strongest offerings. The highly regarded psychology department offers a very comprehensive curriculum with a required internship. The theology program is among a limited number in the nation that follows orthodox Roman Catholic teaching, thereby attracting many prominent theologians to the campus; "the best teachers in the world," boasts a Californian. Every professor in the department must take an oath of fidelity to the Pope, swearing to teach true Catholic theology. Students consider the newest major in religious education (catechetics) to be "awesome" already, in the words of one junior. Nursing students enjoy a fully equipped simulated clinic that enables them to practice their skills; real-world experience is gained at a local Steubenville hospital, at Weirton (West Virginia) Medical Center and at a number of medical centers in Pittsburgh. With such solid training behind them, more than 90% of recent graduates have passed the state board examination on the first try. Other departments drawing praise include philosophy, political science, classics, English, business, and the humanities and Catholic culture program. Biology majors thrive under the tutelage of caring professors and in the state-of-the-art surroundings of a new structure, the Saints Cosmas and Damian Science Hall that opened in August of 2000.

Engineering recently was dropped as a major. Because the math program is small, "some classes are offered only one semester every other year," observes a major. "That makes it very difficult to schedule classes." Many consider the Spanish major less challenging than they would like. The fine arts are "virtually nonexistent," with only a handful of art classes, a music minor, and a small, though excellent theater program. Classes in the education department could use less "busy" work and more rigor, according to some students.

Facilities: Although the beautiful Pope John Paul II Library was dedicated as recently as 1987, students already complain that it is too small and needs more study space. Most, however, find it quiet. The collection of just over 232,000 volumes is especially strong in theology and philosophy. The range of 5874 periodicals (700 paper) is somewhat limited, although database searching helps to compensate. The library provides on-line access to more than 60 research databases. Students also have access to more than 6.4 million books and periodicals through the library's OPAL catalog and the OhioLINK network. Many students, especially those in upper-level courses, travel to the major university libraries in Pittsburgh to conduct more extensive research.

There are 4 computer labs around campus, in the library and in 2 of the academic buildings. Three of the four labs have PCs; 1 has Macs. The lab that is open the latest, in the library, closes at 11:30 p.m. Waits can be quite lengthy during midterms and finals. Says a sophomore, "More computers with extended hours would be a great improvement to our campus." Internet access is available in students' rooms in the residence halls.

Special programs: The university has a study abroad program in Gaming, Austria, that enables 100 students from any major, usually in their sophomore year, to spend a semester studying at a newly renovated 14th-century Carthusian monastery. An accounting or business administration major may take part in a 4 + 1 M.B.A. program in which he or she earns a master's degree in business administration 1 year after earning a bachelor's. Philosophy, theology, and psychology majors may participate in similar accelerated programs.

Campus life: Sixty-one percent of the undergraduates live on the 124-acre hilltop campus overlooking the Ohio River. Only seniors and undergraduates who are married and students over the age of 21 are allowed to live off campus, but few students would rather be anywhere else. Says a senior: "There is an uplifting and positive air that flows through campus." Most residents are members of the university's distinctive "household" system, in which groups of as many as 25 men or women, usually living on the same floor of a residence hall, join together as a family for spiritual, emotional, and social support. Like fraternities and sororities, but based on faith and prayer, the households form, for many, "the backbone of student life," to quote a junior, also joining forces for sports, socializing, and even study. About 55 households exist on campus. The residence halls themselves observe strict quiet hours, and intervisitation between men and women is permitted only on weekend afternoons. Less than 1% of the men and women belong to a single Greek fraternity and single sorority; though their parties are open to everyone, their presence on campus is not welcomed by all students. "Swing dancing is huge on campus," says a sophomore, "and all levels of skill are acceptable!"

A typical weekend is filled with religious activity. "For a Catholic, it's heaven," says a sophomore. Some Saturday mornings are spent praying at local abortion clinics, followed monthly by Saturday evening festivals of praise, 2 hours of worship in song. For most, Sunday Mass is the "focal point," while throughout the week about 700 students attend 1 of 3 daily Masses. The annual January 22 antiabortion March for Life in Washington draws 8 busloads of students for the trip; the Students for Life club is the second largest on campus and works to preserve and enhance life at all ages through campaigning against measures legalizing contraception, abortion, and euthanasia. Nearly 500 students are involved in various community-service programs through Works of Mercy Outreach as well as missionary work through Franciscan Missions of Peace. Crime is rarely a topic of concern, thanks to 24-hour guards on patrol. Students, however, consider the surrounding neighborhood to be less safe and advise caution when walking off-campus.

Serious athletes no longer have to sacrifice to attend this university. which has had no intercollegiate athletics. In 2005 the university's board of trustees unanimously authorized the school to seek membership in Division III of the National Collegiate Athletic Association (NCAA). The first intercollegiate games for the university will begin in 2007 under provisional NCAA membership; the university will be eligible for full membership in 2011. The university plans to field men's and women's teams in basketball, soccer, cross country, and tennis, plus baseball for men and volleyball for women. Until then, club teams in most of those sports plus intramurals in flag football, volleyball, basketball, and Ultimate Frisbee keep the athletically minded challenged. "Club rugby games on the weekend also draw big crowds," adds a senior.

Steubenville itself (pop. 19,000) provides little of cultural or social interest to most students, who prefer to drive 40 minutes east to Pittsburgh. Households sometimes take a break from the books by gathering at area ranches or campgrounds for retreats; Portiuncula Chapel, a simple stone structure with wooden benches on campus, is used by many for private contemplation and prayer.

Cost cutters: In a recent school year, 92% of the freshmen and 87% of continuing students received financial assistance; 61% of the freshmen and 67% of the continuing students received aid that was need-based. The average award for a first-year student with financial need consisted of a need-based scholarship or grant averaging $7190 and need-based self-help such as loans and jobs averaging $3866. Typical debt for a recent graduate totaled $21,616. Students generally are considered for scholarships if they have a 3.6 GPA, a 27 ACT or 1220 SAT combined math and critical reading score. In a recent year, University Scholarships, based on academic performance, paid from $2000 to $8000 annually; upper-class academic awards for juniors and seniors, $1000–$2000 yearly; need-based University Grants, $100–$2300 a year. SWOP (Student Work Opportunity Program) lets students work off part of their college costs by helping with about 600 jobs around campus.

Rate of return: Eighty-four percent of freshmen return for the sophomore year. Fifty-seven percent graduate in 4 years; 64%, in 5 years; 67% in 6.

Payoff: Theology was the major of choice for 21% of recent graduates followed by business at 11% and education at 10%. Many students return to their home regions to find employment in a variety of fields or find jobs with the 35 companies and organizations that recruited on campus in a recent school year. Those who pursue advanced degrees study far afield as well as near to home. Several graduates study for doctoral degrees in philosophy at the International Academy of Philosophy in Liechtenstein, while others seek licensure in theology at the John Paul II Institute in Rome.

Bottom line: Undergraduates advise those considering Franciscan University to visit the campus in order to understand thoroughly the prayerful and faith-filled nature of the community. "The student who benefits most from 4 years here," says an easterner, "is one who is willing to forgo the 'extended childhood' that most other schools seem to foster, and who truly desires to follow the way of the Cross."

Heidelberg College

Tiffin, Ohio 44883

Setting: Small town
Control: Private (United Church of Christ/Congregational)
Undergraduate enrollment: 565 men, 525 women
Graduate enrollment: 5 men, 9 women (191 part-time)
Student/faculty ratio: 16:1
Freshman profile: 0% scored over 700 on SAT I verbal; 14% scored 600–700; 36% 500–599; 50% below 500. 0% scored over 700 on SAT I math; 16% scored 600–700; 34% 500–599; 50% below 500. 5% scored above 28 on the ACT; 5% scored 27–28; 16% 24–26; 23% 21–23; 51% below 21. 28% graduated in top fifth of high school class; 58% in upper two-fifths.

Faculty profile: 77% Ph.D.'s
Tuition and fees: $16,134
Room and board: $7108
Freshman financial aid: 98%; average scholarship or grant: $10,705 need-based
Campus jobs: 65%; average earnings: $450/year
Application deadline: May 1
Financial aid deadline: None (Priority date: Mar. 1)
Admissions information: (419) 448-2330;
(800) HEIDELBERG
e-mail: adminfo@mail.heidelberg.edu
web site: www.heidelberg.edu

Many students heading off to college assume they'll be leaving tender loving care back home. At Heidelberg College, 48 miles south of Toledo, Ohio, however, freshmen simply trade in the family TLC for the college's award-winning TSD, its Total Student Development program. Every new undergraduate is assigned to a team consisting of 8–10 other freshmen, a faculty advisor, and 1 returning student. The groups meet for 1 hour a week throughout most of the freshman year and discuss issues of a personal, cultural, social, or academic nature as students feel the need. The faculty advisor also works with each student individually to develop a 4-year plan covering the full spectrum of goals for his or her time on campus. Completion of the program is required for graduation. Says a recent alumnus: "The TSD program shows students and their parents right away that Heidelberg is a place to grow, not just academically but also socially, culturally, and emotionally. The student and staff work together to foster this growth of the whole person."

And now, students are getting a little more TLC as well; at least their pocketbooks are. In the 2002–2003 school year, Heidelberg cut its tuition rate by 32%. As a result, tuition and required fees for the 2005–2006 school year were $16,134, just $540 more than tuition and fees were in the 1997–1998 school year. With all but a small percent of all undergraduates receiving some kind of financial aid on top of the lower tuition, that's TLC with TNT.

Student body: All but 6% of Heidelberg's students are from Ohio, largely drawn from small towns or suburbs of major metropolitan areas. The vast majority of nonresidents also are midwesterners, though 18 states and 14 foreign countries have undergraduates on campus. Thirty-nine percent of the enrollment attended private or parochial schools. Many students are the first in their families to attend college. Fewer than 10% are members of the United Church of Christ. International students, many from an exchange program in Japan, represent 2% of the undergraduate population, followed by African-Americans at 5%; and Hispanics and Asian-Americans at 1% each. For the most part, students are easy going and fairly conservative in their outlook. Socially, they range from those who are goal-oriented to the pursuers of the perfect party, and in the course of 4 years on campus, there usually are very few people whose faces and habits, if not always their names, are not known to everyone. Students also place a high value on friendliness; as one member observed, "It is unacceptable to walk down the sidewalk and not say hello to someone." Equally unacceptable is being too competitive; though most are concerned about academics, it is considered the "Heidelberg way" to want others to succeed and to actively encourage each other to do better. However, lack of student interest in politics and many campus activities frustrates those classmates trying to promote a more active political and social life.

Academics: Heidelberg was founded in 1850 by members of the German Reformed Church, and until the early 1970s the college required all tenured faculty to be members of a Christian faith. Today's Heidelberg remains church-related but is considerably less rigid, with faculty and students of all religious beliefs and of varying degrees of faith. The school operates on a 2-semester calendar and awards bachelor's degrees in 29 disciplines and the master of arts in education and counseling and a master of business administration. The average class size is 15, with the range extending from 55 in General Zoology to as few as 4 for upper-level computer science courses.

General-education requirements draw courses from the traditional disciplines and fulfill about a third of the semester hours needed for graduation. Included is a 1-semester start-off First Year Seminar, which emphasizes connections between different disciplines and different skills. All juniors must select 1 course from a group of classes on Exploring the Liberal Arts, which further stresses the interrelationships between disciplines. A required senior capstone experience is designed to link learning and doing.

One-on-one after-hours assistance ("for 3 straight hours," 1 troubled student recalls) is the hallmark of most of the 66 full-time faculty members and many of the 53 part-timers as well. All but 4 of the full-time faculty members and all but 9 of the part-time teach undergraduates. Thirty-three percent are women. A majority also takes an active part in campus activities and usually is quite agreeable about participating in student programs. "As a senior this year," says an English major, "I can honestly say that I know at least 75% of the faculty personally. Professors I have had only once remember my name and stop me on the sidewalk to ask how my major is coming along. The caring faculty is a big plus!"

Majors and nonmajors alike rave about the biology department which thrives via top-notch professors, modern equipment (including terrific water-quality, physiology, and human cadaver labs), and challenging courses. Other of the sciences—chemistry, physics, psychology, and water resources that are offered as majors and geology, which is a minor—also are considered outstanding. To insure that the sciences remain at the top of their field, the new Gillmor Science Hall, named for long-time U.S. Representative Paul Gillmor of Ohio's Fifth Congressional District, opened in January 2005. The education major earns a gold star for putting students out in the field every year. Business administration boasts faculty rich in practical experience and makes sure that students get plenty of their own through internships; however, some students wish there were more courses in marketing and sales. Smaller departments such as English and computer science feature outstanding faculties. The music curriculum is dynamic and very demanding, some even think too much so.

Majors in allied health and health service management no longer are available, joining majors in art, French, and sociology that were dropped a few years ago. Foreign language instruction with majors in German and Spanish is hurt by having too few faculty members. Mathematics lacks variety in the courses offered. Students note that while the communication studies and media tracks in communication and theater arts are strong in their instruction of theory, both need more up-to-date equipment.

Facilities: Beeghly Library's unusual design, a 3-story circular structure with lots of glass, makes it "almost fun to be in," says a frequent visitor. As a study center, it offers plenty of rooms for group sessions, individual carrels that can be reserved, and a 24-hour room for night owls. However, the praise diminishes when it's time for extensive research. Students say that the collection of 260,000 volumes (of which just over 150,000 are books) and 829 periodicals is lacking in updated publications especially medical and biological journals. However, an on-line catalog, extensive database searches, and membership in OPAL and OhioLink, 2 consortia of higher education institutions, bring plenty of information to their fingertips.

Computer terminals located in every residence hall are available around the clock, as are units located in the Honors Center. Various microcomputers also are located in computer centers in the sciences complex, the library, the business department, and the administration building. The main buildings on campus and some of the housing facilities are wireless.

Special programs: Juniors may spend a semester or a year at the other Heidelberg, the university in Germany. The college also sponsors a program with the Center for Cross Cultural Study in Seville, Spain and in Havana, Cuba. Internships in Washington, D.C. are available through American University. Engineering students may earn degrees from Heidelberg and Case Western Reserve University after spending 3 years at Heidelberg and 2 at Case; similar joint programs are offered in forestry and environmental sciences with Duke and in nursing with Case Western Reserve.

Campus life: Eighty-six percent of Heidelberg's undergraduates live on the 120 acres of gray limestone buildings, and most of them remain over the weekend. Thirty percent of the men and 36% of the women belong to 4 local fraternities and 4 local sororities. Their dances and parties are usually open to all and attended by many of those who stay around, although students attach little special significance to Greek membership. An increasingly popular gathering place on campus is The Down Under, a nonalcoholic club open until 4 a.m. on Sunday and available Friday nights for use by any college group that wants to sponsor a campuswide dance or other event. Petty theft is the most common crime on campus and usually occurs because students have neglected to lock their dorm room doors. However, one student left her car keys in the car door for 3 days and the car was left untouched!

Football, basketball, and men's and women's soccer draw the best crowds of the 9 men's and 8 women's teams competing in NCAA Division III. Heidelberg's mascot is one of a kind among U.S. colleges and universities: the Student Prince, which comes from a German operetta of the same name. Fifty percent of the men and 40% of the women turn out for 9 men's and 8 women's intramural sports.

Students who love Heidelberg's small size nevertheless find Tiffin (pop. 20,000) limited in its social and cultural options. Bowling Green, Toledo, and Columbus are popular larger alternatives.

Cost cutters: In the 2005–2006 school year, 98% of the freshmen and 99% of continuing students received financial aid; for 84% of both groups, the aid was need-based. The average freshman award consisted of a $10,705 need-based scholarship or grant and need-based self-help aid such as loans and jobs averaging $4268. An average 2005 graduate left with debts of $20,886. The Heidelberg Scholars Competition recognizes and rewards students who are among the top 20% of the high school seniors applying to the college. To be considered, all students must have submitted an application by January 15 of their senior year. Selected candidates will be required to attend 1 of 2 competition events held on campus in February. Students are eligible to receive 1 of 5 awards, ranging from the Heidelberg, which pays full tuition, down to the Merit Award, which pays $3000 annually, with scholarships paying $4000, $5500, and half tuition in between. Minority Achievement Awards pay up to $4000. Music scholarships in varying amounts also are available as is a 10-month interest-free payment plan.

Rate of return: Eighty percent of freshmen return for the sophomore year. Fifty percent graduate in 4 years; 52% within 5 years; 54% in 6.

Payoff: Education at 22% and business at 18% were the most popular majors among 2005 graduates. Psychology followed with 15% of the grads. The vast majority take jobs immediately, primarily in the Midwest, in fields such as business, banking, education, and health care administration. Employers of Heidelberg alumni have included NCR, BP America, Mac Tools, General Mills, and Batelle. About 50 companies and organizations recruited on campus in the 2004–2005 school year. Less than a fifth pursue advanced degrees within 6 months of commencement, although within 5 years of graduating, nearly 50% do so.

Bottom line: Heidelberg students are open and easygoing and welcome newcomers to the fold, provided that they are willing to be friendly and not too academically or socially competitive. Notes a junior: "Heidelberg gives students a chance to explore all of their capabilities without forcing any religion, career, or stereotype upon them. Here students are able to be themselves and to discover exactly what that means."

Hiram College

Hiram, Ohio 44234

Setting: Rural
Control: Private (Disciples of Christ)
Undergraduate enrollment: 405 men, 495 women
Graduate enrollment: NA
Student/faculty ratio: 11:1
Freshman profile: SAT/ACT scores: NA; 31% graduated in top tenth of high school class
Faculty profile: 95% Ph.D.'s
Tuition and fees: $23,510
Room and board: $7610

Freshman financial aid: NA
Campus jobs: NA
Application deadline: Early decision: Dec. 1; Regular: Mar. 15 (Feb. 1 for scholarship consideration)
Financial aid deadline: Mar. 1 (Feb. 1 for scholarship consideration)
Admissions information: (330) 569-5169; (800) 362-5280
e-mail: admission@hiram.edu
web site: www.hiram.edu

There are semesters and trimesters and January terms and one-course-at-a-time, and then there's the Hiram Plan. Under the plan, each semester is divided into a 12-week segment in which students typically take 3 courses followed by a 3-week segment in which they take a single class. That class often involves an off-campus experience enabling almost half of all Hiram students to study abroad as part of programs led by Hiram College faculty. In 2005–2006 trips ranged from a 3-week visit to Trinidad and Tobago in the fall sponsored by the biology and English departments to a spring term trip to Bhutan sponsored by the religious studies department and the ethics center.

Hiram has yet another plan having nothing to do with the academic calendar: a plan to assist families in paying for college. In 2004 Hiram made the pledge not to raise tuition in the course of a student's 4 years at college, enabling parents to know upfront what they will paying each year for their son's or daughter's course of study. Says a sophomore: "The best part of our tuition and financial aid is that the cost of tuition will not increase for a person across the 4 years. The tuition price might increase for the new class, but students already enrolled will not have to pay the increase." In early 2006 the college announced it would freeze fall 2006 tuition at 2005 levels, giving members of the Class of 2010 a price break of their own.

Student body: Although students may end up around the world during their time at Hiram, three quarters of them over the years have come from Ohio. Altogether, Hiram students have homeports in 26 states and 23 foreign countries. In recent years, a fifth have been graduates of private or parochial schools. Forty percent are first-generation college goers. Minority students account for 15% of the undergraduate enrollment, though no breakdown is available to show the portion that is African-American, Asian-American, Hispanic, or Native American. There also is no figure for the number of students who are foreign nationals. Only 3% in recent years have been members of the Christian Church (Disciples of Christ). Students see themselves as socially aware, intelligent, and involved. Politically, "it may feel more liberal at times," says a sophomore, "but generally an equal balance exists between Democrats and Republicans." On a campus so small, most students know or at least know of each other, and because residence halls house a mix of classes, with no separate freshmen housing, there is great unity among students of all levels. While a majority work hard to excel, the focus is more on personal satisfaction than competition. Says a junior: "The academic setting of this college is so phenomenal . . . you're just driven to do your very best."

Academics: Hiram, founded in 1850, awards the bachelor's degree in 30 majors. A weekend college enrolls an additional 300 students in courses every other weekend. The college also offers a small Master of Arts program in interdisciplinary studies that enrolls up to 20 students a year. Undergraduate class sizes recently ranged from 40 in an economics class to just 2 participants in a psychology course on animal behavior. Rather than let classes grow too large, professors generally have preferred to open extra sections of the same course. As a result, the average enrollment has stayed between 15 and 20 participants. "As you could imagine, few people leave a classroom confused," says a senior. "Students get a lot of individual attention—as much as they need."

Incoming freshmen begin their time at Hiram with a 5-day New Student Institute. They meet in groups of 12 to 15 with a faculty advisor to select courses, discuss a common reading sent to them over the summer, and generally become acclimated to college life. The same group of students and advisor stays together for the first-term Colloquium that emphasizes reasoning and communication skills in the discussion of a central theme. Topics have included Order and Simplicity, taught by a physics professor, and the Image of War, led by a professor of art.

The general-education program is built around team-taught sequence courses. Students pick up spring term where the Colloquium left off with the First-Year Seminar, a 12-week course that provides an introductory experience in Western thought, taught from the perspective of 1 discipline. The seminar seeks to improve students' college-level writing and analytical skills. In the remaining years, undergraduates must choose 1 of the following: 2 interdisciplinary courses, 1 of which must be team taught; an integrated 3-course collegium, or an interdisciplinary minor, as well as fairly standard distribution requirements.

Hiram's faculty includes 73 full-time faculty members. No figures are available to show the number of part-time, who in recent years totaled just over 20. Almost half the faculty members in recent years have been women. Nearly all professors are distinguished by a love of students, teaching, and the liberal arts tradition, and view learning as a collaborative endeavor. As one student put it: "The instructors live the liberal arts ideals that they preach, and they enjoy an interest in a variety of subjects." Undergraduates especially appreciate the interest the faculty takes in them. Says a junior: "They get to know your interests along with your strengths and weaknesses so they become better mentors. You also get to know your professors as people and develop a friendly relationship with them."

Biology is clearly one of Hiram's strongest offerings. "Faculty members are diverse, energetic, and progressive," recalls a major. "They don't believe in lecturing to 'vegetables' and often force student participation." The laboratory equipment in the new Gerstacker Science Center is excellent as are opportunities for off-campus learning. Just 3 miles away, the 360-acre James H. Barrow Field Station offers a natural laboratory where students can study and care for primates and exotic birds as well as reptiles and herbs. One result from this experience has been an impressive number of students admitted to the Ohio State Veterinary School, in recent years, 3 times more than from any other Ohio private school. Chemistry is considered outstanding by its majors, too, who also place well in graduate and medical schools.

Education takes a similar approach to the sciences, teaming involvement in the real world with a well-constructed academic program. English and history draw praise as well.

Smaller programs such as foreign languages with majors in classical studies, French and Spanish, philosophy, sociology, art, mathematics, and computer science, suffer mainly because their excellent attentive professors are few in number. The theater department could be improved with better physical resources, though a new black box theater is on the drawing board. Management and political science have gained reputations as easier programs where students can choose to specialize with minimal demands on their time or mind. Says a senior: "If you want to take all 'slacker courses,' they are available. If you want to work hard, you can, but it's not required."

Facilities: The roomy library, which opened just over a decade ago, gets rave reviews from students who like its group study rooms, individual carrels, and comfortable lounge seating. Computerized research aids supplement the local collection of 185,000 volumes and 800 periodicals. The library also is a U.S. government depository, receiving 7000 federal documents annually. Connections with OhioLink, a consortium of more than 70 Ohio colleges and universities plus the State Library of Ohio, make available more than 7 million additional volumes and another 4000 journals. Hiram's library also includes the collections of 2 notable Hiram graduates: former Hiram student, Hiram president and U.S. President James A. Garfield and poet Vachel Lindsay, a member of Hiram's class of 1902 who prepared for a career in medicine at the college.

Computer labs are available in every dorm, the library, and the student center. Labs in the dorms and student center are open around the clock. "A lot of students have computers so it is never really a big problem," says a senior.

Special programs: Students may choose from a wide range of off-campus opportunities. The various 3-week courses offered in the 2005–2006 school year, 3 in the fall and 3 in the spring, ranged in price from $2300 for the trip to Trinidad and Tobago to $4300 for the visit to Bhutan. The college also offers 3 exchange programs with Bosphorus University in Istanbul, Turkey; Kansai Gaidai University in Osaka, Japan; and John Cabot University in Rome. During the summer months, the Northwood Field Station, located in the Hiawatha Forest of Michigan's Upper Peninsula, lets students conduct field research and experience group living in a rugged environment. While biology majors use the station to study the natural habitat, religion students delve into the complexities of human beings and nature. A joint-degree program in engineering is available with Case Western Reserve and Washington universities. Internships and seminars in Washington, D.C. also are possible through the Washington Center.

Campus life: More than 90% of the students reside on the 110-acre rural campus. However, the lines between Hiram College and Hiram Village are blurred since most of the village's 1360 residents consist of faculty members and their families who live in Victorian or Greek Revival homes. Instead of sororities and fraternities, there are 4 coed social clubs that recently involved 30% of the students as members, though they have no separate housing and their parties generally are open to everyone. Few miss the annual toga party hosted by one of the clubs! One of the largest and most popular organizations is the Intercultural Forum that sponsors a widely anticipated dinner and talent show every year. On Campus Day, held once each semester, faculty and staff serve lunch to the students and then everyone participates in volunteer work on and off campus. About a third to half of the students leave campus over the weekend either to work or to go home for a day. Although crime is not considered a problem, as a precautionary measure, the college recently increased police patrols around campus and installed additional lighting and security telephones. .

The Hiram College Terriers usually draw a crowd to whatever sport is on the court or field. Says a senior: "Most people will attend the sporting events because they know somebody on the team and are there to support them." Football, volleyball, soccer, and basketball tend to draw the biggest crowds of the 9 men's and 9 women's intercollegiate sports that compete in NCAA Division III. About 10 intramural sports also are available to each sex; in recent years, at least 30% of the men and women have taken part. The men's and women's rugby clubs also have been popular.

For those with a car, Cleveland, 35 miles away, is the favorite getaway. Without a car, says a junior, "there is nowhere to go as Hiram is the college."

Cost cutters: One hundred percent of Hiram's students receive the basic financial assistance—the guarantee that tuition and fees will not increase during the student's 4 years on campus. In addition to that award, 91% of all undergraduates also received some form of additional financial aid in a recent school year, though no figures are available to show the percentage of first-year or continuing students who received aid. The average award exceeded $21,200 but again there is no breakdown to show the portion that was merit-scholarships or need-based grants or self-help aid such as loans and job earnings. More than 200 merit-based scholarships are available annually. The James A. Garfield and Vachel Lindsay scholarships in varying amounts reward students with GPAs of at least 3.5 and 3.0 to 3.5

respectively. The awards are renewable. The college also offers 2 institutional-loan programs, a non-federal work-study program, and several payment plan options.

Rate of return: Eighty-two percent of the freshmen return for the sophomore year. Sixty percent go on to graduate in 4 years, 66% in 5 years. The Tuition Guarantee that extends for 4 years provides additional incentive for students to earn their degrees in that period of time.

Payoff: English attracted the largest number of graduates in a recent class with 12% earning bachelor's degrees in the field. Next in popularity were biology at 10% and management at 9%. Thirty percent of Hiram graduates attend graduate school within 9 months of receiving their bachelor's degrees. Over 60% pursue further education within 5 years. The majority of graduates find positions in a wide array of employment in such fields as banking, business, coaching, and teaching, as well as with such organizations as Americorps and the Peace Corps.

Bottom line: Hiram offers a tranquil environment in which exciting opportunities for learning abound. Undergraduates interested in learning, rather than just taking courses to pick up degrees, as well as those comfortable without the constant stimulation of a big city, are the best matches for Hiram. "Passive sponges" interested only in absorbing and memorizing information should delete this college from their lists of prospects.

John Carroll University

University Heights, Ohio 44118

Setting: Suburban
Control: Private (Roman Catholic–Jesuit)
Undergraduate enrollment: 1564 men, 1836 women
Graduate enrollment: 800 men and women
Student/faculty ratio: 14:1
Freshman profile: Middle 50% SAT I verbal: 500–600; math: 500–610; Middle 50% ACT: 21–26. Class rank data: NA
Faculty profile: 94% Ph.D.'s
Tuition and fees: $23,630

Room and board: $7526
Freshman financial aid: 97%; average scholarship or grant: $4226 need-based; $3737 non-need-based
Campus jobs: 34%; average earnings: NA
Application deadline: Feb. 1
Financial aid deadline: Mar. 1
Admissions information: (216) 397-4294
  e-mail: admission@jcu.edu
  web site: www.explore.jcu.edu/

As a school where accounting has been among the best and most respected majors, John Carroll University in suburban Cleveland has its own numbers in good order. In a recent year, the Jesuit university ranked as the second least expensive of 21 private colleges enrolling 1000 or more students in Ohio. Yet it ranked first among 38 private colleges in the state for the percentage of its educational and general expenditures devoted to instruction—48%. Students from Ohio and 37 other states regard John Carroll as a small school with a big heart, not just for its own undergraduates but also for residents of the surrounding community, who benefit from the Jesuit emphasis on helping others. Says a senior: "I am proud to say that I go to JCU because of all the good it does within the community as well as abroad . . . I have become a much better person and student since beginning here 4 years ago." At John Carroll, people are never just numbers, and it is personalized education in a professional atmosphere that counts.

Student body: Two-thirds of John Carroll's undergraduate enrollment are from Ohio, with most of the rest from the Middle Atlantic region; altogether, students gather from 38 states. A slight majority, 53%, graduated from public schools. Seventy-three percent are Catholic. African-American students in a recent year made up the largest racial minority on campus at 5% of enrollment, followed by Asian-Americans at 3%, and Hispanics at 2%. Foreign nationals were present from 21 countries. Students describe themselves as generally upper middle class, conservative in attitudes and dress (the J. Crew look is big) and as career-oriented, but also caring and aware of the world around them. Most, says a senior, "value family, academics, church, sports, and friendships." A majority regard the university as academically competitive and maintain that everyone seems to learn much more than his or her grade point average reflects. Students who are openly competitive, however, are frowned upon by their peers.

Academics: John Carroll, founded in 1886 as St. Ignatius College and renamed in 1923 for the first archbishop of the Catholic Church in the United States, offers degrees through the master's. Undergraduate majors are offered in 34 disciplines through the College of Arts and Sciences and the Boler School of

Business. The school year is divided into 2 semesters. Average class size for undergraduates is between 20 and 25, not so large that someone can miss class without the teacher noticing. Courses with the smallest enrollments, from 10 to 15 students, include upper-level physics and foreign languages. An entry-level lecture in speech communication can enroll nearly 90 but breaks down into labs of no more than 25 students. A section of General Chemistry I may enroll 40.

The required core curriculum begins with classes in the Basic Core, consisting of coursework in a first-year seminar, English composition, speech communication, and a foreign language. Students also must take 3 courses each in the humanities, the sciences and mathematics, and philosophy; 2 each in the social sciences, religious studies, and international societies, plus 1 course that focuses on issues of diversity and an additional writing-intensive course.

The teaching staff includes 240 full-time faculty members. No figure is available to show the number of part-time faculty, although in a recent year the number was 167. The teaching staff also includes about a dozen Jesuits. Another dozen Jesuits serve as administrators. Fifty-nine percent of the teachers in a recent year were men. No figures are available to show the number that teach at the graduate level only. However, in a recent year when the faculty numbers were similar, all but 10 of the full-time members and all but about 50 of the part-time taught undergraduates. Graduate students recently taught 4% of the introductory courses. The faculty as a whole is regarded as very approachable, intelligent, and concerned about students' opinions on the subject matter being taught and on life in general. "They promote involvement and discussion, rather than just lecture," says a sociology major. Adds a religious studies major: "Most *do* care about the individual and will spend time 1-on-1 with students."

Accounting is regarded as one of John Carroll's most solid majors; its graduates place well in new jobs, and satisfied employers keep coming back for more recruits. In fact, the Boler School of Business as a whole offers an innovative curriculum with excellent opportunities to develop management leadership skills. The English, religious studies, and psychology faculties are excellent, admirers say; biology, chemistry, and physics carry reputations as especially tough disciplines. The new 265,000-square-foot Dolan Center for Science and Technology dedicated in September 2003 provides the most up-to-date facilities and equipment for use in these challenging programs. Communication is noted for both the high quality of its faculty inside the classroom and the extensive opportunities for field experience outside. However, the lower-division courses carry a stigma of being less challenging. Philosophy offers "an eclectic staff that offers a variety of courses (such as a phenomenal course on the philosophy of women) but holds firm ground on informing students about the philosophy of the ancients," says a senior. The mathematics major is especially demanding but rewarding to those who participate.

Students maintain that the offerings in the fine arts need a boost. While there is a major in art history, there is no major in music and limited classes in music, theater, and studio art, which some students miss. The fine arts and the social sciences, "do not receive as much respect, resources and funding as the true sciences do," notes a sociology major.

Facilities: Grasselli Library doubled its capacity in 1995 with the opening of the Breen Learning Center. "Now it is a very comfortable place to study," says a junior. "It's bright, quiet, and spacious." However, the satisfaction stops for her and for many others once the research process begins. Grasselli may have 616,000 volumes and 1975 periodicals, but students say that much of the information is "20 years behind the times," and what suitable materials it has often are so disorganized that it is hard for users to find what they need. Enter the OhioLINK computerized network for assistance. OhioLINK makes available to students an additional 25 million volumes, 3000+ full-text electronic journals, and use of more than 100 electronic databases from more than 75 academic libraries in the state. Most materials can be obtained within a 2-day delivery time. Those students who can't wait head directly to the public library in downtown Cleveland or to the libraries at Case Western Reserve or Cleveland State.

More than 1000 PCs are located in various buildings across campus. Most labs are open until midnight weekdays, a couple until 3 a.m., and until 5 or 6 p.m. on weekends. "Since when do college students finish a paper before midnight?" asks a sophomore. All residence-hall rooms are wired and students with personal computers may hook directly into the university system as well as the Internet. Wireless access is available around campus. While many students bring their own units to campus, a number who don't wish more general-use computers were available for longer hours.

Special programs: As part of a year-in-Japan program, undergraduates can study at Sophia University in Tokyo, at Kansai Gaidai University between Osaka and Kyoto, or at Nanzan University in Nagoya for the same tuition they pay at John Carroll, including equivalent financial aid. A limited number also may enroll at the Loyola Rome Center of Liberal Arts in Italy. Additional opportunities for study abroad are offered in China, El Salvador, Austria, Australia, Denmark, Germany, and England. Closer to home, a 5-year joint degree program in engineering is available with Case Western Reserve University in Cleveland, University of Detroit Mercy, and Washington University in St. Louis. Opportunities for cross-registration are available at 16 colleges and universities in the Cleveland area. A Washington, D.C. semester also can be arranged.

Campus life: John Carroll's 62-acre campus of predominantly Gothic architecture is surrounded by the shady residential areas of Shaker Heights, University Heights, and Cleveland Heights. Sixty percent of the undergraduates live on campus; and as the number of residents grows, events at the student union, such as comedians and movies, become more popular. A newer organization, the Mongols, works to promote school spirit, which some have found lagging, and sponsors at least 1 alcohol-free activity each week. Participation in Greek organizations is modest, with 13% of the men and 18% of the women in a recent year belonging to 4 national fraternities and 5 national sororities. "Sororities and fraternities are popular," says an easterner, "but by no means do other people feel excluded." In fact, most parties are open to anyone who wishes to attend. Social events teamed with service draw especially high participation, among them the annual dance marathon to benefit a children's hospital. Project Gold, a program to feed the poor, and the Hough Project, which helps to rebuild run-down local communities, draw large numbers of regular student volunteers. Occasional thefts are the most troublesome campus crimes; residence hall doors are kept locked around the clock as a deterrent, and only one entrance to campus is kept open and is patrolled at night to keep tabs on who enters and leaves.

Nearly half of the men and 40% of the women turn out for the 8 men's and 8 women's intramural sports. Blue Streaks football, basketball, women's volleyball, and swimming draw the biggest crowds of the 11 men's and 10 women's sports played in NCAA Division III. The men's basketball team placed third in the NCAA Division III national championships in 2004. The rugby, lacrosse, hockey, and ski clubs, 4 of 10 club sports offered, also attract good showings.

When events on campus pale, students often go to the Flats, an arcade of shops, restaurants, and bars well suited for people watching. Downtown Cleveland, just minutes away, offers a wide range of museums, concerts, and professional sporting events. Undergraduates also take road trips to visit friends at other area universities, among them Ohio State, Miami University, and the University of Michigan.

Cost cutters: Ninety-seven percent of the freshmen and 94% of continuing students received some kind of financial aid in a recent school year; for 76% of the freshmen and 79% of the remaining students, assistance was need-based. The average freshman award for a student with need included a need-based scholarship or grant averaging $4226 and need-based self-help aid such as loans and jobs averaging $4155. Other non-need-based awards and scholarships for first-year students averaged $3737. The average indebtedness of a recent graduate was $12,405. In a recent year, the university awarded to entering freshmen more than 200 partial scholarships based on merit alone or on financial need plus academic merit. Outstanding freshmen are eligible for the President's Honor Award that pays $1000 to $10,000; applicants must have maintained B+ averages and have high SAT or ACT scores. The American Values Scholarship, based primarily on academic merit and demonstrated leadership or volunteerism, pays between $1000 and $3000 to freshmen. The Mastin Scholarship in the Natural Sciences pays $10,000 a year to 3 freshmen planning to major in the natural sciences or mathematics. The university offers a cooperative education program in many majors.

Rate of return: Eighty-six percent of the freshmen return for the sophomore year. Seventy percent graduate in 4 years; 76% eventually graduate.

Payoff: Communications was the major of choice for 14% of recent graduates, followed by biology at 10% and marketing at 9%. A fifth of the new alumni went directly to professional or graduate schools. Those who take immediate employment work in fields ranging from sales and management to communications and teaching, mostly in Ohio, but also in Chicago, Pittsburgh, Buffalo, and Detroit. More than 160 companies and other organizations recruited on campus in a recent school year. Students say alumni are especially helpful in finding jobs for new graduates.

Bottom line: John Carroll may not offer 100 majors or a name recognizable in all 50 states. Undergraduates say, however, that what counts is the opportunities the university makes possible. As one undergraduate noted: "If you want to study abroad, John Carroll makes it possible. If you want to do an internship, you can. If you want to start a group, go ahead. It's a lot like the Master Card slogan—'Master the Possibilities.'"

Marietta College

Marietta, Ohio 45750

Setting: Small city
Control: Private
Undergraduate enrollment: 671 men and 679 women
Graduate enrollment: 46 men and women (part-time)
Student/faculty ratio: 12:1
Freshman profile: 5% scored over 700 on SAT I verbal; 21% scored 600–700; 44% 500–599; 30% below 500. 4% scored over 700 on SAT I math; 22% scored 600–700; 41% 500–599; 33% below 500. 6% scored above 28 on the ACT; 15% scored 27–28; 22% 24–26; 27% 21–23; 30% below 21. 20% graduated in top tenth of high school class; 41% in upper fifth.

Faculty profile: 92% Ph.D.'s
Tuition and fees: $22,879
Room and board: $6448
Freshman financial aid: 96%; average scholarship or grant: $6815 need-based; $6893 non-need-based
Campus jobs: 70%; average earnings: $2000/year
Application deadline: Apr. 15 (Mar. 1 for scholarships)
Financial aid deadline: Mar. 1
Admissions information: (740) 376-4600; (800) 331-7896
e-mail: admit@mcnet.marietta.edu
web site: www.marietta.edu

As the saying goes, leaders are made, not born, and a growing share of them are being made at Marietta College in southern Ohio. As part of the McDonough Leadership program, endowed in memory of Bernard McDonough, a local industrialist, students may take courses that analyze the components of leadership or meet in seminars with leaders of local, state, and sometimes national distinction. Students showing the most potential for leadership participate in internships with local and national corporations and institutions. Those who choose to involve themselves in all aspects of the program may graduate as McDonough Scholars. Others may take just a course or 2 or merely participate in the extracurricular programs offered. Whatever the level of involvement, the program already is distinguishing Marietta from other private, liberal arts colleges. Notes a recent participant: "Marietta's size and campus drew my attention, but neither would have been sufficient to get me here. The McDonough Leadership program is the real reason I came. Its new and experimental nature made me believe that it offered great opportunities for growth, and I was not disappointed."

Student body: Fifty percent of Marietta's undergraduates hail from Ohio. Most of the rest are from Pennsylvania and other Middle Atlantic and northeastern states, though students come from 43 states and 13 foreign countries. Eighty-nine percent graduated from public schools. Marietta's enrollment is predominantly white, with 7% African-Americans, 3% Asian-Americans, 2% Hispanic, and 1% Native Americans; 2% are foreign nationals. Students tend to be conservative (though there are strong pockets of liberalism), conformist, and generally motivated toward reaching postgraduate career goals. A majority are extroverted and quickly become involved in a wide range of campus activities. Politically, few are active although concerning issues close to home, says a senior, "students are quick to voice their displeasure with classes, scheduling, and faculty and to commend them when they are right." Academically, the student pool is varied. Says a sophomore: "There are lots of smart kids who didn't get A's in high school but like to learn. At the other end, there are the usual students who live for the weekends." However, even those who opt simply to "go with the flow" find that, at Marietta, keeping up with the "flow" requires some measure of conscientious studying.

Academics: Marietta, founded in 1835, grants the bachelor's degree in 39 disciplines and the master of arts in liberal learning, education, psychology, corporate media, and a physician assistant program. The school year is divided into 2 semesters. Undergraduate class sizes average 22, but even the largest courses, such as Human Anatomy, top out at 40. Upper-level courses aren't much smaller than the average: about 17 or so for, say, Contemporary Europe, History 349.

A new general education curriculum that was implemented in 2003 bears three components. The beginning First-Year Program requires entering students to take a First-Year Seminar and a College Life and Leadership Laboratory to facilitate the intellectual and social transition from high school to college. The core curriculum itself requires 12 courses of a student's choice from such fields as scientific inquiry (2 courses), social analysis (2 courses), and leadership and ethics (1 course). Within these courses, or elsewhere in the curriculum, students must take 2 classes that are writing-intensive. The requirements conclude with a capstone or culminating course in the student's major.

Ninety-one of the 140 faculty members are full-time. Forty-three percent are women. Faculty members encourage participation in class and often involve themselves in a wide range of outside activities that enable students to see them in a "different" light. Picnics at the home of a professor and leisurely conversations outside the classroom also are not uncommon. Notes a senior: "Any professor is willing to use his or her time to help a student, whether you are in their department or not."

One of Marietta's strongest majors is sports medicine, which attracts a large number of students. The program combines coursework in the sciences, applied nutrition, therapeutic rehabilitation, and pathophysiology with extensive clinical experience, much of it with Marietta sports teams. Participants in the program can be certified by the National Athletic Training Association or can continue their studies in physical therapy, a physician assistant program, or medical school. The sciences in general are a good bet, with faculties who are willing to spend time to explain tough concepts to students and a new science center with ample and well-equipped laboratory space. Undergraduate psychology students have the chance to intern and do research in the state's psychiatric hospitals; a child development learning laboratory was recently added. Another unlikely offering at Marietta, petroleum engineering, draws students from around the globe and provides top-of-the-line laboratories, plenty of real-world experience, and excellent contacts for future jobs. The department of economics, management, and accounting provides solid classes and excellent opportunities for internships with major companies; accounting majors have ranked first or second among students in Ohio in passing the C.P.A. exam. History, while small, offers dynamic professors. The education major also is considered excellent.

The foreign language program, with a major in Spanish only, a minor in French, and classes in Chinese, Japanese, and (Brazilian) Portuguese, lacks sufficient faculty and facilities, such as a language lab. Minors only are offered in philosophy and religion.

Facilities: Dawes Memorial Library has been Marietta's greatest shortcoming, and students have been eagerly awaiting its refurbishment to make it less cold and "stoic" feeling. Entering freshmen won't have long to wait: a new Learning and Library Resource Center is slated to open in fall 2008. In the meantime, the top floor of Dawes is for quiet study, the bottom, for group work. Although the size of the collection is decent, 249,000 volumes and 550 print periodicals (with another 3400 electronic), many students rely on interlibrary loan or various on-line resources. Students applaud Dawes' CD-ROM technology and full-text periodical database. The much used OhioLINK connects Marietta students with resources held at 79 college and university libraries throughout Ohio.

There are 120 PCs, 150 Macs, and 80 terminals spread among 10 academic labs. Labs generally are open until either 10 p.m. or midnight weeknights, longer during finals. The college strongly recommends that students have their own personal computers; residence halls have been wired to provide Internet connection to all student rooms. Many buildings also are wireless.

Special programs: Marietta students may study abroad at any of the college's 5 sister institutions in Thailand, Hong Kong, China, or Brazil, or in numerous other sites around the globe through programs sponsored by other college consortia and institutions. A Washington, D.C. semester can be experienced through American University and a summer in New York City through the Lincoln Center campus of Fordham University. Three-two programs are offered in engineering with Case Western Reserve, Ohio, and Columbia universities and the University of Pennsylvania.

Campus life: Ninety percent of the undergraduates live on the 120-acre campus, which many describe as very "New England" in its appearance. Housing options range from single-sex and coed residence halls to an honors theme house and a house for students with an interest in arts and humanities. In fall 2005, a newly renovated 100-year-old hall complete with stained glass windows and hardwood floors was opened as housing for 55 seniors. Twenty-two percent of the men and women belong to 4 national fraternities and 3 national sororities. Greek parties are open to the entire college and are generally quite popular. Crime is low and many students continue to leave their dorm-room doors unlocked, though several security measures have been instituted. Escorts are available to students who feel nervous about walking alone after dark and emergency phones have been installed around campus. To enter residence halls, students must swipe identification cards.

Sports are big at Marietta. At least a quarter of the students participate in 9 intercollegiate sports for men and 9 for women. Two-thirds of the men and nearly half the women turn out for the 7 intramural activities offered. Varsity crew and baseball, in particular, boast winning histories. The school has been NCAA Division III baseball champion 3 times and national runners-up 7 times in 18 World Series appearances and has won the Dad Vail Grand Nationals in crew 4 times.

Other than the sporting events, Greek functions, and various activities offered in the recently renovated student union, students say there is very little to do around the river city of Marietta (pop. 15,000). A small percentage head home on slow weekends. Parkersburg, right across the Ohio River in West Virginia, provides a nearby change of scenery. Others make trips to Columbus or Pittsburgh, neither more than 140 miles away, "to take in the big city atmosphere." Ohio University in Athens is another attraction.

Cost cutters: In the 2005–2006 school year, 96% of freshmen and 95% of continuing students received financial aid; for 77% of all undergraduates, the aid was need-based. The average freshman award consisted of need-based scholarships or grants averaging $6815 and need-based self-help aid such as loans and jobs averaging $5138. Other non-need-based awards and scholarships for first-year students averaged $6893. The average financial indebtedness of a 2005 graduate was about $17,000. Trustees' Scholarships pay $9000 to $13,000 a year to students with combined math and critical reading SATs of 1350 or a minimum ACT of 30 plus a GPA of 3.75 or higher. One Trustee Scholarship recipient also is awarded the McCoy Scholarship that pays for full tuition, fees, room and board, and a new computer. The scholarship is renewable over 4 years by maintaining a 3.25 grade point average. The President's Scholarship pays $6000 to $9000 annually to students with math and critical reading SATs of 1200 or a minimum ACT of 27 and a GPA of at least 3.5; the Dean's Scholarship, paying $4000 to $6000 annually is awarded for combined SATs of 1150 or an ACT of 25 or higher and a 3.25 GPA. Talent Scholarships in the fine arts are based on an on-campus competition and are valued from $500 to $3500 a year. The Academic Achievement Scholarship pays $5000 to first-year minority students and is renewable. An interest-free payment plan allows undergraduates to spread college costs over 10 months.

Rate of return: Eighty percent of freshmen return for the sophomore year. Sixty-five percent remain to graduate.

Payoff: Among 2005 graduates, 11% earned degrees in management, 9% in elementary education, and 8% in psychology. In the class of 2004, 70% of the class took jobs shortly after doffing their graduation robes, many with the 45+ companies that recruited. Twenty-five percent went on to graduate or professional schools.

Bottom line: Marietta is a college where the individual student is encouraged to be all that he or she can be, as one sophomore discovered shortly after enrolling. She notes: "I walked onto the crew team without ever having been in a boat. I had an office in a Greek house as a freshman. I can be an athlete and a student, a friend, a leader or a follower. I can be anything I want at Marietta, and because of Marietta I can be anything I want in the world."

Miami University
Oxford, Ohio 45056

Setting: Small town
Control: Public
Undergraduate enrollment: 6669 men, 7643 women
Graduate enrollment: 452 men, 590 women
Student/faculty ratio: 17:1
Freshman profile: 9% scored over 700 on SAT I verbal; 45% scored 600–700; 41% 500–599; 5% below 500. 14% scored over 700 on SAT I math; 56% scored 600–700; 27% 500–599; 3% below 500. 23% scored above 28 on the ACT; 23% scored 27–28; 38% 24–26; 14% 21–23; 2% below 21. 41% graduated in top tenth of high school class; 69% in upper fifth.

Faculty profile: 90% Ph.D.'s
Tuition and fees: $21,487
Room and board: $7610
Freshman financial aid: 82%; average scholarship or grant: NA
Campus jobs: 30%; average earnings: $1084/year
Application deadline: Early decision: Nov. 1; regular: Jan. 31
Financial aid deadline: Feb. 15
Admissions information: (513) 529-2531
  e-mail: millsme@muohio.edu
  web site: www.muohio.edu

The playing field supporting in-state and out-of-state students at Miami University just got a lot more level. Throughout the nation, thousands of dollars typically separate the rates that resident and nonresident students pay for state-supported colleges and universities. Miami University is an example of those public institutions whose appeal draws top-ranked students from far outside the borders of their states: just 72% of its undergraduate enrollment is from in-state, compared with over 90% at some institutions, and students attend from every state and from 48 foreign countries. Beginning with the freshmen who entered in fall 2004, Miami charges a single flat rate for all undergraduates, whether they live in Ohio or not. That rate for the 2005–2006 school year was $21,487. But state residents interested in what Miami has to offer have nothing to fear; there are 2 state scholarships designated especially for this situation. In the 2005–2006 school year, all Ohio residents received at least $10,902 a year in Ohio Resident and Ohio Leader scholarships, with a maximum combined total of $12,700 possible depending on the student's financial need. With such assistance, an Ohio resident paid no more than $10,585 in tuition and fees for the 2005–2006 school year. Whether the strategy catches on at other public institutions across the country remains to be seen, but Miami University has boldly taken the plunge into uncharted tuition waters.

Student body: While Miami has managed to achieve a measure of geographic variety, racial and ethnic diversity has been harder to acquire. White American undergraduates make up about 90% of the enrollment, with African-Americans accounting for 3%, Asian-Americans, also 3%, Hispanics, 2%, and Native Americans, less than 1%. Foreign nationals represent 1%. Continuing efforts by the Diversity Affairs Council, which represents all racial and ethnic groups in attendance, have made the campus environment more receptive to minorities. At present, the student body is for the most part conservative to middle of the road, largely Republican, and rather preppy in appearance. "Sometimes I think I'm walking in a J. Crew catalog," says an easterner. "There are exceptions, of course, but this look is the norm." Students caution, however, against letting the outward appearance tell the entire story. Says a junior: "Students must be ready to witness people who on the surface may seem quite 'superficial' but digging deep into their personal beings, they will find the individuals they want under the 'J. Crew' coating." An increasing share of undergraduates is concerned about doing well academically. A growing number, says a senior, "believe they will be the next great surgeon, novelist, CEO, or the President of the United States. They are ambitious and intent on making their mark in their 4 years at school."

Academics: Miami University, founded in 1809, offers degrees through the doctorate. The university is composed of the College of Arts and Science, the Richard T. Farmer School of Business and the schools of Education and Allied Professions, Fine Arts, Engineering and Applied Science, and Interdisciplinary Studies. Undergraduate majors are offered in nearly 100 fields. The academic year is divided into 2 semesters. Freshmen can expect classes that typically range from 20 to 100 participants, although 2 or 3 large lectures such as Survey of American History can enroll almost 370. First-year English classes generally have about 25 and are taught by graduate students. Junior and senior courses are more likely to have between 10 and 40, though there are always some classes with just a handful of students.

Liberal-education requirements known as the Miami Plan are divided into 2 parts, Foundation and Focus. The first section mandates 36 hours of Foundation courses in traditional fields that are meant to introduce college-level skills such as critical thinking and understanding contexts. The Focus requirement consists of 9 hours of in-depth study in a field outside the major plus a 3-hour capstone experience. While students applaud the idea behind the breadth of the program, some of the core classes are considered not very challenging and students with heavy course requirements in their majors have found it difficult to graduate in 4 years.

All of the 842 full-time and 356 part-time faculty members teach undergraduates and generally make an effort to know their students and to provide help where needed. Forty percent of the total pool are women. While research is instrumental, students find faculty dedicated primarily to teaching and, with the exception of the occasional indifferent professor, very willing to help undergraduates in any way that they can. In exchange, faculty have certain expectations of students: to attend classes, complete their assignments, and know the material. Advises a psychology major: "The key is to make the effort to meet the faculty on a personal basis. The education is more beneficial and the teaching is more effective. But it's up to the student to make the first step." In one program faculty members even take the first step, volunteering to pair up with a residence hall corridor and serve as a mentor to the students. Undergraduates' major complaint concerns the faculty's role as advisors. Notes a senior: "Many times faculty assigned as advisors have little knowledge of courses outside their own specialties." Graduate students teach a fifth of the introductory courses and students consider their performances "mixed."

Miami's strongest programs, those of the very liberal-arts-oriented School of Interdisciplinary Studies and the real-world Richard T. Farmer School of Business, represent both extremes of academia. In 1974, Western College, a 120-year-old private institution adjoining the Miami University campus, became Miami's School of Interdisciplinary Studies. The curriculum has revolved around core courses team-taught during the first 2 years by faculty from different academic perspectives. Juniors and seniors complete a program of advanced seminars, a senior project in a research workshop, and 32 semester-hours of advanced coursework from the broader university offerings. During the 2005–2006 school year, the university community was considering a proposal to transform the school into Western Honors College, which would serve as an umbrella organization encompassing all university honors programs as well as any self-designed interdisciplinary majors.

At the opposite extreme, students rave about the Farmer School of Business, especially an interdisciplinary advertising/marketing practicum, called Laws Hall, and Associates. The practicum, which involves the departments of marketing, communication, and art, gives students hands-on experience running their own advertising agency, which does work for Ohio businesses. PR Visions offers similar experience in public relations. As interest in the various business majors has increased, some students have found it increasingly difficult to get into overcrowded required classes. In the College of Arts and Science, the programs in psychology, political science, especially diplomacy and foreign affairs, history, communication, foreign languages, mathematics, and physics also win student approval, though political science and communication have been struggling to accommodate rising student demand for their courses. Within the sciences, chemistry, geology, botany, zoology, and microbiology are all very thorough and competitive with excellent opportunities for student research. The architecture program in the School of Fine Arts also is very intense with high expectations of its majors. The paper science and engineering program in the School of Engineering and Applied Science makes available first-rate technology in the field to undergraduates.

Comparative religion and philosophy in the College of Arts and Science have fewer course offerings than other more popular disciplines. The music, art, and theater programs in the School of Fine Arts could also use more faculty and courses to meet the needs of students who have an interest in these fields but are not majors.

Facilities: Miami University has 4 libraries: King, science, art and architecture, and music which together house nearly 2.4 million volumes, 3 million microform items, and 13,710 periodicals. King Library, the main facility, says a junior, "has a reputation as being a meeting and socializing point. Therefore, it does not always prove conducive to individual study." For research, it rates significantly better, with computerized aids known to track down any material at any of the Oxford campus libraries and at Miami's 2 other branch campuses as well as through OhioLINK to other institutions in-state. King also is open around the clock 5 days of the week, starting at 11 a.m. on Sunday and going until midnight Friday, with shorter hours on Saturday. For a quieter study environment, students head to the Brill Science Library.

The main Gaskill Learning Technologies Center is open like the library around the clock from noon Sunday through 10 p.m. on Friday. There also are 16 departmental and divisional labs with shorter hours; together the center and labs provide about 1000 computers. All dormitory rooms and offices are hardwired to the campus network and E-mail system. There also is wireless computer access in several locations across campus, including the libraries and various academic centers. The university strongly recommends that students have their own personal computers.

Special programs: Miami has its own campus in Luxembourg, open to all students in the sophomore year or beyond who have cumulative GPAs of 2.5 or higher. The university also has exchange agreements with Kansai University of Foreign Studies in Japan, the University of Glasgow in Scotland, and several other universities; students pay the same tuition, fees, room, and board as they do at Miami. A 3-2 program in engineering is offered with Case Western Reserve and Columbia University; in forestry, with Duke University. Cross-registration is available with Cincinnati-area colleges. On campus, an Emerging Leaders Program involves 100 first-year students in a semester-long program that introduces them to the complexities of leadership. Several other leadership programs also are open to new and continuing students.

Campus life: Less than half, 44%, of the undergraduates live on the 1179-acre campus, which doesn't include the university's 300-acre airport or 500-acre wildlife and game preserve. For many undergraduates, as this junior recalls, "Miami looks just the way I imagined a college should: ivy-lined, red brick buildings on a large, tree-shaded campus." Most students discover a lively albeit a bit isolated social life to match. ("We have cornfields surrounding our city on every side," explains a senior.) A fourth of the men and the women are members of 28 national fraternities and 22 national sororities; many Greek-sponsored events are open to all and are extremely popular. Most students also find niches and often excel in 1 or more of 350 organizations ranging from career-related clubs in, say, accountancy or zoology to music, writing, religious, and service groups. For example, Miami's speech team recently won its fourth consecutive Division I national championship at the National Forensics Association National Championship Tournament. "All students are very involved, and if you're not, people think you're weird," observes a senior. "Everyone here lives by the calendar." When the calendar permits, many students frequent the local "Uptown" bars (under-age students are allowed in) to socialize, hear local bands, dance—and drink if they're of age. Although crime has not been a problem, a bus system is available to transport students after dark and an emergency telephone system has been installed across campus. A student watch program helps patrol the campus throughout the night and I.D. scanners have replaced keys in all the residence halls. There also has been an emphasis recently on educating students about the potential for rape.

Miami fields 8 men's and 10 women's intercollegiate teams, which compete in NCAA Division I. Hockey is the big attraction, though basketball and increasingly football also draw crowds. More than 85% of the undergraduates are involved in 25 different intramural sports from power volleyball and inner-tube water polo to the more traditional softball, basketball, soccer, and football. Intramural broomball is especially popular to play and watch. Of the 40 sports clubs available, the equestrian team is ranked in the top 10 nationally.

While Oxford (pop. 8500, excluding students) is a picturesque college town, its small shops and hangouts can feel confining after a while. But it's not always easy to get away for those without cars. For those with wheels, Cincinnati, just 30 miles away, is a popular destination. Hueston Woods State Park, about 4 miles north of Oxford, offers a lodge, a nature center, cross-country ski trails, and a lake with marina and beach.

Cost cutters: In the 2005–2006 school year, 82% of the freshmen and 80% of the continuing students received financial aid; for 46% of the freshmen and 40% of the rest, the assistance was need-based. The average freshman package totaled $13,903, with no breakdown available on the portion in scholarships or grants, loans, or earnings from a work contract. The average financial indebtedness of a 2005 graduate was $21,522. Scholarships generally benefit entering freshmen who scored at least 30 on the ACT or 1320 on the SAT math and critical reading portions and ranked in the top 10% of their high school graduating class. Forty-five percent of recent fall freshmen received at least one scholarship; merit-based awards recently ranged in value from $500 to $22,000.

High-achieving students may be named Harrison Scholars, after Benjamin Harrison, the 23rd president of the United States, who was a Miami alumnus. Harrison Scholars receive awards covering either tuition and fees or tuition, fees, room, and board; each also works with a faculty mentor to design his or her own individual course of study. For these awards, students generally scored at least 32 on the ACT or 1470 on the SAT math and critical reading sections and also ranked in the top 5% of their high school graduating class. A cooperative education program is available in the School of Applied Science.

Rate of return: Ninety percent of the freshmen return for the sophomore year. Sixty-six percent graduate in 4 years; 78%, in 5 years; 80% in 6 years.

Payoff: For the 2005 graduating class, 2 of the 3 most popular majors were predominantly career related: marketing at 8%, finance at 7%, and psychology at 6%. About 340 companies and organizations, many in the fields of marketing, accounting, and retailing, recruited on campus in a recent school year. The Peace Corps also attracts many graduates: Miami was recently ranked 25th in the nation among 3600 colleges and universities in producing Peace Corps volunteers. More than a third of the degree recipients in a recent year headed to graduate or professional school.

Bottom line: When people look for a public university with the academic offerings and collegiate lifestyles of many of the more prestigious private institutions, a number think of the Oxford university located on this side of the Atlantic: Miami University in Oxford, Ohio. "Academically," says an international student, "Miami is right up there with the best yet is much more affordable."

Muskingum College
New Concord, Ohio 43762

Setting: Small town
Control: Private (Presbyterian)
Undergraduate enrollment: 803 men, 782 women
Graduate enrollment: 17 men, 44 women (449 part-time)
Student/faculty profile: 15:1
Freshman profile: 3% scored over 700 on SAT I verbal; 22% scored 600–700; 39% 500–599; 36% below 500. 4% scored over 700 on SAT I math; 18% scored 600–700; 41% 500–599; 37% below 500. 5% scored above 28 on the ACT; 5% scored 27–28; 18% 24–26; 26% 21–23; 40% below 21. 24% graduated in top tenth of high school class; 43% in upper fifth.

Faculty profile: 91% Ph.D.'s
Tuition and fees: $16,450
Room and board: $6520
Freshman financial aid: 98%; average scholarship or grant: NA
Campus jobs: 40%; average earnings: $1000/year
Application deadline: Aug. 15
Financial aid deadline: Mar. 15 preferred
Admissions information: (740) 826-8137; (800) 752-6082
  e-mail: adminfo@muskingum.edu
  web site: www.muskingum.edu

When dog bites man, it is rarely a story, no more so than when yet another college raises its annual tuition and fees, taking a hefty bite out of parents' and students' pocketbooks. However, when man bites dog, that makes the headlines fly, as they did in fall 1995 when Muskingum College in southeastern Ohio announced it was *reducing*, not raising, tuition by $4000 a year. The 29% drop from previous charges would begin with those lucky students entering in the fall of 1996. Nine years later, Muskingum's tuition and fees for the 2005–2006 school year rested at $16,450, more than $2000 lower than rates charged at 16 other Ohio private colleges, and 98% of its undergraduates were receiving financial aid. For parents and students who were convinced that tuition could go nowhere else but up, Muskingum's move was one "Man Bites Dog" story with a satisfying ending.

Student body: Only 13% of Muskingum's students come from outside Ohio's borders. The largest portion of those who do are from the Midwest, although undergraduates hail from 28 states and 15 foreign countries. Minority enrollment has been small but growing, with 4% African-Americans, 1% Asian-Americans, and 1% Hispanics. Less than 1% are Native American. Two percent are foreign nationals. The PLUS program for learning-disabled and disabled students also has helped to expand diversity. Ten percent of the undergraduates are members of the Presbyterian Church. Just 15% attended private or parochial schools. Students describe themselves as moderate to slightly conservative, although a touch of liberalism has begun to make some inroads. Friendliness is a hallmark on such a small campus, with the "Muskie Hi!" extended to all passersby the closest thing to an official college greeting. "Overall, the campus is an excellent mix of being laid back and just serious enough," says a junior; those students planning to attend graduate school add a bit more of a competitive edge to certain majors.

Academics: Muskingum, which was founded in 1837 and adopted an Indian name still misspelled and mispronounced almost 170 years later, offers the bachelor of arts and bachelor of science degrees in 42 majors. Thirty percent of the students carry more than one major. Masters of Arts in Education and in Teaching also are awarded. Students follow a 2-semester calendar filled with few large classes. The largest, Introduction to Art, enrolls about 50. More typical are first-year classes of 30–35 with a maximum of 25 in most upper-level courses.

Muskingum's general-education requirements are known as the LAEs, short for Liberal Arts Essentials. The core requirements, which fill 22–28 hours, demand specific classes in writing, speaking, mathematics, the arts and humanities of Western culture, religion and ethics, and wellness. The area requirements, comprising 26–30 hours, allow students to make choices among several courses that cover certain subject areas. Those areas are broadly defined as Scientific Understanding, with classes in biology, chemistry, geology, physics, and psychology, and Cultural Understanding, which has courses divided into 3 sub-categories pertaining to the Global Society, Western heritage, and the American experience. In addition, all seniors are expected to participate in some kind of capstone experience in their majors, usually either a seminar, individual study, or an advanced field experience.

On such a small campus, students come to know their professors well, and most like very much what they have come to know. Ninety-four of the college's 132 faculty members are full-time; 43% are women. Only 3 of the 38 part-time faculty teach solely at the graduate level. While a few members appear pompous "and forget what it is like to be a student," says a junior, the vast majority get an overall rating of "exceptional." Entering freshmen always are surprised to be handed their professors' home phone numbers with their only admonition being not to call after 11 p.m.

The sciences represent Muskingum's star disciplines, offering highly regarded majors in biology, molecular biology, chemistry, neuroscience, environmental science, conservation science, geology, and physics. Their impressive array of equipment ranges from proton nuclear magnetic resonance spectrometers to ultraviolet-visible light spectrophotometers. The professors are known for being demanding but excellent. "As a previous biology major," says a senior, "I find this department to be the most difficult on campus; it takes a lot of dedication." The social sciences don't lag far behind. Psychology in particular has its own outstanding equipment for both human and animal research as well as extensive opportunities for students to gain experience outside the classroom in substance abuse centers, hospitals, mental health clinics, and programs for people with mental retardation. Political science and history are both rich in personal attention from challenging professors. Education has drawn on a cadre of excellent professors, many of whom themselves were former classroom teachers, to offer a program demanding 300 hours of field and clinical experience.

The new Communication Arts Complex is giving long overdue support to the 3 disciplines, speech communication, theater, and journalism, that are housed within its 32,000 square feet. Although a major in sociology is offered, only a few anthropology courses are included. Four geography classes have been open to those interested in this field.

Facilities: Students frustrated by the lack of up-to-date resources contained in their library's 203,000 volumes have learned to depend on OPAL and OhioLINK, on-line services that provide access to the print collections of more than 70 libraries in-state. Users have fewer problems with Muskingum's 5655 paper and electronic periodicals. Says an international affairs major: "If you're doing a major research paper, like a thesis, your best deal is to go to the Ohio State library system." Muskingum's facility seats 310 and generally can be relied upon to provide a quiet atmosphere.

Six primary computing labs are open, many of them on the campus quad, with a smaller lab in each residence hall. Students also may access the Internet from their individual dorm rooms. While the residence hall labs are open around the clock, the labs on the quad typically close at 10:30 p.m. weeknights.

Students who need to work later may obtain special permission to stay after hours. Limited wireless capability also is available on campus.

Special programs: Opportunities for semester or year-long student exchanges exist with universities in Asia, Australia, Canada, Europe, Latin America, Puerto Rico, and the United States. A term in Washington, D.C. also is possible. Art majors can spend their junior year studying at one of the Art Institutes located in any of 8 different cities stretching from Seattle to Philadelphia. Three-2 and 3-3 cooperative programs in engineering and nursing, respectively, are offered with Case Western Reserve University in Cleveland.

Campus life: All students except seniors with special permission are required to live on the 215 acres of rolling land. After their first year, a number of undergraduates elect to live in program houses grouped according to varying student interests. Among the 14 apartment-style facilities available in a recent year were the English, French, German, and Spanish houses, the Track, Martial Arts, and Sinfonia houses, and the AGORA house, which attracts residents interested in leadership and community service. A footbridge crossing the small lake near the center of campus connects the academic area on one hill with 3 of the residence halls on the other. "The way it's set up," says a junior, "you can tell your kids and grandchildren that you had to walk uphill both ways!" Many say Greek life is basically THE weekend focus for that 25%–30% of the campus who are members of the college's 3 local and 2 national fraternities and 3 local and 2 national sororities. Though many independents join in the frequent fraternity functions, a growing roster of performances by comedians, dances, and other alternative activities have been gaining interest. Says a junior: "Students who are not Greek have more and more to do as time goes on." Few of the 90 clubs and organizations attract substantially more interest than others, though a number are quite active and contribute to a busy campus life. The biggest crimes are alcohol-related offenses, often between fraternities, described as "lame at best," says one campus resident. Residence halls are locked at midnight and someone staffs each hall for each hour that doors are open past noon. New lights and call boxes recently were installed around campus.

Fighting Muskies football, softball, and volleyball lead the way in student sporting events. Forty percent of the men and a fourth of the women took part in a recent year in the 9 men's and 8 women's events played in NCAA Division III. A fourth of the men and 30% of the women take part in the 10 intramural sports offered for each sex.

The village of New Concord is located 125 miles south of Cleveland and 80 miles east of Columbus, which are 2 of students' favorite travel destinations.

Cost cutters: All but 2% of the freshmen and continuing students received some kind of financial aid in the 2005–2006 school year. About 78% of both groups were on need-based assistance. The average financial aid package for freshmen included a need-based scholarship or grant averaging $11,276 and need-based self-help aid such as loans and job earnings averaging $4225. Average debt of a 2005 graduate totalled $17,300. Muskingum sponsors special Scholarship Days on 3 Saturdays in February when top-ranked high school seniors can compete for several lucrative scholarships. To qualify, students must have strong academic records as well as an ACT score of at least 23 or an SAT critical reading and math score of at least 1050 plus a GPA of 3.3 on a 4.0 scale. During the day, students take a written test with both short answers and essays and participate in an interview. Three general academic scholarships are available: John Glenn Scholarships, named for the distinguished astronaut/senator graduate in the Class of 1943, which pay full tuition; Presidential Scholarships, paying $8000 to $12,000 a year, and Faculty Scholarships, worth $5000 to $7500 annually. Science Division Scholarships range from $1000 to $2000 per year. Performance Scholarships in the fields of art, music, journalism (print and broadcast), forensics, and theater also are available. Awards in music pay $300 to $2000; those in the other areas pay up to $1500.

Rate of return: Seventy-six percent of all freshmen return for the sophomore year; 48% graduate in 4 years; 61% in 5 years, 62% in 6.

Payoff: Eighteen percent of the 2005 graduates earned a bachelor's degree in business; 13% specialized in early childhood education; 10% in biology. More than 90% of recent graduates immediately entered the workforce, many with the 25 companies and organizations that recruit on campus. Nearly a fifth pursued graduate study at least part-time within 6 months of Commencement. More than 40% pursue an advanced degree within 5 years of graduation.

Bottom line: Muskingum College is a small college in a small village where students are assured of knowing everyone on campus by the time they graduate. "It's an intimate campus that is truly one big family," says an Ohio resident. "It's perfect for someone leaving home for the first time."

The Ohio State University

Columbus, Ohio 43210

Setting: Urban
Control: Public
Undergraduate enrollment: 17,773 men, 16,044 women
Graduate enrollment: 3312 men, 3505 women
Student/faculty ratio: 13:1
Freshman profile: 8% scored over 700 on SAT I verbal; 39% scored 600–700; 43% 500–599; 10% below 500. 12% scored over 700 on SAT I math; 46% scored 600–700; 35% 500–599; 7% below 500. 23% scored above 28 on the ACT; 18% scored 27–28; 35% 24–26; 19% 21–23; 5% below 21. 39% graduated in top tenth of high school class; 66% in upper fifth.

Faculty profile: 99% Ph.D.'s
Tuition and fees: $8082 in-state; $19,305 out-of-state
Room and board: $7275
Freshman financial aid: 88%; average scholarship or grant: $3764 need-based; $8542 non-need-based
Campus jobs: NA; average earnings: NA
Application deadline: Feb. 1 (Scholarships: Dec. 15)
Financial aid deadline: Mar. 1
Admissions information: (614) 292-3980
  e-mail: askabuckeye@osu.edu
  web site: www.osu.edu

The Ohio State University may be best known as a member of the Big Ten in intercollegiate sports, but it belongs also to a more exclusive group: the Big Two. Ohio State has the second largest total enrollment of any college or university in the United States offering more than a 2-year program—about 2500 students fewer than the first-place school, the University of Texas at Austin. (The 2 campuses go back and forth in first and second place.) Altogether, Ohio State enrolls 47,235, including 3600 part-time undergraduates and 3000 part-time graduate students. Its curriculum includes more than 170 undergraduate majors and more than 200 graduate-level programs, for a grand total of over 10,500 courses. Stretching across 1755 acres of land, Ohio State runs its own traffic, parking, and free campus-bus systems, police service, hospital, long-distance telephone and electric-generating systems, and an airport. In spite of the university's size, Ohio State students, rather than being indifferent to one another, feel a close bond with fellow Buckeye football fans and with those who have waved the scarlet and gray before them, or will do so in the years to come. Notes a sophomore: "Ohio State has the strongest networking program in the country. Anywhere one goes, there is sure to be an OSU alumni association that can help in getting a job."

Student body: All but 13% of Ohio State's undergraduates are residents of the Buckeye State. However, the lure of being part of OSU's network and traditions attracts students from all 50 states, the District of Columbia, Puerto Rico and the Virgin Islands, and 81 foreign countries. Three percent of the students are foreign nationals; 8% are African-American and 5% are Asian-American, with 2% Hispanic, and 1% Native American. Eighty-seven percent are graduates of public schools. Although students tend to be conservative, with a certain sense of midwestern privacy about them, newcomers usually are delighted to find undergraduates so friendly on a campus this enormous. Students are proud of the differences in personality and style such vastness can encompass. Recalls a recent graduate: "Nothing shocks people because you see everything at Ohio State." By the same token, just about everyone is assured of finding someone with similar interests amid the throng. Says a graduate of a small Ohio high school: "I have enjoyed being able to find someone somewhere doing whatever I wanted to do, be that studying, seeing a movie, drinking, getting coffee, etc." Most also enjoy sharing in the university's sense of tradition and spirit and readily get involved in activities outside the classroom. Academically, the atmosphere depends pretty much on the individual program, with honors classes and many of the science-related majors quite competitive and others much more laid back.

Academics: OSU, which was founded in 1870, grants degrees through the doctorate with undergraduate programs spread among 12 schools and colleges. The colleges of Law and Veterinary Medicine have graduate-level programs only. The university follows the quarter system, which means that students must work diligently to keep up in their academics. Average class size in an introductory lecture is about 40, while some freshman lectures such as Biology 101 recently enrolled in excess of 600 students. However, most of the large lectures of over 100 notetakers are broken into discussion groups of 20–40 students, each of which meets 2–3 times a week with a teaching assistant. Eighty-six percent of the freshman-level classes actually have fewer than 50 students; only 6% have more than 100. At the upper level, opportunities exist for research sections with just a handful of participants, although many classes for juniors and seniors still enroll between 10 and 80.

Almost 75% of the students admitted to Ohio State enroll in a major or pre-major program in a particular school or college. The remaining students take part in exploration programs where they can access their talents and discover different areas of interest before selecting a major. Regardless of interest, all students must complete a General Education Curriculum that consists of credit hours from 8 academic areas: writing and related skills, quantitative and logical skills, foreign language and culture/international experience, social diversity in the U.S, natural sciences, social sciences, arts and humanities, and the capstone experience.

The huge faculty includes 2782 full-time and 1023 part-time academics. No figures are available to show the number who teach at the graduate level only. Thirty-four percent are women; 2 members are Nobel Laureates. Thirty-nine percent of the introductory classes, generally the smaller recitations, are taught at least in part by graduate students. While undergraduates say many professors at the upper levels are surprisingly accessible to students who make the effort to approach them, the large-lecture format in the early years keeps many freshmen and sophomores from ever trying. Observes a recent graduate: "In introductory classes, the faculty who do teach leave much to be desired because they usually lecture *at* their students. However, most upper-division classes have professors who are articulate, interested in their subjects, and able to spark interest in their students." In some fields, problems arise when foreign faculty members and teaching assistants have difficulty communicating in English; other full professors are more engaged in their research than in their teaching.

Ohio State's strongest programs are the result of excellent faculties, state-of-the-art equipment, strong state support, and an emphasis on teamwork in student projects. Programs meeting these standards are commonly found in the School of Allied Medical Professions; the College of the Arts School of Music; the College of Mathematical and Physical Sciences; and the colleges of Food, Agricultural, and Environmental Sciences; Business; Education; Engineering; Nursing; and Pharmacy. Special gems offered by these and other divisions, according to students, include the programs in Japanese, classics, geodetic science (surveying and mapping), accounting, marketing, transportation and logistics, physics, animal science, welding engineering, music, dance, women's studies, international studies, and physical and occupational therapy.

The strong programs promise to become even stronger under a selective investment program that since 1997 has identified the university's strongest programs and provided resources to move those programs to the tops of their fields. Recent recipients of such funding include the programs in chemistry, history, neuroscience, political science, electrical engineering, psychology, physics, materials science and engineering, English, economics, and mathematics.

Students' chief complaint focuses on the shaky start some students get in the large-class environment. Notes a biology major: "I think a general need is for smaller classes and more personalized instruction and material. This is my second year and I still feel like I'm just learning the broad basics."

Facilities: The Ohio State library system holds more than 5.8 million volumes, 5.7 million microform items, and about 35,500 periodicals spread over the 11-story main Thompson Library located on the campus oval and 19 other facilities across campus. Though newcomers sometimes find the system confusing at first, all of the libraries, plus those at OSU's branch campuses as well as the state government library and more than 80 other Ohio college libraries, are linked by computer and are accessible by using any terminal on campus. Librarians are willing to have a book delivered to a student's dorm room if it can't be picked up. However, undergraduates complain that they may locate the right book or magazine only to find the appropriate pages ripped out! For studying, most students have preferred the smaller libraries to the large, intimidating central structure but that could change in the future. The main William Oxley Thompson Library is being renovated and returned to its original 1913 architectural splendor with 21st Century digital resources and services added. The library is scheduled to close in the late summer of 2006 and reopen by autumn quarter 2009.

About 4000 Internet-connected computers are located at sites across campus, including in the libraries, laboratories, residence halls, and student centers with the main computer center open 24 hours a day. Students with their own laptops also may connect to the wireless system at gathering places all over campus. For these and other reasons, the university strongly recommends that students have their own personal computers. All students in the Department of Industrial, Interior and Visual Communication Design within the College of the Arts are required to have their own units.

Special programs: More than 80 international exchange and study-abroad programs place students in universities around the globe. Cross-registration is available locally with all central Ohio colleges. Study and research opportunities in aquatic biology are available at Stone Laboratory along Lake Erie. The University Honors and Scholars Center offers high-achieving students smaller classes, special housing options, and extracurricular activities, as well as individualized faculty mentoring.

Campus life: A quarter of Ohio State's undergraduates reside on the grounds of the sprawling campus located just 2 miles north of downtown Columbus. Another 70% live in Greek housing and off-campus apartments located within walking distance of the university, thereby enhancing the feeling that OSU is its own small city. Though just 6% of the men and women belong to 2 local and 35 national fraternities and 2 local and 17 national sororities, that's still more than 2000 Greeks! Greeks and independents alike usually begin the weekend on High Street, at the popular strip of nightclubs with enclosed patios big enough to accommodate hundreds of people. With about 700 student clubs available, just about everybody has his or her own favorite, and the rest find kindred spirits and start another. One of the most successful is the 225-member Ohio State University Marching Band, better known among Buckeyes as "The Best Damn Band in the Land." One of the few college all-brass and percussion bands in the country, its performances are steeped in well-loved traditions, among them the moment when the sousaphone player dots the "i" of the Ohio that has been written in script. Because OSU is located in an urban area, the university police, a community crime patrol for the surrounding neighborhood where students reside, and a crimewatch escort service, run by the undergraduate student government, keep regular watch over the OSU community. The university also has emergency telephones located throughout campus and in the nearby off-campus area that directly connect to the university's own 911 service.

Nobody needs to be told that Ohio State football is big, with its back-to-back Fiesta Bowl wins in 2002 and 2003 and the indoor football facility honoring long-time winning coach Woody Hayes. Crowds of more than 100,000 people turn out for home games, and thousands of them take an active part in the pregame and postgame celebrating that occurs. Men's and women's basketball are played in the new 19,500-seat Jerome Schottenstein Center and maintain strong followings among the 16 men's, 17 women's, and 3 coed sports played in NCAA Division I. In 1999 the men's baskeball team made its first appearance in the NCAA Final Four since 1968 and tied the team's record for wins at 27. The intramural offerings are especially staggering, with 48 sports for men and 47 for women, involving 65% of the men and 35% of the women plus 70 club sports.

Most students' idea of a getaway is leaving campus and exploring what Columbus, Ohio's state capital and largest city, has to offer. By the opposite token, finding a quiet place away from the hordes in a nearby park or along a jogging or bike trail is sometimes the best escape.

Cost cutters: Eighty-eight percent of the freshmen and 78% of the continuing students in the 2005–2006 school year received some form of financial aid; aid was need-based for about half of all undergraduates. The average freshman award for a student with financial need included a need-based scholarship or grant averaging $3764 and need-based self-help aid such as loans and jobs averaging $3571. Non-need-based athletic scholarships for freshmen averaged $15,352. Other non-need-based scholarships and awards for first-year students averaged $8542. Average debt among all members of the Class of 2005 was $17,821. The Presidential, Medalist, and Tradition scholarships are all highly competitive awards for top students. The 3 scholarships pay respectively in-state tuition, room and board, a book allowance, plus miscellaneous expenses; full in-state tuition and half in-state tuition. A scholarship dormitory enables students to work several hours weekly to save 20% in housing costs. Cooperative education programs are offered in the colleges of Business, Engineering, Arts and Sciences, and Agriculture.

Rate of return: Almost 90% of freshmen return for the sophomore year. Though just 35% graduate in 4 years, 63% finish in 5 years and 68% in 6 years.

Payoff: The 3 most popular areas of study for the 2005 graduating class were psychology at 6% and communication and English at 4% each. Within 6 months of graduation, 83% of Ohio State alumni traditionally are employed and 10% have enrolled in graduate or professional school. But wherever a new degree-holder ends up, there usually is a loyal OSU alumnus around to help. Throughout the country by last count, more than 5400 veterinarians, about 10,900 physicians, approximately 33,400 engineers, and over 4600 architects are Ohio State alumni.

Bottom line: For the student who likes variety in people, courses, and extracurricular programs and much-beloved traditions, it's hard to beat what's available at OSU. "You can make a big university small but you can't make a small university big," exclaims a senior. "Ohio State, though large in size, feels like a small school when you are on campus. Larger just means that there are more people to meet and more opportunities available to you as a student."

Oklahoma

The University of Tulsa

Tulsa, Oklahoma 74104

Setting: Urban
Control: Private (Presbyterian)
Undergraduate enrollment: 1338 men, 1297 women
Graduate enrollment: 533 men, 343 women
Student/faculty ratio: 10:1
Freshman profile: 28% scored over 700 on SAT I verbal; 32% scored 600–700; 30% 500–599; 10% below 500. 26% scored over 700 on SAT I math; 34% scored 600–700; 30% 500–599; 10% below 500. 36% scored above 28 on the ACT; 14% scored 27–28; 24% 24–26; 18% 21–23; 6% below 21. 62% graduated in top tenth of high school class; 75% in upper fifth.

Faculty profile: 96% Ph.D.'s
Tuition and fees: $18,860
Room and board: $6488
Freshman financial aid: 94%; average scholarship or grant: $4123 need-based; $11,292 non-need-based
Campus jobs: 23%; average earnings: $3500/year
Application deadline: Rolling
Financial aid deadline: Apr. 1 (priority date)
Admissions information: (918) 631–2307;
  (800) 331–3050
  e-mail: admission@utulsa.edu
  web site: www.utulsa.edu

It was the School of Petroleum Engineering that first brought the University of Tulsa international acclaim more than a half century ago, and it's oil money that keeps the university one of the best financial deals around. Sizable donations from three big energy-industry families in the 1960's laid the groundwork for an endowment of $769.5 million as of mid-2005. That hefty foundation enables Tulsa to charge its students just half the actual cost of their college education; most private colleges charge students two-thirds to three-fourths of costs. And the news gets even better. Since 1994, the university has pledged to increase tuition for enrolled students only the amount of the consumer price index plus 2% maximum. If TU is not the university that "black gold" built, it's close to it.

Student body: Fifty-nine percent of Tulsa's undergraduates are from the Sooner State; Though about 70% of the rest are from the Southwest, seekers of the oil rush at TU, as it is called, come from 43 states and 49 foreign countries. Seventy-two percent attended public schools. One in every 10 members of a recent entering class was a National Merit finalist. Just 4% are Presbyterian; 42% claim no religious affiliation. Thirty-eight percent are members of other Protestant denominations. Foreign nationals, many of them attracted to TU's excellent program in applied mathematics, make up 8% of the enrollment; African-American students constitute 7%, Native Americans 5%, Hispanics 3%, and Asian-Americans 2%. For the most part, students of color have become an active part of the university community, joining integrated Greek organizations as well as ones that are historically black and serving as officers of the student government. Most of TU's undergraduates are politically and socially conservative, and rarely activist. Notes a senior: "People care about their grades and their friends but are really apathetic about politics and events outside their own personal circle." More involved students wish larger numbers of their classmates would get engaged in campus activities. Openly friendly, a majority still keep a firm focus on the solid career goals they have set for themselves. At TU it's not uncommon for Greek organizations, not always noted elsewhere for their academic rigor, to post cumulative GPAs of 3.0 on a 4.0 scale.

Academics: The University of Tulsa, founded in 1894 as a Presbyterian university and now run by an independent board, offers degrees through the doctorate. It has a graduate school and a law school plus 3 colleges: Arts and Sciences, Business Administration, and Engineering and Natural Sciences, which together offer 58 undergraduate majors. The academic year is divided into 2 semesters. Average class size is 20 throughout all 4 years, with the largest course, Biology of Populations, enrolling over 90. However, upper-level courses in religion, sociology, and art may have only 5 students apiece.

All undergraduates must take the university's highly touted Tulsa Curriculum, which includes both a core and general-education requirements. As part of the core, a student must take 3 writing courses and take or place out of at least 1 class in mathematics. Students in the Henry Kendall College of Arts and Sciences must complete or show proficiency in 2 years of a foreign language; students of business administration must do so for 1 year. For the general-education requirement, students take 8 courses from 4 blocks of knowledge: artistic imagination, social inquiry, cultural interpretation, and scientific investigation. Students in the College of Engineering and Natural Sciences typically are exempted from taking general education classes in scientific investigation.

TU's faculty totals 427 members, 308 full-time, 119 part-time. All but 37 members of the full-time faculty teach at the undergraduate level. (The 37 teach at the law school.) Thirty-nine of the part-time members also are exclusively law-school faculty. A third of the faculty are women. Though TU has its mumblers and professors who have trouble getting their points across, most faculty members rate such adjectives as *intelligent, down-to-earth,* and *attentive* in terms of both subject matter and students. Undergraduates especially enjoy the multicultural visiting professors who add different perspectives to the campus.

The College of Engineering and Natural Sciences offers Tulsa's strongest programs. Chemical and mechanical engineering boast a winning combination of state-of-the-art equipment and dedicated students teamed in a close working relationship with top-notch professors. Students in Tulsa's mainstay, petroleum engineering, benefit enormously from many active university/industry cooperative research programs. In the natural sciences, the Melvin Bovaird Center for Molecular Biology and Biotechnology enables undergraduates to participate in basic studies of recombinant DNA, immunology, and cellular communication. Career-oriented programs in speech-language pathology and in deaf education in the Henry Kendall College of Arts and Sciences, and nursing in the College of Business Administration also are well-respected programs, as are most other majors in the business college, marketing and accounting in particular. Team teaching and a progressive curriculum focusing on active learning, team work, and leadership skills, keep the business programs timely and in touch. In the College of Arts and Sciences, English and psychology earn especially high grades.

Communication is regarded by some as an "easy" major. History, political science, and religion feature excellent teachers but tend to attract less competitive students and to suffer from lack of attention beyond that given to the general-education block courses. The theater program also is small. Education programs lose some of the best teachers and students of the subject to Northeastern State University.

Facilities: Tulsa's 3 libraries, the main McFarlin Library, the technical library, and the law library, contain just over 1 million volumes, 3.3 million microform items, and 27,604 paper and electronic periodicals. Students generally like McFarlin, which they consider a bright, pleasant, and quiet place to study with at least 6 of the 9 floors offering rooms reserved for private use. Tulsa's on-line catalog is user-friendly and simplifies book and periodical searches. Students also can access a broad array of national databases, including that of the 250-member Research Libraries Group, Inc., as well as the Internet.

The university's 2 main computer labs plus a lab often set aside for academic instruction are located in McFarlin Library. The 2 main labs, with PCs, are open around-the- weekday-clock, closing at 6 p.m. on Friday, reopening at noon on Saturday, closing again at 8 p.m. and reopening Sunday at 1 p.m. to resume the nonstop weekday schedule. Additional labs are available in nearly every other building on campus, including residence halls. Wireless access is available throughout most areas of the library, in most academic buildings and residence halls, and in most other areas where students congregate such as Sharp Chapel and the fitness centers.

Special programs: Foreign study has not attracted large numbers of students from Tulsa, although opportunities to take part in more than 40 programs are there. In recent years, between 12 and 15 students a semester have studied abroad, largely through TU's own programs in Canada, England, France, Germany, Argentina, Switzerland, Russia, and Spain. In addition, TU's College of Business Administration offers a 4-week summer program in international business. Students meet with European business leaders and visit international banks and financial exchanges in cities like London, Geneva, and Frankfurt and, on occasion, in Russia and in Scandinavian countries. More students take advantage of the wide range of excellent internship opportunities offered right in Tulsa. A Washington, D.C. semester also is available. A 5-year B.A.-M.B.A. program is another option. Students in the College of Arts and Sciences can complete requirements for both a bachelor's degree and a law degree in 6 years instead of the traditional 7. The Tulsa Undergraduate Research Challenge enables undergraduates of all class levels from all 3 colleges to participate in advanced research and coursework.

Campus life: Sixty-four percent of TU's undergraduates live on the 209-acre campus located less than 2 miles from downtown Tulsa. A fifth of the men and nearly a fourth of the women belong to 16 national Greek organizations, 7 for men, 9 for women. Although their numbers are comparatively small, the fraternities provide much of the organized social activity on the weekend, with many of their parties open to independents. Hurricane-Hut, the campus bar, also is a popular hangout and offers frequent entertainment such as comedians. Because TU is "not located in the best part of town," as students put it, security is vigilant, especially at night. Emergency phones around campus and an escort service are available whenever needed. Electronic door locks on all residence halls open only with student identification. Students also stay well informed of any problems that do arise through a regular section in the campus newspaper.

Students say school spirit has started to pick up in recent years, especially as the Golden Hurricane football team has been winning more games. The team appeared in the Jan. 3, 2004, Humanitarian Bowl.

Basketball remains the biggest draw of the 8 intercollegiate sports for men and 10 for women played in NCAA Division I. Most Tulsa students would generally rather play than watch; 70% of the men and women are involved in 25 intramural sports for each sex.

Students describe Tulsa, a city whose metropolitan area numbers 840,000, as "big enough to provide quality entertainment and small enough to still breathe quality air." With downtown Tulsa so close, students like to dance at after-hours clubs, go to the river parks on sunny afternoons, attend performances of the city's own ballet and opera companies, or maybe just drive around and admire the homes of the very rich. Students in search of something bigger make the 5-hour drive to Dallas or Kansas City.

Cost cutters: Ninety-four percent of the 2005–2006 freshmen but just 79% of the continuing students received financial aid; 36% of the freshmen and 41% of the remaining students were given need-based assistance. The average freshman award for a student with need included a need-based scholarship or grant averaging $4123 and need-based self-help aid such as loans and jobs averaging $5922. The average non-need-based athletic scholarship for first-year students averaged $16,224; other non-need-based awards and scholarships averaged $11,292. A 2005 graduate left with debts of $23,824. Merit-based University Scholarships range up to $6000 a year, Honors Program Scholarships pay $1000 annually. The prestigious Presidential Scholarship pays as much as $6000 annually to first-year students who ranked in the top 10% of their high school class and who scored at least 33 on the ACT or 1450 on the math and critical reading portions of the SAT. Departmental and performance (music, art, theater, and musical theater) awards cover up to full tuition; athletic awards, up to full costs.

Rate of return: Eighty-four percent of entering freshmen return for the sophomore year. Forty-three percent go on to graduate in 4 years, 59% within 5 years, 60% within 6.

Payoff: Management and petroleum engineering were the most popular majors among 2005 Tulsa grads, each attracting 7% of the class, followed by mechanical engineering at 5%. Almost a third of the graduates went on to professional or graduate schools immediately. Students taking jobs soon after commencement generally accept positions in public relations, engineering, business, and accounting with such corporations as IBM, Procter & Gamble, American Airlines, and the major accounting firms. Companies in the energy industry also are major employers of TU grads. About 140 companies and organizations recruited on campus in the 2004–2005 school year. Large concentrations of graduates end up relocating to such metropolitan areas as Dallas, Houston, Kansas City, and St. Louis.

Bottom line: The University of Tulsa is an aggressive, small, private university that always has refused to behave like a sleepy, local institution. Notes an out-of-stater: "TU is a small university that offers the advantages of a large one: excellent resources, good social life, and Division I sports. It's a place where I can make a difference."

Linfield College

McMinnville, Oregon 97128

Setting: Small town
Control: Private (American Baptist)
Undergraduate enrollment: 773 men, 935 women
Graduate enrollment: None
Student/faculty ratio: 14:1
Freshman profile: 5% scored over 700 on SAT I verbal; 31% scored 600–700; 46% 500–599; 18% below 500; 7% scored over 700 on SAT I math; 37% scored 600–700; 40% 500–599; 16% below 500. 15% scored above 28 on the ACT; 13% scored 27–28; 23% 24–26; 38% 21–23; 11% below 21. 35% graduated in top tenth of high school class; 59% in upper fifth.
Faculty profile: 92% Ph.D.'s

Tuition and fees: $23,022
Room and board: $6610
Freshman financial aid: 90%; average scholarship or grant: $6801 need-based
Campus jobs: 80%; average earnings: $1010/year
Application deadline: Early action: Nov. 15; regular: Feb. 15
Financial aid deadline: Feb. 1
Admissions information: (503) 883-2213; (800) 640-2287
e-mail: admission@linfield.edu
web site: www.linfield.edu

When students pay tuition to Linfield College in the northwest Oregon community of McMinnville, they're getting more for their money than challenging classes, highly accessible professors, and weekly workouts in the athletic center. Roundtrip air fare for a semester or January term of international experience is built into the supersaver tuition rate, which cruised in the 2005–2006 school year at just over $23,000. As a result, a semester abroad in any of 15+ locations from Nottingham to Seoul, or San Ramon, Costa Rica, costs approximately what a semester in McMinnville would. Costs of the overseas January programs vary according to the location and the class format. It's just another way Linfield tries to encourage as many of its students as possible to gain a world view from this tiny community of 25,000. And the encouragement seems to be working. More than half of Linfield's undergraduates study abroad for at least 1 month before they graduate, creating a culturally rich segment in an otherwise rather homogeneous student body.

Student body: Fifty-seven percent of Linfield students are from Oregon, with most of the rest also from the Pacific Northwest. However, undergraduates come from 26 states and 19 foreign countries. Eighty-five percent attended public schools. Asian-Americans constitute the largest minority group on campus, at 6%, with Hispanics and African-Americans, and Native Americans at about 1%. each. Foreign nationals constitute 4%. One percent of the undergraduates are Baptist; members of other Protestant denominations account for 37% of the total, with Catholics constituting 11%. Undergraduates are generally conservative, although less so each year, members say, as newly offered merit scholarships have widened the base of high school graduates who apply. Other adjectives classmates use to describe their peers are *down-to-earth, morally strong, accepting* of diverse opinions and life-styles, *goal-oriented,* and *involved.* Says a senior: "It is not uncommon for a student to be an academic, an athlete, a leader of an organization, and a participant in a service project. Undergraduates do not limit themselves to 1 specific area; they involve themselves with many." The range of academic abilities is wide as well, says a senior. "The academic atmosphere could be described as a bell curve with 'slacker' and 'Rhodes scholar finalist' at opposite extremes. But the slackers usually phase out or get their act together by the third year."

Academics: Linfield, founded in 1858, offers bachelor's degrees in 39 majors. Students take courses divided into 2 semesters, with a January term in the middle. Throughout all 4 years, most classes range from 20 to 30 members, although a course such as Principles of Biology can enroll almost 100. But, adds a psychology major, "It's not uncommon to be in a class of 10, and I've been in 2 intimate classes consisting of 5 students each!" Business classes tend to be more crowded.

Linfield's core curriculum works to strengthen students' reading and writing skills as they explore courses in a wide range of fields. The program consists of an inquiry seminar that all first- or second-year students must take; 2 courses each from 5 areas of inquiry, ranging from The Vital Past to Images and Arts; a 2-part diversity requirement, and a writing-intensive course beyond the inquiry seminar.

One hundred seven of Linfield's 164 faculty members are full-time; 41% are women. Students sum up their professors in two words: the best. Observes a junior: "There are both easy and hard professors at Linfield. Therefore, students can find an easy path here, but if a student chooses the harder way, that student will be challenged by dynamic professors in more ways than he or she can imagine, professors that teach you how to think, comprehend, and analyze. You can't beat that!"

Among Linfield's strongest disciplines, the economics and business departments feature superb faculties and curricula that are very responsive to changes in the business world. All of the sciences are also strong with excellent faculties and facilities. The sociology/anthropology, political science, religious studies, and history departments get high marks for their stimulating, caring professors. The sociology-anthropology department is a winner, says a major, because the professors "encourage you to think critically and question the structures of society." The psychology major, too, has supportive professors and a strong curriculum, with a new animal laboratory to match. Athletic training majors receive exceptional classroom instruction as well as hands-on training with intercollegiate and intramural athletes. The theater arts program's new facilities in the recently opened James F. Miller Fine Arts Center now match the quality of its productions, which have long won rave reviews. Two recent plays were chosen for performance in a regional competition and a musical was named one of the best 14 productions in a recent season at a national judging in Washington, D.C. One particular math professor dazzles students with his ability to adapt his teaching to different learning styles, making all students feel successful. "Students take a class from him whether it's required for their major or not," says a senior.

Computer science has a limited faculty of just 3 professors. Communication arts could use more than its current 3 professors to handle the increasing number of students who choose this field as a major. Students say the program also lacks sufficient equipment and adequate support for such projects as the yearbook and campus radio station. The excellent foreign language faculty could use more resources to support more classes. Majors are offered in French, German, Spanish, and Japanese.

Facilities: "Our new library is amazing," observes a business major, which sums up the feelings of many students about the newly opened structure. Nicholson Library is more than twice the size of the old facility and provides comfortable study spaces for up to 500 students. It also houses 72 computer workstations, compared to just 15 before, and a full range of electronic resources. Current holdings stand at nearly 174,000 volumes and 1275 periodicals, but there's promise of growth since Nicholson has room for 251,000 volumes. Linfield students also have electronic access to the holdings of both Oregon State University and the University of Oregon, as well as of 20 other colleges.

Eight public PC labs and 10 departmental ones provide 228 computers for student use. At least 2 of the labs are open around the clock. Approximately 45% of the computers are Macintosh and the other 55% are Windows-based. All 19 residence halls also have small labs. "No lines, ever," says a history major. All residences have high-speed Internet access, and wireless network access is available in many classrooms and public areas.

Special programs: Every fall and spring semester, the college sends groups of up to 15 students to each of Linfield's 15 study-abroad centers in 11 countries throughout Europe, Asia, and Latin America. Undergraduates wishing to stay closer to home can cross-register for classes at any of 5 other area institutions, including Reed College and Willamette. January-term courses are offered in a number of locations from Hawaii to Malaysia, depending on the particular courses being given that year. A 3-2 program in engineering is offered with Oregon and Washington State universities and with the University of Southern California.

Campus life: Three-fourths of the undergraduates reside on the 193-acre campus. (A 1998 purchase and donation of land and buildings from the Hewlett-Packard Company more than doubled the original size of the campus. Included in that package was the building transformed into the new campus library.) The campus, says a westerner, "has a 'back East' type setting, brick buildings, oak trees, numerous lawns, pathways." Weekends at Linfield revolve around 3 hubs: school-sponsored events such as dances and movies, Greek activities, and sports. Just over a fourth of the men and 30% of the women are members of 1 local and 3 national fraternities and 1 local and 3 national sororities. Their parties are popular but "not necessary to obtain a social life," says a senior. Most are open to independents by invitation only, although such invitations usually flow fairly freely. Students from both groups tend to congregate at the Catalyst, the campus deli, or turn out for campus-sponsored entertainment on Friday nights. Linfield's affiliation with the American Baptist Church is reflected primarily in a very active and diverse Campus Ministry program that involves students in such community service projects as Habitat for Humanity. Fellowship of Christian Athletes also draws large numbers to its weekly meetings. No chapel attendance is required. One of the most popular of the 60 clubs available is the Hawaiian Club with its annual luau at the end of school. The Oregon Nobel Laureate Symposium held on campus every year attracts distinguished speakers such as former President Jimmy Carter and Oscar Arias, former president of Costa Rica and winner of the Nobel Peace Prize. Crime is not a topic of concern, and usually is limited to the occasional theft of laptops or bikes or CDs from student cars. Safety precautions taken include the installation of external call boxes on each residence hall and dead bolts on the doors, additional lighting throughout campus, an escort program, and the hiring of the college's own security and safety director to coordinate security measures.

Sports are big at Linfield, both to play and to watch. In a recent year, nearly 20% of the men and 12% of the women took part in the 9 men's and 10 women's teams that compete in NCAA Division III. Football is the main attraction, (fans often line the end zone with couches for close-up comfort), though basketball, soccer, and volleyball are well attended, too. Eighty percent of the men and 60% of the women participate in the intramural program, 7 sports for each sex.

Most favorite escapes are fairly nearby: the beautiful Oregon coast, an hour west; the city of Portland (pop. 491,000), an hour north; and the mountains, where good skiing can be had, between 1 ¼ and 2 hours to the east. Salem, the state capital, is just a half hour away. Pack an umbrella, though: the Willamette Valley, where Linfield is located, receives an average rainfall of 42 inches a year.

Cost cutters: Ninety percent of freshmen and 89% of continuing students received some form of financial aid in the 2005–2006 school year. Sixty-five percent of the freshmen and 67% of the remaining undergraduates were given need-based assistance. The average freshman award included a need-based scholarship or grant averaging $7730 and need-based self-help aid such as loans and jobs averaging $5944. The average financial indebtedness of a 2005 graduate was $24,594. A wide range of academic merit scholarships are awarded. The Trustee Scholarship paid $10,300 to $14,400 in a recent school year to entering freshmen with a 3.75 GPA; the Faculty Scholarship paid $5500 to $11,000 to students with a slightly lower GPA of 3.40. Various academic departments sponsor scholarship competitions with prizes of $4000 a year for first place, $3200 for second, and $2500 for third. Leadership Scholarships pay up to $3000.

Rate of return: Eighty-two percent of the freshmen return for the sophomore year. Fifty-nine percent graduate in 4 years; 67% in 5 years; 68% in 6 years.

Payoff: Elementary education was the major of choice for 11% of the 2005 graduates, followed by business and psychology at 6% each. The vast majority of Linfield grads enter the workforce soon after earning their diplomas, mainly in accounting, teaching, and business, predominantly in the West and Northwest. Sixty percent take employment with small business firms, though major employers have included Nike, NCR, Apple, the IRS, Techtronics, Honeywell, and General Dynamics. Twenty-two percent of the recent grads went directly to graduate or professional schools. Within 5 years of graduation about 40% of alumni are engaged in higher education.

Bottom line: A satisfied senior may have offered the best summary of what is possible at a small college in a small Oregon community: "From my major in psychology, I've been able to work at a mental hospital and do an internship at the district attorney's office. As an art minor, I've traveled with Linfield's study-abroad program to the Louvre in Paris and created pottery in Mexico over January term. Linfield is right for anyone who wants an excellent, well-rounded education as well as small classes, participation in athletics and the creative arts, and friendly people."

Pacific University

Forest Grove, Oregon 97116

Setting: Small town
Control: Private (Congregational)
Undergraduate enrollment: 1232 men and women
Graduate enrollment: 1250 men and women
Student/faculty ratio: 13:1
Freshman profile: Average combined SAT I verbal and math score: 1130; average ACT composite: 25. Class rank data: NA.
Faculty profile: 78% Ph.D.'s
Tuition and fees: $21,490

Room and board: $6052
Freshman financial aid: 92%; average scholarship or grant: $10,225
Campus jobs: NA; average earnings: NA
Application deadline: Feb. 15
Financial aid deadline: Apr. 1
Admissions information: (503) 352-2218; (800) 677-6712
e-mail: admissions@pacificu.edu
web site: www.pacificu.edu

At first blush, the name Pacific University in the town of Forest Grove sounds like an idyllic campus created by a television writer. But in reality, few campuses are more in touch with what today's students need to advance in the new century. Although best known throughout the Pacific Northwest for its graduate-level professional programs in health sciences and education, for undergraduates, it's the university's solid liberal arts core and close-knit environment of just 1232 that makes learning here so attractive. Says a biology major:

"I expected the school to provide interactive classes in a personal professor-to-student atmosphere. My expectations have been surpassed by the quality of attention I get in my classes." A "theory to practice" approach to learning nudges students out of the classroom into diverse opportunities for research, internships, study abroad, and community service. Continues the biology major: "Pacific will do what is necessary to make a student's education extraordinary." No TV scriptwriter could express it any better than that.

Student body: Half of Pacific's students in a recent year were from Oregon, with 40% of the out-of-staters also from the West. Undergraduates came, however, from 31 states and 7 foreign countries. In a recent year, 17% were Asian-American, 2% each foreign national and Hispanic, and 1% each African-American and Native American. Ninety-one percent attended public schools. Pacific students see themselves as more liberal and politically aware than their peers on other campuses. Many come from small or even rural towns and suburbs in Oregon, Washington, Alaska, and Hawaii and are often the first generation in their families to attend college. "The small numbers allow students to get to know each other well, without hanging out in little cliques," says a sophomore. Academically, life can get intense as students spend a significant amount of time studying, although classmates generally enjoy working together, which brings students closer together and keeps the competition healthy.

Academics: The heart of Pacific University, which was founded by Congregational pioneers in 1849, is the College of Arts and Sciences, which awards bachelor of arts and bachelor of science degrees in 52 majors plus a bachelor of music degree. Surrounding the college are 6 graduate-level professional schools, 5 in the health professions that students consider a major addition to their liberal arts university: the College of Optometry and the schools of Professional Psychology, Physician Assistant Studies, Physical Therapy, and Occupational Therapy plus the College of Education. The university follows the semester calendar with a Winter III term during the month of January, allowing additional opportunities for internships and travel abroad. General Chemistry enrolls the largest number of students at nearly 70, but most classes top out at less than 25. Upper-level language classes may have just a half dozen.

Pacific's core curriculum begins with the First Year Seminar Program where students are introduced to the standards of the College of Arts and Sciences through study of the college's intellectual heritage. During fall term, groups of 20 freshmen each have a class from a senior faculty member with a student mentor who helps guide students through the study of such classic texts as the Bible and Plato's *Republic*. The entire class participates in a program of co-curricular events that, through a series of performances, films, and lectures, relates the content of the class to contemporary events. The remainder of the core curriculum includes a sophomore composition course, foreign language, crosscultural studies, mathematics, and classes in the natural sciences, humanities, social sciences, and the arts. The core covers approximately one-third of a student's coursework for graduation.

Pacific's full-time faculty is split nearly evenly between those members who teach undergraduates in the College of Arts and Sciences and those who teach in the professional schools at the graduate level only. In a recent year, 87 of the 163 full-time faculty members taught undergraduates as did 34 of the 108 part-timers. Forty-eight percent of the faculty were women. No introductory courses are taught by graduate students. Because Pacific has such a clean split between the undergraduate and graduate-level faculties, students know that their professors are there for them and for no one else. Notes a sophomore: "When I think of the faculty, I am reassured that I made the right decision to come here. Professors are extremely well educated and are available, helpful, funny, and inspiring." Most also are flexible in their approach to teaching and learning and eagerly work to accommodate students' interests. One creative writing major was able to write a screenplay dealing with psychological issues in place of a final exam in an introductory psychology course. Says a junior: "The professors here have a great respect for their students, so I want to succeed not only for myself but also for my professors. They are aware of each of their students' potential and know when they are not meeting that."

The sciences are perhaps the most demanding, most competitive programs on campus and enroll many hard-working undergraduates who hope to be admitted to Pacific's graduate professional programs. "I personally have very close relationships with many of the professors," notes a biology major. "The classes are intimate and challenging." The Strain Science Center, which opened in 1993, provides first-rate facilities to match the quality faculty.

Within the humanities division, the foreign language and English departments are considered standouts as well. The language-learning center was recently remodeled to include interactive videodisc workstations, as well as state-of-the-art audio and video production capability that makes it possible for students to convert and view European videos. A modern language student may concentrate in Chinese, French, German, Japanese, or Spanish as a primary language and as part of the program must complete 12 semester hours overseas. The English faculty includes a variety of "passionate" scholars and courses well respected by students. Says a senior: "The faculty are very open and encourage free thinking. They also take a lot of time to read and consider papers." That environment, says a literature major, "gives students confidence." Business students also praise the willingness of their faculty "to go above and beyond their responsibilities," says a major. Exercise science, physics, and math get an enthusiastic "thumbs up" as well.

Students have found the psychology department to be young but very promising, with a high-energy faculty. However, turnover among faculty members has been high, which has limited the effectiveness of the program and increased the need for more permanent faculty to satisfy student demand. The media arts department could use more faculty and more space. The art program could use better facilities, especially for photography. Students say the music and theater departments offer great programs and faculty but need to expand to become more effective.

Facilities: A new library opened for the 2005–2006 school year with just about every amenity a student could need or want. The 49,000-square-foot structure includes a large reading room with a fireplace, individual study carrels, group study rooms, a coffee bar in the lobby, wired and wireless technology, a self-checkout system, and perhaps most useful to procrastinators, a 24-hour study center. The only thing not new is the collection of about 152,000 volumes and 945 periodicals, which is significantly helped by the extensive computerized resources available.

The library's first floor Information Commons has 24 computers for student use; a classroom set aside for library instruction has another 23 units that can be used if there is no class. A lab located in the lower level of Marsh Hall, where several administrative offices are located, is open around the clock. Every residence-hall room has been networked allowing access to the Internet.

Special programs: Along with extensive student exchange programs in Japan and China, Pacific sends undergraduates to Latin America and Europe to study foreign languages and cultures. Political science students may study and intern in Washington, D.C. Students may cross-register for courses at other Oregon independent colleges and at Oregon Graduate Institute of Science and Technology. The graduate institute also offers a 3-2 engineering degree with Pacific, as does Washington University in St. Louis. A full-time, 1-semester internship is available in all undergraduate programs. The Pacific Humanitarian Center also places students in public service jobs for academic credit. A minor in Peace and Conflict Studies, involving faculty members from 7 departments, explores alternatives to violent resolution of conflicts.

Campus life: For most students, enjoyment of the Pacific life is a mixture of on-campus sporting events and parties with excursions to the Portland clubs or out to the coast or nearby mountains. Fifty percent of Pacific's undergraduates live on the 55-acre campus located in Forest Grove (pop. 13,500); and all but a small percent spend most of their weekends on campus. Just 2% of the men and 6% of the women recently belonged to 3 local fraternities and 3 local sororities. Only 1 fraternity has a house and "you don't have to be a member to be 'somebody,'" says a sophomore. Special-interest clubs, such as the Hawaiian Club, Habitat for Humanity, and Students for Environmental Awareness, attract many members. The university also maintains its own coffee house, The Milky Way, for refreshment and entertainment.

Although Pacific maintains an informal affiliation with the United Church of Christ (Congregational), chapel is not even offered. Campus crime has not been a serious issue on the well-lit, well-patrolled campus; however, the university locks all residence halls around the clock instead of just at night as a deterrent to strangers entering.

The school provides 8 intercollegiate sports each for men and women, played under NCAA Division III. Boxer basketball and men's and women's soccer are the biggest draws though the golf and wrestling teams are nationally ranked. Pacific is 1 of 5 U.S. colleges to field a recognized varsity women's wrestling team. Football was recently dropped as a varsity sport and many students miss its presence. To compensate, energetic members of a soccer fan club dress up and bring noisemakers to soccer and basketball games to help raise school spirit. Altogether, about half of Pacific's undergraduates participate in varsity, club, or the 10 men's and women's intramural sports. The handball club is especially popular and nationally recognized. A group called the Pacific Outback organizes events such as hiking, kayaking, rafting, and mountain climbing in the area, with prime targets the Cascade Mountains to the east and the forested Coast Range to the west. A large new addition to the Pacific Athletic Center offers students aerobic and weight training equipment to help get them in shape for such outings.

The city of Portland, 25 miles east, is the principal off-campus getaway. Year-round skiing at Mt. Hood is just a 90-minute drive east, with the Oregon coast about an hour west.

Cost cutters: Ninety-two percent of the freshmen and 97% of continuing students received financial assistance in a recent school year. Eighty-two percent of the freshmen and 70% of the rest received need-based aid. The average freshman award consisted of $10,225 in a scholarship or need-based grant, and $4674 in self-help aid. The average financial indebtedness of recent graduates was $18,500.

Students automatically are considered for various merit scholarships when they apply. They range from the University Award, which pays $6500 to entering freshmen who averaged a 3.19 GPA and a 21 ACT, up to the Honors Award, which pays $9000 a year to the top students who averaged a 3.85 GPA and a 28 ACT. The Presidential Award pays $8000; the Trustee, $7500. A monthly payment plan allows students, at a cost of $55 a semester, to pay semester fees in 4 installments on the 15th of every month.

Rate of return: Seventy-eight percent of freshmen return for the sophomore year. Forty-four percent go on to graduate in 4 years, 57% within 5 years, 63% within 6.

Payoff: In a recent school year, foreign languages and English claimed the largest portion of bachelor's degrees at 11% each, followed by business and biology at 10.5% each and physical education teaching and coaching at 9%. An annual jobs fair sponsored by the Oregon Liberal Arts Placement Consortium puts students in contact with employers for summer jobs and internships, as well as for full-time work upon graduation. The university has had particular success placing graduates with majors in computer science, accounting, and international studies, as well as finding jobs for prospective teachers. Because of Pacific's cluster of graduate programs in the health professions, a disproportionately large percentage of students pursue degrees in physical therapy, optometry, occupational therapy, physician assistant studies, and professional psychology. A third of recent graduates have pursued some kind of advanced study within 6 months of commencement, about half in the arts and sciences.

Bottom line: Notes a senior from outside the Northwest: "Pacific blends challenging academics with a family-like atmosphere. The professors' passion for teaching is obvious and makes the total experience terrific. A high school student who is not as confident as he or she might be will gain a lot from the Pacific experience."

University of Oregon

Eugene, Oregon 97403

Setting: Small city
Control: Public
Undergraduate enrollment: 14,326 men and women
Graduate enrollment: 6013 men and women
Student/faculty ratio: 16:1
Freshman profile: SAT/ACT scores: NA. Class rank data: NA
Faculty profile: 95% Ph.D.'s
Tuition and fees: $5655 in-state; $18,015 out-of-state
Room and board: $6922

Freshman financial aid: 40%; average scholarship or grant: NA
Campus jobs: NA; average earnings: NA
Application deadline: Jan. 15
Financial aid deadline: Mar. 1
Admissions information: (541) 346-3201; (800) 232-3825 in-state
e-mail: uoadmit@oregon.uoregon.edu
web site: www.uoregon.edu

It's the biggest university in the state, with a student body of politically active and socially aware high achievers who nevertheless show few outward signs of competitiveness, and who subscribe to an "anything goes" philosophy. Sound something like the University of California at Berkeley? Try 8000 undergraduates fewer and 500 miles further north. The University of Oregon in Eugene has been compared with Berkeley, though its national prestige and range of course offerings are considerably lower. But there is more than a touch of Berkeley's liberalism in the air over Eugene. "I am Greek," observes a midwesterner, "but even the Greek system, typically the vanguard of conservatism, is liberal here." For students looking for a diverse, physically active student body with a wide range of academic and professional programs to match, Oregon may be the silver lining in the often cloudy Pacific Northwest.

Student body: Seventy-seven percent of Oregon's undergraduates in a recent year were from in-state, with most of the nonresidents also from the West. Students attend from all 50 states and 86 foreign countries. All but 9% are graduates of public schools. Foreign nationals in a recent year accounted for 6% of total enrollment, with Asian-Americans forming the largest domestic minority group at 6% as well. Hispanics followed at 3%, African-Americans at 2%, and Native Americans at 1%. Though their numbers are small, students say the minority groups have strong organizations on campus and, in tune with the generally activist nature of the university, often make their concerns vocally known. Notes a journalism major: "Most people like to get involved and make a difference." The fact that people dress and act casually, students say, makes Oregon very "nonthreatening," despite its comparatively large undergraduate population and the lack of individual attention. Though recent increases in the academic standards required for admission have made academics more of a concern ("Most serious students are incredibly intelligent," says a state resident), they have not stifled the general *joie de vivre*. Notes a senior: "There is a celebration for some culture, state of being, or awareness every week. Concern for the quality of life rates very highly."

Academics: The university, founded in 1876, awards degrees through the doctorate. Oregon's undergraduate programs with 78 majors are offered in the College of Arts and Sciences and 6 professional schools and colleges. The university also has a graduate school and a school of law. The academic calendar is divided into quarters, of which students normally take 3 in an academic year. An Evolving Earth geology course may enroll 400 underclassmen; however, most classes in the early years range from 50 to 200 with required discussion sections limited to 25 students. In some upper-level major courses there may be only 1 person, although a junior or senior is more likely to share a class with 25–60 other students. One third of all first-year students are enrolled during fall term in Freshman Interest Groups (FIGs), which originated at Oregon and have been duplicated at other large institutions. Each FIG consists of 25 students who take thematically linked courses as well as a faculty-led seminar that offers mentoring and further exploration of the course material. First-year students can continue the FIG experience through 5 Pathways that begin winter term. Pathways are designed to enrich students' general education through integration of courses that satisfy university requirements. Faculty members create a small college experience for Pathway students by collaborating and offering small seminars in which ideas are examined from the perspectives of several disciplines.

Every undergraduate, regardless of which college or professional school he or she plans to enter, must take courses in the 3 broad areas of the College of Arts and Sciences: arts and letters, social sciences, and science. Also required are 2 courses in written English and 1 course in 2 of the following categories: American Cultures; Identity, Pluralism, and Tolerance; and International Cultures.

Oregon's teaching faculty recently consisted of 798 full-time and 338 part-time members. Forty-one percent were women. One faculty member has won a Pulitzer Prize. Like the students, most professors are liberal in their viewpoints and diverse in their styles. "They reach all extremes," observes a business major, "from the great ones who challenge you and make school fun, to the tenured monotone who hasn't changed the syllabus in years." One sophomore tells the story of a professor who made her 9 a.m. grammar class so much fun that almost 130 students opted to attend every session rather than take the option of learning the material on-line. "To me," says that sophomore, "the strength of the faculty lies in their ability to make students want to go to class and learn." In some disciplines, especially the sciences, professors are criticized for devoting more of their time and interest to research and publication than to teaching. The graduate teaching fellows who recently numbered close to 1340, teach 14% of the introductory courses, mainly introductory math and first- and second-year language classes. While many are friendly and helpful, some are disgruntled by their pay or are difficult to understand because English is not their native language, which poses more of a problem in math and other courses than in foreign language instruction.

Architecture, journalism, and music all feature varied curricula and demand top-quality work from their students. Psychology, which enjoys world-renowned professors, also attracts large numbers of interested students who bring energy to their programs. Business, with its own share of blue-chip professors, has an excellent, recently constructed building. A new science complex that houses millions of dollars in new equipment has made these disciplines top-of-the-line as well; molecular biology is especially strong. Biology majors also can use a cadaver lab. Among the liberal arts, English, economics, and geography are winners.

State budget cuts have taken their toll, however, on several programs. The program in education was eliminated a few years ago but has been revived with majors in such areas as educational studies, family and human services, and communication disorders and sciences, and an excellent minor in special education. Some students maintain that the sociology and political science majors in the College of Arts and Sciences are too easy, with limited course requirements, large class sizes, and a poor student-to-faculty ratio.

Facilities: The University of Oregon library system is composed of Knight Library, which is the main facility, and a law library plus branches in science, mathematics, art and architecture, and maps and aerial photography. The combined collection, the largest in the state, totals 2.5 million volumes, 2.9 million microform items, and 17,840 periodicals. Janus, the on-line catalog, provides computer access to all items added to the collection since 1975, as well as to the complete holdings of the architecture, mathematics, and law libraries. Orbis, the newest addition to Janus, provides access to the holdings of other schools in the Oregon University System as well as to private institutions in the state. Selected databases also are available on CD-ROM. Recent expansion of Knight Library almost doubled its original size. As a study center, a junior observes, "the library actually is very quiet, considering 16,000 people use it."

Seven public labs, 5 instructional labs, usually free for use when classes aren't in session, and 9 departmental labs restricted to students in those disciplines provide about 500 Windows-based and

Macintosh computers for undergraduates around campus. At least one lab is open until 2 a.m. on week-nights. The university strongly recommends that students have personal computers; architecture majors are required to purchase their own. Many of the buildings on campus are completely wireless while a majority of the others have most of their high-traffic areas covered.

Special programs: A wide range of study-abroad programs in more than 70 countries are available. In addition, students can spend up to a year at any of about 80 campuses around the United States, including Hawaii and the U.S. territories. An engineering/physics option is offered with Oregon State.

Campus life: Just under a fifth of the undergraduates live on the 280-acre main campus. For those who choose to do so, a wide range of special-interest residence halls are available to suit nearly every possible life-style, from halls for those interested in outdoor pursuits or music to a quiet hall, where serious-minded students set their own no-noise hours. Participants in the Freshman Interest Groups also may live together in 1 of 10 residential areas as a way to build stronger relationships and promote after-hours discussions. A "Faculty in Residence" program in the halls also brings together faculty and students outside of the traditional classroom setting. Although Greek life with 13 national fraternities and 8 national sororities is highly visible over the weekends, its membership claims less than 10% of the student body. "The Greeks at Oregon are different," says a member. "Some students who would not be Greek at Cal or USC are Greek here." Other popular student groups include the Green Garter and Oregon Marching bands, as well as OSPIRG, the Oregon State Public Interest Research Group, which lobbies for environmental concerns. Bike theft on this campus of outdoor enthusiasts is the most common crime, "a HUGE problem," according to 1 junior. Adds a senior: "Nice bikes are taken every day." More lights and call boxes on walkways have been added in recent years. Project Saferide provides transportation for women to discourage them from walking alone after dark. Project Safe-Run recently rented dogs to accompany women joggers.

Men's basketball and football especially since the Duck's Rose Bowl appearance a decade ago are the most popular of the 8 men's PAC-10 sports provided. Says a sophomore: "I can hear the crowd scream during home football games from my residence hall, and the stadium's a mile away!" Volleyball draws the best crowds of the 9 varsity sports for women. Intramurals are big with 19 sports for men and 17 for women, and many also take part in the 27 club sports that provide an alternative form of intercollegiate competition. For students seeking a more adventurous group experience, the university's popular outdoor program offers skiing, backpacking, bicycle touring, and white-water sports. However, most undergraduates prefer to head off on their own to the nearest bike path or running trail readily accessible to the campus. Says a senior: "A weekend can be anything from dinner and a movie to rock climbing, wind-surfing, surfing, skiing, kayaking, and pretty much every other extreme sport one could handle."

Eugene (pop. 125,000) is a "true college town," as a Californian put it, devoted to its university and especially noted for its outdoor activities. In fact, the entire town is accessible by bicycle. When a head-clearing run or bike ride doesn't provide sufficient escape from academic life, Portland, the state's largest city, is just a 2-hour drive north. The Oregon coast and the Cascade Mountains offer different sorts of weekend getaways.

Cost cutters: Forty percent of both freshmen and continuing students received financial help in a recent school year. For about 35% of both groups, the aid was need-based. The average freshman award totaled $7118, with no breakdown provided for the portion that was scholarships or grants or need-based self-help aid such as loans and jobs. A typical recent graduate left with debts of $17,111. Oregon high school students can compete for Presidential Scholarships paying about $6000 a year. Diversity-Building Scholarships pay from partial to full tuition, plus fee waivers. Dean's Scholarships recognize motivated students who have high school GPAs of 3.60 or above. Awards range from $500 to $5000. General University Scholarships, which are one-year awards, pay $1000 to $2700.

Rate of return: Eighty-two percent of the entering freshmen return the following year. Thirty-seven percent graduate in 4 years; 56%, in 5 years; 61% in 6.

Payoff: Business administration, architecture and arts, and journalism/communications each accounted for 10% of a recent graduating class. A fifth of the graduates continued their education. One hundred eighty companies and organizations recruited on campus in a recent school year.

Bottom line: Oregon supporters like to think of their campus as "clean, beautiful, wet, and green." And while the general atmosphere may be laid back, those who get the most out of this university are as activist and vocal in the classroom as they are out of it. Advises a senior: "This university can be challenging, and those who pick up the gauntlet reap the rewards."

University of Portland

Portland, Oregon 97203

Setting: Suburban
Control: Private (Roman Catholic)
Undergraduate enrollment: 1076 men, 1756 women
Graduate enrollment: 50 men, 90 women
Student/faculty ratio: 13:1
Freshman profile: 10% scored over 700 on SAT I verbal; 36% scored 600–700; 44% 500–599; 10% below 500. 8% scored over 700 on SAT I math; 41% scored 600–700; 43% 500–599; 8% below 500. 44% graduated in top tenth of high school class; 74% in upper fifth.
Faculty profile: 86% Ph.D.'s

Tuition and fees: $24, 900
Room and board: $7400
Freshman financial aid: 93%; average scholarship: $13,807 need-based
Campus jobs: 55%; average earnings: $2100/year
Application deadline: Feb. 1
Financial aid deadline: Mar. 1
Admissions information: (503) 943-7147; (888) 627-5601
e-mail: admissio@up.edu
web site: www.up.edu

High on a bluff near the confluence of the Willamette and Columbia rivers in scenic Portland, Oregon, sits the campus of the University of Portland. In a city of just under a half-million people known for its sweeping views of Mt. Rainier, Mt. St. Helens, and Mt. Hood, the university, despite its lofty location, is not among the better-known academic peaks. Among private colleges, highly competitive Reed College and the more traditional liberal arts establishment, Lewis and Clark, are preeminent Portland institutions. Among Catholic colleges affiliated with the educationally focused Holy Cross priests and brothers, the prestigious University of Notre Dame in Indiana comes to mind first. But for students seeking a more reasonably priced, small but comprehensive, Catholic institution, the University of Portland outshines its better-known local rivals by thousands of dollars. All of its faculty members, 86% of whom have doctorates, teach undergraduates. Though its undergraduate enrollment numbers only 2832, it offers majors in 60 fields. Its varsity teams, the Pilots, play as part of NCAA West Coast Conference Division I, and students boast that their extensive sports facilities are the best by far in the conference. Beyond mere boasts, the women's soccer team *is* the best, having won the NCAA Division I National Championship in 2005 and 2002. Thanks to a well-organized volunteer-services program, helping the needy has reached the top of more students' extracurricular lists. In short, the name University of Portland may seem like plain vanilla in a world of exotic academic flavors, but what students get hits the spot.

Student body: Just 46% of the university's students are from Oregon; half of the rest are also from the Northwest, with a total of 44 states and 37 foreign countries represented. Foreign nationals account for 1% of the enrollment. Asian-Americans at 9% are the single largest ethnic minority group. Hispanic students represent 3% of the total, with African-Americans at 2%, and 1% Native American. Fifty-one percent of the students are Catholic. Thirty-eight percent attended private or parochial schools. Students tend to be conservative, "yet still exploring," notes a senior and cover the full spectrum of academic intensity from the very focused to those who care little about studies. A fair number are members of the Air Force and Army ROTC, while a junior describes others as "intellectual social activists." Says a senior: "Since 10% of our student body is in ROTC, 60% of our students are female, and Portland is an extremely liberal city, the average lunch table conversations are often very colorfully diverse." Friendliness and openness to others are traits all students share. "It is hard to be lost or ignored at this school," says an Oregonian.

Academics: The University of Portland, which was founded in 1901, awards the bachelor's degree in 60 majors through its College of Arts and Sciences and its 4 professional schools of business administration, education, engineering, and nursing. Master's degree programs are offered in 12 fields, including business administration, engineering, theology, and drama. Classes are divided between 2 semesters, with the largest introductory lectures in chemistry and biology enrolling about 90 students and the majority of classes having just a third that number.

All students are required to fulfill a general-education program consisting of 48 hours of coursework in the major fields, from literature and science to philosophy and theology. Many students unsure of what to study when they enter discover their majors through exposure to so many disciplines, although a number grumble about the amount of philosophy and theology required (9 hours each).

Two-thirds of the university's 279 faculty members are full-time. Forty-two percent of the full-time faculty are women. The faculty as a whole garners a score of 8, where 10 represents the perfect professor. Many have had real-life experience in their fields, a qualification that students value. "The engineering professors are engineers, the business professors are accountants, and the nursing professors are nurses," says a history major. "The faculty are also able to relate directly to the students, which makes it easier for us to learn." Most also are quite giving of their time. Says a senior psychology major: "I have never encountered a professor, even an adjunct, who has not been able to adjust his or her schedule to meet with me." Acknowledging that approach, the Carnegie Foundation for the Advancement of Teaching recently recognized a professor in the Spanish department as "U.S. Professor of the Year."

The professional fields of engineering, business, and nursing and, in the liberal arts, philosophy, theology, political science, and history top the lists of great programs. Each features faculty members who are especially well educated, dedicated, and demanding; nursing, in particular, offers students the chance to do rotations at all of the various hospitals in Portland. The professionally accredited drama program also deserves an ovation among liberal arts majors. Biology has long been known for having a dedicated faculty with expertise and a willingness to work one-on-one with all levels of students "even freshmen," says a senior. The $15 million science building that opened in fall 1999 lets both the faculty and facilities shine. The social sciences, social work, psychology, sociology, and criminal justice are noted for their excellent opportunities for field experience. The School of Education insures that all majors are placed in a classroom 3 weeks after they arrive on campus, which makes all classes seem so much more applicable.

The communication major could use a greater variety of courses, as well as internship opportunities that would give students more hands-on experience. A major in journalism recently was eliminated. Students say math professors do not work well together as a teaching unit; as a result, undergraduates either end up repeating what they have already studied or floundering in new material that is over their heads. There is no major or minor in art and most of the fine arts faculty for the drama and music majors are adjuncts. The program in foreign languages, with majors in Spanish, French studies, and German studies, needs more faculty to offset increasing class sizes.

Facilities: Wilson W. Clark Memorial Library serves most students' routine needs adequately, but little more, with its 380,000 volumes and 1446 current periodicals. The on-line catalog, along with the periodicals listing, helps locate materials, however, observes a junior, "if you are looking for the actual article, it is a guessing game as to whether it will be in the stacks or not." Others complain that many of the books are dated and resources are stronger in some fields, such as theology and political science, than they are in other more technical areas, like engineering and computer science. Students in need of more up-to-date or specialized sources use "PORTAL," a computerized network to 16 metropolitan area libraries, or Orbis, which provides a computerized guide to nearly 5 million items housed at about 20 public and private libraries in Washington and Oregon. Science majors often pay a visit to the Oregon Health Sciences University. For study, Clark is quiet. "A great place to study when you really need to concentrate," says a sophomore.

More than 375 microcomputers are available in 5 labs for general student use, usually accessible from 8 a.m. to midnight or 1 a.m., and until 2 a.m. during exam periods. "During finals, it's really tough to find a spot," says a marketing and management major. "I usually bring a laptop because there are wireless hotspots on campus." Additional terminals are designated for use by students in certain computer-intensive majors such as computer science, engineering, and education. Residence halls also each have a handful of computers. The university strongly recommends that students have personal computers.

Special programs: Students may study abroad in Salzburg, Austria, for the academic year, or in England or Japan for the summer. Opportunities also are offered in France, Spain, Germany, Ireland, Italy, Mexico, Australia, and Chile. A certificate program in peace studies is available to students from any major or school within the university who complete a specified curriculum of courses. An Entrepreneur Scholars program offers 20 undergraduates with an entrepreneurial spirit a combination of class work, applied experience, and international travel to any of 7 countries. Students need not be business majors to participate. Internships are widespread throughout the university and are set up through individual departments. In addition, students may take classes at any of 14 other private colleges in the state, including Reed College and Willamette University.

Campus life: Dorm life is increasingly becoming the focus of weekend activity at the university, with half of the undergraduates living on the 155-acre campus and no Greek organizations as of the last few years. As a result, residence halls are becoming more involved in sponsoring regular events such as dances and game nights. Those who live off campus also host parties at their houses. Says a junior: "The basic weekend usually includes a balanced diet of beer and books." Though Catholic Mass is offered twice on Sundays and weekly at noon, as well as in the evenings in the residence halls, students are not required to attend, but many do. Crime on campus, other than occasional petty theft and car break-ins, is typically not much of a problem though students must use caution walking off campus. Says a senior: "When I feel nervous late at night, I look over my shoulder to glance at an approaching car behind me, and 9 times out of 10 it's public safety." Public safety also does routine bike and foot patrols around the clock.

Seven men's and 7 women's varsity teams play in NCAA Division I. Pilots soccer for both men and the 2005 Division I champion women's team is the big varsity sport (there is no football) and draws about 3000 people per game to the Harry A. Merlo field on campus. Basketball, too, has gained fan support in recent years as the team has improved. The intramural program in a recent year attracted 75% of both men and women to the 20 sports open to both sexes. "Students ranging from no talent to many talents are able to participate and have fun," stresses a woman senior.

The Oregon coast and the mountains (for skiing) provide the best escapes for students who long to get out of Portland.

Cost cutters: Ninety-three percent of freshmen and 89% of continuing students received some form of financial aid in the 2005–2006 school year. For 65% of the first-year students and 57% of the rest, the aid was need-based. The average freshman award included a need-based scholarship or grant averaging $13,807. Average debt of a 2005 graduate was $18,900. The university offers a limited number of scholarships and grants made possible from income provided by gifts and endowments and based on need and academic excellence. The University President's Scholarship recently paid up to $10,000 based on a student's academic excellence, work experience, and volunteer activities. The Arthur A. Schulte Jr. award recently paid up to $6000 based on similar criteria. Holy Cross Scholarships recently paid up to $6000 to noteworthy graduates of Catholic high schools. Students who do not get aid generally say it is not too difficult to find a job around campus.

Rate of return: Eighty-six percent of the freshmen return for the sophomore year. Fifty-nine percent go on to graduate in 4 years, 68% within 5 years.

Payoff: Nearly half of Portland's 2005 graduates earned bachelor's degrees in 3 professional fields: 18% in nursing, 17% in business, and 9% in engineering. Nine of every 10 graduates usually find employment within 6 months of commencement. About 85 companies and organizations recruited on campus in a recent school year.

Bottom line: Students may choose Portland for its price, size, location, personalized attention, breadth of majors, and overall quality of life, but not for its "big-time" reputation. "Everyone can fit into something here," concludes a Californian, "but I'm disappointed that the school is not nationally recognized."

Willamette University

Salem, Oregon 97301

Setting: Small city
Control: Private (United Methodist)
Undergraduate enrollment: 827 men, 996 women
Graduate enrollment: 340 men, 288 women
Student/faculty ratio: 11:1
Freshman profile: 17% scored over 700 on SAT I verbal; 46% scored 600–700; 30% 500–599; 7% below 500. 13% scored over 700 on SAT I math; 48% scored 600–700; 33% 500–599; 6% below 500. 29% scored above 28 on the ACT; 27% scored 27–28; 28% 24–26; 11% 21–23; 5% below 21. 49% graduated in top tenth of high school class; 74% in upper fifth.
Faculty profile: 93% Ph.D.'s

Tuition and fees: $28,416
Room and board: $7000
Freshman financial aid: 95%; average scholarship or grant: $18,666 need-based; $8340 non-need-based
Campus jobs: 40%; average earnings: $1855/year
Application deadline: Early action I: Nov. 1; early action II: Dec. 1; regular: Feb. 1
Financial aid deadline: Feb. 1
Admissions information: (503) 370-6303; (877) 542-2787 (LIB-ARTS)
e-mail: libarts@willamette.edu
web site: www.willamette.edu/admission

For prospective politics majors, Willamette University's location right across the street from the state capital in Salem, Oregon, puts them right in the middle of the action. Students can't help but become involved in the bustle surrounding the legislative sessions; and the opportunities for internships with the governor's office, the staff of a state senator or lobbyist, a legislative committee, or television, newspaper, or radio political coverage are sure winners. The university itself boasts several members of the U.S. Congress among its alumni, including former Sen. Mark Hatfield, Class of 1943, for whom the university's outstanding library is named. Exclaims a history major: "Willamette is where politicians are created in Oregon." Little wonder Willamette wins the votes of so many satisfied students when it comes time to endorse the college of their choice.

Student body: Forty-one percent of Willamette's undergraduates are from Oregon. About 80% of the out-of-staters come from 13 Western states, although altogether students attend from 41 states and 17 foreign countries. Nineteen percent are graduates of private or parochial schools. Only 3% of the students are Methodist;

66% claim no religious affiliation. Asian-Americans account for 6% of enrollment; Hispanics, 4%, multiracial students, 3%, African-Americans, and foreign nationals, each 2% and Native Americans, 1%. Students' greatest contact with undergraduates from another culture has come through Willamette's sister relationship with Tokyo International University, which has an American campus adjacent to Willamette and involves Japanese students in classes with the predominantly white, middle class student body. Willamette undergraduates generally hold views that cover the political spectrum. Says a sophomore: "Most everyone I've met here is always willing to share his or her views on politics, religion, philosophy, etc., almost any time, and I've never felt pressure to keep any of my views to myself for fear of disrespect." As a group, students tend to be very intelligent, well traveled, articulate, and cooperative rather than competitive in their studies. Notes a senior: "There are high levels of involvement in student organizations, athletics, community service, and other activities. But academics are still the top priority and students log large numbers of hours in the library and other study areas."

Academics: Willamette was founded by Methodist pioneers in 1842, making it the oldest college in the West. The university awards bachelor's degrees in more than 30 fields, master's degrees in management and teaching, and a law degree. A dual degree program in management enables a student to earn a bachelor's degree plus a master's in management in 5 years, instead of 6. Courses are divided between 2 semesters. Half of the undergraduate classes have between 10 and 19 students; only one class has had more than 40.

Willamette's general-education program begins with a first-year seminar involving students in classes averaging 16 participants. Seminars have been focused around a single theme, most recently, in fall 2005, "War and Its Alternatives." Beginning in fall 2006, the seminars will explore a variety of topics ranging from the music of Beethoven to cosmology; some of the seminars are to be clustered around a general theme; others will be independent. In addition to all the writing freshmen do as part of the first-year seminar, undergraduates must take 3 additional writing-centered courses, at least 1 in the major field. Other course requirements include 2 quantitative and analytical reasoning classes; 2 years' study of a foreign language and culture; and completion of coursework in 6 Modes of Inquiry that range from Understanding the Natural World to Interpreting Texts to Creating in the Arts.

Willamette's entire faculty is split between 184 full-time members and 117 part-time. Three-quarters of the full-time faculty, 137 members, teach undergraduates as do 74 of the 117 part-time. Forty-two percent are women. Students value the one-on-one relationships that many have with faculty members and find the majority of professors knowledgeable and devoted both to the students and to the learning process. An English major recalls: "I have noticed a few admit when they didn't know something and then come back the next class period with the answer after having researched it." Adds a politics major: "I have written 10-page papers that are returned with 2 pages of typed comments from my professor."

The program in politics benefits greatly from its working laboratory in the state government, as well as its savvy and dedicated faculty. Music also gives a virtuoso performance, with a program that is rigorous and highly respected in the field, a faculty who in the words of a junior "have an incredible passion for what they do," plus an $8 million concert and recital hall that opened in spring 1999. The English, history, and philosophy faculties are diverse in their perspectives and energetic in their teaching. The biology, chemistry, and physics departments also are excellent, and their small classes ensure plenty of personal attention from distinguished faculties and easy access to up-to-date laboratory equipment. The $7.1 million Olin Science Center has provided even greater opportunities for learning. Business, economics, and psychology are especially strong as well.

Students interested in foreign languages wish there were more professors and a greater variety of courses, although the extensive opportunities to study abroad help make up for the shortcomings. Majors are offered in French, Spanish, German, and Japanese studies, with minors in those same fields plus Russian, and Chinese studies. Budding geologists will find no major, although an environmental science major and geography minor are available.

Facilities: The Mark O. Hatfield Library, which opened in 1986, "is beautiful and makes studying there almost enjoyable," in the words of a user. Two walls of the library are entirely glass, which enables plenty of natural light to pour through. There are plenty of personal study carrels for concentrated work, and a 24-hour study room adjacent to the main library has vending machines for late-night snacking. Hatfield's collection of almost 373,000 volumes and 1623 periodicals satisfies most students' research needs, and what students don't find locally can usually be obtained via access to ORBIS, a shared academic collection of more than 7 million volumes from academic libraries in Oregon and Washington. A computerized catalog and database searching plus access to the Internet also make researching papers quicker and easier. When the Hatfield Library doesn't have what a student needs, he or she can always check the university's law library, as well as the state, county, and city libraries, which all are nearby.

About 400 PCs and Macs are offered for student use in the main computer lab, which is 1 of 2 labs open 24 hours, as well as in the library and departmental labs. Students may access the Internet and campus network from their residence hall rooms. Wireless access is available in all classrooms and public buildings. Over 90% of all Willamette students bring their own computers to campus. E-mail stations also are available in just about every building on campus from the library to The Bistro coffeehouse.

Special programs: Since 1965, Willamette has had a sister-university relationship with Tokyo International University. Every fall around 15 students and a Willamette professor join 30 other American students for a term of study at the campus in Kawagoe City, about an hour by train from the heart of Tokyo. With the opening of the TIU campus adjacent to Willamette in 1989, approximately 120 Japanese come to live for 1 year in Salem, half on TIU's campus and half in Willamette residence halls. Half of Willamette's graduates typically study abroad before graduation. In any given year, students can be found in almost 40 countries and on every continent except Antarctica. A dual degree program in engineering is offered with Columbia or Washington University or the University of Southern California; in forestry, with Duke University; and with Willamette's Atkinson Graduate School of Management. A 2-tier internship program places students in all classes in a wide range of job settings. Students also may spend a term in Washington, D.C. or as part of a Chicago urban studies program. Undergraduate research grants enable students to do original research over the summer.

Campus life: Sixty-seven percent of Willamette's students reside on the 72-acre campus, just a 5-minute walk from downtown Salem (pop. 140,000). Thirty-five percent of the men and 29% of the women are members of 5 national fraternities and 3 national sororities. Since independents are welcome to attend Greek functions, and many do, students report little separation between the 2 groups. The Bistro, Willamette's student-run coffeehouse, is a popular location for impromptu conversations with faculty and the ever-popular weekly open-mike nights. The student events board also can be counted upon to come up with creative entertainment like a hypnotist or giant slip and slide. The food isn't bad, either. Boasts a Texan: "People come over from the capitol to eat in our commons." Theft of unlocked items is generally the biggest crime on campus; bikes are the most common target, and students have been advised how and where to lock up their two wheelers. An escort service also takes students up to 5 blocks off campus and residence halls are locked around the clock. Says a junior: "For the most part, students always feel safe in 'the Willamette Bubble.'"

At Willamette, the athletic emphasis is on participating in intercollegiate and intramural sports rather than on watching an elite few score lots of victories. With that ideal in mind, at least 25% of the students take the court or field for the 10 men's and 10 women's intercollegiate sports offered in NCAA Division III competition. Almost half of the men and a third of the women plus faculty and staff participate in the 10 intramural sports for each sex. Those who prefer to cheer turn out in the largest numbers for men's and women's soccer, football, men's basketball, and women's volleyball. The Willamette Outdoor Club sponsors popular camping, canoeing, rock climbing, and hiking trips.

To relax, some students hang out down by the old Mill Race that runs through campus. The beaches of the Oregon Coast are just an hour west; skiing in the Cascade Mountains, an hour east. Portland also is only a 45-minute drive. The campus organization Off the Block regularly sponsors trips to get students without cars off campus; 200 showed up recently to go to the coast.

Cost cutters: Gifts to Willamette, plus its $228 million endowment as of January 2006, relieve students of one-third of their actual educational costs. In the 2005–2006 school year, 95% of the freshmen and 94% of continuing students received financial aid. No figures show the portion that was need-based, although in recent years, the aid was need-based for just about all. The average freshman award for a student with need included a need-based scholarship or grant averaging $18,666 and need-based self-help aid such as loans and jobs averaging $5130. Non-need-based awards and scholarships for first-year students averaged $8340. An average 2005 graduate had debts of $18,756. Numerous merit awards are available, ranging in value from $2000 per year up to full tuition. All admitted applicants are automatically considered for merit- and need-based scholarships on the strength of their academic GPA, test scores, and course selection from high school. G. Herbert Smith Presidential Scholarships, for example, recently paid $14,000 a year to students with a minimum 3.80 GPA and a minimum math and critical reading SAT score of 1350 or 30 ACT composite. Fifty Goudy Scholarships paid $12,000 to those with a minimum 3.7 GPA, 1200 SAT or 29 ACT.

Rate of return: Eighty-eight percent of the freshmen return for the sophomore year. Sixty-seven percent graduate in 4 years; 74% within 5.

Payoff: Politics was the most popular major for the 2005 graduating class, claiming 12% of the degree recipients. Biology and economics followed at 10% each. Just over a fifth of the graduates generally pursue advanced degrees. The majority enter the job market immediately, most accepting positions in the West and Northwest. More than 100 companies and organizations recruited on campus in a recent school year.

Bottom line: "The personal attention at Willamette cannot be overemphasized," advises a recent graduate, "but a student definitely has to be self-motivated to succeed. The professors are here to make you think, not to spoon-feed you information. If you have been admitted, the professors have no doubt you can do the work and they expect the very best from you."

Pennsylvania

Albright College

Reading, Pennsylvania 19612

Setting: Suburban
Control: Private (United Methodist)
Undergraduate enrollment: 662 men, 961 women
Graduate enrollment: 78 men and women (part-time)
Student/faculty ratio: 16:1
Freshman profile: 1% scored over 700 on SAT I verbal; 16% scored 600–700; 42% 500–599; 41% below 500; 1% scored over 700 on SAT I math; 17% scored 600–700; 44% 500–599; 38% below 500. 19% graduated in top tenth of high school class; 48% in upper fourth.
Faculty profile: 72% Ph.D.'s

Tuition and fees: $26,032
Room and board: $7888
Freshman financial aid: 95%; average scholarship or grant: $5533 need-based; $10,046 non-need-based
Campus jobs: 44%; average earnings: $840/year
Application deadline: Rolling
Financial aid deadline: Mar. 1
Admissions information: (610) 921-7512; (800) 252-1856
e-mail: albright@alb.edu
web site: www.albright.edu

Many students today enter college thinking they know exactly what they want to study: business and management, biology, history. For the undergraduate who doesn't know, however, the first couple of years can be an unsettling experience in which he or she drifts unguided through general-education courses, unsure what major to declare. At Albright College in Reading, Pennsylvania, students undecided about their areas of concentration start out right—in the Alpha program. Alpha provides a structured package of academic guidance, including a faculty member specially chosen to counsel undecided students, peer support from former Alpha members, and special activities in which undecided students exchange ideas and attend programs introducing them to various disciplines. Approximately a third of every first-year class enters as Alpha students; in fact, many of the college's brightest individuals were attracted to Albright because it lets them explore many interests before settling on a major by the end of the sophomore year. From Alpha to Omega, Albright clearly stands up with the best.

Student body: Sixty-three percent of Albright's students are from Pennsylvania, with most of the rest also coming from the Middle Atlantic region; 25 other states and 28 foreign countries are represented. Just over a fourth are graduates of private or parochial schools. Though the college is related to the United Methodist Church, only 23% of the students are members of various Protestant denominations including 5% who are Methodists. Twenty-four percent are Catholic, 1% Jewish, and 1% Muslim, Buddhist, Sikh, Orthodox, or Mormon. Fifty-one percent claim no religious affiliation. Racially and ethnically, Albright remains predominantly white, though diversity has increased steadily in recent years and is impressive for a small liberal arts college. African-Americans comprise the largest minority population at 9%, followed by Hispanics at 4%, Asian-Americans at 2%, and Native Americans at 1%. Foreign nationals comprise 5%. Students describe themselves as friendly, curious, open-minded but generally conservative (more so than the faculty, they say), but definitely strong-willed, academically focused, and involved. While virtually all are goal-oriented, their aims differ between simply earning a degree at the end of 4 years and being intellectually challenged along the way, all while keeping up a high level of involvement in student clubs and organizations. Says a senior: "Albright functions because students are competitive in the classroom and because the students get involved with campus organizations. The busier the student, the better." As busy as many students are, though, academics leads the to-do list of most. Says a junior: "You study, do papers, and go to class before the extra stuff can take place."

Academics: Albright traces its own beginnings to 1856 with the founding of the first of 3 colleges that eventually merged to become Albright College. Albright awards the bachelor's degree in 29 majors along with 5 combined areas of concentrations, 4 preprofessional programs, and 8 special programs. (Albright also offers a masters degree in education.) Half of all students step outside the confines of a single major and graduate with combined, interdisciplinary, or multiple majors. In a recent school year, undergraduates created 200 different combinations of majors, befitting a college that was among the first to create undergraduate programs in psychobiology, environmental studies, and biochemistry. Albright follows a calendar with 2 semesters separated by a January term. Entering freshmen can expect most classes through all 4 years to enroll between 10 and 30 students. "'Larger' at Albright means 25–35 people," says a senior. A freshman-level lecture in biology may just top 100 students, but more advanced courses often enroll fewer than 15.

Approximately half of the 32 courses needed for graduation are general-studies classes in traditional disciplines plus an interdisciplinary course. In addition to the straight academics, students also are required to attend 16 cultural events, preferably by the end of the sophomore year. Admits a junior: "It seems annoying at first to *have* to go to these events, but then you start to understand the program more and actually enjoy the different experiences."

Albright's faculty includes 105 full-time and 46 part-time members. Forty-eight percent are women. Most students have nothing but high praise for the professors who, for many, make Albright a challenging experience. Says an English major: "Every year, the faculty become more exciting, vibrant, nurturing, and inspiring, as new faces are added to the ranks. Personal involvement with them is actually difficult to avoid. I can't think of a single department that doesn't have at least 1 profoundly brilliant individual teaching full-time." There are those professors, however, as 1 sophomore puts it, who "won't give you the time of day." Part-time faculty in particular are harder to meet with outside of class.

A first-rate faculty helps to make biology one of Albright's strongest majors. Its varied offerings include the use of a scanning and a transmission electron microscope, local areas for testing ecology, and a genetics program with a faculty expert in DNA. The chemistry department also is well respected and sends many of its graduates on to good jobs in area industries. The psychology faculty covers the best of both worlds: "Young enough to know new areas of study; experienced enough to share many theories," raves a major. The business and accounting programs also earn triple-A ratings, and many students combine majors in psychology and business as preparation for careers in human resources. Though political science is not a large department, its faculty offers a variety of high-quality courses taken by many students as prelaw concentrations. The philosophy professors, says a senior, "make you think, not just learn."

There is only a combined concentration in music, in which courses in music must be combined with those in another subject area such as business, psychology or education to make a major. International relations, environmental sciences, optics, digital media, women's and gender studies and various concentrations in the education program are other disciplines available only as combined majors. Religious Studies has fewer professors and more limited course offerings than some students would like. Computer science, too, is limited in its course selection by having just two professors, as excellent as those two are. "Mathematics needs more professors," too, says a sophomore in the Alpha program. The modern foreign languages program, with concentrations in French and Spanish and 5 courses in German, needs more faculty members, better advising, and more upper-level courses.

Facilities: Gingrich Library gets no more than a lackluster rating from students. Its collection of 219,000 volumes and 725 periodicals often falls short for the rigorous research expected of undergraduates, who must rely on the availability of materials on-line or through interlibrary loan. Database searching with such aids as Lexis/Nexis and OCLC First Search is particularly helpful. Students are more satisfied with Gingrich's quiet environment for study, especially on the second and third floors, as well as the addition of 2 new group study rooms.

What the library lacks in student enthusiasm, the Center for Computing and Mathematics easily claims. The building houses 5 labs, 3 with IBM-compatible units, 2 with Macintoshes, all networked, providing a total of about 75 workstations. The computer center generally is open until 1 a.m., and until 3 a.m. during finals. Additional networked PCs located in 3 academic buildings raise the total number of workstations open to students on campus to about 200. College officials strongly recommend that students have their own personal computers. Wireless connection is available in all classrooms as well as in many popular public areas of the campus.

Special programs: Albright's January term provides most of the opportunity for study abroad in spots as diverse as Greece and Australia or off the mainland to Hawaii or other islands. Study abroad junior year is also encouraged, and Albright has a resource center with full listings, advice, and assistance. Every summer and each semester, students who wish may complete internships through the Washington Center in the nation's capital. A 5-year, double-degree program is available in forestry and environmental studies with Duke, and in natural resources management with the University of Michigan.

Campus life: Two-thirds of Albright's students reside on campus, which covers 118 acres at the edge of a residential section of Reading. Campus living options are varied, including single-sex and coed dormitories, senior privileged apartments, and 14 special-interest suites in which a dozen students with a common interest or purpose may apply for residency as a group. Recently added to the roster was an Academic Honors Hall and 2 coed "First-Year Experience" residence halls for first-year students who want to share their freshman experience. Twenty-eight percent of the men and 32% of the women are members of 3 national fraternities and 3 national sororities. Though Greek life remains popular, students say there is no pressure to pledge and little rivalry exists between the 2 groups. Student say more alternative programming like DJs, bands, karaoke, comedians, and laser tag, have been added in the past few years to keep on campus the students who used to hang out at the frequent parties in the off-campus frat houses. Although crime other than occasional car break-ins is not considered a problem, various security measures recently have been implemented, including an escort service after dark, 24-hour locks on dormitory doors, and more call boxes around campus. "Security is a definite presence!" says a sophomore. Students still advise not walking alone at night because of higher incidents of crime in the surrounding neighborhood.

Thirty percent of the students take part in the 11 men's and 11 women's intercollegiate sports played in NCAA Division III. Slightly more men but slightly fewer women participate in 7 intramural and 5 club sports offered. Sporting events, especially football, soccer, and basketball, are usually supported enthusiastically by fans.

Reading (pop. 80,000) offers easy access to scenic hiking trails in Berks County. Washington, D.C., Philadelphia, and New York City are the most popular travel destinations.

Cost cutters: Ninety-five percent of the freshmen and 87% of continuing students received financial aid of some sort in the 2005–2006 school year. For about 87% of both groups, the aid was need-based. The average freshman award included a need-based scholarship or grant averaging $5533 and need-based self-help aid such as loans and job earnings averaging $5142. Other non-need-based awards and scholarships for first-year students averaged $10,046. A typical graduate left with debts of $23,000. Several merit scholarship programs are available: the Jacob Albright Scholarship, which pays $15,000 a year to students in the top 5% of their high school graduating class; the Provost's and Presidential awards worth $10,500 and $12,500 a year, respectively, Alumni Scholarships paying $7500 annually and Community Service and Leadership Scholarships paying $5000 a year. Coleman Awards are presented in amounts from $3000 to $5000 annually to students of color; United Methodist awards pay $2500 a year to first-year students who have been active in the Methodist Church. Talent awards paying $1000 to $3000 per year are given to students with talent in the fine arts and journalism. Scholar Awards of $1000 to $3000 go to various types of high-achieving students, among them class valedictorians and salutatorians and members of the National Honor Society. Eagle Scouts and Girl Scout Gold Award recipients are among those eligible to receive Leadership Awards worth $500 to $2500.

Rate of return: Seventy-nine percent of Albright freshmen return for the sophomore year. Fifty-two percent graduate in 4 years; 56% in 5 years; 59% in 6.

Payoff: In the 2005 graduating class, 13% earned degrees in business administration, 11% in psychology/psychobiology, and 7% in biology/biochemistry. Sixty-eight companies and other organizations recruited on campus in a recent school year. The vast majority of Albright's graduates typically take jobs shortly after commencement, many with well-known firms such as AT&T, Hershey Foods, du Pont, and American Airlines and with various departments of the federal government. A fourth continue with their education.

Bottom line: Albright, says a recent graduate, "provides a relatively nurturing yet potentially challenging academic environment. Any student who is dedicated can succeed here."

Arcadia University

Glenside, Pennsylvania 19038

Setting: Suburban
Control: Private (Presbyterian)
Undergraduate enrollment: 482 men, 1266 women
Graduate enrollment: 89 men, 343 women
Student/faculty ratio: 16:1
Freshman profile: 5% scored over 700 on SAT I verbal; 30% scored 600–700; 47% 500–599; 18% below 500. 3% scored over 700 on SAT I math; 28% scored 600–700; 47% 500–599; 22% below 500. 22% graduated in top tenth of high school class; 51% in upper fifth.
Faculty profile: 89% Ph.D.'s
Tuition and fees: $24,270

Room and board: $9300
Freshman financial aid: 99%; average scholarship or grant: $7992 need-based; $8865 non-need-based
Campus jobs: 30%; average earnings: $709/year
Application deadline: Early decision: Nov. 1; regular: rolling
Financial aid deadline: Mar. 1
Admissions information: (215) 572-2910; (877) ARCADIA
e-mail: admiss@arcadia.edu
web site: www.arcadia.edu

Any 4-year college that houses some of its students in a castle surely has to be too expensive for most American commoners, right? Wrong—when the castle is located on the grounds of Arcadia University, formerly known as Beaver College, 10 miles north of Philadelphia, where tuition, fees, room, and board in the 2005–2006 school year totaled just over $33,500. The college is best known for its rigorous physical therapy program and early efforts to make writing a skill that covers all subject matter, not solely papers in English literature. A new First Year Study Abroad Program sends 60 first-semester freshmen to London or Stirling, England, for the same tuition rate as education on the Arcadia campus, including round-trip airfare from Philadelphia. When students return, they find some campus surroundings not so dissimilar. Grey Tower Castle, inspired by the famous Alnwick Castle in England, is but 1 of several old-world stone buildings spread across the former country estate that has been Arcadia's campus for more than 60 years. If Gothic and gargoyles are a student's thing, Arcadia may offer an ideal academic setting, which won't cost a king's ransom.

Student body: Sixty-eight percent of Arcadia's subjects come from Pennsylvania, with all but a fifth of the nonresidents also from the Middle Atlantic region. Altogether, students are enrolled from 24 states and 12 foreign countries. Seventy percent are graduates of public high schools. Though Arcadia is related to the Presbyterian Church, Catholics in a recent year made up the largest religious group on campus: 13% of the total. Protestants of various denominations recently comprised 8% (virtually all Presbyterian), followed by Jewish students, and members of other faiths at 1% each. The vast majority, 77%, claimed no religious affiliation. African-American students constitute 9% of the student body; Hispanics and Asian-Americans each make up 2%, Native Americans, less than 1%. Foreign nationals account for 1%. A branch of the American Language Academy at the university adds to the diversity by involving many international students not enrolled at Arcadia in various campus activities. Students are drawn to Arcadia and ultimately stay there because of the strong sense of community that they find. Undergraduates tend to be quite tolerant of diverse ways of thinking and being but rarely take strong political stands. For many, some of their greatest involvement comes in academics, especially in the highly competitive science and pre-physical therapy programs. However, in keeping with the family spirit of the campus, says a psychology major: "Most students form study groups before exams and get through the tough classes together."

Academics: Arcadia was founded in 1853 as a women's college in Beaver, Pennsylvania, but left the town in the 1920s and acquired its present site in 1928. The school became coed in 1972 and changed its name to Arcadia University in July 2001. (The name change even sparked a question in the 20th Anniversary Edition of the Trivial Pursuit board game.) Arcadia awards the bachelor's degree in 34 majors; students may also participate in special programs that lead to a doctorate in physical therapy 3 years after earning a bachelor's from Arcadia, a master's in genetic counseling 1 year afterward, and a masters in physician assistant studies and in international peace and conflict resolution in an additional 2 years. The university follows a semester calendar. Class sizes generally average 16 participants throughout all 4 years, though science courses tend to be larger. Interdepartmental Science, for example, recently enrolled 78; Conversational French may have only 5.

General education requirements begin with demonstrated competency in thought and expression, mathematics, foreign language, and science. Students may choose a course each in the visual and performing arts and the social sciences from a list of about 20 prescribed classes and 2 courses in history-humanities from a similar list of 24. All students must also take the same 2 courses examining American pluralism and non-Western cultures. Every senior ends his or her years at Arcadia by completing an independent project in the major field of study; a week-long exhibit of the students' work is held the last week of classes and draws parents and alumni as well as other undergraduates.

All but 11 of Arcadia's 114 full-time faculty members teach undergraduates, as do 181 of the 215 part-timers. Fifty-six percent of the faculty are women. Undergraduates find in their professors many individuals who have gained professional experience in the real world and are willing to work one-on-one with students whenever needed. "The faculty treat us as intellectual individuals," observes an education major.

Far and away, the science and psychology programs that prepare students for advanced work in physical therapy are Arcadia's best-known and toughest courses. Instead of earning a bachelor's degree in physical therapy, undergraduates major in another discipline, usually biology, chemistry, or psychology, that enables them to complete the prerequisite courses. Those who perform the best are admitted to Arcadia's graduate-level physical therapy program in which a student can earn a doctorate in 3 years. Many of Arcadia's best and most competitive students are attracted by the "4 + 3" physical therapy program, as it is called. However, biology, chemistry, and psychology are all rich in research opportunities and are excellent as well for students not preparing for careers as physical therapists. The fine arts department is highly regarded and offers one of the few bachelor's degree programs in scientific illustration. Education and computer science have faculty who are knowledgeable about the latest developments and research in their respective fields, which translates into graduates who are very well prepared for the job market. English is considered "wonderful" as well.

Students say the program in business administration needs strengthening. "Most of the faculty are adjunct," says a junior, "so they are not always the best at explaining precisely what needs to be done, and they are hard to get in touch with." Many opt to double-major in business and another field. Students in the math and health administration programs face similar problems. Philosophy could use more classes. Spanish is the only language major; French, German, and Italian are offered as minors only. Religion, music, and physics also are offered solely as minors.

Facilities: The new Bette E. Landman Library, named for the longtime Arcadia University president, features what is sure to be the favorite study spot on campus—the 2-story-high Shenker Grand Reading Room. "Before (in the old library) there was no real room to sit and study or read," says a junior. "Now the biggest room on campus is in the library with leather chairs and laptop connections," as well as built-in window seats that overlook the campus green to the castle. Landman's collection of 148,000 volumes and 7832 paper and electronic periodicals stretches further with extensive computerized research aids (the library is now wireless) and room for an additional 32,000 volumes. With the library closing at 2 a.m., really serious night owls head to the Boyer Hall of Science, where students may study all night, provided that they enter before 11 p.m.

The entire Arcadia campus recently became wireless "so we can sit midpoint on the soccer field and log on," exclaims a junior. In addition, computer labs in 4 academic buildings plus the library are open until at least 11 p.m. or midnight. Hours are extended an hour or two during finals week. Four separate labs in Boyer Hall house IBM PCs and Mac computers. Advises a junior: "Residents should have a computer, though, as labs close before papers get written and aren't open much on weekends."

Special programs: Arcadia sponsors its own study-abroad programs in England, Wales, Northern Ireland, Italy, Greece, Korea, Spain, Scotland, Ireland, Mexico, New Zealand, Australia, and Equatorial Guinea. A special treat for first-year students besides the new first-semester program in London, is the London Preview, which allows more than 250 freshmen to take a trip to London over spring break for a total cost in a recent year of $245, airfare and lodging included. With so much encouragement of and opportunity for study abroad at Arcadia, 75% of Arcadia graduates have had some kind of international experience before Commencement. A semester in Washington, D.C. or in Appalachia also is an option. A student with a B average in his or her major may take a course not offered on campus in his or her field at the University of Pennsylvania. A 3-2 program in engineering is offered with Columbia University; a 3-4 program in optometry, with the Pennsylvania College of Optometry, and a 2-2 program in nursing with Thomas Jefferson University.

Campus life: Sixty-eight percent of Arcadia's undergraduates reside on the 76-acre campus, though many who live close by spend at least part of the weekend, maybe an afternoon or just the dinner hour, at home. There are no fraternities or sororities; informal dances held every few weeks, along with weekly bands, comedians, or other performers, as well as parties in the residential suites, are the chief replacements. Peers, an organization that promotes wellness among students, is an especially active organization on campus, as are PRIDE, an organization supporting gay, lesbian, and bisexual students, and the Arcadia Christian Fellowship, a nondenominational group that meets for Bible study and discussion of relevant issues. The close proximity of Philadelphia is a temptation to many, and groups of friends often take the train for an afternoon of exploring museums, other college campuses, or various historic sites. Despite the close proximity of Arcadia's campus to the city, students say crime is not a problem. A computerized card access system was installed in the dormitories a few years ago. More lighting has helped to brighten campus walkways and video cameras have been installed in all parking lots as well as on buildings throughout campus.

A winning women's soccer team with 4 Pennsylvania Athletic Conference (PAC) championships and 3 NCAA appearances since 1998, the third in 2005, tops the 7 sports for men and 9 for women played in NCAA Division III. Men's soccer also draws huge crowds to the field in the middle of campus, making its mark as PAC champions in 2001, 2002, and 2004, with NCAA appearances in the Sweet 16, Elite 8, and second round, respectively. More than a third of the student body is involved in the 5 intramural sports for men and 5 for women.

Home and the City of Brotherly Love are the favorite escapes.

Cost cutters: Ninety-nine percent of the freshmen and 94% of the continuing students received financial aid of some kind in the 2005–2006 school year; 77% of the freshmen were on need-based assistance. No figure is available concerning continuing students who received aid based on need. The average freshman award for a student with need included a need-based scholarship or grant averaging $7992 and need-based self-help aid such as loans and jobs averaging $5594. Other non-need-based awards and scholarships for first-year students averaged $8865. The average financial indebtedness of a 2005 graduate was nearly

$32,000. A variety of merit-based scholarships are provided. The Landman Scholarship pays full tuition to the very top members of the entering freshman class, based on such qualifications as letter grades, class rank, standardized test scores, and leadership. Nearly 40% of entering students recently were selected for Distinguished Scholarships, which pay $8000 to $18,000 annually based on similar criteria. The Arcadia University Achievement Award pays $1000 to $6000 a year to entering students who have demonstrated leadership, community service, or talent in athletics or some other area. A 10-month interest-free payment plan is available for an annual fee of $40. A co-op program is offered to students in all majors.

Rate of return: Eighty-one percent of entering freshmen return for the sophomore year. Sixty-seven percent graduate in 4 years, with another 2% finishing in a fifth year.

Payoff: Just over 40% of the 2005 graduates majored in 3 fields: 15% in business, 15% in education and 11% in psychology. Many of those who go on to receive their doctorates in physical therapy find jobs in hospitals along the East Coast. About 10% of a recent class pursued advanced degrees directly after graduation, the largest number in the arts and sciences.

Bottom line: Arcadia is a university community rich in opportunities for study abroad and cooperative achievement at home. And there is individual attention, not just when a student needs help, but also when a job is well done. Just take a peek at the proud faces at the annual exhibit of senior projects and theses.

Drexel University

Philadelphia, Pennsylvania 19104

Setting: Urban
Control: Private
Undergraduate enrollment: 6130 men, 4028 women
Graduate enrollment: 1487 men, 1982 women
Student/faculty ratio: 10:1
Freshman profile: 7% scored over 699 on SAT I verbal; 34% scored 600–699; 47% 500–599; 12% below 500. 15% scored over 699 on SAT I math; 42% scored 600–699; 37% 500–599; 6% below 500. 30% graduated in top tenth of high school class; 59% in upper fourth.
Faculty profile: 90% Ph.D.'s

Tuition and fees: $24,280
Room and board: $10,505
Freshman financial aid: 92%; average scholarship or grant: $4388 need-based; $9890 non-need-based
Campus jobs: NA; average earnings: NA
Application deadline: Mar. 1
Financial aid deadline: Mar. 1
Admissions information: (215) 895-2400; (800) 2DREXEL
e-mail: enroll@drexel.edu
web site: www.drexel.edu

Textbook learning Drexel University definitely is not. Students who come here are drawn by 2 features: Drexel's location in Philadelphia and its wide-ranging cooperative education program that involves more than 1500 business, industrial, governmental, and other institutions located in 27 states and 12 foreign countries. All students, except those in a 4-year business and administration program, spend their first year on campus and then begin alternating two 10-week quarters of classroom work with 2 quarters of paid employment related to their major. Average earnings over 6 months starting with the sophomore year recently ranged from $8500 to $11,700. Students don't come to Drexel expecting to be pampered or entertained with extensive on-campus activities; they come to get jobs and they do that, while using to the utmost all that the City of Brotherly Love has to offer academically, professionally, culturally, and socially. Concludes a recent graduate: "The excitement and activity of living in a city like Philadelphia have made me a much more 'streetwise' person and, along with my co-op experience, have provided me with more knowledge than any mere textbook education ever could."

Student body: Fifty-six percent of Drexel's undergraduate students are from Pennsylvania; most of the remaining 44% in a recent year were from other states in the Middle Atlantic region, although students recently were present from 40 states and 121 foreign countries. Seventy percent in a recent year were graduates of public schools. Nearly a fifth of the undergraduates, 18%, are age 25 or older. Asian-Americans, at 12% of the undergraduate enrollment, represent the largest minority group on campus, followed by African-Americans at 9%. Hispanics represent 3% and Native Americans, less than 0.5%. Foreign nationals account for 6.5%. Students list *individualistic, industrious,* and *conservative* as three words that best describe the diverse student body. Although most students had a streak of independence when they entered Drexel, the various cooperative schedules force all students to chart their own career paths and course offerings. The quarter system, paired with the urban environment, also gives the atmosphere an intensity that matures students faster than might happen at a slower paced, more bucolic campus. Warns a senior: "Drexel is *very* competitive in most programs, and competitive in all others."

Academics: Drexel University, founded by Philadelphia financier Anthony Drexel in 1891, awards degrees through the doctorate. Undergraduate programs in more than 60 majors are offered in the 7 colleges of Arts and Sciences; Business; Engineering; Information Science and Technology; Media Arts and Design; Medicine; and Nursing and Health Professions, as well as the 3 schools of Biomedical Engineering, Science, and Health Systems; Education and Public Health; plus the Goodwin College of Professional Studies, which serves all part-time undergraduates. Drexel also was scheduled in August 2006 to admit the inaugural class to its new law school, the first law school to be opened by a major private doctorate-granting university in 30 years. The academic year is divided into 10-week quarters, with most students attending school year-round. During their time on campus, students find classes ranging in size from 18 to 40 students, although usually lectures for the required core classes can have from 100 to 250 note takers. Some more specialized, upper-level courses attract only 5 to 8 students.

Core course requirements, which generally cover the traditional fields, vary by college, as do the number of cooperative units a student must fulfill. Undergraduates in all 5-year programs must complete 6 co-op periods to graduate. Students in the College of Media Arts and Design and in several majors that offer a 4-year program within the various other colleges and schools offer the option of a 4-year program with a 2-quarter paid internship.

The full-time faculty numbers 723. No figures are available to show the total number of full-time and part-time faculty members, although in recent years, about half the total pool has been full-time, half part-time. No data also is available to show the number of faculty members who teach at the graduate level only. Thirty-eight percent of the full-time faculty are women. An emphasis on research sends many engineering and science professors out of the classroom and into the labs, leaving behind too many teaching assistants, some of whom students find are heavily involved in research themselves. Other professors speak little English and are difficult to understand. However, concedes a commerce and engineering major: "Their incredible knowledge earns them tremendous respect." The large contingent of part-time faculty also are still generally very active in the fields they are teaching, which gives them up-to-the-minute knowledge to pass along but also can make them difficult to reach for help outside of class.

Students regard Drexel's programs in engineering, fashion design, and some components in business as the indisputable university leaders. Electrical engineering is particularly challenging with excellent facilities, although some students have found the faculty more detached than they would like. An engineering curriculum designed to develop the 21st century engineer, known as tDEC, provides a more integrated, hands-on approach to the discipline. The Antoinette Westphal College of Media Arts and Design offers excellent equipment and a demanding curriculum, as well as a highly respected student-run fashion show. In the LeBow College of Business, blue-chip programs include the business administration concentration in finance and the major in commerce and engineering. Physics, in the College of Arts and Sciences, has excellent lecturers who also are helpful outside the classroom.

Other business offerings are considered poorer investments. The marketing concentration has had fewer instructors and too many accounting classes have been offered by foreign TAs with limited English skills. In general, programs in the College of Arts and Sciences have not received as much attention from job-oriented students or the administration.

Facilities: Most students find the 570,000 volumes and 8321 periodicals in the W.W. Hagerty Library to be adequate for research, with the greatest volume of materials found in the technical fields that have long been Drexel's strengths. The humanities collection is especially limited, and for these materials, students simply walk 3 blocks to the University of Pennsylvania. To those who prefer to let their fingers do the searching, electronic networks provide easy access to collections throughout Philadelphia and the world.

Every incoming freshman should already own, purchase, or have easy access to a Macintosh or IBM-compatible computer. The computers are used extensively throughout the curriculum, and faculty members often develop their own software programs to incorporate into their coursework. The Korman Center for Computing Services provides additional personal computers, graphics workstations, and access to a mainframe. Altogether, about 600 networked public computers are available around campus. In 2000 Drexel became the first major university to operate a completely wireless campus.

Special programs: Drexel offers many Accelerated Degree Programs for highly driven students. Through these programs, students can earn a bachelor's degree and an advanced degree in a shortened period of time. Accelerated degrees are available in the fields of medicine, nursing, business, and engineering, among others. The Baiada Center for Entrepreneurship in Technology provides mentoring, workshops, and an environment for students interested in transforming their ideas into business opportunities. Undergraduates may spend fall, spring, or summer quarters in Bonn, Brussels, London, or Madrid or other cities. Students in the College of Arts and Sciences may participate in a 12-week Sea Education Association (SEA) academic program that provides an opportunity to study oceanography and the marine environment, including 6 weeks aboard a sailing vessel. Back on land, students may cross-register for courses at Eastern Mennonite College, Indiana University of Pennsylvania, and Lincoln University.

Campus life: A fourth of the undergraduates reside on the 38-acre campus located in the University City area of Philadelphia, a few minutes from the city center. (Freshmen who do not live with their parents are required to live in 1 of Drexel's 4 residence halls.) A third of the undergraduates commute from their homes; the rest live in apartments near the university.

Greek participation is small with 5% of the men and women pledging to the 10 national fraternities and 5 national sororities present. Most hard-working students choose to unwind either with the fraternities or at any of the numerous watering holes in the city. A number also are involved in various media-related organizations, such as the campus newspaper and radio station, as well as in Eye Openers, an environmental group. Most students accept crime, such as thefts and muggings, as a given in the city and use appropriate caution when on and off campus. A 24-hour foot, bike, and vehicle patrol is on duty and call boxes are prevalent.

Dragons basketball is the big event among the 8 men's and 8 women's sports offered in NCAA Division I. More than a dozen intramural and 20 club sports also are offered, although most students prefer just to ride bikes or jog on their own or enjoy a spontaneous game of volleyball on some outdoor field.

The biggest attractions are generally those regularly available in Philadelphia, including professional sporting events and cultural offerings. When students need a break from city life, they often head north to the Poconos or to the Jersey shore, only 90 minutes away.

Cost cutters: Drexel's tuition varies slightly depending on whether the student is a freshman or upperclassman or whether he or she is enrolled in a 4-year or 5-year program. In the 2005–2006 school year, a first year student in a 5-year program paid $22,700 in tuition alone; an upperclassman paid $1000 a year less. A first-year student in a 4-year program paid $28,300 in tuition for the year; an upperclassman enrolled in a 4-year program paid $27,100. Ninety-two percent of the freshmen and 82% of the continuing students received financial assistance of some sort in the 2005–2006 school year. For 68% of the freshmen and 62% of the rest, the aid was based on financial need. The average first-year award for students with need includes a need-based scholarship or grant averaging $4388 and need-based self-help aid such as loans and jobs averaging $3840. Non-need-based athletic scholarships for first-year students averaged $20,127. Other non-need-based awards and scholarships averaged $9890. The average 2005 graduate left with debts of $25,347. Foremost among the various scholarships available is the J. Drexel Scholarship, which recently paid up to $8000 annually. Candidates must have a 3.0 grade point average in high school and typically, math and critical reading SAT scores of 1300 or greater. Performing Arts Scholarships recently paid up to $2000; athletic awards, from $2500 to full payment. Provost room scholarships recently provided for a free room the first 9 months of the first school year.

Rate of return: Eighty percent of Drexel's first-year students return for a second year. Because only a small percent of the students opt for the 4-year plan, just 14% of the students go on to graduate in 4 years. Fifty-four percent finish in 5 years, 60% in 6 years.

Payoff: Among 2005 graduates, business and marketing claimed 28% followed by engineering at 20%, and computer and information sciences at 15%. Three hundred companies and other organizations recruited on campus in a recent school year. However, a third of the degree recipients are hired by one of their co-op employers. Just 14% of recent graduates pursued advanced degrees.

Bottom line: Prospective Drexel students know who they are before you ask them. The guidelines are simple, says a New Yorker: "The high school senior who will benefit most from Drexel schedules his or her time sensibly, functions well under pressure, studies efficiently, knows what field he or she is interested in pursuing, and is very determined."

Duquesne University

Pittsburgh, Pennsylvania 15282

Setting: Urban
Control: Private (Roman Catholic)
Undergraduate enrollment: 2163 men, 3160 women
Graduate enrollment: 1223 men, 1617 women
Student/faculty ratio: 12:1
Freshman profile: SAT/ACT scores: NA. 28% graduated in top tenth of high school class; 48% in upper fifth.
Faculty profile: 89% Ph.D.'s
Tuition and fees: $21,480
Room and board: $8054

Freshman financial aid: 98%; average scholarship or grant: $8361 need-based; $2636 non-need-based
Campus jobs: NA; average earnings: NA
Application deadline: Early decision: Nov. 1; early action: Dec. 1; regular: July 1
Financial aid deadline: May 1
Admissions information: (412) 396-5002; (800) 456-0590
e-mail: admissions@duq.edu
web site: www.admissions.duq.edu

What's new at Duquesne University in Pittsburgh? Just about everything, according to the students. Since 1990, this Catholic university has added new schools of Health Sciences, Natural and Environmental Sciences and Leadership and Professional Advancement. A 21st Century learning center brings class work up to the moment with satellite downlinks, electronic "white" boards, and interactive student response pads. For sports enthusiasts, there's a new combined soccer-football field in the center of this urban campus, while cost-conscious students have enjoyed a 4-fold increase in scholarship funds. And total enrollment, which was just over 6000 full- and part-time undergraduate and graduate students in 1988, has expanded by more than 50% to 9916. "This university has experienced an amazing rebirth," boasts a recent graduate. "Any student would do well to attend Duquesne. The smart ones have ample opportunities to make their mark here and get involved. Those who fall in the middle get the assistance and help that they need without being coddled."

Student body: Eighty percent of Duquesne's undergraduates are from Pennsylvania. Though most of the rest are also from the Middle Atlantic region, students attend from 43 states (up from 28 several years ago) and 55 foreign countries. Forty-nine percent of the students are Catholic. A third claim no religious affiliation. Twenty-one percent of the students attended private or parochial schools. African-Americans constitute the largest minority at 4%, followed by Asian-Americans at 2%, and Hispanics at 1%. The number of foreign nationals stands at 2% of enrollment. Students tend to be politically moderate, motivated, well rounded, and involved in community and social activities. "Most of us are of above-average intelligence," says an out-of-stater, "but we are not nerds. We can have fun as well as work hard." In reality, the personal intensity meter swings widely depending on an undergraduate's area of emphasis. According to students, the School of Pharmacy is easily Duquesne's hardest taskmaster, the School of Business Administration is in the middle, and the College of Liberal Arts is more laid back. The fashion meter is a little more consistent. Says a broadcast journalism major: "An Abercrombie & Fitch photo shoot could occur on Academic Walk between classes." Adds an accounting major: "The usual college jogging pants and a sweatshirt definitely do not cut it for our daily classes."

Academics: Duquesne grants bachelor's, master's, and doctorate degrees in 1 college and 9 schools, including the School of Law. Undergraduate majors in 100 fields are offered in the College of Liberal Arts and the schools of Business Administration, Education, Health Sciences, Natural and Environmental Sciences, Music, Nursing, Pharmacy, and Leadership and Professional Advancement. The academic year is split into 2 semesters, with most classes for freshmen and sophomores having from 20 to 40 participants. A biology I class tops the scale at close to 200 students, but most upper-level courses run from 10 to 30.

To graduate, all students must complete a core curriculum that covers 27 credits in the liberal arts, including 7 specific courses such as Basic Philosophical Questions and Shaping of the Modern World, plus students' choices of classes in science and theology. Reviews on the curriculum are mixed. While some consider the program "excellent," others say the classes are taught by some of the least effective professors.

Duquesne's faculty consists of 452 full-time members and 479 part-time. All but 25 of the full-time faculty and all but 20 of the part-time teach undergraduates. Forty-two percent of the faculty are women. The balance in quality tips well to the side of approachable, often "amazing," professors, although there are exceptions. Observes one junior: "With all of Duquesne's wonderful faculty members who are more than willing to help students, provide aid to students in need, and are motivated in the classroom, there are always the few bad apples who refuse to cooperate with students and put them to sleep." Students say graduate students do help teach some introductory classes "but the ones I have had were exceptional," says an English and journalism major. "One is still my favorite teacher."

Many of Duquesne's academic programs, especially those in its professional schools, shine especially bright. The widely respected Mylan School of Pharmacy, which offers an entry-level 6-year professional doctoral program including 2 years preprofessional study, has just what the doctor ordered in terms of internship opportunities, excellent advising, and a 100% placement record for graduates over the past several years. Observes a business major: "Those who make it through the 6 years are worthy of the best jobs, and usually get them." The schools of Nursing, Health Sciences, and Music also are known for their rigorous preparation, although some former health sciences majors wish there were more support for struggling students. Says an education major: "Instead of constantly trying to weed out students, they should focus on adding support systems, such as tutors or a mentor program, that would aid the students along their difficult years in classes." The School of Business Administration has especially strong offerings in accounting, marketing, and finance and boasts a strong job placement record with Pittsburgh area companies. The School of Education incorporates the latest educational research into its classroom teaching, and gets students out of the university classroom well before student teaching time. Says a major: "The faculty has a true understanding of not only how to teach but what it takes to be a good teacher." The biology program in the Bayer School of Natural and Environmental Sciences also features a supportive faculty, excellent resources, and a competitive atmosphere for learning. In the College of Liberal Arts, English, history, and political science are widely regarded as solid offerings with strong teaching by knowledgeable staffs. The psychology department is a recognized leader in the field of existential phenomenology; sociology thrives on having excellent teachers. The newly reorganized Journalism and Media Arts Department draws praise from journalism students who had previously found the communications program lacking. The changes, says a major, "is a testament to the way in which the university accommodates its student body: Students wanted a more academically serious approach to journalism, and we got it."

Other majors offered by the liberal arts college are judged far less kindly by students. Undergraduates say the Department of Modern Languages and Literatures, which offers a major only in Spanish but minors in French, German, and Italian, needs more direction and funding. French, in particular, says a senior studying for a minor in the field, needs more courses: "Some semesters there are no upper-level French classes offered," she says. Other complaints about the college are broader; some students maintain that advising is poor and that many an undergraduate really does not know either what major to choose or how to establish a career goal. Some students find they are unable to graduate on time because courses they expected to take are not available the semester they need them. Students say that too many of the chemistry professors in the Bayer School of Natural and Environmental Sciences are difficult to comprehend and seem to place their own research above undergraduate teaching or helping students outside of the classroom.

Facilities: Gumberg Library, which was built as a printing plant and later used as a garage, holds almost 691,000 volumes, 332,000 microform units, and 17,500 electronic and paper periodicals but tops most students' list of areas that could stand a tune-up. Says a sophomore: "A new paint job, brighter lighting, and more plush furniture would make for a more student-friendly environment." While most find the study atmosphere to be quiet, undergraduates consider the on-site reference collection to be lacking. That's when students turn to Gumberg's excellent computerized research aids, which put students in touch with the holdings of the University of Pittsburgh and other libraries in the area. Notes a senior, "There is an 'online reference librarian' that can help to answer any questions that you might have even if you are doing research from your bedroom." Two of Gumberg's best features are its wireless Internet environment and the lending of laptops for use in the library complex.

One hundred twenty-three multimedia classrooms and numerous computer labs around campus provide access to more than 850 PCs in most academic buildings, the living-learning centers, and union. Duquesne ranks in the top 5% of all universities in computerization and multimedia applications. Several of the computer labs are open around the clock; some close as early as 9 p.m. The university recommends that students have their own personal computers, a Dell, IBM, or Apple.

Special programs: Duquesne students may take courses from any of 8 other Pittsburgh institutions, ranging from all-female Chatham College to Carnegie Mellon University. Those with a taste for more distant learning may study abroad in any of 21 countries. Intracampus combined 6-year programs are available between the School of Business Administration and the School of Law, as well as between the College of Liberal Arts and the law school. Engineering students can earn joint degrees with Case Western Reserve University in Cleveland or the University of Pittsburgh. A Washington, D.C., semester also is possible.

Campus life: Fifty-six percent of Duquesne's undergraduates reside on the 50-acre hilltop campus, known as The Bluff, which overlooks downtown Pittsburgh. Some students who live in the tristate area go home over the weekends. Those who stay behind listen to regularly scheduled bands in the A. J. Palumbo Athletic Center or attend various functions sponsored by the more than 130 clubs on campus. The Union NiteSpot provides a space for students to "hang out on the couches, play video games, play pool, surf the Internet, and have some free snacks and drinks," says a junior. A steady increase in campus programming over the last few years has begun offering more alternatives to students not involved in Duquesne's lively Greek community. Fourteen percent of the men and 18% of the women belong to 1 local and 8 national fraternities and 8 national sororities. Though their revelry has decreased in size and energy over the past few years, students look forward to the open parties held by some of these organizations. More selective fraternities have guest lists.

One of Duquesne's most treasured extracurricular and cultural attractions is the Tamburitzan performing folk ensemble troupe, which takes its name from the Tamburitza family of stringed instruments indigenous to the folk cultures of southeastern Europe. The troupe, established in 1937, offers wonderful performances, as well as scholarships to deserving students. Undergraduates also look forward to the theatrical productions put on by the popular Red Masquers. Although attendance at religious services is not a command performance, students say Saturday and Sunday masses usually are filled. Duquesne promotes an ecumenical environment, though; for example, a Muslim prayer room is provided. Crime is less of a problem than it might be, given the university's urban location, largely because numerous security guards and police officers regularly patrol the campus. "Residence halls," says a senior, "are secure to the point of annoyance with the front desk aides always wanting to see our picture on the I.D." Video cameras are present in the elevators and doorways of residence halls, in the parking garages, and on the rooftops of most other buildings. Emergency blue-light stations are widespread throughout campus. Students still advise using common sense when walking in the surrounding neighborhoods. When an incident does occur on or off campus, an e-mail alert is sent to all students to notify them of the situation.

The Duquesne Dukes basketball team, which plays in the exciting Atlantic 10 conference, is easily the biggest draw of the 1 coed, 9 men's, and 10 women's teams in NCAA Division I. Football, played in Division I-AA, has drawn increasing fan support since the opening of the Art Rooney Field. Club teams offer intercollegiate play in ice hockey, crew, and men's track and field. Students not of varsity quality but eager to play have their choice of 21 intramural events and 35 aerobics classes. About 60% of the students participate.

As one student has said, "Off-campus activity means everything downtown Pittsburgh has to offer," including museums, restaurants, clubs, and professional hockey, baseball, and football games. Mellon Arena for Pittsburgh Penguins hockey and concerts is right across the street; PNC Park, where the Pittsburgh Pirates play and Heinz Field, home of the Steelers, are a short walk. A popular program known as "Saturday Nights in Pittsburgh" provides discounted tickets to local activities ranging from the symphony to festivals to sporting events. Visiting friends at other local universities is another popular pastime.

Cost cutters: Ninety-eight percent of freshmen and 88% of continuing students in the 2005–2006 school year received financial aid. For 74% of the freshmen and 64% of the rest, the aid was need-based. The average freshman package for a student with need included a need-based scholarship or grant averaging $8361 and need-based self-help aid such as loans and jobs averaging $8023. Non-need-based athletic scholarships for first-year students averaged $466; other non-need-based awards and scholarships averaged $2636. The average debt of a 2005 graduate was $23,205. Academic scholarships include the Chancellor's Award, which pays full tuition; the Founders Award worth $6500, and the President's Award paying $4000. The Laval Award pays $6500 to high-achieving minority students. An Auxiliary Grant program provides some need-based gift assistance to students whose need cannot be met by other sources. Cooperative education programs are offered in business, communications, and pharmacy. Tuition varies by academic program. Students majoring in the liberal arts, education, and business paid $19,721 in tuition (not counting fees) in the 2005–2006 school year. Students in such fields as nursing and natural and environmental sciences paid about $500 more. Majors in prepharmacy paid about $1500 more; in the health sciences, an additional $3400 a year; in music, $4900 extra.

Rate of return: Eighty-nine percent of entering freshmen return for the sophomore year. Fifty-five percent graduate in 4 years; 67% in 5 years; 69% in 6 years.

Payoff: The liberal arts claimed the greatest percentage of majors in the Class of 2005, at 31%, followed by business at 26%, and education at 10%. A fifth of Duquesne grads pursue advanced degrees within 6 months of commencement, most frequently in the arts and sciences and in business. Students enrolled in the university's pre-med program who have been recommended by the pre-health professions program director have posted 100% placement into medical school over the past several years. Graduates in pharmacy, health sciences, and other related health fields usually obtain excellent jobs immediately upon graduation. Business majors find work, many in the Pittsburgh area, with such companies as the major accounting firms, Alcoa, Mellon Bank, Thrift Drugs, Bayer, and Walgreens. Sixty companies and organizations recruited on campus in 2004–2005.

Bottom line: Duquesne, according to its students, is on the move academically and athletically. A winning combination of small classes, available teachers, Division I basketball, and a downtown campus more collegiate than urban in appearance makes Duquesne a sure bet for the new century.

Grove City College

Grove City, Pennsylvania 16127

Setting: Small town
Control: Private (Presbyterian)
Undergraduate enrollment: 1162 men, 1137 women
Graduate enrollment: None
Student/faculty ratio: 16:1
Freshman profile: 23% scored over 700 on SAT I verbal; 47% scored 600–700; 25% 500–599; 5% below 500. 23% scored over 700 on SAT I math; 50% scored 600–700; 24% 500–599; 3% below 500. 42% scored above 28 on the ACT; 20% scored 27–28; 29% 24–26; 7% 21–23; 2% below 21. 42% graduated in top tenth of high school class; 77% in upper fifth.

Faculty profile: 88% Ph.D.'s
Tuition and fees: $10,440
Room and board: $5344
Freshman financial aid: 47%; average scholarship or grant: $5104 need-based; $4919 non-need-based
Campus jobs: 52%; average earnings: $450/year
Application deadline: Early decision: Nov. 15; regular: Feb. 1
Financial aid deadline: Apr. 15
Admissions information: (724) 458-2100
  e-mail: admissions@gcc.edu
  web site: www.gcc.edu

Just over 20 years ago, tiny Grove City College became entangled in a controversy involving a Supreme Court case, nasty battles in Congress, and a seemingly negative future for Grove City students, who could receive no more federal financial aid. The Supreme Court ruled in 1984 that laws barring sex discrimination at schools and colleges affected any of their departments receiving federal dollars, including the financial aid office, which indirectly handles students receiving federal grants. While Grove City contended that it did not discriminate, it refused to sign a federal compliance form to that effect. Rather than play by Uncle Sam's rules, Grove City decided to stop enrolling students who received federal grants, creating its own Student Freedom Fund and replacing the lost government monies with privately funded assistance. What observers in 1984 predicted would be Grove City's fall from academic grace never happened. With the aid of generous alumni and other benefactors, Grove City offers a private, Christian-based education at a price that still rivals the in-state fees of many public colleges, just $15,800 for tuition, fees, room, and board in the 2005–2006 school year. Not quite half of the freshmen also receive financial help. This is not a college for everyone, but those who want a liberal arts education in a strong Judeo-Christian context leave Grove City with a well-respected degree and plenty of change in their pockets.

Student body: The geographic foundation of Grove City is widening, as just half of its undergraduates claim Pennsylvania as their home, compared with three-fourths several years ago. Also, students now come from 3 times as many states, 43 versus 15, although the largest contingent still is from the Middle Atlantic region. Eighty-five percent attended public schools. Almost a fifth, 19%, are Presbyterian, and 7% Catholic; most of the rest are members of other Protestant denominations (12% in a recent year were Baptist), though a fifth claim no religious affiliation. Foreign nationals from 8 countries and Asian-Americans account for 1% and 2% of the enrollment, respectively. African-Americans, Hispanics, and Native Americans each constituted less than 0.5% in a recent school year. Grove City students describe themselves as believers in strong Christian morals and generally conservative to ultraconservative in their political and social views. "Some are sheltered; others are not," says a senior. Undergraduates show respect for the college's administrators and professors and are generally kind-hearted and ready with a smile for one another. A majority are distinguished, too, by an adherence to the "Protestant work ethic" and set high standards for themselves academically and spiritually, on top of those already expected by the college. Twenty-four of the 582-member fall 2005 freshman class were National Merit finalists; 75 were high school valedictorians. Observes a senior: "The student body is primarily type A perfectionist types—needless to say the expectations are high so the students just work harder to exceed those expectations." At some point, many students have to learn to accept getting less than an A in every subject.

Academics: Grove City, founded in 1876, awards the bachelor's degrees in over 40 majors covering the liberal arts, sciences, engineering, and music. The academic year is divided into 2 semesters. Most classes range between 14 and 36 participants, with numerous opportunities for students to meet in courses with fewer than 6 attending. However, some students complain that the class sizes are increasing, with a few 400-level courses still enrolling between 30 and 40 notetakers.

The heart of Grove City's rigorous core curriculum is its Civilization Series, spread over 3 years, 1 course each semester. The humanities sequence begins in the fall semester of freshman year with Civilization, an introductory overview that leads to Civilization and the Biblical Revelation the following term, and ends with Modern Civilization in International Perspective, where second-semester juniors study the major ideas and events since the American and French revolutions. Undergraduates also must take 2 courses each in social sciences and international studies, natural sciences with labs, and quantitative and logical reasoning, as well as demonstrate competency in writing and a foreign language.

The faculty, who include 125 full-time and 59 part-time members, 22% of whom are women, are devoted solely to undergraduate teaching. "Their office doors, as well as their homes, are always open," notes a recent graduate, and professors often host spring get-togethers and Bible studies at their houses. Says a sophomore: "They do their best to keep track of what is going on in their students' lives." A no-tenure policy that keeps everyone on a 1-year contract weeds out poor teachers fairly quickly. Says a southerner: "There are solid values and morals here that affect the way almost every professor presents material and encourages all students, even those who disagree." Many professors lead the students in prayer before class or before exams. "Often this has a calming effect," says a molecular biology major.

The rigorous 4-year engineering program, with concentrations in electrical/computer and mechanical engineering, is the college's strongest offering. "For those who make it through," says an admiring junior, "their education is of such high quality that finding a job is a matter of choosing from many offers." In another triumph, graduates of Grove City's excellent education program recently finished first on the Pennsylvania Teacher's Exam, ahead of students from all other colleges and universities who took the test, and also achieved a 99% passage rate on the National Teacher Exam. Biology, mathematics, psychology, accounting, and business management also are widely respected by students.

While students are proud of the excellent preprofessional programs at Grove City, a number think that the liberal arts courses get short shrift. Says an accounting major: "Religion, English, philosophy, and other liberal arts majors are very limited in what is set up for them. They have excellent faculty but need more labs, books, and space for projects and career development." A new Hall of Arts and Letters, which was dedicated in January 2003, provides additional space for these programs and may give them the attention that students seek. A major in Christian thought says faculty in the religion and history departments in particular is "good but overworked. The members are burdened with teaching core classes and are unable to focus enough attention on classes and students within their majors." Political science would benefit from more opportunities for student internships. The communication program is newer and needs more faculty, funding, and courses to be competitive with programs at larger schools. Music majors could use more opportunities to gain experience performing. There is no major or minor in art, only 9 classes. Some students wish there were a classics program to complement the majors in French and Spanish.

Facilities: Henry Buhl Library is small and "by no means a research center," observes a sophomore. Many users consider the bulk of the 140,000 volumes too dated, with few books on new or controversial issues, though the collection of 1200 periodicals and newspaper subscriptions is much more satisfying. Fifty different periodical and reference databases, plus a computerized catalog, help students identify the materials they need. For serious research, most seek their sources either through the Internet, which is accessible from their dorm rooms, interlibrary loan, or by traveling to other campuses. As a place for study, the main floor of Buhl is especially sociable, though serious studiers can find peace in quiet rooms known as "the cages." Says a biology major: "Many students study in the library because guys and girls can study together there, which we cannot do in our dorms." A smaller curriculum library for education majors offers a wealth of children's literature, teaching aids, and equipment, plus a laminating machine.

Since fall 1994, members of each new freshman class have been issued a color notebook computer, most recently an HP Tablet PC, with the cost included in tuition. The computers have become even more useful to students as increasing portions of the campus have become wireless. Students generally use the campus technology center for computer assistance or to use the laser printers. Many professors have teaching packages on file for students to use as extra learning material.

Special programs: Though Grove City has no study-abroad programs of its own, qualified students may spend the junior year overseas and receive full credit toward a Grove City degree. Internships in Washington, D.C. also are an option.

Campus life: All students, unless married or commuting from their parents' homes, are required to live on the 150-acre campus, which is divided by Wolf Creek. "It's a GCC tradition not to walk on the quad," observes a senior, "so the center of campus has a rich, green lawn surrounded by Gothic-looking brick and stone buildings." Students live on the upper campus in all-male and all-female dormitories and can visit the other sex's rooms only certain hours during the weekend. The 8 local sororities are becoming less popular, though they still attract 17% of the women, down from half a few years ago. The 7 local fraternities enroll 15% of the men, an equally sharp drop from 30% only 6 years before. Says a junior: "More people are realizing what division they (the Greeks) cause, and that at a Christian school, they should be uniting instead of separating themselves into elite groups." Student-sponsored dances and coffeehouses are popular alternative activities. A campus staple is the Salt Company, a Christian organization that meets for fellowship on Friday nights. Warriors for Christ praise and prayer meetings attract 500 students each week. Chapel attendance is required 16 times a semester throughout a student's 4 years at Grove City. The campus is well lit and well patrolled, so crime is not considered a problem. One sophomore reports leaving his Visa card on a table at the student union. "Someone turned it in to campus security and I picked it up the next day," recalls the student. Some women residents grumble, however, that all doors but the main one to the women's residence halls have been locked at 9 p.m., while the men's doors have remained open. Says a junior: "I have found this to be annoying at times, as I might have to walk further to get into my dorm, but I consider it a small price to pay in return for such a safe environment."

As a whole, the 9 men's and 10 women's intercollegiate teams competing in NCAA Division III draw decent-sized crowds to their games; Wolverines football, basketball, and soccer chalk up the best attendance. Club sports, like lacrosse and rugby, also are popular. Three-quarters of the men and 60% of the women take part in the 10 intramural sports for men and the 11 for women.

For getaways, students head out of Grove City (pop. 8000) and point 60 miles south to Pittsburgh.

Cost cutters: Despite the lack of federal financial aid, for 47% of the freshmen and 38% of continuing students in the 2005–2006 school year, Grove City's already low tuition was reduced even further by special institutional financial help. Forty-one percent of the freshmen and 33% of the remaining undergraduates received need-based assistance. The average freshman package for students with financial need included a need-based scholarship or grant averaging $5104. Other non-need-based awards and scholarships for first-year students averaged $4919. An average 2005 graduate left with debts of $23,409. One of the most prestigious merit awards is the Trustee Academic Scholarship, which pays $5000 to up to 24 high-achieving high school students. Presidential Scholarships in varying amounts are available to freshmen who ranked first or second in their graduating class or who are National Merit finalists. Up to 4 high-achieving students planning to major in engineering can reduce their costs with awards paying $2500. A payment plan enables any student to spread a year's tuition and room and board payments over 10 months; the annual fee to enroll in the plan is $50. Since the college does not let students take out federal Stafford and Parent PLUS loans, Grove City also offers its own loan program that enables freshmen and sophomores to borrow up to $8500 a year and upperclassmen to borrow up to the cost of tuition less other financial aid. After receiving their first loan, all recipients must attend a college-sponsored seminar on debt management and an additional seminar on credit during their sophomore year.

Rate of return: Ninety-one percent of the entering freshmen return for the sophomore year. Seventy-seven percent graduate in 4 years; 80%, in 5 years.

Payoff: The largest number of 2005 graduates earned degrees in elementary education (9%), in English (7%), and mechanical engineering (6%). Eighty percent of recent graduates entered the job market, many with the more than 180 companies and organizations that recruited on campus. Employers included all major accounting firms, Mellon Bank, USS/USX, GTE, and Westinghouse plus several smaller organizations and school districts. Twenty percent headed directly to graduate or professional schools, about half of those pursuing advanced degrees in the arts and sciences and the rest divided nearly evenly among medical, law, and business schools.

Bottom line: The student who would be happiest, advises a junior is, "a high school student who truly values a challenging academic environment as well as a Christian environment. Grove City students tend to be overachievers with high expectations of themselves and those around them. They value Christian principles even if they are not Christian and they are willing to live in a very rural area for 4 years. Anyone who doesn't fit that profile can make it at Grove City College, but may not enjoy it as much."

Juniata College

Huntingdon, Pennsylvania 16652

Setting: Small town
Control: Private (Church of the Brethren)
Undergraduate enrollment: 649 men, 740 women
Graduate enrollment: None
Student/faculty ratio: 13:1
Freshman profile: 8% scored over 700 on SAT I verbal; 32% scored 600–700; 51% 500–599; 9% below 500. 7% scored over 700 on SAT I math; 46% scored 600–700; 40% 500–599; 7% below 500. 43% graduated in top tenth of high school class; 68% in upper fifth.
Faculty profile: 91% Ph.D.'s
Tuition and fees: $25,890

Room and board: $7240
Freshman financial aid: 99%; average scholarship or grant: $15,668 need-based
Campus jobs: 54%; average earnings: $626/year
Application deadline: Early decision: Nov. 1; regular: Mar. 1
Financial aid deadline: Mar. 1 (Some scholarships: Jan. 15)
Admissions information: (814) 641-3420; (877) JUNIATA
e-mail: admissions@juniata.edu
web site: www.juniata.edu

At an increasing number of colleges and universities, undergraduates are being required to follow a certain schedule of courses, both in their majors and in the area called general education, to ensure that they graduate with a breadth of knowledge in diverse fields and sufficient depth in at least 1 area. Often, it is only the brightest honor students who are permitted to bypass these mandates and design their own courses of study. That's not the case at Juniata College, a private institution of about 1400 undergraduates in central Pennsylvania, where instead of automatically choosing a preset major, each student with the help of 2 faculty advisors develops his or her own Program of Emphasis (POE). A student may select 1 of more than 65 already developed POEs, combine 2 existing ones into a third course of study, or create an entirely new program. The POE allows every student to tailor a course of study that suits his or her particular interests and to explore the specific aspects of a broader discipline that are important to him or her. The Program of Emphasis is but 1 example of a creative approach to curriculum that continues to attract bright students who wish to combine innovation with campus traditions. As a result, when people ask whether Juniata is just another small liberal arts college, from the campus comes a POE-like chorus: quoth the students, "Nevermore."

Student body: Seventy-two percent of Juniata's students are from Pennsylvania, with the rest mainly from the Northeast; 30 other states and 31 foreign countries are represented. Thirteen percent attended private or parochial schools. In the 2005–2006 school year, there were no members of the Church of the Brethren enrolled as students, although 2 years before, enrollment stood at 6%. Sixty-three percent were Protestant and 32% Catholic, with the rest of other faiths, or none. Students of color constitute 6% of the student body: 2% each African-Americans and Asian-Americans, and 1% each Hispanics and Native Americans. Foreign nationals account for another 5%. Undergraduates view themselves as "politically mixed"; the conservatives may hold the majority in terms of bodies, but the liberals tend to be more vocal. Few cliques exist within the enrollment, though Juniata has its share of students who are actively involved in clubs and other campus activities and those who mainly show up for class and parties. While the vast majority are concerned about getting good grades, they generally remain classmates and friends first, and become competitors second. Notes a premed major: "Students are willing to assist one another in all areas of academics, despite 'the curve,'" and peer tutoring and study groups before tests are commonplace.

Academics: Juniata was founded in 1876 by the Church of the Brethren. The college operates on a 2-semester schedule. Classes average 19 in size; introductory biology or chemistry lectures tend to be larger, with about 120 participants, though discussion sections are much smaller. At the junior and senior levels, classes with 10 or fewer are common.

In addition to the student-designed Program of Emphasis, every undergraduate must follow a curriculum that encompasses a freshman experience emphasizing critical reading and writing and transition to college; 2 cultural analysis courses; 2 courses from each of 5 areas: international studies, social science, natural science, humanities, and fine arts, and a class in math and statistics. Students must also take 4 courses from any discipline that emphasizes writing and/or speech communication.

Juniata's faculty numbers 138, of which 94 are full-time. Forty-one percent are women. Students describe their professors as down to earth, competent, very thorough, and fully engaged in after-hours campus functions. Notes a senior: "For the most part, they encourage us to ask questions and be honest about what we don't understand. They are willing to explain topics during office hours and to conduct supplementary study sessions. Most of all, they are excited by their disciplines and, in turn, excite their students." Some of the part-time professors have had a hard time adjusting their teaching styles to fit a smaller college.

Biology and chemistry are respected as perhaps Juniata's most demanding yet rewarding offerings. Virtually all of the natural sciences offer challenging faculties and exceptional equipment, including an electron microscope, 2 nuclear magnetic resonance spectrometers, and a radiation lab. There is no "cookbook chemistry" here, as a major once put it; rather, emphasis is placed on reasoning and thought. Students also join professors in such collaborative programs as the Science in Motion project; this takes students and teachers to schools throughout central Pennsylvania, where they give lectures and demonstrations on biology and chemistry. The multifaceted approach works. Within the past several years, over 90% of Juniata's applicants to medical, dental, optometry, podiatry, and veterinary schools have gained admission; the college also ranks in the top 2% among all private 4-year colleges and universities in the percentage of graduates who have gone on to obtain doctoral degrees in chemistry. Environmental science, which incorporates both biology and chemistry as well as geology in its coursework, also benefits from having the Raystown Field Station, which encompasses a living laboratory for student and faculty research consisting of 29,000 acres of land and an 8300-acre body of water. All of the sciences were enhanced with the completion in summer 2002 of the $20 million Von Liebig Center for Science, which is devoted to student research.

Nor are sciences Juniata's sole strong suit. Education majors are inspired by good professors on campus, as well as by practicums in the local schools nearly every semester and frequent work with young children at the campus' nationally accredited early childhood education center. Business (which uses the case method in many of its classes), history, and the program in peace and conflict studies also are excellent.

The college planned during the 2005–2006 school year to establish Programs of Emphasis in performing arts management and theater performance. Music has incurred some cuts and the art program continues to need more courses. Says a biology major: "This doesn't affect every student but it does affect the overall liberal arts image Juniata attempts to achieve." Criminal justice could use more professors. The foreign languages, with all levels of instruction using the innovative Rassias method available in French, Spanish, German, Chinese, and Russian, also need more professors and resources.

Facilities: The collection at L.A. Beeghly Library consists of 280,000 volumes and 1000 current periodical subscriptions, numbers many serious students find sufficient for the first level of research but little more. A computerized catalog, database searching, and the Internet help students find materials locally, at area colleges, and at libraries around the world. The massive libraries at Penn State also are just 30 miles north "with more resources than a student could possibly use," says a business major. Studying at Beeghly is usually satisfactory—"the place to be," says a psychology and English major—as the library offers different floors for different noise levels plus couches and chairs that give the air of a comfortable though sometimes crowded living room. The key, students say, is to not get distracted by seeing too many people they know.

More than 300 PCs are located in the main computer center in the science building, in the library, and in other academic buildings around campus, providing a total of 16 labs. Most are available until 1:30 a.m., 5 nights a week and up to 11 p.m. on Fridays and 5 p.m. on Saturdays. All residence-hall rooms are equipped for full Internet access. The college strongly recommends that students bring their own computers, preferably Dell. Many students already do so, which has helped reduce crowding at the labs. Students also may check out laptops and wireless cards to use around campus.

Special programs: About 30% of any junior class at Juniata studies off campus in such countries as Mexico, Japan, Spain, Germany, France, Great Britain, Ecuador, and Greece. Faculty participate in a program that brings professors from other countries to the campus. Students preferring to stay stateside can spend a semester in Philadelphia or in Washington, D.C. through the Washington Center. Several 3-2 engineering programs are offered, with Penn State, Columbia, Clarkson, and Washington universities. A 3-3 law program enables students to complete studies for a law degree at Duquesne in 6 years instead of 7. Cooperative degree programs also are available in the allied health and health professions. A relatively new program in information technology combines courses in business, communications, and computer science, and features internships based throughout the United States and abroad.

Campus life: All but 18% of the full-time students reside on the 110-acre main campus nestled in the foothills of the central Pennsylvania mountains, an area even the most sophisticated city dweller can't help but find lovely. Socially, though, the setting can be deadly for those not ready to make their own fun. There are no Greek organizations, and most students attend Friday Night Live entertainment with comedians and bands, weekly Saturday night dances or movies, and a Sunday afternoon artist series. Traditions such as the Madrigal Dinner, at which faculty and administrators both serve and entertain the students, and Mountain Day, an annual fall activity when classes are cancelled for an impromptu picnic and football game with the faculty and administration, are events anticipated and enjoyed by both new and continuing classes. Petty theft, which occurs primarily when students fail to lock their room doors, is the most troublesome crime on campus.

The intercollegiate program, which competes in NCAA Division III, offers 9 sports for men and 10 sports for women. Volleyball, football, and basketball attract the largest crowds. Juniata's volleyball teams, in particular, have earned a loyal following. "You would, too, if you were national champs," observes a senior. The women's team has competed in the NCAA Division III Tournament 25 times, making it to the semifinals 20 times. In 2004, the team won the national championship. The men's team also won the national title in 2004 as well as in 2005 and in 1998. Ten men's and 6 women's club sports from men's and women's rugby and lacrosse to Ultimate Frisbee also have good followings. The rugby teams also sponsor the Storming of the Arch and Pig Roast, 2 other of Juniata's much-loved traditions. The Laughing Bush Outing Service gets students involved in less structured outdoor activities. Twenty-eight percent of the men and 19% of the women take part in the 4 intramural sports provided for each group.

When students want to get away without going far, many head for the cliffs a quarter mile from campus, where they can sit in peace and look down upon the whole town of Huntingdon (pop. 9000). The Elizabeth Evans Baker Peace Chapel, designed by architect Maya Lin, who designed the Vietnam Veterans' Memorial in Washington, D.C., also is a favorite spot for quiet reflection on the adjoining 315-acre Baker-Henry Nature Preserve. For a livelier outing, Altoona or State College, home of Penn State University, is just 45 minutes away.

Cost cutters: Ninety-nine percent of the freshmen and 98% of continuing students received financial help in the 2005–2006 school year. Seventy-nine percent of the first-year students and 77% of the rest were granted need-based assistance. The average freshman award included need-based scholarships or grants averaging $15,668 and need-based self-help aid such as loans and jobs averaging $4551. The average financial indebtedness of a 2005 graduate totaled $22,131. Various scholarships pay from $2000 to $12,000 to students with exemplary academic credentials. A special merit scholarship program provides opportunities for outstanding students to compete for 1 of 4 awards paying full tuition, room, and board, or 1 of 20 paying full tuition. Fields recognized by the scholarships are the arts, environmental responsibility, leadership, and service and peacemaking. The deadline for applying for these awards is in early January. A Native American Scholarship pays up to $10,000 to entering students of Native American heritage with financial need. There also are extensive opportunities for part-time employment. To assist with financial planning, Juniata offers a conditional guarantee that college-sponsored aid will remain unchanged for a student's 4 years of attendance. A 10-month payment plan also is an option for a nominal fee.

Rate of return: Eighty-five percent of Juniata's freshmen return for a second year. Sixty-eight percent graduate in 4 years; 74% within 5 years; 75% within 6.

Payoff: Biology and pre-health professions majors accounted for 14.5% of the 2005 graduates, with degrees in business and accounting also comprising 14.5%, and degrees in education just over 14%. Thirty-five percent of recent graduates went directly on for advanced degrees. In a recent national study of 518 private institutions that do not grant doctoral degrees, Juniata ranked in the top 60 in the percentage of graduates who go on to earn doctorates. The university's placement record is strong as well, with 97% of the seniors who registered with its placement service receiving jobs or involved in post-graduate education within 6 months after commencement. Graduates accepted positions primarily in the Northeast with firms such as AT&T, the Dow Jones Foundation, Northwestern Mutual, IBM, and Sears. Their pursuits ranged, however, from the Peace Corps to work in high finance. Twenty companies and organizations recruited on campus in the 2004–2005 school year.

Bottom line: From the Program of Emphasis, in which students design their own curricula, to the on-campus weekends, in which they design their own fun, Juniata is a place for the independent scholar at any level. Notes a junior: "Younger students don't need to work their way up some sort of ladder in order to hold leadership positions here. At Juniata, you never feel like a freshman."

King's College

Wilkes-Barre, Pennsylvania 18711

Setting: Urban
Control: Private (Roman Catholic)
Undergraduate enrollment: 1009 men, 840 women
Graduate enrollment: 13 men, 35 women
Student/faculty ratio: 16:1
Freshman profile: 2% scored over 700 on SAT I verbal; 14% scored 600–700; 46% 500–599; 38% below 500. 2% scored over 700 on SAT I math; 17% scored 600–700; 46% 500–599; 35% below 500. 33% graduated in top fifth of high school class; 60% in upper two-fifths.
Faculty profile: 83% Ph.D.'s

Tuition and fees: $21,220
Room and board: $8590
Freshman financial aid: 98%; average scholarship or grant: $5700 need-based; $7964 non-need-based
Campus jobs: 20%; average earnings: $1200/year
Application deadline: Rolling
Financial aid deadline: Feb. 15
Admissions information: (570) 208-5858; (888) 546-4772
e-mail: admissions@kings.edu
web site: www.kings.edu

Any college founded by the Holy Cross Fathers of what many consider to be the premier Catholic university in the nation, the University of Notre Dame, is bound to have the seeds of greatness stored somewhere within it. But King's College in Wilkes-Barre, Pennsylvania, which turns 60 in 2006, didn't wait long to establish its own reputation distinct from that of its founding fathers. Though hardly a household name, this college of Christ the King has gained national recognition for a comprehensive core curriculum that sends majors in the popular fields of accounting, elementary education, and physician assistant into the job market with nearly half their academic credits in the liberal arts. The core consists of instruction and reinforcement of skills in areas from writing to critical thinking, as well as required coursework in fields from human behavior to global awareness. It also mandates that every student take 4 courses under the heading "Informed Believing and Acting." Students taking the classes use such adjectives as *excellent, challenging,* and *intense* to describe the coursework. The college itself has recorded notable benefits from the program in terms of a higher student retention rate, rising LSAT scores for those planning to attend law school, and an increase in both use of the campus library and attendance at on-campus cultural events. But today's career-minded students, more impressed with the college's near-perfect job placement rates in numerous fields, also sense that they are getting something more for their money. Remarks a junior: "King's core provides us with a broad liberal arts foundation that may later be applied to *any* major field of study—and to life!"

Student body: Seventy-seven percent of King's College undergraduates are from the Keystone State; the rest, primarily also from the Middle Atlantic region, represent 16 other states and 7 foreign countries. Two-thirds are graduates of public schools. Fifty-nine percent of the student body are Catholic, 13% Protestant, and 1% Jewish; for 8%, religious affiliations are orthodox, or some other; for 19%, they are unknown. Minority enrollment is low, with 2% each African-American and Hispanic, and 1% each Asian-American and Native American. Seven international students attend. Students see themselves as a politically mixed group, with as many fervent Democrats and Republicans as there are those who are apathetic. Says a sophomore: "Students are free to share their feelings on tough issues in a manner that won't disturb the college community." Undergraduates report a "sense of camaraderie" that crosses class lines: "Whether you're a freshman or a senior, everyone is equal," says a junior. Most are hard workers and are academically motivated by personal choice as well as by the expectations of the school though a number still are content to do the minimum to get by. Observes a state resident: "If you are competitive, you will do all right; if you are laid back, you are in trouble."

Academics: King's College awards the bachelor's degree in 35 majors plus master's degree programs in health care administration, finance, accounting, and education with a concentration in reading. A 5-year physician assistant program leading to a master's degree also is offered. Courses are divided into a 2-semester schedule. There is an average class size of 20–30 in the freshman and sophomore years. As at most colleges, introductory science courses generally are larger, enrolling about 35 students; Psychology Statistics enrolls the highest number, with almost 50. Juniors and seniors can expect most classes to have fewer than 20.

The highly touted core curriculum consists of 18 courses that account for 54 of the 120 credits needed for graduation. Included are 15 credits of free elective options, which temper somewhat student criticism that the core and the major together account for too many required courses.

One hundred ten members of the faculty are full-time, and 69 part-time; all but 2 of the part-time teach undergraduates. Two-thirds are men, including many Catholic brothers and priests. While professors are considered knowledgeable and generally good at transmitting information, their human qualities are what count most with undergraduates. Says a senior: "Our faculty members are willing to go the extra mile for students whether it is editing a résumé, encouraging student-alumni relationships, or just taking an interest in the student outside of the classroom. You find them at our athletic fields supporting our teams, at the campus plays, leading service trips, and noting the accomplishments of our students in so many other ways." Most also uphold strict attendance policies to maximize the learning experience. Adds another senior: "As long as you are willing to work, they are willing to help as much as possible."

The college's preprofessional majors are where students find the most rigor—and a solid promise of postgraduate job satisfaction. In the William G. McGowan School of Business, virtually all accounting grads find employment in the field, and more than half, the product of highly successful internship programs, have been employed over the last several years by the major firms. The McGowan School itself is one of only 36 undergraduate schools of business nationwide to be accredited by the Association to Advance Collegiate Schools of Business. Chemistry and biology, along with an excellent interdisciplinary program in molecular biology, are respected as among the most demanding, research-intensive, and rewarding disciplines on campus; they also have become among the best housed after completion in spring 1994 of the $6.4 million Parente Life Science Center that includes more than $400,000 worth of equipment for new molecular biology and tissue culture laboratories. A $5.5 million reconstruction of the physical sciences building serves the computer science, mathematics, chemistry, physics, and physician assistant programs. Psychology features faculty "who know their field inside out, yet don't make students feel inferior," says a major. A neuroscience major combines the best of biology and psychology; a newer major in athletic training education and an existing program in health care administration are considered especially demanding. The physician assistant major, one of 50 programs of its type in the country, also has 100% job placement in a wide range of medical fields from psychiatry to emergency-room work. The education program gives students opportunities for plenty of experience as early as their sophomore year in public, Catholic, and Montessori classrooms. Among the liberal arts, the English department has doubled in size over the past several years and boasts a faculty that majors consider as inspirational as they are demanding. To help ease the job jitters of prospective English majors, alumni who graduated in the field, now attorneys, reporters, and English professors, return for an English Careers Day to show the range of jobs available.

Other departments in the liberal arts are considerably smaller. French and Spanish are the only foreign language majors offered, and the number of faculty is limited, meaning students may end up having the same professor several times. Spanish also needs more rigorous courses for students with greater fluency in the language. The theater major is small and there is no major in music. Physics was discontinued as a major but remains as a minor.

Facilities: Corgan Library qualifies as a quiet study center, except for a humming air circulation system that lulls some users to sleep. When research time rolls around, however, the library falls short in materials on hand, but stands tall in computerized access to information from around the globe. Corgan's collection of more than 171,000 volumes, 15,750 paper and electronic periodicals, and extensive online databases is generally adequate to meet most students' research requests. Arrangements with local institutions make available an additional 1.2 million volumes and 7100 periodicals. Those who can't wait a few days for the resources to arrive often go to Wilkes Library, 1 of 4 local libraries within 10 minutes of campus.

More than 300 computers located in the McGowan business building and 24-hour computer labs in three residence halls and the campus center are available for student and faculty use. The campus also is networked providing students full access to the Internet; the library, student center, business building, and an area outside also offer wireless access. "Computer availability gets a little tricky during midterms and finals," says a junior, "but you can normally find one if you try a few buildings."

Special programs: Students eager to try new experiences off campus can study abroad in 6 countries through an agreement with Webster and John Cabot universities, spend a semester in Washington, D.C., or cross-register for classes at Wilkes University or College Misericordia. An experiential learning program provides internship opportunities throughout the world in most majors. Recent interns have earned academic credit from placements at the White House, the U.S. Departments of State and Commerce, Walt Disney World, and Calvin Klein.

Campus life: Forty-three percent of the undergraduates reside on the 15-acre urban campus, with an additional 33 acres of athletic fields providing a bit more room to run. In fall 2003, a pedestrian mall area known as Monarch Court replaced a city street in the center of campus, providing a central gathering spot for students. There are no social fraternities or sororities (only 1 service fraternity and 1 service sorority with about 30 members apiece), but no one seems to notice because of the abundance of live entertainment on campus and parties held at off-campus houses and apartments. Connerton's Cafe on campus houses not only a coffee shop but also a stage where local bands, comedians, and other entertainers perform for good-sized crowds. The newly renovated and expanded Sheehy-Farmer Campus Center also provides extensive recreational and entertainment opportunities for students. Still, a number of students from the surrounding area do go home, though fewer than in previous years. Fifty clubs and organizations span the traditional range of student interests; the Accounting Association, with its regular trips and fund-raisers, is quite popular as is Habitat for Humanity and other outlets for community service. Security has increased in recent years, so crime is not regarded as a problem on campus, although off campus, students must use caution as some muggings have occurred. For additional help, security guards are prevalent, emergency call boxes have been installed on as well as off campus and an escort service travels off campus, too.

Basketball and football are the biggest crowd pleasers of the 1 coed, 11 men's, and 10 women's teams that play in NCAA Division III. Seven intramural sports for men and 6 for women involve 55% of the men and 35% of the women.

Within the city of Wilkes-Barre (pop. 43,000), a favorite place to relax is Kirby Park, 2 blocks from campus. Those who are avid sports fans enjoy watching ice hockey at nearby Wachovia Arena, home of the Wilkes-Barre/Scranton Penguins as well as AAA baseball with the Scranton Red Barons at a stadium located within a short drive of campus. Few students make ambitious road trips, other than to travel home or occasionally to Penn State or Temple University. New York City and Philadelphia are each about a 2-hour drive away. Skiing and snowboarding in the Poconos is popular in winter.

Cost cutters: Ninety-eight percent of freshmen and 96% of continuing students received financial aid in fall 2005. For at least 70% of both groups, the aid was need-based. The average freshman award for first-year students with financial need included a need-based scholarship or grant averaging $5700 and need-based self-help aid such as loans and jobs averaging $4400. Other non-need-based awards and scholarships for first-year students averaged $7964. For 2005 graduates, the average debt totaled $17,263. Institutionally funded aid based on merit and need more than doubled over a recent 7-year period from $3.6 million to $8.4 million. Full tuition Presidential Scholarships go to 8 to 12 students who rank in the top 5% of their high school graduating classes and have strong SAT or ACT scores. Moreau Scholarships to those drawn from the top 12% of their high school classes vary in value from $11,000 to $14,000 according to the strength of the SAT scores, extracurricular activities, and personal qualities. Christi Regis scholarships pay $7000 to $10,500 to students from the upper fourth of their high school classes. Deprizio Awards worth $3000 to $6500 go to those entering first-year students drawn from the upper 50% of their graduating classes who do not meet the criteria for the more competitive scholarships. A cooperative education program is offered in special education.

Rate of return: Eighty-one percent of the freshmen return for the sophomore year. Sixty-two percent graduate in 4 years; 69% in 5 years; 70% within 6.

Payoff: Nearly a third of the 2005 graduates earned bachelor's degrees in 3 career-related areas: 12% in elementary education, 10% in business administration, and 8% in accounting. Most of the new alumni find jobs in business and industry, various levels of government, social service agencies, education, and health care, primarily in the Northeast and Middle Atlantic states. In a recent class, 97% found jobs in their field of study. Major employers include the national accounting firms, SmithKline Beecham, Alltel Information Systems, Godiva Chocolatier, Ingersoll-Rand, Blue Cross/Blue Shield, Prudential Investments, and Nabisco. Eighteen percent of recent graduates pursued advanced degrees.

Bottom line: A King's College degree in any of several well-respected professional fields will almost ensure an excellent first job after graduation; a King's College education, through the comprehensive core curriculum, will provide sustenance throughout a graduate's life.

Lycoming College

Williamsport, Pennsylvania 17701

Setting: Small town
Control: Private (United Methodist)
Undergraduate enrollment: 633 men, 822 women
Graduate enrollment: None
Student/faculty ratio: 16:1
Freshman profile: 2% scored over 700 on SAT I verbal; 19% scored 600–700; 49% 500–599; 30% below 500. 1% scored over 700 on SAT I math; 18% scored 600–700; 53% 500–599; 28% below 500. 0% scored above 28 on the ACT; 14% scored 27–28; 43% 24–26; 29% 21–23; 14% below 21. 19% graduated in top tenth of high school class; 36% in upper fifth.

Faculty profile: 92% Ph.D.'s
Tuition and fees: $24,255
Room and board: $6542
Freshman financial aid: 82%; average scholarship or grant: $14,694 need-based; $9504 non-need-based
Campus jobs: 43%; average earnings: $1110/year
Application deadline: Apr. 1
Financial aid deadline: Apr. 15 (Priority date: Mar. 1)
Admissions information: (570) 321-4026; (800) 345-3920
e-mail: admissions@lycoming.edu
web site: www.lycoming.edu

It sounds like the beginning of a well-worn riddle: What did the Presbyterians sell to the Methodists that grew in years through the years? The answer, of course, is Lycoming College, one of the 50 oldest colleges in the United States, which draws its name from the Indian word "Iacomic," meaning Great Stream. The college traces its roots to Williamsport Academy, the first elementary and secondary school in Williamsport, Pennsylvania, which was founded in 1812 and run by a board of largely Presbyterian trustees. Once the community gained its own public school system, the private academy became a financial burden. A visionary circuit preacher persuaded the Methodists to buy the school from the Presbyterians in 1848. Over the next 100 years, the former primary school became a seminary, a junior college, and finally, in 1947, a 4-year degree-granting college of liberal arts and sciences. But while other colleges have sought graduate-level programs and a predominantly preprofessional focus, Lycoming has held true to its liberal arts foundation, and recently was described by a noted educational expert as "one of the 212 true liberal arts colleges in the United States." Few circuit preachers ever reaped such rich and lasting earthly rewards.

Student body: Seventy percent of Lycoming's students are from Pennsylvania, with most of the others coming also from the Middle Atlantic region. Twenty-two states and 12 foreign countries send students to campus. Eighty-one percent of the students graduated from public schools. Protestants make up nearly two-thirds of the enrollment; Methodists alone compose almost one-fifth; Catholics, just under a third. African-Americans constitute 3% of the enrollment; Asian-Americans and Hispanics each make up 1%, as do foreign nationals. "At second glance, the school doesn't seem diverse," observes a junior, "but more than color here, there is a wide range of backgrounds that brings a better mix into the culture." Undergraduates see themselves as fairly conservative, with a general sense of respect for each other and little hierarchy between classes. Most are hard workers, concerned about getting good grades, who stay focused, though not driven, toward their post-graduation plans for either more schooling or a good job. Says a criminal justice major: "Students take their academics seriously, however, an A– is *not* the end of the world." Socially, there are the energetic who take leadership roles in a wide range of campus activities, and the apathetic who are content to party and little more. Students from both ends and the great wide middle, though, especially value the lack of cliques. Notes a junior: "I have friends who participate in sports, theater, Greek life, and many other different areas and it is great to hang out with people with different interests."

Academics: Lycoming awards the bachelor of arts degree in 34 majors. A fifth of all recent graduates had two majors. Classes follow a 2-semester calendar. Class sizes vary, though the range is not very extreme. Says a senior: "An entering freshman can expect to see a class as small as 10 and as large as 100," with introductory science lectures taking the high end. Upperclassmen are more likely to encounter courses with 5 to 25 participants.

Lycoming's distribution requirements include courses in traditional fields, including a class related to cultural diversity. Students must complete 3 writing intensive courses, 1 in the major field of study. Two semesters of work also are required in physical activities courses, varsity athletics, wellness courses, or community service projects.

For many students, close relationships with professors is what keeps them at Lycoming. All but 15 of the 103 faculty members are full-time. Thirty-seven percent are women. "The faculty are great people," comments a senior. "They take the time to get to know you as an individual and know your strengths and weaknesses in the classroom." Adds another senior: "Even those professors with whom I have had differences have been very available and helpful."

Students pick a wide range of liberal arts and professional programs as Lycoming's list of the best. Biology and chemistry have only gotten stronger since the opening of a $10 million building in 1990 that, as part of its standard equipment for undergraduates, provides X-ray, tissue culture, genetics, and nuclear magnetic resonance labs; 2 electron microscopes; and 50 individual Bausch & Lomb microscopes, enough for each student in a laboratory. Adds a chemistry major: "Also, chemistry and biology have many opportunities for research projects on campus during the summer and off campus working for companies. Chemistry in particular offers internships with Merck Pharmaceuticals." The conversion of the old gymnasium into a fine arts building has provided equally wonderful facilities for student painters, sculptors, welders, graphic designers, and others. Says an art major: "The windows of the building are huge and the interior is white so the amount of natural light that comes in is immense, creating the perfect place for an artist to work." Students majoring in the already solid accounting, business administration, and economics programs get an added lift from the Institute of Management Studies that provides expanded opportunities for internships and involvement in faculty research and projects. Psychology features "a knowledgeable core of concerned professors," says a major, although some students would like to see more labs and more opportunities for field experience. The creative writing program attracts bright students and dynamic faculty; history, political science and criminal justice draw kudos as well.

Lycoming's highly respected Bachelor of Science in Nursing degree program was discontinued in August 2003. Communication has suffered the past few years from having too few faculty (just 2 full-time members plus one visiting and one part-tme), too many students, and outdated equipment but majors say opportunities for internships in corporate communications and hands-on work at the campus radio and television stations as early as freshman year are plentiful. The foreign languages program, with majors in French, Spanish, and German, needs more class offerings, though students rate the existing faculty quite highly. Says a Spanish major: "The professors speak the language you are studying outside of the classroom with you for practice and help with study abroad and job opportunities. . . . My Spanish teacher also made us dinner at the beginning of the semester to catch up on things." The music department offers a strong choral program but has no string program. "There is not much room to spread your wings in the instrumental area," says a music major, who instead is able to play with the Williamsport Symphony Orchestra. The criminal justice and political science departments need more full-time faculty and more courses, though the ones they offer are excellent.

Facilities: What John G. Snowden Memorial Library lacks in the breadth of its own collection of 188,000 volumes and 1150 current periodicals, it more than makes up for in the extensiveness of its computerized offerings. Along with its own automated catalog, Snowden offers a wide range of CD-ROM and on-line database searches. Better yet, instruction in how to use this technology is incorporated into numerous courses. What material Snowden does not have usually can be obtained through interlibrary loan, often from nearby Bucknell and Susquehanna universities. At times, Snowden can become a social as well as an informational gathering place. However, night owls are quietly applauding the extended weekday library hours until midnight, in response to results of a student survey asking for more study time.

A total of 5 computer labs with 180 units share extended hours on campus. Says a sophomore: "I have never seen or even heard of anyone waiting in line for a computer. During finals week, the library computers get filled but the other labs are always open." Residence halls also have all been wired for individually owned units, providing access to e-mail and the Internet. The campus also is wireless. The college strongly encourages students to bring their own personal computers, preferably an IBM ThinkPad or Pentium 4.

Special programs: Students wishing to spend a semester off campus can take a term in Philadelphia, Washington, D.C., Harrisburg, Pennsylvania, or at any of 2 colleges and universities in England, 2 in Spain, and 1 each in France and Ecuador. More than 200 opportunities for internships also are available. Cooperative programs are offered in forestry or environmental studies with Duke University, in optometry with the Pennsylvania College of Optometry, and in podiatry with the Pennsylvania or Ohio College of Podiatric Medicine.

Campus life: Eighty-three percent of Lycoming's students reside on the 35-acre campus, whose colonial-style buildings give newcomers their first sense that this is how a college ought to be. Because many of the students' families live within a few hours of campus, about a third may leave for a visit home over any given weekend. However, for those who stay, Lycoming offers much in the way of entertainment. Sixteen percent of the men and 24% of the women belong to 5 national fraternities and 2 national and 3 local sororities. Observes a New Yorker: "When the Greeks have parties, they encourage independents to party with them and most of the time, independents take them up on their offer." For those who don't, the Campus Activities Board offers a smorgasbord of concerts, casino nights, dances, and free movies. United Campus Ministries, Habitat for Humanity, and a student-run tutoring program for adults and school-aged children also get a lot of undergraduates involved in their respective projects. Petty theft, largely from residence hall rooms that have been left unlocked, and vandalism are the biggest crimes on campus. Security patrols each dormitory floor once an hour to continue to keep the crime rate low. An escort service also is available, and call boxes recently were installed outside each residence hall building, and parking lot. Says a sophomore: "I'm more scared of the brave little gray squirrels on campus than anything else."

Warrior football is the main attraction on fall weekends, leading the list of 9 men's and 9 women's intercollegiate sports played in NCAA Division III. Men's and women's basketball, lacrosse, and soccer also draw enthusiastic crowds. Three-fourths of the men and 60% of the women opt to unwind by playing the 2 coed or 6 men's or 6 women's intramural sports offered. The Wilderness Club also involves many in hiking, biking, and other outdoor activities.

Williamsport, with a greater metropolitan population of 75,000, is best known as the birthplace of Little League baseball and site of its annual international championship. For big city action, some students visit such metropolitan centers as New York City, Philadelphia, Washington, D.C., Baltimore, and Pittsburgh, each less than a 4-hour drive. A more frequent destination is the Big Ten campus life of Penn State, just 60 miles away.

Cost cutters: Eighty-two percent of the freshmen and 83% of continuing students received financial aid in the 2005–2006 school year; virtually all the aid was based at least in part on need. The average freshman award for a student with need included a need-based scholarship or grant averaging $14,694 and need-based self-help aid such as loans and jobs averaging $4095. Other non-need-based awards and scholarships averaged $9504. The average financial debt of a 2005 graduate was $23,343. Faculty Scholarships pay up to $16,000 a year to 6 students with combined SATs of at least 1950 (29 ACT), plus good performance on an interview. Departmental scholarships, worth up to $13,500 annually, go to 12 students with SATs of at least 1800 (27 ACT) and a 3.3 GPA. Dean's and Lycoming scholarships pay $8000 to $11,000 and $5000 to $7000 respectively, again based on a student's grade point average and standardized test scores. Trustee Scholarships recognizing valedictorians and salutatorians pay $16,000 a year; music, art, creative writing, theater, and community service scholarships each pay up to $2500 annually.

Rate of return: Eighty-three percent of Lycoming freshmen return for a second year. Sixty-one percent go on to graduate in 4 years; 69% finish within 5 years.

Payoff: Among 2005 graduates, 17% earned bachelor's degrees in business, 15% in psychology, and 12% in biology. A large number of alumni go on to make their careers in business (both management and ownership), accounting, teaching, health services, law, and the ministry. Twenty-five companies and other organizations recruited on campus during a recent school year. Twenty-four percent of recent graduates went on to graduate or professional school.

Bottom line: As Lycoming's long history demonstrates, this college has grown and adapted with the times, without losing its commitment to providing a well-rounded, residential collegiate experience. For those looking for a small college where professors and classmates want to know how you're doing, Lycoming could be the answer. As this junior put it: "Lycoming has given me the knowledge I need to be not only successful but happy in my life after school."

Messiah College

Grantham, Pennsylvania 17027

Setting: Small town
Control: Private (Interdenominational Christian)
Undergraduate enrollment: 1070 men, 1794 women
Graduate enrollment: None
Student/faculty ratio: 17:1
Freshman profile: 12% scored over 700 on SAT I verbal; 41% scored 600–700; 39% 500–599; 8% below 500. 9% scored over 700 on SAT I math; 39% scored 600–700; 41% 500–599; 11% below 500. 24% scored above 28 on the ACT; 20% scored 27–28; 28% 24–26; 17% 21–23; 11% below 21. 39% graduated in top tenth of high school class; 63% in upper fifth.
Faculty profile: 71% Ph.D.'s

Tuition and fees: $22,110
Room and board: $6800
Freshman financial aid: 99%; average scholarship or grant: $4879 need-based; $5906 non-need-based
Campus jobs: 55%; average earnings: $1783/year
Application deadline: Early action: Nov. 15 and Jan. 15; regular: rolling
Financial aid deadline: Apr. 1
Admissions information: (717) 691-6000; (800) 233-4220
e-mail: admiss@messiah.edu
web site: www.messiah.edu

At Messiah College, 12 miles southwest of the Keystone State capital of Harrisburg, the Golden Rule—do unto others as you would have them do unto you—is just one of many precepts that students at this evangelical Christian college are expected to follow. According to a Community Covenant all students must agree to follow, gambling and the use of drugs, tobacco products, and alcohol are prohibited both on and off campus during students' enrollment at the college. Attendance at 24 chapel services per semester is required. Although just 4% of the students are members of the Brethren in Christ Church, which founded the college in 1909, virtually all undergraduates and faculty consider themselves born-again Christians and adhere to the school motto, "Christ Preeminent." The school's former slogan once printed on assorted written materials published by the college, "Rigorously Academic; Unapologetically Christian," reinforced what Messiah expects from the members of its community. While most students find the campus rules tolerable, and even less rigid than many had anticipated, an inner spirituality is what actually unifies the campus. Says a recent graduate: "At meal times, other students will sit down with a classmate who is eating alone, and the whole community hurts when the relative of a member passes on or some other tragedy occurs. Messiah is no place for people who don't care about others."

Student body: Fifty-two percent of Messiah's caring students are from Pennsylvania, with the rest also mainly from the Middle Atlantic region, though undergraduates congregate from 39 states and 28 foreign countries. Seventy-five percent are graduates of public high schools. All but 1% of the students are Protestant; that 1% are Catholic. African-Americans and Hispanics each comprise 2% of the enrollment; Asian-Americans constitute 1%; foreign nationals, 3%. While many undergraduates wish the college were more diverse, they acknowledge efforts are underway to increase understanding. Says a senior: "Messiah recognizes its homogenous nature and strives to expose students to many ideas, cultures, and religions through its push toward cross-cultural study." A number of students have served time with their families on missions overseas or hope to go on ones themselves. Students are generally conservative in their lifestyle and politics, usually tending to the Republican voice on issues. Most come from sheltered backgrounds—"Christian families in small town America," says a student from Nigeria—and are mindful of authority. "We're hard workers who place a high value on interpersonal relationships," says a psychology major. "We all are striving to be our best, yet we avoid comparing ourselves to one another, especially academically."

Academics: Messiah confers the bachelor's degree in more than 50 disciplines. In addition to the standard 2 semesters, the college also offers a 3-week January term. Classes average 22 students, with many seminars enrolling as few as 10 and General Chemistry recently posting over 150.

The 4-part recently revised general-education curriculum begins with a First Year Seminar plus another 3 credits each in oral communication and in "Created and Called for Community," which examines Messiah's Christian approach to education, the Old Testament, and other related topics. Undergraduates also must fulfill 35 credits of courses in the traditional liberal arts and sciences including 9 hours in Languages and Cultures and 2–3 hours in non-Western studies. The program concludes with 6 hours in Affirming the Christian Faith, which includes courses in knowledge of the Bible and Christian beliefs and another 6 hours in Living, Acting and Serving Responsibly, which includes courses in fitness and in understanding a pluralistic world. For majors in at least 6 disciplines, students spend 1 to 3 semesters at Messiah's campus in Philadelphia directly across from Temple University.

Messiah's faculty of 297 consists of 170 full-time and 127 part-time teachers; 35% are women. As professed Christians, most make an effort to relate coursework to Christianity. Professors generally mirror the finer qualities of their students, being described as friendly, caring, intelligent, hardworking, and sincere. "Christian professors tend to be more understanding," says a political science major, "but definitely not easier graders." As 1 senior summarizes the faculty: "Some professors are much better than others, some are more boring than others, some are stricter and give more work. But all professors have made it perfectly clear that they are available for help at anytime."

Students sing the praises of the School of the Humanities, which moved in 2003 along with the School of Education and the Social Sciences, into Boyer Hall, named for the late Ernest L. Boyer, Sr., the Messiah alumnus who served as the first U.S. Commissioner of Education. The 95,000-square-foot structure, the largest on campus, offers technologically advanced classrooms and a modern language lab, top-flight facilities equal to the 5-star faculty within. Says an English education major: "Faculty are excellent in their fields, very dedicated, and class sizes are small." Spanish majors find their faculty especially outstanding and the program strengthened by a requirement that all majors in French, German, and Spanish spend at least 1 semester overseas through the Brethren Colleges Abroad program. Some undergraduates say that the communication program could be more rigorous and its facilities on the Grantham campus more useful. Students majoring in various aspects of communications and broadcasting are among those undergraduates expected to spend at least one semester at the Philadelphia campus or at the Los Angeles Film Studies Center. The visual arts department offers excellent facilities and small classes led by professors who are talented artists who share a deep commitment to their students. Business classes carry "an ethical over-tone," says a marketing major, "which seems to be sought by more companies today." However, some find the degree too "generic" and easy. The engineering major is competitive with programs found at more technically oriented schools, thanks in part to the modern Jordan Science Center. The department's solar car "Genesis" finished in the top 10 in Sunrayce 99, one of the nation's top collegiate solar racing events. For the last few years, the Genesis Solar Racing team has competed in the Solar Splash, and in the 2004–2005 school year won a technical award for its design. Music, nursing, and computer science also thrive on the 4 E's: excellent facilities, exciting curricula, exemplary professors, and easy job placement upon graduation.

Many students view the coursework in psychology, human development and family science, sociology, and social work, as less demanding, although students expect steady improvement thanks to the observation lab and other facilities provided in the new Boyer building. Theater students find the facilities "limited" at the Grantham campus, but say those at the Philadelphia campus more than compensate.

Facilities: Murray Library, say students, is a great place for doing computerized research and adequate for finding sources at hand, but don't expect a quiet haven for study. "The acoustics are poor," says a junior, "and sound often echoes throughout the building." Students needing absolute quiet head to the 1 study section where rules of absolute silence are enforced. Five other areas are set aside for group work. Along with a printed collection of 296,000 volumes and 11,036 paper and electronic periodicals, the center houses a 25-computer IBM word-processing laboratory and a 28-computer Mac lab. The catalog is computerized, and databases in various fields assist greatly in research. Students who find the college collection too limited may borrow materials from the state library in Harrisburg, the Dickinson Law School library in Carlisle, and 18 other regional college libraries.

More than 500 computers are open for student use in the computer center, departmental labs, library, student center, and residence halls. Additionally, dorm rooms are wired for network connections for personal computers. Though technically the labs close at 11 p.m., students can make arrangements to stay longer to complete assignments. Wireless access is available in certain buildings and is gradually expanding across campus. A project extending wireless access during the 2005–2006 school year did not include outside areas, which may follow at a later time. Residence halls were scheduled to gain wireless access by the opening of school in fall 2006.

Special programs: Coursework in 6 majors must be completed at Messiah's Philadelphia campus, but students in almost all majors end up spending 1 or 2 enrichment semesters in the City of Brotherly Love. Undergraduates generally take 1 course at the college's living-learning center there and the others at Temple University. Further afield, students may join more than 2000 African students from more than 10 African nations at Daystar University in Nairobi, Kenya. Additional study-abroad opportunities through Brethren Colleges Abroad are available in England, France, Spain, Germany, Greece, Ecuador, Mexico, Japan, and China. Other programs in Latin American, Central American, Middle East, and Russian Studies also are offered. Students who prefer a closer look at domestic policy can take advantage of an American studies program in Washington, D.C., or internships in Harrisburg, the state capital, or can spend a semester or a year at any of 12 other Christian colleges throughout the United States.

Campus life: All but 16% of Messiah's students live in single-sex housing on the 485-acre campus. Open dorm hours when members of the opposite sex are allowed in the living quarters are restricted to weekends in the residence halls and until 11 p.m. daily in the apartments for upperclassmen. "The policies of no alcohol, no tobacco, designated 'open dorm' times, and respectful language create a comfortable place to live," says a junior. There is no Greek system, and "partying" is kept to a minimum, with ice cream socials, theme dances, lasertag, and concerts with contemporary Christian musicians serving as the most popular all-campus events. More than 750 students extend their Christian commitments through voluntary participation in various service activities and outreach teams that do everything from ministering to the elderly and homeless to street witnessing in Harrisburg. Crime is minimal; the worst crime, says a sophomore, "is people doodling on library furniture." And students say they feel safe walking alone after dark through the well-lit campus though an escort service is offered. Additional public safety officers have been hired who are "really good at giving parking tickets, too!" adds a junior.

Seventy percent of the Messiah men and women participate in 8 men's and 8 women's intramural sports; a much smaller percentage plays on the 10 highly successful NCAA Division III varsity teams available to each. Messiah marks its seasons by a change in playing fields, with soccer and field hockey taking precedence in the fall, basketball in the winter, and track in the spring. The men's soccer team became national champions in 2000, 2002, 2004, and 2005. The women's soccer team were national champions in 2005. The women's basketball team was national runner up in 2001 as was the women's field hockey team in 2001, 2002, and 2005. Lacrosse also has a strong following.

Although the campus seems quite isolated to newcomers, Philadelphia and Baltimore are each just 90 minutes away, with Washington, D.C. only 30 minutes further. Hikes along the Appalachian Trail, which runs near campus, also are popular outlets.

Cost cutters: All but 1% of freshmen and all but 4% of continuing students received financial aid in the 2005–2006 school year; about 77% of both groups were given need-based assistance. The average award for first-year students with need included a need-based scholarship or grant averaging $4879 and average need-based self-help aid such as loans and jobs equaling $5885. Other non-need-based awards and scholarships for first-year students averaged $5906. A typical 2005 graduate left with debts of $23,249. Merit-based awards include 6 full-tuition Trustees' Scholarships; 80 President's Scholarships, worth 60% of tuition per year; Provost's Scholarships, which pay $2000–$10,000; and Dean's Scholarships for Scholastic Leadership, which pay $500–$3000 annually. To be considered for these awards, students must generally rank in the top 15%–20% of their high school graduating classes (10% for the Trustees' and President's Scholarships) and score at least 1100 on the combined math and critical reading SATs or 25 on the ACT (1300 SAT or 30 ACT for the Trustees' and President's awards). Multicultural scholarships pay full tuition to 3 students. Messiah Faculty Scholarships pay from $500 to $7000 to students with merit and need.

Rate of return: Eighty-five percent of entering freshmen return for a second year. Sixty-nine percent earn bachelor's degrees in 4 years; 75% in 5 years.

Payoff: Degrees in elementary education drew 8% of the 2005 graduating class, followed by 7% in nursing and 7% in psychology. Fourteen percent of the new alumni go on immediately for advanced study. Most of the rest take jobs primarily in the Northeast and New England. The largest numbers enter the fields of management, accounting, teaching, and service-oriented professions.

Bottom line: Advises a senior: "Students who enjoy engaging in learning as a conversation would benefit the most from a Messiah College education. Most of the classes involve extensive discussion in place of exclusive lecture, and students should be willing to participate. Writing also is highly emphasized, so those not interested in working to improve and constantly use their writing skills will not succeed as well." Students also must weigh the importance of the Christian component to their education. Observes a sophomore: "The Christian atmosphere at Messiah is very prevalent so it takes someone who wants to be in that environment."

Moravian College

Bethlehem, Pennsylvania 18018

Setting: Suburban
Control: Private (Moravian Church in America)
Undergraduate enrollment: 638 men, 895 women
Graduate enrollment: 18 men, 20 women (191 part-time)
Student/faculty ratio: 12:1
Freshman profile: 7% scored over 700 on SAT I verbal; 27% scored 600–700; 52% 500–599; 14% below 500. 6% scored over 700 on SAT I math; 31% scored 600–700; 51% 500–599; 12% below 500. 31% graduated in top tenth of high school class; 53% in upper fifth.
Faculty profile: 84% Ph.D.'s

Tuition and fees: $25,263
Room and board: $7530
Freshman financial aid: 95%; average scholarship or grant: $7757 need-based; $8663 non-need-based
Campus jobs: 44%; average earnings: $731/year
Application deadline: Early decision: Jan. 15; regular: Feb. 15
Financial aid deadline: Mar. 15 (Priority: Feb. 14)
Admissions information: (610) 861-1320; (800) 441-3191
e-mail: admissions@moravian.edu
web site: www.moravian.edu

In the years before 1750, when the few schools of higher learning in Colonial America were for men only, settlers from Germany and Moravia (which became part of the Czech Republic) founded the community of Bethlehem, Pennsylvania, on Christmas Eve, 1741. That task completed, they then opted to unveil a more radical approach to education. In May, 1742, they founded 2 schools; 1 for young men and 1 for young women. Over the next 212 years, the two schools each changed and evolved, until merging as a single coed college in 1954. The foundation had been laid, however, for what was to become the nation's sixth oldest college, Moravian College, which remains associated with the Moravian Church in America. Just 2% of the students are Moravian (36% are Catholic), and the most visible religious connection is the popular Christmas vespers candlelight service, which attracts more than 6000 participants. However, Moravian remains the only member of the nation's 6 original colleges—Harvard, William and Mary, Yale, St. John's, and the University of Pennsylvania being the other 5—to maintain the church affiliation, however loose, that helped spark its founding. Exclaims a senior: "There's a lot to be said about a college in which you can sit in the same room where John Adams wrote a letter to his wife, or where George Washington was entertained."

Student body: More than half, 59%, of Moravian's undergraduates are Pennsylvanians; the vast majority of the rest also are from the Middle Atlantic region, though 24 states and 10 foreign countries have students enrolled. Along with the 38% of the students who are Catholic or Moravian, 45% are Protestant, 1% are Jewish, and 3% follow various other religious faiths. A fourth of the students attended private or parochial schools. Minority enrollment remains small at 3% Hispanic, 2% each African-American and Asian-American, and less than 1% Native American. Foreign nationals account for just over 1%, although their number seems greater thanks to the influence of the Multicultural Club on campus. Undergraduates tend to be middle of the road politically and adhere to traditional family values. As at many colleges, a small group of dynamic individuals, representing at most a fourth of each new class, coordinate and dominate most campus activities. However, all students generally are receptive to Moravian's strong sense of community, produced by the campus's small size and long history, which provides, in the words of a senior, "a distinct feeling of belonging." Academically, students place Moravian in the middle ranks, competitive enough for each person to try to do his or her best but sufficiently laid back to allow time for friends and after-hours fun. Entrance in fall 2005 of the largest and most academically talented class in the college's history promises to raise the overall dedication to learning yet another notch.

Academics: Moravian confers the bachelor's degree in more than 40 majors and tracks plus a master's in business administration and in curriculum and instruction. The college follows a 2-semester plan plus an optional May term. Two-thirds of all classes have fewer than 20 students.

Moravian offers entering freshmen their choice of 2 general education programs. Twenty first-year students who have demonstrated a clear sense of direction may select the Add-Venture program in which they design their own curriculum and are allowed greater flexibility within the liberal arts curriculum. All other students take part in a Learning in Common program that includes a freshman experience and courses from 3 categories: foundational, multidisciplinary, and upper division. The foundational category offers courses in writing, quantitative reasoning, foreign language, and laboratory science. The multidisciplinary category is comprised of courses in historical studies; literature; ultimate questions; economics, social, and political systems; cultural values and global issues; and aesthetic expression. The upper-division category includes a course on the social impact of science and a course on moral life. Other requirements include writing and speaking across the curriculum, computer literacy, and physical education.

Moravian's faculty consists of 115 full-time and 78 part-time professors. Forty-three percent of all faculty are women. Faculty are valued most for a willingness to listen and learn as well as lecture. Notes an elementary education major: "Students should not be surprised when a faculty member calls them by name or works one-on-one with them during a class...In the Moravian classroom, you are dealing with a friend and a mentor who cares about where your future will take you." For their part, says a senior, "students are expected to take responsibility, attend class daily, and interact with the professors."

In most of the college's strongest majors, students enjoy a diverse range of concentrations within the broader field. Depending on his or her career interest, a psychology major can pursue any of 5 tracks, in clinical-counseling, industrial-organizational, experimental, social-developmental, and individually designed programs. Across the board, faculty members are "consistently challenging and encouraging to the students," says a major. The opening in fall 2002 of psychology facilities in a new 3-story academic complex shared with mathematics and computer science, sociology, and education, raised the academic opportunities even higher. Music, a historical favorite of the Moravian Church, offers 4 areas of emphasis: music education, composition, performance, either vocal, instrumental, or jazz, and sacred music. Art, a solid major attracting about 9% of each new class, features multiple levels of coursework and well-equipped options in studio art, graphic and interactive design, art education, and art history and criticism. "Students receive private studios beginning in their junior year," says an art education major. "Trips to Washington, D.C., and New York are frequent to keep up to date with current art trends and the studying of the old."

Other highly regarded programs that demand excellence but are generous with personal attention include physics, biology, chemistry, history, foreign language, and education. Education's practice of placing students in the classroom as early as their freshman year "allows the student to make the decision very early about whether teaching is right for him or her," says a major for whom it was right. A major in nursing, offered in collaboration with St. Luke's Hospital School of Nursing, easily makes many students' "A" list because of its excellent opportunities for hands-on experience with more than 1000 hours of supervised clinical instruction required.

While students find the 4 full-time political science professors to be first-rate, with expertise in such vital topics as China, the Middle East, and political theory, they say an even broader range of perspectives and courses is needed. Religion, too, could use more professors to teach required courses as well as more variety in the courses it offers.

Facilities: Reeves Library just keeps getting better and better, in the eyes of its student users. In the early 90s, the structure underwent a renovation that doubled its size, providing sufficient space for both group and individual study. "It's comfortable, with lots of cubbyholes in which to hide," says a chemistry major. Undergraduates hope the next step will be continued expansion of the collection, which numbers over 257,000 volumes and 1500 periodicals. Excellent computerized—and human—research assistance usually fills in the gaps. Students needing extra help turn to the library at Lehigh University, also in Bethlehem, which has more than 1 million volumes and 9700 periodicals, or make use of the more than 2 million volumes available through interlibrary loan. (The computer lists the holdings of 5 other area institutions.) Special collections in music and education also are available.

The opening of the Priscilla Payne Hurd Academic Complex brought with it additional computer labs for student use around the clock. Altogether, the college wireless network offers students over 100 PC and Mac terminals in 14 public labs and classrooms. While users may sometimes have to wait for a free unit during finals week at the popular lab in the library, computers at the other labs around campus, including several open around the clock, generally are available. Students with their own computers may access the network, including the Internet, from the residence halls.

Special programs: Students can expand their curricula by taking classes at 5 other Lehigh Valley institutions: Muhlenberg, Cedar Crest, and Lafayette colleges, and Lehigh and DeSales universities. Summer study in Spain, Mexico, or Germany is an option. Students may also spend a year at the Center for Medieval and Renaissance Studies in Oxford, England, or a semester in Washington, D.C. A 3-2 program in engineering is offered with Washington University in St. Louis and in national resource management with Duke. A co-op or transfer program in allied health sciences is offered with Thomas Jefferson University College of Allied Health Sciences. Cooperative programs in engineering and geology also are offered with Lehigh University.

Campus life: Seventy-one percent of the undergraduates reside on Moravian's 2 campuses, connected by a mile-long college bus or van ride dubbed the "Moravian mile." The Main Street campus is the larger. The Church Street site, known as the Priscilla Payne Hurd Campus, located in Bethlehem's historic district, includes 2 residence halls, with buildings dating from 1748 through 2002. Fourteen percent of the men and 22% of the women belong to 1 local and 2 national fraternities and 4 national sororities; students say the growth of nationally affiliated fraternities and sororities in the last few years has put more vigor into the program and increased student interest in their activities. They're "active on campus," says a senior, "but not an overwhelming force." Late Night at the ARC, held from 10 p.m. to 2 a.m. every Friday and Saturday night at the recreation center, offers students an alternative to the party scene. Other undergraduates opt to meet friends and take in whatever live entertainment is being offered at the Doghouse, a nonalcoholic campus pub. On any given weekend, a third of the campus residents opt to go home. Undergraduates find the campus both well lit and well patrolled with emergency call boxes and residence halls locked around the clock, so that crime, other than petty thefts, has not been much of a problem.

Greyhound football; men's and women's soccer, basketball, and track; and women's volleyball are the most popular NCAA Division III sporting events offered, 10 each for men and women. "It should be noted," observes a senior, "that all sporting events do draw crowds." More than a third of the men and a fifth of the women participate. Sixty percent of the men and 50% of the women take part in the 11 intramural sports open to each sex.

Bethlehem (pop. 75,000) is 90 minutes from Philadelphia and New York City, and student programming often sponsors bus trips to these and other nearby cities. Says a state resident: "Before I went to college, I never went to New York City, never went to a concert, never went to a museum. Moravian just opens your eyes to everything there is out there." Skiing and hiking in the Poconos are popular outdoor diversions; the banks of the Monocacy Creek offer a nearby spot for quiet reflection. The other Lehigh Valley colleges provide an easy and usually lively change of surroundings.

Cost cutters: In the 2005–2006 school year, 95% of the freshmen and 93% of continuing students received financial assistance. Help was based on financial need for 68% of the freshmen and 71% of the remaining students. The average award for a first-year student with financial need included a need-based scholarship or grant worth $7757 and self-help aid such as loans and jobs averaging $5008. Other non-need-based awards and scholarships averaged $8663 for fall 2005 first-year students. In a recent year, average debts for a grad totaled $12,505. The freshman class entering in fall 2005 contained a record 54 Comenius

Scholars. The Comenius Medallion Scholarship pays up to full tuition to students who rank in the top 5% of their high school class and achieve a score of at least 1450 on the critical reading and math portions of the SAT exam. Other Comenius Scholarships range in value from $10,000 to $15,000 and are offered to students who ranked in the top 10% of their high school graduating class and have a combined score of 1250 or higher on the critical reading and math portions of the SAT. The Trustee Scholarship recognizes membership in the National Honor Society, and a ranking in the top fifth of the high school class, with an annual award ranging from $6000 to $10,000. The Founders' Scholarship, for students with class rank in the top fourth or an 1150 combined critical reading and math score on the SAT, pays $4000 to $8000 annually. All Comenius scholarships also require a minimum score of 500 on both the critical reading and math portions of the SAT. Other scholarships that recognize leadership potential, challenging circumstances in preparing for college, and superior academic performance and interest in science also are available.

Rate of return: Eighty-six percent of entering freshmen return for the sophomore year. Seventy percent graduate in 4 years; 74%, in 5 years.

Payoff: Majors in sociology comprised 16% of the 2005 graduating class, leading those taking degrees in psychology (15%) and management (12%). Most new alumni remain on the East Coast and take jobs with such firms as AT&T, Dun and Bradstreet, Air Products and Chemicals, Merck, Sharp, & Dohme, and Deloitte and Touche. Almost a fifth of the recent graduates pursued advanced degrees immediately after commencement, nearly half of them in the arts and sciences.

Bottom line: Moravian, say its students, is not a college whose sense of community or whose curricula can be captured through a catalog. "Moravian is a small national treasure," boasts an English major. "If a student is seeking an institution that will not only provide an exemplary education but also opportunities for leadership skills, intellectual growth, and independence, Moravian just might be that school, as it is the school for the varsity athlete, the scholar, the musician, and the artist."

The Pennsylvania State University

University Park, Pennsylvania 16802

Setting: Small city
Control: Public
Undergraduate enrollment: 18,013 men, 15,195 women
Graduate enrollment: 2825 men, 2229 women
Student/faculty ratio: 17:1
Freshman profile: 8% scored over 699 on SAT I verbal; 36% scored 600–700; 44% 500–599; 12% below 500. 15% scored over 700 on SAT I math; 47% scored 600–700; 32% 500–599; 6% below 500. 41% graduated in top tenth of high school class; 78% in upper fourth.
Faculty profile: 77% Ph.D.'s

Tuition and fees: $11,508 in-state; $21,744 out-of-state
Room and board: $6530
Freshman financial aid: 48%; average scholarship or grant: $5033 need-based; $3880 non-need-based
Campus jobs: NA; average earnings: NA
Application deadline: Rolling; Nov. 30 for primary consideration
Financial aid deadline: Feb. 15 (recommended)
Admissions information: (814) 865-5471
e-mail: admissions@psu.edu
web site: http://www.psu.edu

To football fans, Penn State is simply home of the Nittany Lions and longtime coaching great Joe Paterno. But the university's influence extends far beyond 107,000-person Beaver Stadium: the saying goes that 1 of every 700 persons in the United States, 1 of every 77 Pennsylvanians, 1 of every 50 engineers, and 1 of every 4 meteorologists can lay claim to being a Penn State graduate. Altogether, at 454,000 living alumni, Penn State recently ranked first among U.S. colleges and universities for the number of breathing, not to say boastful, graduates. With a full-time undergraduate student body of 33,200 on the main University Park campus and a history that stretches back to its origin as The Farmers High School in 1855, Penn State has come to mean academic, athletic, and social opportunities on a grand scale found at few other public universities. Observes a member of the Penn State alumni network: "There is an inexplicable loyalty to the institution and a love for the 'Penn State experience' that no one deliberately tries to acquire but everyone gains. It's a place where school spirit runs high, and student commitment to academics, cocurricular activities, and the university is unmatched anywhere."

Student body: Three quarters of Penn State's students are from in-state. Though a majority of the nonresidents also are from the Middle Atlantic region, prospective alums come from all 50 states, 3 U.S. territories, and a wide range of foreign countries. The undergraduate enrollment includes 5% Asian-Americans, 4% African-

Americans, 3% Hispanics, and less than 0.5% Native Americans; 7.5% are foreign nationals. If any generalities can cover 33,200 people, the following observations fit best. A majority tend to be moderately conservative and rather traditional in their views and lifestyles, friendlier than might be expected on a large campus, and usually quite gregarious and filled with school spirit. Levels of academic competition range from high pressure among top students in the College of Engineering, for example, to more relaxed among majors in less rigorous programs. The overall barometer can be summed up in the words of a New Englander: "concerned but not obsessed."

Academics: Penn State awards degrees through the doctorate and operates on the semester system. Undergraduate majors in more than 160 fields are spread among 10 colleges. Classes throughout a student's 4 years generally remain quite large, averaging 30 in the lower division and 26 at the upper levels. Many lectures in the freshman and sophomore years can enroll from 200 to 800+ note takers. However, it also is possible to have an upper-level course with 1 other classmate in such fields as art, music, or theater and about half of the 4343 class sections in a recent year counted between 10 and 29 students. Many students opt to avoid the entry-year crush at the University Park Campus by spending their freshman and sophomore years at any of 16 two-year campuses throughout the state, enrolling at the University Park campus as juniors.

General-education requirements that all 33,200 undergraduates must complete comprise 45 of the 120–130 credits needed to graduate. The program includes a First-Year Seminar, classes in basic writing/speaking and quantification skills, and breadth and depth courses across the traditional disciplines. In addition, all students must take a course in U.S. culture, a course in International Cultures, and a writing-intensive course in the student's major.

The Penn State instructional faculty numbers 2546 and is weighed heavily toward its 2233 full-time members. No breakdown exists to show the portion that teaches graduate students only. Thirty-seven percent of all the faculty are women. Penn State's ranking in the top 20 universities nationwide in total research expenditures puts much pressure on professors to "publish or perish." The result is a mixed bag in terms of quality of undergraduate teaching although students are delighted to find many more student-oriented faculty than they expected. As a finance major once observed, "The good teachers motivate students in their classes, enjoy having students come to see them in their offices, and are great counselors for academic, career, and personal issues. Other professors are absolutely dull and uninterested in teaching, and may not even answer a knock on the office door. Of course, most faculty members lie somewhere in between these 2 extremes."

When Penn State's finest faculty and first-rate facilities meet, the result is programs worth cheering about. The colleges whose offerings draw the most vocal support are Engineering, Science, Earth and Mineral Sciences, Business, and Agricultural Sciences. Engineering and business programs, in particular, boast high-quality students who exert positive peer pressure on each other to succeed. Recruitment of these graduates is heavy. Although many science professors are the ones most heavily engaged in research, students are often part of the experience, thereby gaining first-hand exposure to sophisticated research techniques, state-of-the-art equipment, and brilliant minds. The College of Education draws applause for its contributions in the university classroom as well as to improvement of the field nationwide. Also singled out for special approval are the programs in hotel, restaurant, and institutional management in the College of Health and Human Development, meteorology in the College of Earth and Mineral Sciences, and the diverse foreign language options, from Greek to Portuguese, in the College of Liberal Arts.

Other liberal arts programs are less strong because of fewer faculty and less funding than the academic giants on campus. With persistence, however, a student can survive the early enormous lectures and find at least 1 gem of a professor who can make a weaker program acceptable, if not (sometimes) wonderful.

Facilities: Although Penn State's 3 main libraries, 5 subject branches, and 3 special units hold 5 million volumes, 5 million microform items, and 58,459 periodicals, undergraduates complain that on a per-student basis the collection averages about half the volumes that their peers at Temple and the University of Pittsburgh enjoy. Their second biggest gripe is that there is seating capacity for only a small percentage of the students. However, the computerized and user-friendly LIAS (Library Information Access System) is winning friends as it continues to expand, now allowing users to tap into listings of other Big Ten Libraries as well as diverse materials in subject matter ranging from literature to agriculture to engineering. Because the Penn State library network is so huge and is critical to the undergraduate experience, as part of freshman English every student is required to tour the facilities and to complete a workbook concerning what he or she has learned, to demonstrate familiarity with the system.

More than 50 computer labs and 247 tech classrooms house Macintosh, Windows, and UNIX computers around campus. Several of the labs are open around the clock; the waits, primarily during finals, are surprisingly few and short, given the thousands of undergraduates needing to use machines.

Special programs: Penn State's opportunities for study abroad included 150 programs in 46 countries throughout Europe, the Middle East, the Far East, South America, Africa, New Zealand, and Australia. More than 1000 undergraduates a year participate in these overseas experiences. The university Center for Student Involvement and Leadership funds a number of organizations to promote leadership education and student participation in public and community service.

Campus life: Just over a third, 38% of Penn State undergraduates live on the 15,984-acre University Park campus, located geographically in the center of the state. The university's Greek system is among the largest in the country, involving 13% of the men in 59 national fraternities and 10% of the women in 31 national sororities. Tensions between Greeks and independents are generally low since every weekend there usually is 1 major Greek function open to nonmembers. For students over 21, more than 15 bars are located within 1 block of campus; fans of the cinema can choose among several movie theaters downtown, as well as another dozen or so films being shown at various classrooms around campus. Altogether, students have their choice of more than 600 clubs and organizations to tap nearly every interest. And when students pool their efforts, the outcome can be staggering. For example, a 48-hour dance marathon held to benefit the families of children with cancer recently raised more than $3.6 million. Crime is minimal and is confined largely to incidents of vandalism and an occasional bike theft. An escort service is available to walk undergraduates home after dark, and maps of the various lighted pathways are provided for students' convenience. Penn State also has its own police force and student security groups.

The 2005 Big Ten Champion Nittany Lion football team is the mainstay of most fall weekends, complete with tailgating and postgame parties for the fans. The celebrations were especially sweet following the team's thrilling Orange Bowl victory over Florida State in January 2006. Homecoming highlights include a parade and all-night vigil at the Nittany Lion Shrine. Throughout the year, though, other nationally ranked Big 10 teams, recently including those in wrestling, volleyball, fencing, gymnastics, women's basketball, women's field hockey, and men's hockey, draw their fair shares of fans. Altogether, Penn State fields 16 intercollegiate sports for men and 15 for women in NCAA Division I. More than half of the undergraduates, that is, over 16,000 people, turn out for the intramural program, 18 sports for each sex. An additional 52 sports clubs and interest groups meet regularly throughout the year, demanding various levels of competitive experience. For the most adventuresome, the Outing Club sponsors organized trips in rock climbing, spelunking, and mountain-biking.

Because of its central location in the state, the small city of State College (pop. 39,000), where University Park is located, is never more than a 4-hour drive home for in-state students in need of a break. For respite closer to campus, students head to the Stone Valley recreation area, just 20 minutes away, for windsurfing, canoeing, kayaking, and fishing, as well as cross-country skiing in season. Climbing Mt. Nittany also is a popular form of recreation.

Cost cutters: In the 2005–2006 school year, 48% of the freshmen and 50% of continuing students received financial help. For at least 41% of the first-year students and 44% of the rest, the aid was need-based. The average freshman award for a student with need included a need-based scholarship or grant averaging $5033 and need-based self-help aid such as loans and jobs averaging $2826. Non-need-based athletic scholarships for first-year students averaged $20,232; other non-need-based awards and scholarships averaged $3880. Average debt of a 2005 graduate was $22,400. Two in every 10 Penn State freshmen receive a university scholarship; awards typically range between $1250 and $2000 a year. Participation in the University Scholars program, a highly selective, universitywide honors program, is by invitation only, with approximately 1500 students eligible for scholarships recently ranging from $2000–$3000. In addition, Penn State has more than 1000 privately endowed scholarships. A cooperative education program is available for most engineering majors.

Rate of return: Ninety-three percent of entering freshmen return for the sophomore year. Fifty-six percent graduate in 4 years, 81% earn their degrees in 5 years, and 84% in 6 years.

Payoff: In the 2005 graduating class, 21% earned degrees in business and marketing; 13% specialized in engineering, and almost 10% in communication/journalism. A recent study placed Penn State sixth nationally in the number of college graduates who eventually earn doctoral degrees; the university also ranked first among Big Ten universities in producing National Science Foundation Fellowship recipients. About a fourth of new graduates go on to pursue advanced degrees within months of Commencement. On the job front, Penn State is a mecca for corporate and government recruiters. In a recent school year, 1280 employers conducted almost 21,000 student interviews. Half of the seniors who find jobs remain in Pennsylvania, with large contingents moving on to New York, New Jersey, Maryland, and Virginia.

Bottom line: Remarks a New Hampshire native and lifetime Nittany Lion: "There are hundreds of opportunities for different experiences at Penn State: to be involved in athletics even if you are not varsity material, to develop leadership ability, and to interact with different types of people. But you have to make your own way here; no one holds your hand."

Saint Joseph's University

Philadelphia, Pennsylvania 19131

Setting: Suburban
Control: Private (Roman Catholic-Jesuit)
Undergraduate enrollment: 2054 men, 2193 women
Graduate enrollment: 200 men, 201 women
Student/faculty ratio: 15:1
Freshman profile: Median SAT I scores: 570 verbal; 570 math. Median ACT composite: 25. 45% graduated in top fifth of high school class. 76% in upper two-fifths.
Faculty profile: 98% Ph.D.'s
Tuition and fees: $27,455
Room and board: $9973

Freshman financial aid: 85%; average scholarship or grant: $8400 need-based
Campus jobs: NA; average earnings: NA
Application deadline: Early decision: Nov. 15; regular: Feb. 1
Financial aid deadline: May 1 (Priority date: Feb. 15)
Admissions information: (610) 660-1300; (888) BEAHAWK
e-mail: admit@sju.edu
web site: www.sju.edu

As the saying goes, all good things come to those who wait. In the case of Saint Joseph's University in Philadelphia, the anticipation lasted for more than a century. As early as 1741, the first resident pastor of Saint Joseph's Church had proposed starting a Jesuit university. However, 40 years of suppression of the Jesuits, which began in the latter part of the 18th century, as well as dissension within Philadelphia's Catholic community, delayed the opening of the school until 1851. The result, however, was worth the wait, as many of the 4250 undergraduates enrolled at Philadelphia's Jesuit university can attest. It is a place where the student comes first, and teachers' schedules are adjusted to suit an individual's needs. Close student/faculty relationships are a way of life, as is an emphasis on student involvement in the community. Nearly 70% of the students who enter as freshmen go on to graduate in 4 years; at least 80% receive some financial help along the way. Says a sophomore: "If you're looking for a college that will stimulate your mind, St. Joe's is it."

Student body: Not quite two-thirds of the students who attend Saint Joseph's are Roman Catholic. A tenth are Protestant; 1% are Jewish. Six percent are of some other faith. The rest claim no religious affiliation or their affiliation is unknown. Fifty-three percent are Pennsylvanians, with out-of-staters also coming mainly from the Middle Atlantic region; 39 states and 34 foreign countries have students on campus. Foreign nationals constitute 1% of the enrollment. African-American students make up the largest minority at 8%, followed by Asian-Americans and Hispanics at 3% each. Fifty-three percent of the students in a recent year attended private, parochial, or some other non-public schools. Undergraduates tend to be middle-of-the-road in their politics and according to one senior are "somewhat sheltered but excited and willing to learn more about social issues." Many become involved in a wide variety of activities, with community service generally high on their lists. Students estimate that about 20% of their number are intense in their studies, most fall in the middle range, and very few neglect studying completely, though a number like to profess as much. Undergraduates have learned to be skeptical of the classmate who claims not to have studied for a test when actually he or she has been preparing for a couple of weeks!

Academics: St. Joseph's confers the bachelor's degree in 40 majors, the master's degree in business administration and various fields in the arts and sciences, and a doctorate in educational leadership. Five-year B.S./M.S. programs are offered in psychology and international marketing and in education in various subject areas. The university runs on a semester calendar. Classes average 25–30 students but range in size from 10–15 for upper-level classes to maybe 50 for some beginning science courses.

General-education requirements include common courses in English, theology, philosophy, and history. Distribution requirements give students their choice of courses in foreign language, mathematics, natural sciences, social/behavioral sciences, philosophy, and theology.

The faculty has 269 full-time members and 329 part-time; all but 7 of the full-time faculty and 219 of the 329 part-time teach undergraduates. Sixty percent of the full-time faculty are men, 14 are Jesuit priests. Students give the majority of the faculty A's for academic expertise, accessibility, and active involvement in the campus community. Observes a junior: "Faculty members are enthusiastic when they teach, knowledgeable about what they teach, and understand clearly why they teach. They're great!" Classroom absences do not go undetected. Says an education major: "The professors actually know their students' names and are concerned when they are not in class." Some students find the quality of adjunct professors brought in to teach required classes to be "inconsistent," in the words of a junior.

Perhaps Saint Joseph's most distinctive offering is its program in food marketing, which prepares students for careers in the food industry. The program maintains strong ties with corporations, and its board of governors is made up of senior executives from the field. Graduates of the program also enjoy a 100% job placement rate within 3 months of earning their diplomas. The department offers other special treats, among them summer study trips throughout the world and its own specialized library with 2100 titles and 320 periodicals. The library also contains a core collection of more general print and electronic business sources. All business students likewise benefit from Mandeville Hall, the computer-integrated business building with high-tech classrooms, lecture halls, and the building's masterpiece, a 300-seat auditorium known as Wolfington "Teletorium" for its teleconferencing and other audio and video capabilities. Other bread-and-butter disciplines are satisfying as well. Politics and history are strong, largely because of excellent and demanding teachers who offer a wide range of perspectives. The curricula and faculties in biology, chemistry, philosophy, theology, and English also are noteworthy; 2 biology professors live on campus and "answer cries at all hours," says a major, though some students think the older science facilities need an upgrade to stay competitive. Accounting is especially intense, with a well-qualified faculty. The sociology faculty practice what they profess. The programs in international relations and psychology are winners, too.

Undergraduates say math and physics need professors less aloof and more committed to their students. While some students are delighted with the major in education (the department head was recently named state teacher of the year), others wish it had more of both professors and courses. Few complain, however, about the numerous opportunities for field experience, which include time spent in both an urban school and a suburban one. Overall, some students think many of the liberal arts departments lie in the shadow of the business program, in terms of money for facilities and materials.

Facilities: Francis A. Drexel Library may be "bright and comfortable," with a computerized catalog and CD-ROM technology to simplify the research process, but the collection at the end of the hunt can be a letdown. Many undergraduates find that too many of the 352,500 volumes are outdated, though the 8900 print and electronic journals and periodicals more than adequately cover their fields. Complaints don't last too long as students have access to more than 4.5 million volumes through the Tri-State College Library Cooperative, a consortium of 30 regional college and university libraries.

Drexel Library is among the numerous areas around campus that offer wireless computer access. Four general-purpose labs with more than 110 largely Pentium computers and 5 departmental labs also are open for student use. Most labs are open until 11 p.m. The university requires that students in the business school and in the psychology, sociology, criminal justice, and interdisciplinary health departments in the College of Arts and Sciences have their own laptops; the university strongly recommends that all other undergraduates students have some kind of personal computer.

Special programs: Opportunity for study abroad is available in 23 cities around the world, from Tokyo and Beijing to Rome and Galway. Undergraduates may enroll for a semester or 2 at other Jesuit schools throughout the United States. Internships in Washington, D.C. can be arranged for politics majors.

Campus life: Sixty percent of Saint Joseph's students live on the 65-acre campus straddling the western boundary of Philadelphia; a third of the residents go home on weekends though fewer do so every year. Those who stay usually split their time between relaxing on Saturdays with organized day trips, coffeehouses, and parties and studying hard on Sundays. In response to student requests, the university has begun to offer more campus programming, including something called SJU 'Til 2, "a pseudo-party," says a sophomore, "where they show movies and have music and free food." Attending fraternity parties remains a popular way to close out the week on Friday nights. Eight percent of the men and 13% of the women belong to the 3 national fraternities and 4 national sororities, and their parties generally attract wide interest from independents as well. One of the more popular community-service projects matches St. Joe students 1-on-1 with elementary school children in predominantly African-American Gomper's School, adjacent to the campus. The Hand-in-Hand festival for the mentally handicapped is another major campuswide student project. Until recently, Saint Joseph's campus had seemed immune from the crime of inner-city Philadelphia. Remarks a state resident: "In reality, student stupidity has been the biggest crime, since anyone who walks by him- or herself at 2 a.m. is going to run into problems." In response, security has added bicycle patrols, performed more than 30,000 escorts a year, and stepped up educational efforts to make students more aware of the actuality of urban crime. "Security is always there," says a junior. "Neither rain, sleet, nor snow keeps them from their appointed rounds."

Midnight Madness, the event marking the first Hawks basketball practice, officially opens the season of the best loved and most followed of the 9 men's and 9 women's intercollegiate teams playing in NCAA Division I. The team also gained millions of additional fans nationwide following its impressive performance in the 2005 NCAA basketball tournament, only going down to defeat in the round of the Elite Eight. Men's soccer, lacrosse, ice hockey, and coed crew draw enthusiastic crowds as well. Those students not of varsity-level ability who are more interested in playing than cheering can take part in any of the more than 30 men's, women's, and coed intramural sports available. Saturday afternoon rugby, 1 of 7 club sports offered, attracts its own spirited following in the spring.

Those who need a break from student life either take the train into Philadelphia or drive to the Jersey Shore, particularly Atlantic City.

Cost cutters: In the 2005–2006 school year, 85% of all freshmen and 80% of all continuing students received some sort of financial assistance. For 80% of both groups, the aid was need-based at least in part. The average freshman award for students with need included a need-based scholarship or grant averaging $8400 and need-based self-help aid such as loans and jobs averaging $3800. Non-need-based athletic scholarships for first-year students averaged $12,000. The average financial indebtedness of a 2005 graduate totaled $15,734. School-sponsored awards include the Board of Trustees Scholarships, which pay full tuition to students drawn from the top of their high school graduating class with SATs in the 1400–1600 range on the math and critical reading sections. Presidential and University scholarships pay one-half to three-fourths and one-fourth to one-half of tuition, respectively, to students with critical reading and math SAT scores of 1300–1390 and 1200–1290. An installment payment plan is designed to ease tuition payments further.

Rate of return: Ninety percent of freshmen return for a second year. Sixty-eight percent graduate in 4 years; 75%, in 5 years, 78% in 6.

Payoff: The largest percentage of 2005 graduates, 12%, earned degrees in marketing. Eight percent graduated with degrees in finance, 7% in food marketing. A fourth of the new alumni proceed directly to graduate or professional schools. Graduates who take jobs after doffing their robes go into such fields as accounting, insurance, banking, and sales, predominantly in the Northeast, with such firms as Peat Marwick, Core States, Prudential, Mellon Bank, and Del Monte. A number also joined the Peace Corps or other nonprofit organizations. More than 400 companies and organizations recruited on campus in the 2004–2005 school year.

Bottom line: Cautions a recent graduate: "Ivy League types will not be happy here; the feeling is very relaxed and personal because of the size and religious affiliation. Middle-class, average-to-competitive, active, group-oriented students will love St. Joe's."

Saint Vincent College
Latrobe, Pennsylvania 15650

Setting: Suburban
Control: Private (Roman Catholic)
Undergraduate enrollment: 703 men, 768 women
Graduate enrollment: 9 men, 12 women
Student/faculty ratio: 13:1
Freshman profile: 2% scored over 699 on SAT I verbal; 19% scored 600–699; 48% 500–599; 30% below 500. 2% scored over 699 on SAT I math; 21% scored 600–699; 46% 500–599; 31% below 500. 2% scored above 29 on the ACT; 34% scored 24–29; 55% 18–23; 9% below 18. 21% graduated in top tenth of high school class; 53% in upper fourth.

Faculty profile: 78% Ph.D.'s
Tuition and fees: $21,679
Room and board: $6874
Freshman financial aid: 95%; average scholarship or grant: $12,849 need-based; $10,956 non-need-based
Campus jobs: 50%; average earnings: $1600/year
Application deadline: May 1 (Priority: Feb. 1)
Financial aid deadline: May 1 (Priority: Mar. 1)
Admissions information: (724) 537-4540;
(800) SVC-5549
e-mail: admission@email.st.vincent.edu
web site: www.stvincent.edu

When students walk onto the campus of Saint Vincent College nestled in the Laurel Highlands of western Pennsylvania, they experience a tradition of liberal learning that began 1500 years ago in Europe. Benedictine monks established Saint Vincent in 1846 at the site of an already active parish, making it the first Benedictine college in the United States. Until 1983, Saint Vincent was a college for men only; today female full-time students surpass the number of men. However, much of the Benedictine influence remains. Benedictine monks still comprise a fourth of the full-time faculty and reside in a monastery located on the edge of campus. The breathtaking Archabbey Basilica, which took 14 years spanning the turn of the century to complete and was completely restored in 1996, dominates the landscape, creating "a perfect setting for worship, work, and learning," in the words of a recent graduate. Current students value the mix of "tradition and technology" that pervades the campus. Says a senior: "The campus is small but progressive, open-minded but rooted in good traditions, safe but adventurous both for the mind and the body."

Student body: Two-thirds of the Saint Vincent students are Catholic, and the largest portion of the rest, Protestant. Eighty-four percent are residents of Pennsylvania, and all but a small percentage of the nonresidents come from other Middle Atlantic states. Still, 26 states and 18 foreign countries have undergraduates on campus. Twenty-four percent attended private or parochial schools. Enrollment is predominantly white, with African-Americans comprising 2% and Hispanics and Asian-Americans each constituting 1% of the total. In a recent year, there were 25 international students and 5 Native Americans. The Dreamkeepers Society, a group that focuses on building an understanding of racial and ethnic diversity, has become 1 of the most active and influential student organizations in the few years it has been in existence. Undergraduates are warm and enthusiastic toward newcomers and old friends alike. Many are "forward thinking" in regard to their own career plans and generally more conservative than liberal regarding social and political issues. Most also are easily able to balance a commitment to academics with an equally fervent desire to get involved and have a good time.

Academics: St. Vincent awards the bachelor's degree in more than 50 disciplines and a master's degree in education. Majors in music education and theater must be earned at nearby Seton Hill College; a bus runs between the 2 campuses every hour. The academic year is divided into 2 semesters. Average class size for freshmen and sophomores ranges from 25 to 35 participants, although courses for juniors and seniors hover closer to 20. The largest class, Physical Geology, enrolls over 40, while a class in environmental economics meets with only 3.

All undergraduates must take a core curriculum that consists of courses in traditional fields and accounts for approximately half of the 124 credits needed to graduate. Although students may select from a wide range of classes to fulfill some of these mandates, 3 specific courses, Language and Rhetoric, Exploring Religious Meaning, and Philosophy I, are required of everyone. A First-Year Experience program provides freshmen seminars with no more than 20 participants per class that meet an extra hour a week for extracurricular activities, such as speakers and films, that relate to the seminar topic.

Seventy-two of the 167 faculty members teach part-time. Twenty-nine percent are women. Twenty-six members are Benedictines. Students find the Benedictine monks to be especially broadly educated and nearly all members of both the lay and the religious faculty to be challenging, other than a few, says a senior, "who still teach as though we were in high school." The majority, however, are praised for what they teach beyond the textbook. Observes a sophomore: "They are willing to spend time to work with us outside the classroom and to encourage us to live lives of service and good moral standing."

Business and biology are the strongest departments, each having excellent faculty and facilities. A life sciences laboratory provides ample space for collaborative research efforts of faculty and undergraduates. Chemistry and physics are considered rigorous but rewarding as well. The accounting curriculum is the business star, both demanding and in great demand, with small classes that guarantee plenty of personal attention. As a result, the percentage of Saint Vincent graduates who passed all 4 parts of the CPA exam on the first sitting has been 3 times the state average over the past few years. Psychology, anthropology, mathematics, English, and history also rate highly. The departments of economics, business administration, public policy, and political science recently were placed under a single academic structure known as the McKenna School of Business, Economics, and Government that students say has brought cohesiveness and expanded learning opportunities to these already strong fields of study.

In 1998, Saint Vincent initiated its own programs in art history and studio art, Spanish, music, and music performance, thus leaving music education and theater as the only remaining majors that must be taken at Seton Hill. Students' chief complaint about the arrangement is that the facilities at Seton Hill are a 15-minute bus ride away from Saint Vincent, so students who want to do extra work must allow time for the trip. Students find classes in the communication major too easy and say adjustments are needed in the program. Education also could use more faculty, more rigor, and more organization. Minors only are offered in Italian, German, Latin, and religious studies, though there is a major in Catholic theology and religious education. A new minor recently was added in public history and new English concentrations in creative writing and professional writing.

Facilities: The library at Saint Vincent's, ranked by a government study as among the best at Catholic institutions and in the top 5% of the nearly 700 liberal arts colleges studied, houses just over 268,000 volumes, 791 current periodicals, and a rare treasure: a 1478 first edition of Chaucer's *Canterbury Tales*. However, some users say the collection lacks sufficient materials in education, foreign languages, and general fiction and, overall, needs many more recent publications. A computerized catalog and various databases are especially useful and much used. Students may borrow freely from the Seton Hill library; undergraduates involved in extensive research projects also travel to the University of Pittsburgh for materials not found online. As a place for concentrated reading, Saint Vincent's library is described by a sophomore as "a quiet refuge for those needing quality study time."

The new $5.1 million Prep Hall Instructional Technology Resource Center located next door to the library features 3 multimedia classrooms, 2 of them with computer network connections at every student desk, as well as a multimedia production laboratory. Elsewhere across campus, there are 5 Windows PC facilities and 2 Macintosh labs, as well as 5-computer labs in the dormitories, open around the clock. Students' main concern has been that the facilities other than those in the residence halls have not been open sufficient hours over the weekend. There also is 1 Internet connection per student in each residence hall room.

Special programs: Sixty percent of each graduating class generally complete at least 1 internship or cooperative education placement apiece. For those eager to study abroad, Saint Vincent has a sister-college relationship with Fu Jen Catholic University in Taiwan; additional opportunities in 7 European countries and Mexico are available through programs with Central College of Iowa. A semester in Washington, D.C. also is a possibility. A 3-2 engineering program is an option with Boston University, Penn State, or the University of Pittsburgh or the Catholic University of America. Through a cooperative program with Duquesne University, degree programs also are offered in physical therapy, physician's assistant, occupational therapy, pharmacy, law, and business administration.

Campus life: Three-quarters of the students live on the 200-acre campus, which includes fields, woods, a lake, and even a cemetery. A new residence hall that opened in August 2002 houses all first-year students and has spurred a growth of services and activities related to the First Year Experience. Though there are no fraternities or sororities, various groups of undergraduates, such as students who live on the same floor of a dormitory or play intramural football together, regularly sponsor parties and other activities as a unit. The campus nightclub, The Underground, is a popular hangout, and students look forward to a wide range of creative campuswide events that are planned, among them the annual February Beach Party held indoors with sand, sunlights, and seafood. Says a senior: "There is always an upbeat buzz on campus." The opening in September 2003 of the renovated Student Union and athletic facility, now known as the Carey Center, only made the buzz better; a 506-seat theater made its debut as part of the Center in March 2004. Because of the large numbers of business and biology majors, clubs built around these disciplines have strong followings, as does the Environmental Awareness Club. Though attendance at Mass is not required, most students choose to go and many also participate in the various programs sponsored by Campus Ministry. Says a sophomore: "It gives the campus a sense of the Catholic faith lived out by the Benedictine order who leads the school." The crime rate is low, and incidents of theft tend to occur only when students neglect to lock their doors. Over the weekends, however, undergraduates must present identification to enter the dormitories; all visitors are required to register with residence hall personnel.

The party-loving intramural football teams draw some of the best crowds to their games; there is no intercollegiate football. Altogether, 70% of the men and 30% of the women take part in the 9 intramural sports available. Eight men's and 11 women's varsity teams compete in NAIA Division I. Basketball, soccer, baseball, and lacrosse, which is independent, have the best attendance at their games. Ice hockey was added as a women's sport in the 2004-2005 school year. The campus also serves as the summer training campus of the Pittsburgh Steelers.

For escape, there are cabins in the Laurel Mountains for those who enjoy nature. Pittsburgh is just 35 miles west for shopping, Pirates baseball, and the nightlife that Latrobe (pop. 11,000) doesn't offer. Ski resorts are about 45 minutes away.

Cost cutters: In a recent school year, all but 5% of the freshmen and all but 7% of continuing students received financial aid; 80% of both groups were given need-based assistance. The average freshmen award for a first-year student in fall 2005 with financial need included a need-based scholarship or grant averaging $12,849 and need-based self-help aid such as loans and jobs averaging $2718. Non-need-based athletic scholarships for freshmen averaged $4578; other non-need-based awards and scholarships averaged $10,956. The typical debt for a recent graduate was $17,000. The college offers a wide range of merit scholarships that can significantly reduce costs over 4 years for students who perform well on competitive exams. The Wimmer Scholarship, named for Boniface Wimmer, the college's founder, is restricted to students ranking in the top 10% of their high school classes and pays full tuition, room, board, and fees to one first-year student and full tuition to 4. How students rank, and the amount of money they receive, depends on their performance on a competitive exam of general knowledge. All awards are renewable over 4 years. Additional academic awards paying $4000 a year go to students with talent in economics, English, history, mathematics, physics, chemistry, biology, computing and information science, religious studies, and music. All but the economics and music scholarships are based on students' performance on a subject area exam. For the economic and policy scholarship, students write an essay on a public policy issue; for the music award, students must perform at a live audition. Leadership grants pay from $500 to $3000 a year. Cooperative education programs are offered in all majors.

Rate of return: Eighty-nine percent of entering freshmen return for the sophomore year. Fifty-nine percent graduate in 4 years; 67% earn their degrees in a fifth year; 69% in six.

Payoff: Majors in psychology and communication at 12% each, and computing at 8% led a recent graduating class. Nineteen percent of the new alumni went right back to school, many buoyed, in part, by the college's excellent track record of graduates being accepted into professional schools. Acceptance rates over the years have been 100% into law school, 70% accepted to medical school, and 100% acceptance into such health-related schools as dental, osteopathic, physical therapy, podiatry, pharmacy, and veterinary schools. The majority took jobs, primarily in the Northeast, with such firms as Westinghouse, Exxon, Xerox, and USX, and with the Internal Revenue Service. One hundred forty companies recruited on campus in a recent school year.

Bottom line: Saint Vincent is a small liberal arts college that quietly goes about preparing its students to handle both the professional and the moral questions in today's world. The Benedictine community, says a senior, provides "an excellent setting in which to prepare for the world, while experiencing self-discovery."

Susquehanna University
Selinsgrove, Pennsylvania 17870

Setting: Small town
Control: Private (Lutheran)
Undergraduate enrollment: 844 men, 1050 women
Graduate enrollment: None
Student/faculty ratio: 16:1
Freshman profile: SAT/ACT scores: NA. 30% graduated in top tenth of high school class; 55% in upper fifth.
Faculty profile: 93% Ph.D.'s
Tuition and fees: $26,265
Room and board: $7200
Freshman financial aid: 93%; average scholarship or grant: $14,710 need-based; $8435 non-need-based

Campus jobs: 54%; average earnings: $770/year
Application deadline: Early decision I: Nov. 15; Early decision II: Jan. 1; Regular: Mar. 1
Financial aid deadline: Mar. 1 (preferred); May 1 (final)
Admissions information: (570) 372-4260; (800) 326-9672
e-mail: suadmiss@susqu.edu
web site: www.susqu.edu

One of the hottest rooming options at many colleges is the "theme house" that enables students who share similar interests in matters as wide-ranging as science and the arts to live together and attend events centered on their common concern. At Susquehanna University in rural central Pennsylvania, the Project House System, which turned 30 in 2006, brings together 325 students—nearly a fifth of the enrollment—in a very special concern: serving others. As part of the program, groups of students live together on the basis of shared interest in an approved volunteer project of benefit to the college or the community. Past endeavors have included serving as Big Brothers/Big Sisters to children in need, working as computer consultants who help individuals or agencies design suitable computer systems, and participating in Senior Friends to provide companionship and support for the elderly. In return for their services, students live in one of the smaller houses on "the Avenue;" in Seibert Hall, a turn-of-the-century renovated building that one student calls "a palace of a dorm;" or in apartment suites. At about $33,500 for tuition, fees, room, and board in the 2005–2006 school year, Susquehanna stretches the purely pocketbook definition of a "best buy," though the percentage of students receiving financial aid has increased since 1990 from just half of the student body to more than 90% in the 2005–2006 school year. But as programs like the Project House System, easy student-faculty friendships, and required career planning for all demonstrate, what is "best" about Susquehanna is some lessons that money doesn't always buy at other, costlier colleges, but that are very much part of the total education here. "That makes Susquehanna University the best buy in my book," says a satisfied sophomore.

Student body: About 60% of Susquehanna's students are from Pennsylvania, with the largest block of out-of-staters from the Middle Atlantic region. Altogether, nonresidents come from 26 states and 10 foreign countries. Eighty-four percent of the undergraduates attended public schools. Seventeen percent of the students are Lutheran, 35% members of other Protestant denominations, 38% Catholic, and 2% Jewish. Eight percent follow other faiths and the rest claim none. African-Americans account for 3% of the enrollment, Hispanics and Asian-Americans for 2% each, and foreign nationals, 1%. Most Susquehanna students come from conservative backgrounds, as is reflected in their dress, political attitudes (though many are politically apathetic) and commitment to postgraduate career goals. However, an increasing number of students are involved in programs and activities that promote and support diversity and more liberal ideas. The Diversity Council conducts educational programs and social activities to promote cultural awareness; a minor in diversity studies also is in place. Undergraduates relish being involved in a wide range of activities and generally are outgoing and highly sociable although a small fraction, says a senior, "have attitudes of superiority." Honors students, who make up 10% of every class, plus a fair number of other undergraduates work very hard, though few display outward signs of stress. Says a senior: "The student body places a high emphasis on academics and often students work together to ensure that they and their peers are getting the most out of their educations."

Academics: The university, which was founded in 1858, awards the bachelor's degree in 35 majors and follows a semester calendar. Class sizes in the first 2 years generally range from 20 to 30; core courses usually top out at 40, although Issues in Human Biology may enroll 60. Juniors and seniors will find 15 or fewer in many of their classes.

Susquehanna's core covers approximately a third of the courses required for graduation and explores 3 areas: personal development, intellectual skills, and perspectives on the world. To enhance their personal development, all students must take courses in fitness and career planning. A new course added in fall 2005 called Core Perspectives is designed to facilitate students' transition to college by integrating issues of intellectual and personal development and giving them close contact with at least 1 instructor, usually a faculty member. The intellectual skills component covers critical thinking and writing, computer literacy, foreign language competency, and mathematics or logic; perspectives on the world draws from a broad range of disciplines. A required "capstone" experience in each student's major recently was added for the senior year, scheduled to start with the Class of 2008.

All but 72 of the university's 199-member faculty are full-time; 40% are women. Five of the full-time faculty teach at the graduate level only. In recent years the faculty has represented an eclectic mix of experienced academicians, corporate executives, a Legion of Honor recipient, and a sky diver. Though there are a few teachers who qualify simply as "average," most students find at least 1 brilliant faculty member in every department, and value the close relationships shared with many professors. Says a biochemistry major: "They teach because they care, and they care because they are personally involved with the students." Most professors also continually push their charges to question their beliefs and opinions. Adds a public relations major: "The professors want you to get the most out of your Susquehanna experience so they are always willing to give you advice on what classes you should take or which alumni you should contact about a possible internship."

Programs in the Sigmund Weis School of Business are among Susquehanna's best, thanks to superb faculties and facilities and the high standards that majors are expected to meet. The management program, for example, includes in its curriculum math and computer applications that discourage weaker students from enrolling. Accounting emphasizes problem-solving more than balance sheets. A sixth emphasis in entrepreneurship, joining others ranging from finance to global management, was added in fall 2005. The Business and Communications building, which opened in 1999, contains information-technology dataports set up at every seat in the 3 multimedia classrooms, team study areas, and student lounges to enourage students to bring laptop computers. An attentive network of alumni provides ample opportunities for student internships and job interviews upon graduation. All of the sciences, especially biology, biochemistry, environmental science, and psychology, provide excellent opportunities for students and faculty to collaborate on research in the expanded and renovated science building. First-rate faculties make English, political science, communications and theater arts, and music strong as well. A new Center for Music and Art includes more flexible practice and performance space, 7 new Steinway grand pianos, and a 320-seat concert hall. Foreign language students especially like the integration of professors from foreign nations into the program, which enhances the learning experience. An elementary and early childhood education major describes her professors as being "truly passionate about teaching their students and creating the highest quality of teachers."

Students' chief overall complaint is that even in some of the best programs, like theater arts, there is too frequent turnover of faculty after a single year. Some mathematics professors need helping communicating their subject matter. Says a major: "I find professors to be very skilled and knowledgeable in their area but (some) are very poor at conveying it to their students. They tend to talk over our heads." Mathematics also shares faculty with computer science. "All the professors cross back and forth," continues the junior. "I do not think that they are strong in both subjects." Quality of the physics faculty is considered mixed, with 1 dynamic professor and others who are less so. Philosophy, religion, and classical studies constitute a combined department with an uneven curriculum and few majors (classical studies, Greek, and Latin are offered only as minors), although recent new hires in these fields have brought fresh life to the programs. Communications needs a greater number and diversity of teachers.

Facilities: Blough-Weis Library is among the university's most popular, sometimes most frustrating, places, with spaces for quiet study that fill quickly when the common areas get too social, as frequently happens, and a 24-hour study lounge/computer lab that intense studiers and procrastinators value. The collection of more than 292,000 volumes and nearly 16,000 periodicals available in print and electronically is steadily improving. A web-based on-line catalog readable from a computer anywhere on campus, as well as extensive computerized research aids including at least one for every discipline helps to ease any shortcomings. Students also use computers to search the contents of 17 other college libraries in central Pennsylvania and can request needed materials through interlibrary loan. Those who fail to start their search sufficiently early, however, sometimes end up traveling to Penn State or Bucknell.

Students have access to 300 PCs spread among 8 main computer labs, including a 24-hour lab in the campus center; the other labs close at midnight. Although the university does not require students to own personal computers, it does strongly recommend that they do. More than two-thirds of the undergraduates already bring their own units. Wireless access also is provided in all major campus buildings.

Special programs: On this side of the Atlantic, students may spend a semester in Washington, D.C., at the United Nations, or in Philadelphia. Across the Atlantic, a smorgasbord of foreign-study programs is available including 1 or 2 semesters at Yaroslavl University in Russia or the University of Konstanz in Germany. An across-the-Pacific exchange is offered with Senshu University in Japan. The Weis School of Business offers a semester in London for majors in the fall or spring of their junior year. Students may cross-register for courses at Bucknell University. A cooperative 5-year bachelor's degree program in forestry and environmental management is conducted with Duke.

Campus life: All but 20% of the students reside on the 307-acre campus, which is about all there is in rural Selinsgrove (pop. 5300). A fifth of the men and a fourth of the women belong to 4 national fraternities and 4 national sororities. A new social space Trax was nearing completion in spring 2006, providing a club-like atmosphere for Greeks and other student organizations to host theme parties, dances, comedy nights, and other events for the student body. Charlie's, the college's nonalcoholic club, is already a popular weekend night spot. Says a patron: "Past activities Charlie's has hosted include 'Make Your Own Music Video Night,' 'Chocolate Lover's Night,' and 'Who Wants to be a Thousandaire Night?', and much more." Out-of-town comedians, hypnotists, and bands always draw a good crowd as well. Almost two-thirds of the students are involved at some point in a community-service project. A branch of SIFE, Students in Free Enterprise, also is quite popular and enables students to combine work in economics-based research projects with community outreach. Crime is not much of a campus concern. Notes an out-of-stater: "The biggest problem in Selinsgrove is facing a $30 fine for riding your bicycle at night without a light." Nevertheless, all residence halls unless they house academic units are locked around the clock as a precaution and call boxes were installed around campus. The university also recently replaced all exterior locks on residence halls with keyless card-entry programs. A "Walk Safe" escort program is available around the clock.

Sports in some circles rival parties as a popular way to unwind. In a recent year, 40% of the men and 25% of the women participated in the 11 men's and 12 women's varsity teams that compete in NCAA Division III. Spectators most often come to cheer the football and the men's and women's basketball squads. Spectator interest in night games generally has increased with the opening of a lighted multisport field and softball field. The 22-sport intramural program attracts a slightly lower portion of undergraduates. The Crew Club, which has its own devoted following, sponsors 2 men's and 2 women's crews that compete in major eastern regattas. The men's volleyball club and women's rugby teams also have impressive records and student followings.

The Susquehanna River (a 15-minute walk or 5-minute rollerblade from campus), the Isle of Que (located midstream), and drives along the back roads of Amish country are popular for quiet reflection. When students have had enough of peaceful country living, Philadelphia, the nearest big city, is 2½ hours away, and Harrisburg, the state capital, lies 50 miles south. The university sponsors Saturday bus trips to more distant cities such as New York and Washington, D.C.

Cost cutters: In the 2005–2006 school year, 93% of the first-year students and 94% of the others received financial help of some sort. For 66% of the freshmen and 64% of the remaining undergraduates, the aid was need-based. The average freshman award for a student with need included a need-based scholarship or grant averaging $14,710 and need-based self-help aid such as loans and jobs averaging $3525. Other non-need-based awards and scholarships averaged $8435. The average debt for a 2005 grad was $12,500. A wide range of 4-year merit-based awards are offered, among them the $15,000-a-year Valedictorian/Salutatorian Scholarships and University Assistantships, which also pay $15,000 and include a professional work experience averaging 10 hours weekly with a faculty mentor. The assistantships typically go to the highest-achieving students who rank in the top 5% of their high school graduating class with SAT scores in the top 10% nationally. Presidential Scholarships, Degenstein Scholarships for business majors or minors; and Scholarships for Distinguished Achievement in Science and Mathematics pay $12,500 annually. These typically go to new students ranking in the top tenth of their high school classes with SATs in math and critical reading of at least 1250. Susquehanna Scholarships pay up to $10,000 to students drawn from the top 15% of their high school class who score 1150 or higher on the math and critical reading components of the SATs. Richard R. Green Memorial Scholarships are designed to help create a more diverse student body and extend in value up to $15,000 depending on academic ability. Special music scholarships range up to $5000 a year.

Rate of return: Eighty-eight percent of the freshmen who enter return for the sophomore year. Seventy-nine percent graduate in 4 years; 82% within 5 years.

Payoff: Business administration attracted 23% of the 2005 graduates, followed by communications and theater arts at 15% and psychology at 7%. Twenty-one percent immediately converted their degrees into graduate school acceptances. About half of every graduating class returns to school within 3 years of earning their bachelor's degrees. Initially, though, the vast majority head for the job market, primarily in the Middle Atlantic and northeastern states. Major employers include AT&T, CBS News, Citibank, Hewlett-Packard, IBM, Hershey Foods, and various hospitals, school systems, and government agencies. More than 50 companies and other organizations recruited on campus in a recent school year.

Bottom line: Advises a recent graduate from New York State: "Susquehanna is great for the student who wants a liberal arts education in a rural setting. However, those looking for neither of these elements may have problems because the liberal arts and Selinsgrove are the major components here."

Temple University
Philadelphia, Pennsylvania 19122

Setting: Urban
Control: Public
Undergraduate enrollment: 9123 men, 11,813 women
Graduate enrollment: 2173 men, 2527 women
Student/faculty ratio: 17:1
Freshman profile: 2% scored over 700 on SAT I verbal; 23% scored 600–700; 51% 500–599; 24% below 500. 3% scored over 700 on SAT I math; 24% scored 600–700; 52% 500–599; 21% below 500. 4% scored above 28 on the ACT; 8% scored 27–28; 19% 24–26; 37% 21–23; 32% below 21. 40% graduated in top fifth of high school class; 77% in upper two-fifths.

Faculty profile: 82% Ph.D.'s
Tuition and fees: $9640 in-state; $17,236 out-of-state
Room and board: $7798
Freshman financial aid: 70%; average scholarship or grant: $5010 need-based
Campus jobs: NA; average earnings: NA
Application deadline: April 1
Financial aid deadline: Mar. 31
Admissions information: (215) 204-7200; (888) 340-2222
e-mail: tuadm@temple.edu
web site: www.temple.edu

If the University of Pennsylvania is Philadelphia's elite member of the Ivy League, then Temple University, according to its students, is Penn's hard-working, blue-collar cousin. As the city's largest university, with about 24,000 full- and part-time undergraduates, publicly supported Temple is known as "the working-class college in Philly," says a recent graduate. "Most students have 2 jobs and, because they are working their way through school, appreciate the education they are getting." For many in this largely commuter student body, the education they are getting is one that works for them. The well-known School of Communications and Theater brings students into close contact with working professionals from these fields; contemporary specializations such as African-American and urban studies rank at the top of their class. And by having a campus in the city's urban core, students acquire plenty of out-of-the-classroom learning as well. "On a secluded campus in the middle of nowhere, a student is not as ready for the 'real' world," observes the graduate. "The Temple experience includes an invaluable course: street smarts."

Student body: Seventy-five percent of Temple undergraduates are from Pennsylvania. Though most of the rest are from other Middle Atlantic states, students attend from 42 states and 101 foreign countries. About 63% of the undergraduates are Caucasian American and 20% are African-American, with 10% Asian-American, 3% Hispanic, less than 0.5% Native American, and 3% foreign nationals. "It's almost like the United Nations," says a Pennsylvanian. "One can meet anyone from anywhere in the world." In sheer numbers, Temple recently boasted the largest number of African-American and Hispanic students attending any college in Pennsylvania.

Temple is virtually synonymous with diversity—racial, ethnic, cultural, ideological, and lifestyle. "You name it, we've got it: preppies, funk, punk, new wave, snobs, and slobs," continues the graduate quoted above. "With so many cultural groups represented," adds a junior from suburban Philadelphia, "I get a chance to learn first hand about them." Most students are unpretentious and independent, qualities that are almost a necessity at a school where individualized attention is lacking. Dealing with the red tape and frequent "run-around" of a large university alone can be character-building. Says a senior: "I learned to be firm, direct, and not to be satisfied until I got an answer." Students are split between the job conscious and the socially concerned, with the level of academic competitiveness usually a reflection of how many outside activities an undergraduate is attempting to juggle.

Academics: Temple was founded in 1888 by Dr. Russell Conwell as an outgrowth of his ministry at the Baptist Temple. More than 115 years later, the university confers degrees through the doctorate level and offers 130 undergraduate majors. The university actually has 5 campuses in the Philadelphia area connected by a free shuttle bus: the main campus, a center-city campus, the suburban Ambler and Tyler School of Arts campuses, and the Health Sciences Center. Temple follows a semester system. The average class size for undergraduates is 24. Introductory classes can exceed 300 in a psychology lecture, with weekly recitations, run by graduate students, that have 30–40 enrolled. Special learning communities are designed to let groups of first- and second-year students take 2 or 3 courses together in a block plus in some cases a weekly seminar. Students can fulfill many of the core requirements through the learning communities while getting to know a smaller group of classmates and faculty members better.

Temple's core curriculum covers American culture, the arts, the individual and society, foreign language/international studies, quantitative reasoning, science and technology, and studies in race. While students may select the courses they wish in these areas from a list of suggested options, all undergraduates must take the same 2 courses in intellectual heritage in which students read primary texts from the time of Homer to the twentieth century. Students also must complete 1 course in English composition plus 3 additional writing-intensive courses from any disciplines of the student's choice.

The faculty includes 1206 full-time members and 1355 part-timers. No figure is available to show the number that teaches at the graduate level only. Forty percent of the full-time faculty are women. Full-timers, as well as the large part-time staff, are generally as busy as their students in juggling responsibilities—in this case, teaching, research, writing, or other jobs. While students respect professors for their expertise and for staying current in their fields, their outside activities generally make faculty members harder to find and less accessible. "Still," says a journalism major, "after 3 years of schooling at Temple, I can honestly say that I have had only 3 'bad' teachers. Most are fair and willing to help." As at many large schools, however, it is often up to the student to take the first step. Graduate students run the full gamut of quality as well. "In large classes where it is hard to get to know the professors," says a junior, "the recitations for these classes let you get to know some pretty amazing grad students." Others are less skilled and make inferior substitutes for full professors.

The School of Communications and Theater is easily one of Temple's outstanding divisions, with excellent programs in broadcasting; telecommunications and mass media; film and media arts; and journalism and theater. The broadcasting program draws many students to Temple and is described as "intense," with faculty members who are both talented and well connected to the industry. Journalism gains by using reporters from the *Philadelphia Inquirer* as part-time instructors. The theater major is strengthened by a sense of camaraderie within the department as well as faculty who remain active in the local theater community. The Richard J. Fox School of Business and Management is equally impressive. The curriculum incorporates both professional development and information technology into its coursework. Observes a broadcasting major: "The name Fox adds to your résumé; it's a very comprehensive program." Freshmen admitted to the school's honors program receive IBM ThinkPad laptop computers as part of their scholarship package. Geography and urban studies feature a mix of experienced professors and local urban activists. African-American studies "has probably the best faculty of its kind," notes an admiring finance major. The history faculty, too, rate a "fantastic," supplemented by great resources both on campus and in the city. The programs in architecture, sport and recreation management, physical therapy, engineering, American studies, the anthropology/human biology track, and music receive high marks. Landscape architecture and horticulture, based on the suburban Ambler campus, also draws raves.

The English department is limited in its course offerings and relies too heavily on graduate students for instruction. Chemistry suffers from introductory lectures that are too large, even in the honors sections. Too many of the large biology classes are simply used to "weed out" weaker students, a senior observes. The foreign language programs work well as minors but as majors, have too few faculty and courses, with only short-term opportunities for study abroad. "The staff is limited," says a French major, "but the professors who are there, are excellent." Physics and math have had too many instructors who speak poor English. Psychology "is too easy," says a major. "One can easily finish the program in 3 years." Academic advising in the College of Liberal Arts also comes under fire. Says a recent graduate: "There aren't enough advisors, there are long waits, and it's very systematic."

Facilities: Temple's 3 libraries, a main facility, an engineering and science branch, and a library materials center, contain 3 million volumes and 24,000 periodicals; the periodical section is especially well stocked with several computerized databases. Paley Library, the main facility, is big enough for a student to find a quiet spot to hide, though lacking in warmth or even atmosphere. "One complaint is the hard wooden chairs," says a user. The book collection falls short and is often disorganized, though an on-line catalog at least attempts to point users in the right direction. In order to obtain a library card, all new students must complete a self-paced workbook that introduces them to basic library skills. When even that knowledge can't help them, students simply head to the nearby Free Library of Philadelphia.

The Tuttleman Learning Center, which opened in fall 1999, houses about 1900 computer stations as well as 30+ multimedia classrooms and 3 interactive lecture halls within its 2½ acres of space, and dramatically changed the balance of computer accessibility from "insufficient" to "incredible." Altogether, 7 general labs and numerous labs in academic departments and residence halls provide 2200 Windows-based PCs, 400 Macs, and 100 Unix machines for student use. Most labs are open until midnight and extend to 24 hours during finals. In addition, wireless access is available in approximately 95% of the classrooms and common areas.

Special programs: In addition to its extensive Philadelphia area campuses, Temple maintains full-service campuses in Rome and Tokyo. The School of Communications and Theater also offers both semester-long and summer programs in London, open to students in any major. Exchange programs are available with universities in England, France, and other countries. Other summer programs run by Temple faculty take students to places as far-ranging as the Sorbonne in Paris or the University of Ghana in West Africa.

Campus life: Although Temple remains largely a commuter university, with 5130 of its 21,000 full-time undergraduates living on campus, that number has risen steadily over the years, as more new students opt to give campus living a try. Sixty percent of new students in the past few years have requested dormitory rooms, with completion in August 2001 of the third new dorm in 6 years adding to the residential living options. The increase in undergraduates who are Temple residents has boosted involvement in more traditional campus activities, though participation still remains comparatively small. One percent of the men and women belong to 12 local fraternities and 11 local sororities, and fraternity theme parties are popular, with tickets available to anyone. Some find that joining the marching band is an easy way to meet 100 new people before school starts. The university grounds are described by many undergraduates as beautiful and well protected for a city campus; an escort service operates from dusk to dawn. Recently formed "Owl Watch" groups involve students trained with the police who patrol the campus. Nevertheless, despite the fifth largest police force in the state and bright lighting "that makes the campus feel like a big stadium during a night game," says a junior, the campus is plagued by petty crime, such as car break-ins and vandalism, and sometimes muggings. Says a male senior: "I feel pretty safe on campus, but I still try to avoid walking at night." As for the surrounding neighborhood, students are advised to proceed with caution.

Fall Saturdays before a Temple football game are often spent tailgating at Lincoln Financial Field, just a bus or subway ride away. "Basketball season also can create mayhem," notes a New Jersey resident, "if the team is doing well," which it usually does, generally boasting a top ten ranking. Says a senior: "The Owls deservedly earn our reverence and devotion." The Liacouras Center, a new multiplex arena/convocation center, easily accommodates 10,000 excited fans for basketball games, as well as 11,000 for a Bob Dylan concert. Altogether, Temple fields 13 varsity sports for men and for women in NCAA Division I. Eighty percent of the men and 65% of the women engage in intramural sports (12 each for men and for women), and the winners of Temple intramural tourneys compete in the City 6 Tournament against 5 other Philadelphia schools. Nonetheless, apathy still prevails around campus, and many a weekend the university appears abandoned, with little going on.

Center-city Philadelphia (just 10 minutes away), as well as other local universities, provides much of the after-hours action for residents and commuters alike. New York City and Washington, D.C. offer alternative, but more distant, urban escapes, and the Jersey Shore and Poconos provide attractive recreational opportunities in their respective seasons.

Cost cutters: Seventy percent of freshmen and 67% of continuing students received some form of financial aid in the 2004–2005 school year, the most recent year for which figures are available; virtually all the aid was based at least in part on financial need. The total average freshman award for a student with need included a need-based scholarship or grant averaging $5010 and need-based self-help aid such as loans and jobs averaging $2778. Non-need-based athletic scholarships for first-year students averaged $12,828. The average 2005 graduate left with debts of $23,772. Entering freshmen who rank in the top 15% of their high school graduating classes with above-average SAT scores are eligible to become Temple Scholars and receive scholarships that range from $1000 to $10,000 annually. Candidates are urged to apply for admission before March 1 to be considered for these awards. Outstanding Achievement Scholarships pay up to full tuition to approximately 100 top graduating high school seniors from Philadelphia. Cooperative education programs are available in all majors.

Rate of return: Eighty-five percent of the freshmen return for the sophomore year. Twenty percent receive their degrees in 4 years, 38% in 5 years, and 44% in 6 years.

Payoff: Elementary education majors comprised 8% of recent graduates followed by psychology majors at 7%, and criminal justice majors at 5%. Many graduates take jobs in accounting, marketing, and computer science with firms such as Cigna and IBM. A number also go directly into teaching. Two hundred seventy companies and organizations recruited on campus in a recent school year. The M.B.A. is probably the most popular advanced degree that students seek.

Bottom line: Temple, says a senior, "is a school about learning, real life, and real people. Students who are not open to new people and new ideas will have a difficult time." Joining a group or organization also helps give students a sense of belonging on the sometimes impersonal campus.

University of Pittsburgh, Pittsburgh Campus

Pittsburgh, Pennsylvania 15260

Setting: Urban
Control: Public
Undergraduate enrollment: 7368 men, 7732 women
Graduate enrollment: 3068 men, 3608 women
Student/faculty ratio: NA
Freshman profile: 14% scored over 700 on SAT I verbal; 42% scored 600–700; 39% 500–599; 5% below 500. 15% scored over 700 on SAT I math; 49% scored 600–700; 32% 500–599; 4% below 500. 73% graduated in top fifth of high school class.
Faculty profile: 88% Ph.D.'s

Tuition and fees: $11,436 in-state, $20,784 out-of-state
Room and board: $7430
Freshman financial aid: 86%; average scholarship or grant: $7518 need-based
Campus jobs: 19%; average earnings: $1722/year
Application deadline: Rolling (Priority date: Jan. 15)
Financial aid deadline: Jan. 15 (Priority date)
Admissions information: (412) 624-PITT
  e-mail: oafa@pitt.edu
  web site: www.pitt.edu

Students interested in pursuing careers in health-related areas may find just what the doctor ordered among the premedical and predental programs or the undergraduate majors in nursing, emergency medicine, health information management, and similar fields at the University of Pittsburgh. In fact, the university environment is uniquely health-oriented, with 6 schools of the health sciences, Medicine, Dental Medicine, Nursing, Pharmacy, Health and Rehabilitation Sciences, and the Graduate School of Public Health, sharing a campus with the predominant School of Arts and Sciences. The University of Pittsburgh Medical Center (UPMC) Health System has several affiliated hospitals and numerous institutes and clinics where undergraduates can observe as well as gain practical experience. Pitt's School of Medicine is a leader in organ transplantation and cancer research; the Western Psychiatric Institute and Clinic, which houses one of the world's most comprehensive psychiatric libraries, is at the forefront in the diagnosis and treatment of mood disorders. Though these facilities do not represent the heart of the undergraduate experience for most students, they are nonetheless among the attractions that lure bright and ambitious students to Pitt. Smaller than many major state universities, with 15,100 full-time undergraduates and only 6700 full-time graduate students, the university offers students a more manageable size, combined with some of the most extensive facilities imaginable.

Student body: Eighty-five percent of the undergraduates are from Pennsylvania, though students in a recent year were lured to Pitt from all 50 states and 122 foreign countries. Most of the out-of-staters also are from the Middle Atlantic region. Nine percent of the undergraduates are African-Americans and 4% are Asian-Americans; 1% are Hispanics and less than 1% are Native Americans. One percent are foreign nationals. "Pitt has a real mix of people," observes a state resident, "a lot of locals, first-generation college students from Pittsburgh's working class, as well as Philly elitists." Many are politically aware and tend toward the conservative end of the political spectrum. Academically, many students are quite focused on working hard to earn a degree, in order to get a good job or gain acceptance into graduate school. But there also are those willing to do just what is needed, and little more. Says a junior: "You could probably find any type of student you chose to locate on our campus."

Academics: The University of Pittsburgh, whose founding in 1787 makes it one of the oldest institutions of higher learning in the nation, offers degrees through the doctorate, including the bachelor's degree in about 100 undergraduate majors. The campus has 16 schools and colleges, 12 of which offer undergraduate degree programs.

The university follows a semester calendar. Popular introductory classes in psychology and the sciences can enroll well over 100 students but are teamed with recitations of fewer than 25; freshman composition and foreign language classes are limited to 22 participants. Upper-level classes generally range between 35 and 60 students.

The School of Arts and Sciences enrolls about half the undergraduates, including freshmen and sophomores planning to enter the schools of Social Work, Health and Rehabilitation Sciences, Information Sciences and Pharmacy plus the School of Education for its sole undergraduate programs in athletic training and exercise science. While in the School of Arts and Sciences, all students must complete general education requirements that draw courses from the major disciplines. There are 3 levels of writing requirements, and a recent graduate maintains that "a student cannot leave Pitt without writing at least 40 to 60 pages of papers." Freshmen can be accepted directly into the schools of Business, Nursing, and Engineering, which have their own requirements.

Pitt's faculty numbers 3552 full-time and 691 part-time members. No breakdown is available on the number that teach at the graduate level only. Thirty-five percent in a recent year were women. Not surprisingly at a research university of Pittsburgh's stature, a number of professors are heavily engaged in research and writing, which can make them hard to find after class and more willing to rely on impersonal time-savers in the classroom, such as computer graded tests. Nevertheless, many students enjoy boasting to friends at other universities about their professor's research contributions and say that most do their best to keep office hours and are usually helpful when approached. A number make the effort themselves to get to know students in large classes. Says a sophomore: "Some professors even require each student to pick up his or her exam from them so that there is at least a connection between name and face."

The science and health-related fields at Pitt are at the head of their class. The premed, pharmacy, nursing, and other health-related programs offer undergraduates incomparable clinical experience at Presbyterian University and Children's hospitals. Biology, says a premed student, features "an extremely qualified and caring faculty." Chemistry is considered first-rate as well. The School of Pharmacy boasts a 97% job placement rate. The program in neuroscience also is one of the few programs of its kind in the country and boasts very well qualified staff.

Pitt's strengths do not stop with the sciences. Philosophy is among the university's best departments, with challenging classes that explore personal ethics and philosophies taught by a staff trained largely at Yale. The major in history and philosophy of science is distinctive and features interesting classes. Engineering is especially challenging with state-of-the-art equipment. Pitt's programs in Hispanic Languages and Literature and Slavic Languages and Literature offer great faculty and depth, as well as wonderful opportunities for study abroad. Language courses in general acquire a special accent when conducted in any of the 26 authentically decorated Nationality Rooms housed within the gothic, 42-story Cathedral of Learning, considered to be the tallest school building in the Western world. Other highly rated programs include anthropology, art history, creative writing, English literature, political science, economics, and statistics.

Even in some of the best programs, students have their share of complaints. Many of the lower-level science, as well as mathematics and economics courses are taught by teaching assistants whose English is limited, making it difficult for students to understand them and, as a result, the course material. Physics and math "lack enthusiastic faculty that get the students excited and interested in learning," says a junior. "They expect the students to do a lot on their own and reward them little for their work." Computer science needs faculty who can explain and elaborate more clearly on important concepts. Psychology and communication each have superb faculty, just not enough of them, says this psychology major. "These departments are too big and students cannot possibly be given individual attention. Sometimes, it also is hard to get classes in these two majors."

Facilities: Among students, the Hillman Library, the largest library facility, which seats 1530 readers, is known as "Club Hillman," where undergraduates gather to gab rather than to study. For more silence, students hold out until the later hours to hit the books (Hillman is open until 2 a.m.) or head directly to any of the 14 other more specialized libraries on campus. Altogether, the university's holdings include nearly 4.2 million volumes, 4.3 million microform items, and 23,377 periodical subscriptions. The computerized catalog PittCat lists all materials located on the Pittsburgh campus plus those at the university's 4 regional campuses.

Seven computer labs with about 650 personal computers plus numerous e-mail kiosks are open for general student use, 3 of them around the clock. An additional 500 PCs in departmental labs are open to students working in those disciplines. All residence-hall rooms are connected to PittNet, the university's local area computer network, with links to the Internet. "Midterms and finals are chaotic," says a junior, "but it's all about timing." Wireless access also is an option from 6 common areas with high student traffic as well as from selected departmental areas and classrooms. Some individual departments may require students to have their own personal computers.

Special programs: Undergraduates may choose to study abroad in an "unlimited" number of countries or spend a semester in Washington, D.C. The large number of Fortune 500 companies headquartered in Pittsburgh makes available extensive opportunities for internships. Students also may cross-register for classes at any of 9 other colleges and universities in the Pittsburgh area.

Campus life: Not quite half, 44%, of Pitt's full-time undergraduates live in university-owned housing, which includes 14 residence halls as well as fraternity houses and off-campus apartments. The 132-acre campus itself is centrally located in the Oakland community, 3 miles east of downtown Pittsburgh. Six percent of the men and women in a recent year belonged to 16 national fraternities and 11 national sororities. Despite their small numbers, members of these groups are very influential in student government and campus social life, though independents find plenty of fun on their own or through any of the 450 other student groups on campus. The William Pitt Union, a favorite student hangout, contains the usual vast array of recreational and social facilities, as well as a restored grand ballroom with vaulted ceilings, mirrored walls, and crystal chandeliers. At least 12 bars within walking distance of campus serve as magnets to the 21-and-over crowd. Because of Pitt's urban location, crime always is a concern to students. Both the campus and city police watch have been increased and a campus bus system takes students to their homes in the surrounding neighborhoods, as well as on campus. A Study Shuttle goes to each of the libraries late at night; a van call service also is available from 7 p.m. until 3 a.m. Residence halls are manned by security attendants around the clock.

Since the fall of 2001, football fans have watched the NCAA Division I Panthers play in a new downtown stadium that was built for the Pittsburgh Steelers, a move off campus some students have welcomed, others not. Basketball, like the rest of the sports Division I, is nearly as popular among the 8 men's and 9 women's intercollegiate teams fielded. The crew, ice hockey, and lacrosse clubs also draw their share of fans. Others take part in the 12 men's, 10 women's, and 5 coed intramural sports offered. "With 800 intramural sports teams to choose from, you always have something to look forward to," says a junior. The Outdoor Club offers other heart-pumping options such as rock-climbing and whitewater rafting.

Pittsburgh wins high marks as a city to turn to for off-campus excitement. Pirates, Steelers, and Penguins games as well as the ballet, symphony, and opera are popular diversions. Schenley Park, a 10-minute walk from campus, offers an outdoor skating rink, tennis courts, swimming pool, golf course, and hiking trails. The Carnegie Museums of Art and Natural History are within walking distance.

Cost cutters: Eighty-seven percent of the freshmen and 77% of continuing students in the 2005–2006 school year received financial aid. No data is available to show the portion of students receiving aid that was need-based. The average freshman award consisted of a $7518 need-based scholarship or grant, and $4380 in self-help aid such as loans and job earnings. The average non-need-based athletic scholarship averaged $13,247. Average debt of a recent graduate was $20,154. Chancellor's Scholarships, which pay tuition, room, and board, are based on high school achievement, standardized test scores, and performances on written essays and interviews. Students interviewed for the Chancellor's awards who do not receive one may receive Honors Tuition Scholarships that pay full tuition. University Scholarships based largely on high school achievement and standardized test scores pay $1000 to full tuition. Anyone in a recent year who had both a 1350 combined SAT I score (or 31 ACT) and graduated in the top 5% of his or her high school class was guaranteed a scholarship of at least $1000. Helen Faison Scholarships pay full tuition, room, and board to underrepresented students. Full-tuition Honors Challenge Scholarships also go to traditionally underrepresented students. Freshmen engineering students may receive awards ranging from $2000 to $4000. All awards are renewable for up to 4 years. A deferred tuition payment plan also is available.

Rate of return: Eighty-eight percent of freshmen return for a second year. Thirty-eight percent go on to graduate in 4 years; 60% in 5 years; 64% in 6 years.

Payoff: The field of business claimed 14% of the 2005 graduates, followed by social sciences and history with 13% and English language and literature with 12%. In a recent year, 40% of the grads went on for advanced degrees. Four hundred companies and other organizations recruited on campus in a recent school year. Employers of Pitt grads include CVS Pharmacy, Deloitte and Touche, Eckerd Drug, Federated Investors, Lockheed Martin, Mellon Bank, and PPG Industries, as well as the University of Pittsburgh and the UPMC Health System. More than a quarter, 29%, of those employed in a recent class were working out of state.

Bottom line: For students interested in the health-related professions, there may be no more ideal choice than the University of Pittsburgh. For students unsure of what to study, Pitt also offers a breadth of majors with something for almost everyone. And for those times when both kinds of students simply don't want to study, the city of Pittsburgh itself is good-tasting medicine.

University of Scranton

Scranton, Pennsylvania 18510

Setting: Urban
Control: Private (Roman Catholic-Jesuit)
Undergraduate enrollment: 1639 men, 2219 women
Graduate enrollment: 101 men, 204 women
Student/faculty ratio: 15:1
Freshman profile: 3% scored over 700 on SAT I verbal; 24% scored 600–700; 58% 500–599; 15% below 500. 3% scored over 700 on SAT I math; 29% scored 600–700; 52% 500–599; 16% below 500. 47% graduated in top fifth of high school class; 75% in upper two-fifths.
Faculty profile: 86% Ph.D.'s
Tuition and fees: $24,030

Room and board: $9904
Freshman financial aid: 97%; average scholarship or grant: $8715
Campus jobs: 16%; average earnings: $900/year
Application deadline: Early action: Nov. 15; regular: Mar. 1
Financial aid deadline: Feb. 15
Admissions information: (570) 941-7540;
 (888) SCRANTON
 e-mail: admissions@scranton.edu
 web site: www.scranton.edu

The University of Scranton in northeastern Pennsylvania is a school students love for its "Jesuitness." Though the university has been run by the Society of Jesus only since 1942, 54 years after its founding, the influence is as rich as if Saint Ignatius Loyola himself, founder of the order in 1540, had laid the cornerstone of the campus. Though just 8 Jesuits are engaged in teaching, nearly half of the faculty hold at least 1 degree apiece from a Jesuit college or university. The general-education program, which even the most career-focused accounting or physical therapy major must fulfill, covers over half the credits needed for graduation. And while the emphasis is on developing well-rounded individuals, the purely academic accomplishments are worth noting: 70% of the entering freshmen graduate in 4 years; Scranton seniors have been awarded 113 Fulbright and other prestigious international awards since 1972, in some recent years boasting 7 or 8 recipients; in a recent year, 80% of Scranton applicants gained admission to medical schools; 75% were accepted to law school; 57% of accounting majors have obtained jobs in the major firms. And for those planning to remain in the region, an influential alumni network is eager to extend a helping hand: about half of all physicians, lawyers, accountants, dentists, and high school teachers in northeastern Pennsylvania are Scranton graduates.

Student body: All but 16% of Scranton students are Catholic. Slightly over half, 51%, are Pennsylvanians; the largest contingent of nonresidents come from other Middle Atlantic states, though 28 states in all and 9 foreign countries are represented. The enrollment is split nearly evenly, 51%/49%, between public school and private or parochial school graduates, with the edge going to those from the public sector. Minority students comprise 8% of the enrollment: 4% Hispanic, 2% Asian-American, and 2% African-American. Foreign nationals account for another 1%. Scranton students tend to be responsible, enthusiastic, open-minded, and supportive of each other. Notes a recent graduate: "We share a strong value system, and everyone seems concerned about friendship, education, family, and religious issues." The undergraduates believe in balancing their academic and social lives, and while Scranton has its share of preppy students, most do not conform to the "J. Crew" look prevalent on other eastern campuses. Says a junior: "A majority of the students here do not care what other people think of them. (We go to class in pajamas at times.) I love that people feel that they don't have to try to impress others." For the most part, the Scranton style remains "academically inclined" in most majors, but more intense in such fields as physical therapy and biology. Still, professors encourage group projects and students "don't step on each other to reach the top," says a computer science major. "The students really stick together and help each other through problems."

Academics: The University of Scranton awards the bachelor's degree in 57 disciplines and master's degrees in 23 areas. Undergraduates majoring in English, business, chemistry, and biochemistry can earn both bachelor's and master's degrees in 5 years. Classes are divided into 2 semesters with a January intersession and 2 summer sessions. Average class size is 23 students, with a range as high as 50 in some introductory history classes and dropping to 10 in upper-level classes in foreign language and other disciplines.

Scranton's distinctively Jesuit liberal arts foundation requires all students to complete a variety of courses in philosophy and theology (the highest number at 15 credits), the humanities, the social and behavioral sciences, and natural science. Students also must complete coursework emphasizing such vital skills as writing, public speaking, computer literacy, and quantitative reasoning. A class in physical education, as well as courses emphasizing cultural diversity and intensity of writing, a freshman seminar, and 12 credits worth of electives, round out the required program. The core covers, at a minimum, 77 of the 130 or so credits needed for graduation.

All of the 250 full-time and 132 of the 176 part-time faculty members teach undergraduates. Thirty-five percent are women. The faculty's academic breadth is reflected in the members' credentials: degrees recently from 135 different universities in 30 countries on 5 continents, ranging from Cambridge University in England and the University of Calcutta in India to Berkeley, MIT, and Harvard in the U.S. Students complain of some professors who ought to retire and others who appear more comfortable with their books than with people. However, the majority, especially many of the Jesuits who live in the residence halls, thrive on frequent interaction with students and deserve, in the words of a senior, a grade of "A+++— incredible." Adds a junior: "Many faculty want to see their students grow in all ways—academically, socially, spiritually, and emotionally."

The school's impressive medical school admission rate is largely a reflection of Scranton's rigorous biology and chemistry majors, which feature a highly qualified and demanding faculty, an intense curriculum, and steadily increasing opportunities for student research. The equally productive accounting department boasts professors who are both CPAs and Ph.D.'s and regular recruiting at graduation time by representatives of the major accounting firms. Other programs in the well-funded Kania School of Management are wise educational investments as well. Majors recently were added in such 21st-century fields as electronic commerce, enterprise management technology, and accounting information systems. The entire School of Management acquired a higher-tech feel with the opening in 2000 of Brennan Hall, the school's new home. The facility offers the most technologically advanced classrooms and instructional space on campus, a fifth-floor Executive Center, 144-seat auditorium, and more than 500 Internet connections. The nursing and physical and occupational therapy curricula and faculties are known for giving students a workout, doing so in a new 4-story, 65,000-square-foot building. Faculties of philosophy, theology, English, psychology, history, and political science are deeply involved in their subject matter and, in the case of the latter 2 disciplines, draw on extensive personal travel experience in their teaching.

Art and music are offered only as minors in art history and music history and have few faculty and facilities as a result. The physics faculty has difficulty teaching lower-level classes so that students can understand the material. Some students who are not math majors find the professors less approachable. Majors in gerontology and criminal justice need to be developed more as programs and to offer a greater variety of courses and professors. The communication major could be more rigorous and needs more faculty and course offerings to keep pace with increased interest from students.

Facilities: Five-story Weinberg Memorial Library, which opened in 1992, is located in the heart of campus, and in the hearts of many dedicated students in need of a quiet place to study. The library offers a study area for every level of intensity, and while hard chairs prevail in the carrels, comfortable couches beckon in a variety of other places, including a 24-hour reading room with a much loved coffee bar. Altogether, group and individual study space is provided for 1000 users. The collection of almost 474,000 volumes and 16,784 periodicals (nearly 2000 in print) continues to grow yearly. That steady increase, along with combined advantages of a computerized catalog, 100+ Internet index/databases, and the overall pleasant environment silences most critics.

More than 900 PCs are available around campus, in the library, academic buildings, and residence halls, for student use. A lab in the library is open 24 hours a day, all of them are open around-the-clock during midterms and finals. And, as more students have opted to purchase their own computers using a university discount, even short lines during exam and paper periods have diminished. Says a communications major: "There is virtually no line to get 'on line.' " Wireless coverage areas include the library, dining facilities, academic buildings, and some residence halls. One hundred percent of the outdoor areas are wireless.

Special programs: Students can spend a semester or a year at any of 27 other Jesuit colleges or universities from Boston to San Francisco. History and political science majors may participate in a Washington, D.C., semester. Opportunities for study overseas are available at Loyola University's Rome Center, Blackfriars Hall at Oxford University in England, the Bejing Center for Language and Culture in China and elsewhere. A 3-2 engineering degree is offered with the University of Detroit Mercy.

Campus life: Eighty percent of Scranton's students live on the 50-acre campus, with most of the rest residing in apartments no more than 5 blocks away. Students find the typical weekend to be "fun, social, and relaxing," and though there is no Greek system, many flock to comedians or dances sponsored by the student government or to parties off campus. The Commuter and Off-Campus Association (COCA) works to spread the message to "party responsibly" and maintain good relations with university neighbors. For most undergraduates, Scranton is an easy school to get involved in, and a majority do just that. Throughout the week and the weekend, undergraduates divide themselves among 25 honor societies, at least two dozen cocurricular clubs (the Biology Club alone has more than 400 members), 17 special-interest groups, 4 university publications, assorted musical groups, the student radio station, and an active volunteer program. Scranton students log more than 159,000 hours of community service each year. Most students regularly attend Masses held in the university chapel and residence halls. Many also seek out the university conference and retreat center at Chapman Lake, just 20 minutes away, to relax, pray, learn, and revitalize themselves. Students say crime on the urban campus is confined to petty theft and some vandalism. Undergraduates, however, are urged not to walk alone after dark on campus or in the university area and instead to call the escort service. Members of COCA also assist in patrolling the area off campus.

Royals basketball is the biggest of the 10 men's and 9 women's NCAA Division III sports, though soccer and lacrosse also bring out the fans. The Lady Royals basketball team has made 19 NCAA Tournament appearances since 1982 including 2006 and 7 appearances in the Final Four since 1985, including back-to-back showings in 1999 and 2000 and a third place finish in 2006. Rugby matches, a club sport, also are popular. Two-thirds of the men and a third of the women engage in intramurals, 18 sports for men and for women.

Seven other colleges within a 15-mile radius offer alternative diversion. Scranton (pop. 76,000) is located 125 miles west of New York and 125 miles north of Philadelphia, both occasional urban getaways.

Cost cutters: In the 2005–2006 school year, 71% of the freshmen and 66% of the continuing students received financial aid. All but a percent or 2 of both groups were given need-based assistance. The average freshman award included a need-based scholarship or grant averaging $10,771 and need-based self-help aid such as loans and job earning averaging $4070. Other non-need based awards and scholarships averaged $7635. Average debts for a 2005 alumnus totaled $15,800. In a recent school year, the university awarded 9 merit-based full-tuition Presidential Scholarships to students who typically were valedictorians or salutatorians with minimum math and critical reading SATs of 1400. Just over 110 first-year students with SATs of at least 1200 drawn from the top fifth of their high school classes were given Dean's Scholarships ranging in value from $8000 to $13,000. Loyola Scholarships worth from $4000 to $9000 went to 326 freshmen with 1100 SATs and class rank in the upper 30%. Arrupe Scholarships presented to 51 high-achieving minority students with need paid between $6000 and $12,000.

Rate of return: Eighty-nine percent of entering freshmen return for a second year. Seventy percent graduate in 4 years; 80% finish in a fifth year.

Payoff: Communications was the most popular major for 2005 graduates, claiming 10% of the class, followed by elementary education at 9% and biology at 7%. A third of the new alumni pursued advanced degrees shortly after commencement. Historically, more than 40% of Scranton graduates in the arts and sciences eventually continue their education. A majority of all new alumni take jobs almost immediately, primarily in major cities such as Philadelphia, New York, and Washington, D.C., as well as throughout the Middle Atlantic states. Most accept posts in nursing, physical therapy, accounting, and sales with firms like Coopers & Lybrand, AT&T, Prudential, and McNeil Pharmaceuticals. Sixty companies and organizations recruited on campus in a recent school year.

Bottom line: "Scranton offers an excellent academic, spiritual, and social experience," remarks a recent graduate. "The fact that class size is kept small promotes a very personal and intimate learning environment, enhancing the growth of the well-rounded person while leaving room for individualism."

Washington & Jefferson College

Washington, Pennsylvania 15301

Setting: Small town
Control: Private
Undergraduate enrollment: 726 men, 674 women
Graduate enrollment: None
Student/faculty ratio: 14:1
Freshman profile: 5% scored over 700 on SAT I verbal; 26% scored 600–700; 57% 500–599; 12% below 500; 6% scored over 700 on SAT I math; 32% scored 600–700; 51% 500–599; 11% below 500. 11% scored above 28 on the ACT; 15% scored 27–28; 41% 24–26; 25% 21–23; 8% below 21. 24% graduated in top tenth of high school class; 51% in upper fifth.
Faculty profile: 86% Ph.D.'s

Tuition and fees: $26,330
Room and board: $7160
Freshman financial aid: 98%; average scholarship or grant: $5410 need-based; $9724 non-need-based
Campus jobs: 41%; average earnings: $830/year
Application deadline: Early decision: Dec. 1; regular: Mar. 1
Financial aid deadline: Feb. 15
Admissions information: (724) 223-6025; (888) 926-3529
e-mail: admission@washjeff.edu
web site: www.washjeff.edu

When two giants of American history, George Washington and Thomas Jefferson, are combined in the name of one tiny liberal arts college, a freshman there might expect great things to follow. And they generally do, especially to undergraduates preparing to attend law or medical schools. Over the past decade, more than 90% of W & J law school applicants have gained admission to schools as prestigious as Harvard, Yale, and Michigan, as well as to other fine, albeit lesser known schools. Although the national average for admission to health-related professional schools is only 45%, well over 90% of W & J applicants are annually admitted to medical, dental, veterinary, and other such programs. In a recent 6-year period, virtually every candidate seeking admission to schools other than medical school was accepted. In one recent year, W & J medical school applicants went 19 for 19 in the admissions game; the next year, the college struck out only once among 21 applicants. Students enrolled say W & J's programs are so rigorous that slackers are weeded out fast and those who survive are prepared for life, liberty, and the pursuit of advanced degrees at any prestigious professional school.

Student body: Three-fourths of the pursuers are from Pennsylvania, many from the western part, with the rest hailing from 32 other states, largely in the Middle Atlantic region, as well as 2 foreign countries. Fourteen percent attended private or parochial schools. African-American students make up 2% of the enrollment, with Asian-Americans, foreign nationals, and Hispanics each accounting for about 1%. Students are described by the adjectives *preppy, conservative, ambitious*, and very *career-minded*. "Old jeans, T-shirts, and tennis shoes don't cut it here," observes a junior. "J. Crew, Polo, Banana Republic, and Ann Taylor are what we wear." Most are friendly, though a few can be snobbish, and many socialize with their own groups of friends. "The scene can be very cliquish," observes a junior, "and someone not a group member can't just disappear, as is possible at a university of 30 or 40 thousand." Though some undergraduates try to give the appearance of being unconcerned about their studies and many are very involved in extracurricular activities, most work hard and long to do well. "Students cannot get behind in their work, or they will get buried here," advises an administrator. Some admit to finding the competitive environment a bit more "cutthroat" than they had expected at a small college.

Academics: Washington and Jefferson College traces its academic roots back to 1781, making it one of the oldest colleges in the United States and the oldest west of the Allegheny Mountains. It awards the bachelor's degree in more than 20 disciplines with 12 special or preprofessional programs also available, as well as self-designed thematic majors that let students explore the interrelationships between disciplines. The academic calendar is divided into 2 semesters with a January term. Class sizes generally range from 4 to 40, although an occasional science lecture, such as organic chemistry, has been known to push 80.

As professionally focused as many students may be, they must spend much of their first year or 2 getting grounded in the broad foundation of the liberal arts. All first-year students begin their time at W & J with a Freshman Forum that involves both a course and a set of related cultural and intellectual events designed to introduce the newcomers to what the college community has to offer. Students also must engage in a "breadth of study" by taking 1 specially designated general education course in the arts, 2 such courses in the social sciences, 2 in the natural sciences and mathematics, and 3 in the humanities. Additional requirements entail a course in cultural diversity, 2 foreign language classes, and courses that demonstrate mastery of 4 skill areas, writing, oral communication, quantitative reasoning, and use of information technology. Two courses in physical education or wellness also are mandated.

Thirty-three of the 130 faculty members are part-time. Forty percent are women. Although W & J has its share of "bad apples," students view most professors as the pick of the crop, concerned about their students' personal growth and well-being as well as about their academic accomplishments. Says a senior: "Professors will stay later or come earlier to help their students, invite them over for dinner, and become interested in their lives. They allow us to see them as people and not merely as a person of knowledge who controls our grade with the stroke of a pen." However, students say a number of the faculty members are aging and welcome the younger, more enthusiastic professors who are being hired to replace them.

It is tough but dedicated faculty members, rather than state-of-the-art equipment or bountiful research dollars, that make the college's strongest programs, biology, chemistry, political science, and history, superb. In each discipline, the faculty represent a wide range of perspectives that they are delighted—indeed, determined—to share with their students. They also stress the development of "clear and concise speaking and writing skills, which are necessary to succeed in postgraduate life," says a history major. Biology, for one, has been strengthened even further thanks to a recent grant from the Howard Hughes Medical Institute that has brought about renovations to the molecular biology and cell culture laboratories, development of a biology mentoring program, and expanded opportunities for student research, both on and off campus. Psychology, sociology, economics, and English also offer 5-star academics. "If you take the right professors," says an English major, "the program is very challenging, cerebral, and rewarding." Philosophy, adds a major, is "up to date and probably the most helpful and supportive department to its students."

The math department is small, and some courses are offered only every other year. Business needs more inspiring professors and more vigor and rigor. Students find the faculty and classes provided in the music major "outstanding," but say equipment appears nearly as old as the flugelhorn. Art, French, German, and Spanish are majors but limited in their course offerings, though the faculty and classes offered are excellent.

Facilities: U. Grant Miller Library is one area where being smaller at W & J is definitely not being better. Students find the collection of 193,000 volumes and 503 periodicals (not counting about 8000 archived electronic journals and newspapers) to be lacking, especially in more recent science publications, so most head to the Internet, to interlibrary loan, or to the much larger libraries of the University of Pittsburgh, Carnegie Mellon, or West Virginia University for extensive research. Students consider Miller a good place to study "with different environments within itself to accommodate all students," says a psychology major. Users also especially like the library's computer lab with 25 computers and the extended hours of operation for the building and the lab—until 2 a.m.

About 100 Pentium computers are located in 4 computer centers in the library, Old Main, the Technology Center, and the new business and modern language building. The Technology Center lab remains open 24 hours. Access to the computer network also is available from every student room. Because W & J's new restaurant-style cafeteria has been fitted with a video camera linked to the college web site, students may check how long the food lines are before venturing outside their rooms. The college strongly recommends that students have personal computers. Wireless access is available in and around many residence halls and academic buildings, including the library, student center, and all dining halls as well as most outdoor locations.

Special programs: Exchange programs are offered with the College of Higher Studies in Administration, in Bogotá, Colombia, the University of Cologne in Germany, the University of Guanajuato in Mexico, and International University in Moscow. Additional opportunities for study abroad can be arranged for a year, for a semester, or during the January term. A Washington, D.C. semester is available through American University. Back at W & J, an entrepreneurial studies program supplements any regular major with coursework in various aspects of entrepreneurship and brings students into contact with business leaders who reflect the qualities being studied. A 3-2 cooperative program in engineering is available with Case Western Reserve or Washington University as is a 3-4 program in podiatry, with the Pennsylvania and Ohio colleges of Podiatry; and a 3-4 program in optometry, with the Pennsylvania College of Optometry and a 3–3 program in law with Duquesne University and the University of Pittsburgh.

Campus life: Seventy-five percent of W & J students live on the 52-acre campus and are spread primarily among 5 large residence halls and 13 smaller halls. Greek life is enormously popular and involves 43% of the men in 7 national fraternities and 37% of the women in 4 sororities. Since fraternity parties are open to all, most independents simply do their weekend celebrating at Greek festivities. George and Tom's, the student-run nonalcoholic night club, brings in comedians and bands. Monticello, a student-operated coffeehouse, also draws supporters to its poetry readings, live music performances, and opportunities for good conversation, "but most students opt for a livelier atmosphere at a fraternity party," says a junior. The Pre-Health Society and various other academic groups bring together students of like interests. SADD, Students Against Destructive Decisions, which promotes responsible behavior in areas concerning alcohol, drugs, sex and other issues, has gained visibility and respect in recent years. Crime, other than occasional theft from the dorms and cars, is not a problem. Call boxes are located throughout campus although some students have wished there were younger, more vigorous security guards on duty.

Athletic competition is about the only serious weekend rival to the Greek revelry. Twelve men's and 11 women's teams compete in NCAA Division III. Since W & J has traditionally had a strong, highly ranked football team, the Presidents' games almost always draw enthusiastic crowds. Forty-nine percent of the men and 24% of the women turn out for the 20 men's and 19 women's intramural sports played.

Though the community of Washington (pop. 16,000) is very small, its proximity to Pittsburgh, only 30 minutes north, makes it seem less isolated. The Meadows Horse Racing Track is another favorite off-campus diversion, just 10 minutes away.

Cost cutters: Ninety-eight percent of the freshmen and 96% of the continuing students received financial assistance during the 2005–2006 school year. Aid was based on need for 70% of the freshmen and 64% of the remaining students. The average package for a first-year student with need included a need-based scholarship or grant averaging $5410 and need-based self-help aid such as loans and jobs averaging $2865. Other non-need-based awards and scholarships for first-year students averaged $9724. Average debt for a 2005 graduate was $17,500. Howard J. Burnett Presidential Scholarships worth $12,000 to $16,000 a year are awarded to students generally drawn from the top 10% of their high school classes with SAT critical reading and math scores of at least 1200 or ACTs of 27 or higher. W & J Scholars Awards pay $10,000 to $12,000 annually to students also usually from the top 10% of their classes with critical reading and math SATs of at least 1000 or ACTs of 23 or above. Both awards are renewable. Other merit scholarships include the Dean's Scholarship paying $8000 to $10,000 a year, the $4000 W & J Challenge Grant, which doubles in value if a student achieves a cumulative 2.8 GPA or higher, and the Joseph Hardy Sr. Scholarship, which pays $500 to $2000 to selected students in the entrepreneurial studies program.

Rate of return: Eighty-six percent of freshmen return for a second year. Sixty-six percent graduate in 4 years; 68% in 5 years.

Payoff: Business administration claimed 17% of the 2005 graduating class, followed by 14% in accounting and 13% in psychology. A third of the new alums proceeded directly to graduate or professional schools. Most of the rest started jobs almost immediately in retailing, marketing, sales, banking, and accounting, many with major firms such as Goodyear, Procter & Gamble, and Chase Manhattan. More than 30 companies and organizations recruited on campus in the 2004–2005 school year.

Bottom line: Although a student with an eye on law school or a health-related professional school may appear to gain the most from 4 years at Washington & Jefferson, majors in other disciplines rarely feel short-changed. However, newcomers must either want to belong to a small, rather preppy, heavily Greek environment or not mind being different in the ambitious pursuit of the college's academic benefits.

York College of Pennsylvania

York, Pennsylvania 17405

Setting: Suburban
Control: Private
Undergraduate enrollment: 1909 men, 2560 women (936 part-time)
Graduate enrollment: 16 men, 8 women (264 part-time)
Student/faculty ratio: 19:1
Freshman profile: 4% scored over 700 on SAT I verbal; 24% scored 600–700; 55% 500–599; 17% below 500. 2% scored over 700 on SAT I math; 21% scored 600–700; 60% 500–599; 17% below 500. 39% graduated in top fifth of high school class; 76% in upper two-fifths.

Faculty profile: 80% Ph.D.'s
Tuition and fees: $10,050
Room and board: $6500
Freshman financial aid: 84%; average scholarship or grant: $3247 need-based; $6270 non-need-based
Campus jobs: 10%; average earnings: $1500/year
Application deadline: Rolling
Financial aid deadline: Apr. 15
Admissions information: (717) 849-1600; (800) 455-8018
  e-mail: admissions@ycp.edu
  web site: www.ycp.edu

If staunchly independent York College of Pennsylvania holds any spiritual affiliation, it is to the little-known cause of CCC: Cutting College Costs. At York, cutting costs has been akin to a campus crusade, with strict adherence to a policy of keeping administrative overhead low, avoiding debt, and resisting the temptation to set a higher tuition for all and temper it for the vast majority with extensive scholarships, grants, and loans. At $16,550 for tuition, fees, room, and board in the 2005–2006 school year, York rates among the lowest priced of all private colleges in the Northeast. More important, as costs have been suppressed, quality in the form of personal attention from knowledgeable faculty has been preserved. "York," concludes a junior, "is truly a school for the students."

Student body: Fifty-eight percent of York's undergraduates are Pennsylvanians, with the rest from 29 other states, mainly New Jersey, Delaware, Maryland, and New York, and 36 foreign countries. Eighty-six percent are graduates of public schools. Racially and ethnically, the student body is quite homogeneous. Only 2% of the undergraduates are African-American, and 1% each Hispanic, Asian-American, Native American, and foreign national. There also is a large contingent of older, nontraditional students who comprise about a fourth of the full-time and part-time undergraduate enrollment. Students describe themselves by such adjectives as *energetic, goal-oriented, down-to-earth, friendly,* and *involved.* "We are workers," says a New Yorker, "willing to put forth the effort necessary to obtain a result."

Academics: Although York was founded as an academy in 1787, it has been a 4-year college only since 1968; it now awards a bachelor's degree in 67 majors, some with several tracks, and 3 master's degrees. The academic year is divided into 2 semesters. Freshmen can expect class sizes averaging 30–40 students, with the largest introductory course occasionally enrolling over 40 but never more than 50. "No lecture classes, which is awesome," says a sophomore. Courses at the junior level and above usually run from 15 to 20 members, though an advanced history class or an English seminar may have only 8 participants.

York's general-education requirements account for 48 of the 124 credit hours needed to graduate. Students take 5 common courses in writing, communication, math, and information literacy, which teaches students how to use library resources and computer technologies. Students also must choose courses from 5 fields: humanities and fine arts, social and behavioral sciences, laboratory sciences, American civilization/government and Western Civilization, and international studies/foreign language. Two credits in physical education are required as well. Many students find the core courses to be as challenging as classes in their majors.

Although students generally like the flexibility in the core and the breadth of courses it exposes them to, their enthusiasm for the 134 full-time faculty members is much warmer. "A student's problems are never trivial," says a sophomore. "The professors take it upon themselves to help the students better understand the work that is troubling them." One chemistry major recalls how her academic advisor got her "2 summers of internships, a laboratory assistant position, and a departmental tutoring position; she also has been very helpful to me in my medical college decision process." Others cite professors' ability to teach complex material so that it is easily understood and to be receptive to any and all student questions. However, students generally give a much more restrained rating to the 295 part-timers who outnumber full-time faculty 2 to 1, finding many hard to locate after classes and not as qualified. Forty-five percent of the faculty are women.

Many of the academic programs rated most highly by students combine textbook learning with real-life experiences, among them business, nursing, criminal justice, education, and mass communications. Professors in both the business and the criminal justice departments have worked extensively in their fields. Criminal justice majors can gain first-hand knowledge, too, by performing their own detective work with the help of a crime analysis laboratory and by serving as part of the campus security staff. The Business Administration Center provides majors with a sophisticated telecommunications network and modern computer facilities. The mass communication program also has a modern building with top-quality studios and editing booths. At York Hospital, a short walk from the campus, nursing students get to experience first-hand what their future profession is really like. Education majors are required to complete 120 hours of observation, no more than 40 in the same school and in at least 1 city setting, before students can enter the classroom to practice teach. "Many of the adjunct professors are local school officials and administrators with vast experience in the field," says a secondary education student. Among the humanities, English and political science are considered thorough in their coursework, tutoring, and advising. A major in Professional Writing requires classes in areas as varied as Rhetorical Theory to Writing for the Web. Such classes, says an English major, "can make any major more marketable." Political science majors gain experience working on campaigns in New York City. Biology is considered a satisfying major as well. "The department," says a major, "works very hard with each of its students to help them get published in a scholarly journal by their graduation." York's major in mechanical engineering got a boost from its move to a newly acquired facility that it shares with nursing and that houses 4 engineering labs as well as classrooms. A required co-op program gives students a chance to gain valuable real-world experience.

Efforts have been under way to beef up other of the humanities, fine arts, and engineering programs. Students find music especially small and its program, though offered as a major in the new communications center, is regarded "more as a hobby than anything else," remarks a senior. Spanish is the only foreign language major available; various levels of instruction are offered in French and German with introductory coursework available in Italian, Latin, and Russian.

Facilities: The renovation and automation of Schmidt Library in 2004 gave Schmidt such 21st-century technologies as digital scanning, high-speed Internet access in a wireless setting, and licensed databases. And, says a junior, "it looks amazing compared to my freshman year." Two quiet floors provide cubbies where students can work independently. A floor of community workstations encourages studying in groups. "They also have big comfortable couches surrounded by windows that allow for a great reading area," adds the junior. YorCat, the on-line catalog, provides access to a collection of 300,000 volumes as well as the Internet. CD-ROM technology offers similar entry to articles in more than 1500 periodicals. CD-CAT makes available over 3 million additional titles held in cooperating libraries accessible to York students. For even more materials, undergraduates can borrow from the resources of 5 other colleges. Students say the core requirement "Information Literacy" on how to do effective research comes in handy as new technologies are added yearly. And there's no beating the human help. Observes a senior: "And though the facilities and the books may be old, the librarians are on top of their game and will sit down with you until you find the information that you need."

More than 450 computers are available in 6 public and 13 special-purpose labs across campus; all use wireless technology. There are 70 wireless access points in public lobbies and the student union as well as in the library for those students who bring laptops. Most labs are open until 1 a.m. and around the clock during finals.

Special programs: Extensive internship opportunities are available, including programs at Walt Disney World, the Baltimore Zoo, and the state capital at Harrisburg. Some classes sponsor trips to the Bahamas or Jamaica, with extra openings available for students not enrolled in the course. Exchange programs with colleges in York and London, England; Tokyo, Japan; Kwangju, Korea, and Cuernavaca, Mexico also are options. A Premedical Scholars Program allows exceptionally accomplished high school seniors to be assured admission to the Pennsylvania State University College of Medicine at Hershey at the same time as they enter York.

Campus life: Forty-three percent of York's undergraduates reside on the 118-acre campus, located just south of Continental Square, where Congress met from September 1777 to June 1778 and adopted the Articles of Confederation. The campus, however, dates back only to 1961, when the college moved from its downtown location to the site of a former golf course. Ten percent of York's men and women are members of 8 national fraternities and 6 national sororities. The Greeks sponsor off-campus parties just about every weekend and while many members and independents attend, there has been an increase in the number of alternatives, such as an on-campus dance club, comedians, and other live entertainment, to which more undergraduates have responded. Whereas 6 years ago, many students would leave campus for the weekend, "that simply is not the case anymore," says a senior. Among popular clubs, the student-run radio station involves more than 100 active members in its programming. Although crime, to date, has not been a serious problem, the college has placed call boxes throughout campus and routinely checks campus lighting for brightness. Security officers, many now patroling on bicycles, are on duty around the clock and provide an escort service. "Any crime that occurs, occurs off campus," says a senior, "and is mostly the result of students making poor decisions." As a precaution, students advise traveling in groups at night off campus. A Student-Neighbor Task Force meets monthly to discuss concerns about off-campus safety and other issues related to the college and surrounding community.

Attendance at sporting events has picked up since York became a member of the Capital Athletic Conference in NCAA Division III. In the 2004–2005 school year, the men's basketball team, the conference champs, competed in the NCAA Division III Final Four, and the stands throughout the season fairly glowed with the "Screamin' Green" T-shirts students wear to show their support for the Spartans. The Spartans compete in 10 men's and 10 women's sports; men's and women's basketball and baseball draw the most fans, though rugby as a club sport continues to gain in popularity. Nearly two-thirds of both men and women participate in 10 intramural sports for each sex and 5 club sports. The Ski and Outdoor Club also gets many involved in its trips. A new sports and fitness center, nearing completion in the 2005–2006 school year, will add 3 new playing fields, one artificial, plus additional spaces for student recreation as well as intramural and varsity play.

For a quick mental and physical health break, students walk up Reservoir Hill, across the street from campus, and in winter, often sled down. Those seeking to get out of York (pop. 50,000) prefer bus trips sponsored by Campus Programming to the Amish country in Lancaster County, to Baltimore's Inner Harbor, about 45 minutes away, or to Philadelphia or Washington, D.C., each a 2-hour drive.

Cost cutters: In the 2005–2006 school year, 84% of the freshmen and 76% of the continuing students received financial help to attend York. Just 48% of the first-year students and 49% of the rest were on need-based assistance. The average freshman award for a first-year student with financial need included a need-based scholarship or grant averaging $3247 and need-based self-help aid such as loans and jobs averaging $2352. Other non-need-based scholarships or awards for freshmen averaged $6270. The average debts of a 2005 grad amounted to $15,621. York College may be fiscally responsible, but it isn't tight when it comes to rewarding top students. Ten full-tuition renewable Trustee Scholarships are available on a competitive basis for freshmen with class rank in the top 20% and SATs of at least 1210 on the critical reading and math portions or 29 ACT composite. A one-half tuition scholarship per year is awarded to all high school valedictorians and salutatorians with strong test scores. One hundred fifty renewable Dean's Academic Scholarships worth one-third tuition are awarded to new students who rank in the top 40% of their class with math and critical reading SATs of 1150 or better or a 26 ACT composite. Entering freshmen planning to major in education, English, history, humanities, foreign languages, music, philosophy, or speech are eligible for a limited number of $1200 renewable awards.

Installment tuition-payment plans are available too, and students can earn as much as 60 credits, half of those needed for a bachelor's degree, through advanced placement and/or credit by examination. Taking advantage of this opportunity, 15% of a recent freshman class saved both money and time and graduated in 3 years.

Rate of return: Eighty-three percent of the entering freshmen return for the sophomore year. Forty-two percent graduate in 4 years, 61% in 5 years, 62% in 6 years.

Payoff: Ten percent of the 2005 graduates earned bachelor's degrees in elementary education, and 7% each in criminal justice and mass communication. The vast majority put their degrees to work soon after commencement, taking jobs with such businesses as AT&T, IBM, and Haskins and Sells, or as nurses at York Hospital, where many worked as undergraduates. One hundred seventy-three companies and organizations recruited on campus in the 2004–2005 school year. Just over a third of all alumni (36%) eventually pursue advanced degrees.

Bottom line: The average student succeeds here, undergraduates say, because the college is willing to work with anyone who needs extra help to earn a degree. At York College of Pennsylvania, administrators and faculty don't just preach the gospel of academic and fiscal responsibility; they practice it.

Rhode Island

Bryant University

Smithfield, Rhode Island 02917

Setting: Suburban
Control: Private
Undergraduate enrollment: 1802 men, 1210 women
Graduate enrollment: 18 men, 21 women (400 part-time)
Student/faculty ratio: 23:1
Freshman profile: 1% scored over 700 on SAT I verbal; 18% scored 600–700; 60% 500–599; 21% below 500. 3% scored over 700 on SAT I math; 35% scored 600–700; 53% 500–599; 9% below 500. 11% scored above 28 on the ACT; 14% scored 27–28; 33% 24–26; 27% 21–23; 15% below 21. 18% graduated in top tenth of high school class; 43% in upper fifth.
Faculty profile: 86% Ph.D.'s

Tuition and fees: $24,762
Room and board: $9568
Freshman financial aid: 85%; average scholarship or grant: $9485 need-based; $8303 non-need-based
Campus jobs: 18%; average earnings: $1530/year
Application deadline: Early decision: Nov. 15; regular: Feb. 15
Financial aid deadline: Feb. 15 (Scholarships: Jan. 15)
Admissions information: (401) 232-6100; (800) 622-7001
e-mail: admission@bryant.edu
web site: www.bryant.edu

At Bryant College 12 miles outside Providence, Rhode Island, seeing is believing, at least when it comes to students deciding to attend this business-oriented college. Eighty-five percent of the high school students who visit the 420-acre campus apply for admission, impressed by both its "friendly" atmosphere and its very contemporary look. Although the college was founded in 1863, it moved to its present site just 30 years ago and features an impressive array of modern architecture. Foremost and newest is the 72,000-square-foot George E. Bello Center for Information and Technology that contains a mock trading room, electronic classrooms, and a 446-seat library with a data port for a laptop at every seat. Next is the ultramodern, all-glass Unistructure that houses all other classrooms. The Bryant Center, designed like a mall, contains student lounges and study corners, as well as restaurants and shops. But it's not just the buildings that are up with the times; the curriculum also reflects modern trends. All Bryant students must complete a liberal arts core as well as a general business core designed to ensure that they are ready to face a rapidly changing world. Business majors must post a liberal arts minor as well. Observes a management major: "There are so many resources here at Bryant, there is no reason why you cannot achieve your goals."

Student body: Eighty-five percent of Bryant's undergraduates are from the Northeast, including 16% from Rhode Island. Students come, however, from 31 states and 30 foreign countries. Seventeen percent in a recent year attended private or parochial schools. Minority enrollment has been rising; Hispanics comprise 4%; Asian Americans and African-Americans, 3% each; Native Americans, less than 1%. Foreign nationals make up 2%. Undergraduates are relatively conservative and conformist, "with a few free spirits roaming around," says a junior. Notes a New Englander: "We're a clean-cut, well-disciplined, friendly bunch of people. We're probably mostly liberal Republicans who all expect good things out of life." Few are politically aware, and only within the last few years have groups such as the Bryant Hunger Coalition or Amnesty International been active (though still small) on campus. Are undergraduates competitive? "We're nearly all business students, and the nature of business is competition," remarks an accounting major. However, the range extends from students who are always trying to "gain the upper hand," to those who are more concerned about impressing the latest employer interviewing on campus. "There also is a lot of collaborative learning and peer tutoring, so people are concerned with their peer's success," adds a junior.

Academics: Bryant University's College of Business awards the Bachelor of Science in Business Administration in 8 concentrations in Information Technology and in International Business. The university's College of Arts and Sciences awards a Bachelor of Arts in Applied Psychology, in Communication, and in Liberal Studies with concentrations in English and Cultural Studies, history, global studies, and economics. A master of business administration also is offered in 8 fields. Some students may accelerate their studies and earn both the bachelor's and master's degrees in business in 5 years. Bryant operates on the semester system. Classes average 27 students, though a course in History of American Technology may enroll 50. Enrollment also usually doesn't fall much below 20 in popular classes, with Mathematics of Finance, Insurance, and Pensions having just 4.

All students must complete a liberal arts core that fulfills 61 of the 123 credits needed for graduation and draws courses from 5 modes of thought: scientific, historical, cultural, literary, and social science. In addition, undergraduates must complete 31 credits of a general business core, as well as requirements for their particular concentrations. A required interdisciplinary seminar joins the perspectives of the 2 cores in various topics. For example, a seminar in Capitalism: Its Apologists and Its Critics examines the relationship between capitalism and other ideologies such as world religions and forms of Marxism.

Just over half, 133 of the 262 faculty members are full-time. All but 11 of the full-time members and all but 5 of the 129 part-time teach undergraduates. Thirty-two percent are women. A significant adjunct faculty from the working world lends real-life perspective to the subjects being studied. But full-time faculty, many of whom either owned their own companies or held high positions in major corporations, stay timely as well; those who do not keep writing or doing research or otherwise stay active in the field sometimes are asked to do so or leave. Notes a marketing major: "Most faculty are approachable, interesting, and enthusiastic and bring many examples from their outside work into the classroom." Bryant also has its share of professors who keep too busy with research or personal projects, and foreign instructors with limited English who can be difficult to understand. Still, concludes a marketing major, "I personally feel that I could rely on and confide in about 95% of the faculty that I have had."

Management, marketing, and finance all earn A's from Bryant students, thanks largely to excellent equipment, well-versed faculty, and challenging curricula. The mock trading room in the Bello Center enables students to apply financial theory and principles of risk management in a simulated trading environment. Marketing faculty make special room for undergraduates in their research. The management program, says a major, "has group projects that make you actively involved in your learning. They are based on real-life experiences from the professors and a burning desire to research topics that are of your personal interest." Faculties in the rigorous programs in applied actuarial mathematics and computer information systems are among the most willing to provide extra help and attention to serious students. The communication department is marked by innovative courses "and an extremely dedicated faculty that makes learning fun," says a senior with a minor in the field.

The accounting program has many well-trained and intelligent professors who "are good accountants but don't know how to teach," complains a management major. Altogether, the liberal arts offerings draw mixed reviews; while some students praise the quality of the professors, especially those in English and Cultural Studies, and sociology, others think these programs were not sufficiently developed before being added as majors and minors. Some students wish languages other than just Spanish were offered. Says a marketing and management major: "Business is no longer national; it is global."

Facilities: The new Douglas and Judith Krupp Library provides 62,000 square feet of the latest in student-friendly research technology. Students who bring their laptops to the facility will find a data port at each of the 446 seats. (The library also has laptops to lend within the building.) From there, a user can access the holdings not only of Bryant College but also of several university libraries in Rhode Island, including the University of Rhode Island. Bryant's own collection numbers just over 154,000 volumes with access to more than 20,000 electronic journals, largely focused on business-related fields. "As far as electronic resources," says a senior, "we do have many to choose from and they are constantly getting updated and improved. I don't think many students would even know how to begin to take out a book. Many of the books we have are outdated and in dire need of replacement."

At Bryant, as one senior put it, "there are more computers than students." In addition to computers in the library and technology center, all incoming freshmen are provided with an IBM R25 laptop computer, included in the tuition rate they pay. Prior to the beginning of junior year, students exchange this laptop for a new model and are given the computer upon graduation. The entire campus is wireless so "the use of wireless anywhere is a plus," says a sophomore.

All students also are required to take a 15-week course in personal productivity software to familiarize themselves with the campus computer systems.

Special programs: A Learning for Leadership program involves each participating student in a multidisciplinary course on leadership theory and practice, as well as a mentor relationship with a leader in a public or private organization. Opportunities for foreign study offered at universities in at least 21 countries from France to Japan are increasing. Students interested in internships may choose from more than 300 companies ranging from Fidelity Investments to the New England Patriots. Bryant Serves, which was begun in 1998, requires that all freshmen participate in a community service project the week before the start of fall semester. The freshman class is divided into smaller groups of 25 to 30 students who are accompanied by a Bryant faculty member or administrator.

Campus life: Eighty-three percent of Bryant's full-time undergraduates live on the well-kept campus which was recently enhanced by the addition of Hassenfeld Common, a landscaped quadrangle that offers a classic New England "common green" between the academic and recreational facilities. Greek membership has dropped to less than 7% of both the men and the women claiming membership in 5 national fraternities and

3 national sororities. The Greeks, who can arrange to live together within a residence hall, sponsor a good share of the weekend social events, which are attended by independents as well as members. Many non-members, however, soon tire of the party scene and seek diversion in the Providence clubs or other on-campus entertainment, or simply use the weekend to catch up on sleep or work. Crime, for the most part, is kept outside the campus gatehouse, which is manned around the clock. The parking lots also are monitored by cameras 24 hours a day, and scan cards are required to enter all residence halls. "The most common crime probably is parking in the fire lanes," remarks a senior.

The men's basketball team, the Bryant Bulldogs, was the toast of the 2004-2005 school year, winning a record 25 games and becoming NCAA Division II Regional Champion for the first time in school history. The team was runner-up in the national championship game. In addition to the men's basketball program, Bryant supports 10 men's and 11 women's varsity teams in NCAA Division II. Along with basketball, Bulldogs football, which was added in 1998, and soccer, as well as the men's and women's rugby club, draw the most fans. Nineteen percent of the men and 14% of the women take part in sports at the intercollegiate level. The university also offers 8 intramural sports for men, 7 for women, and 9 club sports.

Lincoln Woods and Washington Grove parks offer sanctuary relatively near campus. The urban triumvirate of Boston, about 60 minutes away, Newport, 45 minutes, and Providence, 15 minutes, provides the most popular weekend escapes. The Rhode Island beaches are an especially attractive getaway in the spring.

Cost cutters: Eighty-five percent of the freshmen and 84% of continuing students received financial help in the 2005–2006 school year. Need-based assistance went to 63% of the freshmen and 59% of the returning students. An average freshman award for a first-year student with financial need included a need-based scholarship or grant averaging $9485 and need-based self-help aid such as loans and jobs averaging $5485. Non-need-based athletic scholarships for first-year students averaged $16,355; other non-need-based awards and scholarships averaged $8303. Average debt for a 2005 alumnus equaled $22,340. In a recent year, the university offered merit scholarships to high-ranking students that ranged in value from $3000 to full tuition.

Rate of return: Eighty-eight percent of entering freshmen return for the sophomore year. Sixty-three percent graduate in 4 years; 68%, in 5 years.

Payoff: Majors in marketing at 26%, management at 23%, and accounting at 17% together claimed two-thirds of the 2005 graduates. Nearly 200 companies and organizations, ranging from the major accounting firms to Houghton Mifflin and Texas Instruments, actively recruit on campus each fall. The vast majority of new alumni put their diplomas to work in the job market within months of commencement. "The career services department is incredible," raves a junior. "I have been very excited to find the various career opportunities that lie ahead for me next year." Only 4% of recent graduates pursued advanced degrees in business or law.

Bottom line: A student who is fairly certain he or she would like to pursue a career in business, who is not too radical for Bryant's traditional lifestyle, and who has a solid background and an aptitude in mathematics will benefit most from this college. Concludes a senior: "Bryant teaches you how to make a profit, and to do it professionally!"

Providence College

Providence, Rhode Island 02918

Setting: Suburban
Control: Private (Roman Catholic)
Undergraduate enrollment: 1733 men, 2233 women
Graduate enrollment: 60 men, 72 women (788 part-time)
Student/faculty ratio: 12:1
Freshman profile: 8% scored over 700 on SAT I verbal; 43% scored 600–700; 42% 500–599; 7% below 500. 10% scored over 700 on SAT I math; 48% scored 600–700; 35% 500–599; 7% below 500. 14% scored above 28 on the ACT; 23% scored 27–28; 32% 24–26; 22% 21–23; 9% below 21. 38% graduated in top tenth of high school class; 71% in upper fifth.

Faculty profile: 92% Ph.D.'s
Tuition and fees: $25,310
Room and board: $9270
Freshman financial aid: 81%; average scholarship or grant: $8060 need-based; $12,965 non-need-based
Campus jobs: 20%; average earnings: $1200/year
Application deadline: Early action: Nov. 1; regular: Jan. 15
Financial aid deadline: Feb. 1
Admissions information: (401) 865-2535; (800) 721-6444
e-mail: pcadmiss@providence.edu
web site: www.providence.edu

About a fifth of the recent graduates of Providence College, the nation's only postsecondary school run by the Dominican friars, have majored in 2 practical career-oriented programs: marketing, business administration, and management. But when asked to name 1 of the college's most challenging and stimulating courses of study, the vast majority of these alumni, as well as others, set their sights back hundreds of years and selected a course that meets 5 days a week for 2 full years and has nothing to do with their majors: Development of Western Civilization. The 4-semester Western civilization course takes students on an interdisciplinary tour of Western heritage from its beginnings in Mesopotamia through the fall of communism. The 4 professors from the fields of history, literature, philosophy, and theology who team-teach the course are committed to the program and attend each other's classes in order to better craft and coordinate their own lectures. Undergraduates are committed as well and pull for one another to succeed. It's a challenging course of study in which students, together with faculty, act as if "we're all in this together," says a class member. That sentiment, enforced in the first 2 years, sets the stage for a strong sense of community that lasts throughout an undergraduate's 4 or 5 years on campus and leads to 82% earning degrees in 4 years.

Student body: Two-thirds of the Providence students are Catholic. A fifth claim no religious affiliation. Though only 12.5% reside in the tiny state of Rhode Island, 91% of the nonresidents come also from the Northeast; all but 9 states, plus 17 foreign countries, have representatives on campus. Thirty-seven percent of the undergraduates attended private or parochial schools. Hispanic students make up the largest minority group at just over 2% of enrollment, followed by Asian-Americans at almost 2% and African-Americans at 1.5%. Foreign nationals represent 1%. The student body is described as politically conservative, though largely apathetic when it comes to causes, socially enthusiastic, and usually filled with school spirit, as is evident from the large amount of Providence College clothing the undergraduates wear, along with their Abercrombie & Fitch and J. Crew attire. And though students are highly social and very involved in extracurricular activities, few find they can ignore the books. "Academics come first, are demanding, and aren't watered down with beer," observes a recent graduate. "But there is a balance here not found at a think tank like the University of Chicago. We play hard, we party hard, and we study hard."

Academics: Providence, founded in 1917, confers bachelor's and master's degrees. Undergraduate majors are available in 50 disciplines, including several interdisciplinary programs. The school year is divided into semesters. The average class enrolls fewer than 20 students. Other than the Western civilization courses, which can have as many as 100 participants, lower-division classes rarely top 40, and enrollment may drop below 10 in the upper years.

In addition to the Western civilization program, students must fulfill distributional requirements in social science, natural science, philosophy, theology, fine arts, and math. Altogether, the mandated courses fulfill 50 of the 116 credits needed to graduate.

The 369-member faculty is predominantly full-time, with only 82 part-timers. Thirty-seven percent are women. The faculty and administration include 51 Dominican friars and sisters. Professors are both knowledgeable and accessible, and students value the rapport they have with many, particularly the Dominican friars, most of whom are devoted teachers. Notes an admirer: "Many even get buried here on the campus when they die—that's how dedicated they are to this institution!" Freshmen, in particular, appreciate the fact that many professors, both lay and religious, are concerned whether class members have understood the subject matter, and insist that those who haven't come in after hours for help. Students note, however, that some of the older tenured professors and Dominican friars need to learn from the enthusiastic teaching styles of other faculty members.

While Western civilization rates highest on students' lists of best academic programs, their other choices are more professionally oriented. The various business programs are very well respected for their excellent teachers and well-designed curricula, as well as for a number of extracurricular organizations that support the field. Among liberal arts disciplines, philosophy, political science, English, and history earn high marks, largely because of wonderful teaching. A new major in Global Studies, that draws on faculty and concepts from the humanities, political science, and economics, shows early signs of being a much admired and popular program. The biology and chemistry programs are demanding and send large numbers of their graduates on to medical school. "Most professors do research," says a biology major, "and actively recruit undergraduates to participate." Professors of math and computer science are known for being accessible and helpful. Students also are proud of the major in public and community service studies through the Feinstein Institute for Public Service at the college.

The modern languages department offers majors only in French, Italian, and Spanish. German is offered as a minor only. The anthropology program has a single professor and no major or minor. The major in studio art, offering concentrations in ceramics, digital imaging, drawing, painting, photography, printmaking, and sculpture, could use a larger budget as well as more professors. There is no major in traditional physics, rather a cross-disciplinary program in applied physics.

Facilities: The 2-time architectural award-winning Phillips Memorial Library, which already offered an atmosphere that students found calm and comfortable, became even more inviting following renovation in the 2003–2004 school year. The renovation increased student seating and provided more attractive and functional group study spaces. Its collection of 331,000 volumes and 1600 periodicals with an additional 9000 in electronic format, generally satisfies most students' research needs, and undergraduates say that the professors keep the librarians "on their toes" regarding additional materials that are needed. The library is a member of the HELIN consortium that includes 8 other colleges (including Brown University) making available more than 8 million extra volumes for Providence scholars. Students' chief complaint: a computer shortage. The library, notes a junior, "is a place I find myself studying more and more, (but) there are not enough computers to support the large amount of people who flock to the library at night to write papers and do research." The library currently has 30 wireless workstations, 15 laptops available for checkout, and an 18-unit electronic classroom. Plans are underway to add a second electronic classroom.

Seven labs outside the library equipped with 150 Pentium computers are located throughout campus. Most labs are open until midnight weeknights, although students already in the labs can stay locked in to finish their projects. Access to the Internet is provided in all residential areas. Wireless access for those students with laptops is available in the library, at McPhail's, a coffeehouse and snack bar in the student union, and in the dining room.

Special programs: Students can cross-register for courses with the Rhode Island School of Design or participate in exchanges with Kansai-Gaidai University in Osaka, Japan. Other study-abroad programs enable students to spend a semester or year in Switzerland, Spain, Ireland, Scotland, England, or any other country, based upon a student's academic needs or interests. A 3-2 bachelor's degree program in engineering is offered with Washington or Columbia university.

Campus life: Eighty-three percent of Providence students live on the 105-acre campus in Rhode Island's capital city. Although there is no Greek system, students do not lack for off-campus parties, dances, and other social events and campus traditions. One of the most prestigious organizations on campus is the Friars Club, which gives tours of the campus and represents the school at various functions. Undergraduates must be chosen for the honor; given the number who are interested and the limited membership, the selection process is quite competitive. The 800-member Pastoral Service Organization attracts students committed to performing community service and social outreach. The influence of the much-beloved Dominican Order of Preachers remains very strong on campus. Many of the friars reside in the residence halls, serving not as monitors but as friends and counselors to students. Weekends generally end with Sunday's 10:30 p.m. "Last Chance Mass," complete with acoustic band, which usually is packed. Though crime is not regarded as a problem on campus, where the residence halls are locked and security is tight, students who live off-campus encounter a different situation in which break-ins and personal attacks occur. Undergraduates are cautioned not to walk alone in the surrounding neighborhood and to keep doors and windows locked. A security shuttle assists by transporting students to places off campus, and any incidents, off campus as well as on, are publicized so students can respond accordingly.

Forty-five percent of the men and 25% of the women participate in a very competitive intramural program, consisting of 12 sports for men and 13 for women. The intercollegiate program offers 7 men's and 10 women's sports that compete in NCAA Division I. When it comes to Big East basketball, nearly 100% turn out for the excitement of games played at the city civic center. Ice hockey, soccer, and lacrosse games also are occasions for big social gatherings.

Boston and Cape Cod, each an hour away, are the most popular out-of-town travel destinations, although some undergraduates make the 3-hour trip to New York City. Others simply head to Federal Hill, the Italian section of Providence, or hang out with students at Brown University or the Rhode Island School of Design.

Cost cutters: The contributed services of the Dominican community help hold down tuition costs. In the 2005–2006 school year, 81% of freshmen and 78% of continuing students received financial aid. Need-based help went to 65% of the freshmen and 63% of the rest. The average freshman aid package for a student with need included a need-based scholarship or grant averaging $8060 and need-based self-help aid such as loans and jobs averaging $3625. Non-need-based athletic scholarships for first-year students averaged $13,766. Other non-need-based awards and scholarships averaged $12,965. Average debts for a 2005 grad totaled $23,125. The top merit award is the Roddy Foundation Scholarship that pays full tuition, room, and board for 4 years to students planning to attend medical school and having SAT math and critical reading scores of at least 1350 and high school class rank within the top 10%. Students invited to enter the Liberal Arts Honors Program are eligible to receive one of 3 levels of merit scholarships, the St. Dominic Scholarship that pays full tuition annually, the St. Thomas Aquinas Scholarship, paying $21,000 a year, and the St. Catherine of Siena Scholarship, paying $15,000 yearly. All minority students who have demonstrated academic potential, leadership, community service, and financial need are eligible to receive the Martin Luther King, Jr. Scholarship, which pays up to full tuition. Students who plan to major in public and community service studies may receive a $2000 Feinstein Scholarship. A monthly tuition payment plan is available.

Rate of return: Ninety-three percent of entering freshmen come back for a second year. Eighty-two percent go on to graduate in 4 years, 83% in 5 years.

Payoff: Ten percent of the 2005 graduates earned degrees in marketing, 9% specialized in business administration and management and 7% in English. A fifth of a recent graduating class pursued advanced study. The majority of new alumni, however, take jobs, in accounting with the major firms and in sales management with companies such as Pepsi, Carnation, and General Mills. One hundred firms recruited on campus in a recent school year.

Bottom line: Providence College is a small, Catholic, rather homogeneous New England school that its undergraduates find academically challenging, but not overwhelming. Notes a junior: "At Providence, a student is never thrown into something without sufficient help. The college cares about *all* its students, though those who are free spirits or very liberal in their thinking probably will not fit in as easily."

The University of Rhode Island

Kingston, Rhode Island 02881

Setting: Small town
Control: Public
Undergraduate enrollment: 4293 men, 5473 women
Graduate enrollment: 589 men, 982 women
Student/faculty ratio: 19:1
Freshman profile: 3% scored over 699 on SAT I verbal; 23% scored 600–699; 50% 500–599; 24% below 500. 5% scored over 699 on SAT I math; 29% scored 600–699; 51% 500–599; 15% below 500. 21% graduated in top tenth of high school class.
Faculty profile: 90% Ph.D.'s

Tuition and fees: $7284 in-state; $19,926 out-of-state
Room and board: $8114
Freshman financial aid: 65%; average scholarship or grant: $6353 need-based; $4711 non-need-based
Campus jobs: NA; average earnings: NA
Application deadline: Early action: Dec. 15; regular: Feb. 1
Financial aid deadline: Mar. 1
Admissions information: (401) 874-7100
  e-mail: uriadmit@etal.uri.edu
  web site: www.uri.edu

If Paul Revere were a student at the University of Rhode Island, confronted with the choice of hanging "one [lantern] if by land, and two if by sea," he'd just have to get himself a third lantern. For in the academic world of land-grant and sea-grant colleges, URI is both a 1- and 2-lantern university. Established with 1 lantern in 1892 as a land-grant college set up to train citizens for useful employment, URI is now hanging out 2 more lanterns to mark its additional designation as a national sea-grant college recognized for its extensive marine research. (It also was designated an urban grant institution in 1995.) The prime location of the main Kingston campus near the Atlantic Ocean, 6 miles from Narragansett Bay, has produced distinctive undergraduate programs in chemical and physical oceanography and in ocean engineering. More than 20 majors with a marine or environmental focus are offered by departments in 3 of the colleges. Juniors and seniors can also spend a semester at URI's separate Narragansett Bay campus, home of its much respected Graduate School of Oceanography, working as part of marine research teams in both the laboratory and the "field," or the ocean, as the case may be.

Student body: Sixty-one percent of URI's undergraduates are residents of the Ocean State, with a majority of the out-of-staters also from the Northeast. However, students in a recent year attended from all 50 states and 53 foreign countries; international students account for less than 1% of the undergraduate enrollment. African-Americans and Hispanics each comprise about 4.5%, Asian-Americans account for 2.5%, and Native Americans stand at less than 0.5%. Though in sheer numbers and percentages minority representation is low, in terms of enthusiastic groups on campus their impact is far stronger. More than 14 active multicultural organizations from the Cape Verdean Students Association to groups for Asian, Latin, and African-American students speak up loudly and often to ensure that the interests of their members are being heard and observed. Just over 12% of URI's undergraduate enrollment is 25 or older. Eighty-five percent graduated from public high schools. Rhode Island students are the first to admit that their campus carries a reputation as a "party school" though most insist that that tag was truer a decade or so ago than it is now. Says a junior, reflecting the views of many: "The most visible image of students outside of URI is that of the party animals who compose only 10% of the campus. The rest of the campus is reasonably dedicated to their studies and only party on the weekend. I would guess that 15–20% of the population make a total commitment to education and show outstanding motivation and determination." Socially, the campus has its share of athletes and Greeks, as well as a solid contingent of "earthy hippies." Each type eventually finds his or her own peer group and settles into an environment described as "comfortable" and generally "laid back" in all but a few majors.

Academics: The University of Rhode Island confers the bachelor's degree in over 80 majors, master's degrees in 54 areas, and a doctorate in 38. Undergraduate programs are located in 8 colleges. Classes, which follow the semester system, run the gamut in the first 2 years from as few as 20 or 30 in a math or English class to 471 in Introductory Sociology. Juniors and seniors still can expect some classes with 50, though most usually have between 5 and 30. Just 52 of the 1764 undergraduate class sections offered have more than 100 students enrolled. Eighty-two sections have between 50 and 99 undergraduates; almost 600, between 20 and 29 participants.

General-education requirements comprise 39 credits involving courses from 7 areas: natural sciences, social sciences, foreign language or culture, English communication, mathematics, fine arts and literature, and letters, which includes classes from various fields that examine aspects of human values. Students also must take a freshman seminar, entitled Traditions and Transformations, which introduces first-year students to the traditions of higher education and to societal and personal issues affecting the undergraduate years.

All but 23 of the 691-member faculty are full-time. There is no data to show the portion that teach at the graduate level only. Thirty-eight percent are women. Seven percent of the introductory classes in a recent year were taught by graduate students. Some of URI's professors are faulted for being as disinterested as some students in the classroom. Notes a major in marine affairs: "Many come, lecture, and leave." However, there also are a number who, despite the larger class sizes, relish interaction with students and gladly meet with them after class to provide extra help as needed. Says a junior: "If students show an interest, they are more than willing to help."

In addition to URI's excellent programs in oceanography and marine affairs, courses of study for landlubbers also make the grade. The colleges of Pharmacy and of Engineering are known for their rigor and cutting-edge curricula. Pharmacy's breadth includes courses dealing with the science of the field, as well as programs in such social issues as neighborhood outreach and counseling for the elderly. Pharmacy students, however, must commit to a 6-year entry-level program of study that leads to a doctor of pharmacy degree; a total of 188 credits are required for graduation. A 5-year international engineering program allows students to earn both a B.A. degree in a foreign language and a B.S. in engineering and to participate in international internships. For eight years in a row, until 2004, a team of civil engineering students from URI won the New England regional concrete canoe championship. The program in communicative disorders in the College of Human Science and Services "has a dedicated staff that gives great support to outstanding students," says an admiring engineering major. The environmental economics and management major is a bright spot in the College of the Environment and Life Sciences; within the College of Arts and Sciences, history and psychology, which offers lots of opportunities for undergraduate research and internships, also win student respect.

Other disciplines in the broad liberal arts college are overcrowded and less attentive to individual needs. In political science, for example, students consider the faculty first-rate but say the department needs to provide more classes, as well as additional space in those classes already offered. The mathematics department needs to bring in some higher quality faculty members to replace those who rely too heavily on multiple choice tests. Chemistry needs fewer teaching assistants who speak limited English. Biology, says a biological sciences major, "needs to be improved. We have great researchers but some professors do not know how to teach well, even though they know the material inside and out." The science building and equipment also could be updated. Communication studies is understaffed and would benefit from better-quality equipment and facilities as well. Many classes in the College of Business Administration need more rigor.

Facilities: The university's main library has long had a double identity, being, as a recent graduate recalled, "better than a night club for meeting people, and also providing a quiet place where a lot can get done." Recent remodeling increased the space by 60% to 237,000 square feet and added 465 new study spaces, 10 enclosed group study areas, and 26 individual research carrels. Current holdings stand at 1.2 million volumes, though the goal is to increase holdings to 1.5 million as funding allows. There are 7926 current periodicals. The catalog is fully computerized and lists the holdings of 1 other university (not Brown) and 3 colleges in-state. A number of alternative research aids, such as CD-ROM technology also are available and much used. While students generally applaud the improvements, some wish the main facility were open later on Friday and Saturday nights.

Undergraduates have access to several hundred PCs and Macs located in about 10 labs across campus. The 2 biggest labs that house 175 PCs and Macs between them are located in the main library and student union. Most of the time, finding a free computer is easy though most of the smaller labs are only open until 10 p.m. Plus, adds a senior, "the dorms are computer-ready if students bring their own."

Special programs: Foreign exchange programs are available with universities in 6 countries as well as at 21 English- or French-speaking universities in Quebec and Nova Scotia, Canada. Students may also study at any of more than 150 public colleges and universities in 50 states and U.S. territories, paying either the in-state tuition or URI rates. A University Year for Action internship program lets undergraduates earn up to 15 credits while working during the academic year as well as the summer; they serve under the supervision of qualified professionals in more than 600 placements in such fields as medical research, communications, nutrition, marketing, and administration.

Campus life: Thirty-seven percent of the URI undergraduates live on the 1248-acre campus, located in "its own little world," about 30 miles south of Providence. While the university housing is fairly traditional, one of the most unusual and most popular off-campus alternatives is living "down the line," that is, commuting from any of numerous summer houses, most of them located near the water within a 10-mile radius of the campus, that students rent for the academic year. The houses also are the site of much weekend revelry, for those who have transportation. The Greeks, too, are very big on the party circuit, though most of their social activities are open by invitation only. Ten percent of the men and women belong to the 11 national fraternities and 9 national sororities. About 90 clubs are available to students of differing interests; the multicultural organizations and groups related to academic majors have the largest followings. Those with a love of music, theater, poetry, and the visual arts are delighted by rich offerings from a network of artists in the surrounding community, as well as on campus. *The Good 5-Cent Cigar*, the 4-day-a-week student newspaper, also attracts much undergraduate interest and discussion. As a whole, though, some students wish there were more alternatives to partying on the weekends. "There is *absolutely nothing* to do," grumbles a sophomore. "No fun activities for students to get into." Vandalism, some car break-ins, and petty theft are the most prevalent forms of campus crime. Dorm monitors check in guests who enter at night as a way to gain more control over who is around; campus security also maintains bike and foot patrols and helped to establish a Crime Watch for campus neighborhoods. Safe Ride and Safe Walk escort programs are available as well.

NCAA Division I basketball and Division I-AA football draw the most enthusiastic Ram fans of the 10 men's and 12 women's intercollegiate sports provided. Soccer, field hockey, lacrosse, baseball, and rugby, 1 of 17 club sports, also can stir up the crowds. Both the sailing and equestrian teams, also club sports, are nationally ranked and compete internationally. Forty-five percent of the men but only 10% of the women turn out for the 18 intramural sports for each sex.

Without cars, many students confess to feeling "trapped" on the small-town campus, with Kingston (pop. 5500) 30 miles from Providence, the nearest major city. Newport is only 20 minutes away. Those with wheels sometimes keep going to Boston, 90 minutes away, or to Mystic, Connecticut, 45 minutes.

Cost cutters: For about $10,000 less than the out-of-state rate, students from other New England states can enroll in URI programs that are not offered at their own state universities; tuition was just $2630 more than the in-state rate during the 2005–2006 school year. In the 2005–2006 school year, 65% of the freshmen and 53% of the continuing students received financial help. For 57% of the freshmen and 49% of the rest, the aid was need-based. The average freshman award for a student with need included a need-based scholarship or grant averaging $6353 and need-based self-help aid such as loans and jobs averaging $5966. Non-need-based athletic scholarships for first-year students averaged $1179; other non-need-based awards and scholarships averaged $4711. Average debt of a 2005 graduate was $16,200. Outstanding freshman candidates with minimum math and critical reading SAT scores of 1150 who rank in the top third of their high school graduating class are eligible to be considered for Centennial Scholarships that pay up to full tuition. There were 490 Centennial scholars in a recent freshman class. To be considered, students must have submitted their completed application with all supporting information and application fee no later than December 15.

Rate of return: Eighty percent of the freshmen come back for the sophomore year. Thirty-six percent graduate in 4 years, 53% within 5 years, 56% within 6.

Payoff: Sixteen percent of the 2005 graduates earned bachelor's degrees in business/marketing; 12% specialized in communications/journalism; almost 10% received degrees in engineering. The vast majority of new alumni took jobs soon after commencement in the financial, manufacturing, health, and education sectors. More than 150 companies recruited on campus in a recent school year. Less than a fifth of the new alumni generally enter graduate school.

Bottom line: A disciplined student with an interest in oceanography, marine affairs, engineering, or pharmacy will find some educational pearls to be plucked amid the parties at the University of Rhode Island. Undergraduates with less specific interests can emerge with diplomas and some change from their tuition dollars, but how much else depends totally on their own URI—Undistractible Response to Independence.

South Carolina

Clemson University
Clemson, South Carolina 29634

Setting: Small town
Control: Public
Undergraduate enrollment: 7133 men, 5933 women
Graduate enrollment: 1313 men, 815 women
Student/faculty ratio: 15:1
Freshman profile: 7% scored over 700 on SAT I verbal; 40% scored 600–700; 45% 500–599; 8% below 500. 13% scored over 700 on SAT I math; 50% scored 600–700; 32% 500–599; 5% below 500. 31% scored above 28 on the ACT; 15% scored 27–28; 32% 24–26; 15% 21–23; 8% below 21. 42% graduated in top tenth of high school class; 61% in upper fifth.

Faculty profile: 83% Ph.D.'s
Tuition and fees: $8074 in-state; $16,638 out-of-state
Room and board: $5292
Freshman financial aid: 87%; average scholarship or grant: $3264 need-based; $7075 non-need-based
Campus jobs: 27%; average earnings: $2302/year
Application deadline: May 1
Financial aid deadline: April 1
Admissions information: (864) 656-2287; e-mail: cuadmissions@clemson.edu web site: www.clemson.edu

When you ask undergraduates from 50 states and 84 foreign countries why they chose to attend Clemson University in a small (some say isolated) town of 11,000 residents tucked into the northeastern tip of South Carolina (known also as "the middle of nowhere,") their answers form the stuff from which legends are made. For many, the reasons begin and end with mighty Clemson Tigers football, which draws more than 85,000 spirited fans to home games. For some, such as a freshman from California, it was the allure of friendly people with "southern hospitality." For others, the reason was simply not quantifiable, as a business major observed: "I live in New Jersey and have always wanted to go to school in South Carolina." There also, however, are academic reasons for choosing Clemson, among them 5-star programs in architecture, engineering, and agriculture, though their attraction pales beside the university's better-known athletic and social appeal. Whatever it is, though, that brings undergraduates to Clemson, it doesn't take much longer than the first touchdown of the season to discover that a lot more than southern charm is needed to emerge with a bachelor's degree. Forty percent of the freshmen that enter leave with a diploma in 4 years. Sixty-eight percent graduate in 5 years; another 4% stick around for an extra football season and finish in 6. The legend of the Clemson Tiger may bring many to the classroom door, but when, and if, they get out depends on how badly each wants to score.

Student body: Though Clemson's appeal covers every state in the nation and 84 countries around the globe, 68% of the Tigers fans are homegrown in South Carolina. Eighty-one percent attended public schools. African-Americans constitute the largest minority group at 7% of enrollment; Asian-Americans follow at 2%, Hispanics at 1%. Foreign nationals account for 5%. Newcomers seeking "southern hospitality," are rarely disappointed. Clemson undergraduates are, for the most part, friendly, upbeat, polite, and full of school spirit. "Socially," says a senior, "we have hermits as well as butterflies." Many students describe their peers as conservative, and though there are groups for both young Republicans and young Democrats, neither captures the appeal of the Tigers party. Academics generally are as tough or as easy as the major each student chooses. During the weeks before final exams, a person can find as many all-nighters here as at more competitive schools, but the level of studying throughout the term is considerably more uneven.

Academics: Clemson, which turned 115 in 2004, awards degrees through the doctorate and follows a semester calendar. Undergraduate programs in more than 70 majors are spread among 5 colleges and feature classes ranging in size in the first year alone from 25 in English 101 to about 230 in an introductory biology course. Most classes in the first two years, however, are likely to have between 100 and 150; upper-level classes, usually less than 50.

Clemson's general-education requirements are fairly standard and allow students to choose the courses they want from lists of suggested classes that fulfill requirements in a broad range of fields. The coursework covers 38 of the 132 credits required for graduation.

The university faculty consists of 1018 full-time members and 125 part-time. No breakdown is available showing the number of faculty members who teach at the graduate level only. A third are women. Graduate students teach 18% of the introductory courses, usually the labs related to the science courses. A teacher-training program instituted a few years ago to raise the quality of teaching assistants has helped to reduce the number of complaints from undergraduates. Clemson has its share of professors who are set in their ways and others who couldn't care less whether their students attend class. However, many undergraduates are delighted to find many faculty members who clearly enjoy classroom teaching more than research, who are eager to help students outside the classroom, and who take pride in their charges' accomplishments.

Some of the most satisfying academic experiences emerge in Clemson's highly respected programs in agriculture, architecture, and engineering. For each of these 3, a winning combination of the most focused students, rigorous standards, good funding, excellent equipment, and frequent opportunities for hands-on research keeps its programs at the top of the pack. Students of agriculture generally like the fruits of their labors: employment opportunities that usually exceed the crop of qualified graduates by a third. Accounting, economics, and graphic communications in the College of Business and Behavioral Science also have strong academic programs and faculty "willing to go the extra mile for students," says an accounting major. The program in construction science and management joins the School of Architecture as a standout in the College of Architecture, Arts, and Humanities.

Other programs, especially those with less direct career focus such as the fine arts and foreign languages, lack fiscal and administrative attention. The program in parks, recreation, and tourism management in the College of Health, Education, and Human Development carries a reputation for being easy. And, says a civil engineering major, "if advising can be considered a department, it is by far the weakest on campus." Already overburdened professors, says the junior, often have little time or energy to work closely enough with students and many lack sufficient knowledge of opportunities outside their immediate disciplines.

Facilities: Clemson's system of libraries includes the main Cooper Library, an architectural library, special collections located in the Strom Thurmond Institute building, and a departmental branch in chemistry. Cooper Library alone holds the bulk of the 1.2 million volumes, 1.2 million microforms, and 11,374 periodicals, and generally satisfies the needs of both solitary and social studiers somewhere across its 6 floors. (Generally, talkers head to the top 2 floors, researchers to the fourth, and serious studies remain on the first 3 levels.) Undergraduates also find little to complain about in its research offerings; indeed, students from other colleges in the area come to Clemson to find what their facilities don't have. Users lavish their highest praise on the various computerized research aids and the wonderful staff of professional librarians. The library also is completely wireless; says an agricultural education major: "I can find a corner and connect to the library database and find what I need."

All freshmen are required to own a laptop, specifically an IBM ThinkPad T43 in the 2005–2006 school year. Wireless access has spread with the use of the laptops and is now available at several outdoor locations as well as in almost every building. In addition, about 600 PCs are located in most academic buildings throughout campus. Many are open for 24 hours.

Special programs: Opportunities for study abroad are available in 38 countries. The Clemson Honors Program, for example, has sent students to Genoa, Italy.

Campus life: Not quite half, 46%, of Clemson undergraduates reside on the 1400-acre spread that originally served as the homestead of the southern statesman John C. Calhoun, whose daughter married Thomas Green Clemson. But whether anyone stays there over the weekend depends very much on the season. During winter and spring, students within driving distance are likely to travel home. Seventeen percent of the men and 31% of the women belong to the 19 national fraternities and 17 national sororities, whose year-round parties generally are confined to members only. About 300 clubs appeal to a wide range of student interests. For the past decade, Clemson students have celebrated Homecoming Week by building at least one home for Habitat for Humanity. The Fellowship of Christian Athletes is the largest student organization with its meetings held every Thursday at 7:17 and 9:19 p.m.; the National Society for Black Engineers is among the most influential groups with its professional speakers and voter registration drives. Few students consider crime to be a serious problem although various preventative measures are in force. The university provides students with Rape Aggression Defense training and offers free transportation for students on campus and in the neighboring towns. The student police run an escort service to supplement late-night activities. All buildings on campus also have 24-hour card access. Still, students loosely describe the few crimes that do occur as "auto related." Relates a state resident: "The only crime at Clemson takes place when you have nowhere to park, you ruin your car trying to squeeze into a tight little space, half on the pavement, half on the grass, and a ticket witch still gives you a parking ticket!"

Though the best word to describe Clemson's campus during winter and spring is "quiet," the campus is anything but during fall weekends, when more than 85,000 students, alumni, and other fans from throughout South Carolina and from over the state line in North Carolina arrive for home football games.

"It's outrageous," exclaims a Californian, and the revelry generally extends for several hours, even days, on either side of game time. When the Tigers play elsewhere, the team may be gone but the parties remain, and everyone gathers around the nearest big-screen TV. Though there are other NCAA Division I sports at Clemson, 9 additional ones for men and 9 for women, few undergraduates seem to notice. (More students have been playing golf on the university's 18-hole course after the team won the NCAA National Golf Championship in spring 2003.) Intramurals are offered in 45 sports apiece for men and for women; club sports also are immensely popular.

When it is time for traffic to flow out of town rather than in, students travel to Greenville (pop. 58,000) located about 30 miles east, or make longer trips to much bigger cities such as Atlanta, Georgia, which is 2 hours away, or to Charlotte, North Carolina. Escape to Lake Hartwell or the North Carolina mountains also is popular.

Cost cutters: Eighty-seven percent of the freshmen and 71% of the continuing students received financial aid in the 2005–2006 school year. Aid was need-based for 28% of the first-year students and 31% of the rest. The average aid package for a first-year student with need included a need-based scholarship or grant averaging $3264 and need-based self-help aid such as loans and jobs averaging $3394. Non-need-based athletic scholarships for first-year students averaged $11,925; other non-need-based awards and scholarships averaged $7075. Average debt for a 2005 graduate was $14,307. The National Scholars Program provides extraordinary students with a four-year scholarship covering tuition and fees, room, board, and books. The students also receive an all-expenses-paid summer study experience in Europe as well as a wide range of opportunities to interact with top professors. The Clemson Community Service Grant offers students up to $1200 a year in exchange for 20 hours of community service a semester. In a recent school year, 635 grant recipients provided service in the Clemson area or in their hometown. A cooperative education program is an option in every major except nursing.

Rate of return: Eighty-nine percent of first-year Tigers fans return for a second season. Less than half that number, 40%, go on to complete their degree requirements in 4 years; 68% do so within 5 years, 72% within a sixth year.

Payoff: Three career-oriented majors, management at 6.5%, marketing at 6%, and mechanical engineering at 4.5%, claimed the largest number of graduates in the Class of 2005. In a recent year, between a fifth and fourth of the degree recipients continued their education in graduate or professional schools, many in the fields of engineering and science. A majority enters the job market. About 340 companies and organizations typically recruit at Clemson.

Bottom line: To the average American, Clemson will probably always symbolize Tigers football; to employers in such fields as agriculture, architecture, and engineering, a Clemson degree means a well-prepared graduate ready to do battle on very different turf. Students whose academic interests lie in one of these three fields will gain the most yardage from Clemson but even they should have at least a minimal tolerance for football.

Coker College

Hartsville, South Carolina 29550

Setting: Small town
Control: Private
Undergraduate enrollment: 230 men, 330 women (528 evening)
Graduate enrollment: None
Student/faculty ratio: 8:1
Freshman profile: Average ACT composite score: 1011; class rank data: NA
Faculty profile: 85% Ph.D.'s
Tuition and fees: $17,448

Room and board: $5676
Freshman financial aid: 100%; average scholarship or grant: $4808 need-based; $8565 non-need-based
Campus jobs: 34%; average earnings: $1211/year
Application deadline: Rolling
Financial aid deadline: June 1 (Priority date: Apr. 1)
Admissions information: (843) 383-8050; (800) 950-1908
e-mail: admission@coker.edu
web site: www.coker.edu

As a student at Coker College, you can't hide behind rows of desks or in vast lecture halls. Faculty and students sit together at a round table and share in discussions, rather than lectures, about the topic at hand. The onus is on the students, not the professor, to keep classes moving. While undergraduates may differ in their views on such topics as the poetry of Dryden or modern marketing strategies, on one point there is little dissent: students seated around the tables at Coker are getting an educational banquet for the price of a blue-plate special.

Student body: About three-quarters of Coker's diners are from South Carolina. The remainder are drawn mainly from the South; 23 other states and 5 foreign countries are represented. Minority enrollment rests at 25%, with 20% African-American and Hispanics, Asian-Americans and Native Americans comprising the remaining 5%. Two percent in a recent year were foreign nationals. Boasts a southerner: "The student body is very ethnically and culturally diverse for such a small school." Coker undergraduates find mostly friendly, sincere and motivated learners of all interests and styles seated around their discussion tables, and quickly learn to be open to all types. Says an out-of-stater: "In general, students are not afraid to be different in their political and social beliefs. We don't worry about what others think; we are individuals who respect one another's opinions." The same attitude prevails in students' attitudes toward work: almost everyone tries his or her best but doesn't worry about how table-mates are doing. The vast majority of undergraduates are of traditional college age; the majority of older students attend the evening program, which offers majors in 4 fields only.

Academics: Coker College, founded in 1908 as a college for women, awards bachelor's degrees in 31 fields. The academic year is divided into 2 semesters; a 3-week interim term in May offers opportunities to study abroad as well as intensively at home. Class size at Coker depends basically on how many students the professor can fit around a table: the average seating is 12. Larger courses such as Western Civilization may enroll 20, while classes in Chaucer and modern drama may have just 8 students. It is not unusual, however, to have an intimate discussion with 1 or 2 students and the professor.

All students must complete general-education requirements that include 9 semester hours in the humanities, 7 hours in the natural and physical sciences and 3 in mathematics, and 6 each in creative and performing arts and behavioral sciences. Undergraduates also must take 9 hours of written and oral rhetoric, 3 hours in a nonnative language, and 3 hours of physical education plus attend at least 5 cultural events each semester.

The faculty number 56 full-time and more than 70 part-time; 44% of the full-time faculty are women. What the teachers lack in sheer numbers they score in attentiveness; some have even been known to bring bowls of hot soup to students who are sick. Observes a senior: "The vast majority of professors are very friendly, helpful, and available, respecting us as adults and eager to get to know us as people. They open their knowledge, hearts, and homes to us." They also demand a student's best effort in the classroom. Says a senior: "They make assignments clear and expect them to be finished. Late work means lower grades." It's also hard not to notice when someone doesn't show up for class so attendance is expected and considered in the final grade.

The career-related disciplines of business administration and education rate highly on students' list of Coker strong points. Business offers modern computers and an excellent faculty. However, the concentration in accounting was recently eliminated. Education faculty members who demand at least 200 hours of field work also earn an A+ from their teachers-to-be. The music and art departments win respect from even the most job-oriented students for their superb faculties and personal attention to undergraduates' interests. The art building, which is open around the clock, includes an art gallery, photo and graphics design labs, drawing studios (which face north to get the best light), a ceramics area, and classrooms. History, sociology, and psychology also win praise for demanding but open-minded faculties. Relates a sociology major: "For a final exam, my professor gave me the option of taking the test or spending the night in a homeless shelter and recording my findings. Needless to say, I learned more from my experience with the homeless than any textbook could have offered."

Recently renovated laboratories, classrooms, and equipment have given the sciences a well-deserved boost. "Biology is great," says a major. "The faculty cares about the students, the 1-on-1 attention is amazing, and the courses are challenging yet rewarding." While biology has had 4 full-time professors, chemistry and physics have recently shared 2 "superb" full-time members, limiting the range of courses that can be offered in these fields. Of the 2 disciplines, only chemistry is offered as a major. Dance, theatre, and communication also need more professors, though again students find the 1 or 2 in each discipline to be very good. The opening of the $6 million Elizabeth Boatwright Coker Performing Arts Center in fall 1997, with a 500-seat theater, video and audio editing suites, a black box theater, (usable as a television studio), and 2 dance studios, brought much-needed physical improvements to these departments. Nevertheless, some communication majors still wish there were more opportunities for hands-on experience. French and Spanish have been the only foreign language majors offered though introductory courses have been available in Italian, German, and Chinese.

Facilities: A new campus centerpiece, the Charles W. and Joan S. Coker Library–Information Technology Center, was scheduled to open in December 2006. Combining traditional library resources with the latest in wireless and wired technology, the new facility isn't forgetting the study breaks either, with panoramic windows for daydreaming, art collections for relaxing, and a café for rejuvenating. A million dollars on top of the $10 million construction costs has been set aside to increase the college's library holdings from about 68,000 volumes and 531 periodicals to 120,000 books, periodicals, and audiovisual materials. The former library is being renovated into a new student center.

The computer center, located in the recently renovated science building, plus smaller labs in the business, music, and art departments provide a network of 52 computers to students. Most labs are open until 11 p.m. during the week, with shortened hours on the weekends, which some hard-working students find too short. Coker students share these facilities with students at South Carolina's School for Science and Mathematics, which sometimes means computers are taken when Coker students want to use them. Students also wish the weekend hours were more accommodating to undergraduates' schedules. Many students hook up to the Internet from their dorm rooms; all rooms are wired for access.

Special programs: Students can study abroad through Coker's own exchange programs with universities in Japan and Spain or through programs offered by Central College in Iowa and others. The Esther Ferguson Cultural/Education Center of Coker College and the College of Charleston offer interim, summer, and semester programs in Trujillo, Spain, for those who want to study Spanish language and culture. A special scholarship allows up to 3 students to spend a summer abroad in academic studies. A 3-1 degree program in medical technology is obtainable with McLeod Regional Medical Center in nearby Florence.

Campus life: Seventy percent of the undergraduates live on the tree-lined 15-acre campus, creating a very close-knit community. While half the students may leave on any given weekend to go home, the college ensures that some kind of campus event is planned for every weekend to keep as many around as possible. Without any Greek organizations, Coker's Cobra Den is the focus of much weekend activity, with its nonalcoholic bar, big-screen TV, gameroom, DJ booth, and popular dance floor. Campus life itself, says a sophomore, "is like being part of one big sorority or fraternity." In the cultural sphere, musical, dance, and dramatic performances are well supported by the students, and many undergraduates who participated in few activities in high school find themselves not only members, but also leaders, of various groups at the college. The Coker Players, the popular dramatics club, includes many in its own productions, and sponsors trips to performances in New York City or Atlanta. An annual performing arts series, including a popular jazz festival, provides "big city" entertainment for students. The student group HOWL (Helping Our Way of Living) organizes volunteers for various projects, including an annual trip over spring break to build houses or to perform other services for those in need. Though big-city crime is not much of a problem at Coker or in the greater Hartsville area (pop. 28,000), security guards are stationed at night outside the residence halls. Door locks that can only be opened with swipe cards on student IDs have been installed on all residence halls. Guards patrol the campus around the clock. Brighter lighting also has been added.

Sory Boathouse, located on the banks of Prestwood Lake, just 2 blocks from campus, stores the college's canoes. One of the year's big events is the Coker crew race, pitting freshman and junior rowers against sophomores and seniors. The college fields 6 varsity teams for men and 6 for women in NCAA Division II. Cobra soccer and basketball draw the biggest crowds, though the baseball program brings out many fans in the spring. The Coker Olympics of Winter, known as COW Days, in which the 4 classes compete against each other in zany games, also is a big sporting event. Seventeen intramural sports for men and 18 for women also are available.

Because Hartsville itself (pop. 9000) is so small, many students head for the nearest "big" city still within South Carolina, which is Florence (pop. 30,000), about an hour away. Myrtle Beach, 70 miles away, is also a favorite getaway spot. Charlotte, North Carolina, is about equidistant. Those in need of a shorter break can opt for Kalmia Gardens, a college-owned 30-acre botanical garden 3 miles west of campus.

Cost cutters: One hundred percent of all freshmen and 98% of all remaining undergraduates received help to pay for college in a recent school year; for about 90% of all students, the aid was based on financial need. The average freshman award for a student with need included a need-based scholarship or grant averaging $4808 and need-based self-help aid such as loans and jobs averaging $3851. Non-need-based athletic scholarships for first-year students averaged $3685; other non-need-based awards and scholarships averaged $8565. The average indebtedness of a recent graduate totaled $17,323. President's and Dean's Scholarships, based on standardized test scores, class rank, and high school grade point averages, annually pay up to $8500 and $7000 respectively; departmental awards pay up to $2000 a year. High school valedictorians receive $500; other named scholarships pay from $500 to full tuition, room, and board.

Rate of return: Seventy-eight percent of the freshmen return for the sophomore year. Fifty percent finish in 4 years.

Payoff: Eleven percent of a recent graduating class earned bachelor's degrees in education; 11% also in business/marketing; and 8% in visual and performing arts. In a recent year, 36% went directly to graduate or professional schools, 24% in the arts and sciences and 8% in business. Of those entering the job market, about 70% are employed in fields related to their majors; another fourth have jobs in unrelated areas. Most Coker alumni settle in the East and South. Wherever they settle and whatever they end up doing, a majority of alumni are happy to give back to their alma mater: alumni giving recently reached 52%, highest among all South Carolina colleges and universities.

Bottom line: At Coker's educational table, there is reserved seating for every student, but everyone needs to come with an appetite for learning and a willingness to speak his or her mind. Advises a senior: "At Coker, you'll have help in coming out of your shell and opportunities to lead. It's a place where your ideas are important both in and out of class. But you have to be willing to participate in educating yourself. You can't just slip by at Coker."

College of Charleston
Charleston, South Carolina 29424

Setting: Urban
Control: Public
Undergraduate enrollment: 3230 men, 5825 women
Graduate enrollment: 90 men, 209 women
Student/faculty ratio: 14:1
Freshman profile: 8% scored over 700 on SAT I verbal; 50% scored 600–700; 41% 500–599; 1% below 500. 6% scored over 700 on SAT I math; 52% scored 600–700; 40% 500–599; 2% below 500. 2% scored above 28 on the ACT; 7% scored 27–28; 41% 24–26; 43% 21–23; 7% below 21. 55% graduated in top fifth of high school class; 86% in upper two-fifths.

Faculty profile: 85% Ph.D.'s
Tuition and fees: $6668 in-state; $15,342 out-of-state
Room and board: $6948
Freshman financial aid: NA; average scholarship or grant: NA
Campus jobs: 12%; average earnings: $876/year
Application deadline: Early decision: Nov. 1; regular: Apr. 1 (Nov. 15 for scholarships)
Financial aid deadline: Mar. 1
Admissions information: (843) 953-5670
e-mail: admissions@cofc.edu
web site: www.cofc.edu

When students receive their diplomas from the College of Charleston in South Carolina, they are dressed for the occasion, but not in somber-looking caps and gowns. Although faculty don their long academic robes, candidates wear white dinner jackets or long white gowns as they await the big moment, seated before the columns of a building that predates the Civil War. Tradition runs deep at this state-assisted college founded in 1770 by a group of citizens that included 3 signers of the Declaration of Independence. Having survived the Civil War, an earthquake, and Hurricane Hugo in September 1989, Charleston is well into its third century, looking better than ever at a combined cost of just over $22,000 for nonresidents that northerners and southerners alike can appreciate. Says a Georgian: "Don't let the price tag fool you. C of C offers an education that is just as good, if not better, than many schools that cost 3 or 4 times as much, without the added pretensions that often go along with such schools."

Student body: Undergraduates come from every state and 75 foreign countries to be part of C of C's traditions. Two-thirds are from South Carolina, as is evident, students say, in an overall courtesy and caring among classmates. Notes a recent graduate: "There are plenty of good people here, and you can always find someone to relate to." Seven percent are African-American and 2% each are Asian-American, Hispanics, and foreign nationals. Just under a fifth of all students, 18%, graduated from private or parochial high schools. "Students range from hippies in dreadlocks to business men and women in suits," observes a junior, though "lots of people wear popped collars and pastels," adds another. Their political beliefs cover the same wide span, more so, residents say, than at many other South Carolina schools. Observes a sophomore: "Individuality is highly encouraged everywhere!" Academic competition, in general, is less than intense, but, assures a junior, "one never has to feel as if he or she were a 'nerd' for getting good grades." Adds a senior: "Because of the close contact between faculty and students, most serious class members can find intellectual stimulation." Students note, however, that there is also a healthy portion of classmates who fail to take advantage of the school's academic intimacy and remain apathetic about much other than partying. Says a junior: "The College of Charleston has a reputation as a party school, which is not totally unfounded. That side of campus life is easily accessible if you want to take advantage of it, and many people do."

Academics: The College of Charleston awards the bachelor's degree in more than 40 majors and several master's degrees. Classes, which follow a semester calendar plus a 1-month "Maymester," average 21 students. Elements of Biology, the largest course, has had an enrollment of nearly 100, while some seminars and tutorials enroll as few as 2.

General-education requirements draw on coursework from the traditional liberal arts and sciences, including 4 semesters of a foreign language or passage of a proficiency exam. Students may select courses of their own choosing from suggested disciplines although all undergraduates must take the same 2 courses each in English composition and literature and in European history.

C of C's total faculty numbers 858, with 515 full-time members and 343 part-time. All but 6 of the full-time instructors and all but 69 of the part-time teach undergraduates. Nearly half, 48%, of the total pool are women. "All in all, my professors rated an 8 out of a possible 10," says a recent graduate. "They varied from those entrenched by tenure, despite boring lectures, to bright, innovative professors who made learning stimulating and enticing." Some undergraduates, seeking more challenge in the classroom, found some faculty members "too lenient," though always willing to talk in their offices.

Charleston's biology and chemistry programs are tough and very competitive, in part because the college is located near the Medical University of South Carolina, with which it shares expensive equipment and expertise. In recent years, a higher percentage of students have been admitted to the Medical University from Charleston than from any other college in the nation. An excellent program in marine biology is based at its own laboratory, adjacent to the state's Marine Resources Research Institute on James Island. Excellent faculty with "interactive teaching methods and genteel attitudes," in the words of one major, distinguish Charleston's physics and astronomy department. Likewise, accessible and knowledgeable professors with diverse specialties place the psychology, foreign language, history, political science, and English programs on many students' "A" list. The foreign language department, for example, may offer only majors in classics, French, German, and Spanish, but it has 16 minor programs from Italian to Jewish, Russian, or Japanese studies plus courses in Arabic and Chinese. Majors in the School of the Arts enjoy superb equipment, including the largest sculpture kiln in the southeast, as well as access to wonderful opportunities in Charleston, among them the annual Spoleto arts festival in late May, which features displays of visual arts and performances of dance, music, and theater. Most programs in the School of Business and Economics are considered "blue-chip" educational investments toward great jobs plus the new Beatty Center offers undergraduates classrooms with the latest technology, including a real-time trading desk. Serious students also give an enthusiastic "thumbs up" to the Honors College.

The communication major carries a reputation around campus for being easy. Sociology and philosophy have suffered from lack of student interest. Computer science is a newer major that needs more time to become established. While there are many students who consider the education major excellent, others complain that it lacks sufficient advising to insure that students complete the numerous requirements demanded of the discipline.

Facilities: Students greeted the fall 2004 opening of the Marlene and Nathan Addlestone Library with statements akin to the following: "Absolutely amazing!" The new facility provides space for 1 million volumes, almost twice the current collection, spread over 3 stories that extend over 145,000 square feet. The upper 2 floors are for quiet study while "the ground floor," explains an English major, " which has a café that serves coffee and pastries, is meant for groups doing projects and other tasks that require talking." Addlestone also includes an information arcade, a 260-seat computing lab, a total of 20 group study rooms, network connections at 75% of the 1400 seats provided and a secure study area that is open 24 hours a day as finals approach. Regular hours throughout the term are until 2 a.m. The library's collection of nearly 680,000 volumes and 3818 periodicals already has grown by 140,000 volumes and 500 periodicals thanks to the additional space. Serious students hope the new library continues to be more conducive to concentrated study. The old library became so much of a social spot that, in the words of one male student, "girls actually dress(ed) up for it!"

The 260-computer lab in the new library plus units in the new business building, the student union, and other structures have considerably brightened the high-tech picture on campus. The extra-long hours until 2 a.m. in the library also have stemmed most of students' past complaints. Confirms a senior: "Computers are extremely widespread on campus and thank goodness for that!" Wireless access also is an option in many areas.

Special programs: Charleston's membership in student-exchange programs lets undergraduates study at more than 100 domestic or international institutions for the same price they pay at home. Study-abroad programs with universities in 39 countries from Japan to Holland are also offered. As part of a Sea Semester, students spend 6 weeks in classroom studies at Woods Hole, Massachusetts, and 6 weeks aboard a research schooner. Engineering majors may transfer after 3 years to Case Western Reserve in Cleveland, Georgia Tech, Washington University, or the University of South Carolina for 2 more years of study, earning bachelor's degrees from both Charleston and the other institution. A similar 2-2 cooperative program in nursing and the allied health professions is set up with the Medical University of South Carolina. Cross-registration for more general classes is offered with Trident Technical College, The Citadel, and Charleston Southern University.

Campus life: Just 29% of all undergraduates live on the historic, 52-acre campus, where oak trees draped with Spanish moss and brick walkways lit by street lamps win the hearts of visitors. "A southern version of the Ivy League school," brags a Virginia resident. The 13 national fraternities and 11 national sororities, pledged by 11% of the men and 16% of the women, are a "big deal," especially among resident students, and extremely popular fraternity parties provide the social focus for most weekends. Most academic departments have their own clubs, whose members go on trips and sponsor get-togethers. Activities open to all students generally are scheduled at 3 p.m. Tuesdays and Thursdays when no classes meet to encourage involvement by commuters. More and more students also are becoming involved in community service. The College Activities Board organizes a hyperactive schedule of concerts, lectures, trips, movies, and other events. An increase in crime such as robberies during the 2005–2006 school year brought out additional public safety officers on foot, on bicycles, and in cars as well as greater caution by students. Fraternity members volunteer for night escort duty and call boxes are omnipresent around campus. Still, students caution classmates to be careful walking at night.

The former NAIA basketball champs are the most popular of the 7 men's and 12 women's varsity teams. The equestrian, sailing, and women's tennis teams also have won national honors. The sports program has become more exciting since the college moved up to NCAA Division I competition more than a decade ago though fan support other than for men's basketball remains fairly limited. A small percentage of the men and women avail themselves of the 17 intramural sports available to each sex. However, 90 teams have been known to line up for a game of oozeball, which is volleyball played in the mud.

The college's location in the heart of a renowned historic area offers a multitude of cultural and recreational opportunities from beaches and parks on Charleston Bay to museums or shopping at the Old Square Market. Charleston nightlife has something for every taste and pocketbook, from the symphony to reggae bands, from fast food to fine French cuisine. "There is almost too much fun here," warns an accounting major. More distant getaways take students to major universities, like Clemson or the University of South Carolina, especially during football season.

Cost cutters: No figures are available on the portion of undergraduates who received aid in the 2005–2006 school year. Figures from earlier years show that generally not quite two-thirds of all undergraduates received some kind of financial aid, primarily need-based. No recent figures also are available on the amounts or types of aid provided or the average debt load of graduates. A variety of institutional and departmental scholarships are open to all first-year students in addition to the larger number restricted to South Carolina high school graduates that range in value from $2650 for one-year to $6700 for each of 4 years. Presidential Scholarships, for example, generally go to students who graduated in the top 5% of their high school classes and scored 1300 or above on the math and critical reading portions of the SAT or 29 on the ACT. Students must have been admitted by Jan. 15 to be considered for all such academic scholarships. Cooperative education programs are offered in all majors.

Rate of return: Eighty-three percent of freshmen return as sophomores. After 4 years, 46% will have graduated; after 5 years, 59%.

Payoff: Communications and business administration were the majors of choice for the 2005 graduating class at 15% and 14%, respectively, followed in popularity by elementary education at 3%. Twenty-six percent of the graduates pursued advanced degrees. All but a small percentage of those not enrolled in school were employed within 6 months of commencement.

Bottom line: "The pure age of the school imparts a majestic, solid feeling," notes a junior. "Yet the beauty of this college lies not only in its history but also in the highly intelligent, persevering individuals it turns out." Undergraduates caution, however, that it is up to the individual student to resist the temptation of a great number of parties and the charm of historic Charleston to reach out to willing faculty members and become one of those impressive graduates.

Converse College

Spartanburg, South Carolina 29302

Setting: Urban
Control: Private
Undergraduate enrollment: 571 women (202 part-time)
Graduate enrollment: 1165 men and women (full- and part-time)
Student/faculty ratio: 9:1
Freshman profile: Average combined SAT I: 1114; class rank data: NA
Faculty profile: 89% Ph.D.'s
Tuition and fees: $21,176
Room and board: $6460

Freshman financial aid: 80%; average scholarship or grant: $15,866 need-based; $17,061 non-need-based
Campus jobs: 33%; average earnings: $915/year
Application deadline: Early decision: Dec. 1; regular: Mar. 1
Financial aid deadline: Mar. 15 (Priority); For scholarships: Inquire by Oct. 1
Admissions information: (864) 596-9746; (800) 766-1125
e-mail: admissions@converse.edu
web site: www.converse.edu

Converse College, like many other small women's colleges, offers a celebration of women as a regular part of its everyday routine. But on many special weekends throughout the year, Converse celebrates a wide range of other subjects in a very big way for a very small college. Each fall, Converse hosts an 1889 Celebration, during which it remembers, with class competitions in dancing, skits, fund raising, and dorm decorating, the year the college was founded. The winner receives the much coveted 1889 Spirit Cup. Every other year, the campus chapter of Mortar Board hosts the Probe Symposium, focusing on a controversial issue, for example, censorship in the arts. The nationally recognized Carroll McDaniel Petrie School of Music hosts its own music festival, in a recent year celebrating Mozart, and, college-wide celebrations acknowledge Martin Luther King, Jr., Day as well as Women's History Month. That's a lot of celebrating for a school of fewer than 600 full-time undergraduates, but then Converse has a lot to celebrate. Founded as a school that would "always be truly religious without being denominational," in the words of its founder, Dexter Edgar Converse, this college has always believed in living up to its name: doing just the converse of what people expect it to do.

Student body: Almost two-thirds of Converse's students come from South Carolina, with sister southerners comprising 75% of the out-of-staters. Altogether, in a recent year, women represented 28 states and 14 foreign countries. Thirty percent of the students attended private or parochial schools. African-American students recently constituted 12% of the enrollment, Hispanics and Asian-Americans 1% each. Foreign nationals represented another 1%. Converse women tend to be conservative and rather serious about their studies, yet enthusiastic about campus clubs and activities. "We have really brilliant students and others who make average grades," says a premed major. "But the students here are very outgoing, and it is easy to make new friends." Indeed, on such a small campus, many friendships extend across class lines and young women value the sensitive and supportive atmosphere that results. The large portion of Southern young women also adds a flair for proper etiquette and manners. Says a junior, "The students are competitive, in a polite way."

Academics: Converse offers a bachelor of arts, of science, of music, and of fine arts in almost 40 fields, plus a master's of music, of education and of liberal arts plus an educational specialist degree. Men may enroll at the graduate level only. Coursework at both the undergraduate and the graduate level is offered through the College of Arts and Sciences and the Petrie School of Music. The academic year is divided into 2 terms of 13–14 weeks each. A 4-week January term is usually devoted to internships, study-travel with Converse faculty, and specially designed courses, often with field trips.

Not surprisingly, classes at tiny Converse College are small. Average enrollment in an introductory lecture is 20 students; participation in other courses frequently drops below a dozen. All students must complete the General Education Program, which includes courses in core competencies (writing, foreign language, mathematics, etc.), studies in the academic disciplines (humanities, science, social science, fine arts, and literature), and Ideals and Cultures, a 2-course exploration of the events that have shaped humanity. Freshmen may also take Converse 101, a course which introduces students to the resources of the college and polishes their study and public speaking skills.

The faculty includes 72 full-time members. In a recent year, the faculty also included 16 part-time members. Two full-time faculty members and 3 part-time recently taught at the graduate level only. Fifty-two percent of the faculty are women. "There's no such thing as perfection," says a junior, "but the Converse faculty is as close as you can get." The relationship between faculty and students is quite familial, with undergraduates getting to know professors well and rarely feeling too intimidated to ask for help with academic or personal problems. "The members of the faculty here are always willing to help with any questions you might have," says a sophomore. "They make you feel like you are their only student."

Some of the college's most active professors are associated with the school's academic stars, its excellent Petrie School of Music, education department, and majors in biology and chemistry, history and politics, English, and economics and business. Music is a very competitive major with a rigorous curriculum, extensive library, wonderful practice rooms, many with grand pianos, and an electronic music lab. A new major in music therapy recently was added to the repertoire. The education department offers the state's only undergraduate program in deaf education as well as other strong teacher education programs. Extensive opportunities for fieldwork are available right in Spartanburg. The sciences have long featured very good equipment for a small college, and high acceptance rates into medical school. The new 36,000-square-foot Phifer Science Hall, which opened in fall 2004, has pushed the quality of laboratory equipment from "very good" to "state-of-the-art." The free-flowing architectural design also combines lecture space with fully functioning laboratories, allowing faculty and students to move easily between the 2 areas during classes. History and politics have great professors, as students from across the country competing against Converse's delegation in the Model League of Arab States program know. The Converse team has earned national titles 10 years in a row, defeating teams from powerhouses such as Harvard, U.C. Berkeley, and the U.S. Air Force Academy in recent competitions. Many English majors use their solid academic foundation to gain admission to law school or to enter careers in journalism or public relations. Adds a senior: "I didn't expect the academics to be extremely challenging, however, my mind is about to explode every day I am in the classroom."

The Department of Art and Design is making its way to the "A" list, thanks to the recent renovation and doubling in size of the Milliken Art Building. The expansion provides space for each discipline to have its own area as well as room for an art library, a Computer-Assisted Design lab, kiln and firing yards, a photography lab, and an historic preservation room. While students find the math, chemistry, religion, and philosophy professors to be excellent, there are relatively few of them, resulting in limited class offerings. In fact, across the board in all departments, students wish there were more professors, more courses offered, and more updated equipment available. Philosophy has been offered as a minor only, though an endowed chair in philosophy established in fall 2005 will bring more classes, especially in the area of ethics. Sociology stopped being offered as either a major or a minor in 2002.

Facilities: Mickel Library houses a collection of more than 200,000 volumes and 717 current periodicals, with seating provided for more than 240 students. Those seeking quiet head for the upper floors. Seniors can have their own study carrels. Mickel's on-line catalog is available in both web- and text-based computers formats to aid students in their search for materials. Electronic access to several thousand additional journals, magazines, and newspapers also is provided. The 16,000 musical scores and 17,600 recordings also included in Mickel's collection make Converse's music library one of the largest in the South.

Five general-access labs with 75 PCs and a music lab with 22 Macs are available for student use. All residence-hall rooms have Internet access. To make good use of the access, the college strongly recommends that students bring their own personal computers.

Special programs: Semester or year-long programs of foreign study are offered in France, England, Spain, Costa Rica, Iceland, and other countries. Special opportunities to study abroad during the winter term also are provided. Mile-away exchanges are offered with coed Wofford College, also in Spartanburg. Double majors are strongly encouraged, with every department structured to accommodate a double major with almost any other department so that the student can still graduate in 4 years. The new Julia Jones Daniels Center for Leadership and Service encourages student involvement in community service and leadership. Project Serve, for example, engages students in 1 large service project per month as well as a standing site at a local shelter. "Students at Converse are very willing and enthusiastic about service," observes a vocal performance major.

Campus life: Converse requires that all unmarried students of traditional college age who do not live within a 35-mile radius of the campus with a parent or guardian reside in college housing. As a result, 90% of Converse women live on the 72-acre campus located just 80 miles southwest of Charlotte, but less than half that number remain over the weekend. Explains a sophomore: "Most weekends students leave campus for 'road trips,' where we visit friends on other campuses, go home, or participate in planned activities such as shopping or skiing trips sponsored by the Campus Life Office." Much of the time away also involves mingling with men, who are generally absent for much of the regular work week, although residence hall visitation is allowed during certain hours. Fraternity parties at nearby Wofford College are especially popular. Duke, Davidson, Furman, and the universities of North and South Carolina are also frequent party destinations. There are no sororities on campus, but undergraduates say the all-inclusive

Big Sis/Lil Sis program in which juniors adopt first-year students is a satisfactory substitute. The honor code, more than anything else, binds women together on this campus. Notes a religion major: "There is a real feeling of trust between students and professors. Because of this trust, many students never lock their doors, professors feel free to give take-home exams, and students are allowed the privilege of self-scheduling their classes." To ensure campus safety, cards with access codes are required to enter the residence halls. Call boxes are prevalent around campus and public safety officers escort students who prefer not to walk alone after dark. To date, car break-ins have been the most troublesome problem.

The Converse All-Stars compete in cross-country, volleyball, basketball, soccer, and tennis in NCAA Division II. Soccer games draw the biggest crowds. Half the women participate in 4 intramural sports. There also is an equestrian program with competitors at the A-show level.

Cost cutters: In a recent school year, 80% of the freshmen and 75% of the continuing students received financial aid; for 72% of the first-year students and 69% of those continuing, the aid was need-based. The average freshman award for a first-year student with financial need included a need-based scholarship or grant averaging $15,866 and need-based self-help aid such as loans and jobs averaging $3593. Non-need-based athletic scholarships for freshmen averaged $9488; other non-need-based awards and scholarships averaged $17,061. Average indebtedness of a recent graduate was $18,036. Converse offers a wide range of merit scholarships, which start at $1000 and extend to the full comprehensive fee that covers tuition, fees, room and board. To be considered for most awards, prospective freshmen must have earned a minimum high school GPA of 3.5 on a 4.0 system, have combined SAT scores of at least 1100 on math and critical reading, or an ACT Composite of 24. Music scholarships, ranging in value from $1000 to the full comprehensive fee, are awarded to top applicants who plan to pursue a Bachelor of Music degree. Specialized awards in leadership, athletics, theater and visual arts also are offered; the amounts and number of awards vary from year to year. To aid all students, the college offers a payment plan which allows for payment of tuition and fees in monthly installments. Campus jobs enable about 250 students to work between 5 and 15 hours weekly to help defray college costs.

Rate of return: Seventy-four percent of freshmen return for the sophomore year. Fifty-five percent go on to graduate in 4 years; 56% in 5.

Payoff: Twenty-one percent of Converse graduates in a recent year majored in visual and performing arts, followed by 19% each in business and education. In recent years, nearly three-quarters of the women have entered the job market upon graduation, many accepting offers with firms in the Southeast. One hundred seventy-five companies and organizations recently recruited on campus. One-fourth of the graduates opt to pursue advanced degrees. Those seeking further study in music often stay right at Converse.

Bottom line: "Converse encourages self-esteem, independence, and a place of belonging," says a senior. "It is a difficult thing to be open-minded enough at 17 or 18 to break with the norm and consider a women's college. But those who are willing to make this decision will be challenged academically, mature emotionally, and make the best friends of a lifetime in a welcoming and nurturing atmosphere."

Furman University

Greenville, South Carolina 29613

Setting: Suburban
Control: Independent
Undergraduate enrollment: 1175 men, 1511 women
Graduate enrollment: 13 men, 41 women
Student/faculty ratio: 12:1
Freshman profile: 22% scored over 700 on SAT I verbal; 56% scored 600–700; 20% 500–599; 2% below 500. 18% scored over 700 on SAT I math; 61% scored 600–700; 19% 500–599; 2% below 500. 41% scored above 28 on the ACT; 22% scored 27–28; 23% 24–26; 10% 21–23; 4% below 21. 61% graduated in top tenth of high school class; 84% in upper fifth.
Faculty profile: 96% Ph.D.'s

Tuition and fees: $26,352
Room and board: $6912
Freshman financial aid: 85%; average scholarship or grant: NA
Campus jobs: 19%; average earnings: $1071/year
Application deadline: Early decision: Nov. 15; regular: Jan. 15
Financial aid deadline: Early decision: Dec. 1; regular: Feb. 1
Admissions information: (864) 294-2034
  e-mail: admissions@furman.edu
  web site: www.furman.edu or www.engagefurman.com

Furman University, a liberal arts college of 2690 undergraduates at the foot of Paris Mountain in north-western South Carolina, doesn't just *want* its students to be liberally educated both in and out of the class-room—it *requires* this. A special cultural life program requires every student to attend at least 36 cultural events, such as plays, concerts, lectures, and debates, before graduating in 4 years. An emphasis on what is known as "engaged learning," an experience-based approach to the liberal arts, encourages students to put classroom theory into practice through internships, collaborative research projects, study abroad, and service learning. A third of the enrollment gets caught up in a spirit of helping others and partici-pates in the university's largest extracurricular activity: the Collegiate Educational Service Corps. As part of the program, 800 Furman students go into the Greenville community once a week to tutor under-privileged children, help the elderly and handicapped, or perform some other service through 45 area agencies. At Furman, an education is not complete until students have become involved in learning outside of the classroom, as well as within.

Student body: Twenty-nine percent of Furman's students are from South Carolina. Half of the out-of-staters also are from the South, though undergraduates come from 46 states and 27 foreign countries. Two-thirds of the students attended public schools. Racial and ethnic diversity is low but has steadily increased over the years. African-Americans constitute 6% of the enrollment, Asian-Americans 2%, and Hispanics, 1%. One percent also are international students. Undergraduates describe themselves as *kind, considerate, intelligent, hard-working,* and often *overextended* in activities—"natural leaders," as one member put it. "Organized, type-A personalities," says another. The student body also has been marked by a general polit-ical, social, and religious conservatism, which reflects in large part the university's long ties with the Southern Baptist Convention, which were officially severed in 1992. Undergraduates say, however, that the enroll-ment has gradually become more liberal and more receptive to new ideas with every entering freshman class and with each additional year students spend on campus. Says a sophomore: "Many students' con-servative principles tend to change as they are encouraged to see life from new perspectives thanks to 'engaged learning.'" One area where students are unlikely to change is their academic ability, already regarded as "top of the heap." Some class members are faulted by their peers for focusing on the well-paying jobs at the end of the trail rather than the knowledge to be gained along the way. Whatever the goal, students work hard, are helpful to each other, and keep the level of competition high but healthy. "Furman students also know how to unwind," says a sophomore, "and definitely include 'hang-out' time in their schedules. At Furman, there is always something to do, and college is about balance, decisions, and time management."

Academics: Furman, founded by South Carolina Baptists as an academy and theological institute in 1826, confers a bachelor of arts degree in about 30 disciplines, a bachelor of music in 5 areas, and a bach-elor of science in 8 majors. Master's degrees are awarded in education and chemistry. The school year is divided into 2 semesters of 12 weeks each, split by an 8-week term in the middle. During the fall and spring, students usually take three 4-hour courses; during the winter term, two 4-hour courses. Average class size is 17, ranging from 5 to an occasional 45 throughout the 4 years.

In addition to the cultural events required, students must complete general education requirements (GERs) in a wide range of disciplines from the humanities to the natural and social sciences. Each under-graduate also must take at least 1 course in African-Asian studies. The program takes about half of the students' 4 years to finish, but because students need not choose a major until fall term, junior year, the exploration is valuable to many. Says a senior business administration and political science major: "I came into Furman majoring in undecidedness and found my major by exploring the GERs."

All but 38 of Furman's 257 faculty members are full-time. A third are women. Students value the pro-fessors for their open-minded and stimulating style of teaching, which challenges class members to think and probe, rather than memorize facts. "Some faculty, of course, are pompous and pedantic," observes a senior. "But most are very down to earth and genuinely interested in their students' well-being. Many work very hard to establish special friendships with students, and it is not uncommon for a pro-fessor to invite an entire class over for dinner or a special gathering."

Furman's top departments are among the best in their respective fields at any liberal arts college. Chemistry, biology, political science, history, and psychology, in particular, have outstanding faculties. The chemistry department also boasts nearly $2 million in state-of-the-art equipment—infrared spec-trometers, as well as a nuclear magnetic resonance spectrometer—well used by the undergraduates. Undergraduates, in turn, don't stop their learning after earning a bachelor's degree. Furman ranks among the top 10 undergraduate colleges in the country in producing Ph.D. candidates in chemistry. Political science, in particular, provides opportunities for engaged learning through extensive internships. Its faculty, says a major, "choose to teach by encouragement rather than discouragement. In the classroom, they command respect, but their offices are always open and they always have time to chat with students on any topic from the latest news on Capitol Hill to (professional) football." Psychology, too, is known for being exceptionally rigorous, yet marked by dedicated professors who balance toughness with support and availability. Says a psychology major: "If you are a chemistry or psychology major who wants to do well, just go ahead and kiss your social life goodbye. One of my professors prescribed 3½ hours of studying 6 days a week to succeed in his class. Two textbooks, numerous journal articles, a text of professor notes, and a 40-page paper later, I'm beginning to understand."

Music enjoys its own modern equipment and the good reputation of Furman's performance groups. The conductor of the Boston Pops is a Furman graduate. Roe Art Building has won many architectural awards for incorporating teaching facilities for ceramics, painting, photography, and sculpture into its design, though majors wish there were more professors and more variety in the courses offered. The English department shines with resident experts from concentrations as wide ranging as Chaucer and southern literature. Sociology and Asian studies are considered lesser known "diamonds in the rough."

The communication studies major needs additional faculty members to satisfy increasing student demand for courses in this field. The program in theater arts lacks sufficient facilities, though students marvel at the quality of the performances that are produced. Physics needs more professors and ones who can explain concepts better to students. "The above-average student has little trouble comprehending the subject," says a chemistry major, "but the average student is at a loss." The programs in education and health and exercise science are regarded as less rigorous than others at the school.

Facilities: After about 2 years of noisy renovations, the James B. Duke Library is bigger, better, and quieter than ever. The newly expanded facility, which opened in fall 2004, provides 3 times the number of seats, going from 300 seats to 900, including more than 25 group study rooms, plus space for twice as many volumes, up to 800,000 from 400,000, which suits Furman students just fine. Students have long viewed Duke's collection of 436,000 volumes, 857,000 microforms, and 4230 periodicals to be less than adequate for research in upper-level classes. To complete their research, many students turn to Alcuin, the online catalog, the Internet, numerous periodical searches and a hard-working staff for assistance. "The computers help," says a junior, "but the staff helps more—and they smile at you. When we don't have it, we get it, fast. It's an excellent system." Furman and Wofford College also have shared access to a common database that provides full text of some 1100 scholarly journals and indexes about 2200 more. Serious studiers, night owls, and procrastinators also are thrilled about the new 40-seat study lounge that is open around the clock. The library lounge has everything a late-night studier needs, computers as well as drink and snack machines. The rest of the library is open until 1 a.m.

The new Multimedia Computing Commons, also housed in the expanded library, is the largest computing facility on campus and has raised to 370 the number of computers open to students across campus. Computers also are available in Richard W. Riley Hall, named for the Furman alumnus who served as U.S. Secretary of Education under President Clinton, and other general access labs and various departmental and residential facilities. All but 2% of the students also have their own computers, primarily laptops. Wireless networks are available in 95% of the classroom and administrative buildings and residence halls as well as in most public spaces.

Special programs: The departments of English, political science, history, and economics and business administration cooperatively sponsor a fall term in England. The department of modern languages and literature offers a term in each of three centers: Madrid, Paris, and Bonn, Germany. Winter-term travel opportunities vary; in a recent year, students traveled to the Middle East and the Galapagos Islands. A spring or summer term in Washington, D.C. is conducted through the Washington Center for Learning Alternatives. A 3-2 program in engineering is offered with Clemson, Auburn, Washington, or North Carolina State University or with Georgia Tech; a similar program in forestry and environmental studies is an option with Duke. Opportunities to do original research attract 100 to 150 students every summer, recently placing Furman second to Williams College in Massachusetts among national liberal arts colleges in the number and percentage of undergraduates involved in summer research.

Campus life: Ninety-one percent of Furman students reside on the 750-acre campus, which students admit looks a bit more like a country club with its 30-acre lake with swans, 18-hole golf course, bubbling fountains, and rose and Japanese gardens. The university requires all undergraduates, except those who are married or living at home with a parent, to reside in campus housing. One of the more innovative offerings is Eco-Cottage, an experimental house outfitted with energy-saving devices such as solar panels and low-flow faucets where residents recycle and limit their energy consumption. Restrictions on dorm rooms being open to the opposite sex have loosened in recent years and there are brother-sister residence hall pairings for a week of activities during freshman orientation. Thirty-five percent of the men and 40% of the women belong to 8 national fraternities and 7 national sororities; as there are no fraternity houses, parties usually are held in off-campus apartments. As most parties are open to all, students say there is no rivalry between Greeks and independents. A coffeehouse where students and even the college president perform attracts members from both camps. Students are very trusting. Says a city resident: "I can leave my things in the library, go to dinner, and come back, and they'll still be there." Some vandalism and vehicle break-ins do occur, though. Access cards and codes are mandatory for admission to all residence halls. Campus lighting also was recently improved, and a shuttle service is available from 7 p.m. to 7 a.m., but used, says a senior, "really more for convenience than safety."

It's been over a decade since Furman's football team won the NCAA Division I-AA national championship, coming close in fall 2001 with a loss to the University of Montana in the championship game, but excitement in the program continues with fans clad in purple and even painting themselves the school shade as a show of support. Paladins basketball and soccer also draw good crowds of the 8 men's and 9 women's teams fielded, all but football in Division I-A. Seventy-three percent of the men and 41% of the women take part in the 20 men's, women's, and coed intramural teams offered.

For great escapes, Atlanta is only 2½ hours away, as are Charlotte, North Carolina; and Columbia. Paris Mountain is close by for picnics and hiking, while the Appalachian Mountains are an hour north. The South Carolina beaches are 4 hours from campus. Students also find the city of Greenville itself, with a metropolitan population of nearly 400,000, a dynamic community with "great malls, fun restaurants, and a 'happening' downtown," according to one Southerner.

Cost cutters: Eighty-five percent of Furman's freshmen and 82% of the continuing students received financial assistance in the 2005–2006 school year. For 43% of all undergraduates, the aid was need-based. The average freshman award totaled $17,800, though no breakdown is available to show the portion that was scholarships and grants or loans and job earnings. The typical debt facing a 2005 alumnus was $21,194. Each year, Furman offers more than 100 renewable academic scholarships to students in the freshman class. Four Herman Warden Lay Scholarships cover tuition, room, and board. High-achieving high school juniors may be nominated by their guidance counselors to receive one of 2 to 4 Furman Scholars awards, worth $4000. As high school seniors, recipients may be selected to replace the $4000 scholarship with the full-cost Lay Scholarship or the James B. Duke Scholarship, which pays full tuition. Twenty South Carolina high school graduates are eligible to receive renewable Hollingsworth Scholarships, worth $25,000, plus a $1000 scholarship for study abroad. Numerous music scholarships also pay a maximum of half tuition. A program known as the Furman Advantage pays students to do research projects with professors.

Rate of return: All but 7% of the freshmen return for the sophomore year. Seventy-nine percent graduate in 4 years; 83%, in 5 years; 84% in 6.

Payoff: Thirteen percent of the 2005 graduates earned degrees in political science. Another 9% picked up diplomas in history, 8% in business administration. More than a third of the new graduates proceeded directly to graduate or professional schools, mostly in the arts and sciences. Over the last 5 years, Furman's medical school acceptance rate has been nearly double the national average. The law school acceptance rate is close to 90%. Within 5 years of commencement, approximately 72% of Furman alumni continue their education at the graduate level. A majority of the new graduates take jobs in such fields as teaching and accounting throughout the Southeast and Midwest. Eighty-six companies and organizations recruited on campus in a recent school year.

Bottom line: Furman's faculty and facilities have long been on a par with those at more prestigious and pricier private institutions, but some top students may have steered clear of the university because of its ties to the Southern Baptist Convention. With that relationship broken more than a decade ago, undergraduates say students looking for challenging academics mixed with "Southern hospitality," should give Furman a look. But, cautions a junior: "People need to be their own CEOs: driven, efficient, motivated, well balanced, and good at time management."

Presbyterian College

Clinton, South Carolina 29325

Setting: Small town
Control: Private (Presbyterian)
Undergraduate enrollment: 554 men, 584 women
Graduate enrollment: None
Student/faculty ratio: 13:1
Freshman profile: 5% scored over 700 on SAT I verbal; 30% scored 600–700; 43% 500–599; 22% below 500. 3% scored over 700 on SAT I math; 36% scored 600–700; 44% 500–599; 17% below 500. 10% scored above 28 on the ACT; 8% scored 27–28; 31% 24–26; 31% 21–23; 20% below 21. 31% graduated in top tenth of high school class; 52% in upper fourth.
Faculty profile: 94% Ph.D.'s

Tuition and fees: $23,244
Room and board: $6800
Freshman financial aid: 61%; average scholarship or grant: NA
Campus jobs: NA; average earnings: NA
Application deadline: Early decision: Dec. 5, Regular: rolling
Financial aid deadline: Mar. 1 recommended (Dec. 1 scholarships)
Admissions information: (864) 833-8230; (800) 960-7583
e-mail: admissions@presby.edu
web site: www.presby.edu

To begin with, you don't have to be Presbyterian to attend Presbyterian College in upstate South Carolina, any more than you have to be American to attend American University in Washington, D.C., or be named William or Mary to attend The College of William and Mary in Virginia. In fact, just 31% of PC's students are Presbyterian, although 87% are Protestant; 6% are Catholic, and the rest claim no religious preference or are nondenominational. Faculty members are required to be members of a Christian church, and students must complete 2 religion courses for graduation. Attendance at religious services is optional, however, and the Presbyterian name takes a backseat to a broader Christian ethic that pervades the campus and manifests itself in adherence to an honor code and a code of conduct and in an emphasis on service to the community. Students and administrators point proudly to PC's growth as an academic institution, becoming, in the 1989–90 school year, one of the smallest colleges to produce a Rhodes Scholar, as well as rivaling Harvard for the honor of having 5 students chosen as Rotary International Scholars in a single year. The initials PC may officially stand for Presbyterian College, but in the new century they could also mean Pretty Classy.

Student body: Presbyterian's enrollment is very southern, with 64% of the students from South Carolina and most of the rest also coming from the South. Twenty-six states and 12 foreign countries have members on campus. Twenty-nine percent of the undergraduates are from private or parochial schools. Of the 7% who represent minorities, 5% are African-American and 1% each are Asian-American and Hispanic. Twenty students are foreign nationals. PC students are generally conservative to moderate in their political and social viewpoints. Most are academically oriented ("students want to be the best," observes a junior), but not to the exclusion of participation in extracurricular fun and community-service projects. "Most people here are not 'Bible beaters,'" observes an English major. "They are all-American, clean-cut students with a real willingness to help others." "The boy or girl next door," adds a Georgian, which means, cautions a state resident, that "people who are true individuals that stand out (blue hair, spiked) may not fit into the PC mold."

Academics: PC, which was founded in 1880 as a college for orphans, continues to serve undergraduates only, offering the bachelor's degree in 30 majors. The year is divided into 2 semesters, with an optional "Maymester," during which special opportunities for off-campus experiences are provided that could not be worked around semester schedule conflicts. Recent programs have included studies in the Galapagos Islands, Vietnam, and Australia.

Biology 101 has been the biggest class at PC, with 38 students; the size drops below 30 for most other lower-level classes and rarely tops 20 in the junior and senior years, except in some of the more popular majors such as business and English. PC's graduation requirements include both in-class and out-of-classroom work. In the first 2 years, all students must take general-education courses that cover the full range of academic disciplines from English composition and literature to the natural and social sciences. Students also must fulfill an intercultural requirement through either study abroad, taking a course with an intercultural perspective, or completing an internship. After classes, undergraduates must attend 10 cultural enrichment events a year, 5 performances, 5 lectures, in order to graduate.

Presbyterian's faculty of 112 includes 83 full-time members and 29 part-time. A third are women. Five PC professors have been named South Carolina Professor of the Year, more than at any other school in the state. In the classroom, says a sophomore, "professors do a tremendous job of balancing the imparting of subject material and acceptance of student ideas." Adds another sophomore, "The faculty gets an A for availability." Professors get as involved in outside activities such as intramurals as they do in lecturing about Shakespeare or microeconomic theory. Some students even take breaks from campus life by studying at a professor's house or doing their laundry there! Says a junior: "One of my favorite professors retired after my freshman year, and to this day I still go by his house every couple of weeks to chat." Another junior was thrilled to receive a birthday card over the summer, signed by every member of the English department with a personal note.

The widely divergent disciplines of English, biology, political science, and business are hailed as 4 of PC's strongest suits. All offer dedicated faculties with their own individual styles and diverse coursework. The English department boasts 2 recent consecutive South Carolina Professors of the Year; a political science professor followed as the third. Two biology professors were awarded the statewide honor in 2002 and 2003. Religion/philosophy, history, education, music and psychology also draw good reviews.

The foreign languages department, with majors in French, Spanish, and German, and classes in Portuguese, needs more professors and courses, more up-to-date equipment, and a greater emphasis on speaking the language exclusively in class. Sociology could use a sharper career focus in its approach. The fine arts program, which includes art, theater, and dance, continues to need additional resources, though a recent $1 million dollar gift to establish a visual arts facility and operating endowment fund promises to boost the visual arts program.

Facilities: Thomason Library, named for a local business leader, is a popular place to study, sometimes too popular, though students say they can always find a small space in which to hide. Expansion of the library in the 2005-2006 school year was making room for a new archival and special collections wing that will include extensive materials related to the life of Confederate General Thomas J. "Stonewall" Jackson. Many students find Thomason's regular collection of nearly 155,000 volumes and 684 periodicals adequate, but just barely, and rely on a devoted staff and an excellent interlibrary loan system for help when needed. The computerized research assistance gets 5 stars.

As a whole, computer availability on campus is rated as good. Three microcomputer labs, including about 125 Apple Macintosh and IBM computers, are available to students. Two labs are open until midnight every evening, 1 around the clock, and students find the hours sufficient to meet their needs. All residence hall rooms are wired with 2 computer ports providing students access to the campus network as well as the Internet. Wireless Internet coverage is available from more than 90% of the open spaces on campus as well as in the library and several academic buildings.

Special programs: In addition to traveling over Maymester, students may spend a semester, summer, or year abroad in various programs in western Europe as well as in China, India, Japan, or about anywhere a student wishes. Domestic experience is offered for a semester in Washington, D.C. An engineering student can pick up dual degrees through a 3-2 program at Auburn, Clemson, or Vanderbilt University. A forestry/environmental studies program is offered in cooperation with Duke.

Campus life: Ninety-five percent of PC students live on the 240-acre campus (all single students are required to live in college housing), and three-quarters of the undergraduates find enough to do over most weekends. Greek life is big, with 44% of the men pledging to 8 national fraternities, and 36% of the women joining 4 national sororities, the first of which opened in 1989. Independents as well as Greeks like the life that fraternity band parties bring to the small-town campus. About half of the students participate in PC's volunteer services program, which involves them in more than 30 community-service projects, such as tutoring children or working with the homeless. A college chapter of Habitat for Humanity helps to build decent housing around the state, the nation, and the world. Christian groups such as Fellowship of Christian Athletes also are very popular. "Crime? What crime?" asks a junior. Dorms are accessed through a key card computer system. The college's highly regarded Honor Code and Code of Conduct also help to keep crime in check.

Second in popularity to Greek parties are varsity football, soccer, and men's basketball, which compete under the school nickname, the Blue Hose. Eight men's and 8 women's varsity sports are offered in NCAA Division II play. The newest additions to the varsity roster, men's and women's lacrosse, also have become very popular sports on campus. Intramurals draw almost everybody from the stands onto the playing field, with 85% of the men and 65% of the women turning out for the 10 sports open to each sex. A 31-acre tract adjacent to campus has been developed as a comprehensive intramural complex offering football and softball fields, putting greens, and a lighted running trail.

When campus life in Clinton (pop. 10,000), with its parties or sporting events, palls, students hit the road to the bigger cities of Spartanburg, Greenville, or Columbia (each an hour or less away), to the mountains (2 hours), or to the beach (3 hours).

Cost cutters: In the 2005–2006 school year, 61% of the freshmen and 60% of all continuing students received financial help; for nearly all of those students, aid was need-based. The average first-year award in the 2005–2006 school year totaled $23,791; no breakdown is available on the number of scholarships or grants, either need-based or not, or self-help aid such as loans and jobs. The average financial indebtedness of a 2005 graduate totaled $21,517. PC oversees 5 scholarship programs for entering freshmen that are presented on the basis of academic merit, leadership, and character. These awards include the highly prized Quattlebaum Scholarships, which cover the full cost of tuition, room, board, and fees for 2 entering freshmen; the John I. Smith Scholarship, paying $14,000 a year; the Belk Scholarship which pays $10,600 annually, and the Southeastern and Dillard Elliott scholarships that each pay $7000. Leadership Scholarships pay up to $3000 a year. An interest-free payment plan that enables students to pay their comprehensive fees monthly is available through Academic Management Systems. Concludes a junior: "PC works well for the typical middle-class family."

Rate of return: Eighty-three percent of entering freshmen return for the sophomore year. Sixty-two percent go on to graduate in 4 years, 72% in 5 years, 73% in 6.

Payoff: Economics/business administration was the major of choice for 22% of the 2005 graduates. Biology followed at 14%, psychology at 12%. A quarter of the degree recipients in recent years have opted to continue their educations. The majority of new alumni entered the job market, many with firms that have been popular with PC graduates in recent years, among them Pitney-Bowes, Milliken, Prudential, C & S Bank, and Ernst & Young. Forty-eight companies and other organizations recruited on campus in a recent school year.

Bottom line: "Even though it seems as though PC would be boring, situated in the small town of Clinton, this college is not," declares a sophomore. "You can spend a semester in Wales, Spain, or France, take a Maymester trip to Australia with the biology department, work with the homeless in Atlanta, or be a big brother or sister to an underprivileged child. Anything is possible here!"

University of South Carolina at Columbia

Columbia, South Carolina 29208

Setting: Urban
Control: Public
Undergraduate enrollment: 7425 men, 8974 women
Graduate enrollment: 2009 men, 2819 women
Student/faculty ratio: 19:1
Freshman profile: 8% scored over 700 on SAT I verbal; 31% scored 600–700; 47% 500–599; 14% below 500. 9% scored over 700 on SAT I math; 37% scored 600–700; 44% 500–599; 10% below 500. 17% scored above 28 on the ACT; 15% scored 27–28; 30% 24–26; 26% 21–23; 12% below 21. 49% graduated in top fifth of high school class; 82% in upper two-fifths.

Faculty profile: 84% Ph.D.'s
Tuition and fees: $7314 in-state; $18,956 out-of-state
Room and board: $6083
Freshman financial aid: 95%; average scholarship or grant: $6834 need-based
Campus jobs: 14%; average earnings: $2858/year
Application deadline: Dec. 1 (Scholarships: Nov. 1)
Financial aid deadline: Apr. 15
Admissions information: (803) 777-7700;
(800) 868-5872
e-mail: admissions-ugrad@sc.edu
web site: www.sc.edu

If any college or university has come close to getting divine endorsement, it's the University of South Carolina at Columbia, which turned 200 in 2001. On September 11, 1987, as part of the university's celebration of the ecumenical year, the late Pope John Paul II stopped off at the campus during his travels through the United States. At that time, the Pope proclaimed to a crowd of ecstatic Carolina fans: "It is wonderful to be young. It is wonderful to be young and to be a student. It is wonderful to be young and to be a student of the University of South Carolina." And part of that wonder, for students and their parents in the 2005–2006 school year, was to be paying just over $13,000 for tuition, fees, room, and board if they lived in-state and just over $25,000 if they didn't. Affirms a sophomore from Florida: "Whether in state or out of state, this is an affordable school to begin with, and things just get better from there."

Student body: Seventy-eight percent of the students at South Carolina are from in-state, with half of the rest also southerners. Every state and 67 foreign countries have undergraduates in attendance and it doesn't take long for Carolina's Southernness to work its charm on the newcomers. Says a state resident: "The out-of-state students seem to blend in and turn to the Southern style. Everyone is friendly and will say 'hey' when you walk by, true Southern hospitality!" African-American students represent the largest minority group at 14% of enrollment. Asian-Americans account for 3%; Hispanics, 2%. Foreign nationals comprise 1%. Undergraduates at Carolina tend to be conservative and bound by tradition, although in recent years more members have come alive to concerns outside their immediate domain. Notes a senior from the Middle Atlantic region: "Freshmen arrive with attitudes and beliefs that are somewhat short-sighted. However, the university provides an environment in which those views are challenged and where students are encouraged to discuss difficult topics freely." As a whole, the student body tends to be more socially than academically inspired, although the recently reestablished Honors College, the Moore School of Business, and the College of Engineering and Information Technology provide pockets where competition thrives.

Academics: The University of South Carolina offers degrees through the doctorate, with 74 undergraduate majors spread throughout 10 schools and colleges plus the Honors College. The academic year is divided into 2 semesters. Freshmen and sophomores can expect classes that generally range in size from 100 to 300 members, with Geology 103 topping the 300 mark in a recent year. Courses at the junior and senior levels, however, usually have no more than 50 or 60, and very often enroll just 30.

The general-education requirements, which mandate 31 hours of coursework in the standard disciplines, do not impress most students and provide, in the words of a southerner, "only the most basic overview of major subjects," though their broadness does make switching majors among different colleges a bit easier. Undergraduates hold a much more favorable opinion of University 101, a 3-credit freshman course taught in the residence halls that introduces them to the support services and opportunities available at Carolina. Classes are kept small, 20–25 members, enabling students to get to know faculty members on a more personal level.

Sixty percent of the 1413 full-time faculty and 39% of the 592 part-time faculty members teach undergraduates. Thirty-seven percent of the faculty are women. Nearly a fourth of the introductory classes are taught at least in part by graduate students. While some of the tenured professors are viewed as quite "elitist" in their attitudes toward students, and others opt for research and let their TA's do the teaching, a large number make the effort to be friendly and accessible, even amid large classes. Recalls an advertising major: "I have been in classes of anywhere from 40 to 300 people where the professor would call on many by name." Adds a senior: "Not only are they experts in their respective fields of study but also in the art of relating to students." Mixing the arrogant with the approachable, students give the faculty an overall rating of 7 out of 10.

Programs in the Honors College dazzle many. Says a participant: "It offers small classes, opportunities for diversity in education, flexibility in declaring a major, and an amazing honors housing facility exclusively for Honors College students." The Moore School of Business, especially the international business program, gets an A for an especially astute faculty, intense classes, and a stupendous facility. In the College of Arts and Sciences, students praise the political science faculty for its openness, responsiveness to student needs, and willingness to break new ground in the discipline. Majors also get plenty of real-life experience at the state government offices, within walking distance of campus. The Swearingen Engineering Center, with 100 laboratories that can simulate industrial applications of engineering principles, makes just about every program in the College of Engineering and Information Technology outstanding. The colleges of Pharmacy and of Mass Communications and Information Studies also get the student vote of approval for great faculties and curricula. Graduates of the College of Nursing give their college the nod as well since 100% of USC nursing school graduates have passed the state board exams over the last few years. Other highly regarded programs include those in the School of Music and English language and literature, psychology, geography, marine science, chemistry, and statistics in the College of Arts and Sciences.

The undergraduate program in physics in the College of Arts and Sciences is considered weak by other science majors. Says a biology-chemistry major: "The courses are a jumble of haphazard subjects, the department has too many guest professors who have no unity, and the students are not encouraged to pursue internships and other opportunities in the field." Other students find biology to be the least selective of the science programs. The computer science program in the College of Engineering and Information Technology could use more full-time faculty and rely less on teaching assistants whose limited English speaking skills make learning difficult and frustrating. Exercise science in the Arnold School of Public Health and art and anthropology in the College of Arts and Sciences also could use more funding, space, and additional faculty. Says a media arts major: "The art department, though really great, lacks adequate funding for new equipment so that students can get hands-on experience. Equipment also is lacking in repairs due to money shortages."

Facilities: Thomas Cooper Library is the university's main research and study facility, with additional branches for business administration, law, mathematics, medicine, music, and materials related to South Carolina. Together, the 7 facilities house 3.5 million volumes, 5.1 million microform items, and 23,740 periodicals. A computerized catalog as well as numerous CD-ROM database searches facilitates use of the extensive holdings, although some undergraduates still find the research process a bit overwhelming. The stacks, which students say were neglected for many years, have been updated. Suitable spaces to study can be found in the many smaller branches, as well as throughout the 7 floors, 2 above ground, 5 below, in Cooper Library. However, some students find the subterranean levels not conducive to studying because of the absence of windows.

Public and departmental labs housing hundreds of computers are located across campus and generally close before midnight (dorm labs are open around the clock), although students complain that individual lab times, as well as the quality of units offered, vary widely. All residence-hall rooms are connected to the campus network. The university strongly recommends that students have their own personal computers, and many do. Adds a senior: "The campus is slowly going wireless for laptop users."

Special programs: Off-campus study is available in almost any country that a student desires to see, as well as at about 100 public universities and colleges throughout the United States.

Campus life: Forty percent of all undergraduates live on the 372-acre campus in the heart of Columbia. The historic Horseshoe, much revered by students, contains buildings that date from before the Civil War, which were saved from fire by federal troops. (The campus closed during the war when all students joined the Army of the Confederacy and the buildings were used by the Confederate government as a hospital.) Depending on whether it is a fall football weekend or a Saturday in spring, when most everyone heads to the beach, the grounds range from overflowing with people to fairly deserted. About 15% of the men and women are members of 18 national fraternities and 14 national sororities. A few years ago, the university united its traditionally white and black sororities into a single Greek system that remains a popular social force on campus, "hugely popular," says a male sophomore. Five Points, a district filled with more than 15 bars and nightclubs one-half mile from campus, is popular with Greeks and independents alike. Traditions like Homecoming, the University Tree Lighting, and Greek Week are sacred on this very southern campus and reverently passed on from class to class. Moreover, whether women of the 21st century approve or not, says a female state resident, "the tradition still exists here of the helpless southern belle. There is pressure—we are in the deep South—to date someone steadily." Three hundred student organizations, ranging from the College Republicans to Carolina for Kids, a mentoring and tutoring program, suit a variety of interests. An increase in incidents of crime a few years ago, especially thefts of bicycles and other personal property, led to enhanced security measures. Call boxes and better lighting were installed throughout campus, and an escort service and more foot, bicycle, and vehicle patrols were added.

Gamecock football games played on Saturday afternoons in a stadium seating more than 80,000 screaming fans, and the extensive pre-game tailgating, billed as the biggest party in the state, mark most Carolina weekends in the fall. "We are a football school," confirms a senior. The 9 intercollegiate sports for men and 11 for women compete in the Southeastern Conference of NCAA Division I. Thirty-five percent of the men but only 20% of the women participate in 29 intramural sports open to each sex, as well as in varied club sports, which range from the familiar, such as rugby and lacrosse, to the exotic, say, sport parachuting and windsurfing.

The beaches and mountains provide 2 of the most popular getaways, as does that old standby for those who live near the campus, home.

Cost cutters: Ninety-five percent of the university freshmen and 83% of the continuing students received financial assistance of some sort in the 2005–2006 school year. For 36% of the first-year students and 42% of the rest, the aid was need-based. The average freshman award included a need-based scholarship or grant averaging $6834; no figure is available for the amount that was self-help aid such as loans or job earnings. Average debts for a 2005 grad totaled $18,699. The university offers more than 1000 scholarships each year to entering freshmen. To be considered, students must have applied for admission by November 1 and completed and returned the scholarship application by November 30. The most prestigious merit-based awards are those for Carolina Scholars, 20 in-state students who receive $7000 annually, and for McNair Scholars, 20 out-of-staters who receive stipends of $12,000 a year. Typical candidates have SAT math and critical reading scores above 1300 and impressive high school class ranks. Thirty in-state finalists receive $4000 a year. Twenty out-of-state finalists receive $8000 a year. Coopers Scholars (for non-residents), Alumni, and Trustees Endowment scholarships pay $4000, $3500, and $3000, respectively to students with equally high test scores and class rank. A wide range of athletic scholarships also are given. A deferred-payment plan is available, and cooperative programs are offered in numerous majors.

Rate of return: Eighty-three percent of freshmen return for the sophomore year. Forty percent graduate in 4 years; 59%, in 5 years; 65%, in 6 years.

Payoff: Business administration was the major of choice for 8% of the 2005 graduates, with public relations and experimental psychology each claiming 7% of the degrees awarded. Three-fourths of the graduates take jobs immediately, most remaining in South Carolina with such firms as du Pont and NCR and with the U.S. government. More than 400 companies and other organizations recruited on campus in a recent school year.

Bottom line: The University of South Carolina offers a large but fairly relaxed campus for those who are prepared to become involved in order to avoid feeling isolated and who enjoy campus traditions—and football. Notes a state resident: "If you get chills when you hear the theme from *2001* played at a football game, you belong at the University of South Carolina. If you don't, you'll be happier at Clemson."

Winthrop University

Rock Hill, South Carolina 29733

Setting: Small city
Control: Public
Undergraduate enrollment: 1426 men, 3191 women
Graduate enrollment: 122 men, 205 women (907 part-time)
Student/faculty ratio: 15:1
Freshman profile: 3% scored over 699 on SAT I verbal; 18% scored 600–700; 47% 500–599; 32% below 500. 2% scored over 700 on SAT I math; 20% scored 600–699; 44% 500–599; 34% below 500. 0% scored above 29 on the ACT; 14% scored 24–29; 77% 18–23; 9% below 18. 21% graduated in top tenth of high school class; 56% in upper fourth.

Faculty profile: 82% Ph.D.'s
Tuition and fees: $8756 in-state; $16,150 out-of-state
Room and board: $5352
Freshman financial aid: 78%; average scholarship or grant: $6343 need-based; $4838 non-need-based
Campus jobs: NA; average earnings: NA
Application deadline: Mar. 1 (priority date)
Financial aid deadline: May 1
Admissions information: (803) 323-2191; (800) 763-0230
e-mail: admissions@winthrop.edu
web site: www.winthrop.edu

At Winthrop University, one of the most discussed books around campus isn't a *New York Times* best-seller or even a required text for English or history. It's a small, paper-bound document of about 20 pages, entitled *Vision of Distinction*, that outlines Winthrop's goals for the current school year. Unlike most university blueprints, which are inches thick and usually rest untouched on various administrators' shelves, this handy booklet is meant to be carried around, discussed, and acted upon. Specific goals outlined for completion by the end of one recent school year ranged from improving academic programs to increasing the scholastic abilities and racial composition of the student body. In an 8-year period, Winthrop raised the SATs of its entering freshmen by more than 134 points and increased the level of minority enrollment in its freshman classes to between 20% and 26%, among the highest of any 4-year college or university in the Carolinas that is not historically black. As its 120-year climb from teachers college to university demonstrates, Winthrop is a school determined not to stay in one place; and wherever it goes in the next 100 years, it is determined to take a diverse, academically excellent student body with it.

Student body: All but 13% of Winthrop's students are from South Carolina. The rest are mostly other southerners, but came in a recent year also from 40 additional states and 33 foreign countries. As a result of the steady increase in minority enrollment and retention in successive first-year classes, African-American students now constitute 27% of the undergraduate enrollment, and foreign nationals 2%, with Asian-Americans and Hispanics each accounting for 1% and Native Americans, less than 0.5%. Winthrop students, by and large, are proud of who they are and what kind of people they are becoming. Adjectives frequently used to describe classmates are *well-rounded, energetic*, increasingly politically and socially *aware*, and fairly *laid back* where academics are concerned. Says a senior: "About everyone seems to be somewhat concerned about academics, but don't kill themselves over it." Observes a sophomore: "Winthrop consists of students who dive into the college experience wanting to get involved and make the most of their time here." Still, some of the most committed students worry that a majority of students do not take full advantage of the opportunities for leadership and involvement on campus and display an "apathetic attitude," in the words of a senior.

Academics: Winthrop, which celebrated its 120th birthday in 2006, awards 37 undergraduate degrees in more than 100 fields of study, plus master's and specialist's degrees. The calendar is divided by semesters. Average class size in the first 2 years ranges from 10 to 33 people, although some introductory lectures have exceeded 40. (No class is over 100.) Most courses for juniors and seniors have 20–25 participants.

Freshmen entering in fall 2003 were the first to take courses included in a new general education curriculum known as the foundational program. The emphasis is on approaching coursework through analytical perspectives, often interdisciplinary in nature. High points are required courses in The Human Experience and in Critical Reading, Thinking and Writing. As part of a course titled Academy 101, students prepare for their entry to campus by sharing a common reading; in the 2005–2006 school year; the book was *Hope in the Unseen* by Cedric Jennings, who visited campus as part of the program. The foundational course of study also includes courses in the social sciences, humanities and arts, natural science, intensive writing, and a constitution requirement. In addition, undergraduates are expected to attend 18 cultural events. Says a senior: "With approximately 150 events each semester, it's not hard to get 18 in 4 years."

Winthrop's faculty recently numbered 255 full-time members and 230 part-time; no data is provided to show the number that teach at the graduate level only, although in recent years all but a small number of both groups have taught undergraduates. Nearly half, 46%, of the full-time faculty are women. Because most classes are small, faculty are able to know a majority of their students individually and are generally helpful to them, "from the freshman who feels lost to the senior who needs yet another recommendation written for a graduate school application!" says a fourth-year history major. There also are few passive lecture courses, as this elementary education major notes: "Professors instruct students in how to teach themselves, and they challenge them to learn and to investigate their own interests. They encourage students to find out *why*, not just memorize facts." However few, adds a senior, there still are professors who "walk in and lecture for an hour and then walk out."

Programs in early childhood, elementary, and other areas of education in the bedrock Richard W. Riley College of Education, which is named for the former state governor and U.S. Secretary of Education under President Clinton, feature up-to-date facilities such as a sophisticated computer lab with the latest instructional and presentation software. The technology complements an innovative team-taught curriculum and extensive field experience. Adds a senior confidently: "Superintendents will put my application at the top of the hiring list." The College of Business Administration draws bright, competitive students who are seeking a nationally accredited in-state program but do not want the large campus of the University of South Carolina or Clemson. The College of Visual and Performing Arts also features attentive faculties and recently renovated facilities, including computerized labs for music composition, interior and graphic design, and theater and dance studios. Art students can apply their skills at area businesses or right on campus! Each spring, art and design students are encouraged to use the campus' lawns as exhibition space for sculpture and 3-dimensional work. In the College of Arts and Sciences, psychology, history, social work, political science, mass communication, and English are the clear-cut winners. The sciences combine excellent faculty members with 1 new life sciences building and 1 completely renovated structure. A recent grant from the National Institutes of Health is helping to create more opportunities for undergraduates to engage in research in the biomedical sciences.

Undergraduates say that many of Winthrop's weaker departments are those that the university hasn't yet had a chance to improve. Some members of the mathematics faculty, they note, need to be as good teachers and explainers as they are mathematicians.

Facilities: Students accustomed to studying at Ida Jane Dacus Library follow the proper protocol when they enter, going to certain floors and areas when they want to study aloud with others and to different hideaways when they expect total silence. Undergraduates needing research assistance simply ask, "What's up, DOC?"—short for the Dacus On-line Catalog, which helps users uncover what is up in the collection of 560,000 volumes or volume equivalents, 1.2 million microfilms, and 1446 periodicals. Students complain of too many dated resources and too limited hours, with closing at 11 p.m. or midnight depending on how far into the semester it is. "It should be 24 hours or at least remain open until 2 a.m." says a senior. South Carolina's electronic library program PASCAL that links all of the state's university libraries plus more than 100 databases provide further assistance to students.

About 300 PCs and workstations, all of them networked, are available in more than 20 labs for student use. The main computer lab is open most nights until 1 a.m. Students who wish to work late in any computer lab in an academic building have only to have their professor turn their name into Campus Police for admittance, though again, some students think it just might be easier to have at least 1 main 24-hour lab on campus. The university has pledged that no computer older than 3 years old will be in an academic computer center. For those students who bring their own units, all residence hall rooms have 2 computer outlets allowing for free access to the Internet. Wireless access is available in the library plus numerous other hotspots across campus.

Special programs: Study abroad is offered in countries from Argentina to Vietnam. Undergraduates also may study at any of 184 colleges and universities across the country through the National Student Exchange. On campus, a 6-week Emerging Leaders program targets new students to take on leadership positions around campus. A 9-week Leadership Winthrop program offers sessions on topics ranging from Cultural Diversity to Values, Ethics, and Service Learning.

Campus life: First- and second-year students who are not residing with parents within 50 miles of the university must live on the 425-acre campus, located 23 miles south of Charlotte, North Carolina. To enhance student's sense of community, a new program allows first-year students to live together on floors according to their shared personal or academic interests. Many students from out of the area hope this will help students to bond more and opt to stay on campus once the weekend arrives. Already, more and more undergraduates are staying around for attractive concerts, comedians, or other activities provided by the hard-working Dinkins Student Union programming board. The group's efforts have been recognized and not just in increased student attendance at campus events! The National Association of Campus Activities has named the programming board the best such board in the country 3 times in recent years. Greeks are a vital, but not overwhelming, part of the student body, constituting about 12% of the men, 14% of the women, and many of its leaders. A majority of the Greek events, sponsored by the 8 national fraternities and 9 national sororities, are open to the general student body. The Association of Ebonites, which represents the interests of minority students and offers 2 much-loved dance groups and a gospel choir, is among the more active of the 140 student organizations. Groups such as Fellowship of Christian Athletes, various academic clubs and a new organization named SOAR, which stands for Serving Others and Reflecting, also attract plenty of student interest. "Our students are always visible in the community," notes a senior. "From day cares to nursing homes to art museums downtown, Winthrop students can be found volunteering all over the place." A residence advisor monitors traffic in and out of the residence halls between midnight and 7 a.m. Petty theft and bike theft are an occasional problem, though students generally feel quite safe. A recent increase in car break-ins has produced an increase in surveillance by campus police. Notes a senior: "The police put 'gotcha' tickets on cars that have valuables in easy view or unlocked doors to help students realize what will make their cars a target for thieves."

The university fields 8 men's and 9 women's teams in NCAA Division I. Five teams, men's basketball, tennis, and baseball, and women's tennis and volleyball captured a record number of Big South tournament crowns as well as trips to NCAA post-season play in recent seasons. Some fans say that school spirit, and weekend activity, might improve even more if the university had a football team. However, counters a junior, "having the Carolina Panthers (professional football team) so close (20 minutes away in Charlotte, N.C.) makes up for not having our own football team." A recreational sports program of more than 30 same-sex and coed activities draws higher levels of participation—50% of the men and 35% of the women. Winthrop's 325-acre recreational sports complex includes a world class disc golf course, which is a regular site of both the Professional World and U.S. Golf championships.

To get away from Rock Hill (pop. 50,000), students usually head north across the state border into Charlotte. Columbia, South Carolina, is about 45 minutes south; the Atlantic Ocean, 3 hours east; the Blue Ridge Mountains, 2½ hours northwest.

Cost cutters: Seventy-eight percent of the freshmen and 68% of continuing students received financial help in a recent school year. Sixty percent of the first-year students and 55% of the others were given aid based on need. The average financial award for first-year students with need included a need-based scholarship or grant of $6343 and need-based self-help aid of $3044. Non-need-based merit aid for first-year students averaged $4838; non-need-based athletic scholarships averaged $5230. Average debt among those who borrowed was $17,800. Though some scholarships are restricted to state residents, nonresidents who are awarded a scholarship are charged tuition at in-state rates. A wide range of academic scholarships that pay from $500 to full tuition, room, and board are typically awarded to students with high school GPAs of 3.5 and standardized test scores of at least 1200 on the SAT math and critical reading sections or 27 on the ACT composite. Various talent awards in art, dance, music, theater, and interior design paying up to $2500 in some fields also are available. Parents who prefer may pay a $30 application fee per semester to make 4 tuition payments a term.

Rate of return: Seventy-six percent of the freshmen who enter return for a second year. Thirty-two percent graduate in 4 years; 51% earn bachelor's degrees in 5 years; 56% in 6 years.

Payoff: Twenty-three percent of recent graduates earned bachelor's degrees in business and marketing, 19% in education, and 13% in visual and performing arts. Seventy-four percent of recent alumni found employment related to their academic majors, primarily in corporations and schools throughout the Southeast. Eighty-three percent were employed within 3 months of graduation; 93% within 6 months. Nearly 50 companies, school districts, and other organizations recruited on campus in a recent school year. A growing number of students, a third in a recent year, are deferring job plans and seeking advanced degrees, most of them in business or the arts and sciences.

Bottom line: Add Winthrop's name to those traditionally regional former teachers colleges, now universities, that are expanding their diversity and raising the quality of both their students and their academic programs. Robert Winthrop, the Boston philanthropist who supported the college in its early years, never actually visited the campus named in his honor. The university hopes that bright students across the nation won't be guilty of the same omission. "Come visit," advises a junior, "but you may not want to leave."

Wofford College

Spartanburg, South Carolina 29303

Setting: Small city
Control: Private (United Methodist)
Undergraduate enrollment: 603 men, 555 women
Graduate enrollment: None
Student/faculty ratio: 12:1
Freshman profile: 9% scored over 700 on SAT I verbal; 43% scored 600–700; 43% 500–599; 5% below 500. 11% scored over 700 on SAT I math; 49% scored 600–700; 35% 500–599; 5% below 500. 17% scored above 28 on the ACT; 12% scored 27–28; 33% 24–26; 23% 21–23; 15% below 21. 57% graduated in top tenth of high school class; 78% in upper fifth.

Faculty profile: 92% Ph.D.'s
Tuition and fees: $24,130
Room and board: $6805
Freshman financial aid: 92%; average scholarship or grant: NA
Campus jobs: 26%; average earnings: $1230/year
Application deadline: Early decision: Nov. 15; regular: Dec. 1 and Feb. 1
Financial aid deadline: Mar. 15
Admissions information: (864) 597-4130
  e-mail: admissions@ wofford.edu
  web site: www.wofford.edu

At Wofford College in the mid-sized city of Spartanburg, South Carolina, you'll see students studying in the library, cramming in their rooms, or reviewing their notes while tanning by the baseball diamond. But if you look closely enough, you'll also see a number of them filing past the historic Main Building and rubbing the misspelled word *benificent* on a plaque there, a gesture that for generations has supposedly guaranteed impeccable work on papers and exams. It may be just another example of the "Wofford way," as students call it, but this way has become synonymous with an impeccable academic reputation in the Southeast and a growing recognition of that high standard in other parts of the country. As a bumper sticker pronounces: "There's a right way, there's a wrong way, and there's a Wofford way," and, as a satisfied senior puts it, "The possibilities are up to you!"

Student body: Wofford's student body is becoming less parochial. While 64% of the students still hail from South Carolina, 47% of the 2005 freshman class came from out of state, a number from outside the region. A total of 29 states and 8 foreign countries are represented on campus. The student body is also becoming somewhat more diverse: included are 6% African-Americans, 2% Asian-Americans, and 1% Hispanics. Eight students are foreign nationals. Almost a fourth of the students are Methodist, with 47% members of other mainline Protestant denominations. A third attended private or parochial high schools.

Students use words like *conservative, ambitious, intelligent, energetic,* and *well-dressed* to describe themselves. Says a senior: "Though it's easier to make friends when you're sporting khakis and a starched shirt, there are opportunities for all to find social acceptance and friendship." Adds a female classmate: "Students are primarily Republican, and they will express their opinions. Those who are not Republican voice their opinions as well but are mostly kidded about it." Still, undergraduates speak of a special bond shared by the entire Wofford community, a feeling of pride in the college's history and traditions—plaque rubbing and all. The academic environment is challenging, although not cutthroat. Says a senior: "Students are always talking about what they made on a test or what their GPA is among each other. Students who attend Wofford are people who seek perfection and who genuinely want to make good grades, so the academic atmosphere is very competitive."

Academics: Wofford was established in 1854 by the Methodist Church and named for minister and businessman Benjamin Wofford, who gave the college its first $100,000. A century and a half later, the college awards the bachelor's degree in 25 majors. Students take courses divided into 2 semesters, with a January term in the middle. Most classes have about 20 undergraduates. In a recent year, 67 sections had fewer than 10 enrolled. Biology classes probably enroll the most students; the largest is Introductory Animal Biology, which can have 125 in its team-taught lectures, but much smaller labs. Most upper-division courses, as well as the college's highly respected freshman humanities seminars, generally have between 10 and 15.

The humanities seminars are the most noteworthy part of the college's rigorous but otherwise fairly standard core curriculum. As part of the program, the freshman class is broken into small study groups of 16–18 students that emphasize reading and discussion about values questions and issues, as well as writing skills. Four of the humanities seminars in fall 2005 were linked to science courses, for example Theater Physics and Psychology and the Bible. A career workshop also is required.

Eighty-nine of Wofford's 122 faculty members are full-time; 35% are women. The professors—"awesome," according to an accounting major—are what make the college's academic offerings strong. Explains a biology major: "Being a small, private school, Wofford has not been able to afford 'top-of-the-line' equipment, but our faculty make up for it. They are well informed, concerned about students, and enthusiastic about teaching." Their relationship with students encompasses everything from running extra study or makeup sessions to Thursday night bowling with a class. Adds a senior: "They voluntarily serve as mentors to students who are not even in their academic departments and are ever present at campus events and lectures as well as athletic competitions."

Biology and chemistry are sought out by bright and ambitious students for their reputation of sending all but a small percent of their premed graduates to the medical schools of their choice. The opening in January 2001 of a new 61,000 square foot science building, plus renovations to the existing structure next door, have only enhanced students' success rates in these fields. Wofford's exceptional offerings also include English, accounting, finance, business economics, history, religion, philosophy, government, and foreign languages, again thanks largely to experienced and energetic faculties who demand much work from their students. "The English and history departments," observes an English major, "have knowledgeable professors...who are willing to listen and discuss interpretations other than their own." In a recent year, 11 English students wrote novels; 1 was published. In fact, every year, the best novel written by a Wofford undergraduate is given a limited edition printing of 2000 copies. Since 1995, more than 40 students have written novels. "History," says a major, "is phenomenal . . . The small number of majors and the faculty camaraderie afford the students a very personal experience." The foreign language program, with majors in French, German, and Spanish, expects its students to study abroad and incorporates advanced technology throughout its curriculum.

Among Wofford's weaker programs is art history, which, while offered as a major, is shared with Converse College, a women's college located 1½ miles away. Students say that while the existing faculty is excellent, the program lacks sufficient classes and professors. No majors are offered in music and studio art, though a major in theater recently was added. Students wish all the fine arts disciplines, major or not, would gain more resources to provide a wider variety of courses. The teacher education program has a reputation around campus for being an easy "GPA booster." It provides certification for teachers at the secondary level only.

Facilities: Sandor Teszler Library holds more than 197,000 volumes and 4489 paper and electronic periodicals. Renovations have made it a pleasant place to study, with individual study rooms on the first floor and sufficient carrels scattered throughout. "During exams," observes a senior, "students actually spend the night in the library." A computerized catalog, on-line database search capability, and helpful librarians allay student gripes about searching for sources. Wofford and the library at Furman University also share access to a common database that provides full text of some 1100 scholarly journals and indexes about 2200 more. Many students enjoy studying in Great Oaks Hall in the new science building; the hall seats 200 and offers outlets for laptop computers at every table.

Completed early in 1992, and garnering superlatives from students ever since, the Franklin W. Olin Building houses the departments of mathematics, computer science, and foreign languages; language labs; and a computer center that quickly became the hub of a campus technology network. The Olin building offers 3 rooms that house about 25 computers each. Additional units also are located in the library. Labs generally are open until midnight, later during midterms and finals. About half of Wofford students bring their own computers from home to tie into the campus network. The college strongly recommends that students bring their own computers to school, preferably PCs/Windows. There also are several wireless Internet locations around campus "and laptops abound," says a history major.

Special programs: Every year, Wofford's president selects a Presidential International Scholar to undertake a year-long, all-expenses-paid trip through developing nations to study a specific problem with global importance. Other students can spend their junior year abroad in over 30 countries, mainly through the Council on International Education Exchange. Each semester, an average of 10 Wofford students study in Europe. Year-long and summer programs also are possible. Domestic joint programs are available in engineering with Clemson and Columbia universities. Limited cross enrollment is offered with Converse College and the University of South Carolina, Spartanburg. A Washington semester also is available.

Campus life: All but 10% of the full-time undergraduates reside on the campus, a 150-acre academic island in downtown Spartanburg. Says a sophomore: "Wofford is the epitome of a Southern campus. The huge front lawn, shaded by great oaks, is the perfect place to catch a nap, read a book, or chat with a friend or professor." Fifty-one percent of the men and 59% of the women are members of 8 national fraternities and 4 national sororities, including 2 African-American fraternities and 1 African-American sorority. On weekends, people head down to the "row," the fraternities clustered in a central court on campus. Some independents find too much emphasis is placed on partying at the "row." Notes a senior: "Greek life and social life go hand in hand." Membership in the drama fraternity, Glee Club, or Fellowship of Christian Athletes has traditionally been considered a "big deal" at Wofford; involvement in the Twin Towers volunteer service organization is popular as well. Crime is not considered a major problem on campus, although students use caution walking in the surrounding area. To calm nighttime fears, lights and emergency call boxes have been added around the verdant grounds and the women's dorms are kept locked at all hours. Campus escorts also are available, as is a free "Wofford whistle" to any female student who desires one. Security patrols in the outer parking lots have been increased to combat car break-ins.

Despite Wofford's comparatively small size, its Terriers varsity teams play in NCAA Division I, with football (played in I-AA), men's and women's basketball, and soccer the most popular sports of the 10 men's and 9 women's teams fielded. Wofford also hosts the summer training camp for the Carolina Panthers of the National Football League. An active intramural program attracts 60% of the men to 7 sports offered, and 40% of the women to 7 as well.

Students claim that Wofford's location is within easy reach of the beach, mountains, city—whatever kind of escape an individual needs. In fair weather, Milliken Plant's pond, about 3 miles away, is a popular hangout. Spartanburg (pop. 44,000) is less than ½ hour away from Greenville (pop. 58,000); an hour, max, from The Rock—the mountains around Asheville, North Carolina; and less than 3 hours from the much bigger cities of Charlotte and Atlanta.

Cost cutters: Since 1974, the Annual Fund of donations from alumni, United Methodist churches, and friends has more than doubled, enabling the college to shave off more than $8000 in recent years from each student's tuition rate. In the 2005–2006 school year, 92% of all first-year students and 85% of the rest received financial aid of some sort. For 48% of the freshmen and 51% of the others, the aid was need-based. The average financial aid package included a need-based scholarship or grant averaging $6957 and need-based self-help aid such as loans and job earnings averaging $1882. Non-need-based athletic scholarships for first-year students averaged $17,311; other non-need-based awards and scholarships averaged $13,782. Average debts of a 2005 graduate totaled $14,444. The Wofford Scholars program recently paid $1000 up to full comprehensive fees annually to the best new students. Wofford Academic Scholarships are awarded both on the basis of merit and on merit and need and recently ranged from $1000 to $12,000 a year; not all are renewable. Student activity scholarships were recently worth up to $2000 annually. Other awards go to premed students, science students, and high achievers in other arenas.

Work opportunities in the Spartanburg area are generally good, in part because the many Wofford alumni who live and work in the area are eager to hire students from their alma mater, and in part because the school makes vigorous efforts to find employment for undergraduates. Many students also pick up extra money working as campus tutors. Cooperative education programs can be arranged on an individual basis.

Rate of return: Eighty-nine percent of Wofford freshmen return for the sophomore year. Seventy-four percent graduate in 4 years; 77%, in 5 years; 78% in 6.

Payoff: In the 2005 graduating class, 18% of the students earned degrees in biology, followed by 16% in business economics and 11% in government. More than 60% enter the job market immediately after graduation, the largest number in retailing, followed by banking, manufacturing, teaching/administration, and military service. Most students accept positions in the Carolinas or Georgia. Just over a third go on immediately to graduate or professional schools. In a recent count of the college's nearly 14,500 living alumni, about 700 were physicians, pharmacists, dentists, and veterinarians; 680 were lawyers or judges recently including 3 of the 5 justices of the Supreme Court of South Carolina; and about 1400 were presidents or owners of corporations or other organizations. Wofford alumni also included 5 Rhodes Scholars, 5 Truman Scholars, 2 Goldwater Scholars, and 12 Woodrow Wilson Fellows.

Bottom line: Students see the Wofford name beginning to be recognized outside the Southeast, but realize that the degree's highest value still lies in professional school admittance and the regional job market. Notes a recent graduate: "There are unity and pride among alumni and students of Wofford. The Wofford network is an excellent means of getting a job after college in the Carolinas."

South Dakota

South Dakota School of Mines and Technology

Rapid City, South Dakota 57701

Setting: Suburban
Control: Public
Undergraduate enrollment: 1202 men, 390 women
Graduate enrollment: 109 men, 35 women
Student/faculty ratio: 15:1
Freshman profile: Median SAT I scores: 555 verbal; 555 math. 11% scored above 28 on the ACT: 14% scored 27–28; 26% 24–26; 29% 21–23; 20% below 21. 35% graduated in top fifth of high school class; 62% in upper two-fifths.
Faculty profile: 85% Ph.D.'s

Tuition and fees: $4757 in-state; $9744 out-of-state
Room and board: $3903
Freshman financial aid: 75%; average scholarship or grant: $3093 need-based; $2537 non-need-based
Campus jobs: 23%; average earnings: $1500/year
Application deadline: Aug. 15
Financial aid deadline: Mar. 15 (Scholarships: Feb. 1)
Admissions information: (605) 394-2414
(800) 544-8162
e-mail: admissions@sdsmt.edu
web site: www.sdsmt.edu

The Badlands are due east; the Black Hills, directly west, with Mount Rushmore 25 miles to the southwest. To the northwest lies Deadwood, a town reminiscent of the Old West and notorious today for its gambling and the cemetery where Wild Bill Hickok and Calamity Jane are buried. In the center of all this raw, wild country is Rapid City (pop. 60,000), the state's second largest community after Sioux Falls and home to the Hardrockers, Master Chorale, Greeks, and dorm rats of the South Dakota School of Mines and Technology. As a school that has been training mining engineers since 4 years before South Dakota became a state, Tech, as it is called, has expanded its offerings to encompass 10 different kinds of engineering as well as majors in math, science, and related disciplines. But the resident and the out-of-stater alike pay a total price including room and board that hits the mark as surely as any shot Wild Bill ever made: just under $9000 for South Dakotans, and just over $13,500 for everybody else. English majors and historians will find little at Tech for them, but those whose interests lie buried in the earth may consider the offerings at the South Dakota School of Mines and Technology just about the richest ore around.

Student body: Sixty-nine percent of Tech's undergraduates are from the Coyote State; nonresidents come mainly from the Midwest. In all, 34 states and 12 foreign countries are represented. International students account for 1% of the enrollment with the largest number from Norway in a recent year. Native Americans constitute 3%, and Asian-Americans, Hispanics, and African-Americans, 1% each. Initiatives to convince more Native American youths to study math and science have steadily increased their numbers at Tech. Tech undergraduates see their membership split 3 ways: about one-third commuters, many of them older than traditional college age, who live in the surrounding area; one-third active members and participating nonmembers of the school's Greek system, who also serve as leaders of several organizations; and one-third "dorm rats," highly focused, stereotypical engineering students who stay in their rooms and study or play computer games for what seems like all of the time. Says a midwesterner: "It is easy for someone who is outgoing to be a leader here and excel in several student organizations." Some common traits link the 3 groups: all are politically conservative (many from small towns), smart, and hardworking. The undergraduates, says a state resident, are "willing to work hard and work together with other students. The courses here are demanding and it takes a lot of time as well as collaboration with classmates to succeed in them." Says another South Dakotan: "Intelligence helps, but persistence pays off."

Academics: South Dakota Tech, which turned 120 in 2005, awards the bachelor's in 16 fields as well as the master's degree in 12 disciplines and a doctorate in 4. The school follows a semester calendar. Though a chemistry lecture may top 175 members, most freshman classes enroll between 30 and 50. Courses for juniors and seniors usually have 10–30. Students say, however, that individual class sizes rise and fall with the job market. Observes a senior: "Whichever field is currently paying the highest average salary gets the most incoming freshmen."

Undergraduates in every major find a curriculum that gives them little freedom to choose their courses, between requirements for general education and those for the individual concentration. Regardless of major, every student takes classes in composition, technical communications, information technology, mathematics, natural science, social science including courses in cultural diversity, and the arts and humanities. Each major also has its own very detailed outline of the classes a student needs to take during certain semesters of the upper-class years, leaving little time for electives.

Thirty-three of the 140 faculty members are part-time; 80% are men. Four percent of the introductory classes, many in the math department, are taught by graduate students whom students rate as "average." Faculty encompass many levels of ability and approaches. "Some," says a northeasterner, "want to make this college very difficult and are concerned with weeding out people." Others possess the knowledge but have a difficult time expressing it clearly. A majority, however, are friendly and dynamic in their teaching and take time to meet with students outside of class, provide them with references, and assist in job searches.

Most of Tech's engineering offerings are considered its strong suits, including chemical, mechanical, electrical, and materials and metallurgical engineering, which feature strong faculties and students, labs and curricula. The programs in physics and mathematics also are well structured and very demanding, requiring a lot of work in addition to that assigned in the textbook. Though some undergraduates find the curriculum in civil engineering to be less demanding, its student body is one of the most active and is credited with having constructed several award-winning concrete canoes, placing first in the 1995 National Concrete Canoe Competition in Washington, D.C., and fifth in 1999 and 2001.

The programs in mining engineering and geology are smaller and more limited in the courses they can offer in the classroom, though opportunities for work in the natural laboratories of the Black Hills and the Badlands are endless. The geology department, in particular, uses its small size to advantage. Says a delighted major: "Departmental field trips, picnics, and parties offer a great chance to get to know everyone—graduate students and professors. As a geology major, I have found an incredibly close and caring department." The mining program which has suffered from declining student interest in the field and not from inadequate professors or weak curricula recently expanded its focus to become more up to date. The traditional mining engineering major became a major in mining engineering and management, incorporating more management-related concepts into the regular mining engineering curriculum. Industrial engineering needs more professors and greater rigor, according to majors in other fields of engineering. A newer major in interdisciplinary sciences has found it difficult to command the same respect among students as other professional majors.

Facilities: Though the collection at Henry Devereaux Library is modest, just over 365,000 volumes and 516 periodicals, it is well equipped with material for scientists and engineers; in most other areas, however, it is lacking. The computerized catalog lists books and magazines in Devereaux, as well as in other libraries throughout South Dakota and other Plains states. Access to hundreds of on-line databases also is available, although students complain that locally some issues of periodicals have been either stolen or misplaced. "Devereaux is a good place to study," observes a civil engineering major, "if you like total silence; otherwise it's a good place to sleep." A number of soundproof rooms may be reserved by students who need to work together.

Approximately 160 computers are open for student use in diverse locations, at least 2 of which are accessible around the clock. However, some days, undergraduates may have to search a variety of buildings to find a free unit, and even then waits of up to an hour are common at certain busy times. An additional 50 Internet kiosks around campus have helped to reduce the waits somewhat. Wireless accessibility also is available in a number of locations.

Special programs: Students may study in Freiberg, Germany, while paying the same tuition rate as at Tech. Opportunities for real-world experiences are available in every major.

Campus life: Thirty-two percent of the undergraduates reside on the 120-acre campus located on the edge of the beautiful Black Hills—a source, says a state resident, of "awesome scenery and peacefulness" for many a weary student. Just over a fifth of the men and women belong to 4 national fraternities and 2 national sororities. Greek theme parties are especially popular with members, as well as nonmembers who care to attend. "Don't let the word 'engineering' fool you," says a New Englander. "Other schools in the state think we party too much and don't work hard enough." In addition to Greek festivities, most weekends are well stocked with comedians, hypnotists, musicians, and motivational speakers. However, there are Tech undergraduates who rarely deviate from a routine of either commuting back and forth from home or staying holed up studying in their rooms. Popular clubs generally are related to the academic majors, unless, of course, it is the Master Chorale, who sang at the dedication of the National Cathedral in

Washington, D.C., and recently completed a tour of Austria. Traditions related to M-Week, or homecoming, begin with having freshmen wear green beanies and end with the preparation and placement of a senior plaque on the newly whitewashed "M" on M-Hill. Security doors on the dormitories, with an extra set on each floor of the women's residence halls, help to discourage prospective thieves from entering. Notes a local resident: "People may steal from the library or the snack bar occasionally, but for the most part students feel safe here."

Hardrockers football and basketball draw the most fans of the 5 men's and 5 women's intercollegiate sports, played in NAIA competition. Some of the greatest school spirit displays itself among athletes on the floor or field, unless the school is playing rival Black Hills State University when the stands become as boisterous as anywhere. Fifteen intramural sports for men and 15 for women also are there for those who enjoy being especially active. Perennial favorites for the outdoor set include camping, hiking, fishing, hunting, rock climbing, and skiing and snowboarding nearby in the Black Hills region.

Stage shows, plus a little gambling, in Deadwood, and trips to the haunting Badlands or majestic Mount Rushmore are easy off-campus diversions. The more ambitious, and city-starved, may head to Denver, 350 miles southwest.

Cost cutters: Fifty-six percent of the freshmen in the 2004–2005 school year, the most recent year for which data is available, received financial assistance. No figures are available to show the percentage of continuing students who were given aid. For 33% of the first-year students and 29% of the rest, the aid was need-based. The average freshman award for a student with need included a need-based scholarship or grant averaging $3520 and need-based self-help aid such as loans and jobs averaging $3383. A non-need-based athletic scholarship for first-year students averaged $2515. Other non-need-based awards and scholarships averaged $2465. The debts of a recent graduate averaged $15,475. Scholarship, grant, and prize money provided by the college, alumni, and area corporations for incoming and currently enrolled students recently totaled in excess of $330,000. The most prestigious award, the Distinguished Scholarship, recently paid a minimum of $7000 a year. Presidential Scholarships recently paid at least $1000 a year. One in 5 regular students usually receives some sort of scholarship recognition. A cooperative education program is offered in every major.

Rate of return: Seventy-three percent of the freshmen who enter return for a second year. Twelve percent go on to graduate in 4 years, 28% in 5 years, 40% in 6.

Payoff: Nearly 50% of the 2005 graduates earned bachelor's degrees in 3 disciplines: 22% in mechanical engineering, 13% in civil engineering, and 11% in interdisciplinary sciences. Nearly a fifth of the new alumni continue their education immediately. More than three-quarters enter the job market, many accepting offers with the 116 corporations and other organizations that recruited on campus in a recent school year. Frequent employers of South Dakota Tech graduates include Boeing, IBM, Dow, Shell, Rockwell, Exxon, and Cargill.

Bottom line: Depth in a few key engineering or science-related fields, rather than breadth across the curriculum, is the strength of the South Dakota School of Mines and Technology, as it is at most technical schools. Here, however, there is also a setting amid some of the most inspiring scenery in the nation, as well as a price guaranteed to produce awe of its own. And even better, says a New Englander. "I know I'll get a good job when I get out."

Tennessee

Rhodes College

Memphis, Tennessee 38112

Setting: Urban
Control: Private (Presbyterian)
Undergraduate enrollment: 1705 men, 965 women
Graduate enrollment: 9 men, 7 women
Student/faculty ratio: 12:1
Freshman profile: 19% scored over 700 on SAT I verbal; 50% scored 600–700; 28% 500–599; 3% below 500. 19% scored over 700 on SAT I math; 50% scored 600–700; 27% 500–599; 4% below 500. 37% scored above 28 on the ACT; 23% scored 27–28; 31% 24–26; 9% 21–23, 0% below 21. 50% graduated in top tenth of high school class; 79% in upper fourth.
Faculty profile: 95% Ph.D.'s

Tuition and fees: $25,956
Room and board: $6904
Freshman financial aid: NA; average scholarship or grant: NA
Campus jobs: NA; average earnings: NA
Application deadline: Early decision I: Nov. 1; Early decision II: Jan. 1; regular: Feb. 1
Financial aid deadline: Mar. 1 (Scholarships: Jan. 15)
Admissions information: (901) 843-3700;
(800) 844-5969
e-mail: adminfo@rhodes.edu
web site: www.rhodes.edu

If you're going to have a college president who serves the campus with distinction for nearly 60 years, it's good to have one with an education-connoting name like Rhodes, especially if you decide to rename the college after him. In 1984, the college known then as Southwestern At Memphis, formerly Southwestern Presbyterian University, once Stewart College after another former president, and originally Montgomery Masonic College, decided to undergo yet another name change. This one would honor President Peyton Nalle Rhodes, who had served the college from his earliest days as a physics professor in 1926 through various positions until his death in 1984. The name couldn't have been a happier choice, immediately calling to mind the illustrious Oxford scholarships that the nation's brightest students compete for annually and that one Rhodes College political science major won in the 2003–2004 school year. And for many top-ranking students today, the name Rhodes also brings to mind an increasingly competitive small college in the south that is determined to provide a premier liberal arts education at a less than elite price.

Student body: Twenty-seven percent of these Rhodes scholars are from Tennessee. Nonresidents, although mostly also from the South, convene from 40 other states, as well as 8 foreign countries. Sixty percent attended public schools. Minority and multicultural enrollment has increased slightly over the years, recently standing at 9% with 5% African-Americans, 3% Asian-Americans, and 1% Hispanics. The foreign national population constitutes 3% of the total enrollment. Sixteen percent of the students are Presbyterian and 46% members of other Protestant denominations, with 14% Catholic, 2% Jewish, 4% other faiths, and the rest claiming no religious affiliation. Rhodes students are for the most part moderately conservative in their social and political views, but, adds a student from the deep South, "they're more liberal than where I'm from." The atmosphere is very grade conscious, with undergraduates quickly learning they have joined a pool of students as smart as they are. However, that realization doesn't stop most members from sharing notes or providing help to classmates, and it rarely keeps them from enjoying a good party or becoming heavily involved in a wide range of extracurricular activities. Says a Texan: "Rhodes has a very well-balanced set of students. We are all intelligent, fun-loving people." Adds a junior: "A good conversation isn't hard to come by."

Academics: Rhodes, which turns 160 in 2008, offers bachelor's degrees in 24 disciplines plus 8 interdisciplinary majors. The college also has a master's degree program in accounting. The academic year is divided into 2 semesters. Average class size for undergraduates is 17, with the largest, Botany, enrolling 70 students and dozens of classes yearly having fewer than 5.

Beginning with freshmen who enter in fall 2007, all students must take classes from 12 foundation areas, including 3 courses that examine questions of meaning and value and 2 courses in writing, in order to graduate. In addition, students must demonstrate intermediate proficiency in a second language and engage in 1 for-credit activity that broadens connections between the classroom and world.

Forty-three of the 184 faculty members are part-time; 41% are women. Most professors bring the benefit of varied life experiences to the classroom and are praised for the efforts they make to know students on an informal basis while continuing to demand the best from their charges. *Exceptional, outstanding, personable,* and *knowledgeable* are just some of the adjectives students use to describe them. Observes an economics major: "The professors are all really passionate about what they teach and study, which makes you want to work hard for them!"

International studies rates as one of the Rhodes gems, with an excellent faculty and opportunities for internships in such high-level organizations as the State Department and Central Intelligence Agency. As an added feature, the Mertie Buckman International Internship Program places international studies majors in paid internships abroad during the summer. Professors in economics and business administration, political science, English (especially Renaissance literature), psychology, French and religious studies also expose students to diversified viewpoints and challenging curricula. Says a junior: "The classroom discussions in my upper-level English courses are engaged, thought-provoking, and have left me contemplating a particular work or subject hours after the class has been over." The college's mock trial team, offered through the political science department, has won 4 national championships in the last decade. Says a political science major: "The professors are always well prepared for class and do not mind arguing with you after class until you make your point. No matter how crazy your idea, they treat it with respect." Typically, 100% of the applicants to business and law schools, many majoring in these stellar programs, are accepted. The sciences—biology, chemistry, and physics—offer undergraduates ready access to top-notch equipment, including 2 electron microscopes, a nuclear magnetic resonance machine for chemistry, and a cell culture lab frequently used by premed students. The exposure to demanding faculty and great equipment shows: Rhodes applicants have been accepted to medical school at more than twice the national average. The art program has few faculty and limited resources, though a major is offered with an emphasis in either studio art, or art history. The theater program also could use more support. The computer science offerings are limited as well.

Facilities: The new Paul Barret, Jr. Library, which opened in fall 2005, is literally the centerpiece of the college, located as it is right in the heart of the campus. The enormous 4-story structure, that covers 136,000 gross square feet and offers wireless Internet access throughout, is "amazing," in the words of one user, with furniture to match any style of studier, 20 collaborative study rooms, and a 24-hour cyber cafe. "It's large," agrees an English major, "and prestigious and decorated to the hilt, but it doesn't offer any more resources than we had previously." The collection stands at just over 278,000 volumes and 1683 periodical subscriptions, not counting full-text journals in assorted databases. Hard-working Rhodes students hope the next improvement will be later hours, (the library closes at midnight Sunday through Thursday and earlier the other days), something the student government was working during the 2005–2006 school year to extend.

Three new computer labs are available on the lower and first floors of Barret Library. Some labs are open until 2 a.m, others until midnight, though even here some students would like labs that are open around the clock. Altogether, the college provides more than 220 computers for student use. Along with Ethernet ports in each student room, wireless computing is available in selected locations in the residence halls and in many other public locations throughout campus besides the new library.

The college strongly recommends that students have their own personal computers.

Special programs: Rhodes offers an exchange program with 5 campuses in Europe and 1 in South Africa, plus 5 summer programs, including study at Oxford and in Greece. Fifty percent of Rhodes students participate in some kind of study-abroad program. An internship program sends more than 60% of all students to gain on-the-job experience at firms like Federal Express and Buckman Laboratories, as well as St. Jude Children's Research Hospital. Cross-registration is available with Memphis College of Art and Christian Brothers University. A student may spend a semester studying science at Oak Ridge National Laboratory, also in Tennessee. A 3-2 engineering degree is offered with Washington University in St. Louis.

Campus life: Seventy-seven percent of the students reside on the 100-acre wooded campus, whose impressive stone buildings of Gothic design, complete with slate roofs and lead glass windows, belie the school's location in a residential section of midtown Memphis. The Bryan Campus Life Center opened in April 1997 with a ballroom, a multipurpose space the size of 3 basketball courts, and a fitness center, plus other amenities. Both the BCLC and the new library maintain the campus' distinctive Gothic architecture. Membership in Greek organizations is high: 48% of the men and 53% of the women belong to the 7 national fraternities and 6 national sororities that dominate the weekend social life. Religious faith is expressed through several active service organizations. The Kinney program sends more than 80% of the student body annually into volunteer jobs in hospitals, homes for the elderly, schools for the handicapped, and other facilities. The college also has a very active chapter of Habitat for Humanity, the first in the nation to construct single-handedly a home for a low-income family. A tall, iron fence surrounding the campus plus security cameras help to keep out crime from the outside, while an honor code performs a similar function within. The biggest problem is theft from cars parked along the streets outside campus.

A fourth of the undergraduates play on varsity teams in 10 intercollegiate sports for men and 11 for women in NCAA Division III. Lynx soccer is the best-attended sporting event; football and basketball draw modest crowds each year. Eighty-seven percent of both the men and the women engage in the 16 intramural and club sports for each sex, with most students joining teams representing fraternities or sororities.

Visits to Overton Park Zoo across the street from campus, as well as cookouts along the Mississippi River, are popular diversions. Historic Beale Street, "comparable to a clean Bourbon Street," in the words of one senior, is just 10 minutes away and always has something happening. "Memphis," says an out-of-stater, "is large enough to get lost in, and that usually is escape enough. However, it's easy to organize a road trip to anywhere!"

Cost cutters: To keep the Rhodes name prominent in the minds of the nation's top scholars, the college offers more than 200 merit-based scholarships, renewable annually, to entering freshmen, extending up to full tuition, fees, room, and board. Forty-five percent of a recent class received such competitive awards. To be considered for the most generous award, the full-cost Bellingrath Scholarship, students must have been nominated for the award by a high school official, Presbyterian minister, or alumni or friend of the college. Other competitive scholarships pay $500 to full tuition and beyond; fine arts awards pay $12,500 a year. The Rhodes Service Program provides $12,000 in support to up to 15 first-year students with financial need in exchange for 10 hours of community service a week during the school year and 280 hours during two summers. In a recent school year, 77% of all undergraduates received financial help. Need-based awards ranged in value from $600 to $29,000. The average need-based aid package was at least $22,000; the average merit-based award was over $9800. What helps to make such extensive aid possible is an endowment of $223 million as of October 2005, which provides one of the largest per-student investments in the nation, about $139,000 in a recent year. Still, the average recent graduate left with debts of about $21,000.

Rate of return: Eighty-eight percent of the freshmen return for the sophomore year. Seventy-six percent graduate in 4 years, with an additional 3% earning degrees in a fifth year.

Payoff: Fourteen percent of 2005 graduates earned bachelor's degrees in English. Twelve percent each specialized in biology and business administration. A third of the grads pursue advanced degrees immediately. Half of any graduating class continue their education after 2 years. Most students at least initially take jobs in such fields as banking, accounting, management, government, and education; most settle in major metropolitan areas, for example, Memphis, Atlanta, Washington, D.C., and New York. More than 120 companies and organizations recruited on campus in a recent school year; the top 5 national corporate employers of Rhodes alumni are Ernst and Young, Morgan Keegan, St. Jude Children's Research Hospital, Teach for America, and Youth Villages.

Bottom line: Rhodes works best for the undergraduate "who is studious yet looks beyond the books for a total educational experience," says a southerner. "This is what college was meant to be like."

Sewanee: The University of the South

Sewanee, Tennessee 37383

Setting: Small town
Control: Private (Episcopalian)
Undergraduate enrollment: 632 men, 751 women
Graduate enrollment: 55 men, 31 women
Student/faculty ratio: 10:1
Freshman profile: 13% scored over 700 on SAT I verbal; 52% scored 600–700; 31% 500–599; 4% below 500. 10% scored over 700 on SAT I math; 50% scored 600–700; 37% 500–599; 3% below 500. 14% scored above 28 on the ACT; 43% scored 27–28; 20% 24–26; 22% 21–23; 1% below 21. 49% graduated in top tenth of high school class; 70% in upper fifth.
Faculty profile: 97% Ph.D.'s

Tuition and fees: $27,095
Room and board: $7550
Freshman financial aid: NA; average scholarship or grant: $18,342 need-based; $10,638 non-need-based
Campus jobs: 31%; average earnings: $1000/year
Application deadline: Early decision: Nov. 15; regular: Feb. 1
Financial aid deadline: Mar. 1
Admissions information: (931) 598-1238; (800) 522-2234
w-mail: collegeadmission@sewanee.edu
web site: www.sewanee.edu

A student magically whisked to a mountaintop in Tennessee might rub eyes once or twice to be sure he or she hadn't traveled back a few centuries, and across the Atlantic. The Gothic stone buildings with towers, cloisters, and spires are in the tradition of Oxford and Cambridge. Professors, as well as a small number of students with high grade point averages, wear academic gowns to class. Other students are usually dressed in coats, trousers (not jeans!), and ties or in skirts and blouses or dresses—even at football games. Tradition is important at Sewanee: The University of the South, with its undergraduate liberal arts program, small graduate school of theology and new summer master's degree programs in English and American literature and in creative writing. And though the cost of tuition, room, and board of $34,645 hit the upper limit of a best buy in the 2005–2006 school year, the liberal arts program is so strong that a student saves the cost of traveling to England for a similar academic experience.

Student body: Sewanee: The University of the South, commonly known just as Sewanee, the Indian name of its location, was started as a men's college in 1857 by the Episcopal Church and is still owned by 28 dioceses in 12 southern states. A third of the student body is Episcopalian, and 60% profess some type of Protestant faith. Traces of the all-male heritage have largely vanished, with women outnumbering men by 119 undergraduates. Minority students constitute 7% of the enrollment, 4% African-American, 2% Hispanic and 1% Asian-American. Foreign nationals from 23 countries account for 2%. Twenty percent are from Tennessee, and about three-quarters of the nonresidents traditionally come from the South, although 44 states in all are represented in the student body. Almost half, 45%, graduated from private or parochial schools. Students are described as intellectually curious, socially sophisticated, religiously contemplative, and politically moderate to conservative, though "in truth," says a sophomore, "the student body is overwhelmingly apolitical, and we like it that way since political activism promotes divisiveness." Environmentalism is the one movement acceptable to all. There is no formal dress code, yet students choose to stick with tradition and wear coats and ties or skirts and blouses or dresses to class as a sign of respect. Undergraduates caution, however, that the conformity in dress does not imply any lack of respect for individualism or originality. In fact, the 2 largest groups of students, the boarding school preppies and the "granolas," look in their out-of-class attire about as different as classmates can. While most students are considered friendly, Sewanee does have its share of "stuck-up rich kids," according to classmates. Though Sewanee students have had a reputation for knowing how to party hardy ("and it's deserved," admits a junior), undergraduates are quite defensive about the amount of hard work, and true learning rather than test-cramming, they accomplish. Observes a senior: "Sewanee freshmen act, generally speaking, much like freshmen do in the movies: they drink and party a lot and are not much inclined to study. But during the sophomore year, many start to get serious about their studies. I did. As a freshman, I got a 2.8, sophomore year, a 3.1. My junior year I earned a 3.72, and so far, as a senior, I have a 3.8. I have simply gotten into academics and made learning the focus of my life here, as most students do." And the academic honors prove it. The university has graduated 25 Rhodes Scholars, the latest a religion major in the Class of 2005, 34 Watson Fellows, 6 Fulbright scholars, and 25 NCAA Postgraduate Scholars.

Academics: The university confers degrees through the doctoral level and offers the bachelor's degree in 34 majors. The academic calendar is divided into two semesters. Introductory classes are generally limited to 20 or 25 students; upper-level classes often have 12. Half of all classes have between 10 and 19 students; 5% have 30 or more. Adds a junior: "I took a class as a freshman with 4 other people."

The rigorous Sewanee core requires that students take a total of 13 courses: 1 each from English, mathematics, history, social science, religion or philosophy, and the fine arts; 2 science courses (1 lab); 2 writing-intensive courses; 1 foreign language class at the third-year level of proficiency; and 2 semesters of physical education. Students who prefer may take a 4-course interdisciplinary humanities seminar to fulfill the mandates in English, history, philosophy/religion, and fine arts, plus the 2 writing courses. In keeping with the British tradition, every student also must pass a comprehensive exam in his or her major.

All of the 137 full-time faculty teach undergraduates, as do all of the 38 part-timers. Thirty-five percent are women. Almost all faculty members live on campus, and many of the dogs that roam around are regarded as reincarnations of former professors. Undergraduates hold the faculty in high regard, except for the ones who are a bit "too brainy" to get their points across to young students. Notes a senior: "Professors are excellent, period. Most are from the best academic backgrounds and work very hard to make their classes interesting and challenging. Rarely, if ever, are you given 'busy work'; instead, assignments teach you how to expand your knowledge." And though the academic robes may initially appear intimidating, students generally are won over by professors' infectious enthusiasm for their subject matter and warmth and interest in them as people.

English is considered the strongest department because of its distinguished faculty, solid and demanding curriculum, and strong literary tradition. The highly regarded *Sewanee Review* is the nation's oldest literary quarterly, and the department gained a special bonus several years ago when author Tennessee Williams left his estate to the university. "The professors make sure you know how to write well," says an economics major, "and they know their literature." History also has a popular faculty and solid courses, especially those on the Old South and the Civil War and Reconstruction. Other top choices based primarily on having superb faculty are political science, economics, Spanish, French, religion, mathematics, philosophy, and biology. Since the late 1970s, biology majors and others have enjoyed an acceptance rate of 89% to medical, dental, and veterinary schools. Majors in natural resources and the environment, forestry, and geology enjoy not only excellent faculties but also the school's ideal location on 10,000 acres of mountaintop woodlands. Says a forestry major: "It gives the professors, a few of whom are legendary, the ability to show rather than just say."

The fine arts department, with majors in studio art and art history, is understaffed and lacks the ready access to museums and other artistic outlets found at less isolated colleges. The very small music department suffers from lack of facilities, though students say the areas where instruction is offered, in organ, piano, voice, violin, viola, cello, guitar, and the orchestra I woodwinds, are grand. Theater arts has benefited from construction of the new Tennessee Williams Center, which, along with a new theater, offers a computer-aided drafting and design lab with hardware and software for theater projects. Theater majors also may apply to spend a semester of their junior year in intensive theater study in New York City. Many of the psychology courses are considered too repetitive and too "behavioral" in their emphasis. Too many members of the physics faculty are considered either "indifferent" or "unintelligible."

Facilities: In the case of Sewanee's library, the ties to Oxford and Cambridge run bookshelf-deep. Shortly after the Episcopal university's founding in 1857, Oxford and Cambridge universities both donated books to help start its library. Today, the Jesse Ball du Pont Library holds 648,500 volumes and 3444 current periodicals. The facility seats 900—two-thirds of the student body. Many undergraduates use private carrels that are obtained at the start of each semester. Thanks to the school's highly regarded honor code, students can leave materials in their carrels without anything being stolen. A portion of the library called "Night Study" is open around the clock, and an "absolute silence" reading room is provided, although some students find the general atmosphere a bit "soporific" for more tedious work. A computerized catalog, accessible from students' rooms, is much appreciated as an alternative to heading for the library on a cold or rainy night; database searches, along with access to the Internet, have cut back on the number of trips needed to Vanderbilt University's massive library.

The university has 3 labs and 7 electronic classrooms with more than 250 networked Macs and PCs primarily; most of the facilities are open from 8 a.m. to midnight with the 50-unit Academic Technology Center open around the clock. Says a sophomore: "It is practically impossible not to find a computer even on the busiest of study nights." Students also may access the Internet through wired connections in each dorm room or through a number of wireless hotspots across campus.

Special programs: More than 30% of the undergraduates participate in some study-abroad program. Students may spend a summer or semester at Oxford University in England, or take part in similar foreign-study opportunities in 12 additional countries. An island ecology program is offered on St. Catherine's Island off the coast of Georgia. The Tonya Fellowship, set up through the economics and political science department, provides internships in economics and public affairs during the summer months. A 3-2 program in engineering is offered with 4 institutions, including Columbia University and Rensselaer Polytechnic Institute, and in forestry and environmental management with Duke University.

Campus life: Ninety-two percent of Sewanee undergraduates live in 19 residence halls on the mountaintop campus, known as the Domain. Some consider the university's older stone buildings to be its greatest shortcoming. Others counter, "This is not a state-of-the-art school, and we don't want it to be." Nonetheless, Sewanee has been getting a facelift. A new sports and fitness center was completed in 1994 as remodeling of various facilities was completed throughout the 90's. Greek organizations are a mainstay of the mountaintop social life: 46% of the men pledge to 12 national fraternities, which all have lodges for meetings and activities, although members live in residence halls. The 9 sororities, joined by 39% of the women, are local and have no houses. All Greek events, except formals, are open to the entire campus; and while many independents attend, others are put off by the "elitist" attitude of some Greek members. Still, says a junior: "Many people go Greek here who would not have gone at larger universities because it is so different." The Order of Gownsmen, made up of students who have achieved the grade point average required to wear academic gowns, is easily the most prestigious organization and involves about a fifth of the students. Says a sophomore: "Everyone wants to get his or her gown." The Sewanee Volunteer Fire Department and Emergency Medical Service engages a number of dedicated members. The combination of the university's remote location and honor code makes campus crime a topic of little concern. Driving under the influence down the mountain is one of the more frequent violations, though a student-run taxi service on Friday and Saturday nights is available; nonetheless, whenever a student drives out of the gates of Sewanee, "he or she taps the roof of the car to remind his or her guardian angel to come along," says a westerner.

And what do the residents of an isolated campus in a village of 2500 do on the weekend? Football games are the best attended sport at the school, although, in the words of a student, "they're more like large cocktail parties held in front of a backdrop of football." Soccer generates a more serious group of fans although basketball and other athletic events usually are well supported, too. In a recent year, 40% of the men and 35% of the women participated in the 10 men's and 11 women's intercollegiate sports played in NCAA Division III; 60% of the students turn out for the 15 men's and 16 women's intramurals. All students are members of the Sewanee Outing Program, which features mountain climbing, rafting, hiking, and canoeing every weekend during the fall and spring terms.

Nashville is 90 minutes away. For a minimal charge, the school runs a weekly shuttle to Chattanooga, half as far as Nashville but, students say, also only half as exciting. Atlanta is the big trip, about 3 hours away.

Cost cutters: Sewanee's tuition pays approximately three-fourths of a student's total educational expenses; the rest is made up by endowment and gifts. No data is available to show the percentage of first-year or continuing students who received financial aid of any kind in the 2005–2006 school year; however, about 60% of the entire student body receive some kind of financial assistance. About a third of all students were given need-based assistance. The average freshman package for a student with need included a need-based scholarship or grant averaging $18,342 and need-based self-help aid such as loans and jobs averaging $4720. Other non-need-based awards and scholarships averaged $10,638. Three full scholarships covering tuition, fees, room, and board are available to students named Benedict Scholars. Each year, 25 students are selected as Wilkins Scholars; scholars with need receive awards equal to the amount of need while those without financial need are given half-tuition scholarships for each year. Regents' Scholarships pay no less than one-half tuition to 4 entering freshmen of color. Other merit-based awards range in value from $8000 a year to full tuition. As an incentive for good academic performance, the university agrees to "forgive" $3000 of the loan component of any upperclassman's financial aid package for each year in which the student has maintained a cumulative GPA of 3.0. For parents, the university offers a monthly payment option as well as a loan program for middle-income families in which parents pay no interest on what they borrow while the child is enrolled at Sewanee. Repayment begins 30 days after the student graduates or otherwise leaves the university. Average debt of a 2005 graduate was $13,244.

Rate of return: Eighty-eight percent of the freshmen who enter return for the sophomore year. Seventy-eight percent graduate in 4 years; 79% in 5 years; 80% within 6.

Payoff: The social sciences and history were the most popular majors, accounting for 29% of the 2005 graduating class, followed by English at 13%, and foreign languages and literature at 10%. More than a third of recent graduates immediately pursued advanced degrees; more than 70% continue their educations eventually. The university's high number of Rhodes scholars recently ranked it third among liberal arts institutions. Nearly 30 firms and other organizations recruited on campus in a recent school year.

Bottom line: What kind of student is Sewanee for? Advises a westerner: "The student who comes here should be ready for a very Greek-oriented campus and not feel intimidated by outward manifestations of tradition, such as the academic gowns and voluntary dress code." The University of the South, say its students, should be right for a freshman *before* he or she arrives; a newcomer should not come planning to change its distinctive way of life but rather to revel in its well-rounded approach to learning.

The University of Tennessee, Knoxville

Knoxville, Tennessee 37996

Setting: Urban
Control: Public
Undergraduate enrollment: 9173 men, 9385 women
Graduate enrollment: 1712 men, 2244 women
Student/faculty ratio: 15:1
Freshman profile: SAT/ACT scores: NA; class rank data: NA
Faculty profile: 82% Ph.D.'s
Tuition and fees: $5290 in-state; $16,360 out-of-state
Room and board: $6430

Freshman financial aid: 68%; average scholarship or grant: NA
Campus jobs: NA; average earnings: $2187/year
Application deadline: Feb. 1
Financial aid deadline: Apr. 1
Admissions information: (423) 974–2184; (800) 221-VOLS in-state
e-mail: admissions@utk.edu
web site: www.utk.edu

For years, the image of Neyland Stadium, rising like the Great Pumpkin with rows of 100,000 screaming football fans clad in orange, was center stage at The University of Tennessee, Knoxville. Today, there is another landmark set squarely in the center of the campus, which administrators hope will establish a whole new image for the state's largest university: a 350,000-square-foot library. Under the stewardship of former governor and university president Lamar Alexander, who went on to become U.S. Secretary of Education under the 41st president, George Bush, a university once known for its parties cut its undergraduate student body by 5000, raised its standards for admission, and stepped up recruitment of top honors students. Cautions a recent graduate: "A freshman who expects to attend the old UT of parties and football will not succeed here. Times have changed." What has *not* changed is the university's price tag, just over $5000 for state residents and just about $16,500 for out-of-staters in the 2005–2006 school year, still among the lowest tuition rates in the nation despite hefty increases in recent years. Nevertheless, concludes a sophomore, "UT remains one of the top public universities in America, and one of the best buys as well for your dollar."

Student body: Tennessee residents make up 85% of the student body and most of the rest come also from the South, although all 50 states are represented. Minority groups account for 11% of the undergraduate student body; 8% are African-American, 2% Asian-American and 1% Hispanic. Two percent also are foreign nationals from 94 countries. Many students are the first in their families to attend college. Undergraduates are largely conservative and noted for being warm and friendly to newcomers. Says a state resident: "The average UT student is a true 'Volunteer,' interested in what is going on both on campus and in Knoxville." And though the academic rigor of the university has risen, students say that for many undergraduates, studies remain just a part of the total collegiate picture. Says an out-of-stater: "You have the diehard studying folks and then you have those that study very little, none at all, or the night before."

Academics: The university, which turned 210 in 2004, awards degrees through the doctorate, with 120 undergraduate majors, ranging from agricultural economics to theater, presented in 9 colleges and 2 schools. The colleges of Law and Veterinary Medicine offer graduate degrees only. A few years ago, the university switched from a quarter to a semester calendar to give professors and students more time for longer-range projects; at that time, administrators reviewed and updated every course in the curriculum. Entering freshmen can expect classes that range from 23 in English to about 430 in general psychology. Most classes average 26–40 members.

A new general education program requires all students to take coursework in critical skills and subject areas. The mandates include 3 courses in communicating through writing, with one class that is writing intensive, 1 course in communicating orally, and 2 in quantitative reasoning. The subject requirements comprise 2 courses each in cultures and civilizations, arts and humanities, social sciences, and natural sciences.

The faculty includes 1476 full-time members and 81 part-time. No figures show the numbers who teach at the graduate level only. Women comprise just over a third of the faculty. One faculty member has won the Nobel Prize; 5, the Pulitzer. Many professors share their teaching duties with graduate students, who in recent years have helped lead a quarter of the introductory courses. Students' assessment of their quality ranges from "They're wonderful," to "They don't know what they're doing." While faculty quality runs the same gamut from awful to excellent, students agree that, as a whole, the professors are getting better. Several recipients of national teaching awards are on the UT staff, although the overall faculty rating remains at 8 out of a possible perfect 10. "I have, of course, had some professors who were difficult and not effective," says a junior, "but I have also had twice as many exceptional professors (who) provide organized, challenging material and offer endless assistance to students."

Engineering and science programs are strong, particularly chemistry, physics, microbiology, and electrical and computer engineering, which are characterized by tough faculties, fine equipment, and diverse opportunities for students. Engineering also has a wonderful advising program, focused on freshmen. The College of Agricultural Sciences and Natural Resources, a historic leader, remains well equipped. The accounting and finance majors are among several strong offerings in the College of Business Administration, including a distinctive program in logistics and transportation. In business, too, students meet every semester with both a curriculum advisor and a career advisor. Programs in the colleges of Architecture and Design, Nursing, and Education, Health, and Human Sciences are rigorous but rewarding as well. In the College of Arts and Sciences, students single out for praise programs in the School of Art and the political science department with its "unbelievable teachers," says a major.

The College of Social Work remains much smaller in terms of faculty, students, and funding than better established, more powerful academic divisions. Thoughts on psychology are mixed: some consider it a winner; other majors think its courses could be more challenging, with more emphasis on discussion. English and history have disappointed many because of their lack of enthusiastic teachers, large classes with little personal attention, and heavy reliance on teaching assistants. A recent round of budget cuts resulted in some professors leaving UT and some minors being dropped from the curriculum.

Facilities: Students call the 6-story John C. Hodges Library "unbeatable." Notes a graduate: "You feel inspired to study as soon as you open the door"—exactly the way administrators wanted students to feel when they placed the library in the center of campus. However, so many students have become inspired to study that Hodges has become "a social hangout which is quite noisy," says a history major. His advice: head for a corner table above the fourth floor. Hodges contains most of the university's collection of more than 2.8 million volumes, 3.5 million microform items, and 16,656 periodicals. Branch libraries house materials related to agriculture and veterinary medicine and to music, as well as special collections. The Law Library also is located on campus. In addition to its extensive holdings, Hodges includes a computerized catalog accessible from home and office computers, a microcomputer lab, and a state-of-the-art, fiber-optic-wired audiovisual services department, plus study space for more than 2000 students, 308 graduate carrels, and 200 faculty studies. A 24-hour study area also comes in handy.

More than 250 Macs, PCs, and Sun workstations are available at 15 sites throughout most academic buildings and the library with additional units located in all residence halls and fraternity houses. Again, the labs that are open around the clock best fit students' erratic working hours. "If students use all the labs, everyone has a station," says a sophomore, "but many only use the library labs, causing a back-up."

Special programs: Outstanding students participating in the College Scholars program are heavily involved in designing their own curricula; a College Scholar spends his or her final 2 years doing independent study or research or writing a senior thesis. Cross registration in 11 programs is possible through the Academic Common Market, a 14-state southern consortium. International exchange programs are available in 25–30 countries. The Howard H. Baker, Jr. Center for Public Policy includes a program for undergraduate students who are known as Baker Scholars and wish to pursue a career in public service. Summer internships are an option at the Oak Ridge National Laboratory.

Campus life: The 533-acre campus is home, at least temporarily, for 38% of the university's undergraduates, and these students and people of all ages, from previous and future graduating classes, are guaranteed to be there on fall weekends. While academics are getting stronger, Volunteer football fever is not abating. Notes a recent graduate: "During fall semester, the name of the game is 'Worship the Vols.' Everyone attends the football game and then floods the Strip [Cumberland Avenue] for partying, whether we win or lose." Postgame band parties with lots of dancing can be found at any of the 26 national fraternities on campus, to which 8% of the male students belong. The same portion of women are members of 17 national sororities; students report slight friction between Greeks and independents because the Greeks are prominent in so many of the campus political organizations. However, their open parties are popular with nearly all. More than 300 student clubs accommodate most undergraduates' interests; many students get involved in Team Vols, a multifaceted community-service program. Car break-ins and vandalism are the 2 most troublesome crimes on campus. Students are cautioned not to walk alone after dark, with an escort van available from dusk to dawn to make walking alone unnecessary. More than 150 blue-light emergency phones also are located across campus.

Slightly lower levels of Vols fever mark the other 7 intercollegiate sports for men and 10 for women, with basketball, baseball, and track and field competitions drawing the most response. The Lady Vols won the NCAA Division I women's national basketball championship 4 times in the 1990s and made it to the Final Four 6 times between 1995 and 2000 and also in 2004 and 2005. In 2004, the Lady Vols lost to the University of Connecticut Huskies in the championship game. A fifth of the men and 5% of the women participate in the 22 intramural sports offered for each sex; more than 300 intramural football teams were fielded in a recent year.

Knoxville (pop. 195,000) is a good-sized town with lots of things to do. Moreover, the campus is an hour's drive or less from great hiking, skiing, or sightseeing in Great Smoky Mountains National Park.

Cost cutters: In a recent school year, 68% of the freshmen and 57% of the continuing students received some form of financial aid; the majority received aid based on need. The average freshman award for fall 2005 totaled $5548, although no breakdown is available showing the portion devoted to grants or scholarships, loans, or earnings from a job. Average debt of a recent graduate was $21,689. Ten Whittle Scholars receive $7000 a year plus an extra $3500 for a semester of study overseas. Out-of-state tuition is waived for nonresidents. Manning Scholars, named for football great Peyton Manning, a 1998 alumnus, receive the same amount as Whittle Scholars. Tennessee Scholars, who receive $5000 a year (again, out-of-state tuition is waived for nonresidents), have faculty mentors, attend special honors seminars, and take courses taught by top faculty. Twenty-five Tennessee Scholars are selected annually. Altogether, the university annually offers over 4000 scholarship awards from more than 1400 scholarship accounts. For most merit awards, students must have a GPA of at least 3.5 and an ACT composite of 27 or 1200 combined math and critical reading SATs. Students must apply by Nov. 1 to be considered for the top scholarships. Cooperative education programs are available in a number of majors, such as engineering, communications, and business.

Rate of return: Seventy-nine percent of the freshmen who enter return for the sophomore year. Four years after admission as freshmen, just 24% graduate, though 50% finish in 5 years, and 57% do so in 6 years.

Payoff: Typically, degrees at UT are scattered across a wide variety of majors; for 2005 graduates, the most popular fields were psychology at 8%, English at 5%, and biology at 4%. Many new graduates enter management training programs or take professional positions throughout the Sunbelt, mostly in the southeastern states, with such firms as Procter & Gamble, IBM, du Pont, Dow, and the major national public accounting firms, as well as well-known regional and national financial institutions. More than 370 companies and organizations recruited on campus in a recent school year.

Bottom line: Hodges Library probably never will overtake Neyland Stadium as the site of a most cherished UT memory. But while it's hard for a student to resist joining 100,000 other fans for a football game and postgame parties, at the new, more serious University of Tennessee, bypassing the library too many times may mean a string of personal losing seasons.

Texas

Austin College

Sherman, Texas 75090

Setting: Suburban
Control: Private (Presbyterian)
Undergraduate enrollment: 581 men, 705 women
Graduate enrollment: 5 men, 24 women
Student/faculty ratio: 13:1
Freshman profile: 19% scored over 700 on SAT I verbal; 48% scored 600–700; 30% 500–599; 3% below 500. 16% scored over 700 on SAT I math; 50% scored 600–700; 31% 500–599; 3% below 500. 22% scored above 28 on the ACT; 18% scored 27–28; 33% 24–26; 21% 21–23; 6% below 21. 44% graduated in top tenth of high school class; 75% in upper fourth.
Faculty profile: 98% Ph.D.'s

Tuition and fees: $20,495
Room and board: $7376
Freshman financial aid: 97%; average scholarship or grant: $8352 need-based; $15,094 non-need-based
Campus jobs: 30%; average earnings: $1230/year
Application deadline: Early decision: Dec. 1, regular: Mar. 1
Financial aid deadline: Apr. 1
Admissions information: (903) 813-3000; (800) 442-5363
e-mail: admission@austincollege.edu
web site: www.austincollege.edu

First off, Austin College is not located in Austin, Texas; it's an hour north of Dallas, in a town called Sherman (pop. 38,000) near the Oklahoma border. But once past that small point of confusion, there's no mixup as to why Austin College has become, in the minds of many, the best little liberal arts college in Texas. Even in a setting of fewer than 1300 undergraduates, Austin doesn't take for granted the development of the individual student. Every freshman is assigned, from day 1, a mentor who becomes more than an advisor on which courses to schedule. The mentor helps craft the student's educational game plan and serves as professor for the first required course, Communication/Inquiry, which gets the freshman acclimated to the learning process. At least once a term throughout the 4 or 5 years at Austin, the student formally reports to the mentor on his or her progress toward the educational and personal goals originally laid out. In a state where bigger has traditionally meant better, Austin stands apart from the crowd.

Student body: Ninety-three percent of Austin's students are Texan; all but a small percent come from the surrounding region, though 32 states are represented. Eighty-six percent went to public schools. Fourteen percent are Presbyterian; 18% Catholic. The student body as a whole includes 12% Asian Americans, 8% Hispanics, 4% African-Americans, and 1% Native Americans. One percent are students from 12 foreign countries. Austin students consider themselves "individuals, because AC's atmosphere encourages it," says a recent graduate. Students come here "who do not want to blend in," says a Texan. Ideologically, there is a mixture of liberal and conservative viewpoints, with political, religious, social, sexual, and racial and ethnic organizations to reflect every stance. As one student put it: "The undergraduates at AC are conservative liberals with moderate minds." While students also like to think of themselves as enthusiastic and friendly, at Austin the A clearly stands for Ambitious as well as Academics, with athletic coaches themselves putting education first, sports second. "Though most people give the air of being very laid back," says a sophomore, "we all spend our share of hours over books, in the library, or at the computer." "Without the challenge," observes a junior, "it would not be Austin College."

Academics: Founded in 1849, Austin College awards the bachelor's degree in more than 30 fields and features a 5-year teacher education program that leads to both bachelor's and master's degrees. AC's courses are scheduled in semesters with a January term in between. Students can expect an average class to have about 20 students, even in the first 2 years. The only large lecture course is the first segment of Heritage of Western Culture, which enrolls the entire freshman class spring term, more than 300 students; some lower-level science courses aimed at premed students can have 60 or so diligent notetakers in attendance.

The first-semester freshman course, entitled Communication/Inquiry and taught by the student's mentor, develops the critical thinking, writing, and other skills needed to ensure academic success. During 1 term each in the freshman, sophomore, and junior years, all undergraduates must take a third of the 3-part sequence called Heritage of Western Culture, which is team-taught by professors from various academic perspectives. General-education requirements also mandate that students take 3 courses in the humanities, 2 courses in social science, and 1 in natural science and demonstrate competency in a modern or classical language other than one's own and in quantitative skills, either with an approved course or test. Students also must complete a minor or a second major.

Austin's faculty is largely full-time: only 36 of the 127 members are part-timers. Women make up 34% of the faculty. Undergraduates find professors eager to be innovative and creative in their instruction and happy to be called by their first names. Observes a biology major: "Professors place a lot of emphasis on application, critical thinking, and analysis of knowledge, rather than just the 'plug-and-chug' approach. Most also are open to hearing students' ideas and are genuinely interested in helping students. I feel very comfortable talking to my professors, and they encourage that feeling." Most faculty members also don't just follow an open-door policy in their offices. Adds a religion major: "I have dinner at many professors' houses and know their spouses and kids. They are extremely supportive of campus life and organizations and can often be seen hanging out on the lawn or in our pub or cafeteria or at plays and concerts or fund-raisers with students. I wouldn't change my experiences with my professors for anything!" Students have more concern about the quality of some of the adjunct faculty who are not as strong for the year or 2 they are there.

Austin's preprofessional programs, particularly premed, prelaw, and teacher preparation, are among its strongest offerings. Premed and prelaw benefit from the strong liberal arts courses on which these preparatory programs are based. Biology and chemistry are distinguished by outstanding faculties, rigorous and varied coursework, and excellent opportunities for clinical experience during the annual January term or for summer research through the University of Texas medical schools. The interdisciplinary major in international relations rates highly, along with the more traditional prelaw foundations in history, political science, and business. Austin's 5-year teacher preparation program requires the student to earn a bachelor's degree in the arts and sciences rather than teaching, while beginning work in the classroom as early as freshman year. To receive a master of arts in teaching, the student completes a fifth year of study, including an internship. The education program is housed in a renovated Victorian home that combines 21st-century technological offerings with period reception and seminar rooms. English, religion, and psychology also win applause for their superior faculty and varied courses.

Although many departments at such a small college, such as sociology, anthropology, and exercise and sport science, suffer from a lack of diverse courses, art and music, which share a building, have especially limited facilities. Says an art major: "They are crammed into a small building, not enough space at all to do work, display work, and practice your music." Students say music also continues to have trouble keeping students with an interest in the field because they transfer to schools with bigger, more developed programs. A student whose interest is focused on a single field of business, such as accounting, also may be disappointed to find at least 5 or 6 accounting classes, but no separate major. Computer science and economics could use additional faculty members. Communication needs more up-to-date facilities and equipment, as well as more variety in the choice of courses and professors it offers.

Facilities: Abell Library Center, which opened in 1986, has become the college's jewel, "the greatest thing to happen to our campus," in the words of one user. In fact, Abell's popularity seems too great some evenings when the second floor becomes so noisy that study is impossible. With nearly 240,000 volumes, and 2835 periodicals, the collection still has limitations, which usually can be resolved via the Internet or interlibrary loan, or with a quick trip to libraries in Dallas or Ft. Worth. A computerized catalog and computerized databases are helpful, as is a well-used, all-night study room.

More than 100 PCs and Macs are spread among 3 main labs, at least 1 of which is open 24 hours. Each residence hall also has a computer cluster, open around the clock. Students with their own personal computers can use the Internet from their residence-hall rooms. Adell Library, the science building, the technology center, Wright Campus Center, and a steadily growing number of other locations are all wireless hotspots.

Special programs: More than 70% of Austin's students study abroad, largely through programs in 58 countries with the Institute for International Education of Students, Butler and Arcadia universities, and Central College. There also are Austin College programs in Spain and Mexico for undergraduates who wish to increase their knowledge of Spanish and fluency in the language. A semester in Washington, D.C., is another option. Many students use the January term to study overseas or to perform internships across the United States; 1 undergraduate traveled to New Mexico to learn sign language. A 3-2 engineering program is available with the University of Texas at Dallas, Texas A&M, and Columbia and Washington universities.

Campus life: Sixty-nine percent of the students reside on the 60-acre campus; about a fifth are members of 9 local fraternities and 7 local sororities that are less expensive to join than their national counterparts. Says a senior: "We all hate national fraternities and sororities because they all give us bad names. Fraternities and sororities here study more, are involved in the community more, and aren't as huge on partying and getting trashed all the time." Weekend activities sponsored by the Greeks, beginning with a Friday "happy hour," generally are open to everyone after 10 p.m., and students say that the Campus Activities Board does a good job of bringing in popular, regional bands to play for the entire campus, free of charge or at a minimal cost. The Service Station, which coordinates community service projects for students, and Activators, which stands for Austin College Mobile Youth Ministry Team, are 2 of the most active of the 50 clubs on campus. A card access system for entry into the dormitories has helped to decrease incidents of thefts from students' rooms. However, students are advised not to walk off campus alone after dark; campus security, which patrols on foot and in golf carts, provides escorts to make students feel more secure.

Austin College offers 6 NCAA Division III intercollegiate sports for men, and 6 for women including softball, which was to be added in the 2006–2007 school year. Kangaroo football is easily the most popular sport; "students like to come out and get 'Roo'd'," observes a senior. Supporters also have a new 2500-seat stadium just right for "roo-ing." Men's basketball and soccer do battle for the second largest crowds. Half of the men and a fourth of the women participate in 9 intramural sports for each sex. An athletic/recreation complex, dedicated in 2002, keeps participants happy as well as healthy.

Students looking for excitement that can't be found in Sherman head south for a night in Dallas. The college owns 28 acres of private beach and camping areas at Lake Texoma, 30 minutes north, which becomes a popular off-campus hangout in the spring.

Cost cutters: Tuition revenue represents approximately 40% of the operating budget of Austin College. The difference between the cost of attending Austin and the amount students actually pay is made up by income from endowment, contributions by Presbyterian churches, and gifts from alumni and friends. All but 3% of Austin's freshmen and all but 4% of its continuing students received financial help in the 2005–2006 school year; 59% of the first-year students and 55% of the rest got need-based aid. The average freshman award for a first-year student with financial need included a need-based scholarship or grant averaging $8352 and need-based self-help aid such as loans and jobs averaging $4518. Other non-need-based awards and scholarships for first-year students averaged $15,094. AC graduates in 2005 left with average debts of $26,164. The Presidential Scholarship provides full tuition to up to 10 freshmen who ranked in the top 5% of their high school classes, scored at least 1350 on the math and critical reading SAT or 30 on the ACT, completed a short essay on a specific topic, and survived an interview by an AC scholarship committee. Other merit awards range from $1000 to $5000. Posey Leadership Institute Scholarships pay $11,000 to 15 entering freshmen who, along with demonstrated leadership ability, ranked in the top 10% of their high school graduating class and had minimum standardized test scores of either 26 on the ACT or 1200 on the SAT math and critical reading sections. Those students selected take a series of 4 courses that explore theories and practices of leadership, perform community service, and interact with mentors from outside the college community. To be considered for many of the merit scholarships, students should have submitted admission and scholarship materials by Jan.15. An 8-month payment plan is an option for all undergraduates.

Rate of return: Eighty-eight percent of freshmen return for the sophomore year. Seventy-three percent earn bachelor's degrees in 4 years, 74% within 5 years, 75% within 6.

Payoff: Business administration and psychology were the most popular majors for 2005 graduates, claiming 15% of the class each. Another 9% majored in English. Job offers were snapped up by most of the new AC graduates, usually in such fields as banking, politics, insurance, retailing, real estate, hospital administration, and sales and management, mainly in the Southwest or Washington, D.C. area. Over the last 5 years, 30–40% of each graduating class have pursued advanced degrees. Approximately two-thirds do so within 5 years of graduation.

Bottom line: A motivated student, willing to forgo memorization of facts in favor of higher order critical thinking skills, will find Austin College an A-1 choice. Those considering graduate school can raise the grade to A+.

Rice University

Houston, Texas 77251

Setting: Urban
Control: Private
Undergraduate enrollment: 1483 men, 1403 women
Graduate enrollment: 1246 men, 676 women
Student/faculty ratio: 5:1
Freshman profile: Middle 50% combined math and verbal SAT I: 1340–1510. 86% graduated in top tenth of high school class; 94% in upper fourth.
Faculty profile: 96% Ph.D.'s
Tuition and fees: $23,746
Room and board: $8980

Freshman financial aid: 62%; average scholarship or grant: $12,226 need-based; $4999 non-need-based
Campus jobs: NA; average earnings: NA
Application deadline: Early decision: Nov. 1; interim: Dec. 1; regular: Jan. 10
Financial aid deadline: Mar. 1
Admissions information: (713) 348-7423; (800) 527–OWLS
e-mail: admission@rice.edu
web site: www.rice.edu

To succeed as an undergraduate at Rice University, one of the most selective, academically challenging, and least expensive research universities in the nation, a student doesn't have to be just intelligent, disciplined, and serious-minded. Academically, the air may be intense, but socially, Rice students share an irreverent view of themselves—and their college. At Rice, when students turn out fall weekends for the football games, they do so primarily to see the MOB, the renowned Marching Owl Band, to which 10% of the undergraduates in a recent year belonged. The MOB, whose members dress as Mobsters, run randomly from formation to formation and poke fun at the competing team, often to the tune of the college fight song, "Louie, Louie." Regardless of whether or not there is a touchdown to cheer about (usually there isn't), students strike up the following chant:

Secant, tangent, cosine, sine,
Three, one, four, one, five, nine
Cube root, square root, Btu,
Compass, slide rule, go Rice U.

You don't need a slide rule to know that Rice University is one of the very best buys on the college market today. With tuition, fees, room, and board totaling $32,726 in 2005–2006, about $8000 less than its competitors, and more than 60% of the undergraduates receiving financial aid, bright students quickly see that the Rice equation balances nicely.

Student body: Just over half of the students in a recent year were from Texas, with undergraduates from all 50 states and 37 foreign countries in attendance. Ten percent in a recent year attended private or parochial high schools. Minority students constituted almost 30% of the undergraduate enrollment, with 12% Asian-Americans, 9% Hispanics, 5% African-Americans, and less than 1% Native Americans. Rice students see themselves as bright and quick-witted (77% recently ranked in the top 5% of their high school classes); in many cases, other first-rate private universities were simply too expensive for them. As a result, undergraduates find a group of students who are "very real." Notes a junior from the Southwest: "Feeling left out simply does not occur here. Nothing is elitist, and there are very few cliques." Though students' political views range from the liberal to the conservative, few show sufficient interest in political or social issues to indicate a real preference either way. Hard work is a way of life at Rice. Notes a New Englander: "Declining an invitation for something social on the basis of homework is always acceptable, and 2 a.m. is considered a 'normal' bedtime." Students work hard to get the best marks possible, but even with grading on a competitive curve, notes a senior, "they'll always take time to help out classmates, whether it's explaining a concept to them, providing them with notes, or anything else. Rice emphasizes collaborative work, a great skill to learn for the professional world." Many undergraduates also take exception to the school's slightly nerdy image, which they say is very much off the mark. "Socially," says a westerner, "Rice is made up of a lot of fun people who simply don't have much time to have fun."

Academics: Rice offers degrees through the doctorate; bachelor's degree programs in about 50 fields are spread among 6 undergraduate schools. There also are graduate schools of Management and of Continuing Studies. The academic year is divided into 2 semesters. In the first 2 years, class size can range from 20 to 200, with introductory courses, especially in science and engineering, generally at the higher end. Most other courses in the liberal arts fall below 40. For juniors and seniors, the average class is under 30, with 15–20 the most common size.

All students must satisfy distribution requirements, taking courses from 3 groups: the humanities, social sciences, and natural sciences. In addition, every undergraduate must complete a prescribed number of "restricted" distribution courses in an area or 2 outside his or her major. Science and engineering majors generally praise the required courses in the humanities and social sciences, but students majoring in the humanities and social sciences say the courses in the natural sciences, dubbed Nazi for short, are "too rough and too difficult" for those not exposed to these fields in high school.

Rice's total faculty recently numbered 530 full-time and 272 part-time members. All taught undergraduates; 23% of the full-time faculty were women. Two faculty members have won the Nobel Prize. Undergraduates find most faculty members to be extremely well educated, highly respected by their peers, and generally very approachable and responsive to undergraduates' needs. "Here," says a mechanical engineering major, "is an example of why I go to Rice. Friday afternoon I was working on a homework assignment due Monday. I called my professor, who was just leaving, but he said he would wait to talk with me. We ended up working together for an hour until I understood what was going on. And many of the faculty are like that." As at any research university, there are professors who devote more time to research and publishing than to teaching and others who are too esoteric for students to follow. At Rice, however, the percentage is comparatively small. Observes a junior: "You will see professors at sporting events, eating in the residential colleges, and taking students seriously, which is what we want."

Students consider the science and engineering departments to be "exceptional." Both departments boast outstanding faculties and large budgets, and undergraduate majors enjoy easy access to state-of-the-art laboratories, though majors admit the quality of equipment available improves as a student advances in his or her specialty. Bioengineering, for example, has teaching labs "better equipped than research labs at other schools," says a senior. On the less technical side, the faculty in Rice's history department in a recent year had won more teaching awards than their counterparts in any other department on campus. The English department also receives high marks from students for its terrific, highly accessible faculty and small classes. Says a religious studies major: "The history, English, and religious studies department faculties are flat-out amazing. Not only are they well published and do a lot of major research, but they are all vibrant and knowledgeable teachers." Architecture, with its design-oriented program, sponsors a tour for sophomores during spring break that examines architecturally significant regions, usually in the U.S. but recently in other countries. Fifth-year students spend a year gaining practical experience in architectural offices around the world before returning for a final sixth year at Rice. The 22-year-old Shepherd School of Music offers a conservatory-type program in a beautiful new building, which in music circles continues to gain an excellent reputation.

Since business is not offered as a major, many students turn to economics, which classmates consider among Rice's weaker offerings. The program, say students, has relied more heavily on graduate teaching assistants than other courses of study, which majors say hasn't necessarily been so bad. Says a double major in economics and political science: "They are extremely motivated and excited to be teaching a class, and the material is either material so basic that an upperclassman in the major could teach the course, or it's their specialization so they are truly experts in the material." Psychology, political science, and foreign languages also have tended to rely more heavily on graduate students to do the teaching, or have had faculty members who seem disinterested when they do the teaching themselves.

Facilities: Although Fondren Library contains 2.3 million volumes, 3 million microform items, and has about 37,000 periodical subscriptions, a substantial collection for a university of 2900 undergraduates and 1900 graduate students, it elicits few paeans of praise from Rice's demanding scholars. Complains a user: "It's adequate but not stellar for serious academic research, especially if you're looking for foreign language books or untranslated original documents." Many go online or travel to the University of Houston's library. Rice's computerized system for books and periodicals, which also gives access to the listings of a half-dozen other colleges, is helpful and sometimes turns up those rare volumes students thought it impossible to find. For most users, recent structural renovations have made Fondren more comfortable for studying (and sleeping), although such efforts fail to satisfy some of the building's worst critics. States an English major: "It's like a $1000 paint job on a '73 Chevy. The money should have been spent on demolition."

University officials strongly recommend that students have their own personal computers, although availability is rarely a problem. At least 140 Macs and PCs are spread throughout the Mudd Computer Building (open 24 hours a day), the library (also open around-the-clock weekdays), and various academic laboratories. All residence halls also have computers.

Special programs: Rice has exchange programs with Swarthmore College in Pennsylvania, Cambridge and Lancaster universities in England, and several universities in Germany. Faculty from the departments of Hispanic and Classical Studies conduct a program fall semester at the University of Santiago in Chile and for 6 weeks in the summer in Spain. Students also may spend a semester studying deep-water oceanography in Massachusetts and the Caribbean, or maritime culture and commerce on a sailing vessel off the North American coastline. Fifteen high-ability high school graduates may be accepted both to Rice and Baylor College of Medicine for an 8-year program at both schools.

Campus life: For most students, some of whom traveled from California or Massachusetts to attend, the tree-shaded 300-acre campus surrounded by tall hedges, 3 miles outside downtown Houston, is a welcome sight. "More trees than students," exclaims a New Englander. The "country" campus is outdone only by Rice's well-regarded residential college system, which, students say, takes the place of a Greek system without the elitism sometimes associated with fraternities and sororities. Seventy-one percent of the undergraduates in a recent year resided on campus in 9 residential colleges to which freshmen are randomly assigned. Each college, which is coed and houses approximately 200 students, develops a personality all its own and serves as the dormitory, dining facility, and recreational and study center for its residents. The self-governing colleges compete against each other on and off the playing field and host weekend plays and parties. "Last weekend," says a junior, "we donned bunny slippers and pajamas and watched cartoons at 1 college's 'Night of Innocence' party; then we stripped down to various states of undress for another's 'Night of Decadence.'"

The system also enhances faculty/student relations since every college has 20 faculty associates, who eat and socialize with the students; 1 or 2 resident associates, who live with the students; and a college master, a faculty member who lives for a 5-year term in a house by the college. Other organizations outside the college system also are quite active and as off-beat as the Marching Owl Band. Members of Club 13 streak around campus on the 13th, 26th, or 31st of every month wearing only shaving cream and screaming "13, 13." On a more traditional note, the Rice Student Volunteer Program, which coordinates community-service projects, involves about 70% of the campus. *The Rice Thresher*, the student newspaper, also attracts much interest: editors are elected by the undergraduates every spring. Though the campus is located near downtown Houston, students say that crime, other than car break-ins and occasional thefts, is not a serious problem, in part because of a security force that consists of police, not just security officers. Buildings are locked with keys and ID readers, and an escort service, using a golf cart, is available at night.

About three-quarters of the Rice students participate in 14 intramural sports for men and 13 for women. There also are about a dozen club sports for both sexes. Undergraduates compete in 7 intercollegiate sports for men and 7 for women, in NCAA Division I, and students turn out to root for their teams. Recalls a recent graduate: "The football games have a 75–80% student turnout rate—even after an 0–11 season." Basketball also has a devoted following.

For a break from the books, many undergraduates take advantage of the discounts offered "outside the hedges" to students at many of Houston's cultural attractions for "dirt cheap student prices," says a senior. A 1-hour drive to the beach at Galveston is a favorite afternoon trip in the spring. Other students opt for less drastic measures. "My roommate," says a Texan, "goes to the basement of the physics building. I go to my beanbag chair and read the newspaper."

Cost cutters: Rice's significant endowment of $3.6 billion, as of June 2005, helps keep charges down, and student aid levels high. Sixty-two percent of the freshmen and 67% of the continuing students in a recent school year received financial aid; for 34% of the freshmen and 37% of the rest, the assistance was need-based. A typical freshman package for a student with need included a need-based scholarship or grant averaging $12,226 and need-based self-help aid such as loans and jobs averaging $3386. Non-need-based athletic awards for first-year students averaged $23,239; other non-need-based awards and scholarships averaged $4999. Recent Rice graduates left with an average debt of $12,942. While the average debt is several thousand dollars lower than that found at many private colleges and universities, the amount is becoming lower still for future Rice graduates. For the Rice Class of 2008, the university set a cap of $2625 on student loans in financial aid packages over each of the 4 years with a total debt to be no higher than $10,500 in need-based student loans upon graduation from Rice. For families with less than $30,000 in total income, the university meets all need with grants and work-study—no loans. The school offers approximately 250 merit-based scholarships, recently ranging from $750 to 4 years of tuition. For example, a small number of Dobelman and Sikes Scholarships pay full tuition for 4 years to engineering students who have extensive scientific awards and research experience. Another program, the Rice Century Scholars Program, guarantees 2 years of faculty mentorship and research in addition to a $6000 scholarship renewable for 2 years.

Rate of return: Ninety-six percent of the freshmen return for the sophomore year. Seventy-five percent graduate in 4 years, 89% within 5 years, 92% within 6.

Payoff: Of recent graduates, 7% majored in economics, 7% in psychology, and 7% in electrical and computer engineering. More than 40% of new alumni generally go directly to graduate or professional schools. Nearly 50% take jobs, many with consulting firms, management training programs, and engineering rotation programs throughout the country. More than 135 companies and other organizations recruited on campus in a recent school year.

Bottom line: Rice is a place where smart people enjoy each other's company, don't take themselves too seriously, and feel as though they belong. However, cautions an engineering major, "a student must be able to accept not being the smartest person in class anymore. Also, a person who is all work and no play will hate it here. One who is all play and no work will fail out."

Southwestern University

Georgetown, Texas 78626

Setting: Surburban
Control: Private (United Methodist)
Undergraduate enrollment: 532 men, 754 women
Graduate enrollment: None
Student/faculty ratio: 10:1
Freshman profile: 16% scored over 700 on SAT I verbal; 47% scored 600–700; 31% 500–599; 6% below 500. 14% scored over 700 on SAT I math; 51% scored 600–700; 29% 500–599; 6% below 500. 26% scored above 28 on the ACT; 22% scored 27–28; 28% 24–26; 21% 21–23; 3% below 21. 50% graduated in top tenth of high school class; 73% in upper fifth.
Faculty profile: 99% Ph.D.'s

Tuition and fees: $20,220
Room and board: $6547
Freshman financial aid: 84%; average scholarship or grant: $14,602 need-based; $8121 non-need-based
Campus jobs: 49%; average earnings: $1083/year
Application deadline: Early decision: Nov. 1 and Jan. 1; regular: Feb. 15
Financial aid deadline: Mar. 1
Admissions information: (512) 863-1200; (800) 252–3166
e-mail: admission@southwestern.edu
web site: www.southwestern.edu

Southwestern University likes to tell prospective freshmen that it offers every undergraduate a "hidden scholarship." Actually, the "scholarship" is more like a generous rich uncle who helps to pay part of every student's way. Southwestern's endowment was more than $279 million as of June 2005, which, at about $217,000 for each student, ranks among the highest in the nation on a per capita basis. Income from the hefty endowment allows the university to charge students less than 60% of the true educational costs, just $20,220 for tuition and fees, in the 2005–2006 school year. But if it's the hidden scholarship that first draws students to Southwestern's campus, it's the much more obvious benefits that keep them there, such as its personalized attention, 5-star faculty, and first-rate academic programs. In recognition of its strong liberal arts foundation, the campus was awarded a chapter of Phi Beta Kappa in 1995. That's enviable progress for the oldest university in the Lone Star State, a school founded in 1840, just 4 years after the fall of the Alamo.

Student body: Ninety-three percent of Southwestern's students are from Texas; the rest, from 35 states and 8 foreign countries. Hispanics constitute the largest minority group at 14%, followed by Asian-Americans at 5%, African-Americans at 3%, and Native Americans and foreign nationals at 1% each. Just over a fourth are Methodist, another 40% follow other Protestant faiths, and a fifth are Catholic. Eighteen percent went to private schools. Students are friendly and open-minded, running the gamut "from liberal to conservative, outspoken to quiet, activist to apathetic," according to one junior. "Southwestern students are active thinkers," says a junior. "Everyone is surprisingly interesting." The vast majority also are achievement-oriented, both in their studies and in their involvement outside class. Most undergraduates are very active in 2 or more organizations. Some members think their classmates push themselves too hard, trying to excel at whatever they do. Says a senior: "One does not take courses at Southwestern just for the sake of being a student; the students want to be the best!" However, because there are few, if any, bell curves used in grading, undergraduates gladly work together in their efforts to excel.

Academics: Southwestern offers the bachelor's degree in 36 majors including a self-designed independent major. The academic year is divided into 2 semesters. Average class size for freshmen and sophomores ranges from 15 to 45, with courses such as Fundamentals of Physics enrolling near 50. However, most courses at the upper levels usually have between 15 and 20 participants, while more specialized courses like Latin IV and Computer Graphics, for example, may enroll just 3. "A student who wants to stay unknown will not have much luck here," says a communication studies major.

As part of the core requirements, first-year students must take English composition, a course in mathematics, and a first-year seminar. The seminar begins during fall orientation and ends midway through the first semester. The course combines strong academic content with such skills as critical and analytical thinking, writing, and speaking, which are needed throughout college-level courses. In the 2005–2006 school year, the university added the concept of "living-learning communities," giving students the option to take their first-year seminar with a small group of classmates who live together in a residence hall.

During their 4 years, students must also take classes from 7 groups of courses called Perspectives on Knowledge. Every senior must complete a capstone experience in his or her major, such as a special course, project, or comprehensive written and/or oral examination. Students must also demonstrate computer literacy within the framework of their majors.

Many of the 118 full-time and 49 part-time faculty members are real mind-benders. Nearly half, 47%, are women. As 1 student has said, "Top-notch scholars challenge us to stretch to our mental limits in class, and then sit down for coffee and doughnuts in the union for social interaction with us." As a tangible demonstration of this caring quality, faculty are noted for the midnight breakfast that they cook for the entire campus during finals. One sophomore, now a biology major, recalls doing poorly on several of the introductory biology quizzes and receiving a phone message from the professor asking the student to meet to discuss the problem. "The professors really care how students do," says the student, "even in intro-level classes."

History shines with professors "who are excited about what they do, and their enthusiasm rubs off on their students." Psychology, under an equally fine faculty, offers terrific clinical experience in internships at area hospitals, hospices, and schools, plus opportunities for research projects. Biology and chemistry have their own excellent research facilities that, over the past decade, have helped more than 70% of the premed applicants from Southwestern to gain acceptance to medical school. The dedication in 1999 of a new wing on the science building added new multimedia classrooms and a computer laboratory as well as more advanced research facilities. Says a junior: "Many science students have the chance for hands-on research with professors, often leading to publication." Political science earns kudos as well for an accomplished faculty who is involved in the classroom as well as in activities around campus. Sociology, economics, physics, and theater too, are winners, as are the interdisciplinary majors in women's and international studies, which shine with the best faculty drawn from diverse fields.

The foreign language department has improved, students say, but remains hampered by a tendency toward rigidness rather than innovation, which discourages greater student interest. Communication studies needs more "hands-on" courses to complement its theory-based approach to the subject. High demand for courses in both communication studies and religion have strained the capabilities of their "fantastic" faculty. Computer science, which some students also consider too "theory-based," still needs more staff, equipment, and opportunities for students.

Facilities: A. Frank Smith, Jr., Library Center has more than 312,000 volumes, 1372 periodicals, and, since construction of a roomy addition in 1988, twice the space it originally had. Providing more room has helped to lessen the distracting socializing that once occurred although some students still find the atmosphere a bit too chatty and think it may be time for another expansion. "Sometimes it's so full, it's hard to find a space," observes a junior. Users especially like studying in the alcoves with their overstuffed chairs and desks. There also are "plenty of outlets for plugging in laptops," notes a psychology major. Though Smith's own resources don't always answer students' needs, the on-line catalog hooks into the massive listings of the University of Texas at Austin, 30 minutes away, which only rarely lacks the required source.

About 150 PCs are located in the dorms, the library, and in SMART classrooms and labs around campus. The lab in Smith Library is open 24 hours. Students with their own computers, of whom there are many, have direct Internet access from their rooms.

Special programs: Southwestern's fall semester in London annually serves about 30 students and 2 faculty members. Tuition, room, and board for the London term are equal to those on campus, so the only extra costs are plane tickets and souvenirs. Some Southwestern faculty use their summers to lead programs in such countries as Korea, China, Spain, Turkey, Jamaica, or Mexico. A wide variety of year or semester exchanges overseas also are available. Undergraduates who prefer may spend a semester stateside in the state capital at Austin, in Washington, D.C., or in New York. A 3-2 engineering program is offered with 4 major universities. An initiative known as the Paideia Program enables select students to build connections between their classroom experience and out-of-the-classroom opportunities in such areas as leadership, service, intercultural experiences, collaborative research, and creative works. Students apply to the program early in the spring semester of their freshman year.

Campus life: Eighty percent of Southwestern's students reside on the 700-acre campus, located just a half hour from Austin. Greek life is a staple of the weekend social scene, involving 29% of the men and 31% of the women as members of 3 national fraternities and 4 national sororities. Everyone usually is welcome at the Greek parties and many independents attend. A new Friday Night Live program, sponsored by the Office of Student Activities and the University Programming Council, features a different musician, comedian, or other live performance every Friday though many students, mainly freshmen, still opt to leave campus for visits home. And, says a sophomore, "It isn't unusual for someone to say they have to study on Friday or Saturday night. The weekend's a time to catch up—sleep, work, partying—whatever you need!" About a tenth also are involved in the coed service fraternity. Student leadership groups are very popular as well. Proctors in the buildings at night, campus police, escorts, and a well-lit campus away from urban action help to minimize crime. "We are in our little community for the most part," says a junior.

The Southwestern Pirates compete in NCAA Division III as members of the Southern Collegiate Athletic Conference. One in 5 men participates in the 7 men's intercollegiate teams; without football in the heart of Texas, most fans turn out for the basketball, baseball, and soccer games. One in 10 women competes in 7 women's varsity sports, with volleyball and soccer drawing the best crowds. Lacrosse is a popular club sport; 7 of every 10 students play on the 9 intramural teams for each sex.

Georgetown (pop. 30,000) is located on the edge of the scenic Texas hill country, but doesn't offer much from the student's point of view. Exclaims a senior: "Socially, we're a bunch of college kids trying to have fun in a small, conservative Texas town—desperate!" For students with cars, Austin clubs and parties at the University of Texas provide relief. Closer, more natural escapes are Lake Georgetown and San Gabriel Park.

Cost cutters: Eighty-four percent of the freshmen and 83% of the continuing students enrolled in the 2005–2006 school year received financial aid. For 54% of the freshmen and 52% of the rest, the help was need-based. The average freshman award for a first-year student with financial need included a need-based scholarship or grant averaging $14,602 and need-based self-help aid such as loans and jobs averaging $4709. Other non-need-based awards and scholarships averaged $8121. The average debt of 2005 graduates was $18,393. Southwestern offers a wide range of merit-based awards. Three entering freshmen each year are named Brown Scholars and receive annual tuition, room, and board. To be eligible, students must rank in the top 5% of their high school class or post a GPA of 3.9 if the school does not rank its students and should score at least 1400 on the SAT in math and critical reading or 32 on the ACT. Finalists are invited to campus for an interview in early March. All candidates for admission are automatically considered for general academic scholarships that range from $2000 to $15,000 per year, depending on students' class rank or GPA, standardized test scores, and other achievements.

Rate of return: Eighty-nine percent of freshmen return for the sophomore year. Sixty-seven percent graduate in 4 years; given 1 more year, 77% receive their diplomas; 78% do it in 6 years.

Payoff: In 2005, the 3 top majors among graduates were communication at 14%, and business and political science at 9% each. About 25% of the new alumni went directly to graduate or professional schools. Within 5 years, about 70% of all graduates decide to further their schooling. Most of those who enter the workforce join businesses or the teaching profession, usually within Texas.

Bottom line: "The more I'm here, the more I appreciate the value of a liberal arts education," says a Texan. "This school is great for a highly motivated, intelligent senior who can appreciate and adapt to a small, tightly knit campus in a quaint, lackluster town." Adds another Texan more bluntly: "Those looking for a big school or a huge football tradition should steer clear."

Texas A&M University

College Station, Texas 77843

Setting: Urban
Control: Public
Undergraduate enrollment: 16,787 men, 16,344 women
Graduate enrollment: 3937 men, 2585 women
Student/faculty ratio: 20:1
Freshman profile: 8% scored over 700 on SAT I verbal; 37% scored 600–700; 40% 500–599; 15% below 500. 15% scored over 700 on SAT I math; 45% scored 600–700; 31% 500–599; 9% below 500. 25% scored above 28 on the ACT; 15% scored 27–28; 30% 24–26; 20% 21–23; 10% below 21. 50+% graduated in top tenth of high school class; 80% in upper fourth.

Faculty profile: 93% Ph.D.'s
Tuition and fees: $6399 in-state, $14,679 out-of-state
Room and board: $6952
Freshman financial aid: 73%; average scholarship or grant: $2936 need-based; $3339 non-need-based
Campus jobs: 41%; average earnings: $3824/year
Application deadline: Feb. 15
Financial aid deadline: Apr. 1
Admissions information: (979) 845–3741
   e-mail: admissions@tamu.edu
   web site: www.tamu.edu/admissions

Imagine a college big enough to have its own language and customs, its own foreign relations, and, some would say, its own army. Imagine it set on an 8500-acre campus, with nearly 45,000 students—plus a registered Collie named Reveille—all sporting some item of maroon and white, and you've got Texas A&M University. Opened in 1876, A&M is the oldest public institution of higher education in Texas, and traditions run deep. They range from the serious Silver Taps ceremony held to honor a deceased Aggie to the silly Elephant Walk, in which seniors, 2 or 3 days before the big football game against the University of Texas Longhorns, form a single line and wander around campus like dying elephants seeking a secluded spot to end their days. The highly visible Corps of Cadets, an Aggie mainstay since A&M's earliest days as a military institution, involves between 1800 and 2000 men and women, and historically has graduated more officers than any other institution (other than the military academies) in the nation. But one of the best traditions for the budget-conscious is the low tuition, just $6399 for Texans in 2005–2006 and just under $15,000 for others, providing a value to which a student can say "Howdy," the traditional Aggie greeting.

Student body: Though all undergraduates become Aggies for life, 95% begin as Texans, with classmates coming from every state and 115 foreign countries. Just over 16% are members of minority groups: 10% Hispanic, 3% Asian-American, 3% African-American, and less than 1% Native American. Eight percent are foreign nationals. The student body tends to be conservative and traditional in politics and ideas, as well as respectful and friendly to newcomers. On a campus so large, the hype and tradition give every individual a sense of belonging rarely found in such a huge student community. To further promote the sense of closeness, the Vice President for Student Affairs holds a series of luncheons and "chat and chew" sessions to get to know students better. Says a senior: "This is the closest community of 45,000 students that could possibly exist." Though students clearly are motivated about being members of "Aggieland," not all are as enthusiastic about their studies, though competition is keen in such fields as business and engineering, and the percent of freshmen who ultimately earn degrees is the highest among public universities in-state. Observes a senior: "The academics produce more note takers than true free thinkers."

Academics: Texas A&M offers bachelor's degrees in 139 fields and degrees through the doctorate at 9 colleges. The academic year is divided into 2 semesters. Freshmen can begin the school year in August by attending Fish Camp, a 4-day orientation for first-year students in which they learn about Aggie traditions and receive helpful tips for living a successful collegiate life in Aggieland. Classes in the first year start as low as 24 in English courses and have run as high as 340 in introductory chemistry lectures. Advises a junior: "The large weed-out classes during a student's first year are perhaps the most difficult milestones." Most classes for juniors and seniors fall below 60, and some in more specialized areas enroll only a dozen. The most crowded courses tend to be in the engineering, agriculture, and business colleges.

As part of A&M's core curriculum, students must take 12 hours of American history and government, 8 hours of science, and 4 of physical education, plus 6 each in social and behavioral sciences, speech and writing skills, humanities, and visual and performing arts, and mathematical/logical reasoning. Undergraduates also must demonstrate competency in computer skills and a foreign language. Students' main complaint is that the classes taken to fulfill these requirements are generally very large in size with lesser quality teaching.

The faculty in a recent year consisted of 1898 full-time members and 334 part-time. No figures are available to show the portion who teach undergraduates, though in earlier years fewer than 600 of the full-time members and fewer than 200 of the part-time taught at the graduate level only. Twenty-seven percent were women. A tenth of the introductory classes, down from a fourth in recent years, are taught by graduate students, whose quality varies. The university has its share of top-flight faculty, including 1 Nobelist and 1 Pulitzer Prize winner. Although some faculty are anxious to head for the labs, students still find many willing to talk and help. What makes them great, remarks a psychology major, "is their desire to teach and learn at the same time." That desire becomes more evident to students as they reach the smaller, higher level courses.

Historically strong divisions with high enrollments, solid teaching and research, and cutting-edge facilities include the colleges of Agriculture and Life Sciences, Engineering, Science, and Veterinary Medicine plus the Mays Business School. Although most programs in these colleges are first-rate, a few here and in other divisions are regarded as top tier. Examples include chemistry, entomology, management, anthropology, oceanography, physics, veterinary physiology, pharmacology, and chemical, industrial, mechanical, nuclear, and petroleum engineering.

The colleges of Liberal Arts and Education and Human Development tend to hide in the shadows of the other better-funded colleges, although English, in the College of Liberal Arts, has been among the fastest growing departments on campus. The fine arts have begun to garner some attention as well, with a recently formed music program, though there is still no major in art and the number of art classes remains small. Religious studies and Hispanic studies are available as minors only, though there is a doctoral program in Hispanic studies. Foreign language and literature classes are limited as well, although Spanish, French, German, and Russian are offered as majors. Says a junior: "The liberal arts need to attract more students and find ways to attract more money and distinguished faculty."

Facilities: Sterling C. Evans Library has 3.3 million volumes, 5.4 million microform items, 49,000 periodicals, and seats for 4000 readers spread across its 6 stories, which includes a new addition. The quality of the collection, however, is mediocre, according to users; as tough as it is for an Aggie to admit, "Evans is not as good as the library at the University of Texas," says a history major. Adds a sophomore in general studies: "For a campus of our size we lack a main library to brag about." Nevertheless, various components of Evans are worth at least a mild boast, among them the LibCat computerized system that makes researching more than 3 million books and thousands of journal articles comparatively easy. More than 200 databases and numerous other online catalogs, among them WorldCat that connects students with the holdings of libraries around the world are available. The catalog of UT Austin also is on database and a weekly shuttle is provided. Another bright spot is the Medical Sciences Library, also on campus, which holds an additional 100,000 volumes on biomedical topics as well as 1800 periodicals in the field and is very conducive to silent study. Not to be outdone, the new West Campus Library serving primarily the undergraduate and graduate business programs offers a variety of "awesome research aids," says a marketing major, along with "great group study rooms, couches, and an aesthetically pleasing environment."

About 2000 Macs and PCs are available to students in various locales throughout the campus. Their settings range from the 600-seat student microcomputer facility to the sophisticated Computer Services Center, where specialized software can help students prepare a report with supporting graphics, to the numerous smaller facilities together housing more than 1000 units in most general-access buildings. Some facilities are open 24 hours a day. "They are awesome," says a communications major.

Special programs: For the same low tuition that they pay in Aggieland, students can attend a wide range of foreign universities in 12 countries with which Texas A&M has agreements. An honors program offers more intimate courses and independent study opportunities to students in all majors. A 5-year MBA/liberal arts program also is an option.

Campus life: Just 27% of Texas A&M students actually reside on campus, although the bulk of the rest live in apartments close by that house only students and are connected to the campus by university-owned buses. Six percent of the men are members of 19 national fraternities; 7% of the women belong to 2 local and 19 national sororities. However, says a senior, "we are all Aggies first and foremost, so even if you aren't Greek you still are very much a part of Aggieland." In fact, many Greeks and independents find their special niches in the more than 700 clubs and organizations available. Along with the Greeks and the Corps of Cadets, other popular organizations are the Opera and Performing Arts Society (OPAS), responsible for bringing national ballet and orchestra groups to the land of country western music, and the Aggie Orientation Leader Program, whose members plan and help conduct the special Fish Camp for freshmen. Thefts of books and bicycles are the most common crimes in Aggieland; security measures include a diala-ride program to order transportation after dark and emergency telephones across campus. The Corps of Cadets also runs an escort service at all hours of the night.

Does one need to say that football dominates Aggie weekends in the fall? The ritual actually begins the night before home games with "Midnight Yell Practice," a spirited session conducted at midnight with some 3000 yellers. Sufficiently revved up, the Aggie fans, known collectively as the Twelfth Man, turn out the next day to support the team by standing throughout the game, another Aggie tradition. This ritual actually started with the original Twelfth Man, a onetime player and spectator who donned the team uniform and stood ready to jump into the 1922 game against national champion Centre College in Kentucky if the Aggies lost too many men to injuries.

The Aggie flame may dim somewhat after football season, but it never goes entirely out. NCAA Division I sports are big at A&M, with baseball drawing the second biggest crowds of the 9 intercollegiate sports for men. Of the 12 varsity sports for women, basketball, volleyball, and softball spark the greatest interest. (Riflery is a coed sport.) Nearly half of all undergraduates participate in the two dozen intramural sports available for each sex, everything from flag football and handball to wallyball, pickleball, flickerball, and 16-inch softball.

Students who long to see some non-Aggies can travel to Houston and Austin, each about 2 hours away. Galveston, the site of Texas A&M's coastal campus, San Antonio, and Dallas, also are popular destinations at about 3 hours drive by car.

Cost cutters: In the 2005–2006 school year, 73% of the freshmen and 76% of continuing students received financial aid; for 58% of the freshmen and 71% of continuing students, the aid was need-based. The average freshman award for a student with financial need included a need-based scholarship or grant averaging $2936 and need-based self-help aid such as loans and job earnings averaging $6144. Other non-need-based awards and scholarships averaged $3339. No figure is given for non-need-based athletic scholarships. Average debts of recent grads totaled $15,490. Every year, more than 1000 new scholarship offers are made by the university's Office of Honors Programs and Academic Scholarships. About 200 President's Endowed Scholarships, each worth a total of $12,000 over 4 years, and 200 Lechner and McFadden awards, worth $2500 a year, go to entering students who ranked in the top 10% of their high school class and scored at least 1300 on the math and critical reading SATs (30 ACT). Students who have an admissions application on file by early January are reviewed for other scholarship options. Preference is given to those who have succeeded academically despite difficult circumstances. Out-of-state recipients of college and departmental level scholarships valued at $1000 or more annually qualify for a non-resident tuition waiver. Cooperative education programs are available in all but the College of Education.

Rate of return: Ninety percent of entering freshmen return for a second year of Aggie traditions. Though only 32% graduate in 4 years, 69% do so within 5 years; 76% in 6 years.

Payoff: For the graduates of 2005, the most popular majors were interdisciplinary studies at 6%, psychology at 5%, and biomedical science at 4%. Approximately 1500 companies and organizations routinely recruit at Texas A&M, and new alumni have few fears about finding a job. Notes a senior: "Former students are always looking to hire another Aggie, so that the network for finding jobs is incredible." Aggies end up just about everywhere doing almost anything, but usually find positions in such fields as engineering, computer science, accounting, and finance; employers include General Dynamics and Texas Instruments. A tenth of recent graduates split evenly between medical school and law school.

Bottom line: Undergraduates who lack a sense of independence may have trouble in Aggieland, though the student body is amazingly close for such a large university. The blood of those who stick it out, however, is guaranteed to turn deep maroon as they start talking and acting like an Aggie. And the future looks bright. "We have a riddle here," observes an alumnus. "What do you call an Aggie 5 years after graduation? The answer is 'BOSS.'"

Texas Christian University

Fort Worth, Texas 76129

Setting: Suburban
Control: Private (Disciples of Christ)
Undergraduate enrollment: 2654 men, 4064 women
Graduate enrollment: 303 men, 315 women
Student/faculty ratio: 15:1
Freshman profile: Middle 50% range of SAT I scores: 520–620 verbal; 540–640 math; Middle range ACT composite: 23–28. 53% graduated in top fifth of high school class.
Faculty profile: 91% Ph.D.'s
Tuition and fees: $21,320

Room and board: $6980
Freshman financial aid: NA; average scholarship or grant: NA
Campus jobs: NA; average earnings: NA
Application deadline: Feb. 15
Financial aid deadline: May 1
Admissions information: (817) 257-7490; 1-800-TCU-FROG
e-mail: frogmail@tcu.edu
web site: www.tcu.edu

According to students, getting rid of stereotypes is one of Texas Christian University's biggest problems. Although TCU's name may suggest a college where chapel is required and rules about good, clean living are strictly enforced, that is not the case. TCU is affiliated with the Disciples of Christ, but the church has minimal impact on how the school is run. Nevertheless, as a Texan notes, "there is a TCU stereotype that some students feel they have to fit. Outsiders think we're all rich, upper class, white Texans—not true. And students who come here thinking they can play the social games that were seen on the TV show *Dallas* don't last long." While TCU is 76% Texan and has its share of upper-income students, it also has undergraduates from all but 2 states and 75 foreign countries, drawn largely by total costs of just over $28,000 in the 2005–2006 school year and by well-respected programs in fields such as the natural sciences, business, and communications. To some, TCU may signify a certain set of social standards, but to prospective employers and admissions officers at graduate and professional schools in a wide range of fields, TCU means excellence.

Student body: Of the 14% of the students who are members of minority groups, 6% are Hispanics, 5% African-Americans, 2% Asian-Americans, and less than 1% Native Americans. Four percent are foreign nationals. Ninety-five percent of all undergraduates attended public schools. Five percent are members of the Disciples of Christ Church; 51% are members of other Protestant denominations. Undergraduates are generally conservative, Republican, and quite outgoing and friendly. In the past, many acquired the label "bubble children" because of a lack of awareness of life-styles less fortunate than their own. Some of that narrowness is breaking down, however, as the student body becomes more diversified; many students attracted to the music, dance, radio, and journalism programs are less preppy and more liberal in their thinking. Still there remains some pressure to conform, mostly within the large and influential Greek system. Whatever social pressure exists, however, rarely enters the classroom. Although premed and upper-level business students, as well as those in the honors program, can be quite intense, a majority keep their studies in perspective. While undergraduates note that it is "cool to get an A here," studying to the exclusion of everything else, or at the expense of anyone else, is frowned upon. Says a nursing student: "Our crowded study rooms and library underline the emphasis on academics. The emptiness of the dorms on Friday and Saturday nights proves that students can effectively unwind."

Academics: TCU, founded in 1873 as the AddRan Male and Female College, awards the bachelor's degree in almost 100 majors, plus degrees through the doctorate in about 20 areas. Undergraduate programs are offered in 5 colleges and 2 schools; Brite Divinity School is for graduate work only. Classes average 27 students, and range from 10 for some language courses to between 100 and 150 for science lectures, which break into labs of about 15 participants. Warns a junior: "Incoming freshmen should expect classes so small that skipping them without being noticed becomes difficult."

A new core curriculum that took effect with fall 2005 freshmen structures courses in 3 categories. "Essential competencies" include writing, mathematical reasoning, and oral communication. The Human Experiences and Endeavors section requires classes in the humanities, fine arts, natural sciences, and social sciences. The final area in the Heritage, Mission, Vision, and Values curriculum mandates coursework in such areas as global and cultural awareness and citizenship and social values.

TCU's faculty includes 467 full-time members. There is no data to show the number of part-time members, though in previous years there were about 200. There also are no figures to show the number that teach undergraduates, though, again, in earlier years, the vast majority of full-time members did so. Women comprise 37% of the full-time members. Most students are comfortable with the balance that many faculty members have reached between teaching and research. With few exceptions, as a chemistry major notes, "they are interested in undergraduate learning and don't sacrifice this for research success. The fact that they do maintain impressive research programs, however, is definitely a benefit to us." First-year students, in particular, are delighted to find faculty members so involved with their classes. Says one: "Many of my teachers look for class participation and interaction as opposed to simple lecturing and note taking." A sophomore was delighted when one of her biology professors a year ago e-mailed her about how well she had done on the final exam. "He said he was proud of me," she recalls. "That individual attention is quite the norm here."

TCU's reputation for strength in the natural sciences is well deserved, with demanding faculties and curricula and recently renovated labs helping to place 92% of the premed students into medical, dental, and veterinary schools. Contributions from Tandy Corporation have helped push facilities at the M.J. Neeley School of Business a notch above the competition, with excellent advising and extensive equipment such as computer labs and videotape rooms for classroom recording aimed at developing students' writing and speaking skills. Finance majors get to invest a $1.4 million portfolio in the school's student-run Educational Investment Fund. "The emphasis," says an accounting major, "is on doing and learning, not sitting and learning." Not to be outdone is the building for the colleges of Fine Arts and Communication, which provides excellent equipment, and a site for outstanding tutorials and instruction in disciplines as wide ranging as art history, dance, and journalism and for the radio/TV/film department. The program in speech-language pathology in the Harris College of Nursing and Health Sciences is very highly regarded and offers an on-campus clinic providing valuable hands-on experience. Nursing students at the college also benefit from the integration of computers into the curriculum, as well as from an emphasis on good, old-fashioned hard work. The most distinctive new instructor is Hal, a 6-foot human patient simulator that is controlled by computers and can change size, gender, and age to simulate different types of patients in distress. Hal is preprogrammed with 90 different patient scenarios that allow students to see immediately the consequences of the care they have provided. Religion majors in the AddRan College of Humanities and Social Sciences enjoy nationally recognized scholars and other connections to the Brite Divinity School, while students in English, philosophy, political science, and fashion merchandising and interior design boast their own divinely inspired faculties and curriculum.

Psychology is regarded by students from diverse fields as "among the majors anyone can get through if all else fails," says a science student. "Many do well in this program, but others are able just to slide through." The College of Education also has a reputation for being less demanding than other divisions and could use more space as well as more rigor. The only foreign language major is Spanish, which majors say is a solid program but needs to offer a wider range of courses. Minors only are offered in French, German, and Japanese, plus instruction in Greek and Italian. The engineering department, founded in 1996, has been playing catch-up to the more established engineering departments found at other Texas schools, but watch out! The new $25 million Tucker Technology Center, housing mathematics, engineering, and computer science, offers 6 state-of-the-art engineering labs as well as classrooms, seminar rooms, and senior design spaces and 2 general-use computer science labs with 62 workstations.

Facilities: On such a social campus, it is not surprising that Mary Couts Burnett Library, located near the center of campus, is a favorite meeting place, and not just to read Dryden, Dostoevsky, or Darwin. "It's the place to be after 6 p.m.," says a junior. The newest addition, the Bistro Burnett located in the library lobby, only adds to the social air with its menu of Starbucks coffee and Krispy Kreme donuts that can be brought into the study areas. For those determined to get something done, a designated "quiet area" has become a place for silent companionship. "The best place on campus to study," says one user, "just quiet rows of books and books and books." Students researching papers generally find the collection of just over 2 million volumes and 28,727 paper and electronic periodicals more than adequate for a school of 6700 undergraduates. A computerized catalog and Internet access as well as access to assorted databases and electronic journals make the research process even more satisfying. In fact, says a speech pathology major: "We turn to the computer for most of our information; the library tends to be additional."

You don't hear too many complaints about limited access to computers, especially since the Tucker Technology Center opened. More than a thousand PCs are available for student use in Tucker plus another 12 PC labs, 6 Macintosh labs, and other sites on campus. Labs generally are open until midnight or 2 a.m. most nights of the week. All student dormitory rooms, including fraternity and sorority houses, have been wired as well to provide network connections to each resident, and students say most of their classmates seem to have their own units. Says a sophomore, "I would speculate that many students choose to bring a computer over a car, if they have to choose between the two." The university also strongly recommends that students have their own personal computers. Wireless access is available on many parts of campus.

Special programs: TCU offers study for a semester or a year abroad in 28 countries, including Spain, Italy, and England, as well as in South America, Japan, and Australia. TCU faculty members from various disciplines also lead summer courses in various countries throughout the world; the university's own London Study Centre provides semester-long academic programs. An internship program is offered in London as is a student exchange with the University of the Americas in Puebla, Mexico, or Kansai Gaidai University in Osaka, Japan. A fall semester at the Washington Center in the nation's capital is popular, too. Project PRISM provides leadership skills classes, campus and community service opportunities, international experiences, and a community leader mentor program for those students interested in developing as leaders.

Campus life: Not quite half of TCU's students, 46%, live on the 300+-acre campus, 3 miles from downtown Fort Worth. As a rule, Fridays are date nights, and Saturdays are party nights, but Thursday nights, when the 1 local and 12 national fraternities and 3 local and 13 national sororities have their mixers, are the biggest of all. Fraternities and sororities are quite popular at TCU; 35% of the men and 40% of the women belong. Membership has declined, however, since several years ago, when nearly half the student body pledged. Most Greek activities are held off campus and restricted to members, making some independents feel left out their freshman year, although most eventually find some outlet of interest in the 200 student organizations that are available. Crime is always a concern because of TCU's location in a major city the size of Fort Worth (pop. 480,000). Security measures are plentiful, from keeping all outside residence hall doors locked around the clock, to installing numerous emergency call boxes to maintaining a varied security patrol—the Froggy 5-0—"on golf carts, bikes, and rollerblades," says a senior. "But the main problem we have is students' common sense," says a junior, "like going running wearing headphones at 3 a.m." A recent problem with car break-ins was stemmed by the installation of security cameras and fences.

NCAA Division I sporting events used to be used more as social occasions, where people gathered to see who else was there and to decide where to go that night, rather than as opportunities to cheer on the Horned Frog teams. Enter the student-led HyperFrogs who paint their bodies purple and yell spirited cheers at football and basketball games, generally the best attended of the 8 men's and 9 women's varsity sports. Fifty recreational sports are offered to men, women, and mixed groups.

When students get the urge to dance the two-step, Billy Bob's and other clubs around Fort Worth are the places to go. For bigger clubs, undergraduates drive to Dallas, a half hour away, which also offers true sports fans the Dallas Cowboys and other professional teams. San Antonio, Austin, and Houston are other popular weekend destinations.

Cost cutters: Endowment and gift income enable students to pay just 60% of the real cost of their educations. No financial data is available for the 2005–2006 school year, but in an earlier year, 82% of all freshmen and 63% of the continuing students received additional financial help with their college costs. For 39% of the freshmen and 34% of the rest, the aid was need based. No data is available on the average freshman award for any recent or current school year. Academic Scholarships recently ranged from $4000 to full tuition and are awarded on the basis of scholarship and leadership; to be considered, a student typically has had combined SATs in critical reading and math of 1230 or an ACT composite of 27, and ranked in the top 15% of his or her high school class. Chancellor's Scholarships pay full tuition, and Dean's and Faculty awards were recently worth $8000 and $6000 a year, respectively.

Rate of return: Eighty-four percent of all freshmen return for the sophomore year. Sixty-nine percent go on to graduate in 6 years.

Payoff: Marketing at 9% was the most popular major among undergraduates who earned degrees in a recent year. Finance and advertising/public relations followed at 6% each. Slightly more than half of the graduating seniors in a recent class took jobs right away, many in such fields as education, journalism, radio/TV/film, nursing, the military, government, accounting, marketing, and management. Many remain in Texas, with a large concentration staying in the Dallas/Fort Worth metropolitan area; 135 companies and organizations recruited on campus during a recent school year. No data is available on the number who pursue advanced degrees.

Bottom line: For students eager to become involved in a friendly, largely conservative university community where both Greeks and Horned Frogs are big, Texas Christian just could be the place. Says a southerner: "At TCU, I receive an excellent education, professors who care, a push to get involved in campus activities and leadership positions. Students who are introverted or limited in involvement may not be able to make the most of what TCU has to offer."

Trinity University

San Antonio, Texas 78212

Setting: Suburban
Control: Private (Presbyterian)
Undergraduate enrollment: 1124 men, 1292 women
Graduate enrollment: 52 men, 82 women
Student/faculty ratio: 10:1
Freshman profile: 25% scored over 700 on SAT I verbal; 53% scored 600–700; 21% 500–599; 1% below 500. 20% scored over 700 on SAT I math; 60% scored 600–700; 20% 500–599; 0% below 500. 51% scored above 28 on the ACT; 26% scored 27–28; 19% 24–26; 3% 21–23; 1% below 21. 49% graduated in top tenth of high school class; 72% in upper fifth.
Faculty profile: 97% Ph.D.'s

Tuition and fees: $22,277
Room and board: $7880
Freshman financial aid: 78%; average scholarship or grant: NA
Campus jobs: NA; average earnings: NA
Application deadline: Early decision and early action I: Nov. 1; early action II: Dec.15; regular: Feb.1
Financial aid deadline: Priority: Feb. 1; Regular: Apr. 1
Admissions information: (210) 999-7207;
(800) TRINITY
e-mail:admissions@trinity.edu
web site: www.trinity.edu

When it came to tracking outlaws on the Texas frontier, the Texas Rangers always got their man through dogged determination, self-reliance, and resourcefulness. With a similar single-mindedness of purpose and an independent flair, Trinity University in San Antonio has pursued its goal of becoming one of the best small universities in the nation (not just Texas), and by the looks of things, has gotten its men—and women. Once dismissed by serious students as a country-club college for the rich, Trinity now boasts a first-year class in which a third graduated first in their high school classes, a faculty of whom 97% hold Ph.D.'s or terminal degrees, and a library whose collection of more than 927,000 volumes and 2135 periodicals marks a growth matched by few other colleges or universities, more than doubling its size in one 10-year period. Making all this possible is an endowment that has mushroomed from just $100 million in 1979 to more than $733 million as of May 2005, and that enables Trinity to charge students just half the true cost of their education. As an added incentive to convince top scholars to give Trinity a try, more than three-fourths of students receive some kind of financial assistance on top of the cut-rate tuition. In the battle for top students, Trinity makes it tough for a prospective freshman looking for top quality at a good price to say "no."

Student body: Sixty-nine percent of Trinity's students are Texans (including 10% from the surrounding geographic area), though 44 states and 30 foreign countries are represented. Hispanics comprise 11% of the enrollment, followed by Asian-Americans at 6%, African-Americans at 3%, foreign nationals at 2.5%, and Native Americans at 1%. The Trinity Multicultural Network works hard to educate majority students about all aspects of diversity and acceptance. Twenty-seven percent of the students attended private or parochial schools. Six percent are Presbyterian. Students politically and socially are considered "fairly liberal" for Texas and not as uniformly conservative as some might think. Observes a Texan: "It has been said that Trinity is the most conservative liberal arts school around, but I disagree. While there are many active political and social conservatives, as one would expect for any institution in Texas, there are also a wide variety of liberals and opposing viewpoints. One of the great strengths of Trinity is its political diversity." Undergraduates are described as intelligent, energetic, a bit preppy, and focused on keeping pace with the demanding curriculum, "very GPA driven," says a junior. Students mainly put pressure on themselves to succeed, viewing good grades as the key to enviable jobs and graduate school placements. The fact that the university does not grade on a bell curve allows "everyone to have his or her chance for an'A,' which eliminates much of the competition," observes a senior.

Academics: Trinity, which was founded in 1869, awards the bachelor's degree in 37 majors and master's degrees in education, health care administration, and accounting. Classes, on the semester system, generally are small, with most in the early years ranging from 20 to 40 students, although the largest class, such as Chemistry in the Modern World, may exceed 100. Juniors and seniors are likely to share courses with 10 to 20 classmates.

Trinity's common curriculum is built on a theme of 6 "fundamental understandings," or ways of looking at the world, ranging from understanding the intellectual heritage of Western culture and other cultures to understanding the world through science. In addition to these courses, an undergraduate must take a first-year seminar centered on a specific theme, a writing workshop, and courses or tests to demonstrate competency in a foreign language, computer, and mathematics skills, and lifetime fitness. "Most students think of the requirements as being like vegetables," says an engineering science major. "No one likes to eat them but they're good for you." And sometimes, as students surprised by their own choice of majors will attest, freshmen end up loving the turnips put on their plates and make them part of a steady diet.

Trinity's faculty consists of 240 full-time members and 67 part-time. Women make up a third of the full-time ranks. Students for the most part find the faculty to be knowledgeable and generally quite accessible. Says a Texan: "Most are available and willing to help students even beyond their posted office hours, and I never feel uncomfortable dropping in to any professor's office unannounced. It is also easy to forge personal relationships with most, which is very beneficial in regard to academic advising, recommendation letters, etc." Adds a senior from the Southwest: "They challenge us and then they help us achieve their high expectations."

The combination of top faculties, facilities, and students has produced some outstanding departments. Undergraduates majoring in chemistry, biology, and physics work with equipment, such as 2 high-field nuclear magnetic resonance spectrometers and ultraviolet, infrared, and mass spectral instrumentation, that lets them perform research and present papers on a par with those in some graduate programs. "Sociology and political science are fabulous departments," exclaims a major in sociology and urban studies. Professors with varied expertise and willingness to inspire all students and give special help to those having trouble make both areas so strong. English, economics, and engineering also draw praise for their impressive faculties. Business majors find the coursework challenging and especially enjoy the "Student Managed Fund" course that gives participants hands-on investment experience managing $800,000 from the university endowment fund. Accounting is considered especially strong. The interdisciplinary urban studies program also is viewed as a gem of a small department.

The modern languages and literature department offers majors in Chinese, French, German, Russian, and Spanish, but could always use additional instructors to provide a greater variety of courses within each field. The art department should become stronger following renovation of the Ruth Taylor Fine Arts Center, which was nearing completion in spring 2006.

Facilities: Coates Library may be fast growing but many students find it so quiet and so cozy with overstuffed chairs at every window that they tend to fall asleep while studying. On the whole, the library has become Trinity's increasingly popular study and research center. Says an English major: "Recent banning of cell phones and enforcement of noise policies have made it a much more conducive place to study." Students find the computerized research aids to be constantly improving and especially helpful as are the librarians who, says a senior, "make doing research on a topic outside your major less scary." Many students just wish the library were open later than midnight.

Recent renovations to the library, in the words of a junior, provided "one whole floor dedicated to lounge-style study space with abundant personal computers that is not as cumbersome as a lab setting." The library and most academic buildings as well as most external areas on upper campus also are equipped with wireless connectivity for laptops. "Most students have computers," continues the junior, "but use labs as a convenience rather than walking back to their dorms." Altogether, 2 general-purpose and several departmental labs holding more than 180 computers are usually open until midnight, though some students wish more labs were open later. The university strongly recommends that students have their own computers.

Special programs: Approximately 40% of Trinity students in a recent graduating class spent some time abroad in some 3 dozen countries covering 6 continents. Every year, about 30 to 40 students conduct independent or faculty-supervised research.

Campus life: Because freshmen, sophomores, and juniors are required to live on campus, three-fourths of all undergraduates end up residing on the 117-acre hilltop campus, which overlooks the city of San Antonio. Nine local fraternities and 6 local sororities involve about a quarter of the men and women. The Greek societies sponsor a mixture of all-school functions and events restricted to members. Says a sophomore: "Greek life dominates Trinity social life, especially at night." The absence of Greek houses helps to reduce divisions between members and independents. Still, observes a female student, "It is easier to be an independent as a female rather than a male because parties don't tend to exclude women whereas they do exclude men." Local clubs offer good entertainment alternatives and participation in campus clubs goes without saying. Says a business major: "Although not a requirement, being involved is a big part of being a student at Trinity." Interest in community service has grown from just 50 members involved several years ago in the Trinity University Voluntary Action Center (TUVAC) to at least 45% of the student body. Says a senior: "I haven't met a single person who has never been involved in TUVAC one way or another." Car break-ins and vandalism represent the most serious problems around the Trinity campus. Theft from residence halls is kept low thanks to locked outside doors. Security phones are widespread around campus and an escort service is provided for individuals who need to go out after dark.

The university fields 9 Tiger teams for men and 9 for women; 20% of the men and 12% of the women in a recent year participated. All sports are NCAA Division III. Football and men's and women's soccer and basketball boast the best attendance, with good reason. The women's basketball team won the Division III national championship in 2002–2003, and 4 of Trinity's teams, football, men's and women's soccer, and volleyball, all recently qualified for the Final Four in their respective sports. Seventy-five percent of the students take part in a very active intramural program, with 16 sports for men, 13 for women, and 4 for both, including coed trap and skeet shooting. Each residence hall elects an IM representative to encourage students to play.

For escape, students head to San Antonio's famed River Walk or to San Antonio Spurs games. For more distant getaways, the beautiful Texas hill country is about an hour away, the coast 2½ hours.

Cost cutters: Thanks to Trinity's large endowment, 78% of the freshmen and more than 75% of all students received some type of financial assistance in a recent school year. Need-based aid went to 43% of the undergraduates. In a recent year, the average financial aid package totaled $14,484, although no figures are available to show the amount that were grants and scholarships or loans and job earnings. Almost 50% of Trinity students receive merit-based awards. Trinity awards 3 academic scholarships, the Murchison, President's, and Trustee's awards, that range in value from $4000 to $12,000 a year and are renewable. To be considered, students should have ranked in the top fifth of their high school class, have a GPA of 3.5 or higher, and a combined SAT math and critical reading score of at least 1260 or a 28 ACT. Baker Duncan Scholarships pay $2000 to $10,000 to students planning to major in art or participate in music, theater, or debate. A separate application is required. National Presbyterian Scholarships pay $500 to $1400. A low-interest loan program also is offered.

Rate of return: Students drawn to Trinity generally like what they find. Eighty-nine percent of the entering freshmen return for a second year. Sixty-seven percent graduate in 4 years; 75% in 5 years; 77% in 6.

Payoff: Just over half of all 2005 graduates earned degrees in 3 disciplines: 21% in business/marketing, 20% in social sciences and history, and 11% in modern languages and literature. Nearly a third of Trinity graduates begin work immediately toward advanced degrees in a wide range of graduate and professional programs. Those seeking jobs usually are most successful in such areas as accounting, business management, computer applications, and engineering. One hundred companies and other organizations usually recruit on campus.

Bottom line: Students who are happiest at Trinity share the same drive as their university: to be the best and to have a grand time getting there.

University of Dallas

Irving, Texas 75062

Setting: Suburban
Control: Private (Roman Catholic)
Undergraduate enrollment: 454 men, 616 women
Graduate enrollment: 255 men, 191 women
Student/faculty ratio: 11:1
Freshman profile: 27% scored over 700 on SAT I verbal; 44% scored 600–700; 24% 500–599; 5% below 500. 10% scored over 700 on SAT I math; 44% scored 600–700; 37% 500–599; 9% below 500. 33% scored above 28 on the ACT; 17% scored 27–28; 24% 24–26; 17% 21–23; 9% below 21. 42% graduated in top tenth of high school class; 71% in upper fifth.
Faculty profile: 92% Ph.D.'s

Tuition and fees: $20,406
Room and board: $7026
Freshman financial aid: 98%; average scholarship or grant: $3460 need-based; $8680 non-need-based
Campus jobs: 37%; average earnings: $1200/year
Application deadline: Early action: Nov. 1 and Dec. 1; regular: Mar. 1
Financial aid deadline: Mar. 1 (Scholarships: Jan. 15)
Admissions information: (972) 721–5266;
  (800) 628-6999
  e-mail: ugadmis@udallas.edu
  web site: www.udallas.edu

Welcome to the University of Dallas. Your classmates this year will be a bunch of folks who need no introduction: Plato, Virgil, St. Francis of Assisi. Spend your first year getting to know each other here on your home turf, and then spend some time in Rome, the Eternal City, with side trips to Greece. Tuition, room, and board for a year here—or abroad—are just about the national average for private colleges, but the education you'll get, sponsored by the Roman Catholic Church, is anything but. Though just turning 50 years old in 2005, the University of Dallas goes to the age-old heart of the liberal arts experience. Its prescribed courses use original texts, in translation, of the world's great thinkers. About 85% of Dallas students spend a semester of their sophomore year at the university's campus in Rome. "The Rome experience makes it clear why we study a core curriculum," says a junior. "The semester I was there, I never found another student at a different university who experienced both the intense learning and the travel options that we did. It's the opportunity of a lifetime."

Student body: Fifty-seven percent of the undergraduates at the University of Dallas are Texans. Most of the rest are from the Midwest or California, though students come from 49 states and 18 foreign countries. Sixty-seven percent are Roman Catholic, and 7% are Protestant. Twenty-three percent claim no religious affiliation. Advises a sophomore: "UD is a Catholic university but does not necessarily require the independent-thinking student who would be ideal to attend UC to be Catholic or of any religious affiliation." Forty-two percent attended private or parochial schools. Undergraduates are proud of a student body that is more racially and ethnically diverse than that of many other small, private colleges: 15% Hispanic, 5% Asian-American, 2% African-American, and 1% foreign national. Because so many different kinds of people have such distinct perspectives and viewpoints, undergraduates, most of whom are conservative, soon learn to be more open-minded. Says a student from the southwest: "Most students have formed their personal opinions and philosophies and are quite prepared to defend them. But we all respect each other's views. For example, my best friend and I disagree on everything—politics, religion, philosophy, etc.—but that doesn't hamper our relationship." Many undergraduates come from middle-class Catholic families who expect much from their offspring. "You don't have to look far to see that academics come first here," says a westerner. "Among upperclassmen, the sense of competition is even keener, although as you progress you get to know the system and you find out what works for you, so you can relax a bit more. But classes are tough. All of them."

Academics: Dallas offers bachelor's degrees in 27 majors, as well as master's and doctoral programs in the Braniff Graduate School and the Graduate School of Management. All undergraduates study in the Constantin College of Liberal Arts. The academic year is divided into 2 semesters. Classes for freshmen and sophomores generally range from 20 to 40 participants, although General Biology enrolls almost 80. Juniors and seniors usually experience classes of 10–25 tops; many senior seminars enroll only 5.

The rigorous Dallas core is the heart of its educational offerings, taking students on a journey through the intellectual tradition of Western civilization. The trip involves at least 67 credits of work in fields ranging from the English literary tradition, philosophy, and Western civilization to laboratory sciences, mathematics, economics, and politics. Because of the core, says a junior, "students have a common academic experience and, as a result, discuss and debate *outside* of class as much as inside." Every senior also must pass a comprehensive exam or complete a project in the major field of study.

Ninety-eight of the 122 full-time faculty members teach undergraduates, as do 44 of the 113 part-timers. About 90% of the faculty are lay; women comprise 23%. Students find the entire campus, faculty and staff alike, to be committed to the love of learning. "Where else will the security office open up a lab for you at 3 a.m. so you can finish a project?" asks a recent graduate. Professors, known as tough graders with little tolerance for procrastination, also have a knack of making even the most unappealing sounding subject, such as epistemology, seem dazzling. "The professors have a mission," concludes a politics major, "to instill the liberal arts mentality into all students."

The semester in Rome is for many their own personal age of enlightenment. Classes are taught largely by UD professors at the school's own campus on the outskirts of the city. The semester includes a 10-day group trip through the ancient sites of Greece, and a 10-day study break allows for other travel through Europe. The philosophy department is marked by "premier philosophical thinkers"; the history department, by distinguished church and medieval historians; the English department, by a great faculty and emphasis on the texts of Homer, Virgil, Melville, and Joyce. "Students complete voluminous projects each semester, and the classes demand so much reading on a consistent basis," says an admiring politics major. "English is a *very* respected major here among the student body as well as the faculty." A science center, completed in 1985, offers excellent facilities for use by biology, chemistry, physics and new computer science majors; over 85% of UD premed graduates gain admission to their first-choice medical schools. (Over 90% of pre-law graduates can boast the same acceptance.) In all of these programs, a history major concludes, "The faculty push you as far as you can go, and then some. You always are challenged."

Students admire and respect the professors of politics for their knowledge and their efforts to "teach students to think through the complexity of humanity," as a major puts it. However, those undergraduates seeking a more modern approach to the practical side of 21st-century politics will be disappointed in the heavy emphasis on political theory and early political thinkers like Thucydides and Heroditus. "Political science doesn't exist here," says the history major. "It might as well be called philosophy." Students who wish to gain a more realistic view can spend a term in Washington, D.C., taking courses at Georgetown

University and working as interns in the House or Senate. Undergraduates looking for other more career-oriented majors, such as nursing or communication, will be disappointed because there are no such specialties, although a 6-course concentration in journalism is offered to supplement other majors. A new Bachelor of Arts program in business leadership, which enrolled its first students in fall 2003, provides concentrations in corporate ethics and responsibility, international business, behavioral management studies, and financial accounting. Only business leadership majors can add these concentrations. While majors in art and drama are available, a number of students also would like to see and hear more music, although a concentration plus opportunities for performance are offered.

Facilities: Blakley Library's collection of over 223,000 catalogued volumes in book form, more than 75,000 volumes in microform, and 583 current periodicals "leaves a lot to be desired," as a recent graduate recalls. "However, its shortcomings only motivate the students to leave campus for a while and snoop around the library at Southern Methodist University—mortal sin!—or the Dallas public library." For researchers, computerized assistance is one of Blakley's redeeming virtues, with laptops available for student checkout. For serious studiers, Blakley is quiet, but there are other quiet buildings open all night. Says a senior: "The library's only virtue as a place to study is that it is not your dorm room."

Students have their choice of 4 labs on campus with about 25 computers each and workstations in the library, foreign language and math departments and other sites. Many are open until 2 a.m. All students are given Internet access; the college strongly recommends that undergraduates bring their own personal computers, which many already do. Wireless access also is available in parts of many buildings across campus.

Special programs: Students can supplement their bachelor's degrees with a master's in business administration by following a 5-year plan that includes 1 full-time summer session with the UD Graduate School of Management. A 5-year bachelor's-master's degree program in psychology also is an option.

Campus life: Fifty-nine percent of UD's students reside on the 750-acre campus. There are no Greek organizations, and students consider the Rugby Club "the closest thing we have to a frat," says a junior. "Even if the Saturday afternoon game is not well attended, all students know they are welcome to drink with the team afterwards." Other weekends are filled with dances, assorted performers, and various social events sponsored by the university and different student groups. The Italian Club, College Republicans, and Crusaders for Life, a group supporting the pro-life position, are among the organizations with active memberships. Mass is offered at noon and 5 p.m. daily, and services are well attended, with students of all faiths made to feel welcome. One undergraduate recalls a Mass held during the semester abroad in which the choir was led by "a Jewish singer, a pagan flute player, and a Catholic guitarist." Doors to all Dallas dormitories are locked at all times, one of several measures that keep the crime rate low.

The Crusaders field teams in 6 intercollegiate sports for men and 7 for women, as part of NCAA Division III competition. Basketball games, along with rugby matches, are the best attended sporting events. All but 12% of the men but only 38% of the women participate in a half dozen or so intramural sports for each sex, ranging from flag football to inner tube water polo.

Students say that getting away can be tough for those without cars; the campus is located in Irving (pop. 190,000), about 12 miles west of Dallas but "still in the middle of nowhere," says an out-of-stater. "Even Denny's is 10 minutes away." However, Texas Stadium, home of the Dallas Cowboys, is only 4 blocks from campus. To remedy feelings of isolation, the student government sponsors regular trips to cultural, social, and recreational events in Dallas/Fort Worth.

Cost cutters: In the 2005–2006 school year, 98% of UD freshmen, as well as 95% of continuing students, received financial aid. Fifty-eight percent of all undergraduates were given need-based help. The average freshman award for a student with need included a need-based scholarship or grant averaging $3460 and need-based self-help aid such as loans and work averaging $4080. Other non-need-based awards and scholarships for first-year students averaged $8680. A typical recent alumnus left with debts of $21,700. Students who submit their application for admission by either the November or December Early Action deadline or by January 15 at the latest are automatically considered for 1 of 3 Primary Academic Awards. Students who ranked in the top 1% of their high school class are eligible for full tuition awards through the Partners in Excellence program. Students who have excelled academically while taking a challenging curriculum could receive the renewable Trustee Award paying up to $10,000 a year. Metroplex Scholars Awards recently paid up to $12,000 to Texas residents who ranked in the top 10 or top tenth of their high school graduating class, depending on the size, with at least an 1150 math and critical reading SAT or 25 ACT. Leadership Awards, which pay $1000 to $3000, are available to student leaders with strong academic records and extracurricular participation who perform well in an on-campus interview. Additional scholarships are offered to top talents in art, theater, chemistry, classics, mathematics, physics, and foreign languages.

Rate of return: Eighty-five percent of entering freshmen return for the sophomore year. Fifty-seven percent earn bachelor's degrees in 4 years; 63% in 5 years; 65% in 6 years.

Payoff: English was the most popular major among 2005 graduates, claiming 14% of the class. Politics followed at 12% and biology at 9%. About 30% of the new alumni decide to pursue advanced degrees immediately upon graduation; usually about half in the arts and sciences. Eighty percent eventually go on for further education. Those entering the job market find positions nationwide in such fields as education, sales, management, publishing, and journalism. Almost 40 companies and organizations recruited on campus in a recent school year.

Bottom line: If you're not prepared to give up memorizing in favor of critical thinking or to expand your reading list to include *Beowulf* and Plato's *Republic,* then attending the University of Dallas will only seem like a lot of hard work. But for those who come with open minds, the opportunities for learning at home and in Rome are inspiring.

University of Texas at Austin

Austin, Texas 78712

Setting: Urban
Control: Public
Undergraduate enrollment: 15,973 men, 17,709 women
Graduate enrollment: 6075 men, 5414 women
Student/faculty ratio: 14:1
Freshman profile: 18% scored over 700 on SAT I verbal; 40% scored 600–700; 31% 500–599; 11% below 500. 26% scored over 700 on SAT I math; 43% scored 600–700; 25% 500–599; 6% below 500. 30% scored above 28 on the ACT; 18% scored 27–28; 26% 24–26; 16% 21–23; 10% below 21. 68% graduated in top tenth of high school class; 88% in upper fifth.

Faculty profile: 88% Ph.D.'s
Tuition and fees: $6972 in-state, $16,310 out-of-state
Room and board: $7638
Freshman financial aid: 74%; average scholarship or grant: $6750 need-based; $3500 non-need-based
Campus jobs: NA; average earnings: NA
Application deadline: Feb. 1
Financial aid deadline: Mar. 31
Admissions information: (512) 475-7440
    web site: bealonghorn.utexas.edu/freshmen or www.utexas.edu

It's hard to get 50,000 people to agree on anything, but there is one thing to which most students, faculty, and administrators at the University of Texas at Austin can nod their heads: Some days there are just too many people. With 37,000 full-time and part-time undergraduates, 13,000 full-time and part-time graduate students, and 2730 faculty members, plus another 18,000 administrators and staff members, UT Austin would rank among the state's 40 largest cities. Recalls a recent graduate: "I did not expect the school to be more like a metropolis than a campus. You can't get the classes you need. There's nowhere to park. Lines are long and bureaucracy is at its worst." However, she, like others, used the 900 campus organizations to her advantage, finding a niche as well as professors receptive to her concerns. "I learned to like UT," she reflects. "If you have the patience to overcome the obstacles, you'll get a fantastic education—one that teaches you to deal with all life's frustrations." You'll also get one of the best bargains around: "a Cadillac education at garage-sale prices," boasts another recent survivor.

Student body: In a word, diverse. As a recent graduate describes it, "We have the scholastically intense library lovers, the partying frat rats, the philosophers and stargazers, quiet people, loud people, students with a 'cause,' liberals and conservatives, Bible bangers, and agnostics/atheists. Whatever you're looking for, you can find it—or introduce it." The undergraduate student body includes 14% Asian-Americans, 14% Hispanics, 9% foreign nationals from 125 countries, and 4% African-Americans. Ninety-two percent are Texan, but students come from all states. Though a student body of 33,700 full-time undergraduates is bound to have its share of all-night studiers and all-night partiers, the partiers are less likely to last a full 4 years. Notes a senior: "The overall atmosphere is laid back and pleasant, although classes are all challenging to some degree. Rumors of easy-A classes always prove disappointingly false." Most competitive are the honors programs that "consist of high achievers who could have gone to an Ivy League college," says one participant. About 250 members of the 2005 freshman class were National Merit finalists; more than 300 in a recent year were valedictorians.

Academics: UT, which was founded in 1883, offers more than 100 bachelor's degree programs, plus advanced degrees through the doctorate; undergraduate programs are based in 11 colleges and schools. Graduate programs only are offered in the School of Law, the Graduate School of Library and Information Sciences, and the Lyndon B. Johnson School of Public Affairs. The academic year is divided into semesters. Freshman English and foreign language courses usually enroll about 25 students, and lower-division math classes between 50 and 100; introductory classes in government, economics, biology, chemistry, and history may have 500 students in lectures. All classes with more than 100 students are divided into discussion groups of about 20, led by graduate students, which meet separate from the lecture. Juniors and seniors find their courses ranging in size from as few as 15 to about 80 maximum.

Undergraduates, regardless of major, must complete 14 courses of basic education requirements in the following areas: English and writing, including 2 specific courses in composition and literature; American history and government, including Texas government; social science; natural science; mathematics; and fine arts or humanities. Students must also demonstrate competency in a foreign language or take classes. Some colleges and schools require specific classes to meet these mandates or additional coursework in these or other areas.

The 2482 full-time and 252 part-time faculty members, 36% of whom are women, and 2 of whom have won a Nobel Prize, have varying degrees of involvement with research and undergraduate teaching. Some students, depending on their majors, view research as a positive ingredient that gives undergraduates opportunities, some with $10,000 UT grants, to engage in "real" research with professionals who are nationally known in their fields. However, most undergraduates end up relying on the more than 2400 assistant instructors and teaching assistants, some great, some less so, for help with their coursework. Underclassmen should not give up on getting to know their professors, advises this junior: "Students have to take it upon themselves to get to know their professors individually, which can often be intimidating, considering the large size of some of the freshman and sophomore lecture classes." As for the quality of instruction, undergraduates say it is as varied as the students' commitment to learning. "The good and bad faculty are evenly disbursed," says another junior. "Some are great professors to have, and then some of them you wish would retire *today!*"

Among the top-ranked programs are Latin American and Middle Eastern cultural studies, biology, Spanish, computer sciences, and all disciplines in the College of Engineering with its Texas-size research grants and the top minds in the country leading the teaching. Students particularly like the competitive and realistic learning environment set up by the Red McCombs School of Business, which is housed in a modern building, with its own media and student centers, and also benefits from contributions by corporations and alumni. The 5-year program in the School of Architecture is highly competitive with top-flight students. The music program in the College of Fine Arts has good courses and wonderful facilities.

Students complain that many disciplines such as history and some modern languages in the College of Liberal Arts as well as programs in the College of Natural Sciences have been "slighted" when it comes to funding and have too few professors and too many graduate students leading a plethora of enormous introductory classes. Notes a microbiology major: "While the College of Natural Sciences has its own computer labs and offers some tutoring, the classes are just too large and teachers are not receptive to students. Many, in my opinion, do not care whether the students are learning or not." The journalism program in the College of Communication also has been plagued by problems of size. Despite recent efforts to trim the number of students in the program, journalism students still sometimes find it hard to get into the classes they need and to receive individual attention in the large classes they do get.

Facilities: The UT library system, which holds 8.5 million volumes, 6 million microform items, and 48,100 periodicals, constitutes the ninth largest academic library in the United States, and is considered by one expert to be among the 32 best libraries in the world. Seventeen different libraries on campus specialize in particular areas from architecture and planning to physics/mathematics/astronomy. Most undergraduates, however, spend the bulk of their time studying and socializing in the 2 enormous general libraries: Perry-Casteñada, which contains more than 2.5 million of UT's total volumes and seats 3200 readers, and the Undergraduate Library, with a smaller collection used mostly by lower-division students with seating for 2000. An on-line catalog links all libraries; extensive computerized search engines also are available. The Benson Latin American Collection and the Lyndon Baines Johnson Library and Museum are particularly noteworthy.

Students have access to the libraries' excellent computer system as well as the Internet from their residence-hall rooms. There also are a number of microcomputer labs in the dorms and other campus buildings plus a 200-seat microcomputer laboratory with Macs and PCs; together these units, which add up to several thousand, constitute what students claim may be the largest single grove of Apple computers in the world. Still, there often are long waits in some labs. Undergraduates in the College of Education teacher preparatory program are required to have personal computers. Several public wireless sites also exist.

Special programs: The university offers more than 100 active exchange agreements with institutions around the world, from Peru to The Netherlands. Altogether, undergraduates may study at any of more than 350 programs in 80 countries. A rigorous Plan II Honors program offers top students an interdisciplinary liberal arts curriculum that is structured around year-long courses and small seminars led by distinguished faculty.

Campus life: The UT campus spreads across 350 acres but houses just 19% of the students on the grounds. Nine percent of the men and 13% of the women pledge 27 national fraternities and 23 national sororities. Undergraduates say that "clearly established boundaries" exist between the rest of the student body and the Greeks, who attend their own parties and gravitate toward their own clubs and restaurants. However, nonmembers can easily find private parties, campus parties, concerts, or other cultural events around campus to keep them from singing the blues. The bars, clubs, and restaurants of Sixth Street, a 6-block row of live bands and nightlife, also provides a ready source of entertainment. Nine hundred recognized student groups, among them HBSA, the largest undergraduate Hispanic organization in Texas, and the Orange Jackets spirit and service organization, also provide outlets for students of similar interests. Bike and book theft, predominantly during finals, are the most frequent campus crimes; students generally find the police and lighting systems good. A card-key access security system exists in the residence halls. A SURE (Students United for Rape Elimination) Walk program provides escorts or rides for classmates who need to walk home or to their cars from anywhere on campus. A University Safety Council involves student groups and near-campus neighborhood organizations in a joint effort to enhance safety measures even further.

Not surprisingly, Texas Longhorn football, housed in a stadium seating 80,106, is the biggest event on a big, big campus; "Please, this is Texas," observes a Houston resident. In fact, most students plan trips home for weekends when the team is playing out of town—unless, of course, the Longhorns are playing the University of Oklahoma in Dallas, when all the traffic flows outward. Among other of the 8 NCAA Division I sports for men and 10 for women, men's and women's basketball, women's volleyball, and men's baseball also draw enthusiastic crowds. Thirty-nine percent of the men and 26% of the women participate in the 45 intramural sports open to each sex.

Austin, the state capital (pop. 552,000), provides plenty for students to do. For great escapes, the beautiful Texas hill country is just to the west, and San Antonio is an hour or so south.

Cost cutters: Seventy-four percent of freshmen and 77% of continuing students received financial aid in the 2005–2006 school year. Need-based help went to 57% of the freshmen and 44% of the rest. The average freshman award for a student with need included a need-based scholarship or grant averaging $6750 and need-based self-help aid such as loans and jobs averaging $3650. Other non-need-based awards and scholarships averaged $3500. No figure is available to show the average amount of a non-need-based athletic scholarship. In 2005, new alumni departed with an average debt of $16,850. For those with leadership skills, high academic achievement, and special talent, the low price at UT is cut even further by more than 12,000 competitive scholarships awarded annually and worth over $17.5 million in a recent year. Although many awards are restricted to Texas residents, an out-of-stater who does receive a scholarship of at least $200 in value may pay in-state tuition rates. A cooperative education program is available in all engineering majors and in several other fields. Off-campus housing near the university is expensive, but UT runs shuttle buses to other areas of town where apartments are more reasonably priced.

Rate of return: An impressive 93% of freshmen decide that big-school life is for them and return for the sophomore year. Just under half, 47%, earn their bachelor's degrees in 4 years; however, the number increases to 71% within 5 years and 75% in 6 years.

Payoff: Among 2005 graduates, 16% majored in the social sciences and 13% each in business and communication. Though no figures exist to show the portion of students pursuing advanced degrees or finding jobs, the lack does not trouble most graduates. Notes a recent grad: "A degree from here is a ticket to success. Also, in Texas, many business executives are Longhorns, and the connection is much appreciated."

Bottom line: The University of Texas at Austin is not for the timid or passive. To a much greater degree than at smaller colleges, it is up to the individual student to attend class, turn in assignments, study, and keep up. An undergraduate also needs to remain open-minded. Says a recent graduate: "If you want to spend the entire time in college with people who look just like you and think just like you, there are plenty of places like that in Texas. But if you are willing to open your mind, learn about others, and then come up with your own opinions, UT is the place."

Utah

Brigham Young University

Provo, Utah 84602

Setting: Suburban
Control: Private (The Church of Jesus Christ of Latter-Day Saints)
Undergraduate enrollment: 13,837 men, 13,623 women
Graduate enrollment: 1241 men, 699 women
Student/faculty ratio: 21:1
Freshman profile: 15% scored over 700 on SAT I verbal; 41% scored 600–700; 35% 500–599; 9% below 500. 17% scored over 700 on SAT I math; 44% scored 600–700; 32% 500–599; 6% below 500. 23% scored above 29 on the ACT; 61% scored 24–29; 16% 18–23: 0% below 18. 49% graduated in top tenth of high school class; 99% in upper half.

Faculty profile: 98% Ph.D.'s
Tuition and fees: $3410 LDS, $5116 other faiths
Room and board: $5790
Freshman financial aid: 20%; average scholarship or grant: $1756 need-based; $2762 non-need-based
Campus jobs: 40%; average earnings: $4800/year
Application deadline: Feb. 15
Financial aid deadline: June 30 (Scholarships Feb. 15)
Admissions information: (801) 422-2500
e-mail: admissions@byu.edu
web site: www.byu.edu

Three things can be said with certainty about Brigham Young University in Provo, Utah: it is very big, it is very inexpensive—and it is very Mormon. And it is exactly these 3 qualities that draw most of BYU's students to its campus. With a daytime full-time undergraduate enrollment of more than 27,000, all but 2% of whom are members of The Church of Jesus Christ of Latter-Day Saints, there is, in appearance at least, an unmistakable homogeneity among the students: men sport no beards (but always shoes in public areas) and women wear modest attire (no skirts above the knee) in adherence to the school's dress code. It is not easy to be of a different religious faith at a school that is so thoroughly Mormon, but another important factor—the low tuition—makes some students give BYU a try. LDS students pay just $3410 in tuition; those not of the faith pay 50% more. With room and board, the total for non-LDS members is only $10,906, a fraction of the cost at most big-name universities.

Student body: Just over a fourth of BYU's bargain hunters, 29%, are from Utah; nearly half of the non-residents come also from the West but undergraduates represent all 49 other states and 121 foreign countries. The enrollment includes 2.5% foreign nationals, about 4% Hispanics, 3.5% Asian-Americans, and less than 1% each African-Americans and Native Americans. Students who attend BYU are generally bright, conservative, and industrious and are drawn as much by its spiritual environment and "clean atmosphere" as by its reputation for solid academics. BYU students, says a Californian, "are conservative, good people who want and seek [for] the best out of life, especially from social relationships." As a result, though students sense that the level of competition is rising in certain rigorous disciplines such as accounting, there is little of the stressful academic drive found at some other campuses. One student's hypothesis: "The emphasis on moral goodness helps temper competition."

Academics: BYU, which was founded in 1875, offers degrees through the doctorate, including bachelor's degrees in 194 majors, based in 8 colleges, the David O. McKay School of Education, and the Marriott School of Management. The Clark Law School awards the juris doctor degree only. The academic year is divided into fall and winter semesters that extend from September to late April. Students who wish to accelerate their degree programs can participate in 2 short spring and summer terms. Freshmen should brace themselves for an enormous range in class sizes the first year. While freshman English classes generally are restricted to 20 participants, a few of the required general-education courses can exceed 400. Observes a sophomore, While "I have been pleased with the high morals and standards here on campus, I have been somewhat disappointed with the large classes and poor teachers in some of the general education classes." American Heritage has been known to enroll 900, though students often can get questions answered during much smaller required discussion sessions. Classes for juniors and seniors, however, rarely exceed 40. Newcomers who long for more personal classes can sign up for the Freshman Academy, a first-semester program of small learning communities. As part of the academy, up to 120 students take clusters of classes together that connect them to faculty, to each other, and to the opportunities available at the university.

All undergraduates must take a new University Core of up to 25 courses ranging from American Heritage and Advanced Writing and Oral Communication to Biological Science and Wellness. Also included are a 2-course sequence in the Book of Mormon and 1 course each in the New Testament and Doctrine and Covenants, plus 3 or 4 classes in religion electives.

Of the university's 1762 faculty members, 441 are part-time. All teach undergraduates. Twenty-eight percent of the full-time faculty are women. About 97% in a recent year were Mormon. "They do not always have the best teaching ability," remarks a student who transferred from a more rigorous school, "but they care," a trait students at such a large university especially value. Adds a senior: "The faculty is generally very student-oriented and very accessible." A number also "are excellent at putting what we learn into a spiritual context," says an economics major. The faculty is considered "great" in the honors classes.

The Marriott School of Management offers undergraduate degree programs in management, accountancy, and information systems that are as rigorous as they are popular. Accounting in particular accepts only the best and, this sociology major notes, "is able to weed out less ambitious students through prerequisite courses in a preaccounting core." The School of Education, especially its program in elementary education, also is highly regarded and almost guarantees good jobs quickly for its graduates. The LDS emphasis on family strengthens the family sciences program in the College of Family, Home, and Social Sciences. Communications majors in the College of Fine Arts and Communications become familiar with equipment of a quality not always made available to undergraduates, thanks largely to the student-run NewsNet TV productions. The college's music program also is of prime quality. The Ira A. Fulton College of Engineering and Technology, well funded by area companies, provides top-of-the-line computers and other equipment for its majors. Language enthusiasts find a global feast of well-developed offerings in the College of Humanities, with bachelor degree programs available in French, German, Italian, Russian, Portuguese, Spanish, Japanese, Chinese, and Korean, plus classes in a wide range of languages from Latvian and Lithuanian to Afrikaans. Many of the professors are native speakers. The College of Nursing insures rigorous study to students in the program and good job placement upon graduation.

Some social science disciplines in the College of Family, Home, and Social Sciences have been hurt, students say, by a lack of faculty knowledgeable about the latest research. Sociology classes only "skim the surface of issues," says a major, and need more depth, especially at the 300- and 400-level courses. Some majors such as recreation management and youth leadership in the College of Health and Human Performance carry reputations of being "notoriously easy," says a journalism major.

Facilities: Harold B. Lee Library holds an impressive collection of over 3.5 million volumes, 3.3 million microform items, and nearly 200,000 electronic and paper periodicals. In addition, the BYU Regional Family History Library has access to about 300,000 volumes and 2.5 million rolls of microfilm contained in the Church's Family History Library in Salt Lake City. Student complaints have centered on too little study space in the main facility and the hardship of all-day Sunday closings. Some have found it unfair that only graduate students are given carrels. "If you are in their carrel when they want to use it, you have to move," grumbles a senior. Excellent computer research assistance, as well as a helpful human staff, makes the enormous catalog of books a little less intimidating. "Our library rocks!" concludes a junior.

More than 4600 computers are available for student use around campus. About 850 are in labs designated for general use; the rest are in labs run by individual colleges and departments. Students also have access to 5 supercomputers for research purposes.

Most labs are open until 11 p.m. or midnight. Accounting majors and other students in the business school are required to provide their own personal computers. Wireless access is available in several buildings around campus from the library, the student center, and most academic buildings to the athletic building and field house.

Special programs: Six-month resident programs are offered in Vienna, Paris, Madrid, London, and Costa Rica. Spring/summer programs also are available in Asia, Canada, Europe, Mexico, and South America. Altogether, students may study in any of 55 countries. Students may spend a semester in Washington, D.C. as well.

Campus life: More than 8000 undergraduates live in single-sex housing unless married on the 557-acre main campus. All single LDS students are divided into "wards" of 200–300 members, within which they find most of their social and religious life. Devotionals and firesides are held on a regular basis with various leaders of the Church serving as speakers. BYU's dress and grooming standards are quite detailed; for example, such "grubby attire" as sweat suits, jogging clothes, and bib overalls is restricted to the immediate area around residence halls and informal outdoor activities, and is not permitted in dining areas. In addition, students must abide by an honor code that, among other stipulations, prohibits sexual relations outside of marriage and demands adherence to the "Word of Wisdom," which includes abstention from alcoholic beverages, tobacco, tea, and coffee. Each winter semester, every student who plans to continue must have an ecclesiastical endorsement interview with his or her local ecclesiastical leader to determine the student's commitment to the honor code. Not surprisingly, there are no Greek organizations, and the more popular secular groups are the College Republicans, the Outdoor Adventure Club and the BBQ Club, for those with "a love for grillin'." Dating remains the focus of the average student's social life at BYU. Notes a male senior: "Marriage is important to students and they are as diligent in courting as they are in academics." Although the crime rate is low, emergency telephones are provided around campus for extra reassurance. Some students feel the outdoor lighting could be improved.

Football, basketball, and men's volleyball are the largest of the 10 men's and 11 women's intercollegiate sports that compete in NCAA Division I. The intramural program with 34 sports for men and 32 for women provides plenty of opportunities for student wards to compete against one another. Sixty percent of the men and 39% of the women get involved. Skiing, both snow and water, also is popular.

As a college town, Provo provides students with the closeness of a community of 111,000 people, but more cosmopolitan Salt Lake City is just 45 minutes north. The Wasatch Mountains overlook BYU on the east, and Utah Lake to the west; both offer wonderful, natural escapes.

Cost cutters: Funding from The Church of Jesus Christ of Latter-Day Saints covers nearly 70% of educational costs, keeping the tuition rate low. In addition, 20% of freshmen and 40% of continuing students in the 2005–2006 school year received financial aid. For 13% of the freshmen and 29% of the others, the aid was need-based. The average freshman award for a student with need included a need-based scholarship or grant averaging $1756 and need-based self-help aid such as loans and jobs averaging $837. Other non-need-based awards and scholarships for first-year students averaged $2762. No data is available regarding athletic scholarships. The average 2005 graduate with school loans left with debts of $12,955. A scholarship matrix available to freshmen awards scholarships based on a combination of each student's GPA and ACT/SAT composite score. An entering freshman with a GPA of at least 3.89 and an ACT score of at least 33 (1460 math and critical reading SAT) receives 8 semesters of full LDS tuition. A student with the same GPA but a lower ACT test score of 32 (1410 SAT) would receive 2 semesters of full LDS tuition; an ACT test score of 29–31 (1280–1360 SAT) would warrant 2 semesters of half LDS tuition. Various combinations of GPA and ACT/SAT scores provide scholarships at one of those 3 amounts. The most prestigious award, the Gordon B. Hinckley Presidential Scholarship, pays 150% LDS tuition for 8 semesters to students who in a recent year had an ACT score of at least 33 or 1460 SAT and class rank of 3.85 and were members of the LDS church. Performance and talent awards recently paid from $100 to full tuition and fees for 1 year. BYU offers cooperative education programs in majors as diverse as agronomy, horticulture, Chinese, and accounting. Students may work a maximum of 20 hours a week while attending school.

Rate of return: Eighty-two percent of the freshmen return for their sophomore year. Twenty-two percent go on to graduate in 4 years; 38% in 5 years, and 70% within 6. After freshman year all but 5% of the men serve a mission of approximately 2 years' duration for the LDS Church. Therefore, most students take longer to graduate.

Payoff: For 2005 graduates, the 3 most popular majors were business marketing at 16%, education at 12%, and visual and performing arts at 7%. Nearly a quarter, 22%, of recent BYU graduates have continued their education at some point after earning their bachelor's degrees, although the vast majority seek jobs upon graduation. About 430 companies and other organizations recruited on campus in a recent school year.

Bottom line: Although the environment is not at all hostile to students of other religious faiths, undergraduates must recognize that Brigham Young University is a Mormon school primarily for members of the LDS Church. Advises a junior: "Any student with high academic goals, a positive attitude, and high moral standards would probably love it here. Those who want the freedom to make more liberal choices about their lifestyles would not."

University of Utah

Salt Lake City, Utah 84112

Setting: Urban
Control: Public
Undergraduate enrollment: 8666 men, 6885 women
Graduate enrollment: 2637 men, 2147 women
Student/faculty ratio: 19:1
Freshman profile: 15% scored above 28 on the ACT; 12% scored 27–28; 24% 24–26; 28% 21–23; 21% below 21. 27% graduated in top tenth of high school class; 40% in upper fifth.
Faculty profile: 86% Ph.D.'s
Tuition and fees: $4340 in-state, $13,528 out-of-state

Room and board: $5822
Freshman financial aid: 42%; average scholarship or grant: NA
Campus jobs: NA; average earnings: NA
Application deadline: April 1 (Priority: Dec. 15)
Financial aid deadline: Mar. 15
Admissions information: (801) 581-7281; (800) 685-8856; e-mail: admissions@sa.utah.edu; web site: www.sa.utah.edu/admiss/index.htm or www.utah.edu

Only 3 years after Brigham Young, the Mormon leader and pioneer, first proclaimed, "This is the place" when he laid eyes on Utah's Great Salt Lake Valley in 1847, the University of Utah began existence as the University of Deseret. In 1892, it was given its present name. Now this public university is laying claim to another title: the best all-around school between the University of Chicago and the University of California, Berkeley. While other major universities within that region may quibble with the pronouncement, students at the U are convinced of what they speak, boasting of facilities "comparable to those at Harvard," as well as a campus that encompasses a wide range of viewpoints, including many degrees of liberalism, in a state known for its conservative stance. Though the overall academic air is friendly and easy-going, students who aspire to greatness can, and usually do, reach their educational goals. In 2003, a Minnesota student was named a Rhodes Scholar. Notes a senior, who received a full-ride scholarship to Utah: "I was accepted at Penn, Georgetown, and the University of Michigan and desperately wanted to attend one of those universities. In retrospect, though, I'm very glad I decided to come here. Any student willing to apply him- or herself can achieve a superior education from the U. This is an institution that provides great opportunities for those who seek them."

Student body: Ninety percent of the university's undergraduates are from Utah; just over half of the rest also are westerners, though students come from every state and 100 foreign countries. Just 5% in a recent year attended private or parochial schools. The average age of undergraduates is almost 25 years, reflecting a large number of students older than the traditional 18–22 age bracket. In fact, notes a senior: "My mom is a student on campus, as well as my grandfather." The undergraduate student body remains predominantly white, though racial and ethnic diversity has increased. Asian-Americans comprise 4%, Hispanics 3%, African-Americans and Native Americans, each about 1%. Foreign students also account for 5%. Students estimate that about half the student body is Mormon, with the Latter-day Saint Student Association one of the biggest campus groups. However, undergraduates find the general atmosphere very open and even liberal at times. One result is an eclectic mix of conservatively dressed students and a nearly equal number who, says a local resident, "look as though they just walked out of the 60s." For many undergraduates, the lure of the mountains and especially the great snow skiing or snowboarding proves too strong, and off they go, classes or not. Observes a sophomore: "Some students treat the U as if it were a community college where they go on a trial basis to see if they'll like higher education." A rigorous honors program, third oldest and considered by many to be one of the best in the nation, provides a welcome change of pace for many serious students.

Academics: The University of Utah offers degrees through the doctorate. Undergraduates may choose among more than 70 degree programs in 12 colleges; undergraduate programs in medical laboratory science and prearchitecture also are available through the School of Medicine and the Graduate School of Architecture, respectively.

The university follows a semester calendar. Freshmen and sophomores can plan on encountering some large lectures with anywhere from 100 to 400 classmates. Classic Civilization has had almost 450 enrolled. Upper-level classes can drop below 12, though most have between 20 and 30 participants.

All undergraduates must complete 2 courses from 3 of 4 subject areas—fine arts, humanities, physical and life sciences, and social sciences excluding their major area. Students also must take specific courses in writing, American Institutions, including a class in either history, economics, or political science, and in quantitative reasoning, with 1 class each in mathematics and statistics or logic. Requirements at the upper level include an approved communication writing course in the major and a course that examines diversity. Students seeking a Bachelor of Arts degree must demonstrate competence in a foreign language or sign language; those earning a Bachelor of Science need additional coursework that is considered "quantitatively intensive." Undergraduates complain that most general-education classes are too large and many offer merely average instruction, provided typically by graduate assistants working on their Ph.D.'s. A program entitled LEAP enables a group of first-year students to take many of their general-education classes together as well as a small interdisciplinary seminar in which they stay with the same students and instructor for the whole academic year.

The 1687-member faculty, including those at the School of Medicine, consists of 1175 full-time and 512 part-time members. Of the full-time members, 806 teach undergraduates, as do all but 40 of the part-time. Women comprise 39% of the faculty. Graduate students teach 20% of the introductory classes. Most undergraduates say that, once a student gets beyond the large, often poorly taught general-education courses, the quality of instruction becomes dramatically better—"excellent," maintains a senior. Many professors have managed to strike a workable balance between research to keep their knowledge of their areas on the cutting edge and attentiveness to student needs. However, there are still some faculty in upper-level courses who teach the same way they have for years, with little regard for its effectiveness, or lack of it on students.

Center stage among Utah's star divisions are outstanding ballet and modern dance programs, housed in the beautiful Alice Sheets Mariott Center for Dance. These programs send many of their graduates on to professional companies, among them Ballet West. In fact, many performing groups, such as the Utah Symphony, Ballet West, Repertory Dance Theatre, and Utah Opera Company, had their beginnings on campus. The Marriott Center features among other amenities, 6 studios, costume and scenery workshops, and a 333-seat theater that is steeply raked to permit all audience members to see the dancers' feet.

The College of Engineering and the David Eccles School of Business benefit from the 3 double *f*'s: fantastic faculty, funding, and facilities, although some students think the business school suffers a bit from grade inflation. In the College of Social and Behavioral Science, students find excellent political science professors and opportunities for hundreds of internships through the Hinckley Institute of Politics. The major also offers well-designed certificate programs in international relations, public administration, and practical politics. Biology, chemistry, and physics each provide rich opportunities for undergraduate research. The English department in the College of Humanities shines largely because of stellar faculty, who, says a junior, "are open and assured." An extremely well-equipped communications program also in the humanities college with 2 new buildings, one housing 2 PBS television stations and a National Public Radio station sets high standards for performance for its majors.

Art devotees say the department at the U lacks diversity in its course offerings, with no emphasis in interior design and too few computers for the graphic design program. Math students complain of professors whose limited English is difficult to understand. A recently added spoken-English test requirement and a 2-week academic and cultural orientation for international teaching assistants is aimed at resolving such student complaints. The mathematics building also needs upgrading. Sociology, one of the larger majors, needs more full-time faculty members.

Facilities: Marriott Library has more than 3.1 million volumes, 3.6 million microforms, and almost 41,000 periodicals. Since everything is computerized, students can find out quickly what is available and what is not. Recent expansion of the library doubled the room available for books and student computer labs. For studying, says a senior, "the new addition is great. It is well lighted and the desks and chairs are conducive to studying." Special branch libraries house the university's collections in mathematics, health sciences, and the law.

In a recent year, 900 microcomputers were accessible to students in the library (with more than 260 networked units alone), the engineering, math, and business buildings, the student union, and the residence halls. Some of the centers are open 24 hours a day. More specialized facilities, including an IBM supercomputer, are available largely to graduate students but also to some undergraduates with advanced computer needs. Numerous locations around campus also provide wireless access.

Special programs: Utah students can attend any of about 150 colleges and universities in the United States and numerous foreign institutions in 14 countries, while paying Utah tuition, room, and board. More than 300 faculty members from a wide range of disciplines list research projects with the Undergraduate Research Opportunities Program, seeking students to work one on one with them. Through the very active Lowell Bennion Community Service Center, students may choose from more than 100 service-learning courses that may be integrated into their academic experience.

Campus life: The university is largely a commuter campus, with only 9% of the undergraduates residing in both single-sex and coed housing on the 1535-acre grounds. The developed portion of the campus is largely confined to 670 acres; another 485 acres recently were designated as a nature preserve on which no building can ever take place. The U of U campus is akin to a city within Salt Lake City, recently boasting its own abbreviated version of the "Twelve Days of Christmas": a 9-hole golf course, 8 auditoriums, 7 art galleries, 6 television production studios, 5 restaurants, 4 sports complexes, 3 public museums, 2 movie theaters—and a regional health sciences center where the artificial heart was pioneered. The campus also gained admirers worldwide as it hosted the opening and closing ceremonies and the athletes' village during the 2002 Winter Olympic Games that were held in Salt Lake City.

Just 1% of the men and women are members of 8 national fraternities and 7 national sororities. Though the size of their membership is small, their parties, some wild, others not, are an integral part of the weekend social life, and many Greeks are highly visible also in other campus events and organizations. What social life the Greeks don't provide usually is taken care of by the Latter-day Saint Student Association, which sponsors its own social groups, or the student government. About 300 smaller clubs provide additional alternatives for undergraduates. "Many opportunities exist to be involved," says a senior, "but it takes an effort on the student's part...to create his or her own experience," because so many students on this commuter campus simply attend classes and go home. Students find the campus in general to be well lighted, well patrolled, and essentially free of crime, although bike thefts and stolen wallets and purses can be a problem. An emergency telephone system exists throughout the campus.

Running Utes football is popular, as is men's basketball; both draw spirited crowds. "March Madness" is also usually a biennial event at Utah, as the NCAA men's post-season basketball tournament is played on campus just about every other year. Women's gymnastics has its own strong following, especially since the Lady Utes have won 10 national championships and hold the NCAA attendance record for women's athletics. In all, there are 10 varsity sports for men and 14 for women in NCAA Division I. Skiing or snowboarding is naturally an attraction, with the university offering the largest college ski-instruction program in the nation. Less than 10% of the students find niches in the 60+ intramural sports for each sex, from softball and wallyball to darts and foosball. Personal outdoor recreation, such as mountain biking, hiking, and rock-climbing, also is big as are organized trips led by Campus Recreation. Three U.S. wilderness areas are visible from campus.

Students who still find they need to get away can simply go into Salt Lake City (pop. 193,000), described by a resident as "a big little city that, for its size, provides a lot to do." Professional sports fans can watch the Jazz, the Grizzlies, and the Stingers, representing respectively the men's basketball, hockey, and triple-A baseball teams. Skiing and snowboarding at Park City, Snowbird, and 5 other resorts within 45 minutes of campus, plus trips of all sorts to Jackson Hole, Wyoming, are popular. The truly adventuresome may opt to run the rapids of the Colorado, Yampa, and Green rivers.

Cost cutters: Forty-two percent of freshmen in the 2005–2006 school year received financial aid; for 31%, the assistance was based on need. Among continuing students, 45% received some kind of aid; all but 3% were given need-based assistance. The average first-year award included a need-based scholarship or grant averaging $4414 and need-based self-help aid such as loans and jobs averaging $3860. Non-need-based athletic scholarships for freshmen averaged $13,735; other non-need-based awards and scholarships averaged $2819. Average debt of a 2005 graduate was $12,806. A variety of merit scholarships are available to high-achieving entering freshmen, many for those who intend to major in certain disciplines. A Utah resident with a strong academic record may qualify for a President's, Honors at Entrance, Top Ten, or other private-source scholarship, as well as a variety of departmental awards. A high-achieving nonresident may be eligible for a merit scholarship, a nonresident academic full- or partial-tuition scholarship, or a Leadership Scholarship; these pay resident tuition for 2 semesters. Recipients pay the difference between the out-of-state and in-state rates plus all fees. Cooperative education programs are available in several areas of engineering, computer science, materials science, and metallurgy, as well as in the colleges of Health, Science, Humanities, and Social and Behavioral Science.

Rate of return: Nearly 70% of the entering freshmen return for the sophomore year. Twenty-four percent graduate in 4 years, 45% in 5 years, 60% in 6 years.

Payoff: Economics was the top major for 2005 graduates, claiming 6% of the class, followed by mass communication and political science at 5% each. More than 300 national firms, such as AT&T and General Mills, as well as 150 local companies, recruited on campus in a recent year, enticing most graduates directly into the job market. In a recent year, 27% entered graduate or professional schools.

Bottom line: The University of Utah is "a lot more than just another pretty place," observes a university official. And, as its students attest, it can provide plenty of academic challenge, as well as a beautiful setting, to those who are motivated, self-disciplined, and willing to become involved in campus life. The student who comes to Utah to ski instead of to study, however, is headed for a downhill slide on the grading curve as well as on the slopes.

University of Vermont

Burlington, Vermont 05405

Setting: Small city
Control: Public
Undergraduate enrollment: 3940 men, 4712 women
Graduate enrollment: 400 men, 622 women
Student/faculty ratio: 14:1
Freshman profile: 7% scored over 700 on SAT I verbal; 37% scored 600–700; 45% 500–599; 11% below 500. 6% scored over 700 on SAT I math; 38% scored 600–700; 45% 500–599; 11% below 500. 12% scored above 28 on the ACT; 19% scored 27–28; 32% 24–26; 26% 21–23; 11% below 21. 21% graduated in top tenth of high school class; 45% in upper fifth.

Faculty profile: 88% Ph.D.'s
Tuition and fees: $10,748 in-state, $24,934 out-of-state
Room and board: $7332
Freshman financial aid: 81%; average scholarship or grant: $12,913 need-based; $2684 non-need-based
Campus jobs: NA; average earnings: NA
Application deadline: Early action: Nov. 1; regular: Jan. 15
Financial aid deadline: Feb. 10
Admissions information: (802) 656-3370
e-mail: admissions@uvm.edu
web site: www.uvm.edu

In the world of educational bargains, the University of Vermont presents a problem, an unusual case of a split personality. Not much more than a third of the students, 36%, are from the Green Mountain State; the majority are not. The portion from within pay one of the lowest prices in New England for a premier doctorate-granting university with an emphasis on undergraduate education: $10,748 in 2005–2006. The portion who hail from outside Vermont's borders, however, are charged more than twice as much as their in-state classmates for the same education: $24,934. Add $7332 in room and board, and UVM becomes just $9500 less costly than Harvard and other premier New England institutions. However, the out-of-staters show no sign of staying away, and the in-staters just smile those savvy Yankee grins.

Student body: Though most out-of-state students come also from the Northeast, 49 states and 27 foreign countries are represented in the student body. Increasing racial diversity has been a slow process at UVM, partly a function of Vermont's cultural landscape, in which less than 3% of the population is something other than Caucasian. Still, steady progress has been made with minority enrollment up 21% over the last 2 years, thanks in large part to collaborations with selected urban communities. At UVM, 6% of the students are members of racial and ethnic minority groups; 2% each are Hispanic and Asian-American, and 1% each are African-American and Native American. Foreign nationals also account for 1%. Most undergraduates are bright, energetic, politically engaged, and outdoorsy. Says a New Englander: "We have everything from granola hippies to popped-collar preppies. The campus is very politically active, mostly liberal, but we have a College Republicans group as well." Students describe a very accepting and tolerant environment in which members feel free to express themselves, if that is what they choose to do. Says a New Yorker: "Students are concerned about the world and vocal in the sharing of those thoughts through speak-outs and rallies, a very popular type of setting throughout the year." Many students are involved in and excited about the academic side of college life, and more than 80% are involved in student activities. However, a shrinking but still noticeable portion remains "party oriented" and sometimes push the boundaries a bit far. "Some come thinking they can party from Tuesday through Thursday as well as over a long weekend," says a senior, "but they are out within a semester." Vermont's widening appeal as a place to attend college also is raising the quality of candidates who enter.

Academics: UVM, as the school is commonly called, short for *Universitas Viridis Montis*, the University of the Green Mountains, was chartered in 1791, the same year that Vermont became a state. Philosopher and education reformer John Dewey ("learning by doing") was a member of the Class of 1879. The university offers degrees through the doctorate; undergraduates can earn bachelor's degrees in more than 90 majors through 7 colleges and schools. There also are a graduate college and a medical school. The academic year is divided into semesters. Freshman classes can get rather large, with introductory courses in such areas as psychology research methods enrolling about 300 students. However, recalls a senior, "I took French, philosophy, and English courses my freshman year with 20–30 students and sometimes fewer." Many classes for juniors and seniors may still have 40 participants, although as the senior continues, "my political science seminar has only 15 people, and I had an English seminar with just 8!" In fact, just 3% of all course sections enroll more than 100 students and the vast majority has fewer than 30.

Specific distributional requirements vary by college or school. Most students, however, are required to complete approximately 10 courses in the traditional disciplines, plus a 3-credit course in Race and Culture or an equivalent course exploring race relations and ethnic diversity in the United States. A Teacher Advisor Program known as TAP enables first-year students in the College of Arts and Sciences to combine small interactive courses with attentive academic advising. Freshmen can enroll in small group seminars on topics of common interest, choosing either semester-long departmental seminars or year-long interdisciplinary seminar programs. The seminar professor serves as the student's academic advisor for the year.

The total faculty including professors from the medical school number 1235; of the 1017 full-time members, 564 teach undergraduates; 144 of the 218 part-time members do. Thirty-nine percent are women. Graduate students teach 3% of introductory courses. UVM has both outstanding professors, whose reputations as "really tough" generally mean that their courses are the most interesting and best taught, and others who "aren't so hot" and put little effort into their lectures or in getting to know their students. The overall rating: many more professors in the plus column than on the minus side. Says a sophomore: "I have had amazing professors and not so amazing ones, but the good ones have truly challenged me to think and confront things in our world."

The technologically advanced building for the School of Business Administration is the crowning touch to a division noted for excellent faculty members with innovative teaching styles and real-world connections. Likewise, in the College of Arts and Sciences, political science professors are admired for provoking their students to "think and learn" and for providing them extensive opportunities outside the classroom. Political science is but 1 of several disciplines housed in the Center for the Study of Arts and Sciences, which actually is a refurbishment of the Old Mill building, originally constructed in 1883. History, religion, Russian, anthropology, English, film, social work, and psychology also boast great faculties and intriguing courses. The environmental studies/natural resources program in the School of Natural Resources is excellent, with modern laboratories equipped for research in tree physiology and genetics, wildlife and fisheries biology, water resources, and forest pathology. A research vessel and $4.5 million laboratory are located at Lake Champlain less than a mile from campus. Though small, the geology department is also a gem as is the program in microbiology. The Community and International Development degree program in the College of Agriculture and Life Sciences enables students to assist faculty members in research that stimulates community development. "It is the definition of hands-on learning," raves a major. "As a freshman they hooked me up with a 3-month internship with the U.S. Agency for International Development in Jamaica." Closer to home, the college's major in animal science gives students wonderful opportunities to work in the horse and cow barns. All programs in the College of Engineering and Mathematical Sciences are challenging and prepare their students for real-world situations, not ideal cases. New CAD and math computer labs support a leading-edge approach.

While students find the biology major rigorous, some think the faculty could be less attentive to their research and more attentive to undergraduates' needs in advising. A special course for first-year students assists in their exploration of options in the field. Students hoping to major in journalism at UVM will find no such specific program available, though they may find their interest satisfied in a new public communication major. Undergraduates interested in modern foreign languages would like to see more options in addition to majors in French, Spanish, Italian studies, German, and Russian.

Facilities: Bailey/Howe Library has 1.4 million volumes, 6567 periodicals, 1.9 million microform items, and entirely too much talking on the main floor for students who want to get something done. However, 1 floor up is generally a bit quieter, and the third floor "is like a tomb," says a user. Students generally find the collection more than adequate, with ample access to interlibrary loan, efficient and extensive computerized research aids, and librarians who are "amazingly friendly and helpful," says a senior. "I haven't run into a problem yet." Science students spend more of their time in the separate Cook Physical Sciences Library. Collections in medicine and the health sciences are located in the Dana Medical Library, a very silent study center.

Undergraduates in the School of Business Administration are required to purchase tablet PCs. Other students may use any of 700 PCs and Macs spread throughout a dozen computer labs in the library and other academic buildings. Says a junior: "They are in various locations all over campus and open all different hours to accommodate the needs of students." Every residence hall room is wired for connections to the campus network and Internet, and many portions of the campus are wireless. Most undergraduates have their own computers.

Special programs: Students with a special interest in the sciences may enjoy HELiX, the Hughes Endeavor for Life Sciences Excellence, which provides mini-seminars each semester, as well as grant-sponsored opportunities for participants to conduct individually designed research projects with faculty members. An Integrated Social Science Program enables students to explore important social problems from the perspectives of the various social sciences. Students take 4 semester-long courses, on such topics as Social Inequality and Capitalism and Human Welfare, and may complete an optional thesis. A 3-3 program in veterinary medicine with Tufts University is an option; students apply as a UVM sophomore. Those who wish to study abroad can pursue a semester studying international marketing in Grenoble, France, or a term in Germany, Scandinavia, Russia, Australia, or Japan. Other opportunities are available in 60 countries around the world.

Campus life: Freshmen and sophomores are required to live on the 460-acre campus overlooking Lake Champlain. Nearly 600 students from all classes, along with graduate students, reside in the Living/Learning Center, where groups of up to 7 in a suite plan, direct, and participate in any of 30–35 year-long programs focusing on specific themes, everything from emergency medicine and community service to photography and alternative music. There also are special-interest houses and floors in other living units. All types of housing, especially the new University Heights residences with their many "green" design features, encourage students to be environmentally friendly. Notes a state resident: "Students are all given recycling bins with each dorm room and are encouraged to recycle everything possible. We are a truly green school!"

Just 7% of the men belong to 2 local and 7 national fraternities, and 5% of the women to 5 national sororities. Both groups are active and sponsor many weekend parties open to all "but they are an option, not prevalent," says a sophomore. The cafes and coffeehouses of Burlington also are just a 10-minute walk from campus. With a student body described as "outdoorsy," it's no wonder that many are active in the Outing Club, which sponsors 3 to 5 activities a weekend year-round, and in environmental organizations, although participation is highest in Volunteers in Action, a community service organization. Theft of laptops, iPods, bicycles, and bicycle seats is the most common crime, though emergency call boxes and a vigilant campus police force keep other kinds of incidents in check.

Since the school has no football team, soccer and lacrosse are the fall's most popular sports, followed in the winter by Catamount basketball and hockey, which always pack the stands. In 2003, 2004, and 2005, the UVM men's basketball team advanced to the NCAA Division I tournament and in 2005, advanced to the second round for the first time in the school's history. In 1996, the hockey Cats made it all the way to the NCAA Frozen Four competition. Women's basketball also draws big crowds. A perennial powerhouse on the slopes, UVM's ski team has won 6 national championships in the history of the program and has finished among the top 5 schools in the country for 32 straight years. UVM fields 9 teams for men and 11 for women, which compete in NCAA Division I. Thirty-five percent engage in intramural activities ranging from dodge ball to inner-tube water polo and average participation on 5-6 different teams. It also should come as no surprise that the ski club is extremely popular, as are the clubs in rugby, crew, cycling, sailing, Ultimate Frisbee, figure skating, and snowboarding.

Burlington, Vermont's largest city (metropolitan pop. 149,000), is located approximately 100 miles south of Montreal, 200 miles northwest of Boston, and 300 miles north of New York City, all destinations for students seeking a more cosmopolitan environment. Otherwise, the Adirondacks to the west and the Green Mountains to the east provide natural lures to those needing to "head for the hills." "The location," says a New Englander, "does not get any better, but be ready for a cold winter."

Cost cutters: State appropriations traditionally have made up the smallest portion of UVM's operating budget, recently accounting for just 9% of the total operating budget. The single largest share, about 37%, comes from tuition and fees. In a recent school year, 81% of UVM freshmen and 75% of continuing students received financial aid. Fifty percent of the freshmen and 57% of the remaining students received aid based on need. When aid distribution is viewed according to student residency, more than 65% of Vermont students and almost 45% of out-of-staters receive some kind of financial aid. The average freshman award for a first-year student with financial need included a need-based scholarship or grant averaging $12,913 and need-based self-help aid such as loans and jobs averaging $6280. Non-need-based athletic scholarships for first-year students averaged $15,990; other non-need-based awards and scholarships averaged $2684. Average debt of a recent graduate was $20,142. Every year, a growing number of bright high school seniors from Vermont are named Vermont Scholars and earn renewable scholarships. Those with financial need receive a benefits package that covers all need using grants, scholarships, and work study; those without need receive a $1500 annual scholarship. The best and brightest in the state can receive

Green and Gold Scholarships paying full tuition over 4 years. The UVM Presidential Scholarship recognizes out-of-state residents who generally rank in the top 20% of their high school graduating class and have the highest SAT and ACT scores. Scholarship amounts range from $1000 to $3500. Other superior nonresidents may receive C.V. Starr Scholarships worth $3000 a year. Cooperative education programs are available primarily through the School of Business Administration and College of Engineering and Mathematical Sciences. Budgeted payment plans also are an option.

Rate of return: Eighty-eight percent of the freshmen like what they see and return for the sophomore year. Fifty-five percent graduate in 4 years; after another year of study, the proportion increases to 65%; after 6 years, close to 70% have earned diplomas.

Payoff: In 2005, the most popular majors for graduates were business administration (10%), and psychology and English (7% each). Over 80% of a recent class entered the job market immediately after graduation; major employers include Bear Stearns, Dana Farber Cancer Institute, General Electric, IBM, most of the major accounting firms, and public interest research groups. Large numbers of graduates also find positions in educational systems, hospitals, government and human services agencies, and a variety of agriculturally and environmentally based organizations. More than 190 employers recruited on campus in a recent year. Nearly a fourth, 23%, of recent graduates enrolled immediately in graduate or professional schools.

Bottom line: UVM is great "for the high school senior who seeks a change from an urban environment, but also wants some of the conveniences of a small city," notes a minority student. "If you do well here, you can go almost anywhere. And if you're environmentally conscious, Vermont is for you!"

Virginia

Bridgewater College

Bridgewater, Virginia 22812

Setting: Small town
Control: Private (Church of the Brethren)
Undergraduate enrollment: 639 men, 856 women
Graduate enrollment: None
Student/faculty ratio: 16:1
Freshman profile: 2% scored over 700 on SAT I verbal; 17% scored 600–700; 46% 500–599; 35% below 500. 3% scored over 700 on SAT I math; 17% scored 600–700; 49% 500–599; 31% below 500. 8% scored above 28 on the ACT; 8% scored 27–28; 11% 24–26; 36% 21–23; 37% below 21. 39% graduated in top fifth of high school class; 74% in upper two-fifths.

Faculty profile: 79% Ph.D.'s
Tuition and fees: $18,990
Room and board: $8800
Freshman financial aid: 99%; average scholarship or grant: $3441 need-based; $10,868 non-need-based
Campus jobs: 30%; average earnings: $1108/year
Application deadline: Rolling
Financial aid deadline: Aug. 15 (Priority date: Mar. 1)
Admissions information: (540) 828-5375; (800) 759-8328
e-mail: admissions@bridgewater.edu
web site: www.bridgewater.edu

A decade ago, bustling Bridgewater College in Virginia's Shenandoah Valley was anything but bustling when the weekend rolled around. On Mondays through Fridays, more than three-quarters of Bridgewater's 1000 or so students back then could be found studying and hanging out on the 190-acre campus. (All students who do not commute from home are required to live in college housing.) But very few of those residents stuck around past their 1:15 classes on Fridays, leaving for home or to party at neighboring, bigger universities. Not anymore. "Suddenly, the parking lots are still full on Friday nights," says a senior. On any given weekend, as many as 60% of Bridgewater's residents can be found attending a steady diet of coffeehouses replete with comedians, musicians, or magicians, as well as movies and dances, put on by the student-run Eagle Productions. Student athletes, especially those playing football or men's and women's basketball, are excited to find more classmates, plus a number of faculty members, cheering them on from the sidelines. Restrictions on drinking alcohol and on visits by the opposite sex in student housing still prevail at this college affiliated with the Church of the Brethren, but more undergraduates are discovering that the weekend benefits easily outweigh the detractions. Recalls one basketball player, now a recent graduate, "A lot of students used to leave campus on the weekend but this is changing. The college offers lots of things to do. . . . This school really emphasizes developing the whole person and tries to help you mature during your 4 years here."

Student body: Virginia is home to 77% of the students; most of the rest come from 22 other states, many in the Middle Atlantic region. All but 12% are graduates of public schools. Seventy-six percent are Protestant, and 11% are members of the Church of the Brethren. Twelve percent are Catholic; 4% are other faiths; and the rest claim no religious affiliation. Foreign nationals from 11 countries, about half of whom are members of Brethren College exchange programs, constitute 1% of enrollment. African-Americans account for 8%; Hispanics, Asian-Americans, and Native Americans, each 1%. Students tend to be conservative and traditional in their values, fun-loving, and unpretentious, with a sensitivity and openness that make "fitting in" and becoming close friends relatively easy. On the negative side, the closeness can get a bit excessive. Laments an out-of-stater: "There seem to be no 'secrets' in regard to people and their personal concerns." Grades are generally respected as a private matter, though, and everyone tries to do his or her best without paying too much attention to how a classmate has fared.

Academics: Bridgewater, founded in 1880, awards the bachelor of arts degree in 31 major fields and the bachelor of science in 21. Classes average 16 students. At the extremes, an education overview course, Teaching as a Profession, can enroll 106, while several courses have an enrollment of 1. The college follows a semester schedule, with a January interterm.

As part of Bridgewater's general-education program, undergraduates take coursework in world history and civilizations, cultures of the global community, global diversity, literature, fine arts, Old or New Testament, religion or philosophy, social sciences, natural sciences, mathematics, and integrated learning. In addition, students take core proficiency courses in effective writing, oral communication, critical thinking, and wellness, plus an activity course and either a foreign language or demonstrated competency for the B.A. degree or mathematics and science for the B.S. A comprehensive exam is required of every senior. At least 8 times a semester, undergraduates must attend convocations, held once a week and consisting of musical performances, films, plays, and lectures. To complete his or her Bridgewater experience, every student must compile a Personal Development Portfolio. The portfolio, done with the help of a faculty mentor over 4 years, details the student's accomplishments in citizenship, cultural awareness, aesthetics, ethical development, leadership, social proficiency, and wellness, as well as in the traditional academic areas.

Bridgewater's faculty number 126, with 96 teaching full-time. Forty-four percent are women. Students find most professors quite easy to talk to, either in class or over a snack after hours. "There are a few faculty members," says a junior, "who sometimes are drawn into a research hole and never come out, but most faculty are willing to build a relationship with students." A majority also don't settle for rote learning. Says a junior: "Our professors like to challenge us to think critically and 'outside the box.'"

Thought-provoking and caring faculties make most departments at this small college strong. History, political science, philosophy, religion, sociology, and economics are all distinguished by excellent instructors who enjoy forging 1-to-1 relationships with students. Business administration offers its own diverse and challenging selection of classes with plenty of chances for internships and other on-the-job experiences. The classes in athletic training likewise are "very intense and demanding but rewarding," says a major. "Athletic training requires out-of-classroom observation and clinical affiliation hours as well as the classroom work." The music department is rigorous, and its chorale and stage bands each take spring tours. The newly renovated Carter Center for Worship and Music, formerly the Bridgewater Church of the Brethren, has provided 10 soundproof practice rooms, 2 Reuter pipe organs, and 23 pianos for student use. The biology, chemistry, physics, and mathematics and computer science departments became winners with the opening in August, 1995 of a $10 million Science and Mathematics Center. The new structure brought the facilities in these departments up to the long-time stellar quality of most of their faculties. Also joining the plus column is the major in communication studies, already drawing acclaim for its open-minded and personable faculty members and its opportunities for hands-on learning although some students say the program must increase its rigor to avoid being pegged as a "cop-out" major.

Theater, German, and social work are offered as minors only. Philosophy and religion are offered only as a combined major, though students find the classes rewarding and fun for those involved. The major in Family and Consumer Sciences enrolls few students and lacks the funding of other departments. The foreign language labs, with majors in French and Spanish, need more advanced equipment; the program also needs more professors and more language options for students.

Facilities: Alexander Mack Memorial Library contains just over 189,000 volumes and 650 periodicals, which most students find "okay," but no more. The computerized catalog which connects to various off-campus libraries rates higher in student views. For extensive research projects, most undergraduates use the Internet or the collection of nearby James Madison University, which has more than twice the number of books and 4 times the periodicals. Students say the study environment at Mack has improved over the last year. "The overall feel of the library is welcoming," says a sophomore, and it doesn't hurt that Starbucks coffee recently was added. Couples and even groups sometimes meet at the library for some socializing along with their studying, which means silent studiers need to find a spot tucked away from the chatter. The library also recently extended its weekday hours until midnight and offers laptops for checkout.

More than 175 computers are available in 5 main computer laboratories, 2 located in the science center, and in academic departments. Facilities are open around the clock which students appreciate. Each dormitory room also is wired for access to the campus network with student-owned PCs. Wireless networking is available in the library and campus center.

Special programs: Through Brethren Colleges Abroad, students can study for a year in 16 countries from Greece to Ecuador. A Washington semester is an option with American University. A dual degree program in forestry is offered with Duke University, in engineering with Virginia Tech and George Washington University, in physical therapy with George Washington University and Shenandoah University, and in nursing with Vanderbilt. Those interested in veterinary medicine can complete a dual degree program with Virginia Tech.

Campus life: Amid the flurry of increased weekend activities awaiting Bridgewater students, few express the concern of years ago regarding the college's dorm visitation rules. Visiting hours to the single-sex residence halls by members of the opposite sex have expanded steadily in length over the past few years and currently extend from 10 a.m. to midnight Sunday through Thursday and from 10 a.m. to 2 a.m. Friday and Saturday. There are no fraternities or sororities. Seven percent of the students sing in the Oratorio Choir, which performs every December. All dormitories are locked nightly and have an alarm system that goes off if someone enters after midnight. Students use a magnetic key card to enter whenever they like. Crime, however, is not seen as much of a problem.

Two-thirds of the men and a third of the women participate in the 24 intramural sports offered for each sex, which includes several activities for mixed teams. A third of the men and 15% of the women suit up for the 9 men's, 10 women's, and 1 coed NCAA Division III varsity teams. Bridgewater's winning football team, which was the national runner-up in 2001, draws some of the biggest crowds. The newly completed, 34,000-square-foot Funkhouser Center for Health and Wellness provides eagerly awaited modern facilities for fitness, intramural, and recreational activities. Horseback riding is available for credit and recreation; the college has its own stables and will board a student's horse for $100 a month.

The town of Bridgewater (pop. 3900) is surrounded by the Allegheny Mountains to the west and the Blue Ridge Mountains to the east, with Mennonite farms dotting the immediate area. Harrisonburg, 10 minutes away, and Washington, D.C., and Roanoke, each about 2 hours distant, are popular getaways, as are at least 4 other colleges and universities in the surrounding area. Several ski resorts also are within easy driving distance.

Cost cutters: In the 2005–2006 school year, all but 1% of undergraduates received financial aid; 70% of the first-year students and 68% of the rest were on need-based assistance. The average freshman award for a student with need included a need-based scholarship or grant averaging $3441 and need-based self-help aid such as loans and jobs averaging $4067. Other non-need-based awards and scholarships averaged $10,868. Average debt of a 2005 graduate was $25,780. President's Merit Plus Awards are the most highly coveted scholarships, paying full tuition to incoming freshmen with a 3.8 GPA and a minimum math and critical reading SAT of 1350 or ACT of 30. A maximum of 10 awards are made each year. President's Merit Awards pay $12,000 for a 1200 SAT (27 ACT). McKinney ACE 30-5 scholarships range in amount from $6000 to $10,000 annually, depending upon the GPA of the student. Concludes an out-of-stater: "The financial aid I received made Bridgewater's expenses less than those at any state school I applied to."

Rate of return: Seventy-seven percent of freshmen return for the sophomore year. Sixty-eight percent graduate in 6 years or less.

Payoff: Majors in business administration comprised the largest group of 2005 graduates, at 17%. Thirteen percent earned degrees in biology, 9% in communication studies. The largest portion of graduates start full-time jobs within months of commencement, primarily in the East, with such firms as Dow Chemical and with the U.S. Labor Department and other agencies. About a fifth of a recent class entered teaching.

Bottom line: "Educating and instilling sound values are taken pretty seriously at Bridgewater College," advises a recent graduate. Students prepared to accept some campus rules in exchange for a supportive familial environment will most enjoy the Bridgewater experience.

Christendom College
Front Royal, Virginia 22630

Setting: Rural
Control: Private (Roman Catholic)
Undergraduate enrollment: 159 men, 213 women
Graduate enrollment: NA
Student/faculty ratio: 12:1
Freshman profile: 32% scored over 700 on SAT I verbal; 47% scored 600–700; 19% 500–599; 2% below 500. 6% scored over 700 on SAT I math; 33% scored 600–700; 48% 500–599; 13% below 500. 29% scored over 28 on the ACT; 16% scored 27–28; 23% 24–26; 16% 21–23; 16% below 21. 25% graduated in top tenth of high school class; 38% in upper fifth.

Faculty profile: 81% Ph.D.'s
Tuition and fees: $15,818
Room and board: $5776
Freshman financial aid: 78%; average scholarship or grant: $3715 need-based; $4035 non-need-based
Campus jobs: 40%; average earnings: $1750/year
Application deadline: Early action: Dec. 1; regular: Mar. 1
Financial aid deadline: Apr. 1
Admissions information: (540) 636-2900; (800) 877-5456 e-mail: admissions@christendom.edu web site: www.christendom.edu

For students enrolled at Christendom College, a Roman Catholic school of just 372 undergraduates in Virginia's peaceful Shenandoah Valley, the name of their institution says it all. Christendom refers to a Christianized social order, which is exactly the collegiate environment undergraduates from 43 states and 1 foreign country set out to find. The college was founded in 1977 with a vision of providing a liberal arts education in a setting faithful to the official teachings of the Catholic Church and of the Pope as its leader. Students follow a detailed, 3-year core curriculum rich in theology and philosophy, followed by a year of concentration in 1 of 6 liberal arts majors. Undergraduates are at all times expected to adhere to strict standards of dress and behavior. "Initially, I thought this school would be austere in its bearing," recalls a junior. "Christendom, however, has a splendid balance between social functions and academia, as well as an emphasis on the spiritual life." The college also boasts one of the lowest tuition rates among Catholic institutions, just $15,818 in tuition and fees for the 2005–2006 school year. With a year's room and board bringing the total to about $21,600, Christendom is the answer to many a worried student's prayer.

Student body: "The undergraduates at Christendom are first and foremost strongly Catholic," says a sophomore from the Midwest, and statistics bear this out. One hundred percent of the students are Catholic. Only 14% in a recent year attended public schools; 52% attended private or parochial schools; 34% were home-schooled. Four percent of the students are Hispanic and 2% Asian-American. Eleven students in a recent year were foreign nationals. The students who seek out Christendom's special style of learning tend to be politically conservative and active supporters of the pro-life movement. While serious about their studies, students also consider themselves to be active, fun-loving, and energetic. Says a senior: "You will always find puritans and party animals in this type of school setting, but most students are moderate."

Academics: As much as Christendom students love to have fun, there is no getting around the demanding workload expected of all. With no class larger than the 38 found in a required course on the History of Western Civilization, there are no enormous lecture halls in which to hide. Classes with only a handful of students, such as the 3 enrolled in the Government and Politics of Europe, also are plentiful in the 2-semester schedule and keep participants on top of their assignments.

The foundation of Christendom's academic program is its rigorous, 3-year core curriculum that covers 84 of the 126 credit hours needed to graduate, including 18 hours each of philosophy and theology but only 3 each of math and science. Students start the first-semester freshman year with classes in English Composition and Literature, History of the Ancient and Biblical World, Euclidean Geometry (or another college-level mathematics course), Introduction to Philosophy, Fundamentals of Catholic Doctrine I, and Elementary French, Greek, Latin, or Spanish. Another 6 courses, many of them continuations of the first-semester's work, are required the following term. Sophomores take 6 more required courses in their first semester, and 5 the second, including classes in Metaphysics and in Social Teachings of the Church. The core requirements conclude in the junior year with Literature of Western Civilization III, History of Medieval Philosophy, and Moral Theology in the first term, and classes in History of Modern Philosophy and Catholic Apologetics in the second. It's a trial by fire that is made more bearable because everyone else is enduring it, too. Says a senior: "In the early years, because of the core curriculum, students tend to have tests at the same time and papers due close to the same time, so they usually study together without a lot of temptation to blow things off. Then when you get into your major, hopefully you will have developed study habits to keep you on track and give you the ability to juggle time constraints."

The other benefits students find in the core is its exposure across the disciplines to Christendom's fine faculty, whose members recently numbered 35, all but 14 of whom taught full-time. Underclassmen quickly discover a team of scholars, 90% of whom are men, devoted to their subject matter, to their students, and to the philosophy of the school. To teach at the college, all faculty must affirm their loyalty to the official teachings of the Catholic Church. Public dissent or rejection of the Church's official teachings as interpreted by the Pope or of the Pope as head of the Catholic Church is grounds for termination of the faculty contract. Says a philosophy major: "These are faith-filled men and women who care deeply that each of their students understands the material that is presented. The faculty is very excited about what they teach and is interested in making their students excited as well." Little wonder, given the professors and thought-provoking subjects they teach, that many class discussions are followed up along the walkways or over lunch.

In the junior year, students get the first in-depth opportunity to begin to explore their major field of study, in which they will be required to complete a senior thesis the following year. Seven liberal arts majors are offered in French, classical and early Christian studies, English language and literature, history, philosophy, political science and economics, and theology. (A master's degree is offered in theological studies.) Students generally concur on the 2 strongest academic offerings at Christendom: philosophy and theology. "The teachers in these areas are excellent," says a philosophy major, "and understand the nobility of what they are teaching." They also are rarely too busy to assist with problems a student may be having. Philosophy, in particular, benefits from having faculty members with expertise in different areas so all periods of thought are covered. Students wish there were more theology professors to offer an even greater breadth of courses in this field. History, too, comes alive from a faculty who are "mostly young, energetic, and excellent teachers," says a major, though it, too, could use additional faculty.

Students have mixed views about the political science and economics program. Students interested in these fields may choose between the regular political science sequence and a more career-oriented politics program that includes 9 credit hours of practica, consisting of a special series of lectures, seminars, and workshops plus a 6-credit hour internship. Students generally like the practica and internship opportunities made possible by the college's proximity to Washington, D.C., which takes them to Congress, think tanks, lobby groups, and other organizations involved in public policy. However, some students say that more professors are needed to teach political theory and that those present need to improve the quality of the lower-level core courses to put them on a par with the stronger upper-level offerings. Some students think the professors in classical and early Christian studies are "overworked," and additional faculty is needed to give more attention to both introductory-level and more advanced students. Undergraduates destined to be most dissatisfied with Christendom's offerings are those with serious interest in mathematics, biology, chemistry, physics, psychology, or business. There are no majors and few or no courses offered in these fields. Minors are available in the major fields and in mathematics, science, Greek, Spanish, and Latin.

Facilities: The new 40,000-square-foot St. John the Evangelist Library opened in fall 2004, and its completion didn't come any too soon for students. The new facility seats well over half the resident student population and has room for a collection of 130,000 volumes. The current holdings of about 68,000 volumes and 279 periodicals are strongest in the fields of theology, philosophy, literature, and history. Interlibrary loan, which is easily accomplished through nearby D.C. and Virginia universities, and Internet access help keep the complaint level low. A strict silent-study policy made the old library an efficient place for study and students have come to expect no less from the new structure.

Christendom's new library contains Internet public-access terminals in the Information Commons in the center of the library's main floor. Additional labs in the student center and administration building are for writing papers and checking e-mail. The writing lab is accessible around the clock; the library is open until midnight. Students say the only backup occurs during finals time, though the wait is rarely more than 30 minutes.

Special programs: Christendom provides 3-week summer abroad experiences for students to Rome, Italy; Dublin, Ireland; and Spain, offered in an alternating cycle. A junior experience in Rome begun in fall 2002 enables half the class to spend the fall semester in Rome, with the other half traveling and studying there during spring term. Participation in the program is voluntary.

Campus life: After the rigors of the academic week, Christendom students treasure the weekends and find ways to have fun without fraternities and sororities. All but 10% of the students reside on the 100-acre rural campus, which is surrounded by the Blue Ridge Mountains and bounded on the west by cliffs overlooking the Shenandoah River. In the center of campus is the Chapel of Christ the King where mass is offered daily. Though not required, most students attend. Two of the most popular organizations on campus, the Legion of Mary, an evangelical group that spreads the Catholic faith through ministry in such places as retirement homes and a local prison, and Shield of Roses, which takes students on Saturday bus trips to the D.C. area to pray outside abortion clinics, further reflect the centrality of students' religious faith to their lives. Other popular groups are the Debate Club and the Christendom Choir and Schola Gregoriana, which performs Gregorian chant. There also, says a midwesterner, "are several groups of students who get together with open invitation and play instruments, sing Irish songs, recite poetry, tell stories, and have a campfire by the river." Campus crime is virtually nonexistent, although security guards are present on campus at night for insurance. Says a sophomore: "Students are more afraid of bears and deer on campus than attackers." Adds a junior: "The worst thing that happens here is pranks. You have to watch out for those! But not crimes."

The college fields intercollegiate teams in men's and women's soccer and basketball, baseball, softball, and women's volleyball. A fourth of the men and 14% of the women in a recent year competed. Seventy percent of the men and 50% of the women take part in 7 intramural sports for each sex. Many students burn energy participating in the regularly scheduled swing dances or cultural dances that vary from Irish to Czech to Spanish. A hike along the Appalachian Trail, 5 miles east of campus, or a swim in the Shenandoah River provides alternative study breaks. For those longing for some urban excitement, Washington, D.C., is 65 miles east. The downtown area of Front Royal (pop. 12,000) is 4 miles from campus. Winchester (pop. 22,000) is 20 miles north.

Cost cutters: Because Christendom College accepts no direct federal aid nor participates in such indirect aid programs as the Stafford Loans, students needing aid rely on the generosity of donors to the college. And generous they are. Through their assistance, 78% of first-year students received some form of financial aid in a recent school year; 66% of continuing students did. For 53% of the freshmen and 52% of the continuing students, the aid was need-based. The average award for a first-year student with financial need included a need-based scholarship or grant averaging $3715 and need-based self-help aid such as loans and jobs averaging $4950. Other non-need-based awards and scholarships averaged $4035. Average debt of a recent graduate was lower than at many schools, $11,240. A number of merit scholarships are awarded to students and range in value up to full tuition. To be considered for an award, first-time freshmen must have achieved a score of 1800 or better on the new SAT or a score of 27 or higher on the ACT and submit a high school record demonstrating substantial achievement and a willingness to work. The college offers a family discount when more than one child is enrolled. Financial aid administrators note that the amounts of academic scholarship funds awarded are weighted toward first-year students; they caution that scholarship students in their second through fourth years cannot expect to receive the same amount or level of scholarship funds as in their first year.

Rate of return: Nearly 88% of entering freshmen return for the sophomore year. Seventy percent graduate in 4 years; 75% in 5 years.

Payoff: Nearly two-thirds of recent graduates earned bachelor's degrees in 3 fields: 21% each in political science and history and 20% in philosophy. Eight companies and organizations recruited on campus in a recent school year. Three-quarters of the graduates headed directly into the job market, most remaining on the East Coast. A fourth pursued further study in the arts and sciences, many in philosophy, history, and literature.

Bottom line: Christendom College is most appropriate for those students seeking a close-knit environment steeped in both the official teachings of the Catholic Church and a curriculum heavy in philosophy and theology. Says a student from the Pacific Northwest: "This school lived up to my expectations for academic difficulty but the kind of knowledge and type of teachers here have made it all worth the necessary extra effort."

The College of William and Mary

Williamsburg, Virginia 23187

Setting: Small town
Control: Public
Undergraduate enrollment: 2515 men, 3005 women
Graduate enrollment: 769 men, 727 women
Student/faculty ratio: 11:1
Freshman profile: 44% scored over 699 on SAT I verbal; 42% scored 600–699; 12% 500–599; 2% below 500. 35% scored over 699 on SAT I math; 51% scored 600–699; 13% 500–599; 2% below 500. 50% scored above 29 on the ACT; 43% scored 24–29; 7% 18–23. 79% graduated in top tenth of high school class; 97% in upper fifth.
Faculty profile: 89% Ph.D.'s

Tuition and fees: $7778 in-state, $23,048 out-of-state
Room and board: $6417
Freshman financial aid: 53%; average scholarship or grant: $6978 need-based; $5408 non-need-based
Campus jobs: NA; average earnings: NA
Application deadline: Early decision: Nov. 1; regular: Jan. 5
Financial aid deadline: Mar. 15 (Priority: Feb. 15)
Admissions information: (757) 221-4223
  e-mail: admiss@wm.edu
  web site: www.wm.edu

The College of William and Mary in Williamsburg, Virginia can't claim to be the oldest college in the United States, but that historical distinction, held by Harvard (founded 57 years earlier), is about the only first that William and Mary hasn't earned. The college, which turns 315 years old in 2008, is home to the nation's oldest college building (attributed to Sir Christopher Wren and dating back to 1695) and the oldest school of law. The illustrious Phi Beta Kappa Society was founded by a small group of William and Mary students in 1776, and the nation's oldest honor system is still in place there. Perhaps most significantly for the generations to come, the college counts, among its oldest and possibly most important student/faculty relationships, one between William Small, a William and Mary mathematics professor, and an engaging young student named Thomas Jefferson (Class of 1762). Jefferson later said of Small's influence: "From his conversation, I got my first views of the expansion of science and of the system of things in which we are placed." All this from a college that endures today as the oldest educational bargain around.

Student body: Sixty-seven percent of the students attending William and Mary are from Virginia; the rest in a recent year came from the remaining 49 states and 52 foreign countries. Undergraduates include 6.5% Asian-American, 6.5% African-American, 5% Hispanic, and 2% foreign national students. Thirty students are Native Americans. As significant as the enrollment figures for minorities is the retention rate, which at William and Mary is high; on average, 94% of the minority students at W&M graduate in 5 years, more than double the national average. One of 4 students is a graduate of a private or parochial school. Most undergraduates are moderate in their politics, relationships, and comfortable dress, and down to earth and accepting of personal differences. "We are serious-minded scholars here," says a state resident, "but we believe in being warm, friendly, and socially active, too." Classmates use words like "intellectually curious," "self-motivated," and "go-getters" to describe each other. Says a junior: "Students strive to excel both through the passion they employ in their studies and the compassion they share with friends through countless activities." Competition is more within oneself than against others "and my expectations, like everyone else's, are high," says an English major. And because good grades are hard to come by, students enforce the centuries-old honor code and don't react kindly to those who stray from it.

Academics: The College of William and Mary, named for King William III and Queen Mary II of England, grants degrees through the doctorate. Undergraduate programs in about 30 major fields are offered in the School of Arts and Sciences and the School of Business Administration. Advanced degrees are awarded in the Graduate School in Arts and Sciences, the schools of Education and Marine Science, and the Marshall-Wythe School of Law. The academic year is divided into semesters. The biggest course, Principles of Biology, recently enrolled about 300; students swear that except for a few introductory lectures of this size or slightly smaller, most freshman classes range from 20 to 40 participants. Even in the large settings, faculty make the extra effort to get to know their students personally. Some take photographs to better match names with faces; the head of the biology department, who teaches the large introductory classes for majors and non-majors, recently arranged special "Coffee Talks," where he meets with students in groups of 3, as many as would like, so they can get to know each other better outside of class. All underclassmen also are guaranteed at least one small setting in the required freshman seminar, which has a cap of 16 students and matches student interests with senior faculty members in an intensive experience steeped in reading, writing, and discussion. Juniors and seniors usually find classes of 12–40, though some upper-level courses have only 5.

Regardless of major, all students must complete coursework in 7 broad areas: the biological and physical sciences, social sciences, mathematics and quantitative reasoning, world cultures and history, literature and history of the arts, creative and performing arts, and philosophical, religious, and social thought. Students also must complete 11 courses distributed among 3 broad fields of study. Foreign language and upper-division writing and computing competence specific to each student's field of concentration also is required. Students for the most part appreciate the "flexibility and freedom" they have in choosing their general-education courses while gaining exposure to a wide range of fields.

The faculty consists of 596 full-time professors and 167 part-time; 121 of the full-time faculty and 57 of the part-timers teach at the graduate level only. Women make up 34% of the faculty. Individual relationships with professors are the same staple of the college that they were in Thomas Jefferson's undergraduate days. Observes a government major with a minor in economics: "My economics advisor is a renowned expert on health care economics and industrial organization, and also the hardest professor I've had at the college. And yet I can sit down with him 1-on-1 and discuss the Dodgers' chances to make the World Series." Unlike faculties at more research-oriented universities, the professors at W&M, this student continues, "remember that students are the lifeblood of the institution, and do their utmost to draw out individual strengths." Adds a government major: "The professors have high expectations and challenge students without apologies but are always willing to help."

William and Mary's strongest disciplines, history, government, biology, accounting, and religion, have both changed with the times and remained as solid as Wren Chapel. History and government naturally are enhanced by the college's proximity to colonial Williamsburg and to Washington, D.C., but also benefit from a superb faculty. Biology, a traditionally strong discipline that sends more graduates to Virginia medical schools than any other public biology program in-state, offers a modern new science building with first-rate labs and equipment. Opportunities for research are meaningful and extensive, as this senior who spent the summer collecting samples from the deep-sea submersible *Alvin* relates: "When we do research, we get to work on independent projects, not just wash graduate students' glassware or crunch numbers for a professor." Economics majors have ample opportunities to engage in independent or honors research. Modern language laboratories complement intense individual instruction from professors and extensive out-of-classroom opportunities, some across either ocean, to expand proficiency. A passionate religion faculty makes "enticing" subject matter even more appealing. English, anthropology, art history, international relations, public policy, business, chemistry, geology, physics—each is demanding, exciting, and respected in its own way. The accounting program consistently ranks among the top 20 in the nation, as employers from the major firms who recruit at W&M well know. Graduates of other concentrations in the School of Business Administration also are highly prized by prospective employers.

A list of disappointing departments is harder to come by. Mathematics is known around campus for being fairly incomprehensible. "The teachers know their stuff," says a computer science major, "but have a reputation for being unable to come down to the level of the average student." Visiting professors from the National Aeronautics and Space Administration (NASA) have presented a special challenge in comprehension. The psychology department, while having some exceptional faculty members, has been understaffed, limiting the number of courses available. Some students would like to see a journalism major.

Facilities: Earl Gregg Swem Library, large for a college, small for a university, contains most of W&M's collection of about 2.1 million volumes, 2.3 million microform items, 11,313 periodicals, and more than a half million government documents. Earlier complaints from students that Swem's study environment failed to "match the quality of students or professors at W&M," were swept away in the dust of a recent $35 million renovation and expansion. Says an economics and international relations major: "The new library has ample room to study and its open, fresh atmosphere also contributes to its strength as a study environment." A 24-hour study lounge also is attached to the library. Swem's research capabilities have never *not* been appealing. The LIbraries ONline catalog, LION, is easily king of the Swem and widely used by undergraduates as are other on-line resources. Widely read and enjoyed is *The Throne*, a newsletter posted in Swem's bathrooms, "a favorite among student patrons," says a senior. Libraries for law, marine science, and physics are slightly less capacious, with other, smaller departmental libraries containing materials on biology, business administration, chemistry, education, geology, and music.

About 300 Pentium PCs are available to undergraduates in 17 locations, some open 24 hours. A number of professors routinely log assignments on the computers. However, only those enrolled in the executive M.B.A. program are required to own their own PCs. Computer hookup capability in every dormitory room has encouraged most undergraduates, perhaps 80% of incoming freshmen, to bring their own units, students say. Nearly all of the campus also is wireless, enabling students to use laptops in the library, at the on-campus coffee shop, and even in the Sunken Gardens, as studiers watch their friends toss Frisbees in sunny weather.

Special programs: Foreign exchange programs are available in 40 countries with, among others, Exeter and St. Andrews universities in England and Scotland, respectively; the University of Valencia in Spain; Beijing Normal University in China; and Université Paul Valery in Montpellier, France. Three-2 combined engineering programs are offered with a wide range of universities, including Case Western, Columbia, and Washington. A combined program in forestry and environmental science also is available with Duke University.

Campus life: The college is predominantly residential, with 76% of the undergraduates making their home on the 1200 acres of history. "Knowing that Thomas Jefferson studied in these same spots more than 200 years ago is inspiring," says a state resident. A third of the men and a fourth of the women are members of 15 national fraternities and 11 national sororities, which compete socially, philanthropically, and academically, boasting a GPA among the Greeks higher than that of the overall student body. Many of the Greek parties are open to independents, and feelings of animosity between the 2 groups, says a New Yorker, "are as low as can be expected." The Greeks and the Delis, a row of small sub-shop-style eateries that serve alcohol, are the sites of much Saturday-night socializing, and each locale attracts students from both groups. "Fraternity parties are popular," says a Virginian, "but language houses, cultural organizations, and the University Center's Activities Board also throw popular events for late-night weekend fun." More than 60% of W&M students have been involved in some kind of community service project by the end of their senior year. The Alan Bukzin Memorial Bone Marrow Drive, which raises money and tests potential donors, is considered the largest such drive in the country. Smaller, more specialized activities like the improvisational theater, with its popular 12-hour outdoor "Improvithon" each spring, and *a cappella* musical groups have their own very active participants and fans. The mysterious 13 Club is a secret society whose members do good deeds at the college without ever letting anyone know who they are. "Almost everyone is involved in several clubs," says a junior, "and would like to find time for a few more!" Incidents of crime are low with bike thefts the most troublesome. "Trust in God but lock your bike," says a junior. Minor transgressions may involve 2 fraternity brothers singing the school fight song at 3 a.m. Emergency phones are prevalent, and student escorts from a service fraternity whose phone number is printed on all student ID's are available.

Among the 10 varsity sports offered for men and 11 for women, football and soccer attract the biggest and most spirited crowds. Varsity teams compete in NCAA Division I. There also are 32 sport clubs on campus, ranging from rugby to sailing to martial arts, as well as an extensive recreational sports program, 24 sports for each sex and 11 coed, involving around 70% of the undergraduates; in a recent fall season, 70 football teams and 96 soccer teams competed against one another in their respective sports.

Students can escape in time as well as place to Colonial Williamsburg, across the street from campus. Washington, D.C. is 2½ hours away; Virginia Beach and Richmond are each just an hour's drive from campus. But "if you think you want to leave on the weekends," says a senior from the Midwest, "you'd better be prepared to miss out on a lot. And no one wants to miss out."

Cost cutters: In a recent year, William and Mary boasted the ninth highest endowment per student among public universities; its total value equaled almost $438 million as of June 2005. In a recent school year, 53% of the freshmen and 46% of continuing students received some form of financial aid; for about 26% of all undergraduates, the help was based on need. The average freshman award for a first-year student with financial need included a need-based scholarship or grant averaging $6978 and need-based self-help aid such as loans and job earnings averaging $2540. Non-need-based athletic scholarships for first-year students averaged $13,035; other non-need-based awards and scholarships averaged $5408. The average debt of a recent graduate who borrowed was $19,952. More than 40 merit scholarships are based on academic performance and ranged in value in a recent year from $500 to $3730. Approximately 150 athletic scholarships are presented as well. The brightest and best of the incoming freshmen, approximately 8% to 10% of each class, are named Monroe Scholars and receive $2000 for a summer study project to be completed between the junior and senior years. Ten students who work in food service are eligible for $1500 scholarships presented by the Order of the White Jacket.

Rate of return: All but 5% of freshmen return for a second year. Eighty-one percent graduate in 4 years; 89% in 5 years; 91% in 6. In a recent national comparison of graduation rates among 257 doctorate-granting institutions, the College of William and Mary ranked 16th nationally and 2nd among public institutions.

Payoff: The top majors for members of the Class of 2005 were the social sciences at 24%, business/marketing at 12%, psychology at 10%, and English at 9%. Nearly a third of the new alumni enrolled directly in graduate or professional schools. Each year, approximately 120 seniors apply to law school; of those, 85% are accepted by at least 1 school, often among the most prestigious in the nation. In addition, 85% of graduating seniors with a B average who apply to medical school are accepted. Those who take jobs immediately after graduating join such firms as PricewaterhouseCoopers, American Management Systems, and Ernst and Whinney. More than 400 companies and organizations recruited on campus in a recent year.

Bottom line: A college like William and Mary doesn't get to be 3 centuries old, with a birthday guest list for 1993 that included the Queen of England and the President of the United States, by being 1-dimensional or trendy. "William and Mary is only for the very serious-minded, self-disciplined scholar," advises a recent graduate. "It is not for the party animal or the bookworm, but for the well-rounded, goal-oriented high school graduate. Anyone who doesn't want to study every night, or at least every couple of nights, shouldn't come here."

George Mason University

Fairfax, Virginia 22030

Setting: Suburban
Control: Public
Undergraduate enrollment: 6190 men, 7388 women
Graduate enrollment: 787 men, 1046 women
Student/faculty ratio: 14:1
Freshman profile: 4% scored over 700 on SAT I verbal; 22% scored 600–700; 48% 500–599; 26% below 500. 3% scored over 700 on SAT I math; 25% scored 600–700; 51% 500–599; 21% below 500. 47% graduated in top fifth of high school class; 86% in upper two-fifths.
Faculty profile: 82% Ph.D.'s

Tuition and fees: $5880 in-state, $17,160 out-of-state
Room and board: $4970
Freshman financial aid: 61%; average scholarship or grant: $4929 need-based; $6231 non-need-based
Campus jobs: NA; average earnings: $2149/year
Application deadline: Early action: Nov. 1; regular: Jan. 15
Financial aid deadline: Mar. 1 (Scholarship: Dec. 1)
Admissions information: (703) 993-2400
   e-mail: admissions@gmu.edu
   web site: www.gmu.edu

For a student interested in learning how the federal government does or does not work, George Mason University offers a ringside seat at bleacher prices. The university's location in Fairfax, Virginia, just 15 miles west of the action, is what draws so many students to the school and has helped make it the fastest growing university in the Old Dominion. Although George Mason's rapid growth and high percentage of commuters (79%) bring with them problems of insufficient sections for popular classes and weekends on which the campus has resembled a ghost town, GMU delivers a formidable education. The university is rich in internships, ambitious students, and a growing roster of faculty drawn from prestigious colleges across the nation who want to be part of the George Mason success story. And the Patriots' dazzling run to the Final Four before a national television audience in the spring 2006 NCAA Division I basketball tournament only raised its visibility. Says a freshman: "In contrast with Virginia's old, traditional schools, Mason emphasizes its youth and lack of 'old habits' and reputation. Mason exudes an exciting feeling of opportunity and innovation."

Student body: Eighty-eight percent of George Mason's undergraduates are from Virginia. The rest come from 46 other states, many in the Middle Atlantic region, and 133 foreign countries, reflective of the international community in the Washington area. Seven percent of the total university enrollment are foreign nationals. Says a sophomore: "It is common to wake up and hear 4 different languages being spoken on the way to my first class." Minority students comprise 30% of the total; 14% Asian-American, 9% African-American, and 7% Hispanic. To help improve racial and ethnic relations, all freshmen are required to attend a cultural diversity workshop as part of their orientation. Says a double major in political communication and public relations: "Students here know that the real world is diverse, and that to be successful, you need to be able to understand, appreciate, and communicate with all different types of people." All but 5% of the students attended public schools. The real divisions lie between the students who commute, many of whom are older students, and those who live on campus, predominantly of traditional college age. Says a New Englander: "Lots of Mason students have families at home and work 40 hours a week. Understandably, they are not all that concerned about the quality of life for a full-time undergraduate because they're only on campus for a few hours a week." All undergraduates, however, tend to be politically astute, socially aware, and rather intense about learning and attaining certain career goals, whatever approach to campus life they've taken.

Academics: George Mason, which turns just 35 in 2007, awards about 55 undergraduate, 37 master's, and 9 doctoral degrees, plus a juris doctor. At the undergraduate level, it has been organized into 6 colleges, though in July 2006 that number rises to 7 when the single College of Arts and Sciences becomes the College of Liberal Arts and Human Sciences and the College of Science. There also are a Graduate School of Education and a law school, located in Arlington. The academic calendar is divided into semesters. Undergraduates can expect an average class size of 28 students. Entering freshmen will encounter some rather large classes: introductory courses in psychology and biology generally enroll 350 (Introduction to Cultural Anthropology has topped 410), with the smallest first-year classes rarely below 70. However, the situation improves considerably in the latter years, with juniors and seniors averaging 20–50 in many classes and some upper-division courses having just 2 participants.

As part of recently adopted general-education requirements, all undergraduates must take courses in such skills as written and oral communication, quantitative reasoning, and information technology, as well as a wide range of subject matter from U.S. history and Western Civilization to global understanding and the natural sciences. Additional courses place a special emphasis on English composition and writing.

The faculty of 2180 includes 1202 full-time members, of whom 946 teach undergraduates, and 978 part-timers, of whom 880 do the same. Fifty-five percent are women. Two faculty members, in economics, have won the Nobel Prize, one in 1986, a second in 2002. A second professor, in history, won the Pulitzer Prize. Sixteen percent of the introductory courses in a recent year were taught by graduate students. Over the past several years, many professors have left posts at more prestigious institutions, such as Harvard, Northwestern, and Amherst, to teach undergraduates at George Mason as the university's highly touted Robinson Professors. The schedule of classes printed each semester details which courses these faculty members are teaching. Many students find a distinction between the regular professors, many of whom are "competent but average," and the Robinson ones, who are "excellent." Says a psychology major: "They don't have huge egos and aren't afraid to encourage a student. I've even had teachers who called me at home just to tell me I did well on a test or that I forgot to turn in a paper." Many students like having such a large number of adjunct professors. Says a government and international politics major: "Having people with 'real world' experience, that is they do their job for a living and don't just teach it, brings an added element to the classroom that you wouldn't otherwise get with a tenured PhD."

In the one-time College of Arts and Sciences, psychology, English, economics, history and art history, and international studies have all benefited from having faculties, both Robinson and regular, on the upper side of competent, as well as solid curricula. Government and international politics specializes in excellent front-line internships along with renowned but personable professors who "have some of the best experience in the world," says a major. Continues another: "I have had many classes where the professors worked in a presidential administration, in the State Department, in the Department of Defense, or are fellows at one of the Think Tanks downtown. Having that first-hand knowledge and supplementing the information that we read in books is a huge benefit." Programs in the School of Information Technology and Engineering, especially computer science, have benefited from construction of a second new building in 1991 with such first-rate equipment as robotics and virtual reality labs. Says a senior: "The school has a great reputation for getting students hired as soon as they graduate." The School of Management is regarded as "extremely competitive" and demands high standards for entrance into its programs. The College of Nursing and Health Science draws respect as well. Says a nursing student: "The curriculum, made up of class work and practical experience, provides for a well-rounded student who is comfortable in all aspects of his or her future career." The College of Visual and Performing Arts is distinguished by both the quality of its faculty and the performance venues it offers.

In the College of Arts and Sciences, the natural sciences need better lab equipment, smaller classes and faculty more in tune with its varied students. Says a government and international politics major: "Some of the professors fail to allow for differences in B.A. and B.S. students." Communication lacks challenging professors and, along with social work, students say, could use more attention from the administration. Several of the foreign language and area studies programs, among them majors in Latin American, and Russian studies and minors in Asia Pacific and Islamic studies, have lacked sufficient funding, courses, and faculty members. This is changing, however, with growing student interest in these fields. Though there remain language majors in only French and Spanish, along with those in Latin American and Russian studies, a minor recently was added in Chinese and enrollment in classes in Japanese and Arabic has increased substantially. Students save their chief concerns, however, for the overall problem of inadequate academic advising, which has varied among departments from attentive to essentially nonexistent.

Facilities: Five-story Fenwick Library—"old, musty, but nice and quiet," in the words of a senior—has been steadily adding to its holdings over the past decade to make it a library equal to the stature the university as a whole has been striving to attain. Its collection, now consisting of about 1.1 million volumes, has tripled in size since 1989. The collection of current periodicals, 11,565, also is considered quite adequate. Supplementing Fenwick is its more modern, 10-year-old cousin, the Johnson University Center that houses a larger, though noisier, more computerized and technologically advanced facility. "Fenwick has more of the useful books," says a junior. "The JC Library has good multimedia." Computerized aids in both facilities list materials held at other D.C. area libraries from which students may borrow. George Mason students also may use the nearly 400,000 volumes contained at the law school campus.

Students say networked computer terminals seem to be everywhere. Observes a senior: "George Mason didn't just walk into the 21st century; we pole-vaulted." Indeed, some 1500 terminals are located in student labs, dormitories, academic departments, and the library. The newest addition is Innovation Hall, 100,000 square feet of fully networked classrooms, a 120-seat academic computer lab that is open around the clock, as well as special amenities such as an institutional resource center for the development of online classes. Most other labs around campus are open until midnight or 2 a.m. Students in some programs are encouraged to have personal computers.

Special programs: A year-abroad program sends students to 10 countries, 8 in Europe. Cooperative degree programs are available with 4 Virginia institutions, including Virginia Tech and the University of Virginia. New Century College is an integrated program of study at George Mason that emphasizes collaboration, experimental learning, and self-reflection.

Campus life: Twenty-one percent of George Mason's undergraduates reside on the 806-acre campus, an increase from just 9% who were residents a few years ago but still a small population that can produce an empty feeling when the commuting majority leave shortly after classes are over—and many resident students exit with them. To provide some sense of cohesion for newcomers, George Mason offers what has been dubbed President's Park, in which a group of first-year students live together, take a class together, and are offered several additional benefits to smooth the transition to college. Membership in Greek organizations is low: 5% of the men belong to 15 national fraternities, and 5% of the women to 12 national sororities. Because of the small resident population, Greek influence can seem considerable and closed parties can make a dull weekend seem even more deadly to independents. College Republicans and Young Democrats are both popular as is the Muslim Student Association.

The campus comes alive, however, in 2 spacious structures. The 10,000-seat Patriot Center arena, where basketball games are played, attracts major concert performers, while the 2000-seat Center for the Arts, students boast, "is gorgeous and can compete with the Kennedy Center" in Washington, D.C. Undergraduates especially like the 500 free tickets set aside at Center performances for students. So far, crime has not been a major concern, other than theft of the costly $100+ parking decals which students must display on cars in order to operate and keep them on campus. An on-campus police force using bikes, cars, and their own 2 feet, patrol against this and other incidents of theft or vandalism. Dorms also are locked around the clock and security call boxes are located throughout campus. An escort service is available as well.

If participation in school sports has been limited, with less than a fifth of the men and a tenth of the women taking part in 11 intramural sports for men, 10 for women, school spirit has been anything but. Most students, some with their bodies painted green, turn out for Patriots basketball games. "Basketball is huge," observes a senior and that was before the team's improbable string of victories against long-time basketball powerhouses in the 2006 NCAA Division I basketball tournament. But men's basketball has not been the lone winner among the university's 11 men's and 11 women's varsity sports. George Mason also has had nationally ranked teams in soccer, volleyball, and track and has won a national championship with its coed team in skeet and trap shooting. The lack of a varsity football team bothers few students since the start in 1993 of a club football team that has gone on to gain varsity club status, joined the Seaboard Conference and been conference champs in 2000, 2001, 2003, 2004, and 2005. Crew, lacrosse, and rugby also are popular club sports.

The District of Columbia provides the extracurricular, as well as the academic, focus for many, with plenty of spots for shopping, dining, and sightseeing.

Cost cutters: Sixty-one percent of the freshmen and 54% of the returning students received some financial assistance in the 2005–2006 school year; aid to 35% of both groups was need-based. The average freshman award for a student with need included a need-based scholarship or grant averaging $4813 and need-based self-help aid such as loans and jobs averaging $2808. Non-need-based athletic scholarships for first-year students averaged $11,789. Other non-need-based awards and scholarships averaged $5030. Average indebtedness of a 2005 graduate was $13,607. Mason (in-state) Scholars recently received 4 years of tuition, room, and board, based on academic merit. Presidential (to out-of-state) and Minority scholarships each recently paid a year's tuition and are also based on academic performance. A cooperative education program is offered in most majors.

Rate of return: Seventy-nine percent of the freshmen return for the sophomore year. Thirty-three percent graduate in 4 years, though the number rises to 48% within five years, and 53% in six years.

Payoff: Despite the lure of national politics, which brings so many top students to George Mason, the most popular majors for the 2005 graduating class were communication at 12% and psychology and nursing at 8% each. Nevertheless, many graduates take jobs in the federal government, with agencies like the Central Intelligence Agency and the Office of Management and Budget, as well as the departments of Agriculture and Defense. Others associate themselves with major corporations like TRW, Marriott, and the Giant Food supermarket chain, a sample of the 200 companies and other organizations that recently recruited on campus. While many accept posts nationwide, a number settle in the District of Columbia area. There are no data on the percentage who enter graduate study.

Bottom line: George Mason is a school where a student can have contact with some of the best teachers (Robinson professors), best programs (business, government and international politics, economics, and others), and best opportunities (internships in the nation's capital). Or a less ambitious undergraduate can simply be satisfied with cheering on the Patriots basketball team. Says a proud Virginian: "We are not stuck in tradition here. No one will ever tell you that you can't do something; they will say, 'Well, it doesn't hurt to try it and see what happens.'"

Hampden-Sydney College

Hampden-Sydney, Virginia 23943

Setting: Rural
Control: Private (Presbyterian)
Undergraduate enrollment: 1062 men
Graduate enrollment: None
Student/faculty ratio: 11:1
Freshman profile: 10% scored over 700 on SAT I verbal; 30% scored 600–700; 46% 500–599; 14% below 500. 5% scored over 700 on SAT I math; 37% scored 600–700; 49% 500–599; 9% below 500. 17% scored above 28 on the ACT; 16% scored 27–28; 21% 24–26; 25% 21–23; 21% below 21. 18% graduated in top tenth of high school class; 33% in upper fifth.
Faculty profile: 81% Ph.D.'s

Tuition and fees: $23,410
Room and board: $7738
Freshman financial aid: 92%; average scholarship or grant: NA
Campus jobs: 24%; average earnings: $900/year
Application deadline: Early decision: Nov. 15; early action: Jan. 15; regular: Mar. 1
Financial aid deadline: Mar. 1
Admissions information: (434) 223-6120; (800) 755-0733
e-mail: hsapp@hsc.edu
web site: www.hsc.edu

It's a place where "tradition permeates everything," in the words of a southerner, where "a certain sense of propriety is maintained. It's a friendly campus where such things as honor and gentility still have value." If "it" sounds like an oasis untouched by time or turmoil, meet Hampden-Sydney College in

Virginia's historic Southside, which remains, after 231 years of continuous operation, the tenth oldest institution of higher learning in the nation and oldest of the few remaining all-male colleges. Although its style is largely of another era, its curriculum and the academic interests of the men who mold it are very much up to date. Almost half of recent graduates majored in economics, with another third majoring in history and political science. Nearly three-fourths of the graduates take jobs in such fields as banking, investment, management, and teaching. Within 5 years, about 55% are back in school pursuing advanced degrees, the largest portion in business, law, and medicine. "We are," says a recent graduate, "men in touch with reality who are going to contribute to society," joining a long line of distinguished graduates who have done the same.

Student body: Not quite two-thirds of Hampden-Sydney's men are from Virginia, and the overall atmosphere of the campus is noticeably southern. Although students come from 35 other states, most also are from the South. Fifty-nine percent in a recent year were Protestant (12% Presbyterian) and 14%, Catholic. Twenty-five percent claimed no religious affiliation. Just over half graduated from private or parochial schools. The student body is becoming more racially and ethnically diverse; about 7% are minorities: 4% African-American and approximately 1% each Hispanic, Asian-American, and Native American. Twenty international students also are present from 13 countries. "Conservative is probably the one word that would apply to most people here," says a sophomore. "The only one more appropriate would be southern!" Largely because of that southern quality, Hampden-Sydney men, although generally competitive concerning their studies, are usually too well mannered to show it. The academic atmosphere, observes a senior, "is laid back but puts tremendous emphasis on personal responsibility in and out of class . . . A's are hard to come by here as there is no grade inflation, but earning one is that much more special." The student-run honor code, which presumes that every student is a gentleman who will conduct himself in an honest and trustworthy manner, is a major component of both the academic and the very active social life. "A common slogan," says a Virginian, "is 'where men are men, and women are still guests.'"

Academics: The distinctive name Hampden-Sydney pays tribute to John Hampden and Algernon Sydney, 17th century English supporters of the ideals of representative government. By taking the name of these 2 heroes when the college opened in 1775, Hampden-Sydney immediately became associated with the cause of independence, including such patriots as James Madison and Patrick Henry on its first board of trustees. In fact, the original students organized a militia company and left classes to defend Williamsburg during the Revolutionary War. From their uniforms, gray trousers and hunting shirts dyed purple with the juice of pokeberries, came the school colors, garnet and gray. During the Civil War, another generation of young men engaged in combat; this time they were captured and paroled by General George B. McClellan on the condition that they return to their studies.

Today, life at Hampden-Sydney is considerably tamer. The college awards the bachelor's degree in 27 fields. Men are enrolled in classes by semester, with an optional 1-month short term beginning 1 week or 2 after graduation exercises. The average class has 15 students. Introductory courses in such popular subjects as fine arts may top 40 students, but a 300-level class in history has just 3. Distribution requirements include 4 courses in natural sciences and mathematics, 3 in social sciences, and 7 in the humanities. Students also must take courses or complete a test to demonstrate intermediate-level proficiency in a foreign language. Especially demanding is the mandated rhetoric program, which involves classes in English composition as well as a 3-hour timed essay due by the end of the sophomore year. Writing also is emphasized throughout the curriculum.

All but 19 of the 106 faculty members in a recent year were full-time (25% were women), and most seem to belong at Hampden-Sydney. Many faculty members are as "unique and somewhat eccentric" as the school itself; having students over to dinner with the family is the norm, rather than the exception. The majority teach their respective fields with a passion and thoroughness they are eager to share with students, in any way possible. Says an economics major: "I once had a conflict between 2 evening classes, and a professor taught me the class I missed during the day in one of my free periods, with 3 other students. That professor went out of his way for us."

Economics, history, and political science are popular because of excellent professors and challenging curricula. Remarks a political science major: "The professors are superior and the classics of political science are taught; it's hard to find a course in which Plato and Thucydides aren't on the list of required reading." Courses in chemistry, biology, and physics allow freshmen to work on equipment that is often reserved for graduate students at bigger research universities. Several scientists from NASA and other award-winning researchers serve as challenging professors. The programs in English and rhetoric, as well as in religion and classics, also feature devoted faculties. The rhetoric faculty, whom all freshmen have, "are great and *really* teach you how to write," boasts a sophomore.

At a school where Plato and rhetoric reign, students say that computer science, offered as half of a dual major with mathematics, and a pre-engineering program, part of a 3-2 program with the University of Virginia, are both "not strong at all." A major in fine arts recently was started and offers concentrations in music, theater, and visual arts, though students say the program still needs more space, supplies, professors, and student interest.

Facilities: During the 2005–2006 school year, Hampden-Sydney's library director along with a group of faculty, staff, and students went on a very different kind of road trip: touring other campus libraries in Virginia as well as in Georgia and Pennsylvania, gathering ideas for how to make the college's new library comfortable and aesthetically pleasing. The new structure, which is estimated to be ready for studying and research in fall 2007, replaces Eggleston Library, which after 45 years and one renovation had become too small for its 224,000 volumes and 823 periodicals. (Another 2000 full-text journals and newspapers were available online.) Eggleston also lacked the expanded stacks, group study space, and technology that 21st-century users demand and that will be part of the new building. One holdover from Eggleston students hope will be included: undergraduates needing to spend extended time in the library could reserve carrels for the semester to serve as permanent offices away from their noisy residence hall rooms.

Because computers are "vital" to accomplish the amount of paper writing demanded in the rhetoric program and beyond, entering freshmen are encouraged to purchase a Dell computer that can link them with the various services from their dorm rooms. "Most students have their own," says a senior, "so college computers are used mostly for convenience and when seeking a quiet place to work." For those occasions, 3 general-use and several departmental labs provide a sufficient number of PCs that usually are available from 8 a.m. until 1 a.m.

Special programs: Hampden-Sydney men who want a change of pace can spend a year or semester at any of 4 women's colleges or 2 coed institutions in Virginia. Those longing to travel further afield may participate in approved courses of study throughout Europe, Central and South America, Australia, Asia, and the Middle East. A semester is offered in Washington, D.C., through The American University. A public service concentration enrolls juniors in 12 hours of related coursework and an internship.

Campus life: All but 3% of Hampden-Sydney men reside on the 660-acre campus and "we take our weekends very seriously," says a Virginian. Frequent visits from students at 4 nearby women's colleges create a situation where, says a recent graduate, "on the weekends, no one would know this school was single-sex." Women visitors generally head to the 10 national fraternities, which for many men are the lifeblood of social success at Hampden-Sydney. Roughly 30% of the undergraduates are members, though the Greek parties generally are open to all. Another popular organization on campus is Good Men Good Citizens, named for the school motto, which performs community service. A student-run volunteer fire department garners its own share of respect from fellow students and county residents whom they serve. Crime is of little concern, as is evident from dorm rooms left open, expensive texts left out, and keys left in cars. "The most troublesome crime," says a senior, "is if someone borrows your bike to get to class and forgets to return it." The college honor code as well as the campus's isolated location serves to discourage most crime.

Thirty percent of the men play NCAA Division III athletics. Fall football weekends are enormously popular, with Hampden-Sydney men dressed in coats and ties and their dates in dresses and hats watching the game from the grassy hill overlooking the football field. Fans turn their attention in winter to basketball, with the Tigers well known for their regular appearances in the NCAA tournament. Lacrosse and baseball draw good crowds in the spring. Four other varsity sports are offered. Eighty percent are involved in 8 intramural sports. The rugby and outsiders clubs provide additional physical challenges as does the 300-acre forest and trails surrounding campus, which offer extensive opportunities for mountain biking and hiking. Hunting and fishing are also serious diversions for many.

When the rural, all-male setting becomes too much to handle, Washington, D.C., Richmond, and the nearby women's colleges provide the most common off-campus escapes. Says a senior: "With 4 neighboring women's colleges, there are many choices to make as to destination."

Cost cutters: Hampden-Sydney's healthy endowment, exceeding $113 million in June 2005, helps to keep down costs. In a recent school year, 92% of the freshmen and continuing students received financial aid; for 54% of the first-year students and 51% of the others, the help was need-based. The average freshman award totaled $16,791, although no breakdown was available to show the portion that was scholarships and grants or jobs and loans. A typical recent graduate left with debts of $7071. Several academic scholarships are awarded without regard to financial need. The merit scholarship program includes the Allan Scholarships recently worth $20,000 to men with at least a 1400 SAT in math and critical reading and class rank in the top 5%, Venable Scholarships recently paying $16,000 for SATs of at least 1350 and a top 10% class ranking, and Patrick Henry Scholarships worth $12,000 to those with SATs of 1250 or higher and class standing in the top 15%. Merit scholars who demonstrate financial need greater than the stipend can receive additional grants. Awards that recognize student leadership but lower academic achievement levels than those of the Allan, Venable, and Patrick Henry scholarships recently paid $2000 to $10,000 a year.

Rate of return: Seventy-four percent of the freshmen return for the sophomore year. Sixty-one percent graduate in 4 years; 63%, in 5 years; 64% in 6.

Payoff: Economics was the major of 49% of a recent graduating class. History was next in popularity (17%), followed by political science (15%). No data is available on the portion of graduates who immediately pursue advanced degrees. Most of those who enter the job market so do primarily on the East Coast.

Bottom line: Hampden-Sydney is not a college that young men choose with the idea of radically changing it. Says a junior: "I would recommend Hampden-Sydney to any man who loves tradition and honor as much as we do. If a high school senior is also outgoing, motivated, and fun-loving, this is definitely the place to be." But students caution that the academics are quite rigorous and only those prepared to work even harder than they play will join the historic ranks of Hampden-Sydney alumni.

Hollins University

Roanoke, Virginia 24020

Setting: Suburban
Control: Private
Undergraduate enrollment: 790 women
Graduate enrollment: 14 men, 41 women (220 part-time)
Student/faculty ratio: 10:1
Freshman profile: 14% scored over 700 on SAT I verbal; 32% scored 600–700; 35% 500–599; 19% below 500. 2% scored over 700 on SAT I math; 30% scored 600–700; 42% 500–599; 26% below 500. 10% scored above 28 on the ACT; 18% scored 27–28; 30% 24–26; 38% 21–23; 4% below 21. 30% graduated in top tenth of high school class; 50% in upper fifth.
Faculty profile: 98% Ph.D.'s

Tuition and fees: $22,945
Room and board: $8160
Freshman financial aid: 98%; average scholarship or grant: NA
Campus jobs: 45%; average earnings: $1245/year
Application deadline: Early decision: Dec. 1; regular: Feb. 15
Financial aid deadline: Feb. 1
Admissions information: (540) 362-6214; (800) 456-9595
e-mail: huadm@hollins.edu
web site: www.hollins.edu

What small university has produced more published writers than any other college its size in the United States? If you're all set to say the name of a prestigious East Coast, ivy-covered institution costing about $40,000 a year, repeat after me: Hollins University in Roanoke, Virginia. Hollins, a women's institution of nearly 850 full- and part-time undergraduates and 275 coed full- and part-time graduate students, is the alma mater of Pulitzer Prize winners Annie Dillard and Mary Wells Ashworth and novelists Lee Smith and Elizabeth Forsythe Hailey. Each woman earned her bachelor's and master's degrees in Hollins's small but prestigious program in creative writing. Pulitzer Prize winning poet Henry Taylor and Lamont poetry prize winner Margaret Gibson are other alumni of Hollins's graduate program. Because of the college's small size and emphasis on personal contact, undergraduates work with the same master's-level faculty as the graduate students and often can arrange independent study projects with noted authors who participate in Hollins's writer-in-residence program, which in the past has drawn such authors as Eudora Welty and Howard Nemerov to the campus. Hollins clearly is no southern "finishing" school for young women, except perhaps for a woman "finishing" yet another impressive project.

Student body: Forty-eight percent of Hollins's first-place finishers are from Virginia; the majority, predominantly also southerners, come from 44 other states and 9 foreign countries. A quarter received their high school diplomas from private or parochial schools. The undergraduate student body includes 6% African-American students, 2% Hispanics, 1% Asian-Americans, and 3% foreign nationals. Students describe themselves as being more varied than prospective students might expect. "Many students are legacies from proper southern families," observes a Virginian, "but a majority are active, independent, socially conscious students who come from diverse backgrounds. Financial aid is a must for many of us, shattering the image of our being rich snobs." Adds a nontraditional student: "The social realm of Hollins is broad. We have left-wing extremist feminists, right-wing extremist Republicans, and the in-between students." The women from both ends and the middle also are very sociable and many are involved in the wealth of leadership opportunities open to them on campus. "If you want to be an academic go-getter, you'll find plenty of competition," notes a senior. "There is quite a drive to succeed here, and the faculty are very good at instilling this."

Academics: Hollins, founded initially as a coed college in 1842 but limited to women at the undergraduate level since 1852, offers bachelor's degrees in 29 majors, as well as a master's degree in teaching, English and creative writing, children's literature, dance, screenwriting and film studies, and liberal studies. The academic year is divided into semesters plus a January term. Freshmen can expect classes that generally range between 15 and 25 participants, although 3 courses, such as Introduction to Film as Art, enroll 50 to 58. A linear algebra class can have as few as 2 women, but most upper-level classes have 10–20.

Hollins requires all students to complete one 4-credit course from each of 5 perspectives: Aesthetic Analysis, Creative Expression, Ancient and/or Modern Worlds, Modern and/or Contemporary Worlds, and Social and Cultural Diversities. Students also must take up to 6 credits in Scientific Inquiry and an amount that varies in Global Systems and Language, depending upon a student's placement. Also required are courses in writing, oral communication, quantitative reasoning, information technology, and physical education. Independent study projects are encouraged for juniors and seniors.

All but 40 of Hollins's 108 professors are full-time, and just over half, 51%, are women. A majority combine the best of 2 elements: a superb education, evident from the high percentage with doctoral degrees, and a love of teaching, obvious to many young women the moment they step into the classroom. "The thing that makes them even more outstanding," says a sophomore, "is the level of personal attention they are not only willing but also *want* to give you. They are excellent!"

English, psychology, and history are the stand-out departments. The English faculty are as illustrious as the graduates; included are a nationally known poet and a prize-winning novelist; the diversity of courses recently ranged from Holocaust Literature to Modern Southern Writers to Children's Literature. The history professors are "passionate and engaging." The psychology department's stuttering clinic is but one area where psychology majors specializing in speech pathology can gain hands-on experience. Other students participate in research projects that complement their interests in areas ranging from psychobiology to child psychology. The Dana Science Building provides special laboratories for the study of perception, motivation, learning, and behavior. Students find the science equipment in other areas to be up-to-date as well and very accessible. Economics, philosophy, political science, art history, and French feature attentive faculty and solid curricula. The major in dance also draws applause from students. Says a junior: "Students come to dance and often leave with opportunities to continue their careers." The interdisciplinary women's studies program, though small, is stellar as well. Says a senior: "The professors are incredibly educated and offer classes that change your way of thinking and challenge you to explore yourself. All of the professors also are available to talk, advocate, and educate outside of the classroom."

As at most small colleges, limited student enrollment in certain programs—at Hollins, music, physics, religious studies, classical studies, and German—means fewer professors and fewer course offerings. Communication studies needs to continue to grow and add more professors to keep pace with rising student demand.

Facilities: Wyndam Robertson Library, which opened in 1999, isn't just a high-tech respository for books. In recognition of Hollins writers' contributions and influence on American literature, the $14 million facility has been designated one of just 36 National Literary Landmarks in the country. Among the authors honored are 1932 Hollins graduate Margaret Wise Brown, who wrote the beloved children's classic "Goodnight Moon." Current holdings stand at 174,000 volumes and 14,500 periodical titles, many with electronic full-text access. Undergraduates find the librarians especially helpful in guiding students through the various computerized research aids available. A computerized catalog, providing access to Robertson's holdings as well as those of other libraries, joins numerous other databases and on-line resources that are in heavy use. The building offers Internet access for each of the 500 seats in the library. It also features large, naturally lit seating and study areas, a student-faculty coffee commons, as well as a multimedia editing, composition, and screening suite.

The Hollins computer system includes 100 terminals located around campus, many available 24 hours, as well as several personal computer laboratories housing more than 30 additional units. Many undergraduates have their own personal computers. Every residence hall is wired for Internet access. Hollins strongly recommends that students bring their own PC's or laptops. Because so many students do, those who do not have little trouble finding a free unit when they need one. Wireless networking also is available around campus.

Special programs: Every year, about 60 students spend a semester at Hollins's campus in London, while another 35 study for a semester or year at the Hollins center in Paris. Hollins students also can participate in a semester in Greece, Italy, Ireland, Japan, Mexico, or Spain. Altogether, more than 40% of Hollins' young women study abroad before they graduate. Closer to home, undergraduates may study at any of 6 other Virginia colleges or spend a semester in Washington, D.C., or at the United Nations. Art history majors may spend a year at Christie's in London. A 3-2 program is offered in engineering with Washington University and Virginia Polytechnic Institute; a 4-2 program in architecture also is an option with Virginia Tech.

Campus life: Ninety-one percent of the students reside on the 475-acre campus, which feels very "homey and old-fashioned" with its acre of green surrounded by 19th-century buildings. Many of the residents take off for the weekend, to parties or sporting events at coed colleges, such as Washington & Lee, or at all-male Hampden-Sydney. Oftentimes, parties with bands playing on campus bring students from the neighboring colleges to Hollins. Although there are no sororities, the women find a variety of other groups to suit their interests. About a third participate in SHARE (Students Helping Achieve Rewarding Experiences), a community service organization. The literary society, Grapheon, sponsors very popular student poetry and fiction readings. The Black Student Alliance organizes numerous events on campus to expand education about black culture and history. One-fifth of the women are active in student government; a fourth, in the school's leadership development program. Around-the-clock security patrols, emergency "panic" buttons located along walkways and in laboratories, and locks at dusk on the dormitory doors help make the students feel safe on campus.

Hollins women compete in 7 intercollegiate sports, played as part of NCAA Division III. Field hockey, cross country, and volleyball were dropped from the roster at the end of the fall 2004 season. Soccer and basketball draw the biggest crowds. Half of the students take part in other recreational activities. Since many students ride horses, the Riding Club is also popular. Over the last 2 decades, Hollins women have captured 15 national individual riding championships. In 1993 and 1998, Hollins won the national championship in intercollegiate riding and since 1993, the Hollins team has placed in the top ten 11 times. The Hollins Outdoor Program offers weekly trips off campus to suit lovers of both nature and natural thrills, including activities as peaceful as hiking or camping and ones as exciting as white-water rafting or windsurfing.

Roanoke (pop. 225,000) is located in a valley surrounded by the Blue Ridge Mountains and offers plenty of shopping, restaurants, and theaters. Washington, D.C., Richmond, and the surrounding colleges all are favorite travel destinations.

Cost cutters: Hollins graduates remember their alma mater; about 40% give to the annual fund drive, helping to keep fees low. About 98% of both first-year and continuing students received financial aid in 2005–2006; 65% of the first-year students and 47% of the rest were on need-based assistance. The average freshman aid package totaled $18,826, although no breakdown is provided for the amounts given as scholarships and grants or as loans and job earnings. The average college debt of 2005 graduates was $19,592. To the very best students usually drawn from the top 10% of their high school graduating classes with SATs of at least 1700 (24 ACT), the Batten Scholars program issues awards ranging up to and including full tuition plus special leadership opportunities. Eligible candidates not selected as Batten Scholars may receive other Scholar Awards paying $8000 to $16,000 a year depending on standardized test scores and GPA. Founders Awards pay $5000 to $10,000 a year to students who have excelled in high school extracurricular activities and clubs. Creative Talent Awards also pay $5000 to $10,000 for distinguished achievement or outstanding promise in visual arts, photography, creative writing, music, or dance. A family may pay for 4 years' tuition in one blow at the rate in effect when their daughter enters Hollins. A 10-month interest-free tuition payment plan also is an option.

Rate of return: Seventy-nine percent of freshmen return for the sophomore year. Fifty-five percent graduate in 4 years; 61% in 5 years; 62% in 6.

Payoff: Twenty-one percent of recent graduates earned bachelor's degrees in English/creative writing; 10% each graduated in psychology and communication studies. A fifth of recent graduates went on to graduate or professional schools. The majority, however, take jobs soon after graduating, many as administrative assistants and management trainees at such firms as Merrill Lynch and North Carolina National Bank. A number settle in Washington, D.C., Atlanta, New York, Charlotte, or other cities.

Bottom line: "Hollins," says a sophomore, "remains both a women's college and a *true* liberal arts college that has not succumbed to the preprofessional trend. But the young woman who comes here should want an education different from 'the norm.' Already I can see a difference in me from when I graduated from high school. I am more confident, more motivated, even more organized!"

James Madison University

Harrisonburg, Virginia 22807

Setting: Small town
Control: Public
Undergraduate enrollment: 5800 men, 9085 women
Graduate enrollment: 186 men, 503 women
Student/faculty ratio: 20:1
Freshman profile: 3% scored over 700 on SAT I verbal; 29% scored 600–700; 53% 500–599; 15% below 500. 3% scored over 700 on SAT I math; 34% scored 600–700; 50% 500–599; 13% below 500. Class rank data: NA
Faculty profile: 80% Ph.D.'s
Tuition and fees: $5886 in-state, $15,322 out-of-state

Room and board: $6124
Freshman financial aid: 56%; average scholarship or grant: $6035 need-based; $2747 non-need-based
Campus jobs: 19%; average earnings: $1920/year
Application deadline: Early action: Nov. 1; regular: Jan. 15
Financial aid deadline: Mar. 1
Admissions information: (540) 568-5681
e-mail: admissions@jmu.edu
web site: www.jmu.edu

In a state that boasts colleges named for George Washington's mother (Mary Washington), George himself and Robert E. Lee (Washington and Lee), and even King William III and Queen Mary II of England (The College of William and Mary), it was only a matter of time before the State Normal and Industrial School for Women at Harrisonburg went with the flow. Thirty years after its founding in 1908, the women's teachers college became Madison College and then, in 1977, James Madison University, a name change that celebrated both the nation's fourth president and the college's history of revolutionary change and growth. No longer a women's college with a single-career orientation, James Madison has become a comprehensive, coeducational institution enrolling almost 17,000 students in bachelor's, master's, and doctoral degree programs. In 2 decades, both the enrollment and the faculty have more than doubled. But one factor has remained fairly stable: the price. For just over $12,000 for in-state and about $21,500 for out-of-state tuition, fees, room, and board in the 2005–2006 school year, James Madison offers a solid mix of liberal arts and preprofessional programs that does credit to the school's illustrious name.

Student body: Seventy percent of James Madison's undergraduates are from Virginia, and the others also are mainly from the Middle Atlantic region. Though students come from 43 other states and 52 other countries, undergraduates still make jokes about whether members are from the "state" of northern Virginia, the more cosmopolitan area around Washington, D.C., or the less bustling southern "state" of Richmond, the capital. Asian-Americans constitute 5% of the enrollment; 3% are African-Americans, 2% Hispanics, and 1% foreign nationals. All but 5% graduated from public high schools. As a whole, undergraduates have a "conservative twang" to them, says one member, but their involvement covers all ranges of the spectrum, from those who are aware and active concerning many social and political issues, to others content to remain far removed. Few are *laissez faire* about their studies, however, and most students are described as "motivated" and "hard working," but "balanced" in their approach to academics and student life. The resulting atmosphere around campus is fairly relaxed, says a senior, "Each person tries to do better than he or she did before but doesn't step on anyone else's toes."

Academics: JMU awards bachelor's degrees in 45 fields, including more than a half-dozen specialties within such areas as art, biology, and music. The undergraduate program is spread over 6 colleges; advanced degrees are offered in more than 26 disciplines. The academic year is divided into semesters. Freshmen should expect to attend lectures with 50–150 classmates, although the largest course, General Psychology, recently enrolled about 230. English courses are kept to no more than 20 students; labs also average 20. Upper-level courses average about 28.

A general-education program maps out 40–43 credit hours of coursework that all undergraduates, regardless of their major, must take. Mandates fall under a unifying theme, the Human Community, with 5 academic clusters for students to complete. Students take their choice of prepackaged sets of courses within each cluster. All students complete Cluster 1: Skills for the 21st Century, which includes such skills as reading, writing, and language proficiency, during their freshman year; many at least start Cluster 3: The Natural World, which offers various science and math courses. Most also tackle Cluster 5: Individuals in the Human Community, with its classes in psychology and wellness. Some students opt to postpone until their sophomore or junior year work on the remaining 2 clusters: Cluster 2: Arts and Humanities, which features classes in history, English, and the fine arts, and Cluster 4: Social and Cultural Processes, with varied offerings in history and the social sciences. Reaction to the requirements is mixed; some love them, some don't.

All but 70 of the 795 full-time faculty members teach undergraduates. All but 12 of the 293 part-time members do. Women comprise 42%. Three percent of the introductory lectures are taught by graduate students. Undergraduates as a whole are pleased with a faculty whose members generally are accessible and interested in their charges, despite some large class sizes. Recalls a junior: "Most professors make the effort to have an impact on students' lives. They serve as advisers to clubs and organizations in order to get to know students on a personal level."

James Madison's strengths are as wide ranging as its course offerings. The already strong College of Business, whose programs attract a fifth of the undergraduates, was bolstered a few years ago by the opening of a $9 million building with additional staff to match. The courses that are offered stress application, involving students in work with actual companies, as well as in developing strategies for imaginary firms. The excellent School of Music in the College of Visual and Performing Arts is housed in a $7 million complex complete with the finest computers and other facilities. New equipment for the radio and television programs is but 1 attraction in the much-praised School of Media Arts and Design in the College of Arts and Letters. Sociology and anthropology are considered strong as well. James Madison's founding focus, education, remains strong in the College of Education. A well-respected program in communication sciences and disorders in the College of Integrated Science and Technology offers a speech and hearing clinic where students can learn by doing and also provide a service to the community. Majors in psychology and integrated science and technology, with its advanced equipment and emphasis on technological problem solving in a larger context, draw praise from course participants. Says a junior: "The ISAT professors are generally very experienced in their fields and have a passion for teaching."

Students say that other health-related programs need better professors. Spanish and other of the foreign languages offered need to demand more thinking and discussion from their students. The major itself is in modern foreign languages with 4 years of instruction offered for a concentration in French, German, Italian, or Spanish, and 2 years in Russian, Latin, Chinese, and Japanese.

Facilities: Carrier Library, which holds more than 627,000 volumes, 1 million microform items, and 7393 periodicals, continues to battle the university's rapid growth, with a major addition completed in 1982 and a new floor added for the 1994–95 school year. Students complain of an insufficient supply of research materials, many of them outdated, as well as excessive demand to use the computerized search systems available for both books and periodicals. Many undergraduates seek what they need at the University of Virginia or use interlibrary loan from other Virginia institutions. Because many sections of the library are noisy, serious studiers head for the "stacks," which, they warn, can be "quiet, but spooky, dark, and intimidating," or leave Carrier to work in vacant academic buildings. Restrictions on the use of cell phones and talking are helping to reduce the noise level.

The opening of the new business building and renovation of the science building, both with plenty of computers, helped to alleviate overcrowding in other laboratories throughout campus. Computer clusters with more than 300 Windows and Macintosh units are located in a dozen sites, in most classroom buildings as well as the residence halls. Most facilities are open until midnight, though at least a couple are open 24 hours. Wireless access also is available. The college strongly recommends that all undergraduates have their own computers; students in the College of Business and the College of Integrated Science and Technology are required to have their own.

Special programs: James Madison conducts semester abroad programs in London, Antwerp, Florence, and Salamanca. The programs, open to students in all majors, are led by a JMU faculty member who teaches at least 1 course. All others are taught, in English, by native professors. Students may participate as early as the second semester of their sophomore year; selection is based on academic level and grade point average.

Campus life: Thirty-eight percent of the undergraduates reside on the 605-acre campus, which includes a 31-acre farm. The structures are a mixture of old blue limestone buildings on the front campus and more modern red brick buildings on the back, all surrounded by the breathtaking Blue Ridge Mountains. Newman Lake, a favorite study spot, is strategically based at the entrance to the university. Nine percent of the men belong to 13 national fraternities, and 11% of the women to 8 national sororities. While the Greeks play an active part in JMU's social life, the weekend partying is not exclusive and has been "toned down" in recent years. (Parties in off-campus housing are popular as well.) Nevertheless, members of the Greek organizations tend to be the students most involved in activities and leadership. There also are 287 academic, music, honorary, religious, service, and sports clubs that students can become involved in. Incidents of crime generally are limited to petty theft; the names of students or others caught stealing are printed in the school newspaper, thereby serving as a deterrent to others considering such action, with possible embarrassment before their peers. A Campus Police Cadet program involves undergraduates who patrol campus, issue parking tickets, and escort other students after dark; the cadets work from 7 p.m. until 2 a.m. weeknights and until 3 a.m. weekends.

James Madison posts teams in 13 sports for men and 15 for women in NCAA Division I (football is I-AA). Men's soccer and men's and women's basketball are the most popular. Football gets a good turnout of fans, as much to watch the 325-member Marching Royal Dukes, one of the top marching bands in the country, perform at half time as to cheer on the team. Two-thirds of the men but only a third of the women engage in 18 intramural sports, from horseshoes and bowling to faster-paced tennis and volleyball.

Harrisonburg (pop. 40,500) is located in the heart of the scenic Shenandoah Valley. Many students head for relaxation to the Blue Ridge Mountains or for excitement to Richmond, Roanoke, or Washington, D.C., each just a 2-hour drive.

Cost cutters: In the 2005–2006 school year, 56% of the freshmen received financial aid, as did 39% of the continuing students. Thirty-six percent of the first-year students and 28% of the rest were on need-based assistance. The average freshman award for a first-year student with financial need included a need-based scholarship or grant averaging $6035 and need-based self-help aid such as loans and jobs averaging $2330. Non-need-based athletic scholarships for first-year students averaged $11,734; other non-need-based awards and scholarships averaged $2747. The average debt of a 2005 graduate was $10,642. Approximately 150 scholarships, some annual, some 4-year, generally based on financial need, academic merit, and/or other factors, are awarded. A majority are in the $500 to $2000 range. Fifty in-state students with solid academic credentials and high financial need are named Centennial Scholars and receive a package covering tuition, fees, room, and board. The program also provides for interaction with a faculty mentor, community service, and various cultural enrichment activities and career-oriented workshops. Scholarships for talent in athletics and in the fine arts also are available. A Degree in Three plan enables the efficient student to complete work toward the bachelor's degree in 3 years by taking courses during the summer session.

Rate of return: Ninety-one percent of the freshmen who enter return for the sophomore year. Sixty-four percent graduate in 4 years; 78%, in 5 years; 80% in 6.

Payoff: For the 2005 class, psychology at 7%, marketing at 6%, and media arts and design at 5%, were the most popular majors. In recent years, nearly a fifth have gone on to graduate or professional schools. A majority of those seeking jobs found positions along the East Coast, primarily in Virginia. More than 160 companies and other organizations recruited on campus in a recent school year.

Bottom line: Boasts a political science major: "We have the environment of a small university but are large enough to be very competitive. James Madison is an institution where innovation is taking place. This is the school to beat!"

Mary Baldwin College

Staunton, Virginia 24401

Setting: Small town
Control: Private (Presbyterian)
Undergraduate enrollment: 1074 women (353 part-time)
Graduate enrollment: 32 women
Student/faculty ratio: 10:1
Freshman profile: 9% scored over 700 on SAT I verbal; 26% scored 600–700; 32% 500–599; 33% below 500. 3% scored over 700 on SAT I math; 13% scored 600–700; 41% 500–599; 43% below 500. 3% scored above 28 on the ACT; 18% scored 27–28; 24% 24–26; 12% 21–23; 43% below 21. 33% graduated in top fifth of high school class; 59% in upper two-fifths.

Faculty profile: 93% Ph.D.'s
Tuition and fees: $20,605
Room and board: $5860
Freshman financial aid: 99%; average scholarship or grant: $6500 need-based; $7000 non-need-based
Campus jobs: 69%; average earnings: $2000/year
Application deadline: Early decision: Nov. 15; regular: Apr. 15
Financial aid deadline: May 1
Admissions information: (540) 887-7260; (800) 468-2262
e-mail: admit@mbc.edu
web site: www.mbc.edu

Few stronger role models exist for 21st century young women than 19th-century educator Mary Julia Baldwin. When nearly every other school in the Shenandoah Valley was closing its doors during the final years of the Civil War because of intense fighting in the area, Miss Baldwin, who served as principal of an all-female seminary from 1863 to 1897, used both her courage and her wits to keep the school open. Emerging stronger than ever after Reconstruction, the seminary went on to become a 4-year college in 1923, 81 years after its founding. Today, Mary Baldwin College remains firm in its commitment not just to stay open but also to prepare the approximately 820 women in its residential bachelor's degree program, plus other women enrolled in a nonresidential, individualized adult degree program, for contemporary conflicts involving careers, family, and community. In the opinion of its satisfied students, the college is winning the war of well-prepared graduates as well.

Student body: More than half of Mary Baldwin's students, 62%, are from Virginia, with the remainder from 38 states, mostly in the mid-Atlantic region, and 4 foreign countries. Eighty percent graduated from public high schools. Twenty-three percent of the enrollment is African-American, 5% Hispanic, 6% Asian-American, and 2% foreign national, including a large number from Mary Baldwin's sister school in Japan. One percent is Native American. The Black Student Alliance is not only one of the newest but already one of the most active and visible organizations on campus. Forty percent of the undergraduates are Protestant, and 41% are Catholic. Five percent are Presbyterian. The age span is wide, with students ranging from older women enrolled in the adult degree program to younger girls in a program for the exceptionally gifted that combines high school and college work. Nevertheless, most Mary Baldwin students form a close community unto themselves. A feeling of trust and camaraderie links the undergraduates, born at least in part from the highly valued honor pledge all of them sign. Students are mainly conservative, though some "ultraliberals" are present, quite opinionated on current issues, and serious about their work, but not so serious as to overlook parties and other extracurricular activities.

Academics: Mary Baldwin offers the bachelor's degree in about 24 standard majors and 8 combined fields of study. Students also may develop their own independent majors. A master of arts in teaching and a master's in Shakespeare and Renaissance Literature in Performance are awarded as well. The calendar includes 2 semesters followed by a 1-month spring term. Classes average 17 students, ranging from 44 in an introductory chemistry lecture down to 4 for a course in intermediate accounting.

The college's extensive general-education program covers 62 of the 132 semester hours needed for graduation. Along with 36 hours in the arts, humanities, social sciences, and natural sciences, the coursework covers writing excellence and mathematical reasoning, international education, either through study of a foreign language or culture or an overseas experience; experiential education, usually through an internship; physical education, and the contributions of women through a women's studies course. Students also must demonstrate competence in oral communication through completion of specified courses or testing out.

Many of the faculty members, the 76 full-time, all but 3 who teach undergraduates, and 53 part-time, most of whom teach in the Adult Degree Program, are noted for going out of their way to help students without coddling them. Observes a political science major: "The faculty are the glue that keeps the students on campus. They are highly dedicated to the achievements of all students, and overall, students honor and respect their work." Others speak of a deep trust that extends between faculty and student. Recalls a senior: "I lost a paper and turned it in late but my professor believed that I really had finished it on time and accepted it without a late penalty." Women comprise 53% of the faculty.

Political science is the "go-getter" major, attracting a majority of young women who are student leaders, which keeps the program very competitive. The programs in business administration, psychology, and communications, with its radio and television studios and desk-top publishing system, offer up-to-date equipment and experienced faculties. Biology and chemistry are "hands-on" majors as well, providing undergraduates with frequent access to very modern equipment. The major in health care administration is "intense," requiring 47 hours of coursework compared with fewer than 40 in most disciplines, but majors find the program rewarding because of the extensive on-the-job experiences and dedicated faculty. English, art, international relations, sociology, and Asian studies also are especially demanding, with creative and helpful faculties.

Students find the music major lacking, largely because there is a limited variety of courses available and women with a strong interest in the field can find larger programs at nearby James Madison University and Shenandoah Conservatory. Art also has limited faculty and facilities. Math relies more than many other departments on adjunct faculty members for instruction. Majors are offered in French, Spanish, and German, though instruction in Japanese and Russian has been available. Students who wish to major in

German must take some of their classes at Washington and Lee. The physics major also requires that some classes be taken at Washington and Lee. There is no single major in religion or social work, although combined majors including these fields, or minors in them, are offered.

Facilities: Students searching for a quiet place to study head for Grafton Library on the south end of campus, which, at least in its peaceful atmosphere, is all that a library should be. One of its best features is the study carrels, each wired for Internet access, which students sign up for at the beginning of the semester, and where, because of the honor code, they can leave important books and papers unattended. However, Grafton, with its 140,500 volumes, is less satisfactory for research, though a computerized catalog, numerous database searches, 11,900 paper and electronic periodicals, and the Internet usually fill in the gaps. Students often rely on materials, especially periodicals, obtained from surrounding colleges.

Nearly 230 PCs are available for student use around campus, including public workstations in each classroom building. The main computer center is open 24 hours a day; though the door is locked at 11 p.m., students may use a 3-digit code to enter anytime afterward. The campus also offers wireless access to those with laptops.

Special programs: In August 1995, Mary Baldwin inaugurated the Virginia Women's Institute for Leadership (VWIL), a joint public-private venture designed to immerse women in an around-the clock leadership education program. In addition to the regular requirements in general education and the major, VWIL students must complete additional courses in the arts and sciences, physical and health education, and military leadership (ROTC), plus a cocurricular program and a minor in leadership studies. Students not involved in VWIL may elect to complete the interdisciplinary leadership minor. A 2-year Carpenter Quest program combines academic study, spiritual exploration within a student's faith, service, and a variety of enrichment activities that support the individual's efforts to make sense of life, learning, and faith. Opportunities to study abroad range from May-term courses in Renaissance art in Italy or in the English judicial system in London to a year or semester at Mary Baldwin's sister school in Kyoto, Japan. Students may also spend the junior year at any of 6 other private colleges in Virginia, including 3 that are all female, and 1, Hampden-Sydney, that is all male. Two 3-2 joint degree programs are offered, in engineering with the University of Virginia and in nursing with Vanderbilt.

Campus life: Although students not residing with their families are required to live for all 4 years on the 54-acre campus, the combination of being nearly all female and being housed in a town of 23,500 sends most young women onto the road when the weekend comes, usually to coed or men's colleges within a reasonable drive. "If I could change anything about Mary Baldwin," says a sophomore, "I would change the social life. There just really isn't one here." The most popular stop is all-male Hampden-Sydney, Mary Baldwin's "brother school." Students also travel to Virginia Military Institute, Washington and Lee, or even the University of Virginia. Those who stay behind can get a lot of studying done—and even, with the willing help of the security office, get into the few facilities that are locked over the weekend. Observes a Virginian: "I would say the average student spends about half of her weekends here and half of her weekends traveling."

Occasional mixers from such popular groups as the Caribbean Student Alliance and other major events at the school reverse the flow of traffic and bring male and female visitors to Mary Baldwin. Though there are no sororities, plenty of other organizations, ranging from the judicial council to the *Bluestocking* yearbook, afford women the opportunity to assume positions of authority. At any given time, more than 200 of the 1100 full-time students hold leadership posts in campus groups, and leadership seminars and other training programs are offered regularly on topics ranging from time management to decision making. Crime is not considered an issue on campus, with highly visible 24-hour security guards willing to serve as escorts or otherwise help to make the women feel safe.

Less than a quarter of the students are involved in the 8 intercollegiate, 4 club, and 4 intramural sports available. Squirrels lacrosse and field hockey played in NCAA Division III draw the best home crowds, although the addition of food catered by the dining hall for tailgating at soccer games is boosting enthusiastic attendance there as well. Many prefer independent hiking and camping in the Blue Ridge Mountains.

The community of Staunton provides an off-campus atmosphere many students find relaxing. For the most mobile, Washington, D.C. and Richmond are each a 2- to 3-hour drive from campus.

Cost cutters: All but 1% of the first-year students received financial assistance in the 2005–2006 school year; for 78%, the aid was based on need. For continuing students, the comparable figures were all but 5% and 60%. The average freshman award for a student with need included a need-based scholarship or grant averaging $6500 and need-based self-help aid such as loans and jobs averaging $2000. Other non-need-based awards and scholarships for first-year students averaged $7000. Graduates left with an average debt of $18,625. More than 40 special scholarships are awarded on a competitive and need basis in such areas as leadership, fine arts, humanities, and science. Baldwin Scholarships recently paid $4500 to entering freshmen and transfer students with a 3.0 grade point average. Freshmen with a 3.0 GPA and an SAT I score of at least 1000 or ACT of 23 received up to $9300 in a recent year. Augusta Awards given to those students not eligible to receive a Baldwin Scholarship recently paid $2700 to $7300. Honor Scholar Awards paid $3500. One-third of the students use a monthly tuition payment plan.

Rate of return: Sixty-nine percent of freshmen return for the sophomore year. Fifty-two percent graduate in 4 years; 57% in 5 years.

Payoff: Psychology majors comprised 16% of the 2005 graduating class; 13% left with degrees in business administration, 11% in sociology. Twenty-five percent went immediately on to graduate or professional school. Forty-five percent eventually pursue advanced degrees. The vast majority immediately enter the job market, principally in the Southeast and the Middle Atlantic region, in such areas as management, banking, and sales. The job hunt for many is made much easier as the college's placement center mails a student's resume to 30 companies and then contacts each firm for follow-up and feedback.

Bottom line: "A student who needs her self-image raised should come to Mary Baldwin," advises a junior. "It's a place where she can become involved and be heard. I really don't want to leave when I graduate. My ultimate career goal is to be the president of Mary Baldwin."

Randolph-Macon College

Ashland, Virginia 23005

Setting: Suburban
Control: Private (United Methodist)
Undergraduate enrollment: 541 men, 561 women
Graduate enrollment: None
Student/faculty ratio: 11:1
Freshman profile: 3% scored over 700 on SAT I verbal; 23% scored 600–700; 54% 500–599; 20% below 500. 2% scored over 700 on SAT I math; 18% scored 600–700; 59% 500–599; 21% below 500. 34% graduated in top fifth of high school class; 67% in upper two-fifths.
Faculty profile: 93% Ph.D.'s
Tuition and fees: $23,945

Room and board: $7305
Freshman financial aid: 99%; average scholarship or grant: NA
Campus jobs: 22%; average earnings: $1100/year
Application deadline: Early decision: Nov. 15; early action: Dec. 1; regular: Mar. 1
Financial aid deadline: Mar. 1 (Priority date: Feb. 1)
Admissions information: (804) 752-7305;
  (800) 888-1762
  e-mail: admissions@rmc.edu
  web site: www.rmc.edu

Among America's premier families, alma maters have been handed down like fine ancestral china, with sons and daughters following their parents and grandparents to Harvard, Yale, Vassar, West Point—and tiny Randolph-Macon College in Ashland, Virginia. One recent graduate trod in the steps of his brother, 2 uncles, grandfather, and great-grandfather, all the way back to before the Civil War. Notes the family's latest Randolph-Macon alumnus: "The fact that 6 generations of my family have attended has created an unspoken feeling of trust that the college has something substantial and unique to offer." For students with or without family connections, Randolph-Macon continues to offer, 176 years after its founding, a rigorous liberal arts education, lots of personal attention, an easy southern social life—and one of the best values in small liberal arts colleges around.

Student body: Virginia is home to 68% of Randolph-Macon students. Another fourth typically come from Maryland, Pennsylvania, and New Jersey; the rest from 31 other states and 19 foreign countries. More than half, 54%, are Protestant, including the 14% who are Methodist, the school's historic affiliation. Another 17% are Catholic. Seventy percent graduated from public schools. The minority enrollment is 7% African-American, and 1.5% each Asian-American and Hispanic. Twenty-two students are foreign nationals. Students are proud of the openness and warmth felt on campus, and in an effort to make the atmosphere even more inclusive the college has instituted a number of courses and events to increase students' appreciation of racial, ethnic, and cultural differences. Undergraduates are rather conservative in their dress and attitudes, value campus traditions, and are described as being academically motivated but socially relaxed, generally able to maintain a good balance between weekly work and weekend partying. Says a senior: "Randolph-Macon is a very close-knit community where everyone knows each other. This at times can be either suffocating or accommodating, depending on someone's particular personality."

Academics: Randolph-Macon, founded in 1830, was the first college in the nation to move from a curriculum based on Latin and Greek to one based on the English language. It offers a bachelor's degree in 29 major fields of study. The academic year is divided into semesters plus an optional January term, which provides special time for overseas travel and internships. Average class size for undergraduates is 15. A few classes for freshmen may top out at 30. It is also very common to have several upper-level classes in the single digits. The small class sizes, says a junior, "allow for a lot of individual attention, but you better do your work or the professor will know."

To graduate, every student must participate in a 3-course First-Year Experience program devoted to developing the skills of writing and argumentation. The program features yearlong courses team-taught by 2 professors, each specializing in a different discipline, plus an associated seminar. Among courses in the 2005–2006 school year was one titled Wine, Science, and Society that incorporated lessons from science and literature. The remainder of the college's core curriculum is made up of areas of knowledge and cross-area requirements that draw connections among various academic disciplines.

A faculty of 137 includes 88 full-time and 49 part-time members. Women constitute 41% of the team. Undergraduates consider the close, easy-going student/faculty relationships at Randolph-Macon to be among the college's most enduring qualities. Most professors are described as "accommodating," "understanding," "helpful," "concerned," and as just about the most thought-provoking and challenging friends a student could ever have. "They don't let you just get by," says a senior. "They ask you to take responsibility for learning but are always there for you to answer questions and offer advice."

The top-rated department, to majors and nonmajors alike, is biology, which requires every student to complete a research project that lets him or her experience to the full extent the patient work, frustration, and ultimate thrill of scientific inquiry. The equipment available rivals that of larger state universities but is always accessible to undergraduates. The psychology department also is known for having professors who are both intelligent and good teachers, plus a curriculum that is very diverse in its offerings. English, too, provides a wide range of challenging courses from Shakespeare and Renaissance Drama to History of the English Language and Modern Novels on the Screen. The economics/business program offers a wealth of courses and an excellent internship program, including 1 in public policy in Washington, D.C. Most professors, says a major, "were business professionals prior to teaching and effectively incorporate real-world applications to their courses." Political science, which offers an internship at the United Nations, international relations, and history also are extremely well taught.

Majors in computer science and sociology are small with limited course offerings. While this sociology major feels his department could definitely benefit from increased funding, size and money don't necessarily determine quality. "My professors are very supportive," he notes, "and are always challenging me to work my hardest, try new things, and pursue research in my area of interest." Language enthusiasts will find majors in French, German, Spanish, Latin, and Greek, though elementary- and intermediate-level instruction is offered in Chinese and Japanese.

Facilities: McGraw-Page Library, which opened in 1987 at twice the size of the previous structure, remains students' favorite place to study, with its private "no-noise" study rooms, and vast array of online research services available. A computerized catalog and assorted databases as well as access to the Internet all bolster the collection of more than 182,000 volumes and 1455 periodicals.

Students have access to 350 PCs on campus. The largest clusters of units are based in labs in the library and science buildings and are open until 1 a.m. Though waits can occur at midterms or finals, most are no more than 15 minutes. Since all dormitory rooms have been wired for computer access, many residents bring their own units, which the college strongly recommends. Wireless access is available in the library and adjoining quad.

Special programs: Randolph-Macon offers study abroad programs in the United Kingdom, Ireland, France, Spain, Italy, Germany, Mexico, Korea, Japan, Australia, and New Zealand. Undergraduates also may study for a year or less at 1 of the other institutions in a 7-college consortium. The Summer Undergraduate Research Fellowship program (SURF), begun in 1996, provides 10 students with a $2000 stipend and on-campus accommodations during the summer for 10 weeks of intensive research. Joint programs are available in engineering with Columbia University and with the University of Virginia, in forestry and environmental studies with Duke, and in accounting with Virginia Commonwealth University.

Campus life: Eighty-nine percent of the students live on the college's 115-acre campus and generally stay there once the weekend arrives. Residential options include a newly renovated freshman village, special-interest housing, and townhouse apartments. Almost 40% of the men and women belong to 7 national fraternities and 4 national sororities. Though Greek life is extremely popular, students report almost no division between Greeks and independents. A growing number of student-sponsored events such as dances, comedians, or concerts keep both independents and Greeks involved, with the new "Macon College" coffee shop becoming a popular gathering place for all students. Forty percent of the students participate in one or more community-service activity, including work through such groups as Big Brother Big Sister, Habitat for Humanity, and Amnesty International. Although crime, other than thefts of bicycles or laundry, is not much of a concern, dorms are kept locked around the clock with a card access system, and emergency telephones have been set up throughout campus.

R-MC competes in NCAA Division III in 7 men's and 8 women's sports. Yellow Jacket basketball games were the place to be in the 2004–2005 school year as the men's team won the Old Dominion Athletic Conference championship and the women's team placed second in the nation. Football and soccer also consistently draw enthusiastic crowds. Half of the men and women are involved in the intramural program, which offers 12 sports for each sex.

When Ashland (pop. 7000) begins to feel a bit closed in, students needing to break away drive to Washington, D.C. (1 hour, 15 minutes), Virginia Beach (1 hour, 40 minutes), or nearby Richmond (just 15 minutes south). The Blue Ridge Mountains and Virginia Beach also beckon.

Cost cutters: Ninety-nine percent of entering students and 93% of continuing ones received financial aid in the 2005–2006 academic year; for 54% of the entering students and 48% of the rest, the help was based on need. The average freshman award totaled $21,037; three-fourths of that total consisted of gift assistance, one fourth of self-help aid, such as loans and job earnings. Recent graduates left with an average debt of $15,130. A variety of merit scholarships, recently ranging from $5000 to $20,000, are offered to outstanding entering students. To be considered, students should apply for admission by February 1. In a recent year, 46% of the entering class received a merit-based scholarship. Students with the highest level of achievement are eligible to receive awards contained within the Presidential Scholars Program. Most scholarship recipients will have combined SAT scores of 1650 or above on the new scale with at least 500 on each section or comparable ACT scores and are ranked in the top 25% of their high school classes. Recipients of the highest level awards usually have an academic record that greatly exceeds those norms and they are among the top students in their classes. All scholarships are renewable over 4 years. The college also offers grants of up to $8000 to siblings of current students, regardless of the family's financial need. Parents with incomes between $30,000 and $75,000 who are creditworthy may borrow up to $15,000 a year from the college's parent loan program. The interest rate was 5% in 2005. Repayment begins 1 month after the loan is made. Parents and students also may pay tuition on a monthly basis over a 10-month period.

Rate of return: Seventy-eight percent of freshmen return for the sophomore year. Sixty-five percent graduate in 4 years; 70% in 5 years.

Payoff: Sixty percent of the Class of 2005 majored in 5 disciplines. Sixteen percent graduated with degrees in economics/business; 13% majored in sociology; 12% in psychology, 11% in political science, and 8% in English. Twenty-seven percent opted to pursue advanced degrees immediately at least part time. Two-thirds of R-MC alumni do so within 5 years. Eighty-five percent of the graduates initially enter the work force, many in retail management and sales, banking, and finance with firms on the East Coast and throughout the Southeast.

Bottom line: "A high school senior who wants to explore various areas of academia in an atmosphere of cooperation with professors and peers can have that experience at Randolph-Macon," advises a recent graduate. "For anyone who wishes to specialize in an area such as engineering, however, a larger university may provide more opportunities."

Randolph-Macon Woman's College

Lynchburg, Virginia 24503

Setting: Suburban
Control: Private (United Methodist)
Undergraduate enrollment: 760 women
Graduate enrollment: NA
Student/faculty ratio: 9:1
Freshman profile: SAT/ACT scores: NA; class rank data: NA
Faculty profile: 92% Ph.D.'s
Tuition and fees: $23,030
Room and board: $8610

Freshman financial aid: 99%; average scholarship or grant: $15,490 need-based; $14,470 non-need-based
Campus jobs: 63%; average earnings: $981/year
Application deadline: Early decision: Nov. 15; regular: Mar. 1
Financial aid deadline: Mar. 1
Admissions information: (434) 947-8100; (800) 745-7692
e-mail: admissions@rmwc.edu
web site: www.rmwc.edu

The best advertisement for the tough academics, great leadership opportunities, and close student/faculty relationships to be found at Randolph-Macon Woman's College is a recent R-MWC graduate, or so say students who have met these alumnae. Recalls a northern Virginia resident: "I decided to attend Randolph-Macon Woman's College because I was impressed by the professional, career-minded attitude that I had seen in several alums. They were not only personable and very bright but also in control of their lives." Adds a Georgian: "There's a self-confidence that you gain from attending R-MWC. It's easy to spot a graduate." For both these young women there was a happy ending: after 4 years at Randolph-Macon Woman's College, they became similarly impressive graduates and role models for high school seniors. Remarks one of these recent graduates: "Randolph-Macon has enabled me to feel comfortable in a wide range of difficult situations where once I would have been intimidated. It's hard to put a finger on the actual mechanism of the attitude building, but whatever it is, it works wonders!"

Student body: Just 41% of R-MWC's works-in-progress were drawn in a recent year from within Virginia's borders; more than half of the out-of-staters typically are from the South. Undergraduates as a whole came in a recent year from 43 states and 39 foreign countries. The enrollment included 8% African-American, 4% Hispanic, 3% Asian-American and 2% multi-racial students. Nine percent were foreign nationals. A tenth of the women typically are 24 or older. Twenty percent graduated from private or parochial high schools. Sixty-nine percent in a recent year were Protestant (14% Methodist), 19% Catholic, 3% Jewish; most of the rest claimed no religious affiliation or their affiliation was unknown. Because students are drawn from so many parts of the United States, they tend to be more liberal than the typical central Virginia student, accepting "everything from Laura Ashley to purple hair," in the words of one woman. A majority are friendly, with few obvious "snobs." Most also are very career-oriented and involved in a wide range of activities. Competition, however, is generally self-competition, with each woman deciding how much, or how little, she wants to challenge herself. "Every individual has a place here," says a junior from the Northwest, "which is why it is Randolph-Macon *Woman's* College, in the singular."

Academics: Randolph-Macon Woman's College, founded in 1891 by the president of the original Randolph-Macon College as a rigorous alternative to then all-male R-MC, awards the bachelor's degree in more than 25 majors. The college recently added master's degree programs related to teaching special education and English for second-language learners. Semester classes average 12 women, and even first-year courses rarely exceed 30; a course in Introduction to Psychology with 45 enrolled has been the biggest students ever encounter. However, with classes so small, students learn quickly that participation is a must, and the final grade often is based on how much a woman contributes to the class discussion.

The general-education program consists of coursework drawn from 3 areas: skills, including expository writing, mathematics, and a foreign language; distribution, with 6 courses representing the traditional academic fields; and dimensions, including a course involving the study of women and 1 course each focusing on the social, intellectual, and cultural traditions of the United States, of 1 or more European countries, and of either Asia, Africa, the Middle East, or Latin America. Students also must complete 1 semester hour in physical education and an interdisciplinary forum taken the first semester of freshman year that examines a single subject from the perspectives of diverse academic fields.

The faculty numbering 96 in a recent year included 19 part-time teachers; 53% of the total were women. The professors provide a wonderful mix of the brilliant, the eccentric, and the dedicated, most of whom students grow to admire. "They have energy and spunk beyond compare," notes a first-year student. Because classes are so small, says a junior, "faculty members get to know every student very well and as a result are able to challenge each one to increase her strengths and decrease her weaknesses."

Across the departments, there are many programs vying for the superlative "best." Psychology majors find their course of study first-rate, with superb professors, up-to-date equipment, and a research-based workload that is often "overwhelming," but worth it. Biology and chemistry also benefit from excellent equipment and enthusiastic faculties; the politics department, says a nonmajor, "is outstanding in every sense, particularly faculty." Economics, too, is characterized by a strong set of professors and a fantastic senior seminar. English, history, and international studies also draw high praise for varied offerings and good resources, although history, says an otherwise satisfied major, "could benefit from historians who specialized in African, Middle Eastern, and/or South American history." Foreign languages are intense with very small classes that enable professors to work closely with individual students; majors are available in French, Spanish, German Studies, Russian Studies, and Classics with an emphasis in classical languages.

Several departments, among them music, theater, art, and physics, have had fewer professors and more limited course offerings than some undergraduates would like. Music, in particular, needs an overhaul, says a sophomore still weighing potential majors. "The music department has a very strong faculty but needs more updated equipment and technology. Listening devices are old and the pianos are often not in tune." Computer science is offered as a concentration within the mathematics major, though some students would like to see it offered as a separate major.

Facilities: Lipscomb Library has a reputation around campus as being "a practical place to study"—if not always the most aesthetically pleasing, says a New Englander. "Our library is a little outdated, besides the furniture looking and smelling like it's from the early 1970s." Other users find that the comfortable couches offset most concerns. The collection of almost 200,000 volumes and 618 periodicals seems adequate for the enrollment but, for a college of this rigor, often starts to fall short during a student's junior year. When that happens, students turn to the on-line computer system that connects them to the appropriate sources at Lipscomb or at the libraries of neighboring Sweet Briar and Lynchburg colleges. Additional on-line research aids as well as the Internet are especially helpful.

Students have 24-hour access to about 100 mainly Dell Pentiums and some Macintosh computers, all of which are networked and located in 7 clusters around campus. Students also may connect a personal computer from their individual rooms to the campus network. About two-thirds of R-MWC students bring their own computers to campus. Every classroom also is wired and there are 6 common areas equipped with wireless technology.

Special programs: About 35 students annually spend the junior year at the University of Reading in England. Cultural exchanges also are offered with about 10 universities across the globe, ranging from Kansai University of Foreign Studies in Japan to Universidad de las Américas in Puebla, Mexico. Summer study tours are offered every year. In a recent summer, students and faculty traveled in London, Japan, and South Africa. A special American Culture program enables students to visit American historical and cultural sites, such as Colonial Williamsburg, Monticello, and Roanoke Island, in order to understand more fully the culture on this side of the Atlantic or Pacific Ocean. A student also may spend a full semester in Washington, D.C. Undergraduates can take courses at Lynchburg and Sweet Briar colleges without paying additional fees. A 3-2 program is offered in nursing with Johns Hopkins University and in engineering with the University of Virginia and with Virginia Commonwealth, Vanderbilt, and Washington universities.

Campus life: All but about a tenth of the women live on the 100-acre campus encircled by a red brick wall. On many weekends, however, a majority of residents hop over the wall to seek social excitement at the football games and parties of other nearby colleges, among them all-male Hampden-Sydney or coed Washington and Lee or the University of Virginia. For on-campus diversion, most students attend a Saturday coffeehouse or comedian, a Sunday picnic, or possibly a special exhibit at the college's own Maier Museum of Art, which houses works by Winslow Homer, Mary Cassatt, and Georgia O'Keeffe. There are no sororities; however, "secret" societies offer a similar intimate social environment for women interested in this type of organization. B.I.O.N.I.C. (Believe It or Not, I Care) and other service organizations involve every student at least once in some kind of project. Odd/even class rivalries are a popular tradition, as are events like the annual Pumpkin Parade. Although within the red-brick wall crime is not usually a problem, the dorms generally are locked at 5 p.m. weekdays or at darkness, whichever comes first, and all the time on weekends. Security recently was upgraded with the switch to electronic key cards. Escorts are available from the parking lots to the dorms, and enclosed walkways connect most of the main buildings. "There is practically no crime," says a senior, "unless you count parking violations!"

A fifth of the women participate in 8 intercollegiate sports played in NCAA Division III. "Field hockey and volleyball draw some students," says a junior, "but most students find little time to attend games." The college has a 100-acre riding center, 10 minutes from the main campus. The Randy-Mac Pac club provides plenty of opportunities for women who prefer hiking, camping, and other forms of noncompetitive outdoor recreation.

Though other colleges in the area with men are the favorite over-the-wall destinations, students also enjoy drives or hikes along the Blue Ridge Parkway, just 20 minutes away.

Cost cutters: Financial help in a recent school year went to 99% of all undergraduates; for 70% of the freshmen and 66% of the rest, the aid was based on need. The average freshman award for a student with need included a need-based scholarship or grant averaging $15,490 and need-based self-help aid such as loans and jobs averaging $4118. Other non-need-based awards and scholarships for first-year students averaged $14,470. More than 20 merit scholarships for freshmen, ranging in value from $5000 to full tuition, are awarded for superior scholastic achievement without regard to financial need. The Trustee Scholarship pays $13,000 to students of high academic achievement and leadership skills. The Theodore Jack, Founders', and Conway scholarships pay $10,500, $9000, and $5000 respectively. Students with the highest academic profile are eligible to receive awards that are part of the Presidential Scholars Program. The most prestigious awards, the Lindner and Nichols scholarships, pay tuition, room, and board for 4 years plus a one-time $2500 stipend for study abroad to a single student each. The full-tuition, renewable Gottwald Scholarship also pays a 1-time study abroad fellowship worth $2500 to 3 students. Other Presidential Scholars awards pay at least $17,500 a year. To be considered, students must apply by December 1. Daughters of ordained Methodist ministers receive a $1000 tuition reduction. General scholarships are awarded based on a combination of a student's grade point average and standardized test scores. For example, a student with a 3.8 GPA and a combined math and critical reading SAT score of between 1100 and 1190 could receive a scholarship worth $10,500; that same GPA combined with an SAT ranging from 1350 to 1600 would bring a scholarship of at least $13,000 and at most full tuition. A loan program for middle-income families and a 10-month, interest-free payment plan also are available. The average recent graduate left with a college debt of $21,992. Alumni don't forget their alma mater, though. Nearly 50% make donations to the college, placing Randolph-Macon Woman's College in the top 1% of colleges in terms of alumni participation in giving.

Rate of return: Eighty percent of freshmen return for the sophomore year. Sixty-one percent graduate in 4 years; 63% in 5 years.

Payoff: Biology majors comprised 15% of a recent graduating class, followed by majors in psychology at 12% and English at 11%. Soon after commencement, just over a third of R-MWC graduates pursued further study. Within 15 years of commencement, a full two-thirds of a graduating class have earned advanced degrees. The college also ranks in the top 10% of baccalaureate-granting institutions in the percentage of students who go on to earn a Ph.D. Those taking jobs settle primarily in the East and Southeast and tend to work most often in sales, marketing, and banking, though such fields as education, journalism, and politics also attract R-MWC alumnae. Just over 100 companies and other organizations recruited on campus in a recent school year.

Bottom line: "Any woman, whether from a small, private school or a large, public one, who wants to succeed, who wants to participate, and who really wants to like herself should attend Randolph-Macon Woman's College," concludes a recent graduate. "Once prospective students see our wonderful old dorms and the rolling lawn of Front Campus, and feel the warm sense of community here they won't want to go anywhere else."

University of Mary Washington

Fredericksburg, Virginia 22401

Setting: Small town
Control: Public
Undergraduate enrollment: 1205 men, 2323 women
Graduate enrollment: 1 man, 25 women
Student/faculty ratio: 15:1
Freshman profile: 17% scored over 700 on SAT I verbal; 52% scored 600–700; 28% 500–599; 3% below 500. 7% scored over 700 on SAT I math; 47% scored 600–700; 41% 500–599; 5% below 500. 39% graduated in top tenth of high school class; 65% in upper fifth.
Faculty profile: 83% Ph.D.'s
Tuition and fees: $5634 in-state, $14,776 out-of-state

Room and board: $6002
Freshman financial aid: 65%; average scholarship or grant: $2245 need-based; $1550 non-need-based
Campus jobs: 25%; average earnings: $1600/year
Application deadline: Honors admission: Jan. 15; regular: Feb. 1
Financial aid deadline: Mar. 1
Admissions information: (540) 654-2000;
   (800) 468-5614
   e-mail: admit@umw.edu
   web site: www.umw.edu

If Mary Washington, George Washington's mother, sometimes stood in the shadow of her famous son, so, too, has the new university named for her done its share of shadow sharing. Started in 1908 as the women's division of the University of Virginia, Mary Washington long deferred to her more illustrious brother, even after becoming coeducational in 1970. Over the last decade, however, Mary Washington has gained recognition of her own, first, as a high-quality, highly selective liberal arts college known as Mary Washington College that concentrated on teaching undergraduates and now, since July 2004, as a small university, the University of Mary Washington, that still puts undergraduates first on its Fredericksburg campus. (A separate campus in nearby Stafford known as the James Monroe Center for Graduate and Professional Studies has the bulk of graduate and continuing education programs.) Application levels for a freshman class of 914 have increased by more than half since 1985, to 4635 applicants for fall 2005 from 2671, with about 2 of every 3 applicants being offered admission. Mary's son, George, may have tossed his coin across the Rappahannock River running near campus, but that's about the only money deposited here that doesn't increase in value over the years.

Student body: Three-fourths of the students are from Virginia, and 17% of the nonresidents are from the Northeast, but undergraduates attend from 42 states and 18 foreign countries. Seventeen percent in a recent year graduated from private or parochial schools. And though Mary Washington has been coed for over 2 decades, women students still outnumber men by a 2 to 1 margin. Asian-Americans and African-Americans comprise the largest minority groups on campus, at 4% of enrollment each, with Hispanics following at 3%. Twenty international students are enrolled as well. The college's Bachelor of Liberal Studies program, which graduated 150 students in a recent year, enrolls undergraduates who are at least age 24 in classes with 18-to-22-year-olds. Undergraduates generally see themselves as rather conservative in their views, but open to new ways of thinking. "I'm very unconventional," says a sophomore, "and I get lots of respect for being different." In fact, some students wonder whether there may actually be more liberal students than conservative, "but the conservative students are very vocal so it feels pretty even," notes a Virginian. Other adjectives used to describe the student body are *creative, unassuming, well-rounded, motivated,* and *extremely friendly.* Upon entering, freshmen sign an honor pledge, promising not to lie, cheat, steal, or break their word of honor. The result is a deep sense of trust and openness on campus, which keeps the level of academic competition stressfree but far from laid back. Says an historic preservation major: "We work hard to get the A's that a good number of professors refuse to give." Adds a psychology major: "It is a pleasure taking classes with people who want to be there; sometimes I have trouble getting a seat in the front row."

Academics: Mary Washington's focus on its Fredericksburg campus is on its 30 majors for undergraduates, though the university has offered a master's of liberal studies to a small number of graduate students enrolled there. The university operates on a 2-semester calendar. Freshman classes range from 20 to 35 students, with some popular courses, such as the Psychology of Human Sexuality, enrolling as many as 187. Junior and senior classes are smaller, from 8 to 20 students.

General-education requirements are organized into 8 goal areas and 5 areas across the curriculum. The goals constitute understanding such fields as writing, mathematical thought, science, the arts, the development of Western civilization, social sciences, a foreign language at the intermediate level, and physical well-being; students take their choice of prescribed courses in these fields. Those requirements that extend across the curriculum may be filled by suitable general-education courses, electives, or work in the major; they include 1 course in environmental awareness, 2 in global awareness, 1 that is race-and gender-intensive, 2 that are speaking-intensive, and 4 that are writing-intensive. The breadth of courses, notes a senior, "eventually help you stumble upon your passion."

For many students, the 5-star faculty, consisting of 231 full-time members and 107 part-timers (39% women), sets Mary Washington apart from other small public institutions. Students are impressed by the superior credentials and the professional and life experiences many professors bring to the classroom. All but 21 members of the full-time faculty and all but 22 of the part-time teach undergraduates. A majority of the faculty members are dedicated as much to teaching as to their subject matter and usually are very willing to meet with students to provide additional help, regardless of whether or not the student is a major in his or her field. Observes a junior: "The professors put a lot of time into their classes, and expect the same in return from their students."

Without a doubt, the college's unusual historic preservation major is a standout. The curriculum is innovative, the faculty excellent, and 300-year-old Fredericksburg itself is a living laboratory. Students and faculty also put their skills to work on modern-day problems as they arise. The political science and international affairs, and economics departments get a boost from both experienced faculty and the college's locale just 50 miles from the capitals of both the nation and the state of Virginia, which provide plenty of opportunities for internships. Psychology emphasizes learning by doing, and many undergraduates get involved in research. Explains a major: "A research symposium is held at the end of each academic year, providing a forum for students to share with others their research findings. Internships and community service are also actively encouraged as a method of applying knowledge and skills learned in coursework to different environments." In English, majors and nonmajors alike struggle for A's from young professors who demand independent, critical thinking; history features many great faculty members who relate history "by telling it in stories," observes an admirer. The classics, philosophy, and religion departments offer a broad curriculum from a diverse faculty "who truly seek an intellectual ideal," says a political science major. Geography, with its small classes led by attentive professors, the sciences, with their greenhouse, science literacy center, and up-to-date instruments, and the foreign language departments offering courses in Arabic, French, German, Italian, and Spanish, are all winners.

Some undergraduates think the business administration department provides "a less than adequate or challenging agenda for its students," in the words of an economics major. The university does not offer other career-oriented majors in such fields as communication or journalism, nursing or social work. Students interested in elementary education must earn a Master of Science degree in education after a fifth year of coursework. A new major in anthropology was added in fall 2005.

Facilities: Simpson Library, which opened in 1989, gives undergraduates no excuse not to get their studying done; there are plenty of carrels, private rooms (including a 24-hour room), tables, and a generally quiet atmosphere. The collection consists of nearly 367,000 volumes and 5782 periodicals, all available through a computerized catalog plus technology to check through journal articles. "Depending on your major," says a senior, "our resources are adequate to excellent, but our computer technology makes up for any less-than-excellent areas."

Several computer labs are available around campus, many specific to a certain major. At least 3 labs in 1 building with Macs, Windows, and Unix computers, are open around the clock. Students with their own computers can access the Internet from their residence-hall rooms. Nearly all students own their own computers. Wireless access also is available.

Special programs: Juniors and seniors may participate in more than 500 internships available each semester, many in the capital cities of Richmond and Washington, D.C.; about a third of the internships are paid positions. More than a fifth of the students take part before graduating. An executive-in-residence program brings top-name professionals, among them investor Warren Buffett, to campus to meet with and teach undergraduates. Study abroad is widely available for a year, a semester, or a summer in more than 40 countries. A Summer Science Research Program, underwritten by a grant from the duPont Fund in 1999, allows majors in natural science to work with faculty mentors on undergraduate research during the summer months.

Campus life: Seventy-one percent reside on the 176 acres of red brick and white columns. The fact that only upperclassmen now can have cars has helped to keep more students on campus over the weekend. There are no Greek organizations. Instead, most students use the residence halls as they would fraternities or sororities, electing their own officers and sponsoring parties and events. The campus "Underground" regularly features bands and programs in a coffeehouse setting. Community Outreach and Resources (COAR), a student-run volunteer program, has picked up tremendous interest since its founding in 1990; the Historic Preservation Club also has a solid membership. Crime is kept in check by several security measures, among them requirements that all student visitors to other residence halls sign in and out and that every nonstudent visitor be checked into the particular room he or she is seeking. Blue lights and emergency phones are prevalent around campus and a student-run escort service provides rides to and from the Battleground Athletic Complex, about 2 blocks from campus.

More than 300 men and women compete in the 23-sport NCAA Division III varsity athletic program that consists of 1 coed, 12 women's, and 10 men's teams. Soccer matches draw the largest number of fans. Observes a junior: "Though there are many sports teams that actually do very well, there isn't much school spirit and students don't frequent such events." UMW's newest varsity sport, rowing, competes in some of the top regattas in the nation. Fifteen intramural sports also are open to each sex; about a fifth of the men and a tenth of the women take part. The men's and women's rugby club is especially popular, as is a noncompetitive group, the Trek Club, which provides opportunities for students to participate in various outdoor sports, from hiking to skydiving.

To escape college pressures, students often like to go back in time by walking through historic Fredericksburg (pop. 22,300) or lounging by the Rappahannock River. Washington, D.C. and Richmond both offer bigger city excitement, just 50 miles away.

Cost cutters: In the 2005–2006 school year, 65% of the freshmen and 63% of the continuing students received financial help. Forty percent of the first-year students and 45% of the rest received aid based on need. The average freshman package for a student with need included a need-based scholarship or grant averaging $2245 and need-based self-help aid such as loans and jobs averaging $2400. Other non-need-based awards and scholarships for first-year students averaged $1550. Average debt of a 2005 graduate was $13,100. Alumni Scholarships, which go to students offered honors admissions, recently ranged from $500 (most are $500 or $1000) to a maximum amount equal to in-state tuition and fees and are renewable over 4 years. During a recent school year, 250 entering students received Alumni awards totaling nearly $202,000. Tuition payment plans also are available.

Rate of return: Eighty-five percent of entering freshmen return for the sophomore year. Sixty-four percent graduate in 4 years; 72% in 5 years.

Payoff: Fourteen percent of the 2005 graduates received degrees in business administration; 10% specialized in English, 8% in biology. Thirty percent of the new alumni went on immediately to graduate or professional schools, at least part-time, half of them in the arts and sciences. Over 80% of the graduates take jobs directly after graduating, many with large firms such as IBM, Xerox, and PricewaterhouseCoopers, or in education, computer science, law, and medicine, primarily in the Northeast or Middle Atlantic states. Ninety companies and organizations recruited on campus in a recent school year.

Bottom line: Mary Washington is "what a college ought to be!" enthuses a recent graduate. "Beautiful, sprawling lawns, with wide porches and large wooden neoclassical columns on red brick buildings. Challenging, stimulating, and full of southern charm and vitality." George's mother would have been proud.

University of Virginia

Charlottesville, Virginia 22904

Setting: Small city
Control: Public
Undergraduate enrollment: 6137 men, 7258 women
Graduate enrollment: 3258 men, 2730 women
Student/faculty ratio: 12:1
Freshman profile: 32% scored over 700 on SAT I verbal; 46% scored 600–700; 18% 500–599; 4% below 500. 39% scored over 700 on SAT I math; 44% scored 600–700; 14% 500–599; 3% below 500. 43% scored above 28 on the ACT; 21% scored 27–28; 21% 24–26; 8% 21–23; 7% below 21. 86% graduated in top tenth of high school class; 95% in upper fifth.

Faculty profile: 91% Ph.D.'s
Tuition and fees: $7370 in-state, $24,290 out-of-state
Room and board: $6389
Freshman financial aid: 53%; average scholarship or grant: NA
Campus jobs: 25%; average earnings: NA
Application deadline: Early decision: Nov. 1; regular: Jan. 2
Financial aid deadline: Mar. 1
Admissions information: (434) 982-3200
 e-mail: undergradadmission@virginia.edu
 web site: www.virginia.edu

If Thomas Jefferson, founder of the University of Virginia, had had his way, students wouldn't be able to earn bachelor's degrees from this highly esteemed university started in 1819. Jefferson considered degrees "artificial embellishments" to learning, and it wasn't until 1831 that the Board of Visitors agreed to grant a master of arts degree. Finally, in 1899, to make the university conform to what other schools were doing, the bachelor's degree was established as a prerequisite for the master's at Mr. Jefferson's University. Just over a century later, a bachelor's degree from the University of Virginia has become one of the most valued artificial embellishments in the land. And at a tuition rate in the 2005–2006 school year of just $7370 in-state and $24,290 out-of-state, any graduate can also declare independence from financial stress.

Student body: "I expected a very preppy and fun school," confesses a Southerner, "but I found UVA to be much more diverse and academically oriented." The undergraduate student body is 8% Asian-American, 7% African-American, 7% foreign nationals, and 3% Hispanic. Seventy percent of the "Wahoos," as the students are called, are from Virginia; students come, though, from every state, the largest number from several states in the Middle Atlantic region, and from 110 foreign countries. One-fourth graduated from private or parochial schools. Newcomers fearful of finding "an elite, snobbish institution" are delighted to discover a campus where many viewpoints are aired in campus-wide debates organized by different groups. Students tend to be conservative though there are a noticeable number of liberals, very intelligent, and involved. "Students are extremely well-rounded here," says a junior. "The whole place buzzes with energy." And while Wahoos are competitive and vie for membership in honor societies and good placements after graduation, the very active social life attracts many, although UVA's party school image has toned down considerably in recent years. "Even the bookworm will blossom here," says a sophomore. "There is a fun intellectualism about UVA." Adds a senior who turned down Stanford for UVA: "Most students take their classes very seriously and pride themselves on competitive GPAs, yet few would be found studying on a Saturday night."

Academics: The University of Virginia awards bachelor's degrees in 46 fields, master's degrees in 64 fields, and doctorates in 54. The College of Arts and Sciences, the McIntire School of Commerce, and 4 other professional schools of Architecture, Education, Engineering and Applied Sciences, and Nursing have programs for undergraduates. The Darden Graduate School of Business and schools of Medicine and Law have graduate-level programs only. The academic year is divided into 2 semesters. The range in class sizes is fairly typical: basic first-year courses in psychology, astronomy, and chemistry can enroll 500, while some required freshman English composition courses are limited to 15. More than 50 university seminars give freshmen the chance to study in small groups with some of UVA's best professors. Most classes for juniors and seniors drop to between 40 and 60, and some upper-level English, engineering, and architecture courses may have only 10 enrolled.

General-education requirements vary among the 5 undergraduate schools and 1 college. In the College of Arts and Sciences, the largest of UVA's undergraduate divisions, students must take 4 courses in a foreign language, 4 in mathematics and natural science, 2 each in humanities, social science, and composition, and 1 each in historical studies and in non-Western perspectives. Students with high standardized test scores may be exempted from certain requirements. Applicants to the McIntire School of Commerce and Curry School of Education must complete 2 years of study in the liberal arts before enrolling in the schools as juniors. Prospective teachers must earn a bachelor's degree from the College of Arts and Sciences and a master's of teaching degree from the Curry School of Education, both degrees awarded simultaneously at the end of 5 years of study.

Just over a third, 36%, of the 2792 full-time professors, 1012, teach undergraduates, as do half, 135, of the 282 part-time faculty. Thirty-seven percent of the total teaching staff are women. Three faculty members have won Pulitzer Prizes. Across the board, students find the faculty to be highly knowledgeable and "every department has at least 1 national figure," says a sophomore. However, many first-year students do not come into close contact with a number of Virginia's star professors who dazzle them in lecture hall, as 32% of the discussion sections of introductory lectures are taught by graduate students. Once into smaller classes for the major, however, a student often finds him- or herself encouraged to drop by a professor's office for extra help, or invited to a faculty member's home for dinner. Says a religious studies major: "The professors truly care about their students, get to know them socially, and challenge them intellectually on a daily basis." As at most major research universities, though, there also are professors who spend considerable time in their laboratories or offices doing research with graduate students.

At Virginia, the liberal arts disciplines are among the strongest on campus. English, history, government/foreign affairs, psychology, and religious studies appear on nearly everyone's list as examples of programs where first-rate faculty place teaching ahead of research, or at least intertwine the two, and the students win. Notes a sophomore: "In these departments, the introductory-level courses are taught by some of the best professors, so that students get a strong grasp of the basics. While these departments are very challenging, a great deal of help also is provided." Religious studies is especially noteworthy for the "wide variety of classes offered in multiple religious traditions," explains a major. Smaller, interdisciplinary majors like political and social thought "offer lots of room for creative thought," says an East Asian studies major. Physics has great research opportunities open to undergraduates. Architecture is highly respected, as is the McIntire School of Commerce, where classes emphasize group work among students often having them develop marketing plans or accounting portfolios for actual companies, and the competition between groups can be intense. Several programs in the School of Engineering, chemical and systems engineering in particular, are especially challenging with excellent job placement for their graduates.

The widely respected economics program lacks sufficient professors to meet student demand for its excellent classes. "Though professors in the department are talented teachers and researchers," notes a major, "they typically face average class sizes of 40+ students, even in 400-level courses." Students majoring in Spanish and other language programs find the professors and coursework "fabulous," just hard to get. Says a Spanish major: "Class size is restricted and the classes taught per semester are limited due to the number of professors in the department. As a result, third-year Spanish majors are unable to enroll in classes they need for their major." The math department suffers from too many professors who teach above Wahoos' heads and often have limited English speaking skills. While students consider programs in the fine arts to be "adequate," dance in particular lacks classes and facilities. Art and music also lack sufficient funding.

Facilities: The university has 2 main undergraduate libraries and 15 departmental ones, which, all told, give students direct access to 5 million volumes, 5.5 million microform items, and 52,192 current periodicals. Clemons Library offers the most frequently used books and periodicals and serves primarily for study—and socializing, although students who need absolute silence can head for the quiet zones in the bottom levels. "Students fondly refer to the fourth floor as Club Clemons as it is always bustling," says a junior. Clemons is open for both bustle and study around the clock on weekdays. Alderman Library which houses the principal collection in the social sciences and humanities gives undergraduates easy access to material here and around the world through an on-line electronic text center. A frequent user offers these insights: "Alderman has the more serious study cubbyholes throughout the mazelike stacks; red phones at various points in the stacks can be used to call the main desk and get directions out of the maze." VIRGO, the computerized library catalog, likewise guides students through the university's enormous collection of books, periodicals, manuscripts—you name it. As an extra help, it also provides alternative sources for materials that the university does not have.

Students may access the university network as well as the Internet from their residence-hall rooms, if they own personal computers, or from any of more than 30 public computing facilities housing more than 900 Windows, Apple, and Unix computers around campus. A wireless network is available in about 75% of all buildings around campus. There are 5 major computer facilities, 3 of them open around the clock. The university strongly recommends that students have their own personal computers; a majority of freshmen entering in a recent fall brought their own units to campus. The university also has 200 computers that can be borrowed for free by students with demonstrated financial need.

Special programs: Study abroad in UVA's own programs is offered in 13 countries. In a recent year, about 10% of graduates in the College of Arts and Sciences received some credit for study abroad. The best of the brightest new first-year students may be named either Echols Scholars in the College of Arts and Sciences or Rodman Scholars in the School of Engineering and Applied Science. An Echols Scholar is exempted from area requirements, need not declare a major, and under careful faculty advisement may choose courses from any disciplines. Rodman Scholars take 4 special courses in design, communications, and computers.

Campus life: Nearly half of the students (46%) reside on the historic "grounds" that Thomas Jefferson designed, now spread over 1160 acres. The most treasured rooms, awarded to outstanding seniors and by lot to graduate students, are the 108 in Jefferson's famed "academical village," where 2 colonnades of rooms flank a lawn, interspersed between 10 "pavilions" in which faculty and academic leaders live. At one end is the Rotunda, a red-brick pantheon set against the Blue Ridge Mountains, that has always been UVA's centerpiece. Notes an Echols Scholar: "Thomas Jefferson's intellectual spirit remains here as inspiration to those seeking knowledge." When it's time to seek some good times, many students head to Rugby Road, where UVA's fraternity houses are located. Twenty-eight percent of UVA men and women are members of 37 national fraternities and 23 national sororities. There are a predominantly white and a predominantly black Greek system with little interaction between them. Until a few years ago, the Rugby Road fraternity parties were open to all students, but because of complaints from neighbors and liability problems, Greeks now use guest lists. Independents, as well as fraternity and sorority members, frequent the Corner, a strip of restaurants and shops within walking distance of the campus. "Low key progressive types," says a junior, "have their own hangouts and private parties." More than 550 clubs and organizations provide niches for students of every avocation, from polo or croquet to writing for the

Skandeline or the *Yellow Journal*. Madison House, a volunteer center, has one of the strongest and most devoted followings.

If Jefferson felt that the government that governs best, governs least, he would be pleased with the emphasis on self-government at his university. Because of a long-standing honor system, under which students pledge not to lie, cheat, or steal, or tolerate those who do, all Wahoos can take unproctored exams, as well as cash checks anywhere in Charlottesville simply by showing their IDs. Students accused of honor code violations may either admit guilt and leave the university or claim innocence and appear before a jury of their peers. Wahoos credit the honor code with cutting down on incidents of petty crime from inside the university system. To deter crime from the outside, members of a student watch program patrol the grounds, and an escort service operates until 3 a.m. to take students home. Lighted emergency phones are located in heavily traveled parts of campus. Students also are urged not to walk alone at night.

Coat and tie or dresses are becoming less *de rigueur* for attendance at Cavaliers football games in NCAA Division I. Students also gladly stick around campus to watch basketball, soccer, and lacrosse games, the most popular of the 12 men's and 13 women's varsity sports fielded, or to take part for themselves in the extensive intramural sports, 18 each for men and women. Cavaliers fans generally have a lot to cheer about. Over the past 16 years, Virginia has won 5 national championships in men's soccer, 2 in women's lacrosse, and 1 in men's lacrosse. The football team has made more than a dozen bowl appearances in the last 18 years; men's and women's basketball have each made at least 20 postseason appearances over the last 26 seasons.

For a natural escape, students drive to scenic Skyline drive in the Blue Ridge Mountains. Another example of Mr. Jefferson's neoclassical design can of course be studied at his home in nearby Monticello, just outside town. Students seem fairly happy with what Charlottesville (pop. 40,000) has to offer, although Washington, D.C. has all that and more just 2½ hours away.

Cost cutters: Fifty-three percent of UVA freshmen and 43% of continuing students received financial aid in the 2005–2006 school year; for about 23% of all undergraduates, aid was based on need. The average freshman award totaled $10,299 although no breakdown was provided for the portion that was scholarships or grants, need-based or not, or self-help aid such as loans and jobs. Average debt of a 2005 graduate was $13,919 for an in-state student and $17,869 for a nonresident. In an effort to help reduce student debt, beginning with fall 2005 freshmen, for any student who qualifies for any form of need-based financial aid, the university will provide additional grants so that the individual will not have to take out loans that total more than 25% of the amount that it costs an in-state student to attend the University of Virginia for 4 years. Since fall 2004, the university has given grants in place of all loans that are offered to students whose families earn at or below 150% of the federal poverty line. Some hefty merit awards are offered as well, among them the Jefferson Scholars program that pays a full 4 years' tuition for superior students regardless of financial need.

Rate of return: Once students enter UVA's grounds, they generally like what they see: 97% of entering freshmen return for the sophomore year. After 4 years, a remarkable 83% have earned diplomas; after 5 years, the figure rises to 92%. The graduation rate of African-American students, at 87%, was recently cited by the *Journal of Black Issues in Higher Education* for being 20 percentage points higher than at any other state university in the nation and higher than at 5 of the 8 Ivy League universities.

Payoff: The most popular majors for the class of 2005 were economics at 10%, commerce at 10%, and psychology at 9%. A large number of former Wahoos go on to pursue advanced degrees in finance, banking, law, business, and medicine. In fact, as a fourth-year student notes, "Many people love this place so much that they become doublehoos," meaning they stay right on campus for their graduate education. Forty-five UVA graduates have been named Rhodes Scholars, the highest number for state universities nationwide. For those seeking employment, more than 500 companies and other organizations recruited on campus during a recent school year.

Bottom line: The UVA experience works best for students who are high academic achievers but also want to take advantage of the very energetic social life the university offers. Those seeking a well-rounded education who are willing to make opportunities happen without prodding from faculty also will perform well. But, warns a northerner, "you have to like red brick and white columns because every building on the 'grounds' has 'em."

Virginia Polytechnic Institute and State University

Blacksburg, Virginia 24061

Setting: Rural
Control: Public
Undergraduate enrollment: 12,384 men, 8701 women
Graduate enrollment: 2321 men, 1411 women
Student/faculty ratio: 17:1
Freshman profile: 5% scored over 700 on SAT I verbal; 41% scored 600–700; 46% 500–599; 8% below 500. 11% scored over 700 on SAT I math; 50% scored 600–700; 36% 500–599; 3% below 500. 14% scored above 28 on the ACT; 16% scored 27–28; 33% 24–26; 28% 21–23; 9% below 21. 36% graduated in top tenth of high school class; 68% in upper fifth.
Faculty profile: 87% Ph.D.'s

Tuition and fees: $6378 in-state, $17,837 out-of-state
Room and board: $4456
Freshman financial aid: 65%; average scholarship or grant: NA
Campus jobs: 43%; average earnings: $1500/year
Application deadline: Early decision: Nov. 1; regular: Jan. 15
Financial aid deadline: Mar. 11
Admissions information: (540) 231-6267
  e-mail: vtadmiss@vt.edu
  web site: www.vt.edu

At Virginia Polytechnic Institute and State University, commonly known as Virginia Tech, there's nothing hokey about being a "Hokie," that is, a member of the school's athletic team, except maybe the designation itself, which was coined by a student in the class of 1896 to foster school spirit. (The official mascot is the gobbler.) In fact, nothing could be less contrived than the job offers graduates of this highly technical public university receive every year, and come to expect. Notes a sophomore: "I came because of the school's excellent reputation in engineering, relatively low tuition, diverse student body, and challenging curriculum. I expect my degree to bring me a high-paying job with opportunities to move up. And I don't see much problem getting accepted into higher level educational programs either." And while Virginia Tech students are prepared to work hard for their degrees, and generally do, more than a fair share of fun comes with the academic environment. Continues the sophomore: "Considering all the 'enginerds' here, it's not as geeky as I expected. Students are studious when necessary, but always willing to skip classes on a beautiful day."

Student body: Seventy-two percent of Virginia Tech's students come from in-state; most of the rest are also from the Middle Atlantic region, although all but 1 state is represented. Asian-Americans at 7% and African-Americans at 5% constitute the largest minority groups on campus, followed by Hispanics at 2%. Foreign nationals from 69 countries make up another 2%. Although the university was primarily a male military college until the mid-60s, in recent years about 40% of the undergraduates have been women, and just 3% of the entire student body has been enrolled in the Corps of Cadets. Because the student body is so large and so diverse, freshmen who apply themselves generally have little problem finding niches into which to fit. Many students are intelligent and creative, but not driven; conservative; and apathetic concerning issues outside their personal concerns. "This place really should be called Virginia Apathe-Tech," says an electrical engineering major. "But that indifference makes this a good place for someone who is energetic and active to rise quickly because no one else is acting." Engineering, business, and architecture tend to attract the largest number of serious workers. Notes a major in international studies: "If you want intense, competitive classes they are available, but so are the easier classes."

Academics: Virginia Tech, founded as the state's land grant college in 1872, offers degrees through the doctorate. Undergraduate majors are offered in 60 disciplines through 7 academic colleges. A college of veterinary medicine and a graduate school offer advanced degrees only. The school year is divided into 2 semesters. In their first year, freshmen will encounter the full range of class sizes: Psychology of Learning lectures may reach 500 students, while English courses are held down to 25. At higher levels, a few specialized courses, such as Feminist Theory and Readings in Latin Literature, may enroll only 4, but juniors and seniors usually can count on classes of 30–150 members, depending on the major and the course. Students complain that recent budget cuts across the state have raised class sizes for all 4 years.

Virginia Tech's core curriculum consists of courses in 7 areas: writing and discourse; ideas, cultural traditions, and values; society and human behavior; scientific reasoning and discovery; quantitative and symbolic reasoning; creativity and aesthetic experience, and critical issues in a global context. Some colleges require "depth studies" in certain of these areas, which means students must choose one of several course combinations outlined.

The 2237-member faculty includes 267 members who are part-time; 238 of them teach undergraduates. Among the 1970 full-time members 1265 do. Twenty-nine percent of the total are women. One faculty member has won a Nobel Prize. Twelve percent of introductory courses are taught by graduate students, some more ready to teach than others. While students respect their professors' intelligence and commitment to teaching as well as to research, they find too many faculty members less than exciting. Notes a liberal arts major: "Most lecture, ask for questions (of which there are very few), and leave. Blah." There are, however, notable exceptions, among them a leading Civil War historian and the superb faculties in the more technical disciplines. Students also credit faculty members with maintaining their enthusiasm for teaching as class sizes have increased. Notes a senior: "There are times when you'll be in a class with 20 people; there are other times you'll be with 500. But the faculty are always there for their students, personally or through TA's. With E-mail, it is even easier to ask questions, so you're always in touch."

Engineering, architecture, agriculture, chemistry, biology, business, and political science are among Virginia Tech's strongest suits. Engineering, particularly aerospace and electrical engineering, is the university's "jewel," with excellent lab facilities, millions in research contracts annually, and some of the brightest freshmen in the nation; however, majors say the engineering college could use more room. Many freshmen who begin as prospective engineering majors find the course load too rigorous and leave for less strenuous disciplines. An excellent 5-year architecture program offers all students the chance to complete a 1-semester internship or experience abroad, usually in their fourth year. Notes a major: "Architecture has incredibly high personal attention and contact with professors, if you want it. Students and faculty work together like colleagues." The program in agriculture benefits from an extensive farm and good lab equipment. The computer science and business majors, among them business information technology and accounting and information systems, incorporate technology into their everyday programs and offer extensive co-op and internship opportunities.

In the shadow of the larger, better funded giants, such smaller departments as physics, music, and theatre arts, and interdisciplinary programs such as religious studies have lacked the necessary dollars, students say, that are needed to make them stronger. Psychology relies too heavily on using teaching assistants in the classroom. Communication, while a solid major, would be enhanced with additional funding and space.

Facilities: Tech's libraries are good-sized, holding 2.2 million volumes, 6.3 million microforms (the fourth largest collection in the country), and 31,365 current serials and journals. The collection is spread among the main Carol M. Newman Library and 3 local branches in art and architecture, geology, and veterinary medicine. Newman is open around the clock during exams. It's big enough to offer space for just about every study—and nonstudy—mood, and generally quiet enough to get work accomplished. Extensive databases and on-line catalog are available and can be accessed from student rooms.

Where are computers at Virginia Tech? Everywhere, say students, and their numbers have done nothing but grow over the years. Since fall 1998, all freshmen have been required to have their own personal computers, the type varying by major. High-speed Ethernet connections are available in all residence halls, laboratories, and lecture rooms as well as wireless access in all academic buildings. There also are 912 university-owned workstations available for general student use.

Special programs: University faculty members regularly conduct summer courses in the United Kingdom, Spain, and Switzerland. Direct student exchanges with some 70 universities in 36 different countries also are available for an academic year. The university's Center for European Studies and Architecture, in Switzerland, provides a broad offering of core courses plus specialized programs in architecture and in business. A Washington semester is another option, and independent study, undergraduate research, special small-group study, and field study can be arranged at the Blacksburg campus. Students also may cross-register with member schools in the Architecture Consortium: Miami University in Ohio, Oxford Polytechnic Institute, Cal Tech, and Florida A&M.

Campus life: Forty-one percent of the undergraduates, including all freshmen, reside on the 2600-acre campus which contains an airport, a farm, experimental plots, and an orchard, all stretched over a scenic plain between the Blue Ridge and Allegheny mountains. "A world of its own," exclaims a state resident. Most of the nonresidents commute from apartments within a mile or two of the school. Thirteen percent of the men belong to 34 national fraternities, and 15% of the women pledge to 16 national sororities (including several historically black Greek groups). Some hold parties, sometimes beginning as early as Thursday evenings, most of which are closed to outsiders. Independents, however, have little trouble arranging or attending parties on their own, so that a visitor to the rural Blacksburg campus is likely to hear live bands with great music almost any day of the week. Several of the service organizations, among the 600 or so groups available, have won national awards for the hours of volunteer work provided annually. The German Club, considered by many to be the oldest fraternal organization on campus, includes a majority of the male leaders on campus and sponsors numerous popular activities, among them the Midwinter's Dance. A 36-member police force, as well as student patrols and bright lighting, helps to keep the environment fairly crime-free, though vandalism, often alcohol-related, is a problem.

The Corps of Cadets, a holdover from the 92 years when Virginia Tech was known primarily as a military college, still attracts a small percentage of highly disciplined men and women who live in designated dormitories and are readily identifiable by their distinctive uniforms. However, interest in the cadets has been growing, especially since the addition in fall 1995 of a concentration in leadership available only to cadets. While cadets participate in all regular academic, athletic, social, and cultural programs, membership in the cadet regimental band, the Highty-Tighties, remains restricted to the corps.

The drill field serves as the center for most outdoor sports and activities. Nineteen intramural sports, including more than 400 basketball teams in a recent year, are available to men and women. Only a quarter of the men and 10% of the women take part. Student clubs in weight lifting, skiing (both water and snow), and spelunking are popular, as is golf on the campus course and skating on the campus pond. NCAA Division I football, 1 of 11 men's and 10 women's sports available, draws huge crowds; the pregame tailgate parties for football are especially well attended and are outdone only by the all-day parties that start sprouting with the first spring flowers.

Mountain Lake, where the movie *Dirty Dancing* was filmed, and the Cascades are popular student retreats when the weather is warm; tubing at New River Junction and hiking in the Cascades also are great. Roanoke (pop. 100,000), 40 miles northeast, is the closest city to Blacksburg (pop. 38,000), which, according to students, is itself "a pretty partying place."

Cost cutters: In a recent school year, financial aid went to 65% of the freshmen and to 63% of all other undergraduates. For 49% of the first-year students and virtually all of the rest with aid, the assistance was need-based. The average freshman award in a recent year totaled $6625, though no breakdown is available to show the portion that was scholarships or grants and jobs or loans. The average college debt of recent graduates was $15,049. Alumni Presidential Scholarships recently paid $8000 to first-year students with superior academic records. A number of departmental, individual college, and athletic awards are available. A budget plan allows students to spread tuition and fee payments over a series of months without interest charges. Cooperative education programs are offered in 48 majors.

Rate of return: Eighty-eight percent of the freshmen return for the sophomore year. Forty-four percent graduate in 4 years, 70% within 5 years, and 74% within 6.

Payoff: The most popular majors for 2005 graduates were biology at almost 6% and psychology and finance at about 5% each. The vast majority of students find jobs within 6 months of graduation, many with the more than 250 companies and other organizations that recruited on campus in a recent school year. Major employers in recent years have included American Management Services, the U.S. Navy, Army, and Air Force, Lockheed Martin, Allied Signal Aerospace, KPMG Peat Marwick, as well as Virginia Tech itself. A large number also opt for self-employment. Almost 15% generally go directly on to graduate or professional schools.

Bottom line: Advises an architecture major: "Tech is big—and acts big—but if you are self-motivated and involved, you will get all the benefits of a big school (diversity, facilities, etc.) without becoming lost in the crowd." However, classmates warn that those who are easily seduced by the party life may find too many opportunities to socialize rather than study.

Washington and Lee University

Lexington, Virginia 24450

Setting: Small town
Control: Private
Undergraduate enrollment: 889 men, 877 women
Graduate enrollment: 237 men, 170 women
Student/faculty ratio: 10:1
Freshman profile: 40% scored over 700 on SAT I verbal; 56% scored 600–700; 4% 500–599; 0% below 500. 39% scored over 700 on SAT I math; 58% scored 600–700; 3% 500–599; 0% below 500. 85% scored above 28 on the ACT; 12% scored 27–28; 0% 24–26; 2% below 24. 76% graduated in top tenth of high school class; 91% in upper fifth.

Faculty profile: 94% Ph.D.'s
Tuition and fees: $28,655
Room and board: $7225
Freshman financial aid: 36%; average scholarship or grant: $19,728 need-based; $12,091 non-need-based
Campus jobs: NA; average earnings: NA
Application deadline: Early decision: Nov. 15; regular: Jan. 15
Financial aid deadline: Feb.1
Admissions information: (540) 458-8710
e-mail: admissions@wlu.edu
web site: www.wlu.edu

East Coast travelers commonly encounter dozens of inns and taverns boasting that "George Washington slept here." But students at Washington and Lee University in Lexington, Virginia, can make a claim few undergraduates at other colleges can top: George Washington helped pay for their education. In 1796, George Washington gave Liberty Hall Academy, founded in 1749, an endowment gift valued at $50,000, in its day the largest donation ever made to a private educational institution in America. That gift, which has remained part of the former academy's endowment, has produced income that helps to make what is now Washington and Lee University one of the most affordable selective colleges in the country.

The school's other founding father, General Robert E. Lee, was no less generous. Lee served as W&L's president from the end of the Civil War until his death in 1870 and laid the groundwork for the curriculum design the university follows today. Its undergraduate business school, graduate law school, and journalism and science courses all began with Lee and help to render Washington's share in the enterprise, the tuition, well worth paying.

Student body: Just 15% of Washington and Lee's students come from the Old Dominion; another third are also from the South. In all, 49 states and 36 foreign countries are represented. Forty percent of the students graduated from private or parochial schools. Forty-five members of the fall 2005 freshmen class were valedictorians or salutatorians; 30 were first-generation college students. Minority enrollment remains low; 4% of the undergraduates are African-American, 3% Asian-American, and 1% Hispanic. Four percent are foreign nationals. Says an easterner: "This school needs to work on diversity a litttle—no, a lot." However, minority students have risen to positions of leadership on the largely WASP campus. Although Washington and Lee remained all-male until the fall of 1985, women already comprise 50% of the student body and have become increasingly integrated into campus life. Says a female senior: "The men now accept the women better socially and feel challenged by them academically." As a whole, students are friendly and greet all passers-by, in keeping with the W&L "speaking tradition" established by Robert E. Lee; they generally are conservative in their dress and their social and political views. " 'Country Club' conservatives," remarks a southerner, "Very preppy, very proper." Adds an economics major: "Few of us are concerned about real issues, but we are aware and know we soon will be called upon to act." Most come to W&L with a determination to succeed in college in order to do well after graduation. However, there are few outward signs of competition, which is tempered both by students' love of a good time and by the highly valued honor system, also a legacy of General Lee, which says no student shall lie, cheat, steal, or act dishonestly. Any student found guilty of violating the honor system must withdraw permanently from the university. In a recent year, 8 students were forced to leave because of honor system violations, but, says a sophomore, "the system also allowed hundreds to take unproctored, self-timed, take-home exams. Not everyone agrees with the way things work here, but things still work." Students are known for being extremely social and ready to party once the week's classes are done. Remarks a junior: "When the weekends come, we act like we are on vacation and have no care in the world. But Sunday through Thursday, everyone is so businesslike it is hard to believe we are the same people you saw Friday and Saturday."

Academics: Washington and Lee confers bachelor's degrees in 40 majors, including 1 for independent work in a student-designed major, plus the juris doctor degree. Exceptional W&L undergraduates may participate in a 3-3 program with the law school under which students receive a B.A. or B.S. degree in combination with first-year law studies. The academic year is made up of two 12-week terms, followed by a 6-week spring term that allows opportunities for special coursework, internships and study abroad in places like England, the Galápagos Islands, Germany, Greece, and Japan.

Classes in the first 2 years generally have 20–35 participants, although an introductory biology class can enroll nearly 60. A fourth of all class sections have fewer than 10 participants; just 1% have more than 40; none more than 50.

Distribution requirements that every student must fulfill draw 37 credits of coursework from four areas: literature; fine arts, history, philosophy and religion; science and mathematics; and social sciences. Second-year foreign language and English composition proficiencies are also mandated. Students usually complete most distribution requirements by the end of the sophomore year, although many, says a philosophy major, "even go beyond the required classes because they have piqued an interest that the student would never have experienced or known about otherwise."

All but 9 of the 215 full-time faculty members teach undergraduates, as do both of the 2 part-timers. Thirty percent are women. Three faculty members have won Pulitzer Prizes. Students use such descriptive adjectives as *phenomenal, top notch,* and *a perfect 10,* "teachers as well as scholars," raves a senior. Adds a classmate: "The professors expect us to challenge ourselves in our thinking, and they certainly help. Most of the faculty members I have had here have been amiable and knowledgeable men and women of good character, as General Lee was." Most students can count on having shared dinners, racquetball games, movies, plays, and/or trips with a good number of these teacher-scholars before they graduate.

Two of W&L's strongest majors are economics and business administration, offered in The Williams School of Commerce, Economics, and Politics, where faculty and facilities are both first-rate and attract some of the brightest students on campus. A board of advisors composed of CEO's and other leaders in the business world helps to keep the school's academic offerings in touch with the demands of the workplace. History, befitting the university's roots, has a highly skilled faculty with a popular following. English, journalism, politics, and geology also are rated as "outstanding" and are only enhanced by extensive program opportunities provided by the school's proximity to Washington, D.C. The journalism program in particular offers both one of the oldest journalism ethics programs in the nation and some of the most up-to-date digital media technology in recently renovated Reid Hall. The philosophy faculty reflect every interest "from Plato to cognitive science," says a major, "and are very willing to work out special classes for special interests." Though the sciences have been smaller departments, biology and chemistry consistently send many students on to medical school. The recently constructed $25 million science center, housing a library, instrumentation rooms, an animal care facility, and computer laboratories as well as additional teaching and research space has only enhanced these already impressive disciplines.

According to students, the highly intelligent math faculty has trouble sometimes bringing material down to students' level. Some undergraduates find the religion department filled with too many opinionated professors, which can make objective learning more difficult. Music and art students who have eagerly awaited the same upgrade of facilities that the sciences received are waiting no more with the scheduled fall 2006 opening of the new John and Anne Wilson Art and Music Center. Engineering seems sometimes lost among the more visible liberal arts offerings.

Facilities: James G. Leyburn Library, built in 1979, is "excellent all around" and designed to hold a half-million volumes. The university as a whole currently has 907,000 volumes, as well as access to 8027 periodicals divided between Leyburn Library and the Law School library, which many find a more silent place to study than Leyburn. The new science library houses collections in 7 science-related fields. There also is a reading room in the Commerce building. Each facility is open around the clock when classes are in session. Computerized research assistance is available including an on-line information system named Annie, after a longtime librarian. Just about every student who wants a reserved study carrel can have one. Civil War buffs find the rare books collection particularly inviting. Observes a sophomore: "Our library has impressive resources so we never have to venture to the University of Virginia's libraries."

There are about 320 computers in 12 locations throughout academic buildings and in Leyburn Library, nearly all open around the clock. All units are networked, and many students bring their own computers. The university strongly recommends that students have personal computers, preferably a Dell laptop. Wireless connections are available around campus.

Special programs: A number of recently added programs is helping to expand undergraduates' world view. The Shepherd Program for the Interdisciplinary Study of Poverty, begun in 1997, involves students in courses as well as living and working experiences as a way to expand participants' understanding of the complex issues related to domestic and international poverty. Students serve in summer internships across North and South America with other undergraduates from Berea, Spelman, and Morehouse colleges. A new Global Stewardship Program focuses on the issues and responsibilities of world citizenship. The program features an expanded international curriculum on campus and more foreign professors as well as wider opportunities for study abroad. Among other opportunities, students wishing to study abroad for a longer period than the 6-week spring term can participate in a full-year exchange with Chung Chi College of the Chinese University of Hong Kong, Kansai and Rikkyo universities in Japan, or University College of Oxford University, paying the same tuition, room, and board charges as at Washington and Lee, plus travel costs. W&L students also can spend the junior year at any of 7 other Virginia colleges or attend Bates College in Lewiston, Maine, or Spelman or Morehouse colleges in Georgia. Cooperative 3-2 degree programs are available in engineering with Renssalaer Polytechnic, Washington University, and Columbia.

Campus life: Sixty-one percent of W&L students reside on the historic grounds, which consist of a 55-acre main campus, 40 acres of playing fields, and 210 acres of unimproved lands. Several of the historic structures, including the President's house and the chapel where General Lee is buried, were built to Lee's specifications. All first-year students as well as sophomores are required to live on campus. Sixty percent of the freshman dorm rooms are singles. Says a Californian: "The ghosts of both Washington and Lee give the campus a history and character that is ultimately unique." To mark the 125th anniversary of the death of General Lee on October 12, 1870, the campus colonnade was draped in black ribbon, further enhancing the aura. Many upperclassmen live either in fraternities or in private homes or apartments. Fraternities *are* the social life at W&L; 83% of the men are members of 14 national fraternities, although independents generally are welcome at any of the numerous Greek parties. A sorority system established in 1989 offers 6 national chapters, to which 77% of the women pledge. Students entering in fall 2003 were the first to enjoy the newest white-columned building on campus, the John W. Elrod University Commons complete with a movie theater, lounges, dining facilities, and other amenities to further enhance student life.

Student autonomy is a trademark of Washington and Lee. A committee composed of student class officers has jurisdiction in cases of alleged student misconduct on the W&L campus, in Rockbridge County, and on other campuses. Except for regulations pertaining to health and safety, dormitory residents make their own house rules. Because of the student-run honor system, undergraduates leave out books, calculators, and other items without fear of their being stolen. Says a sophomore: "I remember seeing a $10 bill tacked to a bulletin board; it stayed there for over a week." Security measures such as a card-swipe system in the freshman dorms to keep out non-students have recently been instituted as extra precautions.

Sports may take a back seat to fraternity events at W&L, but they are still quite popular. About a fourth of the men and a fifth of the women participate in NCAA Division III intercollegiate sports (12 for men and 11 for women). Intramural sports, 15 for men and 7 for women, attracted more than 80% of the men and 45% of the women in a recent year. There also are 10 men's and 5 women's club sports. Fall football—the Generals, naturally—and men's and women's lacrosse in the spring draw the biggest crowds, though football tends to involve more socializing than game-watching.

Those needing escape from the historic campus can drive to House Mountain and enjoy the gorgeous scenery of the Shenandoah Valley, or to Goshen Pass to swim in the Maury River and relax in the sunshine. The Blue Ridge Parkway is minutes away. Charlottesville, home of the University of Virginia, can be reached in just over an hour. The town of Lexington itself has 7300 residents.

Cost cutters: In 2005–2006, financial aid of all sorts went to 36% of the freshmen; need-based assistance was provided to 27%. Thirty-one percent of the continuing students received some type of aid, 24% received aid that was need-based. The average freshman award included a $19,728 need-based scholarship or grant, and $3874 in need-based self-help aid such as loans and job earnings. Other non-need-based awards and scholarships averaged $12,091. The most prestigious awards, the George Washington Honor Scholarships, range in value from $2000 to full tuition, room, and board and recognize a select group of entering freshmen who are chosen, regardless of financial need, based upon character, academic record, and particular promise of leadership. An academic scholarship program in conjunction with the Americorps program provides assistance to designated Bonner Scholars who perform at least 900 hours of community service during their first 2 years at Washington and Lee. The average 2005 graduate left W&L with $17,374 in college debt from need-based loans.

Rate of return: Ninety-five percent of the freshmen who enter W&L return for the sophomore year. Eighty-four percent graduate in 4 years; 87% within 6 years.

Payoff: Business administration at 11%, economics at 10%, and politics at 9% were the most popular majors for 2005 graduates. Nearly a fourth of a recent class went on immediately to professional or graduate schools.

An estimated 75% of all graduates pursue advanced degrees within 5 years of commencement. Two-thirds opt to take jobs immediately after earning their bachelor's degrees, most in such fields as banking, accounting, investment, management, and sales; journalism and education also are popular. Graduates are aided by an enthusiastic network of alumni who are more than willing to hire another W&L grad. In a recent survey by Standard & Poor's, W&L ranked 8th in terms of the percentage of alumni who serve as presidents, vice-presidents, or board members of the most prestigious corporations.

Bottom line: Washington and Lee is a college that combines a challenging liberal arts curriculum with a spirited social life, all wrapped in a mantle of honor and tradition handed down from its early president, General Robert E. Lee. Says a recent graduate: "The size, environment, and 'work hard, play hard' ethic are magical!"

Washington

The Evergreen State College

Olympia, Washington 98505

Setting: Small city
Control: Public
Undergraduate enrollment: 1663 men, 1992 women
Graduate enrollment: 55 men, 89 women
Student/faculty ratio: 23:1
Freshman profile: 11% scored over 700 on SAT I verbal; 42% scored 600–700; 32% 500–599; 15% below 500. 2% scored over 700 on SAT I math; 24% scored 600–700; 42% 500–599; 32% below 500. 14% scored above 28 on the ACT; 14% scored 27–28; 27% 24–26; 24% 21–23; 21% below 21. 16% graduated in top fifth of high school class; 47% in upper two-fifths.

Faculty profile: 73% Ph.D.'s
Tuition and fees: $4337 in-state, $14,747 out-of-state
Room and board: $6924
Freshman financial aid: 50%; average scholarship or grant: $4635
Campus jobs: 23%; average earnings: $2652/year
Application deadline: Mar. 1 (Priority: Feb. 15)
Financial aid deadline: Mar. 15
Admissions information: (360) 867-6170
  e-mail: admissions@evergreen.edu
  web site: www.evergreen.edu

Imagine a school with no letter grades, just personal evaluations that faculty and students complete about each other, and students do about themselves, and then spend finals week discussing. Imagine a school without traditional majors or departments, but rather a series of team-taught interdisciplinary courses, centered on a problem or theme, that students take for a full year. The watchword in these classroom discussions: question authority. Imagine a campus with neither fraternities nor sororities, where one of the biggest clubs is WashPIRG (Washington Public Interest Research Group), the biggest sporting event is soccer, recently overtaking boomeranging in popularity, and the campus mascot is the geoduck (pronounced gooey-duck), an oversize clam that serves as a symbol of the unofficial campus motto *Omnia Extares,* loosely translated as "Let it all hang out!"

You are not imagining some private, experimental college from the '60s. Just set your compass to points northwest, and discover a very public member of the Washington state university system, The Evergreen State College. Notes a westerner: "Evergreen is an institution that prizes intellectual and educational freedom. Because there is no official version of the 'truth,' there are many opportunities for students to 'slide by'; however, few choose to do this. Evergreen is an island of innovation among the trees of the Pacific Northwest."

Student body: Seventy-nine percent of the Greeners are from Washington State; many of the out-of-staters also come from the Northwest as well as the Midwest, but students hail from all 50 states and U.S. territories. People of color, referred to by Greeners as "First Peoples," constitute 17% of the undergraduate enrollment. Asian-Americans, Hispanics, and American Indians each comprise 4% of the student body and African-Americans constitute 5%. Professors of color in 2005 made up 25% of the full-time faculty. Less than 1% of the undergraduates are foreign nationals from 14 countries. Over the last couple of years, 15% of the total enrollment has been aged 25–29; 10%, 30–39; and 13% over 40, which makes for some lively class discussions. Greeners see themselves as liberal, concerned, community-oriented, creative risk takers who function best in a collaborative rather than a competitive atmosphere. Says a senior: "Evergreen students find what motivates them and use their passions to fuel their education." Although a student must be self-motivated and self-directed to survive academically, there is little overt competition, given the emphasis on co-operative learning and individual evaluation rather than letter grades. For this reason students who need to be at the head of the pack or must have structure to perform to their optimum abilities have trouble adjusting to "Evergreen time," which, say students, is about 7 minutes behind everywhere else.

Academics: Evergreen, which turned 35 in 2006, confers the Bachelor of Arts, of Science, and of Arts and Science. All degrees are in liberal arts and sciences rather than in separate subject areas. The school also awards master's degrees in environmental studies, public administration, and teaching. The academic year is divided into quarters, with full-time students earning at least 12 but no more than 20 credits per quarter. Class size can range from 1 to 100 students. However, because several courses are team-taught, and often subdivided, the maximum student/faculty ratio in any class is 21:1.

Evergreen State operates under the assumption that every student knows best what subjects and styles of learning he or she needs in college. Thus, there are no required courses or subjects that must be covered. However, the college recently adopted "Expectations of an Evergreen Graduate," that were set by the faculty as a way to aid both students and faculty in planning an appropriate course of study. By the end of their 4 or 5 years on campus, Evergreen graduates are expected to be able to: articulate and assume responsibility for their own work; participate collaboratively and responsibly in a diverse society; communicate creatively and effectively; demonstrate integrative, independent, and critical thinking; apply qualitative, quantitative, and creative modes of inquiry appropriately to practical and theoretical problems across disciplines; and as a culmination of their education, demonstrate depth, breadth, and synthesis of learning and the ability to reflect on the personal and social significance of that learning. Even then, how students choose to get to these ends may still rely on an individual's discipline, motivation, and willingness to take diverse classes, even ones he or she doesn't particularly like. Says a senior: "For those not committed to getting a liberal arts education, it's not so great. People can take 4 years of art and graduate, and I don't like the idea of that." Most Greeners not earning a Bachelor of Science degree tend to graduate without having taken any math.

Interdisciplinary, team-taught "coordinated studies" are the dominant mode of instruction; students are led by 2–4 faculty members in a set of integrated courses centered around a common theme. Undergraduates and professors average 16 hours a week of contact time in the classroom or in workshops. Large group meetings generally occur at least twice a week and then break into smaller discussion groups of 15–25 people. These smaller groups may meet as frequently as 4 times a week. The faculty leader and students read the same materials and write and share brief reports.

In a recent coordinated studies program entitled "Love and Work," 66 students and 3 faculty members discussed the roles that love and work play in defining people's lives, examining the personal histories and professional contributions of people from various cultures and time periods. The 48-credit, year-long course emphasized the development of such skills as reading, writing, perceiving, listening, speaking, and contemplation, and awarded academic credit in literature, art, music, gender studies, cross-cultural studies, and writing. Although many coordinated studies programs are focused on specific subject areas, many first-year students are encouraged to take coordinated core courses such as Love and Work, which introduce them to the interdisciplinary approach and emphasize skills that will be used throughout their education at Evergreen. At the intermediate level, many students move into "group contracts," which operate in a similar fashion, but in smaller groups of 20–40 participants and 1–2 faculty members. Coursework is still interdisciplinary but more narrowly focused. Individual learning contracts are available for juniors and seniors who need to complete upper-division research or to cover material not contained in any of the prepared programs.

Instead of letter grades, students receive narrative evaluations from their professors and write their own evaluations of their professors and themselves. Notes a Greener hoping to attend law school: "With written evaluations instead of grades, people who don't work can't slide through the system and you're evaluated only on what you did and not in comparison to other students."

All of the 160 full-time and 64 part-time faculty members teach undergraduates, and they follow an egalitarian approach to learning; though most have doctorates (49% of all faculty are women), they prefer to be called by their first names rather than addressed as "doctor" or "professor." Says a sophomore: "They are kind and welcome conversation, academic or otherwise." The fact that professors cannot gain tenure encourages them to spend less time in research for publishing and more on designing and teaching courses. However, students caution that Greeners must investigate professors carefully before investing a year's worth of time in a particular course. Notes an easterner: "The faculty range from being incredibly knowledgeable, inspiring mentors to being flaky types. A student's entire academic experience here depends on the quality of the faculty. So much time and money can be wasted if a student is not lucky—and careful. You have to ask around before you register."

Although there are no individual subject departments as such, students feel that 3 broad offerings—Society, Politics, Behavior, and Change; Environmental Studies, and Scientific Inquiry—are particularly enhanced by the interdisciplinary approach and, in the case of the sciences, by modern equipment such as a scanning electron microscope, gas chromatograph, and mass spectrometer. Many of the core programs also win student respect for their focus on the development of strong writing, reading, and thinking skills. The program in film/video is considered outstanding as well. Says a senior studying media production: "At Evergreen, starting my first year, I would have full access to media equipment and all the facilities, including everything from darkrooms, video-editing suites, and recording studios to checking out microphones and video cameras."

Some students wish more courses were available in the Expressive Arts, especially music, though, the building in which the program is housed draws rave reviews for its excellent lighting. Courses in specific career-oriented fields such as communications are practically nonexistent, and students must design their own curricula. Courses in business and management have been folded into the area of Society, Politics, Behavior, and Change, concentrating on such issues as organizational management and behavior, entrepreneurship, and ethics in an approach probably not recognizable to most traditional business majors.

Facilities: Online is the way to go at Daniel Evans Library, which contains just over 471,000 volumes and 2731 periodicals. Although students find it a comfortable place to study, they complain that the holdings aren't always adequate. "Lots of feminist literature but few conventional classics," says a senior, though students say most professors require a lot of online research. The much-used online catalog shows the holdings of other Washington facilities, including the State Capital Library. Also offered on loan are 4500 items of media equipment, ranging from cameras and projectors to tape recorders and video/audio equipment. The helpful staff earns 5 stars as well.

Twelve computer labs and classrooms are open to students. All of the classrooms used for undergraduate instruction allow for wire connectivity between laptops and the Internet. In 15% of the classrooms, wireless connectivity is possible. Network access also is available in dorm rooms. The main computer center is open 18 hours a day. "The computer center usually is full," observes a senior, "especially during evaluation week because the final form is online at the center."

Special programs: Students participate in study-abroad programs in 25 countries worldwide through Evergreen academic offerings, internships, and individual contracts as well as through programs with partner institutions. Internships are available in all fields. The Center for Community Based Learning and Action established in 2003 links students and faculty with organizations working on a wide range of community issues. Students who commit to 1 of 3 terms of service are eligible for Education Awards that range in value from $1000 to a 300-hour term to $2362 to a 900-hour term.

Campus life: Seventy-nine percent of the Greeners live off campus, but those, including many first-year students who make Evergreen their home, rave about the student apartments, mostly with private bedrooms and full kitchens. Although the college has no fraternities or sororities, parties and potlucks are fairly regular events. In fact, much of the weekend social programming, if such a thing exists, depends upon the weather. Whenever the sun shines in this predominantly rainy climate, students are happy to entertain themselves outdoors, playing hackysack or listening to music. When the weather is inclement, the Housing Community Center is a favorite hangout. Groups come and go in tune with student interests; a recent list ranged from Evergreen Students for Christ to the Union of Student Workers. On Monday and Wednesday afternoons, faculty, students, and staff meet for governance meetings to discuss administration of the college; undergraduates regularly are assigned to DTFs (Disappearing Task Forces), designed to tackle and, hopefully, solve specific problems and then go out of business. Students say that crime is rare, though bothersome whenever it happens, most commonly minor theft; emergency telephones and extra lighting keep it in check. For the most part, however, students look out for one another and their belongings. Says a Greener: "I even had trouble giving away some old graduate school catalogs because people kept seeing the stamp of the Evergreen department and returning them."

Evergreen offers 5 varsity sports that are affiliated with the NAIA: soccer, basketball, cross-country, track and field, and women's volleyball. There are 10 intramural sports for each gender, though students don't just rely on organized activities for their recreation. The college's 1000-acre campus is located "out in the woods," with its own beach, just a short stroll through the forest down to the water. On the beach, students can dig for the campus mascot, a giant burrowing bivalve that is edible only after a great deal of pounding and cooking. Other outdoor activities such as hiking and rock climbing are more satisfying. Skiing and snowboarding are big in winter, as is kayaking in the spring.

Students seeking more urban diversion head for Seattle, the nearest big city, which is 70 minutes away; Portland, Oregon, is a 2-hour drive. Downtown Olympia (pop. 42,500), located 7 miles east, is described as "very quaint" with restaurants, cafes, and a movie theater that recently charged $1.50 for a double feature. Olympia is also the state capital.

Cost cutters: Fifty percent of recent freshmen and 58% of continuing students received financial aid; for 28% of the first-year students and 45% of the rest, aid was need-based. The average award for a first-year student with financial need included a need-based scholarship or grant averaging $4635 and need-based self-help aid such as loans and jobs averaging $3315. Non-need-based athletic scholarships for first-year students averaged $833. Scholarships of a few hundred dollars to $4100 are available to students in various academic disciplines. Waivers of in-state tuition are given to students of color, various ethnic backgrounds, and exceptional academic merit. Cooperative education programs are available in all fields. The average recent graduate left with a diploma and $13,000 in college debt.

Rate of return: Sixty-nine percent of entering freshmen return for the sophomore year, up from 55% several years ago. Administrators point to the start of the first-year core programs designed to introduce students to Evergreen's unusual approach to learning as a primary reason for the improvement in the first-year retention rate. Thirty-nine percent go on to graduate in 4 years, 49% in 5 years, and 52% in 6 years. Just 37% finished in 5 years several years ago.

Payoff: The most popular areas of interest for recent graduates were the fields of social science, education, and environmental studies. More than two-thirds of all graduates take jobs shortly after commencement. The 3 most popular areas of postgraduate employment are business and management, education and counseling, and environmental and life sciences, each of which attracted 25% of the graduates. Nearly 30% of new alumni pursue advanced degrees within the first year of receiving their diplomas. More than 50 employers and 60 graduate school representatives typically recruit Evergreen graduates. Evergreen students also participate in a job fair in which about 160 organizations are represented.

Bottom line: "Evergreen is special," says a westerner, "because the structure of the education here makes the student responsible for what is learned. We become active participants rather than passive recipients in the pursuit of knowledge. Anyone who wants to be told how to think will have a difficult time at this school."

Gonzaga University

Spokane, Washington 99258

Setting: Urban
Control: Private (Roman Catholic-Jesuit)
Undergraduate enrollment: 1866 men, 2140 women
Graduate enrollment: 489 men, 652 women
Student/faculty ratio: 14:1
Freshman profile: 10% scored over 700 on SAT I verbal; 36% scored 600–700; 45% 500–599; 9% below 500. 10% scored over 700 on SAT I math; 43% scored 600–700; 40% 500–599; 7% below 500. 29% scored above 28 on the ACT; 19% scored 27–28; 30% 24–26; 18% 21–23; 4% below 21. 28% graduated in top tenth of high school class; 65% in upper fifth.

Faculty profile: 86% Ph.D.'s
Tuition and fees: $23,518
Room and board: $6700
Freshman financial aid: 95%; average scholarship or grant: $8235 need-based; $5520 non-need-based
Campus jobs: 33%; average earnings: $1773/year
Application deadline: Feb. 1
Financial aid deadline: Feb. 1
Admissions information: (509) 323-6591, (800) 322-2584
e-mail: admissions@gonzaga.edu
web site: www.gonzaga.edu

What college student, numb from lack of sleep during finals week, can't identify with the 16th-century Italian Jesuit saint, Aloysius Gonzaga? While a seminarian in Rome, young Gonzaga took time out from his studies to care for the sick and dying in the plague-stricken city. As a result of this extracurricular activity, though students may claim it was the books, Gonzaga died of exhaustion at the age of 23, no doubt leaving a trail of incompletes in his coursework. Gonzaga was designated the patron saint of youth in 1726, and 161 years later, in plague-free Spokane, Gonzaga University was named in his honor. In the intervening years, the university has become known in its own right for its humanitarian concern for students, giving many respite through periodic retreats and an annual pilgrimage (or 15-mile hike) which attracted 120 students in a recent school year, plus a faculty of lay and religious members always eager to listen and help. "Gonzaga prides itself on its sense of community," says a senior. "For a great many people, Gonzaga becomes home."

Student body: Just under half of the undergraduates, 49%, are from Washington State with the rest from 46 other states, many in the west, plus 21 foreign countries. Thirty-five percent graduated from private or parochial schools. Foreign nationals comprise 1% of the enrollment. Not quite 5% of the students are Asian-American, 4% Hispanic, and about 1% each African-American and Native American. Catholics constitute 47% of the undergraduates. The Gonzaga community consists of students who are liberal as well as conservative, city dwellers and country folk, fervent partygoers and full-time studiers, and members who remain as apathetic as others become overinvolved. Undergraduates also are noted for being quite outgoing. "With such a small campus it's not impossible to know everyone," remarks a recent graduate, "and people actually make the attempt!"

Academics: Gonzaga offers degrees through the doctorate, including the juris doctor. Bachelor's degrees are offered in 43 majors through the College of Arts and Sciences and the schools of Business Administration, Education, Engineering, and Professional Studies. The academic year is divided into 2 semesters. The average class size for all undergraduates is 23. Introductory lecture classes for freshmen and sophomores generally range from 20 to 50 participants. Classes in the business school have an average enrollment of 33. The average engineering course has only 15.

Gonzaga's general-core requirements cover 31 of the 128 semester hours needed for graduation. The curriculum draws on blocks of courses from 5 areas: philosophy, religious studies, thought and expression, mathematics, and English literature. Many students think that some of Gonzaga's best courses are included in this basic curriculum. The core, concludes a mechanical engineering major, "has helped to broaden my perspective of the world as a place not where only money matters, but where culture also has a vital role."

In a faculty numbering 625 members, all but 44 of the 325 full-time members plus 290 of the 300 part-timers teach undergraduates. Forty-three members of the faculty and administration are Jesuit priests, some of whom live in the halls with students. Thirty-seven percent of the faculty are women. The faculty are valued for stressing individual development more than competition between peers and for being sympathetic to student problems while maintaining high standards for performance. "They make us think for ourselves and won't just let us get by with textbook knowledge," says a civil engineering major. Adds a mathematics major: "They are passionate about not only their subject matter but about teaching students. They value students' input and genuinely want students to succeed."

According to undergraduates, Gonzaga maintains the "best engineering school in the Jesuit system." A new computer-aided design and engineering facility keeps students, as early as their freshman year, involved in true-to-life projects using the latest technology, under the watchful eye of faculty who are regarded as demanding but "humane." Likewise, the high quality of the professors in philosophy and religious studies demonstrates why these disciplines have remained cornerstones of the Gonzaga curriculum. English, history, and political science also receive ratings of "outstanding," although some students think additional political science professors are needed to give students more options. History also could use more upper-division classes. Biology and chemistry, already rich in first-rate faculty, are benefiting from extensive renovations to Hughes Hall, including a new 3-story chemistry wing as well as a cell and molecular biology suite, greenhouse, and aquatics lab. In the School of Education, the program in special education wins a gold star for getting students out of the college classroom and into public and private schools, as well as group-home environments; student research also is encouraged throughout the school's programs. Accounting is the star program in the School of Business Administration, as its graduates demonstrate with consistently high scores on the CPA exam.

Though most of the business programs are excellent, the finance and economics departments in particular have been uneven in faculty quality and in the amount of preparation they give students for work after graduation. Foreign language devotees wish that more upper-division courses were offered; the university has majors in French and Spanish and minors in German and Italian. "The teachers, though dedicated, have limited resources to work with," remarks a junior. Communication arts needs additional faculty and a broader range of courses, although the service-learning practicum within the public relations program, which gives students experience in a nonprofit setting, is satisfying just as it is. Some students, however, find the quality within the communication arts program uneven, with a strong major, for example, in broadcast studies and a less satisfactory one in journalism. The department also struggles to keep pace with rapidly advancing technology in the communications field. The theater arts program also part of communication arts needs a better theater which is planned and more funding. The music facility is small and dated as well.

Facilities: For years, students had cried, rather than crooned, over Crosby Library, a gift from Bing Crosby, Class of 1924, that always seemed noisy and overcrowded. However, the opening of the $22 million Ralph E. and Helen Higgins Foley Center in fall 1992 immediately put former Crosby users and newcomers in a holiday mood. The Foley Center, which covers about 140,000 square feet and is 4 times the size of the Crosby building, greatly expanded the amount, variety, and comfort of student seating available, even providing a 24-hour study lounge. "It exudes academia," says a senior. Adds a sophomore: "Most students use the library to study because of the view and comfy couches." With the additional space, books held in storage plus new purchases have raised the size of the collection to about 259,000 volumes and 4612 periodicals, with an additional 200,000 volumes of legal materials housed at the Gonzaga Law Library. Foley contains several computerized research aids ranging from an online catalog and extensive databases in several subject areas to the ability to have documents faxed from other facilities; the computer network is accessible from all academic buildings and residence halls on campus.

Students may access the university computer system from more than 300 computers spread throughout 11 computers labs. One main lab is open around the clock. The university strongly recommends that all undergraduates have personal computers. Wireless access is available in several buildings on campus.

Special programs: Students may take courses at Whitworth College, also in Spokane. Gonzaga's own campus in Florence, Italy, enables students who are fluent in Italian as well as those who are not to spend the junior year in the student home of St. Aloysius Gonzaga, "a must," raves a senior. One- or 2-semester programs are offered in Paris and in Granada, Spain, for undergraduates fluent in modern foreign languages and in London and Watford, England, for those whose fluency stops with English. Student exchanges also are an option with universities in Mexico, China, and Japan. Gonzaga's newest program, the School for Field Studies, enables biology majors to spend a summer session or fall or winter term at sites in the British West Indies; Australia; Baja, Mexico; Costa Rica; and Kenya.

Campus life: Just over half of the students, 51%, reside on the 110-acre campus on the banks of the Spokane River. Although there are no fraternities or sororities, 30 sophomore men and 30 women are invited annually to be members of the Knights and Setons, a service organization. Off-campus houses serve as the predominant weekend party sites, but student-government sponsored events such as dances, comedians, and laser tag also draw enthusiastic crowds. Many students turn out with equal zeal for the Sunday evening Masses, as well as for spiritual "search" retreats held 4 times a year, faith and intimacy retreats, silent scripture retreats, and freshman retreats. Community service also is high on most students' "to do" list. "I'm excited about Gonzaga's emphasis on social justice," says a Montanan. "There are numerous opportunities to volunteer my time and energies." Crime, other than bike stealing, has not been a serious problem on the urban campus. Over the last few years, security measures have increased; residence halls are kept locked around the clock, lighting has been improved, bike patrols have been added, and an escort program is available for students out walking after dark. When incidents do occur, campus security sends out e-mails as a warning to students.

While baseball has its following, Bulldog basketball is *the* sport at Gonzaga, which competes in NCAA Division I. The team has appeared in the NCAA tournament for at least the last 8 seasons. Fans stand in line for hours for tickets to the games, which usually are sold out. Student supporters known as the Kennel Club see that the decibel level at games stays high and also organize pre-game and post-game parties. Seven varsity sports are available for men, and 7 for women. The crew team, open to both men and women, competes throughout the western United States and Canada. Club sports in men's and women's rugby, alpine skiing, and ice hockey also have spirited participants and fans. Eighty-five percent to 90% of the student body participate in intramural, club, and/or varsity sports.

When students want off-campus diversion, they seldom have to look further than the Spokane metropolitan area (pop. 420,000) for the usual city cultural offerings. Seattle is 270 miles west. For closer, more natural experiences, 76 mountain lakes and 5 ski areas are located within a 90-mile radius of the campus.

Cost cutters: "GU is incredibly generous in giving aid," exclaims 1 recipient, and indeed it is. Twenty-eight percent of the operating budget in a recent year was returned to students in the form of financial aid. As a result, all but 5% of the 2005 freshmen received financial help; 60% were given aid based on financial need. Ninety-three percent of continuing students also received financial assistance; 62% received need-based aid. The average financial indebtedness of a 2005 graduate was $23,140. The average freshman award for a first-year student with financial need included a need-based scholarship or grant averaging $5291 and need-based self-help aid such as loans and jobs averaging $6156. Non-need-based athletic scholarships for first-year students averaged $16,793. Other non-need-based awards and scholarships averaged $6226. Need-blind Gonzaga Merit Scholarships recently ranged in value from the Trustee, paying $7000 annually, to the Achievement, paying $1000 a year. There is an unlimited number of these merit awards, and all high school students who qualify, based largely on GPA, difficulty of curriculum, test scores, extracurricular activities, recommendations, and quality of the application essay, will receive a scholarship. Diversity Scholarships, recognizing significant ethnic and/or cultural experiences, recently paid $2500 a year; a graduate of Catholic high schools may receive 1 of 10 Joseph Cataldo Scholarships recently worth $5000 annually.

Rate of return: Ninety percent of freshmen return for the sophomore year. Sixty-three percent graduate in 4 years. Given 1 more year, 77% finish; 78% do so in 6 years.

Payoff: More than half of the 2005 graduating class earned degrees in 3 popular fields of study. Twenty-four percent majored in business and management, 23% in social studies and history, and 8% in engineering. Within 5 years, half of recent Gonzaga alumni enroll in graduate or professional schools. The vast majority of graduates, however, use their degrees to find jobs, many with large employers like

Boeing, Microsoft, Washington Water Power, IBM, and Seafirst. Most settle in the Northwest, though a number also pursue opportunities with the federal government in Washington, D.C. About 100 employers and organizations recruited on campus in a recent school year.

Bottom line: "Gonzaga fosters an atmosphere of diversity and free opinion, with the Catholic perspective in the background," observes a recent graduate. "The Jesuit liberal arts education is invaluable, and the attitude conveyed to students is one of caring and nurturing."

Pacific Lutheran University

Tacoma, Washington 98447

Setting: Suburban
Control: Private (Evangelical Lutheran)
Undergraduate enrollment: 1213 men, 2156 women
Graduate enrollment: 311 men and women
Student/faculty ratio: 15:1
Freshman profile: SAT/ACT scores: NA; class rank data: NA
Faculty profile: 90% Ph.D.'s
Tuition and fees: $22,040
Room and board: $6765

Freshman financial aid: 95%; average scholarship or grant: $6966 need-based; $5502 non-need-based
Campus jobs: 41%; average earnings: $2145/year
Application deadline: Rolling; Feb. 15 (priority)
Financial aid deadline: Jan. 31
Admissions information: (253) 535-7151;
  (800) 274-6758
  e-mail: admissions@plu.edu
  web site: www.plu.edu

When undergraduates across the country are asked to describe their classmates, many use the *a* word: *apathetic*. Although Pacific Lutheran University admittedly has its share of indifferent individuals, students are more apt to pick an *i* word: *involved*. Some of the fastest growing and most popular groups on campus are the social justice clubs that focus concern on a range of such serious world issues as global recycling. By graduation, more than a quarter of the undergraduates have taken part in varsity athletics, compared with just 4% nationally. Others find a home in numerous choral and religious groups. Says a senior: "PLU has an old-fashioned, spirited atmosphere. Frankly, it's still cool at PLU to have a lot of school spirit." And, after paying less than $29,000 in tuition, room, and board for the 2005–2006 school year, no wonder the undergrads are so full of PLU pride!

Student body: Seventy-six percent of PLU undergraduates come from Washington, and most of the rest are from the surrounding region, including Oregon, Montana, Idaho, California, and Alaska. Altogether, students in a recent year came from 38 states and 24 foreign countries. All but 3% are graduates of public high schools. Minorities in a recent year constituted 11% of the student body, including 6% Asian-Americans, 2% each African-Americans and Hispanics, and 1% Native Americans. International students accounted for another 5%. Twenty-seven percent are Lutheran. Undergraduates use words like *curious, caring, open-minded, fun,* and *hard working* to describe their peers. While students find the academic climate challenging, strong encouragement and support from classmates and faculty keep the atmosphere from becoming intense. "Nonthreatening," is how one undergraduate describes it. Students value that their classmates, for the most part, are down-to-earth and people-loving. Notes a Midwesterner: "A student that is preppy, uninvolved, and close-minded will not succeed at PLU."

Academics: Pacific Lutheran, which turned 115 in 2005, awards the bachelor's degree in 36 fields of study and the master's in 5 fields. Undergraduate programs are offered in the College of Arts and Sciences and 5 schools: Arts and Communication, Business, Education, Nursing, and Physical Education. The calendar includes 2 semesters of 14 weeks each and a January term. Freshmen can expect to have classes that average between 20 and 25 participants, although the largest course, Cell Biology, can enroll more than 120. Juniors and seniors generally average 14 to a class, though many courses have fewer than 10 participants.

Students have a choice of 2 core curricula. The more traditional requires 32 credit hours, 4 each in art, music, or theater; literature; anthropology, history, or social science; economics, psychology, sociology, or social work; natural science, computer science, or mathematics; and philosophy and 8 in religious studies. The alternative International core: Integrated Studies of the Contemporary World, mandates 28 hours of interdisciplinary courses that explore a central theme. The International Core opens with 2 introductory courses in Authority and Discovery and in Liberty and Power and follows with 4 thematic courses at the 200-level and an additional 300-level course. Courses in this program stress critical thinking and writing. Students in both cores take a freshman-year program that has a writing seminar and an inquiry seminar plus additional courses in mathematical reasoning, science, writing, diversity, physical education, and a senior seminar or project.

Just over three-quarters, 242, of PLU's 312-member faculty is full-time. All but 1 or 2 members of the full-time and part-time faculty generally teach undergraduates. Forty-six percent in a recent year were women. Faculty at the university win points for their dedication to teaching over research, their desire to know and understand PLU students, and their determination to see their charges learn and succeed. The fact that many are PLU alumni enhances their love of and commitment to the university and its students. However, there have been a few older professors "who are very content being tenured," says an education major.

The schools of Business and Education earn respect for the quality of their faculties and the experiences available to students in these fields. Says an education major: "From the start, you get to be in the classroom observing and teaching." The School of Physical Education, says a recreation major, offers "amazing professors" and an excellent teacher-placement rate. In the School of Arts and Communication, music offers a diverse and rigorous program for talented students under superb faculty. Communication majors like the approach of the program, which gives students a broad base of knowledge and then enables them to specialize in such concentrations as conflict management, journalism, media performance and production, and public relations/advertising. In the College of Arts and Sciences, biology, chemistry, geosciences, economics, history, philosophy, sociology, and psychology all feature stimulating professors who encourage many of their students to pursue advanced degrees in these fields. The School of Nursing is very competitive and majors enjoy close relationships with their professors and plenty of hands-on training.

Recent cuts in PLU's engineering programs reduced its major in engineering science to a 3-2 program in which students must complete the last 2 years of coursework at another campus. The majors in computer engineering and applied physics also have been trimmed, although students can still complete the full 4 years' coursework at PLU. Women's studies and global studies are both complementary majors, which means a student must take a second major from any other discipline within the university in order to graduate with a major in either of these 2 fields.

Facilities: Students looking for a quiet place to get some work done head to Robert A.L. Mortvedt Library. On days when research is on the agenda, however, students generally go online. Mortvedt's collection of 597,000 volumes and 4732 periodicals seems sufficient in quantity but draws mixed reviews on its quality. "Some students," says an education major, "maintain that the library has whatever they need, while others complain there is nothing of substance for them to use in their papers." Most users consider the computerized catalog, Internet access, and database searches to be among Mortvedt's best features. PLU students also have direct access to the libraries of 4 neighboring colleges, including the University of Puget Sound, and may borrow materials from the University of Washington as well.

Four computer labs, 2 used for teaching and 2 open plus departmental labs, give undergraduates up to 16 hours daily access on weekdays to IBM PC and Macintosh microcomputers. Wireless access also is available on many spots around campus. Students with their own computers may connect to the Internet from their dorm rooms.

Special programs: Fifty-five different study-abroad programs are available in 28 countries. PLU sponsors its own spring semester in Trinidad and Tobago. Students may also participate in PLU featured programs in China, Tanzania, Norway, Spain, Mexico, and England. Extensive off-campus courses are conducted during the January term. A 3-2 engineering program is offered in cooperation with Washington and Columbia universities, where many of PLU's engineering science majors opt to complete their coursework.

Campus life: Half of PLU's undergraduates reside on the 126-acre campus in suburban Parkland, 7 miles south of Tacoma. Most live in coed dorms, although 1 all-women's residence hall is available. There are no fraternities or sororities, but more than 60 student organizations from Dirt People for the Earth, an environmental club, to the Knitting Club and numerous Christian Bible study or singing groups, provide a sense of community to students of varying interests. Although off-campus parties are popular, many students simply enjoy "hanging out," talking with friends in a lounge or attending a campus dance, movie, or play. A problem with vehicle break-ins prompted construction of a fenced and gated parking lot, which has cut down on auto-related problems. An escort program is well run and widely used. Students refer to PLU as the "Lutedome," a safe haven in a sometimes risky neighborhood, which requires caution off-campus.

"We are big sports fans," says a recreation major, reflected both in the heavy student involvement (recently 60% of the men, 40% of the women) in NCAA Division III competition, and in the spirited turnout for games. Lutes football is the most popular of the 10 men's and 10 women's sports, although soccer, men's basketball, softball, and baseball also are well supported. Sixty percent of all undergraduates are involved in the intramural program, 12 sports for each sex. The Ultimate Frisbee team the PLU Reign, a club sport, generally draws about 70 participants. Trips sponsored by the Outdoor Recreation Organization also are well attended.

For off-campus diversion, students can choose the urban delights of Seattle, 40 miles north, or the magnificent outdoors of the Pacific Northwest, including nearby Puget Sound, Mt. Rainier (20 miles as the crow flies), and the rest of the Cascade Range.

Cost cutters: All but 5% of the freshmen and all but 7% of the continuing students received financial aid in a recent school year. For 69% of the freshmen and 72% of the continuing students, the aid was need-based. The average freshman award for a student with need included a need-based scholarship or grant averaging $6966 and need-based self-help aid such as loans and jobs averaging $5821. Other non-need-based awards and scholarships averaged $5502. The average debt of recent graduates was $22,190. Regent's Scholarships (full tuition) and President's Scholarships (that pay $13,000 in year 1 and increase each year up to $14,500 in year 4) are awarded annually. Students who apply by Dec. 13 with a GPA of at least 3.8 and critical reading and math SATs of 1250 or an ACT of 28 or higher are invited to apply. Academic Scholarships recently paid up to $6000. Artistic Achievement Awards are available to students who stand out in forensics, drama, art, music, or dance. Payment plans also are available. A cooperative program is an option in all majors.

Rate of return: Eighty-three percent of freshmen return for their sophomore year. Though just 45% graduate in 4 years, 65% do so in 5 years, 68% in 6 years.

Payoff: Business, education, and nursing were the overwhelming choices of majors for a recent graduating class with 16%, 13%, and 7% of the seniors respectively. The vast majority of PLU alumni enter the job market soon after commencement, many accepting employment in the Northwest with such firms as Ernst & Young and Safeco. More than 50 companies and organizations recruited on campus in a recent school year. Of recent alumni, 11% went directly to graduate or professional schools. In a recent year, 23 of 25 pre-med students were accepted into medical school.

Bottom line: Observes a senior: "One who tries hard, has a positive attitude, and is very involved—that's a future Lute."

University of Puget Sound

Tacoma, Washington 98416

Setting: Suburban
Control: Independent
Undergraduate enrollment: 1069 men, 1496 women
Graduate enrollment: 37 men, 147 women
Student/faculty ratio: 11:1
Freshman profile: 19% scored over 700 on SAT I verbal; 50% scored 600–700; 27% 500–599; 4% below 500. 11% scored over 700 on SAT I math; 48% scored 600–700; 35% 500–599; 6% below 500. 32% scored above 28 on the ACT; 20% scored 27–28; 31% 24–26, 14% 21–23; 3% below 21. 38% graduated in top tenth of high school class; 59% in upper fifth.

Faculty profile: 86% Ph.D.'s
Tuition and fees: $28,460
Room and board: $7140
Freshman financial aid: 87%; average scholarship or grant: $11,000 need-based; $7649 non-need-based
Campus jobs: 39%; average earnings: $2000/year
Application deadline: Early decision: Nov. 15 and Dec. 15; regular: Feb. 1
Financial aid deadline: Feb. 1
Admissions information: (253) 879-3211; (800) 396-7191
  e-mail: admission@ups.edu
  web site: www.ups.edu

There are few better jumping-off points to the Pacific Rim countries than the shores of the Pacific Northwest. And there are few colleges better positioned from which to make the leap than the University of Puget Sound on aptly named Commencement Bay, in Tacoma, Washington. Every 3 years, the university's Pacific Rim/Asia Study-Travel program takes 20–30 students through a series of courses in various Asian countries, including the Republic of Korea, Japan, the People's Republic of China, Thailand, and India. Each student is required to develop a research project that involves bibliographic research on-site during the year in Asia. Upon return, the student presents the project for critical review by others in the group.

The program, most recently held in the 2005–2006 school year, is open to undergraduates of all academic interests and majors, although students must survive a rigorous selection process and have had adequate preparation in the university's Asian studies program before going. This far-flung program is but one of many leaps forward that UPS has successfully taken in the last decade. With SAT scores up 170 points in 10 years, a Phi Beta Kappa chapter since 1986, and a student-retention rate that has increased to 73% from 52% since 1984, this university is uniquely positioned to command attention on the mainland as well as overseas.

Student body: Thirty percent of Puget Sound's students are from Washington; 55% of the out-of-staters are from the West. Altogether, 44 states and 12 foreign countries have representatives on campus. Nine percent of the undergraduates are Asian-American; 4% Hispanic, 2% African-American and 1% Native American. Foreign nationals account for 1%. Twenty-three percent of all undergraduates attended private schools. While students recognize that the enrollment is not very diverse racially, ethnically, or financially, they say that they cover the spectrum in attitudes. "There are the job-oriented, here to get marketable degrees, which they will," says a psychology major. "Others are here for the education and steer clear of taking courses that just look good on a graduate school application or résumé." Students' political views are too liberal for some and too conservative for others and span all levels of involvement as far as issues off campus are concerned. The presence of many overachievers keeps the campus stress level high at times; nevertheless, students describe UPS as a generally friendly and outgoing place with an environment that is "challenging but not confining."

Academics: The University of Puget Sound, which turned 115 in 2003, offers undergraduate majors in more than 40 fields, and master's degrees in teaching and education and in occupational and physical therapy. A special interdisciplinary major allows students to create their own field of concentration by combining academic offerings. Courses are divided into 2 semesters, with classes averaging in size all 4 years between 20 and 30 members. Introductory science or economics lectures may have 90 in attendance; upper-level philosophy and literature seminars, just a handful of students.

Freshmen begin their time at Puget Sound with Prelude, Passages, and Perspectives, an unusual orientation program that combines a rigorous outdoor experience with an introduction to college-level reading and writing with involvement not just in the campus community but in the Tacoma-Seattle area as well. A new core curriculum that took effect in fall 2003 mandates 2 first-year seminars in Argument and Inquiry, courses through the junior year in the standard academic areas known as "Five Approaches to Knowing," and an interdisciplinary connections seminar in the junior or senior year.

All but 10 of the 235 full-time faculty teach undergraduates, as do all but 9 of the 59 part-timers. Forty-five percent of the faculty are women. Students say professors cover the spectrum of quality, from individuals who are enthusiastic about their subjects and convey that fervor in their teaching to "a few," says a sophomore, "who you wonder how and why they were hired." On the plus side, there are few pompous Ph.D.'s at Puget Sound. Says a senior: "These professors have no problem being real people with their students and don't hide behind their academic degrees." The student development office encourages students to take faculty to lunch by providing meal cards for this purpose.

Though it is hard to beat Asian studies for in-class thoroughness and out-of-the-classroom excitement, many other programs also make the list of Puget Sound's best. Students in biology and chemistry regularly use specialized equipment such as an electron microscope, as well as spectroscopy labs and a marine cold room, under the close guidance of caring professors. A new environmentally friendly science lab building, scheduled to open in fall 2006, offers excellent new facilities and equipment for programs in chemistry, biology, geology, physics, and environmental studies, and some distinctive features as well. Included among them: a Foucault pendulum in the central lobby and a floor tile pattern displaying a border of *pi* translated into binary code. Politics and government are noted for their lively classroom atmosphere and economics and international political economy for their distinguished professors "who are highly active with their students," says an economics major. English boasts a diverse faculty of poets, authors, and journalists who share their real-world experiences along with their literary insights. Some students, however, consider the quality of instruction from this eclectic blend of professors to be uneven. Music, with its excellent faculty and extensive opportunities for performance, "is almost a conservatory-style program without actually being as overwhelmingly intense as a conservatory," says a major.

There are no separate majors in what Puget Sound considers "applied subjects" such as journalism. Newer programs in gender and environmental studies, both minors only, need time to broaden and become stronger. Classics is a newer major. The communications studies major needs to grow to meet increasing student demand for courses.

Facilities: A $7 million renovation to Collins Library in the summer of 2000 moved out the faculty offices and classrooms that provided noisy distractions and created a quieter facility more conducive to serious study. "It's probably where I get my best work done," says a major in international political economy. Students especially like the 2 grand reading rooms at the entrance with their large tables and leather couches and armchairs. Also drawing rave reviews is the electronic commons for enhanced student research as well as "Ethernet ports installed *everywhere* for laptop use," says a sophomore. The collection of nearly 550,000 volumes and 23,800 paper and electronic periodicals satisfies most students' research needs. For those who want to know more, membership in the Orbis consortium enables UPS students to borrow materials from libraries at 27 other colleges and universities in Oregon and Washington. Thanks to Orbis, says a senior English major, "I had the benefits of a major research library."

More than 400 computers are available to students in labs across campus. One lab is open 24 hours; others are open until 2 a.m. most days or during regular building hours. The residence halls also have small computer clusters. Internet access is available in all residence-hall rooms, in classrooms, "and even in the dining hall," says an English major. As of the 2005–2006 school year, wireless access was available in the library, the Wheelock student building, residence halls, science labs, and in some classrooms. Work was underway to expand wireless access to the entire campus. The university strongly recommends that all students have personal computers, preferably Dell or Apple.

Special programs: In addition to participating in the Asian studies program, students can spend a year in England, Germany, Scotland, Wales, Australia, The Netherlands, or Japan, or a semester in England, France, Germany, Spain, or Chile. Another option is an 8-week summer course in Taiwan. Altogether, undergraduates can study at their choice of over 100 sites in 50 countries. Back home, a Business Leadership program enables 30 freshmen to combine 4 years of traditional business courses with classes in the liberal arts and to take part in seminars that prepare them for leadership positions in the corporate sector; each student also is assigned a mentor from the business world. A 3-2 engineering program is offered with Columbia, Washington, Boston, or Duke University or with the University of Southern California.

Campus life: Sixty-two percent of the undergraduates reside on the 97-acre campus, which charms prospective freshmen with its 32-year-old, ivy-covered Tudor Gothic buildings sporting red brick arches and porticos amid towering fir trees. Twenty-two percent of the men and women belong to 4 national fraternities and 4 national sororities. Independents maintain, however, that being Greek is not essential for having fun and most parties are open to all who are interested. Also, a deferred rush system allows classmates time to form solid friendships regardless of fraternity or sorority membership. Popular student organizations include the Repertory Dance Group, which puts on sold-out student-choreographed performances, Hui-O-Hawaii, which involves the large island population in various activities; and the Outhaus, which sponsors weekend canoeing and hiking trips. Seventy-five percent of all undergraduates participate in community service. Among the most popular activities is Kids Can Do!, a mentoring program for disadvantaged youth. The occasional bicycle theft or car break-in is the biggest campus crime. Nonetheless, residence halls are locked around the clock, and a vehicle escort service transports students to areas within 3 miles of campus. Students say crime in the surrounding area is more worrisome so everyone needs to use caution when walking off-campus.

Eleven varsity sports for men and 12 for women draw 20% of the men and 15% of the women as participants in NCAA Division III competition. Most Logger events attract a core of devoted fans, with varsity football, soccer, and basketball playing to the largest groups of spectators. Says a Californian: "It's fun to laugh at all the people who dress like Loggers for the games." The women's volleyball team has been national champions and draws a good-sized crowd as well. About a fourth of the undergraduates take part in the 7 intramural sports for men and 6 for women. Crew is a popular club sport.

A favorite off-campus getaway is nearby Port Defiance Park, which offers a great beach, Japanese gardens, nature and bike trails, and huge grassy areas for stretching out and relaxing. Seattle has much more to offer students than does Tacoma (pop. 186,000) and is only 30 minutes away. Mt. Rainier and the Olympic National Forest provide a different kind of recreational environment.

Cost cutters: Eighty-seven percent of freshmen and 85% of continuing students received financial help in the 2005–2006 school year; 59% of the freshmen and 55% of the rest were given need-based assistance. The average freshman award for a student with need consisted of a need-based scholarship or grant averaging $11,000 and need-based self-help aid such as loans and jobs averaging $5665. Other non-need-based awards and scholarships averaged $7649. Graduates in 2005 who had borrowed funds had an average college debt of $25,842. A wide range of merit scholarships are available, among them Wyatt Trustee and Trustee Scholarships paying $8000 and $9000 a year, respectively, President's Scholarships worth $6000,

$4000-a-year Chism Scholarships for freshmen planning study in the arts or humanities, $3000 Dean's Scholarships, Howarth Scholarships worth $4000 to freshmen intending to major in the sciences, and scholarships of varying amounts based on performance in specialized areas such as art, forensics, music, and theater. Seven $3000 Leadership/Community Service Scholarships are presented to incoming freshmen, and a limited number of awards, averaging $1500 a year, go to students enrolled in the Business Leadership program. Cooperative education programs are available in all majors. Two deferred-payment plans and an institutional loan program for upperclassmen also are offered.

Rate of return: Eighty-seven percent of entering freshmen return for the sophomore year. Sixty-five percent graduate in 4 years; 72%, in 5 years; 73% in 6.

Payoff: Eleven percent of the 2005 Puget Sound graduates earned bachelor's degrees in business; 8% each specialized in English and biology. The majority of recent graduates entered the job market shortly after commencement, accepting positions in computing with such firms as Microsoft, in accounting with Ernst & Young, in aerospace with Boeing, and in marketing with Procter & Gamble, Gallo, and Xerox. Most alumni remain in the Pacific Northwest. More than 120 companies and other organizations recruited on campus in a recent school year. Thirty percent pursued advanced degrees in graduate and professional schools. About half of UPS alumni in a recent year were working in business, 20% were in medicine and science, 15% in education, 9% in government, and 6% in law. Over the past dozen years, the university has graduated 2 Rhodes Scholars, plus several recipients of Watson Fellowships and Fulbright Scholarships.

Bottom line: "Students must be self-starters and willing to get the help that they *will* need," declares a former fraternity president. "Puget Sound is a good place for students to showcase their talents or to develop abilities they were unaware they possessed."

University of Washington

Seattle, Washington 98195

Setting: Urban
Control: Public
Undergraduate enrollment: 11,227 men, 11,989 women
Graduate enrollment: 4503 men, 5196 women
Student/faculty ratio: 11:1
Freshman profile: 11% scored over 699 on SAT I verbal; 37% scored 600–699; 37% 500–599; 15% below 500. 18% scored over 699 on SAT I math; 45% scored 600–699; 30% 500–599; 7% below 500. 17% scored above 29 on the ACT; 55% scored 24–29; 25% 18–23; 3% below 18. 82% graduated in top tenth of high school class; 96% in upper fourth.

Faculty profile: 93% Ph.D.'s
Tuition and fees: $5610 in-state, $19,907 out-of-state
Room and board: $6846
Freshman financial aid: 37%; average scholarship or grant: $5000 need-based; $2500 non-need-based
Campus jobs: NA; average earnings: NA
Application deadline: Jan. 15 (Priority: Dec. 1)
Financial aid deadline: Feb. 28
Admissions information: (206) 543–9686
  web site: www.washington.edu

To followers of Pac-10 football and basketball, the term *Huskies* may simply refer to the University of Washington's winning teams. But to Washington freshmen encountering introductory courses of 500 or more students, the word better describes the role they must assume to plow through the pack in the big, big world of Seattle's largely commuter university. "Boy, was I shocked," recalls a Tacoma freshman, "when I walked into my first fall-quarter class, a lower-level math course, to see about 500 other students already there." Such shock, in a school of more than 23,000 full-time undergraduates, can sometimes land students on the early dropout list. But the university has taken steps to make the world smaller. An autumn-quarter program called Freshman Interest Groups divides new students interested in certain majors into FIG clusters of 20–25 classmates. Freshmen in a cluster take 3–4 courses together; at least 2 courses are the regular large lectures, but for the other the members meet in just their small group. Professors in several large introductory lectures have noticed that a normally reticent Husky is more willing to ask for help as a member of a small group than as 1 person in a class of 500. From just 10 groups in 1988, the program mushroomed to 115 by a recent fall, involving about half of the 4500-member freshman class. As one recent participant observed: "The program really helps you get into the swing of things. In the first 2 weeks of school, I made many new friends that I otherwise might not have. You just can't let the big size of this school scare you."

Student body: Eighty-six percent of the undergraduates are state residents; although 44 states in a recent year were represented, the largest numbers are typically from the West. Asian-Americans constitute the single biggest minority group on campus at 26% of total undergraduates, followed by Hispanics at 4%, African-Americans at 3%, and Native Americans at just over 1%. Foreign nationals from 68 countries recently added another 3%. About a fifth of the undergraduates in a recent year were older than 25. According to students, the university has its share of members who are politically active (to some, politically extreme) and enjoy voicing their opinions and discussing timely issues. Those who are not active at least tend to be environmentally and socially aware, more so than on other large campuses; undergraduates in general are described as "natural," "easy going," and "stimulating." While the atmosphere appears laid back, except in certain high-pressure disciplines such as engineering and the sciences, students emphasize that the shrinking violet is liable to wither into oblivion. "A student must be independent and outgoing, not shy," advises a recent graduate. "It takes incredible self-discipline to survive."

Academics: The University of Washington, founded in 1861, grants degrees through the doctorate. Undergraduate programs in 140 majors are offered through 17 colleges and professional schools. The regular academic year is divided into three 11-week quarters, with a fourth (summer) term available for those who wish to accelerate their studies. Average class size for undergraduates is 40, but survey courses, as mentioned, can exceed 500. Altogether, 7% of all undergraduate courses have more than 100 students; 9% have 50–99. Upper-level courses in some majors may enroll fewer than a half dozen, and many junior- and senior-level classes range between 20 and 30 participants. Some, however, still extend as large as 50 to 200.

The university has fairly minimal general education requirements that undergraduates in all colleges and professional schools must fulfill. They consist of 40 credits of Areas of Knowledge, with at least 10 credits from each of 3 areas, Visual, Literacy and Performing Arts, Individuals and Societies, and the Natural World. All students, also, must fulfill certain skills requirements, including an English composition course, a course in quantitative or symbolic reasoning, and an additional writing course.

The faculty consists of 2879 full-time members and 639 part-time; no figures are available to show the percentage who teach at the graduate level only. Just over a third are women. Five faculty members have won the Nobel Prize. Students find most of the professors to be intelligent, and enthusiastic about their subject matter, and very willing to help their charges learn when they have the time. However, problems generally arise with the teaching assistants, who end up doing most of the one-on-one with students while professors are heavily engaged in research. At Washington, 40% of the introductory courses in a recent year were taught, at least in part, by graduate students. Here, as at many other major universities, undergraduates complain about foreign TAs who do not speak English well enough to get their points across in class or to follow up with help for those who need it. Some problems are also reported with older tenured professors who have difficulty relating to younger students.

The Henry M. Jackson School of International Studies, in the College of Arts and Sciences, is noted for its interdisciplinary language and area studies programs on major world regions. The College of Engineering, which offers perhaps the university's most competitive area of study, has lots of grant money and top-of-the-line equipment, including computer systems rated nothing short of "exceptional." Majors single out chemical engineering, in particular, for its "great teachers and explainers who care about students' personal growth."

Undergraduates majoring in UW's first-rate programs in biological and life sciences and hoping to attend medical school after graduation benefit from access to state-of-the-art microscopes, opportunities for research, and a chance to take courses at the UW School of Medicine. The School of Nursing, the Business school, and the computer science program in the College of Arts and Sciences, also are characterized by committed faculty of excellent quality, a wide selection of courses, dedicated students, first-rate equipment, and good library resources. The college's music program features attentive faculty who still manage to maintain active professional performing careers at venues throughout the nation.

Other programs in the College of Arts and Sciences, primarily in the social sciences and humanities, have taken a back seat in funding and administrative attention to the sciences and other more technological fields. In a recent school year, the communication department, applied mathematics, and Slavic languages all suffered major funding cuts.

Facilities: Students have their choice of 4 major libraries and 15 branch facilities, which together hold almost 6.5 million volumes, 7.5 million microform items, and 48,300 serial titles. Odegaard Undergraduate Library is the coziest—and noisiest—of the study centers, open around the clock from Sunday at 1 p.m. through Friday night. Students desiring concentration often head for the Suzzallo (main) Library, with its superquiet graduate reading room, or adjoining Allen Library for the natural sciences, completed in 1990 and described as both huge and "incredible." The other major facilities contain materials related to the health sciences and East Asian studies. Though newcomers often find the research process initially overwhelming, a computerized catalog connecting the main facilities with the departmental ones is helpful, as are the human librarians. More than 500 databases in business, the sciences, and the humanities and social sciences also are available. Concludes a sophomore: "If you can't find it here, it doesn't exist."

Laboratories housing about 5000 public computer terminals, largely Macintoshes and PCs are located in at least 20 places around campus, including most residence halls. Three of the major centers are open around the clock. Wireless access is available in all or part of many buildings across campus and was continuing to expand throughout the 2005–2006 school year and summer.

Special programs: UW students may participate in international study programs in over 50 countries in Latin America, Europe, the Middle East, Africa, and Asia. A semester in the other Washington—D.C.— also is an option. Programs are available for a quarter, a semester, or a year.

Campus life: Just 17% of the undergraduates live on the university's 703-acre campus, located between Lake Washington and Lake Union. The vast majority of the students commute from the neighborhood or other parts of Seattle. As a result, the university can feel comparatively abandoned during weekends when no major sporting events draw a crowd. Twelve percent of the men are members of 28 national fraternities; 11% of the women belong to 16 national sororities. Greeks sponsor numerous events on campus, but admission to their parties is restricted to members and their guests; also some animosity exists between members and independents who think the Greeks have "an attitude." The university offers more than 350 student organizations, recently ranging from the Feminist Theory Colloquium to the Direct Selling Club, and the "hopping" Seattle night life, especially the bars and clubs along "the Ave," keeps most independents, and others, entertained. Campus crime is regarded as a problem, ranging from occasional attacks to flashers to bike thefts. "Even U-locks are being defeated," says a junior. "Now the thieves cut the racks." An escort service known as UWCares and a night shuttle for those who live off campus are available. The outside doors to residence halls are either locked at 10 p.m. or secured around the clock. Dozens of new lights and emergency telephones have been installed around campus over the past few years.

Husky competition has always been huge, with 11 men's and 12 women's teams competing in the PAC-10 conference of NCAA Division I. Football games "are almost mandatory," notes a recent graduate, as are the assorted dances and social get-togethers that go with them; women's basketball also brings out a crowd. The women's volleyball team won its first-ever national championship in December 2005. About half of the Husky fans, some 10,000 individuals, take to the field or court themselves, enjoying 20 intramurals for men and 18 for women that recently ranged from squash to Ultimate Frisbee. The waterfront activities center offers water sports. Sport clubs exist for everything from aikido and archery to water polo and weightlifting.

UW students don't have to go far to escape campus life. Seattle, says a student from Singapore, is a city with a comfortable pace, "neither too slack nor too intense," with lots to do. Mountains for hiking and skiing and lakes for sailing and boating also are within easy reach. Mount Rainier is a 90 minute drive; Canada, 2 hours distant.

Cost cutters: The fact that Washington's out-of-state tuition hovers in the low range for major doctorate-granting universities is good, since nonresidents will find few scholarships available. As at most state universities, scholarships, both merit-based and need-based, are offered to state residents, with about 500 awards presented every year. About 125 scholarships recently were awarded to non-residents. An estimated 37% of 2005 freshmen and 56% of continuing students received financial aid, all but a few percent need-based. The average freshman award for a student with need included a need-based scholarship or grant averaging $5000 and need-based self-help aid such as loans and jobs also averaging $5000. The average non-need-based award and scholarship totaled $2500. The average for a non-need-based athletic scholarship was $9000. Average estimated debt of a 2005 graduate was $15,700. Cooperative education programs are available to students majoring in business administration and engineering.

Rate of return: Despite the large size of their first-year classes, 93% of entering freshmen return for the sophomore year. Just 46% graduate in 4 years, but 70% gain their diplomas in 5 years and 74% in 6 years.

Payoff: Seventeen percent of the 2005 graduates earned bachelor's degrees in social sciences, followed by 13% in business and marketing and about 7% each in biological sciences and engineering. Graduates who seek employment directly after commencement are hired mainly by corporations throughout the Pacific Northwest, among them Boeing, Rockwell International, Eddie Bauer, and the major accounting firms. Six hundred companies and organizations recruited on campus in a recent school year. Those seeking advanced degrees, 38% in a recent year, do so most often in various fields within the liberal arts and sciences, followed by engineering and business.

Bottom line: The University of Washington is a big-name school where rain is plentiful but personal attention is sparse. "To be successful, an undergraduate must be willing to go after whatever he or she wants," says a state resident. "The student who needs hand-holding will bomb out here."

Whitman College

Walla Walla, Washington 99362

Setting: Small city
Control: Private
Undergraduate enrollment: 682 men, 798 women
Graduate enrollment: None
Student/faculty ratio: 10:1
Freshman profile: 37% scored over 700 on SAT I verbal; 46% scored 600–700; 15% 500–599; 2% below 500. 31% scored over 700 on SAT I math; 56% scored 600–700; 12% 500–599; 1% below 500. 60% scored above 28 on the ACT; 20% scored 27–28; 11% 24–26; 8% 21–23; 1% below 21. 60% graduated in top tenth of high school class; 91% in upper fifth.

Faculty profile: 84% Ph.D.'s
Tuition and fees: $28,640
Room and board: $7470
Freshman financial aid: 47%; average scholarship or grant: $16,850 need-based; $4250 non-need-based
Campus jobs: 96%; average earnings: $1126/year
Application deadline: Early decision: Nov. 15 and Jan. 1; regular: Jan. 15
Financial aid deadline: Feb. 1 (Priority date: Jan. 5)
Admissions information: (509) 527-5176; (877) 462-9448
e-mail: admission@whitman.edu
web site: www.whitman.edu

For a wide range of high-achieving students from 50 states and 31 foreign countries, the 5 W's that must be considered in any great educational search—who, what, where, when, and why—can be accounted for simply by saying: Whitman in the Wheatfields of Walla Walla, Washington. Whitman College has distinguished itself among small and selective national liberal arts colleges, not only for its location in the Pacific Northwest but also because of its rock-solid, unpretentious, and exceptionally rigorous programs in the liberal arts. Though about a third of the students are Greek and two-thirds play intramural sports, this is no campus of party animals. Eighty-three percent of the freshmen who enter go on to graduate in 5 years; three-fourths of the graduates pursue advanced degrees within 5 years of commencement. At just over $36,000 for tuition, fees, room, and board in 2005–2006, Whitman pushes the upper limit of best educational buys, viewed simply in monetary terms. But compared to its academic peers, most of which can cost several thousand dollars more, "the Whitman experience," says a southerner, "is definitely worth living."

Student body: Forty-two percent of Whitman's student body are from Washington State, with almost three-quarters of the rest also from the Northwest. The largest portion of out-of-staters come from Oregon, Colorado, and California. Minorities make up 15% of the undergraduates, including 8% Asian-Americans, 4% Hispanics, 2% African-Americans and 1% Native Americans. Foreign nationals constitute 3% of the enrollment. A fourth of the students graduated from private or parochial schools. Students describe their classmates as eclectic and open to new ideas, though most maintain fairly traditional values and are described as only "moderately liberal" in their political views, "with a few hippie-wannabe's," adds a senior. However, there's always some point that can be debated, and many classmates enjoy nothing better than a lively discussion of politics over dinner. Others would rather avoid real-life issues altogether. Outwardly, says an easterner, "there tends to be a good deal of fleece vest and J. Crew wearing." Though socially laid back and rarely outwardly competitive about the academic side of life, most "work hard at their studies and sometimes burn out," says a sophomore, "but that's Whitman." Saying "I have to study" is respected by peers as an acceptable excuse for not attending a social event and many join together in study groups and opt to hit the books together. "It's a running joke," says a senior, "that if the senior class reapplied, only half of us would get in, because the entrance standards go up so much every year. Because the freshmen are smarter every year, it gives us upperclassmen that much more incentive to stay sharp."

Academics: Whitman, which was founded in 1883 and named for pioneers who ran a local mission station, awards the bachelor of arts degree in 42 majors. Classes, which follow a semester schedule, average 14 students. A popular geology course may enroll 48, but even in classes of this size, says a junior, "there is nothing to preclude a student from asking questions." Most other freshman and sophomore classes top out at 30 participants. Upper-level seminars may have only 6.

Freshmen are required to take a core course common to all called Antiquity and Modernity, which is taught in sections of 14 students. A 1-semester extension of the core, titled Critical and Alternative Voices, offers students the opportunity to study non-Western world views. Says a history major: "The intellectual climate of the campus has been enhanced by the common knowledge all of the freshmen share." In addition, students must earn a minimum of 6 credits each in social sciences, humanities, fine arts, and science (including 1 course with a laboratory); 1 course of 3 or more credits in quantitative analysis; and 2 courses designated as fulfilling the requirement in Alternative Voices.

Full-time faculty members number 115, with an additional 72 part-time instructors. Forty percent are women. Whitman professors are noted for being intelligent, enthusiastic, and wonderfully accessible, "great people, not just great teachers," says a sophomore. Most engage students in active dialogue rather than rely mainly on passive lecture in the classroom "and are also good about teaching in multiple ways," says a senior. "On a given day, a professor might use a chalkboard, slides, overhead projector, and computer to present concepts to a class." Such ingenuity comes in part from the work of The Center for Teaching and Learning, based in the library. The center enables faculty new to Whitman as well as veterans to collaborate on ways to make subject matter more meaningful and exciting to students; it also helps acquaint faculty with the latest technological tools that might help to explain difficult material more clearly. Faculty members also encourage group work outside of class to develop further analytical and interpersonal skills and build self-esteem. Adds a senior: "Their commitment to the lives of their students in and out of the classroom is phenomenal."

Politics, English, history, math, music, philosophy, sociology, and psychology all feature terrific faculties. "In politics, it just has to do with the professors," says a major. "They engage you personally as well as intellectually. You do the reading, not just because you're worried about your grade, but because you don't want to embarrass yourself in class in front of someone you respect and admire." Biology is regarded as a "very, very tough program but a good crucible in which to test your stuff." Student research opportunities in both biology and chemistry were enhanced by completion of a new science building in the 2002–2003 school year. Astronomy and geology make great use of their equipment and location. Says a science major: "Astronomy labs visit our 16-inch telescope in the wheat fields; geology field trips explore the surrounding terrain." Environmental studies is "well rounded, expanding, current, and relevant to our world," says a major. Theater is a very intense major that in addition to rigorous classroom work, puts on 9 productions throughout the school year, giving students hands-on experience in everything from directing to casting, as well as acting. Japanese, says a sophomore, "has one of the best professors a student will ever encounter."

Though some departments like Asian studies and anthropology are smaller and rely on just a handful of professors to teach all courses, students say the quality of what is provided generally makes up for any lack in quantity. Undergraduates seeking such career-oriented majors as accounting, business, communication, or journalism will be disappointed, as Whitman does not offer them.

Facilities: "I love our library!" says 1 double major, a sentiment echoed by many in this very academic community. Penrose Library contains a healthy collection of just over 374,000 volumes and 2200 electronic and paper periodicals spread over 3 stories. The newly renovated facility provides space for an expanded collection of up to 600,000 books along with additional study rooms with large windows and a cafe. Students already find the book collection to be "excellent, varied, and modern," in the words of a geology major, and easy to access using the online catalog system. Various electronic and online databases assist in periodical searches. The library also is a popular study spot. Unoccupied seats are sometimes hard to find at exam time, though the fact that the building stays open 24 hours usually insures sufficient study space sometime. The science building also houses several special collections in astronomy, biology, chemistry, geology, and physics.

Four labs and 41 classrooms around campus have a total of over 270 microcomputers, mainly IBM-compatible PCs. Some labs close around 1 a.m. but with 24-hour access to the library, all computers there are available around the clock. Students with their own units also can be hooked into the campus network for access anytime of the day or night. Says a senior: "I was nervous about coming to campus without a computer, but I never once had a problem."

Special programs: Over 40% of Whitman juniors study abroad, a number in 2 affiliated programs sponsored by the college at the University of Manchester in England and at St. Andrews University in Scotland. Whitman students may also join a group of 45 undergraduates from 16 other liberal arts colleges for a year in Kyoto, Japan. Additional opportunities are available throughout Europe, Asia, and Australia. Urban semester programs in Chicago, Philadelphia, and Washington, D.C. are an option. Three-2 joint degree programs are offered in engineering with the University of Washington and with Cal Tech, Columbia, Washington, and Duke universities; in environmental management and forestry with Duke and in oceanography and biology or geology with the University of Washington. A 3-2 program also is an option with the Monterey Institute of International Studies. A 3-3 law program is available with Columbia and a 4-1 teacher education program is offered through Bank Street College of Education. Students in a wide variety of disciplines can collaborate with faculty on research projects over the summer. In one such program in a recent school year, 13 faculty members and 22 students pursued research projects in such fields as language studies, history, geology, music, and computer technology.

Campus life: Sixty-three percent of Whitman students live on the 117-acre campus, 3 blocks from downtown Walla Walla (pop. 30,000). Among the residential options are 11 special-interest houses covering areas from Chinese or Japanese language and culture to environmental concerns or the fine arts. Thirty-four percent of the men and 26% of the women are members of 4 national fraternities and 4 national sororities. The presence of Greek organizations at Whitman has been a source of much student debate, though no serious division, in recent years. Observes a junior, "Because the Greek system is so closely monitored by independents on campus, their unity gives the independents something concrete to agree or disagree with. The point is that there is a place here for both Greeks and non-Greeks alike; you get a feeling of belonging no matter what side of the fence you fall on." Undergraduates describe their calendars as "pleasantly intense," fitting in everything from a dance to a coffeehouse to programs sponsored by the excellent Residence Life staff, but most weekend bookings include some time for studying. "Everyone seems to have at least 1 sport/activity/interest that they are passionate about, and many other activities they also enjoy," says a senior. The Coalition Against Homophobia is one of the most active and respected organizations on campus. The opening of the Reid Campus Center in January 2002 has given students a new place just to hang out or continue to be active. Incidents of crime are low, though bike theft is a problem every year. "Bring a bike lock and use it," advises a junior. The "yellowjacket" security force provides an escort service at night; emergency call boxes with sirens and lights are also posted around campus, though they rarely have been needed.

Intramural sports are especially popular, with 4 single-sex and coed activities, involving two-thirds of the students. Teams of Greeks and independents facing off in flag football or Ultimate Frisbee always draw cheering crowds to the central playing field. Some fans even line the main quad with couches to watch the hugely popular intramural flag football games. The most committed players convert to Fighting Missionaries in the 8 varsity sports for men and 8 for women, played in NCAA Division III competition. Though basketball, soccer, and volleyball draw bigger crowds, the college's alpine and cross-country ski teams have won numerous national titles. Club sports also boast a following.

A highly developed outdoor program takes advantage of Whitman's setting close by the wilderness. Skiing, snowboarding, rafting, hiking, rock climbing, and kayaking are all popular weekend pastimes. The college also owns a cabin on Mill Creek, about 20 miles from campus, which students can reserve. A favorite source of relaxation is heading to the nearby wheat fields to "watch the sunset and drink wine—very romantic," says a recent graduate. The nearest major city, Spokane, is 150 miles north; Portland, Oregon, 235 miles west; Seattle, 260 miles northwest.

Cost cutters: In 2005–2006, 47% of all freshmen and 35% of all continuing students received some form of financial aid; for a majority of those students, help was need-based. The average freshman package for first-year students with financial need included a need-based scholarship or grant averaging $16,850 and need-based self-help aid such as loans and jobs averaging $5975. The average non-need-based scholarship or grant for freshmen averaged $4250. The Paul Garrett Scholarships for Men and the Claire Sherwood Memorial Scholarships for Women reward outstanding academic achievement, leadership, and contributions to school and community. Awards range from $2500 to $30,000 a year, depending upon financial need. The scholarships include a trip to New York City in the student's senior year to visit the headquarters of major corporations and graduate schools in the east. President's Scholarships also provide from $2500 to $30,000 annually—again depending on financial need—to entering students based upon exceptional performance in art, debate, or theater. Whitman Achievement-based Scholarships pay $6000 to $10,000 based primarily on a student's GPA and test scores, the rigor of courses taken, and extracurricular interests. All students, regardless of financial status, receive a hidden scholarship of sorts. Whitman's total endowment of almost $312 million, as of June 2005, the largest among private colleges and universities in the northwest, provides income that helped reduce tuition by nearly $3800 in a recent year. Assistance in holding down costs also comes from alumni; Whitman has had the highest percentage of annual alumni giving of any college west of the Mississippi, with over 50% of graduates contributing on a yearly basis. Nonetheless, the average financial debt of 2005 graduates was $16,200.

Rate of return: Ninety-five percent of freshmen return for the sophomore year. Seventy-nine percent graduate in 4 years; 83% in 5; 86% in 6.

Payoff: Psychology and biology were the most popular majors for 2005 graduates, declared by 11% of the class each. The third-place choice was politics at 10%. More than half of recent grads used their diplomas as admission tickets to graduate or professional school, 13% each in business and law, 12% in arts and science, 8% in medicine. A majority of new alumni stay in the Pacific Northwest and northern California, although a number move to Boston, New York, and Washington, D.C. Major employers include Honeywell, IBM, Great West Life Insurance, and Microsoft; the Peace Corps also is popular. One hundred twelve companies and organizations recruited on campus in a recent school year.

Bottom line: "Whitman is a comfortable, insular, and generally great place to avoid (while profoundly debating) the real world for 4 years—but you better know your stuff," warns a recent graduate. "After the very intense attention from professors and the competitive but supportive atmosphere here, I feel I can take on anything."

West Virginia

Bethany College

Bethany, West Virginia 26032

Setting: Small town
Control: Private (Disciples of Christ)
Undergraduate enrollment: 408 men, 487 women
Graduate enrollment: None
Student/faculty ratio: 14:1
Student profile: 4% scored over 700 on SAT I verbal; 11% scored 600–700; 37% 500–599; 48% below 500. 4% scored over 700 on SAT I math; 10% scored 600–700; 42% 500–599; 43% below 500. 3% scored above 28 on the ACT; 6% scored 27–28; 21% 24–26; 40% 21–23; 30% below 21. 29% graduated in top fifth of high school class; 55% in upper two-fifths.

Faculty profile: 59% Ph.D.'s
Tuition and fees: $14,370
Room and board: $7025
Freshman financial aid: 97%; average scholarship or grant: $5900 need-based; $6200 non-need-based
Campus jobs: 79%; average earnings: $820/year
Application deadline: Rolling
Financial aid deadline: May 1 (Priority date: Apr. 1)
Admissions information: (304) 829-7611; (800) 922-7611
e-mail: admission@mail.bethanywv.edu
web site: www.bethanywv.edu

As a recent graduate aptly put it, "Bethany may not be the most selective school in its admissions, but once here students have to *earn* their degrees." This rural West Virginia college of 900 undergraduates accepts about 70% of the students who apply, with just over half of the freshmen who enrolled in fall 2005 drawn from the upper two-fifths of their high school classes. Once in the door, however, Bethany students are expected to fulfill requirements that ensure they will leave as solidly prepared as their peers at more selective colleges. To begin with, undergraduates must complete 9 liberal arts courses in fields ranging from Mathematical Understanding to Cultural Awareness. Required also is a freshman seminar, a seminar in Biblical literature, and a senior project such as a research paper, creative endeavor, or laboratory research, plus a senior comprehensive exam in the major field. Thanks to such breadth and depth in the program, boasts a junior, "Undecided majors can experience a wide range of fields, while a student with more focus can jump right into a fantastic department." As an extra, many departments suggest or mandate internships during the January term or over the summer. For students still unsure about all that Bethany has to offer, a recent drop in tuition should quell any doubts. From fall 2001 to fall 2002, the tuition rate was cut 42%, dropping from just over $20,000 to $12,000, as a way to make a private college education more affordable to future students. At total costs in 2005–2006 of $21,395, about $8000 less than they might normally have been, a bachelor's from Bethany is worth more for a whole lot less.

Student body: A fourth of Bethany's students are from West Virginia. Typically, one-third come from the East Coast and New England states, another third from the Middle Atlantic region, and the rest from other areas, totalling 23 states and 15 foreign countries. Eleven percent belong to the Disciples of Christ, 33% to other Protestant faiths, 36% to the Catholic Church. Minorities make up about 4% of the student body: 2% African-Americans, 1% each Hispanics and Asian-Americans. Foreign nationals constitute another 3%. About 70% graduated from public high schools. "My fellow students," notes a senior, "are overwhelmingly kind, yet strongly opinionated." Their political views run from liberal to conservative. The student body as a whole is hard-working but not as intellectually curious as some individual members would like it to be, although the percentage of academically oriented students increases in each advancing class, from freshman to senior. Notes a sophomore: "It is getting ready for the senior comps and projects that has Bethany students' attention," and steps up the work pace accordingly.

Academics: Bethany, which turned 165 in 2005, awards the bachelor's degree in more than 30 fields of study. The school year is split into 2 semesters plus a 2-week January term, which students are not required to take. The typical Bethany class averages 20 participants, although introductory courses can extend to 30. Classes in the major are more likely to have 20 or fewer participants.

All of Bethany's 63 full-time and 23 part-time faculty members, a third of whom are women, act like full-time teachers. At Bethany, it's not unusual for a professor to call a student if he or she has missed class a few days in a row; small student/faculty get-togethers also are common. "Faculty see it as their goal to challenge us and work us to our best potential," says a communications major. Nevertheless, undergraduates have been concerned that some of the most talented young professors leave after just a short time in pursuit of higher salaries elsewhere. Says a sophomore: "The professors are not paid enough but they do not show it. They love their jobs and love the students they serve. In one word, they are dedicated."

Talk about campus ranks the communication department at the top of the pack, thanks to great faculty and advanced equipment for the student-run radio and television stations and newspaper. Some students worry, however, that there is an insufficient number of professors to meet the needs of the increased number of students who choose this field as a major. The economics and business department, which offers majors in economics and accounting, has fine instructors and challenging coursework. The economics major offers tracks in financial economics and managerial economics and in international economics, with or without study abroad. English rates an A for the well-rounded experience of its faculty, including a noted Hemingway scholar, and varied course offerings. Political science professors, says a major, "welcome questions and discussion in class and always have open doors outside of class." Physics is described as "difficult and demanding, the best!" Chemistry and biology have knowledgeable and helpful professors who provide plenty of hands-on experience to students, in a recently renovated building. History, physical education and sports studies, and religious studies round out the list of noteworthy programs, featuring both wonderful professors and high standards and, in the case of physical education and sports studies, excellent equipment.

Students say some lower-level foreign language classes lack rigor, although the advanced classes are more challenging and satisfying. Programs in music, theater arts, and visual art are small.

Facilities: Until computerized research became ubiquitous, "inadequate" was probably one of the kinder words that research-weary students used to use to describe T. W. Phillips Memorial Library's collection of almost 117,000 volumes and 302 periodicals. The online catalog, extensive databases, and link to the Internet have raised students' spirits, giving them access to holdings across the country. The entire facility also was renovated in 1995, which made it a much more satisfying place to study. Students who like to study in the library find its 10 p.m. closing too early.

Students have 24-hour access to 2 main computer labs, a 30-seat PC lab and a second lab with 25 PCs. The only times students may not use the labs is if a class is using them. Departmental mini-labs and 10 PCs in the library also are available. The college strongly recommends that undergraduates have their own computers.

Special programs: Study abroad options include programs in Europe, as well as in Canada, Puerto Rico, Argentina, and Japan. A Washington semester with American University enables undergraduates to study the workings of the federal government, while a semester in Charleston, through West Virginia University, provides a similar glimpse of the state government. A 3-2 engineering program is offered with Columbia, Washington, or Case Western Reserve University.

Campus life: Ninety-five percent of Bethany students live on the 300-acre rural campus, in the foothills of the Allegheny Mountains in West Virginia's northern panhandle. The Greeks keep Bethany's social life moving, with 44% of the men and 53% of the women belonging to 5 national fraternities and 3 national sororities. Since some Greek activities are restricted to members, independents of all ages have tended to hang out at their own "club," a popular local bar, named Bubba's Bison Inn. An increase in alternative weekend programming, such as comedians and bands, has given independents other options. Maxwell's Coffeehouse attracts many students who simply desire good conversation and relaxation, as well as music, entertainment, and a weekly movie. Many undergraduates get involved in running the campus radio and television stations and the newspaper, *The Tower;* others join clubs that are related to their majors or that perform community service. Active clubs range from the International Students Association to the Political Awareness Society and Amnesty International. Although students say the campus has a very "safe" feeling; doors to all residence halls and other buildings are locked at 9 p.m. and for all day on the weekends.

NCAA Division III intercollegiate sports, 9 for each sex, involve a third of the student body, while 40% opt to participate in the 7 intramurals each for men and for women. Bison soccer games are the focus of many fall weekends although football draws near equal crowds. Softball and baseball games take over in the spring. For the truly adventuresome, the Outdoors Club offers such thrilling activities as scuba diving, sky diving, and rock climbing.

For urban excitement, students with cars head northeast to Pittsburgh, less than an hour away, or to Wheeling, just a half-hour's drive. Others simply "take a hike" in the nearby woods.

Cost cutters: In the 2005–2006 school year, 97% of the freshmen and 96% of continuing students received some form of financial aid; for 68% of the freshmen and 64% of all other classes, aid was need-based. The average freshman award for a student with need included a need-based scholarship or grant averaging $5900 and need-based self-help aid such as loans and jobs averaging $6135. Other non-need-based awards and scholarships for first-year students averaged $6200. Average debt of a 2005 graduate was $18,000. The Bethany Merit Scholarship program offers awards based on standardized test scores and grade point averages. Awards range in value from $3500 to $7500. The Kalon Leadership Award pays $2500 to students who have demonstrated leadership within their school, community, church, or other organization. The Disciples Student Award pays $1500 to Disciples of Christ church members; the children of Disciples of Christ ministers may receive $2500 scholarships.

Rate of return: Of the freshmen enrolling, 88% return for a second year. Fifty-six percent graduate in 4 years; 58%, in 5 years; 59% in 6.

Payoff: The 3 most popular majors for the 2005 graduating class were communication at 18%, psychology at 16%, and biology at 9%. More than 80% of recent graduates have gone on immediately to jobs; half were employed in the Ohio-Pennsylvania-West Virginia area, a quarter in Maryland and Virginia, just under a fifth in New England. In a recent graduating class, 35% continued on to graduate or professional schools at least part-time. Almost half of all alumni attend graduate school within 10 years of earning bachelors degrees from Bethany.

Bottom line: Bethany is a small college where everyone soon knows whatever another student does, right or wrong. But it is also a place where those who wish to make up for little effort or poor grades in high school can get a second chance. Says a junior: "The only student who would not do well here is someone who doesn't want to get involved. It's hard to be isolated on such a tightly knit campus and community."

Shepherd University

Shepherdstown, West Virginia 25443

Setting: Small town
Control: Public
Undergraduate enrollment: 1294 men, 1655 women
Graduate enrollment: 11 men, 12 women
Student/faculty ratio: 29:1
Freshman profile: 2% scored over 700 on SAT I verbal; 10% scored 600–700; 47% 500–599; 41% below 500. 0% scored over 700 on SAT I math; 8% scored 600–700; 48% 500–599; 44% below 500. 3% scored above 28 on the ACT; 6% scored 27–28; 21% 24–26; 33% 21–23; 37% below 21. Class rank data: NA.
Faculty profile: 88% Ph.D.'s

Tuition and fees: $4046 in-state, $10,618 out-of-state
Room and board: $6020
Freshman financial aid: 77%; average scholarship or grant: $3627 need-based
Campus jobs: 19%; average earnings: $1225/year
Application deadline: Early action: Nov. 15; regular: Rolling
Financial aid deadline: Mar. 1
Admissions information: (304) 876-5212/5213; (800) 344-5231
e-mail: kscranag@shepherd.edu
web site: www.shepherd.edu

Few universities have had more democratic beginnings than Shepherd University, formerly Shepherd College in Shepherdstown, West Virginia. The school got its start when the county seat was moved to Charles Town in 1871, and the townspeople, in the days before empty buildings were converted into trendy boutiques, decided to use the vacant courthouse for educational purposes. Seven town fathers drew up the articles of incorporation and gave themselves the power to select instructors, pay salaries, and prescribe the courses of study. Less than a year later, Shepherd College became part of the state system of higher education, where it has remained. West Virginians keep coming to their college of the people, pushing the school's enrollment up by 200% over the last 2 decades, and making Shepherd the fastest growing institution in West Virginia. In March 2004 Shepherd College became Shepherd University. The road to West Virginia finances is never smoothly paved, and students have come to expect lack of supplies and faculty departures for higher salaries elsewhere. On balance, however, most find the quality of education available for such a low tuition—just over $4000 for in-staters and less than $11,000 for nonresidents in the 2005–2006 school year—too good to pass up.

Student body: Sixty percent of Shepherd's students are from West Virginia. The largest portion of out-of-staters comes from the Middle Atlantic region although 47 states are represented. Ninety-four percent of the students graduated from public schools. Minorities comprise 10% of the student body—5% African-Americans, 2% each Hispanics and Asian-Americans, and 1% Native Americans. Thirty international students from 22 foreign countries attend. While the average age of freshmen is a fairly typical 19 years, that of the overall undergraduate population recently held at 23, reflecting a significant number of nontraditional students. The undergraduates are mostly conservative but apolitical, friendly, and fairly laid back about their studies; a small group of overachievers run the majority of campus organizations. "It is play time for many students," observes a recent graduate, "and they are the ones who are here for 5 or 6 years" or never make it through.

Academics: Shepherd offers the bachelor's degree in 70 different fields plus various recently added master's degree programs. The academic year is divided into semesters. Freshmen can expect classes of between 20 and 45 students, although a music appreciation class can enroll 60. Most courses for juniors and seniors rarely top 30, and upper-level seminars have as few as 12.

The general-studies program at Shepherd accounts for 47 of the 128 hours needed for graduation, with courses from the humanities, social sciences, life or physical sciences, mathematics, and physical education. Students generally like the structure but wish a wider choice of courses were available.

Just 43% of Shepherd's 242 faculty members are full-time; 42% are women. Some are too bright to be approachable, and others rarely stray from the textbook in their teaching. Most, however, fall in the middle range of caring, intelligent friends; in the words of an education major: "Overall, most of my professors have done more than simply present subject matter to their students. They have opened their doors to make sure they have done their part in encouraging the success of their students." Adds a senior: "They like it when students ask questions and show up during office hours." Their overall rating, according to 1 sophomore: "Above average, but not great."

Shepherd's programs in art, especially graphic design, music, and theater are thorough and demanding, and enhanced by their location in the beautiful and roomy Frank Creative Arts Center. Theater, though the only 1 of the 3 fine arts programs that is a minor, not a major, has become one of the college's fastest growing programs. The professional Contemporary American Theater Festival, instituted by the program's director and held during the summer at the college, provides excellent opportunities for students to observe, participate, and learn. The English department is distinguished by faculty who maintain active publishing careers outside the classroom while also making time to take classes on field trips to the Folger Shakespeare Theater and the Library of Congress in Washington, D.C., about an hour away. Accounting, business administration, and environmental studies benefit from top-notch faculties and strong curricula. Nursing, psychology, sociology, math and a challenging education program also win applause.

The mass communication major has been criticized for being "vague and unfocused" and in need of better organization. It also is becoming increasingly overcrowded, with too few full-time professors to handle the rapid growth in student enrollment. Engineering, physics, historic preservation, journalism, Spanish, and French as well as theater are offered as minors only. Classes in German and Russian also are available. Courses only, too, are offered in religion and philosophy.

Facilities: Undergraduates studying in the 3-story Ruth Scarborough Library are using words they never considered before to describe its interior: "plenty of room," "top of the line," "absolutely beautiful." The reason is completion in 2002 of an $18 million dollar wing that tripled the size of the existing structure and increased seats for studiers to 600 from just 200. Amenities include a high-ceilinged reading room, a 24-hour study room and various new computerized research aids. Students hope the collection, currently standing at 189,000 volumes and 539 periodicals, will be the next feature to grow.

The university maintains more than 300 computers for student use in labs and public areas. Labs are generally open from 8 a.m. to 11 p.m. Students wish that there were more units in favorite labs, such as the one in the library, and that all labs were open later. As of the 2005–2006 school year, there was no wireless access on campus.

Special programs: Internships in all fields are possible. A semester in Washington, D.C. also can be arranged as part of the Washington Gateway Program, which provides a variety of lectures, workshops, seminars, and field trips that make the most of Shepherd's proximity to the nation's capital. Undergraduates who wish to go farther afield may study abroad in any of at least 8 foreign countries. A 2-2 engineering program is offered with Marshall and West Virginia universities.

Campus life: A quarter of Shepherd's full-time students live on the rolling, 323-acre campus, and residents with cars often head out for the weekend. On the bright side, observes a recent graduate, "Those who stay every weekend can get a lot of studying done," though student center coffeehouses, touring comedians, and socials in the residence halls offer some diversion. About 5% of the undergraduates belong to 4 national fraternities and 3 national sororities, all of which are fairly active. Although concerns about liability keep most parties restricted to members or guests, there is friendliness between the Greek and non-Greek communities. Some students would like to see the Greeks become a larger presence in the campus social life but it's not an easy sell. Note 2 juniors: "There are so many commuters that it makes it difficult to convince them that they can still participate in Greek life." Crime, such as petty theft, occurs mainly because students fail to lock their doors; even after the rare incidents many residents still do not lock up on the assumption that historic Shepherdstown (pop. 2500) is small and safe.

One of the best ways to keep homebound travelers on campus is a Rams football or basketball or soccer game, which usually draws a crowd. Football fans were out in full force during the 2005–2006 season as the Rams won game after game. In November 2005, on the 50th anniversary of Shepherd's only previous undefeated football season, the Rams repeated by beating West Virginia State 51–10, ending the regular season 11–0. A total of 6 intercollegiate sports for men and 6 for women are played in NCAA Division II. There are 12 intramural sports for men and women, though less than a fifth of the men and just 5% of the women take part. The Shepherd Outdoor Club keeps a large number of students fit through regular weekend trips canoeing, hiking, and horseback riding.

Baltimore and Washington, D.C., each about 70 miles away, are attractive weekend getaways when Shepherdstown begins to seem too quaint. The surrounding area, with Harpers Ferry and Antietam battlefield nearby, is steeped in Civil War history.

Cost cutters: One of the original traditions of the town fathers has been maintained: keeping Shepherd's education financially accessible. The college's charges are among the nation's lowest, though the average debt of 2005 graduates was $14,887. Seventy-seven percent of 2005–2006 freshmen and 67% of continuing students received financial assistance; for almost half, about 47%, of all undergraduates, the aid was need-based. The average freshman award consisted of a $3627 need-based scholarship or grant and self-help aid such as loans and jobs averaging $2530. An athletic scholarship averaged $4465. No figure is available for the average amount of merit-based awards and scholarships not based on financial need. Foundation Scholarships recently paid $5000 a year to 4 exceptional students who had a minimum 3.5 grade point average in high school and a 28 ACT composite or 1270 math and critical reading combined SAT. Students with a 28 ACT or 1270 math and critical reading SAT also are eligible for Alumni Association Scholarships that pay $2200 a year to 2 West Virginians and $4400 to 2 out-of-staters. Presidential Scholarships worth $1500 annually go to entering students who have at least a 3.5 GPA, a 26 ACT composite or 1200 math and critical reading SAT, and a quality academic course load. Cooperative education programs are available in all major fields of study.

Rate of return: Sixty-nine percent of the entering freshmen return for the sophomore year. Twelve percent graduate in 4 years; 35% within 5 years; 40% within 6.

Payoff: Of 2005 graduates, 11% earned degrees in business administration, 9% in secondary education, and 8% in recreation and leisure studies. In recent years more than 80% have taken jobs soon after commencement with major business firms such as Marriott, IBM, and Unisys and with U.S. government agencies in various states throughout the Northeast and Southeast. About 140 companies and organizations recruited on campus in a recent school year. About 15% of the degree recipients enroll in graduate school within 6 months of commencement.

Bottom line: "Shepherd is a lot like a more mature high school," says a recent graduate. "If you want a great education, you can get it here, but you can also slide through if you want to."

Wisconsin

Alverno College

Milwaukee, Wisconsin 53234

Setting: Urban
Control: Private (Roman Catholic)
Undergraduate enrollment: 1515 women (661 part-time)
Graduate enrollment: 2 men, 14 women (180 part-time)
Student/faculty ratio: 12:1
Freshman profile: 1% scored above 28 on the ACT; 5% scored 27–28; 10% 24–26; 22% 21–23; 62% below 21. Class rank data: NA.
Faculty profile: 89% Ph.D.'s
Tuition and fees: $15,418

Room and board: $5670
Freshman financial aid: 96%; average scholarship or grant: NA
Campus jobs: 38%; average earnings: $2500/year
Application deadline: Aug. 1
Financial aid deadline: Apr. 15
Admissions information: (414) 382-6100; (800) 933-3401
e-mail: admissions @alverno.edu
web site: www.alverno.edu

In a typical American history course taken to fulfill a general-education requirement, students usually demonstrate their knowledge of the causes of World War II by filling page after page of a blue book. At all-women's Alverno College in Milwaukee, a woman is more likely to have to demonstrate her knowledge by pretending to be a United States senator in 1939 and explaining in a classroom speech why events in Europe and Asia will inevitably involve America in a global conflict. The speech, unlike the blue book exam, does not receive a grade; rather, it is assessed not only for its content but also for such skills as communication and analysis. Often the performance is evaluated by the student, who assesses her own persuasiveness as captured on videotape, as well as by the professor. To graduate from Alverno, a student needs more than a broad base of subject knowledge. In addition, she must have acquired a certain level of competency in each of 8 abilities ranging from communication and problem-solving to social interaction and effective citizenship. This is an unusual approach to learning, applauded by education experts around the country, although adopted by few other institutions. And it's one that has put this small, Catholic women's college at the forefront of discussions on what a graduate should have gained from his or her college experience.

Student body: While Alverno's program may be nationally known, its student body is drawn from a much narrower base. Ninety-seven percent are from Wisconsin, many of them commuting from the greater Milwaukee area. Other students come mostly from the Midwest, with a total of 10 states and 12 foreign countries represented. African-American women constitute the largest single minority group at 20% of enrollment, followed by 11% Hispanics, 5% Asian-Americans, and 1% Native Americans. There are 13 international students. A third of the women are Catholic and 32% are Protestant. Although undergraduates vary in age from 18 to past 50 (a third in a recent year were 25 and older), many of them are first-generation college students who are serious about their learning. However, the atmosphere on campus is caring and supportive rather than intense, again because of Alverno's approach to education. More than at most colleges, each student is truly competitive with herself alone, since there are no letter grades and assessments are designed to measure each student's progress against her previous achievements, and not in comparison with others. "This approach encourages us to help each other learn without feeling threatened," observes a recent graduate, and group projects are commonplace. The diversity of races, ethnicities, ages, and associated life experiences also widens the opportunities for the women to learn from each other. Says a junior: "Everyone's differences bring something special and unique to class discussions and individual work."

Academics: Alverno awards the bachelor's degree in more than 30 majors and master's degrees in business administration, education, and nursing. Students take courses divided by semesters, with the average course enrolling 28. The range is small: the largest course, U.S. History 1607-1900, recently enrolled just 33; Fundamental Concepts of Mathematics II, 5. "We are never faced with a lecture-hall-type scenario," boasts a senior. "It would be too hard to teach the interactive, ability-based curriculum to such a large group."

Alverno, founded by the School Sisters of Saint Francis, celebrated its centennial in 1987, but the competency-based educational program for which the college is best known has been in place only since 1973. As is required at most schools, all Alverno students must complete general-education courses in a broad range of subjects from history and English to math and science. Classes offered in every discipline at the college are designated not only by their subject matter but also by the types and levels of skills that they teach. Competence in each of 8 abilities, communication, analysis, problem-solving, valuing in decision making, social interaction, global perspectives, effective citizenship, and aesthetic responsiveness, is required for graduation. Periodic assessments during each course, involving written, oral, or hands-on demonstrations of competence, enable student and faculty to evaluate thoroughly how much progress has been made in each ability, although no grades are ever given. First-year students take a preprofessional seminar that assists them in selecting a major and understanding the career options that can follow. Students in every major also spend at least 1 semester in a field internship, which includes a weekly seminar in which participants share off-campus experiences. Every student also must create a diagnostic digital portfolio that includes information that demonstrates her competencies.

A total of 225 faculty members—104 full-time, 121 part-time, and 75% women—makes this program work. Students call all instructors, laypersons, and religious sisters by their first names. Observes a recent graduate: "I really appreciate the faculty and their respect for students. Anytime you are willing to be a teacher and a learner in the same position, you're a true professor." Students note, however, that some new faculty have a hard time adjusting to Alverno's approach.

For the most part, students find the overall approach to learning more distinctive than any single academic department. However, 2 large preprofessional majors, nursing and business and management, are considered to be among the best. Their emphasis on practical learning, which easily encompasses the competency-based approach, prepares students more than adequately for the outside world. The education faculty, says a major, "is very in tune with individual development, open to suggestions and responsive to student needs." Majors in professional communication and psychology and a minor in integrated arts and humanities with coursework in English, history, religious studies, and philosophy, also are winners. The sciences rank highly thanks to a $12.7 million Teaching, Learning, and Technology Center built in 1999 that houses, among other facilities, a 2-story wing with science, computer, and multimedia laboratories. Music and math are smaller programs, with fewer faculty members and more limited course offerings. The art department "is stuck in the basement," says a junior, and the dance and movement studies program, offered as a minor, is still adjusting to changes in its floor space brought about by the return of varsity athletics. There are no foreign language majors, though a minor is available in Spanish language and cultures. A minor also is an option in theater arts.

Facilities: Alverno's Library/Media Center is low on published materials, including about 92,000 books, 115,000 bound periodicals, and 2487 paper and electronic periodical subscriptions, although there are also over 273,000 microforms and 31,000 audiovisual items, such as videotapes, sound recordings, and films. Students find the overall collection limited in scope, dated, and suitable only for minor research; for more extensive projects, most rely on the Internet and interlibrary loan as well as the "great reference librarians," says a senior. Alverno students have access to books, videos, journal articles, and additional materials from 7 other small Wisconsin colleges. As a place to study, the newly furnished center wins points for being clean, quiet, and comfortable "with an atmosphere that lends itself to learning," says a senior. The library closes early, however, at 9:30 p.m. weeknights and at 5 p.m. or sometimes 6 p.m. on Sunday nights.

More than 450 desktop and notebook computers are available for student use in a variety of locations, in computer labs and classrooms, discipline-specific labs, and residence halls. Internet access is present in all locations; wireless access is an option in the library, the student commons/cafeteria, and student coffeehouse. The larger labs are open until just 9 p.m.; those in the dorms never close.

Special programs: Engineering students may cross-register at Marquette University. Study abroad is offered in England, France, Mexico, and Japan through Alverno's own exchange agreements, as well as in a dozen other countries through programs provided by other institutions. More than 100 businesses and organizations provide student internships in the Off-Campus Experiential Learning program.

Campus life: Just 13% of Alverno's students live on the 46-acre campus, though much of the social life is focused off school grounds, in the city of Milwaukee. Sorority life remains minimal but is growing with 3 local sororities enrolling 1% of the women. Options for the sports-minded have expanded considerably in just the past few years. Four intramural sports also returned to campus after an absence of a quarter century. The Alverno Inferno took the court in fall 2000 with varsity teams in basketball and volleyball. Soccer, softball, and cross country were added a year later, with all sports part of NCAA Division III. New athletic fields will be ready for play in spring 2007. The college encourages students to become involved in community events, many centered at the campuses of Marquette University and the University of Wisconsin, Milwaukee. A program called "Alverno Presents" brings various performers to campus over some weekends. Popular clubs are major-related, among them Women in Communications and Students in Free Enterprise, or reflect personal situations, such as

Hispanic Women of Alverno or the Single-Parent Support Group. Though the college is located 20 minutes from downtown Milwaukee, students say big-city crime rarely affects the campus. The residence halls are well secured and security guards walk women who wish escorts to various places after dark.

The city of Milwaukee (pop. 636,000), with its professional sports teams and active cultural life, satisfies most student urges to get away.

Cost cutters: Alverno's below-average tuition is the direct beneficiary of the contributed services of the School Sisters of Saint Francis, who teach and serve as administrators. Tuition is slightly higher for nursing students, just $744 more a year for fall 2006. Ninety-six percent of first-year students and 83% of continuing students received financial help in the 2005–2006 school year. For 87% of the first-year students and 81% of the rest, the assistance was based on financial need. The average freshman award totaled $14,333, though no breakdown is available to show the portion that was scholarships and grants or loans and job earnings. Alverno offers a full range of academic scholarships extending from $3000 to $7500 a year. The scholarships can be renewed for an additional 3 years. Extended payment schedules also can be arranged.

Rate of return: Seventy-six percent of first-year students return for the sophomore year. Thirty-five percent graduate in 4 years; 42% in 5 years; 47% in 6 years.

Payoff: For 2005 graduates, nursing was the most popular major, attracting 23% of the class, followed by elementary education at 13% and psychology at 10%. Ninety percent of Alverno graduates are hired within 6 months of commencement. Most accept posts with midwestern firms such as Allen Bradley, Ameritech, and Miller Brewing, as well as with the Medical College of Wisconsin and local hospitals and schools. Almost 50 companies and other organizations recruited on campus in a recent school year. Nearly 30% of Alverno alumni eventually pursue graduate studies though just 17% of the graduates do so immediately.

Bottom line: Alverno women won't find the traditional campus life with men, lots of clubs, or even letter grades. On the other hand, as a recent graduate offered a permanent job by her field internship employer reports, the ability-based curriculum guarantees recruiters a lot more than A's, B's, or C's on a transcript. "My abilities to communicate effectively, interact socially, analyze, and solve problems, among other skills, are evident in my work," she says. "There is no doubt in my mind that Alverno was the best choice for me."

Beloit College

Beloit, Wisconsin 53511

Setting: Small town
Control: Private
Undergraduate enrollment: 551 men, 779 women
Graduate enrollment: None
Student/faculty ratio: 13:1
Freshman profile: 28% scored above 700 on SAT I verbal; 43% scored 600–700; 23% 500–599; 6% below 500. 10% scored above 700 on SAT I math; 51% scored 600–700; 32% 500–599; 7% below 500. 39% scored above 28 on the ACT; 23% scored 27–28; 24% 24–26; 11% 21–23; 3% below 21. 37% graduated in top tenth of high school class; 60% in upper fifth.
Faculty profile: 95% Ph.D.'s

Tuition and fees: $26,884
Room and board: $5924
Freshman financial aid: 80%; average scholarship or grant: $15,676 need-based; $14,025 non-need-based
Campus jobs: 82%; average earnings: $1300/year
Application deadline: Early action: Nov. 15 and Dec. 15; regular: Jan. 15
Financial aid deadline: Mar. 1
Admissions information: (608) 363-2500;
(800) 9-BELOIT out-of-state
e-mail: admiss@beloit.edu
web site: www.beloit.edu

You can count on most colleges to have Homecoming in the fall, Winter Carnival in the snow season, and some kind of rites of spring to mark the end of ice and cold. But at Beloit College, 50 miles south of Madison, Wisconsin, sophomores add another set of dates to their spring calendar: Declaration of Major Days. The celebration, filled with social hours and symposia to mark each undergraduate's selection of a major, also draws to a close 2 years of curricular and outside events designed to help students make more informed choices about their fields of study. A year-long First-Year Initiatives program, known naturally as FYI, uses small seminars and coursework from diverse disciplines to develop skills of inquiry, writing, and speaking common to all majors. A 2-day retreat during November of the sophomore year introduces students to opportunities for internships and study abroad. During Exploration Month, otherwise known as February, academic departments hold informational meetings and social events to inform sophomores of the campus and career opportunities available in various majors. By the time Declaration Week arrives, almost every sophomore knows not only what subject matter interests him or her but also what skills that major requires, what internship and study abroad opportunities it provides, what careers it makes possible, and so on. Declaration of Major Days may never rival Homecoming as a nationwide campus event, but Beloit has never done things just to be fashionable, only forward-thinking.

Student body: Just under a fifth, 17%, of Beloit students are from Wisconsin; 43% of the nonresident undergraduates are from the region, although 48 states and 41 foreign countries are represented. One-fifth of the students graduated from private or parochial schools. Foreign nationals make up 7% of the student body. Asian-Americans and African-Americans each constitute 3%, Hispanics 2%, and Native Americans 1%. At Beloit, observes a recent graduate, "it's the 'in' thing to be an individual. Sometimes people take individuality to the point of being a 'clique' in itself, but for the most part the attitude is genuine." As a southerner puts it more bluntly: "You can go to class in your pajamas. No one cares about externals." Beloit students see themselves as "open minded" rather than adhering to any set political philosophies; the enrollment as a whole is more liberal in its thinking than are undergraduates at most other campuses. Says a southerner: "The students are very liberal and eager to explore issues concerning politics and academics. Social awareness is a concern to all students as well." The secret to getting along, students say, is learning to respect the opinions of others as well as being willing to stand up for your own beliefs. As socially laid back as most are, they are equally intense in their academic endeavors, although motivated more by the desire for knowledge than by the grade at the end of the semester. Nevertheless: "If you don't study, you fail," says a junior simply. "No one, no matter how smart, breezes through Beloit."

Academics: Beloit, which observed its sesquicentennial in 1996, awards the bachelor's degree in more than 50 majors. Students take courses divided into semesters, with the average class enrolling 15 students. Popular courses such as Introduction to Astronomy can have 40; beginning language classes like Elementary Hungarian may have only 3.

Along with the various first year seminars, Beloit students must complete distributional requirements in 3 broad areas of the curriculum: natural sciences and mathematics, social science, and arts and humanities. A basic writing class and a writing-intensive course also are on the "must do" list. Students round out their choices of major with study or experience of a language or culture not their own; an experiential learning component; and a unit of interdisciplinary studies or 2 units of paired courses.

Twenty-four of the 127 faculty members are part-time (43% are women), but few members of the total faculty take a part-time approach to their students. Although a small number can intimidate undergraduates with their brilliance or freeze them out with their cool indifference, the majority are understanding as well as intelligent. "Many professors encourage students to do more than they ever have before," says a senior. "But because faculty members always make themselves available to help and because they really seem to care about us, we push ourselves to try harder." Adds a Californian: "They seek to challenge your ideas—not to prove you wrong or 'give' you the right answer, but to make you question the established and to always be open for different solutions."

Two less common undergraduate majors, anthropology and geology, are widely acclaimed as Beloit's outstanding offerings. Anthropology features faculty who excel in teaching, research, and approachability and superb facilities such as the Logan Museum of Anthropology, whose equipment and collections as well as ancient Indian mounds located throughout campus are available for student use. The department offers advanced courses in 3 fields—cultural anthropology, archaeology, and biological anthropology— a rare display of breadth at a small undergraduate school. Geology likewise provides superb faculty with excellent equipment and opportunities for extended field trips following spring term that take students throughout the United States as well as overseas to such locales as Iceland and the Italian Alps. Five-story Chamberlin Hall has well-equipped laboratories on every floor, including a roof-top observatory, for students majoring in biology, chemistry, physics, biochemistry, astronomy, mathematics and computer science, and geology. The department of modern languages and literature also shines, with majors in French, German, Russian, Spanish, and East Asian Languages and Culture (Japanese and Chinese), as well as coursework in Hungarian and Italian. English's creative writing program features a faculty whose "attention, insight, and enthusiasm are amazing and encouraging," says a major. "Anyone can leave Beloit a writer, and everyone can benefit." Economics, too, rates favorable mention, as do the majors in studio art and art history. Both disciplines have blossomed with new faculty and staff as well as new computer labs and studio space and renovations of existing classrooms.

While Beloit's weak spots are few, they do exist. While the theater arts major as a whole thrives, with excellent theaters and equipment as well as an inspiring Young Artists in Residence Program, dance devotees would like to see a greater number and variety of courses offered within the theater arts curriculum. Music also needs more classes and more space.

Facilities: After a $5.25 million renovation in the 1990–91 school year, Col. Robert H. Morse Library became a much more "user-friendly" facility, with soundproof study rooms equipped with tables, chairs, and blackboards, individual desks with outlets for computers, and plenty of lighting and comfortable armchairs and couches. "Unfortunately," notes a junior, "the white noise of the fans leaves bobbing heads on all 3 floors," unless, of course, another student finds a friend from this small campus to chat with, in which case, "you just have to move to a study room," says a junior. Undergraduates complain that for most research beyond the freshman year many of the 253,000 volumes are too dated and the 1666 periodicals a bit narrow in scope to meet students' most intense research needs. Relief is two-fold. The first stop is the reference librarian, says a sociology major. "She is brilliant and many, many students use her as their first research tool." From there come the various computerized systems that provide access to the holdings of all libraries in the state of Wisconsin, including the 7 million volumes housed in Madison as well as libraries in other parts of the United States and the world.

Most of the academic and cultural buildings on Beloit's campus offer wireless access, and the wired campus network is accessible from every campus building. Students who need computers find plenty among the more than 250 PCs and Macs in the library, dozen departmental labs, and 24-hour labs in academic and residential buildings. Every residence hall room also has data ports.

Special programs: The college's World Outlook program provides opportunities for study abroad in seminars led by Beloit faculty members; recent destinations included France, Germany, Scotland, Australia, and Ecuador. Beloit also has exchange programs with universities in 12 countries from Turkey to Hong Kong; additional study abroad and domestic study options through other college programs also are available. The Center for Language Studies on campus offers 9-week intensive language programs during the summer in Arabic, Chinese, Czech, Hungarian, Japanese, Korean, Russian, and Spanish. As a result of such opportunities for language study and travel, more than 40% of all Beloit undergraduates end up studying abroad. Washington Semester and Washington Economic Policy Semester programs are offered through American University in the nation's capital. Cooperative 3-2 programs in engineering, forestry and environmental management, nursing, medical technology, and social work are available with a number of major universities. More than 150 internship positions are provided on a regular basis in the Beloit region. Cross-registration for courses is offered with the University of Wisconsin, Madison. Eighty percent of Beloit students complete some kind of independent study during their 4 or 5 years on campus.

Campus life: Because undergraduates are not allowed to live off campus until their senior year, all but 7% reside on the 40-acre campus, which was modeled after early New England colleges. After the first year, students may choose to live in special-interest housing, which recently accommodated residents with interests in French, Spanish, Russian, women's issues, anthropology, environmental issues, gay and lesbian issues, Latino issues, and music, or in Greek housing. In keeping with Beloit's emphasis on individualism, just 15% of the men belong to 3 national fraternities, and 5% of the women join 1 national and 2 local sororities. Independents are welcome at most Greek functions. "Greeks are neither popular nor unpopular," observes a junior, "because here at Beloit they are so different from the fraternity stereotype that people aren't sure what they represent." More than 100 students are involved in the FM radio station, 60 in the Beloit Science Fiction Fantasy Association, and smaller numbers in such diverse groups as the International Club, the Juggling Club, and the Alliance, which focuses on gender issues. The student pub, known as the Coughy Haus, is a favorite hangout on Friday night. Undergraduates say crime in the economically depressed neighborhood surrounding the college is a problem and students, male and female, are advised not to walk alone after dark. Over the past few years, the college has improved lighting throughout the campus, locked residence halls around the clock, added emergency telephones, and increased security patrols as deterrents. However, says a midwesterner, "students always are leaving their backpacks unguarded in the library and at the entranceway to the cafeteria. Crime by students against one another is rare."

The Buccaneers football team attracts the best and most exuberant crowds, though basketball, soccer, and men's and women's lacrosse also have good followings among the 10 NCAA Division III sports offered for each sex. Fewer than a third of the students participate in the 15 men's and 13 women's intramural sports.

Beloit (pop. 36,000) doesn't offer many stimuli for college students, so most in need of a break road-trip to the University of Wisconsin at Madison (45 minutes by car or an hour and recently about $6 by bus directly to the campus) or to Chicago (90 minutes by car, recently $22 round trip by bus).

Cost cutters: More than 40% of Beloit alumni contribute to the college annually. That continued support, along with a healthy endowment of more than $106 million as of June 2005, helps to keep down costs. In the 2005–2006 school year, 80% of freshmen and 77% of continuing students received financial assistance. No figures are available to show the portion of students who received need-based aid, although in previous years, just over 70% of both freshmen and continuing students did. The average package for a first-year student with need included a need-based scholarship or grant averaging $15,676 and need-based self-help aid such as loans and jobs averaging $3482. Other non-need-based awards and scholarships for first-year students averaged $14,025. Graduates in 2005 who had financial need left school with an average debt of $18,783. Moral Obligation Scholarships, based on financial need, are awarded with the expectation that, as alumni, recipients will return to the college amounts equal to or greater than the initial awards. In addition to need-based aid, Beloit offers approximately 60 specially funded merit scholarships. Presidential scholarships pay $10,500, $12,000, or $13,500 a year over 4 years; candidates for the award must rank in the top 10% of their high school classes (or have GPAs of at least 3.5), have a 1200 critical reading and math SAT or 26 ACT, and present evidence of significant extracurricular activities. Candidates for the Presidential award must be interviewed on campus during one of two weekends in January and February. Other academic scholarships pay from $4000 to $13,500 a year.

Rate of return: Eighty-nine percent of the freshmen who enroll in Beloit return for the sophomore year. Sixty-two percent graduate in 4 years; 70%, in 5 years; 72% in 6.

Payoff: No single major claims an overwhelming percentage of Beloit graduates; for the 2005 class, the most popular choices were psychology at 11%, anthropology at 10%, and economics at 8%. In a recent year, 74% entered the job market shortly after graduating, in fields ranging from business and government service to teaching, advertising, and the arts. More than 60 companies and organizations recruited on campus in a recent school year. More than 60% of alumni complete graduate or professional degrees within 10 years of commencement. Among recent graduates, 20% have opted to pursue advanced degrees immediately.

Bottom line: Advises a senior: "Beloit is a very open-minded school where there is little pressure on students to look, act, or talk the same. It is a relaxed community that maintains a strong interest in improving its students. However, those who come must be willing to be tolerant of other's opinions and to sample a wide range of classes. Beloit expects its students to want to get an education; and if that is not your first priority, you won't be happy here."

Marquette University

Milwaukee, Wisconsin 53201

Setting: Urban
Control: Private (Roman Catholic-Jesuit)
Undergraduate enrollment: 3423 men, 4107 women
Graduate enrollment: 1055 men, 1112 women
Student/faculty ratio: 15:1
Freshman profile: 11% scored over 700 on SAT I verbal; 40% scored 600–700; 40% 500–599; 19% below 500. 15% scored over 700 on SAT I math; 38% scored 600–700; 39% 500–599; 8% below 500. 28% scored above 28 on the ACT; 23% scored 27–28; 29% 24–26; 12% 21–23; 8% below 21. 34% graduated in top tenth of high school class; 56% in upper fifth.
Faculty profile: 88% Ph.D.'s

Tuition and fees: $23,346
Room and board: $7720
Freshman financial aid: 90%; average scholarship or grant: $8449 need-based; $8825 non-need-based
Campus jobs: 32%; average earnings: $1500/year
Application deadline: Dec. 1
Financial deadline: Feb. 1
Admissions information: (414) 288-7302; (800) 222-6544
e-mail: admissions@marquette.edu
web site: www.marquette.edu

Marquette University, a 125-year-old Catholic university run by the Society of Jesus in Milwaukee, pays tribute in its name to the renowned Jesuit priest Jacques Marquette, who explored the upper Middle West and the Mississippi River in the 17th century. Whereas Marquette fended off unfriendly Indians and coped with unnavigable waters in his quest for knowledge, the challenges confronting today's Marquette students are decidedly urban. A recent graduate recalls: "While the city life offers many outstanding attractions—

concerts, professional sports, theater, ballet—it also has its bad side—transients, crime, and limited housing. But the Jesuit education forces us to look further than our future earning potential and makes us aware of our community." Thanks to that Jesuit commitment and to the combined efforts of the university, the city of Milwaukee, and local community groups, the neighborhood around Marquette is a safer, more economically vibrant place than it was several years ago. Crime is down 53% and the university alone at last count, has invested almost $50 million in new and rehabbed housing, attracting a dozen new businesses to the area in the process. The result has been not just a better life for the university and the people in its surrounding neighborhood, but also an education for Marquette's middle- and upper middle-class students about being involved in the renewal of a community. Says a senior: "We live in an urban environment where it is essential that students become more than campus aware, but socially aware as well. The students may be more conservative politically, but we are liberal towards opening our minds to new ideas and various values of other individuals."

Student body: Undergraduates see themselves as a spirited bunch. Says a senior: "We do not shy away from questions/conversations about faith, justice, identity, mission." Nearly two-thirds, 63% are Catholic, 17% Protestant. Minority enrollment at Marquette includes 5% African-Americans, 4% Asian-Americans, 4% Hispanics, and less than 0.5% Native Americans. International students from 77 countries comprise 2% of the undergraduates. Students come from all states, but 48% are from Wisconsin, with large numbers also from the Chicago area. Forty-five percent graduated from private or parochial schools. While a majority of undergraduates tend to be conservative and to adhere to mainstream values, a broad variety of political philosophies, extending to the very liberal, are represented. The academic range is wide as well, "from those who are upset with anything less than a 4.0 to those who are here more for the fun and consequently are barely getting by," remarks a junior, though most tilt toward the hard-working end. At Marquette, say its students, competition is much more a struggle with oneself than with peers.

Academics: Marquette grants the bachelor's degree in 58 fields of study, plus postgraduate degrees through the doctorate in 6 colleges and 7 schools and programs. All but the Graduate and Law schools offer programs for undergraduates. The academic year is divided into 2 semesters. Average class size for undergraduates is 28, although freshman history lectures may have 600 students. Most other first- and second-year courses enroll fewer than 50; classes for juniors and seniors usually have about 30 but can dip as low as 10 or 15 participants.

A new core curriculum common to students across all colleges and programs requires 36 credit hours in 9 subject areas. Three credit hours each are required in mathematical reasoning, individual and social behavior, science and nature, histories of cultures and societies, literature and performing arts, and diverse cultures. Six credit hours each are expected in rhetoric, human nature and ethics, and theology.

Marquette's entire faculty numbers 1046 members, 592 full-time, 454 part-time. Of the full-time faculty, 80 teach at the graduate level only as do 194 of the part-time members. Thirty-eight percent of the total pool are women. Graduate students in a recent year taught 3% of the introductory courses. Students find the heavy reliance on part-time faculty somewhat undesirable, although, as 1 critic notes, "even the most popular and busiest professors are excellent in terms of accessibility and willingness to work with undergraduates." However, it is up to the student to speak up when he or she needs help and the student may be surprised at the response. Observes a junior: "I would say 9 out of 10 faculty members are friendly, caring, and concerned about the success of their students."

Some of Marquette's strongest programs are those that emphasize hands-on learning. In the College of Arts and Sciences, political science "has a most involved, most excellent faculty," raves a major, "with a real emphasis on guest speakers and internship programs." The university's Les Aspin Center for Government, for example, offers students an opportunity to live, learn, and work for a semester or summer in Washington, D.C. History and biology also are excellent, with dedicated teachers who remain active in their fields. The College of Engineering continues to uphold its strong reputation with a long-standing cooperative education program that involves about 40% of the qualified majors, a recently remodeled building, and new equipment. Its program in biomedical engineering, which combines courses in biology, chemistry, mathematics, computers, and engineering, is touted as the largest in the country. The College of Communication, which includes programs in journalism and the performing arts, provides many courses and state-of-the art equipment for budding television, radio, and print reporters. A campus speech clinic likewise gives speech pathology majors in the College of Health Sciences first-hand experience. In the College of Business Administration, accounting gets high scores from students who value the savvy faculty, well-rounded curriculum, and high job placement record. The international business program which requires proficiency in a foreign language as well as study abroad, also is much admired. The College of Nursing, the School of Education, and the Program in Physical Therapy, which enrolls all students in a 6-year curriculum leading to bachelor's and master's degrees, also draw respect from students both in and out of the fields.

The dental hygiene program, after years of high maintenance costs and dwindling student interest, was terminated with the Class of 2004. The social work major also was recently cut. There already are no majors in either art or music.

Facilities: John P. Raynor, S.J. Library, named for Marquette's late former president who served from 1965-1990, opened in September 2003 and already is popular with students who like its emphasis on 21st-century research technology. "Very modern and nice—and very busy," observes a sophomore. Adds a senior: "It is probably one of, if not the busiest, places on campus easily." The $47 million 3-story structure is filled mainly with reading rooms and group-study areas as well as reference desks and computer workstations designed to assist students in finding resources. The bulk of the university's collection, which stands at 1.3 million volumes, 1.5 million microform items, and 15,868 periodicals, is housed next door, in the old Memorial Library. (Additional volumes are housed in the Law Library.) An elevated bridge connects the two structures. Students seeking quiet tend to gravitate toward the older structure "where it is always silent," says one patron. Night owls especially like the new hours: the first-floor Information Commons in Raynor is open around the clock and well used after the rest of Raynor is closed. In the first semester after the library opened, 35,000 students entered the library between midnight and 8 a.m. Marquette's dual library system also houses 1 of the true gems of fantasy literature: the original manuscripts of J.R.R. Tolkien's masterpieces, *The Hobbit* and *The Lord of the Rings*.

About 1200 university-owned PCs and Macs are available for general student use throughout campus: The 2 most popular spots are the Information Commons in Raynor Library and the first floor computer lab in the computing and mathematics building, both of which are open around the clock. Labs also are located in other academic buildings, the student center, and the residence halls, where labs are open around the clock to their residents only. All rooms in the residence halls are wired for high-speed Internet access. A number of buildings across campus, including Raynor Library, have wireless access.

Special programs: Foreign study includes summer programs in Mexico, Germany, and Belgium; intersession in Russia; and terms in Oxford or in Madrid or Strasbourg, France, for those who are fluent in each language. Altogether, 24 programs for foreign study are available in 16 countries. A semester in Washington, D.C. is an option as well. Cross-registration is possible with the Milwaukee Institute of Art and Design. The Freshmen Frontier Program provides support to selected entering freshmen who do not meet regular admission requirements but show potential for success. A Service Learning Project integrates community service with academic coursework in more than 3 dozen courses.

Campus life: Fifty-five percent of all undergraduates but 90% of the freshmen and sophomores reside on the 80-acre urban campus, located close to Lake Michigan. Many others live within easy walking distance of campus. The city's principal thoroughfare, Wisconsin Avenue, intersects the campus, while Milwaukee's major expressway interchange frames the south and east borders of the university. Two safety programs help to make the immediate area around the campus safer for undergraduates: LIMO (Local Intercampus Mobile Operation) provides free transportation to students and employees between the campus and the adjoining residential areas; and the university safety patrol, known as the "yellow jackets," involves students in teams, each carrying a two-way radio for quick access to campus safety officers, city police, and paramedic units, that patrol the campus and nearby residential area. Both programs also provide escorts 7 nights a week for Marquette students, faculty, and staff. Students give Marquette's public safety department a gold star for its efforts. Says one female undergraduate: "The public safety department is one of the best in the nation and is absolutely wonderful at protecting and serving students' safety and well-being."

Fraternities and sororities attract 5% of the men and 7% of the women to 11 national fraternities and 11 national sororities. Greek and independents alike also gravitate to the popular bars on Wells Street. University Ministry is very active and sponsors numerous retreats and spiritual development activities. The Marquette University Community Action Program involves hundreds of students in local volunteer efforts. Together students, faculty, and staff devote 150,000 hours to community service each year. Midnight Run, an organization that focuses on issues of hunger and homelessness, and JUSTICE, a group dedicated to examining issues of social justice throughout the world, have been especially prominent about campus. Musical performing groups such as the ever popular band as well as orchestra, choir, and gospel choir and various ethnic student organizations also are very active.

The word *big* doesn't begin to describe Marquette basketball games, which are played off campus at Milwaukee's Bradley Center, home of the NBA's Bucks, and are the high point of the 7 men's and 7 women's intercollegiate sports played in NCAA Division I. New recreational fields adjacent to the campus are the home of Golden Eagles men's and women's soccer as well as a variety of club and intramural sports. Thirty-nine intramural sports, in which 30% of the men and 18% of the women participate, also are hugely popular. True sports fans can put in overtime watching Milwaukee Bucks basketball and Brewer baseball.

The Milwaukee Zoo, the "Domes" botanical gardens, rock concerts, stage shows, and Lake Michigan are other popular off-campus diversions.

Cost cutters: In the 2005–2006 school year, 90% of Marquette freshmen and 86% of continuing students were awarded financial aid; 54% of the freshmen and 51% of the continuing students received need-based assistance. The average freshman award in 2005–2006 for a student with need included a need-based scholarship or grant averaging $8449 and need-based self-help aid such as loans and jobs averaging $5762. Other non-need-based awards and scholarships, not counting those for athletics, averaged $8828. The average non-need-based athletic scholarship totaled $19,129. The average debt of 2005 graduates was $26,345. A number of scholarships and awards based on academic merit are available to entering freshmen. Ignatius Scholarships pay $6000 to $9000 to entering freshmen based upon their academic performance, standardized test scores, leadership, and community service. The full-tuition Raynor Distinguished Scholarship goes to 3 high school seniors who ranked at or near the top 5% with an ACT of at least 29 or a combined math and critical reading SAT of 1300, as well as significant leadership experience in and out of the classroom. A 10-month tuition payment plan is available. A cooperative education program is offered in engineering only.

Rate of return: Ninety percent of the freshmen return for the sophomore year. Sixty-two percent graduate in 4 years; 78%, in 5 years; 80%, in 6 years.

Payoff: For 2005 graduates, the most popular majors were business and marketing at 22%, communications at 14%, and engineering at 10%. Sixty-seven percent of a recent graduating class went on to jobs soon after commencement; many accepted offers with the 320 companies and other organizations that recruit on campus. Major employers included Procter & Gamble, Ameritech, and Kimberly-Clark. Twenty-nine percent of the new alumni pursue advanced degrees within a year of earning their bachelor's at Marquette.

Bottom line: Says a senior: "A student who is academically dedicated but also has other interests, particularly in community service and social justice-type issues, would benefit most from Marquette. Not only do we learn about new ways of looking at the world through philosophy and theology and other classes but we receive lots of opportunities and encouragement to go out and change the world we live in to make it a better place."

Ripon College
Ripon, Wisconsin 54971

Setting: Small town
Control: Private
Undergraduate enrollment: 477 men, 476 women
Graduate enrollment: None
Student/faculty ratio: 13:1
Freshman profile: 14% scored over 700 on SAT I verbal; 41% scored 600–700; 18% 500–599; 27% below 500. 8% scored over 700 on SAT I math; 36% scored 600–700; 36% 500–599; 20% below 500. 17% scored above 28 on the ACT; 13% scored 27–28; 26% 24–26; 23% 21–23; 21% below 21. 21% graduated in top tenth of high school class; 41% in upper fifth.

Faculty profile: 92% Ph.D.'s
Tuition and fees: $21,550
Room and board: $5610
Freshman financial aid: 99%; average scholarship or grant: $15,713 need-based; $10,465 non-need-based
Campus jobs: 38%; average earnings: $766/year
Application deadline: Aug. 1
Financial aid deadline: Mar. 1
Admissions information: (920) 748-8185; (800) 94RIPON
e-mail: schuetzs@ripon.edu
web site: www.ripon.edu

Familiarity, it is said, breeds contempt. For 1 native of Ripon, Wisconsin, close proximity to the hometown college sent her to another school. After 1 semester, though, she was back where she knew she belonged. "I thought all liberal arts schools had the same atmosphere as Ripon. WRONG. Ripon is very student oriented, and professors 'hang out' with undergraduates; they play in the orchestra, they play intramural sports. They get to know so much about you they can custom fit you with an education." And at Ripon, founded in 1851, custom tailoring doesn't cost extra. Tuition, fees, room, and board were just over $27,000 in 2005–2006, a far cry from the 1873 tuition rate of $8 a term but still several thousand dollars less than comparable costs at other small, highly selective Phi Beta Kappa colleges on the East and West coasts.

Student body: Ripon draws the majority of its students from the Midwest; 74% are from Wisconsin, but undergraduates come from 35 states and 13 foreign countries. Forty-three percent graduated from private or parochial schools. Minorities comprise 9% of the student body—3% Hispanics, 3% African-Americans, 2% Asian-Americans, and 1% Native Americans. Foreign nationals add another 2%. Undergraduates describe themselves as friendly and enthusiastic, academically motivated and involved. "Students are willing to help out a classmate, without worrying that the one who was helped may outscore them on a test," observes a recent graduate. Also, grading is not done on a curve, further reducing any need to "beat out" one other. Students consider themselves diverse in their thinking reflecting a mixture of liberal and conservative viewpoints. "Political debates take place all the time," says a history major, "and everyone is accepting of others' opinions and beliefs."

Academics: Ripon offers bachelor's degrees in about 30 disciplines. The academic year is divided into 2 semesters with an optional 2-week Maymester. Most classes for freshmen and sophomores range from 15 to 30 participants, although an introductory lecture may creep toward 40. Most courses for juniors and seniors have from 8 to 15 participants; various independent study projects, as well as 1-on-1 scientific research with professors, ensure that every student gets plenty of personal attention.

A First-Year Studies program immediately launches students into what Ripon expects of them academically with a 4-credit interdisciplinary seminar offered fall term. Among the 17 different topics offered in a recent school year was People, Prairies, and Populations, in which students used readings, field trips, and activities to explore how the disciplines of art, biology, economics, English, history, mathematics, music, philosophy, and politics could all be involved in prairie management programs in Wisconsin and the Ripon area. All students also take a developmental writing course as freshmen and later an upper-level writing-intensive class selected from any discipline. Six credits each in the behavioral/social sciences, fine arts, humanities, natural sciences/mathematics, and global studies; 2 credits in physical education, and third-semester competency in a foreign language also are required. Some of these distribution requirements are taken care of through the First-Year Interdisciplinary Seminar, depending on its academic emphasis.

Forty-five of the 97 faculty members are part-time. Women comprise 39% of the faculty. Professors at Ripon recognize and encourage a spirit of individualism in their students by giving them assignments that encourage incorporation of personal interests and information from other classes. Cooperative efforts are promoted as well, and many faculty members show up for study groups over a pizza the night before a test. It is not unusual for students who rate faculty on a scale of 1 to 10, to give them a "20," or to grade them from A to F, with an A+. Observes a junior: "Faculty care more truly than I could have ever expected at a collegiate level. They are ethical and brilliant and often sacrifice their free time in extracurricular activities or in helping students." Adds a senior: "Since Ripon's classes are so small, it's impossible not to know professors on a personal level. That helps you to learn more in your subject area and also helps when they're later referring you for jobs, etc., because they really know you as a person and as a student."

Biology and chemistry are exceptionally strong, with excellent equipment and faculties very willing to ask students to assist them 1-on-1 in their research. Biology also sponsors diverse field trips studying marine ecology or desert ecology during the Maymester. Recalls a sophomore: "Ripon offers the Ceresco Prairie and my freshman class spent more time there than in the classroom." History is a department "dedicated to 'doing history' and not just memorizing dates," says a major. "Professors emphasize the use of primary sources, and we're encouraged to look at the perceptions and motivations behind the actions of historical personages." Senior business management majors complete a semester-long project in which they start and run every aspect of a company from finance to marketing. English is noted for its stimulating faculty members who bring a diversity of experience and perspectives to the department. The psychology faculty, says a major, simply "are wonderful. They will do almost anything to help you out if you need it. They also are willing to listen to constructive criticism and are looking to improve constantly." The communication program is described by a senior as being "very vigorous," giving students "an all-around liberal arts education and the confidence to get any job they want." Religion, though it has a single full-time faculty member, supplements his excellent teaching with presentations from other religious figures in the area.

Although Ripon counts actors Spencer Tracy and Harrison Ford among its alumni, students have found the theater major lacking in courses and facilities; nevertheless, its faculty is excellent and its productions generally are of high quality and well supported by the undergraduates. The music major also is considered small but lacks the quality and variety in performance groups many students desire. Departments of such majors as philosophy, sociology, and politics and government, each need an additional professor to present greater variety in the courses being offered. Physics was dropped as a major and replaced with a broader major in physical science.

Facilities: Lane Library, built in 1930 and last expanded in 1974, is small: 161,000 volumes and 800 periodicals, but offers students a range of study options from the cold and austere to the comfortable. Says a politics major: "There is a ton of tucked-away areas to find quiet and solitude so you can focus." Students who wish may reserve personal study carrels by the semester. One of Lane's chief assets is its wonderful staff. Says a sophomore: "The librarians and student staff workers are awesome helpers when it comes to students needing resources and help finding various items in the library." A computerized system for both books and periodicals quickly tells users what materials Lane has and which ones are available where through interlibrary loan. Periodicals unavailable at Ripon can be obtained from almost any library in the state via WILS (Wisconsin Interlibrary Services). Students also can borrow more up-to-date books from the University of Wisconsin, Oshkosh, library, just 20 minutes away.

Computers seem to be everywhere, with about 100 Macintosh and IBM PC microcomputers in the library, dorms, and classroom buildings, as well as the computer center. Most labs are open until midnight or 1 a.m. with extended hours at midterm and finals times. Wireless hotspots are available in Lane Library, the commons, and several other locations around campus.

Special programs: Ripon students can study in 13 foreign countries from Budapest, Hungary to Pune, India, as well as at the college's own international study center in Bonn, Germany. Joint programs are offered in engineering with Rensselaer Polytechnic Institute, University of Minnesota, and Washington University; in forestry and environmental studies with Duke University; in social welfare with the University of Chicago; and in nursing with Rush University. Students may cross-register with members of the Associated Colleges of the Midwest. An exchange with Fisk University, an historically black college in Nashville, Tennessee, also is an option, as is a semester in Chicago or Washington, D.C.

Campus life: For those needing plenty of elbow room, Ripon's the place, offering 250 acres to its 953 full-time students, nearly all of whom live on campus. Twenty-eight percent of the men are members of 2 local and 3 national fraternities; 14% of the women belong to 1 local and 2 national sororities. There is no separate Greek housing so fraternities generally host "lounge" parties with dancing in the residence-hall lounges, and independents attend as they wish. Some undergraduates join together as members of 2 coed living groups. About 50 students a year have weekly shows on the campus radio station. The *College Days* student newspaper has a strong following as well. The Cultural Diversity Club and the Community Service Coalition also have active supporters, as do groups as diverse as Campus Christian Fellowship and The Network, a gay, lesbian, bisexual, and transgender awareness group. For most students, Ripon remains a place where students can leave their backpacks and jackets in the lobby of the student commons to go to dinner, and return to find everything still there. Residence halls are equipped with a key card system and locked around the clock. An escort service is available and used.

Sports are popular at Ripon. About 40% of the men recently played on the 9 varsity teams that are part of NCAA Division III. Twenty-nine percent of the women participated in the 9 intercollegiate sports available for them. Men's and women's basketball and soccer, women's volleyball, and men's football and baseball draw the biggest crowds. A slightly lower proportion of the students participate in a wide assortment of intramural sports, 15 each for men and for women. "We have everything from 'gerbils' (indoor soccer) to inner tube water polo!" raves a senior. Hockey and fencing are the most popular club sports. There also is plenty of stickball, Frisbee, and hackysack at the quads, the 4 dorms that house the fraternities and other upperclassmen.

Those longing to rip out of Ripon (the college, that is) can go south to the South Woods Wildlife Sanctuary, located 1 block from campus. Once winter ends, 20 lakes within 25 miles of Ripon offer students the chance to swim, boat, bike, hike, and camp. An outdoors club involves many students in activities that make the most of the area's natural offerings. Oshkosh and Fond-du-lac are just 20 minutes away. Occasionally, students leave the 7100 residents of Ripon behind and make a longer trek to Milwaukee, Madison, or Chicago.

Cost cutters: In the 2005–2006 school year, 99% of Ripon freshmen and 88% of continuing students received financial help; 78% of the freshmen and 71% of the rest were given need-based aid. The average freshman award for a student with financial need included a need-based scholarship or grant averaging $15,713 and need-based self-help aid such as loans and job earnings averaging $5255. Other non-need based awards and scholarships averaged $10,465. Among recent graduates, the average debt was $16,210. The top academic award for 1 lucky freshman is the full-tuition Pickard Scholarship; 10 awards paying $15,000 a year go to Pickard finalists. Candidates, who enter a competitive interview process, generally come from the top 5% of their high school class with ACTs of 30 or above and combined math and critical reading SATs of at least 1340. The Presidential Scholarship pays $12,000 annually to students with a minimum 3.8 GPA and similar class rank and test scores. Other renewable awards paying $5000 to $10,000 a year are given to students with lower test scores and GPAs. Students with talent in music, theater, or art can receive yearly awards of up to $5000; for forensics, up to $10,000. The Knop Scholars Program pays full tuition to 1 top student planning to study science or math. Diversity Awards worth $15,000 a year go to high-achieving students who will contribute to the cultural, ethnic, geographical, and socioeconomic diversity of the student body; an interview is required and demonstrated financial need is considered. High school valedictorians receive $6000 annually. Monthly tuition payment plans are available. A student can earn a bachelor's degree in 3 years with no summer study, but he or she must elect more courses and achieve higher grade point averages in the second and third years. There is no charge for the extra courses. Two percent of the 2005 graduates finished early.

Rate of return: Eighty-five percent of freshmen return for the sophomore year. Sixty-one percent graduate in 4 years; 71%, within 5 years; 74% within 6.

Payoff: For the class of 2005, the top majors were biology and history at 10% each, followed by psychology at 9%. Twenty-two percent of the recent graduates went on immediately to graduate or professional school, with the largest portion pursuing advanced degrees in the arts and sciences. After 2 years, about half of Ripon alumni have pursued or are pursuing advanced study, with the largest number in business school. The majority of recent graduates took jobs directly after commencement, most in banking, sales, teaching, and public relations/communications, with such firms as Northwestern Mutual Life, IBM, 3M, and First Chicago Bank, as well as the *Milwaukee Journal*. Most alumni settle in the Midwest and find that the college's senior survival workshops in everything from apartment hunting to buying a car or insurance facilitate the transition from Ripon to the real world.

Bottom line: "Depending on whom you talk to," notes a philosophy major, "Ripon's small size is either its best quality or its worst. For the high school senior who feels that he or she will do well in small, personal, challenging classes and who wants to get involved on campus, I recommend Ripon. The personal attention here is conducive not just to academic growth, but to personal growth as well."

St. Norbert College

De Pere, Wisconsin 54115

Setting: Suburban
Control: Private (Roman Catholic)
Undergraduate enrollment: 829 men, 1093 women
Graduate enrollment: 63 men and women (part-time)
Student/faculty ratio: 14:1
Freshman profile: 12% scored above 28 on the ACT; 10% scored 27–28; 29% 24–26; 30% 21–23; 19% below 21. 24% graduated in top tenth of high school class; 50% in upper fourth.
Faculty profile: 92% Ph.D.'s
Tuition and fees: $22,509

Room and board: $6068
Freshman financial aid: 98%; average scholarship or grant: $11,136 need-based; $1866 non-need-based
Campus jobs: 54%; average earnings: $1150/year
Application deadline: Rolling
Financial aid deadline: Mar. 1
Admissions information: (920) 403-3005; (800) 236-4878
e-mail: admit@snc.edu
web site: www.snc.edu

When Abbot Bernard Pennings, a Norbertine priest and educator, decided to open a college near Green Bay, Wisconsin, that would "perfect the personal, moral, and intellectual development of each student," the abbot didn't have to worry about such problems as expanding student/faculty ratios or getting across his message in a lecture to several hundred undergraduates. Pennings opened St. Norbert College in 1898 with a single student. More than a century later, the coed Roman Catholic college enrolls nearly 2000 full-time undergraduates and has 161 full- and part-time faculty members, but it still manages to adhere to Abbot Pennings's commitment to the individual. Over and over, students cite a hallmark of Pennings' legacy: personal attention provided by friendly and concerned professors, by college staff, including financial aid and career counselors, and most of all by other students. "I have never seen so much concern for the other person," marvels a senior in political science. "This kind of atmosphere gives one the confidence and the self-esteem to reach for the stars."

Student body: The universe of St. Norbert is quite homogeneous, though the college is working to expand diversity: Three percent of the students are foreign nationals from 13 countries. Another 2% are Hispanic and 1% each are Native American, Asian-American, and African-American. Seventy-one percent of the undergraduates are from Wisconsin, with large numbers also from Michigan, Iowa, Minnesota, and Illinois—the Chicago area in particular. A total of 22 states are represented. Catholic students make up 51% of the school population. Thirty percent graduated from private or parochial schools. Students say the economic span ranges from students whose wealthy parents pay for everything to those who work hard to pay for everything themselves. One senior assesses her peers as follows: "Students here tend to be intelligent, friendly, eager to learn, fairly knowledgeable about our world, and politically conservative." Academic competition varies by major, with the range extending from the "highly intellectual," in the words of one junior, to the "extraordinarily laid back."

Academics: St. Norbert offers the bachelor's degree in more than 30 majors plus a master's degree in theological studies and in education. The academic year is divided into 2 semesters. Average class size for undergraduates is 24. Business and general-education classes are the largest, but rarely exceed 50 students. Raves a business and economics major: "In 4 years here, I have only had 1 class in a lecture hall; the rest of my classes have been about 20–25 students."

St. Norbert's general-education program is split into 2 levels. In the lower biennium for freshmen and sophomores, 1 course is mandated from each of 9 subject areas ranging from religious studies and human relationships to foreign heritages and quantitative skills. In the upper biennium, juniors and seniors take 1 course each in religious studies, Western tradition, and global society plus a general-studies capstone course. There also is a focus on writing across the curriculum.

The St. Norbert faculty is composed of 109 full-time members and 52 part-time, and just about all demand full-time commitment from their students. Thirty-seven percent are women. Students describe their professors as "all around quality people" who know their stuff and keep the classroom atmosphere relaxed to encourage questions. Says a sophomore: "Professors provide a safe academic environment for students, where there are no stupid questions and every student comment deserves some sort of attention by the class."

Business administration offers a wide variety of courses and an excellent faculty to teach them. Accounting is especially rigorous. The International Business and Language Area Studies program prepares students to enter the global marketplace through advanced language instruction, study abroad, and diversified coursework at home in economics, mathematics, and political science; in the senior seminar, students operate a business corporation (Discoveries International) and conduct extensive research projects related to the foreign market. The teacher education department turns out "the best teachers in the state," in part because of the emphasis on experience; majors are required to student-teach in their sophomore and senior years. English and the social sciences win student approval for the quality and friendliness of their teaching staffs. Psychology, in particular, stresses experimental study by students. Mathematics also is excellent. Student/faculty research projects in the natural sciences, particularly biology and chemistry, have gotten a boost from National Science and Kresge foundation grants directed at undergraduate, not graduate, research efforts, though students wish that some of the equipment were a bit more up-to-date.

Students interested in modern foreign languages wish there were more professors and more variety in course offerings. Majors are offered in French, German, and Spanish, and a minor in Japanese. A personal Japanese language major also is an option when faculty staffing is available.

Facilities: Walk into Todd Wehr Library and you'll immediately learn the source of the building's greatest pride and downfall. Observes a senior: "On any given night, a person could walk into the library and not be able to find a place to study because it is so packed with students either researching or studying." Such popularity, however, also can mean elevated noise levels, especially between the hours of 8 p.m. and midnight. Adds the student: "If you're lucky enough to get a study room, then it is not really a problem, but those are scarce." The third floor also is designated for total silence. Users engaged in serious research have learned to overlook the shortcomings of Wehr's collection of 220,000 titles, which has become steadily larger and more up to date in recent years, and its 652 periodicals, which a number find too limited. However, full-text database subscriptions increase students' access to periodical literature to over 5000 titles. In addition, the library subscribes to several specialized databases plus online catalogs to libraries at numerous other Wisconsin colleges and universities, at Northwestern University and at the University of Texas at Austin.

More than 220 computers housed in public labs and in the library and campus center are available for student use. Labs generally close by midnight weeknights and at 7 p.m. Fridays and Saturdays but are extended by 2 hours a night during the last few weeks of the term. Internet access is available from all residence hall rooms, classrooms, offices, and laboratories. Wireless computing is an option in the library and campus center as well as in several instructional areas. Additional wireless availability was planned following the 2005–2006 school year.

Special programs: Among a wide range of study abroad programs, in 20 countries, 2 of the more far-flung involve student exchanges with Sophia University in Tokyo and the Australian Catholic University. Education majors may do their student teaching in 1 of 12 different countries. Undergraduates may also study for a semester in Washington, D.C. The Leadership Service and Involvement Program offers courses and activities that help boost self-confidence.

Campus life: Most of the students, 75%, live on St. Norbert's 92-acre campus bordering the Fox River, 5 miles south of Green Bay. "The college is very compact," says a state resident, "which is definitely a selling point in the cold northern Wisconsin weather." Its setting creates a peaceful atmosphere conducive to both learning and relaxation. It has become even closer knit, since the opening in September 2000 of the Ray Van Den Heuvel Family Campus Center, a home for various student organizations as well as offices related to community involvement and cultural diversity. The idea, says a recent graduate, "was first conceived and for the most part planned by a group of students, who envisioned the center as giving a new sense of community to campus." As a Catholic college in the Norbertine tradition, St. Norbert emphasizes the importance of community and shared values. Students who are not practicing Catholics generally find the atmosphere welcoming rather than restrictive. Just 6% of the men and 8% of the women belong to 1 local and 3 national fraternities and 3 national and 2 local sororities. More students belong to a wide range of independent social groups, among them NoNonsense and CC Hams for women, and Admar and Big for men. Some of these groups boast memberships of over 200; others have fewer than 20. Independents and Greeks spar in friendly competition during major festivities like Homecoming and Winter Carnival, and all host dances over the weekend. Community service programs also are very popular, giving students a choice among 27 service organizations. Campus crime is of little concern to most students. "There are usually 1 or 2 'major' crimes each year—one year's was the theft of someone's CD collection," a senior recalls. As safety measures, however, residence-hall outside doors are locked and there is a Safe Walk escort service and emergency call boxes.

With a few exceptions, sports are low-key at St. Norbert. The college offers 10 NCAA Division III varsity sports for men and 10 for women. Hockey draws the biggest weekend crowds to cheer on the Green Knights, followed by football and basketball. Thirty percent of the men and 13% of the women engage in intramural sports, 7 for each sex.

For off-campus diversion beyond De Pere (pop. 20,000), many students head for the malls, restaurants, and cafes in Green Bay or go home for the weekend. The Door County tourist area near Green Bay is a popular day trip in autumn and spring. Some students road-trip to the University of Wisconsin, Madison, or to Minneapolis.

Cost cutters: St. Norbert guarantees a diploma and no more than 4 years of college bills to students (except education majors) who enter as freshmen, enroll in 4 courses per semester, do not fail or withdraw from any classes, and maintain a cumulative 2.0 grade point average. If students qualify for the guarantee but can't complete their degree requirements (because courses are unavailable, for instance), the college will waive tuition for the courses the student needs to graduate. Tuition will remain the same over the 4 years a student attends St. Norbert if a premium is paid. There are guaranteed jobs for all freshmen who want to work, and tuition assistance if a wage-earning parent dies. An endowment of more than $52 million, as of June 2005, helps the college to hold down costs and provide more than $32 million in scholarships, grants, loans, and about 1300 campus jobs. In a recent school year, all but 2% of St. Norbert's freshmen and all but 4% of its continuing students received financial aid. For 68% of the freshmen and 70% of the rest, the assistance was based on need. The average freshman award for a student with need included a need-based scholarship or grant averaging $11,136 and need-based self-help aid such as loans and job earnings averaging $4583. Other non-need-based awards and scholarships averaged $1866. Three main merit scholarships, renewable over 4 years, are based on SAT and ACT test scores, high school grades, and class rank. The Trustees Distinguished Scholarship pays $8000–$9500 each year; the Presidential Scholarship, $7000–$7500; and the John F. Kennedy Leadership Award, $4500–$6500. Music scholarships are obtainable through audition only. The average college debt of recent graduates was $20,770.

Rate of return: Eighty-eight percent of entering freshmen return for the sophomore year. Sixty-four percent graduate in 4 years, 70% in 5 years; 71% in 6. Observes a recent graduate: "The college expects students to graduate in 4 years, and advisers do everything they can to get you through in that period of time."

Payoff: Twenty-eight percent of 2005 graduates majored in business administration. Tied for the second most popular majors were communication, media, and theater and elementary education at 12% each. The college boasts a 95% placement rate in jobs and graduate school. A third of all graduates typically pursue advanced degrees within 5 years of graduation; less than a fifth pursue advanced degrees within 6 months of commencement. More than 60 companies and other organizations recruited on campus in a recent school year.

Bottom line: "Students who need or desire close contact with professors, and students who want a smaller, more comfortable atmosphere should look into St. Norbert College," says a sophomore. It's a place where Abbot Pennings' sense of individual attention still reigns.

University of Wisconsin, Madison

Madison, Wisconsin 53706

Setting: Urban
Control: Public
Undergraduate enrollment: 12,728 men, 14,713 women
Graduate enrollment: 4608 men, 4751 women
Student/faculty ratio: 13:1
Freshman profile: 16% scored over 700 on SAT I verbal; 44% scored 600–700; 30% 500–599; 10% below 500. 29% scored over 700 on SAT I math; 50% scored 600–700; 19% 500–599; 2% below 500. 56% graduated in top tenth of high school class; 91% in upper fifth.
Faculty profile: 92% Ph.D.'s

Tuition and fees: $6284 in-state, $20,284 out-of-state
Room and board: $6500
Freshman financial aid: 52%; average scholarship or grant: NA
Campus jobs: NA; average earnings: NA
Application deadline: Feb. 1
Financial aid deadline: Mar. 1
Admissions information: (608) 262-3961
   e-mail: on.wisconsin@admissions.wisc.edu
   web site: www.wisc.edu

When asked to describe her school's student body, an Ohio undergraduate at the University of Wisconsin, Madison answered this way: "Think of a large city, say New York City, and imagine every type of person you would find there. Now think Madison." The same goes for the university's curricular and extracurricular life. Think of 4300 courses offered each semester, including instruction in more than 60 foreign languages, and of resources ranging from a nuclear reactor to a mastodon skeleton, then think Madison. Think of a major university in the midwest with about 27,500 full-time undergraduates, more than 9000 full-time graduate students, 2975 faculty members, more than 160 undergraduate majors, and more than 700 student organizations—and you've got the University of Wisconsin's main campus in Madison. Intimidating? Many who fear being trampled in the rush change their minds after they've enrolled. "I expected the school to be much too large," recalls a recent geography graduate. "I found quite the opposite. It was easy to find my own niche because there are so many academic and social organizations available."

Student body: Minority and foreign national students make up about 15% of the total undergraduate enrollment. Foreign nationals constitute 3%; Asian-Americans, 5%; Hispanics and African-Americans, each 3%; and Native Americans, less than 1%. In a recent year, a third of the undergraduates had attended private or parochial schools. Students repeatedly cite the "phenomenal" range of UW's student population. Though 70% are from Wisconsin, students come from every state and 110 foreign countries. The student body mixes the midwestern conservatives with the liberal "earth muffins and deadheads who brought the school to the headlines in the '70s," observes a Minnesotan. Still, there is great spirit and cohesiveness among students. Exclaims a senior: "Wisconsin is a world-class institution and we are all proud to be Badgers." Undergraduates tend to be articulate, open minded, and socially involved. "Hardly a day goes by without a rally of some sort," a junior from Minneapolis observes. Adds a state resident: "If there is a cause, you can always find a group of students fighting for it." The academic atmosphere is fairly competitive; "not neurotic, but self-motivated," says a recent graduate, especially since so many programs, such as Education and Engineering, require certain GPA's for entrance.

Academics: UW-Madison, founded in 1848, grants bachelor's degrees in more than 160 majors and offers advanced degrees through the doctorate; 3 colleges and 6 schools offer programs for undergraduates. The Graduate School and the schools of Law and Veterinary Medicine award advanced degrees only. The academic year is divided into 2 semesters. Not surprisingly, the range in class size is enormous, from 5 in certain seminars and language courses to 300 in introductory-course lectures.

   The university-wide general education requirements are broad. They include coursework in communication, quantitative reasoning, natural science, humanities/literature/arts, social studies, and ethnic studies. Many schools and colleges, as well as individual programs, have subject requirements that go beyond those of the university-wide mandates.

Wisconsin's 2975-member faculty consists of 2365 full-time members and 610 part-time. All but 198 of the full-time members teach undergraduates; there is no corresponding figure for the number of part-time faculty who do. A third are women. Four former faculty members have won the Nobel Prize. The faculty's high quality is appreciated by students, who use such words as *outstanding, world class,* and *provocative* to describe their professors. Undergraduates express dissatisfaction, however, with some faculty members, especially those in the natural sciences, for slighting their teaching tasks in favor of research. "Imagine," says a psychology major, "No science professor, chemistry as well as zoology, asked me for my name even though I came to their offices maybe 5 times." In general, the quality of student/faculty relationships depends largely on the student, though many professors welcome closer bonds. Notes an accounting major: "Many of the professors strongly urge students to come talk to them. They are happy to help and like getting to know their students."

Recent surveys have rated 70 undergraduate programs at Madison, from bacteriology and dairy science to physical education and zoology, as being among the top 10 in the nation in their respective fields. Madison's political science department benefits greatly from the university's setting in the state capital, which lets students roam the halls of government as legislative aides or lobbyists. The business school stands out for its prominent and experienced faculty and its "great job placement," according to a recent journalism graduate. Journalism students enjoy an old-fashioned newspaper war, with 2 competing daily student newspapers, the *Daily Cardinal* and the *Badger Herald*; in some areas, however, the newsroom equipment is more old-fashioned than students would like. The creative writing program, though small, is very competitive and boasts a stimulating faculty; in fact, the English Department overall is a winner. Other first-rate programs noted for a good balance of teaching and research include German, biochemistry, chemical engineering, women's studies, sociology, agricultural studies and several of the area studies disciplines, such as Scandinavian and Latin American, Caribbean, and Iberian. The School of Education and the undergraduate programs in the School of Medicine are stellar as well. Students in the School of Human Ecology, which includes majors in such programs as interior design, consumer science, and human development and family studies, enjoy its smaller size. "You really get a lot of one-on-one help from professors," says a major in interior design.

Math professors are considered knowledgeable and they publish a lot, but "many simply do not know how to teach the material," notes a recent graduate. Lower-level math classes too often rely on teaching assistants who are difficult to understand or do not explain concepts sufficiently well. Many of the sciences, while academically rich and rigorous, tend to have more impersonal professors engaged intensively in their research rather than their undergraduate students. Physics seems overly tough to many majors in the other sciences.

Facilities: Each of Madison's 43 campus libraries has its own distinct personality. Memorial Library, the main graduate facility, with extensive humanities and social science collections, is "classic sturdiness with its dark stacks," notes a senior, and many students find it intimidating. College Library is the most social and, consequently, not too great for studying. The engineering and medical sciences libraries offer the best environment for serious students. "There is a library for everything, and they all have the best views on campus of the lake," exclaims a recent graduate. The latest facility closes at 2:45 a.m. The 43 libraries altogether have more than 7.2 million volumes and 55,000 periodicals. Those numbers don't include the collection in the State Historical Society Library in Madison, whose 2 million volumes students also turn to for research.

One thousand Windows XP and Mac computers are located in 13 labs around campus, from the libraries and academic buildings to private dorm study areas. Dataports are available in all dorm rooms. Most labs are open until around midnight, though a few are open 24 hours a day, 7 days a week. Labs closer to housing can have lines at exam time, but students willing to walk a bit further usually find a free unit. More than half of Madison's students in the 2005-2006 school year reported owning laptop computers. To accommodate students' increasing use of laptops, the university planned to expand its existing wireless coverage to make the entire campus wireless by the summer of 2006, a job that entailed creating 2600 access points in 130 buildings.

Special programs: Undergraduates may go abroad to study in more than 40 countries in Europe, Asia, and South America. Some programs, including the ones for Nepal, India, and Thailand, require students to successfully complete an intensive 10-week language program before they go. Nearly a fifth of Madison's undergraduates study abroad. The Institute for Environmental Studies offers a 26-credit certificate program with more than 100 courses. Under the UW Medical Scholars Program, 50 Wisconsin high school seniors are provisionally admitted, as college freshmen, to the UW medical school and may complete their undergraduate work in as little as 3 years. Political internships are available in Washington, D.C. and at the state capitol in Madison.

Campus life: All but a small percent of the undergraduates, plus a few cows along the western end, reside on the 933-acre campus on the shore of Lake Mendota, or in private dorms, Greek houses, and apartments within a mile of the university grounds. Although only about 10% of undergraduates are members of Greek organizations, parties at the 26 national fraternities and, less frequently, at the 11 national sororities are popular. Nonmembers often attend, but not as frequently as in past years; alcohol-related liability problems have forced many social fraternities to close parties and check IDs. The State Street bars, which form a horseshoe around the state capitol, are equally alluring. Memorial Union, facing the lake, draws huge crowds every weekend for concerts, movies, and speakers or simply for chatting on the terrace while sipping beer, munching popcorn, and feeding the ducks. The Hoofers, the oldest outing club in the nation, sponsors incredible skiing, sailing, and climbing trips. Environmental groups such as UW Greens and WISPIRG are very popular—but so are College Republicans. In short, Madison's size provides opportunities for all types of students to live (and socialize) as they please. Remarks a journalism major: "More solitary people can choose to get lost in the shuffle; the gregarious can talk to a thousand people daily." Few worry about crime. Frequent walking patrols by campus police officers, a well-illuminated "light-way" for nighttime, emergency telephones, and SafeWalk/SafeRide/SafeBus transit options help allay student fears.

The SERF (Southeast Recreational Facility), sort of a "high-tech gym," wows all but the most confirmed couch potatoes. Equally awesome to many alums are the Badgers' back-to-back Rose Bowl victories in 1999 and 2000; the team continues to pack the 77,000-seat football stadium. Students stick around after the game for a "5th quarter" to dance to the haunting strains of UW's Band. Wisconsin's Badgers compete in 11 other Big Ten Conference varsity sports for men; women also can choose among 12. The women's hockey team won its first national championship in March 2006 after chalking up a school record-setting 36 victories in the 2005–2006 season. The national championship was the year's second for the Badgers after the men's cross-country team won the national crown in fall 2005. There is also a wide range of intramural sports, 14 each for men and women. Sailing and windsurfing on the lake are very popular, as are jogging and bicycling on the trails at Picnic Point. Sledding on cafeteria trays down Liz Waters hill along Observatory Drive attracts 300–400 students after the first snowfall.

For those who can't find what they need on campus or in town, a road trip to Chicago, 125 miles south, or Milwaukee, 75 miles east, may be the ticket.

Cost cutters: In the 2005–2006 year, 52% of freshmen received financial aid; 25% got help based on need. No corresponding figures are available for continuing students. The University of Wisconsin has hundreds of scholarships for the bright, the talented, and the needy. About 500 honorary freshman scholarships paying up to $5000 are awarded each year to students from Wisconsin and other states as funding permits who are selected as Kemper K. Knapp Scholars; selection is based on performance in the National Merit competition and high school record. Students from Minnesota may pay about $1500 over the in-state tuition rate. The FASTRACK aid program provides freshmen from Wisconsin whose family incomes fall below a certain level with a 4-year structured aid package that includes work-study and grants plus loans of up to $1500 a year, with no loans the first year. Cooperative education programs are available to majors in engineering and agriculture. The average recent graduate who borrowed left Madison with $18,630 in college debts.

Rate of return: Ninety-four percent of entering freshmen return for their sophomore year. Forty-six percent graduate in 4 years, jumping to 75% within 5 years, 78% within 6.

Payoff: In the 2005 graduating class, 6% earned degrees in political science, 5% in psychology and 4% in English. Just under half go on to graduate or professional schools immediately after graduating. More than half of the students enrolled at Madison's Medical School are graduates of the university. Many of those seeking jobs accept positions with Fortune 500 companies. In a recent school year, 900 companies and other organizations recruited on campus. Over the years, the University of Wisconsin, Madison has produced 24 Pulitzer Prize winners, 17 Nobel laureates, 10 winners of the National Medals of Science, and 6 Rhodes Scholars. The Madison campus also is second, behind the University of California, Berkeley, in the number of graduates who become Peace Corps volunteers, totaling more than 2600 since 1961. In a recent year, the campus led all other colleges and universities with 142 graduates joining the Peace Corps.

Bottom line: "If you want a fun 5 or 6 years, Madison is as good as things come," remarks a recent graduate. "If you want a quality 4-year program, you have to know where you are going when you get here and be willing to sacrifice more than those around you. However, if you do make the effort, you may just be getting the biggest bang for the buck in American education."

University of Wyoming

Laramie, Wyoming 82071

Setting: Small city
Control: Public
Undergraduate enrollment: 3921 men, 3841 women
Graduate enrollment: 669 men, 621 women
Student/faculty ratio: 12:1
Freshman profile: 3% scored over 700 on SAT I verbal; 23% scored 600–700; 43% 500–599; 31% below 500. 3% scored over 700 on SAT I math; 26% scored 600–700; 42% 500–599; 29% below 500. 10% scored above 28 on the ACT; 10% scored 27–28; 24% 24–26; 27% 21–23; 29% below 21. 20% graduated in top tenth of high school class; 39% in upper fifth.

Faculty profile: 82% Ph.D.'s
Tuition and fees: $3426 in-state, $9816 out-of-state
Room and board: $6240
Freshman financial aid: 61%; average scholarship or grant: $3823 need-based; $1955 non-need-based
Campus jobs: 7%; average earnings: $1175/year
Application deadline: Aug. 10
Financial aid deadline: Mar. 1
Admissions information: (307) 766-5160; (800) 342-5996
e-mail: why-wyo@uwyo.edu
web site: www.uwyo.edu

If you long to go to school in the Equality State, where the Great Plains meet the Rockies, you've already narrowed your choice to the 13,207-student University of Wyoming. As the only game in town, in a state where "everyone knows everyone," the university doesn't have to contend with other state universities, or smaller 4-year colleges, for that matter, for its share of the state funding pie. Nor do wealthy individuals and organizations have to choose among competing institutions when funding scholarships. The low cost of tuition, fees, room, and board for in-state residents, less than $10,000 in 2005–2006, has made attendance at the University of Wyoming a tradition in many families. Nonresidents, who come from every state, also find a warm welcome with total costs of just over $16,000, often more affordable than their own state universities. Notes a third-generation Cowboy: "We're very friendly—Wyoming people usually are—and out-of-state students easily become part of the student body." Adds a business major: "The size here is perfect—you can be a somebody or a nobody, depending on what you feel comfortable with."

Student body: Seventy-three percent of Wyoming students are from in-state with the largest group of out-of-staters from the West. While numbers are still low, minority enrollment has increased by more than a third since 1986. Minorities account for about 6% of the student body—3% Hispanic and about 1% each African-American, Native American, and Asian-American. International students from 71 countries comprise about 3%. A high proportion of older students lends a fairly serious, career-oriented aspect to a generally fun-loving student body. Undergraduates tend to be conservative, though apolitical, "relaxed, happy, and easy to get to know," in the view of a student from Alaska. Many come from outdoor, ranching, or farming backgrounds. Like most Wyoming residents, students are "individualistic but cooperative and always ready to lend a hand to a friend," observes a 5th-year pharmacy student.

Academics: The University of Wyoming, which was founded in 1886, awards bachelor's degrees in about 75 majors, offers advanced degrees through the doctorate, and has 6 undergraduate colleges. The academic year is divided into 2 semesters. Average class size in introductory lectures is 41. The largest course, Fission, Fusion, and Psychosis, a geology class, recently enrolled 253; the smallest, Biblical Greek, had 2. Average class size for juniors and seniors shrinks to 20 students, with courses in commerce and industry and biology the most crowded. Students who want more personal interaction than some of the larger first-year courses can provide may participate in Freshman Interest Groups, which bring together no more than 20 students who take 3 or 4 classes together their first semester while living on the same residence hall floor.

A rigorous University Studies program requires all students, regardless of college or major, to take courses from across the curriculum. The basic skills component includes a first-year seminar dealing with various topics to assist in the transition to university life; 3 levels of a writing requirement, including 1 writing-intensive course in the student's major; 3 levels of mathematics courses, ranging from basic math to problem-solving to a course that applies quantitative reasoning to a subject area, 1 computer course and 1 in oral communication. Students may test out of only the first-level courses in math and writing. The other areas include 2 lab courses from 1 or more different branches of science; 3 courses from the humanities, social and behavioral sciences, and fine arts, touching all 3 areas; a course in the Wyoming and U.S. Constitutions; and 1 course each in U.S. diversity and global awareness.

The faculty is predominantly full-time: just 49 of the 692 faculty members are part-time. All but 13 members of the full-time faculty teach undergraduates as do all but 4 of the part-time members. Women comprise a third of the faculty. Student reviews range from "mediocre" to "excellent." Says a senior: "Most of my professors were imaginative, and most important, easy to talk to." Graduate students teach a tenth of the introductory courses.

Departments highly rated by students include molecular biology in the College of Agriculture, boosted by the animal science/molecular biology complex, pharmacy and nursing in the College of Health Sciences, and political science, international studies, and wildlife management in the College of Arts and Sciences. Astronomy and astrophysics, also in Arts and Sciences, are backed by good research, as well as access to the largest infrared telescope in the continental United States, located at Jelm Mountain Observatory, just outside Laramie. The geology department, too, makes excellent use of an ideal location and a new Minerals Research and Reclamation Center; a hard-to-be-missed mounted skeleton of the huge dinosaur *Apatosaurus,* commonly known as brontosaurus, adorns the university's geological museum. In a state particularly dependent on engineering talent for such major industries as mining and petroleum, it's no surprise that programs in the College of Engineering benefit from considerable corporate support and are considered strong with excellent faculties. Outstanding professors with real-life as well as academic experience more than satisfy job-conscious undergraduates in the College of Business. Opportunities for internships and extensive job listings upon graduation are satisfying as well.

The College of Education offers practical classroom instruction at the Lab School and has earned recognition for offering an innovative program, but students say that its curriculum is not sufficiently challenging and recently changing requirements have kept students in flux. Concerns about teaching assistants with limited English-speaking skills, employed in such fields as mathematics in the College of Arts and Sciences, continue to be addressed. Foreign teaching assistants are tested on their English-speaking skills and take an intensive course in American educational culture before being allowed to teach.

Facilities: The library system has 2.4 million volumes (including 1 million government documents) and 11,642 periodicals and is hailed by students as among the university's "best assets," good for studying, above the noisy main floor and basement, that is, and generally satisfactory for researching. It offers the latest computerized research assistance though not always the most up-to-date books or diverse periodicals. In addition to the main William Robertson Coe Library, the university features science and technology, geology, and law libraries, and undergraduates quickly learn which places tolerate the most socializing.

Approximately 1300 Windows workstations are readily available in all college residence halls, several classroom buildings, the student union, and the library. "There are sufficient computers," says a senior, "but their hours are not always long enough." Most labs are closed by 11 p.m. (the lab in the library is open until midnight) with fewer hours over the weekends. One lab is open 24 hours. Wireless access is available in many of the main academic buildings and the library with plans in the 2005–2006 school year to expand the system as funding permitted.

Special programs: Student-exchange opportunities range from a semester program in England to time in countries as diverse as Spain, Korea, Colombia, and Russia. Internships as well as a semester in Washington, D.C., also are available; so is a semester at the United Nations.

Campus life: One-fifth of the undergraduates live on the 785-acre campus, which, students claim, boasts the highest elevation of any college campus in the United States. Laramie, the university's southeastern Wyoming home, has a population of about 30,000 and is located on a plain more than 7200 feet above sea level between 2 mountain ranges, 44 miles east of the state capital of Cheyenne. Although a college catalog once described the climate as "clean, cool, sunny, dry, sheltered, and invigorating," one Casper resident translates this as: "It can get a bit chilly in the winter." Another junior gives more explicit advice: *"Don't come if you hate the cold weather."*

Seven percent of the men belong to 9 national fraternities, and 5% of the women pledge to 4 national sororities. Independents have their own private parties, and little socializing occurs between the 2 groups. Says a senior: "Many non-Greek students resent the Greek system for their attitudes and domination of campus activities." Many others opt simply to live and let live. Many students go to nearby bars to unwind. The Cowboy Bar offers live bands and western swing dancers nightly; the Buckhorn has a bullet hole in the mirror (the result of a domestic dispute), and the Ranger draws folks in tie-dye and Birkenstocks. The College Republicans and various environmental clubs are most active on campus. Campus crime, save for the occasional bike theft, doesn't seem to be of much concern, and women students feel relaxed about personal safety. "I frequently jog or cross-country ski in Laramie streets at night and feel very safe," says a female pharmacy student. There is an escort service, and increased lighting and emergency phones are posted around campus.

Whereas only a small proportion of the students participate in intercollegiate athletics, 7 for men and 8 for women in NCAA Division I, intramural sports, ranging from touch and flag football to trapshooting and Frisbee, are far more popular. Close to 6000 students, faculty, staff, and spouses compete in the 45 different sports. Cowboy football is big, so big, in fact, that the university's football stadium seats about as many people as live in the city of Laramie. Basketball and rodeo are popular, too.

Wyoming is not for the city slicker, and students are drawn by the opportunity to do great fishing, hunting, hiking, and skiing. All these activities are available in the Snowy Range, 30 miles from campus. Vedawoo, a rock formation 30 minutes away, is a great place to learn rock climbing or just to picnic. For a change of pace, many students go to Cheyenne, to Fort Collins, Colorado (an hour's drive), or to Denver (2½ hours distant) for weekend shopping, dinner, concerts, or visits with friends.

Cost cutters: Sixty-one percent of 2005–2006 freshmen received financial aid; for 49%, the aid was based on need. Nearly 48% of the continuing students received some kind of aid; for 47% the aid was need-based. The average first-year award for a student with need included a need-based scholarship or grant averaging $3823 and need-based self-help aid such as loans and jobs averaging $3875. Non-need-based athletic scholarships for first-year students averaged $3428. Other non-need-based awards and scholarships averaged $1955. In a recent year, a minimum of 2 President's Honors Scholarships, worth full tuition, were awarded to students in every Wyoming high school, plus 25 Trustee's Superior Student scholarships, which paid full tuition, room, and board. A nonresident incoming freshman with a GPA of 3.5 or higher was eligible for 1 of 125 Wyoming Excellence Scholarships that recently paid $1000; an out-of-stater with a GPA between 3.0 and 3.499 was eligible for 1 of 125 Wyoming Achievement Scholarships, recently worth $750. Federal work-study is provided to about 400 students. Cooperative education programs are available in engineering and business. Room and board can be paid in 8 or 10 installments. The average college debt of 2005 graduates was $15,250.

Rate of return: Seventy-six percent of the freshmen return for the sophomore year. Just 26% graduate in 4 years; 50% in 5 years, 56% in 6 years. Observes a senior communications major: "I have found it easy to graduate in 4 years and it's doable, as long as people take the most direct route. There are many shortcuts if you look."

Payoff: The largest numbers of students in the class of 2005 majored in elementary education at 9%, 6% in business administration, and 5% in psychology. A fifth of the graduates go directly on to graduate or professional schools. More than 150 companies and other organizations recruited on campus in a recent school year. Most graduates take employment immediately in fields related to their majors, primarily in the Rocky Mountain and northwest areas.

Bottom line: "It's easy to shine at the University of Wyoming," notes a resident who came after rejecting offers of admission from more prestigious but pricier schools. "Actively seeking out and taking advantage of the learning and extracurricular opportunities here will lead to success and satisfaction."

Alphabetical Index of the Colleges

Agnes Scott College, GA, 81

Alaska Pacific University, AK, 10

Albertson College of Idaho, ID, 101

Albion College, MI, 262

Albright College, PA, 489

Alma College, MI, 264

Alverno College, WI, 681

Appalachian State University, NC, 425

Arcadia University, PA, 491

Assumption College, MA, 245

Augsburg College, MN, 281

Augustana College, IL, 107

Austin College, TX, 590

Bellarmine College, KY, 217

Beloit College, WI, 689

Berea College, KY, 219

Berry College, GA, 84

Bethany College, WV, 682

Birmingham-Southern College, AL, 1

Blackburn College, IL, 109

Bluffton College, OH, 446

Bradley University, IL, 112

Bridgewater College, VA, 623

Brigham Young University, UT, 613

Bryant College, RI, 543

Buena Vista University, IA, 186

Butler University, IN, 145

California Polytechnic State University, CA, 25

Calvin College, MI, 267

Canisius College, NY, 391

Capital University, OH, 448

Carroll College, MT, 337

Centenary College of Louisiana, LA, 231

Central College, IA, 189

Centre College, KY, 222

Christendom College, VA, 625

City University of New York/Hunter College, NY, 374

Clemson University, Clemson, SC, 552

Coe College, IA, 191

Coker College, SC, 554

College of Charleston, SC, 559

The College of New Jersey, NJ, 361

College of Saint Benedict, MN, 284

College of St. Catherine, MN, 286

College of the Ozarks, MO, 314

The College of William and Mary, VA, 628

Colorado School of Mines, CO, 42

Concordia College, MN, 289

Converse College, SC, 560

The Cooper Union for the Advancement of Science and Art, NY, 377

Cornell College, IA, 194

Creighton University, NE, 345

DePauw University, IN, 147

Drake University, IA, 197

Drexel University, PA, 494

Drury University, MO, 316

Duquesne University, PA, 497

Earlham College, IN, 150

Eckerd College, FL, 70

Elmira College, NY, 380

Elon College, NC, 428

The Evergreen State College, WA, 664

Florida Institute of Technology, FL, 72

Franciscan University of Steubenville, OH, 457

Franklin C. Olin College of Engineering, MA, 247

Furman University, SC, 562

George Mason University, VA, 631

Georgetown College, KY, 225

Georgia Institute of Technology, GA, 86

Gonzaga University, WA, 667

Gordon College, MA, 250

Goshen College, IN, 153

Grinnell College, IA, 200

Grove City College, PA, 500

Guilford College, NC, 431

Gustavus Adolphus College, MN, 292

Hamline University, MN, 295

Hampden-Sydney College, VA, 634

Hanover College, IN, 156

Hastings College, NE, 348

Hawaii Pacific University, HI, 98

Heidelberg College, OH, 454

Hendrix College, AR, 19

Hiram College, OH, 456

Hofstra University, NY, 383

Hollins University, VA, 637

Hope College, MI, 270

Houghton College, NY, 386

Illinois College, IL, 114

Illinois Wesleyan University, IL, 117

Indiana University Bloomington, IN, 158

Ithaca College, NY, 388

James Madison University, VA, 640

John Carroll University, OH, 459

Juniata College, PA, 503

Kalamazoo College, MI, 272

Kettering University, MI, 275

King's College, PA, 506

Knox College, IL, 120

Le Moyne College, NY, 392

Linfield College, OR, 476

Loras College, IA, 203

Luther College, IA, 205

Lycoming College, PA, 509

Lyon College, AR, 22

Macalester College, MN, 298

Manchester College, IN, 161

Marietta College, OH, 462

Marist College, NY, 394

Marquette University, WI, 692

Mary Baldwin College, VA, 642

Mercer University, GA, 89

Messiah College, PA, 511

Miami University, OH, 464

Millikin University, IL, 123

Millsaps College, MS, 311

Monmouth College, IL, 125

Montana Tech of the University of Montana, MT, 339

Moravian College, PA, 514

Mount Saint Mary's College, MD, 237

Muskingum College, OH, 467

Nebraska Wesleyan University, NE, 351

New College of Florida, FL, 75

New Mexico Institute of Mining and Technology, NM, 368

North Central College, IL, 128

North Dakota State University, ND, 443

Northeastern University, MA, 253

Oglethorpe University, GA, 92

The Ohio State University, OH, 470

Pacific Lutheran University, WA, 670

Pacific University, OR, 478

The Pennsylvania State University, PA, 517
Presbyterian College, SC, 566
Prescott College, AZ, 13
Providence College, RI, 545
Purdue University, IN, 164
Quincy University, IL, 130
Randolph-Macon College, VA, 645
Randolph-Macon Woman's College, VA, 648
Rhodes College, TN, 581
Rice University, TX, 593
Ripon College, WI, 695
Rochester Institute of Technology, NY, 397
Rockhurst University, MO, 319
Rose-Hulman Institute of Technology, IN, 167
Rutgers, The State University of New Jersey, Brunswick/Piscataway, NJ, 364
St. Bonaventure University, NY, 400
Saint John's University, MN, 301
Saint Joseph's College, IN, 170
Saint Joseph's University, PA, 520
Saint Louis University, MO, 322
Saint Mary's College, IN, 172
St. Mary's College of Maryland, MD, 239
St. Norbert College, WI, 698
Saint Olaf College, MN, 304
Saint Vincent College, PA, 522
Sewanee: The University of the South, Sewanee, TN, 583
Shepherd College, WV, 684
Shimer College, IL, 133
South Dakota School of Mines and Technology, SD, 578
Southwestern University, TX, 596
Spring Hill College, AL, 4
State University of New York at Albany, NY, 414
State University of New York at Binghamton, NY, 408
State University of New York, College at Geneseo, NY, 402
State University of New York, College at Potsdam, NY, 405
State University of New York, College of Environmental Science and Forestry, NY, 411
Stonehill College, MA, 256
Suffolk University, MA, 258
Susquehanna University, PA, 525
Taylor University, IN, 175
Temple University, PA, 528

Texas A&M University, TX, 599
Texas Christian University, TX, 602
Thomas Aquinas College, CA, 27
Transylvania University, KY, 227
Trinity University, San Antonio, TX, 605
Truman State University, MO, 325
United States Air Force Academy, CO, 49
United States Coast Guard Academy, CT, 61
United States Merchant Marine Academy, NY, 417
United States Military Academy, NY, 420
United States Naval Academy, MD, 242
University of Alabama, Tuscaloosa, AL, 6
The University of Arizona, AZ, 15
University of California, Berkeley, CA, 30
University of California, Davis, CA, 33
University of California, Los Angeles, CA, 35
University of California, San Diego, CA, 38
University of California, Santa Cruz, CA, 41
University of Colorado at Boulder, CO, 52
The University of Connecticut, CT, 64
University of Dallas, TX, 607
University of Delaware, DE, 67
University of Denver, CO, 55
University of Evansville, IN, 178
The University of Georgia, GA, 94
University of Idaho, ID, 104
University of Illinois at Chicago, IL, 135
University of Illinois at Urbana-Champaign, IL, 138
The University of Iowa, IA, 208
University of Kansas, Lawrence, KS, 214
University of Maine, ME, 234
University of Mary Washington, VA, 651
University of Michigan, MI, 278
University of Minnesota, Morris, MN, 307
University of Missouri, Columbia, MO, 328

University of Missouri, Rolla, MO, 331
The University of Montana, MT, 342
University of Nevada, Reno, NV, 354
University of New Hampshire, NH, 357
University of North Carolina at Asheville, NC, 433
University of North Carolina at Chapel Hill, NC, 436
University of North Florida, FL, 78
University of Northern Colorado, CO, 57
University of Oregon, OR, 481
University of Pittsburgh, Pittsburgh Campus, PA, 531
University of Portland, OR, 484
University of Puget Sound, WA, 672
The University of Rhode Island, RI, 548
University of Scranton, PA, 534
University of South Carolina, SC, 568
The University of Tennessee, Knoxville, TN, 587
University of Texas at Austin, TX, 610
The University of Tulsa, OK, 473
University of Utah, UT, 616
University of Vermont, VT, 619
University of Virginia, VA, 653
University of Washington, WA, 675
University of Wisconsin, Madison, WI, 701
University of Wyoming, WY, 704
Valparaiso University, IN, 180
Virginia Polytechnic Institute and State University, VA, 657
Wabash College, IN, 183
Warren Wilson College, NC, 439
Wartburg College, IA, 211
Washington & Jefferson College, PA, 537
Washington and Lee University, VA, 660
Webb Institute, NY, 422
Westmont College, CA, 44
Wheaton College, IL, 142
Whitman College, WA, 678
Willamette University, OR, 486
William Jewell College, MO, 334
Winthrop University, SC, 571
Wofford College, SC, 574
York College of Pennsylvania, PA, 539